planet earth home

by Mel Moench

---------------Introducing the

functional,
efficient,
ecologically balanced,
need-oriented,
energy-independent,
food-independent,
simple,
durable,
non-polluting,
single family,
universal,
minimal existence,
living system

------------built in the image of nature.

This is the complete story of over 32 years research into designing the most technically advanced, mass-producible, self-sufficient home in the world that could be located anywhere on Earth—and also maintain a 20th century lifestyle……

……….Mel Moench

LONGWOOD PUBLIC LIBRARY

Copyright © 1994 by Mel Moench

All rights reserved. No part of this book may be reproduced or transmitted in any form or by any means, electronic or mechanical, including photocopying, recording or by an informational storage or retrieval system--except by a reviewer who may quote brief passages in a review to be printed in a magazine or newspaper--without permission in writing from the publisher. For information, contact **Osprey Press**, 2107 Ibis Drive, Buffalo, MN 55313 or ospreypress@charter.net.

First edition, book format, February 1995.
Second edition, book with cover jacket, August 1995.
1997 edition, book with simplified format and "12-Volt Advantage"
-----1997 edition new ISBN
1998 edition, expanded diet section, home page on Internet.
1999 edition, reorganized, reformatted T/C and index, updated
2000 edition, updated, www.planetearthhome.com
2003 edition, reformatted T/C, updated
2003e eBook edition (pdf)
2003emr eBook edition (lit)
2004 edition, expanded, updated thermal mass, T/C
-----2004 edition ISBN 0-9673711-6-3
2005 edition, updated T/C and index, articles, expanded text
2007 edition, updated biomass/gasification and expanded index

Although the author and publisher have exhaustively researched all sources to ensure the accuracy and completeness of the information contained in this book, we assume no responsibility for errors, inaccuracies, omissions or any inconsistency herein. Any slights of people or organizations are unintentional.

Library of Congress Control #2003095144----ISBN 978-0-9673711-6-3

<u>HOW TO SCAN THIS BOOK</u>

This book can be scanned or speed read in *less than two hours* by reading the ***<u>bold/underscored/italicized text.</u>***-----They highlight key concepts or ideas. A more complete look at individual sections of interest can follow. The main points are discussed at length using more details.

For the most in-depth study, the yellow pages bibliography can be referenced. They are a complete source for the <u>mountains</u> of scientific and technical information that were condensed into the text of this book. See the table of contents for index to them.

Note that "Earth Home" is abbreviated "EH" throughout. For starters, page lxxii explain "prototype" and "methology of text."

HOW TO SCAN THIS BOOK

This book can be scanned or speed read in *less than two hours* by reading the ***bold/underscored/italicized text.***-----They highlight key concepts or ideas. A more complete look at individual sections of interest can follow. The main points are discussed at length using more details.

For the most in-depth study, the yellow pages bibliography can be referenced. They are a complete source for the mountains of scientific and technical information that were condensed into the text of this book. See the table of contents for index to them.

Note that "Earth Home" is abbreviated "EH" throughout. For starters, page lxxii explain "prototype" and "methology of text."

READ FIRST

1. System Approach

<u>The text that follows is broken down by systems</u>. It often describes products I used and tested, as well as the reasons why they didn't work out. It tells what I am presently using and the products/methods that I'm looking into for future use. I have included a very comprehensive list of suppliers of products at the end of the text. In most cases, the appropriate reference files are referred to in the text.

2. Writing Style/Humor

I am sometimes criticized for the dry, humorless textbook/termpaper style of writing. I acknowledge that on the wit/humor scale--I am not even on it. The subject matter is extremely lengthy, technical, and difficult to understand by an average reader. I wish to lay a foundation for future projects, research efforts, and any cooperative efforts that may spring from this work. I did not write this in the hopes of being on the bedside reading list of Joe American. I wrote this to be a reference book for future generations and forward-looking people in the hope that it will be of some use. I hope this is of some value to you---It would have been for me.

3. Scanning the Entire Text Quickly-Again

This book can be scanned or speed read in ***less than two hours*** by reading the ***<u>bold/underscored/italicized text.</u>***-----They highlight key concepts or ideas. A more complete look at individual sections of interest can follow. The main points are discussed at length using more details.

For the most in-depth study, the yellow pages bibliography can be referenced. They are a complete source for the <u>mountains</u> of scientific and technical information that were condensed into the text of this book. See the table of contents for index to them.

Again, note that "Earth Home" is abbreviated EH throughout.

4. Articles Written on the Earth Home Philosophy

Translations, explanations, descriptions, and communications about this book and the Earth Home philosophy can be seen in magazine article reprints. See Table of Contents for location.

5. A Note On Technology

Much of the world's research, products, technologies, and effort have generally been aimed at markets that exist already and not toward emerging technologies and lifestyles. For this reason, many technological advances are sometimes overlooked or played down as marginally important. I feel there are many existing technologies that may be revisited in the future in order to complement Earth Home-style projects and purposes.

READ FIRST

1. System Approach

<u>The text that follows is broken down by systems</u>. It often describes products I used and tested, as well as the reasons why they didn't work out. It tells what I am presently using and the products/methods that I'm looking into for future use. I have included a very comprehensive list of suppliers of products at the end of the text. In most cases, the appropriate reference files are referred to in the text.

2. Writing Style/Humor

I am sometimes criticized for the dry, humorless textbook/termpaper style of writing. I acknowledge that on the wit/humor scale--I am not even on it. The subject matter is extremely lengthy, technical, and difficult to understand by an average reader. I wish to lay a foundation for future projects, research efforts, and any cooperative efforts that may spring from this work. I did not write this in the hopes of being on the bedside reading list of Joe American. I wrote this to be a reference book for future generations and forward-looking people in the hope that it will be of some use. I hope this is of some value to you---It would have been for me.

3. Scanning the Entire Text Quickly-Again

This book can be scanned or speed read in *less than two hours* by reading the ***<u>bold/underscored/italicized text.</u>***-----They highlight key concepts or ideas. A more complete look at individual sections of interest can follow. The main points are discussed at length using more details.

For the most in-depth study, the yellow pages bibliography can be referenced. They are a complete source for the <u>mountains</u> of scientific and technical information that were condensed into the text of this book. See the table of contents for index to them.

Again, note that "Earth Home" is abbreviated EH throughout.

4. Articles Written on the Earth Home Philosophy

Translations, explanations, descriptions, and communications about this book and the Earth Home philosophy can be seen in magazine article reprints. See Table of Contents for location.

5. A Note On Technology

Much of the world's research, products, technologies, and effort have generally been aimed at markets that exist already and not toward emerging technologies and lifestyles. For this reason, many technological advances are sometimes overlooked or played down as marginally important. I feel there are many existing technologies that may be revisited in the future in order to complement Earth Home-style projects and purposes.

DEDICATION/ACKNOWLEDGMENT

I would like to dedicate this work to a number of people who have made a contribution to the project.

I'd like to dedicate this to Linda Rainbolt, my first wife, who was very understanding and tolerant of this project in its early stages.

I would also like to dedicate this project to my second wife, Claudia Grinnell Moench, without whose patience, tolerance, and understanding this could never have been written. She is what I consider to be a perfect companion for me, and she has contributed greatly to this project. She has allowed me to continue working on the project, always keeping me on the light side of life. This project has been particularly hard on relationships, and has slowed down during periods of unstable relationships. I hope I never meet wife #3. I feel that a stable family relationship is necessary to a project of this scope, especially in light of the fact there is no clear substantial monetary reward at the end of the project, such as comes from marketing a product or service. This project was meant to be a design project: to develop the technology needed to mass-produce this type of home. I feel that the actual mass production could be left to another person, contemporary, family member, or acquaintance using the technology that will be developed.

This is also dedicated to my children, Nathan, MeLea, and Kessie, with whom I have a special relationship. I'd also like to thank my immediate family members. My mother Betty Wilbur, my sister Laurell Moench, my brother Larry Moench, and my father Lyle Moench who had to deal with my bent personality all these years. I would especially like to thank my brother Babe (Lyle Moench). He was at my side doing hands-on work during much of this project, and was invaluable to the development of this project. He was more than a brother: he was a friend, advisor, and confidante during this entire project.

I'd especially like to thank Ron Quittem, Scott Quittem, Tom Nelson, Eric Pike, Steve Hanka, and Levi Hanka for their special help and insights into the project. They have been a constant source of friendship, help, and support throughout the 30 plus years of this project.

I'd also like to thank Al Tabery for the use of his sheet metal shop over the years. He was like a combination father/brother to me, and allowed me the use of his shop to build many prototypes and test many ideas. His light attitude seemed to remind me of the saying "No man is a failure who is enjoying life". I'd also like to thank Luke Markve and Richard Scott for their special influence on me during this project. They kept my feet on the ground in the early years.

I'd also like to thank my grandfather, Louis Cihlar, who taught me "efficiency" and "recycling" decades before it was fashionable. Thanks also to my uncle, Johnny Frey, for his direct, honest, courageous, outspoken manner--and hardworking philosophy. He said that *learning is a matter of listening more and talking less.*

I would also like to thank the hundreds of people whom I call friends or advisors, who fed me information/criticism that they thought appropriate and continue to do so today. This information network was of particular help to me in researching some of the more unusual products, methods, and ideas related to Earth Home (EH) research.

A special thanks to the Buffalo, Minnesota Library staff, their network in St. Cloud, and the University of Minnesota. They put up with thousands of requests over the years. Their help and support was ***indispensable.***

I would also like to thank all the people who have helped me over the years who think they should be mentioned here. They do belong here. Their help and emotional support have been greatly appreciated.

I would also like to thank the God of Abraham for the guidance and patience shown to me. I have come to feel a sense of direction and purpose in this project. It has made my life both challenging and peaceful.

Mel

Favorite sayings:

Max Planck once said that "an important scientific innovation rarely makes its way by gradually winning over and converting its opponents; it rarely happens that Saul becomes Paul. What does happen is that its opponents gradually die out and that the growing generation is familiarized with the idea from the beginning."

Schoepenhauer said that "all truth passes through three stages: first it is ridiculed; second, it is violently opposed; third, it is accepted as being self-evident."

Albert Einstein also wrote that "The significant problems we have cannot be solved at the same level of thinking with which we created them."

Mahatma Gandhi said, "We must be the change we wish to see in the world."

Max Feffer said, "The life we want depends on what we do."

The Arctic explorer Fridtjof Nansen said that "the history of the human race is a continuous struggle from darkness toward light. It is therefore no purpose to discuss the use of knowledge. Man wants to know, and when he ceases to do so, he is no longer man."

I agree that regardless of race, religion, or gender, we should not pass less useful knowledge to our children that we have received from our ancestors.

Edmund Burke once said that "Nobody makes a greater mistake than he who did nothing because he could only do little." Yet another Chinese proverb says, "Knowing and not doing is equal to not knowing."

The hardest part of any task is simply starting.

Albert Schweitzer once said, "Whoever is spared personal pain must feel himself called to help in diminishing the pain of others."

George Ohsawa said that "Fasting in the true sense means to eat and drink "simply" in accord with those principles which are at the core of the infinite order of the universe."

Heracleitus said, "It is in changing that we find purpose".

Churchill also said, "Men stumble over the truth from time to time, but most pick themselves up and hurry off as if nothing happened."

TABLE OF CONTENTS

*Used in Earth Home

*Used in Earth Home

*Used in Earth Home

*Used in Earth Home

*Used in Earth Home

*Used in Earth Home

*Used in Earth Home

*Used in Earth Home

*Used in Earth Home

*Used in Earth Home

*Used in Earth Home

*Used in Earth Home

*Used in Earth Home

*Used in Earth Home

*Used in Earth Home

*Used in Earth Home

*Used in Earth Home

V. HEATING SYSTEM 277

*Used in Earth Home

*Used in Earth Home

*Used in Earth Home

*Used in Earth Home

*Used in Earth Home

*Used in Earth Home

*Used in Earth Home

*Used in Earth Home

*Used in Earth Home

*Used in Earth Home

*Used in Earth Home

*Used in Earth Home

*Used in Earth Home

*Used in Earth Home

*Used in Earth Home

*Used in Earth Home

*Used in Earth Home

*Used in Earth Home

*Used in Earth Home

*Used in Earth Home

*Used in Earth Home

*Used in Earth Home

*Used in Earth Home

*Used in Earth Home

*Used in Earth Home

*Used in Earth Home

*Used in Earth Home

*Used in Earth Home

*Used in Earth Home

LIST OF FIGURES

*Used in Earth Home

*Used in Earth Home

*Used in Earth Home

*Used in Earth Home

*Used in Earth Home

*Used in Earth Home

PREFACE/INTRODUCTION

A. History of Self-Sufficient Structures

1. Evolutionary Efforts

Historically, tribal groups were the earliest forms of self-sufficiency. In this tribal society, tasks were spread out among the members at very early developmental stages. Self-sufficiency meant tribal self-sufficiency and not individual or family self-sufficiency. Certain members were specialized in grinding corn for bread, hunting, and for cleaning or tanning of hides. This is similar to how the Indians, Eskimos, and the African tribes have evolved.

Traditional self-sufficiency typically was a family trying to make or grow everything it needed to survive. It had the connotation of a "hermit" lifestyle; stuck in the north woods chopping wood and feeding the fruits of their garden. Minimal amounts of money supported the family, and they did without many comforts or luxuries.

In order to be a self-sufficient family, you typically had to have a certain amount of land, tools, equipment, and farm machinery. A family had to have an ample water supply to grow food and to wash with. Much time and hard work was necessary to provide for their needs. They had to barter in order to procure many necessities. ***Self-sufficiency as a lifestyle was traditionally very difficult and time consuming -- one of the reasons that the industrial revolution caught on quickly.*** It freed the family from the necessity of providing everything for themselves. They could simply work a job outside and buy most of their necessities.

2. Self-Sufficiency Projects (Energy Emphasis)

Many people refer to self-sufficiency as having the ability to generate all power for the home. The following summarizes some significant efforts.

a. Advanced Houses of the World

One book, Advanced Houses of the World, by Stephen Carpenter, prepared by CANMET (CADDET-Center for the Analysis and Dissemination of Demonstrated Energy Technologies) compiles much of the recent experiments done on energy efficiency of homes. This organization in Netherlands has put the world's energy test homes all in one book. Note: this book uses the term "autonomous" for energy only and may be confused with this work's usage of autonomous to mean stand-alone completely from society. However this book goes into much technical detail on homes built and monitored around the world on their energy use.

These houses typically cut their energy needs by two-thirds to about 50 kwh/sq. m. They use technologies such as super insulation, air-tight construction, ventilation with heat recovery, high-performance windows, transparent insulation, passive solar design, high-performance heating systems, solar domestic hot water systems, integrated mechanical systems, high-efficiency lighting, energy-efficient appliances, photovoltaics, and eco-management strategies.

These houses are scattered all over the world with different climates, regional practices, project motivations, and economic considerations. They study energy interrelationships but do not go into the home as a system to benefit the family in areas of food production.

b. University/College Projects

The U.S. Department of Agriculture Rural Housing Research Unit, in connection with Clemson University, has been experimenting with low energy conservation houses since 1977. Similar work was done in early 1980's by the Minnesota-based Mid-American Solar Energy Complex and the Small Homes Council of the University of Illinois.

c. Government Projects

On a per capita basis, I believe Canada leads the world in research on energy-efficient homes. They not only have encouraged projects such as the Waterloo Green Home, but also published many reports and studies. In-depth studies such as the booklet, "Energy and Power Needs and Availability in Housing," through the Canada Mortgage and Housing Corporation, have made home design a "science." The CMHC has many projects and publications on the subject of housing design such as, "Biological Toilets and Greywater Systems," "Towards an Investigation of Sustainable Housing," "Efficient and Effective Residential Air Handling Devices," and the Healthy Housing Design Competition.

Researchers in Sweden have also done a lot of work in energy conservation in housing with over 30 homes built under the Pilot and Demonstration Programme. They have also developed the ELAK 1984 codes, which is the standard for energy-efficient homes. They have a modular approach to homes using 8 inches of insulated walls. The homes are built in these modular sections, assembled, and completely sealed. The Swedes are probably leading the world in the manufacture of energy efficient homes. I also give them high marks for other areas of self-sufficiency, especially in toilet and wind generator design.

In Wales, the National Center for Appropriate Technology (NCAT) does research to identify products and processes that would be of benefit to developing countries. This extensive research center covers most areas of low and intermediate technology for self-sufficiency.

Germany probably has the best controlled experiments on energy efficiency by placing all homes to be tested in one geographical area. This avoids the complexities with extrapolating data to a different climatic region. See Advanced Houses of the World book for more details.

Also, the Division of Energy Technology in Australia has worked on a low-energy consumption house. Japan has an R-2000 program and the Sunshine Project.

d. Alberta Sustainable Home

In 1994 the Alberta Sustainable Home was completed in Calgary. It receives much publicity from around the world. Jorg and Helen Ostrowski and others tried and tested many new technologies and products in this home. Some of the techniques used include; 5-pane windows, a waterless toilet, 3 greywater recycling systems, slab-on-grade construction, shallow foundation, airtight drywall technologies, recycled materials, organic fiber boards, solar hydronic heating, and several forms of lighting products. This home concentrates on resource efficiency (recycling) and autonomous power generation and they continuously test and publish.

*Used in Earth Home

e. International Center for Sustainable Development

John Spears and his group in Maryland have been working on promoting sustainable development for over 30 years. The organization has tested many concepts including; compressed earth brick, straw board insulation, earth lime plaster, rainwater collection, composting toilets, PV, active solar hot water collectors with heated floors, floor geo cooling and others.

f. Earthships

One of the most widely known terms of late is "earthship". Mike Reynolds has written four books on the philosophy of making low-impact homes with recycled materials-predominantly automobile tires. They use many water and energy-conserving techniques. Each earthship is unique and they have been built all over the world. Many have even been built with significant food-producing capabilities.

g. Zero Energy/Passive Homes (ZEH)

There are a limited number of homebuilders in the world that have built homes that are net producers of electricity. They are typically connected to the electricity grid and sell energy back when production exceeds demand. Two popular areas for such homes are Florida and northern California where photovoltaic energy was emphasized.

European homes are also being built without central heating systems. These homes are also referred to as passive homes, body-heat homes, and homes without heating. Passive heat inputs are delivered externally by solar irradiation through the windows and provided internally by the heat emissions of appliances and occupants. This essentially suffices to keep the building at comfortable indoor temperatures throughout the heating period.

h. Home Alive Project

In Canada, there is a home dedicated to green living and conservation of energy on a whole home basis. The "Home Alive" project uses a vast number of technologies in the construction and operation of this unique home.

i. Solium House

This house features solar panels and wind turbines as an alternative energy source and lithium-powered energy for storage. It also has a geothermal system for heating and cooling. Located south of Calgary, Alberta, Canada, it utilizes lithium batteries charged by solar panels and roof-mounted wind turbines. It supplies DC power for all home energy requirements and is independent of the grid.

3. Self-Sufficiency Projects (**Both** Food and Energy)

a. Autonomous House Book

The book Autonomous House, by Robert and Brenda Vales, was one of the earliest documentation of scientific developments/conceptions of designs for family independence, which would generate all of the family's needs within or near the home. It's noted in the book that there are no completely self-sufficient homes, because our technology is not advanced enough to make such an item, and there is no concerted effort to advance technology in this area.

b. NASA CELSS and Russian Bios-3

Some universities and NASA (National Aeronautics and Space Administration) have developed the "alternative technology theme". A few universities are doing research on a "smart" house. (This is an effort to automate the house by using computer control.) NASA is probably the largest and the most well funded developer of certain

*Used in Earth Home

areas of self-sufficiency such as in the "CELSS" system (Closed Environmental Life Support System). In many various and scattered publications, NASA publishes research efforts, for example, on showers to be used in space stations and water saving/conservation schemes. They do work on filtering soap out of water, growing plants using accelerated photo intensities, and growing selected species of plants in special ways. They also do research on intensive growing, different soils, and CO_2 enrichment. They do the most extensive research in self-sufficiency for specialized applications such as extended space travel or space colonization.

The Russians have researched closed systems and at one time were the world leader in this technology. At the Institute of Biomedical Problems in Moscow, Yevgeny Shepelev became the first human to live with biological life support in 1961 when he spent twenty-four hours in a chamber where chlorella algae regenerated his air and purified his water. At the Institute of Biophysics in Krasnoyarsk, Siberia, these algae-based systems were further developed with the Bios-3 experiments in the 1970's and 1980's, where they achieved six-month closures with a dozen food crops supplying half the food and providing nearly all the air and water regeneration for crews of two and three people.

c. New Alchemy Institute

At the New Alchemy Institute in New England, John Todd and his group have done work with environmental houses. They called their experimental self-sufficient home "The Ark." They've done quite a bit of work on survival methods, and I consider them to have been leaders in the United States in this type of research.

d. Publications

Mother Earth News magazine had a research facility in North Carolina that has been working on self-sufficiency projects for many years. Mother Earth News is probably the most familiar name associated with self-sufficiency in the United States -- especially by laypeople. Another magazine, Homepower, is another example of articles about choices that homeowners have to be more self-sufficient.

The book that contains a huge amount of information is the Encyclopedia of Country Living by Carla Emery. This reference book tells as much information about self-sufficiency technologies as a person could ever want. How to Be Food Self-Sufficient by Glenn and Viola Andrews gives good insight into the traditional self-sufficient lifestyle and is a complete work in a small package.

Also, many people are researching the field and building new homes based on that research. (Incidentally, other good starter sources of information are The Efficient House Sourcebook by Robert Sardinsky and the staff of Rocky Mountain Institute, and Real Goods Solar Living Sourcebook edited by John Schaeffer.)

e. Biosphere II

The huge Biosphere II project in Arizona has drawn a great deal of publicity. It has cost millions of dollars to enclose approximately 3 acres under glass. Included with the plant growing area for food is a large portion devoted to aesthetics. The Biosphere II has a mountain, a savanna, a rain forest, a desert, an ocean and many different climates in one huge glass structure. About one-half acre of space is devoted to self-sufficiency, and overlaps into the Earth Home research. Researchers started out with approximately 3,800 species of plants and animals to research while being sealed inside (of which 156 are edible). Their air conditioning and air movement power needs were horrendous. If they were out of power for more than two minutes, the temperature rise would kill off most of their plants and animals. However, their research on food production has direct application in the Earth Home field, and I have researched many of their printed materials. Especially informative was the book Life Under Glass by Abigail Alling and Mark Nelson with Sally Silverstone.

f. Individuals/Retrofits

I believe there are only a handful of individuals around the world who are experimenting with a completely self-sufficient home. There are many hundreds of thousands more interested in lowering their cost of living in specific areas by using solar energy or wind energy, for example.

*Used in Earth Home

Most people who are involved in self-sufficiency research are in a specialty field, such as wind generators, solar energy, or water filters. The volume of self-sufficient products is still low, and there is no complete experimental or commercially available system. Most people are using the home they have while gradually modifying it to be more efficient or more self-sufficient.

g. Bioshelters

There are a few homes built with plants on the inside that "work" with the interior environment and occupants. These bioshelters are on the way toward the Earth Home philosophy of providing all food and power.

h. The Earth Home System

The Earth Home System differs significantly from all other similar projects in that the end result is a mass-producible product. I would like to put special emphasis on the words "mass-producible." There have been many projects over the years that deal with similar topics, such as energy-efficient homes and self-sufficient living styles. None of these are goal-oriented towards a cost efficient, mass-producible model that can be used anywhere. (Also, note that the project is independently funded without subsidies from any governmental body or affiliation/membership with any academic organizations, home builder lobby groups, or any professional associations.)

B. Earth Home Project Description and Purpose

1. Earth Home Project Goal

a. Goal Description

This is a collection of over 32 years research into what I believe to be the world's most technically-advanced, independent living system. ***The goal, as I've stated previously, is to develop the technology to be able to mass produce food- and energy-independent living shelters for any location on the planet Earth and be ecologically compatible***. The home must also maintain 20th century comfort standards.

If you were to graph the self-sufficient quality of homes, at the far left would be a conventional home (0% self-sufficient), and at the far right would be the Earth Home system (near 100% self-sufficient). In-between are super-insulated homes, underground homes (which, incidentally, are many times referred to as Earth Homes), solar homes, wind-generated homes, solar-wind retrofits, envelope homes, etc. All of these homes are in transition, or on the way to complete self-sufficiency. ***The goal of this project is to develop the most technically advanced self-sufficient home possible (100% self-sufficiency)***. I believe the world needs a norm to which comparisons can be made.

In actuality, complete 100% self-sufficiency is unattainable, because of the maintenance on the structure or components, and because salt has to be imported. No known plant produces salt, although some plants do take salt from salt-laden soil and store it in their leaves and stems (salt-tolerant). (See Plants - Salt files.) Also yeast/enzymes for alcohol/vinegar production would be easier to purchase than to make in a typical home.

If each Earth Home owner developed specialized skills and specialized tools, they would naturally form a sort of "collective" where technology and products could be obtained from each other. Such "cottage industries" are a common part of our culture, and will likely play an important part of Earth Home proliferation.

b. Other Descriptive Titles for this Work

The following are other possible titles for this collection, with a brief description following.

1. Autonomy in Housing. The word "autonomous" means completely stand-alone or self-sufficient. Autonomous House was the original title of a book by Robert and Brenda Vale from Cambridge, England.

2. Self-Sufficient Living System. The word "self-sufficiency" is interwoven in many conversations involving this home, because the purpose is to provide all the needs of the family within the confines of the walls and immediate surroundings. "Self-sufficient" means providing for one's self -- without having to be dependent on other people, other societies, or other technologies.

3. Family Food Factory. This was a term used in one newspaper article on the Earth Home. The word "family" means, of course, the designed-around unit, and "food factory" may as well have been called "food/energy factory." It is a generator of food and energy -- an active manufacturer of products that a family needs.

4. Microfarm System. In essence, the Earth Home is actually a miniature or microfarm--a place to grow food and provide for a family's needs in one location.

5. Battery Operated Home. This title could have been used because it illustrates one of the major design points of this home. It is not dependent on 110-Volt electricity from a utility company (grid system). Batteries store the necessary electricity. Even though this is only one of the elements necessary to make a completely self-sufficient home, it is a term that is easily understood.

6. Ultimate Human Habitation, or Treatise on an Ideal Home for the Earth. These idealistic titles take into account my own opinions and hopes for the future.

7. Long-Range Survival Home. This title could have been used because of the home's ability to stand-alone: to survive without outside aid. It has the quality of being able to provide basic necessities for a family of four, regardless of the outside social, cultural, technological or climatic conditions at the time.

8. Habitation for Sustainable Society. The word "habitation" means dwelling or home. The word "sustainable" has been used to denote a society that will exist regardless of outside influences such as oil from the Mid-East and products unique to a region, a political entity, or a country.

9. TO: Mel. I thought of this title because it is written to myself when I was 23 years old. A specific intent of this book is to completely document the project from A to Z, so that this can be used as reference material for someone starting a similar project or interested in a project such as solar energy, wind energy, or non-polluting appropriate technologies.

10. In Search of 100% Self-Sufficiency in Home Design. 100% self-sufficiency is impossible to attain, but the word "self-sufficiency" is probably the most-used word when talking about a project of this nature.

11. Independent Living System. This is what I call the Earth Home system of living. Independent Living System, or ILS, means a living system that will provide a choice between dependency and independence. The word "system" means that the individual parts are often dependent on other parts. Even though a component of the Earth Home may not, in itself, be an ultimate design -- or best, stand-alone design -- it is the entire system that I describe as an ultimate design.

12. Eco Shelter. This was a term that was used throughout the late 1970's and early 80's, meaning a home that is in tune with the ecology or nature.

*Used in Earth Home

13. Environmentally Friendly Home. This connotes a home that is in tune with the environment. The words "recycling," "non-polluting," and "Earth-friendly" also come to mind.

14. Recycling Home. The Earth Home is designed to re-use most foodstuffs, water, and wastes. It is a key quality of the system.

15. Biosphere. This early 1970's term is attached to a project in Arizona known as "Biosphere II." (Biosphere I is the planet Earth.) The project simulates the Earth's environment inside of a closed system.

16. Alternative Energy Home. Following the oil embargo of 1975, the phrase "alternative energy" became popular, especially following the publication of E.F. Schumacher's book, Small is Beautiful. The phrase "alternative energy" became part of the titles of many projects and programs throughout this country, and is a term that, even though dated, does have a recognizable meaning and is still used.

17. In Search of Independence. This could have been used because of the independent nature of the Earth Home. The phrase "in search of" means "a quest for," and that's what the project has been over the years. I believe this independent/dependent choice is a central theme for Earth Home development. I feel that it's the very nature of humans to be independent, rather than dependent on other people for their needs and wants.

18. Intermediate Technology Home. The word "intermediate technology" has been used more in the late 1980's. Intermediate technology is a compromise between the low technology of the developing world and high technology of the developed nations. Another synonym might be "appropriate" technology.

19. Evolving Technology. This evolution of products and services is what fuels continued research in the Earth Home.

20. The "Unplugged" Lifestyle. The term has meant, "not connected to electricity" in popular titles. This underscores "independent" as a goal in one's life.

21. Encyclopedia or Self-Sufficiency in Housing Design.

22. Textbook for Self-Sufficient Homes.

23. Design Manual for Self-Sufficient Homes.

These last three titles suggest that every conceivable subject related to the design and building of self-sufficient homes has been researched, categorized, described, and summarized.

c. Prototype Explained

As of September 1, 2005, the Earth Home project is between the first and second prototypes. A prototype is an experimental model of a finished product used to test various qualities before proceeding with mass production. Even with advanced simulation techniques and modeling methods, a prototype is desirable to get the "feel" of the final product. Prototypes are typically expensive, but they save money by eliminating production problems later on. Industry often enters the market too quickly with a product, only to have the consumer complain about the quality. They may then correct the problem and re-issue the product as a "new" or "improved" model. In this way, industries use the consumer as their "Research and Development" department.

2. Qualities Desired for the Earth Home

The Earth Home is designed to approximate an average, comfortable lifestyle in the 1990's. I'm not interested in drastically altering living patterns in order to live in this house, although I do think most people would change their lifestyles somewhat when living in a house of this nature -- adapting a more eastern or oriental style, especially in cooking and diet. This house is designed as an option -- a choice for beyond 2000. This house is also designed for handicapped access. I feel that it is the house that will allow people to choose their own level

*Used in Earth Home

of self-sufficiency. ***They will then have the choice of complete dependence on our society or complete independence from society.***

To summarize, this goal is an attempt to: grow 100% of the family's food requirements; generate 100% of power requirements; recycle water and wastes; get rain water from the roof, filter it, and use it for washing needs; further filter water for use in cooking and drinking; and provide for all of the family needs within the confines of the home and immediate surroundings. This would greatly reduce a family's need for extra income.

I looked at what I wanted the home to do. ***The qualities that I built into the Earth Home are as follows:***

a. Functional

This home had to work as the prime ingredient to the design. How it looks comes second. A good design will make the item work most of the time, and if it does break down, makes it easy to fix (user-maintainable).

b. Efficient

The world belongs to the efficient -- the qualities light and small are becoming a world trend. Efficiency is something that we will be living with throughout the 1990's and into the 21st century as a prime consideration in many things we do, read about, talk about, and purchase. The word "efficiency" never really got going until the oil embargo of the early 1970's that launched the "solar era." Recycling went from "trendy" in the 1980's to big business in the 90's.

c. Ecologically-Balanced

The Earth Home attempts to recycle nearly all of the products that are taken into the home. It recycles water, waste, and some air by the design of the Earth Home CO_2/O_2 balance. (CO_2 is carbon dioxide, which comes from the animals and O_2 is oxygen that comes from the plants.) The Earth Home seeks to allow humans to live lightly on the land, being much more environmentally responsible.

d. Need-Oriented

I wanted to develop a needs list that I could go by when designing a feature. ***Earth Home seeks to satisfy basic human needs, as shown in the following figure.***

e. Energy-Independent

The home generates all the electricity it needs by the combination of wind, photovoltaic (PV), and event/time-dependent generator backup. I've cut the electrical requirements inside the Earth Home to a minimum so that the batteries will store electricity for approximately three days if the wind isn't blowing and the sun is not shining. Note: The design takes into account energy throughout the entire process, from construction to maintenance and operation of the home.

An average U.S. house in 1996 used approximately 100 million Btu's of energy to construct. This figure is very large and can be substantially reduced by using natural materials and techniques that would use less resources.

*Used in Earth Home

NEEDS (Earth Home seeks to satisfy these)	WANTS
SHELTER protection from animals protection from rain, etc. protection from lightning protection from fire cool from heat heat from cold lights from darkness sleeping area shelter maintenance CLOTHES protection from elements clothes maintenance FOOD methods of securing (growing) methods of preparation methods of storage WATER drinking water cooking water washing water method of heating water methods of washing dishes clothes shelter self hair	TRANSPORTATION (needs when traveling) SOCIAL ORGANIZATION (politics) LONG RANGE COMMUNICATION EDUCATION LEISURE ENTERTAINMENT (arts, crafts, theater, music, recreation, sports) HOBBIES HEALTH CARE (major)

Figure 1-NEEDS/WANTS LIST

*Used in Earth Home

f. Food-Independent

The home fulfills the requirements of a food producer, in that the entire south side is used as a plant growing area with an attached animal protein/fish area on the west side. This area in combination with a small exterior garden is designed to produce all the needed food for a family of four. Again, it does this by a combination of producing food and modifying the needs of a family. (See Chapters on Food) Salt that a family needs cannot be generated; however, studies are underway on the kinds of recycling that can be done with salt already inside the system.

g. Simple

Simple is beautiful, and it has always been a quality that's good to design into any piece of equipment. The more complex it gets, the more chances for it to break down. Keep It Simple, Stupid (KISS) is a designer's "buzz" word.

h. Durable

1. Storm- and Earthquake-Resistant

Very few people on this planet are working on homes that resist fire, storms, high winds, earthquakes, bullets, bombs, and any other disruptive influence on a home. The increased cost of any such home might be prohibitive. The Earth Home is meant to be resistant to all of the above activities to some degree. These natural and man-made disasters will be taken into account when designing the Earth Home—and intended to make it as good or better than any other popular building style or combination of materials.

2. Low Maintenance

The home is designed to last over 100 years. In Europe the typical design life is closer to 300 years. The components are meant to last from 20 to 100 years-depending on the type. Maintenance of the home is a prime consideration in the total cost of a home. For example, the exterior skin is ferrocement (a reinforced cement), so that it needs very little maintenance. The Earth Home is also designed to be user- maintained with simple hand tools, enabling a person to be able to repair almost anything that breaks. (See also Maintenance section)

i. Non-Polluting

The word "recycling" is being used more and more. This home uses recycling as a central theme to its design. Wastewater is to be recycled using an aerobic digester. The heat and even the smoke (sub-micron aerosols) from the wood burning stove are designed to be recycled by a "scrubber system" as technology becomes available.

j. Single-Family/Adaptable to Communities

The Earth Home is designed around four people (two adults and two children) but it can be modified to accommodate more or fewer people. It can be used as a model for housing larger numbers of people, such as family groups or small communities. The design of the Earth Home should lend itself easily to larger units.

k. Universal

This home is designed to be used anywhere -- the desert, mountains, north country, and coastline cities -- regardless of the climate. Slight modifications in design would enable the home to be used anywhere on the planet (or even on a craft on the ocean). Living in Minnesota with temperature extremes and four climates assisted testing greatly. The materials from which the Earth Home is constructed were chosen for their universal availability (cement, steel, wood). Renewable materials, renewable technologies, low energy technologies, and organic materials were stressed in the design.

*Used in Earth Home

l. Minimal Existence

I designed the Earth Home, not around the frills of 21st century life, but on a combination of the minimal existence of the 18th and 19th centuries, and most of the comforts of 20th century living. It is need oriented, not want driven, as are many of our products and lifestyles in the 20th century. A basic healthy diet and basic comforts are first and foremost.

m. Living System

I believe a complete system approach is necessary in order to succeed. In this endeavor I don't believe a typical 20th century home could be retrofitted with all the qualities of the Earth Home. However, if the occupants decided to change the Earth Home into a typical 20th century home, they would have the capability to do so themselves.

n. Built in the Image of Nature

I feel that nature is our best example of how to live on this planet. For example, the deer bends over high grass and lies down, thus insulating them from the cold of the ground. "Nature's way" is the common sense, logical approach. I intended to copy nature as much as possible in the design. Traditional homes are designed to be in opposition to nature, and a lot of our current technology is not Earth-compatible. This home is designed to be a low cost home. I am trying to keep the price of this home below $150,000 in 2005 U.S. dollars. This is designed to be a home for the masses, similar to the Model T Ford of the early 1900's. Also, building materials were selected to minimize the following environmental impact:

- Energy and water use
- Ozone depletion
- Natural resource depletion
- Manufacturing emissions
- Total energy to produce, transport, install and disposal at the end of life
- Off-gassed emissions

It is interesting to note that to manufacture a solar collector requires more energy that the collector can gather in 6 ½ years!

C. World Issues Driving the Project

Why set a goal to design and develop a mass-producible home that produces all the food and power for a family of four?

1. Unproven Theory.

It has never been accomplished before and I feel that it is possible. Throughout history, the first step to any goal is to get a clear vision of the end result and gradually work toward that end. This goal was set on March 3, 1975 and I had just completed a goal that took me 18 months to accomplish. I had had an interest in the area of alternative technology and a suitable background. ***In the United States there are some housing styles that approach self-sufficiency, such as the attached greenhouse, the envelope home, and the solar home of the mid-1970's***. I felt that making a home 100% self-sufficient would be a lifetime goal. A small goal would be accomplished quickly, but a massive goal would test the limits of my capabilities. In the event that I didn't accomplish the goal, it would keep me occupied for the rest of my life. I remember the saying "Don't gamble if you cannot afford to lose!" I felt and still feel that even if the project never comes to fruition, I will have put my lifetime effort into a worthy cause.

*Used in Earth Home

2. Energy and Resource Conservation.

a. Pollution Reduction

Buildings, not cars, are the major damagers of the Earth. Pollution from the heating and cooling of buildings exceeds that from cars, even in the U.S. The pollution happens at the power plant and where the materials are made. The construction sector of the economy is huge. After agriculture, construction is the second largest industry in the world.

b. Energy Use Reduction

In the United States, approximately 20-30% ***of all energy is consumed in the home***. Space heating and hot water is around 14% alone. If you add food processing, clothing industries, house maintenance, and construction energy, the ***figure climbs to around 60%***. This is the lion's share of the entire United States energy requirement, and we use the lion's share of the world's energy. Even though Americans make up only 4.5% of the world population, we consume five times the world's average per capita in energy! And another statistic is that, according to the World Watch institute, buildings account for one fourth of the world's wood harvest, two fifths of its material and energy usage, and one sixth of its fresh water usage. This is a lot of resources!

So by targeting the largest users of energy and resources in the entire world, I would have a maximum impact on society and future generations. Note that there is a difference between simply making more and conserving what we have. Energy can be either conserved or generated. The total cost of conserving-energy technologies are usually less expensive than energy-generating technologies. Also it is commonly believed that in order to achieve very energy-efficient buildings, it is necessary to adopt a "house as a system" approach.

c. Garbage Reduction/Plastic-Based Litter

It is no secret that we are amassing tremendous amounts of garbage that is filling our landfills at an alarming rate. Simply dealing with the mountains of trash is a significant portion of the tasks of cities. Plastic-based litter is being found in the world's oceans and in virtually all terrains.

d. Wood Scarcity

1. Staggering Statistics

One of the worst problems for 2-3 billion people on the world is cooking on wood fires. Half of humanity cooks over wood fires—the poorer half. Nearly half the world's wood supply is used as fuel. More than 2 billion people are facing fuelwood shortages. Forests in the developing countries are shrinking by more than 15 million hectares a year. The ratio of forests-to-people is less than half what it was in 1960. For most, there's little alternative to burning wood.

2. Sustainability Issue

Woodstoves cook slowly, the smoke causes glaucoma and lung diseases for the women and children, the children get burned in the fire, and they burn much too much fuel that must be gathered from greater and greater distances. At this rate of consumption, it's not sustainable. Most wood fires and cooking stoves are also very inefficient.

3. Health Issues of Wood Cookstoves

Indoor smoke pollution now ranks 8th in health burden worldwide (lost years of healthy life), and ranks fourth in the "least-developed" countries (which make up about 40% of the world population) according to the World Health Organization's World Health Report 2002.

*Used in Earth Home

Smoke in the home from cooking on wood, dung and crop waste kills nearly one million children a year. The total annual death toll is 1.6 million—a life lost every 20 seconds. Acute respiratory infections, ear and eye problems, breathlessness, chest pains, headaches and giddiness are just some of the symptoms that poor woman and children suffer in their rural homes.

3. Economic Reasons.

I have always felt that a home should be more to a family than just a pretty heated box. I felt that the amount of money that an average person pays for a home should be a benefit for the present and an investment for the future. It should be a home that works for you. The trend in the United States has been toward a two-income family, which was a gradual departure from the one-income family of the 1960's and 70's. ***I feel that the two-income trend can be reversed***. I believe that this technology will begin to reverse that trend, so that a smaller amount of household income will be necessary to maintain a home and a family.

4. Soil Problems around the World.

a. Desertification

I feel that if Earth Homes were to proliferate over the world, it would slow the amount of pollution from our industries. It is estimated that the annual global loss to desertification is an area about the size of the state of Maine. Our planet is drying up and the soil quality is deteriorating. Of the one-ninth of the earth's land was considered arable in 1900, little remains healthy: most is stressed and losses are accelerating.

b. Salinization

As rocks and soils are worn away by the effect of water, small amounts of the mineral salts they contain are carried into rivers and aquifers, and therefore into irrigation water. If either too little water or too much water is applied to the crops, salt will remain on the soil.

Salinization can reduce yields in the early stages and eventually lead to the destruction of fertility in the soil. Although salinization can be improved, there is no economical way to remove the salt from soil. The Food and Agriculture Organization of the UN estimates that steady increase in soil salinity is reducing the world's irrigated area by 1-2 percent every year or roughly 3 hectares per minute.

c. Soil Compaction

Soil compaction is also a problem, because plants constantly break down organic matter. The soil particle size gets smaller, actually compacting the soil. Organic humus of unplanted soil is loose and spongy, thus resisting compaction.

d. Erosion

Soil erosion is a problem caused by the effects of weather upon the soil. Some people view the soil of the world as a never-ending commodity. It is, however, a finite substance, and the quality is variable.

*Used in Earth Home

You can notice soil erosion when driving through the countryside, especially after a rain or after the soil has been plowed. The tops of the hills appear lighter in color than the valleys. The humus and the decayed plant matter are washed from the top of the hills into the valleys. Farmers typically spread fertilizer mainly on the high spots in their fields.

A third of the original topsoil in the United States is now gone. It is estimated that the world has from 50 to 100 years of farmable soil, using current farming practices.

e. Soil Depletion

Of the sixteen or more elements that are essential for plant growth, only three are commonly put back (Nitrogen, Phosphorous, and Potassium or NPK). Plants that are grown on the same soil over the last 30 or more years have experienced a drop in the mineral level. This depletion can take as little as 10 years and be significant enough to cause errors in the Composition of Foods Chart first published in 1948 and updated in 1963. (See VII. Diets and Foods-Nutritional Information Section) The soil is depleted of selenium in most parts of the country, and often only marginal levels of zinc, magnesium, calcium, and other minerals. The Earth Summit Report in 1992 said that the levels of soil-based minerals in North America have dropped 85% in the last 100 years.

f. Stopping Use of Hydrated Lime

About the turn of the century, we created machines that could grind limestone to a small enough particle size so that it was effective in adjusting the pH of our farm soils. Because it was cheaper than "burnt" lime, government agents recommended it over the chemical burnt lime (calcium oxide and calcium hydroxide). Limestone will adjust the pH, but has no effect on the soil particle structure or does it have any disinfecting action, as does hydrated lime (calcium hydroxide).

Hydrated lime (both dolomitic and high calcium), agglomerate the clay soil particles, improving the tilth (breathing) of the soil. Because of the larger particle size and elimination of the "hard pan", the soil is less likely to erode-both from water and air. The particles are sand size instead of dust size. Thus the larger particle size helps to prevent air erosion, and spread of the pathogens. It also absorbs water to a greater extent. The disinfecting action on virus, bacteria, fungus, and the supply of calcium and magnesium nutrients, all have a beneficial effect in achieving a natural balance to the soil.

g. Irrigated Land Decrease

Irrigated land comprises only about 16% of the world's cropland, but contributes about 40% of the world's food production. In the 1980's, as major rivers began to run dry for parts of the year, and most of the best sites for dams and reservoirs were already developed, the per capita net world irrigated area began to shrink for the first time in modern times.

h. "Modern Agriculture"

"Modern agriculture" is at present based on the intensive use of industrial inputs (chemical fertilizers, pesticides, machinery), non-renewable energy sources and "high-yield varieties" of agricultural crops. The complete "artificialization" of nature in the attempt to control all factors influencing farm production has led to the over-exploitation of resources and hence degradation of former high potential land.

The negative ecological impact of such agricultural industries (large farmers) focusing on monoculture crops for export and high-income markets has been near catastrophic and the horrendous costs resulting have never been born by those who caused them. Hundreds of millions of hectares of fertile land have been degraded and rivers and water reservoirs polluted with chemical wastes. In India alone, 160 million hectares (i. e. ten times the area of arable land in Germany) are so severely degraded that they cannot be used for food or feed production.

5. Increasing the Total Food Supply.

a. World Hunger

More than half the world's present 6 billion people live in perpetual hunger! 40,000 children starve to death each and every day. 60 million people will starve to death this year. Eight hundred million people do not have enough food to eat. If we were suddenly to join the less fortunate, our next meal would be a small bowl of rice and perhaps a piece of fish an inch square the day after tomorrow.

Scientists have categorized the global food situation by separating the issues into food shortage, food poverty, and food deprivation. Food shortages occur when total food supplies within a designated area are insufficient to meet the needs of its population. Food poverty refers to the situation in which households cannot obtain enough food to meet the needs of all their members. The last category is food deprivation that means inadequate individual consumption of food or specific nutrients. This can also be termed undernutrition. Studies indicate that in 1992, there was enough food in the world to feed all inhabitants *if* they were vegetarian. The global food situation is, however, much more complex and interconnected than most people realize.

b. World Food Production

Of the 160 or so nations of the entire world, 140 of these are dependent on North American grain exports. There are only four food grain exporters in the world -- United States, Canada, Argentina, and Australia. Over 23 billion bushels of corn is produced in the world and only 13 percent of the total production is exported. ***I feel that proliferation of the Earth Home technology would increase the food supply by making each family a producer of food, rather than having a single American farmer produce food for some 400 people.***

Over the next 30 years, as weather patterns continue to destabilize due to global warming, population adds another few billion to the planet, and oil supplies begin to lag behind demand, an ability to grow, forage and hunt for one's own food may become increasingly important. If long-term disruptions in central services ever occur, a stored supply of food and the ability to generate more food will be of utmost importance.

c. Food Distribution

Even in the U.S. there is only about three weeks' supply of food in supermarkets and food stores. Grain stocks have been down to 62 days of consumption.

Most foods do not store well-even peanut butter, popcorn, and sunflower seeds go bad after a few years or so. Only a couple canned foods—beef stew and tuna--last 5 years or longer. The emergency preparedness/survival companies advise the optimal conditions to store food, but it is difficult to keep food very long under average conditions.

6. Slow Down Climate Changes.

a. Plants/Animals Reduction

It is estimated that approximately 200 species of plants and animals become extinct each year, never to be seen again.

b. Ocean Changes

It is also estimated that an approximate 4°C rise in the ocean temperature would virtually eliminate commercial fishing, because of the dependence of the fish on the lower forms of life, which cannot exist in a warmer ocean. El Nino is a good example.

*Used in Earth Home

The oceans of the world have started so-called "dead zones". There are about 150 areas off inhabited coasts that are formed from fertilizer, sewage, and vehicle emission runoff. This nitrogen triggers the proliferation of plankton, which in turn depletes oxygen in the water. Some fish might flee this suffocation but slow moving, bottom-dwelling creatures like clams, lobsters, and oysters are less likely to escape.

The world now gets approximately 17 percent of its animal protein from fish according to the UN. Commercial overfishing and bottom trawling is endangering this supply.

c. Aquifer Depletion

Also, the entire world's aquifers (underground water supplies) are being depleted rapidly. (The aquifers are also being polluted by chemical waste dumps and toxic contaminants of various kinds.) Africa is a good example of the drought conditions due to the lowering of the water table. As of 1993, Africa has experienced an almost continuous drought for seven years. Some eighty countries are experiencing water shortages enough to threaten agriculture, such as northern China, southern India, Pakistan, Zimbabwe, Mauritania, and Mexico. The western U.S. including California's water supply is also critically low. (See also Drinking Water Quality Section)

In the Earth Home System, most of the wastes and water are recycled for further use, so the drain upon the existing water supply would be much less.

d. Global Warming Issues

1. Temperature Extremes and Results

Approximately 30,000 Europeans died from record heat in one summer, some of the worst heat in over 500 years. The Midwestern heat wave of 1995 killed 669 people in Chicago. The 1996 and 1997 season of record heat spells, extreme rainfall and drought, Caribbean hurricanes, and winter storms are signals that we must act on the results of climate change.

With record-high temperatures throughout the south during the summer of 1998, Disney World had to shut down its water parks because of the threat of a viral encephalitis outbreak. Global warming is creating a breeding ground for diseases. (See Increased Health section)

2. Overview of Global Warming/Predictions

Global warming is another critical environmental problem. The book, Global Warming: The Greenpeace Report, by Jeremy Leggert, is a very knowledgeable book in the area of environmental problems. After reading this book, UK Prime Minister Margaret Thatcher said of it:

"We have an authoritative early warning system, an agreed assessment of some 300 of the world's leading scientists of what is happening to the world's climate. A report of historic significance, what it predicts will affect our daily lives."

This report is an extensive compilation of studies regarding the environment of the planet. The book goes on to say that many scientists agree that the emissions resulting from ***human activities are substantially increasing the atmospheric concentration of the greenhouse gasses***. These increases will enhance the greenhouse effect, resulting in warming of the Earth's surface. In 1990, the scientists predicted that, if greenhouse gas emissions are not sharply decreased, we might experience a 1°C to 3°C rise in global temperatures. This temperature increase is predicted to occur between the year 2030 and the turn of the next century, 2100.

3. Global Temperature Changes Statistics/History

The ten hottest years in recorded history have all been in the last 15 years! The 1990's were the hottest decade on record! 1997 was the warmest year on record until 1998 shattered global temperature records! 2005 repeated 1998 records as well and 2002 and 2003 coming in second and third. We recently now know that ***the***

three warmest years on record have come in the last five years. The temperature is rising and that the rise is gaining momentum.

There is a decrease in the amount of snow that covers the northern hemisphere, a simultaneous decrease in Arctic Sea ice, continued melting of alpine glaciers, and a rise in sea level--all consistent with global warming. Rain has even been reported for the first time in Antarctica and an ice-free patch of ocean about a mile wide has recently opened near the North Pole! The continued ice melt may make the Northwest Passage a reality.

The following figure estimates the amount of temperature rise that will be experienced shortly after the turn of this century. We have recorded instances of global temperature changes of less than 1°C. During 1816, the average global temperature was less than 1°C below today's average. There were frosts in June as far south as New England, and disastrous crop failures. ***Thus, we have some historical indication of what a slight global temperature change will bring about***. I feel that many of the results of this imbalance are being felt in our climate today. I feel that our climate swings, record-breaking temperatures, and unpredictable weather are all a direct result of human activities.

4. Greenhouse Gasses

The author/scientists suggest(s) that we, as a species, must reduce our emissions of greenhouse gasses to about 60% of today's concentration. Basically, we will have to cut in half our use of coal, oil, and gas to maintain the concentration of greenhouse gasses at today's level. In 2004, the National Center for Atmospheric Research revised estimated global warming to 4.7 degrees instead of 3.6 degrees in the coming century. When will the next revision occur?

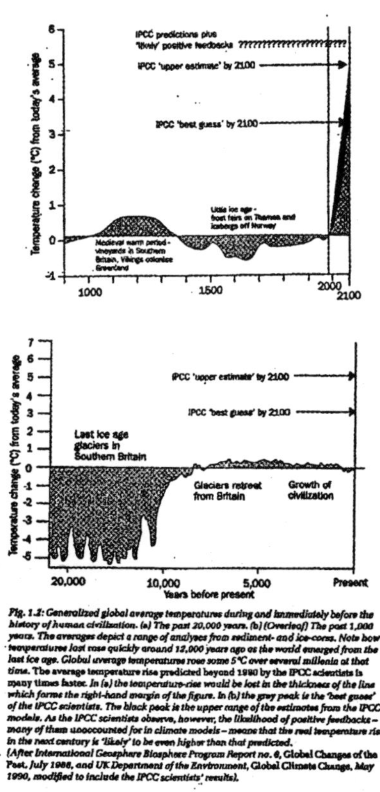

Fig. 1.2: Generalized global average temperatures during and immediately before the history of human civilization. (a) The past 20,000 years. (b) (Overleaf) The past 1,000 years. The averages depict a range of analyses from sediment- and ice-cores. Note how temperatures last rose quickly around 12,000 years ago as the world emerged from the last ice age. Global average temperatures rose some 5°C over several millenia at that time. The average temperature rise predicted beyond 1990 by the IPCC scientists is many times faster. In (a) the temperature-rise would be lost in the thickness of the line which forms the right-hand margin of the figure. In (b) the grey peak is the 'best guess' of the IPCC scientists. The black peak is the upper range of the estimates from the IPCC models. As the IPCC scientists observe, however, the likelihood of positive feedbacks – many of them unaccounted for in climate models – means that the real temperature rise in the next century is 'likely' to be even higher than that predicted.
(After International Geosphere Biosphere Program Report no. 6, Global Changes of the Past, July 1988, and UK Department of the Environment, Global Climate Change, May 1990, modified to include the IPCC scientists' results).

Figure 2-GLOBAL TEMPERATURE THROUGH HISTORY

*Used in Earth Home

5. Melting Permafrost

Any rock or soil remaining at or below 0 degrees C for two or more years is permafrost. Permafrost can contain over 30 percent ice or practically no ice at all. About 14 percent of the world's carbon is stored in Arctic lands. There is emerging evidence that this ancient carbon is starting to be released as rising temperatures cause the permafrost to melt and its organic material to be broken down by bacteria. There has already impacted roads, buildings, pipelines, and other infrastructure occurring in Arctic areas like Alaska and Siberia as a direct result of decades of climate change. The following figure illustrates this graphically.

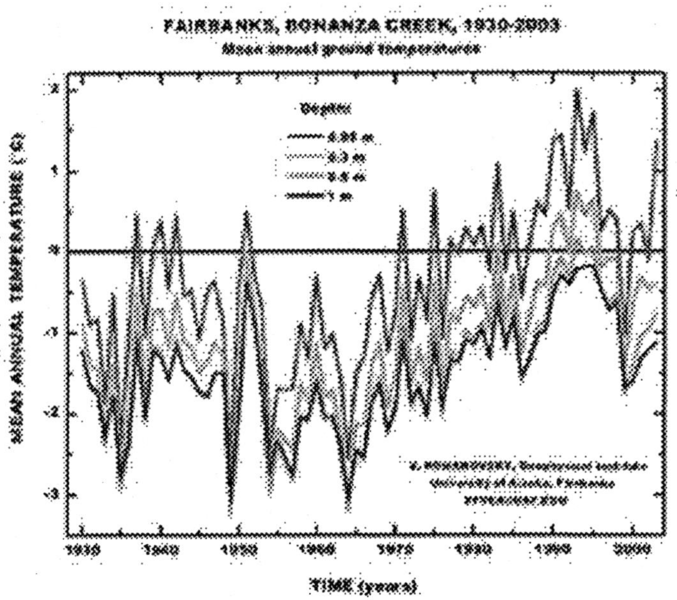

Figure 3-PERMAFROST TEMPERATURES

e. Carbon Dioxide Concentration

Besides temperature, carbon dioxide and ozone are also indications of climatic change. The following figure shows that the carbon dioxide concentration in our atmosphere has been increasing almost linearly since 1958. Even though the rate of emissions from fossil fuels has been reduced, there is a consistent rise in CO_2 concentration. Over the last 200 years or so, levels of carbon dioxide in Earth's atmosphere have risen from about 280 parts per million to over 360 parts per million.

In 2005, carbon dioxide density hovered around 379 parts per million as compared with about 376 just one year ago. That year-to-year increase of about 3 parts per million is considerably higher than the average annual increase of 1.8 parts per million over the past decade, and markedly more accelerated than the 1-part-per-million annual increase recorded a half-century ago, when observations were first made. It is thought by a number of scientists that significant fuel burning in China and India is largely responsible.

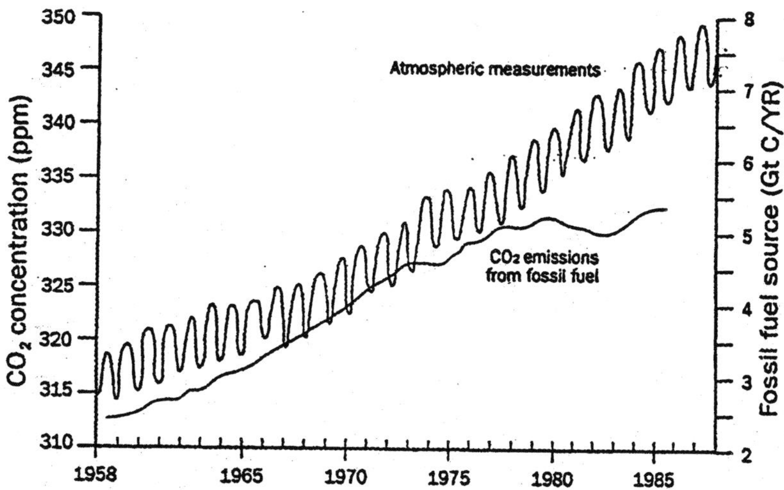

Fig. 1.4. Atmospheric CO_2 concentrations (as measured at Mauna Loa, Hawaii, since 1958). They have increased more or less linearly. Note how the CO_2 emissions from fossil fuels increased less rapidly after the oil-price hike in the early 1970s, yet the concentration of CO_2 in the atmosphere has continued its steep rise. This could be due to an escalation of tropical deforestation, or release of carbon dioxide from soils warmed by the removal of forest cover, or possibly a decreasing ability of the oceans to draw down CO_2 from the atmosphere, or a combination of factors. Note also the annual expression in the data of seasonal changes in photosynthesis and respiration.
Source: *D. A. Lashof and D. A. Tirpak (eds.),* Policy Options for Stabilizing Global Climate *(US Environmental Protection Agency, 1989).*

Figure 4-ATMOSPHERIC CO_2 CONCENTRATION

f. Ozone Thinning

Also, the rate of ozone depletion has recently been reported to be twice the previous estimate. The following figure shows how the ozone has thinned in one location. In the U.S., between a third and a half of all cancers are skin cancers. Studies show that a 1% decrease in ozone in the stratosphere produces a 2% increase in ultraviolet radiation reaching the ground. Some authors have suggested that the effect on the aquatic food chain, fish production--especially in the southern oceans, and oxygen output from the ocean could dwarf the risks to human health. The ozone hole in Antarctica doubled in size in 1995 to the size of Europe! NASA has measured 40% ozone depletion over the Arctic in March-April of 1987. Studies on the effects of increased UV (ultraviolet) radiation on plants have only gone as high as 25% above normal. Sensitive crops include cotton, peas, soybeans, cabbages, and many species of trees and grasses.

*Used in Earth Home

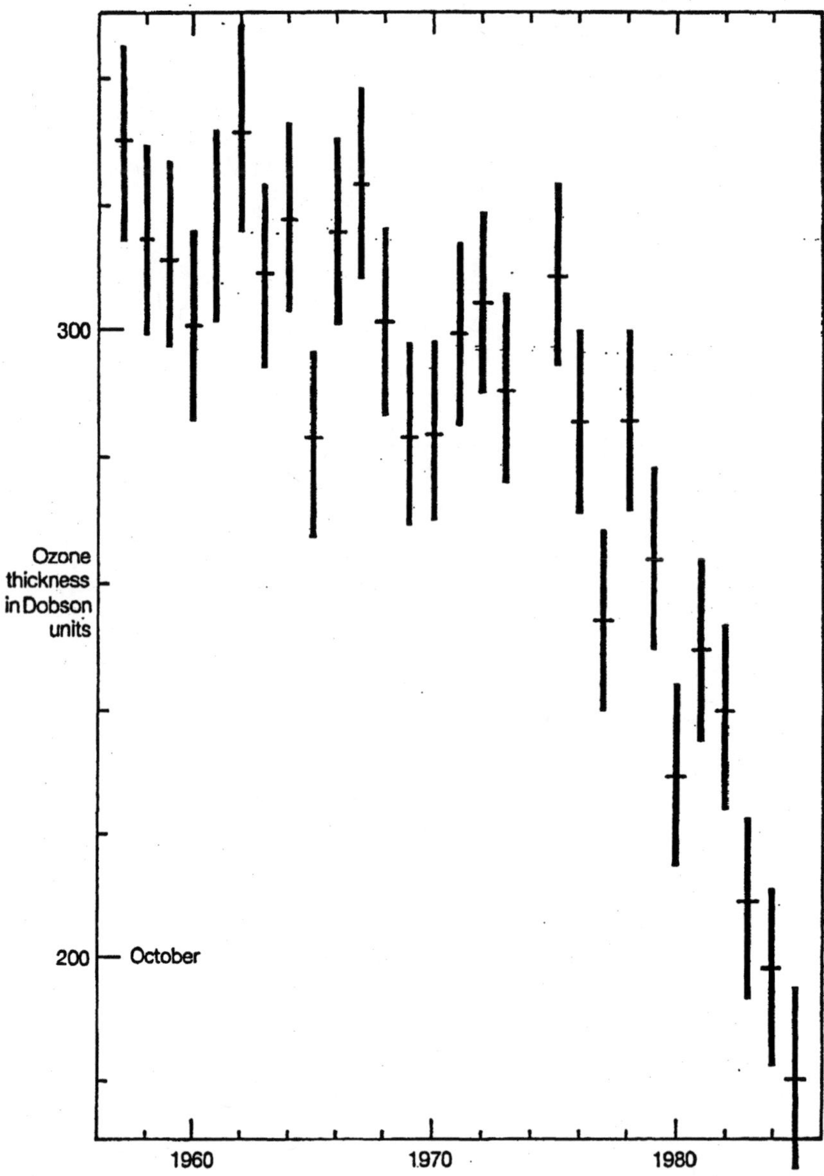

Formation of the ozone hole. Data on the thickness of the ozone layer over Halley Bay in Antarctica each October, as plotted by Farman and published in 1985.

Figure 5-OZONE THINNING

*Used in Earth Home

g. Weather-Related Changes/Issues

1. Overview

In 2002, unusual weather is blamed for 9,400 deaths and $56 billion in damage, according to the United Nations and insurers. As the costs of weather-related disasters rise, unease about climate change rises, also. Many people are starting to realize that we live in a changing world and that these changes may not be cyclical as many have believed. Some believe that unusual and extreme weather may be a permanent part of life on earth.

2. Hurricanes/Tornados

In the U.S. during May 2003 a record 562 tornadoes formed over the Midwest. Hurricanes Katrina and others have severely ravaged the southern states in 2005. There is an increase in frequency of hurricanes worldwide.

3. Floods

In 2005, Central and Eastern Europe have been hit by a deluge of rain, causing widespread flooding, many casualties, and severe structural damage. The state of Bavaria, in southern Germany is one of the worst affected areas. Flood defenses have been washed away after the Danube burst its banks, submerging last areas of flood plain, turning roads into rivers and inundating homes across the region.

4. Droughts/Heat

As of 2004, the western U.S. is entering a sixth year of extreme drought. Portugal and parts of the Mediterranean suffer the effects of one of the fiercest heatwaves on record.

7. Slow Down Pollution

a. Fertilizers and Pesticides

Excess use of fertilizers and pesticides have almost destroyed our environment. The Chesapeake Bay is almost dead, infested with fisteria; the Mississippi River has been declared dead due to excessive fertilizer and animal waste runoff. Many more lakes and rivers are endangered due to this runoff. (see also Soil Problems section)

A U.N. report estimates that some 2 million tons of waste per day are disposed of within waters. This waste includes industrial trash and chemicals, human waste, and agricultural runoff, such as fertilizers, pesticides, and pesticide residue. The U.N. also estimates that 50 percent of the population of developing countries depends on polluted water sources.

b. Dead Zones in Oceans

Each year a swath of the Gulf of Mexico becomes so devoid of shrimp, fish, and other marine life that it is known as the dead zone. Scientists have identified agricultural fertilizers as a primary culprit behind the phenomenon. The dead zone forms each April and generally grows throughout the summer, reaching a peak in late July. At its peak, the nearly lifeless water can span 5,000 to 8,000-plus square miles (13,000 to 21,000 square kilometers), an area almost the size of New Jersey.

The nutrients that flow into the Gulf of Mexico allow microscopic organisms called phytoplankton to bloom. When these algae die, they sink to the bottom of the ocean. There, they are decomposed by oxygen-consuming bacteria. In the process, the bacteria consume most of the surrounding waterborne oxygen, leaving little oxygen for the other life-forms that depend on it.

Fish, shrimp, and all other marine organisms that require oxygen to survive either flee the zone or die. The phenomenon is triggered by excess nutrients in the Mississippi and Atchafalaya River Basins. The main source of excess nutrients is agricultural runoff, namely chemical fertilizers and animal manure. Nitrogen and phosphorus also come from human waste, via wastewater treatment plants and septic systems; domestic animal waste; and industrial sources. Additional nutrient sources include power plants, cars, and agricultural and industrial ammonia emissions.

Dead zones are not unique to the Gulf of Mexico. There is evidence for more than a hundred dead zones worldwide. They range in size from 0.3 to 26,000-plus square miles (1 to 70,000-plus square kilometers). In the U.S. these oxygen-depleted zones develop annually in western Long Island Sound off New York and Connecticut, the Chesapeake Bay off Maryland and Virginia, and the Neuse River in North Carolina. Dead zones are also found in the North, Adriatic, Baltic and Black Seas and Japan's Seto Inland Sea.

I believe that a proliferation of Earth Homes will begin to revolutionize the impact of food production on the environment, and slow this environmental damage.

8. Increased Human Health.

a. Malnutrition Background

It has been said that there is only one major disease, and that is malnutrition. Some say that all ailments and afflictions that we inherit are directly traceable to this major disease. There are also many scientific studies that deal with diet-related health problems in the U.S. To sum up, they say that heart disease has now reached epidemic proportions-claiming half of all men over forty. Cancer takes one third, and arthritis plagues 97% of all adults. 32 million Americans are overweight and a majority has defective vision and decayed teeth. Americans spend the most money on health care, yet ranks 16th in the world in life expectancy. (see A Note on Modern Medicine section)

b. Spread of Old Diseases

Malaria, once thought of as a strictly tropical disease, has been reported as far north as New York, New Jersey, and Michigan. Malaria now kills 2 million people worldwide every year. More mosquito-borne tropical diseases are occurring in the northern United States. In the summer of 2000, West Nile fever, a rare and encephalitic virus that is endemic in parts of the Middle East, Asia, and Africa, was linked to the encephalitic deaths of four people in the state of New York. Dengue fever, Hantavirus, and viral encephalitis are also more common.

c. "Transporting" Infectious Diseases

We are seeing a tremendous outbreak of old and new diseases throughout the world, with diseases that were under control, rebounding with biocidal resistant strains. These outbreaks are disturbing as more and more medicines seem to no longer work. The underlying fear is that we will experience a world wide epidemic of a size and virulence, previously unknown. This is mainly due to the quick transportation of infected persons and animals throughout the world. Many infected persons, animals and insects can be transported and infect others long before they are determined to be sick.

d. New Ailments/Pandemics

History also shows an increase in the number of "new ailments" that have surfaced, such as Reyes syndrome, Lyme disease, Legionnaire's disease, AIDS, herpes genitalis, Ebola filovirus, Marburg, Machupo, Lassa, swine flu, SARS, Foot and Mouth disease (FMD), mad cow disease (BSE), and the flesh-eating virus. Less contact with other humans would also help to lessen the danger of many infectious diseases.

In the 20th century, there have been three global flu pandemics. The first, the 1918 Spanish flu, was the worst. After World War I, it killed between 20 million and 40 million people. Milder outbreaks in 1956 and 1968 (Hong Kong flu) killed about 1 million each. All three times, a bird flu evolved a way to spread among humans. For decades, experts have predicted another outbreak. Birds can carry 15 known types of type A influenza, the most serious kind of flu virus.

History has shown that there have been 10 pandemics in the past 300 years. As of this printing, the bird/avian flu H5N1 is threatening to be the next pandemic. WHO says it is reasonable to prepare for 2 million to 7.4 million deaths.

e. Parasites

1. Parasites: The Problem

A recent nationwide survey conducted by the Centers for Disease Control in 1976 revealed that one in every six people selected at random had one or more parasites. An estimated 85-95% of North American adults had at least one parasite in them but don't know it. According to the World Health Organization, 3.5 billion people suffer from some type of parasitic infection. Numerous studies say that nearly 85% of Americans have parasites in their bodies.

Projections for the year 2025 suggest that more than half of the 8.3 billion people on Earth will then be infected with parasitic diseases. Worms may be the most toxic agents in the human body. They are one of the primary underlying causes of disease and are the most basic cause of a compromised immune systems.

Tests often do not show the presence of parasites because the testing procedures are by and large outdated and inadequate. Parasites are a serious public health threat and there are few people who talk about them.

2. Spreading Parasites:

Some of the possible reasons for the rising number of parasitic infections include:

1) Rise in international travel.
2) Contamination of municipal and rural water supplies.
3) Increasing use of day-care centers.
4) Influx of refugee and immigrant populations from endemic areas.
5) Return of armed forces from overseas.
6) Continued popularity of household pets.
7) Increasing popularity of exotic regional foods.
8) Use of antibiotics and immunosuppressive drugs.

There are 4 basic methods through which we can get infected:

--Via food or water which are sources of the roundworm, amoebae, giardia.
--Via a vector - the mosquito is a carrier of dog heartworm, filaria, malaria; the flea is a carrier of dog tapeworm; the common housefly transmits amebic cysts; the sand fly carries leishmaniasis.
--Via sexual contact where partners can transmit trichomonas, giardia, amoebae.
--Through the nose and skin where pinworm eggs and Toxoplasma gondii can be inhaled from contaminated dust, hookworms, schistosomes, and strongyloides can penetrate exposed skin and bare feet.
--Airplanes/Extensive international travel has exposed people to a whole range of exotic diseases never before encountered in their homeland.

*Used in Earth Home

3. Parasitic Symptoms

-Feel tired most of the time (Chronic Fatigue)?
-Have digestive problems? (gas, bloating, constipation or diarrhea which come and go but never really clear up)
-Have gastrointestinal symptoms and bulky stools with excess fat in feces?
Suffer with food sensitivities and environmental intolerance?
-Developed allergic-like reactions and can't understand why?
-Have joint and muscle pains and inflammation often assumed to be arthritis?
-Suffer with anemia or iron deficiency (pernicious anemia)?
-Have hives, rashes, weeping eczema, cutaneous ulcers, swelling, sores, papular lesions, itchy dermatitis?
-Suffer with restlessness and anxiety?
-Experience multiple awakenings during the night?
-Grind your teeth?
-Have an excessive amount of bacterial or viral infections?
-Depressed?
-Difficulty gaining or losing weight no matter what you do?
-Did a candida program which either didn't help at all or helped somewhat but you still can't stay away from bread, alcohol, fruit, or fruit juices?
-Just can't figure out why you don't feel really great and neither can your doctor?

Some medical experts believe that every patient with disorders of immune functions, including multiple allergies (especially food allergy), and patients with unexplained fatigue or with chronic bowel symptoms should be evaluated for the presence of intestinal parasites.

4. Definition and Testing for Parasites

A parasite is an organism which lives off the host, the host being you or me. The parasite lives a parallel life inside our bodies, feeding off either our own energy, our own cells or the food we eat. The nature of a parasite is to not make itself known. A smart parasite lives without being detected because if it is detected, of course, something is going to be done to eradicate it. Parasites are "clever" in their ability to survive and reproduce, which is of course, the purpose of any organism on this planet. Parasites can occur anywhere in your body. No organ is immune from their infestation.

Unfortunately medical testing procedures only catch about 20% of the actual cases of parasites.
There exist over 1,000 species of parasites which can live in your body, however tests are available for approximately 40 to 50 types. This means physicians are only testing for about 5% of the parasites and missing 80% of those which are present. This brings the ability to clinically find parasites down to 1 %.

How, then, do you determine whether or not you have parasites? In order to understand how to make this determination, you have to understand what a parasite does. A parasite eats, lays eggs and secretes. Depending on the kind, parasites will eat different things. Some parasites love sugar, for instance. If you are a person who craves sugar, you may have a sugar loving parasite. These parasites live off the food that goes into your body. They exist mainly in the digestive tract, but can also be found in the liver, as well as throughout the body.

Other parasites actually get their nutrition directly from the cells of the body. They can literally attach themselves anywhere and suck nutrients out of the cells. These parasites are significantly more dangerous because they can travel to areas in the body where they can do a lot more damage than a parasite living exclusively in the digestive tract.

The parasites eat your nutrients before you do! They grow healthy and fat, yet your organs and skin starve for nutrition. What's more, parasites can remain in your body for 10, 20 or even 30 years. This means you could have eaten meat 10 years ago that was contaminated and still be hosting the tapeworms or other types of parasites which were in that meat. Parasites also reproduce very quickly!

*Used in Earth Home

5. Categories of Parasites

There are two major categories of parasites: large parasites, which are primarily worms, and small parasites which are mainly microscopic in size, including what are called protozoa and amoebae. Parasites can be further categorized by junction. Some groupings of parasites include; Giardia, genital protozoa, nervous system protozoa, intestinal nematodes, liver & lung trematodes or flukes.

--Small Parasites
Despite their being almost invisible, small parasites can be dangerous. Microscopic parasites can get into your joints and eat the calcium linings of your bones. This can lead to arthritic tendencies. They can also eat the protein coating on your nerves (the myelin sheath) and this can cause a disruption in the nerve signal from the brain. One type of tiny parasite which infects the colon is called "Entamoeba Histolytica". This type of infection can also be found in the liver, the lungs, and the brain. The disease is called amebiasis, and is often transmitted via contaminated food or water.

The smaller parasites, the protozoas and amoebas, can function almost like bacteria by traveling through the bloodstream to virtually any part of the body. They reproduce without laying eggs and behave more like an infection in the body than do the larger parasites. The smaller parasites reproduce without the process of laying eggs—they reproduce by duplicating themselves in a manner similar to bacteria or viral reproduction.

--Large Parasites
Large parasites, which are the worm type, are usually large enough to be seen with the naked eye. Some can be up to 10 or even 15 inches long and in most cases cannot travel to other parts of the body, other than the digestive tract.

The larger parasites are worms which reproduce by laying eggs. Eggs are deposited into the intestinal tract, where they stick to the walls of the intestines. When the eggs hatch, the young feed on the food that we eat and eventually grow into adults. The adults then repeat this process. Some of the larger parasites include tapeworms, pinworms, :hookworms, roundworms, and threadworms.

6. The Dangers of Parasites

1) Parasites Secrete Toxins
All organisms secrete something, whether it be lubricants, waste materials, protective liquids for warding off viruses, bacteria and other harmful organisms, or secretions to help attract food. No matter what the secretion is--the secretion can be a toxin to the host organism. Simply put, the secretions from parasites into our bodies are poisons and toxins which our bodies are forced to deal with by increasing the process of detoxification. As anyone who has ever maintained an aquarium knows, ammonia is extremely toxic, yet it is one of the gases excreted by parasites living within human and animal hosts.

2) Strained Immune System
On the other end, a chronic parasitic infection secreting low levels of toxins can create an extremely strained immune system which may allow varied health problems to develop. When the immune system is strained over a long period of time, it of course, becomes weak. People with a weakened immune system tend to feel tired all the time. Some people refer to this as "Chronic Fatigue Syndrome".

When the immune system is weak, our bodies become susceptible to infections of all kinds. This can be an extremely dangerous situation in this day and age because we are exposed to more viruses than ever before. Also, they are changing and adapting at a very fast rate as are the bacteria, many of which are now resistant to antibiotics and other artificial measures which used to combat them.

3) Parasites Create Toxic Overload
If parasites secrete toxins into our bodies which our bodies need to neutralize, and we happen to be one of those people who drinks alcohol, smokes cigarettes, eats junk food and breathes polluted air, the extra stress and strain on the body's cleansing system can be enough to push the body into what we call toxic overload. Toxic overload

*Used in Earth Home

occurs when the 4 cleansing systems of the body have been pushed too far by an overload of toxins in the body. Parasite toxins in the body are one more thing a toxic body does not need.

7. Getting Rid of Parasites:

Once you've determined that you do have parasites, taking drugs to get rid of them may not always work. This is because a drug will often drive a parasite from one organ of the body to another. It's like people moving to better climates to make their living conditions more pleasant, or birds flying south for the winter.

Therapy to remove entire tapeworms from the small intestine is only successful if the whole worm is expelled. If the head remains, the entire worm will grow back.

f. Nutrition-Related Health Issues

Many books deal with fresh fruits, vegetables, and juices as "medicine" for the body. Studies have shown that vegetables and fruits start losing vitamins and minerals from the very moment they are picked, even though methods of cooking are used to ensure that they remain nutritious. ***I believe that food that is raised and eaten as close to fresh as possible is the best source of nutrition for human beings***—as well as a deterrent to disease and health-related problems. (See Nutrition Information-Industrialized Food Problems section and Vitamins/Minerals-Trace Minerals section)

g. Obesity

An estimated 31% of Americans are obese! The Amish people have an estimated obesity rate of around 4%. The generally accepted reason is their active lifestyle. They plant, harvest, maintain, prepare, and do many other manual chores around the home. Exercise is paramount to maintaining one's weight.

9. Moral/Religious Viewpoint.

I believe that we human beings are stewards of the Earth, and that it is our responsibility to give this Earth to future generations in the same or better condition than we received it. Another moral obligation we have is to help those less fortunate than ourselves. ***Approximately one-half of the world's 3 billion people have no fresh water to drink, and another one-third have no adequate food or housing***. Some people say that the poor will be with us forever. This may be true, but I believe that the developed nations of the world need to take a leadership role in ensuring that all people's basic needs are met. Confucius once said that ***"The strength of a nation is derived from the integrity of its homes."***

*Used in Earth Home

10. Population Issues.

The following figure shows the population of the Earth in the years 1900, 1950, 1970, and 2005 (projected). We see population growing exponentially. Simply due to this population explosion, ***there will be more of a burden upon the Earth in order to meet everyone's needs***. (The CO_2 increase closely correlates to the population growth curve.) In 1994, 88 million people were added to this planet! Globally over 800 million people suffer from malnutrition; with 7 million children under the age of five dying each year. As of 1999, there are over 6 billion human beings on the planet!

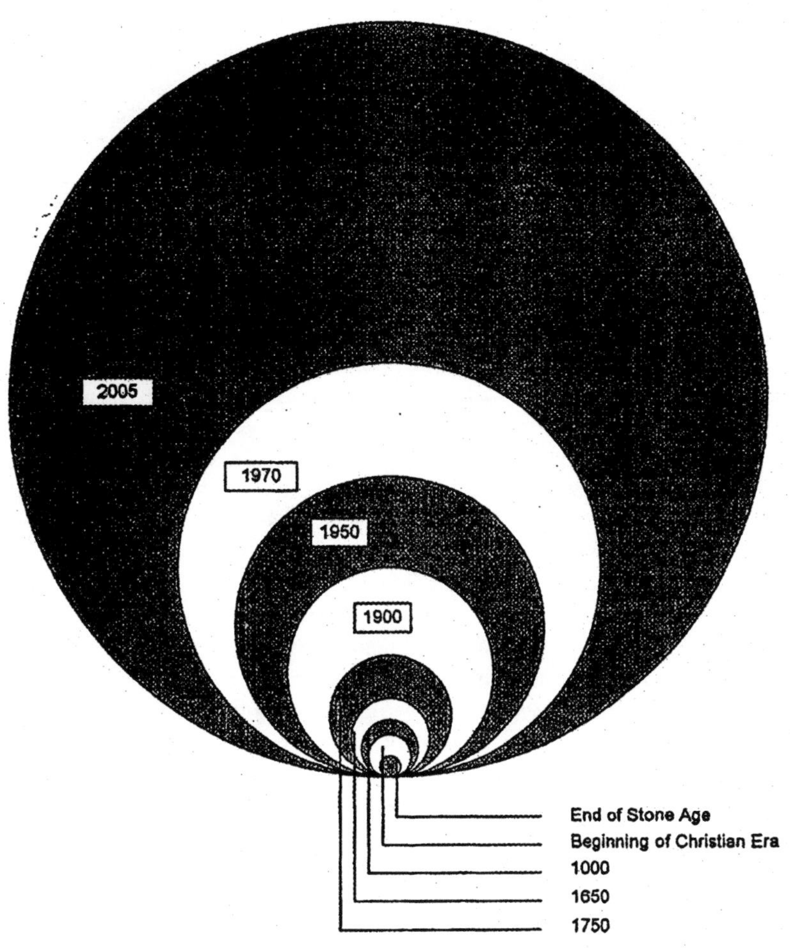

Figure 6-WORLD POPULATION GROWTH

*Used in Earth Home

11. World Security.

a. Wars

There are approximately 50 wars going on at any one time around the world—and the vast majority have religion as a major issue. I believe that because of this volatile situation, the entire Earth is at risk, especially due to the nature of the weapons that we human beings have developed. A saying goes, ***"We human beings have never built a weapon that we have not used against another human being."*** We are the only species that kills our own members for reasons other than to obtain food, territory, the opportunity to reproduce, or to protect offspring.

b. Oil Shortages

In 1975 we experienced an oil shortage that was potentially severe enough to cause a departure from the status quo in the United States. I feel that another such oil shortage could easily happen as a result of international political conflicts. To prevent continued dependence on oil, I think Earth Home technology should be developed. I don't think we should continue to spend 20 calories in petroleum energy to produce 1 calorie of food. The ecological and political balance of the world is much more fragile than most people think, and I believe humans are capable of tipping that very easily.

c. Natural Disasters

Add to this scenario the possibility of natural disasters such as volcanic activity and earthquakes that could drastically affect world security. ***It has been said that the only real security for people is self-sufficiency.*** There is a list of disasters requiring shelter that includes: chemical-biological warfare, conventional warfare, earthquake, explosions, fallout, fire, heat wave, high winds, home invasion, hurricane, meteor, local nuclear attack, nuclear power plant accidents, pole shift, power outage, terrorist attack, tornado, and winter storm. There seems to be no shortage of potential disasters for the planet.

d. Asteroid Strikes, Meteor Showers, Comets, Solar Flares

Some people think the greatest natural threat to the human species is impacts from outer space. Only in the last decade, once the dinosaur-killing asteroid was accepted as fact, have geologists taken impacts seriously. There is evidence from various ancient sources that whole civilizations have been destroyed by comets before the invention of writing. Noah's Flood and Atlantis could very well be the result of a real geologic event.

And the spectacle of comet Shoemaker-Levy smashing into the planet Jupiter in 1994 got a lot of people thinking. An estimated 2,000 near-Earth objects are orbiting out there, only a couple hundred of which have been found, that could collide with Earth and wipe us out.

12. Maintain Current Lifestyle.

I believe other options for self-sufficiency would require more drastic or lowering of one's standard of living and increased labor/equipment inputs and/or a more communal style of living. Also, there would be a much increased learning/transition curve. ***The Earth Home lifestyle would be similar to an average 20th century lifestyle***.

13. Sustainability/Renewable Energy Goal

Sustainability redefines the relationship of humanity to the planet from one of open-ended exploitation to one of dynamic balance between short- and long-term human needs. Sustainability efforts will be helped greatly by proliferation of Earth Homes on the planet.

Renewable energy in the future has also received much attention and will likely continue to do so. For example, a new law in China stipulates the responsibilities of government and society in developing and applying renewable energy. At the same time as the law was passed, the Chinese Government set a target for renewable energy to contribute 10% of the country's gross energy consumption by 2020, a huge increase from the current 1%. Seeing this as a future stimulus of renewable energy development, many Chinese and international observers are very excited, expecting a tremendous growth in the renewable energy market in the next 15 years as the result of the implementation of this law.

14. Future Unknowns/Instability

Some people think that many things are a threat to their survival-financial collapse, diminishing food reserves, political instability, terrorism, oil threats, and the new millennium. There are many more reasons for setting this goal that is related to global instability such as the planetary alignments; Hopi, Mayan, and pyramid prophesies; notable increase in hurricane activity; volcanic eruptions; solar winds and sunspot activity; and earthquakes. However, I do not dwell on the prophecies of the Bible nor other people such as Nostradamus, Edgar Cayce, and Richard Noone. I rather try and concentrate on existing technologies and choices we still have available.

D. FAQ (Frequently Asked Questions)

1. Why a Mass-Produced Completely Self-Sufficient Home System?

a. The Importance of Buildings

Human beings' lifestyle is very dependent upon buildings. I don't think we realize that most of us spend most of our life in buildings that protect us from the changing outdoor climate and give us space to live and work. For this comfort we expend a vast amount on energy and resources. In fact, the construction sector in many industrialized countries is by far the most important energy user.

b. The "Science of Home Construction"

The major purpose of documentation of over 31 years' research is to advance the science of self-sufficiency and mass-producible self-sufficient homes. I believe that a home should do more for a person than simply being a heated box so people can throw their money into the stove. I feel that the great amounts of effort necessary to purchase a home should justify receiving more in return.

"Une maison est une machine - à-habiter."

A house is a machine to live in.

--Charles Jeanneret
1887 - 1965
(architect)

*Used in Earth Home

c. A Model for Future Generations

I would particularly like to direct the terminology and sentence structure to "another" Mel Moench at age 23 in 2005. That is, I would like to direct this to a person just starting serious research, as I did in 1975. If I had this documentation in 1975, it would put me years ahead. I had very little written information and documentation on which to start my research. About the only book I had was Autonomous House, by Robert and Brenda Vales.

I wish to address young people with an interest in this area, especially those who are just starting a family. I feel that information of this nature would be helpful in planning alternative/energy-efficient homes that would suit a family for many years. Lifestyles are constantly changing, and I hope to make Earth Home technology another choice for young people.

Another audience I wish to address is the elderly and people who have an interest in making their own lives much more self-sufficient. I feel that this is a valuable source book for self-sufficient home research. I have also included sources of information of a very specific nature, such as air cylinders, DC motors, solar cells, etc., to aid the person who is interested in a specific area of energy conservation, product development, or alternative energy.

On March 3, 1975, I wrote the following paragraph:

> **"This project is an attempt to concentrate 20th century technology into a universal plan that will begin to restructure the living ways of the peoples of the world."**

This statement still describes the purpose of my project today. I sincerely believe this technology could have a world-wide influence not unlike the introduction of the potter's wheel some 6,000 years ago.........This is the complete story of that plan.

d. Auto and Aviation Industry Example

What would happen if you wanted a new car? Would you look through the yellow pages and pick out a car fabricator? Would he then contact component manufacturers and specify each component based on your interests, needs, and financial situation? Would he then proceed to make your car unique to your needs? I don't think so. If planes and cars were custom made, I think we would be generations behind in evolution.

I feel the home industry should parallel the mass-production mentality of the car and airplane industry that offers basic models and then slightly customizes them to suit individual tastes. The home would function the same, but would reflect the unique tastes of the individual families.

2. What Is Unique About This House?

First of all, it is the only house designed to be 95% to 100% independent. The individual components are integrated for a complete "system" approach. It is not designed to be taken apart and used independently, even though some of the products could be used in that manner. This is the only house designed to provide most food inside the structure, using very little of the outside environment. It is a structural system that fully integrates making food and power for a family of four. It can also be adapted for larger units such as a village.

3. Who Would Benefit?

I believe that the Earth Home philosophy and structure would give future generations a new choice. The only practical choice today is a dependent lifestyle. People are dependent on the rest of the world for their food source and livelihood. I feel that an additional choice of complete independence would be beneficial to human

*Used in Earth Home

beings. If they wanted to increase their independence, they could produce more food, power, and most needs themselves. They would then need to acquire less money, as their outside needs decreased.

I believe that the nature of humans has always been to attain some form of independence. I also believe that people do not choose dependence from want; they choose it because it is available and easy.

For developing countries, the United States has always been the role model of the "ideal" lifestyle. I believe that another example such as the Earth Home system should be offered to developing countries. ***The water-conserving quality of this home by itself could be especially useful in arid climates***.

I believe the elderly could be kept active as well with low-impact harvesting and food preparation. Fixed income food budgets would be less affected by price increases.

4. Why Hasn't Government Tried This Before?

a. Politics in General

One answer to this question could be politics. I don't believe countries can get together for a united effort, especially taking into account the vast complexities of this technology. Also, the energy shortage is not yet critical, so a goal of this nature is not seen as practical. Some people also feel that this type of technology is somewhat "alarmist," because of the survivalist implications: one family excludes the entire world. Typically, successful politicians would never mention an issue unless there is benefit gained. As a result, voters are moved emotionally instead of intellectually.

Many people do not consider the level of pollution and global warming critical. Pollution is a problem that goes unnoticed for many years, unless you live around a source, where its effects are more visible.

Entrepreneurs are not generally given grants and developmental money like larger businesses to develop a product that may contribute to society. Also, funds for experimentation usually go to companies with products that will clearly make more money or more jobs, rather than to a project whose goal is merely to develop technology (as in pure research).

It seems that governments tend to "sell" energy. They prefer to control electricity, utilities, communication, and many other services. I feel that somehow the government, as an entity, may be slightly threatened by a technology that reduces its control of the individual.

b. Science and Technology Budget

The proposed budget for 2005 in the Science and Technology area include: NIST 20%, NSF 3%, NIH 3%, NASA Space Science 2%, NASA 1%, DOE Science Programs, U. S. Geographical Survey 2%, Defense 4%, NASA Earth Science 8%, NOAA 11%, Defense Science and Technology 11%, and Defense Applied Research 13%. I think there should be room in this huge budget for independent living schemes as well.

5. Why Hasn't Private Business Tried This Before?

Businesses do not generally try a "package deal" because of their own product lines. They may deal in special products involving solar, wind, or other aspects of Earth Home technology. It is easier and more efficient for them to stick close to their specific product lines. Management of business has never had a great track record for rewarding creativity inside individual companies. It is sometimes said that employers don't hire people that have the ability to replace them. Creativity seems to be a threat to companies, similar to a departure from normal business practices.

Industry has guidelines, codes, and standard business practices by which it operates. It would be very difficult for a new company to leap into this field with a product such as an entire home and contents.

*Used in Earth Home

Another reason is that control of many businesses is in the hands of older, established people with seniority in the company. They may have an extensive but somewhat narrow vision of their own products, and hesitate to be open to new projects. ***There is also a tremendous amount of research and development time involved in a project of this nature.*** Many companies would simply go broke if they invested the huge resources necessary to complete a research project of this scope. Also there is a limited number of final decision-makers due to the disparity of wealth. Five percent of the people own 95% of the wealth in the U.S. And on a world basis, about 140 billionaires own 40% of the entire earth's wealth!

6. Why Haven't Other People Tried this Before?

First of all, it is being done on a single product approach (windmills, low flush toilets, solar cells, solar heating panels, etc.). I have seen steady increases in the amount of interest and economic support given to products that save energy or recycle. It is being done by various advanced houses in bits and pieces. (See Advanced Houses of the World by Stephen Carpenter) For example, the following technologies are being experimented on to a greater degree:

1. water conservation/rainwater use by Southwell house in England
2. non-refrigerant cooling and pier footings by the Waterloo house in Ontario
3. DC and battery technology by the Castricum house in the Netherlands
4. hydrogen technology and storage by the German Autonomous House
5. controlled scientific study by the German houses at Heidenhein and the SSSH
6. water conservation and recycling by the Earthship organizations

However, the "total approach" research and development is too costly for most individuals to undertake. I estimate that about 200 individuals around the world are working on the theory of completely self-sufficient homes. I find that people involved in this type of research are very individualistic and fiercely independent. ***Given these qualities, there is little organized effort, cooperative research, or shared information between them.***

Few banks will lend money for an experimental effort. Banks must have collateral, a clearly defined goal, and a clearly defined benefit or outcome. Even venture capitalists must see "a light at the end of the tunnel."

7. Why Aren't Technologists Headed in This Direction?

Technologists are primarily employed by government or by private business, because it's about the only way they can make a living (not too many door-to-door scientists). Typically, most people cannot make enough money to support research for very long. This is even true when the research does not involve making more money.

Typically, technologists are told what projects to work on for the company, so they can't work full-time on Earth Home-related technology. It is also naturally much easier to accept things as they are.

Trade secrets and patents also play a part in restricting technology. For example, unless you know the chemical composition of a product, it is difficult to find a cheaper and more Earth-friendly product. Patents discourage "technology-sharing" as well.

8. Is This Technically Possible to Achieve?

There have never been calculations showing that it is impossible to provide enough food for a family in a small space. In fact, the efficiency of food production has never been critically looked into as a "system" until the previously mentioned Biosphere II project in Arizona. The Earth Home system allows interaction with the outside environment, full contact with fresh air, and full sunshine without most of the glass covering. These effects would increase the food production efficiencies. I have often said that given appropriate time and money, most technically challenging projects can be accomplished.

*Used in Earth Home

9. Wouldn't This be Like "Turning Back Time"?

This modern self-sufficient home technology is not turning back the clock into the Middle Ages, but a modern response to a changing world. The techniques used are cutting-edge sustainable technologies that are combined into a home system that would improve the future for all people. This technology offers another lifestyle that offers increased health, security, and peace of mind to those who choose it. The world stands to benefit greatly from the proliferation of the modern self-sufficient homes.

10. Wouldn't This be Too Complex and Too Expensive?

Some have said that this system is too complex and costly. To respond to this, I would say that many products intended for mass production have this criticism in common. As the products are gradually incorporated into the marketplace and the sales volume starts to increase, many changes happen. New processes, designs, and/or materials are incorporated into the product—making them less costly, able to be produced faster, more efficient, or contain enhanced features. By far, the biggest expense for any product occurs in the design, tooling, and setup phases of development.

To counter this argument, I would also ask, "What is the cost of not developing self-sufficient homes?"

E. Mel Moench's Activities/Chronology/Successes

1. Early Beginnings/History

I began working on this project on March 3, 1975, in Waverly, Minnesota. I started breaking ground in the back of a 50' x 200' lot. At that time the plans were drawn to revision #18, which was a geodesic dome. This structure was going to be erected in the back of the lot. However, I found that space was a problem, and that the zoning ordinances did not permit this type of structure. I was, at the time, so involved in accomplishing my goal that I began to build in complete ignorance of the local laws and ordinances. Although I had already compiled an extensive inventory of materials, the possibility of legal problems compelled me to find a new site further away from civilization.

2. Scope of Research - Prototype Explained

These are the numerous sources of information I used in researching and developing the Earth Home system:

a. 7,500 Books Read/Scanned.

Approximately ***7,500 books were read since 1975*** -- sometimes as many as 10 a day. Private collections of alternative energy books were explored when the opportunity arose.

b. 3,500 Magazines Read/Scanned.

Approximately ***3,500 magazines were read*** that contained articles relating to appropriate technology or similar projects.

c. 8,000 Phone Calls.

Approximately ***8,000 telephone contacts*** were made with individuals who had expertise in related areas.

*Used in Earth Home

d. 3,000 Letters.

Approximately ***3,000 letters were written*** over a 28-year period, looking for information or technical product literature.

e. Foreign Contacts.

Many foreign publications were scanned to find out if they had application for this type of research. I've had articles and books translated from Korean and French languages. I've read books or articles from Russia, Denmark, Sweden, Finland, Japan, Canada, Mexico, and Australia.

f. Thomas Registers/McMaster-Carr.

There are two books that have had especially extensive use during this project. One is ***the McMaster-Carr Supply Catalog, and the other is the Thomas Registers***. I've scanned them both ***from cover to cover***.

g. NASA.

I regularly scan *NASA publications*, to find out what researchers are doing in this area.

h. Newspapers.

Newspapers were read by the thousands, and other people sent many articles to me. They were constantly keeping me updated on technology related to this project.

i. Visits.

I visited ***hundreds of people*** who had expertise or product knowledge in a particular field.

j. Technical Journals.

Thousands of technical journals or papers were read to explore deeply into selected subjects. The University of Minnesota, through the library system, was a prime source for technical journals and articles. People who were in industry, working on their doctorate degrees, or continuing their education usually wrote these articles. These subjects were researched extensively, and usually contained excellent bibliographies for further research.

k. Massive Internet Research.

I have spent *thousands of hours* looking for information on the Internet. The "net" is increasing in value to research efforts because of the increasing number of websites and links to other sites. The information is also very current.

Research and development is often completed by companies first making a product and putting it into the marketplace, and then getting the complaints from returned goods. They then sometimes change the product based on these returns, and reintroduce the product as a "new" or "improved" model. Research and development happens in every manufacturing company in the world. However, due to market pressure, companies often issue a product many months or years in advance of perfecting it.

Japan has a more extensive method of developing products than we do in the United States. The Japanese government encourages inventors to develop a product, and actually assists them in bringing it forward to the market much more than in the United States.

*Used in Earth Home

In the United States, inventors are discouraged both in the marketplace and financially. I theorize that after an inventor brings a product to market, the maximum time they can safely market the product is approximately 18 months. In those 18 months, the inventor must bring a product to market and prove its marketability. By that time, they have developed a market base, and larger companies see this as an opportunity. They can immediately develop a look-alike of that product and bring it to the market themselves. I believe that the U.S. patent laws do not protect companies adequately. Changing one minor detail in a patent will allow larger companies to enter the market with a similar product. Also, the litigation involved in patent infringement cases is lengthy, and smaller companies may not be able to afford lengthy court battles.

3. Laws/Jail Time

Land was then obtained in a rural portion of Wright County, near Howard Lake. When I broke ground, I still felt strongly about building this structure. I felt there was nothing that would stop me from doing it, at any cost. The home construction was going along quite well until the local building authorities found out what I was doing and demanded that I get a permit. Knowing that the permit process was a lengthy one, and that this was a radical departure from building codes, ***I felt that it was more expedient to ignore the authorities, go ahead with construction, and put my time into the actual building of the home***.

The Wright County building code officials "red-tagged" me to stop construction until I received a permit. I ignored the red tag. The next step was a court injunction -- a temporary restraining order stopping me from building until I received a permit. I went to court and explained that this was an experimental structure, and that I would like an experimental permit.

The next step was a permanent injunction, which forbade me to continue work on the project. Ignoring all of the court orders, I found myself in contempt of court, and ***was sentenced to 60 days in jail***. I was in jail for three days in Buffalo, Minnesota before I reached an agreement with the building code officials and the judge, stating that I would apply for a building permit. A certain amount of pressure was exerted, and I was given a building permit. The agreement allowed me to continue working on the Earth Home, but not to receive its certificate of occupancy until it met the building code. I was free to leave on that basis. I am still working under this condition today. I have had no communication with Wright County planning and zoning personnel since then. It is possible that court orders and contempt of court action could be initiated at some point in the future. ***I could go back to jail for the heinous crime of living in my own home***.

4. Building Codes/Morality

Building codes of various kinds are in effect in all 50 states, even though people may sometimes hint that a certain area allows non-restrictive and/or unusual construction styles. Houseboats on a navigable body of water are about the only exception and the legal holes are slowly closing on that creative lifestyle. There are experimental airplanes being developed by the military or private companies, and experimental cars being built by Detroit. . There is even an organization called the Experimental Aircraft Association (EAA). ***I feel that experimental homes should have a place in the legal realms of the government***. Even codes and environmental standards were completely put aside for testing nuclear weapons in the 1940's.

I further believe that experimentation of this nature should not only be allowed, but should be encouraged. I feel we as a people should use time and resources to test new living schemes such as the Earth Home concept.

—Plato believed that "the test of truly knowing what is right is to act on what you know."

..........and Albert Einstein had the following said about him**........"Great spirits have always been met with violent opposition from mediocre minds."**

*Used in Earth Home

5. Successful Testing to Date

I'd like to highlight the successes I've had with Earth Home I through the 28th year of design and testing (2003):

a. Electrical Lighting Efficiency.

-- I tested lights in various rooms of the Earth Home and found that natural lighting should be used as much as possible. Different types of light bulb filaments are used for specific areas of the Earth Home.

b. Super Water-Efficient Toilet.

-- I have designed/developed a six-ounce flushing toilet with an odor control system, which makes it one of the lowest flushing toilets in the world.

c. Water Efficiency-Handwashing.

-- I have developed a foot-activated hands-free hand washing system that uses 2 ounces of water or less. This system allows children as young as 18 months old to easily wash their hands. (Incidentally, hands and face are the leading disease carriers and transmitting mechanisms for young children.)

d. Water-Efficient Shower

-- I have designed a .75 gpm (gallons per minute) demand shower -- This ultra-low water-use shower uses less than 1/2 the water of the most efficient showerhead on the market in 1996.

e. Utility Cube

-- I have developed a compact utility system in one unit that contains almost all the utilities a human being needs in a space of approximately 3'x3'x3'. It includes a toilet, an electrical system, controls, battery, propane supply, demand heater, water pump, freezer, and sink all in one compact area.

f. Water filtration

-- I have developed a two-stage water filtration and purification system that uses very little power, and is reusable.

g. Irrigation

-- I have developed a controlled plant watering system under the soil so the water is evenly distributed down long lines of indoor plants.

h. Space Utilization and Lifestyle Flexibility

-- The spaces in the Earth Home system have been designed, tested, and re-designed over an extensive period. The interior spaces are designed for convenience of use for a wide variety of human activities, with most of the south side used for natural lighting and plant growing.

*Used in Earth Home

i. Ultra-Low Maintenance Exterior Skin

-- I've developed a very low-maintenance ferrocement to allow the exterior skin to "breath" and to provide structural support. The skin is a thin mixture of concrete and fibers that can be sprayed onto the house using conventional methods.

j. "Spin-off" Technologies

The following is a list of related gadgets that I have developed over a period of time, that may have applications for other projects;

a. 12-volt DC inflatable structure pump with 0 to 5 psi pressure switch. This is a small air pump that could be used to inflate a portable structure, such as an army tent. It could inflate a complete greenhouse with as little as 150 milliamps of 12-volt current.
b. The cool tube technology with a 12-volt DC circulating pump is an example of water being circulated through the ground with as little as 150 milliamps of current. This system, which is still in the experimental stage, could potentially be used to cool a small space or cabin.
c. The utility "unit" is a 3' cube, as mentioned earlier. It contains all of the utilities people need for comfortable living. This has possible application in airplanes, campers, or as a portable unit for military applications.
d. I've designed lightweight, inflatable-member camping tents that set up quickly, and take up very little space when packed.
e. I've developed a fish pond aerator that aerates a 500 gallon tank with 150 milliamps of 12 volt DC electricity.
f. I developed a tiny freezer that can be carried on your back. This portable pack could be used to freeze foods or medical supplies.

6. The Reasons for Developing Earth Home II Prototype

I have been designing and developing another prototype since 1992, based on a number of reasons. They include the following:

a. Thermosiphon Testing

The Earth Home I was two stories--the thermosiphon heating method did not work as designed because of the quantities of hotter air that had to be moved. I feel that one story should be used to allow greater mobility among children, the elderly, and the handicapped. Air movement would be accomplished with a central, super-efficient fan and a large "over-room" duct system.

b. Airflow Options.

There are more airflow options using the new design. "Envelope" or "shell" construction could be used with this system because of the new roof design.

c. Ground Contact.

There is more shaded ground contact for summer cooling. Summertime cooling is affected by the amount of surface exposed to the ground. I am doubling the "footprint" of the Earth Home to approximately 2,800 square feet (including garage and greenhouse).

*Used in Earth Home

d. Lighting.

There is more natural lighting in the new prototype. I am increasing the optional sunlight above the south side, and increasing the natural lighting above the high-use kitchen, dining, and living areas.

e. Flax.

I will be using a thicker, flax bale insulation system on Earth Home II.

f. Construction.

Earth Home II will be much easier to construct. It is closer to the ground and does not require extensive equipment to construct. In third world countries, a one-story structure is still the logical choice.

g. Roof.

I have eliminated all asphalt and asbestos products from the roof to eliminate/reduce contamination of the water supply. Asphalt and asbestos products "leach out" over time and get into the water supply, making it very difficult to filter.

h. Rainwater.

I have increased the rain gutter volume. I found that small rain gutters available in lumberyards are too small for the very heavy rainfalls that occur sporadically. I am finding that all rainwater must be collected for use.

i. Western Sun.

I have added western sun exposure for certain plants. For example, tomatoes with basil prefer a western sun in order to ripen fully. Fish raising could also benefit by longer sunlight in the evening for better algae growth.

j. Cool Tubes.

Cool tubes with moistening tubes were added to increase ground contact for cooling.

k. Atmospheres.

There is optional plant atmosphere mixing in the new design. I have added two doors so a person can walk into the greenhouse from the living spaces.

l. Underfloor heating option.

Under-floor heating similar to "Ondol's" of Korea would be an option in the new design.

m. Handicap/Elderly.

It will be easier to care for plants because less stooping and bending would be required to tend the plants.

*Used in Earth Home

n. Overhead Water Option.

An additional long south side water supply for thermal mass could be installed, in addition to the storage system in the utility area.

F. Published Articles/Papers

1. The Futurist May-June 2004 Issue

Self-Sufficient Homes

By Mel Moench

Self-Sufficient Homes

Welcome to the self-sufficient home. Its inhabitants make their own energy, produce their own food, and do their part to save the world's environment.

Get ready to live in a totally self-sufficient home, one that is specially constructed and equipped to generate all its power and raise all your food.

A home that is self-sufficient should not be confused with an "independent home," which typically refers only to its energy use. Most so-called independent homes are still dependent on food distribution systems to sustain its occupants.

Modern self-sufficient homes--also known as autonomous homes, bioshelters, or independent living systems--use an immense number of appropriate technologies. They generate and store their own power using solar energy, wind generators, photovoltaic panels, and renewable energy. They maximize usable power by using battery electrical storage, direct current controls, high-efficiency lighting, energy-efficient appliances, super-insulation, natural lighting, passive ventilation, thermal mass, heat recovery ventilation, and high efficiency woodstoves. They minimize negative impact on their surroundings because they can be built with green or alternative construction. They employ low-water toilets, wastewater treatment, water reuse, graywater systems, smoke scrubbers, and recycling to reduce pollution and conserve water. And, after ensuring the land stays healthy, they provide the best possible conditions for efficient food production, including intensive organic agriculture, undersoil irrigation, aquaculture, greenhouse food production, and composting. A basic and reliable home control system saves effort, eliminates mistakes, and helps coordinate all the activities and functions.

So why don't we all live in self-sufficient homes right now? Because there aren't any. The fact is that a completely self-sufficient home system supporting twenty-first-century lifestyles has yet to be built and tested in its final form. So far, I have built a prototype and a second prototype is in the works. My first prototype Earth Home tested many aspects of the design and showed that the concept could indeed be realized. The second prototype will become the first modern home in history to sustain human occupants indefinitely using concepts, technology, products, diets, and systems from all over the world.

Complete Self-Sufficient Technologies

Space program research was probably the first place where complete self-sustaining technology was sought that incorporated both food production and energy-independence in a limited enclosure. NASA's early Closed Environmental Life Support System looked into intensive plant growing, carbon dioxide enrichment, soap filtering, and extreme water conservation for extended space travel and/or colonization.

*Used in Earth Home

The Russians also researched closed systems, and at one time may have been may have been the world leader in this technology. At the Institute of Biomedical Problems in Moscow, Yevgeny Shepelev became the first human being to live with biological life support. In 1961, he spent 24 hours in a chamber where chlorella algae regenerated his air and purified his water. Siberia's Institute of Biophysics in Krasnoyarsk further developed algae-based systems with the Bios-3 experiments in the 1970s and 1980s. These experiments enclosed crews of two or three people for six months with about a dozen food crops supplying half the food and providing nearly all the air and water regeneration.

In the United States, John Todd and his group at the New Alchemy Institute did pioneering work with their experimental self-sufficient home, The Ark, in the early 1970s. This group was one of the first to emphasize aquaculture in self-sufficient home designs. Arguably the best known self-sustaining project was the huge Biosphere II structure in Arizona that completely sealed eight people for two years beginning in 1991. It cost millions of dollars to enclose approximately three acres under glass, about half an acre of which was dedicated to food production using 156 edible plant species. This experiment forms the most in-depth documentation on efficient food self-sufficiency in a confined space.

The Self-Sufficient Home Evolves

The oil embargo of the mid-1970s prompted many projects dealing with energy efficiency and conservation. My Earth Home system project began in 1975 and attempted to develop the technology to mass-produce food and energy-independent living shelters for any location on the planet while being ecologically compatible with the requirements of each region.

The early Earth Home goal was to be a functional, efficient, ecologically balanced, need-oriented, simple, durable, non-polluting, single-family, universal, minimal existence living system. I emphasized nature as a model, using a complete system approach. As this ultimate self-sufficient home design came into being, I drew inspiration from cultural information from around the world. The plan would implement ideas, materials, foods, and methods that have stood the test of time, as well as newly emerging technologies. At the time, I planned that the technology would first lead to the creation of mass-producible self-sufficient homes, which would then inspire the development of plans, kits, and components for the owner-builder.

Throughout the design process, I considered it important that the home be able to maintain an average twentieth-century lifestyle with all of the accompanying conveniences and comforts. This meant that the home essentially had to become a living, sensing, and reacting mechanism, needing no significant human intervention other than planting, harvesting, food preparation, and maintenance--a kind of automatic mini-farm. This 29-year project culminated in my book Planet Earth Home (Osprey Press, 1995; fifth printing 2004), which documents the entire project and totally encompasses the field of complete self-sufficient home technologies.

Even though the goal was to make this mini-farm completely self-sufficient, 100% self-sufficiency is technically unattainable in the purest terms. Everything will break at some point because sun, water, friction, heat, and other forces are constantly at work. Routine component replacement and maintenance requires some materials that may not be available locally as yet. Also, dietary salt, yeast, and enzymes for alcohol and vinegar production are much easier to purchase than to make or recycle.

The basic design of an Earth Home would remain the same if built in any climatic region, though it would have to be adjusted or modified slightly depending on local conditions. Factors that would affect the fine-tuning of the design include soil conditions, solar/wind ratio for power generation, altitude, tropical/cold climate species potential (trees, oil plants, and other species), rainfall, and average temperature. In a rainforest, for example, an Earth Home would use more photovoltaic panels to generate energy from the sun and rely less on wind generators. In colder locations, generating energy from wind power would be more important. Earth Home construction in the tropics would favor foliage to help keep the sun's rays off the surface of the home by using wall or roof lattices, while heating the home would be a primary consideration in cold locations, requiring greater insulation systems for the primary heating zone or core rooms.

Benefits of Self-Sufficiency

A variety of significant, attractive short-term benefits will drive the development of modern self-sufficient homes. These include security from severe weather, climate changes, and natural disasters; security from

*Used in Earth Home

infectious diseases and related health problems; a fresh and nutritious diet; a dependable food supply; and security from global unrest.

But the real benefit of Earth Himes will be the long-term sustainability of our planet. It should be no secret that the planet is experiencing unusual weather and climate abnormalities. The 10 hottest years in recorded history have all been in the last 15 years; the 1990s were the hottest decade on record. The Midwestern heat wave of 1995 killed 669 people in Chicago. In 1996, we had a season of record heat spells, and 1997 was the single warmest year on record--until 1998 shattered global temperature records. Record-high temperatures throughout the southern United States during the summer of 1998 forced the shutdown of Walt Disney World's water parks because of the threat of a viral encephalitis outbreak. The United Nations and insurers blame unusual weather for thousands of deaths and billions of dollars in damage.

"Many scientists agree that the emissions resulting from human activities are substantially increasing the atmospheric concentration of the greenhouse gasses," writes Jeremy Leggett in his book Global Warming: The Greenpeace Report (Oxford University Press, 1990). "These increases will enhance the greenhouse effect, resulting in warming of the earth's surface." In 1990, scientists predicted that, if greenhouse gas emissions are not sharply decreased, we might experience a 1°C to 3°C rise in global temperatures. They suggest that we would have to cut in half our use of coal, oil, and gas in order to lower our emissions enough to maintain concentrations of greenhouse gases at current levels.

Proof of warming includes a decrease in the amount of snow that covers the northern hemisphere, a simultaneous decrease in Arctic Sea ice, continued melting of alpine glaciers, and a rise in sea level. Rain has even been reported for the first time in Antarctica and an ice-free patch of ocean about a mile wide has recently opened near the North Pole.

Meanwhile, studies have shown that the carbon dioxide concentration in our atmosphere has been steadily increasing since 1958. Even though the rate of emissions from fossil fuels has been reduced, concentration has risen consistently.

In 1995, the size of the ozone hole over Antarctica doubled to about the size of Europe. For the first time in recorded history, the hole stretched over populated areas, exposing residents in southern Chile and Argentina to very high levels of ultraviolet (UV) radiation. Studies have shown that a 1% decrease in ozone in the stratosphere produces a 2% increase in UV radiation reaching the ground, posing more risks to humans. In the United States, for instance, between a third and a half of all cancers are skin cancers widely blamed on UV exposure. Australia has the highest rate of skin cancer in the world, with estimates that two out of three people will get at least one skin cancer in their lifetime.

Add to this scenario the possibility of natural disasters such as volcanic activity, comets, solar winds, sunspot activity, or earthquakes that could drastically affect world security. How long is the stability of the planet going to be immune from these types of significant occurrences? Winter storms and random weather extremes such as record-breaking extreme hot, cold, and winds are signals that we should act on the results of climate change. Through its innovations, the self-sufficient home is one way of helping limit human environmental degradation and increasing resource sustainability.

Health Benefits of Self-Sufficiency

An increase in the numbers of modern self-sufficient homes would also offer more security from infectious diseases because of less-frequent air travel and interactions with other people. Many diseases such as malaria, dengue fever, Hantavirus, and viral encephalitis have reemerged recently. In the summer of 2000, West Nile fever, a rare and encephalitic virus that is endemic in parts of the Middle East, Asia, and Africa, was linked to the deaths of four people in New York state and has been increasing in many other states.

A number of new ailments have also surfaced, such as Reyes syndrome, Lyme disease, Legionnaire's disease, AIDS, Ebola, swine flu, and SARS. This is primarily due to the quick transportation of infected persons and animals throughout the world, where they may infect others before they are diagnosed as sick.

Besides helping to reduce these health-damaging impacts of climate change, Earth Homes themselves would be health-enhancing by helping people improve their diets and lifestyles. Many nutritionists agree that disease and

*Used in Earth Home

health-related problems can be reduced or deterred if people eat fresh food. Studies have shown that vegetables and fruits start losing vitamins and minerals from the very moment they are picked, even though methods of cooking are used to ensure that they remain nutritious. Many of the foods we purchase today differ significantly in vitamin and mineral value from the same ones a generation or two ago. Part of the reason is that many essential vitamins and minerals no longer make it back into the soil that grows our food.

Long-Term Global Benefits

A gradual transition to self-sufficient home technologies will also have significant worldwide, long-term benefits. It will help prevent malnutrition by increasing food production, reduce the energy needs for agriculture and housing, slow the advance of global soil problems, reduce the burden on world water supplies, help slow environmental and climate changes, and even slow or reverse the two-income family trend.

Land and energy use would also be more efficient with self-sufficient homes. The United States uses half of its agriculture energy to produce animals, and spends three to 12 calories in petroleum energy to produce one calorie of food. In addition, almost a quarter of all food produced in the United States is wasted because of harvesting losses, storage losses, processing losses, transportation losses, and kitchen and plate waste. In addition to U.S. agricultural energy outputs, approximately 20% to 30% of all energy is consumed in the home. Adding the energy used for food production, processing, and distribution, this is an enormous amount of resources used in a typical U.S. home. In contrast, the self-sufficient home produces its own energy, freeing families from dependence on outside sources.

Our planet is also drying up and its soil quality deteriorating. Roughly a third of the original topsoil in the United States is now gone, and the world has an estimated 50 to 100 years of soil that is farmable with current, irrigation dependent farming practices. And 80 countries, including China, India, Pakistan, and Mexico, have experienced water shortages severe enough to threaten agriculture. Earth Homes recycle most of their water for further use, resulting in much less drain upon the existing usable water supply.

Power-Generation in the Home

In the last decade or so, significant products and development efforts have reached the marketplace that fit well into self-sufficient home development needs. Battery and energy demand research, DC (direct current) circulating pumps, hydrogen production and storage technologies, CHP (combined heat and power) units, and the popular healthy food trend are among many developments that may speed the evolution of modern self-sufficient homes.

Since completely self-sufficient homes must now store electricity in batteries, in batteries, higher power densities and lower cost is very important. The electronics and automotive industry are primarily driving research into small, light, and power-dense batteries. The issues of automotive fuel economy and emissions are also demanding that the load on the alternator be reduced. Many scientists and engineers are looking at conserving power and efficiently managing energy drains.

The average home in the United States contains approximately 60 different electric motors--virtually all of which are inefficient. A large portion of electricity is used in the motors that circulate hot and cold air inside the home to maintain comfortable temperatures. Much research effort on electric motors has resulted in ECM (electronically commutated motor) technology that draws an amazingly small amount of electricity when it needs it. This motor technology has been applied to liquid circulating pumps in the solar heating industry. Laing Thermotech in Denmark and Wilo Stratos have recently introduced continuous duty DC circulating pumps that draw less than 10 watts of electricity.

A home could use hydrogen technologies in a number of places. Gaseous hydrogen is similar to natural gas or propane with less heating value per cubic foot. However, when gaseous hydrogen burns, pure water is the result. This makes it a unique nonpolluting technology that can be generated by electricity and stored for later use. As this generation and storage technology comes of age, hydrogen will be useful as a clean fuel source for cooking, hot water heating, and many other uses.

*Used in Earth Home

Hydrogen can also be used for CHP units that are chest-freezer-sized and can be used in residential applications. When electricity is needed, a gaseous fuel is pumped directly into the fuel cell to produce both DC electricity and heat. There are at least five companies in the world developing residential CHP units.

Health-related technologies are also helping to evolve self-sufficient homes. This field of products and services for maintaining one's health is a significant share of the gross national product in the United States. A substantial portion of the industry is dedicated to promoting the body's natural ability to maintain health, stamina, and weight, such as through nutritious eating, fresh air, exercise, and adequate vitamin and mineral intake. These qualities are very easy to implement in a self-sufficient home lifestyle, since virtually all foods can be raised on-site--controlling all soil, plant, and animal inputs.

Toward a Better Future for All

Human beings are stewards of the earth, and it is our responsibility to give this earth to future generations in the same or better condition than we received it. We also have a moral obligation to help those less fortunate than ourselves. Approximately one-half of the world's 6 billion people have no fresh water to drink, and another one-third have inadequate food or housing.

More than half my life has been dedicated to the cause of modern self-sufficient homes. My wish is that this technology will mature while resources and conditions are favorable to its development--if not for single-family use, then for extended family or village use. This technology may stay on the back burner and simmer in the minds of many creative independent thinkers on the planet, but I believe it will become forefront in time--I hope not too late for the human species……Mel

----

About the Author--Mel Moench designs and develops self-sufficient homes. His recently updated book Planet Earth Home (Osprey Press, 2004) is available electronically or as a bound volume and may be ordered from www.planetearthhome.com. His address is 7245 15th Street SW, Howard Lake, Minnesota 55349. E-Mail mel.moench@charter.net.

A longer version of this article is posted on the World Future Society's Global Strategies Forum, www.wfs.org/gsforum.htm.

2. Sustainable Building Conference

a. Abstract

MASS-PRODUCED SELF-SUFFICIENT HOMES
MEL MOENCH

Earth Home Project, Osprey Press, Buffalo, MN 55313 USA.
E-mail: mel.moench@charter.net

Purpose—It is common knowledge that the Earth's inhabitants are growing faster than resources or the technologies necessary to feed and clothe them all. While the poor will always be on this planet, I feel another model of lifestyle should be explored. Relying on hybrid seeds of a limited number of crops and a limited number of animals to produce the world food supply may not be viable in a changing world. Heavy reliance on food distribution systems and political processes have historically had problems in the past feeding a hungry world.

Results—A mass-producible home design using low impact materials and technology could be developed. This home would be capable of operating anywhere on the inhabited Earth and provide for its occupants similar to a "mini-farm" or small "food factory." The home would generate its own power needs using renewable energy and make use of efficient food production and food storage techniques. Efficient (high feed-to-food ratio)

*Used in Earth Home

animals and disease-resistant strains of plants would be chosen to provide a healthy and nutritious diet in and around the home. Optimized methods of planting, watering, harvesting, storage, and preparation would be chosen that would maximize benefit.

Conclusions—A project should begin that would prove the feasibility of a low-impact home that provides all food and power for a family, extended family, or village. This testing and technology for this "product" could be a model for other variations of the home that would be slightly modified for different climatic regions and local food cultivars. Each country or organization could choose a variation of the basic model for development and testing, based on regional preferences and social customs. In this way, another choice for human lifestyle would emerge—independent living as opposed to dependence on many other systems and people. See www.planetearthhome.com for more information.

TOPICS + KEYWORDS: Self-Sufficient Homes, Autonomous Homes, Sustainable Housing, Sustainable Development, Independent Homes, Natural Building, Appropriate Technology Development, Organic Building.

b. Full Text of Paper

MASS-PRODUCED SELF-SUFFICIENT HOMES

Author: Mel Moench
Organization: Earth Homes Project and Osprey Press

Why Develop Self-Sufficient Homes?
Introduction to Completely Self-Sufficient Homes
Self-Sufficient Home Definition

I define modern self-sufficient homes as an attempt to: 1) grow 100% of the family's food requirements, 2) generate 100% of power requirements, 3) recycle water and wastes, 4) get rain water from the roof, filter it, and use it for washing needs, 5) filter/distill water for use in cooking and drinking, and 6) provide for all of the family needs within the confines of the home and immediate surroundings. Special methods to dry, store, process, and cook foods are used to save energy, time, and effort.

Modern self-sufficient homes are specially designed and equipped to maintain a comfortable lifestyle as experienced by the US, Europe, and other industrialized countries. Drastic alterations of lifestyle are not needed. A family's need for extra income outside the home would be greatly reduced.

Background/History

It is common knowledge that the Earth's inhabitants are growing faster than resources or the technologies necessary to feed and clothe them all. Many well-educated people are searching for solutions to many of society's problems. The flow of goods and services world-wide is necessary for the health and well-being of its occupants. With virtually no exceptions, people are dependent on other people for their basic existence. The "Western World lifestyle" is predominant in most mass media.

I believe that another lifestyle model should be created that would be an option for both developed and developing countries. There are many reasons why an independent lifestyle option supported by a completely self-sufficient home should be investigated.

Global Uncertainties
Commodity Distribution System

There are many global uncertainties affecting the flow of goods and services to the individual and family. This flow involves the transportation system (shipping lines, roads, highways, bridges, tunnels, gas stations, and refineries, etc.) communication systems, plumbing systems, electrical transmission lines, and many other methods. Heavy reliance on existing food distribution systems and political processes have historically had problems in the past feeding a hungry world. Disaster relief efforts highlight problems distributing food in non-

*Used in Earth Home

ideal conditions. According to the Earth Policy Institute, world grain stocks have been down to 59 days of consumption.

Avenues to deliver goods and services are highly dependent on stability of many forms. This stability can be disrupted by many factors that have been on the increase for years. Some of these disrupting influences include wars, regional conflicts, and political instability. The causes of these instabilities are many such as; ethnic differences, socio-economic disparities, hardships, feelings of inequalities, and poverty.

Oil dependence and terrorism can also have drastic destabilizing effects on society. Arguably, the only real security for people is self-sufficiency.

Unusual Weather/Natural Disasters

It should be no secret that the planet is experiencing unusual weather and climate abnormalities. The 10 hottest years in recorded history have all been in the last 15 years and the 1990's were the hottest decade on record. The United Nations and insurers blame unusual weather for thousands of deaths and billions of dollars in damage. Add to this scenario the possibility of natural disasters such as volcanic activity, comets, solar winds, sunspot activity, or earthquakes that could drastically affect world security. How long is the stability of the planet going to be immune from these types of events?

Infectious Disease Increase

Many diseases such as malaria, dengue fever, Hantavirus, West Nile fever, and viral encephalitis have re-emerged recently. A number of new ailments have also surfaced such as Reyes syndrome, Lyme disease, Legionnaire's disease, AIDS, Ebola, swine flu, SARS, and avian flu. A self-sufficient home lifestyle would require much less travel and personal interrelationships and thus limit contact with communicable diseases.

Agricultural/Food Issues

Agricultural Problems

There are many significant agricultural issues that adversely affect world food sources including; desertification, arable soil nutrient depletion, deforestation, irrigated land decrease, hydrated lime use issues, soil salinization, soil compaction, erosion, and aquifer depletion. Self-sufficient homes can continue to improve their own soil quality by composting and recycling.

Africa is a good example of drought conditions due to lowering of the water table—as of 1993 it had experienced an almost continuous drought for seven years. Some eighty countries are experiencing water shortages enough to threaten agriculture, such as northern China, southern India, Pakistan, Zimbabwe, Mauritania, and Mexico. Self-sufficient homes capture rainwater from the roof, provide adequate storage, use it efficiently, and then recycle most of the water for further use.

Food Plant Species Issues

The vast majority of the foods that human beings consume come from only 11 plant sources and 7 animal sources. This reliance on a small number of species of plants and animals has a potentially catastrophic effect, as was experienced in the Irish Potato Famine of 1847. This phenomenon is further evidenced by the blight throughout the single-variety coffee plantations in Britain's Asian and African colonies that transformed the British into a nation of tea drinkers.

Hybrid Seed Issues

The eight major world food grains are all hybrids, requiring farmers to purchase seeds every year. However, hybrid plants produce infertile seeds, or they produce qualities in the second and third generation that are drastically different from the first generation hybrid plant. These hybrids are also often dependent on more water and fertilizers for their higher yields. Self-sufficient homes are designed to use non-hybrid or open-pollinated food plant cultivars and further improve the plant variety by gathering seeds of improved plants for planting the next season.

*Used in Earth Home

Industrialized Food Problems
American Diet Example?

There are specific nutritional issues associated with the Standard American Diet (SAD) such as; high calorie, low nutrient, low fiber, high fat, excess saturated fat, excess hydrogenated oils, high protein, excess salt, excess sugar, excess alcohol, excess milk foods, excess meats, high vitamin D, and excess phosphorus. The American diet has also been described as hydrogenated, de-fibered, de-germinated, defatted, re-fatted and manipulated by the food industry.

If we feed the American supermarket diet to a colony of young monkeys, within a few years these monkeys will develop all the modern diseases. Also, when the industrial (mass produced/factory processed/refined) foods diet was introduced to various tribal cultures throughout the world, a general degradation of their health followed, usually within one generation. Tooth decay and diseases such as diabetes, cardiovascular disease, and cancer increased to levels that correlated with those industrialized societies. Amusingly, a sign posted near the junk food machines in a major U.S. city zoo warns "DO NOT FEED THIS FOOD TO THE ANIMALS OR THEY MAY GET SICK AND DIE!"

The China Health Project has basically demonstrated the health benefits of a diet based on plant foods. We spend many more calories in oil energy to get one calorie of food in a meat diet than with a vegetarian diet. This is one reason that the self-sufficient home diet stresses vegetable foods with smaller amounts of meat and fish—similar to the Eastern diets.

Specific Food Issues
Sugar, Wheat, and Antibiotics

Refining of sugar has been implicated in a variety of diet-related illnesses such as; fuelling cancer cells, calcium depletion, causing tooth and gum decay, and creating extra cholesterol that hardens arteries and fattens the liver. Every year millions of pounds of antibiotics are consumed by humans, livestock and poultry. The overall effect has not only been destruction of the healthful bacteria in the human intestinal tract, but also the establishment of strains of harmful bacteria that are resistant to antibiotics.

Processing wheat into white flour, cooking, canning, and other food processes involves losing significant vitamins and minerals as well as other nutrients. It has been estimated that there are from 30 to 140 chemical food additives or preservatives in an average American meal. Food processors have an estimated ten thousand chemicals they may add to what we eat. Flavorings are the largest group of all additives—over 500 natural and 1500 synthetic.

Food Additives

Other additives to food include preservatives, acids, alkalis, buffers, neutralizers, moisture content controls (humectants), coloring agents, dyes, physiologic activity controls (such as ethylene gas), bleaching agents, maturing agents, bread improvers, processing aids, sanitizing agents, emulsifiers, emulsion stabilizers, texturizers, fortifiers, antioxidants, deodorants, drying agents, extenders, gassers, hydrolyzers, hydrogenators, disinfectants, neutralizers, anti-foaming agents, anti-caking agents, curers, waxes, and coal tar. Many people have some kind of sensitivity to specific chemicals.

Diseases of Food Deficiency

There are specific diseases attributed to deficiencies in food; beriberi, goiter, scurvy, rickets, eye trouble, and liver poisoning. The following are generally accepted diseases attributed to diet; cancer of the breast (one in three develops cancer of some kind), cancer of the colon, diverticulitis, heart disease, high blood pressure, irritable bowel syndrome, non-insulin-dependent diabetes, and obesity. Nutritional problems have been linked to the following problems and diseases; heart attacks, strokes, vascular insufficiency, diabetes, prostate cancer, other cancers, arthritis, behavior problems such as crime, tooth decay, and atherosclerosis.

Choosing an Independent Lifestyle

*Used in Earth Home

Other than all the negatives that warrant a look at a new independent lifestyle, let's look at positive characteristics of interest.

Dependent vs. independent is the two basic choices to acquire food, shelter, and other needs. I believe that it is the nature of human beings to choose independence if given the chance. Whether we want to generate our own needs ourselves or to work to buy them is a choice that only recently may become a possibility.

I feel that it is the self-sufficient home that will allow people to choose their own level of self-sufficiency. They will then have the choice of complete dependence on society or complete independence from society. In this way, another choice for lifestyle would emerge—independent living as opposed to dependence on many other systems and people.

Self-Sufficient Home Systems as a "Product"

I think that a self-sufficient home with all its components and systems should be developed and marketed as a unit to consumers. This product would be slightly different—depending on location and many other factors. But the basic self-sufficient functions and space allocations would all be very similar.

Self-Sufficient Home Evolution

Research into completely self-sufficient homes logically first looked at all the relevant previous research and projects. Smaller portions of a complete system had been looked at over the years in many places.

Background/History/Technologies

Space program research was probably the first place where complete self-sustaining technology was sought that incorporated both food production and energy-independence in a limited enclosure. NASA's early Closed Environmental Life Support System looked into intensive plant growing, carbon dioxide enrichment, soap filtering, and extreme water conservation for extended space travel and/or colonization.

At the Institute of Biomedical Problems in Moscow, Yevgeny Shepelev became the first human being to live with biological life support. In 1961, he spent 24 hours in a chamber where chlorella algae regenerated his air and purified his water. Siberia's Institute of Biophysics in Krasnoyarsk further developed algae-based systems with their Bios-3 experiments in the 1970s and 1980s. These experiments enclosed crews of two or three people for six months with about a dozen food crops supplying half the food and providing nearly all the air and water regeneration.

New Alchemy Institute Projects

In the early 1970's, John Todd and his group at the New Alchemy Institute did pioneering work with their experimental self-sufficient home, "The Ark". This was one of the first projects that emphasized aquaculture in self-sufficient home designs.

Biosphere II

Arguably the best-known self-sustaining project was the huge Biosphere II project and structure in Arizona that completely sealed eight people for two years beginning in 1991. It cost millions of dollars to enclose approximately three acres under glass, about half an acre of which was dedicated to food production using 156 edible plant species. This experiment forms the most in-depth documentation on efficient food self-sufficiency in an enclosed and confined space.

The Earth Home Project

Brief Description of the Earth Home Project

The oil embargo of the mid-1970's brought many energy conservation and alternative energy projects to the centre stage. On March 3, 1975, I defined the goal of the Earth Home Project as "developing the technology to mass-produce food and energy-independent living shelters for any location on the planet" while being ecologically compatible with the requirements of each region.

*Used in Earth Home

29-Year Research History

I wanted the end result to be a functional, efficient, ecologically balanced, need-oriented, simple, durable, non-polluting, single-family, universal, minimal existence living system. I emphasized nature as a model using a complete system approach to create the ultimate self-sufficient home design.

Drawing inspiration from cultural information from around the world, the plan would implement ideas, materials, foods, and methods that have stood the test of time as well as newly emerging technologies. At the time, I planned that the technology would first lead to the creation of mass-producible self-sufficient homes which would then inspire the development of plans, kits, and components for the owner-builder.

Throughout the design process, I considered it important that the home be able to maintain an average modern lifestyle with all of the accompanying conveniences and comforts. This meant that the home essentially had to become a living, sensing, and reacting mechanism, needing no significant human intervention other than planting, harvesting, food preparation, and maintenance—a kind of "automatic mini-farm". This three-decade project culminated in my book Planet Earth Home (Osprey Press, fifth printing 2004), which documents the entire project and totally encompasses the field of complete self-sufficient home technologies in the world.

Even though the goal was to make this "mini-farm" completely self-sufficient, 100% self-sufficiency is technically unattainable in the purest terms. Everything will break at some point because sun, water, friction, heat, and other forces are constantly at work. Routine component replacement and maintenance requires some materials that may not be available locally as yet. Also, dietary salt, yeast, and enzymes for alcohol and vinegar production may be easier to purchase than to make or recycle.

Independent Home vs. Self-Sufficient Home

At the time there were many projects involved with energy conservation of many forms. Homes and automobiles logically seemed to receive most of the attention. A completely self-sufficient home went much further. A home that is self-sufficient should not be confused with an "independent home," which typically refers only to its energy use. Most so-called independent homes are still very dependent on food distribution systems to sustain its occupants.

Modern self-sufficient homes—also known as autonomous homes, bio shelters, or independent living systems use an immense number of appropriate technologies and systems. The fact is that a completely self-sufficient home system supporting twenty-first-century lifestyles has yet to be built and tested in its final form.

Earth Home Prototypes I and II

So far, I have built a prototype and a second prototype is planned. My first prototype Earth Home tested many aspects of the design and showed that the concept could indeed be realized. The second prototype may become the first modern home in history to sustain human occupants indefinitely using concepts, technology, products, diets, and systems from all over the world.

Earth Home II Images—Northern Hemisphere Temperate Shown

Following are images of one variation of the Earth Home for Northern Hemisphere locations in a temperate climate. Other variations such as tropical climate and desert locations are in the process of development. The images were generated from CAD files of the basic plans of Earth Home II. (See Images in Text)

Structural Overview

Framing, Roof, and Skin

The structure is designed to be a one story post-and-beam construction with flax bales on their sides insulating the core rooms. Flax bales would be coated on the outside with a stucco-like mixture of "Ferro-cement" or a lime alternative and the inside walls would be a compounded lime plaster. A corrugated steel slanted roof to the south (Northern Hemisphere) enabled water collection and snow/ice melting. The floor is fabricated of a poured concrete/lime mixture over flax bales on their sides that can be adapted to in-floor heating options. Other materials such as adobe could also be used for the floor.

Exterior Features

Small bio-intensive raised mounds allow for easier weeding and undersoil watering. Edible shrubbery and grapevines on trellis systems provide shade relief. The home is all on grade except for a cool storage area under the kitchen/living rooms for items such as food, water, and batteries.

Interior Spaces

An attached animal area on the western end (Northern Hemisphere) is intended for fish, fowl, and animal production. A long and narrow attached greenhouse area on the south side is designed for intensive vertical plant production combined with passive solar heating. There is also a special food dehydration area with grain storage capabilities. A natural-lighted central living area/kitchen in the centre of the home has access to windows on the south side. Three bedrooms are located off the central kitchen/living area to the rear of the home.

Energy Overview

The home would generate its own power needs using renewable energy. Emphasis is on passive solar, wood burning, wind energy, and photovoltaic panels.

Energy Reduction and Conservation

A logical first step in typical energy projects is to reduce the need for energy. The Earth Home has been designed around minimizing the use of all forms of energy. The central core area is designed to be constructed of thick bales of organic fibers which are a form of "super insulation" because the R-value is much higher than typical homes require. The ceiling is also designed to be made with lighter weight insulation sandwiched between two durable sheets of organic board such as strawboard, hardboard, or particle board.

Where the heat build-up is more significant, exterior shading is utilized more to block the sun's energy from getting into the building envelope in the first place. Energy-efficient appliances and compressors are also utilized to minimize energy use and reduce the electrical storage requirements.

Generation and Storage of Electricity

Photovoltaic panels generate electricity and send it to the central controller. An appropriate small tilt-down wind generator model is chosen (depending on location) and the output is also fed to the controller. This controller regulates inputs and keeps the deep cycle storage batteries charged. A small multi-fuel generator is designed as a back-up supply of electricity. Direct current (battery) controls are used because of their higher efficiencies.

Wood and Wood Burning Efficiency

A wood cultivation and harvesting technique called "coppice and pollard" produces more useable firewood than other methods. This method harvests the faster-growing shoots from the main tree trunk that grow back. Fast-growing species of indigenous trees are meant to be planted nearby and specially harvested for a continuous supply of wood for cooking and heating as needed.

A special draft control system on the ultra high efficiency woodstove efficiently burns each piece of wood for maximum heat efficiency. A special downstream smoke scrubber option can greatly increase efficiency and greatly reduce emissions. The stove has the option to be used for cooking at the same time as for space heating or hot water. Only a small amount of wood is necessary for a typical meal using efficient heat transfer techniques.

*Used in Earth Home

Lighting Systems

The use of natural lighting was emphasized wherever possible. Efficient and/or specific task lighting techniques are used wherever the natural lighting is inadequate. A specific type of light bulb for each location was chosen using the criteria cost, lumen level, and hours needed each day.

Earth Cooling and Thermal Mass

Although the underground temperature of the earth varies considerably over the planet, it can be used for natural cooling and/or relief from high temperatures. Water can be circulated through buried coils of tubing and into many water containers. These water containers act as a thermal mass and help to keep the living areas at a comfortable temperature. An efficient low-head, high-flow circulating pump keeps the water flowing through the system. Special plumbing methods prevent leakage from the low-pressure storage "tube-tanks".

Food Systems

After ensuring the self-sufficient home energy needs are met, it provides the best possible techniques for efficient food production, including intensive organic agriculture, undersoil irrigation, aquaculture, and greenhouse trellis system.

Food Production Overview

The Earth Home must use efficient food production techniques. An example of efficient commercial methods of producing food can be seen in large commercial chicken/egg operations. They house 60,000 to 100,000 chickens in a special building that uses conveyors to deliver feed and collect the eggs. This highly mechanized process can be adapted on a much smaller scale for self-sufficient homes.

Fast-growing/efficient animals are chosen and incorporated into the internal "food cycle" or "pyramid" system of production. The waste products from some plants, animals, and/or processes are used as input for other plants and animals until the people are the ultimate consumers.

Disease-resistant strains of open-pollinated plants would be chosen to maximize yield in highly variable conditions. Optimized methods of food preservation are also chosen to minimize labor, resource, and energy use.

Raising Fish

Research has shown that an average family could provide all its animal protein requirements in a 3,000 gallon covered and heated pool full of Tilapia fish. Bass, catfish, carp, or other appropriate species could be used in non-tropical regions.

Air from a wind-powered air compressor is meant to be used to keep the fish tanks aerated with oxygen. Insects are designed to be fed to the fish using a black light capture system to blow them against the surface of the water. Special "fish chow croutons" can be made from some waste products mixed with specific foodstuffs. Fish are one of the most efficient converters of feed to flesh, requiring only 2 to 4 pounds of basic feedstuffs to produce 1 pound of fish.

Animal Raising

One of the requirements of the animals is that they have a high feed efficiency. Many feed-to-food studies have been completed on domesticated agricultural animals commonly used for food. However, some other animals not currently in widespread use have been found to have a much higher feed-to-protein efficiency.

High feed efficiency animals such as fowl, piglets, and chevrotains (small deer) are to be used for the Earth Home system. Note that there approximately a whopping 90% (average) loss of energy when plant food is turned into herbivore meat! This is another reason that vegetarian or near-vegetarian diets are more efficient for any self-sufficient home scheme.

*Used in Earth Home

Plant Production

All non-hybrid open-pollinated plant species are chosen for the following traits; small size, all or most plant parts edible, high nutrient content, local plants for local cultural food groups, adaptable for multiple cropping, low-light tolerant, high growth rate, stores well, sproutable seeds, and tastes good eaten raw. These qualities make the plant more efficient in a smaller space so more high quality food can be produced in a limited area.

Food Preservation Techniques

Self-sufficient home food preservation favors drying because of the low energy input and easier storage characteristics. Fermented foods such as cabbage, Kim chi, and other vegetables are also stressed for many reasons. By fermentation, the food may be made more nutritious (especially B_{12}), more digestible, safer, and/or have better flavor. Fermentation is a relatively efficient low-energy preservation process which can increase product life and reduce the need for refrigeration or other energy-intensive processes for food preservation.

The least-favored method is freezing and refrigerating because of higher energy use. A low energy use refrigerator and freezer are used with special modifications to increase efficiency.

Typical Diet

Typical diet in the self-sufficient home includes vegetables, raw fruits, raw juices, protein, and carbohydrates. Protein from fish, fowl and small mammals are meant to be utilized. Carbohydrates from root crops and grain production would be used for most meals. Oil for salad dressings and cooking is meant to be produced from local oil crops such as soybeans, sunflower, and/or rapeseeds (canola). Estimates indicate that a balanced diet should provide over 1600 calories per day per person.

Water System and Technologies

Even though water is the most common substance on Earth, only 2.8% of the planet's water is fresh water (not salty), and the UN estimates that agriculture uses from 2/3 to 3/4 of the available supply.

Rainfall Cycle/Background

Water from rainfall is eventually evaporated back up into the atmosphere. Rainfall can be divided roughly into thirds. One third evaporates as soon as it hits the Earth because the ground temperature is usually warmer than the rain. The splashing water spreads over great amounts of surface area and speeds evaporation. Another one-third of the rainfall runs off the soil into creeks, rivers, lakes, and finally into the ocean. The last one-third soaks into the ground, gets filtered by the soil, and becomes part of underground water systems, or "aquifers".

In arid regions, approximately two-thirds of the rainfall is evaporated back into the air immediately. Another third runs off into streams, leaving only about 3% actually replenishing the groundwater supplies in those areas.

Rainwater Collection/Filtration History

Rainwater contains virtually no bacteria count before it hits the surface, so it's very clean. It's very similar to distilled water because it contains very little chemicals, minerals, salts, rust, etc. It's also naturally softened, which means that soap will easily make suds. This makes it easier to clean clothes, dishes, and bodies.

Many countries currently use substantial amounts of rainwater. In Hawaii, Greece, much of the Caribbean, Korea, Japan, and Israel, for example, the major part of the water supply comes from rainwater.

Rainwater is meant to be used in the self-sufficient home after filtration. To make the home self-sufficient, it is necessary to use water filters that can be reused. A natural pre-filter system made of screens, gravel, and finally sand traps any roof debris before going into the storage tank. Final filtration is accomplished by reusable water filters that contain serrated disks stacked on top of one another. The fine serrations between the disks let the water through and trap the particles.

*Used in Earth Home

Metal Roof/Gutter Catchment System

Corrugated steel roofing material is commonly used throughout the world because of its durability and reasonable cost. It also stands up well to intense sunshine. In a self-sufficient living scheme, any rainfall must be fully utilized. Special oversized rain gutters and piping is designed to fully utilize any torrential rains of short duration.

Pure Drinking Water Production

Rainwater should be purified before human consumption. Excellent water quality can be obtained using the distillation process. The ancient Greeks used the distillation process on their ships to convert seawater into drinking water. Distillation is one of mankind's earliest forms of water treatment and is still popular throughout the world. Distillation can be accomplished with a small amount of heat or solar energy.

Water Recycling with an Aerobic Digester

Major energy would be expended in pumping any "new" groundwater to the surface for every use in the home—especially where animal watering and plant irrigation is needed. Water re-use is very important for self-sufficient home systems. Water can be re-used in two major ways; graywater from washing, and treated blackwater (toilet water) after treatment. A specially modified aerobic digester takes in used water and begins the purification process.

A wind-powered air compressor system is used to bubble air through the digester to make it work. Water coming out of the digester is recycled to under-soil irrigation and the natural air conditioning system.

Indoor Air Quality

There are many different chemicals used in modern building materials that are potentially unhealthy for the occupants. Reliance on non-outgassing natural and local materials are preferred for health and cost reasons.

Passive Ventilation Techniques

Passive ventilation is used to adjust the home to variable weather conditions that may come up. For example, as the wind changes direction, doors open and close to allow maximum venting of hot air from the home and greenhouse. This system avoids the high energy use of powered fans and duct systems. Roof openings and built-in vents allow the lighter hot air to escape the home envelope when needed.

Natural Cooling

Swamp coolers are low-impact devices that cool by evaporation or by using groundwater to cool the air in order to reduce the air temperature. Typical evaporating swamp coolers work best in low-humidity environments. However, fully enclosed coolers can re-circulate the lower temperature groundwater to provide relief from the heat even in humid environments. A series of cool water tanks acts as a thermal mass to buffer the effects of outside temperature fluctuations.

Air Filtration and HRV's

A heat recovery ventilator (HRV) is a method to exhaust stale inside air and replace it with fresh outside air. As the stale air goes out and the fresh air comes in, they pass close to each other and heat is exchanged between them. This is a method to mix indoor and outdoor air without significant energy inputs other than the small fan necessary to move the air.

Reusable air filters are meant to be used in self-sufficient home systems. These filters have a permanent coating that catches dust and particles and are cleaned by soap and water. The air quality inside the home is also improved by mixing with the oxygen-rich attached greenhouse air when appropriate.

Electronic Systems

*Used in Earth Home

Optimized methods of planting, watering, feeding, harvesting, storage, and preparation would be chosen that would maximize benefit and minimize human effort. These methods would require a large number of different functions that rely on regularly scheduled events or occurrences. For example, environmental controls that would respond to changing weather would need adjusting on a constant basis.

Simple manual controls and tasks that would operate the home and food production process could be utilized, but it would require more people, hours of labor, and very close attention to details virtually 24 hours a day. We humans make mistakes and those mistakes could be very costly in a complete self-sufficient home scheme.

A basic and reliable home control system that is adapted and programmed to each location would save much effort and attention, eliminate errors, and help to coordinate all the activities and functions of the home system. This more extensive automated electronic system could be installed and programmed at any time.

Adaptability to New Technologies

The Earth Home is meant to be adaptable to new technologies as they emerge. Flexibility in regards to design changes saves much effort. New technologies could include breakthroughs in hydrogen storage, biomass technologies, new solar technology, fuel cell breakthroughs, alternative energy storage technologies, and many more.

Recent Technological Advances Aiding SS Home Development

In the last decade or so, many significant products and development efforts have emerged that fit well into self-sufficient home development needs. Battery and energy demand research, DC (direct current) circulating pumps, hydrogen production and storage technologies, CHP (combined heat and power) units, and the popular healthy food trend are among many developments that may speed the evolution of modern self-sufficient homes.

Storage Battery Technology

Presently, completely self-sufficient homes store electricity in various types of batteries. High power densities and lower cost are very important. The electronics and automotive industry are primarily driving research into small, light, and power-dense batteries.

Efficient Motors, Pumps, and Fans

The average home in the United States contains approximately 60 different electric motors—virtually all of which are inefficient. A large amount of electricity is used in the fan motors that circulate hot and cold air inside the home to maintain comfortable temperatures.

Much research effort on electric motors has resulted in ECM (electronically commutated motor) technology that draws an amazingly small amount of electricity when it needs it. This motor technology has been applied to liquid circulating pumps in the solar heating industry. The companies Laing Thermotech in Denmark and Wilo Stratos have recently introduced continuous duty DC circulating pumps that draw less than 10 watts of electricity!

Hydrogen Evolution and Advancements

Gaseous hydrogen is similar to natural gas or propane with less heating value per cubic foot. However, when gaseous hydrogen burns, pure water is the result. This makes it a unique non-polluting element that can be generated by electricity and stored for later use. As this generation and storage technology comes of age, hydrogen could be useful as a clean fuel source for such tasks as cooking and heating domestic hot water.

Combined Heat and Power Units (CHP)

ACEEE estimates that conventional thermal power plants waste about two-thirds of their input energy. CHP systems can cut this waste roughly in half. CHP systems, also known as cogeneration, generate electricity and thermal energy in a single, integrated system.

*Used in Earth Home

Some CHP units are chest-freezer-sized and are designed to be used in residential applications. When electricity is needed, a gaseous fuel is pumped directly into the fuel cell to efficiently produce both DC electricity and heat. Hydrogen, propane, natural gas, methane, and some other fuels can be successfully used as a power source for CHP units. There are at least five companies in the world developing residential CHP units.

Health/Organic Food Industry

Health-related technologies are also helping to evolve self-sufficient homes. This field of products and services for maintaining one's health is an increasingly significant share of the gross national product for many developed countries. A substantial portion of the industry is dedicated to promoting the body's natural ability to maintain health, stamina, and weight through nutritious eating, fresh air, exercise, and adequate vitamin/mineral intake. These qualities are very easy to implement in a self-sufficient home lifestyle since virtually all foods can be raised on-site—controlling all soil, plant, and animal inputs.

Mass-Production Implementation Options

While the poor will always be on this planet, I feel another model of lifestyle should be explored. A mass-producible self-sufficient home design using low impact materials and technology could and should be developed by all nations of the world on all continents. This "mini-farm" or small "food factory" would be self-sustaining and ecologically compatible.

Planning and Design Phase

I believe each nation should begin projects that would prove the feasibility of a low-impact home that provides all food and power for a family. Countries could adapt the complete self-sufficient home techniques to their unique situation, climate, indigenous food/fuel crops, and social/cultural customs.

Natural Construction Alternatives
Low-Impact Materials

Each project could use local natural or low-impact materials. Home construction alternative materials include papercrete, cob, adobe, rammed earth, light clay, straw-clay, earthbag, flax-bale, straw-bale, and many others. Some of the natural home component and wall materials include; bamboo, straw panels, pozzolans, Carrizo, lime plaster, and various organic fibers. Indigenous floor materials can include earthen floors, adobe, and various concrete variations—with infloor heating options. Bamboo and other materials could be used for components such as gravity water pipes.

Roofing Durability

Aluminum is a very long-lasting roofing material, but it has very high embodied energy. Recycled aluminum from the soft drink industry could be used for durable roofing, but recycled aluminum is now being re-used for more beverage cans. Corrugated steel contains lower embodied energy, lasts for a very long time, and is in common use world-wide. Steel also does not contaminate any collected rainwater.

Minimizing Timber Use

It is usually a surprise to learn that lightweight wood framing or "stick-frame" has become the predominant building method in the U.S. only since the end of World War II. Returning GI's and a flourishing economy embraced it because it was fast and cheap. To minimize lumber use, post and beam construction techniques that have been used for hundreds of years should be used in self-sufficient home schemes. Substantial wood use in the walls, interior partitions, and floor has been avoided.

Self-Sufficient Home Variations for Other Climates

The basic design of an Earth Home would remain the same if built in any climatic region, though it would have to be adjusted or modified slightly depending on local conditions. Factors that would affect the fine-tuning of the design include soil conditions, solar/wind ratio for power generation, altitude, tropical/cold climate species potential (trees, oil plants, and other species), rainfall, and average temperature.

Examples for Other Locations

In a rainforest, for example, an Earth Home would use more photovoltaic panels to generate energy from the sun and rely less on wind generators. Earth Home construction in the tropics would also favor foliage to help keep the sun's rays off the surface of the home by using wall and/or roof lattices.

In colder locations, generating energy from wind power would be more important as well as requiring greater insulation systems for the primary heating zone or core rooms. Wind generator and wind air compressor models would be chosen that is more resistant to damage from high winds.

Hot and Dry Climate Variation

In dry climates more rainwater storage tanks would be filled from the over-sized rain gutters from the roof. Special solar distillation, solar cooking, and food dehydrator adaptations could also be employed. More underground tubing would be required as well as increasing the capacity of the natural cooling circulation system for indoor comfort.

Local and Cultural Variations in Food Plants

Local diets would be copied as much as possible. Traditional cultural cuisine and foods that support the existing diet would take precedence in order for the home to gain acceptance.

Owner/Builder Options

After the concept is proven for each location by testing mass-produced models, kits could be made available. The owner-builders should have access to the technology, products, and systems. These could be purchased as needed and assembled using family or village help. In this way proliferation would happen more quickly.

Self-Sufficient Home Potential Models
Extended Family/Village Model

The basic floor plan of Earth Homes could be easily modified by additions to either end or rear. Rooms could be attached to the basic shell without significantly affecting the operation of the main structure. Even whole villages could use the Earth Home as a food production and storage facility. Each family could concentrate on specific food or animal production techniques of interest.

High-Rise Urban Model

The Earth Home could very well be the top floor of a multi-family dwelling. The lower areas could be individual residences that are heated and cooled by the central woodstove in the centre of the main self-sufficient home. The wind generator/photovoltaic system would have to be larger for the increased capacity.

Urban Location Model

It is designed that the self-sufficient home functionality is dependent on only a small amount of outside land in order to support its occupants. The bio-intensive raised mounds do not require a huge amount of land like other farming techniques. The Earth Home could fit nicely into an urban setting providing there would be unrestricted access to the sunshine for the interior plants.

Effect of World-Wide Proliferation of Self-Sufficient Homes

A variety of significant, attractive short-term benefits may drive the development of modern self-sufficient homes. These include security from severe weather, climate changes, natural disasters; and related health problems. I feel self-sufficient homes would provide increased security from the effects of global disturbances.

Human Health Benefits

*Used in Earth Home

A healthy, nutritious, and most importantly—dependable food supply is a very strong benefit of the self-sufficient home.

More Security from Infectious Diseases

An increase in the numbers of modern self-sufficient homes would also offer more security from infectious diseases because of less-frequent air travel and interactions with other people. If many people did become sick, more effective long-term isolation would be possible.

Significant Diet Improvement

Self-sufficient homes would be health-enhancing by helping people improve their diets and lifestyles. Many books deal with fresh fruits, vegetables, and juices as "medicine" for the body. Many nutritionists agree that disease and health-related problems can be reduced or deterred if people eat fresh food.

Studies have shown that vegetables and fruits start losing vitamins and minerals from the very moment they are picked, even though methods of cooking are used to ensure that they remain nutritious. Many of the foods we purchase today differ significantly in vitamin and mineral value from the same ones a generation or two ago. Part of the reason is that many essential vitamins and minerals no longer make it back into the soil that grows our food. Self-sufficient homes would add composted nutrients back into the soil supply.

Reduction in Obesity and Malnutrition

It has been said that there is only one major world disease, and that is malnutrition. Some say that all ailments and afflictions that we inherit are directly traceable to this major disease. Some 31% of Americans are overweight and obesity has become a world-wide health problem.

The Amish have a significantly less rate of obesity (4%) than the average American which is commonly attributable to more physically active lifestyles. Self-sufficient home owners would commonly be more active also due to the routine planting, weeding, harvesting, preserving, preparation, and cooking of food. In addition, the lifestyle would enjoy a healthy and nutritious diet in and around the home.

Environmental Benefits

A gradual transition to self-sufficient home technologies will also have significant worldwide, long-term benefits.

Increase Sustainability

Self-sufficient homes would minimize negative impacts on their surroundings because they can be built with green or alternative construction. They can employ low-water toilets, wastewater treatment, water reuse, graywater systems, smoke scrubbers, and recycling to reduce pollution and conserve water. By composting and water recycling, they reduce the burden on world water supplies and slow the advance of global soil problems.

But the real benefit of Earth Homes will be the long-term sustainability of our planet. Through its innovations, the modern self-sufficient home is one way of helping limit human environmental degradation and increasing resource sustainability. Fewer natural resources are also required for packaging foods, transportation, and other aspects of dependent living.

Slow Global Warming

"Many scientists agree that the emissions resulting from human activities are substantially increasing the atmospheric concentration of the greenhouse gasses," writes Jeremy Leggett in his book Global Warming: The Greenpeace Report (Oxford University Press, 1990). "These increases will enhance the greenhouse effect, resulting in warming of the earth's surface." In 1990, scientists predicted that, if greenhouse gas emissions are not sharply decreased, we might experience a 1°C to 3°C rise in global temperatures. They suggest that we would have to cut in half our use of coal, oil, and gas in order to lower our emissions enough to maintain concentrations of greenhouse gases at current levels.

*Used in Earth Home

Proof of this warming includes a decrease in the amount of snow that covers the northern hemisphere, a simultaneous decrease in Arctic Sea ice, melting of alpine glaciers, and a rise in sea level. Rain has even been reported for the first time in Antarctica and an ice-free patch of ocean about a mile wide has opened near the North Pole.

Slow Carbon Dioxide Rate of Increase

Studies have shown that the carbon dioxide concentration in our atmosphere has been steadily increasing since 1958. Even though the rate of emissions from fossil fuels has been reduced, concentration has risen consistently. There are 100 million cattle in the U.S. and approximately 1.2 billion large ruminants in the world. Many studies have implicated these animals in carbon dioxide increases. Self-sufficient homes would help to slow the increase by decreasing the number of methane-generating cattle that are raised for food. Higher feed-to-food ratio animals that also use less water would typically be used in self-sufficient home schemes.

Slow Ozone Rate of Increase

Ozone is also a significant environmental issue. In 1995, the size of the ozone hole over Antarctica doubled to about the size of Europe. For the first time in recorded history, the hole stretched over populated areas, exposing residents in southern Chile and Argentina to very high levels of ultraviolet (UV) radiation. Studies have shown that a 1% decrease in ozone in the stratosphere produces a 2% increase in UV radiation reaching the ground, posing more risks to humans.

Australia has the highest rate of skin cancer in the world, with estimates that two out of three people will get at least one skin cancer in their lifetimes. Self-sufficient lifestyles would use much smaller amounts of products that contribute to ozone depletion.

Energy Use Reduction

A gradual transition to self-sufficient home technologies would slow the increased dependence on central energy production. The United States, for example, uses half of its agriculture energy to produce animals, and spends 3 to 12 calories in petroleum energy to produce one calorie of food.

In addition to agricultural energy outputs, an estimated 20% to 30% of all energy is consumed in a modern home. Adding the energy used for food production, processing, and distribution, this is an enormous amount of resources! In contrast, the self-sufficient home will produce its own energy, freeing families from dependence on outside sources.

Economic and Social Benefits
Efficiently Producing Food/Helping to Prevent Malnutrition

The Food and Agriculture Organization of the UN estimates that from 10 to 40 percent of the world harvest is wasted because of harvesting losses, storage losses, processing losses, transportation losses, and kitchen and plate waste. Self-sufficient homes would be designed to produce the maximum amount of food using the minimum amount of energy and labor. Self-sufficient homes will help prevent malnutrition by increasing total food production.

Slow the "2-Income Family" Trend

In the U.S. there has been an increasing trend to have two people support a family. This trend has been on the increase for a long time—probably starting sometime in the late 1970's. I feel that Earth Home technology is capable of slowing and even a reversal of the two-income family trend.

Create Jobs

The testing and technology for this "product" could be a model for other variations of the home that would be slightly modified for different climatic regions and local food cultivars. This continuing research, testing, and manufacturing have the capability to create another industry that will begin to perpetuate itself.

*Used in Earth Home

Cottage Industry Possibilities

Some possible trade items that may be generated by Earth Home families include: compost, fertilizer, seed, specialty dried or portable foods, vinegar, medicinal products, home components, natural building materials, and other foodstuffs. Some home maintenance and tool repair services may also be possible.

Develop Rural/Marginal Use Areas

There are many areas in the world that are marginally used for agriculture, housing, or other human activities. This land could be utilized for Earth Homes because quality arable land and abundant water supplies are not necessary—only intermittent water obtained to supply the water storage tanks.

Global Benefits

International Cooperation on Technology

There would be common design intent, components, sub-assemblies, and methodology to all the designs. However, each country could choose a variation of the basic model and/or components for development and testing, based on climate, regional preferences, natural resources, expertise, and social customs among many others.

International Trade Potential

Components could be used in commerce for importation and export. These components would be made in each country and be used to trade for other components needed by self-sufficient homes.

Generate New Research Projects

Any research and development (R&D) efforts on self-sufficient homes would theoretically never end. R&D efforts by major corporations are simply ongoing. The only variables are the focus and budget from year to year.

Lower Cost Component Research

It is widely known that higher production volumes mean lower cost. These volumes would drive improvements in design very similar to manufacturers of automobiles, wash machines, and most mass-produced consumer items.

More System Integration

Total system design would also improve because of international cooperation. There could be competitions for the lowest impact components, products, and processes. This would result in specialized expertise in all areas of the design.

To simply begin thinking about a self-sufficient home as a mass-producible product would open up new and interesting thought patterns in the creative minds. Louis Pasteur once said, "Chance favors a prepared mind".

Answering Criticisms

Technical Impossibility?

There have never been calculations showing that it is impossible to provide enough food for a family in a small space. In fact, the efficiency of food production has never been critically looked into as a "system" until the previously mentioned Biosphere II project in Arizona. The Earth Home system allows interaction with the outside environment, full contact with fresh air, and full sunshine without most of the glass covering. These effects would increase the food production efficiencies. I have often said that given appropriate time and money, most technically challenging projects can be accomplished.

Turning Back Time?

*Used in Earth Home

This modern self-sufficient home technology is not turning back the clock into the Middle Ages, but a modern response to a changing world. The techniques used are cutting-edge sustainable technologies that are combined into a home system that would improve the future for all people. This technology offers another lifestyle that offers increased health, security, and peace of mind to those who choose it. The world stands to benefit greatly from the proliferation of the modern self-sufficient homes.

Too Complex and Too Expensive?

Some have said that this system is too complex and costly. To respond to this, I would say that many products intended for mass production have this criticism in common. As the products are gradually incorporated into the marketplace and the sales volume starts to increase, many changes happen. New processes, designs, and/or materials are incorporated into the product—making them less costly, able to be produced faster, more efficient, or contain enhanced features. By far, the biggest expense for any product occurs in the design, tooling, and setup phases of development.

To counter this argument, I would also ask, "What is the cost of not developing self-sufficient homes?"

Conclusion

Human beings are stewards of the earth, and I believe it is our responsibility to give this earth to future generations in the same or better condition than we received it. I also believe that we have a moral obligation to help those less fortunate than ourselves. Approximately one-half of the world's 6 billion people have no fresh water to drink, and another one-third have inadequate food or housing. Albert Schweitzer once said, "Whoever is spared personal pain must feel ... called to help in diminishing the pain of others."

My sincere wish is that modern self-sufficient home technology will mature while resources and conditions are favorable to its development—if not for single-family use, then for extended family or village use. I would love to still be alive when I see international cooperation in this endeavor.

Thanks for listening............Mel
See www.planetearthhome.com for more information.

3. Other Publications

As of publication date, there are 2 other conferences and one video production in the making.

G. EH Tabs/Modifications for Other Locations & Uses

1. Koppen Climate Classification System

a. History and Description of System

Many attempts have been made to classify the climates of the earth into climatic regions. One notable example is that of Aristotle's Temperate, Torrid, and Frigid Zones. However, the 20th century classification developed by German climatologist and amateur botanist Wladimir Koppen continues to be the authoritative map of the world climates in use today.

The Koppen system has been modified by several geographers since his death. The following modified Koppen classification uses six letters to divide the world into six major climate regions, based on average annual precipitation, average monthly precipitation, and average monthly temperature. After the general climate description, a description of the general vegetation follows.

A for Tropical Humid
B for Dry
C for Mild Mid-Latitude
D for Severe Mid-Latitude
E for Polar
H for Highland

b. Koppen Chart

A	**Tropical humid**	Af	Tropical wet	No dry season
		Am	Tropical monsoonal	Short dry season; heavy monsoonal rains in other months
		Aw	Tropical savanna	Winter dry season
B	**Dry**	BWh	Subtropical desert	Low-latitude desert
		BSh	Subtropical steppe	Low-latitude dry
		BWk	Mid-latitude desert	Mid-latitude desert
		BSk	Mid-latitude steppe	Mid-latitude dry
C	**Mild Mid-Latitude**	Csa	Mediterranean	Mild with dry, hot summer
		Csb	Mediterranean	Mild with dry, warm summer
		Cfa	Humid subtropical	Mild with no dry season, hot summer
		Cwa	Humid subtropical	Mild with dry winter, hot summer
		Cfb	Marine west coast	Mild with no dry season, warm summer
		Cfc	Marine west coast	Mild with no dry season, cool summer
D	**Severe Mid-Latitude**	Dfa	Humid continental	Humid with severe winter, no dry season, hot summer
		Dfb	Humid continental	Humid with severe winter, no dry season, warm summer
		Dwa	Humid continental	Humid with severe, dry winter, hot summer
		Dwb	Humid continental	Humid with severe, dry winter, warm summer
		Dfc	Subarctic	Severe winter, no dry season, cool summer
		Dfd	Subarctic	Severe, very cold winter, no dry season, cool summer
		Dwc	Subarctic	Severe, dry winter, cool summer
		Dwd	Subarctic	Severe, very cold and dry winter, cool summer
E	**Polar**	ET	Tundra	Polar tundra, no true summer
		EF	Ice Cap	Perennial ice
H	**Highland**			

Figure 7-KOPPEN CHART

*Used in Earth Home

Each Koppen category is further divided into sub-categories based on temperature and precipitation. For instance, the U.S. states located along the Gulf of Mexico are designated as "Cfa." The "C" represents the "mild mid-latitude" category, the second letter "f" stands for the German word feucht or "moist," and the third letter "a" indicates that the average temperature of the warmest month is above 72°F (22°C). Thus, "Cfa" gives us a good indication of the climate of this region, a mild mid-latitude climate with no dry season and a hot summer. The following figures are various maps to illustrate these geographical areas.

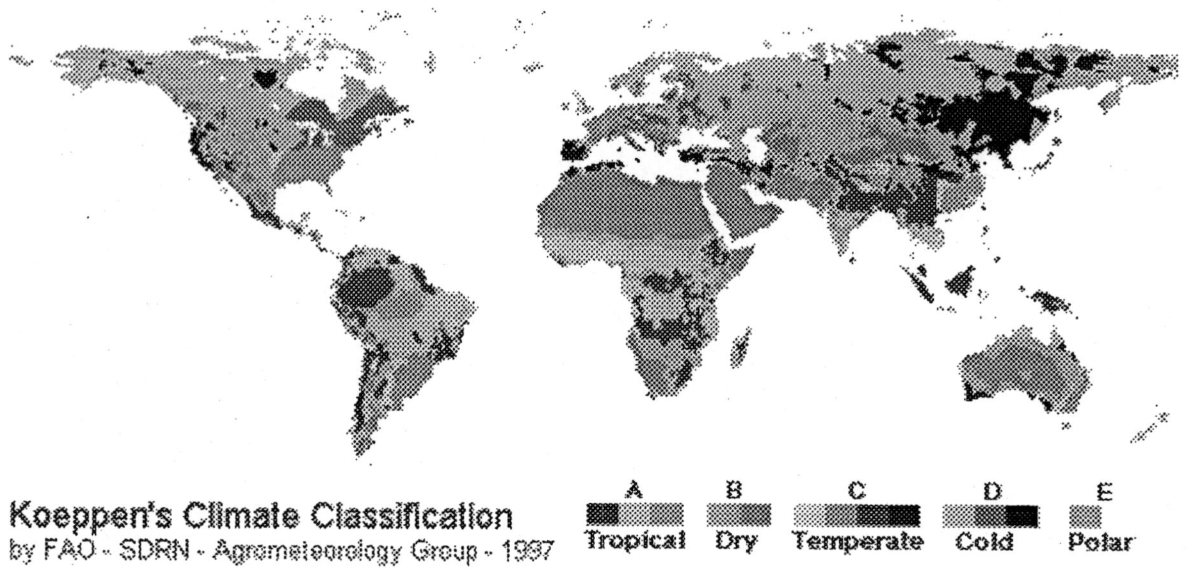

Figure 8-GLOBAL BIOME MAP

*Used in Earth Home

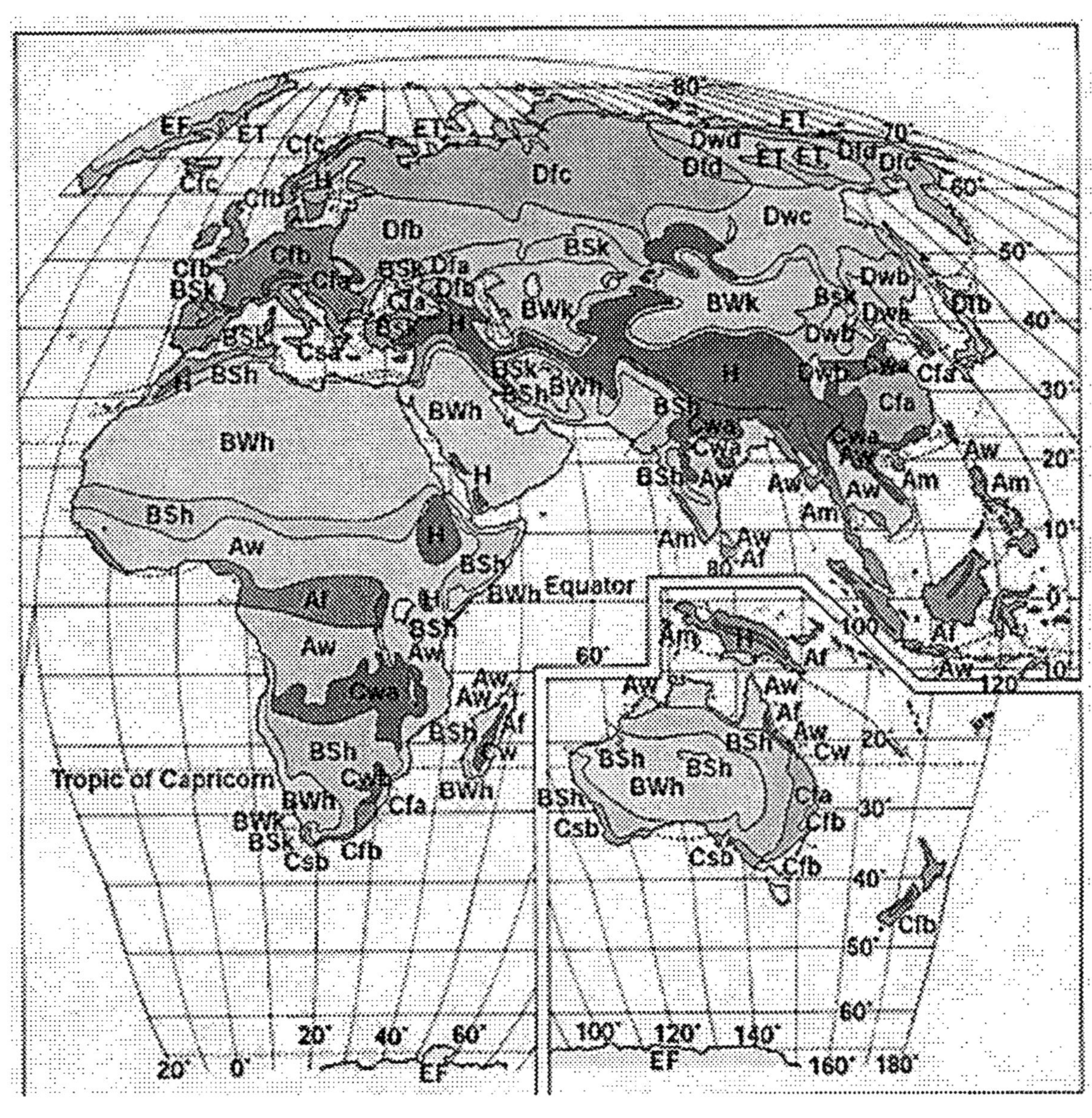

Figure 9-KOPPEN-EASTERN

*Used in Earth Home

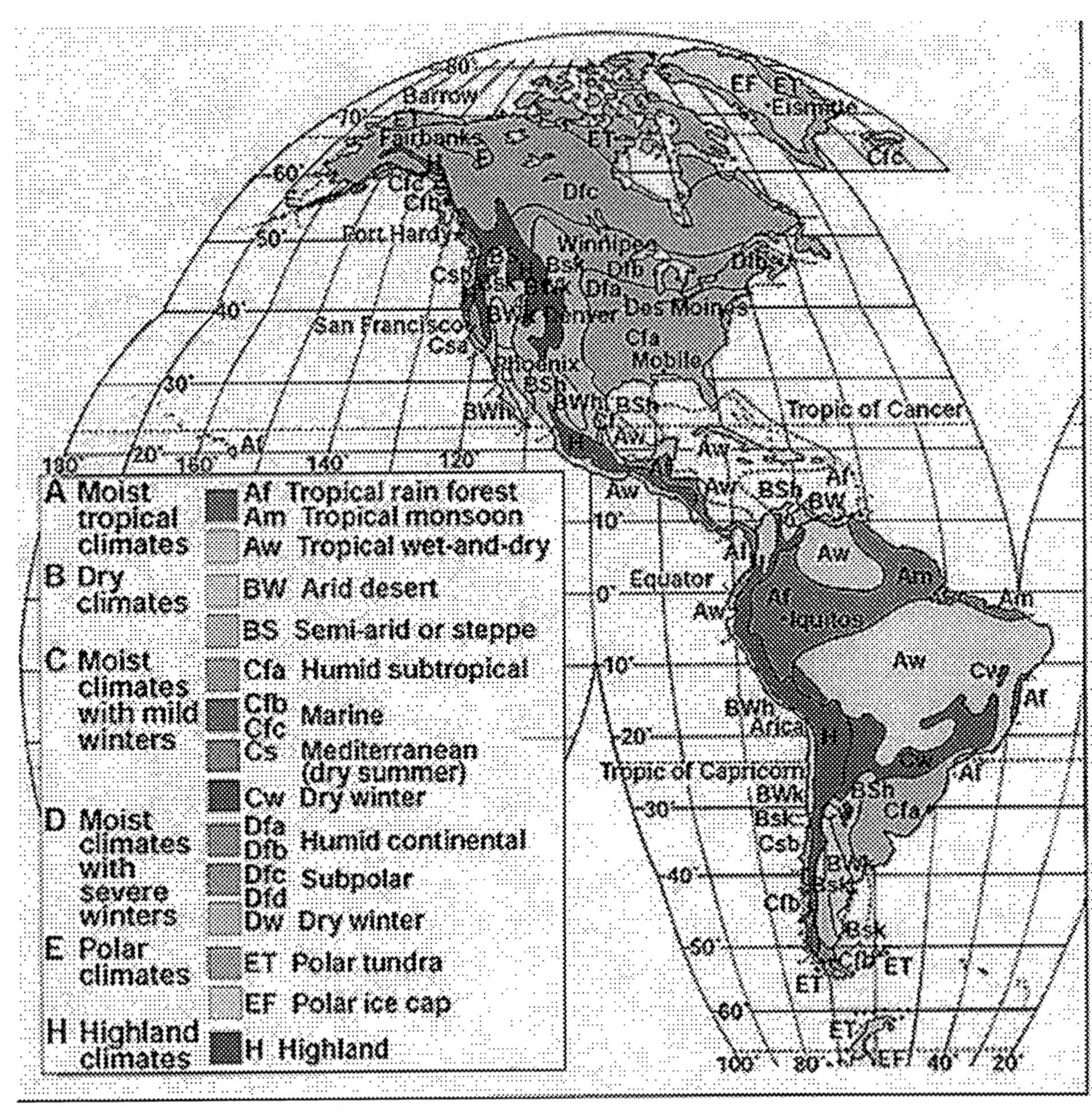

Figure 10-KOPPEN-WESTERN

*Used in Earth Home

c. A for Tropical Humid/Moist

Tropical moist climates extend northward and southward from the equator to about 15 to 25 degrees of latitude. In these climates all months have average temperatures greater than 18 degrees Celsius. Annual precipitation is greater than 1500 mm. Three minor Köppen climate types exist in the A group and their designation is based on seasonal distribution of rainfall. Af or tropical wet is a tropical the climate where precipitation occurs all year long. Monthly temperature variations in this climate are less than 3 degrees Celsius. Because of intense surface heating and high humidity cumulus and cumulonimbus clouds form early in the afternoons almost every day. Daily highs are about 32 degrees Celsius while night time temperatures average 22 degrees Celsius. Am is a tropical monsoon climate. Annual rainfall is equal to or greater than Af, but falls in the 7 to 9 hottest months. During the dry season very little rainfall occurs. The tropical wet and dry or savanna (Aw) has an extended dry season during winter. Precipitation during the wet season is usually less than 1000 millimeters—and only during the summer season.

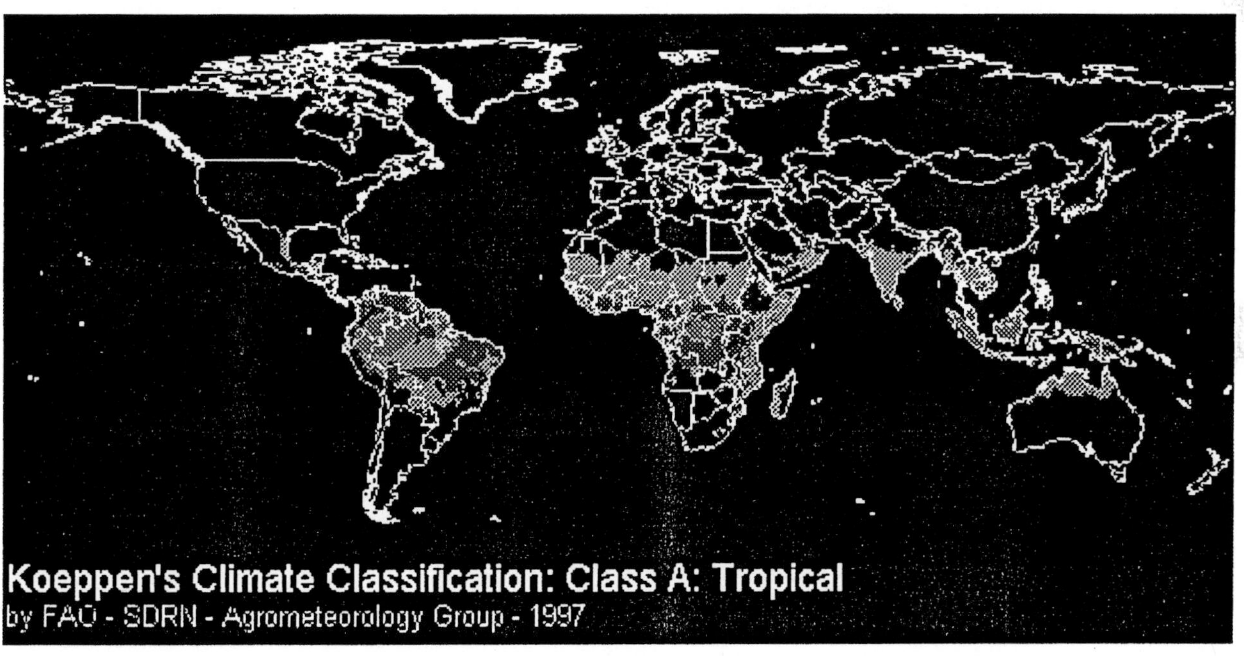

Koeppen's Climate Classification: Class A: Tropical
by FAO - SDRN - Agrometeorology Group - 1997

Figure 11-A REGIONS

d. B for Dry Climates

The most obvious climatic feature of this climate is potential evaporation and transpiration exceeds precipitation. These climates extend from 20 - 35 degrees North and South of the equator and in large continental regions of the mid-latitudes often surrounded by mountains. Minor types of this climate include:

--Bw - dry arid (desert) is a true desert climate. It covers 12 % of the earth's land surface and is dominated by xerophytic vegetation.

--Bs - dry semiarid (steppe) is a grassland climate that covers 14% of the earth's land surface. It receives more precipitation than the Bw either from the intertropical convergence zone or from mid-latitude cyclones.

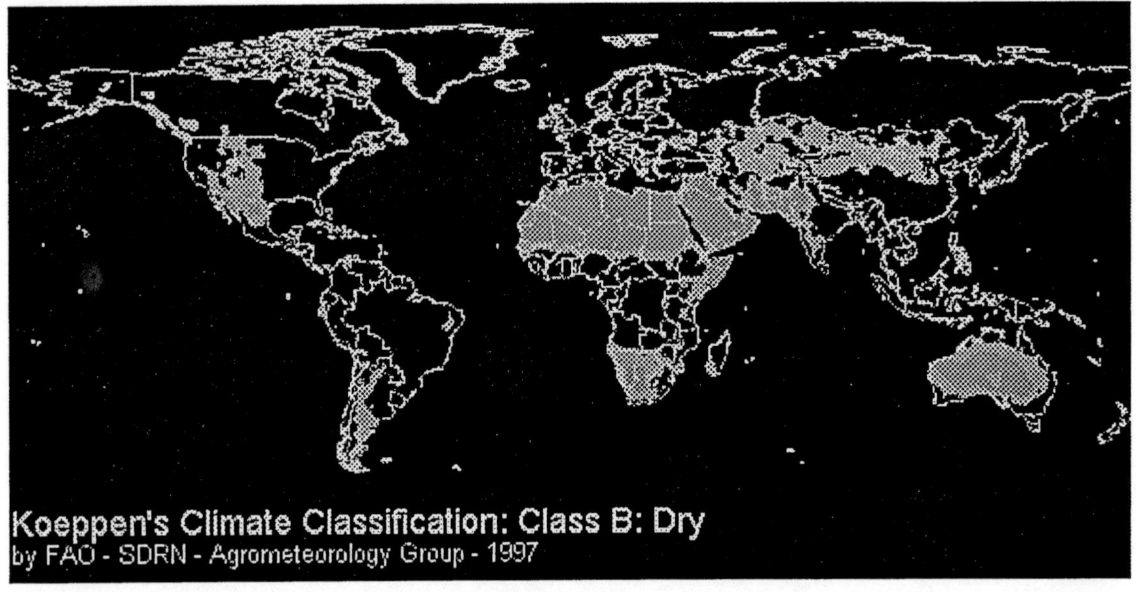

Figure 12-B REGIONS

*Used in Earth Home

e. C for Moist Subtropical Mid-Latitude Climates

This climate generally has warm and humid summers with mild winters. Its extent is from 30 to 50 degrees of latitude mainly on the eastern and western borders of most continents. During the winter the main weather feature is the mid-latitude cyclone. Convective thunderstorms dominate summer months. Three minor types exist: Cfa - humid subtropical; Cs - Mediterranean; and Cfb - marine. The humid subtropical climate (Cfa) has hot muggy summers and mainly thunderstorms. Winters are mild and precipitation during this season comes from mid-latitude cyclones. A good example of a Cfa climate is the southeastern USA. Cfb, marine, climates are found on the western coasts of continents. They have a humid climate with short dry summer. Heavy precipitation occurs during the mild winters because of continuous presence of mid-latitude cyclones. Mediterranean climates (Cs) receive rain primarily during winter season from the mid-latitude cyclone. Extreme summer aridity is caused by the sinking air of the subtropical highs and may exist for up to 5 months. Locations in North America are from Portland, Oregon to all of California.

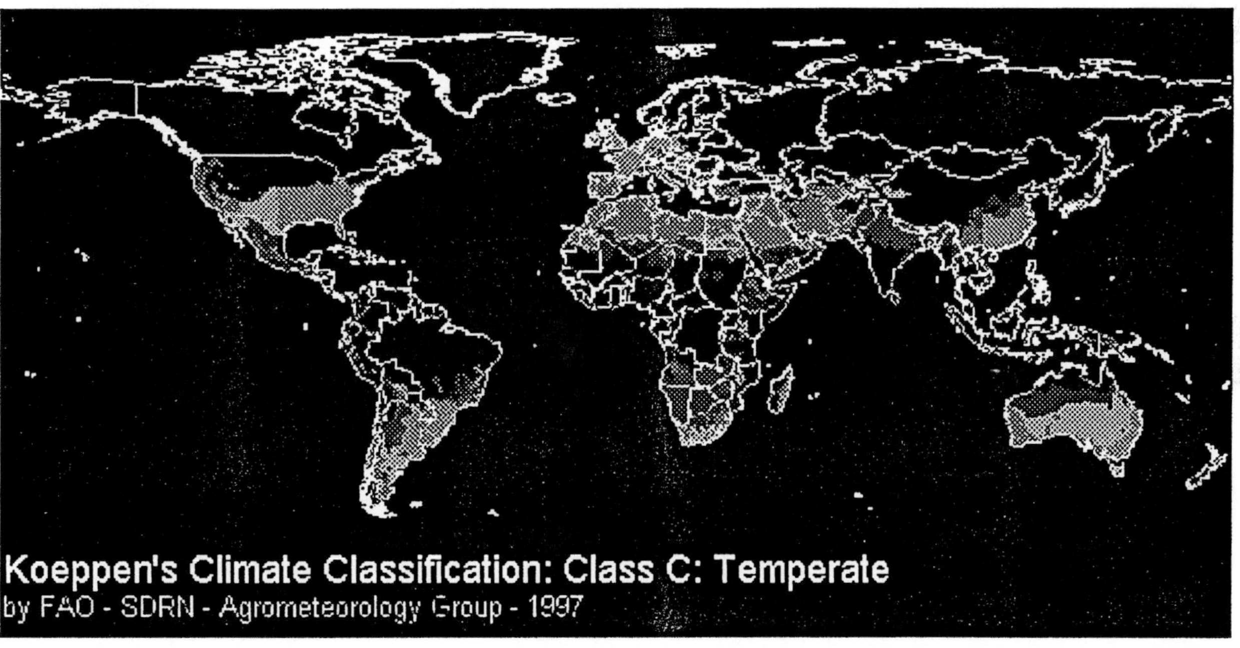

Figure 13-C REGIONS

*Used in Earth Home

f. D for Moist Continental Mid-latitude Climates

Moist continental mid-latitude climates have warm to cool summers and cold winters. The location of these climates is pole ward of the C climates. The warmest month is greater than 10 degrees Celsius, while the coldest month is less than -30 degrees Celsius. Winters are severe with snowstorms, strong winds, and bitter cold from Continental Polar or Arctic air masses. Like the C climates there are three minor types: Dw - dry winters; Ds - dry summers; and Df - wet all seasons.

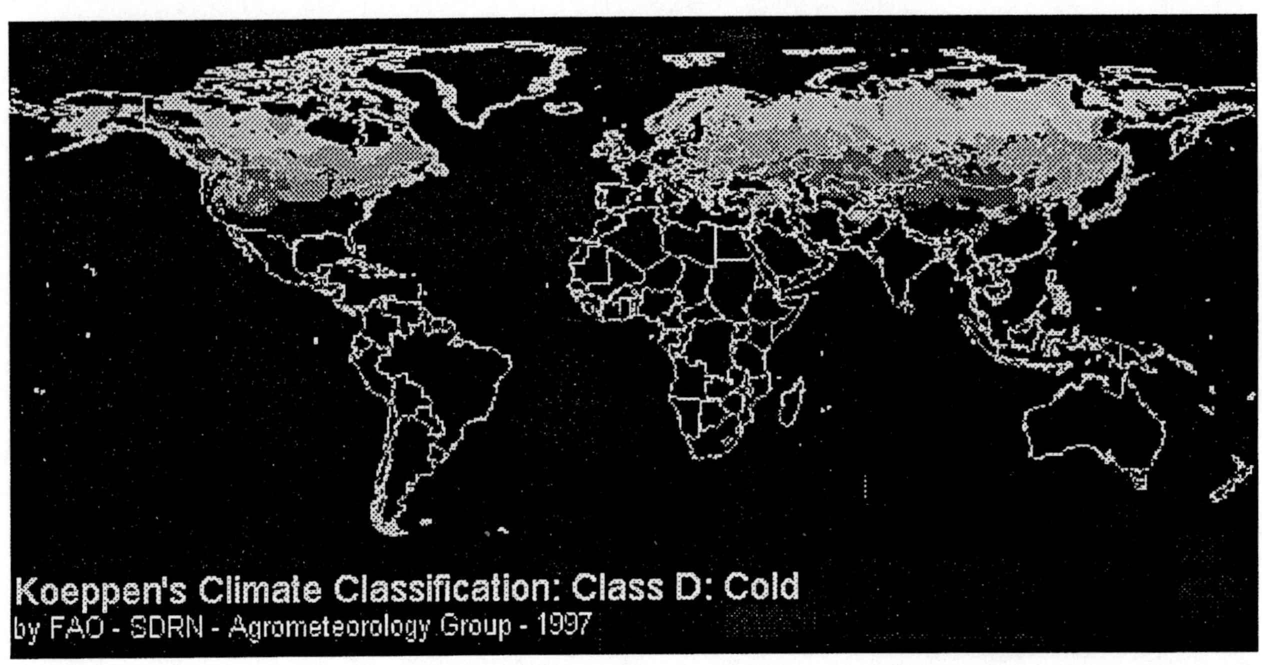

Figure 14-D REGIONS

g. E for Polar Climates

Polar climates have year-round cold temperatures with warmest month less than 10 degrees Celsius. Polar climates are found on the northern coastal areas of North America and Europe, Asia and on the landmasses of Greenland and Antarctica. Two minor climate types exist. ET or polar tundra is a climate where the soil is permanently frozen to depths of hundreds of meters, a condition known as permafrost. Vegetation is dominated by mosses, lichens, dwarf trees and scattered woody shrubs. EF or polar ice caps has a surface that is permanently covered with snow and ice.

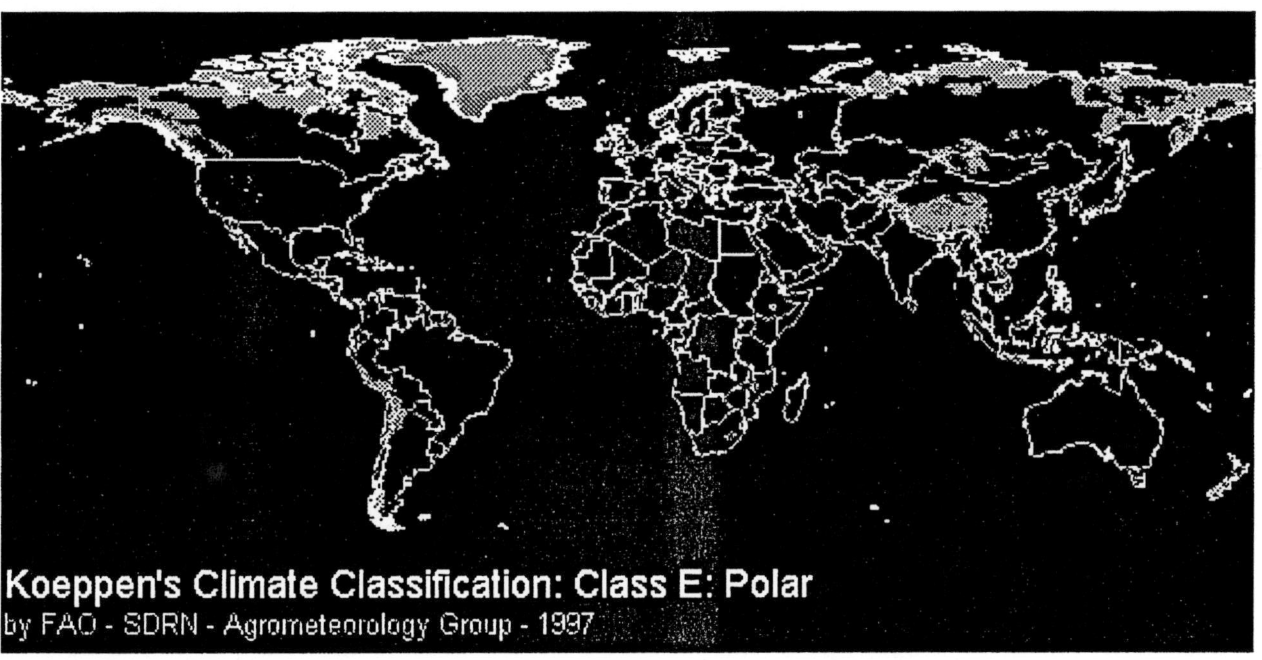

Figure 15-E REGIONS

2. Climate and Vegetation Groups

a. Description of Groups

More detailed information helps to differentiate between climatic regions/groups. Koppen used vegetation groups to aid in climate classification. Definite temperature and precipitation criteria are used to distinguish between climate types.

A climates are hot and moist.
C climates are warm and moist.
D climates are cool and moist.
B climates include a wide range of temperature and a range of moisture.

b. Tropical (A) Climates

All tropical climates are warm; the subdivisions are based on differences in precipitation. Tropical Rainforest (AF) Climate is located in the ITCZ (10-15 N/S). Diurnal range in temperature is greater than the difference between the warmest and coolest months (annual range). Every month has precipitation and no month is deficient in rainfall. This high amount of rainfall keeps the soil moisture at capacity. EVT occurs at potential rate.

c. Tropical Rainforest (Af) Climate

Vegetation Tropical rainforest vegetation is very closely associated with the tropical rainforest climate. Representative areas include: Amazon Basin Congo Basin in Africa, parts of the Indo-Malaysian area of Asia. The tropical rainforest is densely forested. Three levels of vegetation are frequently recognized in the typical rainforest:

-The high level consists of solitary giant trees that reach heights of 200 feet extending far above the rest of the forest.
-The middle layer of trees grows to heights of 100-130 feet and makes a massive canopy which sunlight has difficulty penetrating.
-Beneath the middle layer is the bottom portion of the forest which has little undergrowth because of lack of sunlight.

The tree trunks are slender with few branches.
The crowns begin at great heights where sunlight is available.
70% of all plant species growing in the tropical rainforest are trees.
There is great diversity of species with no pure stands of trees.
A single acre may contain 50 species of trees.

A number of other plants other then trees have adapted themselves to the environment:

-Lianas - plants that do not have rigid stems, vine-like. They use trees as support to grow towards the sunlight.
-Epiphytes - such as bromeliads and orchids make homes in the trees deriving moisture from the air. Although the ground in the rainforest is clear from undergrowth it is difficult to get around. The soil is always wet so tree roots do not go deep into the soil.
-Buttresses fan out 10-15 feet on all sides as support.

The soil in tropical rainforests is extremely poor, and is very acid. The luxuriant vegetation grows in infertile soil. Nutrients are locked up in the vegetation that falls to the forest floor. Since there are no temperature or precipitation seasons here, leaves fall when they die throughout the year. Thick layers of plant material collect on the rainforest floor. This material decays quickly in the hot, humid climate and releases its nutrients immediately. Extensive root systems close to the surface soak up the nutrients quickly. If the rainforest is not disturbed, growth can go on indefinitely. As soon as an area is deforested, intense leaching of the soil begins and remaining nutrients can be depleted in several years. If these fields are abandoned, secondary forest moves in that may take centuries to return to rainforest.

d. Tropical Monsoon (Am) Climate

This climate is always hot, seasonally excessively moist. It is similar to tropical rainforest (Af) climate in temperature conditions. It is distinguished from Af by its rainfall regime. The winter/summer reversal of airflow brings dry and wet seasons to the Am climate. This climate is best developed in SE Asia. As warm, moisture-laden air flows form the Indian Ocean in summer, a wet season develops. In winter, when a high pressure system develops over the continent, the air is very dry. The dry season is short and is followed by heavy rain so there is rarely a soil moisture deficit. The water balance is in a surplus state and EVT occurs at the potential rate.

Am vegetation - as you move to tropical climates with a dry season, the vegetation changes. The forest becomes less dense with individual trees more widely spaced. Ground cover is heavier because more light penetrates to the ground surface. The forest is semi-deciduous, i.e. some trees drop their leaves during the dry season and some retain their leaves. The trees that retain leaves have adaptations to dry weather that include: deep or extensive roots, small leaves, and thick cuticles. Many of the trees found in the rainforest are also found in the semi-deciduous forest but drop their leaves during the dry season. Somewhat pure stands of trees occur including: teak, ebony, mahogany, cacao, rubber and banana.

e. Tropical Wet and Dry (Aw) Climate

North and south of the Af climate are areas where the ITCZ penetrates during the high sun period bringing convectional precipitation. During the low sun period the trade winds dominate bringing a distinct dry season.

As you move form the equator-ward side of the Aw climate to the pole-ward side the dry season becomes longer and longer. The water budget varies from a year-round surplus on the equator side to year-round deficit on the pole-ward side of the Aw climate.

Aw associated vegetation - as you move pole-ward to tropical climates with less annual rainfall and longer dry seasons, the vegetation shows xerophytic adaptations. Xerophytic adaptations include low growing trees to reduce water loss from wind, thick bark, and/or small leaves or thorns. On the equator side of the Aw climate trees are present and this forest can be very luxurious during the wet season but life less during the dry season. As trees become more and more scattered because of the increasing dry period, grasses become dominant. This is Savanna vegetation and is found in the drier Aw climates and well into the BS climate. The grasses have dense root systems and can absorb moisture rapidly so very little rain makes it past the roots deep into the soil. During the dry season the tops of the grasses die but the roots remain viable. The dead grasses insulate the roots form cold and drought. Trees are found in the Savanna but are widely separated because of lack of moisture and need for extensive root systems. Root systems are oriented either vertically (very deep to tap deep soil moisture, typically 10 times height of tree), or horizontally (close to surface to absorb maximum amount of rainfall, typically 5-7 times height of tree). Deep-rooted trees have a shortened dormancy period because they can tap deep soil moisture during dry season. Tree/shrub species found on Savanna: Acacia, Eucalyptus.

f. Desert Climates (Bs, Bw)

Semi-arid Hot Climate (BSh) or Low-latitude Steppe - This climate is found surrounding the low-latitude deserts. You cannot distinguish between Bsh and BWh climates by temperature only, but consider precipitation also. Although the precipitation in the BSh climate is not very much, it is greater than the deserts. The typical steppe has 10" precipitation per year and always less than 30". Seasonal distribution varies. BSh climates on the equator side receive 80% of rainfall during the high-sun period when the ITCZ migrates to the region. The steppes on the pole-ward side of the low-latitude deserts experience maximum precipitation during the low-sun period. Precipitation is mainly from cyclonic fronts that occasionally swing far south. The water balance shows a deficit throughout the year.

g. Low-Latitude Deserts (Bwh)

These deserts lie approximately between 18-28 in both hemispheres. They coincide with the equator-ward edge of the subtropical high pressure belt and trade winds. This includes the world's great deserts: Sahara, Sonoran, Thar, Kalahari, and the Great Australian. Environmental conditions are harsh; searing heat is present most of the year. Air flows generally downward so air masses that cause rain rarely penetrate the area. There is a general lack of precipitation with no pattern developed.

Desert Vegetation - deserts are regions where PEVT is much higher than annual precipitation. The name desert was originally a term describing vegetation that was coined in North Africa. Desert means "plants that are evenly spaced". Western civilization applies the term desert to both vegetation and climate.

All deserts have some plant life. Even the driest deserts, which appear without plant life most of the time, contain dormant seeds that come to life after rare showers. The rain showers may be years apart. In the world's deserts there are two major types of plant life.

The first are species nourished directly by rain and may be dormant for long periods of time and are annuals and perennials. Other plants live in protected areas, e.g. valleys and depressions and seek water through their extensive root systems. Desert plants have to survive extreme dryness and drastic diurnal and annual temperature ranges. For example:

Location/Temp.	Average max. temp.	Average min. temp.	Range
Lima, Peru	89F	51F	38F
Yuma, Ariz.	113	31	89
Reno, Nev.	98	-1	99
Kazalinsk, Russia	103	-21	124

Many desert plants are adapted to use dew for moisture and can take in water through leaves and stem. Xerophytic plants have adapted by:

-Having extensive root systems oriented either horizontally or vertically.
-Above ground plants have compact growth with leaves hugging the ground.
-Leaves have thick cuticles.
-Leaves are small or absent or have hairs that raise wind off surface.

Growth Forms of Desert Plants:

-Leafless Evergreen Shrub - e.g. Cactus, which is found in the Americas or Euphorbia found in Africa. They have shallow, poorly developed root systems but can store a lot of water. Leaves are absent but trunk is green and can photosynthesize.
-Deciduous Shrubs - major component of desert vegetation. They leaf out only when sufficient water is present and can leaf out more than once a year. Growth is very fast in wet periods.
-Ephemerals - only present when enough water falls to ensure a complete growth cycle. e.g. grasses annuals - have fragrant, colorful flowers to ensure pollination. Seeds know when to sprout because outer covering is abraded or chemical is washed off.

h. Mid-Latitude Climates ("C"- Cs/Cf/Cm)

These climates (C) are located in the belt of the prevailing westerlies. They are characterized by seasonality in temperature and have mild winters. Different "C" climates based on seasonality of precipitation (f,w,s), and severity of winter (a,b,c). Precipitation regimes depend upon their position relative to the subtropical high pressure belt and the polar front.

i. Dry Subtropical Climate (Csa) or Mediterranean

The Mediterranean basin contains the largest area of this climate. This climate is found on the west coasts of middle latitude continents in for example, California, Central Chili, South Africa, and Western/Central Australia. This climate (Csa) has long, hot, dry summers and mild, rainy winters. The climate is affected by the subtropical high pressure cell in the summer producing arid conditions. The wet winter occurs when the westerlies with cyclonic storms move in. The annual water balance varies from a surplus in winter to a deficit in the long summer.

-Sclerophyll Forest - largest area of development in Mediterranean Basin. Associated with Cfa climate. The vegetation of this forest is dominated by an evergreen, leathery, drought-resistant foliage. Heights range from 18 inches to 10 feet. The woody vegetation varies depending upon the length of the dry season. In the wettest areas of this climate tree species include cork, pine, oak and olive. These trees provide an open canopy. In drier areas trees tend to disappear and shrubs form a dense covering over the ground. In the drier areas the shrub cover is discontinuous and lower, reflecting the lack of water.

Fires are common in the Sclerophyll forest and the plants here are adapted to live in this environment. Many species of shrubs/trees have seeds that can be dormant for years and will germinate only after their structure is altered by fire.

j. Subtropical (Cfa) Climate

Found on the Southeastern side of continents (primarily between 30-40), this climate is hot and humid during the long summers and cool and humid during the short winter season. This climate is a transition between the tropical rainy (A) climates and the more severe continental climates (D) towards the poles. In the U.S. and China, polar air masses bring cold "spells" in winter. During the winter season, frontal precipitation from cyclonic storms dominate. This frontal precipitation is replaced by convectional precipitation during the summer.

The water budget for most of this climate is a surplus and the deficit at the remaining locations usually occurs for no more than 2-3 months.

-Mid-Latitude Deciduous Forest - this forest community is generally associated with the Cfa and Dfa climates, i.e. continental climates with mild winters. This forest is found in eastern U.S./southern Canada, NW Europe, southern tip South America, and East Asia. Approximately 5000 different species of plants here compared with 50,000 in Tropical Rainforest. Pure stands of one species is common so lumbering is very active.

There are 2-3 layers of vegetation present; canopy layer (100'), understory of bushes not well developed, thick ground cover in early spring when trees have not leafed out yet. The Mid-latitude Deciduous Forest has great extent both latitudinally and longitudinally. This forest is not homogeneous but has dominant species in different areas because of the wide range of temperature and precipitation that is experienced in this forest. The center of the Eastern Deciduous Forest is located in the Smokies and Cumberland mountains. There are as many as 25 different dominant species in the Eastern Deciduous Forest, all dominant in different areas.

k. Marine West Coast (Cfb) Climate

This climate lies pole-ward of the dry subtropical climates on the western sides of continents and can extend quite a distance. The prevailing westerlies constantly bring in moisture from the oceans and if a warm ocean current is present off-shore the climate is even more moist and mild. The degree to which this climate extends inland depends on the presence or absence of mountain barriers. Locations include:

-The west coast of U.S. from N. California to the panhandle of Alaska.
-Southern Chile (narrow band because of mountains).
-NW Europe - extends far inland because of lack of North-South trending mountains.

This climate (Cfb) is very mild because of the modifying effects of the ocean. This climate does not have large seasonal extremes of temperature, summers are cool and winters are mild. Average summer temps are 60-65F.

*Used in Earth Home

Average winter temps are 30-45F. Freezing temperatures are more frequent and more severe then in the Humid Subtropics but the growing season is still quite long (6-8 months) considering the latitude. Rainfall is adequate throughout the year, the water budget always shows a surplus. Places such as Europe get 25-30 inches per year. Evaporation rates are low so rainfall is very effective. In areas with mountain barriers precipitation can be high (40-100"/year) on the windward side.

l. Moist, Severe Winter (D) Climate

These climates are found pole-ward of the "C" climates. The "D" climates have longer, colder winters and greater annual range of temperature as compared with "C" climates. The boundary between C/D climates is where the coldest month averages below 32F. As you move from coastal areas toward the continental interior, winters become much colder and longer. Large landmasses are required to produce the "D" climates which is lacking on the southern hemisphere.

Boreal Forest (assoc. with Cfa, Cfb, Dfa, Dfb) / Tiaga - the Boreal Forest occurs under a number of climatic regimes. The Boreal Forest is associated with climates having cool summers and cold winters. The trees are evergreen and are conifers. They have special adaptations to the severe climate. The air is dry here so plants need adaptations for temperature and precipitation fluctuations. Small leaves have thick cuticles. Trees are conical shaped to allow snow to fall off branches. The canopy is closed and is low to the ground. There is little ground cover. There are few species of trees in the Tiaga but you find extensive pure stands. Representative species include spruce, larch (tamarack), fir birch, pine.

m. Polar (E) and Tundra (Et) Climate

This climate lacks a summer. Its southern boundary is the northern limit of the forest. This boundary occurs approximately with the July 50F isotherm which means the warmest month, in the Tundra, averages 50F. The dividing line between the ET and EF climate is 32F for warmest month. The ET climate has long, cold winters and short summers similar to Alabama in January. Only 2-4 months have average temperatures above freezing. The daily temperature range in the Tundra is small. In summer daily maximum is around 60F and minimum is approximately 35F. Annual precipitation is only 10-12 inches.

Tundra Vegetation - the transition from Boreal Forest to treeless Tundra is very gradual with tree species thinning out and becoming dwarfed. Although the tundra receives little precipitation (some call it a frozen desert) it remains as snow and insulates the ground in winter. The tundra is underlain by permafrost which produces poor drainage in summer.

3. Unique Weather Considerations

While the Koppen system doesn't take such things as temperature extremes, average cloud cover, number of days with sunshine, or wind into account, it's a good representation of our earth's climate. With only 24 different subclassifications, grouped into the six categories, the system is easy to comprehend.

Koppen's system is simply a guide to the general climate of the regions of the planet, the borders do not represent instantaneous shifts in climate but are merely transition zones where climate, and especially weather, can fluctuate. The following takes into account many other fluctuations that are important in making decisions regarding home modifications that are better suited to a specific location.

a. Wind Speed Maps

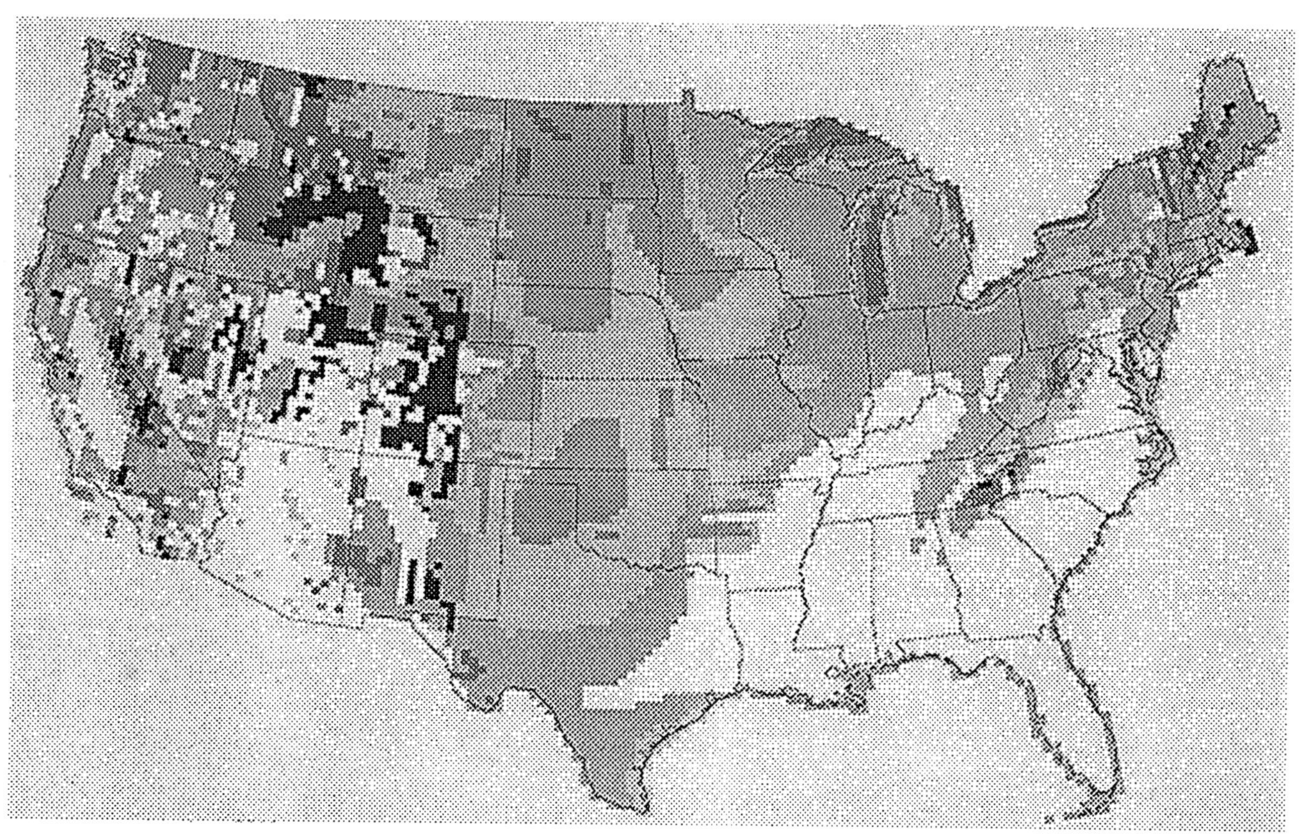

Figure 16-US WINDSPEED MAP

*Used in Earth Home

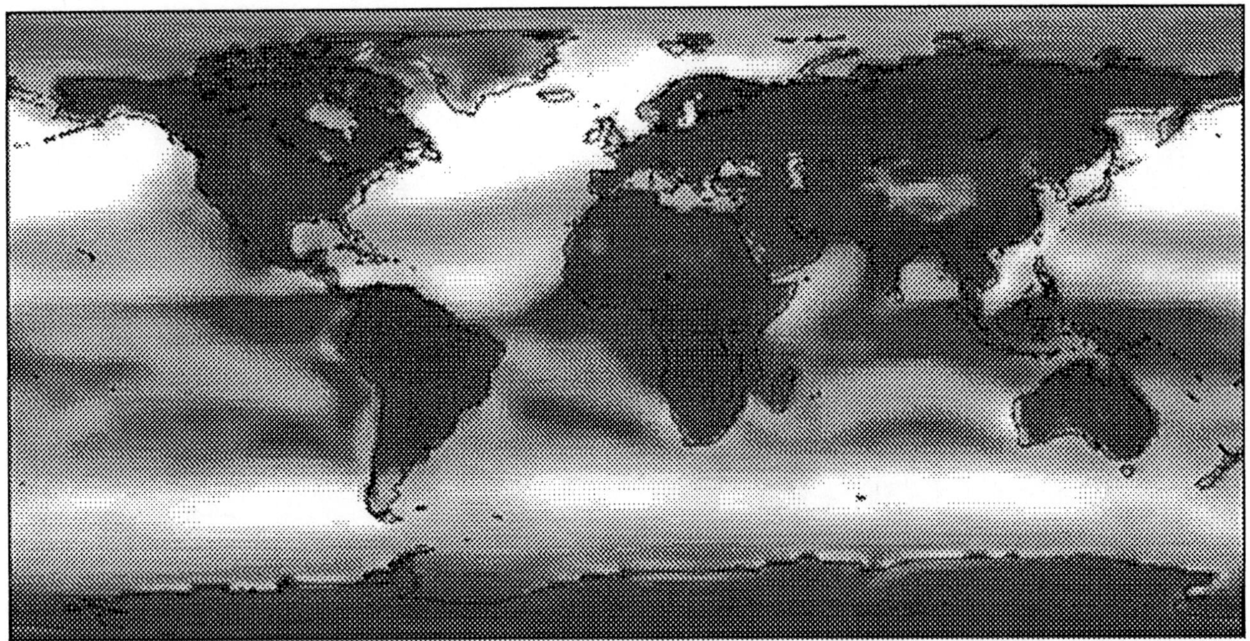

January

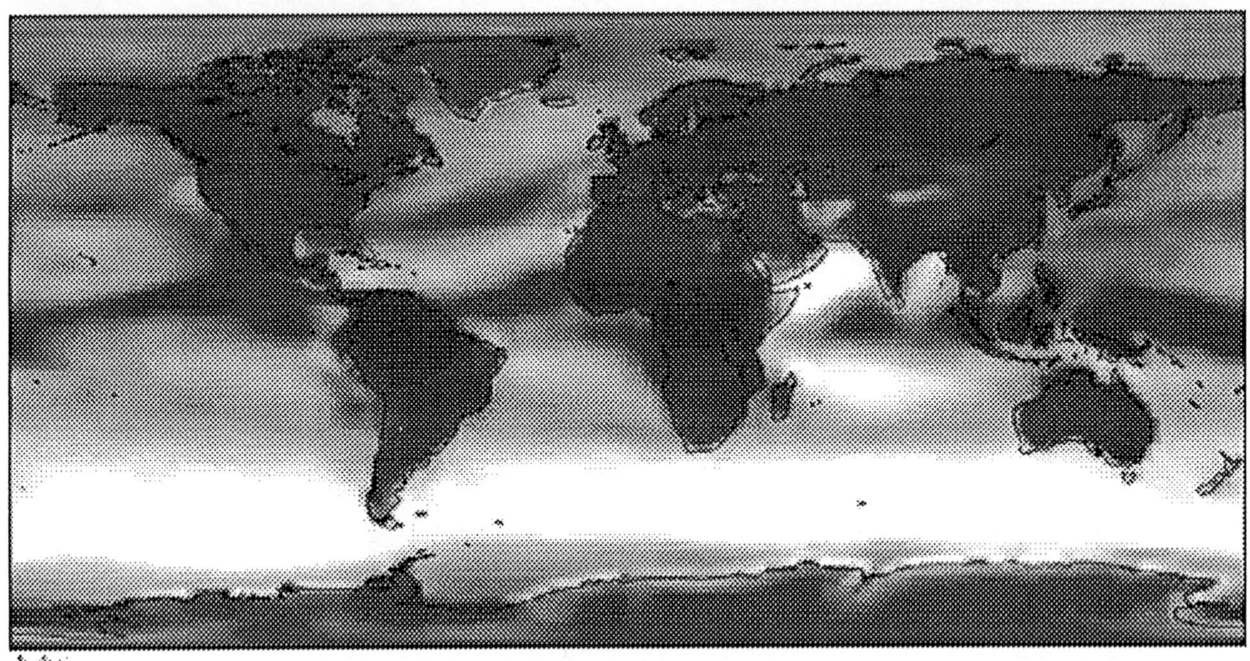

July

Wind Speed (meters/sec)

0 7 14

Figure 17-WORLD WINDSPEED MAP

*Used in Earth Home

1. Wind Consistency of Direction

In Iran, people used what is called "wind towers". These wind towers were tall, chimney-like affairs built up on top of homes to channel air in and out of the structures. This was done using a twin-scoop arrangement up to two stories above the house. The people (builders) in Iran were able to design their architecture this way because of the **very <u>consistent</u> wind direction and speed.** Wind scoops are also used in Egypt, Peru, Afghanistan, and Pakistan.

2. Considerations

If consistency in direction is the predominant wind style, wind generators can be designed differently than is the case with variable wind direction. Knowing the prevailing direction allows use of larger and more "aimed" wind machines. The apparatus can capture wind more effectively when a "funneling" approach is used.

b. Solar Insolation

1. Southwest U.S. "Hot Zone" Exception

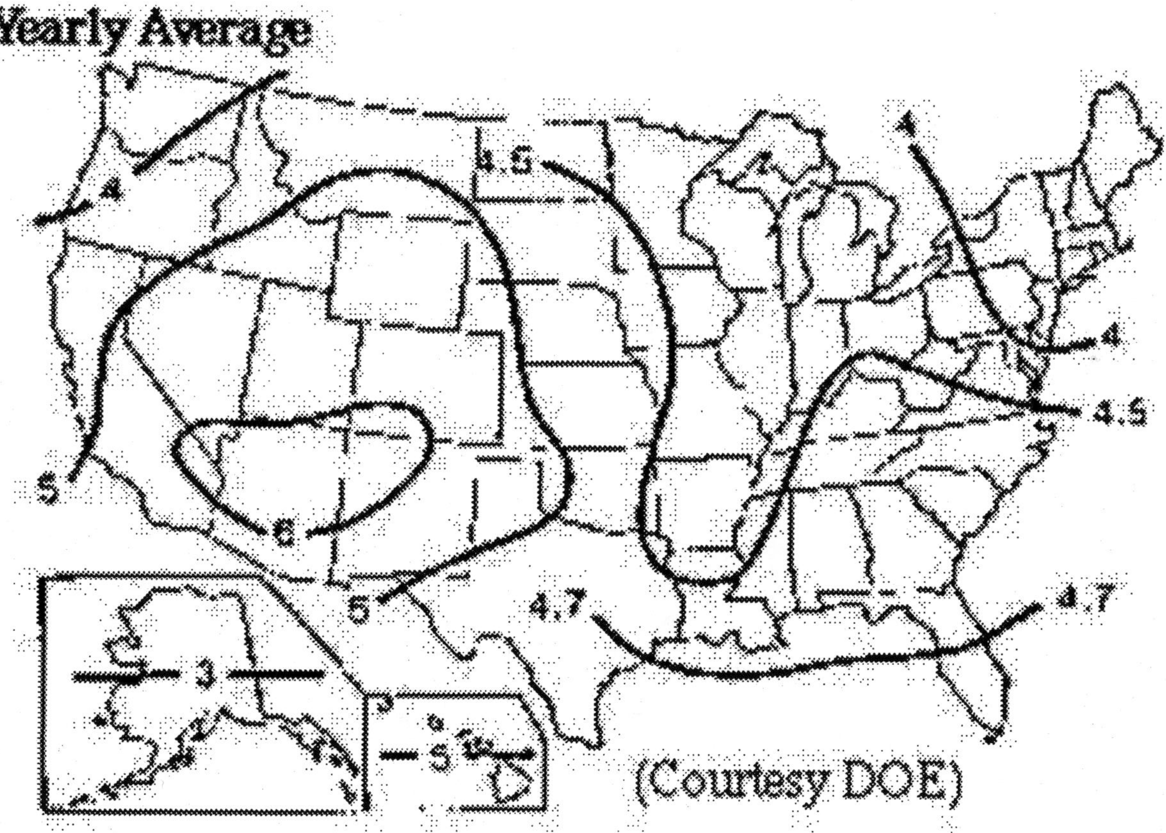

Figure 18-SOUTHWEST US "HOT ZONE" SOLAR INSOLATION MAP

*Used in Earth Home

2. <u>Australia Insolation Area</u>

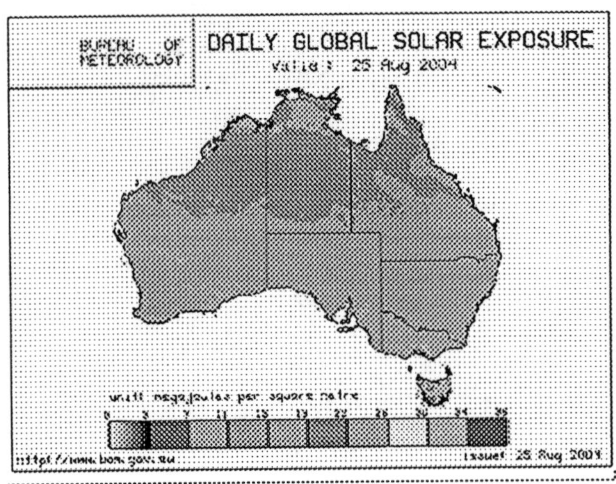

Figure 19-AUSTRALIA SOLAR INSOLATION MAP

c. Rainfall Data

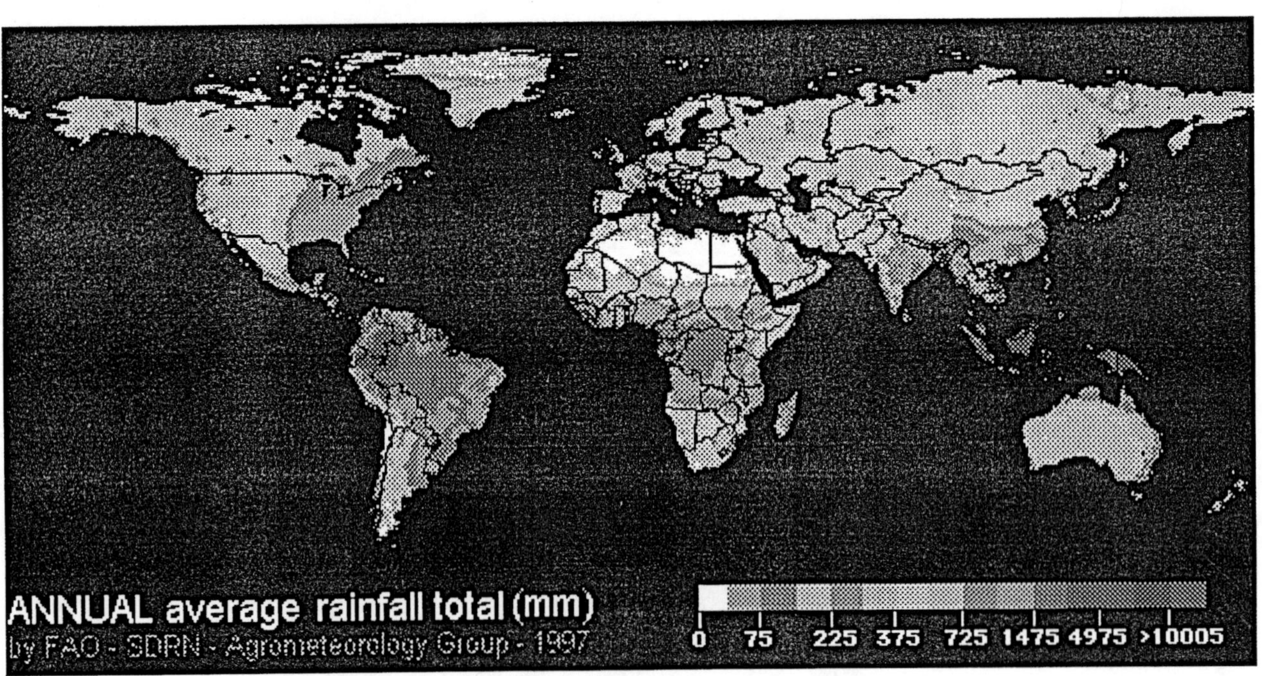

Figure 20-GLOBAL RAINFALL MAP

(See also Alternative Water Supply section)

d. Humidity Classification (Dewpoint)

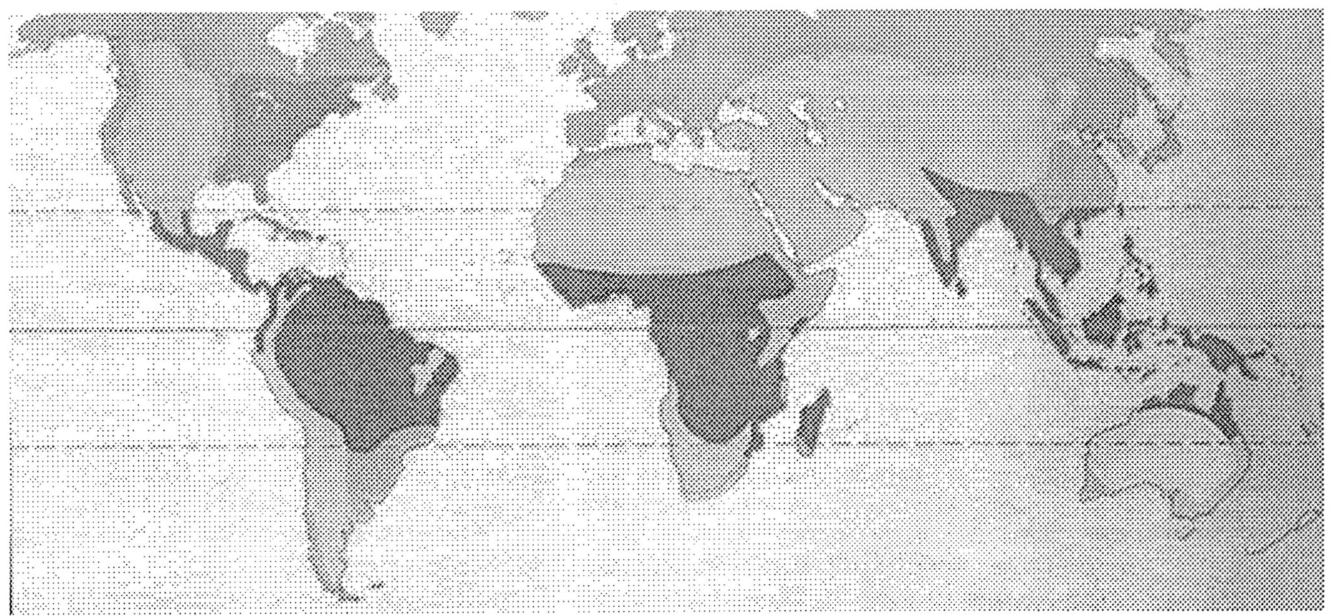

Figure 21-GLOBAL DEWPOINT MAP

e. Day-Night Temperature Swing

(See Central Heating and Central Cooling sections)

f. Soil Data/Oil Plant and Cereal Grain Potential

g. Degree-Day Heating Requirements

h. Degree-Day Cooling Requirements

*Used in Earth Home

i. Biomass Potential (See Woodgas section)

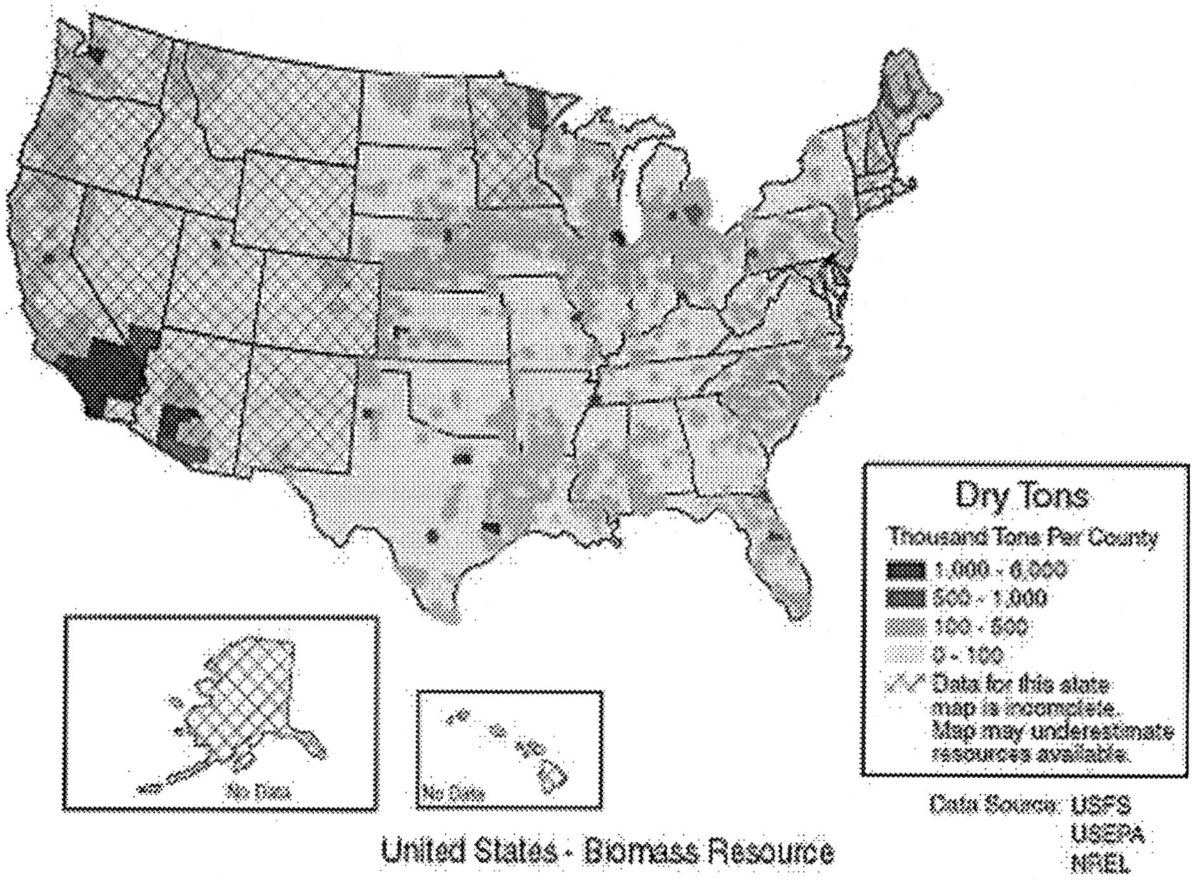

Figure 22-US BIOMASS RESOURCES MAP

Figure 23-GLOBAL BIOMASS RESOURCES (NO DATA)

j. Freeze Protection

(No data on frost footings and/or plumbing modifications.)

k. Growing Season Length in Days

*Used in Earth Home

1. High Altitudes (Elevation)

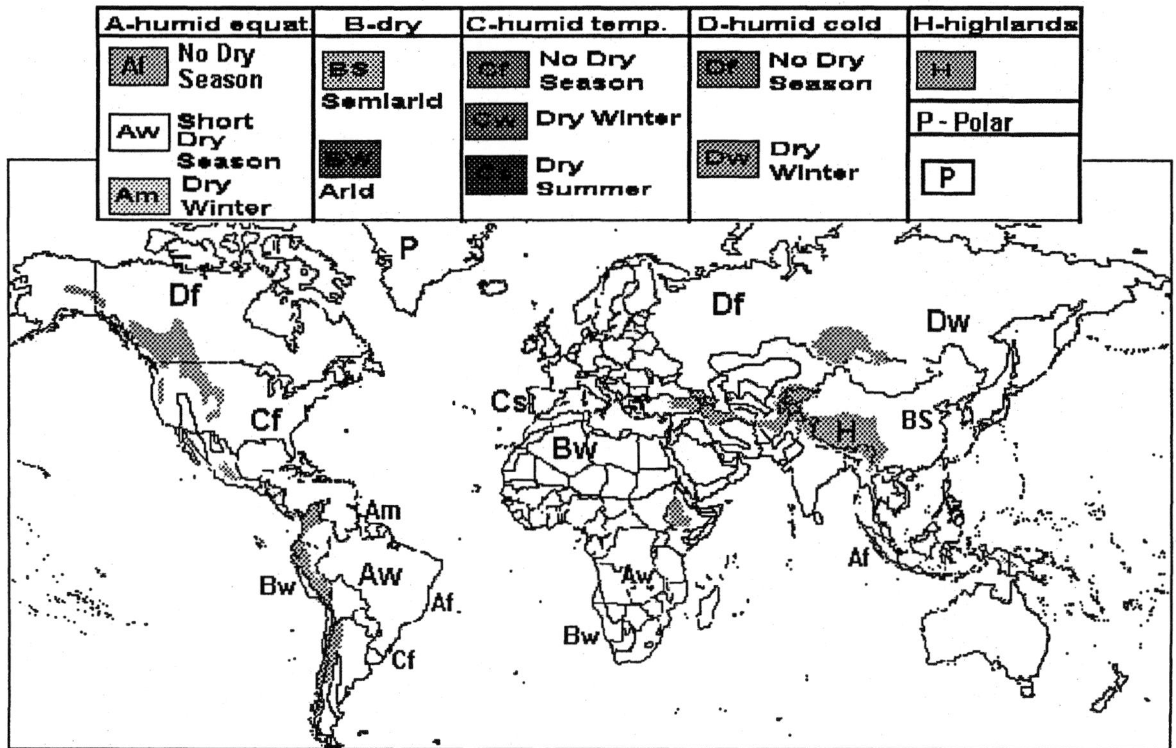

Figure 24-HIGH ALTITUDE AREAS

4. Alternative/Indigenous Construction

a. Indigenous Materials Background/Availability

A home can be made out of many different materials. Often the selection of a material is based upon the geographic region in which the house is built. For example, in the southern climates the materials may be tile, concrete, brick, or adobe to take advantage of the nighttime "cool." Northern houses are more often wood frame structures with fiberglass, cellulose, or, more recently, polyurethane insulation. Natives of Africa may use a grass hut construction. Corrugated steel over a wood frame is often used in southern regions, where it rains more frequently. In the eastern countries, stucco or concrete architecture is favored.

*Used in Earth Home

b. Materials Used in Home Construction

1. World's Building Materials

At the turn of the century, only about 2 million of the Earth's 6 billion inhabitants live in buildings of manufactured or industrially processed components. Approximately another 2 billion live in structures of earthen materials and the other 2 billion live in other types or no building at all. Taking this into account, low-impact construction alternatives have definite advantages.

2. Long-Lasting Materials

Many times, the choice of housing materials depends on how long the builders wish the house to last. Throughout history the longest lasting homes have been made of a ceramic material such as brick, stone, stucco, and concrete block.

3. Sidewall/Skin Materials

The "skin" of the structure is what is normally called a sidewall, or the outside of the home itself. This skin must resist the wind forces on the structure called uplift, overturn, racking, and shear. It must also be resistant to rain and sun degradation. There are many ways to block air from entering a structure by using such things as Styrofoam insulation, aluminum siding, Masonite siding, cedar siding, and various other materials. I wanted a material that would last at least one hundred years and would "breathe" somewhat.

c. Popular Alternative Construction Style Background

During the design of the Earth Home I looked at many different housing designs including geodesic domes, rammed-earth adobe, papercrete, structural insulated panels, post and beam, and many others.

There are many other alternative methods including; cob (sand, clay, straw, and water), adobe, bamboo, hemp, living roofs, thatch, wattle and daub, earthbag, light straw-clay (light loam, light clay, straw clay, straw loam), straw panels, earthship, timberframe, superadobe, and many more. There seem to always be someone who wants to make a home another way. Most of these techniques are more suited to one location, society, and/or climatic region and are outside the scope of this text.

d. Exterior High Mass Walls

1. Background/History of Exterior High Mass Walls

In southern and central Europe, the vast majority of residential buildings have been built using massive wall technologies. For centuries, massive building materials have been making life without air conditioners relatively comfortable even in countries with hot climates, such as Spain, Italy, or Greece.

Controlling indoor comfort through high thermal mass walls has been used for centuries on every continent in the world. In the U.S., frame houses and cheap energy slowed the popularity of the method for many years. The early solar passive homes of the 70's (with their rock beds and water drums) proved to be effective at reducing heating costs. In the late 70's and early 80's the rammed-earth wall construction techniques enabled much more heat storage.

In certain climates, massive building envelopes such as ceramic masonry, concrete, earth, and insulating concrete forms (ICFs) can be one of the most effective ways of reducing building heating and cooling loads. Several comparative studies have shown that in some US locations, heating and cooling energy demands in buildings containing massive walls can be lower than those in similar buildings constructed using lightweight wall technologies.

2. How High Mass Walls Work

A thermal-mass wall can be thought of as a giant flywheel that continuously rotates with power supplied by thermal energy or heat. There is a cyclical quality from day to night swings, and a climatic quality from the seasonal temperature changes.

During the winter, the wall mass works to maintain warm temperatures in the living spaces, using the heat fed to it by both sunlight and, in most cases, a supplemental source of heat. In the summer, the wall mass maintains cool temperatures inside the house by extracting heat from the home's air during the day and releasing it during the cool night.

e. Rammed-Earth/Adobe

The rammed-earth method involves packing soil into a form and using them like bricks. I decided not to use this method because it did not have world-wide applicability. More insulation against the cold weather was needed in the Northern Hemisphere, for example. Adobe and/or rammed earth could be used in some locations and are included in the "Tabs" Section for international applications.

f. Lime in Home Construction

1. Lime vs. Portland Cement

Most forms of building construction require a cementing agent or binder. Lime was the most commonly used cementitious binder until about a century ago, when its use started to decline. It was replaced by Portland cement, a material essentially developed for structural purposes in the era of the industrial revolution. Portland cement has certain advantages over lime when strength and rapidity of hardening are required, and because there are agreed quality standards. It has now become the dominant cementitious binder, thanks in part to aggressive marketing.

Cement mortars crack and craze because of their rigidity and brittle nature, as well as the daily expansion and contraction due to the variations in the weather and temperature. Cement mortars have the added disadvantage that there is no free lime solution to seal the cracks. If a crack did seal, it would break again because of the continued movement of the mortar.

2. Lime Uses through History

Survivals from ancient Rome include the structural core for walling, floors, cisterns, baths, aqueducts, dams, vaults, and domes. The Romans developed lime concrete for structures that have not been surpassed, examples of which date from 300 B.C. Probably the most recognized Roman building that was build using stone rubble walls cemented together by "Roman concrete' (lime and imported volcanic soils from Pozzuoli, Italy now "pozzolans") was the Pantheon in Rome.

Harbors, canals, bridges, and the foundations for large structures in the eighteenth and nineteenth centuries made extensive use of lime concrete. In the cold northern regions of Scotland and Wales lime plasters protect even stone walled buildings from harsh weather and fierce rains

Many of the most important historic buildings regularly visited and in use today owe their presence and continued stability to lime concrete foundations. Examples in the UK include the Houses of Parliament, Westminster Bridge, Lincoln Crown Court, and the British Museum. Also many of the heritage buildings in Australia were built using lime. They include decorative fronts of the buildings in Fremantle, country towns, and the few left in Perth, as well as Government house and Treasury Building. These moldings are still in good condition and most are around 100 years old.

*Used in Earth Home

3. Alternative Builders Using Lime

Some alternative builders are eliminating cement altogether. They are using quicklime, slaking it, and adding prickly pear cactus gel (nopal) to mixtures as a binder. Most builders can use hydrated lime soaked in water to make a plastic, workable mix. Straw bales perform well with lime based plasters and earthen plasters. Lime plasters dry more slowly, gaining strength over time, which is their advantage for owner-builders.

4. The Advantages of Lime—Versatility

Lime is a very versatile material which can be used for many purposes in construction. Lime-based renders allow walls to breathe so that moisture can disappear without damaging the structure. Lime mortars are much more suitable than cement mortars for use with earth-based building techniques, because they are less rigid and more permeable. They are also very suitable for decorative purposes. Architects and builders are beginning to realize that there are advantages in having a choice of binders for different applications; even where cement is preferable for structural purposes, lime often makes a better render. In Europe, the conservation sector is a prime mover in the resurgence of lime s a building material. In developing countries this role is often taken up by development agencies.

5. Lime as a Versatile Binder

When it is used well, lime is quite simply the best and most versatile binder in the world. There is a wide variety of limes which might be produced from differing materials and with various production methods.

Building lime has been used as a binder for building work for thousands of years, due to its unique setting properties and the exceptional smoothness which it offers when it is worked. Its versatility is shown by the wide variety of uses to which it is put. Structural elements for which lime mixes may be used, in appropriate designs, include foundations, walls, floors, vaults and roofs. Lime is also used for many finishes including paints, plasters, renders, and decorative work such as cornices and hand-modeled stucco.

6. Lime as a Render/Stucco for Exteriors

Architectural historians tend to use the work stucco to denote an exceptionally hard, durable, fine-textured plaster render for exterior finishes. Exterior walls can be made using building limes with various formulas and the "breatheability" of the wall can be adjusted. There is current debate on how best to make protective stuccos and plasters on strawbale houses, for instance.

The base of the wall is the most vulnerable part, being exposed to frequent contact with surface water, abrasion and impact. Care must be taken to protect the base of the wall from moisture using a buffer material such as concrete blocks or other materials. The basic Welsh saying of "a good boots and cap", meaning a water proof foundation or footing, and a wide overhang roof, will protect most walls. Wicking moisture from the ground will carry salts into the walls, mortar, and plaster.

7. Lime as a Plaster for Interiors

Interior coatings or plasters, make rooms easier to clean, reduce the risks of vermin and insects, and generally make a significant improvement to hygiene. The plaster gives a surface which can be bright and attractive by itself or can form a base for decoration. It is also incombustible and can be used to improve fire resistance, an attribute particularly useful for timber-frame buildings.

8. Lime Mortar Render over Strawbales

Lime mortars have been used on almost all the strawbale houses and structures in Western Australia and have proved very successful. There are two forms of lime used in these strawbale buildings, hydrated and hot or lump. At present hot lime either as putty or in a dry form is preferred for plastering strawbales. Hot lime is well known as being the best and safe plasticizer. The addition of hot lime into cement and sand mixes makes

*Used in Earth Home

mortars not only easier to work but flexible. These mixes that have the addition of hot lime are known as composition mortars (compo).

Lime mortar render is essential in allowing the passage of air and moisture to pass through the walls. When walls become saturated from leaky roofs, water-pipes, or from flooding, the strawbales have to lose the excess water very quickly. Lime mortar is the only cladding to provide this advantage.

Lime mortar is applied to strawbales in three coats similarly to plastering onto any form of lathing. The first coat covers the straw ends and lath to form a base to which it is keyed. This coat is often called a "pricking up" coat or "scratch coat". There is a six week minimum between coats to allow mortar to carbonate.

The second coat is a strengthening or float coat. Its purpose is to shape and straighten the walls and ceilings.

The third is the finishing coat. It provides the desired surface finish or "fining up", a process of finishing the surface rendering with a teak float to provide a compact and water resistant surface. The lime mortar as a protective cladding over straw bales has the additional advantage that it is vermin resistant and a disinfectant.

g. Alternative "Concrete-Like" Skin Materials

h. Papercrete Construction

5. Identified Categories of Modifications

a. Tab Listing

The tabs are an easy way to keep track of the variations on the Earth Home-depending on location on the Earth. Each of the tabs will involve slight modifications to the basic design. These modifications are easily implemented into the design without significantly affecting the core layout, function, and purpose. The exact tab details continue to evolve. ***The identified tabs to date include:***

a. Tab 1-Solar/Wind Ratio
b. Tab 2-Tropical Species
    1. Tropical Tree Species-Leuciana/Algarrobo
    2. Oil Plant Species
    3. Other Plant Species
c. Tab 3-Reduced Rainfall/Arid Climate
    1. Water Storage/Reduced Aquifer Options
    2. Condensate Water Collection
    3. Softened Water Modifications
d. Tab 4-Increased Earth Temperatures
    1. Solar Hydronic Heat
    2. Thermal Mass Capacity
    3. Clay Stove Option
    4. Swamp Cooler Option
e. Tab 5-Decreased Earth Temperatures
    1. Frost Depth Modifications
    2. Night Coolers/Thermal Mass for Refrigeration
    3. Short Season Plants
    4. Greenhouse "Curtain Wall"
    5. Lower Ceiling Height
f. Tab 6-Heating/Cooling Load Ratio
g. Tab 7-Wet Environments
    1. Tropical Species
h. Tab 8-Underfloor Insulation/Heating Options
    1. Wood-Fired Heat
    2. Solar Hydronic Heat
i. Tab 9-Hemisphere/Orientation

*Used in Earth Home

1. Mirror Image Footprint

j. Tab 10-Exterior Soil Chemistry Options

1. Irrigation Options
2. Plant Species Options

k. Tab 11-Roof Coloration Scheme

l. Tab 12-Southwest US "Hot Zone"

m. Tab 13-High Altitudes

b. Alternative Water Supply-General

1. Condensation from Roof

2. Condensation from Soil

3. Air Wells

4. Fog and Dew Collectors

c. Central Cooling Options-General

1. Degree-Day Cooling Requirement

2. Evaporative ("Swamp") Cooler Overview

An evaporative cooler is the scientific name for "swamp coolers." These evaporative coolers work by pushing air past a cool, damp surface, so that evaporation of water is what cools the air. ***Evaporative coolers or swamp coolers are at their most efficient when working in an atmosphere between 35% and 40% relative humidity***. They became very popular in the southwest part of the United States, Arizona, Texas, Nevada, New Mexico, Colorado, and Utah. Typically, evaporative coolers cool the air to 60% to 80% of the span between wet bulb and dry bulb temperature. (Dry bulb is normal air temperature and wet bulb uses a moistened pad over the mercury bulb to take humidity into account.) In a typical home in the southwest, they push enough air through the home so that the entire air volume of the home is completely changed about every three minutes.

Over a number of years, evaporative cooler manufacturers have developed new types of pad material to blow air through. Some of these pads include Kool pads, cool cells, and various cellulose papers. The cellulose is impregnated with a special salt to prevent rotting. The pads are also designed to be cross-fluted, so that the air speed stays constant at 250 feet per minute. These are scientifically designed so that a maximum amount of air comes in contact with the water. (See Cooling/Dehumidifying file.)

There are also manufacturing techniques that protect the leading edge of the media from the hot, dry air that first enters. The leading edge is where the most concentration of minerals and contaminants begin to deposit. By protecting this part of the cooling pad, the use of harsh biocides and cleaners can be avoided.

One disadvantage of this type of cooler that they typically evaporate or use roughly 8 gallons of water per hour in order to achieve enough cooling for an average home in the Houston area, for example. This water would need replacing and energy would be needed.

d. Arid Climate Modifications

1. Water Considerations (See Water section)

2. Evaporative ("Swamp") Cooler (See Cooling section)

e. Central Heating Options

1. Masonry Stoves/Tile Stoves

*Used in Earth Home

Tile stoves have been used for 500 years in Russia, Scandinavia, and German-speaking countries where it is known as a kachelofen. About two-thirds of Finland's new homes have built-in masonry stoves. Masonry stoves take longer to heat up, but they hold their heat better.

There are aspects to a masonry stove that bear mention. ***It is difficult to use a masonry stove with a central heating system in a cold climate***. Most of the masonry installations are in situations where the air can circulate freely to all living areas—no privacy bedrooms. Also, masonry stoves transfer heat over 30 times more slowly than iron stoves, thus taking much longer to begin heating. They also require wood of 3" diameter or less which means more work putting up wood.

2. Woodgas Stoves

3. Solar Heating (See separate section)

f. Passive Solar Heating

A popular renewable energy source is called "passive" solar. Passive means no energy inputs such as pumps or fans. ***Most often, passive solar consists of many south-facing glass or plastic windows and a storage medium (mass) immediately behind them***. Sun shines through the glass and heats up the surface of the heavy items. Shades or insulated blinds are drawn at night to prevent the heat from radiating back outside. Passive solar heat has been very successful in the southern part of the United States. Northern applications of passive solar are not as cost effective because of the increased heat loss at night through the windows. Double panes of glass helps prevent this loss but is more costly to build. (See Energy/Power Section for more complete discussion of solar energy.)

g. Solar Hydronic Heat

Liquid flat plate solar collectors can be used to provide hot water to in-floor heating systems. The 100 to 125 degree F. water is not hot enough to harm the feet when walking on the floor.

A solar heating system designed to provide all of a home's heating requirements is prohibitively expensive. Solar space heating systems are usually designed to provide 30% to 80% of heating, depending on the geographical location, the system type, and its size.

Active solar space heating systems are most feasible in climates that have extended heating seasons with many sunny days. Areas that should not utilize solar hydronic space heat are areas with cloudy conditions during the winter, such as the coastal Northwest, in areas with short heating seasons, such as Southern California and Florida. Collectors must be within 30 degrees of true south orientation. Typically, two 4 foot by 8 foot collectors would provide all the domestic hot water for a family of 4.

i. Heating/Cooling Hardware and Design Options

1. High Mass Masonry Stoves

2. Korean Ondol/Infloor Heating

About the same time, the Koreans developed the "Ondol" system. This was a system of "smoke plenums" or channels underneath the floor of a home. They built the floor as an integral part of the chimney. The smoke traveled in these channels under the floor, through a collection plenum, and up a chimney stack at the other end of the home. In this way they were able to heat the entire floor from a stove located a little lower than the floor level. The Chinese K'ang, the Afghan Tawakhaneh, and the German Steinofen are variations of the same principle.

*Used in Earth Home

j Miscellaneous Techniques

1. Night Cooler

A night cooler is defined as thermal mass for the refrigerator/freezer functions. A standard refrigerator has only insulation, but a night cooler also has mass. In northern locations, the mass would be cooled down at night and used during the day. About half of the earth's surface would benefit from the night cooler option.

2. Concentrating Solar Cooker

3. Other Technologies

6. Unique EH Applications

a. Urban Settings

Approximately ¾ of the world's population lives in areas of high density or urban areas. The Earth Home is designed around minimizing the "footprint" of the home and outside growing areas, making it suitable for densely packed housing units.

b. Local Materials/Construction Method Flexibility (See Alternative/Indigenous Construction section)

The Earth Home can be built with any number of indigenous materials such as lime, cob, bamboo, straw, and many more. Since it is a one story home, it requires limited structural support from the walls. The posts support the trusses, and the walls supply insulation and protection from the elements.

The Earth Home can be constructed using alternative methods such as pouring the walls around the bales/windows and hoisting the entire wall up in one section. This allows much faster construction and better control of flatness of the exterior. A "gin pole" type of arrangement could be used to hoist all 4 walls into a vertical position using cables from the central support pole. There are many other alternative construction methods that are still in the design phase at present.

c. Multi-Family Unit

The late Margaret Mead and others have suggested that the Earth needs more plans for communal-style independence because the entire world's population can never afford single-family dwellings-especially third world countries. I feel that the earth's massive population is an unnatural occurrence and should not be used as a basis for future technological planning on a broad scale. ***Nature has shown through the ages that it keeps its numbers of any one species in check by many means such as starvation or disease.***

I also believe that people would be physically and mentally healthier if they were spaced farther apart on the Earth's surface. I feel that 1/8 to 1/4 mile distance between homes would be an improvement over the current arrangement of crowded cities. Scientists have conducted experiments in overcrowding with rats. They found that rats develop ulcers, cancer, and more aggressive personalities when competing with other rats for limited space. I believe that spacing people out would also drastically reduce crime.

d. Tribal/Extended Family Use

Even though this text is geared to single-family dwellings, it can be adapted to larger structures or groups by following the same technologies and proportions. I feel that the system should be developed, tested, and refined in a 4 person application before gearing up for larger projects like extended families, tribes, or even villages. Some additional technologies would be necessary because of the simple laws of physics and material strengths. Tribal systems of living have some advantages.

e. Village Systems

1. Water Hyacinth for Sewage Treatment and Food

Water hyacinth has been studied as a method for filtering wastes out of water, and as a food source for human beings. ***It is calculated that 3 kilograms of fresh water hyacinth contains all the nutrients and minerals that a human body needs for one day.*** However, there are considerable limitations to its use because of its bad taste. There is much more research that must go into the water hyacinth system to make it practical for a self-sufficient homestead.

2. Trout Ponds

Trout ponds can also be used at the village level for both food and as a post-treatment mechanism.

f. High Electricity Production Areas

1. Greenhouse "Grow" Lights

2. Water Ionizers

People realized years ago that many of the long-lived cultures shared at least one common quality-they all drank highly alkaline water from oxygenated streams. Years of research and testing conducted by Japanese and Asian scientists has found that drinking alkaline water daily neutralizes the acidity produced internally as a result of improper diet and daily stress.

Ionized water is made by passing an electric current through water. The result is acidic water used for plants, washing, etc. and alkaline water for drinking. Water molecules naturally tend to bond in groups of 10-13, whereas ionized water molecules are in groups of 5-6. There are 3 extra electrons on the outer orbit of ionized water molecules. These smaller particles of ionized water pass through body tissue more efficiently making hydration more effective.

The health benefits from using alkaline water for drinking include detoxification, blocking free radical damage, and making food taste better. One of the drawbacks of ionizing water is the significant amount of energy that it takes to produce it. To date, all of the ionizers on the market are 110 volts A.C., but more D.C. models are being developed.

3. Ozone for Drinking Water Production

Ozone has been used for disinfection of drinking water in the Municipal Water Industry in Europe for over 100 years. Many commercial water companies use equipment that can manufacture over 200 pounds of water per hour. Ozone has a very good safety record with no deaths in over 100 years of use. Ozone typically requires significant amounts of 110 volt electricity and most units are larger than home-sized.

g. High Biomass Areas

1. Charcoal Production

Charcoal can be made by burning wood in a trench until the wood is burning in the center and then putting a corrugated sheet of steel over the fire. Dirt is quickly put on the steel and allowed to cool for a week. This produces a good quality charcoal for general filtering or burning.

2. Gasification (See Woodgas section)

h. Miscellaneous Areas

7. Conclusion/Future Research

This section represents the latest revision of the optional technologies that may be used in conjunction with constructing an Earth Home at other locations on earth. This is by no means all of the available technologies. These listed are the most popular and successful at the present moment. No attempt has been made at this point to "tailor" an Earth Home to any other location other than Minneapolis, MN area. This is the area most familiar to the author and is the subject of the book, *Planet Earth Home Minneapolis.*

This section will continue to be updated to reflect new techniques, products, and technologies as they become known or available. This will also be updated as new locations for Earth Homes are being tested. Readers are invited to contribute to future revisions as well.

I. ENERGY/POWER OVERVIEW

A. Energy Background/Issues/Data

The only energy sources I consider for long-term self-sufficiency is of a renewable nature. Propane is used as an interim fuel until hydrogen production and storage technologies are improved. Note that there is more detailed information available in each particular section. Consult table of contents for exact page numbers.

1. Renewable Energy Sources

a. Non-Repeatable Over the Earth

1. Hydropower

Water has been harnessed with Pelton Wheels, Kaplan propellers, Harris Wheels, Turgo Wheels, Banki turbines, and Tyson Turbines among many others. Even though there is a great deal of interest in harnessing the power of flowing water, this subject has not been covered in this text because of the non-universal access to these sources of power.

2. Other Non-Repeatable Sources

There are many projects that deal with energy sources that occur only at certain locations over the earth. Some of these include geysers, waterfalls, ocean currents, and tides. The purpose of this project is not to use those sources that are not accessible to all.

b. Repeatable Over the Entire Earth's Surface

I chose the energy sources that are repeatable over the entire Earth's surface, rather than sources that would be better suited to one locale, such as hydropower or geysers. This distinction separates some of the "specialized" homes from the ones that can be copied/duplicated or mass-produced. Examples are wind and sunshine that occurs at varying intensities all over the planet. (Note that alternative fuels provide only about one percent of the world's energy as of 2000.)

***Used in Earth Home**

2. Energy and Conversion "Technologies"

a. Mechanical

One basic type of energy involves movement of something such as the blades of a wind generator against the wind or the movement of a piston to compress air. Mechanical motion must first happen before it can be transformed into electricity, for instance. Each time a transformation happens, energy is lost in the form of heat. The early machine shops were examples of pure mechanical energy. One driveshaft ran through the entire shop and belts powered each machine as it was needed.

b. Electrical

Electricity can be produced directly using chemical activity such as a battery, photovoltaic cells, or the not-so-familiar thermovoltaic process directly from heat energy. Mechanical motion can produce electricity when a crystal is squeezed as in the piezoelectric effect in some cigarette lighters.

c. Heat

Heat is more easily understood, because we all deal with it. Typically, something had to be burned in order to be useable by humans. Heat can also be produced by transforming electricity using resistance heating elements. But this transformation is not efficient because the heat produced is of less quality or "usability" by humans.

Another example is the Stirling heat engine that produces mechanical motion from the addition of heat to a confined gas.

d. Common Energy Conversions

The following chart may help to understand the various most commonly discussed energy sources related to self-sufficient homes. There is constant research going on in each area below.

Biofuel (matter) into heat energy..........burn wood
Biofuel (matter) into liquid storage.........................alcohol production
Biofuel (matter) into gaseous fuel.....methane production

Heat energy into mechanical motion.................expanding wax cylinder
Heat energy into mechanical motion..........................bimetallic strips
Heat energy into mechanical motion...............Stirling heat engines
Heat energy into mechanical motion...........................steam engines
Heat energy into electricity.....................thermoelectric

Sunshine into electricity.....................photovoltaic
Sunshine into heat energy....................solar heating panels
Sunshine into mechanical motion................solar powered Stirling engines

Mechanical motion into electricity....................wind generators
Mechanical motion into electricity................piezoelectric crystals
Mechanical motion into storage.......wind-powered air compressor

Electricity into heat..................resistance heating elements
Electricity into cold...................thermoelectric elements
Electricity into gaseous fuel........................hydrogen production
Electricity into mechanical motion.......................electric motors

*Used in Earth Home

3. Fuel Data/Statistics Charts

a. Gaseous Fuel Chart

The following chart gathers information on gaseous fuel types. The chart that follows concentrates on other fuela that are non-gaseous fuels.

Gaseous Fuel	/Gallon	/Cubic Foot	/Pound	Notes
Propane	92,000 Btu/Gal. (*72,000 Btu/gallon net)			
Natural Gas		1,000 Btu/cubic foot		100,000 Btu/therm * .820 million Btu/1000 cubic feet (net)
Biogas		500-600 Btu/cu. Ft.		Requires 50% methane to burn. Usually mixed with CO2
Methane		39 Mj/cubic meter or 1,000 Btu/cu. Ft.		
Hydrogen	6,500 Btu/Gal Gas	279 Btu/cubic foot		

*After efficiencies of combustion are taken into account.

Figure 25-GASEOUS FUELS CHART

*Used in Earth Home

b. Fuel Statistics Chart Chart

The following chart is basic statistics on many fuel types. Gaseous fuel data can be found in the Gaseous Fuels section.

Fuel	/Gallon	/Cubic Foot	/Pound	Bulk Density (kg/liter)	Mass Energy Density (kJ/kg)	Volume Energy Density (kJ/liter)	Notes
Vegetable Oil	130,000 Btu/Gal.		8,500 Btu/lb.				
Soybean -------Soybean Oil	------ ------117,000-120,000 Btu/Gal			0.77 ----------	21?? -------------	16.2	
Shelled Corn			7,500 Btu/lb.	0.76	19.1	14.5	
Wheat Straw							
Ethanol	6,500 Btu/Gal.						
Seasoned Firewood							*15.4 Btu/cord (net)
Softwood chips (dry—7% MCWB)				0.19	20	3.8	
Pellets (1/4" sawdust pellets)				0.68	20	13.6	*13.6 million Btu/ton (net)
Pellets (3/8" peanut shell)				0.65	19.8	12.9	
Pellets (Switchgrass)					18.5 Gj/ton		
Coconut shell (broken to 1/4 inch pieces)				0.54	20.5	11.1	
Biodiesel				0.92	41.2	37.9	
Diesel				0.88	45.7	40.2 (42.6-45.0 Mj/kg)	
Jatropha Oil						(39.6-41.8 Mj/kg)	

*After efficiencies of combustion are taken into account.

Figure 26-FUEL STATISTICS

B. Solar Energy

1. History of Solar Energy

People have harnessed solar energy for centuries. As early as the 7th century B.C., people used simple magnifying glasses to concentrate the light of the sun into beams so hot they would cause wood to catch fire. Over 100 years ago in France, a scientist used heat from a solar collector to make steam to drive a steam engine. In the beginning of this century, researchers came up with a remarkably efficient solar boiler.

The solar water heater gained popularity at this time in Florida, California, and the Southwest. The industry started in the early 1920,s and was in full swing just before World War II. This growth lasted until the min-1950's when low-cost natural gas became the primary fuel for heating American homes. The public and world governments remained largely indifferent to the possibilities of solar energy until the oil shortages of the 1970,s. Today people use solar energy to heat buildings/water and to generate electricity.

2. Solar Heating-Active

Another source of energy that became much more popular in the mid 1970's was solar heat. Solar energy became very popular after the 1973 Arab oil embargo and the formation of the OPEC alliance. I feel this was one of the incentives for launching the "appropriate technology era." Another factor was a book by Robert Schumacher called Small is Beautiful. This book underscored the concept that human beings should become much more efficient in the future.

This era began with the passive solar work in the "Southwest Heat Zone". This is a zone where the solar insolation is higher than anywhere else in the continental United States. (Solar insolation is a number that reflects the relative amount of sunshine striking the earth's surface.) Many people began researching and developing products such as solar panels that could be put on virtually any home. In the beginning, the United States government funded some research into solar panel designs. Interestingly enough, they also funded the purchasers of those same panels. I feel that there was not enough incentive to develop low cost solar systems. It was not until later that some of these less expensive systems became available. (See Solar files - all.)

a. Direct vs. Indirect Systems

This system uses a pump to circulate potable water from the water storage tank through one or more collectors and back into the tank. The pump is regulated by an electronic controller, an appliance timer, or a photovoltaic panel.

In indirect systems, a heat exchanger heats a fluid that circulates in tubes through the water storage tank, transferring the heat from the fluid to the potable water.

b. Thermosiphon

A thermosiphon solar water heating system has a tank mounted above the collector. As the collector heats the water, it rises to the storage tank, while heavier cold water sinks down to the collector.

c. Draindown/Drainback Systems

In cold climates, this system prevents water from freezing in the collector by using electric valves that automatically drain the water from the collector when the temperature drops to freezing. A drainback system is a variation of this approach that automatically drains the collector whenever the circulating pump stops.

*Used in Earth Home

d. Flat Plate/Hydronic

The most common collector for solar hot water is the flat plate collector. It is a rectangular box with a transparent cover, installed on a building's roof. Small tubes run through the box and carry fluid—either water or other fluid, such as an antifreeze solution. The tubes attach to a black absorber plate. As heat builds up in the collector, it heats the fluid passing through the tubes. The hot water or liquid goes to a storage tank. If the fluid is not hot water, water is heated by passing it through a tube inside the storage tank full of hot fluid.

The surface that heats up is called an "absorber" plate. The absorber plate could be any number of materials, including aluminum, steel, black plastic, or even wood. The color of the absorber plate is generally black, though there are some studies suggesting that a geranium leaf green is more efficient at picking up solar radiation.

Some examples of clear surfaces are acrylic, polycarbonate, Plexiglas, vinyl, and the most long-lasting: glass. The tilt angles for the panels are normally 45° to 60° from horizontal depending on the season and latitude. ***In Minnesota, the best "sun hours" are from approximately 10:45 a.m. to 3:15 p.m.***

e. Concentrating Solar Power (CSP)

Another application of solar energy is "concentrating" collectors. This concept uses mirrors or a polished surface to reflect the sun's rays onto a collection surface, fluid, or pipe. In this way, the temperature of the fluid is raised higher, which can be used and stored more efficiently.

Concentrating Solar Power (CSP) is employed whenever higher temperatures are needed. There are basically four applications when concentration of the sun's energy is used.

1. Dish Systems

Dish systems are very similar to satellite TV dishes. They have a highly reflective surface that concentrates solar energy on the focal point. This focal point gets extremely hot and the heat is transferred from there to a useable area such as a storage tank.

2. Parabolic Troughs

Parabolic troughs are similar to the dish system, but a continuous pipe is the collection media. The reflective surface is typically a parabolic shape with the fluid collection pipe at the focal point of the parabola. Both of these collectors must always be pointed at the sun in order to achieve the high temperatures. (see Non-tracking Concentrating Collectors also)

3. Solar Power Towers/Solar Thermal Electricity

Most solar thermal systems use solar collectors with mirrored surfaces to concentrate sunlight onto a receiver that heats a liquid. The super-heated liquid is used to make steam that drives a turbine to produce electricity in the same way that coal, oil, or nuclear power plants do.

Solar thermal systems may be one of three types; central receiver, dish, or trough. A central receiver system uses large mirrors to reflect sunlight onto a receiver on top of a high tower. Computers and motion control devices keep the sun's rays directed at the collection point. This type of installation is very expensive and more difficult to maintain. However the LUZ in the Mojave desert of California had produced energy at comparable prices to the other alternatives until its closing at the end of 1992.

Another solar thermal electricity system uses a dish-shaped solar collector to collect sunlight. This system resembles a television satellite dish. A third system used mirrored troughs to collect sunlight. Until recently, trough systems seemed the most promising.

4. Concentrating Photovoltaic (See Photovoltaic Section)

5. Non-Tracking Concentrating Collectors

Argonne Laboratory in Illinois has experimented with a double concentrating compound parabolic collector. Twin parabolic surfaces on either side of a pipe reflect light on the pipe from large angles.

Typically, concentrating solar collectors have to be "tracked" or pointed at the sun the entire day, as the sun moves across the sky. Tracking gains some efficiency, but at the expense of operating the motor and/or the tracking mechanism. (See Solar files.) However, the twin parabolic collectors do a similar job without the need for tracking.

f. Vacuum/Evacuated Tube Solar Collectors (ETS)

These collectors consist of rows of parallel transparent glass tubes, each containing an absorber and covered with a selective coating. Sunlight enters the tube, strikes the absorber, and heats the liquid flowing through the absorber. These collectors are manufactured with a vacuum between the tubes, which helps them achieve extremely high temperatures (170-350 degrees F); so they are appropriate for commercial and industrial uses.

1. Four Concepts

There are four different concepts for vacuum tube solar collectors. (They are also referred to as evacuated tube solar collectors or ETS). The first is the heat pipe variation. This technology involves using many small heat pipes and delivering heat to a copper water pipe. One company, Thermo Technologies, calls the system "evacuated heat pipe technology". (See also Heat Pipe Section) With the direct-flow vacuum tube, the fluid flows through the tube. The collector is comparable to a small flat-plate collector which is fused into a vacuum tube.

The CPC collector is based on the so-called Sydney tube, which is a thermos flask type of design. The absorber coating is on the inner glass pipe of the thermos flask. Heat transfer from absorber to copper pipes with fluid inside the thermos flask is via a metal sheet. Since the absorber is a cylindrical design, a reflector allows the sunlight to get to the rear side too.

The Schott tube is a combination of different concepts. There is a glass pipe inside the tube, onto which the absorber has been vapor-deposited. The fluid flows directly through this glass tube, and no metal-glass junction or transition is required. The half-reflector is inside the vacuum tube.

2. Advantages of ETS Collectors

Manufacturers of evacuated tube solar collectors claim many advantages including:

1) Glass is cheaper than copper or aluminum.
2) Full 360 degrees of sun allows for up to 94% sun tracking which would capture heat longer each day.
3) Suitable for hard water use.
4) Easy installation and cleaning.
5) Can be added on more easily.
6) Effective on cloudy or low radiation days.
7) Light weight.
8) Non-mixing design allows for more uniform water temperature.

g. Other Solar Heating Methods

1. Batch or Breadbox Heaters

This system is also referred to as a batch heater and a breadbox. It consists of an approximately 40-gallon insulated tank, lined with glass on the inside and painted black on the outside. It is mounted on the roof, or on the ground in the sun. Plumbing from the house supplies the box with cold water through an inlet that extends down to the bottom of the tank. The box itself acts like a collector, absorbing and trapping the sun's heat and heating the water. An outlet supplies the house with heated water from the top of the tank.

2. Transpired Solar Collectors

A transpired collector is a south-facing outside wall covered by a dark sheet metal collector. The collector heats outside air, which is then sucked into the building's ventilation system through perforations in the collector. They have been used for pre-heating ventilation air and crop drying. A transpired collector is inexpensive to make, and commercially, have achieved efficiencies of more than 70 percent.

h. Hybrid Combinations

One hybrid product combines concentrating photovoltaic (electricity generating) panels with water circulation to remove excess heat build-up in the panels. The water is usually routed to a heat exchanger to preheat domestic water. This concentration of sunlight significantly boosts the output of the PV cells. (See Water Heating Section)

i. EH Use of Solar Hydronic

One of the tabs in the Earth Home design is to use solar-heated water pumped into the floor mass. In-floor heating systems use moderate water temperatures which coincide with the temperatures easily reached in solar water heating systems. Typical inlet water temperatures range from 100 deg. F. to 125 deg. F., which is precisely the range where active solar systems excel. Rather than heating a large water or rock storage tank, a concrete slab floor can be used to store the heat and slowly release the heat as needed.

3. Solar Heat Storage (see Thermal Mass section)

a. Air

The storage of solar energy is a little more difficult if air, for example, is heated. Air cannot hold much heat because its density is so low. (See Thermal Mass Section also)

b. Water

The black absorber plates are more often constructed using water channels. A pump is used instead of a fan to circulate the warmed fluid into a storage area. Water storage systems (hydronic) are most often used for domestic hot water use. These commercially available systems use a small pump to circulate water through channels in the solar panels and into a storage tank inside the home at night. Water or hydronic systems are typically used for heating or preheating water for showers and bathing. (See Thermal Mass Section also)

c. Rock

A rock storage system was also sometimes used for solar-heated air systems. (See Cooling/Dehumidification - Cooling Batteries section.) A major drawback is that the temperature of the air coming out of the rock storage was not high enough to circulate into an entire room and cause the structure to become heated. ***A minimum***

*Used in Earth Home

plenum temperature for a hot air system is approximately 140°F. Any lower temperature makes it difficult to heat up a room in cold weather. (see Thermal Mass Section also)

4. Passive Solar Energy

a. Passive Background

Passive solar commonly means "without active pumps or fans of any kind". Many homes have been built to take advantage of the sun's rays entering a space and heating it up. (See also Solar History Section)

b. Transparent Insulation

A recent higher technology improvement is to use small glass tubes and stack them against a brick wall, for example. These glass tubes are called transparent insulation and have been used in the Self-Sufficient Solar Home at Freiburg, Germany.

c. Passive Solar Use in EH

Passive solar is the method used to heat the greenhouse portion of the Earth Home as well as the western end designed to contain the fish tanks. Passive solar is more thoroughly discussed in the Heating Section.

d. Thermosiphon Systems

Thermosiphon systems do not use powered pumps, but work by the fact that hot water is less dense than cold water. This hot water rises inside a pipe loop and puts the warmer water at the top of the system or in the storage tanks.

5. Solar Air Conditioning/Solar Cooling

a. Solar Cooling Chart/Overview

One possible alternative to the mechanical refrigeration/cooling equipment is solar cooling. Also known as solar air conditioning, this thermally-powered equipment is less efficient than mechanical systems, but it uses less primary energy for operation. There are many variations of this equipment, but they all use either solar heat and dehumidification or both together.

The following chart shows how solar cooling is progressing. It shows various configurations of solar technology and products. Solar cooling is still in its infancy compared to other solar technologies.

*Used in Earth Home

Solar-Operated Refrigeration Technology	Single-Stage Absorption	Double-Stage Absorption	Adsorp-tion	Solid Sorbents	Liquid Sorbents
Ready to Market?	Many large products but few small products	No small products—mostly direct-fired	A few products	Many sizes of sorption rotors	A couple systems in pilot plants.
Working fluid/sorbent	Water/LiBr or ammonia/ water	Water/LiBr	Water/ Silica gel	Water/LiCl or Water/ Silica gel	Water/LiCl
COP (Coefficient of Performance) or Efficiency	.7	1.1	.6	.5-.8	>
Operating Temperature (C)	75-110	140-160 (steam, pressurized water)	65-95	60+	60+
Notes			Larger and very heavy	Mods. for each climatic condition	Not needed with regeneration facility

Figure 27-SOLAR COOLING CHART

*Used in Earth Home

b. Air Conditioning Technology/Background

Air conditioning is the dominating energy consuming service in buildings in many countries and in many regions in Europe the demand for cooling and dehumidification of indoor air is growing due to increasing cooling loads.

Two different refrigeration technologies are currently used for building air conditioning systems: electric vapor-compression (Freon type) and heat-driven absorption cooling.

Absorption chillers are driven by steam, hot water, or fossil fuel burners. The technology is mature, as it has been used for the past 100 years. The refrigerant in a LiBr absorption chiller is water, so the lower temperature limit is about 40F. The refrigerant in an ammonia-water absorption chiller is ammonia, so the lower temperature limit is about 20F. This cycle can be used for low-temp refrigeration.

c. Liquid-Desiccant Air Conditioning

A liquid-desiccant air conditioner has three major components: (1) a conditioner, (2) an interchange heat exchanger, and (3) a regenerator. The conditioner cools and dries the process air. The regenerator removes the water that the liquid desiccant absorbed in the conditioner, restoring the desiccant to a concentrated state. The interchange heat exchanger preheats the cool, weak desiccant that is flowing to the regenerator using the hot, concentrated desiccant that is leaving the regenerator. A liquid-desiccant is ideally suited for a high humidity climate with long cooling seasons.

Some research projects are attempting to develop an energy efficient air conditioner to be able to compete with conventional vapor compression systems. These liquid desiccant air dehumidifier/indirect evaporative coolers use cross-flow type Plate Heat Exchangers (PHE) as dehumidifiers. It removes moisture form the air and provides 100% fresh air without the application of Chlorofluorocarbon (CFC) refrigerants. Low grade energy such as waste heat or solar energy could be used for the liquid desiccant regeneration.

d. Issues with Solar Air Conditioning

All conventional chillers and air conditioners dry air by cooling the air below its dewpoint temperature. This includes chillers and direct-expansion (DX) systems that use electric vapor-compression technology and chillers that use absorption technology. Once below the dewpoint, water vapor in the air will condense on the heat exchanger of the chiller or air conditioner. When drying air, these systems must run with a wet cooling coil and the air that leaves this coil must be close to saturation. Both these conditions favor the growth of mold, mildew and other biological organisms.

If a cooling system dries air by condensing the water vapor, it will have trouble meeting a building load that has a large latent component. (The heat released when water vapor condenses is referred to as the latent heat of condensation. Approximately 1060 Btu are released per pound of condensing water. A building's need for dehumidification is referred to as its "latent" load.) Approximately 25% to 30% of the cooling provided by a conventional DX air conditioner will be latent (i.e., dehumidification). However, in humid climates, the latent load can be between 30% and 60% of the total load, the larger latent loads tending to occur when ventilation is greatest.

If a homeowner ignores the fact that his air conditioner is not providing sufficient dehumidification, he will create far greater problems. When a building is inadequately dehumidified, people are uncomfortable. A common response is to turn down the thermostat. This creates a cool but clammy indoor environment. And, the high indoor relative humidity that results will promote the growth of mold, mildew and other harmful organisms. The property damage caused by this will cost the building owner more than if he had installed a cooling system that could have prevented the problem.

Several good options exist for meeting high latent loads that retain the basic electric vapor-compression cooling system. In all options, the process air is overcooled to remove extra moisture, but then reheated to maintain

*Used in Earth Home

comfortable indoor conditions. The method for reheating differentiates these systems. In some, reheating is done using heat from the refrigerant circuit (e.g., heat from the condenser). In others, an air-to-air heat exchanger (either a heat-pipe device, a run-around coil, a heat wheel or a plate-type heat exchanger) is used to move heat from the warm air entering the air conditioner to the cool air leaving.

6. Photovoltaic(PV)

a. Background of PV

Photovoltaic (PV) panels or modules have been used for many years to generate electricity from sunlight. They are now being mass-produced in sufficiently high quantities to begin to lower the price per watt. (See Photovoltaic files.) There are over 100,000 homes in the U.S. that use PV panels. The first completely energy independent home has been built in Germany with the use of many PV panels along with an array of other technologies.

Photovoltaic panels contain layers of rare earth elements that are excited by sunshine. The electrons move to another layer, setting up an electrical potential. These panels are usually covered with glass, and have positive and negative connections on the back. They generate most of their electricity under direct sun conditions, but can also be used in cloudy or hazy conditions with reduced output. Efficiency actually improves with colder temperatures.

PV panels are typically "ganged" in arrays, and faced directly <u>true</u> south (in the northern hemisphere). They can be "tracked ", or moved to follow the sun with a tracking mechanism similar to solar concentrating panels. Solar panels can be mounted on a pole or rack for better access to sunshine between 9:00 a.m. and 4:00 p.m. Traditional roof-mounted PV panels may eventually have to be moved when a typical roof is re-shingled. Recently the Japanese have introduced roof tiles that produce electricity!

Stationary panels are normally adjusted to gain efficiency about twice a year, depending on the sun angle. It has been estimated that from 10% to 40% more average efficiency can be gained in tracking, especially south of 45° latitude. PV panels produce rated output about 5 hours per day on the average. Solar insolation maps are available from merchants of photovoltaic panels.

b. Flat Panels

PV panels generate different voltages, depending on the manufacturer. They vary from 15.9 volts DC to about 17.1 volts DC. (It is acceptable to mix PV panels of varying voltages.) A typical panel, such as the M-75 by Arco, produces 15.9 volts DC. PV panels of a slightly higher voltage are often used to compensate for losses due to high temperatures and long wire runs to the controller.

A PV panel has to produce less than 1-5% of a battery's capacity before a charge controller is not necessary. Any greater output from the panels into the battery bank (unregulated) would cause gassing and could damage the battery.

c. Bifacial

Recently, bifacial or double-sided solar panels have come on to the market. These panels produce energy by both sides. Claims of 15-20% more output using the backside scatter caused especially by snow, water, and desert sands. Currently Solmecs from Israel is the only supplier of these panels. (See Solar Heating Manufacturers)

Bifacial panels use a sort of "double compound" reflector systems to direct some of the side insolation onto the back of the panel. A similar system has been worked on using hydronic panels at Argonne Labs. (See concentrating above)

d. PV Roof Panels

Many companies now offer photovoltaic roof panels in many variations. They are still relatively expensive, but are gaining in popularity. (See PV files)

e. Concentrating PV Systems

Concentrating photovoltaic solar systems use mirrors or reflective surfaces to direct sunlight onto photovoltaic surfaces. The idea is to increase the number of "suns" striking the surface, so the electric output is dramatically increased. This system allows many times the output of the solar panel. However, due to the greatly increased solar energy striking the surface, the lifetime of the PV panel is greatly reduced.

f. Hybrid Combinations

See section of text on Solar Heating-Active for combination concentrating PV and hydronic (heating) panels. It is also interesting that the Japanese are using special roof tiles to collect electricity at a slightly higher efficiency than typical flat panels.

Another hybrid produces electricity and also hydrogen. This product is in the experimental stages as of 2004. (See PV files.)

g. Future PV Materials

1. Plastic Solar Cells

Scientists have recently developed cheap plastic solar cells flexible enough to paint onto any surface and potentially able to provide electricity for wearable electronics or other lower-power devices. This technology could be expanded to other surfaces such as a wall or roof.

Hopes for plastic solar cells have been dangling before scientists for decades, since a U.S.-Japanese research team discovered that plastic can be made to conduct electricity. Among the plastic materials that are being looked at from numerous sources includes Lepcon or Lumeloid. The new materials may be able to turn 70 to 80 percent of the energy from sunlight they receive into electricity. Most photovoltaic cells are only about 15 percent efficient.

Some new photovoltaics are made from "organic" materials, which consist of small carbon-containing molecules, as opposed to the conventional inorganic, silicon-based materials (24% efficient). The materials are ultra-thin and flexible and could be applied to large surfaces. Organic solar cells (3% efficient at present) could be manufactured in a process something like printing or spraying the materials onto a roll of plastic.

2. PV Photoelectrochemical

There is also experimental work going on in the field of converting sunlight directly into hydrogen and oxygen. The cells are immersed in water and when the sun shines on the cell, water is split similar to hydrolysis. (See PV files)

7. Thermal Photovoltaics (TPV)/Thermophotovoltaic

Thermal photovoltaic or thermovoltaics is an energy conversion procedure in which thermal radiation in special photovoltaic cells is transformed directly into electric energy. Most significant are the very high power densities in proportion to photovoltaics. While a solar cell the size of a postcard can produce around 1.5 watts in the sunlight, a thermal photovoltaic generator of the same size could theoretically produce 300 watts! They typically use infrared radiation and are placed just a few centimeters from the radiant source.

*Used in Earth Home

There is also significant research in the field of complete thermovoltaic (TPV) generators. To generate power, fuel is contiguously burned in a ceramic tube which glows red-hot. The photovoltaic cells which surround the tube receive the infrared (IR) photons from this emitter and convert them to electric power. These "solar" cells are used with this tiny "sun" created by burning a gaseous fuel (presently methane). However, because this tiny "sun" is very close to the cell, IR power intensities at the cell are one thousand times higher than outdoor sunlight. Fuel is burned cleanly, completely, and continuously without periodic explosions like an internal combustion engine.

This TPV generator technology is likely to have many other applications such as vehicle power, heat and electricity for remote cabins, recreational vehicles, or boats. (See also Automobile section)

C. Wind Energy

1. Wind Power Throughout History

A major subject of interest has been harnessing the wind for human use. The wind is still used today to grind grain in Iran, as it has been for thousands of years. Vertical axis wind turbines are used to turn stones against one another to grind grain into flour.

Another early use of natural forces to assist human beings in their tasks was in the massive wind-powered grain mills in the Netherlands. The wind that blows across the Dutch countryside is very steady and unchanging. The huge blades rotated slowly, but with great power.

Wind was also used in early United States history to pump water from the ground. The multi-bladed wind pumps were common on farms throughout the Midwest, and many are still used today. The wind pumping mechanism had to be "feathered", or turned out of the wind, in order to avoid overspeed damage from high winds. Also wind normally comes from varying directions in a relatively short period of time. (See Wind files.)

2. Windmill Background

a. Windmill/Wind Turbine Types

1. Vertical axis

Vertical-axis wind turbines (VAWT) can be categorized according to two basic principles: pushed or pulled by the wind. The push principle is the oldest with multiple vertical sails or paddles were blown around the vertical axis by the wind. A key advantage of Darrieus and Savonius-type of wind system is that they can draw wind from any direction without the need for a yaw system.

Another advantage is that they are quieter than horizontal axis machines. They also claim to produce 50% more electricity in a year's time because they can make electricity in turbulence and changes in wind direction.

2. Horizontal Axis

Conventional horizontal axis wind turbines (HAWT) with three blades can be regarded as the industry standard. Wind turbines can be further categorized by size. For example, small wind turbines are commonly called SWT for short. Wind turbines less than 1 kw in size are categorized as "micro". The following figure shows the various kinds of windmills used to assist human efforts throughout time. They include the Savonius rotor, Cretan windmill, Darrieus rotor, and the high speed rotor of present.

b. Wind Machines—Make or Buy?

A person can construct any and all sorts of wind machine that the human mind can dream up. However, one of the simplest wind machines to construct is a slow-moving sail-type such as the Cretan. More than one book can be obtained to show a person how to construct these types of wind machines. However, one drawback is that they must be tended in order to be useful to the family. In order to more fully understand wind and its effects, it is useful to take a look at wind machines that are used to make electricity.

3. Wind-Generated Electricity

a. History

Wind generators became popular in areas not suitable for hydraulic power from streams that were used to turn water wheels for grinding grain. The history of wind generated electricity goes back many years. Most of these early windplants powered farm lights with 32 volts D.C. and glass batteries.

Wind powered generation of electricity began to decline in the 1920's, when the REA (Rural Electric Authority) began stringing electric lines. Only a few of the 32-volt DC generators are still around. Home voltage was raised to make it cheaper and easier to make long wire runs to the barn and other outbuildings.

b. Wind Generator Basics

Electricity is generated when a magnetic field passes across a coil of wire. This is the basis of most electrical generation in the entire world. There are two kinds of electrical generators. One is a permanent magnet generator and the other is an alternator. In an alternator, the electrical field is generated by weak electric signals going through a coil of wire, thus making its own magnetic field with a small amount of electricity. The alternator must use electricity to generate more electricity. A magnet generator uses the rotating permanent magnetic field to create electrical potential in coils of wire.

Today some of the most efficient wind generators are the alternator type, using as many as 12 "poles" and specially wound fields to increase efficiency. However, permanent magnet generators are more reliable because they do not require electrical energy to excite the field. (See Generator files) the most important maintenance item on wind generators are the bearings. It is important to ensure that the main bearings are lubricated and rotating freely.

The power in the wind is proportional to the cube of the wind speed. Typically wind generators operate from 1/4 to a maximum of 2/3 of the time in windy sites. The Battelle Pacific Northwest Lab has maps of annual windpower for the entire world.

Electricity can be readily stored in 12-volt DC batteries or "changed" to provide 110 volts AC. A device called an inverter can be used to transform electricity from the batteries into the household current commonly used in the United States. Some of the newer inverters are extremely efficient and do not lose much power upon conversion or in idle mode. ***The Earth Home is not designed to need an inverter***. (See Converters/Inverters file for the reasons discussed in "12-Volt Advantage") (See Electrical Power section for more discussion of wind generators.)

c. Wind Tower Terminology

Wind machines can be vertical axis types like a merry-go-round or horizontal axis models that rotate into the wind using a tail. Most wind power equipment today utilizes a horizontal axis and an upwind rotor. More electricity is generated as the tower gets higher, but it is not a consistent increase. However, the wind direction is more uniform causing less wear on the bearings.

The tower that the wind generator sits on should be at least 30 to 40 feet above the ground to avoid some of the turbulence created by air passing over the ground. Air does not travel exactly horizontally, but actually rolls, similar to the way a fluid such as honey spreads out on when poured on a surface. The actual direction of the wind is tilted down about 6° from horizontal. The wind generator axis has to be tilted slightly up and into the approaching wind.

Most wind generators sit on top of a tower made of steel, fiberglass, wood, and sometimes pre-stressed concrete. A major drawback is the effort required in servicing or troubleshooting the generator.

*Used in Earth Home

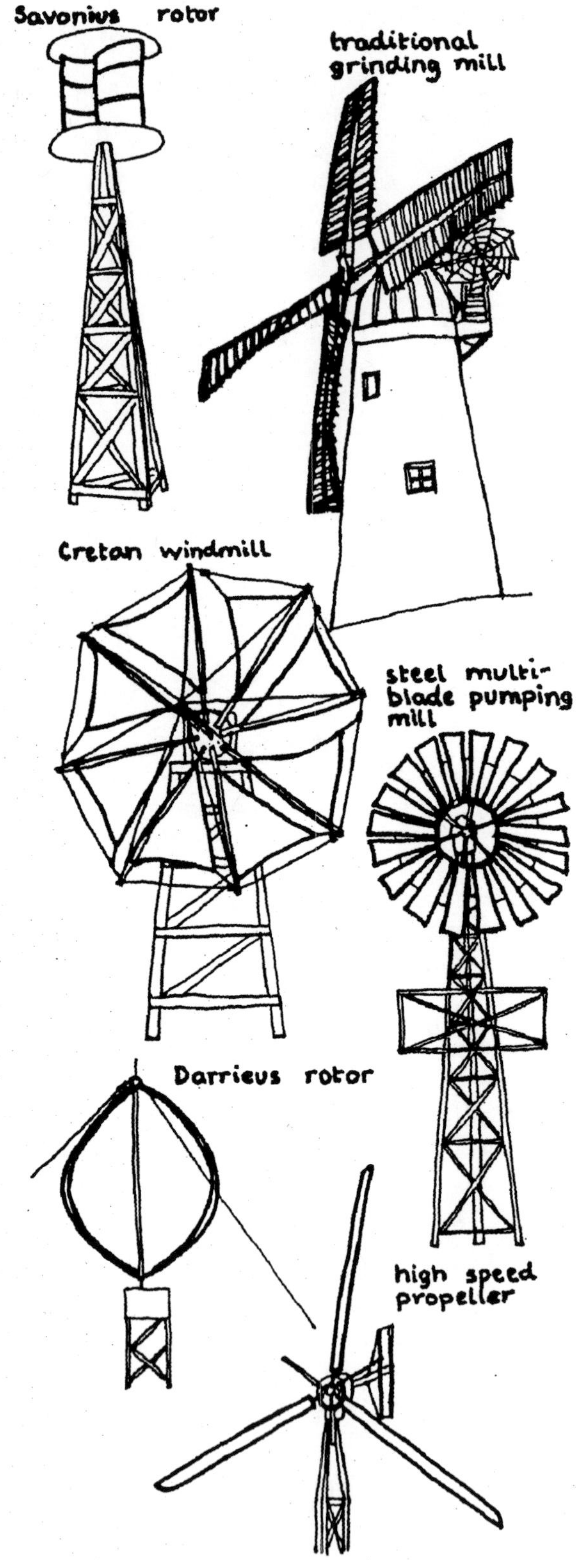

Figure 28-WINDMILL TYPES

*Used in Earth Home

d. Wind Tower Height vs. Power Output

Wind generators should be high enough to avoid the excessive turbulence that obstructions create. The following figure explains the connection by using a graph.

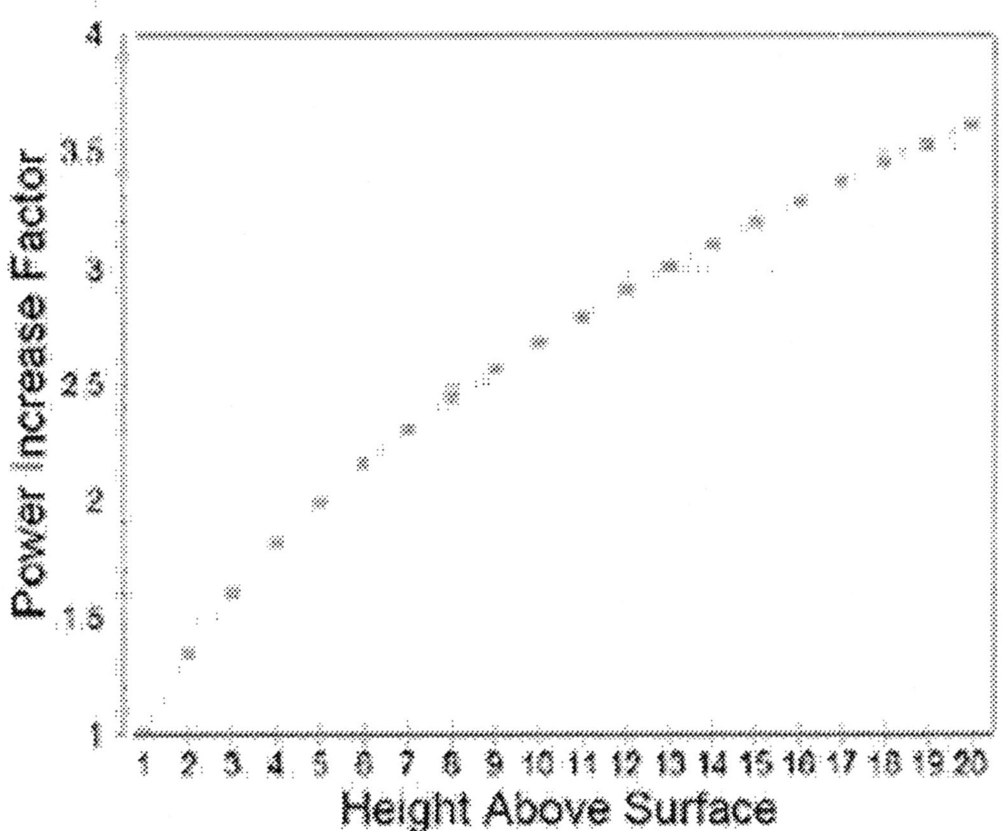

Figure 29-WIND GENERATOR HEIGHT VS. POWER OUTPUT

4. Compressed Air From Wind Machines

Along with providing electricity, the wind is also capable of compressing air. Compressed air is a storage medium that is not often thought of by alternative energy enthusiasts. Compressed air has been used in industry for many years for a multitude of applications. Most major manufacturing companies consider compressed air to be as important as running water. There are numerous uses for compressed air including tools, pumps, motors of various kinds, and water pumps. Storage of compressed air requires simply a tank with a check valve (to let air in but not out). Regulation and use normally require a regulator, filter/dryer, lubricator, and valving. There is, however, a slight loss of pressure over time through the valves and pipe connections. This is one drawback to using this system for long-term power storage.

There are a few commercially available wind machines that compress air. The "Bowjon" uses compressor-coupled blades on the top of a tower, similar to electric wind generators currently on the market. This wind generator compresses air into a storage tank located away from the tower. In the typical Bowjon application, compressed air is used to pump water by means of a "jet" system. Air is injected down the well pipe under the water, and the rising bubbles actually force the water and air mix to a higher level above the ground. There are also at least two Danish companies now making wind air compressor devices. (See Wind Generator files.)

D. Biomass Basics

1. Definitions—Biomass/Biomatter

Biomass is defined as complex polymers composed primarily of carbon, hydrogen and oxygen that have been created by metabolic activity of living organisms. Biomass is called a renewable resource since green plants are essentially solar collectors that capture and store sunlight in the form of chemical energy. Biomass resources are potentially the world's largest and most sustainable energy source.

2. Biomass Background

a. Biomass History and Statistics

The name “Biomass” was invented about 1975 to describe natural materials used as energy sources. It occurs in a wide variety of forms (wood, paper, trash, etc.) Approximately one percent of all biomass is used as food by humans and other animals. Globally, it is estimated that biomass supplies about 6 or 7 percent of total energy, and it continues to be a very important energy source for many developing countries. In the last two decades, interest in biomass has greatly increased even in countries where its use has drastically declined.

Biomass varies widely in both mass and volume fuel density, as well as varying in chemical composition. It often has high water content, and the different methods of recording and measuring MC can be confusing. While biomass can be used directly (mostly in wood fires), it can be converted to higher forms of fuels. Biomass is converted to various fuel forms in thermal (combustion, pyrolysis, and gasification) processes and biological (fermentation and digestion) processes. There are many various biomass conversion processes.

Biomass accounts for about 14 percent of the world’s energy supply. It is the most important source of energy for ¾ of the world’s population living in developing countries. In the U.S. alone, there are over 9000 MW of biomass power plants. Sweden derives over 14 percent of its energy from biomass.

b. Biomass Problems and Issues

While biomass is a great renewable energy source, it is not a good fuel, because it typically contains more than 70% air and void space. This low volumetric energy density makes it difficult to collect, ship, store and use.

Despite its wide use, biomass is usually used so inefficiently that only a small percentage of useful energy is obtained. It can also be a health hazard in some circumstances. For example, cooking stoves can release particulates, CO_2, NO, formaldehyde, and other organic compounds in poorly ventilated homes.

Also, the overall energy efficiency in traditional use is only about 5-15 percent, and biomass is often less convenient to use compared with fossil fuels. Solid fuels are not as convenient or versatile as liquids or gases, and this is a drawback to the direct use of biomass. Fortunately, a number of techniques are known for converting it to liquid or gaseous forms.

c. Wet Biomass

Biomass includes wood and is usually discussed as such. However wet biomass and waste products that contain significant water is a large part of a potential fuel source. At least one company is working on efficient burning of wet material using dual chambers. (See Woodstoves-Biomass files)

3. Definitions—Biofuel/Bioenergy

Bio-fuel is defined as biomass (or materials derived from biomass processing) that are utilized for generation of energy via combustion. Biomass fuel or biofuel is an energy source derived from living organisms. Most commonly it is plant residue, harvested, dried and burned, or further processed into solid, liquid, or gaseous fuels. It also includes wood waste, wood liquors, peat, railroad ties, wood sludge, spent sulfite liquors, agricultural waste (cereal straw, seed hulls, corn stalks and cobs), fish oils, soybean oil, sludge waste, waste alcohol, municipal solid wastes, food leftovers, landfill gases, industrial wastes, and ethanol (alcohol from fermented sugar) blended into motor gasoline. Another source of biomass is our garbage, also called municipal solid waste (MSW). Trash that comes from plant or animal products is biomass. Food scraps, lawn clippings, and leaves are all examples of biomass trash.

However, the most familiar and widely used biomass fuel is wood. Native shrubs and herbaceous plants are potential sources as well. Animal and/or human waste can also be used—typically to make methane. This text will concentrate on wood and vegetation.

4. Bioenergy Statistics

Bioenergy (total) covers about 15% of the world's energy consumption. Sweden and Finland supply 17% and 19% respectively, of their energy needs with bioenergy.

In the United States rising fuel prices led to a large increase in the use of wood-burning stoves and furnaces for space heating. Impending fossil fuel shortages have greatly increased research on its use in the United States and elsewhere. Because biomass is a potentially renewable resource, it is recognized as a possible replacement of petroleum and natural gas. Biomass is not as concentrated an energy source as most fossil fuels even when it is thoroughly dry.

5. Background-Gasification Processes

There are basically three methods of gasification—Producer, Synthesis, or Pyrolysis.

a. Producer Gas (Covered in this Text)

Or it can be <u>gasified with air</u> to make "producer gas" (typically CO 22%; H_2 18%; CH_4 3%, CO_2 6% and N_2 51%). When biomass is gasified with air the resulting gas has approximately 50% nitrogen, and is <u>good only for use at the point of origin</u>. Producer gas typically has an energy value of 5-10 MJ/m2. It is this producer gas which is the focus of this text.

b. Synthesis Gas

Biomass can be gasified with steam or oxygen to make "Synthesis Gas" (typically 40% CO, 40% H2, 3% CH4 and 17% CO2, dry basis) which can be used to make methanol, ammonia, and diesel fuel with known commercial catalytic processes. Oxygen gasification produces a gas with twice the energy (~12 MJ/m3) and can be put into pipelines, storage, or for chemical synthesis. This process can be used for larger plants and will not be extensively covered in this text.

c. (Flash) Pyrolysis and Limitations

1. Pyrolysis Background

Chemical decomposition through pyrolysis is the same technology used to refine crude fossil fuel oil and coal. Pyrolysis has been used since the dawn of civilization. If some means is applied to collect the off-gasses (smoke), the process is called wood distillation. The ancient Egyptians practiced wood distillation by collecting tars and pyroligneous acid for use in their embalming industry. Pyrolysis of wood to produce charcoal was a major industry in the 1800s, supplying the fuel for the industrial revolution, until it was replaced by coal.

In the late 19th Century and early 20th Century wood distillation was still profitable for producing soluble tar, pitch, creosote oil, chemicals, and non-condensable gasses often used to heat boilers at the facility. The wood distillation industry declined in the 1930s due to the advent of the petrochemical industry and its lower-priced products. However, pyrolysis of wood to produce charcoal for the charcoal briquette market and activated carbon for purification systems is still practiced in the U.S.

2. Pyrolysis Technology

Pyrolysis is a roasting process, also known as retorting, destructive distillation, or carbonization. In the pyrolysis process, organic materials such as wood or other biomass, is heated in a oxygen-free reactor. This causes the material to breakdown into new compounds, usually a hydrocarbon mixture. The result of the reaction usually appears to contain an oil like liquid, a carbon rich solid residue and some gaseous fumes.

3. Processing Differences

The mixture of solids, liquids, and gases depends on the time taken, and the temperature of the process: high temperatures and long reaction times produce more gas while lower times and temperatures produce more liquids and solids. Many of the products are the same as those available from petroleum refining, and can be used for similar applications.

4. Flash Pyrolysis

Flash pyrolysis is a process in which organic materials are rapidly heated in absence of air. Biomass can be gasified pyrolytically by quickly heating to 400-600 degrees C, yielding also 25% charcoal and lots of condensables such as tars. Under these conditions, organic vapors, gasses, and charcoal are produced. The vapors are then condensed to bio-oil. Typically, 70 percent of the feedstock is converted into oil and the resulting gas has an energy value of 17-20 MJ/m2.

A number of organic materials have successfully been processed in the current pilot plants such as bagasse, palm residues, rice husks, straw, pine wood, olive husks, beech wood, oak wood, switchgrass, and poplar. Most of the work centers on agricultural waste or forest waste that can be procured in large quantities. Pyrolysis is undergoing research and several technologies have been used to date including rotating cone flash pyrolysis, rotating cone reactor, and flash pyrolysis plants.

Before processing organic materials in a fast pyrolysis plant, the feedstock must have the following requirements: particle size less than 6 millimeters, moisture content less than 10 percent. Both of these require time and energy inputs in any self-sufficient living scheme and may make it impractical to use pyrolysis for energy production. Pyrolysis will not be covered extensively in this text because of the high temperature input and cost of equipment that is necessary.

6. Gasification/Gasifiers

a. Techniques and Raw Materials

1. Gasification Defined

Gasification is defined as the conversion of a feedstock to a combustible gas (with negligible char residues). The gas can then be used as a fuel. A gasifier is an automated biomass combustor system that uses the products of gasification as a fuel. Larger gasifiers typically have mechanical fuel delivery from a storage bin to the refractory lined gasification chamber where partial combustion (usually of the char) generates sufficient heat to cause volatilization of the incoming fuel.

2. Wood as Raw Material

Woodgas is gases that can be made from wood, other biomass and waste for heat, power and synthesis of ammonia and fuel (it is also called "producer gas", or "synthesis gas") When biomass decomposes at elevated temperatures, three primary products are formed: gas, bio-oil, and char. The following is related technologies and projects dealing with the technology.

3. Sewage as Raw Material

Using sewage and landfills to produce gas are the subject of the Methane section and will be covered there.

b. Gasification History (Wood, Charcoal, and Coal Gas)

1. Fuel Gas in Europe—1790

Making a combustible gas from coal and wood first began around 1790 in Europe. Such manufactured gas was used for street lights and was piped into houses for heating, lighting, and cooking. Factories used fuel gas for steam boilers, and farmers operated their machinery on wood gas and coal gas. Woodgas has been used for decades where clean heat is required. These produced gas which combusted so clean it was used in chimney-less household appliances such as cookers and heaters, without adverse effects.

The Industrial Revolution was fueled by gas starting in 1800 (primarily from coal by pyrolysis) initially used for city and home lighting, then for cooking and power generation. Coke for steel making was a useful by-product. By 1850, the major cities of the world had "gaslights". ***The internal combustion engine was invented to make electricity from producer gas about 1880.***

Fuel gas, produced by the reduction of coal and peat, was used for heating as early as 1840 in Europe, and by 1884 it had been adapted to fuel engines in England. After the discovery of large petroleum reserves in Pennsylvania in 1859, the entire world changed to oil—a cheaper and more convenient fuel. Thousands of gas works all over the world were eventually dismantled.

2. World War II

Wood gas generators have been a proven emergency solution when other fuels become unobtainable in case of war, civil upheaval, or natural disaster. There was a widespread use of woodgas generators during World War II, when petroleum products were not available for the civilian populations in many countries. In occupied Denmark during World War II, 95% of all mobile farm machinery, tractors, trucks, stationary engines, fishing and ferry boats were powered by wood gas generators.

Petroleum shortages during World War II led to widespread gas generator applications in the transportation industries of Western Europe. Even in neutral Sweden, 40% of all motor traffic operated on gas derived from

*Used in Earth Home

wood or charcoal. All over Europe, Asia, and Australia, millions of gas generators were in operation between 1940 and 1946. Charcoal-burning taxis were still common in Korea as late as 1970.

3. Advent of Oil (Again)

However, because of the wood gasifier's somewhat low efficiency, the inconvenience of operation, and the potential health risks from toxic fumes, most of such units were abandoned when oil again became available in 1945. Except for the technology of producing alternate fuels, such as methane or alcohol, the only solution for operating existing internal combustion engines, when oil and petroleum products are not available, has been these simple, inexpensive gasifier units.

7. Gasification Technologies/Equipment

Design of gasifier depends upon type of fuel used and whether gasifier is portable or stationary. Gas producers are classified according to how the air blast is introduced in the fuel column. History of gasification reveals several designs of gasifiers. The most commonly built gasifiers are classified as either updraft, downdraft, twin-fire, or crossdraft gas producer.

a. Updraft Gasifier

An updraft gasifier has clearly defined zones for partial combustion, reduction, and pyrolysis. Air is introduced at the bottom and act as countercurrent to fuel flow. The gas is drawn at a higher location. The updraft gasifier achieves the highest efficiency as the hot gas passes through the fuel bed and leaves the gasifier at low temperature. The sensible heat given by gas is used to preheat and dry fuel. Disadvantages of updraft gas producers are excessive amount of tar in raw gas and poor loading capability. Hence it is not suitable for running vehicles.

b. Fixed-Bed Gasifier History

In the updraft gasifier, gas leaves the gasifier with high tar vapor which may seriously interfere with the operation of internal combustion engines. This problem is minimized in downdraft gasifiers. In this type, air is introduced into a downward flowing packed bed or solid fuel and gas is drawn off at the bottom. A lower overall efficiency and difficulties in handling higher moisture and ash content are common problems in small downdraft gas producers. The time (20-30 minutes) needed to ignite and bring the plant to working temperature with good gas quality is shorter than updraft gas producer.

Down draft gasifiers in the 5-100 kw level were widely used in World War II for operating vehicles and trucks because of the relatively low tar levels. However, since hot gases naturally rise, it is necessary to supply power to draw the gasses down through the gasifier. (See also Automobile section)

c. Twin-Fire Gas Producer

The advantage of co-current and counter-current gasifiers are combined in a so a called twin-fire gasifier. It consists of two defined reaction zones. Drying, low-temperature carbonization, and cracking of gases occur in the upper zone. Permanent gasification of charcoal takes in the lower zone. The gas temperature lies between 460 to 520 degrees C. The total process takes place under pressure to produce fairly clean gas.

d. Crossdraft Gas Producer

Crossdraft gas producers, although they have certain advantages over updraft and downdraft gasifiers are not ideal either. The disadvantages such as high exit gas temperature, poor carbon dioxide reduction and high gas velocity are the consequence of the design. Unlike downdraft and updraft gasifiers, the ash bin, fire and reduction zone in crossdraft gasifiers are separated. These design characteristics limit the type of fuel for operation to low ash fuels such as wood, charcoal and coke. Start up time (5-10 minutes) is much faster than that of downdraft and updraft units and they operate well on dry air and dry fuel.

e. Fluidized-Bed Gasifiers (Not Covered in this Text)

Fluidized bed gasifiers require high power input, and exact controls, and are suitable only for large installations. They will not be covered in this text.

f. Modern Stratified, Downdraft Gasifier Operation

Until the early 1980's, wood gasifiers all over the world (including the World War II designs) operated on the principle that both the fuel hopper and the combustion unit be airtight; the hopper was sealed with a top or lid that bad to be opened every time wood was added. Smoke and gas vented into the atmosphere while new wood was being loaded; the operator bad to be careful not to breathe the unpleasant smoke and toxic fumes.

Over the years, a new gasifier design bas been developed. This simplified design employs a balanced, negative-pressure concept in which the old type of sealed fuel hopper is no longer necessary. A closure is only used to preserve the fuel when the engine is stopped. This new technology has several popular names, including "stratified, downdraft gasification" and "open top gasification."

During operation of this gasifier, air passes uniformly downward through four zones, hence the name "stratified." The uppermost zone contains unreacted fuel through which air and oxygen enter. This region serves the same function as the fuel hopper in the Imbert design.

In the second zone, the wood fuel reacts with oxygen during pyrolysis. Most of the volatile components of the fuel are burned in this zone and provide heat for continued pyrolysis reactions. At the bottom of this zone, all of the available oxygen from the air bas completely reacted. The open top design ensures uniform access of air to the pyrolysis region.

The third zone is made up of charcoal from the second zone. Hot combustion gases from the pyrolysis region react with the charcoal to convert the carbon dioxide and water vapor into carbon monoxide and hydrogen. The inert char and ash, which constitute the fourth zone, are normally too cool to cause further reactions; however, since the fourth zone is available to absorb heat or oxygen as conditions change, it serves both as a buffer and as a charcoal storage region. Below this zone is the grate. The presence of char and ash serves to protect the grate from excessive temperatures.

g. Downdraft Gasifier Disadvantages

The foremost question about the operation of the stratified, downdraft gasifier concerns char and ash removal. As the charcoal reacts with the combustion gases, it eventually reaches a very low density and breaks up into a dust containing all of the ash as well as a percentage of the original carbon. This dust may be partially carried away by the gas; however, it might eventually begin to plug the gasifier, and so it must be removed by shaking or agitation. Both the Imbert gasifiers and the stratified concept have a provision for shaking the grate; when they are used to power vehicles, they are automatically shaken by the vehicle's motion.

Another important issue in the design of the stratified, downdraft gasifier is the prevention of fuel bridging and channeling. High-grade biomass fuels such as wood blocks or chips will flow down through the gasifier under the influence of gravity, and downdraft air flow. However, other fuels (such as shredded wood, sawdust, and bark) can form a bridge that will prevent continuous flow and cause very high temperatures. Obviously, it is desirable to use these widely available biomass residues. Bridging can be prevented by stirring, shaking, or by agitating the grate or by having it agitated by the vehicle's movement. For prolonged idling, a hand-operated shaker has been included in the design.

h. Stratified, Downdraft Gasifier Advantages

The stratified, downdraft design has a number of advantages over the World War II, Imbert gasifier. The open top permits fuel to be fed more easily and allows easy access. The cylindrical shape is easy to fabricate and permits continuous flow of fuel. No special fuel shape or pretreatment is necessary as any blocky fuel can be used.

8. Gasifiers and Stirling Engines

Some of the newer updraft gasifiers produce gas with a high tar content which is then used to power Stirling engines that can use such fuel. Producer gas containing tar and particles can be used directly in a Stirling engine without further cleaning. This technology is continuously being developed and modified. (See also Stirling section)

E. Biomass—Solids

1. Wood/Solid Fuel (see also Heating section)

a. History/Cost Comparisons

A major repeatable source of heat is burning wood or vegetation matter. Woodfuel accounts for about 10 percent of the total energy used in the world. It provides about 20 percent of all energy used in Asia and Latin America, and about 50 percent of total energy used in Africa. It is estimated that a third of the world population scrambles daily to obtain woodfuel to meet domestic needs.

A full 75% of Earth's peoples burns wood for cooking and heating. Half of all trees cut are used for fuel and in the U.S.-wood provides more energy than nuclear power. There are over 11 million woodstoves in use in the U.S. ***Theoretically, it takes approximately seven acres of well managed woodland to supply the continuous heating and cooking needs for one family in the northern U.S.***. I believe this figure will drop as newer, more efficient methods of wood heating are developed. Heating with wood is also less costly than all conventional methods. (See the following figure)

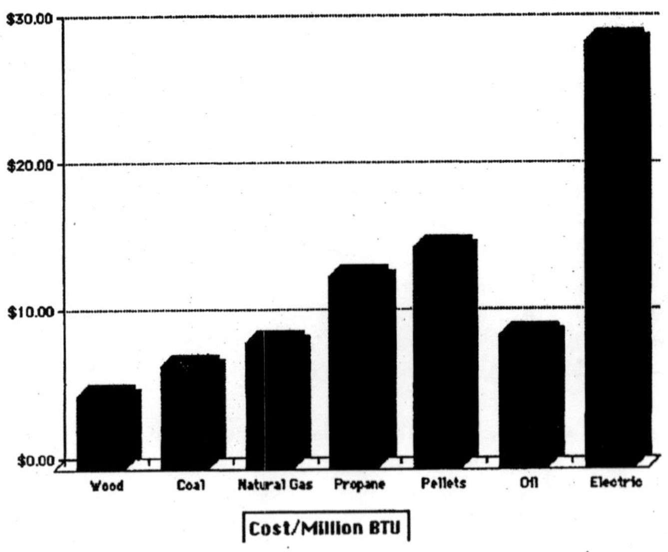

Figure 30-WOOD HEATING COSTS

*Used in Earth Home

b. CO_2 Issues

There is an ongoing debate whether wood burning contributes significantly to higher carbon dioxide levels in the atmosphere. If a person heats with wood, I believe it will not contribute to higher global CO_2 concentrations leading to global warming or the greenhouse effect. The amount of CO_2 given off by burning wood should be the same amount that would be given off if the wood were simply allowed to rot on the forest floor. The soil, however, does not have the benefit of the decaying organic matter.

c. Wood for Steam Generation (see Electricity-Generation section)

d. Wood for Gasification Boilers (see Woodgas section)

2. Wood Pellets/Densification

Biomass density may be increased by milling and compressing dried residues. The resulting briquettes or pellets are also easier to handle, store, and transport. Compression has been used with a variety of materials including crop residues, herbaceous native plant material, sawdust, and other forest wastes.

a. Pelletizing/Densification Process

Densification is a relatively new process in which the air is squeezed out at very high pressure to make pellets (using feed type machines), cubes (using alfalfa cubes), or logs. Best of all, for many applications almost any biomass can be used provided it is chopped fine: sawdust; agricultural residues and even municipal solid waste. (See Alternative Pelleting Materials section)

b. Pelleting Background/History

The residential wood pellet fuel industry in North America was created in the early 1980s as a response to the energy crisis. The modern pellet stove dates from 1983. Today, almost one million tons of pellets are sold each year – to heat nearly 500,000 pellet stoves and fireplace inserts in homes the United States and Canada. Consumption is greatest in the Pacific Northwest and Northeastern states where pellets are manufactured from sawmill and wood product residues and where heating energy requirements are significant.

Interestingly, the vehicle units of the World War II era were equipped to gasify blocks of wood. The gasifiers had ample vibration to jar the carefully sized wood blocks through the gasifier. In fact, an entire industry emerged for preparing wood for use in vehicles at that time. (See Woodgas section)

c. Pelleting Technology

Soft wood waste has to be dried to about 10% moisture content and reduced in size to below 10x10x100mm before it can be processed into pellets. The core process of the wood pelleting plant comprises 5 stages: milling, conditioning, pressing, cooling and screening. The raw material is first reduced to a particle size of about 3mm with a hammermill.

The material is conditioned with dry steam and water to the required temperature and moisture content to activate the lignin as a pellet binding agent and to obtain the necessary malleability of the product. This is the most critical stage of the process to achieve an optimum performance of the pellet press and to minimize wear on the press die and rollers. Wood pellets leave the pellet press at a temperature of about 100°C and need to be cooled down to about 25°C to harden the wood pellet and to maintain the quality of the product during storage and handling.

*Used in Earth Home

d. Wood Pelleting Process and Machines

A number of properties are commonly known to affect the success of pelleting including: moisture content of the material, density, particle size, fiber strength, and lubricating characteristics. The main factors that have been studied to improve the pelleting process are die geometry, steam conditioning temperature, moisture optimization, length of the grind, and binding agents.

Most machines have been designed for sawn or planed wood residue or other forms of wood machining. It gives them a means of turning their waste streams into a valuable renewable fuel product. Most machines are supplied with a die designed for softwood material.

3. Biomass Pelleting Alternatives

a. Switchgrass Pelleting

Switchgrass is a perennial prairie grass native to North America. One acre of a switchgrass plot can grow the energy equivalent of about 2-6 tons of coal per year. Switchgrass can also be pelletized and behaves similarly to alfalfa pellets. When switchgrass is pressed into pellets and burned in specially designed space-heating stoves, the efficiency is claimed to reach 85%.

b. Alfalfa Pelleting

The alfalfa crop is cut at the early flowering stage to optimize yields and nutritional quality. The alfalfa is partially field dried, picked up, chopped, and rushed to a processing plant where it's dehydrated, ground into meal, and processed into pellets. Sun-cured alfalfa pellets are produced by similar methods except that the hay may be somewhat more mature when cut and either partly or fully field dried before processing. Alfalfa cubes are made from coarsely chopped alfalfa hay that has been partly or completely field dried.

c. Corn as Pellets

Corn is being used in the Midwestern U.S. to fuel modified pellet stoves. Corn for pellets or pellet stoves will not be covered in this publication because of the high value of the corn for human and animal food.

d. Other Biomass Crops

There are a growing number of crops being looked at for biomass including hybrid poplar trees. Waste agricultural residue such as sunflower hulls is also being looked at for pelleting. Hops, pine needles, and many other herbaceous energy crops (HEC) like switchgrass can be pelletized.

4. Burning Pellets/Pellet Stoves

Del-Point close coupled gasifier stove burns switchgrass, but requires a cleaner grate setting. Two dies are available: one producing pellets of 8mm diameter (for pellet stoves and boilers); the other pellets of 11mm diameter which burn in unmodified solid fuel stoves.

5. Pelletizing Future

a. Pelletizing Issues

Industrial palletizing equipment is usually either rind die mills or flat die mills. They got their start from palletizing feed for animals. Sweden Power Chippers (SPC) is one company specializing in small pelletizing plants. A 150 kg/hr unit is currently under development. Another company from Australia, Falkner Maschinenbau is also developing 70 kg/hr. units.

b. Pellets in Earth Home?

There are a growing number of companies that pelletize wood for burning in woodstoves. Claims of higher efficiencies and cleaner ash is common. Wood pellets will not be covered in this text because of the energy required to pelletize and the lack of small pellet presses.

6. Charcoal (See Woodgas section)

F. Biomass Liquids (Oil Crops/Biodiesel)

1. Biomass Liquid Conversion Efficiency Issues

Liquid biofuel is usually bioalcohol such as methanol, ethanol, and biodiesel. The efficiency with which biomass may be converted to ethanol or other convenient liquid or gaseous fuel is a major concern. Conversion generally requires appreciable energy. If an excessive amount of expensive fuel is used in the process, costs may be prohibitive.

2. Alcohol (see separate Alcohol section)

3. Oil Crops

a. Common Oil Crops and Data

There are over 350 species of oleaginous, or oil-producing plants and thousands of sub-species. Plants that are commonly found in different regions of the world include the oil palm, coconut, rapeseed, peanut, sunflower, safflower, soybean, hemp and corn. The following figure lists production data for them.

b. Jatropha

1. Jatropha Background

Jatropha is a large shrub (up to 8 meters) well distributed in Africa and Asia. It is widely cultivated for its edible green pods and its fried seeds taste like peanuts. Edible oil is extracted from the seeds and the seeds are used in curry powders. The black Jatropha plant seeds contain from 30% to 80% oil. Seed yields of 5 tons per hectare have been routinely achieved. Jatropha starts producing seeds within 12 months but reaches its maximum productivity level after 4 to 5 years. It grows in marginal soil and is being looked at for the mass production of biofuel The fruits, seeds and flowers are all considered to be nutritious vegetables. The leaves are extremely rich in essential nutrients such as ß-Carotene, Vitamin C (ascorbic acid), iron and free leucine. For example, the ß-carotene content of the leaves is three times as high as in carrots. Members of the genus Jatropha are known to be very toxic. However, a non-toxic variety has been found in the Papantla region of Veracruz State in Mexico which is suitable for human consumption after roasting.

2. Uses for Jatropha Oil

Jatropha curcus is unusual among tree crops because the dry fruits and seeds will remain on the tree for some time before falling to the ground, especially under dry conditions. The plant lives, producing seeds, for over 50 years. It is a perennial that can grow without irrigation in arid conditions where corn and sugar cane could never thrive. Jatropha naturally repels both animals and insects and is typically planted along the circumference of farms to protect other crops. Jatropha requires minimal inputs, stabilizes or even reverses desertification, and can be used for a variety of products—even after the biofuel is extracted.

Jatropha is a source of renewable energy for fuel (pre-combustion chamber diesel engines), edible oil, animal feed, and pharmaceutical products—ideal trees for increasing cash income. Jatropha is used for lamps (lighting), cooking, in engines, and for soap making. Other parts of the plant are also useful: dark blue dye and wax can be produced from the bark, the stem can be used as a poor quality wood, and the roots help in making yellow dye. The flowers of Jatropha curcas and the Jatropha stem have well-known medicinal (anti-cancerous) properties, and the leaves can be used for dressing wounds. All these things can be used or sold. Alternate uses of the oil also include varnishes, illuminants, organic insecticide, and medicine. Jatropha curcas oil cake is also rich in nitrogen, phosphorous and potassium and can be used as protein-rich livestock feed or organic manure. See following figure for more complete uses for jatropha.

3. Jatropha Oil Extraction

Jatropha oil extraction can be done with hand- or engine driven expellers. These are simple machines, which can be operated on village level and built within the country. Some examples of extraction equipment are: the Sayari Expeller, the Bielenberg Ram Press, the Komet Expeller, Hexan-Extraction, and the common traditional hand method.

4. Jatropha Issues

There are still some inherent problems with Jatropha and research work is still required. Scientists are learning more and more about the properties of Jatropha. Some of the issues include:

1) Jatropha oil is hydroscopic in that it absorbs water and needs nitrogen blanketing on steel tanks. Jatropha is high in acid and it has the tendency to degrade quickly—particularly if not handled properly.

2) Right from the time of expelling, the oil needs to be kept in storage conditions that prevent undue degradation. Exposure to air and moisture must be minimized.

3) The oil must be fully degummed before it can be made into biodiesel!

4) Some of the contents of edible Jatropha seem to be quite different compared to these contents in non-edible Jatropha.

5) Seeds degrade as soon as they are picked and so careful storage and handling is required.

c. Moringa Trees

Moringa is similar to Jatropha and can be used to produce oil. Moringa is also a drought-tolerant, multipurpose tree. It grows very fast under favorable conditions (2-3 meters in 6-8 months) and yields up to 120 tons dry matter per hectare per year when planted very densely and used as forage. It can survive in harsh regions on stony, infertile land.

Moringa seed kernels contain about 40% oil by weight. The oil can be extracted by hand or machines. Ram and Spindle presses are some of the mechanical methods of extracting oil from seeds. The oil can be used for soap making and consumption. After pressing, the cake can be dried, stored and be used for water purification or as a fertilizer. Moringa seed coagulants are a viable alternative to expensive and toxic chemical coagulants such as aluminum sulphate (alum) for purifying drinking water. (See also Jatropha section)

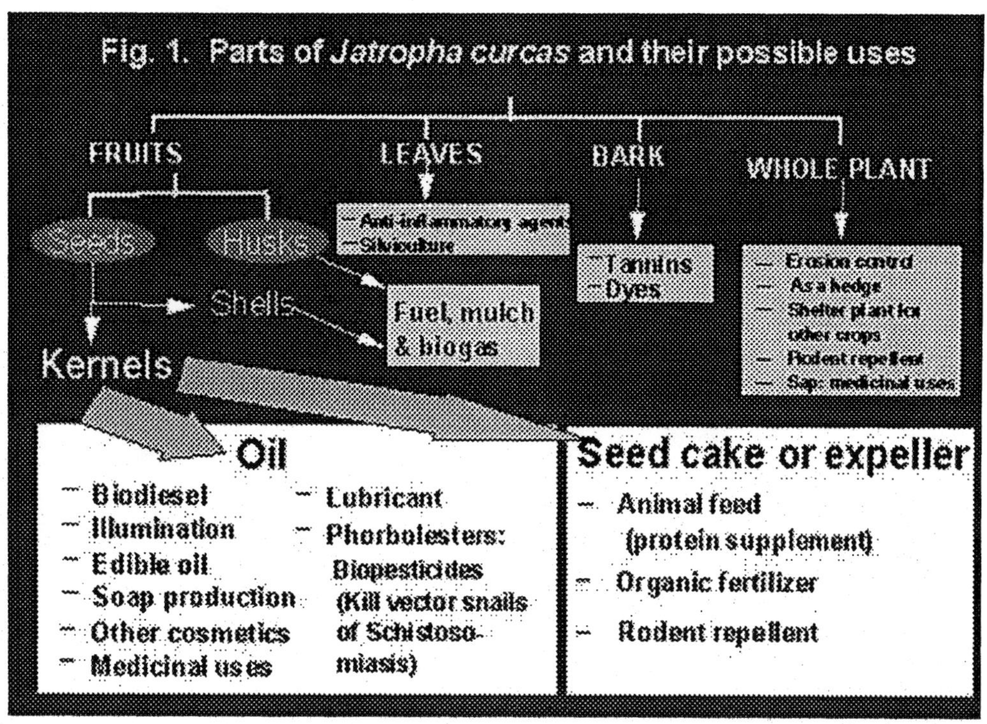

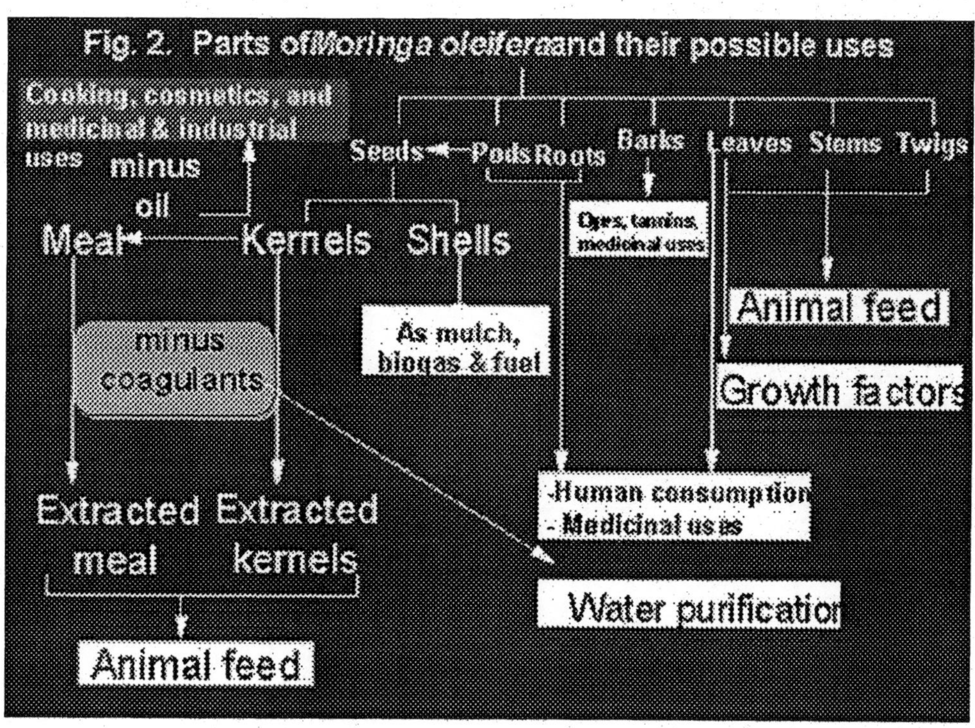

Figure 31-JATROPHA AND MORINGA USES

*Used in Earth Home

d. Other Oil-Producing Plants (with Charts)

Throughout history, people have been searching for an alternative to petroleum fuels. The Chinese Tallow Tree (Sapium sebiferum) is an ancient and valuable oil seed producing tree with a long history of large scale commercial production in China and parts of Asia. It is one of nature's most prolific producers of renewable hydrocarbons. Pongamia has also been investigated as an oil-producing plant.

The large shrub, Euphorbia tirucalli, is typically used as a hedge in Brazil. Along with a similar plant from Morocco, Euphorbia resinifera, they have long been investigated as sources of energy. Most of the research that has been done centered on large acreages and mass harvesting and processing. The following figures gives a glimpse into other oil-producing plants and how much oil they produce in various units.

4. Biodiesel Technology

Biodiesel is a fuel made with vegetable oils, animal oil and fats, or greases - such as recycled restaurant grease and can be used in diesel engines without changing them. The legal definition of biodiesel is that it is a diesel quality liquid fuel that is produced from either biomass or waste cooking oil, which has an ester content of at least 96.5% by weight and sulphur content which does not exceed 0.005% by weight or is nil. Biodiesel can be used in modern diesel vehicles with little or no modifications. It is the fastest growing alternative fuel in the United States.

Oil Crop	Latin Name	Pounds of Oil per Acre	Kilograms of Oil per Hectare	Gallons per Acre
Oil Palm	Elaeis guineensis	4585	5000	635 gallons
Coconut	Cocos nucifera	2070	2260	287 gallons
Jatropha	Jatropha curcas	1460	1590	202 gallons
Rapeseed (canola)	Brassica napus	915	1000	127 gallons
Peanut	Arachis hypogaea	815	8900	113 gallons
Sunflower	Helianthus annuus	720	800	102 gallons
Safflower	Carthamus tinctorius	605	655	83 gallons
Mustard	Glycine max	345	375	61 gallons
Soybean	Cannabis Sativa	280	305	48 gallons
Corn	Zea mays	135	145	18 gallons

Figure 32-OIL CROP PRODUCTION DATA

*Used in Earth Home

Plant	Latin Name	kg oil/hectare
corn	Zea mays	145
cashew nut	Anacardium occidentale	148
oat	Avena sativa	183
palm	Erythea salvadorensis	189
lupine	Lupinus albus	195
rubber seed	Hevea brasiliensis	217
kenaf	Hibiscus cannabinus L.	230
calendula	Calendula officinalis	256
cotton	Gossypium hirsutum	273
hemp	Cannabis sativa	305
soybean	Glycine max	375
coffee	Coffea arabica	386
linseed	Linum usitatissimum	402
hazelnut	Corylus avellana	405
euphorbia	Euphorbia lagascae	440
pumpkin seed	Cucurbita pepo	449
coriander	Coriandrum sativum	450
mustard	Brassica alba	481
camelina	Camelina sativa	490
sesame	Sesamum indicum	585
crambe	Crambe abyssinica	589
safflower	Carthamus tinctorius	655
buffalo gourd	Cucurbita foetidissima	665
rice	Oriza sativa L.	696

Plant	Latin Name	kg oil/hectare
tung oil tree	Aleurites fordii	790
sunflower	Helianthus annuus	800
cocoa	Theobroma cacao	863
peanut	Arachis hypogaea	890
opium poppy	Papaver somniferum	978
rapeseed	Brassica napus	1000
olive tree	Olea europaea	1019
piassava	Attalea funifera	1112
gopher plant	Euphorbia lathyris	1119
castor bean	Ricinus communis	1188
bacuri	Platonia insignis	1197
pecan	Carya illinoensis	1505
jojoba	Simmondsia chinensis	1528
babassu palm	Orbignya martiana	1541
jatropha	Jatropha curcas	1590
macadamia nut	Macadamia terniflora	1887
brazil nut	Bertholletia excelsa	2010
avocado	Persea americana	2217
coconut	Cocos nucifera	2260
oiticia	Licania rigida	2520
buriti palm	Mauritia flexuosa	2743
pequi	Caryocar brasiliense	3142
macauba palm	Acrocomia aculeata	3775
oil palm	Elaeis guineensis	5000

Figure 33-OIL CROPS

*Used in Earth Home

a. Diesel/Biodiesel History

Ironically, the first diesel engine ever made, in 1893, was powered by peanut oil—a biofuel. By the 1920's the petroleum industry had all but eliminated the biofuel infrastructure and usurped the market with diesel fuel because it was cheaper to produce. Even then, the engine's inventor, Rudolf Diesel, maintained that "the use of vegetable oils for engine fuels may seem insignificant today, but such oils may become, in the course of time, as important as petroleum and the coal-tar products of the present time."

b. Rapeseed Biodiesel (See Vegetable Oil section)

c. Biodiesel (Vegetable Oil)

Biodiesel is a blend of diesel fuel and vegetable oil. Usually the vegetable oil must be heated to lower its viscosity. Internal combustion engines can also run on 100% vegetable oil with the correct conversions. Vegetable oil production from Spirulina is being investigated for an answer to the continuing oil shortage for transportation. Many different kinds of oil presses are being used to extract the oil from the plant source.

d. Biodiesel Future

In India, the Supreme Court has recently banned the use of undiluted diesel fuel for commercial vehicles in Delhi due to its adverse effects on health, and other cities are reported to have followed suit. According to most sources, biodiesel can be used in any diesel engine or burner without adaptation. Tests have shown that biodiesel has similar or better fuel consumption, horsepower, and torque and haulage rates than conventional diesel.

e. Biodiesel in EH?

Most of the vegetable oil production will be consumed for foodstuffs in the self-sufficient home. (see Biodiesel files). Also, most of the biodiesel testing is on waste vegetable oil (WVO) from fast-food restaurants.

G. Biomass Liquids (Alcohol/Ethanol)

1. Ethanol vs. Methanol—the Chemistry

a. Ethanol Background

Ethanol, also known as ethyl alcohol or grain alcohol, is a flammable, colorless chemical compound, one of the alcohols that is most often found in alcoholic beverages. In common conversation, it is often referred to simply as alcohol. Its chemical formula is $C2H5OH$, also written as $C2H6O$.

Humans have been making ethanol from sugar and starch for over 10,000 years—mostly very dilute (<12% with most yeasts). The Arabs discovered distillation about 1000 AD and more concentrated beverage alcohols proliferated. In the 1800s the French began pioneering the use of ethanol for commercial purposes, mostly as solvents. During WWII ethanol was widely used as a blend fuel at ratios from 10 to 30%. Because of its high octane it was also used in small planes. Unfortunately blends require 100% ethanol and distillation can only produce 95% without having to "break the azeotrope", which adds expense. This is also referred loosely to "drying".

In 1980 farmers discovered that they could market excess corn as the ethanol blend fuel "gasohol". They could also in principle produce the ethanol on the farm.

b. Methanol Background

Early in the 19th century it was discovered that the "smoke" generated during charcoal making contained all sorts of chemical goodies like acetic acid, acetone, and methanol (1.5% from hardwoods, 0% from softwoods). As a byproduct of charcoal making these chemicals were quite cheap and could be used commercially. So, depending on place, production, and price, the two alcohols have been used more or less interchangeably.

In 1923, chemists discovered a catalyst that could make methanol (50%) yield from coal gasification, and that methanol was much cheaper than methanol from wood distillation (wood alcohol) or ethanol from corn/potatoes/starchy and sugary products. Woodgas or "syngas" may also be converted to methanol, a one carbon-alcohol that can be used as a transportation fuel. Because methanol is a liquid, it is easy to store and transport. (See Woodgas section)

c. Ethanol Preferred for Earth Home

Methanol from natural gas is presently much cheaper than ethanol. Methanol from wood is potentially much cheaper than ethanol from corn—but requires gasification, compression and a catalyst. Until the need becomes more critical, it is anticipated that methanol will continue to be made from natural gas.

Ethanol is a "better" alcohol compared to methanol because the former is derived from agricultural products, is a renewable fuel, and is relatively harmless to the environment. (Methanol has half the energy per gallon of gasoline and ethanol has 2/3 the energy of gasoline.)

2. History of Alcohol

a. Background/Overview

Another potential source of energy is alcohol. Alcohol (or ethanol as is the correct definition) is produced by fermentation of starches, sugars, and yeast. Alcohol for human consumption goes back thousands of years. The Babylonians brewed beer and the Germanic tribes of Europe fermented apple juice. Many references to wine are found in historical accounts. The Romans knew how to do it as did the Egyptians, the Greeks, the Phoenicians, and even the barbarians. Archaeologists have unearthed simple clay stills from ancient Mesopotamia, the "cradle of civilization." It is interesting to note that some people postulate that the driving force to early man starting to farm was that he desired excess grain from which to produce alcohol.

b. Fuel Alcohol History

Fuel alcohol or ethanol is a pure substance, unadulterated by contaminants (unless denatured by addition of a small amount of gasoline), and relatively harmless. Ethanol has many advantages as a fuel source, but it does not compete in most countries with other liquid fuels on an economic basis for two basic reasons. First, raw materials for alcohol use are more valuable for food or other uses. Secondly, alcohol requires more energy to produce than it will deliver in any use. Currently, the technology for making alcohol is well understood and the basic procedure is quite simple. (See also Methanol vs. Alcohol section)

The amount of labor and time involved in producing large quantities of alcohol is quite extensive. Sugarcane is the world's largest source of fermentation ethanol and Brazil has produced over 90 billion liters of ethanol from sugarcane. Some of the alternative sources of alcohol that have been suggested include switchgrass or hybrid poplar.

3. Alcohol Production

a. Basic Process Chart

To do this, a starch (from foodstuffs, grains, food wastes, and/or biomass) must be converted into a sugar and, in the presence of an enzyme, fermented into alcohol. The following figure shows simple alcohol production equipment. Complete discussion follows.

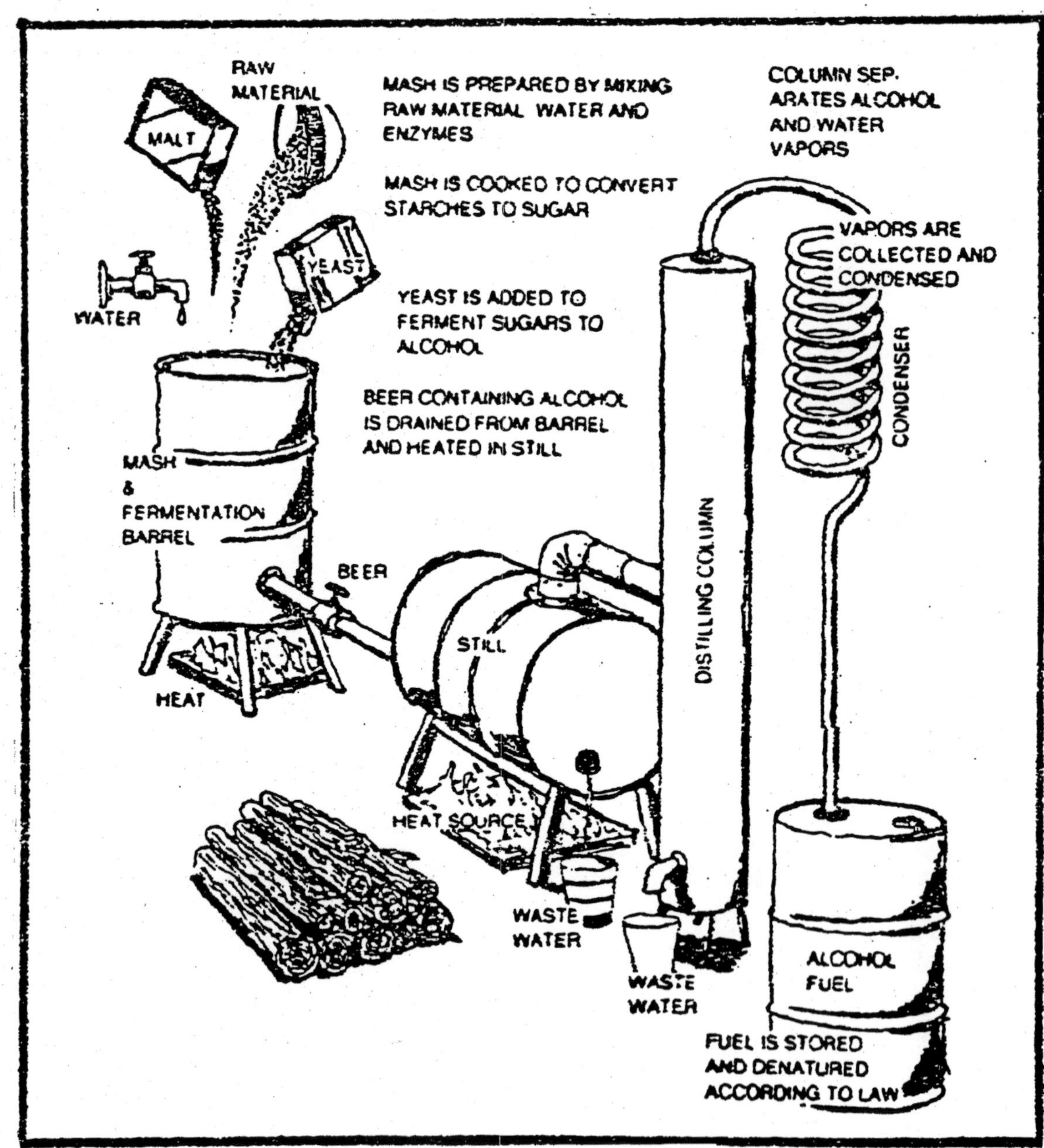

Figure 34-BASIC PROCESS OF ALCOHOL PRODUCTION

*Used in Earth Home

b. Sugar, Starch, or Cellulose (Carbohydrates)

Because yeast need a supply of simple sugar in solution to make alcohol, raw materials are needed that can supply sugar in sufficient quantities to make the process worthwhile. The most abundant source for this sugar is plant matter. Cellulose from kudzu, for example, can be used for alcohol production.

Plants are mostly water, carbohydrate, and protein—with differing amounts of these ingredients concentrated into different portions of the plant. It is the carbohydrates we are interested in. Carbohydrates fall into one of three basic categories:

1) Sugars. Glucose, fructose, and maltose are found in large concentrations in such plants and plant products as sugar beets, sugar cane, cane sorghum, molasses, fresh or dried fruits, and whey and skim milk.

2) Starches. These are larger, more complex molecules formed from groups of simple sugars joined together. Starches include potatoes, sweet potatoes, corn, wheat, milo, grain sorghum, barley, rye, artichokes, cacti, manioc, arrowroot, and pumpkins.

3) Cellulose. Composed of long chains of sugars and lignin, cellulose is the basic building block of all plant fiber. It is found in such things as corn stalks, corn cobs, hay, straw, grass, and wood. Cellulose is also the primary ingredient in paper (from wood pulp) and manure (from undigested plant fiber).

Although nearly any crop or plant residue can be used in the manufacture of alcohol fuel, some provide far greater yields than others or are easier to process. The easiest materials to make alcohol from are the high sugar content group. This includes sugar cane, sugar beets and molasses. By mulching, pressing, or washing, most of the fermentable sugar in these raw materials can be recovered. Figure 10 shows basic flowcharts of possible carbohydrate sources for alcohol production.

c. Enzyme Sources

As stated above, the ingredients for alcohol fuel production fall into one of three basic categories: sugars, starches, or cellulose. Sugars are the easiest to process, starches are next easiest, and cellulose is fairly difficult. Sugars are the easiest because they can be extracted and fermented with a minimum of effort. Enzymes are not required since there are no starches to be broken down. Starches and cellulose requires enzymes which must be purchased or cultured. Brewers yeast is a common purchased enzyme used to turn the sugar into alcohol.

Furthermore, history shows that in order to make an alcoholic beverage from cereals the starch must first be converted to sugars by enzymatic action. ***This conversion may be done by one of three methods-germination, salivation, or fermentation.*** In the first method the sprouting grain furnishes its own enzyme, diastase; in the second the primitive brewer supplies the enzyme ptyalin from his (or her) own saliva; in the third the enzyme is derived from the fermenting organism, usually a fungus. In all three methods the enzymes would be destroyed by excessive heat.

It may come as a surprise to some readers to know that in ancient times saliva was used as a source of diastase (amylase) for conversion of starch to sugars in some fermented alcoholic beverages such as Japanese sake' and South American chicha. This method is still used to make chicha in the Andes regions of Bolivia and Peru. (See also Alcohol Production Section)

The best overall source of enzymes for the self-sufficient home is sprouting seeds. Barley produces an abundance of enzymes in its sprouts. Sprouted barley or malt is chopped up and added to the ground starch solution to "hydrolyze" or decompose the starch into sugar.

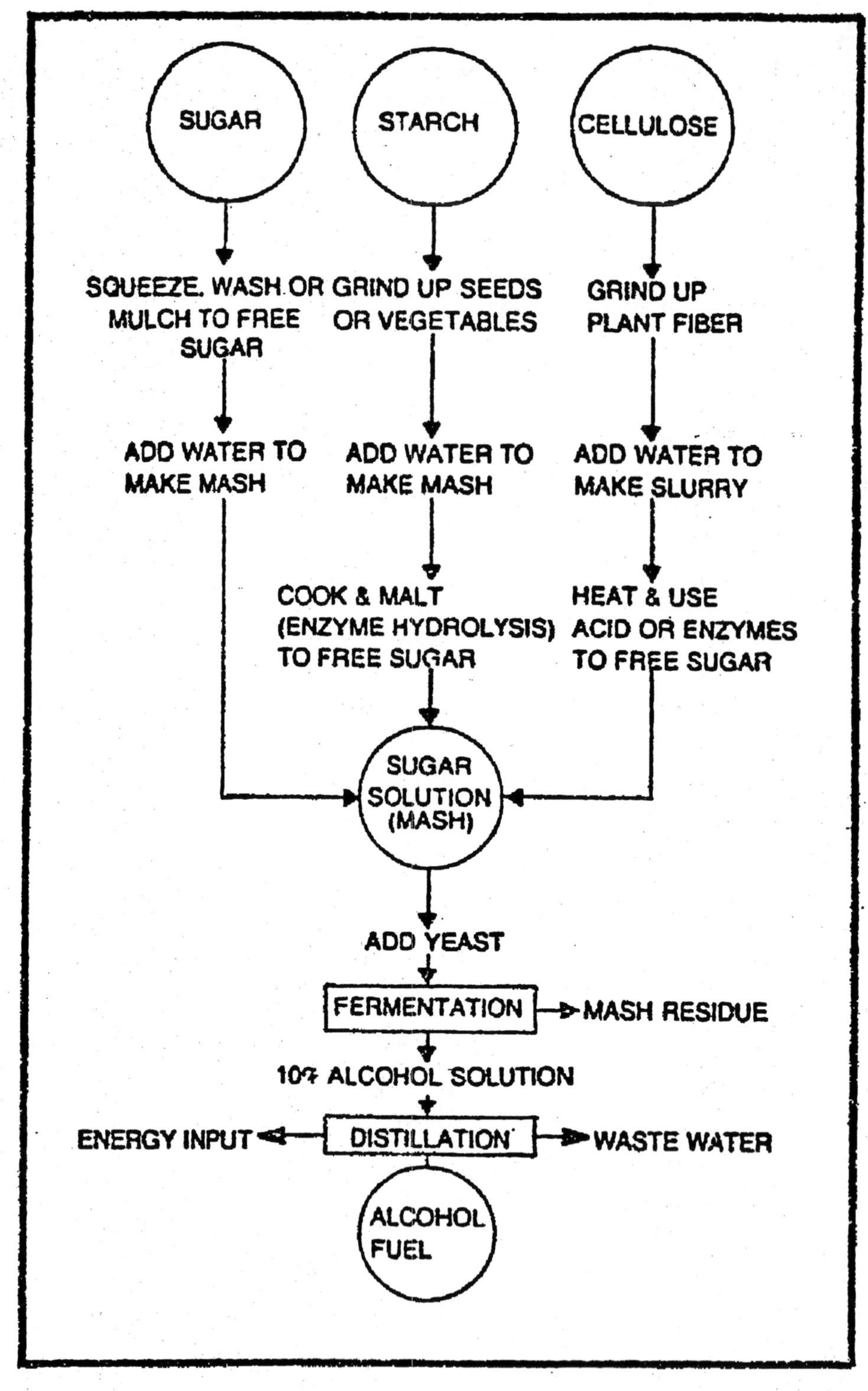

Figure 35-ALCOHOL RAW MATERIAL FLOWCHART

*Used in Earth Home

d. Yeast Discussion/Sources

Yeast is a general word that describes any of several species of single-celled fungi. The two species of interest to brewers are Sccaromyces cerevisiae, the original top-fermenting ale yeast, and Saccharomyces uvarum, the bottom-fermenting lager yeast. Both of these closely related species live their entire lives as single cells. During their lives, yeasts gain energy for continued life by eating sugars. Fermentation is the sum total of all the chemical reactions used by yeast to gain energy from sugar. As far as the yeast is concerned, alcohol and carbon dioxide are simply byproducts of the fermentation process.

Yeast can be cultured by any homebrewer, but it is a difficult process. A high degree of cleanliness is required besides some specialized equipment.

The basic steps to manufacture of quality yeasts are:

1) Make wort--------------------culture preparation
2) Make solidified wort---------culture preparation
3) Inoculate some slants for storage------------------master culture
4) Inoculate from a slant to a petri plate------------------working culture
5) Make flasks of sterile wort-------starter preparation
6) Make a small starter culture-----starter preparation
7) Make a large starter culture------starter preparation

To ensure long-term success in maintaining sterile cultures, three variables must be mastered:

1) Temperature
2) Measurement of Contamination
3) Recognition of Mutations

The Earth Home System does not get into an elaborate discussion on slanting yeasts. At this point in time, yeast is included with items that are best purchased in small quantities similar to table salt.

e. Recipes/Commercial-Scale Fuel Production Techniques

The following describes the conversion process used by the Archer Daniels Midland alcohol production plant near Decatur, IL. The process starts with corn and yields ethanol alcohol, corn germ meal, corn oil, and high protein gluten. Note that all 13 steps are not required if simple fuel production is the goal. Steps 3 through 7 would be omitted and step 12 would not be necessary if you were using straight alcohol fuel in a converted engine.

1) Steeping to loosen various parts of the corn kernel
2) Grinding to break the corn kernel apart. (3/16” screen or sandlike)(mix at 16 gallons of water per bushel)
3) Germ separation to recover the corn oil and corn germ meal.
4) Fine grinding to separate the starch and gluten fractions.
5) Removal of fiber for corn gluten feed which is 21 percent protein.
6) Removal of protein for corn gluten meal which is 60 percent protein.
7) Concentrating the starch by removing excess water.
8) Cooking the starch in the presence of the liquefying enzymes which convert the starch chains to dextrins. (slow boil for 30 minutes with agitation)
9) Cooling and adding saccharifying enzymes to convert the dextrins to glucose.
10) Yeast is then added to convert the glucose to ethanol alcohol and carbon dioxide. (2-4 ounces per bushel)
11) The alcohol (10 percent in the fermenter) is distilled to a concentration of 96 percent to 96.5 percent pure.
12) The purified alcohol is then redistilled to 99.75 percent to 100 percent pure.

13) The anhydrous alcohol is denatured with gasoline to make gasohol.

Research is ongoing to simplify techniques for family sized plants and also to obtain/substitute enzymes and yeast for ongoing alcohol production. Barley malt, for example may be substituted for commercial enzymes. Other ingredient substitutes for hops are wood sage, sarsaparilla, mugwort, or horehound.

f. Alcohol Yields

Yields of alcohol vary widely due to their chemical make-up. According to Brazilian estimates, a ton of sugar cane, for example, yields 94 kg of sugar and 70 liters of alcohol. Corn and wheat will yield roughly 2.6 gallons of alcohol per bushel.

g. Alcohol Production from Food Wastes

Alcohol can also be generated from waste food and biomass. Jerusalem artichoke stalks and maple sap can be sources of carbohydrates that can be used for small-scale alcohol/vinegar production. (See Vinegar Files)

h. Distillation

Distillation involves heating the alcohol/water mix after fermentation to a temperature of about 180 deg. F. At this temperature, the alcohol evaporates and the vapors are allowed to come into contact with a cold surface such as a copper tube or stainless steel. This method is used to separate higher "proof" alcohol from weaker alcohol mixes such as beer.

i. Large-scale Alcohol Plants

The amount of labor and time involved in producing large quantities of alcohol is quite extensive. There is a great deal of pumping and mixing involved in the process, and the ingredients must be temperature-controlled. The great energy requirements of heating a house would not be conducive to using alcohol as a primary heating method. (See Alcohol files.)(See Alcohol Production section) Too much vegetation would be required as raw material for the fermenter.

j. Small-scale Alcohol Plants

As of 1993, an <u>automated</u> method of producing alcohol in <u>small</u> manufacturing plants has not been successfully developed and marketed. However, tiny batch alcohol plants have application for small engine fuel and/or vinegar production. (See Uses for Food Waste section) This much smaller alcohol plant could make use of waste vegetation and a small amount of crop that is raised to supply the fermentation unit. (See Back-up Generator Options)

k. Vinegar Production (see Diet-Vinegar Section)

Since vinegar is the next step in the alcohol production process, a small amount of alcohol production capability has been designed into the Earth Home System. (See Diet-Vinegar section)

4. Using Alcohol

a. Using Alcohol in Engines

<u>1. Moisture in Alcohol</u>

Alcohol that comes from most distillers is 85-95% pure. This hydrous ethanol is alcohol that comes straight from a relatively simple still and contains some water. This sounds fine, but the small amounts of water remaining in the alcohol does not burn efficiently and can cause cold-weather problems--especially in engines.

Ethanol that has not been dried is typically heated slightly before being injected into an engine cylinder, for example.

Alcohol must be very pure to be able to use it in most instances without problems. An overall purity of 95% or higher guarantees that the alcohol could be used without much difficulty. After drying or moisture removal, the purer grades are used to mix with gasoline. This allows it to be burned much easier.

2. Data—Btu/Orifice Size

Engines can be modified or converted for alcohol use. Since gasoline is about 115,000 Btu per gallon and alcohol is about 67,000 Btu per gallon, more alcohol must be burned in any given amount of time to get the same performance from the engine. Thus it is necessary to open up the fuel ports that lead into the cylinder through the carburetor. The opening must be made larger by the same ratio of areas--or about 60-65% larger by volume or 30-35% larger by diameter. Some engines require that the timing must be advanced 4-6 degrees to compensate for the higher octane of ethanol.

3. Back-up Generator/Small Engine Fuel

Alcohol can be used for small engine fuel such as a back-up generator. The carburetor will have to be specially modified to enable it to burn alcohol efficiently and run at a high R.P.M. If dual-fuel use is desired, then the carburetor must be further modified to use both fuels because of the lack of lubrication and dual fuel switching option.

Small engines such as a chainsaw and rear tine tiller for loosening/blending of garden soil can also be modified to use straight alcohol. They typically do not use much fuel.

4. Other Alcohol Converted Engines/Brazil

There is some patented techniques for using hydrous alcohol more efficiently in engines. The Hansen cycle technology (U.S. Patent no. 4509464) has been patented, but as yet no commercial applications have been marketed.

Alcohol conversions for larger engines such as automobiles are beyond the scope of this text. (See Transportation Section) However, neat alcohol (95% impure grade) is widely used in Brazil in cars fitted with special parts. They currently mix 18%-22% alcohol in with their gasoline. Brazil probably leads the world in ethanol use per capita.

b. Burning Alcohol for Heat

1. High Temperature Refrigeration Fuel

Alcohol can be used for a heat source to drive an absorption cycle device. Systems have been developed to concentrate the flame on a pipe or point source for absorption refrigeration mechanisms. Note that other sources such as electricity, propane, kerosene, methane, and solar heat can also be used to generate the high heat necessary to power the absorption refrigeration cycle. (See Alcohol and Propane file.) (See Refrigerators file.)

2. Cooking Fuel

Using alcohol for cooking is not feasible because it takes more heat (Btu's) to produce alcohol that it returns. It is this concept that points toward wood rather than a high quality energy such as alcohol or electricity as a primary cooking fuel—similar to the way most of the rest of the world cooks.

c. Using Alcohol for Hydrogen Production (see Hydrogen section)

*Used in Earth Home

d. Alcohol to Produce Vinegar

After alcohol is made, it is allowed to ferment longer in the absence of oxygen to yield vinegar. A special culture of "mother of vinegar" is added to alcohol to begin the process. (See also Vinegar Section) Alcohol strength from 5.5% to 7% is typically used.

Vinegar is used as a salad dressing and as a cleaning agent. It has many other uses around the home. (See also Vinegar files)

5. Future for Alcohol—Ethanol from Cellulose?

Cellulose is the single most important component of plant biomass. Like starch, it is made of linked sugar components that may be easily fermented when separated from the cellulose polymer. The complex structure of cellulose makes separation difficult, but enzymatic means are being developed to do so.

There is significant research going on in the field of "enzymatic hydrolysis of biomass cellulose to sugars" for many years. Since cellulose is a polymer of the sugars needed to make ethanol, scientists have been working on "cracking the cellulose nut" since about 1910. This process should ultimately create an "enzyme cocktail" that breaks down the cellulose in biomass to glucose, which then serves as a platform chemical for producing fuels, chemicals, and other products. This promises to greatly reduce the production cost of alcohol (ethanol). However, scientists have been promising cheap ethanol from cellulose by enzymatic or acid hydrolysis for 100 years. Perfection of this technology will create a large potential for ethanol production using plant materials that are not human foods.

H. Biomass Gas (Woodgas)

(Note that this text will treat woodgas separately from methane because of the different raw materials that they begin with. Separate sections are provided for each.)

1. Woodgas Gasification Technology

a. Woodgas Matchstick Example

Light a wooden match; hold it in a horizontal position; and notice that while the wood becomes charcoal, it is not actually burning but is releasing a gas that begins to burn brightly a short distance away from the matchstick. Notice the gap between the matchstick and the luminous flame; this gap contains the wood gas which starts burning only when properly mixed with air (which contains oxygen).

In a sense, gasification is a form of incomplete combustion; heat from the burning solid fuel creates gases which are unable to burn completely, due to insufficient amounts of oxygen from the available supply of air. In the burning matchstick, as the wood was burned and pyrolyzed into charcoal, wood gas was created, but the gas was also consumed by combustion (since there was an enormous supply of air in the room).

b. Gasification—Clean Combustion Technology

Gasification is the cleanest, most efficient combustion method known. The hot fuel gases are ducted to a low energy gas burner which fires cleanly in the boiler combustion chamber, maintaining radiant heat transfer. While some gasifiers can operate on wet fuels, the small-scale units that have been used to successfully retrofit existing boilers typically utilize dry, particulate wood residues.

In a gasifier, minimal air is supplied to avoid combustion of the volatiles. As a result, the fuel gases produced have a heating value sufficiently high that they can be cooled, ducted to a separate unit and then ignited and burned with a self-sustaining flame. Most of the biomass gasification efforts have been to produce gas with a very low content of particles and tar. This can then be fed into an internal combustion engine to generate power.

c. Woodgas Statistics

By weight, this gas (woodgas) from the charring wood contains approximately 20% hydrogen (H_2), 20% carbon monoxide (CO), and small amounts of methane, all of which are combustible, plus 50 to 60% nitrogen (N_2). The nitrogen is not combustible; however, it does occupy volume and dilutes the wood gas as it enters and burns in an engine.

As the wood gas burns, the products of combustion are carbon dioxide (CO_2) and water vapor (H_2O). Thus, the aim of gasification is the almost complete transformation of these constituents into gaseous form so that only the ashes and inert materials remain.

d. Gasification Schematics

The following figure shows various methods of constructing a wood gasifier. Wood gasifiers being developed can be classified as 1) fixed bed (updraft and downdraft), and 2) fluidized bed. (See Biomass Basics section) The next figure illustrates the various types of gasifiers using drawings.

2. Woodgas Cookstoves

a. Woodgas Cookstove Technology

Woodgas cooking stoves are perhaps the best application of woodgas technology so far. These are gasifiers that produce gas from wood and then burn the gas, leaving charcoal (itself a useful fuel). They're clean, fast and efficient. They burn small pieces of wood, sticks, wood chips, corncobs or nutshells, producing a clean, blue flame and no smoke.

b. Woodgas Cookstoves/Parishad Ovens

In Kerala, India, more than half a million homes now have Parishad ovens. These ovens are high-efficiency wood burning stoves which use at least 50% less firewood, saving 0.6-0.8 million tons of firewood a year.

c. Charcoal Gasifier Cooking Stoves

Charcoal gasifiers were generally more popular than wood gasifiers during the producer gas era in Sweden in the days of WWII, even as the wood gasifiers improved in design. Wood gas was cheaper, but charcoal gasifiers were so much easier to handle, easier to maintain, and had much more fuel economy.

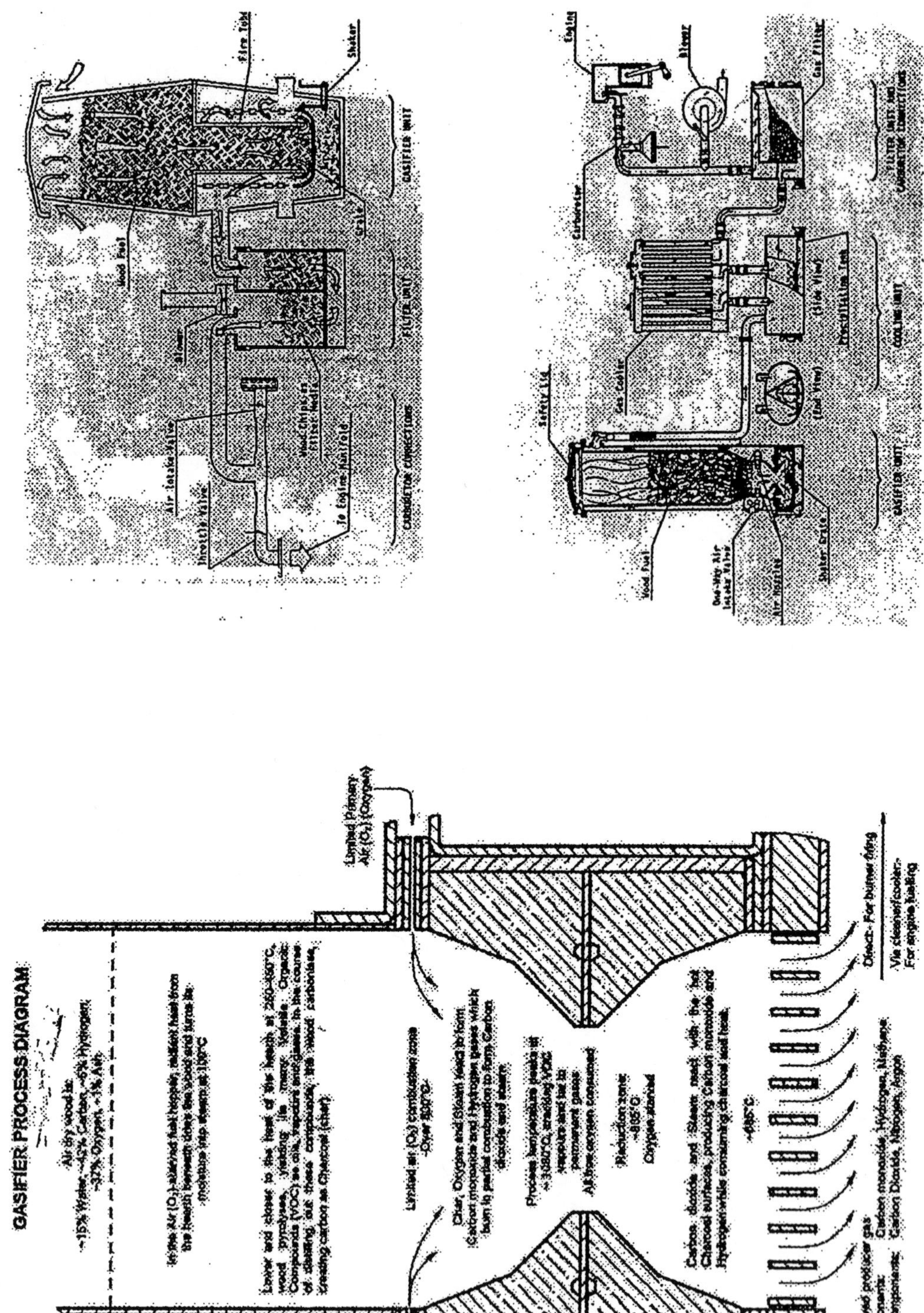

Figure 36-GASIFICATION SCHEMATICS

*Used in Earth Home

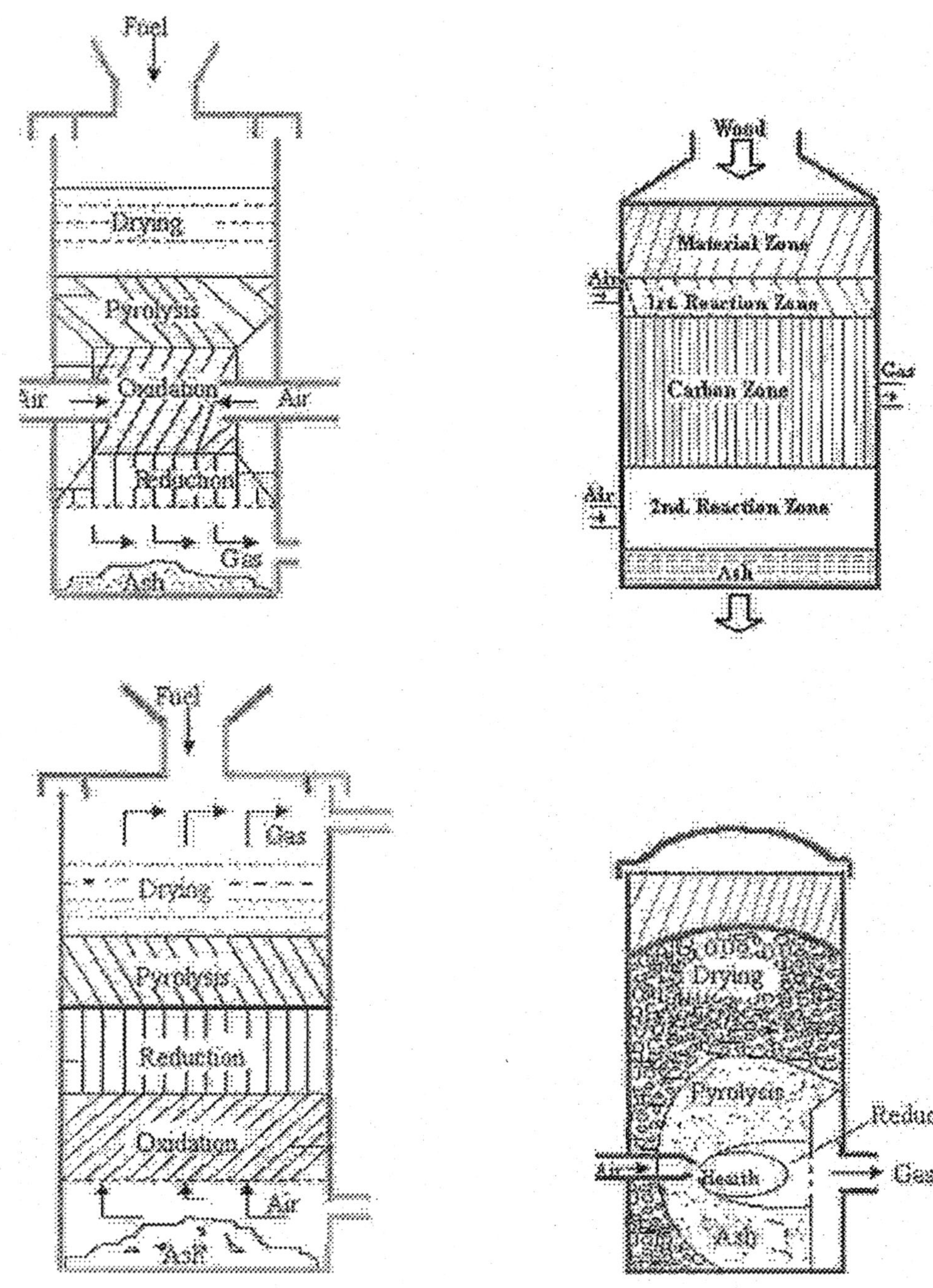

Figure 37-GASIFICATION TYPES

*Used in Earth Home

3. Charcoal/Charcoal Gas

a. Charcoal History

Charcoal is second only to wood as a Third World fuel. It's half the price of kerosene and a quarter the price of LPG or electric power. It burns without smoke and stores well without rotting. For the producers it's much lighter than wood, easier to transport, and producing it keeps many thousands in work. And it's also a high-energy fuel—ideal for local blacksmiths' forges and for small industry.

But it's a very wasteful fuel—cooking with charcoal uses much more wood than cooking with firewood. Burning wood to make charcoal wastes a lot of energy and creates a lot of pollution, and most Third World charcoal production is inefficient.

Charcoal is an important household fuel and to a lesser extent, industrial fuel in many developing countries. It is mainly used in the urban areas where its ease of storage, high energy content (30 Mj/kg as compared with 15 Mj/kg for woodfuel), lower levels of smoke emissions, and resistance to insect attacks make it more attractive than wood fuel.

b. Production of Charcoal

The production and distribution of charcoal consists of; preparation of the wood, drying, pre-carbonization, carbonization, ending carbonization, and cooling/stabilization. There are two basic methods of making charcoal: direct and indirect. The direct method uses heat from the incomplete combustion of the organic matter which is to become charcoal. The rate of combustion is controlled by regulating the amount of oxygen allowed into the burn and is stopped by excluding oxygen before the charcoal itself begins to burn. This is the ages old method used to make charcoal in a pit, pile or, more recently, in metal or masonry chambers (kilns).

The indirect method uses an external heat source to "cook" organic matter contained in a closed but vented airless chamber (retort). This is usually carried out in a metal or masonry chamber (furnace). The indirect method results in a higher yield of high quality charcoal with less smoke and pollutants and requires less skill and attention than the direct method.

The production of charcoal spans a wide range of technologies from simple and rudimentary earth kilos to complex, large-capacity charcoal retorts. Good charcoal contains 5 percent ash, 75 percent fixed carbon, 20 percent volatiles with a bulk density of 250-300 kg per cubic meter.

c. Charcoal Vehicles

Note that charcoal-burning taxis were still common in Korea as late as 1970. (See Automobile section)

d. Charcoal Gasifier Cooking Stoves (See Cookstoves section)

4. WWII Imbert Gasifier

a. WWII Imbert Gasifier Details

The upper cylindrical portion of the Imbert gasifier unit is simply a storage bin or hopper for wood chips or other biomass fuel. During operation, this chamber is filled every few hours as needed. The spring-loaded, airtight cover must be opened to refill the fuel hopper; it must remain closed and sealed during gasifier operation. The spring permits the cover to function as a safety valve because it will pop open in case of any excessive internal gas pressure.

About one-third of the way up from the bottom of the gasifier unit, there is a set of radically directed air nozzles; these allow air to be injected into the wood as it moves downward to be gasified. In a gas generator for vehicle use, the downstroke of the engine's pistons creates the suction force which moves the air into and through the gasifier unit.

The cooling unit required for the Imbert gasifier consists of a water-filled precipitating tank and an automotive radiator type gas cooler. The precipitating tank removes all unacceptable tars and most of the fine ash from the gas flow, while the radiator further cools the gas. A second filter unit, containing a fine mesh filtration material, is used to remove the last traces of any ash or dust that may have survived passage through the cooling unit. Once out of the filter unit, the wood gas is mixed with air in the vehicle's carburetor and is then introduced directly into the engine's intake manifold.

The Imbert gasifier is, in many ways, self-adjusting. If there is insufficient charcoal at the air nozzles, more wood is burned and pyrolyzed to make more charcoal. If too much charcoal forms, then the charcoal level rises above the nozzles, and the incoming air burns the charcoal. Thus, the combustion zone is maintained very close to the nozzles.

Below this combustion zone, the resulting hot combustion gases—carbon dioxide (CO_2) and water vapor (H_2O) pass into the hot charcoal where they are chemically reduced to combustible fuel gases: carbon monoxide (CO) and hydrogen (H_2). The hearth constriction causes all gases to pass through the reaction zone, thus giving maximum mixing and minimum heat loss. The highest temperatures are reached in this region.

In summary, the World War II Imbert gasifier design bas stood the test of time and has successfully been mass produced. It is relatively inexpensive, uses simple construction materials, is easy to fabricate, and can be operated by motorists with a minimum amount of training.

b. Imbert-Style Woodgas/Gasifier Issues

1) During startup of the gasifier, a blower needs to be used to create the proper airflow.

2) Fine char and ash dust can eventually clog the charcoal bed and will reduce the gas flow unless the dust is removed. The charcoal is supported by a movable grate which can be shaken at intervals. Ash buildup below the grate can be removed during cleaning operations. Usually, wood contains less than 1% ash (by weight). However, as the charcoal is consumed, it eventually collapses to form a powdery charcoal/ash mixture which may represent 2 to 10% (by weight) of the total fuel mass.

3) Storage of gas is difficult. Most gasifiers are "producer gas" oriented. The term, "producer gas generation," is used because no storage system is used; only that amount of gas demanded by the engine is produced. The gas is introduced into the engine and consumed a few seconds after it is made—when the engine is shut off, the production of gas stops.

4) The World War II Imbert gasifier requires wood with a low moisture content (less than 20% by weight) and a uniform, blocky fuel in order to allow easy gravity feed through the constricted hearth.

5) Twigs, sticks, and bark shreds cannot be used. The constriction at the hearth and the protruding air nozzles present obstructions to the passage of the fuel and may create bridging and channeling followed by poor quality gas output, as unpyrolyzed fuel falls into the reaction zone. The constricted hearth design seriously limits the range of wood fuel shapes that can be successfully gasified without expensive cubing or pelletizing pretreatment. It is this limitation that makes the Imbert gasifier less flexible for emergency use.

5. Other Uses for Wood/Charcoal Gas

a. Tractors/Mobile Applications (See also Automobile section)

The following figure shows various engine and tractor modifications that were fabricated and tested.

*Used in Earth Home

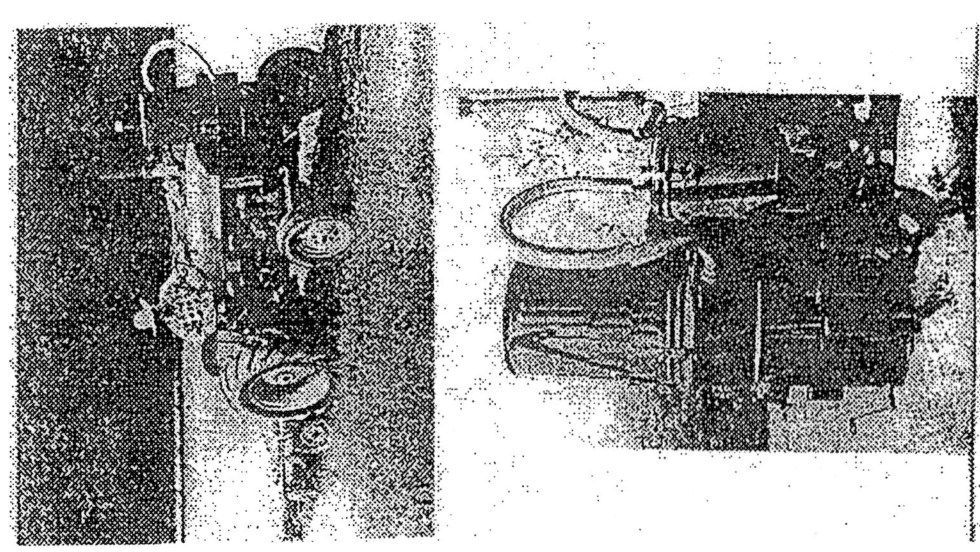

Figure 38-WOODGAS GASIFICATION TESTING

*Used in Earth Home

b. Woodgas for Engine Fuel

Of all indigenous, renewable energy sources, biomass in the form of wood or agricultural residues is the most readily available in many developing countries. In those developing countries, internal combustion engines are widely used in stationary applications such as electric power generation and operation of water pumps and mills. Technologies such as gasification, which allow utilization of biomass fuel in such engines after minimum preparation, are therefore of particular importance.

c. Stationary Engines/Generators

Woodgas/gasification technologies are suited to production of gas on an intermittent basis until the producer gas supply runs low. Generators are ideal applications because energy is only needed when the battery bank runs low. (See EH Gasifier section)

d. Cookstoves in Third World Countries (See Cookstoves section)

e. Wood Gasifier Boilers

The following figure shows a boiler powered from woodgas. Such units are increasing in popularity due to their significant increase in efficiency.

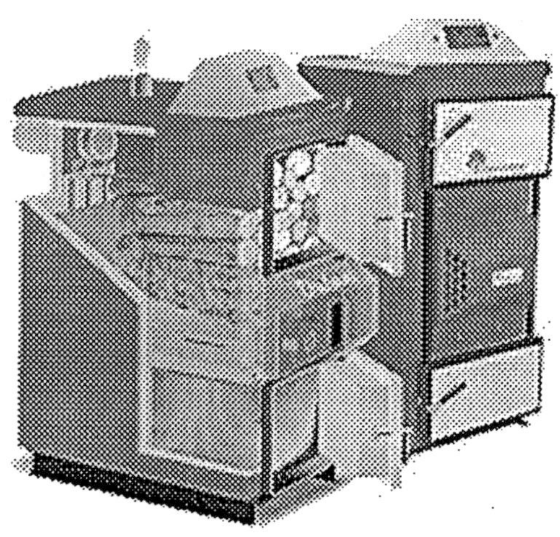

Figure 39-WOOD GASIFICATION BOILER

6. Global Research on Gasifiers

Substantial technological development and demonstration programs have been carried out in the past two decades in a number of developing countries, e.g. China, India, Philippines, Thailand, etc. In India alone some 1,700 small units have been installed since 1987, with a current installed capacity of about 35 MW. This is one of the most comprehensive biomass gasification programs in the range of small- to medium-scale gasifiers in the world. The major focus has been on the use of modified diesel engines to run in a dual-fuel mode. Dual-fuel mode means that these gasifiers produce gas from wood and then burn the gas, leaving charcoal (itself a useful fuel).

7. Gas from Dry Fermentation (See Methane section)

8. Combination Woodgas/Charcoal Production in EH

The Earth Home is intended to use woodgas to power the stationary back-up generator. A by-product of woodgas is charcoal and will be used for energy or water filtration.

I. Biomass Gas (Biogas/Methane)

1. Biogas/Methane Background

a. Biogas Production (Anaerobic Digestion)

Anaerobic digestion is another method for forming gases from biomass. It uses microorganisms, in the absence of oxygen, to convert organic materials to methane. Biogas or methane is produced when plant vegetation is anaerobically digested. The carbon-based gas is then collected, stored, and burned. This method is particularly suitable for animal and human waste. Animal feedlots faced with disposal problems may install microbial gasifiers to convert waste to gaseous fuel used to heat farm buildings or generate electricity. In landfills, biomass rots and releases methane gas, also called biogas or landfill gas.

b. Chinese Biogas Programs

The Chinese are leaders in this field with over 5 million biogas plants in working order. About 25 million Chinese people use biogas mainly for cooking and lighting. Most of the biogas facilities are family-sized and suitable for cooking purposes only. Larger facilities would be necessary to produce electricity from the gas. Most of the biogas plants are either fixed dome or floating drum varieties that use cattle dung as the substrate.

c. Methane Toilet Systems

Domestic toilet wastes is another source of energy that has been considered for self-sufficient systems. Biogas is produced when a warm manure mixture, for example, is allowed to "ferment" in the absence of oxygen. There are "batch" methane production units that use toilet waste, but an automated, continuous method has not been developed. (A continuous system would cycle the toilet wastes in one end and continuously produce methane at the other.)

d. Methane Issues

Great amounts of vegetation are needed to produce any significant quantities of useable gas. The material needs the correct solids ratio and a constant 100 degrees F. in order to continue to produce. The gas is highly corrosive as well. In addition to aesthetic concerns, the problems with methane production are similar to automated alcohol production in that substantial equipment and controls are necessary.

2. Composting Organic Matter (see Composting Section)

3. Methane from Dry Fermentation

a. Dry Fermentation Technology

Both the dry and liquid methods for turning biomass into biogas use anaerobic fermentation. Biomass is fermented to produce biogas. However, dry fermentation has been developed to simulate what happens inside a cow's stomach in batches. This means that a typical gas plant requires less piping, storage capacity and process energy.

Dry fermentation extracts energy from biomass by anaerobic fermentation (biomass gasification) in the form of methane (CH4) and heat. This controlled process is typically executed in biomass power plants, where the methane is used to run engines generating electrical power. The process also generates heat. The dry fermentation process is not geared towards the production of bio fuel.

Biomass is introduced to the dry fermentation plants fermenter chambers in batches. This means there is no continuous flow of materials or liquids to be pumped into the plant via a pumping system but rather a pile of biomass, up to 50% solid, brought into a fermenting chamber and left alone for about 30 days. This type of biomass conversion is run automatically by the biological fermentation phases, given the balanced mix of required substrates and bacteria.

After the batch production period, another batch of biomass will be processed. The processed biomass can be used for composting purposes. Dry fermentation units can be "fed" with a variety of different biomass components. These substrates comprise of seasonally and constantly available raw materials.

b. Dry Fermentation Advantages

Dry Fermentation achieves the same end product as liquid fermentation but it has many advantages including:

1) Less manual work is involved—dry fermentation only requires one person—to fill the batch vat and a biomass replacement operation every 4 weeks or so.

2) No smell—traditional liquid fermentation processing of biomass causes intense odors every time the biomass has to be added to, which is frequently. However, dry fermentation processing requires additional biomass only infrequently and the most odorous parts of the process occur within the plant that cannot be opened during fermentation.

3) No single point of failure—by having a series of smaller fermentation vats, if your biomass does experience an unsuitable acid level, the single vat involved can be cleaned out and replaced, without affecting the rest of your process.

4) No biomass input separation—the dry fermentation process can use both wood and plastic. As such, your raw material does not have to be separated out. This means a lower operating cost.

5) Less water required—dry fermentation is just that, dry. As such the process does not depend on a regular input of water. This reduces input costs and minimizes the use of another valuable resource, water.

6) Hygienic Operation—Heat which is a by-product of the process, can be used to sterilize the plant. No cleaning is necessary!

7) Energy can be stored—the input biomass can be stored quite easily. This is good for supply in winter or in case biomass is needed in a hurry.

8) Less processing energy—as the dry fermentation plant has only a small requirement for energy to initiate and maintain the process, operation costs are low.

Simulating the digestion of a cow sounds easy but, dry fermentation has taken some time to be developed. Refining the process to its current level has made it commercially sound and easier to run. It does, however, still require some know-how to initiate and maintain the production process. Development continues on this process.

*Used in Earth Home

J. Gaseous Fuels/Hydrogen

1. Gaseous Fuels Data (See Fuel Statistics/Overview Chart)

2. Methane/Biogas/Gasification (See Biogas/Methane section)

3. Propane/Natural Gas

Another heat source is petroleum-based gaseous fuels such as propane and natural gas. These are not renewable and are discussed here to compare to hydrogen. Natural gas is rated at one thousand Btu's per cubic foot and propane is about 2,500 Btu's per cubic foot (hydrogen has 279 Btu per cubic foot). Propane is a mixture of approximately 90% pure propane, 5% propylene, butanes, and other ingredients. Propane is widely used because it compresses easily and is available worldwide. There is a good world supply of both at present. (Natural gas is actually burned off at some facilities.) However, another gaseous fuel-hydrogen has many advantages over both these petroleum-based fuels for self-sufficient homes.

4. Hydrogen

a. Hydrogen Production

Hydrogen is both the best of fuels (because it burns fast and clean) and the worst of fuels (because it is difficult to store.

1. Electrolysis Background

There is virtually no free hydrogen that exists by itself. Presently, it is made by hydrolysis or from fossil fuels. Hydrogen is a non-polluting fuel that has enormous potential both for the Earth Home System in the future, and for transportation fuel worldwide. I feel that hydrogen research will accelerate in the future. There are a number of reasons why hydrogen is interesting. Hydrogen burns by combining with oxygen, so the only waste product is pure water (zero pollution).

Hydrogen is typically produced by passing direct current through distilled water and collecting the gas that collects at the cathode(hydrolysis). (See Hydrogen files). Washing soda can be used as a catalyst in the electrolyte. Potassium hydroxide (KOH) and stainless steel electrodes are normally used. Hydrogen is collected at the anode (+) and oxygen at the cathode (-). Many high school science classes use a 6-volt dry cell to produce hydrogen even though 1.24 - 2 volts are all that is needed. About 100 watt/hr. of electricity is needed to produce 1 cubic foot of hydrogen gas.

2. Alternative/Hybrid Hydrogen Production

There are also papers written on hydrogen production by algae and isolated chloroplasts, and by using microbial photosynthesis. These are very early in the development stages and to date, have not received significant funding for research.

Hydrogen can also be produced with hybrid solar collectors. These experimental PV collectors produce both electricity and hydrogen. (see PV files)

3. Future "Combination" Battery

I believe a hybrid battery may be developed in the future to function as a "combination" battery. Since hydrogen is produced at the cathode terminal of a lead acid battery when it is overcharged, I feel that a hybrid battery

*Used in Earth Home

could be developed to use this hydrogen as the battery "gasses." (See also Hydrogen files.) This hydrogen could then be used as a fuel source.

4. Hydrogen Production from Ethanol

There is considerable work going on at the University of Minnesota and elsewhere on a new extraction process to get hydrogen directly from ethanol. This has not been commercialized at present, but the research looks promising.

b. Hydrogen Storage

1. Hydrogen Storage Challenges

Storage of hydrogen is very difficult, which is the main problem with using it. If hydrogen is stored as a gas, it has to be pressurized from 200 psi (thin wall) to 5,000 psi (thick wall) before it can be put into pressurized storage vessels. If hydrogen must be stored as a liquid, it must be cooled to minus 423 degrees F. in order to stay in a liquid phase.

It is such a small atom that it permeates almost all materials. Hydrogen will gradually pass through glass, steel, and many other substances. (See Hydrogen files.) In some systems, a platinum or palladium hydride is used to store hydrogen. Slightly pressurized hydrogen is pushed into the lattice, which soaks it up like a sponge. Heat is then applied to drive off the hydrogen for use. However, these special metal hydrides are very expensive to manufacture at present.

Another potential problem with hydrogen is its explosive qualities. It was a hydrogen explosion that destroyed the Hindenberg blimp. Since the Hindenberg explosion, hydrogen has not been used for any lighter-than-air craft.

The Self-Sufficient Solar Home (SSSH) in Freiburg, Germany uses a 15 cubic meter tank for the hydrogen and a 7.5 cubic meter tank for the oxygen. They used a pressure of 30 bar in both tanks. They continue to use and monitor the system.

2. Future Hydrogen Storage Technology

Hydrogen generation, storage, and use have been investigated extensively by Billings Energy Corporation, in Provo, Utah, which has used hydrogen to power buses, entire homesteads, tractors, and mail vehicles. (See also Storage of Electricity/Batteries section.) Work is also being done on more elaborate storage schemes such as high-pressure tiny glass microspheres.

3. Future Earth Home Hydrogen Storage

Even if the technology may not be available for Earth Home use today, research suggests that it soon will be. Since hydrogen is lighter than air, it necessitates locating any future hydrogen systems designed for the Earth Home above any potential ignition sources or outdoors.

c. Hydrogen Uses

1. Hydrogen Burning

Hydrogen can be burned like any gaseous fuel such as natural gas or propane. The only by-products are water vapor. Hydrogen is more efficiently burned by using a porous sintered metal as a "wick" for the fuel. It burns more completely and can be controlled better. This system is used in the SSSH (Self-Sufficient Solar Home) in Freiburg.

2. Future Hydrogen Developments

Hydrogen continues to make inroads in the energy field. Major vehicle manufacturers have announced that they will have hydrogen-fueled cars and busses on the market starting in the years 2003 and 2004. Siemens-Westinghouse is offering solid oxide fuel cells for electricity generation with efficiencies of 70%. PEM and other fuel cells are being prepared for in-house electricity and heat generation with overall efficiencies of 85%. The hydrogen hydride electric batteries are commercially available for laptop computers and electric cars. The shell Oil Company has established a Hydrogen Division. By all outward appearances, hydrogen is quickly becoming of age. (See Transportation section)(See CHP section)

5. Use of Gaseous Fuel

a. Fuel Cells

1. Fuel Cell Technology

There are other ways to generate electricity such as fuel cells as used in the space program. Fuel cells generally consist of a positive electrode (cathode), a negative electrode (anode), and an electrolyte that conducts ions between them. Figure 11 illustrates how a fuel cells work. Fuel cells are clean and quiet devices that generate electricity through an electrochemical process involving fuel and air. Similar to batteries, each individual fuel cell produces approximately one-half volt. Multiple cells in a "stack" configuration produce higher voltages and power. Fuel cells are twice as efficient as combustion engines at converting fuel energy into electricity and therefore provide more power with less fuel.

All fuel cells require the hydrogen atom for operation--whether supplied from electrical hydrolysis of water, petroleum products, or ethanol. Fuel cells operate like a battery except they don't run down. They produce energy in the form of electricity and heat for as long as fuel is supplied.

2. Types of Fuel Cells

The five or so different kinds of fuel cells each use a different electrolyte, but the most popular is the Proton-Exchange Membrane (PEM). Other types are the alkaline fuel cell (which has been used on NASA space missions), alkaline, the regenerative fuel cell, and the direct methanol (DM) fuel cell, which offers efficiencies of about 40 percent for use in light vehicles. Automotive research is also looking at phosphoric acid (PA) fuel cells, molten carbonate fuel cells, and recently solid oxide fuel cells (SOFC).

The solid oxide fuel cell is also suitable for large-scale electrical generating stations. A key benefit of the solid oxide fuel cell is its ability to operate directly on a variety of available fossil fuels including natural gas, liquid propane, gasoline, diesel, and now renewable bio-fuels.

3. Fuel Cell Drawbacks/Limitations

All fuel cells have the drawbacks of being expensive and complex. The proton exchange membrane cells are very finicky about their fuel stream. Just about everything contaminates a PEM.

b. Future Fuel Cell Technologies

1. Fuel Cells Combined with Electrolyzer

Proton Energy Systems has combined with the U.S. Navy to test a fuel cell used with a unit to generate hydrogen. Electricity generated during the day from photovoltaic panels powers an electrolyzer, to make hydrogen fuel from water. This hydrogen is stored and used at night to make electricity when the sun is not shining. This combination system could lessen the need for large battery banks as the hydrogen would then function as an electrical storage device. (See also Hydrogen section)

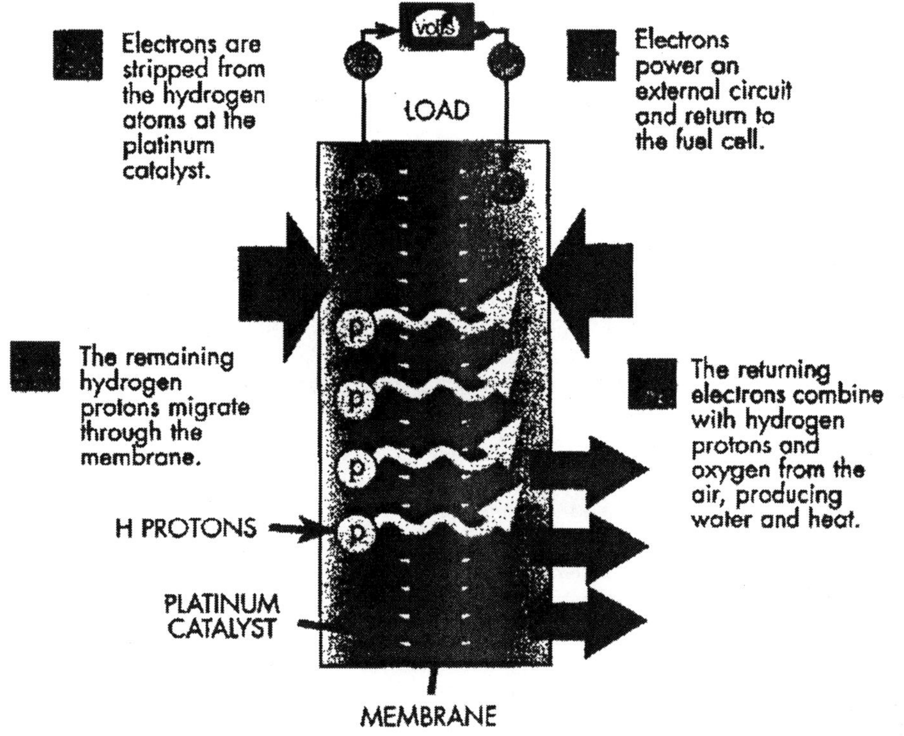
HOW A FUEL CELL WORKS
Electrons are stripped from the hydrogen atoms at the platinum catalyst.
volts
LOAD
Electrons power an external circuit and return to the fuel cell.
The remaining hydrogen protons migrate through the membrane.
The returning electrons combine with hydrogen protons and oxygen from the air, producing water and heat.
H PROTONS
PLATINUM CATALYST
MEMBRANE

Figure 40-FUEL CELL DIAGRAM

2. Fuel Cell Research

However, the Germans have been working on fuel cell technology in the last few years to lower the cost and improve performance. There is also much work being done on fuel cells for automobiles that convert other fuel sources such as gasoline into hydrogen. Mercedes-Benz and Chrysler are putting much money into the technology. However, they are all very expensive yet. One company-Energy Related Devices in Los Alamos, NM is developing a small fuel cell designed to power a cell phone or a laptop computer. Methanol or ethanol is being used as a fuel source.

Another recent development is the zinc/air fuel cell. This new fuel cell is regenerative and not discarded, like a primary battery. Regenerative fuel cells are suitable for applications where a closed-loop form of power generation is needed. It separates water into hydrogen and oxygen through the use of a solar-powered electrolyser. The gasses are then pumped into the fuel cell, which generates electricity, heat, and water.

3. Fuel Cells and Ultracapacitors

Ultracapacitors can deliver up to 10 times the power with 10 times the expected life of a battery and offer lower weight. In addition, ultracapacitors also operate more reliably at high- and low-temperature extremes. Maxwell technologies are working on a combination to combine fuel cell output with ultracapacitors to provide longer continuous power. This technology has the capability to expand to larger power applications. (See also Future Batteries section)

6. CHP (Combined Heat and Power) (See also Alternative/Future section)

a. Micro-Power (or CHP) with Gasifiers

Micro power is also known as distributed generation, on-site generation, small-scale generation, and/or self-generation. For the two billion people who remain without electricity, micro-power may be an alternative. There is a trend towards more open, decentralized, competitive electricity systems. Proponents of micro-turbines believe that this technology will revolutionize the power industry.

Micro-power technologies can use renewable sources, e.g. small gasifier applications, as is the case in China and India. Ranging from 15 to 500 kW, these turbines have the advantage of being low-cost, easy to manufacture, long-lived, and simple to operate and maintain. The current biomass-based technology mostly used for distributed power is a fixed downdraft gasifier coupled with an internal combustion engine. (See also Woodgas section)

b. CHP Woodgas Output/Production

Some calculations suggest that a gasifier/micro-turbine unit should consume wood at a rate of slightly less than 1 kg per kilowatt-hour of electricity generated. That translates to around 13 kg of wood a day to meet a typical household's average electricity demand - less than 5 tons a year.

c. CHP Woodgas Issues

1) The process needs to be tuned to ensure that the wood gas meets the thermodynamic requirements of the micro-turbines.

2) Another research priority will be to ensure that the gas is clean - free of ash - when it enters the turbine. No gritty material can get into the unit.

3) The CHP needs to run with minimal attention, like a petrol generator. There needs to be a method for an automated handling system that provides a constant supply of chipped wood to the gasifier.

K. Earth Home Energy Choices

1. Qualities of Energy Sources-Discussion

a. Temperature Discussion

1. Useful Temperatures of EH Functions

Different functions in a home require specific temperatures. For example; underfloor heating requires 29 degrees C. for room temperatures of 25 degrees C, hot water heating requires 58 degrees C. duct temperature, herb/vegetable drying requires 50 degrees C, and clothes dryers require 30-40 degrees C. Of course, cooking and food preservation requires boiling water.

*Used in Earth Home

2. High Temperatures More Useful

A higher temperature heat source is more versatile because it can always be lowered in temperature and used other places. Some technologies such as refrigeration require higher temperatures for the absorption cycle to happen.

b. Easily Stored

The ability to be conveniently put aside for another time is a valuable asset. Some energy storage devices deteriorate significantly over time such as compressed air. Also some energy sources require great expense to store them safely.

c. Easily Transformed/Minimize Efficiency Losses

Many times the exact mix of energy must change. This can happen from summer to winter or from day to night. When one form of energy is changed into another form, the result is a loss of efficiency--usually in the form of heat. This heat is not always a desirable effect.

d. "Quality" of Energy-High or Low

Electricity is considered a higher quality of energy than low temperature heat because it can be used for many more tasks in the self-sufficient home. Also alcohol contains much more Btu per pound than wood and is more versatile.

e. Hours/Day Available

Choosing the right combination of energy sources is dictated by geographic location. The right mix of solar, wind, and PV would be chosen by assembling data on availability of these sources at certain times during the day. For wind power, it can be determined how long (on average) the wind will blow and the average wind speed. The mix of energy sources for Albuquerque would be different for London, for example.

f. Alcohol/Vinegar Production Options

This last feature was put in because of the many interdependencies in the Earth Home System. The many tasks in the system as a whole must be taken into account. Vinegar is necessary in the diet of the Earth Home family due to the reduction in flavors that they will experience when adapting to the new diet. (See Diet-Specific Cultivars-Vinegar section)

Vinegar (made from alcohol) as a cleaning agent is also very beneficial to the overall system. (See Related Items-Household Section) As mentioned previously, alcohol also has uses for fuel for small engines such as a modified chainsaw, back-up generator, and tiller for loosening/blending of soil. (See Energy/Power section on Alcohol)

2. Cooling (Space)

The earth is used to provide massive amounts of cooled water that is designed to be stored inside the living spaces. Special tanks will be placed in mostly unused spaces so not to interfere with the normal movement and comfort of the family. Low wattage circulating pumps will be used to keep this cooled water circulating through tubing under the ground.

*Used in Earth Home

3. Heating (Space)

One potential source of space heating that has been discussed is wind energy. Typically, using a wind generator for a source of space heating is a waste of energy because of the high value of the energy produced. The self-sufficient home could better use electricity to power electric motors, pumps, fans, and lights. Common smaller wind generator systems use electrical resistance heating only as a way to "shunt" or control/use the excessive capacity on very windy days. The European countries have for years led the world in the design and development of larger wind generators which is commonly used to sell back to the electric companies.

The Earth Home is designed to use wood as a primary source of heat. Efficient burning of wood and accompanying smoke scrubbing will boost the efficiency of the stove to a higher level. The heat will be distributed via larger diameter ducts to greatly lessen the energy supplied to a typical furnace fan.

4. Lighting (Electricity)

It's often said that when the sun doesn't shine, the wind blows. Most alternative energy schemes (including the EH) use a combination of both wind power and photovoltaic arrays to ensure an energy supply almost all of the time. An adequately sized battery storage and control system integrates both systems.

5. Refrigeration/Freezing

The food refrigeration compressor is designed to use electricity for power. The control system is designed to take advantage of high energy production times to drop the temperature of foods. A control mechanism takes advantage of those times when the outside temperature is lower than the freezer compartment insulation casing.

6. Domestic Hot Water Heating (DHW)

a. Background

After space heating, water heating is often the largest energy demand in residences. Any home needs hot water for a variety of needs. Efficient transfer of energy from an energy source to water is critical for maximum efficiency. The EH is designed to pre-heat all water that flows through the last or demand heater for maximum energy efficiency. This way, most of the Btu's will come from the easier-to-obtain sources such as solar or wood. (See also Heating Water section.)

The Earth Home system is designed to use a separate solar hot water system when the location is south of Denver, Colorado latitude (See EH tabs section). North of that latitude a coil of tubing above the greenhouse area is used to preheat water in the warm season for domestic use.

b. Primary Domestic Water

The Earth Home system is designed to use a gaseous fuel for cooking, heating water, and also as a back-up for the lighting system. An optional use would also be for the back-up generator. Propane is presently used in the experimental Earth Home I prototype for final heating of the water (See Propane files). However, another gaseous fuel-hydrogen has advantages over both petroleum-based fuels and will be phased into the Earth Home System. (See Hydrogen section)

c. Dehydrator

Hot water from the demand heater will be circulated through the dehydrator to keep an even heat to dry out foods for preservation. A separate loop of water containing antifreeze will be used for the following uses and routed through the separate heat exchanger option in the demand heater.

*Used in Earth Home

d. Clothes Dryer

This small, efficient heater will also be the final heat supply for the clothes dryer also. A coil of tubing inside the dryer will contain the water recirculated through the demand heater heat exchanger as above. Note that the demand heater model was chosen so this option could be utilized in both places.

e. Distillation Unit

A small flame also keeps a continuous supply of distilled water for drinking purposes. By using a small chamber for boiling eliminates the high energy input and losses associated with common distillation apparàtus. A back-up high intensity UV light and silver-impregnated ceramic/activated carbon filter is designed to be used should the main distiller go down for any reason. (See Drinking Water Production section) The distillation unit can also be used to distill alcohol from the low-proof beer. A quick changeover is required to batch load the beer into the distiller. (See Energy/Power section on Alcohol also)

f. Greenhouse Soil Heating in Colder Weather

Long tubes inside the soil in the V-trough will allow the planting of plants much sooner than without supplemental heat. Using the demand heater as a final regulation for the woodstove or generator jacket-heated water will allow much greater control over the soil temperature as well as a back-up system.

7. Cooking

Cooking with a gaseous fuel has the great advantage of being able to control temperatures very precisely down to just a simmer. Cooking very slowly has advantages in efficiency and not having to be tended constantly. Propane is presently used in the experimental Earth Home I prototype. (See Propane files) It has been estimated that it takes 16 million Btu's a year to cook for a family of four. This breaks down to approximately 15 thousand Btu's per meal.

Woodgas generation and hydrogen will gradually be phased into EH cooking because it is clean and able to be manufactured on-site. Hydrogen has approximately 279 Btu's per cubic foot, and would take approximately 55 cubic feet to cook each meal. This amount must be generated three times a day or about 7 cubic feet per hour on average. (See Hydrogen section.) A woodgas generator similar to the WWII styles will be used as well. (See Woodgas section)

8. Back-up Generator/Small Engine Fuel

A gaseous fuel <u>and</u> alcohol are designed to be used for the back-up generator. The carburetor will have to be specially modified to enable it to use both fuels because of the lack of lubrication and flexibility of having dual fuel capabilities.

As mentioned previously, small engines such as a chainsaw and tiller are designed to use straight alcohol because of the portability of these items. They typically do not use much fuel. (See Energy/Power Section on Alcohol)

Woodgas will also be used to generate producer gas and used as needed without storage. The woodgas generator will be sized to make gas at exactly the rate of consumption by the stationary generator. Small blocks of wood and/or compressed vegetation will be used as the fuel.

*Used in Earth Home

9. Aerobic Digester/Fish Tank Aeration

The aerobic digester and fish tank share a common need: air. Oxygen must be available so the fish don't die and so the digester will not go "septic" for a very long period of time. An electric backup is provided in case the wind does not blow for more than a few days. (See Fish section.)

10. Exercise-Generated Energy

Through 99 percent of our evolutionary history, humans have had an active lifestyle. Today, humans are approximately one-third as fit as our ancestors. Exercise has been recognized as a prime ingredient to good health.

a. Grain Grinder/Generator Option

The Earth Home is designed to have a built-in method to grind grain using a device similar to an exercycle. Human power can also be used to replenish the batteries in times of unusual weather caused by periods of calm and cloudy weather.

b. Meat Grinder

Grinding meat is equally as important and may be accomplished with a separate attachment or unit. Grinding meats allow much more efficient use of small quantities and more thorough digestion for higher end use.

c. Manual Cultivator for Raised Mounds

This equipment has yet to be designed.

d. Soil Mixing and Blower Attachment

This equipment has yet to be designed.

L. Alternative/Future Power Options (See also Biomass section)

1. Stirling Engines

A Stirling engine is not an energy source, but a way to transform heat into mechanical motion to turn a generator or alternator, for instance. (See Stirling files.) This is a heat engine that generates mechanical movement directly from heat. The advantage of the engine was that the combustion chamber and the cylinders were separated, so that virtually any type of fuel could be used. It does this by expanding and contracting air contained in a piston. A typical heat source for a Stirling engine is coal, alcohol, oil, propane, or gasoline.

The first Stirling engines pumped water out of mine shafts. At present, Stirling engines are being used experimentally for automotive propulsion systems and refrigerators. In the past they've also been used in such things as fans and small engines to perform work around the farm.

One of the problems with Stirling engines for self-sufficient home systems is that the heat source should be <u>hotter</u> than a wood fire, though there are experimental wood-fired Stirling systems being tested. This would necessitate providing a "higher quality" of fuel.

There is also work being done on solar power and Stirling engines that work on a much smaller temperature differential. These may have application for solar and ground-contact uses. I feel that the future holds promise for Stirling engines because of their simplicity. (See Refrigerator Options section)

2. Thermoelectric/Thermovoltaic

Another option to generate electricity directly from heat is called the thermoelectric, "thermopile", (Seebeck, or Thomson effect). A bank of thermoelectric cells is placed directly on the sidewall of a woodstove, for instance. It generates electricity proportional to the amount of heat that it receives. (See Thermoelectric file.) This technology is quite expensive at present and much development needs to be completed to make it cost-effective.

A newer technology is Alkali Metal Thermoelectric Converter (AMTEC) using an electrolyte membrane to separate high and low pressure chambers. As heat is applied, sodium in the high-pressure chamber ionizes, enters, and passes through the electrolyte membrane. The neutral sodium then evaporates into the low pressure chamber, condenses on its cooled inner surface, and is returned to the hot high pressure chamber by a capillary structure to complete the cycle. There needs to be temperature ranges of 900-1,100 degrees K. and 500-750 degrees K. respectively. DOE and Northwestern University are working on this system.

A similar future technology just emerging is the thermovoltaic (TPV) concept. This concept uses the longer wavelength infrared radiation to excite converter cells and generate electricity. (See Thermoelectric files.)

3. Geothermal (see Thermal Mass section)

4. Steam Engines (see Electrical Power-Generator Options section)

Steam will be discussed in Electrical Power-Generator Options section.

5. Biodiesel (see Biomass section)

The above choices are based on today's technology. I believe that breakthroughs in other branches of self-sufficient homes will speed development. Two such possible technologies follows.

6. Computer-Controlled Combustion Draft/Scrubber

There have been many attempts to make wood stoves more efficient. As mentioned previously, some of these include burning the smoke in a double chamber inside the stove by introducing outside air to re-start combustion of the smoke. Other types of draft controls try to minimize the effect of wind on the chimney. ***I believe the future for wood stoves will see extensive draft control using a computer microprocessor, or programmable logic controller (PLC).*** This will be done to increase efficiency and decrease emissions. Sensors may include flame detectors, stack temperature sensors, air pressure sensors, smoke detectors, moisture sensors, timers, and stepper motor controls on dual-draft openings. I feel these types of technologies will begin to emerge when another oil shortage occurs, or if "socio-economic" conditions make these technologies more popular.

7. Gas-Driven Heat Pumps

Significant research is being done by several countries into gas-driven heat pumps. One of the most efficient ways to use electricity in a new conventional home is a water-source heat pump. Using an alternative fuel for a fuel source could have possibilities for self-sufficient homes of the future.

8. "Uni-Engine"

Another possibility of mechanical power is a "one engine fits all" engine. In the early U.S., tiny one-cylinder kick-start engines were developed. This was about the same time as the early machine shops used one engine to power all the machines in a shop using an overhead shaft and belts connected to each machine. This way they avoided the expense of buying a power plant for each piece of equipment. This uni-engine could theoretically be used for vacuum cleaner, grain grinder, central air distribution, washer, dryer, generator, and even portable power for transportation.

9. Distributed Generation—The Concept

a. Distributed Generation (DG) Background

Distributed generation provides an industrial or commercial electricity user with an alternative to getting its power from the grid. It "distributes" the financial burden instead of a utility floating bonds to build huge megawatt generating stations. DG consists of generator sets, small microturbines, or fuel cells. Thomas Edison had distributed generation in mind when he first wired New York City in 1882. He did not envision huge power plants distant from the point of consumption.

b. Home-Sized Power Plant/Water Heater Combinations (CHP)

The term CHP means combined heat and power with the emphasis on residential applications. It is estimated that approximately two-thirds of the fuel used to generate electricity in the U.S. is wasted in the form of discarded heat. CHP is also known as cogeneration. When electricity is needed, hydrogen gas or other gaseous fuel source is pumped directly into the fuel cell to produce both DC electricity and heat. There are about 5 companies developing CHP units for residential use. (See Fuel Cells section, Microturbines section, and Fuel Cells files)

I foresee much more development with home-sized power plants or CHP. These power plants can provide electricity <u>and</u> heat by utilizing the waste heat from an internal combustion engine. The fuel could be almost any source, and the generated electricity could be fed directly into the home. An efficient "boiler-style" water jacket could surround the cylinders as well as the waste gas stream. Super-heated fluid could then be used to power cooling equipment for both refrigeration <u>and</u> air conditioning. (See Heating-Future section)

Recently Sunpower began to attempt commercial development of small biomass-fired Stirling generators/water heaters. (See Generators Files). I believe that small scrubbers are not far behind.

c. Microturbines

Microturbines are small power plants that use natural gas or low grade gasoline to make electricity and heated water as a by-product. Currently there are about 6 companies that are developing units in the 30 to 250 kilowatt size. Microturbines have not been developed to use biofuels at present. There is one company using the microturbine technology and applying it to low-head stream flow to make it a renewable source. I expect microturbines to continue to approach the home size. (See Generators files).

II. THERMAL MASS OVERVIEW

A. Thermal Mass Technology

1. Thermal Energy Storage (TES) Background

The oldest form of energy storage involves harvesting ice from lakes and rivers, which was stored in well insulated warehouses and sold or used throughout the year. Uses included almost everything we use mechanical refrigeration for today, including preserving food, cooling drinks, and air conditioning. The Hungarian Parliament building in Budapest is still air conditioned with ice harvested from Lake Ballaton in the winter.

In modern times, thermal energy storage or TES allows surplus energy to be stored for later use. Energy can be stored in the storage medium either by changing its temperature (heating or cooling) or by changing its "phase" (e.g. from solid to liquid). The energy is released when the process is reversed. TES may be short term, e.g. storing "coolness" for later use to reduce peak air conditioning demand, or long term, e.g. between seasons. This text only discusses the short term energy storage methods.

Approximately 87% of the cooling systems using TES in the U.S. uses ice, 10% used water, and 3% uses eutectic salt as the storage medium. When heating is involved, water or water-antifreeze solutions are the most common TES method used.

2. Specific Heat

Specific heat is defined as the measure of how much energy a substance can store. If the scale was from 0-1, then water would top the list with 1.0. Following water, wood (oak) .6, glass .2, stone .2, brick .2, sand .2, concrete .15, and iron .1. Eliminating oak as being too costly, water and concrete are the effective winners for heat storage material.

3. Thermal Conductivity

Thermal conductivity is the measure of efficiency of heat transfer. Another way to look at it is the ease of getting energy back from the material. (See individual sections for discussions on thermal conductivity)

4. Sensible Heat vs. Latent Heat

Most heat storage materials are sensible. This means as they absorb heat, their temperature increases and they become warm to the touch. Examples are water, rock, soil, and concrete. Another form of thermal storage

*Used in Earth Home

material is latent heat storage (LHS) that uses chemical bonds to store and release heat. This means that they absorb heat without an increase in temperature. All phase change materials (PCM) are in this category since they change from a solid to a liquid and back indefinitely.

B. Natural Thermal Storage Materials

There have been many attempts to use a "thermal storage area" or "thermal battery" of one kind or another. The least costly materials are those that are natural.

1. Water Storage Overview

a. Density/Temperature Background

The efficiency of any thermal mass system depends of the specific heat of the material and its thermal conductivity. The specific heat of water is five times that of rock. Therefore it takes only 1/5 as much mass of water to store the same amount of heat as rock storage.

b. Water Storage Applications

By far, most of the thermal storage systems in use are water or water/antifreeze systems. Water is heated in boiler or stove jackets and pumped into water tanks. This heated water can then be used at a time of peak demand to satisfy heating requirements.

c. Antifreeze Considerations

To protect from freezing temperatures, additives are put into the water. Commonly available additives include polypropylene glycol, silicon oil, and methanol. Some systems use automotive anti-freeze but it is poisonous.

d. Water Tank Fabrication Techniques (See also Fish Tank section)

Water tanks have been used in many energy storage schemes--especially since the mid-1970's. Construction methods include welded steel, wire-wound concrete, reinforced concrete, fiberglass, and plastic. Many of these have been buried and insulated with water plumbed to and from them. Most of these systems use solar energy from flat panels on the roof or ground. The massive thermal storage capabilities of these systems are the draw for designers/builders. In practical applications, though it is difficult to maintain the high temperatures needed for adequate heating when used as an only source of heat. (See also Solar-Storage files)

Very inexpensive water tanks can also be fabricated from polyethylene sheeting, non-woven polypropylene fabric, and agricultural fence wire/mesh. The wire is wrapped several times around the desired shape and fastened together. This forms the sides of the tank. The nonwoven polypropylene is added to even out the pressure and plastic is then put inside the fabric/wire frame to hold the water. As the tank fills with water, the plastic is pushed against the fabric/wire structure, holding the water inside.

Another way to fabricate inexpensive water tanks is to use cardboard tubes that are used to pour concrete into footings for decks and pilings. The tubes are very strong and lightweight. Plastic in the form of layflat tubing is put inside the cardboard with the end crimped or tied securely. Again, the plastic keeps the water inside and the cardboard tubing contains the plastic. Tanks made with this method are tall and slim.

It is also possible to fabricate phase change material (PCM) containers and fill/seal them. However, this technology is outside the scope of this text. (See also Thermal Storage section)

2. Rock Storage Overview

a. Density/Temperature Background

Thermal storage of solar-heated air using rocks was looked at seriously in the late 1970's after the oil embargo. Rocks have a high density, but not as high as water. However, rocks can get to a higher temperature than water (maximum of 212 deg. F. under normal atmospheric pressure). (see High Temperature Storage Section)

b. Rock Storage Techniques (Solar)

Experiments have been done blowing air through rock beds for nighttime or daytime cooling. Rock size has to be exactly right so that the static pressure drop through the rock bed is reasonable. Also, larger rocks take more time to cool to a suitable temperature.

One of the problems with a rock bed system is also that moisture collects on the surface of the rocks and causes mold and odor problems. Due to this issue, rock storage installations have become very rare.

3. Soil Storage Overview (See separate Soil Thermal Mass section)

C. Other Thermal Storage Materials

1. Latent Heat Storage Materials (PCM)

a. Phase Change Materials (PCM) Overview

Latent heat storage uses a phase change material as a storage medium. This concept is particularly interesting for lightweight building construction. While undergoing phase change-freezing, melting, condensing, or boiling- a material absorbs or releases large amounts of heat with small changes in temperature. Phase change applications typically involve liquid/solid transitions. The Phase Change Material (PCM) is solidified when cooling resources are available, and melted when cooling is needed. PCM's have two important advantages as a thermal storage media; they can offer an order-of-magnitude increase in heat capacity, and for pure substances, their discharge is almost isothermal. However, most PCM applications are for industrial applications and not for the building sector.

b. Eutectic Salts

Another method used to store the sun's energy (heat) called "Wolmen salts". This was a "eutectic" solution sealed in plastic cylinders. The sun heated these cylinders directly and the fluid inside went through a phase change. Thus, the heated solution took on many Btu at a fixed temperature before it began to show a temperature increase. At night, air was blown across these tubes and the stored heat given back to the living space. (See Solar – Storage section also.)

c. Density/Temperature Advantages

Phase change materials store up to 8.5 times the energy as water by itself. There are over 70 different latent heat storage materials on the market today.

d. PCM/Water Hybrid Systems

Water tanks with PCM-filled plastic capsules have been developed to combine the best qualities of each system. This system consists of salts and hydrates contained in plastic capsules, where the thermal energy is stored during hydration of the thermally dehydrated salt. This method allows higher thermal capacities than just using water. Different phase change materials can be used for different storage temperatures.

e. Future Phase Change Materials

Glauber's salt (sodium sulfate decahydrate), calcium chloride hexahydrate, and paraffin wax are the most commonly used as PCMs in solar heating systems. Although these compounds are fairly inexpensive, the packaging and processing necessary to get consistent and reliable performance from them is complicated and costly.

Research on solid-liquid phase change materials has concentrated on the following materials: linear crystalline alkyl hydrocarbons, fatty acids and esters, polyethylene glycols, long alkyl side chain polymers, the solid state series of pentaerythrithol, pentaglycerine, and neopentyl glycol, low melting metals and alloys, quaternary ammonium clathrates and semi-clathrates, and salt hydrides. Also recently, a PCM-graphite composite material has been developed and tested that combines the high heat storage capacity of the PCM and the large thermal conductivity of graphite. These are all high-tech compounds that require much more research to be useful in reasonable-cost residential applications.

2. Heated Paraffin Wax

Paraffins have much lower thermal conductivity both in solid and liquid phase than other PCMs. They also have a lower density which makes them have less thermal capacity per unit volume. Another disadvantage is that it is flammable and more expensive than PCMs such as inorganic hydrated salt. To date, there is few installations that and little information available on heating paraffin for thermal storage medium.

3. Salt Hydrates (See Phase-Change Materials (PCM) section)

4. Future Thermal Storage Methods

a. High Density Desiccants

Another method of constructing thermal batteries is the previously mentioned desiccant bed with high density. Having two large masses of high density desiccants that can be used one at a time is advantageous. The dry desiccants can be used at night, while the other bed is being regenerated using solar heat. These systems show promise, especially if a desiccant material can be found that is organic or recyclable.

A fundamental problem with any thermal battery system is that it is difficult to do any airflow adjustments or modifications once the system is built. Also, a large mass of material must be used because of the small temperature changes. (See also Solar.)

b. PCM-Treated/Encapsulated Wallboard

At the present time, research is continuing on putting layers of phase change materials onto gypsum wallboard for thermal storage. This material would increase the heat capacity of standard wallboard immensely. This material is being tested in combination with hydronic loop systems to effectively remove heat as necessary.

*Used in Earth Home

There is also work ongoing with plaster impregnated with tiny spheres. Inside the spheres is a phase-changing paraffin wax that acts like any other phase change material. Only a quarter inch of this mixture on walls can have as much effect as a brick wall.

c. Ionic Liquids

Most of the familiar liquids (e.g., water, ethanol, benzene etc.) are molecular. That is, regardless of whether they are polar or non-polar, they are basically constituted of molecules. However, since the early 1980s, an exciting new class of room-temperature liquids has become available. These are the ambient-temperature ionic liquids. Unlike the molecular liquids, regardless of the degree of association, they are basically constituted of ions. This gives them the potential to behave very differently to conventional molecular liquids, when they are used as solvents.

Ionic liquids are organic salts with melting points under 100 degrees. Ionic liquids are attractive solvents as they are non-volatile, non-flammable, have a high thermal stability, and are relatively inexpensive to manufacture. They usually exist as liquids well below room temperature up to a temperature as high as 200 degrees C. The key point about ionic liquids is that they are liquid salts, which means they consist of a salt that exists in the liquid phase and have to be manufactured, they are not simply salts dissolved in liquid. Usually one or both of the ions is particularly large.

The most common ones are imidazolium and pyridinium derivatives, but also phosphonium or tetralkylammonium compounds can be used for this purpose. Lately, environmental friendly halogen-free ionic liquids have been introduced. Ionic liquids are highly solvating, non-coordinating medium in which a variety of organic and inorganic solutes are able to dissolve.

d. Other Research

At the present time, there is little significant research being done on thermal storage materials and/or chemistry. There must usually be an underlying reason to do applied or pure research. Some of these reasons include filling a need for society that can lead to manufacturing a product, finding more uses for a new material, and/or government-subsidized research for the common good of society. In this case, there appears to be a lack of reasons for research in this area.

D. Soil Thermal Mass/Storage

1. Earth as Source of Heat Background

The Earth has been used for a source of heat and thermal storage ever since the first cavemen sought shelter in caves. These first uses were rock caves, but much interest is being shown to using the earth to extract/transmit heat. This heat movement is influenced by many variables.

a. Soil Types

There are ten different kinds of soil on Earth, each of which is formed by the breaking down of a different type of rock. As soil if formed, it settles into layers. The top layer consists of decayed organic material and is called humus. Below that is the topsoil, which is also composed primarily of plant and animal remains. Underneath the topsoil is the subsoil. The subsoil is much lighter in color than the topsoil because it consists primarily of minerals.

b. Groundcover Influences

The influences on temperature variations in the earth above 26-30 feet deep includes season (annual air temperature), vegetative cover (groundcover), snowcover, soil types, and moisture content. As one would

*Used in Earth Home

expect, the earth's temperature changes in response to weather changes, but there is less change at greater depths.

If there is vegetation on the surface of the soil, the temperatures will be lower than when covered with soil only. The farmers take advantage of this when they leave the dark soil exposed to the sun's rays in the spring. This allows the soil to heat up faster, so the seeds will germinate faster.

2. Earth Temperature Overview

a. Soil Temperature Influences

Annual air temperature, moisture content, soil type, and vegetative cover all have an effect on underground soil temperature. As you would expect, the earth's temperature changes in response to weather changes, but there is less change at greater depths.

b. Soil Temperatures on the Surface

Most of the soil data comes from sources that measure temperature at depths of 2,4, and 8 inches below the surface. Typical agricultural extension organizations measure 4 inch soil temperatures. In Europe, they measure at 20 centimeters and 50 centimeters depth. In Russia, some studies have gone down over a meter to collect their data.

Temperature on the surface of the earth is probably monitored and studied more by farmers than any other occupational group. They plant crop seeds on the basis of the soil reaching a certain temperature. Even within an individual crop type such as soybeans, there are certain strains that prefer warmer soil temperatures for successful germination.

c. Soil Temperature Time Lag

When burying tubing (earth coils) for heat transfer, the time lag must be taken into account. The earth temperature several feet deep reaches its coldest or warmest temperature several weeks after building loads peak, with an annual swing ranging from 18 to 26°F for most sodded surfaces. At depths of twenty feet or more, there is no significant change from summer to winter, and the mean ground temperature approaches the annual average air temperature plus 2°F—down to about 200 feet. Thus, deep vertical loops generally require much less pipe than horizontal loops closer to the surface, but require more specialized excavation equipment.

d. Temperature Data 2-30 Feet Deep

This range of depth under the earth is an area of much interest and concern because of the potential to extract heat energy from it. Literature is scattered in many sources. This data has been compiled in specific locations and are made public through services such as the Soil Conservation Service Soil Survey. However, this data usually stops at the 6 foot depth level because it is no longer of any interest to farmers and agricultural companies. Thus the temperature from about 6 feet to the 30 foot level is an area that has not received much research.

e. Groundwater Temperatures/Chart

The ground itself is colder than some people realize. Studies have shown that about 26' beneath the surface, the soil maintains an even temperature of approximately 50°F in the Minnesota area. The ground temperature over the United States varies considerably, as shown in the following figure. As mentioned previously, these ground temperatures vary slightly depending on terrain, shading, and moisture content surrounding the immediate area. Earth temperatures are closely approximated by the temperature of water in shallow wells. Both heat energy and cooling energy have been extracted from the earth beneath our feet and much research has been put into this subject.

*Used in Earth Home

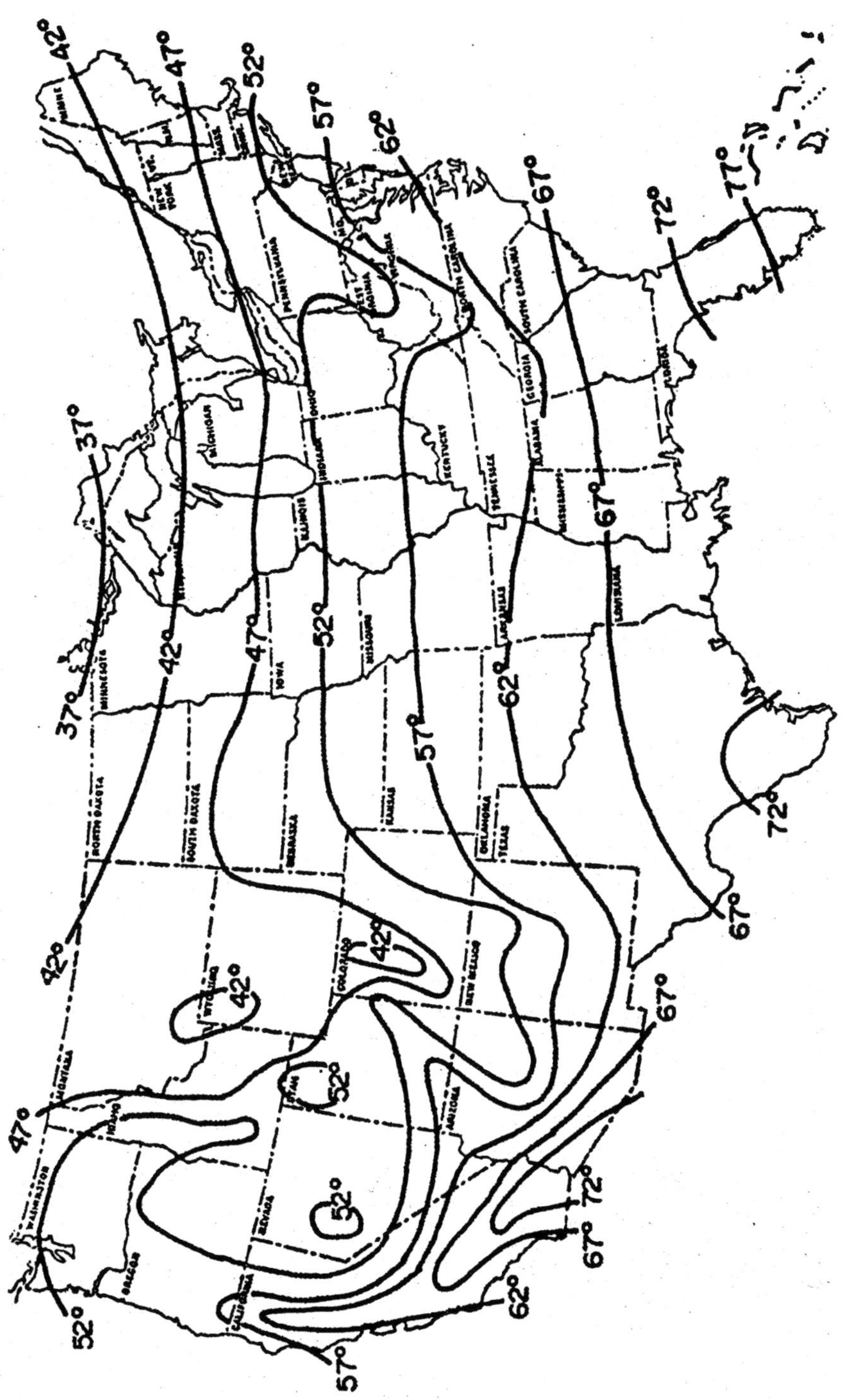

Figure 41-MEAN GROUNDWATER TEMPS.

(deg. F. at 30-60 ft. depth)

3. Soil Thermal Mass/Storage Issues

a. Moisture Influences on Heat Transfer Rates

Heat moves through soil slowly and is measured by its thermal conductivity. The major influence on thermal conductivity is moisture content. Moist soil transfers heat much faster than dry soil. Studies show that dry ground has an R factor from 5 to 10, but wet ground has an R factor from .5 to 1.43. This proves that moist soil conducts heat much more readily than dry soil. This is a 3 to 20 times greater thermal conductivity for the wet soil. The wet soil also dissipates heat into the surrounding soil for much larger distances. The drier the soil, the more it acts like insulation, and the wetter the soil, the more it acts like a conductor of heat.

Knowing exactly the moisture level and thermal conductivity of the soil helps to predict the actions of any storage scheme. Another method is to control the moisture inside the soil by using soak hoses or other irrigation technique. This method would help to predict the influence of the thermal mass on the structure. (See Controlling/Adjusting Moisture section)

Another great variable on the ability to transfer heat is the soil makeup. Soil thermal properties vary by a factor of ten and the thermal performance of rocks also varies widely. For example, these factors must be individually tested before ground source geothermal loop design can be finalized for a heat pump application.

b. Controlling/Adjusting Moisture

In a controlled situation, the amount of moisture can be controlled by adding moisture from a water source. The actual delivery of the moisture can be above or below the surface of the soil. When water is applied to the surface, it is prone to much more evaporation.

Below ground moisture-adding techniques are identical to the methods of irrigation. Sub-surface tubing can be made of porous rubber, perforated Tyvek, or tubing with punched holes in it. There is also special water emitters that may be employed. (See Irrigation section also)

c. Density Background

As stated previously, there are ten different types of soil and each of them has a slightly different density and thermal characteristic. (See also Thermal Mass Walls section)

d. Temperature Swings of the Soil

How well the mass contributes to a reduction in heating loads depends on climate, design, occupancy type, and building orientation. The amount of sunlight coming into the home is a significant factor as well. There are areas climates where nighttime temperatures do not fall low enough to fully discharge the stored heat from the mass walls, as well as climates where daytime temperatures are too high for the mass to work independently.

The temperature of any thermal mass tends to cycle like any material exposed to the cyclical day-night/seasonal changes that occurs as the earth spins on its axis. The farther into the earth you go, the slower the changes. At just a couple feet under the surface, any temperature changes in the day-night cycle are lost, and only long-term or seasonal changes are left. It is this seasonal cycle that must be understood for each location for effective use of thermal mass.

e. Soil Storage Applications

Most of the thermal mass applications are involved with high thermal mass walls that use earth berms. This system creates a high mass situation that makes the temperature swings much less.

Heat pump applications are also much interested in soil characteristics. They require good heat transfer between the pipes and the soil. Most heat pump manufacturers will advise testing of the soil to ensure good thermal

*Used in Earth Home

performance. The thermal qualities of soil are not as defined as water and rock systems, and make for more unpredictable performance.

E. Low-Tech Soil Heat Extraction Techniques

1. Cool Tubes/Air Extraction

a. Cool Tubes Background

In the early 1970s, a technology called "cool tubes" became popular. This technology brings air into the home by means of long, buried underground tubes that cool the air as it passes through the ground. Some of them used 400 feet of 12-inch diameter tubes.

After looking at many of these systems in operation, and related test data, I find that there are substantial problems associated with this method. The major problem was the cost to excavate huge amounts of soil to bury the large tubing. A second problem with this system is that moisture accumulates inside the tubing. After awhile the incoming air had a "musty" smell to it that could not be removed. It is possible that the tubes could harbor harmful bacteria and other organisms. There are some cool tube systems still being tested and used. (See Cooling/Dehumidification)

b. Plenums in Rocks (see Rock Storage Overview)

2. Water Pipes in the Ground (See Cooling-Dehumidification section)

3. Basement Wall Cooling (See Cooling-Dehumidification section)

F. High-Tech Soil Heat Extraction Techniques

1. Heat Pump Technology

A ground-source heat pump uses the earth or ground water or both as the sources of heat in the winter, and as the "sink" for heat removed from the home in the summer. For this reason, ground-source heat pump systems have come to be known as earth-energy systems (EES). Heat is removed from the earth through a liquid, such as ground water or an antifreeze solution, upgraded by the heat pump, and transferred to indoor air. During summer months, the process is reversed: heat is extracted from indoor air and transferred to the earth through the ground water or antifreeze solution.

See geothermal files for various methods used to coil the tubing underground. (Also see EH Ground Source Cooling section.)

a. Heat Pump Background/Applications

Some heating systems such as electric heat pumps use water/refrigerant-filled underground tubing to reheat the water. A direct-expansion (DX) earth-energy system uses refrigerant in the ground-heat exchanger, instead of an antifreeze solution. Geothermal heat pumps use the constant temperature of the earth as the exchange medium instead of the outside air temperature. This allows the system to reach fairly high efficiencies (300%-600%) on the coldest of winter nights, compared to 175%-250% for air-source heat pumps.

Since the introduction of air-source heat pumps to the marketplace in the 1950's, nearly one-third of all homes built today in the U.S. have at least one heat pump. Geothermal heat pumps (sometimes referred to as earth-coupled, ground-source, or water-source heat pumps) have been in use since the late 1940's. There are approximately 40,000 geothermal and water source heat pumps installed in the United States each year. Heat pumps can be powered by solar and can extract heat from soil, water, or air.

*Used in Earth Home

b. Heat Pump Tubing Options

Most of these geothermal heat pump systems involve vertical, horizontal, or under-pond tubing. The choice of how the tubing is buried (and where) has a great influence on the efficiency and maintenance of heat pump systems. Under-pond or water-source systems are the most efficient because the tubing comes in direct contact with a water source and allows good heat transfer. (See Geothermal files.)

c. Heat Pump Innovations

One of the more notable innovations in heat pump technology is the Reverse Cycle Chiller (RCC). It offers the advantages of allowing the homeowner to choose from a wide variety of heating and cooling distribution systems from hydronic radiant floor to multiple zones for forced air. The system consists of a standard air source heat pump, a large, heavily insulated tank of water; a fan coil: and some controls. This system allows the heat pump to operate at peak efficiency most of the time rather than only at above freezing outdoor temperatures like an ordinary heat pump would.

Other innovations include two speed compressors, variable speed fans, desuperheaters, and scroll compressors. Some systems also add dehumidifying heat pipes and new designs for heat exchangers. Still other variations are gas-fired heat pumps, ductless heat pumps, and heat pumps with gas back-up heat (dual fuel).

d. Disadvantages of Heat Pumps

Of course, the heat pump requires electricity-and lots of it. It is often compared to electric heating elements for space heating. The installation price of a geothermal system can be several times that of an air-source system of the same heating and cooling capacity. Many heat pump owners complain about noisy operation and inadequate heating performance.

2. Heat Pipe/Future Heat Extraction Technologies

a. Heat Pipe Technology/Background

The development of the heat pipe originally started in about 1839 and were first used with water as the fluid and relied on gravity to return the water to the evaporator (later called a thermosiphon). This Perkins Tube was a system in which a long and twisted tube passed over an evaporator and condenser, which caused the water within the tube to operate in two phases. They were in widespread use in locomotive boilers and baking ovens.

The concept of the modern heat pipe, which relied on a wicking system to transport the liquid against gravity and up to the condenser came about at General Motors in about 1944. By 1969 there was a great interest in heat pipes, especially for NASA. They were interested in regulating the temperature of a spacecraft. This research and application expanded the use of heat pipes into all fields. Heat pipes are routinely used to cool electronic components-especially for small devices like notebook computers. They have been considered for a wide variety of applications, ranging from heat rejection in space to cooling of gas turbine vanes.

b. Heat Pipe Basics (See also Heat Pipe Dehumidification section)

The heat pipe is a device for transporting heat from one point to another with quite extraordinary properties. Heat transport occurs via evaporation and condensation, and the heat transport fluid is recirculated by capillary forces which automatically develop as a consequence of the heat transport process. With this mode of heat transfer, the heat pipe has the capability to transport heat at high rates over appreciable distances, virtually isothermally and without any requirement for external power. It may be regarded as a "passive" heat transport system with an extremely high effective thermal conductivity in the direction of heat transport.

A metal cylinder (copper for instance) is sealed with a fluid (water for instance) within it creating a closed system. One end of the tube is heated and the other is cooled. The heat source (the evaporator) causes the fluid to boil and turn to vapor (this is absorbing energy as heat). This also creates a pressure difference that causes the vapor to flow towards the cooler end of the tube. Once the vapor reaches the cold end of the tube (the condenser), the fluid changes phase again from vapor back to a liquid (releasing the energy as heat). This liquid returns to the hot (evaporator) end by means of a wick so that the liquid can repeat the process. This process is capable of transporting heat from a hot region to a colder region. It requires no addition of external energy and can be manufactured to have any geometry or property desired. (See the following figure) Probably the most important heat pipe feature is the ability to transport heat along the direction of fluid flow with a very small temperature drop.

c. Heat Pipe Components/Construction

A heat pipe has three different components; the casing, the working fluid, and the wick. The casing can be made out of a variety of different materials, depending on the application and the working fluid. Most heat pipes currently used have copper, stainless steel, or aluminum casings.

The wick is often a woven wire mesh that is composed of very small pores. Stainless steel is easiest to work with but copper is also used. Aluminum on the other hand, is difficult to weave and therefore in using this material it is difficult to achieve a small pore size. The pore size is important because the wick operates under the principle of capillary action. Capillary action describes how fluid in a very small tube will be forced up through this tiny opening causing the fluid to rise. The wick is usually located against the inside walls of the heat pipe and can have various geometries. (See the following figures) (See also Cooling/Dehumidification/Heat Pipe Dehumidification)

There are many working fluids available—especially those with a high latent heat of vaporization to absorb a lot of energy. Heat pipe fluids range from liquid hydrogen and nitrogen at cryogenic temperatures, to water, ammonia, and alcohol at near-ambient temperatures, to liquid metals such as sodium and lithium at elevated temperatures. The problem with using many of these working fluids is that some are flammable and some may be toxic. For those reasons, the most common fluid is water.

d. Heat Pipe Variations

There are specific types of heat pipes developed for very individual applications. Variations on the basic design include heat pipes with thermal diodes/thermal switches, variable conductance heat pipes, and flat plate heat pipes. Recently heat pipe technology has been combined with solar hydronic heating. (See Solar Heating section)

e. Heat Pipe Earth Applications

There are many applications for heat pipes involving the heat/cool of the earth. One application is for melting of ice on concrete walks. Another application is the reverse where they try and preserve the permafrost so no thawing occurs. This could be useful in specific Arctic driveway locations and far northern airport runways. (See the following figure)

There is also experimentation on the use of heat pipes in Trombe walls to heat an area. As of yet, thermal mass heat extraction has yet to be extensively researched.

A traditional heat pipe is a hollow cylinder filled with a vaporizable liquid.

A. Heat is absorbed in the evaporating section.

B. Fluid boils to vapor phase.

C. Heat is released from the upper part of cylinder to the environment; vapor condenses to liquid phase.

D. Liquid returns by gravity to the lower part of cylinder (evaporating section).

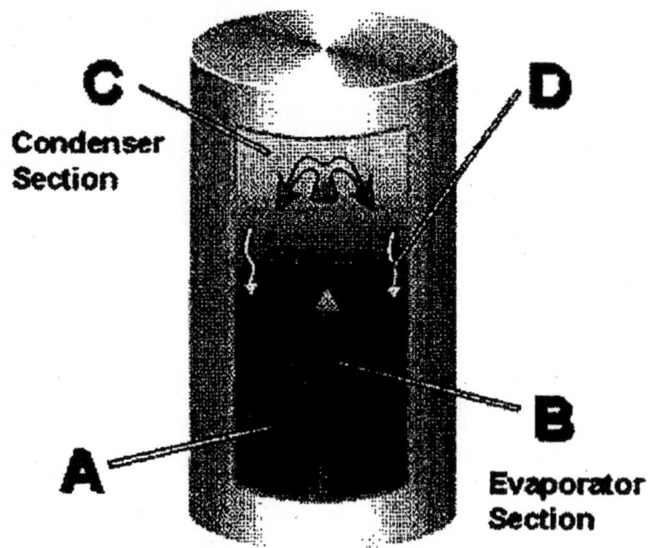

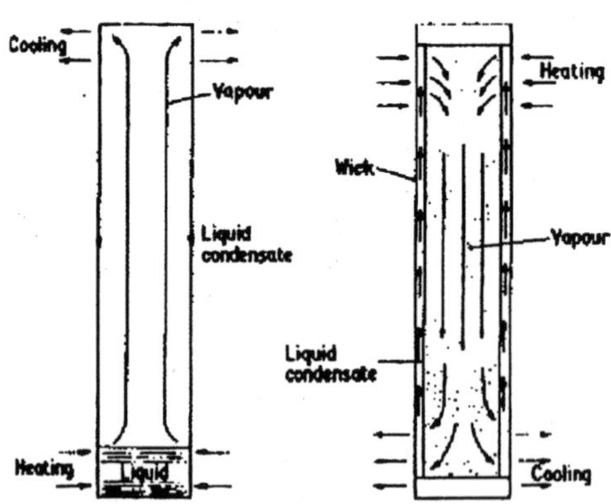

Figure 42-HEAT PIPE BASICS

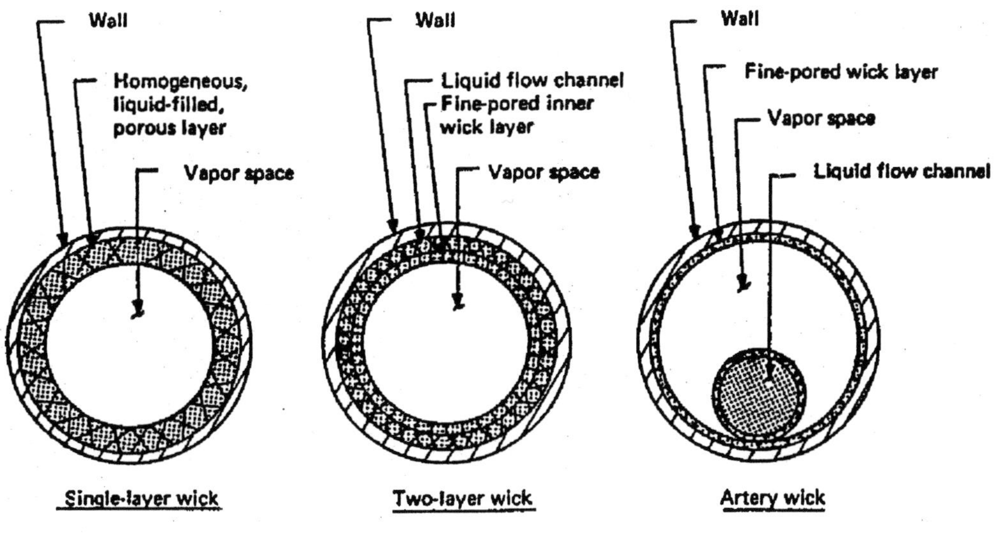

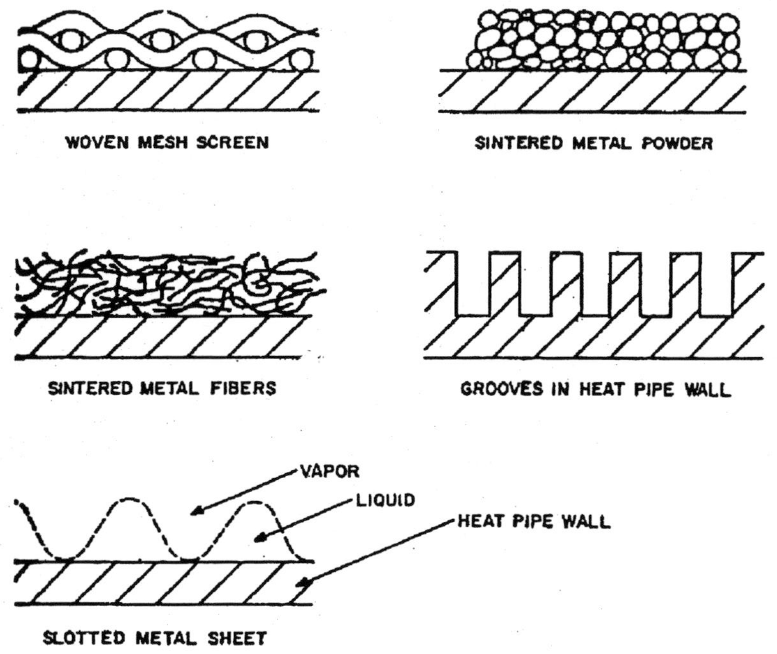

Figure 43-HEAT PIPE CONSTRUCTION

*Used in Earth Home

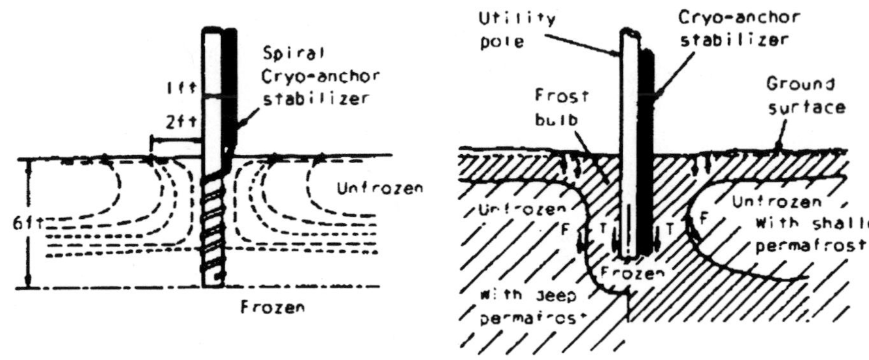

Figure 44-HEAT PIPE GROUND APPLICATIONS

*Used in Earth Home

G. Home Thermal Heat Storage Techniques

1. Optional Locations for Mass in Homes

a. In Sun-Facing Living Areas

There have been many designs at putting high thermal mass materials in direct contact with the sun's rays. This would heat up the mass during the heating hours and release the stored heat at night. Insulation can be used to minimize the heat loss through the windows at night. Trombe walls have been used successfully in southern locations for many years. Even massive block floors have the effect of storage of energy, provided the slab is insulated from below to keep the heat inside the building envelope.

b. Interior Walls

There is a large amount of literature and research into thermal mass walls of one kind or another. Some designs use the outside of the wall as the storage medium and others say that the interior high mass wall section is the most critical. There is ongoing research on this subject. (see Thermal Mass Wall section)

c. Inside Spaces

It is generally agreed that putting thermal mass materials inside the insulated fabric of buildings is one of the best places to put them. There is no contact with surfaces or materials that can transmit heat energy out of the structure except air which is basically an insulator. The disadvantage is that it takes up space that is normally reserved for occupants and other necessary living systems.

d. In-Floor Heat (See Solar section)

e. Structural Thermal Storage

Large thermal storage devices have been used in the past to overcome the shortcomings of alternative cooling sources, or to avoid high demand charges. Buildings designed to make use of thermal storage include features which increase thermal mass. These may be used for storage only, or may serve both as storage and as structural elements. Several structural materials satisfy the requirements for sensible heat storage; these include concrete, steel, adobe, stone and bricks.

f. Combination Methods

There have been many attempts to use some of each storage method and combine them into a hybrid system. Examples include using heated water pipes to circulate inside of a rock bed, and air plenums in the soil.

Much construction, design, and testing have been done on hybrid systems. To date, none of the hybrid systems has been touted as the ideal storage system for homes. There continues to be significant interest in new storage techniques.

2. Exterior High Mass Walls

a. Background/History

In southern and central Europe, the vast majority of residential buildings have been built using massive wall technologies. For centuries, massive building materials have been making life without air conditioners relatively comfortable even in countries with hot climates, such as Spain, Italy, or Greece.

Controlling indoor comfort through high thermal mass walls has been used for centuries on every continent in the world. In the U.S., frame houses and cheap energy slowed the popularity of the method for many years. The early solar passive homes of the 70's (with their rock beds and water drums) proved to be effective at reducing heating costs. In the late 70's and early 80's the rammed-earth wall construction techniques enabled much more heat storage.

In certain climates, massive building envelopes such as ceramic masonry, concrete, earth, and insulating concrete forms (ICFs) can be one of the most effective ways of reducing building heating and cooling loads. Several comparative studies have shown that in some US locations, heating and cooling energy demands in buildings containing massive walls can be lower than those in similar buildings constructed using lightweight wall technologies.

b. How Mass Walls Work

A thermal-mass wall can be thought of as a giant flywheel that continuously rotates with power supplied by thermal energy or heat. There is a cyclical quality from day to night swings, and a climatic quality from the seasonal temperature changes.

During the winter, the wall mass works to maintain warm temperatures in the living spaces, using the heat fed to it by both sunlight and, in most cases, a supplemental source of heat. In the summer, the wall mass maintains cool temperatures inside the house by extracting heat from the home's air during the day and releasing it during the cool night.

c. Concrete "Sandwich" Walls

Insulated concrete sandwich walls are typically made with a center of foam with a layer of concrete on each side. (Industrial buildings of pre-stressed concrete also utilize a similar method.) A typical sandwich wall would consist of a 2 inch exterior layer of concrete, 2 inches of foam, and 4 inches of additional concrete on the interior. The material R-value of this wall would be 11.33.

However, the actual performance of this wall is several times greater than the material R-value. By placing a highly effective layer of Styrofoam extruded polystyrene insulation between the two concrete layers, the interior temperature can stabilize the interior layer of concrete. While the climate temperature seeks to warm the interior of the building, the insulation prevents rapid swings in temperature.

All materials have intrinsic mass based on their specific heat capacity. This feature of including the wall construction in the R-value is called mass performance R-value or the equivalent wall performance R-value. ***The degree of improvement in R-value (equivalent R-value) in a given structure is greatly dependent upon the climate location, the occupancy type, the orientation, as well as the overall building design.***

d. Climate Variations on Thermal Mass Wall Applications

1. Sun Belt/Altitude Challenges

The equivalent R-value of residences constructed with Styrofoam T-Mass technology in the Midwest U.S. will see an equivalent R-value roughly twice that of the material R-value.

2. Midwest/Northern Climate Challenges

The equivalent R-value of residences constructed with Styrofoam T-Mass technology in the Southern U.S. will see an equivalent R-value that can be as much as three times or greater than the material R-value.

*Used in Earth Home

3. Ongoing Testing/Research on Whole-Walls

Wall systems with significant thermal mass have, depending on the climate, the potential to reduce building annual heating and cooling energy requirements below that of a standard wood-frame construction with similar steady-state R-value. In 1991 fundamentals were developed for a procedure for measuring and generating metrics that reflect thermal mass benefits. This procedure now incorporates dynamic R-value evaluations.

ASHRAE is developing models to test the performance of thermal-mass wall styles in several locations. This system allows for dynamic R-value evaluations. Oak Ridge National Laboratory (ORNL) has performed a significant amount of research into the dynamic thermal performance of wall technology.

3. High Temperature Stove/Furnace Applications

a. Off-Peak Electricity Example

Electric off-peak systems take advantage of high temperature thermal storage. They use a special insulated container that is slowly heated during the night to a very high temperature. During the day, when heat is needed, the control system switches over and draws heat off the storage medium as needed. This high temperature system assures that the air drawn off has a high enough temperature in the incoming plenum to efficiently heat using the existing fan and ductwork.

Furnace or stoves that heat other materials have also been tried. An example is the typical Swedish sauna stove that is surrounded by small rocks. As the stove heats up the rocks are also heated to a high temperature. This high temperature storage is what keeps the temperature high even though occupants are applying water to the stove/rocks to make steam.

b. High Mass Masonry Stoves (See Heating System/Masonry Stoves section)

c. High Mass Chimney (See Heating System/Draft/Chimney section)

d. Other High Temperature Storage Methods

Calcium chloride (salts) has been used to store energy for later retrieval using high thermal mass. The salt can be heated to a much higher temperature than many other materials. This method is a high-tech alternative and uses Stirling engines or other methods to recover the energy.

4. Cold/Refrigeration Storage (See Refrigeration Options-Nite Cooler Tab section)

*Used in Earth Home

H. Earth Home Thermal Mass (Dual-Use) Techniques

1. Massive Water Storage Method (See Cooling/Dehumidification section)

    a. Water as Medium (see EH Ground Source Cooling section)

    b. Radiator Effect (see EH Ground Source Cooling section)

    c. Efficient Pumping/Control Techniques (see EH Cooling Water Circulation section)

2. Greenhouse Soil "Trombe Wall" (see EH Trombe Wall Soil V-Trough System)

*Used in Earth Home

III. STRUCTURES OVERVIEW

A. Background/History of Human Dwellings

1. Dwelling/Shelter Types on the Earth

Human beings, over thousands of years, have chosen many different sizes and shapes for their dwellings. They have lived in tents, huts, lodges, igloos, tipis, kivas, yurts, domes, cliff dwellings, cluster dwellings, castles, reed houses, thatched houses, sod houses, stone houses, tree houses, mound houses, earth lodges, grass houses, KI's, ramadas, wigwams, pit houses, hogans, wickiups, chickees, lean-to's, plank houses, longhouses, and pueblos. They range from the earliest caves to the later cabins, tarpaper shacks and "modern" homes of today. Humans have sought shelter from the elements, comfort, and beauty in a great variety of structures.

Our shelter fantasies begin when we are very young. Put some children into a room with a chair and a blanket and what will they do? They'll drape the blanket over the chair and create their own little shelter, along with a fantasy world to go with it. After we become adults, our shelter fantasies become more substantial, and much more expensive. The home is typically the most valuable possession that we own. At the same time, it reflects our creativity and our own personality, especially if we had input in the design or construction.

2. Overview of Materials Used in Home Construction

a. Building Materials and Human Beings

At the turn of the century, only about ***2 million of the Earth's 6 billion inhabitants live in buildings of manufactured or industrially processed components.*** Approximately another 2 billion live in structures of earthen materials and the other 2 billion live in other types or no building at all. Taking this into account, low-impact construction alternatives have definite advantages.

b. Indigenous Materials (See also EH Tabs section)

A home can be made out of many different materials. Often the selection of a material is based upon the geographic region in which the house is built. For example, in the southern climates the materials may be tile, concrete, brick, or adobe to take advantage of the nighttime "cool." Northern houses are more often wood frame structures with fiberglass, cellulose, or, more recently, polyurethane insulation. Natives of Africa may use a grass hut construction. Corrugated steel over a wood frame is often used in southern regions, where it rains more frequently. In the eastern countries, stucco or concrete architecture is favored.

*Used in Earth Home

c. Long-Lasting Materials

Many times, the choice of housing materials depends on how long the builders wish the house to last. Throughout history the longest lasting homes have been made of a ceramic material such as brick, stone, stucco, and concrete block.

d. Green/Natural Building Materials

It is advantageous to use recycled and more Earth-friendly components when constructing a home. It is sometimes difficult to locate such components. A good source of information is the Green Building Resource Guide by John Germannsson and The Natural House Book by David Pearson.

e. Sidewall/Skin Materials

The "skin" of the structure is what is normally called a sidewall, or the outside of the home itself. This skin must resist the wind forces on the structure called uplift, overturn, racking, and shear. It must also be resistant to rain and sun degradation. There are many ways to block air from entering a structure by using such things as Styrofoam insulation, aluminum siding, Masonite siding, cedar siding, and various other materials. I wanted a material that would last at least one hundred years and would "breathe" somewhat.

3. Modern U.S. Home Overview

a. Wood Framing History

To most Americans, it is usually a surprise to learn that lightweight wood framing has become the predominant building method in the United States only since the end of World War II. Returning GIs and a flourishing economy embraced it because it was expedient and cheap. Stick-frame, as it is popularly known, has only very recently been adopted to any extent in other parts of the world. Wood frame residential construction in the United States is a leading cause of global deforestation because so much of it is needed.

b. U.S. Home Size History

Since the turn of the century, average house size in North America has been going up almost as fast as family size has been going down. An average new house in 1912, for instance, was 1,500 square feet. During the Depression, the few houses that were built were small, less than 1,000 square feet, but sizes began to climb again after the war. In the 1960's the average was 1,450 square feet and in 1989 it jumped to nearly 2,000 square feet.

Modern American homes are the largest of any single family type in the world. Americans spend much time in and around their home. The term "sculpted environment" is sometimes used to describe the way some people mold the home to their needs.

c. Indoor Pollution Issues

The modern home is not the safe haven we think. There are many hazards including; lumber treatments, petrochemical paints, formaldehyde, polyurethane foams, polyvinyl floor tiles, electromagnetic radiation, hydrocarbons from combustion, household chemicals, insulation materials, and radon. As the house ages, some of these hazards will be reduced.

*Used in Earth Home

4. Popular Alternative Construction (See also Concrete-Based Construction and Earth Architecture sections)

During the design of the Earth Home I looked at many different housing designs. I systematically eliminated them one by one in order to fulfill the requirements of the Earth Home System. (See Goals and Qualities desired).

a. Geodesic Dome

The early design for the EH was a truncated geodesic dome. This shape provided very good structural support at reasonably cost. I decided to pursue other options because of rainfall collection, plant growth inside, and privacy spaces. I decided to put rooms into the design instead of a loft system with central heated/cooled air distribution. One of the earlier designs was a "thermos-bottle" style made of two huge clear glass domes. The air space between the domes would be evacuated to provide a nearly perfect insulation. This technology would involve a super kiln and heating the glass to drape into a below-ground form before being slowly cooled.

b. Earthship/Used Tire Berming

The concept of an earthship uses used auto tires to berm the soil and/or use thermal mass as a thermal collector/damper for heat energy. There is a great interest in this style of construction and has become very popular. Since the goal of the Earth Home is to locate a home anywhere in the world, and there is a limited supply of tires, this method was not used for the Earth Home. The EH uses water as a thermal storage medium and local grown flax bales as a shell insulation material.

c. Poured Membrane (See also Concrete-Based Construction section)

One of the early designs was also a form onto which concrete was sprayed on. I was planning on inflating a membrane and freezing it in wintertime. This could then support the weight of the concrete. This was also abandoned because of the temperature requirements of concrete. The alternative was to use a plastic or fiberglass-type of covering for an inflated structure. I felt that the cost of such a structure was prohibitive and would require massive amounts of technology and petrochemicals.

d. Structural Insulated Panels (SIP)

Structural insulated panels or SIP for short, consist of two outer skins and an inner core of an insulation material to forma a monolithic unit. Most structural panels use either plywood or oriented strand board (OSB) for their facings. OSB is the principal facing material because it is available in large sizes. Some manufacturers offer fiber-reinforced plastic (FRP) or a cementitious plank outer skins. A special gypsum-like coating is available for finishing high ceilings.

Other names for similar products are foam-core panels, stress-skin panels, nail-base panels, sandwich panels, and curtain-wall panels. Some of these building panels are nonstructural, while some have no insulation. Long self-tapping screws called panel screws are often used to mount the panels.

The cores of SIP's can be made from a number of materials, including molded expanded polystyrene (EPS), extruded polystyrene (XPS), and urethane foam. Most of the manufacturers use EPS for the insulation, but urethane has a higher R-value. These panels are somewhat expensive, but save on labor cost for homes. One great advantage of their construction is that they are lightweight.

A similar building technique is called TridiPanel. This system uses a foam core, but puts steel wire mesh on each side. After the panel is in place, concrete is either troweled into place or pumped on with special concrete pumping machinery. This system can use concrete, Gunite, Portland cement, plaster, or stucco.

The Earth Home will use similar panels on the ceiling where weight is of paramount importance. I believe the future is bright for this method of construction and that more earth-friendly and green materials will eventually be used for the insulation.

e. Post and Beam/Pole Building (See EH Post and Beam section)

5. Earth Architecture (See also Concrete-Based Construction section)

a. History of Earth Architecture

Approximately 15% of the French population, one half of the world's population, approximately 3 billion people on six continents, lives or works in buildings constructed of earth. Earth is universally and easily available. It has been used as a building material throughout history and in most cultures around the world.

b. Cob Construction

Cob is made from clay, sand, straw, and water. Cob building was for centuries a staple of British and Western European home architecture. Cob was used as a building material in Canada by early immigrants from the British Isles. Into the 1930's cob was promoted by the Roosevelt administration.

Cob is mixed into a dough-like consistency and then placed onto the walls up to two foot thick and worked in to create a monolithic wall structure. No forms are used, making any shape possible. Clay acts as the glue, sand hardens the structure, and the straw works like rebar to give the walls tensile strength. Cob structures can withstand earthquakes, won't catch fire, is energy efficient and inexpensive to build. Cob earthen walls are sustainable and can last for centuries.

c. Rammed-Earth/Adobe

The rammed-earth method involves packing soil into a form and using them like bricks. Rammed earth buildings have been with us for over 10,000 years and little has changed in the technology. The western 2/3 of the Great Wall of China is made of rammed earth and it is said to be over 2,000 years old.

d. Adobe/Wattle and Daub

Early adobe used clay as the binder but modern adobe uses about 6% cement in the formula.

e. Earth Architecture and EH

I decided not to use this method for all EH locations because it did not have world-wide applicability. More insulation against the cold weather was needed in the Northern Hemisphere, for example. Adobe and/or rammed earth could be used in many locations and is included in the "Tabs" section for international applications.

B. Overview of Concrete as Construction Material

1. Concrete Background/History

The history of cement goes back to the Egyptian lime and gypsum mortar that were used on the pyramids. (Limestone is the only type of stone that becomes harder when exposed to the elements of nature.) The Romans perfected the technique with their aqueducts—being in excellent state of preservation today.

Concrete or Portland cement was developed during the nineteenth century to be a fast setting and durable material. Over the years technology has included additives for strength and other needed features. Concrete is particularly useful when the strength is needed for multi-story buildings (highly stressed or pre-stressed), as became popular as urban land prices increased dramatically.

2. Concrete-Based Construction Methods (See also EH Tabs section)

a. Insulated Concrete Foundation (ICF)

Insulated concrete foundation construction is similar to concrete block construction, except the concrete is in the middle of a sandwich of foam. The foam blocks are assembled first with rebar inside the hollow spaces. The concrete is then poured into the space to form the backbone of the wall. The foam acts as an insulation material and is permanently kept in place by the concrete. ICF construction has one limitation vs. concrete block construction. It requires the application of a durable finish material whereas concrete block can be painted or left bare.

b. Underground Homes

Sometimes underground homes are called earth homes. The underground home is also popular today. One of the big reasons I chose to avoid earth berming (soil covering) is the cost factor. The home must be braced extensively in order to resist the inward and downward forces of the soil placed high on the sidewalls or directly overhead. An alternative to massive bracing is Spancrete (extruded pre-stressed concrete sections) placed side-by-side on the roof to form long spans of roof material. However, this is very expensive and needs to be sealed completely on top of the concrete in order to resist water pressure and the effects of frost.

c. Cordwood-Concrete

One of the styles I looked at was the cordwood designs. This method used a cut piece of split firewood and wrapping fiberglass insulation around it. It is then piled up to form a wall. Stucco lath is then nailed to the ends of the wood and concrete stucco mix is applied. I abandoned this method because of the cost of the lath and extensive labor requirements. I also had doubts about the wall integrity.

d. Papercrete Construction

Papercrete is basically a type of industrial strength paper mache' made with paper and cardboard, sand, and Portland cement. Other names include paper adobe, fidobe, fibrous cement, and padobe. Papercrete was originally patented in 1928. Since it was cheap and simple, it did not reach significant profitability and it was essentially abandoned until recently. In the early 80's several people began to experiment with it again.

The concept of papercrete starts with a mixer similar to a huge kitchen blender. In short, they add and mix the dry ingredients with water to form a slurry, cast the slurry into blocks or panels, and let it dry out. Each batch requires approximately 1 shovel of cement, 3 shovels of sifted sandy dirt, and 1-55 gallon drum of newspapers and magazines. Glossy magazines are preferred because the "slick" paper contains clay, which is beneficial to the mix. The newspapers and magazines are soaked until they are soft before adding to the mixer. They then cast the slurry into a form and let it air dry in the sun.

When it hardens up, papercrete is lightweight (it is 80% air), an excellent insulator (R 2.8 per inch), holds its shape even when wet, and is remarkably strong (compressive strength of 260 psi). And, since it contains paper fibers, it has considerable tensile strength as well as compressive strength. Also, since the individual paper fibers are saturated with cement, oxygen doesn't have a chance to penetrate, and combustion cannot be sustained. In summary it has been touted as having low cost, high strength, good insulating characteristics, fire-resistance, and high thermal mass.

Experimenters have saved elaborate foundations because the weight of a wall section is only one pound per square foot! They have constructed powerful mixers with custom blades and hydraulic "squish boxes" to remove excess water before air drying. Work is being done on adding other fillers to the mix and finding ways to speed the drying process.

The drying process is the huge drawback because it takes forever. Also the end product is susceptible to damage by absorbing water again either from the humidity or "wicking" moisture from the ground. The papercrete must be waterproofed in order to last many years. Most of the papercrete structures are in very dry climates.

e. Straw-Bale Construction w/Stucco

There were straw-bale houses built in the Sandhills area of the Nebraska prairies in the early 1900's. Three-string straw-bale construction has attracted interest recently as a building technique. (Incidentally, the National Research Council of Canada has carried out fire safety tests on plastered straw bales, and found them to be better than most conventional building materials.) Rice straw has also been used because its high silica content makes it decay very slowly. Most of the straw bale homes are covered with a stucco of some type.

3. Disadvantages of Portland Cement

The exacting nature of Portland cement manufacture requires some 80 separate and continuous operations, the use of a great deal of heavy machinery and equipment, and large amounts of heat and energy. The capital investment per worker in the cement industry is among the highest in all industries.

Portland cement is very rigid and it may not be the ideal material for applications requiring some flexibility. It is also relatively expensive to produce and often in short supply in developing countries. Typically, an African laborer may need to work for up to a week to earn enough money to buy one bag of cement. In comparison, alternative binders such as lime can often be produced locally, on a smaller scale and at a lower cost. (see also Lime Advantages-Environmental Section)

There are other disadvantages of cement and strong composition mortars when used for straw bale construction:

1) Poor bond strength to mating surfaces.
2) Rigid and brittle render does not allow for structural movement.
3) Cracking and crazing.
4) Will not allow the wall to breathe.
5) Expands and contracts on a daily basis, breaking the bond to straw ends.
6) Cracks become rivers when shedding water.
7) Expands, cracks, spalls, and explodes in fires.
8) Creep, with daily expansion and contraction.
9) Cracks become chimneys in the case of fire.

4. Future Concrete Replacements/Developments

Over the years there was increasing need to replace concrete with other alternatives because of cost and environmental issues (see Lime Advantages-Environmental Section). Some of these included adobe, pozzolans, lime, geopolymers, and rammed earth materials. This text will concentrate on building lime because it offers world-wide availability, can be made resistant to moisture, and can be successfully used virtually anywhere on the planet.

a. Lime as Concrete Replacement (See Building Lime as Alternative section)

b. Geopolymer Technology

Geopolymers are flexible ceramics which transform like plastics at low temperatures. This technology has been used to manufacture fly ash-based geopolymer concrete. This new construction is tougher, more cost effective, and environmentally friendly than Portland cement concrete and does not use cement. In addition, geopolymeric cement manufacture emits 80% less CO_2 than Portland Cement.

c. Hybrid Adobe/Combination Methods

There are many other alternative methods including; cob (sand, clay, straw, and water), adobe, bamboo, hemp, living roofs, thatch, wattle and daub, earthbag, light straw-clay (light loam, light clay, straw clay, straw loam), straw panels, timberframe, superadobe, and many more. There seem to always be someone who wants to make a home another way. Most of these techniques are more suited to one location, society, and/or climatic region and are outside the scope of this text.

Hybrid adobe construction is combination of papercrete, adobe, and fiber adobe (or fidobe) construction. It is still in the development stages and poses possibilities for concrete replacement. Hybrid adobe is also known as hydradobe, hybridobe, and hyperadobe. It is a mixture of papercrete and fibered adobe (aka fidobe). It may also include fibers such as hemp, glass, and jute. (See also Concrete-Based Construction section.)

d. Marl as Concrete Substitute

Marl is a clay-like material found under many bogs and swamps. Marl could be incinerated to form caustic lime, which is an important component of mortar and Portland cement. A low magnesium content of some marl make it ideal for creating firebrick, which was used to line furnaces and build fire-resistant structures.

e. Ceramicrete/Grancrete Concrete Substitute

Grancrete is a liquefied concrete-like mixture consisting of 50% sand or sandy soil, 25% ash, and 25 % binding material. The binding material is composed of magnesium oxide and potassium phosphate, the latter of which is a biodegradable element in fertilizer. Grancrete sets up in hours instead of days for traditional concrete. Grancrete descends from Ceramicrete, a product developed in 1996 to encase radioactive waste at Argonne. Ceramicrete thus prevents pollutants from leaking into the environment

It is being evaluated to construct low-cost housing in Third World countries. Grancrete is typically sprayed with a special gun over a frame of wood, metal, and Styrofoam sheets. In 20 minutes it sets up to form a waterproof, fire-resistant structure that has more than twice the strength of traditional concrete and can withstand extreme temperatures without cracking. The material can be applied over other materials such as woven sugarcane stalks as well.

f. Isochanvre Concrete Substitute

Many products can be made from hemp including a cement-like material. It is being successfully used in Europe and is available as a commercial product called "Isochanvre". French-made products use natural lime and water for binding agents. Processed hemp can be used as cement and poured directly onto soil. Unlike cement, the hemp-based product is very flexible, doesn't crack, is water-resistant, and seven times lighter than concrete.

5. Concrete Binders/Fibers/Reinforcement

a. Hemp as a Concrete Binder (See also Hemp as Concrete Substitute section)

Hemp is one of the oldest useful plants. Its fibers are used in all sorts of textiles and for many other purposes. It is being looked at for a binder because of its strong fibers and renewable nature. However, hemp contains silicic acid, which is not alkali resistant.

b. Steel as a Concrete Binder

Steel fibers are available unperforated, corrugated, matted, or with a wide end for better bending. They must be purchased because they are difficult to fabricate using common tools and equipment. Steel also has the effect of increasing the tensile strength of concrete and resisting cracking.

c. Glass Fibers in Concrete

Specific glass fibers have the capacity to resist chemical attacks in an alkaline environment as would be experienced in the hydration of cement. However, glass fibers are better in mortar because of their notch sensitivity.

d. Polypropylene Fibers as a Concrete Binder

Short fibers of polypropylene is commercially available for concrete as a filler. It adds crack resistance as well as toughness to concrete. Various lengths of fibers are available. The only issue is the mixing of the fibers into the batch of concrete. It must be uniform for maximum benefit.

e. Carbon Fibers

Carbon can be used in small shapes, little sticks, and shredded. Carbon is very resistant to corrosion and greatly benefits the concrete mix. However, a good source of carbon has yet to be developed.

f. Other Organic/Natural Materials for Concrete Reinforcement

Fiber reinforcement options can also include natural fibers such as bamboo, sisal, and jute (burlap) in low-tech countries. These fibers can degrade over the years and are not specifically approved materials. Bamboo, however, has been used successfully in place of rebar in developing countries for decades. Other natural fibers that has been used in hybrid adobe include sawdust, dried weeds, grass clippings, straw, and hemp.

g. Mixing/Working with Fibers

The ratio of Portland cement to fine aggregate (sand) can range from no filler to all to 1:2. Fibers of all kinds have been used in cement to prevent cracking in ratios of up to 2% by weight, when mixed at the batching plant. But with that small a percentage, no tensile structural reinforcement is gained, only toughness. Fibers need to be added at least 5-7% by weight to gain structural advantage. The problem is that fibers in that quantity cannot be mixed in a mixer because they ball up. Commercially, they are add to a Gunite spray with a chopper gun. Another method is to use open weave fabrics and build with layers of fabric and cement. Simply lay the open-weave fabric, pour cement from a bucket, and spread it out.

C. Hemp Technology as Concrete Alternative

1. Background/History of Hemp

Thought to have originated in the area just north of the Himalaya mountains, the hemp plant was used by the Chinese to produce fiber as early as 2800 BC. By 500 AD the plant had spread to Europe, and eventually it was brought to the New World by the explorers. Now it is a common plant found wild or cultivated over much of the world. Hemp was grown on virtually every early farm in Pennsylvania and considered a vital necessity.

There are over a dozen broad categories (and upwards of 25,000 specific applications) for industrial hemp: textiles; cordage; construction products; paper and packaging; furniture; electrical; automotive; paints and sealants; plastics and polymers; lubricants and fuel; energy and biomass; compost; food and feed. Henry Ford

*Used in Earth Home

used hemp, wheat, straw and synthetic plastic for the fenders and hemp and other agricultural materials in the fuel of his early prototype Ford automobiles. Farmers in Europe have been growing hemp for over 20 years without any problems related to marijuana.

Until the late 1800s, almost all of our cloth was made from hemp, and virtually all of our paper was made from hemp rags. From 1631 to the early 1800s, hemp was such a valued commodity that it was considered legal tender (money). Regions of Kentucky and Wisconsin were among the largest hemp producers. Hemp production seemed destined to increase substantially in the 1930s when an invention called the decorticator began getting wide attention. The decorticator strips the hemp fiber from the stalk. This had been the most labor-intensive and expensive part of producing hemp and would revolutionize production similar to the way the cotton gin did.

2. Hemp in Construction

a. Construction Material Background

Hemp-based construction products can be used in place of cement, timber, gyprock (sheetrock), plaster, insulation and acoustic tiles. Washington State University's Wood Composite Laboratory has tested hemp for use as medium density fiberboard. It found that hemp is twice as strong as wood. French, German, Hungarian, Polish and US companies now make hemp-based construction and insulation products. Many other countries grow the raw material and/or manufacture hemp paper, and could adapt to more diverse production when demand is sufficient.

b. Isochanvre (Direct Concrete Substitute)

The newest and best product to be created from Cannabis Sativa Hemp, "Isochanvre", comes from France. Hemp, or 'Chanvre', is cultivated by French farmers under government contracts, as is tobacco. It is sold as two different products: Isochanvre Insulation and Isochanvre Construction.

The best way to describe this product is to call it a non-toxic replacement for cement, lumber, sheetrock, plaster, insulation and acoustic tiles. Isochanvre is non-flammable, fungicidal, antibacterial, waterproof and inedible by rodents and termites. Due to the high silica content of hemp and the ability of Isochanvre to retain the plant's qualities, it has the ability to store warmth and give it back after a while, making for very energy-efficient buildings. Because of its strength and flexibility, Isochanvre is an ideal construction material for areas susceptible to earthquakes, tornadoes and hurricanes. Isochanvre worked with lime is supple, water-resistant, and seven times lighter than concrete. It can be poured directly onto an existing floor to raise the level, repair, and insulate.

Molded walls can be poured in framing. For a rough finish, wood forms can be used. For a finer surface, smooth or plastic casings should be used. After the forms are removed, the surface can be smoothed with a roller and a lime wash. The color of Isochanvre is a creamy ochre (the color of hemp). After it's completely dry, it can be painted, textured or wallpapered - but this will interfere with its acoustic qualities. It can be troweled on in thicknesses less than 10cm. which should be an excellent product to finish straw-bale construction. Isochanvre petrifies itself, the hemp fibers, bound with lime, become mineral over time, making a building stronger and more valuable with age. So hemp seems to be a totally sustainable, non-toxic building alternative to wood and concrete.

3. Hemp in Insulation (See Isochanvre section)

4. Hemp Fibers for Clothing

The hemp stalk is composed of 20% fiber. Hemp is the strongest natural fiber in the world. It is valued for its strength and durability when used for textiles, cordage, and paper. The fiber can be made into any type of cloth, from the finest linen to the coarsest canvas. Cloth made from hemp fiber is stronger, warmer, more durable, more absorbent, and softer than cotton.

*Used in Earth Home

Hemp stalks produces long, strong bast fibers that make clothing with good insulating and absorbing properties. Clothing made from hemp is having a resurgence in the U.S. and consumer options are expanding greatly.

5. Hemp for Concrete Binder (See Concrete Binder section)

6. Other Hemp Products (See also Paint files)

Hemp consists of three principal raw materials: fiber, seeds, and hurds. Hemp is principally grown for the bast fiber it produces from its stalk. However, the seeds and hurds are also important economically.

French hemp manufacturers also make ropes, bags, textiles, paints, heating and lubricating oils, pharmaceutical products, animal food and abrasives from the sap, which is rich in silica. Hemp seed oil made into paint/varnish dries quickly and leaves a thin elastic film. Hemp-based paints have already proved their superior coating and durability characteristics. Surfboard makers in Sydney, Australia are making fiberglass-free surfboards, which are instead sheathed in a knitted hemp fabric, sourced from Eastern Europe, Nepal and China, and knitted in Melbourne.

Hemp rope (cordage) has been valued throughout history for its superior strength and resistance to deterioration in salt or fresh water. Hemp can also be made into paper. Paper made from hemp is known as the "archivist's perfect paper" because it lasts much longer than tree pulp paper and does not harden, crack, yellow, or crumble with age. Hemp fiber can be used to make every grade of paper.

The hemp seed is composed of 30% oil. Hemp seed oil for food contains over 70% cholesterol-fighting essential fatty acids, the highest of any seed oil. The seed cake is the solid part of the seeds that remains after the oil is expelled and makes a nutritional, high-protein supplement to wheat flour. The hemp seed can be eaten as a nutritious snack, like sunflower seeds.

Hemp seed oil can also be chemically combined easily with 15% methanol to provide a very good diesel fuel substitute.

7. Legal Status of Hemp

Industrial hemp means those parts of the Cannabis sativa plant which contain less than 1.00% tetrahydrocannabinols (THC). THC is the psychoactive chemical found in Cannabis sativa. Industrial hemp is not to be confused with marijuana. Marijuana comes from the flowers of the Cannabis sativa plant and contains more than 1.00% THC.

Hemp is illegal to grow in the United States, but not to wear. Industrial hemp is grown in nearly 30 countries, and as of October 2005, legislators in 22 U.S. states have introduced bills calling for a re-examination of the law prohibiting its cultivation in the United States. The legislation essentially requires a legal distinction between hemp fiber and marijuana by defining/classifying any cannabis sativa with less than 0.3% THC as hemp fiber.

D. Building Lime as Concrete Alternative (See EH Tabs section)

NOTE: There is some duplication in this section from the EH Tabs section due to the importance of lime and other concrete substitutes as an alternative building material.

1. Lime vs. Portland Cement

Lime is a remarkable and versatile material. It has a long tradition of use in building and agriculture and in many other industries; it can be make from a great variety of raw materials, some of which are abundant; and its

*Used in Earth Home

manufacture is essentially simple and can be carried out economically on a small scale. Yet the value and potential of lime is today strangely underestimated, particularly in the building industry, where it is most needed.

Most forms of building construction require a cementing agent or binder. Lime was the most commonly used cementitious binder until about a century ago, when its use started to decline. It was replaced by Portland cement, a material essentially developed for structural purposes in the era of the industrial revolution. Portland cement has certain advantages over lime when strength and rapidity of hardening are required, and because there are agreed quality standards. It has now become the dominant cementitious binder, thanks in part to aggressive marketing.

Cement mortars crack and craze because of their rigidity and brittle nature, as well as the daily expansion and contraction due to the variations in the weather and temperature. Cement mortars have the added disadvantage that there is no free lime solution to seal the cracks. If a crack did seal, it would break again because of the continued movement of the mortar.

2. Lime Uses

a. Historical Lime Construction

Historically, the most important cement was unquestionably lime, used the world over for thousands of years. Before Portland cement became available, lime concretes were used for many applications in building works and in civil engineering. One of the earliest lime concrete floors discovered is dated about 5600 B.C. This was one of a number found adjacent to the river Danube at Lepenski Vir in Yugoslavia.

Survivals from ancient Rome include the structural core for walling, floors, cisterns, baths, aqueducts, dams, vaults, and domes. The Romans developed lime concrete for structures that have not been surpassed, examples of which date from 300 B.C. Probably the most recognized Roman building that was build using stone rubble walls cemented together by "Roman concrete' (lime and imported volcanic soils from Pozzuoli, Italy now "pozzolans") was the Pantheon in Rome.

Harbors, canals, bridges, and the foundations for large structures in the eighteenth and nineteenth centuries made extensive use of lime concrete. In the cold northern regions of Scotland and Wales lime plasters protect even stone walled buildings from harsh weather and fierce rains

Many of the most important historic buildings regularly visited and in use today owe their presence and continued stability to lime concrete foundations. Examples in the UK include the Houses of Parliament, Westminster Bridge, Lincoln Crown Court, and the British Museum. Also many of the heritage buildings in Australia were built using lime. They include decorative fronts of the buildings in Fremantle, country towns, and the few left in Perth, as well as Government house and Treasury Building. These moldings are still in good condition and most are around 100 years old.

b. Present Lime Construction

After more than a century of eclipse, building limes are coming back into favor, not only with conservationists but also with architects. Sir Michael Hopkins' new Glyndebourne Opera House in Sussex, England uses lime mortar throughout. In more recent times, lime-ash mixes have been used to make upper floors in mills, factories and homes.

c. Alternative Builders Using Lime

Some alternative builders are eliminating cement altogether. They are using quicklime, slaking it, and adding prickly pear cactus gel (nopal) to mixtures as a binder. Most builders can use hydrated lime soaked in water to make a plastic, workable mix. Straw bales perform well with lime based plasters and earthen plasters. Lime plasters dry more slowly, gaining strength over time, which is their advantage for owner-builders. (See Lime Uses-Strawbales section)

d. Other Uses for Lime

Up until the mid 1960s the wood stove and copper were always built in with lime rich mortar because it was unaffected by intense fire and didn't expand or contract whether fired or cold. The lime mortar always outlasted the life of the wood stove or copper. Lime is also very important for soil enhancement. (See Soil section)

3. The Advantages of Lime

a. Versatile

Lime is a very versatile material which can be used for many purposes in construction. Lime-based renders allow walls to breathe so that moisture can disappear without damaging the structure. Lime mortars are much more suitable than cement mortars for use with earth-based building techniques, because they are less rigid and more permeable. They are also very suitable for decorative purposes. Architects and builders are beginning to realize that there are advantages in having a choice of binders for different applications; even where cement is preferable for structural purposes, lime often makes a better render. In Europe, the conservation sector is a prime mover in the resurgence of lime s a building material. In developing countries this role is often taken up by development agencies.

b. Abundance/Lower Cost

The abundance of limestone world-wide means there is a high probability that this valuable low-cost resource will be available in geological formations not too distant from wherever it is required.

c. Environmental Advantages

The many environmental benefits to be gained by a return to appropriate uses of building limes are significant. These include the ability to manufacture locally on a small scale and to produce a binder at lower temperatures, using less energy than most currently available binders. In addition, by increasing local production and availability, associated transport, pollution, and cost may be correspondingly reduced. ***It is estimated that the production of Portland cement accounts for 7-8 % of the total greenhouse gases produced on earth by human activity!***

d. More Reasons to Use Lime

--Lime allows buildings to breathe
--Lime provides a comfortable environment
--Hygroscopic materials such as lime plasters, mortars and renders stabilize the internal relative humidity by absorbing and releasing moisture
--Free lime enables autogenous healing by precipitation
--Lime provides good adhesion because the fine particle size of lime are far smaller than cement.
--Lime mortars can protect adjacent materials. Lime mortars with high free lime content have the benefit of high porosity and high permeability. These characteristics allow lime mortars to protect other adjacent materials by handling moisture movements through the building fabric and protecting masonry materials from harmful salts.
--Lime renders can assist drying out by evaporation
--Lime mixes have good workability
--Lime binders can be durable and have stood the test of time. When used carefully, lime is exceptionally durable. Caesar's Tower at Warwick Castle has stood the test of time for over 600 years, and many cathedrals have stood longer. An outstanding example is the Pantheon Temple in Rome which has a lime concrete dome spanning over 43 meters (142 feet). This has survived for nearly 2,000 years.
--Lime finishes are beautiful
--Lime contributes to a healthy environment. Due to its alkalinity fresh lime is caustic and has been used, often in the form of limewash, for its disinfectant qualities. Lime is also used for water purification.

--The use of lime has ecological benefits. Lime stone can be burnt at relatively low temperatures to achieve full calcinations. Kilns need to reach 900 to 1,000°C as opposed to 1,300 to 1,400 for OPC. Free lime absorbs carbon dioxide in the setting process of carbonation. It is possible to produce lime locally on a small scale and if this is done the consequent reduction in long distance transport also has ecological benefits.

4. Lime Technology

a. Naturally-Occurring Forms of Lime

Calcium carbonate occurs in many forms, of which one of the most common is limestone. The formation of limestone often involves a sedimentary process. Sediment may contain widely varying quantities of silica, alumina, and other minerals and compounds. In using limes, one must consider which limes are available and the most suitable, in order that the appropriate classification is selected and specified for the use.

b. Lime Manufacture

Lime does not occur naturally but must always be manufactured. Quarried lime is burned in special kilns at high temperatures. Wood was the original fuel used for lime-burning and wood firing still produces some of the best quality limes. In the manufacturing processes the material passes through several stages, as follows.

The raw material is calcium carbonate which is usually quarried as limestone, but may also be found as chalk, coral rocks or shells. When this is heated in a kiln it undergoes a chemical change, giving off carbon dioxide gas and forming calcium oxide. This is commonly known as quicklime or lump-lime. When quicklime is combined with water it changes to calcium hydroxide, commonly known as slaked lime, hydrated lime or often just "lime".

c. Lime Cycle

This lime can slowly absorb carbon dioxide from the air to form calcium carbonate. As this is chemically the same as the raw material, the whole process is often seen as a cycle, but in practice the carbonated lime which is finally achieved may be very different physically from the limestone or other original material.

Thus, lime from many different sources all have one thing in common and that is the cycle of heating, setting, and return to the same chemical makeup. The following figure shows this in graphic form.

d. Lime Characteristics

Although each lime is different, and some may perform in very special ways, there are certain characteristics which are typical of most limes and set them apart from other binders such as cement, gypsum, and clay. Lime possesses the following characteristics;

1) Stickiness
2) Workability (plasticity and water retention)
3) Durability
4) Soft Texture
5) Breathability (high porosity, high permeability)
6) Low thermal conductivity
7) Autogenous healing
8) Protection

*Used in Earth Home

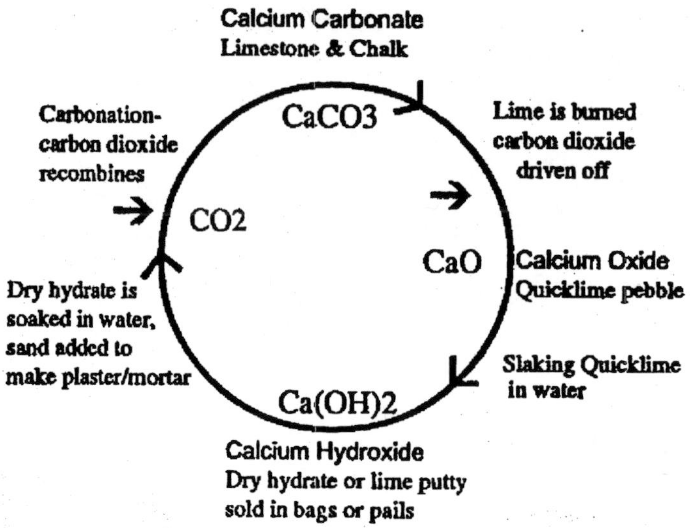

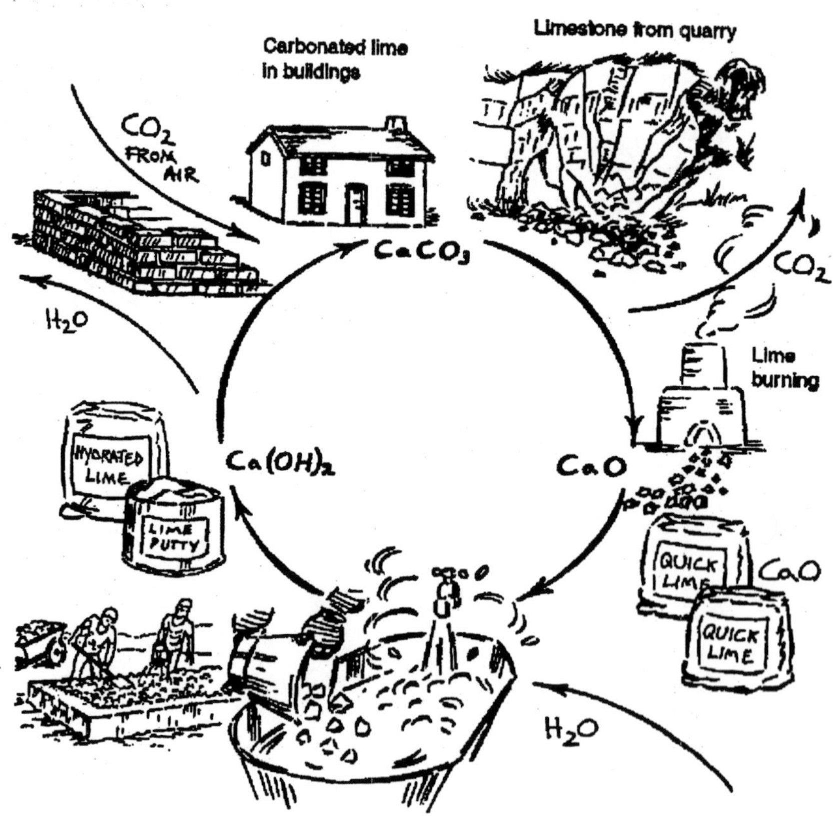

Figure 45-LIME CYCLE

*Used in Earth Home

e. Two Basic Ways to Set Limes

There are two ways in which limes may set. The first is a slow combination with carbon dioxide gas (a component of the air) in a process called carbonation. Limes that set using the air are called air limes. Nearly all limes set to some extent by carbonation, which is the only way that the purest limes gain strength. The air limes hold more water in their pastes (lime putties) that gives it the workability needed for mortars. They also hold their water against the suction of porous backings. Air limes are also slow to set, which are the properties needed for plastering work.

Limes may also be set by combination with silicates and aluminates in the presence of water in what is called hydraulic set. The hydraulic set is a property exhibited by limes which contain active clay impurities. In many cases the proportion of these impurities is low and carbonation remains important, but for some limes the hydraulic set is predominant. Hydraulic limes are most appropriate where strength is important or where lime must set in permanently damp conditions.

f. Workmanship/Issues with Lime

The raw materials available, production methods used, and the standard of workmanship will all have a major effect on final quality. One has to understand the requirements of a certain construction use as well as local conditions before finalizing a specification for a lime. It is quite possible that local materials, although not "standard", will be suitable-provided appropriate methods of preparation and application are employed.
The use of untried local materials can be both exciting and rewarding provided serious failures are avoided. If well tried and tested principles are followed through, it is possible that untried local materials may be used with success. If this is the intention, then small-scale trials will be essential. An example might be to make sample wall panels for artificially accelerated weathering tests, or to watch the natural weathering over several years.

g. Forms of Purchased Lime

The type of lime available in the US, whether high calcium or dolomitic, hydrated or hydraulic, can be made into many forms. Lime can be crushed or ground, sold as lump or pebble quicklime, or wet quicklime putty in containers, and also sold as dry hydrated lime. The forms of lime include bagged quicklime, lime putty in cans, dry hydrated lime in bags or bulk, or dry hydraulic hydrated lime in bags.

5. Using Lime in Construction

a. Lime as a Versatile Binder

When it is used well, lime is quite simply the best and most versatile binder in the world. There is a wide variety of limes which might be produced from differing materials and with various production methods.

Building lime has been used as a binder for building work for thousands of years, due to its unique setting properties and the exceptional smoothness which it offers when it is worked. Its versatility is shown by the wide variety of uses to which it is put. Structural elements for which lime mixes may be used in appropriate designs include foundations, walls, floors, vaults and roofs. Lime is also used for many finishes including paints, plasters, renders, and decorative work such as cornices and hand-modeled stucco.

b. Lime as a Render/Stucco for Exteriors

Architectural historians tend to use the work stucco to denote an exceptionally hard, durable, fine-textured plaster render for exterior finishes. Exterior walls can be made using building limes with various formulas and the "breatheability" of the wall can be adjusted. There is current debate on how best to make protective stuccos and plasters on strawbale houses, for instance.

The base of the wall is the most vulnerable part, being exposed to frequent contact with surface water, abrasion and impact. Care must be taken to protect the base of the wall from moisture using a buffer material such as concrete blocks or other materials. The basic Welsh saying of "a good boots and cap", meaning a water proof foundation or footing, and a wide overhang roof, will protect most walls. Wicking moisture from the ground will carry salts into the walls, mortar, and plaster.

c. Lime as a Plaster for Interiors

Interior coatings or plasters, make rooms easier to clean, reduce the risks of vermin and insects, and generally make a significant improvement to hygiene. The plaster gives a surface which can be bright and attractive by itself or can form a base for decoration. It is also incombustible and can be used to improve fire resistance, an attribute particularly useful for timber-frame buildings.

d. Lime Mortar Render over Strawbales

1. Lime Mortar Render Importance/History

Lime mortars have been used on almost all the strawbale houses and structures in Western Australia and have proved very successful. There are two forms of lime used in these strawbale buildings, hydrated and hot or lump. At present hot lime either as putty or in a dry form is preferred for plastering strawbales. Hot lime is well known as being the best and safe plasticizer. The addition of hot lime into cement and sand mixes makes mortars not only easier to work but flexible. These mixes that have the addition of hot lime are known as composition mortars (compo).

Lime mortar render is essential in allowing the passage of air and moisture to pass through the walls. When walls become saturated from leaky roofs, water-pipes, or from flooding, the strawbales have to lose the excess water very quickly. Lime mortar is the only cladding to provide this advantage.

Lime mortar is applied to strawbales in three coats similarly to plastering onto any form of lathing. The first coat covers the straw ends and lath to form a base to which it is keyed. This coat is often called a "pricking up" coat or "scratch coat". There is a six week minimum between coats to allow mortar to carbonate.

The second coat is a strengthening or float coat. Its purpose is to shape and straighten the walls and ceilings. The third is the finishing coat. It provides the desired surface finish or "fining up", a process of finishing the surface rendering with a teak float to provide a compact and water resistant surface. The lime mortar as a protective cladding over straw bales has the additional advantage that it is vermin resistant and a disinfectant

2. Advantages of Lime Mortar Render with Water

Lime mortar render is essential in allowing the passage of air and moisture to pass through the walls. When walls become saturated from leaky roofs and/or water-pipes, or from flooding, the strawbales have to lose the excess water very quickly. Lime mortar is the only cladding to provide this advantage.

Lime mortar will withstand the variation in daily temperature and movement of the structure. It is flexible enough not to form large cracks on the surface and is assisted by the consistent insulative properties of the straw on the internal surface of the render.

Cracks that occur due to structural movement seal through a process known as homogeneous healing. Cracks become rivers during storms or wet weather and the water carries a solution of lime that deposits along the cracks and eventually seals with a pure lime similar to the formation of a stalagmite/stalactite in a cave.

Lime mortar as a protective cladding over straw bales has the additional advantage that it is vermin resistant and a disinfectant. Mice dislike boring holes through it because lime burns eyes and skin. Although mice may take advantage of damaged areas and make a home inside, they would not be able to live off the straw material. Lime has been used as a disinfectant for centuries, usually as a whitewash.

*Used in Earth Home

Lime mortar as a protective cladding over straw bales has the additional advantage that it is vermin resistant and a disinfectant. Mice dislike boring holes through it because lime burns eyes and skin. Although mice may take advantage of damaged areas and make a home inside, they would not be able to live off the straw material. Lime has been used as a disinfectant for centuries, usually as a whitewash.

3. Applying Lime Mortar Render

Lime mortar is applied to strawbales in three coats similarly to plastering onto any form of lathing. The first coat covers the straw ends and lath to form a base to which it is keyed. This coat is often called a "pricking up" coat or "scratch coat". There is a six week minimum between coats to allow mortar to carbonate.

E. EH Stucco on Flax Bales/Post and Beam Construction

The Earth Home is designed to be a combination flax bale (with ferrocement coating) and post and beam construction.

1. Post and Beam Overview

a. Post and Beam Background/History

Pole construction has been popular since the 1930's with a global tendency to build on poles or stilts going back thousands of years. Although pole building is a very old system of construction, building with poles and posts has become increasingly popular in modern times. A basic pole/post and beam structure frame consists of the following:

-Vertical supports, which are either circular poles or rectangular posts embedded in the ground;
-Horizontal members, often called nailing girts, fastened to the sides of the poles to anchor the wall covering;
-Rafters or trusses supported by horizontal girders and diagonal braces;
-and supports, usually referred to as purlins, fastened to the rafters or trusses to anchor the roofing frame together and to provide a fastening surface for the roofing.

The poles are embedded in the ground and extend to the top of the building to support the roof, providing a structure quite like skyscrapers in engineering and design.

b. Comparison with Other Methods Discussion

Stud-frame structures, as well as most post-and-beam or timber-frame buildings, must first have a poured concrete slab or foundation to support the great weight of the home itself. Traditional homes use a concrete footing approximately 1' x 2' underneath all the block walls. The frame structure is then constructed on top of and anchored to the foundation or slab. The additional cost, time, labor, and skill needed for the concrete portion of the building is a major disadvantage with these building techniques.

c. Post and Beam Advantages

I chose pole-barn-type or post-frame construction for many reasons. The inherent design of pole buildings offers increased fire safety and wind resistance, which is a prime factor for their use in hurricane-prone areas. The poles transfer wind, snow, and building loads directly into the ground. This style is easily adaptable to the most difficult sites: steep hills, rocky soils, marshy or floodland areas, sand beaches, hurricane or earthquake zones.

This construction method is also easy and cost-effective. To sum up, the advantages of post-beam construction include:

- Eliminating foundations
- Replacing footings with pier footings
- No concrete forms
- Posts form the main framework
- Bracing is greatly reduced
- Lower-cost construction/maintenance

Poles themselves spread flame slower than smaller wood sections and they can be made to last 50 years or more. A preservative is pressure impregnated in the wood fibers--especially in the top 12 inches of soil where most decay and insect attacks occur. Concrete "pads" under the poles effectively carry the weight of the home—the roofs and walls.

2. Flax Bale Advantages

a. Flax History

The first recorded uses of flax come from Southern Mesopotamia where flax was grown as long ago as 5,000 B.C. Flaxseed was once a staple food source utilized by the ancient Greeks, Romans, and Egyptians. By the 8th century, the Roman emperor Charlemagne ruled that every citizen of the Roman empire had to consume flaxseed daily to maintain health.

b. Nearly Indestructible Organic Fiber

First off, the difference between hay and straw is that hay is cut when the plant is about to form seed, or has just formed seed and is at its highest protein content. Straw is the stalk left after the grain has been harvested and has no protein content. It may provide a home for creatures if unprotected, but they would be unable to live on it.

I have decided to use flax fibers instead of straw because of more flexibility with flax and the durability of the fiber. Also, I believe that any organic fiber must be placed in a vertical orientation to stand the test of time for settling purposes. I also chose flax because the concrete sticks to it better and acts as an organic stucco lath. It also was easier to fireproof.

c. Flexibility to Vary Consistency of Fibers

Flax has the unique quality of being able to vary the actual consistency of the fibers. After the flax is cut down and begins to age on the ground, it changes. It begins to take up water and organisms begin to break it down. After many months, the fibers are soft and "spongy-like". The farmers describe it as more "wool-like". After it is baled, the mass looks as if all the air is out of it and it appears to take on a more cloth-like appearance. The color changes from a light brown to gray. The R-value may also change, but no testing has been carried out to my knowledge.

d. Fiber Orientation Q & A/Discussion

Most of the bale construction orients the fibers in a horizontal position. Following is typical comments expounding the horizontal orientation and counterarguments for vertical orientation:

1) The strings last longer.

Counterargument: the strings are not what gives strength to a wall. It is the concrete in the final cured form that is the lion's share of the structural support.

2) Bales are stronger in horizontal orientation.

*Used in Earth Home

Counterargument: Actually compression strength along the grain of wood, for example exceeds the compression strength sideways by a huge margin. An organic fiber is much less compressible in the long grain orientation. There are countless stories of a a piece of straw being imbedded into a tree by the force of a tornado. Also, when a fill material is used between bales to transfer load from one to another, a continuous column is created which can handle heavier loads without deflection or settling.

3) Horizontal orientation allows notching and curving.

Counterargument: If one were interested in making a wall into artwork or spending more time making an exterior wall more beautiful, this argument would stand up. Any adjacent interior walls will most likely be dealt with similar to any other wall in that shelves are hung from the wall and decorations put upon them. If the argument is that the lime, concrete, or plastered wall cannot be attached to with commonly available fasteners, then a counterargument would be that whatever is put on the wall can be moved as opposed to permanent notches cut into the wall.

4) Bales are more stable when laid flat as the wall rises.

Counterargument: This is a simple gravity and geometry case and is true. Vertical orientation would need pinning for structural integrity until the concrete stucco is cured. Actually horizontal bales are most often pinned as well to keep them in position.

5) Pinning is more difficult.

Counterargument: this is simply untrue. Would it be harder to drive a steel pin sideways into a bale against the grain or sideways parallel to the stalks of flax? The only disadvantage is that the pins may have to be slightly longer in length.

e. Fireproofing Flax Bales

I've experimented with making the flax material fireproof. There are two methods I've worked with that are both successful. One is to spray a mixture from U.S. Borax Corporation, making the flax fireproof after drying. Another material I used was borax in a 5 mol. granular form. I mixed it up with water and sprayed it using a little larger nozzle size. Either method fireproofs the flax fibers very well. Future plans call for the flax to be fireproofed as it is baled to get more penetration on all the fibers.

3. Earth Home Ferrocement/Flax Skin Construction

The material formulation I chose was "ferrocement" which became popular in boat building days. A structure is built with a wire-mesh skin, and cement is troweled onto the wire mesh. When the concrete sets, it contains the steel similar to rebar. Ferrocement boats were constructed with an amazingly waterproof concrete. These boats lasted a very long time and were very seaworthy.

Ferrocement is also known as ferro-fiber cement or composite shell construction. It is a very low-cost composite material made of ordinary Portland cement, sand (or even better, microfine rock dust filler), and distributed fiber reinforcement. It is typically used to create shell structures. (See Concrete-Based Construction section)

a. Stucco Lath Alternative

On Earth Home I a special wire mesh called "stucco lath" was used and troweled over with a rich mixture of concrete called stucco. This expensive stucco lath will be replaced with flax fibers directly on Earth Home II. Testing showed that the concrete stucco held onto the fibers very strongly with the other ends of the fibers still interwoven in the baling process.

b. Ferrocement Over Flax

In Earth Home II, I decided to use flax as both an insulator and structural support for the outside skin. This combination seemed to have the best qualities that I was looking for.

The flax is placed sideways on the top of the containment footing. This way, the flax fibers have a vertical orientation for maximum structural support. This also increases insulation value as opposed to "flat" bale construction. The rounded ends of the flax bales are removed, so they may be placed tightly end-to-end to prevent air leakage from the inside wall to the outside wall. After a course of flax bales is laid down, a thin bead of fiberglass insulation will be put on top of the flax. If any settling occurs, the fiberglass expands to take up the air space. Before the next course is laid down, a special tie-wire will be inserted from the inside to the outside to bind the interior wall to the exterior wall. The courses will be laid in this manner all the way to the top section, with the exception of the windows. These will be 2" x 14" treated wood construction with the windows set into this frame. ***The flax bales are 14" thick and give an approximate R factor of 32-42***. (University of Arizona research puts R factor of straw bales at R-3 per inch across the grain.)

I've been working with a method to spray the concrete onto the side of the flax bale, thus imbedding the concrete particles between the flax fibers for a natural stucco lath. I've mixed a very rich mixture of stucco using washed silica sand and Portland cement. The small particle pushes easily between the flax fibers, and the sharp particle hardens to form a durable material. The concrete can be colored easily, for example, by the addition of ferrous sulfate to get a yellowish-reddish brown.

c. Base of the Walls Protection

The base of the walls are the most critical part of the wall because of the moisture that collects there. It is important to keep this section as dry as possible. Some straw bale home builders are experimenting with a layer of car tires under the wall to keep them dry. The car tires are very resistant to rotting and degradation.

d. "Breathability" to the Exterior

It is important to construct the exterior walls to have the ability to trap moisture on the inside of the interior wall and to allow the exterior to "breathe". Any moisture that gets trapped inside the walls must have sufficient paths for the moisture to travel when the humidity on the outside gets lower. Failing to do this can result in black mold, which can be devastating to not only the structure, but the inhabitants as well. (See Black Mold Section)

e. Window Details (see Windows section)

F. Roofs

1. Roofing Background

Historically, roofs have been made of almost any material that water cannot permeate. The qualities I looked to include: durability, Btu's to produce and maintain, weight, fire rating, coating degradation, and resistance to insects and fungus.

2. Modern Roofing Materials Chart

The following figure summarizes modern roofing materials.

*Used in Earth Home

Type	Price $/sq.	Fire Rating	Life Years	Min. Slope	Weight lb./sq.
1. Asphalt Shingles (Organic)	90-175	C to A	15-25	2-in-12	235-390
2. Asphalt Shingles (Fiberglass)	90-175	A	20-30	2-in-12	210-390
3. Asphalt Roll	55-75	C to A	10-15	1-in-12	45-110
4. Asphalt Sheet (Corrugated)	55-65	C	20-25	2-in-12	80-120
5. Cedar Shingles	300-400	C	15-30	4-in-12	160-250
6. Cedar Shakes	300-400	C	20-50	4-in-12	200-300
7. Clay Tiles	250-500	A	45+	3-in-12	750-1500
8. Concrete Tiles	250-400	A	50+	4-in-12	850-1050
9. Slate Shingles	500-700	A	50+	4-in-12	700-1000
10. Steel	125-200	A	25	1-in-12	120-170
11. Copper	400-500	A	50+	1-in-12	100
12. Aluminum	150-300	A	35-50	3-in-12	35-65

Figure 46-MODERN ROOFING MATERIALS

*Used in Earth Home

3. Metal Roofs

a. History of Metal Roofing

Metal roofing has been used in Europe for thousands of years. The Holy Bible records the installation of metal roofing on the temple in Jerusalem by King Solomon around 970 BC (I Kings 6:22). Paul Revere handcrafted copper roofs in New England. The oldest aluminum roof in the world was installed in 1880 on the Chief Secretary's office building in Sydney, Australia, and it is still in sound condition. The cap of the Washington Monument, also aluminum, was installed in 1884 and has likewise experienced no problems.

b. Aluminum Roofing

Aluminum is similar to galvanized steel in many ways. Recycled aluminum started out as the first choice in roof coverings, but the recycled aluminum can companies use virtually all of the recycled aluminum cans to make more beverage containers. (Used beverage containers (UBC's) are 98% of the content of 3105 H24 aluminum). Virtually none of the recycled aluminum is available for roofing or other aluminum needs.

Aluminum (.050") roofing is lighter weight and has a much longer life. Also coatings such as "Kynar" add life to the roof. This lighter weight roof allows less static load bracing than the heavier galvanized steel. Even though aluminum is much more long lasting and may ultimately be the world's choice for roofing, it is expensive and consumes much energy at present. Steel roofing is used almost exclusively for this reason.

c. Galvanized Steel Roofing

Galvanized steel has become the most widely used roofing material in third world or low-income areas. It has worldwide availability and does not require huge amounts of energy to manufacture. Another advantage is that it can resist high temperatures. Sunshine can heat up roofs immensely.

The coatings that have been developed for steel make it more resistant to sunshine and moisture. Manufacturers are adding ceramic particles to simulate the skin of a tile. Also, they're increasing the structural strength and experimenting with different profiles. (See Roofing - Metal Roofing files.)

4. EH Roofing Details

a. Roof Design

1. Roof Materials

Galvanized steel roofing was chosen over aluminum because of the cost and world-wide availability. Newer painted and plated coatings such as "Kynar" add much more life to the roof.

2. Roof Air Channels

The roof of the Earth Home II will be sloped to the south to drain the water to the gutter system and into the cistern. The roof will be typically white in color, to reflect the intense summer heat. (See Roof Coloration Section) The southern edge may be black in the extreme north, to prevent ice build-up near the rain gutters. I found that a sloping metal roof to the south does not collect snow. In many cases the snow will melt as it lands. It has to be extremely cold for snow to stay on the roof. The corrugated roof of Earth Home I have air channels underneath, so the heated air flows from the south side upwards to the north side. In designing Earth Home II, I used no roof openings such as vents or stacks, other than the chimney. History has shown that whenever a roof opening is made, it increases the chance that the roof will leak at that point.

*Used in Earth Home

b. Scissor Truss System

I used a 5-12 pitch, or 5" rise for every 12" of run (or horizontal distance). The roof truss system for Earth Home II is a "scissors truss." (See Roofing - Trusses files) There is a slight pitch on the north side so that the north "roof" can be opened. The slanted north roof can become a vertical surface so the greenhouse area may be naturally vented through the roof cavity. (See EH Heat Prevention Details section)

c. Ceiling/Roof Insulation

The roof insulation I chose was stress-skin expanded polystyrene (E.P.S. foam). This material was *chosen because it does not contain CFC's, can be recycled, and has an R-value of up to 4.0 per inch. Eight (8) inches of EPS would total R-32 for the roof. The next choice was shredded newsprint with borax, commonly called cellulose.

5. EH Heat Prevention Details

a. Preventing Heat Build-up Under the Roof

1. Reflective/Radiant Foil

A reflective foil barrier is sometimes used immediately under a roof. This thin aluminum foil product reflects radiant energy back to the outside, thus lowering the temperature of the attic space. Aluminum reflects 94.5% of UV radiation. Radiant foils are just emerging in the marketplace, having their beginnings in Florida, Texas, and the Southwest. A perforated foil helps to prevent moisture build-up on the underside of the roof. (See Roofing - Reflective Foil file and Cooling-Humidification System-Preventing Heat Build-up section)

2. Roof Coloration

Colors of a roof can affect heat build-up immensely. Dark colors absorb the sun's energy faster and light colors reflect energy. The Earth Home uses a similar color scheme as awnings. Some awning manufacturers have learned that a dark band near the eave will heat up and begin to draw heat away from the eave. The rest of the awning is light color to reflect the sun's rays. As the heated air moves away from the eave, it brings in cooler air under the awning. This system is used in the EH and allows the heated air to move along the air channels built into the roof construction.

b. "Passive Ventilation"

1. Reasons for Passive Design

The term passive generally refers to having no fans or pumps that can draw electricity. Many homes use *fans to exhaust great amounts of heated air from the greenhouse area. History has shown that greenhouses expend a considerable amount of energy in removing great amounts of the built-up summer sun shining on the clear material. If the heat is not removed fast enough, the plants will wilt, stunt, or die completely in only a short time. The design of the roof of the Earth Home uses the shape and thermosiphon effect to allow the great amounts of heat that enters through the clear panels to escape easily and without continuous fans or blowers.

2. Passive Vents Overview

The roof design includes a high ceiling in the greenhouse area with large hinged vent doors. These vent doors are connected to large plenums inside the scissor trusses. These passages rise up to the peak of the roof where they exit through the peak of the roof when the passive vents are in the open position.

*Used in Earth Home

The passive vent doors are large portions of the roof that are on hinges and can be simply tilted back to allow heated air to exit from the scissor truss plenums. The passive vent doors are designed to be opened with small motors that move slowly. The weight of the doors is balanced so that a small amount of energy is required and that gravity will return them to the closed position.

3. Wind Tunnel Testing

The top of the passive vent doors are exactly even with the top of the roof when in the open position. This will prevent eddy currents from the wind from pushing air back down into the home. Wind tunnel testing has proven that air exits the passive vent doors when the wind blows from any direction. The lower pressure at the opening created by the wind velocity also helps the airflow considerably. Sensors near the openings warn of impending rain or high winds that will harm the home.

G. Construction Details Overview

1. Foundation/Slab

a. Foundation Basics/Discussion

Foundation assemblies in conventional housing are often un-insulated. This is because during the heating season the ground is warmer than the outdoor air, and thus the heat loss to the ground is only a small percentage of the total heat loss. However, in an energy-efficient design, the percent heat loss would be too great. Thus it is necessary to use insulated foundations to decrease heat loss to the ground. *A notable exception to the foundation types above are the Finnish foundations. They use extremely heavily insulated slab-on-grade systems.*

b. Foundation Categories/Types

Foundations provide the structural support for the building. In cold climates, it is necessary to place the house footings below the frost line to prevent building shifts caused by ground freeze/thaw cycles. The basic three types of foundations are:

1. Slab on Grade

Slab-on-grades are used in warm climates and is the cheapest method. Since they are climate-specific, they will not be covered here.

2. Unheated Crawlspaces

Unheated crawlspaces are used in moderately cold climates where shallow excavations are necessary to prevent frost heave.

3. Full Basements

Full basements are used where excavations exceed 3-4 feet deep.

c. EH Foundation Details

1. Frost Discussion

The Earth Home uses a "frost curtain" around the north and west sides of the home. This one-layer flax bale groundcover with a concrete cover extends 6 feet from the base of the exterior wall. The reason for the curtain is to move the winter frost away from the base of the wall in order to avoid any shifting from the freezing ground. In this manner, deep frost footings are avoided at much lesser cost.

2. Full Basement Issues

I feel that a full basement is not necessary. Most people use them for seasonal storage, mechanical equipment, or playrooms. I feel they are not an economical use of resources. They came about because the need for frost protection went 3-4 feet deep and we humans are more than 4 feet tall!

I believe the need for below-grade space is for protection of mechanical and water systems, food storage, a stable temperature environment for batteries, and certain food products in common storage. ***The Earth Home foundation will copy the Finnish system except for a much smaller basement area to take advantage of the temperature stability that the soil offers.***

3. Basement Utility Area

In the new designs for Earth Home II compared to Earth Home I, I'm using the ground to protect the plumbing and water system from freezing. I also reduced the entire under-the-floor surface in Earth Home II and concentrated all the plumbing and water systems in one small area. The basement/utility area underneath the floors is very small, accounting for only 8' x 20' of area. This area holds the waste disposal, food storage system, battery storage area, cistern water storage, recycled water storage system, and most of the plumbing system. Most of the vulnerable utilities are kept at or below ground level in order to prevent freezing, should the house malfunction and lose the ability to heat in cold climates.

e. Floor/Slab in the Earth Home

1. Cascading Floor Levels for Water Flow

Ideally, water should cascade through the home and outside garden by gravity, from the highest vertical level and degree of purity to biological land treatment at the lowest level. The Earth Home attempts to use slight differences in floor levels, plumbing techniques, and gravity flow to attempt to simulate nature's way for water to flow naturally.

In addition to conserving water, there are other good reasons to cascade water and use it ultimately for irrigation—conserving dissolved nutrients, conserving the energy used to heat water, and eliminating what is otherwise a tricky disposal problem.

In the home, drinking is the highest use, followed by cooking, bathing, hand washing, dish washing and clothes washing. The last use in the cascade would be to dump feces into water if there are no other alternatives.

2. EH Floor Slab Details

The EH floor is designed to be a one-piece concrete "pier-like" slab poured over flax bales for heavy insulation. Similar slabs are being tested in Kitchener, Ontario. A corrugated steel sheath will be placed on the bare ground before the flax and concrete is poured. This gives the EH access to the stable ground temperatures for ventilation and pre-heat.

The slab or floor of the Earth Home is designed to be flax bales with vertical fiber orientation that is "encased" in concrete. The concrete webs give it structural support and the flax gives it insulation. Insulating the living space from the ground helps to stabilize temperatures and prevent moisture build-up from the soil. Above-mentioned testing in Canada has proven the principle and provided encouraging results. (See next section.)

d. Flooring Surfaces in the Earth Home

1. Cork Material

The EH flooring is designed to be made from natural cork or linoleum materials. Cork contains millions of enclosed air cells that make the floor very quiet, fire retardant, and very comfortable. Cork is a natural material made from the bark of one species of tree. Other recycled materials can be used to manufacture carpet such as

*Used in Earth Home

recycled pop bottles. This material also will be used in the living room. Hard flooring resists dust mites that have been known to cause allergies in many people. Bamboo flooring has also been recently developed and marketed.

2. Linoleum

Linoleum is a felt or canvas coated with linseed oil, cork, and resins. The Latin root of the word linoleum means flax or linen combined with oil. Linoleum is flooring that is manufactured by oxidizing linseed oil to form a thick mixture called linoleum cement. The cement is cooled and mixed with pine resin, and wood flour to form sheets on a jute backing. Linoleum is a flooring product that may develop into cottage industries for Earth Home inhabitants.

3. Reflexology Floor Surface (See also TCM Reflexology section)

In nearly every village in Taiwan they have built special paths of pebbles and every morning at 3 or 4 o'clock, people walk barefoot around the pebble path for a half hour before they go to work. Hundreds, even thousands do this and it has become a way of life. China has hundreds of the paths as well. In addition to China, cobblestone or reflexology paths exist in public areas in a variety of countries, such as Malaysia, Korea, and Germany. The Earth Home will include a cobblestone path (floor surface) to simulate smooth river rocks 1/2" to 2 1/2" in length with a height of 1/2" to / 1/2". A flip-down mat will be used in the bathroom floor in front of the sink. The following figure illustrates one model.

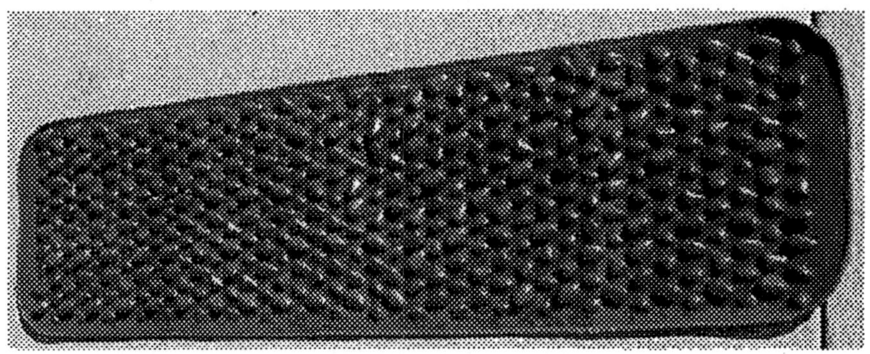

Figure 47-MANUFACTURED REFLEXOLOGY SURFACE

2. Basement/Utility Area

a. Water Storage and Processing

1. Storage Tanks and Filtration (See EH Rainwater section)

2. Aerobic Digester (See EH Digester section)

b. Food Processing/Storage

1. Vinegar Production (See also Food Preservation section)

The vinegar production area must be separated from any fermentation activities because of the organisms that cause the vinegar. These organisms can spoil any alcohol fermentation—which is the mechanism of vinegar production.

*Used in Earth Home

2. Fermentation Crocks (See Food Preservation section)

c. Composting/ CO, Area (See Air Quality section)

3. Internal Spaces

a. Efficient Use of Spaces

The shape I chose for this home is a one-story structure. I experimented earlier with two-story structures, thinking that the thermosiphon loop principle could be used to move the lighter and warmer heated air from the heat source below into the upper rooms. I found, however, that this method by itself could not move sufficient quantities of air to heat or cool the structure quickly enough to keep up with the outside temperature variations. Thus it was necessary to mechanically move air inside the structure to obtain uniform temperatures throughout.

Another advantage gained from moving air besides uniform temperature distribution was more personal comfort by mixing the plant oxygen-laden air with the carbon dioxide-laden air from the humans. The humidity from the plants could also be used to replace the humidified air going up the chimney. Using a one-story design also enabled much more use of solar energy through the greenhouse translucent panels as well as nearly doubling the rainwater collection potential.

In past experiments, I put fish tanks in the basement, hoping they would be kept from freezing. I found, however, that placing the fish tanks underneath the foundation made it more difficult to maintain them. Harvesting and feeding of the fish was more difficult, and the amount of natural sunlight was insufficient. The cistern (water storage tank) was left under the foundation to keep from freezing.

b. Internal Wall Construction

The internal walls will be a gypsum/lime mixture troweled directly on the inner surface of the flax bales. On top of that will be a vinyl coating to act as a vapor barrier. Other tabs can include adobe interior walls or other natural materials. (See EH Tab section)

c. Interior Space Allocation Overview

The underside of the roof trusses is sloped, so that the rooms can be independently moved around more easily without contacting the ceiling. The Japanese have actually used a system of spring-loaded walls so walls can be moved around inside of the home. This system was designed to take advantage of a family's changing needs for space, as children grow and gradually leave the home. Another advantage of the under-roof-heated space is that the HVAC system is inherently insulated.

Another concept to increase flexibility is the extra bed that is enclosed vertically in a large cabinet or "the fold-down guest room." In this way, additional space is created as needed, similar to storing a mattress or futon in a closet. Chests of drawers located under the beds are another way to increase usable space.

Non-gypsum products for the walls are preferred because of the "moisture-flywheel" effect. This is the long amount of time necessary to thoroughly dry out gypsum wallboard. Also, the large thermal mass of the walls makes it more difficult to heat up or cool down. A product just coming onto the U.S. market uses recycled paper and gypsum pressed into a wallboard. Metal studs for framing are also becoming more cost effective as their volume continues to rise. However, the "thermal bridging" effect has been shown to have a substantial negative effect when used on outside walls.

*Used in Earth Home

d. Ceiling Height

The ceiling height of the rooms are meant to be a standard 8 feet. However, the kitchen/living area has the ceiling elevated to meet the underside of the rafters. This could exceed 15 feet at the peak. Higher ceilings improve the feeling of openness and spaciousness inside a home. The high ceiling makes it easier to route the HVAC ducts also.

Ceiling height can be made any height within reason by using a tab in the design. (see Methology of Text-Tab section) In colder climates, a lower ceiling would help to hold the heat near the occupants. (See also Floor Elevations in Earth Home).

e. EH Loft Area

The top of the enclosed rooms in the earth home is available for a loft. Lofts can be used as storage, food storage, children play areas, and many other uses. By designing the truss system for more headroom has created a dual-use area without the cost of another full floor level. The loft cannot support the weight of a full floor joist system, but can support lighter loads. If the room ceilings were strengthened with stronger floor joists, more weight could be supported.

G. Sunlight Control and Uses

1. Exterior Shading Techniques

a. Edible Shrubbery

Shrubbery such as Rosa Rugosa and tall plants will be used for shading. No trees would be placed within 15 feet of the south glass and should be no more than 10 feet high to allow a certain amount of sunlight. (See Blueprints) The plants would be undersoil irrigated with treated water from the aerobic digester.

b. Edible Flowers

Edible flowers could also be used for ornamental purposes. Examples of edible flowers include marigolds, violets, lavender, nasturtiums, roses, hollyhock, honeysuckle, chrysanthemum, hibiscus, primrose, day lilies, daisies, gladiolus, marguerites, lilacs, sweet peas, and rose geraniums. Most of the dried petals from these flowers make delicious tea. Tender center violet leaves are very rich in Vitamins A and C.

c. Trellised Food Plants-Grapevines and Hops

Grapevines and hops plants will be used on the north side of the Earth Home. Shading from these trellised plants would shade the screened-in porch from the hot evening sun.

The hop cones can be used in beer brewing, but are not the only part of the plant that the farmers found useful. It was a common vine in the settler's kitchen garden. The young shoots in the spring were eaten as a special treat in salads, a wax extracted from the tendrils was used as a reddish-brown vegetable dye, the fibers were used in textiles as a substitute for flax, the stalks were used for basket and wicker-work, and the leaves and spent hops were an especially excellent food for sheep. Other uses for hops include using the natural resins for pellet binders. There is also one German patent for adding hops to sausages as a “natural” preservative and the Romans ate the young shoots of hops like asparagus. Hops has also been used as a treatment for acidosis

Other edible wild plants can also be used around the structure. American Indians used lamb’s quarters for greens and shepherd’s purse seeds for snacks much as we eat peanuts today. Gold miners avoided scurvy and created very elegant salads with miner’s lettuce. There are many more wild edible plants that can be used around the yard.

d. Mechanical Shading

Mechanical methods to provide shading are covered in Cooling/Humidification section.

2. Natural Lighting/Skylights

Natural sunlight will be allowed through the roof through fiberglass, "filon" or acrylic panels. These translucent roof panels match the profiles of the roof sections for a better fit. I found that natural sunlight near the center of the home is very desirable in terms of energy savings from lighting. In the typical 20th century home, lighting is a major source of power consumption. Reducing power usage will reduce the battery bank necessary for power storage. (See Electrical System section)

3. Windows

a. High Performance Windows Background

High performance windows can be defined as any window system that has a U-value of 1.5 W/sq.m.K) or lower, which is half of conventional double-glazed windows. These values are achieved through a combination of multiple glazing, low-emissivity coatings, inert gas fills, insulating edge spacers, low-conductivity frames and insulating shutters. The benefits are lower heating costs; reduced capital costs for heating and cooling equipment; reduced drafts; and elimination of condensation on windows.

b. EH Windows

The windows will be set into the 2" x 14" treated wood frame sections that form openings in the flax bales. The windows will be three layers of glass that disassembles for cleaning. They open casement-style for fresh air. There will be a small protrusion from the wall that will cover the top of the window opening. This small "roof" will protect the window from excessive moisture from rainfall. This system has been used successfully on stucco homes for centuries.

4. Sunshine Effects on Exterior (See Roofing section)

H. Ergonomic/Maintenance Features

1. Built-In Low Maintenance Features

a. Floor Grates

The Earth Home is designed to have a floor grate just inside all exterior entrances. This grate would capture soil and particles from shoes before they are tracked into the home. This would save cleaning time. Also, a grate system will be used near the woodstove to capture debris when wood is handled.

b. Raised Platform for Washer and Dryer

The washer and dryer are on raised platforms to make it easier on the back to bend over and take out clothes.

*Used in Earth Home

c. Exterior Lever-Style Door Handles

Ergonomic features such as lever handles on exterior doors will be used. Lever handles are much easier to unlatch when carrying other items and if the hands are cold or wet.

d. Handicap Access Ramps

Handicap ramps are used for the garage entrance and all access points.

2. Floor Maintenance and Cleaning

a. Central Vacuum Floor Maintenance and Cleaning

The floor on the Earth Home is meant to be cleaned with a central vacuum cleaner. This option allows efficient cleaning with a minimum of effort. One high speed motor uses a bagless system for low-impact operation. The final filter is user-cleanable with soap and water similar to the central HVAC filter.

b. Fabric Mops

Mops use recycled fabric as the mop material. Spring-loaded clamps hold the fabric in place when the mop is used.

3. Comparisons with Conventional Homes

a. Painting Exterior

Since the Earth Home is ferrocement with or without color added, it never needs painting. Some stucco-style homes have been virtually maintenance-free for 50-100 years.

b. Shingling Roof

The Earth Home roof is corrugated steel and has a lifetime much greater than asphalt shingles. Also, because the roof is sloped towards the south (in Northern Hemisphere), snow is melted off almost immediately. This does not give ice and moisture a chance to build up.

*Used in Earth Home

IV. COOLING-DEHUMIDIFICATION SYSTEM

A. Cooling Background

1. Ancient Cooling Techniques

a. Caveman Cooling

In prehistoric times, cave dwellers had little need for cooling because their caves were already cool. The rocks and the soil temperatures remained constant because of the even temperatures inside the earth itself. As humans became more civilized, sophisticated cooling systems evolved.

b. Ancient Roman Cooling

Cooling systems have changed greatly over the past thousands of years. The Romans built some of the earliest recorded cooling systems. They built their homes with very thick walls of stone, which is a natural "thermal battery." The temperature of the entire structure was lowered at night, and this massive rock dwelling remained fairly cool during most of the next day.

c. Iranian Wind Towers

In Iran, people used what is called "wind towers". These wind towers were tall, chimney-like affairs built up on top of homes to channel air in and out of the structures. This was done using a twin-scoop arrangement up to two stories above the house. The twin scoops were on opposite sides of the prevailing winds. As the wind blew from one side, the scoop channeled the air down into the home. The exhausted air then traveled back up the opposite side of the channel, and was released on the downward side of the wind tower. In this way, the homes kept a natural breeze going through them so that they were much more comfortable. The people (builders) in Iran were able to design their architecture this way because of the very <u>consistent</u> wind direction and speed. Wind scoops are also used in Egypt, Peru, Afghanistan, and Pakistan.

2. Cooling Technology

Humans can detect extremely small changes in temperature, humidity, and odor. This makes it more difficult to find optimal conditions for comfort. The human body produces about 75 watts (250 Btu/hr.) of heat all by itself.

a. Human Body's Cooling Mechanisms

What keeps a person cool is a function of many different conditions. The two main ingredients are temperature and humidity. A cool temperature keeps you cool simply because it's lower than your body temperature. Lowering the humidity keeps a person cool by increasing the rate of evaporation of perspiration from the skin. The skin has to give up energy to lose particles of water, and this evaporation causes the skin temperature to lower. This principle is the same as the "wind chill index" in the colder climates.

Various points on the human body sense the cooling effect much more quickly. The sensitive areas on the human body are the ankles, wrists, and head. When you are inside a building, your ankles are the most critical, because heat near the ceiling makes your head seem warmer, but even though your head is warm, your ankles are actually a trigger mechanism that causes your body to feel cold.

b. Basic Human Comfort Chart

The following figure shows the comfort chart for optimal comfort at various air speeds. ***Human comfort is a function of relative humidity, air speed, and temperature***

c. Categories of Cooling Employed

The following figure shows how cooling methods may be categorized.

d. Active vs. Passive Cooling Methods

In a passive cooling system, no energy is used for power. Air typically flows past a colder surface and then into the home. An active cooling system requires heat or electrical input to move the fluid. Common fluids involved in cooling are air, water, and refrigerants. ***Water was emphasized in the Earth Home system because of the higher amount of Btu's that it can hold per unit volume and earth-friendliness***. Most cooling systems in the United States and around the world depend on electrical energy to move air, water, refrigerant, and/or heat in some way or another.

In many places of the earth, standard cooling methods are twice as expensive as the heating methods, so cooling is a very important part of the energy needs of society.

B. Using the Earth for Cooling

1. Early American Architectural Cooling

a. Soddies

In the early pioneer days in the United States, settlers built sod homes with exterior walls up to two feet thick. The walls of these "soddies" would consist of moist dirt packed together with a clay material to resemble a finished wall. They were a good example of natural air conditioning because the high thermal mass of the walls kept the home cooler during the day.

*Used in Earth Home

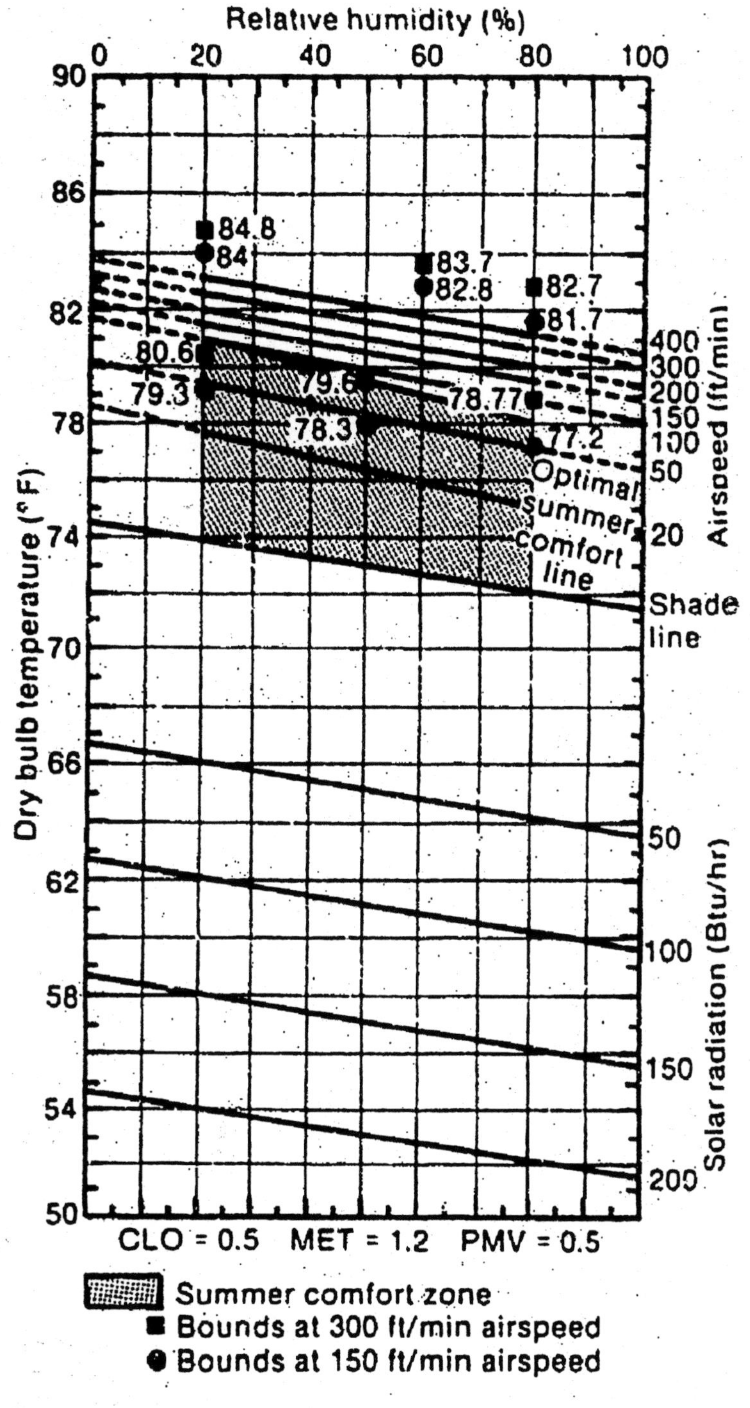

Figure 48-HUMAN COMFORT CHART

*Used in Earth Home

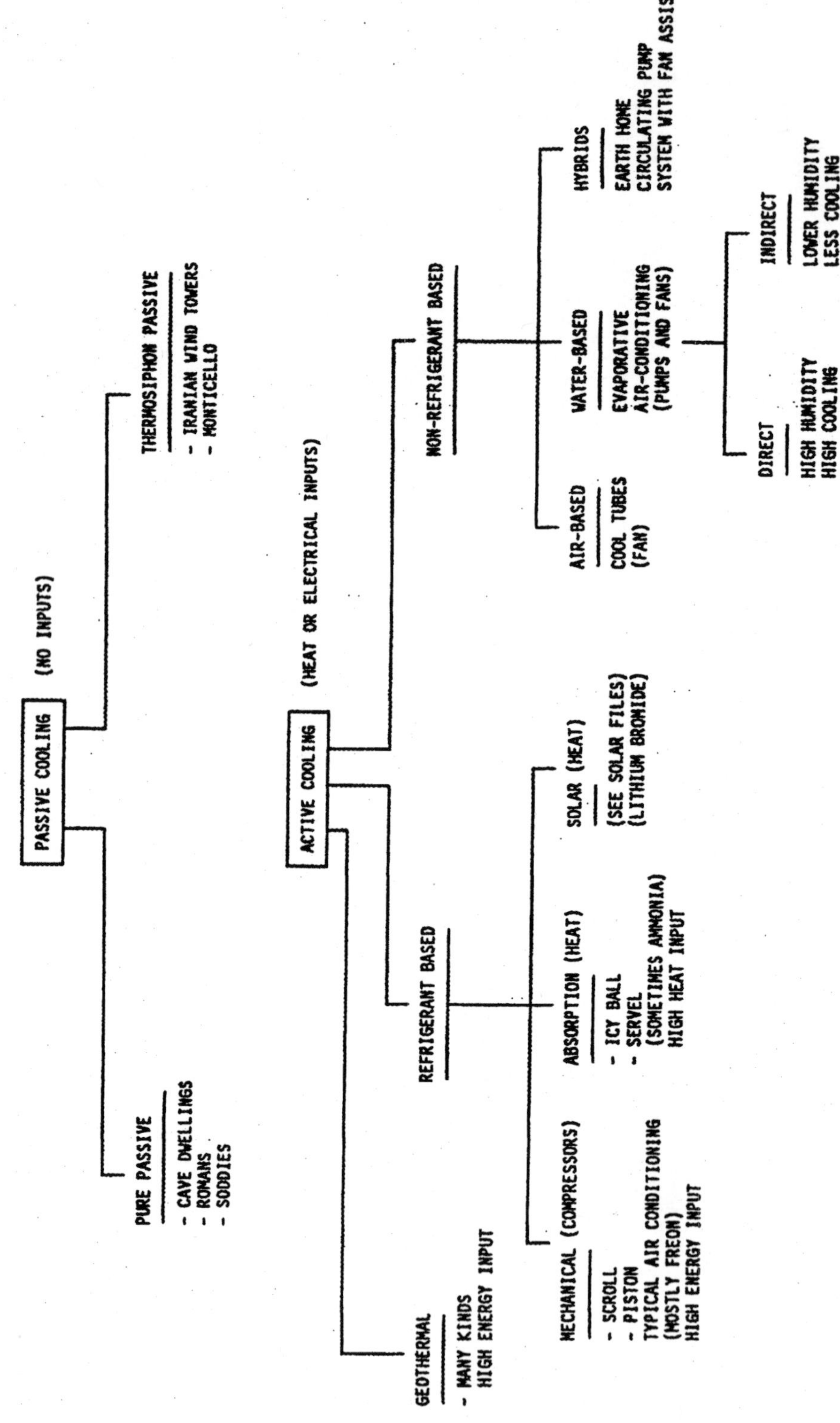

Figure 49-CLASSIFICATION OF COOLING METHODS

*Used in Earth Home

b. Jefferson's Monticello

Thomas Jefferson's home, Monticello, is a unique example of an early cooling system. A long central subterranean hallway that led out to a separate structure fed the hallways inside the home. The air was continually drawn into the home through this cool underground hallway, and drawn out through the upper windows on the second story of the home. This is an early example of the "thermosiphon loop" principle.

2. Modern Architectural Cooling

a. Underground Homes

Another method used for cooling is to bury or sink the house completely or partially into the ground. These homes were called underground homes or basement homes, and were wholly or partially built of concrete. The sidewalls stayed cool because they were shaded from the sun and in direct contact with the ground, very similar to a cave. One of the main advantages of underground homes is the lack of air conditioning costs. However, they are <u>more</u> than offset by the expensive concrete decking and materials/labor that are needed to waterproof the cement, such as bentonite, Bituthene, or urethane.

b. Basement Testing

I have done similar tests with older homes by opening up the basement door and closing all the other doors and windows except for a fan blowing out of an upstairs bedroom window. This cools for a couple of hours, but the limitation is the amount of "coolness" that you can extract from the surface of the basement walls. I found that the cooling is extracted in a very short period of time, and then the basement walls begin to heat up. Another drawback of this system is that the air that enters this structure is much more humid than the air that is inside the home already. The basement walls are wet and moist, and the incoming warm air evaporates this moisture off the walls and carries it throughout the home.

c. Cooling "Batteries" (See Thermal Mass section)

3. Cool Tubes (see Thermal Mass section)

C. Using Groundwater for Cooling

1. Evaporative ("Swamp") Coolers

An evaporative cooler is the scientific name for "swamp coolers." These evaporative coolers work by pushing air past a cool, damp surface, so that evaporation of water is what cools the air. ***<u>Evaporative coolers or swamp coolers are at their most efficient when working in an atmosphere between 35% and 40% relative humidity</u>***. They became very popular in the southwest part of the United States, Arizona, Texas, Nevada, New Mexico, Colorado, and Utah. Typically, evaporative coolers cool the air to 60% to 80% of the span between wet bulb and dry bulb temperature. (Dry bulb is normal air temperature and wet bulb uses a moistened pad over the mercury bulb to take humidity into account.) In a typical home in the southwest, they push enough air through the home so that the entire air volume of the home is completely changed about every three minutes.

Over a number of years, evaporative cooler manufacturers have developed new types of pad material to blow air through. Some of these pads include Kool pads, cool cells, and various cellulose papers. The cellulose is impregnated with a special salt to prevent rotting. The pads are also designed to be cross-fluted, so that the air speed stays constant at 250 feet per minute. These are scientifically designed so that a maximum amount of air comes in contact with the water. (See Cooling/Dehumidifying file.)

There are also manufacturing techniques that protect the leading edge of the media from the hot, dry air that first enters. The leading edge is where the most concentration of minerals and contaminants begin to deposit. By protecting this part of the cooling pad, the use of harsh biocides and cleaners can be avoided.

One disadvantage of this type of cooler that they typically evaporate or use roughly 8 gallons of water per hour in order to achieve enough cooling for an average home in the Houston area, for example. This water would need replacing and energy would be needed.

2. Indirect Evaporative Coolers

Another type of evaporative cooler is called an indirect evaporative cooler. In this type of evaporative cooler, the water is not in direct contact with the air, but rather is separated by a system of heat exchangers, tubes, or fins. The cool water is dripped around a tube and the warm air is blown through the center of the tube. In this way, the air loses its heat to the inside of the tube without picking up the humidity. In some installations all air is actually recycled inside the home using this system, so that the air is never in contact with the outside atmosphere. Studies have proven, however, that the indirect cooling does not work very well if the wet bulb temperature is above 65°F.

3. Radiant Cooling Systems

A recent study in radiant cooling has recently been demonstrated in a Kitchener, Ontario office building. Radiant panels cover some 30% of the ceiling. These panels absorb radiant heat and make the people "feel" comfortable. The same panels were used for heating. Condensation issues were dealt with using a dehumidifier system to keep the dew point low.

4. Heat Pumps (see Thermal Mass section)

D. Dehumidification Issues (See also Humidification under Heating section)

1. Relative Humidity Basics

Keeping the humidity from 35-50% inside the home is advantageous and cost-effective for reducing moisture damage. (See also Heating/Humidity section for humidity discussion.)

Blowing cold air around the home is only one aspect of cooling. Another very important aspect of cooling is called dehumidification. ***Dehumidification is the process of removing water vapor from damp air.*** The four generally accepted ways of lowering the relative humidity of moist air are: increasing the temperature, dehumidifying with a heat pump, removing moisture with sorbent systems, or simply mixing the moist air with dry air. If possible, it is better to get some of the moisture out of the air, rather than the other methods. There are three different methods of doing this: sorbent dehumidification (adsorbent/absorbent), refrigerant dehumidification, and air cycle dehumidification.

2. Sources of Moisture in the Home

Moisture in a home can come from many sources such as perspiration, gas stove gasses, showers, dishwater evaporation, and heat recovery ventilation (HRV) condensation. Other sources of evaporated moisture are houseplants, floor washing, framing lumber, furnishings, gypsum board, and concrete. (See the following figures) NASA has determined that as much as 4 lb. of moisture is given off by an adult human being in one 24-hour period. This moisture is a combination of perspiration and respiration. This moisture deserves special consideration because of the following problems that it can cause. ASHRAE says that 90% of all building failures are moisture related!

3. Problems of High Water Vapor Content

a. List of Problems

Any problematic high water vapor content in air can:

1. Create psychological stress and discomfort;
2. Encourage ill health;
3. Germinate mold and spores;
4. Accelerate the corrosion of metals;
5. Reduce the electrical resistance of insulators;
6. Spoil surface finishes;
7. Introduce premature chemical breakdown, including dry rot.

b. Black Mold/Toxic Mold and Sick Homes

When toxic molds such as stachybotrys, aspergillus versicolor, and some species of penicillium are involved, it can create serious problems. These molds—which grow in damp, dark places and often are hidden behind walls, under floors and above ceilings—produce dangerous airborne "mycotoxins." Many doctors believe they cause a raft of serious ills, including flulike symptoms, chronic fatigue, memory impairment, dizziness, and bleeding in the nose and lungs, while others say the science isn't there yet to make that claim. Molds have been linked to several illnesses. They are primary suspects in the tripling asthma rate over the past 20 years.

Many states do not have any "mold standard" for buildings, but efforts are underway. In any event the "sick home" syndrome is likely to become a much greater issue in the future.

4. Moisture Retention in Furnishings

The processes of cooling and dehumidifying assume that there is already a certain amount of moisture inside the home. I believe that the furniture, draperies, carpets, and wall furnishings should be made of materials that will not absorb much moisture. In this way, cooling and dehumidifying are accomplished much more easily. For example, rattan could be used rather than upholstered furniture and low permeability paints/finishes could be used. This would reduce the amount of humidity that could be absorbed inside furniture.

*Used in Earth Home

Moisture Balance

Every building operates under a **moisture balance strategy**, ie: the rate of moisture removal from the living spaces **must equal** the rate at which it is generated. As more moisture is generated, it must be removed in order to maintain a constant humidity level.

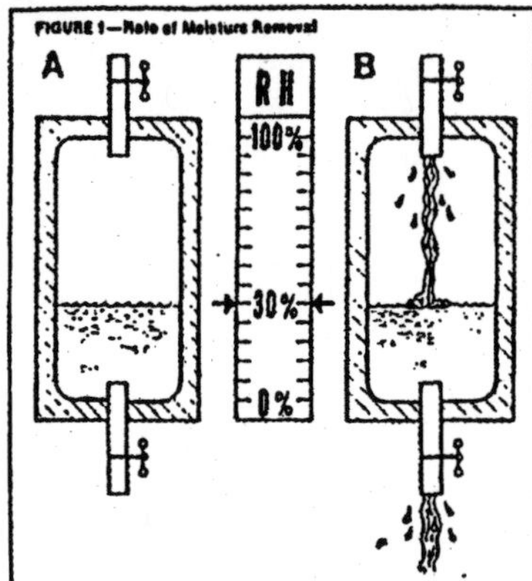

Notice in Figure 1 that containers A and B represent the building and its humidity level. Building A has no moisture input and no removal, while building B has high moisture input and removal. The humidity level in both buildings remains constant. This demonstrates that humidity levels can be controlled by either reducing the source of moisture or increasing the rate of moisture removal by means of ventilatin.

Moisture Balance

The most common source of moisture in houses are people and their activities, plants, unvented or poorly vented combustion appliances, humidifiers, wet building materials and surrounding soil. The first two sources are the most difficult to predict and control. Remember that code requires a bathroom to have an exhaust fan to control moisture generated in that room. A kitchen fan is designed to ventilate cooking odors, grease and moisture if used regularly.

Yet no ventilation is required to handle the constant sources of moisture like plants, people and activities, ground moisture, dishwashers and floor washing. Notice in Figure 2 how well this is shown.

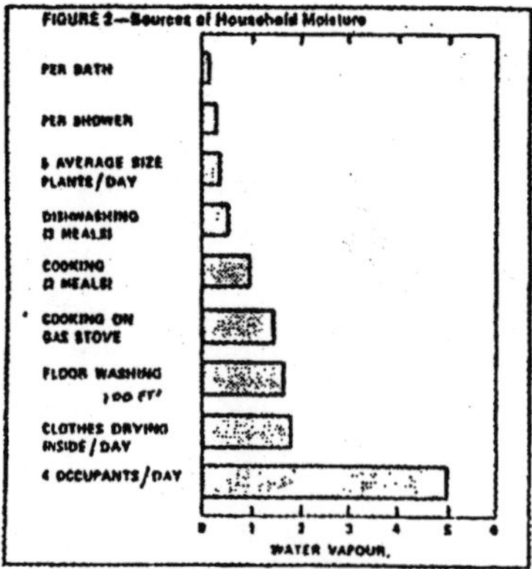

Air Leakage

In the past, we have depended on dealing with the variables in moisture generation by hoping the building has enough natural air leakage to handle these concerns. As you may note, it is hard to guess which house will have moisture problems. Trying to engineer leaks and cracks is an impossible task that can leave a home cold and drafty or tight and stale. What drives air leakage is pressure differences between inside and outside, wind pressure, temperature differences, combustion equipment and the stack effect of heat rising, leaving and being replaced.

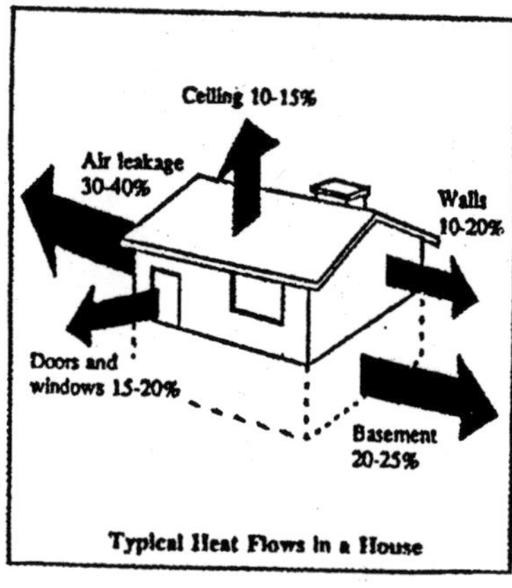

Typical Heat Flows in a House

The various paths for air leakage are: junctions between building materials, windows, doors, soffits, cantilevers, floor and wall junctions, electrical wires, outlets and fixtures, plumbing stacks and chimney chases, to name a few. Along with exiting warm air is moisture and the potential for concealed condensation in walls and attics.

Window Condensation

Window condensation is generally not the fault of a bad or low quality window. There are four basic variables involved with window condensation:

1). **Outside temperature** (not controllable).

2). **Indoor temperature** (slightly variable).

3). **Window R-value** (slightly variable, only at time of purchase)

4). **Humidity level** (both variable and controllable).

We cannot do much about the first, second or third condition, but we can effectively control the fourth. By allowing the homeowner a means by which to increase or decrease the humidity level, you have put the responsibility of moisture control where it belongs — in the homeowners hands.

A humidifier is the accepted method to add humidity. A heat recovery ventilator is the accepted method to dehumidify a home, as well as improve the air quality inside through continuous, controlled ventilation that preheats the fresh; dry air with the exhausting stale, humid air.

Figure 50-MOISTURE IN THE HOME

*Used in Earth Home

MOISTURE SOURCE BY TYPE	ESTIMATED MOISTURE AMOUNTS (PINTS)
Household Produced	
Aquariums (fish tanks)	Replacement of evaporative loss
Bathing: Tub (excludes towels and spillage) Shower (excludes towels and spillage)	0.12/standard size bath 0.52/5-minute shower
Clothes washing (automatic, lid closed, standpipe discharge)	0+/load (usually nil)
Clothes drying Vented outdoors Not vented outdoors or indoor drying line	0+/load (usually nil) 4.68 to 6.18/load (more if gas dryer)
Combustion--unvented kerosene space heater	7.6/gallon of kerosene burned
Cooking: Breakfast (family of four, average) Lunch (family of four, average) Dinner (family of four, average) Simmer at 2030F, 10 min., 6" pan (plus gas) Boil 10 min., 6" pan (plus gas)	0.35 (plus 0.58 if gas cooking) 0.53 (plus 0.68 if gas cooking) 1.22 (plus 1.58 if gas cooking) less than 0.01 if covered, 0.13 if uncovered 0.48 if covered, 0.57 if uncovered
(CONTINUED NEXT PAGE)	

Figure 51-HOUSEHOLD MOISTURE CHART, PAGE 1

*Used in Earth Home

MOISTURE SOURCE BY TYPE	ESTIMATED MOISTURE AMOUNTS (PINTS)
(CONTINUED FROM PREVIOUS PAGE)	
Dishwashing (by hand): Breakfast (family of four, average) Lunch (family of four, average) Dinner (family of four, average)	 0.21 0.16 0.68
Firewood storage indoors (cord of green firewood)	400 to 800/6 months
Floor mopping	0.03/square foot
Gas range pilot light (each)	0.37 or less/day
House plants (5 to 7 average plants)	0.86 to 0.96/day
Humidifiers	0 to 120+/day (2.08 average/hour)
Pets	Fraction of human adult weight
Respiration and perspiration (family of four, average)	0.44/hour (family of four, average)
Refrigerator defrost	1.03/day (average)
Saunas, steam baths, and whirlpools	0 to 2.7+/hour
Vegetable storage (large-scale storage is significant)	0+ (not estimated)

Figure 52-HOUSEHOLD MOISTURE CHART, PAGE 2

E. Mechanical Cooling/Dehumidification Technology

1. Refrigerant Dehumidification

Refrigerant dehumidification is illustrated in the following figure. This figure shows the method in which moisture is extracted from air and cooled. Discussion will not be repeated here because it is the same process as refrigerators and air conditioners use. (See Food Preservation section and Mechanical Cooling section) Also, in refrigerant dehumidification, power needs are substantial. It is one of the reasons that many people in the southwest part of the United States prefer "evaporative cooling."

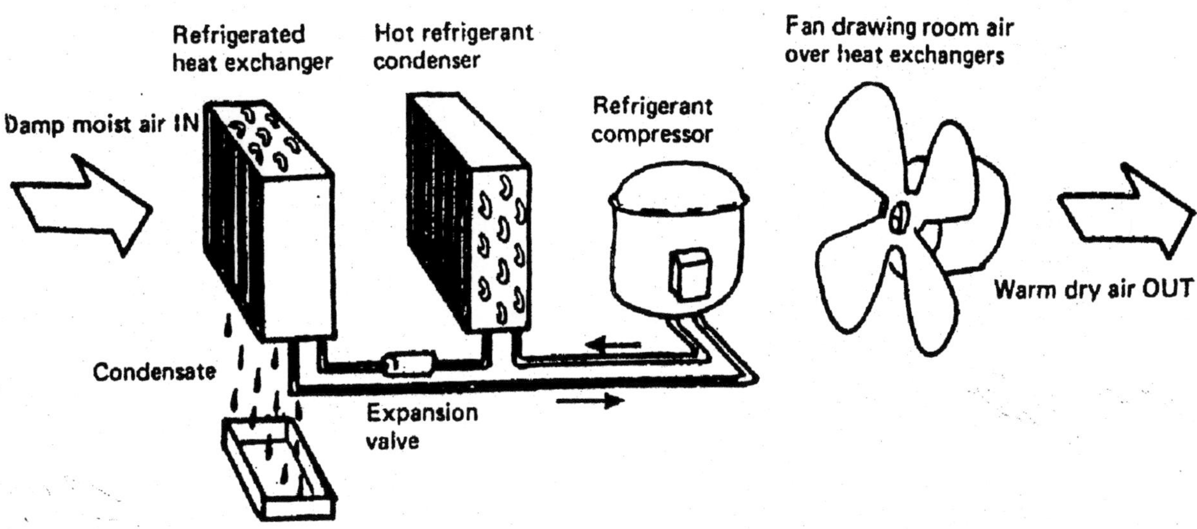

Figure 53-REFRIGERANT DEHUMIDIFIER BASICS

2. Heat Pumps (see Thermal Mass section)

3. Absorption Systems (Refrigerant)

The absorption cycle uses a very high heat source to generate cold (see note below). Absorption systems were the first mechanical systems developed to cool food. One of the earliest methods of absorption cooling was the "Icy Ball" system. Servel (absorption) refrigerators were later used to cool food in the 1920s. These refrigerators used a small propane pilot light to heat up a refrigerant inside a copper coil. This refrigerant could be ammonia or one of the new refrigerants, Freon. Basically, high starting torque and excessive electrical needs prevent mechanical space cooling use in a self-sufficient living scheme such as the Earth Home system. ***(Note: The technology and the principles of mechanical cooling using the absorption and mechanical cycles are virtually identical to freezing of foods, and will be covered later in Food Preservation section.)***

*Used in Earth Home

Even though space cooling using the absorption cycle was never popular, it has been reliably used for small refrigerators. The absence of moving parts brings complete silence, and these coolers are much more reliable than compressor-type mechanical refrigeration. The cost is slightly higher at first, but the operating cost is only about half as much as a compressor. A drawback is the combustible fuel it must use.

There is also some work being done on solar-powered adsorption refrigeration systems. One uses a lithium bromide and water absorber that can be regenerated at about 88°C. These systems, however, are still quite expensive.

4. Mechanical Compressors

a. Compressor Types

Mechanical cooling involves pumping compressed refrigerant through a tiny tube and into the cooling cavity. As the refrigerant expands, it cools and extracts heat from the cooling compartment. Air moves across the coils to produce cooled air. There are many different kinds of mechanical compressors used to compress these refrigerants, including piston compressors and scroll compressors. At present, the scroll compressor is the most efficient on the market.

b. Refrigerants

In the future, the freons (CFC's) will be completely banned by international agreement, because of the damaging effects to the ozone. Refrigerants such as MP 39, 409 A, and 134 A were developed to comply with international standards. All of these are still hurting the earth's ozone layer, but at slower rates. This has forced many scientists and companies to look for a substitute refrigerant altogether.

c. Future Refrigerants

Helium is one of the substitutes for these chemicals because it can be compressed readily. Ford and Chrysler cars have come out with a helium cooling system. Also, the Japanese use many ammonia refrigerants in their commercial buildings. One U.S. company is scheduled to start up production of helium-cooled refrigerators in Shanghai. Refrigerant research continues today.

F. The Earth Home Cooling System

1. Preventing Heat Build-Up (See also Structure section)

a. Background/Basics

The entire cooling theory assumes that the home has already started to get hot and the people feel uncomfortable. ***It is much easier to prevent the heat from entering the structure in the first place, so that less mechanical cooling is necessary.***

Many people plant shade trees around their homes to keep the sidewalls and windows cooler. (See also Structure-Shading Section) The wind is also used in many cultures to cool structures depending on the site and orientation. Homes are sometimes situated on the side of a cliff, on the edge of a hill, or high elevation to take advantage of prevailing winds to keep air moving through the home.

b. Heat Build-up Studies

The design of a low-energy home should first take into account external surfaces on the home in an attempt to prevent the sun from raising the temperature of living spaces. In Australia, a study was conducted on the effects of window shades, blinds, and drapes of many different colors and materials. The researchers used wood materials, laminated steel, laminated foam, and many other shading methods. They concluded that the most efficient way to shade a home is to stop the sunshine on the outside of the home. The best method was found to be a white metallic surface a few inches from the exterior of the glass. The sun would heat up the metallic surface and cause it to give up the heat by convection on both sides of the surface. They reported a 90% blockage of heat using this system. Some companies, including Sears Roebuck and Company, use a similar system on their shutters today.

If a little sunshine is needed, as in a greenhouse, a shading material such as diluted white latex paint or wet mud thrown against the glass does a good job of preventing heat build-up. A newly developed "smart glazing" helps to self-adjust light transmittal. (See Solar - Glazing file.)

c. Roof Heat Build-up

A radiant foil will be used on the roof. (See Roofs-Reflective/Radiant Foil section)

d. Earth Home Heat Build-up

The Earth Home uses a system of south blinds and plant shading on the east and west sides to prevent heat build-up. South side garden plants near the glass will help block the sunshine during the hottest months. Jerusalem artichokes, which grow approximately six to eight feet tall with wide leaves, are to be used to help shade the greenhouse. The roofing will reflect the vast majority of solar radiation and prevent the attic spaces from overheating. (See Roofing, Reflective Foil file.)

The greenhouse is to be vented separately through the roof. I'm using a figure of 30 seconds as the length of time in which to completely replace the greenhouse air. This is done in order to try and keep the temperature within 5°F of outside temperature. (Plants should not get over 85 degrees F.) I've used a slight overhang on the east and west sides to allow shading. Overhangs block the effects of the sun in the same way a straw hat shades a person's face.

2. EH Ground-Source Cooling

a. Construction Details

The Earth Home II system is designed to use the ground as a source of cooling. It is said that cooling systems should be 90% comfort and 10% relief from the heat, in those situations where the air temperature is too hot. ***The Earth Home II cooling system will be based upon a water cool tube technology with modifications***. I have designed and built a series of buried water tubes to extract the "coolness" from the soil. I have buried additional perforated tubing above the main cooling tubing with the sole purpose of wetting the ground. Studies show that dry ground has an R factor from 5 to 10, but wet ground has an R factor from .5 to 1.43. This proves that moist soil conducts heat much more readily than dry soil. The wet soil also dissipates heat into the surrounding soil for much larger distances. Also, a study showed that wetting the soil surrounding the cool tubes allowed the water to exchange its heat faster than if the ground was dry.

b. Burying Water Tubing Overview/Details

Geothermal heat pump manufacturers are now finding out that a single tube in a trench is not cost effective. If they drop a complete coil of tubing inside the vertical trench (slinky-style) and backfill, they can increase the water volume and heat transfer dramatically.

Inside the underground tubing will be fastened static mixers at about 50 foot intervals where the sections are joined. (See the following figure) These one-piece plastic or stainless static mixers will "destratify" or mix the water to prevent a thin film of cooled water on the inside surface of the tubes from staying at one temperature. In essence, it stirs the water slightly so most of the water comes into contact with the tubing surface for a much better heat exchange process.

Figure 54-STATIC MIXER

3. Earth Home Cooling Water Circulation

a. Circulation Basics

Circulation of water is to be accomplished via a non-pressurized, or "gravity" system using a low head circulating pump such as the Hartel. A circulating pump is a low head or low-pressure pump. (See Pumps - Water files.) If the tubing in the ground is all filled with water, it is only necessary to lift the water a slight distance from one tube and put it into the other tube to get this water to flow slowly. The circulating pump would be modified with a venturi device to enable it to pump much greater volumes of water with the same energy input.

The main resistance to flow would be the "smoothness" of the inside of the tubing, any sharp corners, the length and diameter of the tubing, and the velocity of the water. The diameter of the tubing should be large enough to prevent significant resistance to flow. There would not be any corners, and the tubing would be black polyethylene-which has a very smooth interior surface. (See Plumbing files)

b. Cooling Water Requirements

To summarize, water would be cooled through the moisture-laden soil and circulated through a radiator, and the cool air would then be blown around inside the home to supply 1/2 to 3/4 ton of cooling. The average house in temperate climates requires only two to three tons of air conditioning, but the Earth Home needs less because of the insulation and design. The amount of cooled water stored in the Earth Home and coil size would vary depending on climatic conditions. Warmer climates would necessitate built-in water tanks in the corners of rooms or part of specialized furniture for more "cool" storage. (see EH tabs section) Any condensation would be collected just below the coils with special troughs. Dripping condensation is one of the major problems with using colder water pipes to cool a home because of the humidity in the air.

4. Earth Home Air Circulation (See Heating-Air Distribution section)

This heated or cooled water would then flow through a radiator system in the main air distribution plenum above the stove. This radiator system will also be used for heating -- using valves to adjust the flow through the stove.

*Used in Earth Home

G. Future Cooling/Dehumidification Technologies

1. Solar Cooling/Air Conditioning (See Solar Air Conditioning section)

2. Solar Dehumidification

a. Sorbent/Desiccant Dehumidification

Sorbent dehumidification uses solids that have a large internal surface area on which water molecules can condense without changing the nature of the solid. Absorbents are hygroscopic materials, or water-seeking materials, which change their nature (vapor pressure) when taking up moisture. Typically, an absorbent dehumidifier is a slowly rotating drum of a desiccant material (the adsorbent), through which moist air is blown (see the following figure). The most commonly used adsorbent is a strong concentration of salt. Another strong absorbent is lithium chloride, which is also very popular.

Other desiccants include calcium, aluminosilicate clay, zeolite compounds, montmorillonite clays, superabsorbent (hydrophilic) polymers--or SAP for short, titanium gel, activated alumina, molecular sieves, and the new type one M (1M) materials. (See Desiccant Files)

Most installed desiccant systems use solid desiccant materials. However, there is much interest in liquid desiccant technologies that have the potential to be 50% smaller and 40% less costly than solid desiccant systems. However, one disadvantage of the liquid systems is that they need a pump and a regenerator, whereas the solid systems require only a fan to blow air against the solid adsorbents.

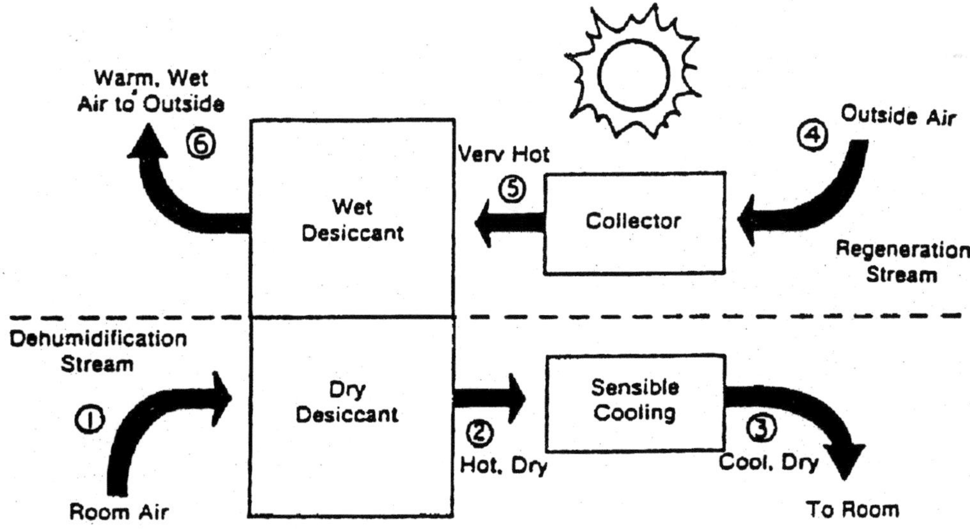

Figure 55-ADSORBENT DEHUMIDIFIERS

*Used in Earth Home

b. Solar Assist Desiccant Dehumidification

The use of a desiccant system is the most promising low energy-consumption dehumidification alternative currently available. Heat from a solar collector can be used to regenerate the desiccant bed, and the only electricity need is to move the small amount of air through the system. Typically 40 pounds of water per day (from a San Antonio residence) would require 4 cubic feet of silica gel and 75 square feet of flat plate solar collector. This same solar collector could also be used to provide part of the winter heating requirements. The following figure shows an example of a desiccant bed dehumidifier. To regenerate a desiccant, it is heated to allow it to release the moisture it contains. Typically, desiccants are regenerated in the temperature range of 194°F to 500°F.

Most of the commonly available commercial desiccant dehumidifiers use a solid absorbent. This absorption process takes place on the surface of the absorbent, and the amount of the moisture absorbed is directly proportional to the available surface area. At the present time, the previously mentioned desiccant rotary dryers are the most popular because they are space efficient, and they do a good job of dehumidifying.

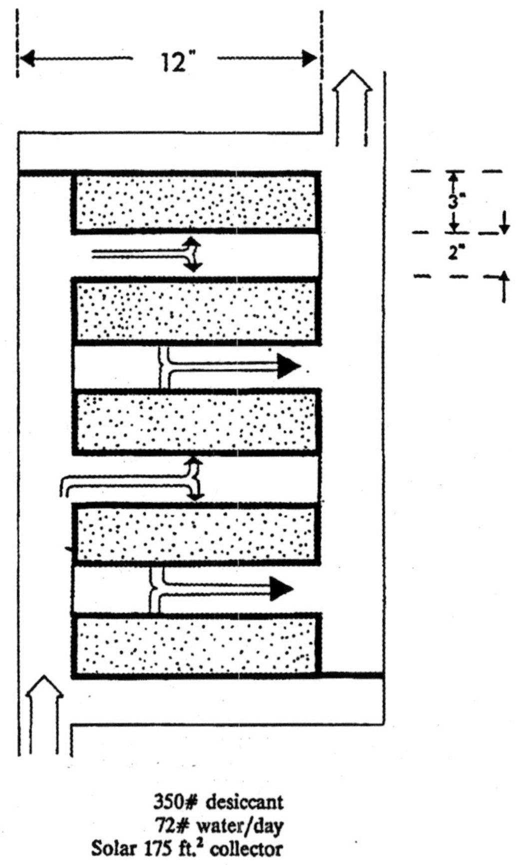

350# desiccant
72# water/day
Solar 175 ft.² collector

Figure 56-DESICCANT BED DEHUMIDIFIER

*Used in Earth Home

3. High Density Desiccant/Thermal Mass Battery (see Thermal Mass section)

4. Heat Pipe Dehumidification Systems (see also Thermal Mass section)

a. Heat Pipe Dehumidification Technology

A heat pipe dehumidification system is a passive device which uses a series of closed tubes filled with refrigerants to transfer heat from the outside supply air to the supercooled post-cooling coil air. Because the heat pipe pre-cooling coil provides initial air cooling, the total cooling and dehumidification capacity of the system is increased during peak load conditions. During off-peak conditions, the heat pipe pre-cooling coil replaces part of the load on the cooling coil necessary to provide a given level of dehumidification, and the reheat coil replaces part of the reheat load necessary to provide a comfortable supply temperature, with no energy input. As a result, heat pipes provide both enhanced dehumidification and energy savings.

b. Heat Pipe Dehumidification Benefits

Because heat pipes are passive, with no moving parts, they are virtually maintenance free. (See the following figure) Below are some benefits of dehumidifier heat pipes:

--Less operational costs/quick payback on investment
--Dehumidification and superior indoor air quality
--Comfort greatly enhanced
--Prevents costly damage to interiors by moisture/saves remodeling costs
--Prevents odors caused by moisture (mold growth)

Below are some benefits of heat recovery heat pipes:

--Tremendous energy savings
--No cross-contamination of air streams
--No "Tilt" mechanism to break down or maintain
--Ventilation in all seasons
--Controllable heat pipes
--Very efficient and effective

Note: see also Thermal Mass/Heat Pipe section.

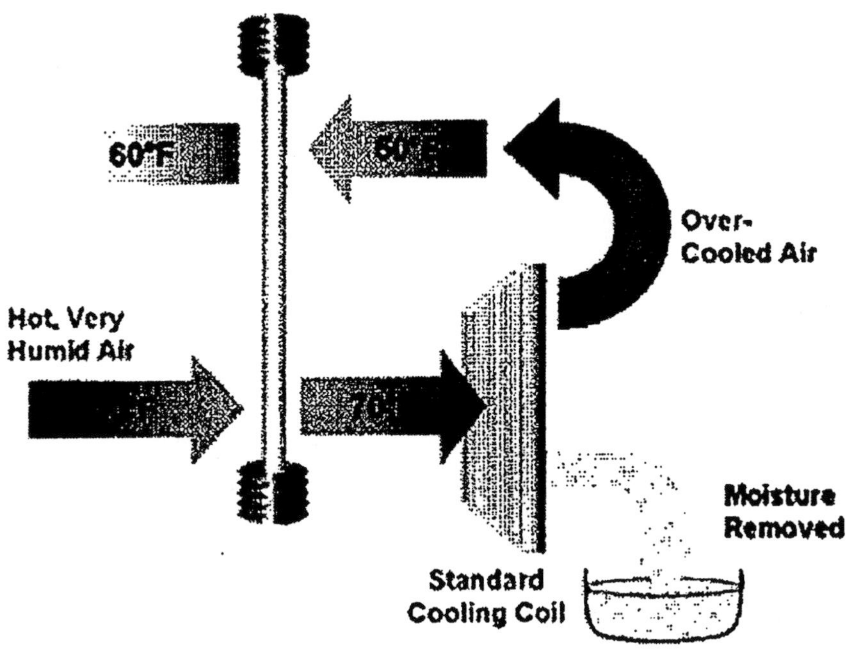

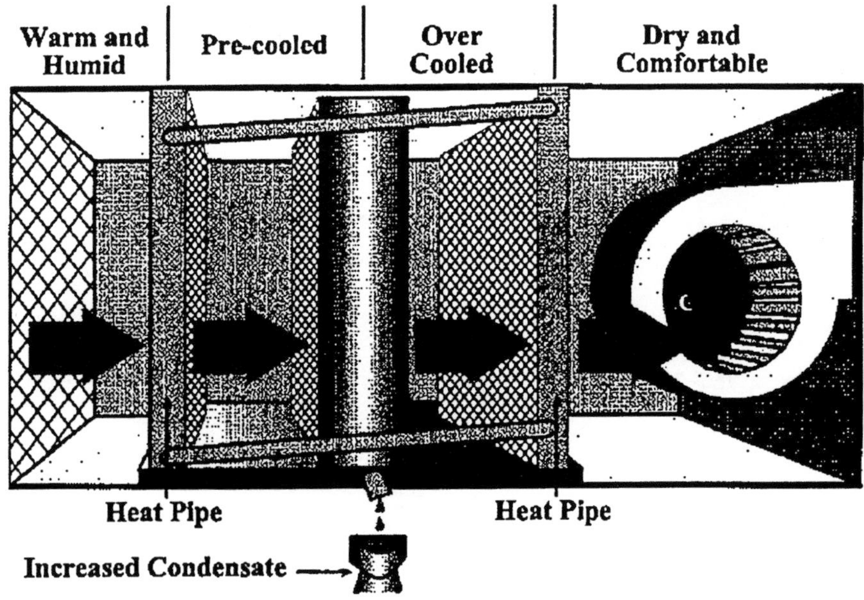

Figure 57-HEAT PIPE DEHUMIDIFICATION

*Used in Earth Home

V. HEATING SYSTEM

A. History of Home Heating Systems

Early humans used fire in their caves, and later may have partially relied on fermenting manure and/or animals for warmth.

1. Roman Systems

The earliest recorded drawings of heating systems are from the Roman era (Hypocaust). The Romans (See following figure) used a system of ductwork underneath the floor and through the walls of larger buildings to circulate heated air. In this way the heat was perceived to come from all around the room, because the floor and the walls would both be warm.

2. Korean Ondol

About the same time, the Koreans developed the "Ondol" system. This was a system of "smoke plenums" or channels underneath the floor of a home. They built the floor as an integral part of the chimney. The smoke traveled in these channels under the floor, through a collection plenum, and up a chimney stack at the other end of the home. In this way they were able to heat the entire floor from a stove located a little lower than the floor level. The Chinese K'ang, the Afghan Tawakhaneh, and the German Steinofen are variations of the same principle.

3. Kivas

Another method of heating was discovered in the southwest part of the United States. Very early Native American tribes in Arizona used what's called a "kiva." A kiva is an underground chamber for meetings and ceremonial purposes. They used an air channel with a stone slab "draft blocking system" so the falling incoming cold air would not disturb the fire in the center of the underground chamber.

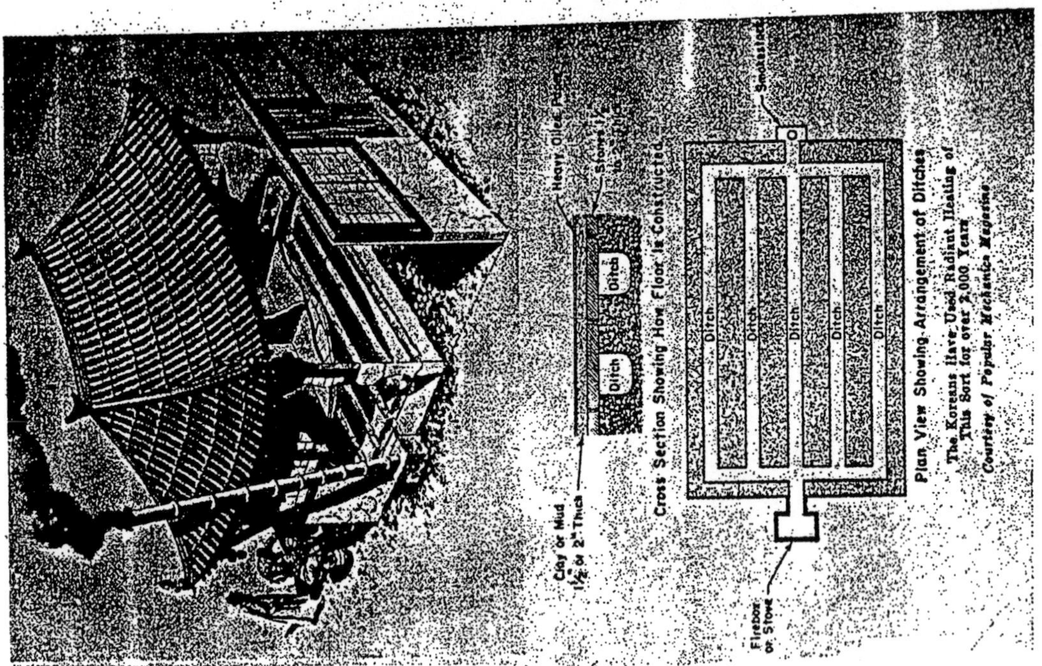

Figure 58-EARLY HEATING SYSTEMS

*Used in Earth Home

4. Native American Tipi

The Native Americans of the plains used thermosiphon methods to heat their tipis. (See next section). They knew that the smoke went straight up and out the top of the tipi, so they devised a method to channel incoming cooler air along the sides to replace the smoke as it exited. In cold weather they sometimes also used a liner that extended completely to the ground. The cold air would enter through the space left at the bottom of the main tipi, hit the liner, travel over the top of the liner, and mix with the outgoing hot air. This way the cold air would not go directly to the center and out the top. This channeling method created a "pocket" of warm air and protected the occupants from cold air drafts.

5. Developing Countries

A very common heating system of many developing countries is the 3 stone fire. This was basically 3 stones arranged in a circle with a rock or steel plate on top. Fuel was put into the sides of the fire and the smoke bellowed out around the top

6. Early American Homes/Thermosiphon Loop

From earliest known times, people were aware of the fact that hot air rises and cold air sinks (thermosiphon loop). A heated fluid rises because it has a lower density than colder fluids-colder fluid has its molecules are more closely packed together. This thermosiphon loop principle has been used in many applications such as window box solar collectors, natural gravity solar heaters, and it is the process that drives the heating systems in most of the older homes in the United States. These systems typically had a stove on the lower floor with central floor registers that allowed the heat to rise into the upper rooms. Cold air returns were located near the walls to return the cooler air and complete the loop.

B. Earth Home Solar and Heat Storage (See also EH Thermal Mass section)

1. Passive Solar Heating

A popular renewable energy source is called "passive" solar. Passive means no energy inputs such as pumps or fans. ***Most often, passive solar consists of many south-facing glass or plastic windows and a storage medium (mass) immediately behind them***. Sun shines through the glass and heats up the surface of the heavy items. Shades or insulated blinds are drawn at night to prevent the heat from radiating back outside. Passive solar heat has been very successful in the southern part of the United States. Northern applications of passive solar are not as cost effective because of the increased heat loss at night through the windows. Double panes of glass helps prevent this loss but is more costly to build. (See Energy/Power Section for more complete discussion of solar energy.)

2. EH Solar Applications

a. EH Greenhouse Area

The entire southern wall of the Earth Home is a vertical glass wall for plant growth. The Earth Home has door openings from the kitchen/living area to each of two separate greenhouse areas, so that air can circulate as desired. The south-facing glass on the Earth Home gets the most heat during the 10:45 a.m. to 3:15 p.m. time period.

*Used in Earth Home

Sunlight entering through the southern glass will heat up the plant soil, benefiting the plants, but excess heat will inhibit plant growth. The solar gain is tremendous, so the greenhouse needs cooling of some sort. The plants will wilt if they are not ventilated properly.

b. EH Roof Truss Ventilation

The roof truss system in the Earth Home is designed so that the southern space can be ventilated by opening up vents in the greenhouse ceiling. This will allow heat to flow from the greenhouse area through the roof cavity and out the roof vent. (See Roof section)

c. EH Hydronic Soil Heating/Soil Trombe Wall

An auxiliary hydronic heating system for the greenhouse soil is also built into the south wall, so it can be heated independently from the central stove. This will extend the growing season because soil temperature is often more critical than air temperature for growing plants.

The plumbing is flexible, so heat can also be withdrawn from the soil using the same pipes. In this way it can act as a Trombe wall.

C. Heating with Wood

1. Wood Burning Statistics

Wood accounted for 25 percent of all energy used in the United States at the beginning of this century. With increased use of fossil fuels, its significance rapidly declined. By 1976, only 1 to 2 percent of United States energy was supplied by wood, and burning of tree wastes by the forest products industry accounted for most of it.

Although the same trend has been evident in all industrialized countries, the decline has not been as dramatic everywhere. Sweden, for instance, still meets 8 percent of its energy needs with wood, and Finland, 15 percent.

The use of wood to provide heat is as old as mankind; but by burning the wood we only utilize about one-third of its energy. Two-thirds is lost into the environment with the smoke. Gasification is a method of collecting the smoke and its combustible components. (See Woodgas section)

2. Wood Background

a. Wood Cultivation

Wood needs vary with the climate and species of tree used, of course. But a good rule of thumb is that about 1/8 acre of trees should be used each heating season. Thus a 5 acre wood lot would have to have a species of tree that matured in less than 40 years. Most of the time 15 to 25 years from planting to first harvest is all that is necessary.

Presently, wood is prepared for use by sawing down the tree, cutting it in sections, splitting the larger pieces, and allowing the wood to dry out. In many countries throughout history a method of wood "cultivation" was practiced called "coppice and pollard" (see the following figure).

Using this method, the tree was cut when they were about 9 inches in diameter. The runners that grew from the old root system were harvested regularly every 12 years or so. Ten feet of new growth could be possible in one year. This way, the young leaves could also be fed to animals and no chain saws or wood splitters would be necessary.

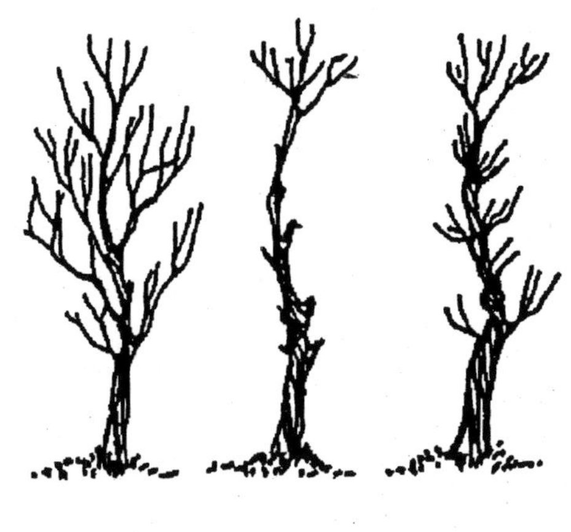

Pollard trees (bottom) were cut well above ground level. In a coppice (middle drawings) trees were cut approximately at ground level. Shredding (top drawings) was the practice of removing branches from standing trees, for fuel or fodder.

Figure 59-WOOD CULTIVATION METHODS

*Used in Earth Home

b. Wood Harvesting/Drying

Typically, wood is cut to length and stacked as close to point of use as possible to eliminate transportation costs. Larger sections of wood should be split into smaller pieces in order to burn completely. Wood sections should be split with a splitting maul from the trunk end towards the top of the tree, following the natural growth pattern in the trunk. Small hairline cracks in each section are a telltale sign where to strike the wood in order to split it with the least amount of effort. The wood should be split to sizes smaller than 6 inches in the longest diagonal dimension for most efficient wood stoves.

Wood should be piled in a single row to allow wind and sun to continually dry out the pieces. If another pile is needed, keep it a couple feet away from the first row in order to allow good airflow. Covering the wood keeps the rain from re-wetting the wood and helps the bottom layer of wood dry out completely.

All wood should dry out (seasoned) before they are burned. It takes fresh cut wood about 8 months to reach 20% moisture content. Wet wood will burn eventually, but it takes a great amount of Btu's from your wood stove to dry it. This "boiled off" water causes problems in the chimney system by creating more creosote. Symptoms of poor performance related to wet firewood include; difficulty getting a fire going and keeping it burning well, smoky fires with little flame, dirty glass, rapid creosote buildup in the chimney, low heat output, smell of smoke in the house, short burn times, excessive fuel consumption, and blue-gray smoke from the chimney. Chimney stack temperature should be above 250°F to eliminate creosote formation. (See Wood/Woodstoves files)

c. Species/Btu Discussion

If no dry wood is available, ash wood is preferable to any other type of wet wood because it burns more readily. ***Dry wood gives roughly the same Btu value per pound (about 8,600).*** For example, a 60 lb. piece of oak has the same heating value as a 60 lb. stack of lighter wood such as pine or basswood. Wood varies in heating value from hickory having 30 million Btu per cord to poplar at 17.5 million Btu per cord. The tropical tree algarrobo is used extensively in the tropics for a source of wood, construction, and nitrogen fixer of the soil. However, it only grows in specific areas.

It is interesting to note that wood ashes make excellent fertilizer (in moderation) and can also be used for icy walkways and soap making.

3. Wood Stoves

a. Wood Stove Background

Humanity has kept itself warm with wood heat for thousands of years. Benjamin Franklin invented the first enclosed woodstove. Prior to this time, people kept themselves warm by standing in front of open fireplaces that sent most of their heat up the chimney and only radiated a small portion of this heat back into the room. An open fireplace constantly sucks large volumes of cold outside air into the house to replace the hot air that flows out the chimney. Heating a home with 30 cords of wood each winter was not uncommon for fireplace-heated homes. (One cord of wood measures 4 feet wide by 4 feet tall by 8 feet long.) The Franklin Box probably cut wood consumption by three-quarters and made for better-heated homes with fewer drafts.

b. Basic Wood Stove Types

There are six basic wood stove types: airtight, old non-airtight, recent catalytic, boilers, recent non-catalytic, and masonry. Generally, stoves are made of heavy steel with a tight-sealing door and draft control mechanism of some sort. Wood stoves have traditionally been of steel and cast iron construction here in the U.S. ***Around the world the situation is different—masonry stoves were in use long before steel stoves.***

*Used in Earth Home

c. Outdoor Wood Stoves

1. Outdoor Wood Stoves Background

An outdoor furnace resembles a small utility building. The stove is water-jacketed and insulated. The water in the jacket is heated and pumped underground through insulated pipes to the building that is heated. This system also provides domestic hot water as well. Some outdoor woodstove/boiler combinations can be operated as gravity systems (without power). See Bibliography section on Woodstove Manufacturers.

2. Outdoor Wood Stoves Data

The following figure shows technical data for selected outdoor woodstove models.

MANUFACTURER	MODEL	BTU/L.B. OF WOOD	AVERAGE STACK TEMP
Central Boiler	CL-17	4448.80	131.8°F
Taylor®	T450	3072.44	151.0°F
Wood Master	WM434MF	2908.05	198.7°F
Heatmor	200CSS	2553.22	259.6°F
Hardy	180	2502.90	330.6°F

Figure 60-OUTDOOR WOODSTOVE DATA

d. Masonry Stoves/Tile Stoves

Tile stoves have been used for 500 years in Russia, Scandinavia, and German-speaking countries where it is known as a kachelofen. About two-thirds of Finland's new homes have built-in masonry stoves. Masonry stoves take longer to heat up, but they hold their heat better.

These "Russian fireplaces," as they are sometimes called, have thick walls of either stone or masonry with a main channel going up and out, similar to a brick chimney lined with ceramic tiles. After the fire gets started and a good draft is established, twin dampers are used to close off the updraft, causing the smoke to take a longer path through the masonry chimney. This heats up the bottom part of the masonry fireplace. When the smoke heats and picks up speed again, another set of twin dampers are turned and allow the air to take yet another serpentine path through the chimney. This procedure is repeated until the entire masonry lattice becomes a hot chimney. This method keeps the temperature of the outgoing smoke as low as possible, heating up this "thermal battery".

There are aspects to a masonry stove that bear mention. ***It is difficult to use a masonry stove with a central heating system in a cold climate***. Most of the masonry installations are in situations where the air can circulate freely to all living areas—no privacy bedrooms. Also, masonry stoves transfer heat over 30 times more slowly than iron stoves, thus taking much longer to begin heating. They also require wood of 3" diameter or less—which means more work putting up wood.

e. Steam/Boilers (See Electrical Power/Generator Options)

Some homes generate heated water using "boilers". ***A boiler is a stove designed specifically to heat water***. In this method, any one of the heat sources could be used with a water jacket surrounding it. Water is then pumped into special tanks in each room called radiators.

Steam boilers heat water hot enough to turn it to steam. (See Steam files.) Steam generation and use is very specialized and involves condensate feed pumps, controls, and high-pressure components. It was not used because of the technicalities encountered. (See Electrical Power/Generator Options section)

Some work has been done on a high efficiency internal combustion steam engine. This technology, however, never got past the development and patent stages. (See Hansen cycle engines-Herbert, N.W. Hansen)

f. Woodstove Efficiencies/EPA

Woodstove efficiencies are not very scientifically determined. The Environmental Protection Agency of the U.S. Government lists woodstove manufacturers and corresponding efficiencies. However, after inquiring about methods and procedures of the Environmental Protection Agency, I found it does not actually test wood stoves for efficiency. It merely categorizes stoves based on EPA estimates of efficiency. There is no testing being done at this point, and a test protocol has not been developed as of 1990. At least one private outdoor stove company has attempted to compare efficiencies of competitors' stoves in their sales literature. However, the exact testing protocol could not be obtained from the company. (See Wood /Woodstoves files)

g. Clean-Burning Wood Stoves

The following figure shows a typical clean-burning woodstove. The predominant features are the air-tight door, firebrick lining, and secondary air jets.

4. Woodstove-Related Technologies

a. Catalytic Combustors

Another technique used to enhance a wood stove's performance is called a "catalytic combustor." It is similar in function to the catalytic converters used on automobiles to curb emissions. One combustor is made from a ceramic material in a honeycomb shape. It is then plated with platinum to form the catalyst. Hot smoke comes in contact with the combustor, re-ignites, and burns the particles of smoke. ***One drawback to catalytic combustors is that they can't withstand sudden temperature changes, and they only work at high temperatures***. Therefore, a certain amount of attendance is required.

b. Draft/Chimneys

The chimney is what carries the smoke out of the living space. Draft can be described as the updraft "suction" effect from the combination of a heated chimney column and wind blowing across the top. Natural convection for open wood stoves without adequate chimneys provides poor mixing of air with fuel gases and can result in incomplete combustion, soot and emissions. A chimney can supply 1 mm water pressure per meter of height.

Draft is difficult to control on a stove because of pressure differences in a home and varying stack (stove) temperatures. Draft control devices include a simple bimetallic damper, threaded air vent, slide damper, or other mechanisms for controlling air intake to the stove.

A wood stove smokestack/chimney should be at least three feet higher than the highest point on a house to allow good draft. Modern chimneys are usually lined with three materials for durability—thermal concrete, 304 stainless steel, or clay tile. Dry wood, good draft, and a well-designed wood stove all contribute to efficient use of wood for space heating.

Figure 61-CLEAN-BURNING WOOD STOVE

*Used in Earth Home

c. Scrubbers/Heat Exchangers

Wood stoves would be much more efficient if the heat in the smoke could also be utilized. ***Approximately 50% of wood Btu's are lost up the chimney in the smoke***. There are industrial "scrubbers" that clean pollution particles from exhausted smoke. One scrubber is a tank through which the smoke travels before it gets released from the stack. Inside the tank are water jets that spray through the chamber. The water particles carry a slight static electrical charge. The oppositely charged smoke particles attach to the water particle and fall to the bottom of the scrubber to be collected. The water is also heated and could be used to assist space heating. (See Scrubbers file.)(See Future Woodstoves section)

Another method that has been used is a stainless steel heat exchanger in the chimney. This exchanger saves heat from the hot stack gasses and puts it into the clean air supply. The exchanger needs to be stainless to resist corrosion from the condensate. A German house recovers heat in this manner. The Waterloo Green Home has a similar system but uses two containers of rocks alternatively to reclaim heat.

d. "Top Down" Fire-Building Technique

The conventional approach to build a fire is to crumple some newspaper, put some fine kindling on that and some heavier kindling on top, light the paper and watch as the whole affair collapses into a smoldering mess. Or, as sometimes happens, it catches enough that you can begin to add bigger pieces until you have a respectable fire. However, since the early 1990s, it has become more common to build fires top down.

The top down technique is the counter-intuitive opposite: put down three or four full sized pieces of firewood, then a layer of coarse kindling, then some fine kindling on that and top off the pile with a couple of sheets of crumpled paper. The paper is lit and, believe it or not, the fire builds progressively, gaining intensity, down through the layers to the biggest logs on the bottom!

For steel stoves, cast iron stoves, or fireplaces, a true top down fire is impossible because the fireboxes are limited in height. A modified "front-to-back" approach works in these cases. Put two or three full size split pieces towards the back of the firebox, then a few pieces of heavy kindling, then lean a dozen thumb size pieces of kindling against them and add a few crumpled sheets of newspaper at the front of the firebox. Light the paper and watch the fire build steadily towards the back of the firebox.

The advantages of the top-down fire building method are: minimal start-up smoke; no chance that the fire will collapse and smother itself; and no need to open the loading door to add larger pieces once the kindling fire is established.

5. Earth Home Wood Burning

a. Earth Home Woodstove

In the United States, most self-sufficient home designs use wood as a primary heat source, and back-up heat sources such as fuel oil, propane, natural gas, or electricity. The Earth Home will use an efficient wood-burning stove as a primary heat source. ***The centrally located stove is to be of stainless steel construction with a built-in cooking area on one side. The stove is a "gravity-boiler" design with built-in water jacket***. A boiler water additive such as sodium nitrite will be added to resist corrosion inside the system. Large pipe diameters, smooth elbows with large radii, and "smooth" valves will keep the water circulation energy draw to 4-10 watts. (See Circulating Pump section) Additives can also help to lessen pipe friction so the pump will not have to work as hard.

*Used in Earth Home

b. EH Woodstove/Options/Accessories

An optional curtain is designed to be drawn around the stove to function as a sweat bath area or sauna. It is interesting to note that many cultures throughout history have used the sweat bath/sauna for therapeutic purposes. Benefits claimed include reducing stress, toning the skin, relieving arthritis/lower back pain, and enhancing sleep. (See Wood/Wood Stoves files.)

In many countries a woodstove provided additional functions of cooking, baking, smoking meat, drying grain, hops, malt, and flax. It was also used for heating water for washing and cooking. ***In the Earth Home design, an optional combination boiler/smokehouse/barbecue is designed to be located just outside the north (summer) entry inside a screened-in deck.*** This outside stove would eliminate using small quantities of wood for cooking or early morning heat. The woodstove could also be used as a primary heat source so none of the smoke will mix with the family's breathing air and cause respiratory problems in sensitive individuals. Locating the wood stove outside has at least one disadvantage, however, in that there are some reports of significant increases in wood usage in outside installations.

6. Future Woodstoves

a. Woodstove Improvement Options

A virtual pollution-free, ultra-high efficiency wood stove could be developed using scrubber technology. I have analyzed many of the drawbacks with wood stoves and wood stove technologies and feel that the future may bring testing on a stove that burns wood in smaller pieces such as the end only. This concentrated hot combustion area could be surrounded with heat transfer/scrubber technologies and "smoked" as one would smoke a cigar. I feel the firebox should be somewhat vertical to take advantage of gravity. Ash insulates the fire and prevents air from getting to the wood. The ash control mechanism should be trouble-free and automatic. This would happen independently as the fire is normally burned.

b. Woodstove Draft Control Improvements

Draft would not depend on the prevailing winds, but a blower placed downstream from the scrubber or a "venturi-style" blower just downstream from the combustion chamber. ***I feel a system that combines scrubber technology, computer draft control, electricity generation, and water heating will be developed to be the central power source for homes.*** (See Energy/Power section)

c. Wood Gasification Boilers (See also Woodgas section)

Wood gasification boilers use the combustible gasses produced by the gasification process. Because the boilers use wood gasification combustion, they give unusually high overall heating efficiency. They use substantially less wood than conventional boilers and .outdoor water stoves with no visible smoke when fully operating. Wood gasification boilers burn so clean that they are much safer with virtually no risk of a chimney fire.

D. Distributing Heat/Heated Fluid

1. Water as a Heat Transfer Medium

a. Hot Water Circulation Background

After combustion and heating, the distribution of the heated fluid can be accomplished in many different ways. One option is to use water as a transfer medium inside the home. A common method is to pump the hot water to radiators located inside the rooms. Radiators would give up heat to the room air, and the water would flow back to the central heat source where it is reheated and re-circulated. ***Hot water heating systems heat more evenly***

and more comfortably than any air systems I've encountered. I think this is due to the more gradual temperature change with water heating systems, and the subtle radiation effects on the skin.

Also to be noted is that it takes less circulation energy to heat with a water system than an air system. In Europe, hydronic heating is used much more that here in the U.S. and accounts for less overall energy use per home.

b. In-Floor Heat/Water Tubing

1. In-Floor Background/History

Another way to distribute hot water is water pipes in or under the floor. (See Concrete files.) Although the Romans used wood-fired in-floor heating systems 2,000 years ago, systems for modern homes have not been popular until recently.

2. In-Floor Heating Technology

There are companies that specialize in putting tubing underneath the concrete slab so the entire floor is heated. (See HVAC files.) This puts heat right where it is needed the most—on the ankles. Water pipes can also be installed between the floor joists in conventional-type construction. This system can be used to retrofit existing homes with underfloor heating.

3. In-Floor Issues

Fifty years ago, many systems were installed using copper tubing. Unfortunately, prospective customers shied away because of leakage problems resulting from poor soldering and shifting slabs. Water still slightly permeates through some tubing, creating moisture problems. Special tubing has been developed to solve this problem. With the proper design and installation, in-floor systems can be among the most efficient and comfortable heating systems available.

It has the disadvantage, however, of not being able to deliver quick heat. In the fall and spring when it gets a little chilly and the thermostat calls for heat, heated water begins to flow. By the time the whole slab is warm, the "flywheel effect" slightly overheats the home. Some in-floor homes also use an auxiliary method to provide quick heat when needed.

c. Earth Home Hot Water Circulation System

A low-head, high volume, energy efficient circulating pump will be used using the "venturi' principle. This system is the same as the one used to cool the home. For complete discussion, see Cooling section under Water Circulation.

Recent innovations in advanced houses have also used oversized radiant heating systems so that a lower delivery water temperature can be used. In one system the entire floor is a radiator and the temperature only has to be 26 deg. C.

2. Air as a Heat Transfer Medium

a. Air Circulation/Ducting Background

1. Ducts

In traditional air-moving systems, a "duct" system is used underneath the floor to transfer the air in and out of the rooms. In a cold climate, if there is a basement underneath, most of the air-moving ductwork is located in the sub-floor area between the basement and the first floor space. Studies have shown that about 20% to 25% of the heat loss in a traditional house is through the basement walls. There is a loss of heat when the air comes into contact with a cooled plenum surface. In a traditional house, however, it is about the only practical way to circulate heated air into rooms.

***Used in Earth Home**

2. Air as Media

Most heating systems use air media to move heat around, or provide an open area to mix the heated air with the cooler air. The most common form of heating is to heat air and blow it throughout the home. ***I find that air sooner or later gets heated anyway, regardless of the system used***. Even in the radiant heating systems where infrared energy heats the object itself, it would re-radiate this energy back to the room and heat the air by conduction.

b. Earth Home Hot Air Circulation System

1. Coils/Ducts/Enclosed Rooms

I've decided to enclose the rooms as much as possible for privacy, rather than having one large open area, as in a loft system. ***In the Earth Home II, I have designed privacy spaces (bedrooms) and allowed air to move in and out for more controlled ventilation and comfort***.

2. Hot Water Coils

In the Earth Home II, the central air-moving system will assist the heated water system. ***I've tried to locate the source of heat (coils) as close as possible to the center of the home. This distribution center is designed to have one large air-moving fan (a larger version of a backwardly inclined fan).*** (See Cooling section for complete discussion)(See also Fan Technology section.) ***Connected to this fan are large-diameter air ducts leading to each room from above***. Large-diameter ducts are used to reduce the friction of air on the walls of the ducts. (See Air Fans files.)

3. Mechanical Damper Control Options

Air is blown into the rooms and controlled in each room with an adjustable bimetallic damper. A bimetallic damper is two dissimilar strips of metal laminated together. When the damper is heated, different rates of thermal expansion of the two metals cause the strip to bend in one direction, creating mechanical motion. (See HVAC files.)

Another example of producing mechanical motion directly with heat is a "heat piston." This consists of a movable piston in a cylinder that is partially filled with paraffin oil that has a high coefficient of expansion. The oil expands and contracts through a selected temperature range, causing the piston to move. This movement can exert a force on a lever to open windows or ducts. This is the way that the greenhouse louvers will be opened to let the hot air into the ceiling cavity and out the vents in the roof. (See following figure) Manufacturers of heat pistons are listed in the Greenhouse - General files.

A shape memory alloy (SMA) spring can also be used. An SMA spring is currently used in an electrical kettle switch to automatically switch off the kettle when the water contents boil. SMA gives a larger force and deflection output for a given temperature change, thus enabling the SMA spring to be positioned at the shortest distance to the steam path.

*Used in Earth Home

Figure 62-HEAT PISTON

E. Air Quality Inside the Home

1. Air Quality Overview

It is estimated that we humans spend up to 90% of our time indoors. A recent federal survey reported that air pollution inside American homes might be ten times worse than outside. There are at least 27 recognized indoor air pollutants (not including negatively charged ions in the air).

a. Air Changes per Hour (ACH)

1. ACH Background

The term ACH refers to the number of times the entire volume of air in a home is completely replaced by fresh air from the outside. Natural air leakage rates (normal pressures) for conventional homes vary between .2 and .48 air changes per hour. The total air change rate for conventional homes (at 50 Pa pressure) ranges from four to seven! Note that natural ventilation is reliant on wind and temperature differences to move the air. On mild and calm days, natural airflow may be insufficient to dilute indoor pollutants to an acceptable level.

The actual amount of air that needs to be brought into and out of a house is a subject of continuing debate. ***Different air change per hour (ACH) figures have been recommended over a number of years from many sources***. Canadian standards suggest 1.5 air changes per hour as adequate in a home of this design. Extremely "tight" homes are .5 ACH. The typical range on the Advanced Houses project went from .5 to 2.3 with the average around 1.5. (This was at 50 Pa pressure also.) The new R-2000 standard is 1.5 ACH which roughly means .5 ACH under normal conditions. The recent Minnesota Energy Code mandates .35 ACH to all habitable rooms.

2. Earth Home Air Changes

I am using .85 air changes per hour at 50 Pa as a design figure. If moist air were exhausted from point sources such as the kitchen hood exhaust or a bathroom exhaust without replacement, a situation could develop called "backdraft". The house would have a negative pressure and air would try to enter the home through the chimney, causing problems with combustion sources that need to be supplied with fresh air such as the propane demand heater.

b. Air Filtration/Cleaning

1. Air Filters

The air inside a home should also be filtered; otherwise the home stays dirty from dust and lint particles. Typical 110-volt electrostatic filters require too much electricity because of their continuous draw and higher voltage requirements. According to industry experts, about 80% of all air conditioning system failures have as primary cause "restricted airflow" which means clogged filter.

2. Electronic Air Cleaners

Electronic air cleaners are sometimes also used to "clean" the air. These electronic air cleaners are not HRV's. (See Below) They use a charged grid to collect particulate matter. These devices are mainly effective for actual particles, whereas a large fraction of room pollutants are gases. They do nothing to exhaust moisture, CO_2, and gases such as radon. Because they are not ducted to the exterior, they cannot replenish the supply of oxygen for the home, either.

3. Earth Home Air Filter

I have located non-electric electrostatic air filters that use permanently charged neoprene material imbedded on fibers to collect dust using the electrostatic principle. These filters are reusable and washable, so only one set of filters is needed in the home (see following figure). Another option is to use silver particles in the filter to kill viruses.

4. Future-Soil Bed Reactors

Air quality can be increased using a soil bed reactor. Basically this involves piping the air into the soil where the microbes eat the impurities from the air. This method can be adapted from a commercially available product called an Airtron. The Airtron uses a combined activity of houseplants and soils to filter the air.

2. Air Leakage/Airtightness

a. Vapor Barrier Background

Since a home uses 30%-40% of its heating cost to compensate for air leakage, it's necessary to make a house as air tight as possible. A vapor barrier is one material used to stop air filtration into a home. ***A home needs a vapor barrier surrounding the living area to prevent moisture from getting into the wall space and to prevent excess air infiltration***.

There are four methods commonly used to achieve airtight building shells:

1) Sealed polyethylene sheets
2) Airtight Drywall Approach (ADA)
3) Exterior air barriers
4) Airtight pargings (stucco)

Normally, a good vapor barrier such as cross-laminated polyethylene is used behind the interior finish to prevent house moisture from condensing in the insulation. (See Films file.) A special sealing tape is used at the seams and around light fixtures, so that the home is almost completely sealed. A large emphasis on detail was needed to prevent as much infiltration as possible.

The ADA system gaskets and seals the gypsum board against each other. They then paint with low permeability paints or use metal foil to complete the vapor barrier.

*Used in Earth Home

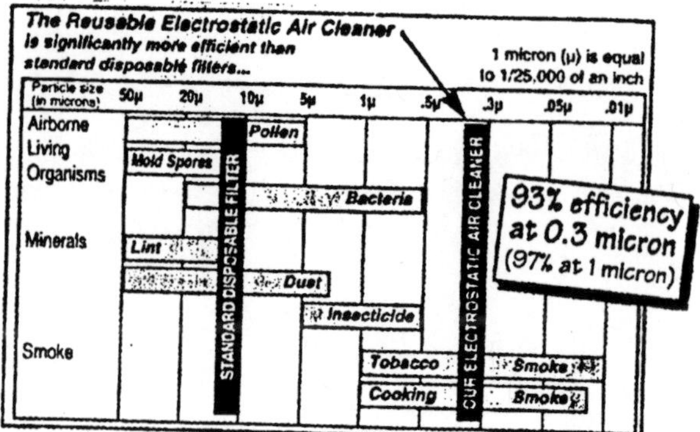

Your Lungs Deserve Better! These Furnace Filters Electrostatically Clean Air, Without Wiring!

Problem: Your respiratory system must eliminate 2 heaping teaspoons of pollutants each DAY. But the typical disposable furnace filter removes only 5-10% of indoor pollutants.

Solution: Our Electrostatic Air Cleaner **removes up to 93%** of pollen, dust, allergens, smoke and other pollutants, and does so efficiently—so allergies and respiratory problems are relieved, and your home's air is as fresh as can be. Prescribed by doctors.

The Best Part: It's as easy to use as your current filter—permanently replaces it, with no **electrical hookup or installation.** The fiber materials used in its exclusive 3-stage filtration system have an **inherent** static electrical charge. The friction of the air passing through increases that charge, attracting and holding particles as they enter. That's why there's no need for electrical hook-up.

Permanent Washable Air Filters

Rigid filters need no frame. Extremely high dust holding capacity. Low resistance to air flow. Easily washable.

Available in standard sizes and in bulk rolls for cutting to size. Cuts with regular scissors.

Filtering is by the electrostatic principle. Made of natural hairs that are cured, treated and permanently coated with a plastic and neoprene compound. This coating creates an electrostatic attraction for dust without the need of oil. Sanitized. Resist odors, mold, and mildew. Class II UL Listed for fire resistance.

Standard size filters are sold in carton quantities as listed.

Figure 63-REUSABLE AIR FILTERS

*Used in Earth Home

The third approach is to separate the functions of air barrier and vapor barrier and use an interior vapor barrier and an exterior air barrier. Vapor permeable but airtight sheets (usually spun-bonded polyolefin) are placed under the exterior cladding to achieve an exterior air barrier.

Masonry houses can be made completely air-tight. The concrete or stucco layers can provide an effective air barrier. Polyethylene sheeting or foam insulation can act as a vapor barrier.

Many of the custom homes that were built immediately following the oil embargo were built extremely tight with extra insulation. This created moisture problems and dry rot because they included no means to vent this excess moist air. (See also Wintertime Dry Air - Humidifiers.)

b. Earth Home Vapor Barrier System

As mentioned earlier, the interior walls of the Earth Home will be impervious to moisture so that the flax would not pick up moisture from inside. Vinyl paint applied over the interior cement/plaster walls will slow water transmission greatly. The exterior skin will be rich "stucco-like" mixture that would not saturate but allow moisture to go through slowly.

3. HRV/ERV/Air Ventilation

a. Types of Ventilation Systems

There are three types of ventilation systems; balanced ventilation; exhaust only; and natural. Supply-only systems are usually not used because of the danger of driving moist building air into the building shell. Balanced ventilation systems are often the system of choice because they provide the best control of incoming and outgoing airflow. It is easier to put heat recovery on these systems also.

b. HRV—Air-To-Air Heat Exchangers

Excess moisture and indoor air quality points to a need for an "air-to-air heat exchanger" or heat recovery ventilators (HRV's). A heat exchanger is a device that takes heat away from outgoing air and gives it back to incoming air. Heat is "exchanged" between inside and outside air. Some heat exchangers have efficiency ratings of over 80%. (See Heat Exchangers - Air-to-Air/HRV file.)

A home should be under slight <u>positive</u> pressure to exhaust pollutants. HRV's not only greatly increase the energy efficiency of the heating and cooling cycles by preconditioning the fresh air, but they also help control humidity levels, thwarting the growth of many kinds of bacteria, fungi, and other molds.

Many of the ventilation systems can operate at two speeds: low for normal operation, and high speed for peak periods. This is a manual switch that controls speed.

c. ERV/Types of Exchanger Cores

Energy Recovery Ventilators (ERV) also regulates humidity levels and can be connected to most forced-air heating systems. During the summer, the heat exchanger works in reverse to expel heat from the incoming air as it heads toward your air conditioner. Heat recovery ventilators (HRV) have no humidity control.

There are basically 4 types of cores used in the industry. They include:

--Cross flow plate cores
--Counter flow flat-plate cores
--Heat pipe cores
--Rotary wheel cores.

*Used in Earth Home

Rotary wheel exchangers offer the best advantages for homes with air conditioning as they can regulate humidity with a rotary wheel core plus a desiccant wheel. However, they are more expensive.

d. HEPA Option

A HEPA (high efficiency particulate) filter could also be added as an option to filter incoming air for sensitive people. HEPA filtration was developed by the Atomic Energy Commission during World War II to remove radioactive particles from the air in manufacturing plants. By definition, a HEPA filter must remove at least 99.97% of all airborne particles by particle count at a size of .3 microns which is one 300th the diameter of a human hair. Thus they remove all known organisms harmful to humans.

An activated carbon pre-filter is often used to absorb vapors such as organic solvents and odors. A pollutant switch (humidity, CO_2, or occupancy) can be used to switch to high speed if sensors indicate high levels of these contaminants.

e. Typical HRV Installation/Ducting

The following figure is a schematic of a typical HRV installation. ***Incoming air is ducted into the bedrooms, where high oxygen-content air is needed, and exhausted in places of high humidity and stale air such as the bathroom and kitchen***. Heated air will also be removed from the EH refrigerator compressor and demand heater areas.

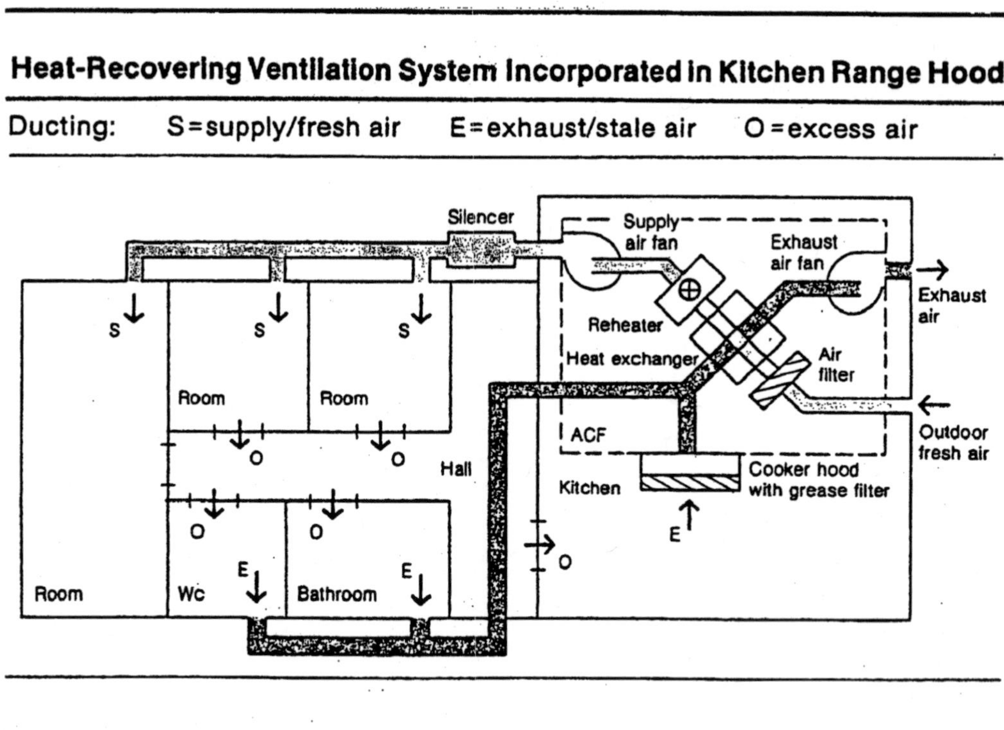

Figure 64-AIR-TO-AIR HEAT EXCHANGER INSTALLATION

*Used in Earth Home

f. Humidity Map of U.S.

The following is a map showing areas of the United States that are more appropriate for a heat recovery ventilator and energy recovery ventilator installation. HRV's are recommended to be installed in the regions shown. (See also EH Tabs section)

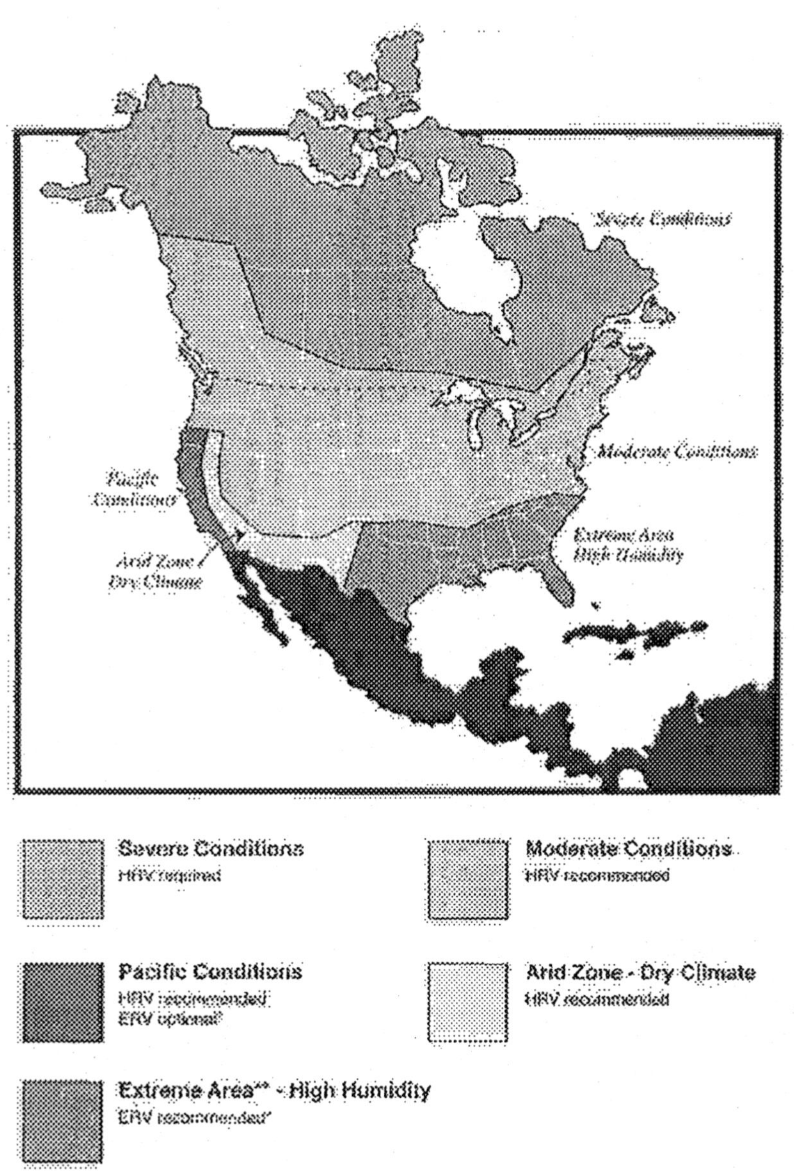

* ERV not recommended where temperatures fall below 25°F (-4°C) for more than five days.
** ERV's are recommended in regions where high outdoor humidity is cause for operating air conditioning/dehumidification more frequently than heating system.

Figure 65-HUMIDITY MAP OF U.S.

g. Earth Home HRV

1. CO_2/O_2 Mixing

Air inside the Earth Home is a combination of air that is being used by the people and air that is being used by the plants. Human beings give off carbon dioxide as waste products of their respiration. Plants, in contrast, give off oxygen as a waste product of photosynthesis. This beneficial oxygen is available in small quantities for the home as needed. (Air changes for greenhouse ventilation is accomplished separately.) (See also Roof section)

So, plants and humans sharing the same atmosphere are a good combination--benefiting by each other's waste products. A good rule of thumb is to maintain indoor carbon dioxide levels at 600 to 1,000 parts per million. Higher levels of CO_2 is better for plant growth. (See Plants section) (Also see HVAC files and Cooling - Dehumidification section.)

2. HRV Details

The Earth Home HRV would constantly bring in fresh air to force out the stale air and pollutants. The slower the air speed through the exchanger, the higher the efficiency. Aluminum construction was chosen because they last longer than treated paper methods. Moisture that condenses on the core of the HRV needs to be drained off in times of extra high humidity. The fan will move air more slowly to gain as much efficiency as possible through the oversized exchanger.

4. Humidity in Air (See also Cooling/Dehumidification section)

a. Humidity Regulation Background

Proper indoor humidity is recognized by ASHRAE (American Society of Heating, Refrigeration, and Air Conditioning Engineers) to be 35%-50%. If it gets much drier than this, the body's mucous membranes start to dry up and cause discomfort. Homes are especially apt to be drier during the heating season when the outside air that enters is low in humidity. Wood stoves remove moisture from the air by creating a negative pressure with the draft of the stove, so that moisture-laden air goes up the chimney and is replaced through cracks and crevices by drier outside air.

b. Effects of Humidity on Health

The amount of moisture in the air or humidity has significant effects on our health. The following figure shows some of the effects of various levels of humidity.

c. Humidification Chart

A common way to help with wintertime drying of air is to install a humidification device. ***There are basically six types of humidifiers--impeller, evaporative wick-type, misting steam, hot steam, ultrasonic, and floor register covers***. (See Humidifiers files.) The following figure shows some of these typical ways in which homes are humidified.

d. Earth Home Humidification

A frequent problem with all humidification systems is water impurities. ***Filtered rainwater in the Earth Home system is immune to these problems of water impurities because of the higher purity of the water.*** A good low-energy choice is the pan-type humidifier with ceramic plates. It will be placed in the main air stream, where water "wets" the surfaces by capillary action.

A separate fresh air intake to the stove and demand heater areas through the HRV should eliminate any pressure problem by using dry outside air as the stove intake directly. Moisture then remains in the home and helps the sinuses stay moist.

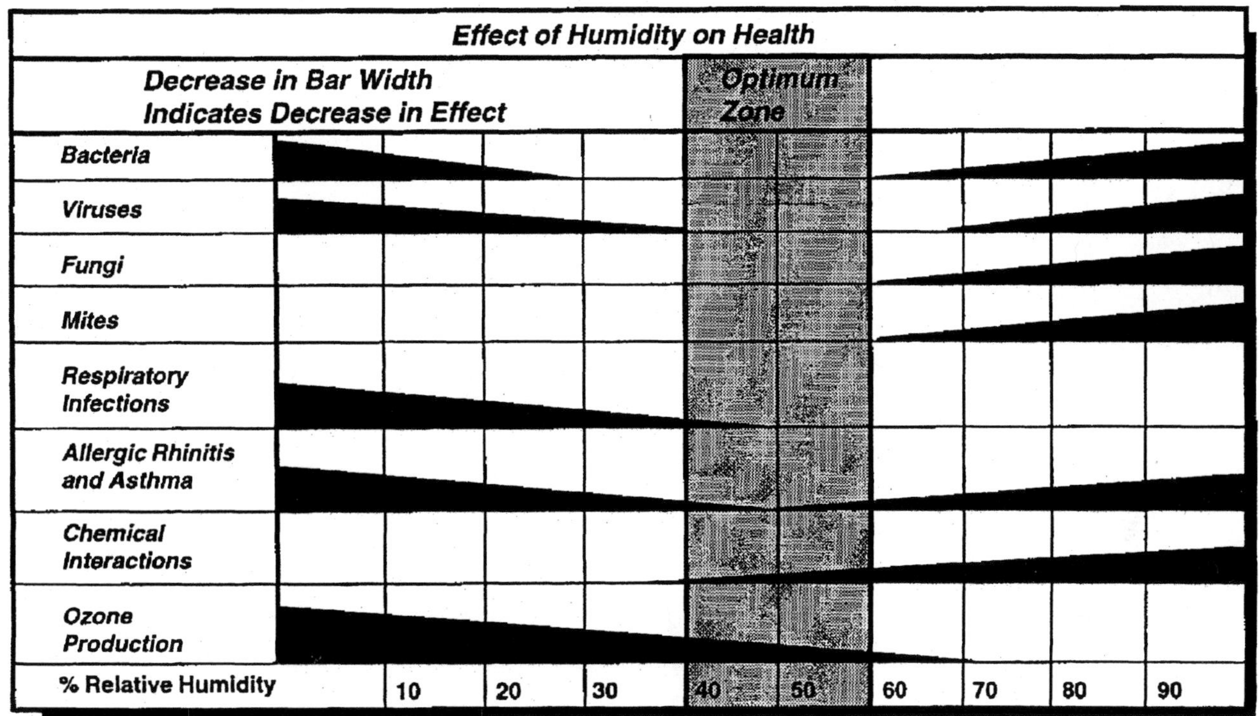

Figure 66-EFFECT OF HUMIDITY ON HEALTH

e. Humidity from Clothes Drying

1. Clothes Drying Background

Clothes drying typically has been accomplished by either clothes dryers (30%) or simply clotheslines. About 80% of electricity consumed by a typical tumble clothes dryer is used to heat the air. Modern clothes dryers attempt to dry the clothes in the least amount of time. Space considerations account for the small capacity of commercially available dryers.

There are several methods to cut the cost of drying clothes. For example, spinning the clothes at 3,000 RPM with a centrifuge can cut the drying energy in half because it removes most of the water. It is interesting to note that many of the dryers in older peoples' homes are located on a raised platform. This makes it easier to put clothes inside them without bending over so much.

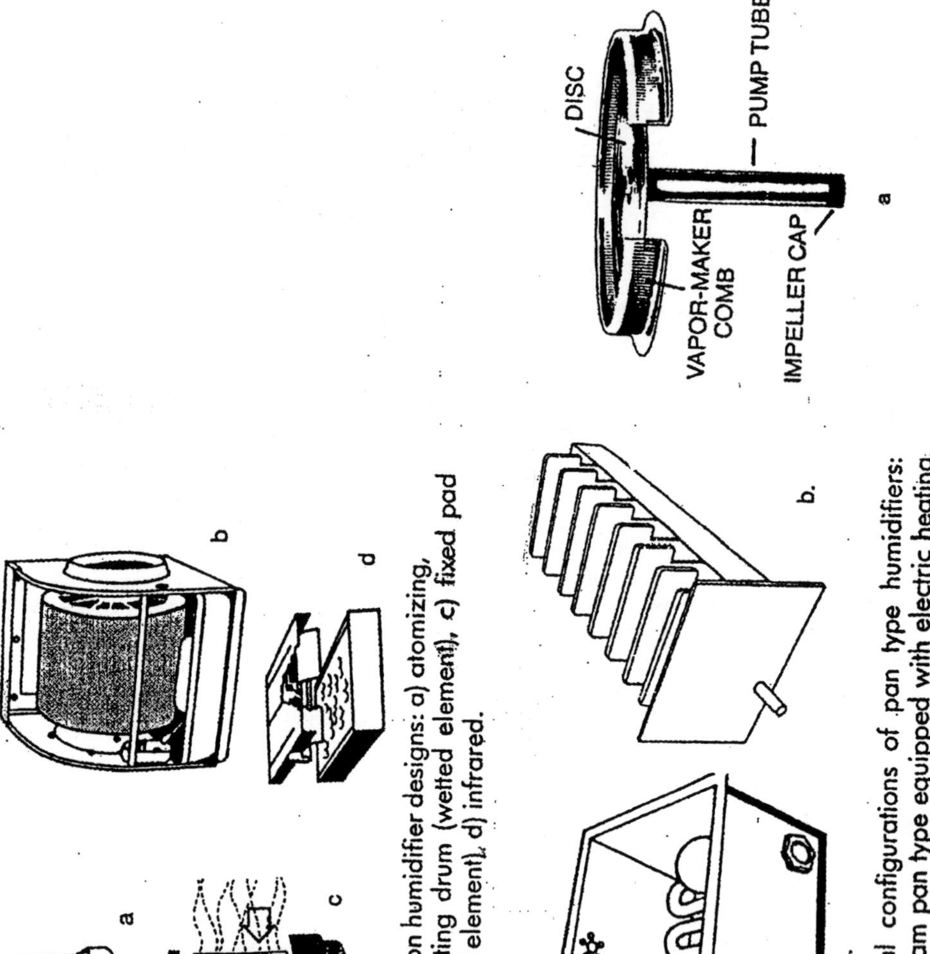

a
b
c
d
Common humidifier designs: a) atomizing, b) rotating drum (wetted element), c) fixed pad (wetted element), d) infrared.
a.
b.
Typical configurations of pan type humidifiers: a) steam pan type equipped with electric heating element (steam coil), b) pan type with plates that are wetted by capillary action.
DISC
PUMP TUBE
VAPOR-MAKER COMB
IMPELLER CAP
a
b
Some atomizing type humidifiers utilize a spinning disc (a) to cast water against a vapor making comb which atomizes water so it can be dispersed directly into the distribution system; b) high pressure nozzle sprays water through a pad or at a splash plate to atomize water.

Figure 67-TYPICAL HOME HUMIDIFICATION SYSTEMS

*Used in Earth Home

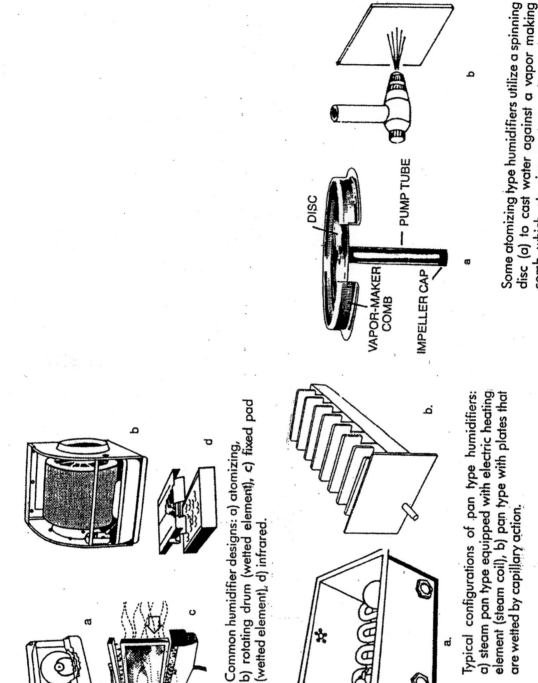

2. Earth Home Clothes Drying

The Earth Home II will use a slower large tumble system to increase natural evaporation and to greatly decrease the need for heated air. There will be more space between the clothes to allow for more natural evaporation. A longer dwell time can be maintained also. The large dryer will be placed above the living spaces under the rafters. The dryer will swing down for loading and unloading. This system takes advantage of the attic space that is wasted in typical homes.

5. Air Distribution

a. Moving/Exhausting Air Effects

Another way to prevent heat build-up is to exhaust the air using fans. Studies have shown that a fan moving air allows the thermostat setting to be increased 4°F without any decrease in comfort whatsoever. After about 11:00 pm., windows are opened on many homes in warm climates to capture some of the cool night air. A study found that small fans were preferred to larger fans, moving air at approximately 160 feet per minute. Above that speed, papers are disturbed on a table.

b. Earth Home Central Air Circulation Fan

After the buried cool tubes deliver cooled water to the radiator system, air is blown across the finned radiator and heat is exchanged. ***The fan I plan to use is very similar to a ceiling fan, except modified to look like an efficient, large-diameter backwardly-inclined fan***. The following picture is similar to the type that will be used.

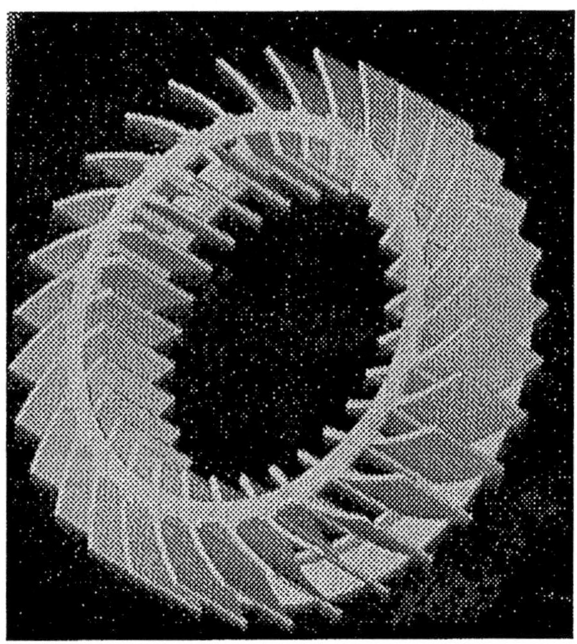

Figure 68-EARTH HOME CENTRAL AIR CIRCULATION FAN

*Used in Earth Home

The air in the ducts should be circulated at 1,000 to 1,200 feet per minute (maximum) in order to eliminate any whistling noises from inside the ducts. Larger ducts would be used because they require less wattage per CFM for the air-moving motor. Ducts made of E.P.S. foam with a foil surface are far more cost effective than steel or galvanized metal. Cheap, flexible ducts have also been made of Mylar and stainless steel wire coils.

*Used in Earth Home

VI. WATER SYSTEM

A. Sources/Uses of Water

1. Water Facts

H_2O or water is what makes planet Earth unique among the other planets. It is this chemical compound which makes life possible. ***Even though water is the most common substance on Earth, only 2.53% of the planet's water is fresh water (not salty), about 2/3 of that is locked up in glaciers and permanent snow cover, and agriculture uses 75% of the available supply***. To look at the entire water cycle, I first looked at where water comes from in the first place.

2. Rainfall

Water from rainfall is eventually evaporated back up into the atmosphere. ***Rainfall can be divided roughly into thirds. One third evaporates as soon as it hits the Earth*** because the ground temperature is usually warmer than the rain. The splashing water spreads over great amounts of surface area and speeds evaporation. ***Another one-third of the rainfall runs off the soil into creeks, rivers, lakes, and finally into the ocean. The last one-third soaks into the ground, gets filtered by the soil, and becomes part of underground water systems, or "aquifers".*** In arid regions, approximately two-thirds of the rainfall is evaporated back into the air immediately. Another third runs off into streams, leaving only about 3% actually replenishing the groundwater supplies in those areas.

3. Groundwater

a. Groundwater Background

There are two water supplies for human use (when you're not located near a lake or a creek): rainwater and groundwater. Groundwater can be pumped up to the surface by driving a pipe into the ground with a special filter tip known as a "sandpoint". Groundwater can be found as little as 20 feet below the surface, but better water quality may be obtained further down, as far as 400 feet below the surface. Going down even further you may hit "artesian " water, which is under pressure and sometimes contains more minerals such as calcium.

b. Aquifers

One advantage of underground water is that it is usually very clean, having been filtered through many feet of soil. If you drive a sandpoint or bore a well several hundred feet deep, you can obtain clean drinking water almost anywhere on the planet. Aquifers and underground rivers have defined borders, so one area may be much better for sinking a well than another area just a few feet away. A disadvantage of groundwater from aquifers is that it contains minerals. Iron oxide (known as rust), calcium, and other minerals are picked up as it seeps through the ground.

Another disadvantage is that the aquifers are drying up across the United States and areas such as Africa, China, former Soviet Union, and India. We human beings have put such a strain upon our natural resources that it becomes necessary to go deeper and deeper for good water supplies.

c. Pumping Energy

Another disadvantage of pumping water from the ground is the power required to bring the water to the surface. There are many ways of pumping water up, but they all require substantial power. It is first necessary to get the pump started (the technical term is starting torque) and it then requires a huge, steady energy input. (See Pumps - Water.) (See also Motors.) ***For these reasons it is advantageous to use rainwater as a source of water for the self-sufficient home.***

4. Rainwater (See Separate Rainwater section)

5. Water from Condensation

a. Condensing Water from Air—the Technology

If groundwater or rain is not available, there are several little-known alternative methods to obtain fresh water by condensing atmosphere humidity. We live in a dilute "ocean" of aerial moisture and/or "sky rivers" full of fresh water from which we can draw fresh water. Depending on the temperature and partial pressure (p), air contains varying amounts of water vapor. When the partial pressure at a given temperature exceeds a certain level of saturation (saturation pressure, ps), then condensation occurs. The term "relative humidity" (RH) is the ratio of the partial pressure to saturation pressure. The saturation pressure (and the carrying capacity) of air increases with the air temperature/pressure.

When a suitable substrate is available and its temperature is below the dew point, dew can form and be collected. The substrate can be cooled to various degrees by radiation or conduction to the ground or atmosphere, best during the night. The process of cooling by radiation is of course inhibited during daylight hours.

The essential principle in obtaining water from the air has thus been shown to be: a great water condensing surface which must be well protected against the heat of the sun and at the same time it is necessary that the air should pass to the condensing surface slowly, in order that it may cool properly and so deposit its water.

b. Ancient Air Wells

The collection of atmospheric humidity is an ancient technology that has been rediscovered in modern times. In 1900, Russian engineer Friedrich Zibold discovered 13 large conical tumuli of stones, each about 10,000 feet square and 30-40 feet tall, on hilltops near the site of the ancient Byzantine city of Feodosiya. Because there were numerous remains of 3-inch diameter terracotta pipes about the piles, leading to wells and fountains in the city, Zibold concluded that the stacks of stone were condensers that supplied Feodosiya with water. Zibold calculated that each "air well" produced more than 500 gallons daily, up to 1000 gallons under optimal conditions.

In the Sahara Desert there exist many miles of ancient underground passages called "foggaras" that have been dug into the sides of mountains. The tunnels connect with the surface through an air vent every 75 feet or so, serving to collect humidity and seepage. Similar excavations exist in Afghanistan, and have served to hide the movement of troops from observation by Soviets and Americans.

c. Air Wells Science/Fabrication

In 1931 Achille Knapen succeeded in condensing and extracting water from warm air to irrigate fields and vineyards in southern France with what he called, an "air well". Looking like a 40-foot concrete beehive, it was possible to produce as much as 6,000 gallons of water daily for every 1,000 square feet of condensing surface. Air wells are also known as dew condensers or aerial wells.

An air well can be built on practically any scale, and the wall materials can be concrete blocks, bricks or concentric hollow shells filled with sand or earth. A small air well 12 feet high and 12 feet across with walls 2 feet thick can supply a generous output of daily water. It can be fitted with top and bottom air pipes, and a multitude of condensing plates on the inside. Warm air circulates and gives up moisture on the cool inside condensing plates angled downward toward a catch basin at the bottom were it is collected.

With such principles in mind, the Belgian inventor Achille Knapen built an air well on a 600-foot high hill in France. The unique structure was described in Popular Mechanics Magazine. Other air wells have been written about or constructed over the years by Beysens, Leon Chaptal, Wolf Klaphake, Maimonides, and the non-profit organization OPUR.

d. Modern Dew Condensers

In the 1960s, Israelis irrigated plants with dew condensers constructed of polyethylene. A similar method was developed in the 1980s using specially prepared foil condensers to irrigate saplings. In 1982, Calice Courneya patented an underground air well that employs the same principle of using the ground as a heat sink:

Modern research conducted by the non-profit (OPUR) shows that the best materials for the collection of atmospheric humidity should be light weight, thermally insulated radiative condensers that radiate heat quickly. Such materials were not widely available until recently.

There are also several patents extant for glorified air conditioners that dehumidify the air to produce potable water, but they all require electrical power. Soviet cosmonauts aboard space station Mir used a system that recovered water from the air.

e. Dew Ponds and History

The water collectors known as "dew ponds" were invented in prehistoric times, but the technology is nearly forgotten today. A few functional dew ponds can still be found on the highest ridges of England's bleak Sussex Downs and on the Marlborough and Wiltshire Hills, and connected to castle walls. They always contain some water that apparently condenses from the air during the night. Gilbert White described a dew pond at Selbourne, England only 3 feet deep and 30 feet in diameter that contained some 15,000 gallons of water which supplied 300 sheep and cattle every day without fail.

f. Capturing Dew—the Technology and Research

The ability of materials to capture dew depends on their specific heats. The best material is swan's down, followed by flax or cotton, silk, paper, straw, wool, earth, charcoal, silica sand, and powdered chalk. Other researchers that have done work on capturing dew include Aristotle, Arthur J. Hubbard, Edward A. Martin, C. J. Cornish, Gilbert White, Clement Reid, S.B. Russell, Pacey and Cullis, UNEP, Edward A. Martin, and John Aitken.

g. The Technology of Capturing Fog—Fog Fences

The Roman author Pliny the Elder mentioned the Holy Fountain Tree, growing on the island of El Hierro in the Canary Islands. For thousands of years (until about 100 years ago) the people there obtained most of their water from the trees, the leaves of which captured fog.

Fog contains from 0.05 gram of water per cubic meter, up to 3 grams. The droplets are 1 to 40 microns in diameter. Fog has a very low settling rate, and it is carried by the wind wherever it may go. Fog collectors therefore require a vertical screen surface positioned at right angles to the prevailing wind. The collector must be a mesh because wind will flow around a solid wall and take the fog with it. A fog collector captures about half of the water passing through it. The efficiency of fog collectors depends on the size of fog droplets, wind speed, and the size of mesh (about 1 mm is optimal), which should fill up to 70% of the area. Two layers of ultraviolet-protected mesh, erected so as to rub together, causes the minute droplets to join and drain into PVC pipes attached to the bottom of the nets.

The ideal location for fog collectors are arid or semi-arid coastal regions with cold offshore currents and a mountain range within 15 miles of the coast, rising 1,500 to 3,000 feet above sea level. Collection varies with the topography and the density of the fog. Ocean or lowland fog usually lacks sufficient water or wind speed to yield a substantial amount of water, so careful evaluation studies must be made to determine the suitability of any particular microclimate.

Fog fences have the advantages of being passive, requiring no artificial energy input for operation. Claims include the quality of simple to design and can be constructed quickly and easily with little skill. The water quality from appropriate areas usually is good, though some treatment may be necessary for human consumption.

The Canadian organization FogQuest is the international leader in development of fog collectors. In the past few years, FogQuest has conducted several successful projects in Yemen, Guatemala (Lake Atitlan), and Haiti (Salignac Plateau). More have been planned in the Sultinate of Oman, Ethiopia, and Nepal. The yield at the best sites in Haiti is about 5.5 liters/m2day. In other words, each square meter of mesh produces about 165 liters/month. A large collector (50 m2) would produce about 175 liters daily, which is sufficient to supply the needs of nine people. Fog collectors in the Sultanate of Oman have yielded as much as 70 liters/sq meter/day.

Many other schemes for capturing fog have been proposed, including using electricity on wire screens. The U.S. Patent Office has many device descriptions in their files for fog dispersal and capture systems. However, very few have been built and/or tested to date.

6. Human Water Use

a. Water Use History

In early times, villages were founded near water supplies because water is heavy and difficult to move. Early Eastern civilizations ingeniously used bamboo pipes to transport water great distances. In the Roman era, water delivery systems became quite complex. Some of these huge stone aqueducts are still in working condition today. Many other ancient civilizations developed sophisticated systems for transporting water.

b. Modern Water Use around the World

Today most industrialized nations use large amounts of water for domestic and industrial use. For example, some studies suggest that the average Canadian now use about 72 gallons of fresh water per day at home for drinking, cooking, washing, and sanitation. This is an excessive amount when compared to other countries such as Sweden and the United Kingdom, where average water use is less than 50 gallons per person per day. In Germany and France, it is only about 37 gallons per person per day.

B. Rainwater Overview

1. World-Wide Rainwater History

For centuries, people have relied on rainwater harvesting to supply water for household, landscape, livestock, and agricultural uses. Before large centralized water supply systems were developed, rainwater was collected from roofs and stored on site in tanks known as cisterns. With the development of large, reliable water treatment and distribution systems and more affordable well drilling equipment, rain harvesting systems have been all but forgotten, even though they offer a source of pure, soft, low sodium water.

Rainfall is highly variable over the entire planet, but when you consider recycling and reuse of the water, one large supply of water will last a long time. (As a safety measure, water can even be purchased from a local fire department for a modest fee.) It rains almost all over the planet at <u>some time</u>.

Rainwater contains virtually no bacteria count <u>before</u> it hits the surface, so it's very clean. It's very similar to distilled water because it contains very little chemicals, minerals, salts, rust, etc. It's also naturally softened, which means that soap will easily make suds. This makes it easier to clean clothes, dishes, and bodies. Many countries currently use <u>substantial</u> amounts of rainwater. ***<u>In Hawaii, Greece, much of the Caribbean, Korea, Japan, and Israel, for example, the major part of the water supply comes from rainwater</u>***.

2. Harvesting Rainwater

a. Conveyance—Water Flows Downhill

Gutters, downspouts and pipes convey roof runoff to the storage tank, called the cistern. Gutters need to be sloped at least 1/16 inch per foot of run. They should be suspended from hangers no more than three feet apart. Aluminum or galvanized metal are recommended because of their sturdiness, although inexpensive plastic gutters may serve beneath small roof areas. The downspout should be sized to provide at least one square inch of opening per 100 square feet of roof area. Provide a downspout for each 50 feet of gutter run.

If there are tall trees near the roof, cover the gutter with 1/2-inch hardware cloth, and place simple wire baskets in each downspout opening to keep leaves and twigs out of the runoff. The pipe leading to the cistern should be a minimum of 4 inches in diameter (assuming the most common layout--gravity flow). It need not be buried beneath the frost line, but must have a slope of at least 1/4 inch per foot. Sharp pipe bends should be avoided, and cleanouts should be incorporated where horizontal runs exceed 100 feet.

b. Keeping the Water Clean

<u>1. Roof Washers</u>

Dust, leaves and bird droppings accumulate on roof surfaces between rainstorms. A simple device known as a roof washer is often used to filter the largest material from the roof runoff. The roof washer diverts the first flush of runoff (containing most of the contaminants) away from the cistern.

<u>2. Gutter Strainers</u>

A gutter strainer is a key item in any rainwater harvesting system that may seem simple enough. A gutter strainer is an important tool in the first step of the process of harvesting rainwater which is the removal of debris, leaves and host of other particles and solids that could easily end up in the rainwater harvesting storage tank making it much more difficult to take the water to the next stage of the filtering process. There are molded assemblies and spring models that filter larger particles from the rainwater.

*Used in Earth Home

3. Downpipe Filters

Downpipe filters are the simplest method of collecting rainwater as it flows through the downpipe. The unique construction of the vertical fine filter rinses out dirt particles larger than 0.28mm, moss, leaves and insects away into the drain. The filter will extract over 90% of available water without any obstruction of the downpipe.

c. Rainwater Storage/Cisterns

1. Cistern Background

In the (North) American Colonial days, many homes had rainwater storage tanks or "cisterns". These cisterns were generally made out of a coated concrete material. They usually held 500 to 5,000 gallons, with some holding over 10,000 gallons. To maintain a fresh cistern, the settled particles were cleaned out every couple of years and a fresh ammonia/bleach solution (at least 50 parts per million) was washed on the walls to prevent bacteria build-up.

An excellent cistern coating is used on the dolphin and seal tanks at the Como Zoo in St. Paul, Minnesota. The builders trowel this rich cement mixture on the wet concrete and let it harden to end up with a liner that is impervious to water (waterproof). (See Concrete files.)

To keep rainwater fresh, it has to be kept cool in order to keep the bacteria count as low as possible. ***One of the reasons that early cisterns were located in the lower part of a home was that contact with the ground kept them cooler***.

2. Primary Filter Options

Vortex filters connect to standard storm water pipes below ground. They come in a range of sizes to and deliver 90% collection efficiency on roof areas up to 3000 sq. m. There is no restriction or obstruction of water flow through the filter. They minimize maintenance by removing anywhere for debris to collect.

3. Cistern Construction Details/Options

The cistern can be of nearly any size and material. Any watertight tank of non-toxic material will serve: bulk milk tanks, never-used, lined fuel tanks, or precast fiberglass, polyethylene or concrete tanks, including those designed as septic tanks. Large cisterns are often made of concrete cast in place. (Lined concrete-block vaults are not recommended, as it is very difficult to make them waterproof.) The cistern inlet and outlet should be designed to minimize stirring the solids settled on the tank bottom, and the tank should include a manhole, a vent, a cleanout sump and an overflow pipe. If the cistern is to store potable water, a vertical fill pipe for use by water haulers is also desirable.

3. Cistern/Downspout Filters

There are many kinds of water filters from low-tech primary filters to higher-tech secondary filters. The low-tech primary filters separate large roof debris such as bird droppings, twigs, leaves, and organic vegetation of various kinds. The following figures show many kinds of primary cistern filters that have been designed and used.

These filters generally use a coarse grid system such as wide mesh steel grate, finer mesh screens, and finally a fine sand filter. Water trickles slowly through the sand into a storage tank. I found that simply allowing the water to “settle” filters out most of the fine particles after some time.

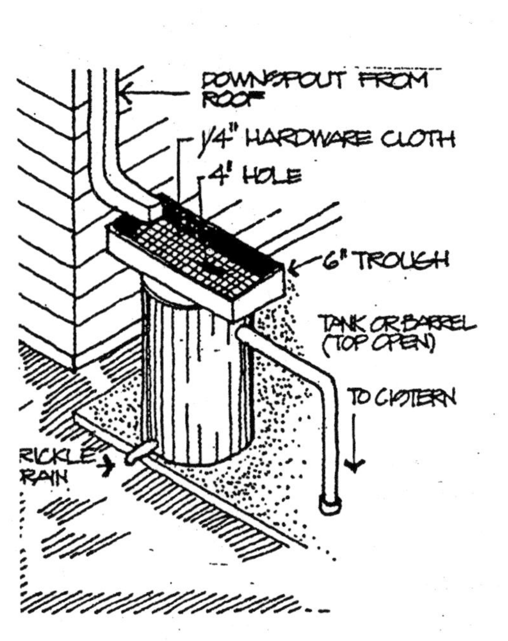

ROOFWASHER

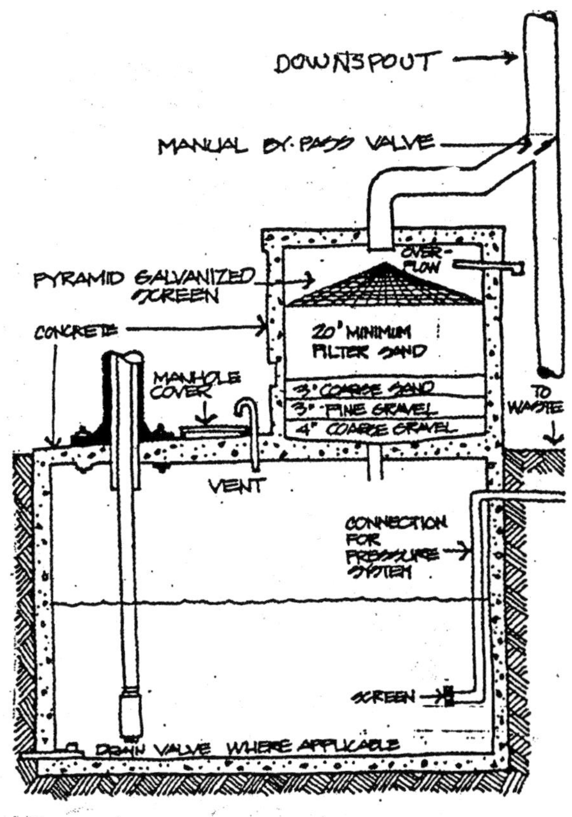

CISTERN WITH SAND FILTER

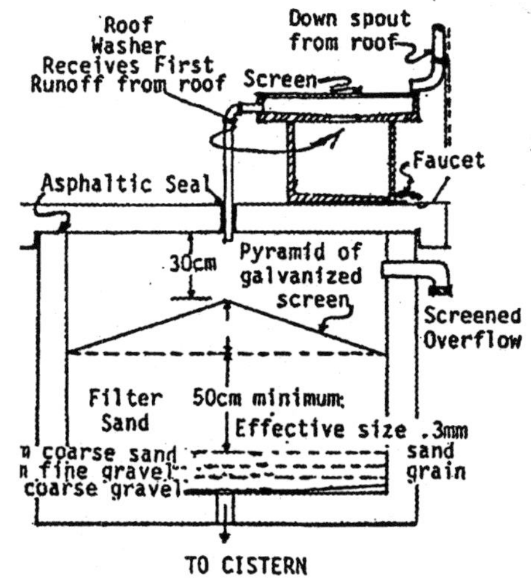

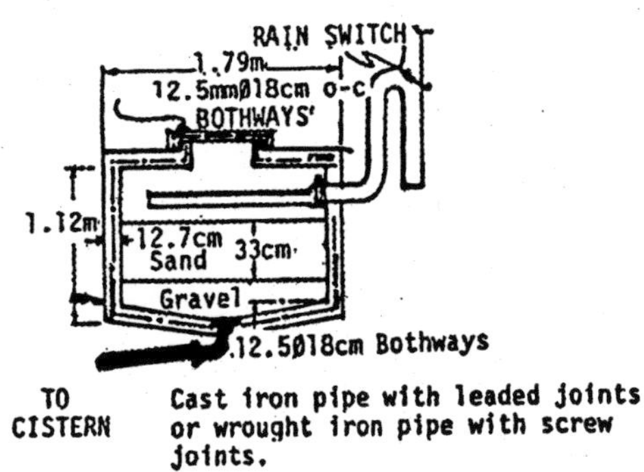

Figure 69-CISTERN FILTERS, PAGE 1

*Used in Earth Home

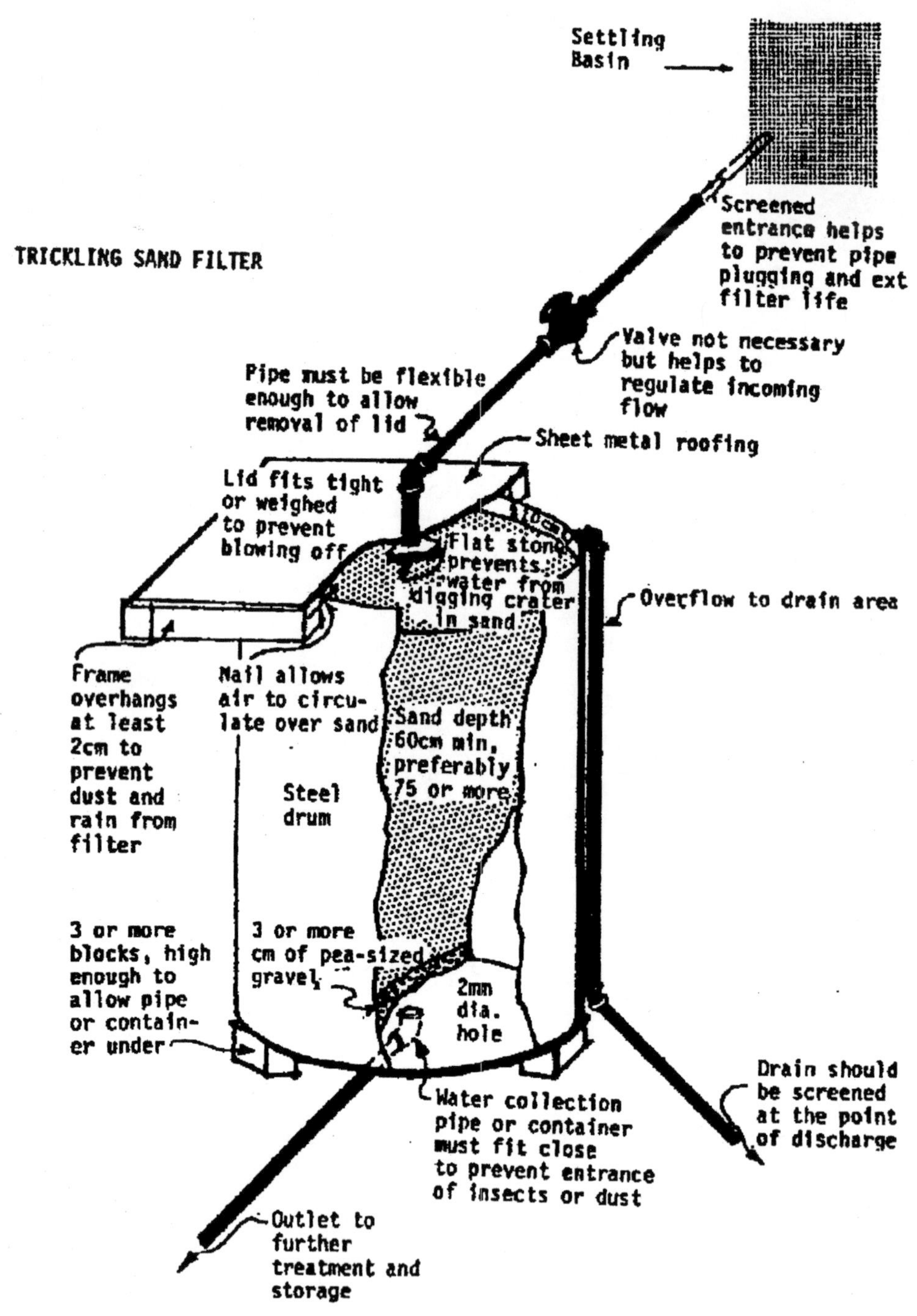

Settling
Basin
TRICKLING SAND FILTER
Screened
entrance helps
to prevent pipe
plugging and ext
filter life
Valve not necessary
but helps to
regulate incoming
flow
Pipe must be flexible
enough to allow
removal of lid
Sheet metal roofing
Lid fits tight
or weighed
to prevent
blowing off
Flat stone
prevents
water from
digging crater
in sand
Overflow to drain area
Frame
overhangs
at least
2cm to
prevent
dust and
rain from
filter
Nail allows
air to circu-
late over sand
Sand depth
60cm min,
preferably
75 or more
Steel
drum
3 or more
blocks, high
enough to
allow pipe
or contain-
er under
3 or more
cm of pea-sized
gravel
2mm
dia.
hole
Drain should
be screened
at the point
of discharge
Water collection
pipe or container
must fit close
to prevent entrance
of insects or dust
Outlet to
further
treatment and
storage

Figure 70-CISTERN FILTERS, PAGE 2

*Used in Earth Home

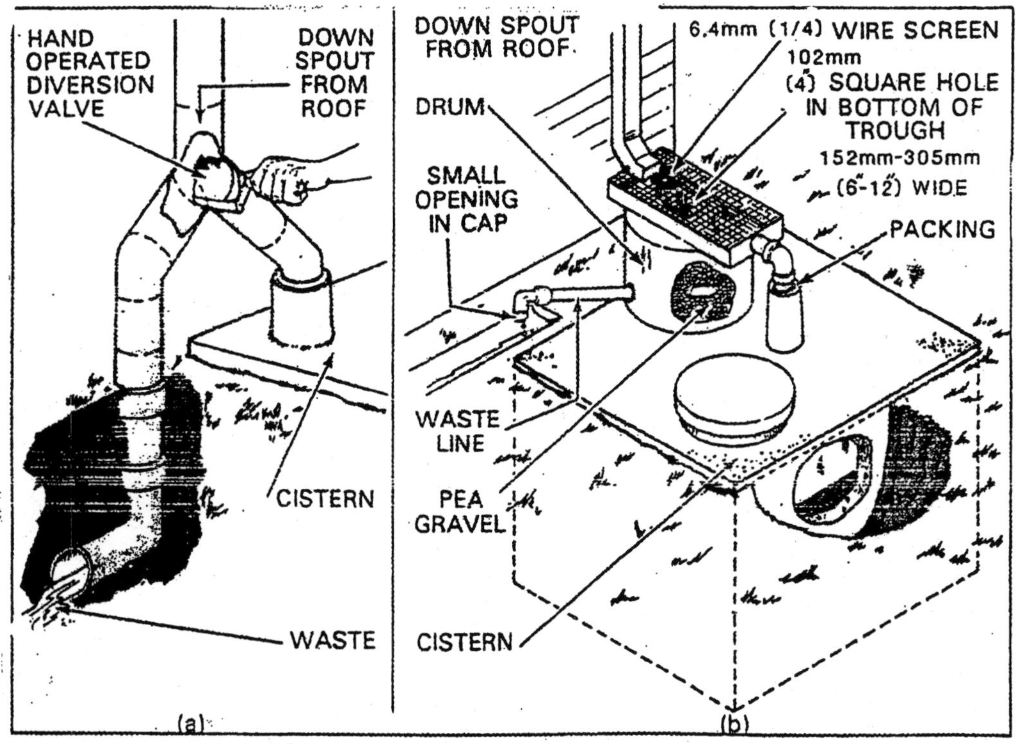

SOURCE: AAUIM, "PLANNING FOR AN INDIVIDUAL WATER SYSTEM", 1973

Methods of roof washing for cistern water. (a) Hand-operated diversion valve used to waste first rainfall. After roof is washed, the valve is changed so water will enter the cistern. (b) Automatic roofwash. The first rainfall flows into the drum. After the drum is filled, the remaining water flows into the cistern. During a period without rainfall, water dripping from the opening in the waste line empties the drum.

Figure 71-CISTERN FILTERS, PAGE 3

*Used in Earth Home

4. Floating Suction Filters

Floating suction filters are used to filter water as it is pumped from a storage tank prior to use in the home or garden. This protects the pump against drawing up sediment and helps ensure the quality of the rainwater by extracting water from just below the surface where it is cleanest. These are typically stainless steel filters that float below a polyethylene ball and incorporate an integral non return value.

3. Earth Home System of Rainwater Collection

a. Rainwater Supply

The Earth Home system relies on an initial and intermittent rainwater supply followed by filtering and recycling as much as possible. About 1 mm of rain produces 1 liter of water per square meter of catchment area. The initial water flow contains dirt, bird droppings, and leaves from the roof and gutters. Many devices have been made to discard the first batch of roof rainwater that comes into the gutters.

In addition, it is possible to get small amounts of water from the air itself by condensation on a metallic roof surface in days of high humidity. The condensed water flows into the gutters around sunrise.

b. Gutter System

I have found that the rain gutters purchased in hardware stores or lumberyards are not large enough to catch the high volume of water during a good downpour. A larger gutter system has to be used to handle these periods of peak supply. There are some gutter and downspout manufacturers that specialize in custom aluminum fabrication of this kind. ***In the Earth Home, rainwater is collected in an extra large gutter on the south eave, allowed to flow through central collection pipes, and drops into a filtered storage tank below the floor***. To the north a smaller rain gutter system will collect the rain from the smaller slope of the roof and deliver this to the storage tanks via the fish tanks. The fish tanks are fed first and any excess goes to the main storage tank.

c. Storage/Debris Trap/Settling

It has been estimated that a storage tank equal to 25% of the yearly requirement is necessary to be sure that enough water is available. This size varies depending on the climatic conditions. As the water flows from the roof, it is rough filtered by using a debris trap to remove all the large contaminants. This filter is large enough so it will not become clogged, and it contains an overflow so as not to disrupt supply. The rainwater goes into a large primary storage container and begins to settle out the small particles that may shorten the time between filter changes after it is pumped into the piping system.

d. Reusable Primary Filters

A system of filtration is necessary to obtain cleaner water. (See Water System-Filtration section) To make the home self-sufficient it is necessary to use filters that can be reused. At least two companies make *reusable* water filters. (See Filters files.) These companies include Arkal from Israel, and the Amiad Company. Both of these filters contain serrated disks stacked on top of one another. The serration between the disks lets the water through and traps the particles. These filters are available down to 200-mesh size and have various flow rates. I've found, however, that any rust in the water or steel plumbing pipes makes them difficult to clean. Plumbing pipes and fittings should always be made of a non-rusting material to eliminate this problem.

e. Pressurization vs. Gravity System

At one time I attempted to use a gravity system for all the household water needs, such as washing hands and operating a demand shower system. I found that about 35 psi (pounds per square inch) minimum pressure was necessary to do these tasks efficiently and quickly. I added a small bladder-filled tank and pumping system that has a pressure switch to turn off the pump when a preset pressure is reached. (See Plumbing files.)

*Used in Earth Home

A pressurized water system enables one to do many more tasks, such as pumping great distances, pushing water through a heating system, washing clothes, and irrigating. After pressurizing, it resembles a typical house system. An urban system uses pressure generated by aboveground water towers. Even though the point of use may be a great distance from the tank, the pressure created by the great height of the water tower makes the water pressure inside a home 40 to 80 psi.

f. Pumping Water (see Electricity-Water Pumping section)

C. Drinking Water

1. Definition of Drinking Water

There are many definitions of drinking water that can be used. Humans are now drinking many different waters around the world. As a benchmark, there are three characteristics of ideal drinking water:

1) Total dissolved solids of about 300 ppm (parts per million)
2) Hardness approximately containing at least 170 mg./l. of calcium carbonate. (0-60 ppm is soft, 61-120 ppm is moderately hard, 121-180 ppm hard, 181 ppm and more is very hard where hardness is expressed as CaCo3.)
3) Alkaline pH over 7.0 (neutral) to reduce leaching of metals from pipes
Spring and well waters usually fit into these categories.

2. Nature's Purification Methods

In the natural water cycle, water is purified in two ways: 1) Distillation, where evaporation from the ocean leaves behind particles and dissolved salts; and 2) Biological land treatment, where the action of microorganisms in topsoil biodegrades biological contaminants into nutrients, which are removed by plant roots before groundwater recharges.

3. Well Water

a. Problems with Well Water

A disadvantage of well water is the increasing health risk of groundwater contamination from a variety of sources. Well water can become contaminated by industrial pollutants in the groundwater, toxic contaminants, and heavy metals. Some of these possible sources include dumps, waste chemical storage areas, and cattle feed lots. Some estimates say groundwater contains up to two thousand trace toxic chemicals. EPA reports organic chemicals, inorganic chemicals, toxic metals, and pesticides in over **half** of the United States' groundwater. There is a full spectrum of water quality available from a private well supply. (See Aquifers section)

b. Chlorine in City Well Water

City supplied tap water comes in many different qualities. In order to kill bacteria and microbes, they put chlorine in the water. Chlorine is a good disinfectant, but it is harmful if ingested in large quantities. Not only that, but it combines with hydrocarbons in the water to form carcinogenic chlorinated hydrocarbons. This has been called the most common pollution problem throughout our country.

4. Filtration/Purification Options

As mentioned earlier, rainfall is very pure if you catch it before it hits the ground. When it hits the ground, it splashes around and picks up bacteria, making it necessary to purify it before drinking. There are many ways of doing this. One way is to boil and filter it, which requires great amounts of energy and will not be covered here. Another way is to add chemicals to it, which is also will not be covered here. (See Filters file - complete

***Used in Earth Home**

comparison chart.) Note that the following purification methods are used after the sand filter and disc filter system has completed their jobs and the water is in the plumbing system for general use.

a. Disposable Filter Systems

1. Reverse Osmosis (RO)

Reverse osmosis units use pressure to push the water molecules through a selected membrane. The membrane wears out and must be replaced and it takes energy to pressurize water.

2. Cartridge Systems

There are many cartridges that will purify water, but they all must be periodically replaced. For a self-sufficient home system, a purification system must be recycled or have a much longer service life.

b. Permanent (Non-Disposable) Filter Systems

1. Silver-Impregnated Ceramic Filters

Silver is the only metal that kills bacteria on contact. The history of silver used to disinfect and keep pure goes back many generations. Alexander the Great used silver urns to store water for his troops on extended sea journeys.

Ceramic with silver in them is used as a filter material. The fine silver particles are imbedded into the clay and fired to a hard ceramic consistency. The finished ceramic filter removes particulate down to .2 micron particle size, which is the size of the smallest bacteria.

More than one-half of the world's airlines use silver water filters. Silver-impregnated ceramic filter are manufactured by the Katadyn Company and Berkefeld, among others. The filters must be brushed periodically to remove built-up material. With care not to brush too briskly, the filters should last a very long time. An automated brushing system is already offered on some ceramic filters.

2. Activated Carbon

Activated carbon is made commercially by heating wood to a high temperature (1200°F - 1800°F) and injecting steam in the absence of oxygen. To date, activated carbon cannot be easily recycled or re-activated using at-home technology. Steam and pressure are required with losses of 10% being normal. Charcoal can be made by burning wood in a trench until the wood is burning in the center and then putting a corrugated sheet of steel over the fire. Dirt is quickly put on the steel and allowed to cool for a week. This produces a good quality charcoal for general filtering or burning.

5. Distillation Methods

a. Distillation Overview

1. Distillation Background

Another method of obtaining drinking water is the distillation process. This method is the same method to separate higher "proof" alcohol from weaker alcohol mixes such as beer. (See Energy/Power Section on Alcohol)

The ancient Greeks used the distillation process on their ships to convert seawater into drinking water. Distillation if one of mankind's earliest forms of water treatment and it is still popular throughout the world. Water is heated and driven onto a cold surface such as a copper tube or a stainless steel surface, where the pure water condenses. The impurities stay in the boiling water.

It is also possible to distill drinking water directly from the soil by sealing a film over a hole in the ground. When the sun shines on this film it condenses any moisture inside the soil onto the surface of the film and the water drips to a collection container below the low point in the film (small rock placed on top). However, this method has limitations for a dependable year-round supply.

2. Distillation Myths

Distillation yields the highest quality pure water. There is, however, an ongoing debate whether drinking distilled water actually leaches minerals from the body. The basic process of distillation is responsible for the hydrologic cycle of evaporation from surface water to form rain. Nature purifies 99% of all the water on this planet through the distillation process—consistently. Distillation normally removes 99% of the dissolved minerals in water. Carry-over is primarily a concern with volatile organic chemical contaminants. Filtering the distilled water through a carbon filter removes these contaminants.

It is actually oxygen in water that gives it its taste and not the minerals. Most people now know that water is an unreliable source of minerals because they are of the inorganic variety and the body has difficulty absorbing them. A better source of minerals is the food that we eat, because the minerals are much more readily assimilated. Looking to the animal kingdom suggests that they drink close to distilled water in the form of rainfall, snowmelt, and morning dew without any apparent harm. Hundreds of thousands of people drink distilled water every day.

b. Solar Stills

1. Solar Still Technology

The water from the oceans evaporates, only to cool, condense, and return to earth as rain. When the water evaporates, it removes only pure water and leaves all contaminants behind. Solar stills mimic this natural process. Energy from the sun heats water inside a still to the point of evaporation. Water vapor rises, condenses on the inner glass surface of the still, and drips into a collection bottle. This process removes impurities such as salts and heavy metals as well as eliminates microbiological organisms. The end result is ultra-pure water cleaner than the purest rainwater. Only solar energy is required for the still to operate. There are no moving parts to wear out.

2. Solar Stills Background

Solar distillation is a tried and true technology. The first known use of stills dates back to 1551 when it was used by Arab alchemists. Other scientists and naturalists used stills over the coming centuries. The first "conventional" solar still plant was built in 1872 in what is now northern Chile. This still was a large basin-type still used for supplying fresh water using brackish feedwater to a nitrate mining community. The plant used wooden bays which had blackened bottoms using logwood dye and alum. On a typical summer day this plant produced 4.9 kg of distilled water per square meter of still surface.

3. Solar Still Issues—High Water Use

As water evaporates from the solar still basin, salts and other contaminants are left behind. Over time, these salts can build to the point of saturation if the still is not properly maintained and flushed on a regular basis. Properly operating a still requires about three times as much make-up water as the distillate produced each day. If the still produced 3 gallons of water, 9 gallons of make-up water should be added, of which 6 gallons leaves the still as excess. The excess water flushes the still basin through the overflow to prevent salt buildup. If this is done on a daily basis, the flushed water is of approximately the same quality as the original feedwater that was added to the still. The excess water is of suitable quality that it can be used to water landscaping, wash pots and pans, etc. No sediment or sludge will buildup if the still is properly operated and flushed daily.

*Used in Earth Home

6. Other Water Purification/Treatment Systems

a. Ultraviolet (UV) Lights

A high intensity ultraviolet (UV) light source is used to kill bacteria with close contact with water. Specially constructed tubes allow close contact between the water and the light source for more efficient purification. This germicidal lamp kills a large percentage of the bacteria present in the water. There are 12 volt varieties of UV lights available and are only on when there is water flow. The Aqua-Project involves two companies that offer solar UV water treatment for rural locations in developing countries.

b. Ozone Disinfection

Ozone has been used for disinfection of drinking water in the Municipal Water Industry in Europe for over 100 years. Many commercial water companies use equipment that can manufacture over 200 pounds of water per hour. Ozone has a very good safety record with no deaths in over 100 years of use. Ozone typically requires significant amounts of 110 volt electricity and most units are larger than home-sized.

c. Water Ionizers

People realized years ago that many of the long-lived cultures shared at least one common quality-they all drank highly alkaline water from oxygenated streams. Years of research and testing conducted by Japanese and Asian scientists has found that drinking alkaline water daily neutralizes the acidity produced internally as a result of improper diet and daily stress.

Ionized water is made by passing an electric current through water. The result is acidic water used for plants, washing, etc. and alkaline water for drinking. Water molecules naturally tend to bond in groups of 10-13, whereas ionized water molecules are in groups of 5-6. There are 3 extra electrons on the outer orbit of ionized water molecules. These smaller particles of ionized water pass through body tissue more efficiently making hydration more effective.

The health benefits from using alkaline water for drinking include detoxification, blocking free radical damage, and making food taste better. One of the drawbacks of ionizing water is the significant amount of energy that it takes to produce it. To date, all of the ionizers on the market are 110 volts A.C.

7. EH Water Purification System

a. Distillation System

Distilling water in any self-sufficient scheme could be easily accomplished in combination with domestic hot water production. Problems of mineral/scale build-up would be greatly lessened by using rainwater (soft water) for the water source. Research is continuing on simplified distillation methods that minimize heat inputs.

The Earth Home will use a "demand-heater-style" water distillation unit to slowly produce clean distilled water. A small flame heats a small chamber to force steam onto a cold surface. The by-product of this system is heat for the washing water system. It typically takes 3000 watts to produce 1 gallon of distilled water when using electricity. A back-up system is used for safety purposes. The distilled water system is primary because any filter must be replaced at regular intervals, however long that might be.

*Used in Earth Home

b. UV Light/Silver-Impregnated Ceramic Filter Back-Up

The Earth Home back-up drinking water filter uses a two-stage system. The first is the primary high intensity 12 VDC ultraviolet light that kills bacteria in the water.

After the UV lights have killed any organisms in the water, it is put through a silver-impregnated ceramic filter. ***This second stage is a silver-impregnated ceramic filter with a self-cleaning brush to remove any built-up particles that would inhibit water flow through the filter.*** Any remaining giardia or cryptosporidium would be eliminated in this stage. With care not to brush too briskly, the filters should last a very long time.

c. Distilled Water Uses

Distilled water is used for drinking purposes and as an additive for any lead-acid batteries. Distilled water ensures that no contaminants can shorten the life of the battery.

D. EH Washing Water

1. EH Plumbing Details (See Separate Plumbing Section)

2. EH Body Washing

a. EH Showering/Bathing

The Earth Home shower system is a modified low flow shower system-using about .75 gpm of water. This is roughly half the rate of the most efficient showerheads that are currently available.

b. EH Handwashing

For washing hands, I use a very small "spray" system. I can wash my hands thoroughly using about 2 ounces of water. A fine spray of water is directed down into the sink where the hands are gently rubbed with soap to clean them. Specialized spray nozzles were used to achieve precise spray patterns so a minimum amount of soap and rubbing was necessary. Research has shown that spray taps use about half the water as a running tap.

3. Clothes Washing

a. Background

Any cleaning process requires the interaction of a cleaning solution (soap), dwell time, heat energy, and mechanical agitation. Generally good cleaning requires a balance of these four factors. Decreasing one of these factors requires an increase in one or more of the other factors for proper cleaning. For example, using less soap would require more agitation.

Clothes cleaning involve the removal of a wide range of soil materials from clothing. They include water-soluble materials (e.g., perspiration), pigments (e.g., oxides, carbonates), fats (e.g., sebum), proteins (e.g., blood, egg), carbohydrates (e.g., starches), and dyes (e.g., tea, fruit). In order to perform these cleaning tasks and others such as whitening and foam regulation, complex detergents have been developed for use in water.

To wash clothes it is necessary to first de-wet the water, shake the clothes around to extract the particles, and final rinsing. De-wetting means using a chemical to reduce the water's tendency to stick to itself or cohesion. This makes the water more willing to flow into small spaces such as between the fibers of fabrics. ***The rinsing is important for hygiene reasons.***

b. Hot Water for Washing Clothes?

It is estimated that 2/3 of the average washing does not require hot water. Significant further savings can be realized by using cold water detergents and by advanced washing techniques such as "spray washing". This hot water saving technique uses a detergent solution continually sprayed onto the clothing while it is agitating. (See Heating Water section) (See Washing Machine Types) Better detergents, less dirty work, and more frequent washing are generally causing less use of hot water in developed countries.

c. Soap and Detergents

1. Soap and Detergent Definitions

Soaps, on the whole, are made of materials found in nature, and detergents are labeled synthetic (although some of their ingredients are natural). Soaps have been around for centuries and they are better overall for our health and easier on the environment than detergents.

2. Soap/Detergent Options

There are many soap options when looking at the method of "de-wetting" water to provide cleaning action. De-wetting is generally accomplished by adding a chemical to water to decrease surface tension and cohesion. The category of chemicals are called "surfactants". There are phosphate soaps, biodegradable soaps, lye soaps, and also some plant sources for de-wetting water.

3. Phosphate Soap

Phosphate soaps make up the majority of soaps that are on the market today. Interestingly enough, phosphate soaps are the most damaging to the environment, but they are also the easiest to reclaim. The phosphate-dirt particle can be coagulated with a special agent to form larger particles that can be filtered through a diatomaceous earth material. The complete system for re-use, however, has not been thoroughly developed for domestic use.

4. Biodegradable vs. Biocompatible

Most people don't know that so-called biodegradable soaps can actually be toxic to plants. Something "bio-degradable" breaks down into pieces. These pieces may or may not be good for the environment.

"Biocompatible" means the pieces are beneficial or not harmful to an environment. This means you can use the resulting greywater to water your plants. The product actually breaks down into valuable plant nutrients.

5. Biodegradable Soaps

Biodegradable soaps de-wet water by using less environmentally harmful chemicals. I haven't seen any successful applications to recycle biodegradable or aqueous soaps. They are, however, easier on the environment after disposal.

Homemade soap or lye soap is made with lard, which is an animal fat, and lye, which comes from caustic material such as wood ashes. It is possible to make soap at home using these two materials. (See Soap file.)

Some plants have soap-like qualities and can be used for shampoo including soapwort or bouncing bet, saponica, grapevine sap, clematis, yucca, and others. Some of these can be successfully grown outside in temperate climates.

d. Washing Machine Types

The following figure shows modern wash machine types. There is a vast difference in washing machine types. Horizontal axis, European-type models use far less hot (and cold) water per cycle and normally less than 50% of the energy.

There is a 12-volt wash machine available, but it does not have the capacity of the normal larger units. It is possible to modify an existing modern wash machine to use 12-volt electricity. (See Appliance file.) There is also a way to enhance the operation of a modern wash machine by using a "soft start" mechanism. This is a newly developed technology for starting a wash machine motor, for example, using a smaller amount of energy.

Wash Mach. Type	Cycle	Hot Water Energy (MJ)	% of Total	Agitation/ Spinning Energy (MJ)	% of Total	Total * (MJ)	Eff. Comp. to Hand-wash
Handwash	cold/ cold	0.0	0	0.12	100	0.12	100.0
Vert. Axis	hot/ warm	13.9	97	0.43	3	14.3	0.8
Vert. Axis	warm/ cold	6.7	94	0.43	6	7.1	1.7
Horiz. Axis	cold/ cold	0.0	0	0.50	100	0.5	24.0
Horiz. Spray	warm/ cold	1.8	78	0.50	22	2.3	5.2
Vert. Axis**	warm/ cold	3.3	89	0.43	11	3.7	3.2

*To 50% to 70% moisture content.
**This machine makes use of a "suds saver" or hot water reuse to recover 50% of the hot water heat inout.

Figure 72-WASHING MACHINE TYPES

*Used in Earth Home

e. Fabric Discussion

1. Cotton

Wash performance is highly sensitive to textile properties, soil type, water quality and temperature, washing technique and detergent composition. Cotton material is the easiest material to wash, and is also the closest to being recyclable of any common fabric. Cotton meets half of all the world's textile needs. It washes clean easily but has limitations.

It also shrinks, fades, and bright colors are unavailable. Another drawback is while growing cotton only takes up 3% of the world's arable land, it uses a full 25% of all the pesticide used in the U.S.! Also cotton production takes a heavy toll on soil fertility.

2. Fabric Options

A more earth-friendly fabric that has been developed is called Tencel. Tencel fabric is made from a specially grown tree, and has qualities very similar to cotton. (See Fabric file.)

Also, a new technology has been developed to enable hemp fibers to be used for clothes. The hemp plant (cannabis sativa) is illegal to grow in the U.S. because it is the source of marijuana. However, a number of states have made the growing of hemp legal. A huge clothing and fabric industry will most probably come from this versatile plant. (See also Hemp section)

f. Future Clothes Washing

The Japanese have hit upon the idea of applying ultrasound to washing machines. Sanyo Electric Co. recently put on sale a washing machine that doesn't require detergent to clean lightly soiled clothes. Instead, electrodes on the side of the tub electrolyze the water. An ultrasonic wave generator at the base of the machine uses sonic waves to generate millions of tiny air bubbles to help loosen grime and grit on clothes in a purely mechanical action. The future also shows a new enzyme that dissolves fat in cold water.

E. Recycling Water (Greywater)

1. Greywater/Wash Water Overview

"Greywater" means water other than toilet water (black water) that has been used in such areas as bathroom sink washing, kitchen sink, washing machine, and shower. It normally contains particles, soap, hair, skin flakes, and can be slightly warmed. Dish, shower, sink and laundry water comprise approximately 80% of residential "wastewater."

a. Greywater Background/History

The warmer greywater usually also contains substantial quantities of chemical pollutants, pathogenic and indicator organisms. There have been many ways to deal with greywater which include: 1) pretreatment and undersoil perforated pipes; 2) leeching chamber with no pretreatment; 3) gravel-filled seepage pits with no pretreatment; 4) pretreatment filter alone; 5) intermittent sand filter; 6) recirculating trickling filters; 7) evapo-transportation schemes; and 8) raised soil planting beds.

Greywater systems have been around for some time, but have not been generally discussed or included in typical home schemes. This is due to the health issue and the unproven nature of less complicated greywater systems.

b. Sources of Greywater

The following figure shows how much greywater is produced in a typical suburbia home that could be utilized. Note that the Earth Home will generate much less than this chart show.

Fixture	People	Uses/ person/week	Gallons/ use or minute	Liters/ use or minute	Gallons per week	Liters per week
Washing machine	4	1.5	32	119	192	714
Inside Bathtub	1	1.5	20	74	30	112
Inside shower	2	7	13	48	182	677
Bathroom sink	4	21	0.5	2	42	156
Subtotal-Inside bathroom				0	254	945
Toilet	3.5	14	1.6	6	78.4	292
Kitchen sink	4	21	2	7	168	625
Outside shower	1	4	20	74	80	298
Outside bath	1	0.25	40	149	10	37
Subtotal-Outside bathroom				0	90	335
Handwash tap	1	14	0.25	1	3.5	13
R/O purifier reject water	4	7	1	4	28	104
Blackwater					78	292
Greywater					1080	4016
Total					1158	4307

Figure 73-GREYWATER SOURCES

2. Greywater Treatment

a. Greywater Filters

The following figures show many various ways that greywater has been filtered. They resemble the filters used for rainwater.

A peat filter can also be used to pre-treat septic tank effluent by filtering it through a two-foot-thick layer of sphagnum peat before sending it to a soil treatment system. Peat is partially decomposed organic material with a high water-holding capacity, large surface area, and chemical properties that make it very effective in treating wastewater. Unsterilized peat is also home to a number of different microorganisms, including bacteria, fungi, and tiny plants. All of these characteristics make peat a reactive and effective filter media.

*Used in Earth Home

ABOVE GROUND USE OF GREYWATER

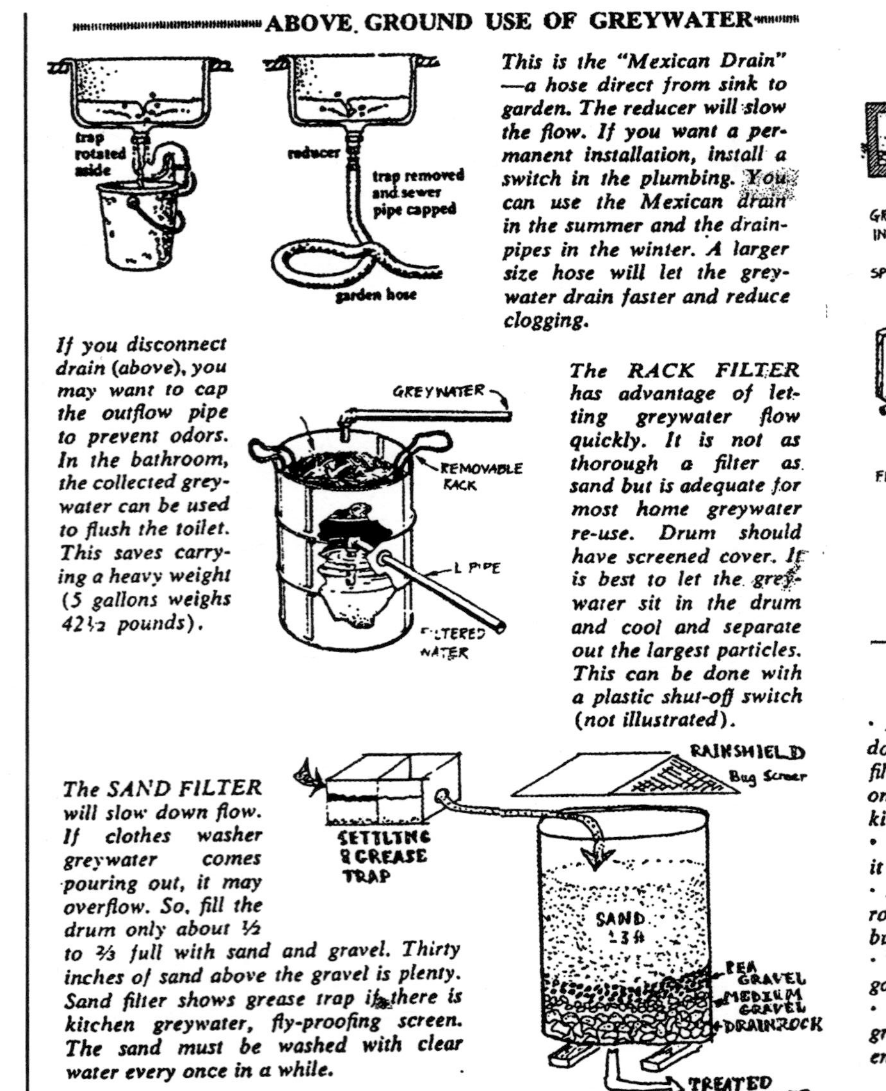

This is the "Mexican Drain" —a hose direct from sink to garden. The reducer will slow the flow. If you want a permanent installation, install a switch in the plumbing. You can use the Mexican drain in the summer and the drainpipes in the winter. A larger size hose will let the greywater drain faster and reduce clogging.

If you disconnect drain (above), you may want to cap the outflow pipe to prevent odors. In the bathroom, the collected greywater can be used to flush the toilet. This saves carrying a heavy weight (5 gallons weighs 42½ pounds).

The RACK FILTER has advantage of letting greywater flow quickly. It is not as thorough a filter as sand but is adequate for most home greywater re-use. Drum should have screened cover. It is best to let the greywater sit in the drum and cool and separate out the largest particles. This can be done with a plastic shut-off switch (not illustrated).

The SAND FILTER will slow down flow. If clothes washer greywater comes pouring out, it may overflow. So, fill the drum only about ½ to ⅔ full with sand and gravel. Thirty inches of sand above the gravel is plenty. Sand filter shows grease trap if there is kitchen greywater, fly-proofing screen. The sand must be washed with clear water every once in a while.

GREYWATER INLET

SPLASH PLATES

SAND

PEA GRAVEL

GRAVEL

FILTERED WATER

THE BOX (of redwood or concrete) can handle larger flows than a single drum—although a series of drums side-by-side will serve the same purpose. Again, a cover is needed, especially to keep out rain which saturates sand and hinders filtration.

This sandbox design allows half of the filter to rest and to aerate—which reopens pores—while the other half works.

GREYWATER CAUTIONS

- *Kitchen sinks contain grease in warm water. The grease must cool down to harden and then be removed by a grease trap—an ordinary filter will become clogged and rapidly produce odors. Some people only re-use bath, laundry, and lavatory greywater. They let both kitchen and toilet go to the septic tank.*
- *Do not use greywater on potted plants or seedlings unless you dilute it or alternate it with fresh water.*
- *Avoid using greywater on crops to be eaten raw, such as lettuce. On root crops, use both grey and fresh water to avoid any pollutant build-up.*
- *To avoid build-up of harmful ingredients, move greywater around garden. Don't leave it in one spot.*
- *Use on crops like tomatoes where edible part is not in contact with greywater. Fruit trees, artichokes, and ornamentals are also fine recipients of greywater.*

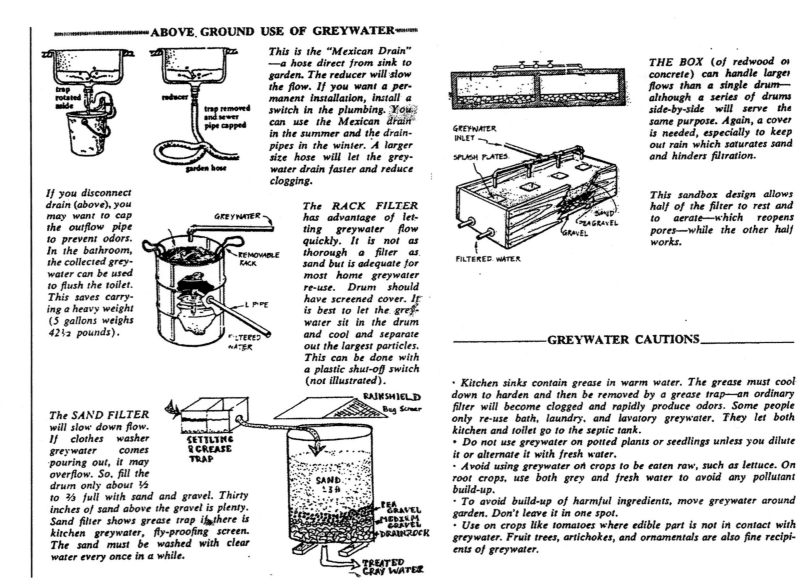

Figure 74-GREYWATER FILTERS, PAGE 1

*Used in Earth Home

INFILTRATION BED

5' Infiltration Pipe

5/16" Holes on 6" centers

Consists of two concentric pipes

Mulch
Topsoil
Sand
Gravel
Wire Screen
Stones

Stabilized, Storable Greywater to irrigation or disposal

A large sand filter using modified septic tank.

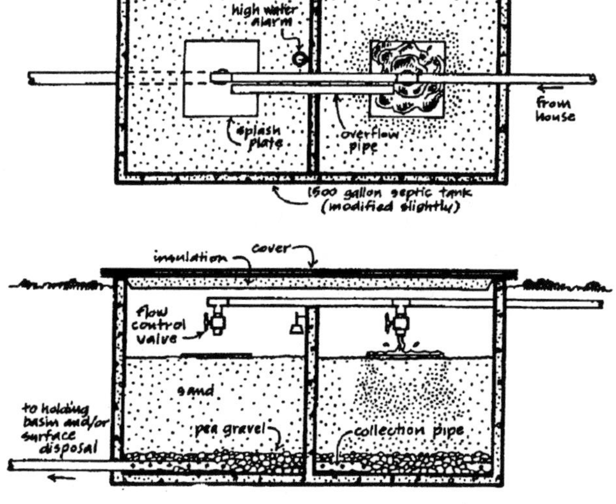

Figure 75-GREYWATER FILTERS, PAGE 2

*Used in Earth Home

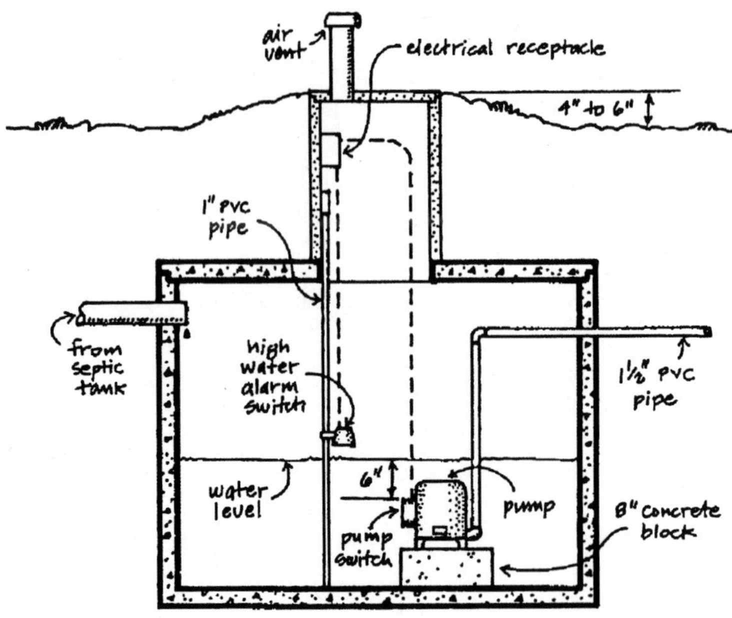

Section through greywater holding tank with pump for irrigation.

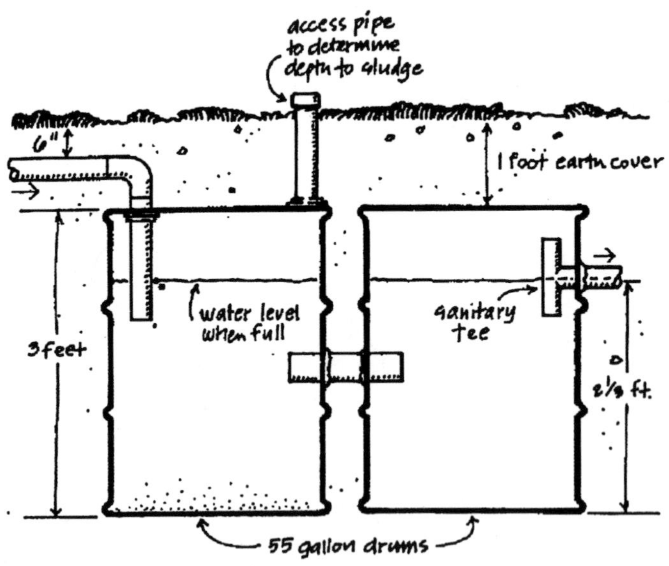

A greywater holding tank can be made by connecting 55-gallon drums in series.

Figure 76-GREYWATER FILTERS, PAGE 3

*Used in Earth Home

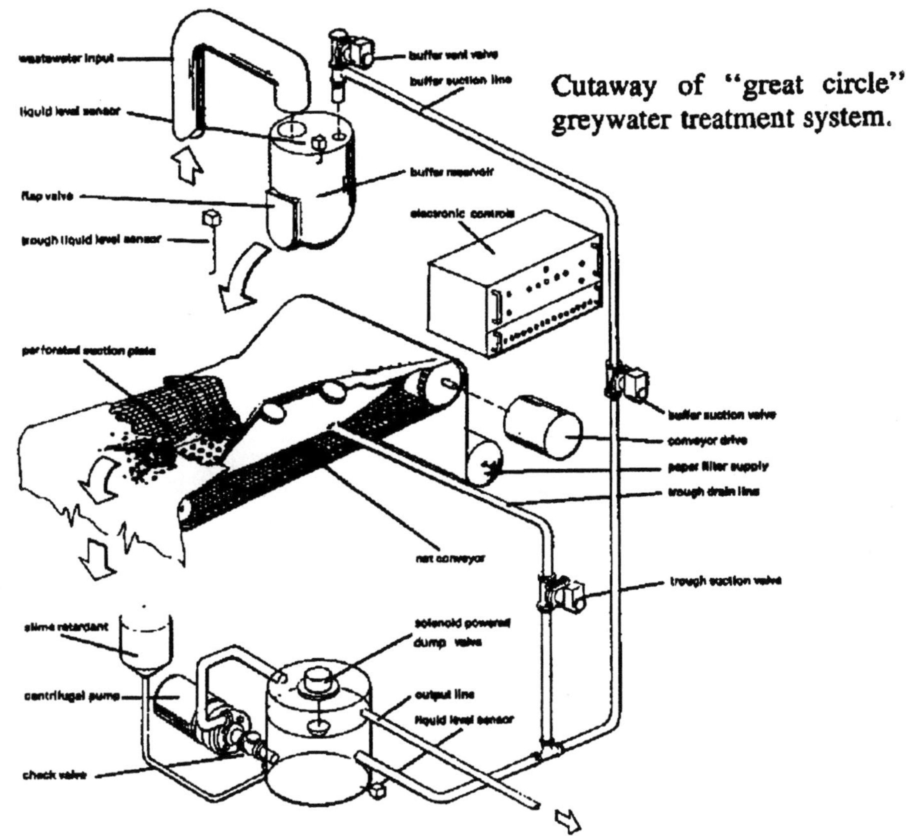

Cutaway of "great circle" greywater treatment system.

Schematic of Aquasaver greywater system.

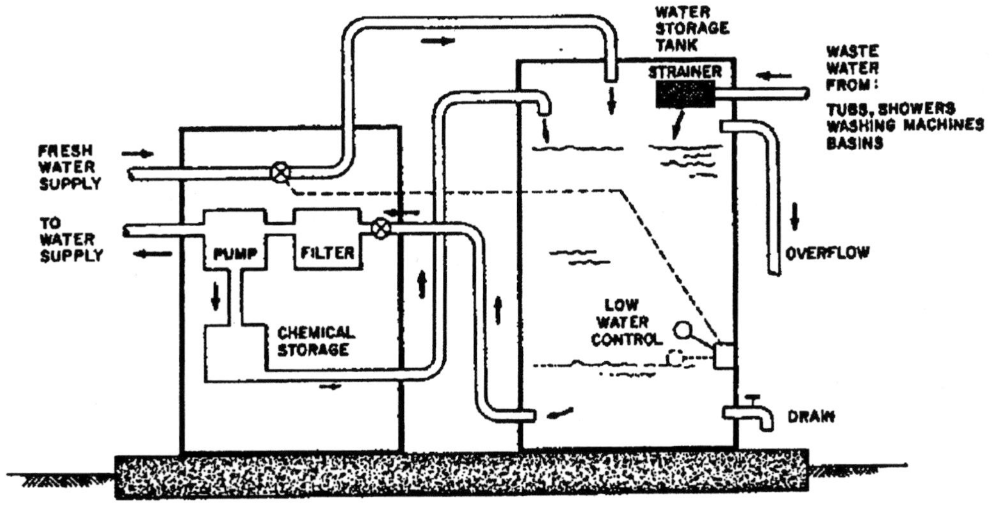

Figure 77-GREYWATER FILTERS, PAGE 4

*Used in Earth Home

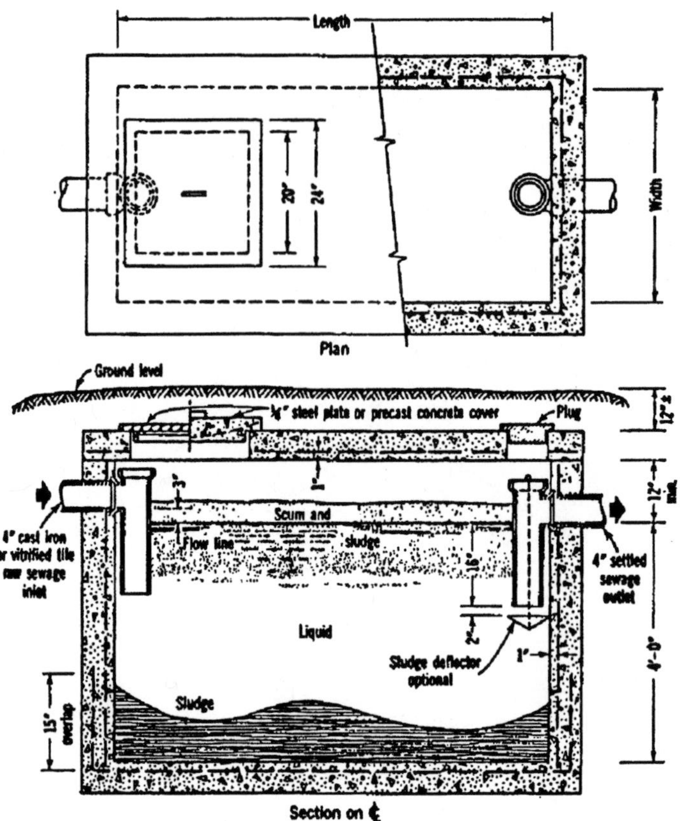

Small concrete septic tank suitable for holding greywater.

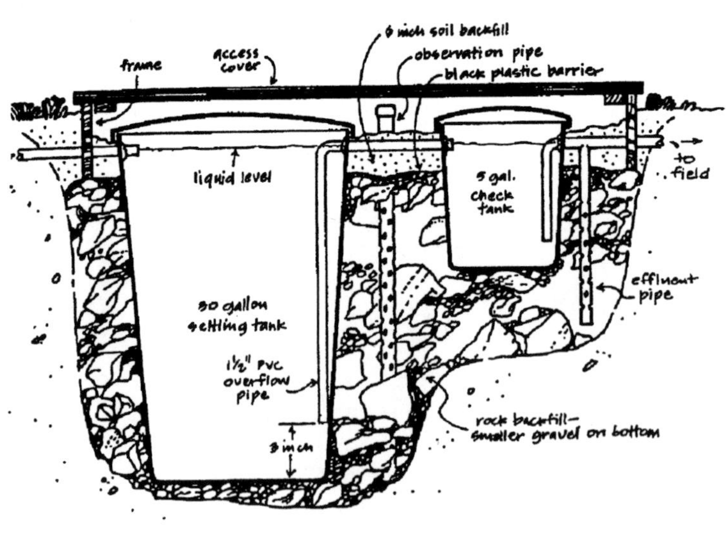

Low flow greywater tank

Figure 78-GREYWATER FILTERS, PAGE 5

*Used in Earth Home

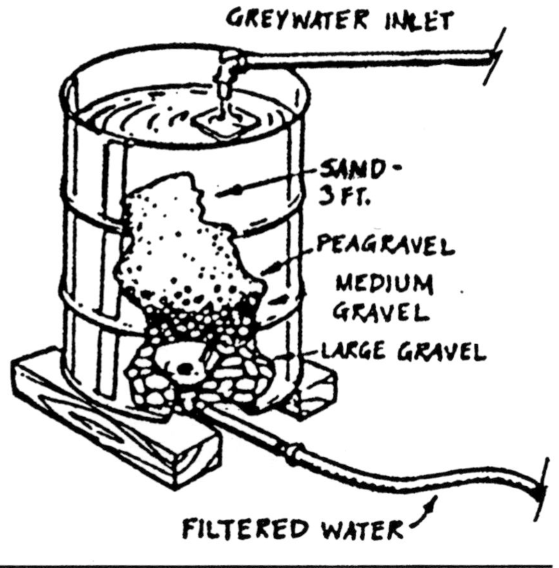

Figure 79-GREYWATER FILTERS, PAGE 6

b. Domestic Greywater Treatment Systems—Background

A domestic grey water treatment system (DGTS) collects, stores, and treats grey water to a high standard. It includes components such as wetlands, intermittent sand filters, soil filters, grey water septic tanks, and aerated wastewater treatment systems. The treatment process varies according to how the grey water is used and includes settling of solids, floatation of lighter materials, anaerobic digestion in a septic tank, aeration, clarification and finally disinfection.

As primary treatment will only reduce the solids in the wastewater, secondary treatment is necessary to remove pollutants from the remaining liquid. Grey water can be diverted to plants via a grey water diversion device or a DGTS. Grey water diversion devices do not treat grey water, while a DGTS treats your grey water to a higher quality standard for use in your garden and possibly your toilet or washing machine. (See Aerobic Digester section)

3. Greywater Diversion Devices

There are two types of greywater diversion devices: gravity and pump. A gravity diversion device diverts grey water from plumbing fixtures directly onto your garden. The flow of grey water is usually activated through a tap or a switch and must be piped to plants through sub-soil irrigation. During wet weather, the tap or switch directs grey water to a drainfield. A diversion device must be installed taking into account any sewer gasses and traps.

A pump diversion device has a similar set up to a gravity diversion device but includes a surge tank to control the flow of grey water to your garden during sudden surges. Kitchen water should not be diverted through a surge tank unless it passes through a treatment system (DGTS) or a grease trap/arrestor. The reason is that fats, oils and food particles in the water can clog the system, create odors, and cause the sub-soil irrigation system to malfunction. (See Kitchen Waste Water section)

4. Health Considerations of Greywater

a. Direct Contact or Consumption

It is best to label all pipes and tanks as greywater. Carefully avoid cross connections that might get mixed up. Always wear gloves when cleaning greywater filters.

b. Breathing of Microorganisms

Sprinklers or spray nozzles can disperse droplets a great distance. People can then breathe them along with the particles. These droplets can also evaporate and leave harmful microorganisms behind on surfaces.

c. Microorganisms on Plants

Direct application to foliage can leave untreated microorganisms on surfaces. Do not apply greywater to lawns or fruits/vegetables that are eaten raw. Fruit trees can accept greywater only to the roots.

d. Contamination of Surface Water

If greywater does not percolate through the soil, it can flow into creeks or other waters untreated. Only discharge greywater underground or into a mulch-filled basin. Do not apply greywater to saturated soils. Intermittent applications allow it to soak in and aerate between waterings.

e. Contamination of Groundwater

It is pretty difficult to contaminate groundwater with a greywater system. But wells should be stayed away from, because the water can follow the pipe down to potable water sources.

f. Chemical Contamination

Biological purification does not usually remove industrial toxins. Toxins either will be absorbed by plants or will pollute groundwater. Many household cleaners are composed of chemicals what are unsuitable for introduction into a biological system Do not buy products that you would not want in your greywater system Divert water containing those you can not avoid to poison the sewer or septic instead.

g. System Overload

Greywater systems are safest when using water that is fairly clean initially. Greywater should not contain water used to launder soiled diapers or by anyone with an infectious disease. Do not store greywater—use it before bacteria multiply. If you have a party and have a "beverage overload", divert it to the sewer.

h. Two Design Principles to Remember

The first principle is that greywater must pass <u>slowly</u> through healthy topsoil for natural purification to occur. The second principle is that an effective greywater design so that no contact takes place before purification. Keeping these in mind will greatly reduce the problems that any greywater system will have.

5. Earth Home Greywater System (See EH Digester section)

*Used in Earth Home

6. Greywater Heat Recovery?

Continuous flow greywater sources—such as the shower (hot source) is sometimes used in an attempt to reclaim some of the heat from the discarded water. Non-continuous sources such as the bathtub and clothes washer have been considered as warm sources. However, virtually none of the systems intended to reclaim heat have been proven to be cost-effective because of the small amount of heat recovered from the water. Most of the testing has concluded single-digit savings of hot water. For this reason and the much more extensive plumbing and controls necessary, no greywater heat recovery is intended for the Earth Home.

7. Kitchen Waste Water

a. Kitchen Waste Background

Kitchen wastes can contain solids such as vegetable matter, soil, soap, and many cooking by-products. In many farmhouses of the past, kitchen dishwater was dumped through a hose in the side of the wall and into the lawn. That was the spot where people dug their worms for fishing, and where the grass grew much faster and greener. Many nutrients are lost down the kitchen sink. Kitchen sink waste water poses special problems for any greywater system. Sometimes the rinse water side of the sink is plumbed into the greywater system and the washwater is put directly into the blackwater system.

Kitchen waste water can also contain grease in liquid or solid form. This grease can cause problems with any digester mechanism and must be dealt with. Kitchen waste water is especially rich with nutrients and should be treated separately when discussing water recycling plans.

b. Grease Traps/Arrestors

The following figure shows a typical grease trap or grease arrestor.

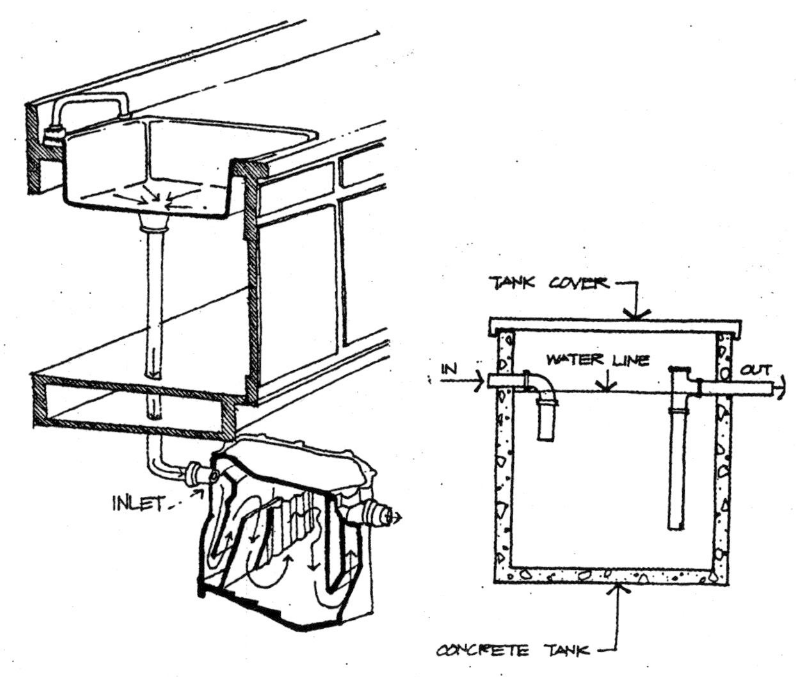

Figure 80-GREASE TRAPS

c. Earth Home Kitchen Waste Water (See also EH Digester section)

The kitchen wastewater will first pass into a grease trap, worm beds, greywater storage area, and finally to the underground plant irrigation system during growing season. Any excess is routed to the aerobic digester to be broken down.(See Earth Home Greywater System)

F. Toilet Wastes (Blackwater)

1. Background/History

a. Sewage Chemistry

1. Feces Chemistry

The feces of an average healthy adult varies in size from 4 to 8 inches by 1 to 1 ½ inches and in weight from 100 to 200 grams. Feces consist of 65% water, 10 to 20 percent ash, 10 to 20 percent soluble substances and 5 to 10 percent nitrogen. The consistency and odor as well as size and weight may vary considerably. Food residue account for only part of the total bulk of feces. The remainder is made up of bacteria and dead cells. The origin of those 10 trillion bacteria is concentrated at both ends of the alimentary canal, the mouth and the large intestine, where more than 100 different anaerobic species reside.

2. Urine Chemistry

Humans pass, on the average, a quart of urine per day. The dry solids in urine-everything left when all water is removed-weigh about the same as the solids in feces. Urine is rich in nitrogen (10-15%) which means that you lose about 10 pounds of pure nitrogen each year.

b. Squatting Position for Defecation

1. Squatting Position History

The natural position for defecation assumed by every mammal in the natural world and primitive human races is the squatting position. When the thighs are pressed against the abdominal muscles in this position, the pressure within the abdomen is greatly increased so that the rectum is more completely emptied. Sitting, on the other hand, has been shown to contribute to many bowel and bladder ailments, such as hemorrhoids, constipation, prostate problems, and incontinence. American Indians and many other cultures did not have any rectal problems or hemorrhoids. The sitting posture evidently "kinks" the anal sphincter, and hinders full emptying of the bowel.

The squatting position is still used in Greece, Italy, Turkey, and throughout the Orient. 75% of the world's population still squats, and young children naturally adopt this position. The followint figure shows the squatting position and intestine support advantages and the next figure shows the normal squatting position for men and women.

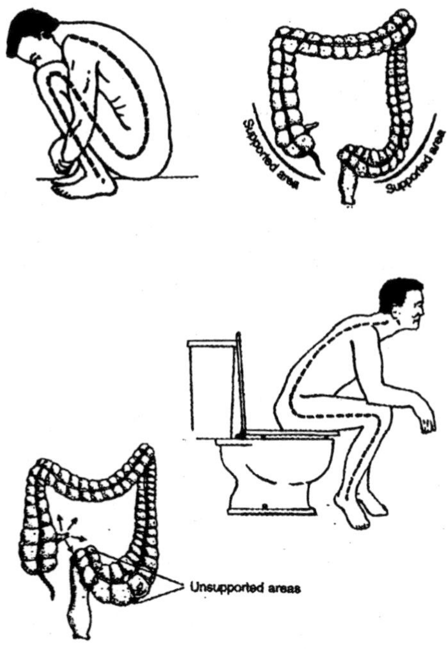

Figure 81-SQUATTING POSITION INTESTINAL SUPPORT

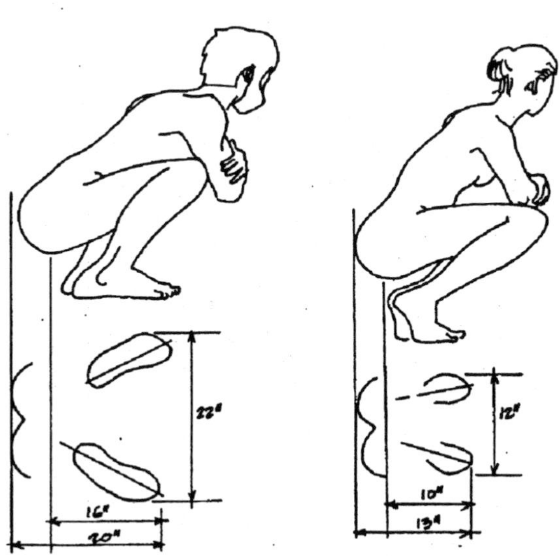

Normal squatting position for men and women.

Figure 82-NORMAL SQUATTING POSITION (MEN & WOMEN)

*Used in Earth Home

2. Modern Sitting Toilet Problems

The first known sitting toilet was crafted from limestone over 3000 years ago, but sitting toilets in those days were rare. It has been only during the last 150 years when sitting toilets, as we know them, have became commonly accepted. This was because sewer mains were installed in London. Sitting toilets represent only a small percentage of the world's population.

Our modern toilets have been criticized as not being constructed according to physiological requirements. They are too high and are often blamed for unsatisfactory results and conditions including ileocecal-valve dysfunction, incomplete elimination, strictures in the sigmoid, constipation, hernias, varicose veins, and appendicitis. A modern answer to this issue is to use a footstool next to the toilet to simulate the natural squatting position. The sitting position evidently "kinks" the sphincter, and hinders full emptying of the bowel.

3. Squatting Position Advantages

Over 75% of the world's population still squats, and young children naturally adopt this position. The above ailments associated with sitting toilets can be greatly eliminated by adopting the squatting position. Improvements in the pelvic and bowel area becomes evident sometimes in as little as a few days after adopting the position.

4. EH Squatting Position Option

The Earth Home will use a product developed in Australia called the "In-Lieu" toilet converter. It is a one-piece plastic molded product that sets in front of a typical sit-down toilet bowl. It allows the user the choice of squatting or sitting to defecate.

c. History of Toilets

In nature, water carries off wastes, and excreta is just another nasty waste. Early sewerage systems emulated natural process. Some cultures disposed of their wastes in water while others used the land. South Sea islanders built their privies over the ocean. The western tradition of sewage comes from the Romans who built both aqueducts for water supply and sewers leading to the Tiber. Perhaps the earliest known water-based fixture was the squat-type toilet used in the Palace of Knossos four thousand years ago—similar to those used all over the Mediterranean area today.

In the cities, waste was dumped haphazardly in the streets. Nobility did somewhat better. Their castles were equipped with garderobes, simple privies built into castle walls and often emptying into a stenchy moat. Sewer and water closet devices made their appearance in the min-nineteenth century in Europe, although types of dry toilets remained in use for many years. The open gutters, washed clean only by rain, were gradually put underground to minimize the appalling stench and mess.

The earth closet is simply a toilet seat with a bucket below to receive the waste matter. After every use, fine dry soil is added or manually flushed from a container; the bucket is emptied periodically. The advent of sewers in the 19th century, and health problems resulting from water borne treatment, sparked an interest among medical people and sanitarians in earth closets.

d. History of Toilet Paper

Humans are the only animals that have the dexterity to actually wipe themselves after each defecation. Currently, it is believed that the original material used for cleaning was leaves and sticks.

1. Roman Methods

In ancient Rome public toilets, they used a sponge with a handle which was put into a small dish with salt water. At home, Roman's also took a piece of cloth and put in into a cutting on the end of a small stick. The richer people used pink (rose) water.

*Used in Earth Home

2. Middle Ages

In the middle ages, the rich Europeans used a piece of sheet, wool, or lace. The monks used some scrap cloth from old frocks. On the Hawaiian Islands people used shells from coconuts. Other coastal people used Mussel shells.

3. Asia

In Asia, the Hindus and Muslims used their left hand, which was washed with water from a jug nearby. Some say the custom never eating with the left hand and shaking hands with the right hand was produced from this custom. Islamic tradition prescribes that you should wipe with stones or clods of earth, rinse with water, and finally dry with linen cloth.

Many Arabs consider the Western practice of using paper to be disgusting. They feel that you always leave a residue by following the practice of wiping with paper.

4. Paper Invented

In the 17th century, newspapers were spreading and they were used accordingly. This led to major problem in England because the landscape was littered with paper. They did not have modern sewers to take the stuff away from sight.

5. Colonial America

Corn cobs and the early Sears catalog were favorites back then. The catalog was free and it had hundreds of pages of blotter and non-smooth paper. The catalogs were favorites for many years until they started printing on glossy, clay-coated paper that was no longer absorbent. If colonists were out and about or in the farm fields, leaves and/or grass were handy substitutes.

6. Toilet Paper Marketed

The first toilet paper was produced in 1857. England was the first place where paper was manufactured just for use in the toilet, but it was not until the 1920's that toilet paper came into general use in the United States. Many people were still using their old catalogs.

The first toilet paper was very coarse--the type the British prefer today. Americans like the soft, fluffy type, which was introduced in 1907.

7. Bidets

During the middle ages, the French invented the bidet for rinsing of both sexes. During WWI, British and American troops found these devices in the brothels that they frequented, leading them to assume that they were only used by women for vaginal douching. When the men returned home, they felt they were of no use.

e. East vs. West Views of Excreta

The East and West developed very different attitudes and practices in relation to the human body and its processes. In China and Japan, "night soil" has been scrupulously collected for centuries to fertilize the fields. A nineteenth-century visitor to Japan tells us that in Hiroshima, in the renting of poorer tenement houses, if three persons occupied a room together the sewage paid the rent of one, and if five occupied the same room no rent was charged. Farmers vied with each other to build the most beautiful roadside privies in hopes of attracting the favors of travelers who needed to relieve themselves. Rational disposal systems in the Orient grew out of the importance of excreta to agriculture. Carts traveled through the cities collecting the precious stuff and carrying it off to dung heaps where it decomposed.

In the West no such practice existed. Chamber pots were emptied into the back yard or street. Some of the streets were designed so that gutters would carry off the filth during a rain. Most of the time, city streets were not pleasant places to be: it is easy to smell how feces got a bad name.

f. Flushing Toilets

1. History of Flushing Toilets

In the 1800's, it was discovered that many then-common epidemic diseases were transmitted through microorganisms in feces. But by then the psychological and technological die had been cast. The basically unsound practice of dumping excreta into any convenient body of water was rationalized. Mr. Crapper's water closet was perfected in the twenties-a period noted for its crusade against germs. The flush toilet eliminated direct contact with excreta. The smell and mess were removed from city streets and put into underground pipes. Methods to treat sewage by settling out solids, adding chemicals to kill bacteria, and, more recently, aerating to speed decomposition, were invented.

2. Toilet Water Facts

The average human being in North America generates 130 gallons of body waste per year. The average toilet in North America uses 5 gallons of water per flush, which means that each of us uses 9,000gallons of water a year-about half our total domestic use of potable water-to get rid of 130 gallons of waste, a ratio of about 70 to 1.

3. Sewage Facts

Sewage is 99.9% water. We typically use huge amounts of water to flush away those 16 to 100 grams (per person per day) of solid matter (feces). Major reasons for this are: 1) the large water surface reduces cleaning "skid marks" on the porcelain plumbing fixture; and 2) the submerged waste greatly lessens offensive odors.

4. Sewage around the World

We humans have a long history of using huge amounts of water to flush our toilets. For example, while about half the average Canadian's daily water supply is flushed away in toilets using upwards of 5 gallons per flush, German toilets use as little as 2.4 gallons per flush, and those routinely installed in Scandinavia since 1975 get by with as little as 1.5 gallons. There are also high efficiency toilets on the market today which function with as little as 3 quarts, sometimes by using a high-pressure jet of air along with the water.

2. Sewage Pumping Issues

Unless all of the waste-generating sources are directly above the container, it is necessary to move or pump the wastes. There are specialized augers and belts to do this, but they clog up and are difficult to maintain. A more efficient approach is to use a pump. (See Electricity-Water Pumping Section)

a. Macerator Pumps

One way to move human wastes through plumbing pipes is a "macerator" pump. They grind up the human waste into a slurry form, which makes it easier to pump. However, macerator pumps clog up quite frequently and they require noisy, high-amperage motors.

b. Diaphram Pumps

A better system to pump small amounts of human wastes is a diaphram pump, which is very similar to a bilge pump on a ship. They have a very high reliability for pumping difficult fluids. Also new materials have made the pump diaphrams last much longer. (See Pumps-Water files)

3. Common Sewage Systems

The following figures list qualities of the four common sewage treatment methods. Note that newer aerobic units and a modification of the Multi-Flo unit address most of the original arguments against aerobic digesters. (See Aerobic/Anaerobic Digesters section)

ISSUE	PIT PRIVY	COMPOST PRIVY	SEPTIC TANK/ DRAINFIELD	AEROBIC UNIT
POLLUTION AND SANITATION	If not near or in water, no pollution or sanitary problems.	No pollution. No sanitation problem with proper composting. Overloading may be a problem when daily use exceeds 4-6 people (55-gal. drum), 8-12 people (Clivus), 15 people (Farallones).	Larger pollution and sanitation problems because of water-feces mix. Soils, groundwater, slopes and overload can be problems outside property line because of in-soil discharge.	Larger pollution and sanitation problems because of water-feces mix. "Shock" loading, mechanical breakdown, power blackout, and inadequate treatment can be problems. Above-soil discharge has more dangers than in-soil. In-soil has negligible pollution potential outside property line.
RECYCLING	Ultimately by burial and planting a tree. Adds nutrients and humus.	Great fertilizer for gardens, etc.	Subirrigation in drain field ultimately fertilizes plants and may recharge water supplies.	ABOVE GROUND: Water and nutrients recycled by irrigation. IN GROUND: Recycled by absorption. In watercourses, nutrients can be pollutants.
(CONTINUED NEXT PAGE)				

Figure 83-COMMON SEWAGE TREATMENT METHODS-PAGE 1

*Used in Earth Home

ISSUE	PIT PRIVY	COMPOST PRIVY	SEPTIC TANK/ DRAINFIELD	AEROBIC UNIT
(CONT. FROM PREVIOUS PAGE)				
COMMUNITY	Accommodates high densities in cities--if away from water. Politically, not available for city use. Discouraged even in rural areas.	Can accommodate high densities in cities. Need pick-up of compost. Politically, new to city and rural health departments. Rarely accepted with ease.	Low densities only--need green space for drain field. Rural use. Accepted home-site system but many badly designed.	Low densities with in-soil discharge. High-density with above-soil discharge. Rarely accepted by health departments because of erratic behavior.
RELIABILITY	Aerobic and anaerobic composting with some infiltration. Very stable.	Most aerobic composting. Stable when proper carbon/nitrogen balance maintained.	Settling, flotation, and anaerobic digestion in tank. Aerobic and anaerobic filtration and digestion in drain field. Very stable if not overloaded.	Aerobic digestion least stable due to "shock" loading and mechanical complexity.
(CONTINUED NEXT PAGE)				

Figure 84-COMMON SEWAGE TREATMENT METHODS, PAGE 2

*Used in Earth Home

ISSUE	PIT PRIVY	COMPOST PRIVY	SEPTIC TANK/ DRAINFIELD	AEROBIC UNIT
(CONT. FROM PREVIOUS PAGE)				
MAINTENANCE	Very easy. Minimal labor.	Not so easy. Proper amounts of vegetable matter must be added to feces. Manual labor required weekly in some models.	Easy. Labor minimal. Needs checking for pumping about every 2-4 years. If dual-field, needs yearly manual switching.	Difficult. Many mechanical parts needing specialist labor. Outside energy source can be a problem. Needs cleaning each year.
COSTS	INITIAL: Very inexpensive ($50). Greywater system may be required. OPERATIO N: None. MAINT.: None.	INITIAL: See illustrations. Greywater system may be required. OPERATION: None. MAINT.: None.	INITIAL: Pretty expensive ($800-$4,500) depending on size, contractor, and materials. Homemade can be cheaper. Greywater system used to advantage. OPERATION: Water costs. MAINT.: Pumping every 3-10 years ($40-$85).	INITIAL: Very expensive ($1,600-$3,000+; drain field, and filtration and chlorinating not included). Greywater system used to advantage. OPERATION: Water costs. Electricity costs ($150+ each year). Filtration and chlorinating ($300+ each yr).
LIFESPAN	About 10 years for a family of 4.	As long as materials last (Farallones, 20 years; Clivus, 60 years?; drum, 10-15 yr.).	10-75 years depending on soils and design.	Less than 10 years before major parts replacement necessary.

Figure 85-COMMON SEWAGE TREATMENT METHODS, PAGE 3

*Used in Earth Home

a. Septic Tanks/Drainfields

Septic tanks are commonly used outside metro areas where there is no city sewer system. A septic tank holds waste until it fills and flows into an area of underground tubing with perforated holes in it. This allows the waste water to evaporate through the soil. The solid matter must be periodically pumped out if the digestion process is insufficient to turn the solids to a liquid. The mound system is a variation where pumping is used instead of gravity draining.

b. Dry Toilets

1. Background/History

Another toilet system that has interest in alternative or homestead use is the composting privy or "dry" system. These dry toilets, or "biological toilets" as they are sometimes called, were introduced in the early 1970s. They originally came from Scandinavia where they were mainly limited to seasonal use. There are basically two types of biological toilets now commercially available. The large type is marketed for year-round use because of its large capacity and few moving parts. There is also a smaller type that sits directly in the bathroom with the toilet seat directly on top of the treatment tank. This type requires electrical heating coils and a fan to promote rapid aerobic decomposition and evaporation.

When the dry toilets started to become popular in the United States, there were concerns over the aggressive marketing tactics designed to promote these dry toilets for year-round use. Tests were conducted and ultimately showed that these units were not true composting units, as they didn't achieve high enough internal temperatures to assist composting. They were found to be more aptly described as biological toilets (the term used throughout this text) because they operate under aerobic conditions to achieve waste degradation and liquid loss through evaporation.

2. Issues with Dry Toilets

Some of these tests also pointed to a number of problems. The first problem is that biological toilets cannot accommodate greywater; that is, all of the household wastewater cannot be included. If you use a dry toilet, a greywater system must also be used to recycle this water.

Another problem associated with the dry system is that the overall solids content of human body wastes is less than 10%. Without some sort of bulking agents and without some kind of moisture loss system, biological action would be anaerobic--giving off few calories for evaporation and producing offensive odors. The toilet's two main functions are evaporation of excess liquid and degradation of organic materials. The biological toilet does not truly compost, because this heat loss from evaporation through the venting is too great to reach the high (lethal) temperatures characteristic of true composting.

Still another problem with the dry system is that the carbon and nitrogen (C/N) ratio of human body wastes needs to be supplemented by the addition of kitchen or garden wastes to avoid overproduction of ammonia. This ammonia emanates from the mass at the bottom of the tank, and this smell can be very offensive to users. Also, numerous creatures in the treatment tank may climb up the chute to the toilet seat to escape this ammonia toxicity. The amount of bulking agent required for maintaining good porosity of the mass is more important, however, than the C/N ratio. Sometimes lime is added to adjust this ratio.

Originally the end product of the dry toilets was claimed to be safe humus or a soil-like material. In actual practice there has been a reluctance to use this end product in the garden except for burial around shrubs and other non-edible or ornamental plants. End products of poorly operating biological toilets have been tested positive for specific pathogens--parasitic, bacterial and viral. Even the better operating toilets can exhibit positive samples for parasites.

*Used in Earth Home

Some of the smaller units have also exhibited problems such as hydraulic overloading (due to substantial amounts of beverage drinking), insufficient mass to sustain composting, aerobic odors, and mechanical or electrical failures. Some of these problems can be associated with poor installation at first. Neglected maintenance can also cause problems.

I believe that more applicable uses for dry toilets would be seasonal uses such as cottages, public recreational facilities, institutions, and small commercial buildings. Another more applicable use would be in very dry climates where the water supplies are scarce and water is at a premium. Even the most technically advanced dry toilet requires one cupful of peat mix per person per day and a rotation of the drum every third day.

I am not using a dry toilet because of this extra care and attention that they require. I believe that a 20th century family should not have to provide the great care and attention necessary to use a toilet of this kind. There are also many other alternatives that have been tried.

c. Aerobic/Anaerobic Digesters (See also EH Digester System)

Aerobic means with oxygen and anaerobic means in the absence of oxygen. There are many different styles of aerobic digesters from many different countries. Aerobic digesters are commonly used in 22 states. The Biocycle (aerobic and anaerobic) from Australia is perhaps the most efficient, at about 99.9% removal of pathogens. The water exiting from this system is almost clean enough to drink. (See Earth Home Toilet/Digester System)

The toilet waste system is perhaps one of the most complex and crucial components of the Earth Home system (see Toilet files).

4. Alternative/Future Toilet and Wastewater Systems

a. Water Hyacinth/Potential Food Source

Water hyacinth (See following figure) has been studied as a method for filtering wastes out of water, and as a food source for human beings. It is calculated that 3 kilograms of fresh water hyacinth contains all the nutrients and minerals that a human body needs for one day. However, there are considerable limitations to its use because of its bad taste. There is much more research that must go into the water hyacinth system to make it practical for a self-sufficient homestead.

b. Trout Ponds

Another alternative sewage system uses trout ponds. I feel that systems of this sort will not be widely accepted unless they are used for entire villages. It must also become much more efficient, less labor intensive, and faster at processing waste. The Earth Home II system is designed for a family of four, which is too small a group to justify the cost of constructing ponds.

c. Methane Digesters (see also Biogas section)

In the United States there have been many studies aimed at making use of the toilet wastes from human beings to generate methane. These methane digesters can be used as a cooking fuel source or limited space heating. The digesters must be kept warm so the biological activity can continue. ***The Earth Home II does not use a methane digester at this point because there is no continuous system available.*** (See Heating - Methane section for more complete discussion.)

*Used in Earth Home

The remarkable wetland water hyacinth (above) is an effective pollution filter. Considered a nuisance in many countries because it spreads rapidly over open water (right), it can filter out toxic metals and pesticides, often in a matter of hours. It can also be used for compost, animal feed, conversion to biogas or to make paper and board.

...water hyacinth could be an excellent source of proteins, vitamins, and minerals, and could be of particular value as a dietary supplement in countries where human diets are generally deficient in these nutrients. The high water content of E. crassipes (95%) makes utilization of this species difficult on a large-scale commercial basis; however, we feel that this fast-growing plant species would be beneficial to human diets on an individual basis, since less than 3 kg of harvested fresh water hyacinth leaves could provide essentially all of the protein, minerals, and vitamins required daily in the human diet. We are currently experimenting with low-cost harvesting and processing methods which should make the utilization of water hyacinth nutrients more feasible on a large-scale basis.

Figure 86-WATER HYACINTH

*Used in Earth Home

d. Ongoing Testing of Spirulina Systems

One Japanese philosopher, Toru Matsui, has fed himself for over 15 years on algae grown on denatured human excreta. There is work going on to use waste products of humans to produce the blue-green algae Spirulina. Spirulina seems to do better in a culture of modified urine and CO_2 than in a mixture of all human wastes. A domestic household toilet waste system such as the Earth Home design is much better at separating the human wastes into solid and liquid portions (urinal-style) and therefore positioned for more research into this important subject. (see Spirulina files) Another by-product of Spirulina production (oxygen) could benefit the aerobic digestion of wastes and the aeration of fish tanks. (See also Future Food Production Technologies, Spirulina/SCP, and Urine Separation sections)

e. Wastewater Gardens

The Planetary Coral Reef Foundation (PCRF) has developed wastewater gardens that effectively treat sewage. This method basically involves a well-sealed two-chamber septic tank and a two-compartment wetland garden containing gravel, plants, wastewater, and mulch. Both the septic tank and the wetland garden are sealed with compacted clay and a geo-membrane liner or cement to prevent any untreated wastewater from seeping out into the groundwater.

They use local plants adapted to wetland habitat. They minimize electrical use by designing gravity flow. This system is ideal for tropical countries, coastal communities, and has been used for single-family residences as well as multi-family units.

f. Human Waste as <u>Resource</u>

I believe we must start to think of human waste as a "resource" similar to the sewage sludge that has been applied to land in Europe and the U.S. for over 40 years. Many eastern countries use the toilet waste from human beings to put on field crops. In Vietnam, the word "honey well" means a special collection spot in the fields where liquid human waste was kept to fertilize rice paddies. This was a valuable commodity, since feces contain approximately 82% organic substances and 18% inorganic materials.

g. Urine Separation/Urinals

1. Separating Toilets—Background and Technology

In an ordinary toilet, both urine and feces are mixed with potable water and then flushed. A source separating toilet keeps the water free from unnecessary pollution from the solids. The notion of source separating toilets is not new. Such devices have been used in eastern Asia for nearly 5,000 years.. Source separating toilets should not be confused with composting toilets which actually mix urine and feces, and often other things, and compost it all.

Because of the large difference in volume and other properties between urine and feces, they can be kept separate, ant treated as the different things they actually are. Source separating toilets occur in two principal forms, the dry and the wet. The following figure shows different urine separating systems.

2. Dry Type (See also Composting Toilet section)

In the dry type, urine and feces are never mixed, but the urine is flushed with a small amount (about 2 deciliters) of water after each usage in order to avoid crystallization in the pipes. Feces are collected in a mini-composting chamber, which might be supplied with compost worms for a better sanitation and decrease of the volume. An advantage with this type of toilet is that the toilet room becomes free of the odors common in an ordinary toilet room. This is because the air is sucked out from the composting chamber by a small fan or natural ventilation to prevent odors.

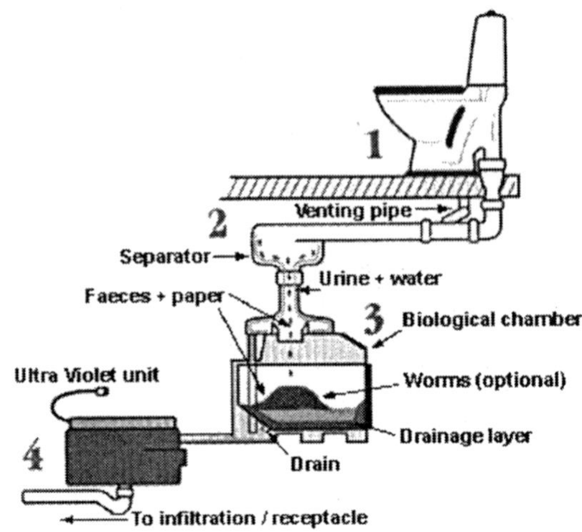

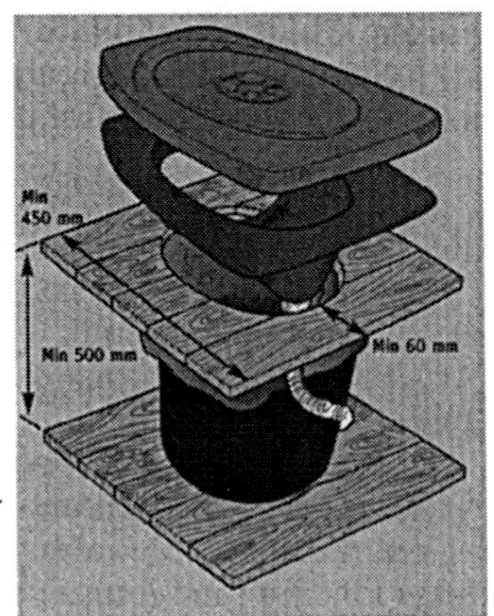

Figure 87-URINE SEPARATION TOILETS/SYSTEMS

3. Wet Type

The wet type of source separating toilet also separate the urine, but feces are mixed with some water for the transport of the material. In some cases, feces are separated by a passive centrifuge-like action.

Source separating toilets are somewhat in-between these two types. In this type, a small amount of water is needed for transport of the feces to a tank. This water is drained off and sanitized with burnt lime.

4. Nutrients in Urine

The following chart summarizes the chemistry of urine compared to feces.

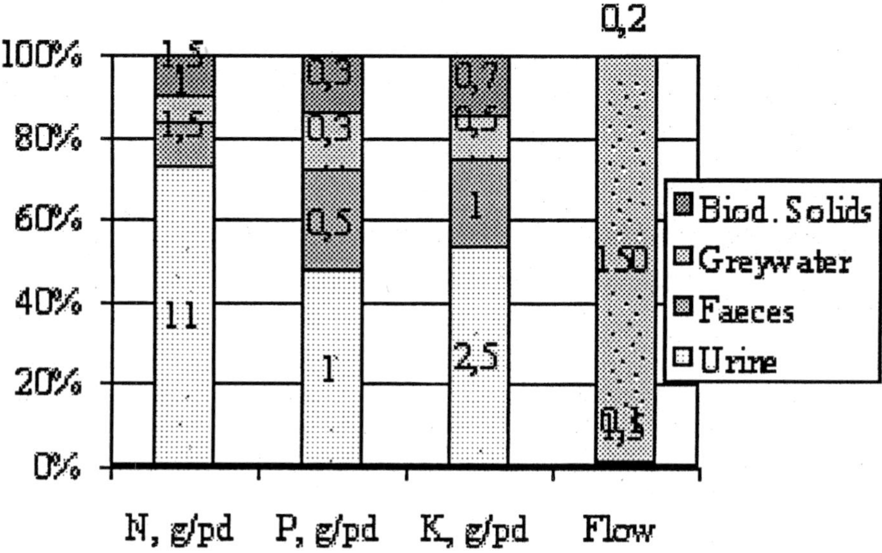

Figure 88-NUTRIENTS IN URINE

Urine is the urban waste fraction containing the largest amounts of nutrients. It contains approximately 70% of the nitrogen and 50% of the phosphorus and potassium in all household waste and wastewater fractions, while the flow of urine is comparatively small. This means that it is interesting to separate the urine at the source, i.e. the toilet. The urine separating toilets were re-invented in Sweden in the 1980-ies, made the construction of urine separating systems possible. In these, the urine is source separated. The urine is then piped to collection tanks, stored and used as a fertilizer for agricultural and horticultural crops.

5. Earth Home Toilet/Digester System (See separate EH Digester System section)

*Used in Earth Home

G. Earth Home Digester System

1. EH Greywater Overview

a. Greywater Storage

In the Earth Home II system, all used wash water (except kitchen sink grease trap) first flows to a temporary storage system to settle out particles of hair, lint, and food particles. ***In the Earth Home system, water is recycled and reused as much as possible to eliminate using up stored water or pumping more from the ground***. Mild low phosphate soaps are preferable because of ease of recycling and/or filtration. (See Soap files.) Strong cleaners containing boron, lanolin, perfumes, ABS, and bleach should be avoided.

b. Plant Undersoil Irrigation

The greywater is then available as needed to the plant undersoil irrigation system. (See Irrigation files.) ***The greywater is delivered directly under the soil to the plant roots so that no possibility of contamination to the plant leaves or to edible surfaces of any kind***. A weekly application of fresh water helps to eliminate accumulation of pollutants in root crops. This undersoil hose is especially designed not to clog up from organic materials. (A greywater heat exchanger will be used to preheat incoming water to the water heater.) There is a 1/4 gallon per square foot per week practical limit on how much greywater that can be used for irrigation. (Theoretically, rich, loamy soil is better for using greywater.) In other words, a 100-foot by 4-foot area would use up to 100 gallons per week. (See Plumbing/Greywater.)

c. Digester Input

Any overflow from the storage/settling tank system will go into the digester, which is a tank that digests human wastes from the bathroom. This is done to ensure that the digester has sufficient liquid in addition to the effluent from the low-flush toilet. (See Toilet Wastes section.)

2. EH Toilet

a. Toilet Choices (See Blackwater Section)

b. EH Toilet/Micro Low Flush

The Earth Home system uses a modified Sealand toilet system with a spray flush and aerobic digester. This toilet has a ball valve on the bottom part of the bowl to release waste into a storage tank to slowly "dissolve" before being pumped out. In this manner, I've been able to use an average of 6 ounces of water per flush, using a circular, high-pressure sprayer. A special small air fan removes offensive odors from the toilet bowl through the air-to-air heat exchanger to the outside.

c. EH Urinal Option

The Earth Home is ideal for a urinal system because of the uses to which the liquid waste can be put. Urine is much easier to dose the digester and would use much smaller and less complex valves. Urine can also be used in Spirulina research systems. Separation of urine from feces also saves water by not flushing the toilet every time that the toilet is used. (See Plumbing Fixtures file) (See also Spirulina section)

3. Aerobic Digester

a. EH Aerobic Digester

The Earth Home II Multi-Flo aerobic digester (before modification) is pictured in the following figure. It uses washable polyester membranes as a culture medium for aerobic bacteria. A Multi-Flo* system will have to be modified for the smaller volume of waste that is generated by Earth Home II. Also, dosing is paramount to proper design and maintenance of any aerobic digester. Dosing is putting measured quantities of effluent into the main digester at controlled intervals. This is done to allow proper dwell time for the bacteria to properly break down the sewage components. (See Dosing Section)

b. EH Digester Effluent Dosing

1. Dosing Background

Enough "batch fed" water would have to enter the aerobic digester so that the volume of outgoing effluent would be fairly constant (thus eliminating "shock loading").

2. Dosing/Dipper Methods

There are several ways to accomplish efficient loading for the digester. Dosing siphons, dipper boxes, or electronic valves can accomplish this by mechanically adjusting the rate of liquid entry into the digester tank. Dipper boxes were originally designed for leach field distribution systems.

The next figure shows 2 typical dosing systems. Dosing siphons are similar to other surge devices such as the dipper box. A "dosing siphon" is a way of turning many small doses of greywater into one large one, without the use of a pump. It is considered tricky to get a dosing siphon to work reliably. It works similar to a flush toilet in that it will not drain until a certain amount of water is introduced into the storage area. The sizing must be right and the outlet must be small enough so that an average surge can activate the siphon.

3. Dosing Siphon Issues

Dosing siphons are not generally designed to split the flow, only collect a lot and then distribute it all at once. The water can easily sit long enough to become anaerobic, and unlike the dipper they will collect crud which must be cleaned out periodically. They also cost more fall—the height difference between inlet and outlet is typically a few feet.

4. Back-up Effluent Sources

A steady and reliable supply of water should be supplied to the aerobic digester. A potential steady water source for the digester is overflow from the fish tanks. The fish tank overflow has value as plant fertilizer as well. Also, the elimination of detergents with "binders" will help to alleviate past problems encountered with similar digesters. (See Soaps/Detergent section)

5. Exit Water from the Digester

When water exits the digester, it can be directed to three places. It could first flow into the tubing directly above the cool tubes system to keep the ground wet for air conditioning in the summer time. The second place that it could go is the undersoil irrigation system for both the plants in the greenhouse and the outside south side plants. (Note that filtered rainwater is used for <u>aboveground</u> spray irrigation, which is the other half of the irrigation system for the plants.) The third undersoil destination for the digester effluent would be the edible shade shrubs and grapevines on the east and north sides of the house. (See Irrigation section.)

*Used in Earth Home

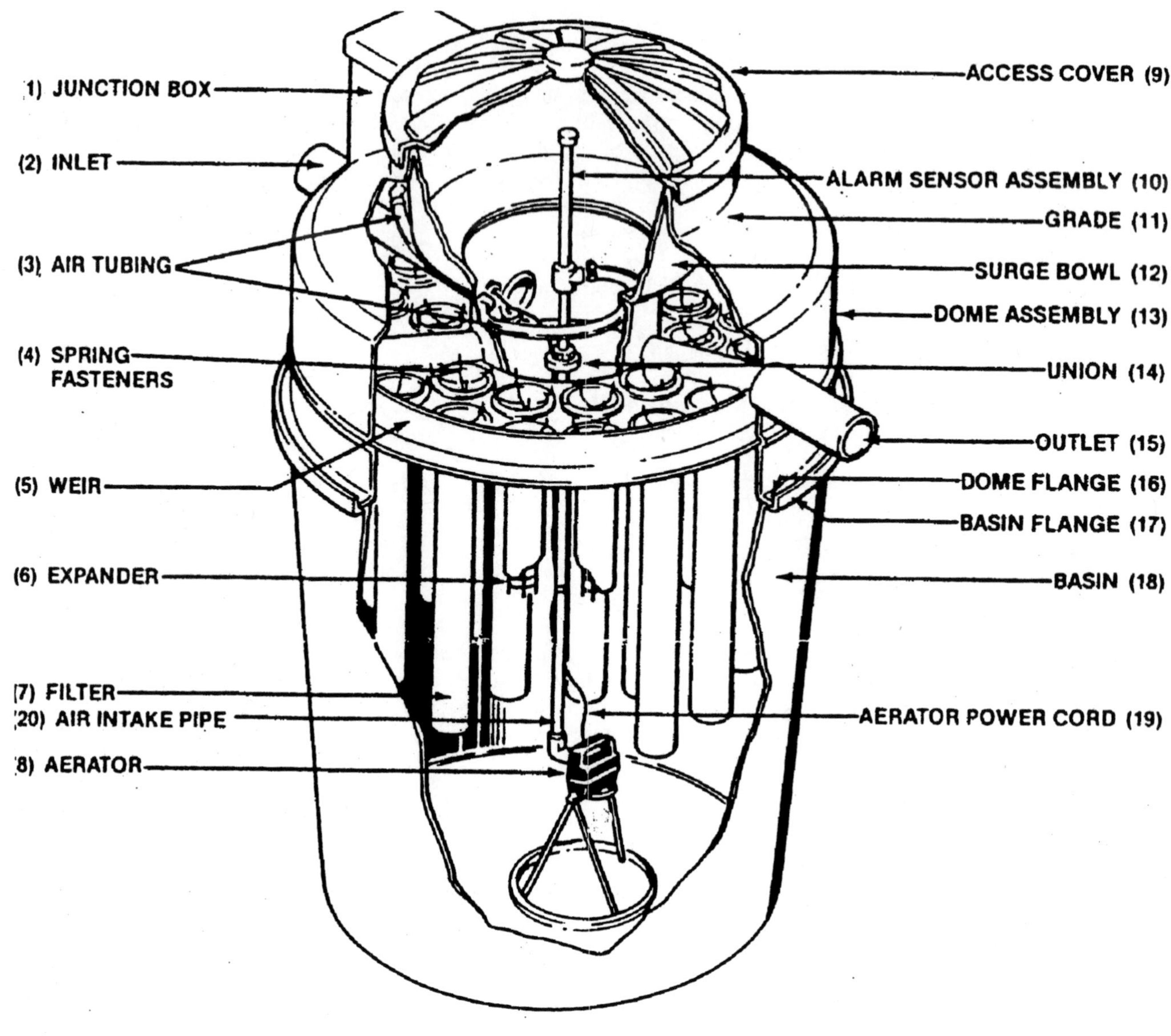

Figure 89-AEROBIC DIGESTER FOR TOILET WASTE

*Used in Earth Home

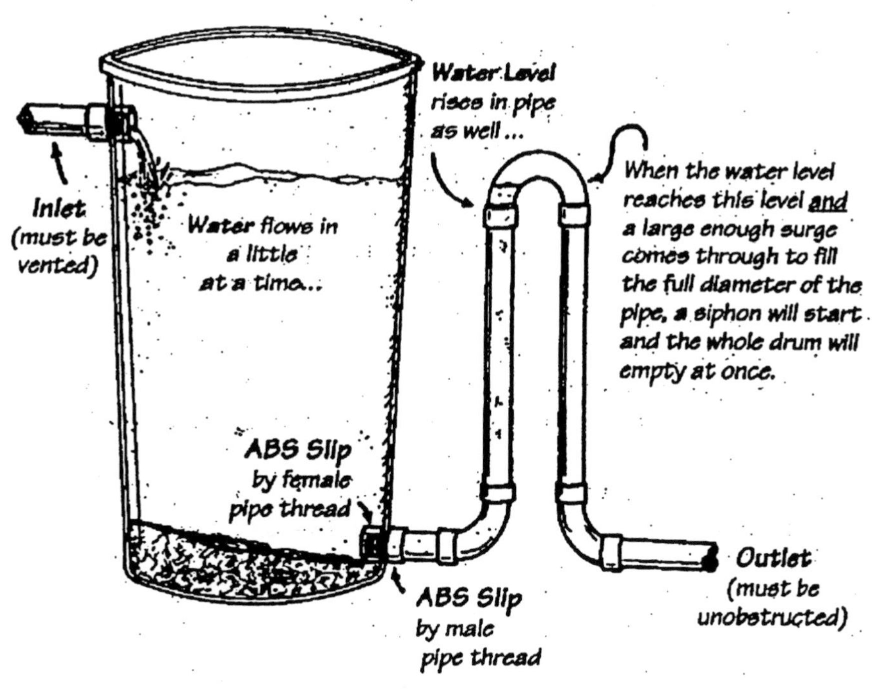
Water Level
rises in pipe
as well ...
When the water level
reaches this level and
a large enough surge
comes through to fill
the full diameter of the
pipe, a siphon will start
and the whole drum will
empty at once.
Inlet
(must be
vented)
Water flows in
a little
at a time...
ABS Slip
by female
pipe thread
ABS Slip
by male
pipe thread
Outlet
(must be
unobstructed)

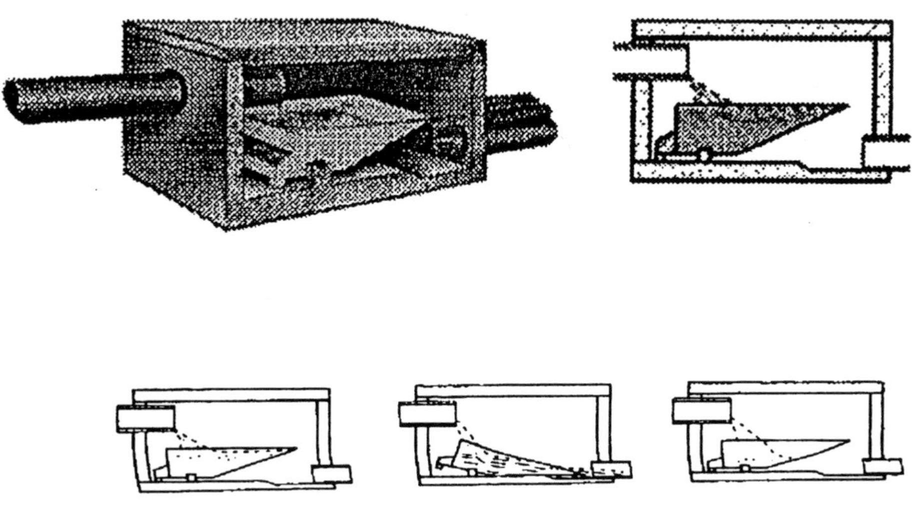

Figure 90-DOSING SYPHON/DIPPER BOX

*Used in Earth Home

4. Wind-Powered Air Compressor for Digester

a. Background/Technology

A wind-powered air compressor (currently available from several countries) is designed to pump air into the aerobic digester as well as the fish tank. Considering the low RPM requirements for this system, a rotary vane or scroll compressor may be more suitable than a piston type compressor. (See Wind Generator files.) Compressed air is used to complete digestion of the waste without using electricity to aerate the wastes.

b. Oxygen-Rich Intake Air

Intake air to the digester could benefit from an oxygen-rich source such as an enclosed plant growing area, or, in the future, from the by-product of hydrolysis (hydrogen generation) or Spirulina production. Quick-growing grasses in an enclosed chamber could also be used as a source of intake air because they produce the most oxygen per unit of time.

c. Control System

Using this system, a batch could go unstirred (septic) for a few days without damage to the system. When the wind begins to blow, it will start compressing air and aerobic digestion would continue.

H. Plumbing Overview

1. Water Heating Overview

a. Background/History

Heating water accounts for approximately 80% of the energy used for washing clothes. Heating water efficiently is at the very heart of overall energy use in the home.

Domestic hot water heaters are usually either a tank type or a "demand" type. The tank type heats water to a pre-set temperature (such as 120°F) in a closed vessel. They are by far the most common type in the U.S.

b. Demand Hot Water Heaters

A demand heater, on the other hand, only heats water as it goes through the unit. They are also known as tankless or instantaneous heaters They don't have to keep water hot and they never run out of hot water. Demand heaters are commonly used in Europe and Japan. ***In fact, the U.S. is one of the few countries that still routinely installs tank-type water heaters***.

c. Earth Home Water Heating

Earth Home I has a Paloma water heater with a built-in warmer. A tank of water is pre-warmed above the small pilot light and is used to wash hands and face. This slightly warmed water can also be used as shower water on hot summer days.

The Earth Home II system is designed to use an Aquastar heater with optional coil. This recirculating option will also final heat water to the built-in dehydrator area, distillation unit, greenhouse soil heating system, and clothes dryer. An Aquastar* is one of the few hot water heaters that will accept the pre-heated water from the woodstove and/or southern solar hot water.

***Used in Earth Home**

d. EH Hot Water Distribution

After the water is filtered and heated, it will be delivered to the kitchen sink, bathroom shower, clothes washer, dehydrator coil, or supplemental greenhouse soil-heating coils as needed. The plumbing system is modified to include flow restrictors and pressure regulators to precisely control the water flow before and after the demand heater. (See Plumbing files.) This is done to minimize water use throughout the home.

2. Future Water Heating Systems

a. CHP Options (See Power-Future Power section)

I think that hot water should be a by-product of electricity generation. I think heating in general should take advantage of the many ways that electricity can be generated since friction or heat is the inefficient part. I foresee home power plants that smoothly integrate these functions. (See Power-Future Power section)

b. Direct-Fired Systems

Another concept that is being worked on is the direct-fired hot water heater. This novel device uses a blast of fire to instantly heat up small rings of stainless steel inside a chamber. Water is then sprayed on the rings and collected at the bottom. Developers say hot water can be provided within 20 seconds of start-up.

c. Hybrid PV Panels Producing Hot Water

Hybrid PV modules have also recently come onto the market. These concentrating hybrid collectors generate electricity <u>and</u> hot water using the same panel. (See Solar Misc. files.) (See Solar Heating-Solar section.)

3. Plumbing Mechanics

a. Background/History

How water and wastewater flows from point of use to ultimate recycling is important because of the energy needed to pump uphill. Gravity must be used as much as possible. Future versions of this text will explore this more in detail.

b. Plumbing Data

The following figure illustrates some of the data necessary to efficiently plumb various water pipes inside a home.

c. Water Pipe Freeze Protection

In many locations on the planet, water must be protected from freezing temperatures and the resulting pipe damage. In the Northern U.S. cattle stock tanks are filled from electrical pumps that are under the surface of the ground. The pipe that feeds the water to the above-ground tank is surrounded by another larger pipe. There is an inch or so of air space surrounding the water pipe that is somewhat heated by the warmer ground. Because of the slight air circulation in the air space, heat is transferred between the earth and the air. This slight warming of the air (and subsequently the pipe) keeps the water inside the pipe from freezing. This method is used instead of electrical "heat tape" on the pipe.

Contents in Cubic Feet and U. S. Gallons of Pipes and Cylinders
One Foot in Length

Diam. in Inches	For 1 Foot in Length		Diam. in Inches	For 1 Foot in Length		Diam. in Inches	For 1 Foot in Length	
	Cubic Feet	U. S. Gallons		Cubic Feet	U. S. Gallons		Cubic Feet	U. S. Gallons
¼	0.0003	0.0025	6¾	0.2485	1.859	19	1.969	14.73
5/16	0.0005	0.0040	7	0.2673	1.999	19½	2.074	15.51
⅜	0.0008	0.0057	7¼	0.2867	2.145	20	2.182	16.32
7/16	0.0010	0.0078	7½	0.3068	2.295	20½	2.292	17.15
½	0.0014	0.0102	7¾	0.3276	2.450	21	2.405	17.99
9/16	0.0017	0.0129	8	0.3491	2.611	21½	2.521	18.86
⅝	0.0021	0.0159	8¼	0.3712	2.777	22	2.640	19.75
11/16	0.0026	0.0193	8½	0.3941	2.948	22½	2.761	20.66
¾	0.0031	0.0230	8¾	0.4176	3.125	23	2.885	21.58
13/16	0.0036	0.0269	9	0.4418	3.305	23½	3.012	22.53
⅞	0.0042	0.0312	9¼	0.4667	3.491	24	3.142	23.50
15/16	0.0048	0.0359	9½	0.4922	3.682	25	3.409	25.50
1	0.0055	0.0408	9¾	0.5185	3.879	26	3.687	27.58
1¼	0.0085	0.0638	10	0.5454	4.080	27	3.976	29.74
1½	0.0123	0.0918	10¼	0.5730	4.286	28	4.276	31.99
1¾	0.0167	0.1249	10½	0.6013	4.498	29	4.587	34.31
2	0.0218	0.1632	10¾	0.6303	4.715	30	4.909	36.72
2¼	0.0276	0.2066	11	0.6600	4.937	31	5.241	39.21
2½	0.0341	0.2550	11¼	0.6903	5.164	32	5.585	41.78
2¾	0.0412	0.3085	11½	0.7213	5.396	33	5.940	44.43
3	0.0491	0.3672	11¾	0.7530	5.633	34	6.305	47.16
3¼	0.0576	0.4309	12	0.7854	5.875	35	6.681	49.98
3½	0.0668	0.4998	12½	0.8522	6.375	36	7.069	52.88
3¾	0.0767	0.5738	13	0.9218	6.895	37	7.467	55.86
4	0.0873	0.6528	13½	0.9940	7.436	38	7.876	58.92
4¼	0.0985	0.7369	14	1.069	7.997	39	8.296	62.06
4½	0.1104	0.8263	14½	1.147	8.578	40	8.727	65.28
4¾	0.1231	0.9206	15	1.227	9.180	41	9.168	68.58
5	0.1364	1.020	15½	1.310	9.801	42	9.621	71.97
5¼	0.1503	1.125	16	1.396	10.44	43	10.085	75.44
5½	0.1650	1.234	16½	1.485	11.11	44	10.559	78.99
5¾	0.1803	1.349	17	1.576	11.79	45	11.045	82.62
6	0.1963	1.469	17½	1.670	12.49	46	11.541	86.33
6¼	0.2131	1.594	18	1.767	13.22	47	12.048	90.13
6½	0.2304	1.724	18½	1.867	13.96	48	12.566	94.00

One cubic foot of water at 39.1 degrees F. weighs 62.4245 pounds.
One cubic foot of air at 32 degrees F., atmospheric pressure, weighs 0.08073 pound.
One pound of water at 39.1 degrees F. has a volume of 0.01602 cubic foot.
One pound of air at 32 degrees F., atmospheric pressure, has a volume of 12.387 cubic feet.
One gallon of water at 62 degrees F. weighs 8.336 pounds.
One pound of water at 62 degrees F. has a volume of 0.1199 U. S. gallon.

Contents of Cylindrical Tanks in U. S. Gallons

Depth of Tank, Feet	Diameter of Tank, Feet								
	5	6	7	8	9	10	11	12	13
	Contents of Tank, U. S. Gallons								
5	734	1058	1439	1880	2379	2,938	3,555	4,230	4,965
6	881	1269	1727	2256	2855	3,525	4,265	5,076	5,957
7	1028	1481	2015	2632	3331	4,113	4,976	5,922	6,950
8	1175	1692	2303	3008	3807	4,700	5,687	6,768	7,943
9	1322	1904	2591	3384	4283	5,288	6,398	7,614	8,936
10	1469	2115	2879	3760	4759	5,875	7,109	8,460	9,929
11	1616	2327	3167	4136	5235	6,463	7,820	9,306	10,922
12	1763	2538	3455	4512	5711	7,050	8,531	10,152	11,915
13	1909	2750	3742	4888	6187	7,638	9,242	10,998	12,808
14	2056	2961	4030	5264	6662	8,225	9,953	11,844	13,801
15	2203	3173	4318	5640	7138	8,813	10,664	12,690	14,894
16	2350	3384	4606	6016	7614	9,400	11,374	13,536	15,887
17	2497	3596	4894	6392	8090	9,988	12,085	14,383	16,879
18	2644	3807	5182	6768	8566	10,575	12,796	15,229	17,872
19	2791	4019	5480	7144	9042	11,163	13,507	16,075	18,865
20	2938	4230	5758	7520	9518	11,750	14,218	16,921	19,858

Figure 91-PLUMBING DATA-PIPES AND TANKS

*Used in Earth Home

It was desirable from a standpoint of safety and flexibility to design a plumbing system that was freeze-resistant. In conventional homes in the north, if the heat goes off for any length of time in the winter, pipes will freeze. They expand and burst, causing extensive damage to the home. ***In the Earth Home II system, the piping system was designed so that the entire home could be frozen for extended periods of time without damage to the system***. The pilot light on the demand heater would slightly warm the plumbing pipes that were located in a concentrated area in an underfloor utility area. (See Earth Home blueprints.)

Plumbing pipes were laid out so gravity will do most of the work. Pumping was only used to pressurize the system, enabling water to be moved greater distances. I attempted to use as few pumps as possible inside Earth Home II. A venting system was also designed to vent the plumbing systems directly from a sidewall rather than penetrating the roof.

d. Pumping Waste Issues (See Toilet Waste/Sewage Pumping section)

4. Digester Greywater Surging Issues (See EH Digester section)

*Used in Earth Home

*Used in Earth Home

VII. ELECTRICAL POWER

A. Electricity Overview

1. Electricity Basics/Background

Electricity comes in two types -- AC (alternating current), and DC (direct current). The official standard line voltage of the U.S. is 115 volts--commonly referred to as 110 AC. This voltage was chosen because it could be conducted in a small wire for considerable distances without much line loss. Other countries use different voltages and a different frequency. The United States uses 60 cycles per second, while European countries use 50 cycles with different voltages. ***I use 12-volt DC power because it is easy to store, safe, and there are many appliances available from the recreational vehicle, automotive, and alternative energy industries***. (Note: It would be relatively easy to power the Earth Home alternatively with a conventional power line hooked to a battery charger system. I decided to design to the most efficient scenario and allow the end user the option to modify. This way they could choose the degree of self-sufficiency they desired.)

To answer the many questions about common AC electricity, inverters, and the more available methods expounded by vendors of alternative energy equipment, I have addressed the issue with a separate article. ***The following section contains the article, "12-Volt Advantage". This was written to expound the many virtues of direct current use for new homes.***

*Used in Earth Home

2. 12-Volt Advantage Article

THE 12 VOLT ADVANTAGE

...The argument to use 12 volts direct current as a future world voltage in new alternative, off-the-grid, independent, or energy-efficient homes.

I sincerely applaud the buyers and sellers of energy-saving products. There is, however, a trend in the U.S. to remain stubbornly attached to typical 110-volt alternating current when incorporating energy-efficient or energy-generating equipment into alternative homes. The equipment usually involves photovoltaic panels and/or wind generators with a battery bank for storage purposes. The whole process is an educational experience and may take some time. You can't simply buy some solar panels and expect to save some money. I believe many people with an interest in this technology are not given the whole picture regarding voltage and control options by merchants of solar and alternative energy equipment for two reasons: First, it is much more profitable to sell design services and readily available equipment. Even if the products are not as energy efficient as their 12 volt counterparts, it is easier to convince prospective customers to invest thousands of dollars in a new or modified home system if they can make the transition with as little hassle as possible. An energy generation system is a very <u>complex</u> undertaking for the average person, and much has to be learned simply in order to make decisions on selection, options, "expand-ability," and installation.

Secondly, the choices available for battery-powered equipment and controls for homes are much more limited than their 110-volt a.c. counterparts. There are much fewer sources of information on pure 12-volt installations and high-tech battery control technology generally available to the public. This information has only recently been compiled into a single source of information. The progression to use 110 v.a.c. has taken place relatively recently in history.

Early windplants used 32-volt direct current to charge the large glass batteries on many farmsteads. Rural Electric Authority was a major player in determining early voltage for homes. They needed a higher voltage so the farmers/ranchers could afford the long wire runs all the way out to the barn and/or other outbuildings. Also a larger wire size would have necessitated heavier hardware on the poles to support the increased weight.

The current official voltage for the United States is 115 volts alternating current at 60 cycles per second sometimes referred to as 110 v.a.c. 60 cycle. Higher voltages are used in industrial applications and utility transmissions. Other countries use different voltages and cycles. As the alternative energy industry began to grow, customers were encouraged to use inverters to make 110 v.a.c. from their battery bank. The selection of 12 VDC equipment and appliances began to get smaller. The increased sales of inverters fueled research into better and more efficient inverters that had smaller standby power losses. I believe the inverter industry has grown not from logical choices about earth-wise energy conservation-but from convenience similar to the use of disposable lighters. Alternative energy merchants use the following arguments to encourage 110 v.a.c as opposed to 12 VDC for home power use. A rebuttal argument follows each main topic.

<u>Wiring</u> - Using an inverter for the power supply requires the home to have only one type of wire-cheap and readily available 12-2 or 14-2 Romex. Inexpensive outlets and switches are used. It is difficult and expensive to work with the heavier #10 wire. Cigarette lighter plugs are expensive. Long wire runs to a barn are prohibitively expensive.

<u>Wiring (Rebuttal)</u> - Using twice as much costlier, heavier, and difficult-to-work-with wire seems at first to be a huge advantage that outweighs all others. However, let us look at each item separately. Cost is greatly influenced by quantity sold. Options that have been barely looked at are using twin strands of 12-2 for higher amperage runs. While it is true that the #10 stranded wire is hard to work with using existing receptacles; options could include "neck-down" of the strands before making the last connection to the receptacle. In the future, wiring may include sensing and communication wires among others, which would mean special mass-produced, multi-run, extruded wire. I do agree that cigarette lighter plugs and receptacles are **bad!** They are very cheaply made and should not be used. A better plug/receptacle combination is a (typical) 240 v.a.c.

*Used in Earth Home

receptacle with the connectors in a horizontal configuration instead of vertical. Yes, it is more expensive, but it launches 12 VDC into the 21st century and the economics of volume may soon apply.

Long wire runs to a barn should be avoided. Remember that I am talking about new construction and not retrofits. Building a barn hundreds of feet from the home is wasteful anyway. Look at the European system of sharing a common wall with the barn in order to save heating dollars. I have never seen an appropriate cost comparison for strictly materials and labor for new home wiring not even taking into account future "home bus" or wire harness innovations. Any more costs could be more than offset by the decreased energy needs and/or a smaller battery bank for 12 VDC home wiring. I believe having a "home energy remote monitor/control" in the master bedroom will become commonplace and also warrant taking a fresh look at "status quo" electrical wiring. Also testing such as remote batteries near point-of-use has never been done.

Lighting - A 110 v.a.c. compact fluorescent light costs 40% of a comparable 12 VDC model and selection favors AC.

Lighting (Rebuttal - Granted, the economics of scale favors typical 110 v.a.c. fixtures and bulbs. Remember, they both use similar materials in their manufacture. However, the aforementioned downsizing of the battery bank and battery charging system may significantly offset this seemingly larger cost. There is some generator fuel savings because 12 VDC chargers are typically more efficient. Also some off-the-grid retailers recommend back-up DC lighting in case of inverter failures. **Everything fails at some point in time.** In many instances it is within our lifetimes. AC light dimmers will not work on power from most inverters (non-pure sine wave) and some inverters ("load demand start") will not turn on some small fluorescent lights. (More on those inverter creatures later) Central single-source fiberoptic lighting schemes are also being looked at.

Entertainment equipment - Your existing TV, stereo, CD player, VCR, satellite equipment, computer equipment, printer, and others will work on inverter-supplied 110 v.a.c.

Entertainment equipment (Rebuttal) - Yes, **but** special wiring and filtering will more than likely be necessary. Because of what is called "phantom" loads, the energy drain could be intolerable. You may have to remember to switch off each unit with a special switch **in addition** to the on-off switch on the front. Another option is to use one complete circuit linking all these units that has to be manually switched off. Also special ferro-resonant or other filtering may have to be added to some AC audio systems to help with the "60 cycle hum" or background buzz. Add up the special switches, wiring, and filtering when figuring the "savings" of your inverter system. Also remember that a DC stereo will consume only a tiny fraction of its AC brother. And it is also a fact that most DC electronic equipment uses less power than their AC counterparts.

Also some of the modified square wave output inverters with high surge capacity may destroy some low cost rechargeable tools, flashlights, laser printers, and copiers.

Refrigerators/freezers - These will run fine on inverters, but virtually all off-the-grid merchants say scrap them out and replace them with the new super-efficient models or go gas-powered.

Refrigerators/freezers (Rebuttal)-Again, the points go to DC because the DC motor that powers the super-efficient compressor is inherently more efficient than the AC version. (More about motors later.)

Appliances/kitchen and laundry - Microwaves, toasters, mixers, coffee makers, blenders, garbage disposals, food processors, trash compactors, many washing machines, gas dryers and many more modern appliances run fine on inverter power.

Appliances/kitchen and laundry - (Rebuttal) - This is correct, but in the vast majority of independent homestead starts, a change of lifestyle begins to happen. The "power hog" appliances turn into garage sale items. These items typically are heating element types such as toasters, deep fat fryers, roasters, electric ranges, and all 220 v.a.c. appliances. A transition takes place and the occupants ask themselves if they really want an appliance enough to warrant the extra planning and expense. Off-the-grid residents evolve into a pattern of looking for high-energy-use chores to do in periods of high winds or full sunlight such as vacuuming or running the clothes washer. In this way they better manage their energy resources. Most appliances higher on the "wanted" list can be obtained in 12 VDC if a person shops around. In fact, at least one company only sells 12-volt products.

*Used in Earth Home

Remember that selection, features, and cost are very dependent on sales volume and are determined by our consumer dollar "votes" to direct research efforts.

Water pumps - There is very little to say positively about pumping water using inverter power.

Water pumps (Rebuttal) - AC submersible water pumps are not only inefficient, but they are very difficult to start up. This "high starting torque" is a **big** reason inverters have to be oversized so much. DC booster pumps can use as little as 40% of the power of AC models.

Power tools - Hand-held power tools will run fine on a 2,000-watt inverter or larger.

Power tools (Rebuttal) - Rechargeable hand tools are not only common but also preferable in many instances. Most off-the-grid merchants recommend 12-volt rechargers for the battery packs due to their speed and much higher efficiency. Some AC rechargers fail to come off full charge on modified sine wave inverters and destroy the battery pack. A generator rather than an inverter is generally recommended to run larger tools such as table saws, radial arm saws, band saws, larger sanders, large drills, mills and the like. This category of power comes under the heading of "occupation" and deserves separate attention. An individual's tools necessary in order to make a living are very specialized and should be considered as a separate cost item. For example, a business generator should be looked at from fuel efficiency and cost-to-maintain basis that should be figured into the price one charges for their services. Another example is the business computer printer. A quality laser printer would require a much larger generator than an ink jet printer and print jobs should be "batched" to minimize generator run time. The generator for business use and back-up generator for the home could be, of course, one and the same unit. I feel that electric starting will become the favored method to use in both instances. The generator will automatically start when the battery bank sensor reads low battery voltage.

Motors/fans - There is a huge selection of AC motors and air movers available.

Motors/fans (Rebuttal) - This category is where battery-powered motors really shine. Virtually all DC motors are more efficient than their AC brothers. It has been estimated that over 50% of U.S. electricity is used in motor drives. Just imagine what a 15% improvement in motor efficiency would do for the planet! Another advantage of DC motors is that they can be speed-regulated by simply using resisters in series. This way many more adjustments in performance are possible along with the possibility of using standard motors for multiple uses. Some off-the-grid merchants recommend DC ceiling fans because of the huge amount of energy that they save. There are also some problems with overheating and a buzzing noise when running on non-sine wave inverters.

Resale value - Conventional-wired homes have a higher resale value.

Resale value (Rebuttal) - If resale value is a major concern, simply run a single strand of #14 wire with the two strands of #10. (This strand could be used as LED indicators when current is being used.) The home could then be run on AC after changing the receptacles and connecting the #14 wire as the ground. The control panel(s) and fuses would have to be changed, but the in-wall wiring could remain the same. I believe that a dual-voltage home wired in this way would have a higher resale value because of the additional options it provides.

But now I would like to turn my attention to a main player in this issue--**inverters**--and discuss some of their shortcomings.

1. Full-time phantom loads-As mentioned earlier, they could be a pain in the rear. Some merchants have suggested that people buy a more expensive inverter that handles these loads more easily. I don't feel homeowners should keep buying the latest inverter to avoid some of the pitfalls. Some merchants have recommended avoiding these loads, for example, by using battery-operated or wind-up clocks.

2. Reliability-If inverters are really that trouble-free, then why do some of the merchants recommend a back-up inverter for critical loads such as refrigerators and/or freezers? Remember the inverter is a very complex electronic gadget. Ever heard of homeowners repairing their own? Industry sometimes uses MTBF (Mean Time Between Failures) data for design and to project returned goods. Generally, the greater number of individual components, the less the MTBF and hence reliability.

*Used in Earth Home

3. An additional sine wave inverter must be used for a small percentage of AC loads. These units are not as efficient as the modified sine wave ones and should not be used on the same circuit. Also, some people recommend stacking inverters for redundancy to avoid a complete power outage when an inverter fails.

4. Inverters should be matched to the load to ensure reliable system operation. If a substantial change occurs in power needs, then a reassessment of the inverter situation should be undertaken.

5. Safety-Inverters make a much more hazardous form of electricity from a relatively safe form. Many people work with battery electricity without bothering to shut down the circuit. I don't think inverter systems can ever match the safety record of pure 12 VDC systems such as automotive.

6. All inverters broadcast radio static when they are operating. The good old ball game just doesn't sound the same on the radio. Also there is the recently debated EMF/health issue of surrounding our families with 60-hertz electrical fields.

7. Inverters are typically 90% efficient unless they are the more expensive units that can be 98% efficient. In essence it "costs" up to 10% of a battery bank for the option of 110 v.a.c.

8. Resale value of inverters is not good because of the speed at which the technology is changing. The demand is much higher for the latest inverters with all the bells and whistles. The situation is similar to used electronic equipment such as 386 computers.

So you can see that inverters have their share of technical problems. A huge investment in time and money is usually necessary to learn about the complete system and have it installed correctly. Then if the family's needs change, so does the inverter system. I think it would be wiser to look seriously at the low voltage alternative. Here is what others have said about low voltage DC in general:

- A fundamental way to reduce power is to reduce the supply voltage of the electronics inside of portable devices. Over the past several years 3.3 volts has been the dominant supply voltage of most IC's. But 1.8 volts is becoming the supply voltage of choice for manufacturers of low-power devices. For makers of laptop PCs, where battery life is a key selling point, 1.2 volts and even sub-1 volt parts yield further power savings.
- Pacemaker companies have continued to lower the voltage of their units for many years for the same reason.
- Advanced automotive controls may soon give us all electric steering on cars. Battery control mechanisms have been highly developed for wheelchairs and radio controlled toys.
- There is a huge and growing industry in the manufacture of battery-powered toys, appliances, and tools. We consumers seem to like the portability of these items.
- Imagine the benefit of having a controlled area in your home where junior could experiment with electricity like it was a toy! I believe children should be raised to think of electricity as an opportunity and not simply something that gives shocks and should be avoided (I am sure most of have a near-miss childhood electrocution story we'd love to share). If a whole generation of children were raised in this manner we may now have had microprocessor-controlled woodstoves and many more earth-wise electrical products. I think we should look at the 12-volt industry the same way we looked at the solar industry 20 years ago and keep an open mind. I think inverters are part of the "transition" necessary with the end result being DC-powered homes.

Many of us are beginning to pay a premium for our health and making more intelligent choices on products we purchase for our homes such as recycled paper and plastic. I believe we should phase out 110 v.a.c. as the dinosaur that it is and replace it with safe DC voltage whenever building a new home in this day and age-especially if the goal may be complete self-sufficiency at some point In fact, the National Association of Home Builders (NAHB) had originally specified DC power for the "Smart House" project for ease of central control, flexibility, and efficiency. Let's base our decisions on efficiency and not tradition! People still look to the U.S. for innovations and trends. Most of the world hasn't learned our wasteful ways yet. I say let's be world citizens and start a more logical ideal voltage for our homes of the future.

Sincerely,

Mel Moench, author, Planet Earth Home–(Written May 6, 1995, updated Feb. 2003)

*Used in Earth Home

As noted from the above article, this work favors 12 volts DC as the voltage of choice. In order to get the most efficiency from the system of batteries, chargers, and controllers, it was first necessary to look at where electricity is used. Next, it was advantageous to find viable options for some of the heaviest users of electricity in typical homes.

3. Average Home Electrical Use List with Alternatives

A typical energy-conscious American family uses about 10,000 watt-hours per day of electricity. A typical low energy-use self-sufficient homestead reduces usage to 2,000 watt-hours per day.

There are a number of problems associated with 12-volt DC electrical use and generation. It is difficult to operate most high current devices with DC power, such as dishwashers, clothes washers, refrigerators, air conditioners, and dryers. All of these devices require high starting torque and high currents. The computer-controlled generator starter and soft-start modifications would make it easier to operate some of these high-current devices with 12-volt DC power.

The following is a list of most of the modern appliances that use electricity in a typical home. (See the following figures). I have suggested substitutes for high current devices. The idea is that now that the uses of electricity have been looked at and ***minimized,*** I looked to how to generate adequate supplies for the home needs. One of the most popular renewables for alternative homesteads is the wind power/photovoltaic option.

B. EH Wind/Solar Combination

1. Earth Home Wind Generator

a. History/Prototype Testing

One electrical generation scheme that I have personally tried was a 48-foot vertical axis wind generator. I tried to reduce the cut-in speed to 3 mph by using a large-diameter wind machine. The cut-in speed refers to the minimum wind speed at which the generator will begin to generate electricity. I found through experimentation that the wind does not blow consistently in any one direction, but creates turbulence from many directions. The vibration from turbulence caused the generator to shake excessively and lose structural integrity. The aluminum members weakened and the stainless steel cable stretched.

b. Automotive Generators

I also attempted to use an automobile alternator to charge extra batteries located inside a vehicle, and then "up-charge" to the house using a drive-in socket configuration. This does work, but it has some disadvantages. Batteries can be charged from a moving car, but the alternator must work a little harder, causing a slight loss in gas mileage. Plus, some mileage was lost in carrying around three extra lead acid batteries, which are quite heavy. Lighter battery technology may make this technology more feasible.

CATEGORY	TYPICAL WATTAGE	ALTERNATIVES
CLIMATE CONTROL		
Air conditioner (room)	1,400 or 1,500/ton	Room cooling accomplished with architectural design in combination with cool tubes.
Air conditioner (central)	5,000	Same as above.
Dehumidifier	257 - 1,200	High efficiency air-to-air heat exchanger venting prevents moisture buildup.
HRV	70 - 300	
Fan (attic)	370	Attic opens to atmosphere and thermosiphon method clears hot air.
Fan (circulating) Fan (furnace) Fan (roll-about)	88 282 - 1,000 171	Air circulation accomplished by one central backward curved fan and distribution system.
Heat lamp (infrared) Heat pump Heater (radiant or space) Oil burner or stoker Resistance heaters Induced draft blower	250 11,848 1,322 266 15,000 50 - 150	A wood stove heat coil accomplishes central heating with air circulation inside ducts using above-mentioned fan. Natural draft intake.
Humidifier Vaporizer	177 480	Excess humidity loss is prevented by fresh air intake to the wood stove. Extra humidity can be added by opening doors to greenhouse area or gravity humidifier in HVAC air stream.
(CONT. NEXT PAGE)		

Figure 92-ELECTRICAL USE CHART, PAGE 1

*Used in Earth Home

CATEGORY	TYPICAL WATTAGE	ALTERNATIVES
(CONTINUED FROM PREVIOUS PAGE)		
ENTERTAINMENT/ TELEPHONES		**May need to expand battery bank or extend generator use if wants are extensive.**
CB	10	
Cellular telephone	20 - 24	Rechargeable battery.
Electric player piano	30	
Laser disk player	30	
Movie projector/slide projector	150	
Radio - phonograph	71 - 75	
Radio telephone	10 - 25	
Satellite system, 12 ft. dish with auto orientation/remote control	45	
Stereo/hi-fi	15 - 100	
TV (25-inch color) TV (19-inch color) TV (12-inch black and white) TV (black and white tube) TV (black and white solid state)	130 - 332 60 - 80 15 160 - 237 55	Solid state more efficient than tube type.
VCR (CONT. NEXT PAGE)	30	

Figure 93-ELECTRICAL USE CHART, PAGE 2

*Used in Earth Home

CATEGORY	TYPICAL WATTAGE	ALTERNATIVES
(CONTINUED FROM PREVIOUS PAGE)		
GENERAL HOUSEHOLD/MISC.		
Alarm/security system	3 - 6	Can be included in microprocessor.
Bed covering (electric blanket)	177 - 400	12V DC models available.
Central vacuum Upright vacuum	750 - 1,500 500 - 950	Central vacuum included in Earth Home system--use when high-energy availability.
Clock radios (2)	10	12V DC models available.
Curling iron	40	12V DC models available.
Electric clocks (3)	12	12V DC or battery operated units--rechargeable.
Floor polisher/waxer	305 - 350	Manual model.
Hair clipper	10	Razor works fine.
Hair dryer	400 - 1,500	12V DC models available at lower wattages.
Hair rollers	350	
Heat lamp	250 - 260	
Heating pad	65	Hot water coil units.
Intellevision	27	
Massager	15	
Sewing machine	75	Treadle models or modified unit.
Shaver	14	Use straight razor or battery-operated model--recharge in peak power time.
Bath exhauster	30 - 150	To air-to-air heat exchanger.
Sun lamp	250 - 279	
Toothbrush	7	Use manual model.
Waterbed	400	Can be plumbed to demand heater.
(CONT. NEXT PAGE)		

Figure 94-ELECTRICAL USE CHART, PAGE 3

*Used in Earth Home

CATEGORY	TYPICAL WATTAGE	ALTERNATIVES
(CONTINUED FROM PREVIOUS PAGE)		
FOOD PRODUCTION (Earth Home)		These are ultra-low energy-use items in the Earth Home, for comparison purposes.
Fish tank aerator Irrigation timer Solenoid valves (irrigation)	4 - 100 10 15	
ILLUMINATION		
Christmas tree lights	50 - 480	12V DC models available.
Compact fluorescent (60W equiv.) Krypton-filled incandescent Tungsten-halogen incandescent	15	The Earth Home concentrates on these three sources for maximum efficiency and only uses incandescent for small use areas.
House number light	15	
Incandescent light	60	
Insect light	100	
Porch light	75	
Whole house average	340	Less for Earth Home.
(CONT. NEXT PAGE)		

Figure 95-ELECTRICAL USE CHART, PAGE 4

*Used in Earth Home

CATEGORY	TYPICAL WATTAGE	ALTERNATIVES
(CONTINUED FROM PREVIOUS PAGE)		
KITCHEN APPLIANCES/ FOOD PREPARATION		
Baby food warmer	165	12V DC models available.
Broiler Hot Plate Oven Range, small burner Range, large burner Roaster Toaster oven	1,436 - 1,500 1,257 3,000 1,250 2,000 - 2,400 1,335 1,200 - 1,400	Propane/gaseous fuel stove with wood backup.
Can opener (electric)	100 - 285	Quality manual models are just as fast.
Carving knife	92 - 100	Manual model.
Coffee grinder Food blender Food mixer Food processor Ice crusher Juicer	100 - 150 350 - 720 100 - 127 370 - 400 300 300	Food processor replaces many other appliances, and it is useful for food preservation.
Coffee maker	850 - 1,500	Alternative methods/hot water and reusable filters.
Corn popper	550 - 575	Pan on stovetop.
Deep-fat fryer	1,448 - 1,600	Low fat diets encouraged.
Dishwasher	700 - 1,500	Can be converted to 12V DC but hand wash best alternative with air dry.
Egg cooker	516	Stovetop method.
Exhaust fan	100 - 300	To air-to-air heat exchanger.
Pressure cooker	1,300	Stovetop method.
(CONT. NEXT PAGE)		

Figure 96-ELECTRICAL USE CHART, PAGE 5

*Used in Earth Home

CATEGORY	TYPICAL WATTAGE	ALTERNATIVES
(CONTINUED FROM PREVIOUS PAGE)		
Slow cooker on low (crock pot)	75	Pilot burner on stove.
Toaster	1,150 - 1,200	Fry toast on pan on stovetop.
Waffle iron	1,116 - 1,200	
Warming tray	140	Pilot burner on stove.
Wok pan	1,000	Stovetop method.
LAUNDRY/UTILITY		
Clothes dryer (electric) Clothes dryer (gas)	4,100 - 8,200 75 - 500	Earth Home system uses a slower rotating drum and hot water for heated air source.
Incinerator	605	
Iron (hand) Iron (mangle)	1,200 - 1,500 1,525	
Sump pump	85	12V DC models available.
Washing machine (automatic) Washing machine (non-automatic)	500 - 1,450 195 - 280	Some washing machines can be converted to 12V DC and "soft start" mechanism.
OFFICE/DEN		
Adding machine	8	Battery-powered calculators.
Computer/modem Monitor - 14" color Monitor - 14" black/white FAX machine - standby FAX machine - receiving Adding machine Dot matrix printer Ink jet printer (DeskJet, Bubblejet) Laser printer	55 - 80 100 25 10 400 - 650 8 200 25 - 35 1,000 - 1,500	Computers are getting more efficient with electricity. At least one company has addressed off-grid computer use. See Electricity Converters/Inverters. Use computer calculator.
(CONT. NEXT PAGE)		

Figure 97-ELECTRICAL USE CHART, PAGE 6

*Used in Earth Home

CATEGORY	TYPICAL WATTAGE	ALTERNATIVES
(CONTINUED FROM PREVIOUS PAGE)		
Electric eraser	100	
Electric pencil sharpener	100	Battery-operated models.
Phone dialer	4	
Typewriter	200	Use computer word processing programs.
REFRIGERATION/ FOOD PRESERVATION		
22 cu. ft. auto defrost (approximate run time 14 hrs. per day) Food freezer (15 cu. ft.) (14 hrs. per day) Refrigerator Refrigerator-freezer (14 cu. ft.)	490 - 700 341 - 750 250 325	OPTIONS: Newer/efficient refrigerators and compressors run less often (6-10 hours/day). See Refrigerators files. Less space is required because of food dehydration method.
WATER HEATERS	Gals.	**(IN AVERAGE GALLONS OF HOT WATER)**
Baby bath	5	
Clothes washing Dishwashing (hand) Dishwashing (automatic) Meal preparation	15 - 25 4 - 5 10 - 15 3	These numbers will be lower for the Earth Home due to natural lifestyle changes.
Hand/face wash Shower Tub bath	1 8 - 15 10 - 15	A combination shower/bath leaves the option open for both a .75 GPM shower and bath. 2 oz./10 sec. handwashing system conserves water.
(CONT. NEXT PAGE)		**NOTE: Electric water heaters average 4,219 watts.**

Figure 98-ELECTRICAL USE CHART, PAGE 7

*Used in Earth Home

CATEGORY	TYPICAL WATTAGE	ALTERNATIVES
(CONTINUED FROM PREVIOUS PAGE)		
WATER PUMPING		
AC jet pump (1/4 hp), 165 gal. per day, 20 ft. well depth DC pump for house pressure system (typical use is 1-2 hr. per day) DC submersible pump (typical use is 6 hr. per day)	460 - 500 60 50	Earth Home uses 12V DC pumps--estimate 1/2 hr./day maximum.
Water pump (deep well)	1,080	Not necessary in Earth Home.
WORKSHOP/ GARAGE/YARD		
Circular saw Drill (1/4" - 3/8") Jig saw Sander Soldering gun Table saw	1,150 - 1,800 287 - 400 287 287 - 300 120 1,380 - 1,800	A larger battery bank will be needed; or upsizing of the generator. Special tool needs must be taken into account separately.
Garage door opener	350 - 550	Manual type.
Hedge trimmer	288	
Lawn mower (electric)	700 - 1,200	Gas-powered models and rechargeables.
Snow blower	1,200 - 3,000	Gas-powered models.
Chain saw		Gas-powered.
Leaf blower	850 - 1,200	Gas-powered.

Figure 99-ELECTRICAL USE CHART, PAGE 8

*Used in Earth Home

c. EH Wind Generator

The Earth Home II is designed to use a more current model of the Windseeker from Southwest Windpower Company. It is a reasonably priced wind generator that has a cut-in speed of approximately 6 mph. One of the problems with early generators was that the cut-in speed was as high as 8 to 9 mph. (See Wind Generator files.) In the Earth Home I prototype, the Windseeker is mounted on top of a 2" diameter steel tower. Copper cables run underground from the wind generator to the control panel inside.

The Earth Home II model is designed to use two wind machines on a single tower. The side-by-side blades are designed to rotate in opposite directions to stabilize the centrifugal forces that are encountered.

The Earth Home II wind generator tower is designed to use a combination lattice and pole configuration for efficiency. The lattice section will be the first 30' bottom section and a 35' aluminum light pole will be clamped to it for the top section. A tilt-down wind generator tower is much easier to maintain than guyed towers that have to be climbed. Remember the saying that ***"everything wears out or breaks at some point."*** A heavy counterweight and a manual/motorized hydraulic system will make it easier to lower it for maintenance.

2. Solar Photovoltaic (PV) Panels

PV modules come in many different configurations. The efficiencies have steadily increased and the costs have come down. Longer-lasting versions are chosen for the Earth Home system that has a glass cover. (See Photovoltaic section.)

3. PV/Wind Ratio

The Earth Home uses a combination of photovoltaic (PV) panels and wind power to generate enough electricity. The previous statement "when the wind isn't blowing, the sun is shining," is fairly correct. So between the wind and the sun there is usually enough supply of energy for electricity a large percentage of the time. A device called a universal controller manages this automatically. It has been estimated that a 70-30 wind/solar split is appropriate for most areas with a 50/50 split in high solar insolation areas.

4. Hydrogen/Woodgas Phased into Earth Home (See also Hydrogen and Woodgas sections)

The Earth Home will ultimately use hydrogen as a means to use any excess electrical generation. In other words, hydrogen gas will be split by hydrolysis and stored for use as a cooking fuel or backup generator fuel. In this way any excess electrical capacity from high winds or windy *and* sunny day will be utilized. (See Energy/Power section on Hydrogen for complete discussion)

Woodgas will be used to fuel the generator—produced and used directly. Other alternatives mentioned in the Energy/Power section will be evaluated based on technology improvements. In this way, the most efficient and appropriate mix of technologies are used in the Earth Home System. ***"There is only one thing that remains constant in the entire universe and that is change itself."***

C. Engine-Driven Back-up Generators

1. Background

Electricity can be made any time a generator is turning at a specified minimum R.P.M. (revolutions per minute). ***Most alternative energy schemes include a generator back-up system, in case the wind or sunlight is unavailable for any length of time.***

*Used in Earth Home

2. Gas and Propane Generators

a. 2 stroke vs. 4 stroke

Most of the generators on the market are 2 or 4 stroke gas-powered units. Four-stroke engines give cleaner and more efficient burning of fuel. (See Engines file) Some of these generators can also be equipped with electric starts, such as Onan, Wisconsin, Briggs and Stratton, Honda, etc.

b. Fuel Efficiency Chart

Some studies suggest 12 VDC gas generators are more efficient at charging batteries than their 115 VAC counterparts because the engine is more appropriately sized to the alternator. They also save energy by charging directly without going through a battery charger first.

There is a wide variation in fuel efficiency of commercially available units. (See the following figures)

3. Generator Engine Options

a. Propane Converted

Four-cycle engines can be modified to burn propane or a gaseous fuel, whereas the 2-cycle cannot. Propane is a "dry fuel," as is hydrogen. Dry fuels require lubrication of the cylinder walls in order to ensure long life and trouble-free operation. Lubrication is achieved in 4-cycle engines splashing around the oil in the crankcase. Some propane-powered generators have a longer useful generator life potential than other generators. Some estimates say 50% longer life. For longer life, a generator should run at 1800 RPM and not the cheaper 3600-RPM construction site models.

b. Alcohol Converted Engines (See Energy/Power section)

c. Woodgas-Powered Systems (See Woodgas section)

d. Diesel Generator Sets

Diesel gen-sets can last three times as long as a gas-burning unit. Diesel fuel is also generally available around the world. However, due to the carburetor and fuel-mixing technology, they cannot be retrofitted with a gaseous fuel or woodgas. Diesel engines are only covered briefly in this text.

*Used in Earth Home

Mfr./ Sizes/ Model	Generator Volt Range/ Avail. Watts	Fuel Efficiency Start Options	Engine 2-Stroke or 4-Stroke	Gas Tank Size	Cont. Rating RPM/ Output	Hours Run Time or Rate	Watt-Hrs/ Gal.
Honda Honda Motor Corp. 4,000 W 406 CL EMS 4000	120/240 .5-6.5 Kw	Recoil/ Electric	4-Stroke	4.4 Gal. Gasoline	3,800 W Rate	6 Hrs.	5,197
Cold-Power ACME North America 4,000 W AD4000R	120/240 2.8-7.5 Kw	Recoil	4-Stroke	1.5 Gal.	3,700 W Cont.	.6 Gal./Hr. 3/8 Gal. LP/Hr.	6,167 974 W-Hrs./ Gal. LP
Generac Corp. 3,500 W #9441 3500XL	120/240 12 VDC 2.4-10 Kw	Recoil	4-Stroke	4 Gal.	1,750 W Cont.	15 Hrs. 60% Duty	3,937
Sentry Pro Gillette 9,000 W SP-90	120/240 12 VDC 2.8-11 Kw	Electric/ Recoil	4-Stroke		8,500 W	1.6 Gal./Hr. 133 Ft.^{3} LP/HP	5,312 LP
(CONT. NEXT PAGE)							

Figure 100-EFFICIENCY OF GENERATORS, PAGE 1

*Used in Earth Home

Mfr./ Sizes/ Model	Generator Volt Range/ Avail. Watts	Fuel Efficiency Start Options	Engine 2-Stroke or 4-Stroke	Gas Tank Size	Cont. Rating RPM/ Output	Hours Run Time or Rate	Watt-Hrs/ Gal.
(CONT FROM PREVIOUS PAGE)							
Coleman Coleman Powermate 4,000 54A4302 4000 ER	120/240	Electric	4-Stroke	5 Gal.	4,000 W	8 Hrs. 50%	3,200
Kohler Kohler Co. 6,500 W 6.5RMY	120/240	Electric	4-Stroke	--	6,500 W	1.27 GPH	5,118
Onan Onan Corporation 7,500 W 7.5JB 60 Hz	120/240	Electric	4-Stroke	--	7,500 W	1.2 GPH 68 $Ft.^3/Hr.$ LP	6,250 110 W-Hrs./ FT^3 LP
Pow'r Gard T&J Manufacturing 8 Kw AE8	120/240	Electric	Vanguard 4-Stroke	--	8,000 W	LP 1.7 GPH	4,705 W Hrs./ Gal.
(CONT. NEXT PAGE)							

Figure 101-EFFICIENCY OF GENERATORS, PAGE 2

*Used in Earth Home

Mfr./ Sizes/ Model	Generator Volt Range/ Avail. Watts	Fuel Efficiency Start Options	Engine 2-Stroke or 4-Stroke	Gas Tank Size	Cont. Rating RPM/ Output	Hours Run Time or Rate	Watt-Hrs/ Gal.
(CONT FROM PREVIOUS PAGE)							
Winco Winco Inc. 8 Kw PSS8000	120/240	Electric	Vanguard 4-Stroke		8,000 W	LP 2.2 Gal./Hr.	3,636 W Hrs./ Gal. LP
Yamaha Yamaha Motors 850 W EF-1000	120/240	Recoil	?	?	850 W 1000 max.	5 Hrs./Gal.	4,250 W Hrs./ Gal.
Kubota Kubota Tractor 3,500 W AE 3500	120/240 12 VDC	Recoil	4-Stroke	2.11 Gal.	3,000 W	3.5 Hrs./Tank	5,000 W Hrs./ Gal.
(CONT. NEXT PAGE)							

Figure 102-EFFICIENCY OF GENERATORS, PAGE 3

*Used in Earth Home

Mfr./ Sizes/ Model	Generator Volt Range/ Avail. Watts	Fuel Efficiency Start Options	Engine 2-Stroke or 4-Stroke	Gas Tank Size	Cont. Rating RPM/ Output	Hours Run Time or Rate	Watt-Hrs/ Gal.
(CONT FROM PREVIOUS PAGE)							
Kubota Diesel 4 HP	12 Volt 80 Amp. 24 Volt 40 Amp	Recoil/Electric	Diesel	?	1,000 Watt	8-12 Hr./ Gallon	8-12 Hr./ Gallon of #2 Diesel
Lightning Charger ATI Power Prod. 900 W 12/24	120 12 VDC	Recoil	Tecumseh TC 300 2-Stroke	20 Oz.	NR	NR	NR

Note: 1) Air cooled unless specified;
2) Assume 36 Cu. Ft./Gal. LP and 1 Gallon LP = 4.23 lbs.;
3) NR = Not Rated

Note; No data available on Hatz 3.6 kw, Isuzu 8.2 kw, Perkins 4 kw, or Mitsubishi generators.

Figure 103-EFFICIENCY OF GENERATORS, PAGE 4

*Used in Earth Home

e. Steam-Driven

Steam generation and use is very specialized and involves condensate feed pumps, controls, and high-pressure components. It was not used in the Earth Home System because of the technicalities encountered.

Some work, however, has been done on a high efficiency internal combustion steam engine. This technology, however, never got past the development and patent stages. (For more information, see Hansen cycle engines-Herbert, N.W. Hansen)

The following figure shows the complexity of a dependable steam system.

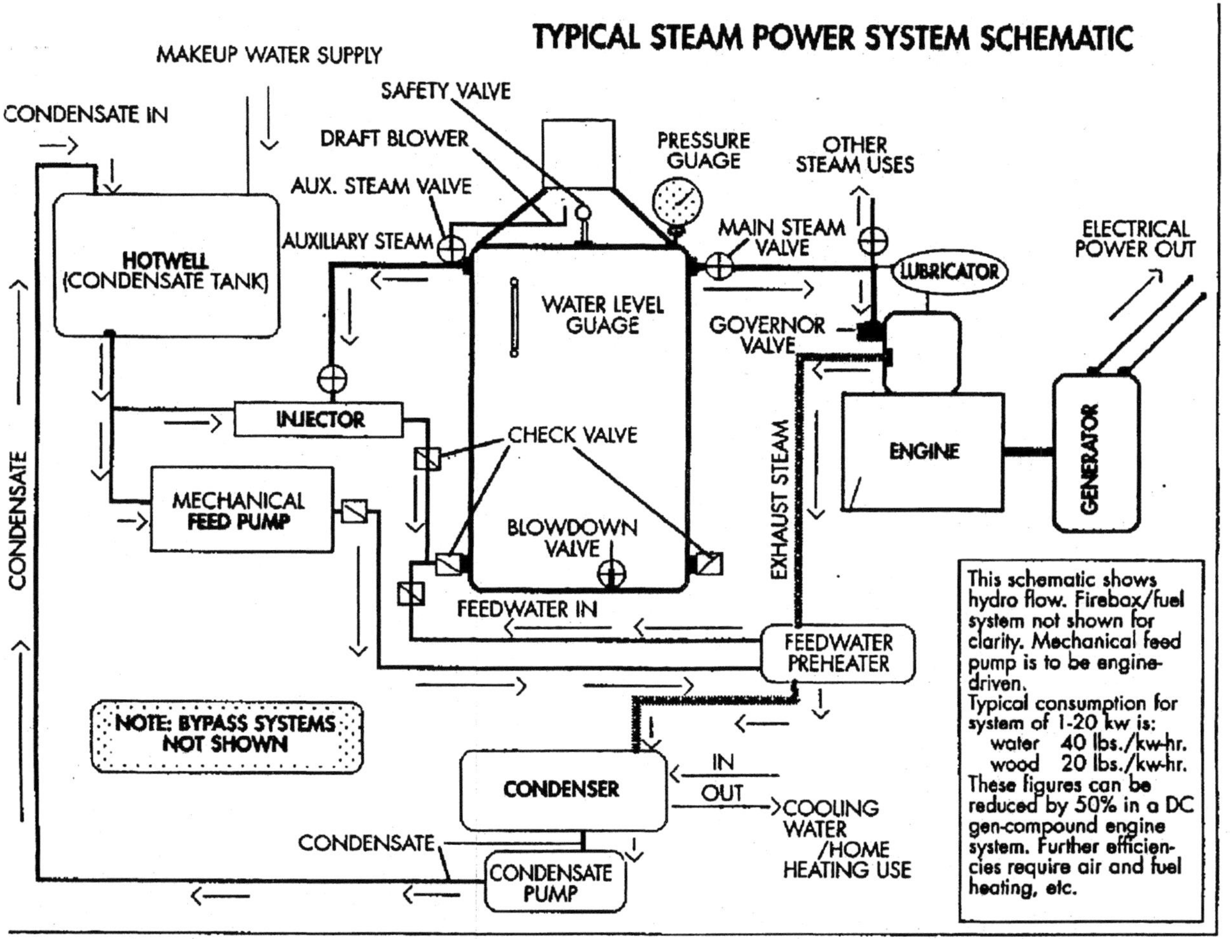

Figure 104-STEAM POWER SCHEMATIC

*Used in Earth Home

4. Earth Home Back-up Generation System

a. Electrical Overview

Generators have been used as backup power supplies in remote homes for many years. ***In the Earth Home system, a generator is used in order to reduce the size of the PV array, wind generator, and battery bank***. The generator will automatically be started based on a reading of battery voltage at 10.6 volts, or a rise in freezer temperature.

b. Simultaneous Tasks

Besides backup battery charging, it can be used for simultaneous tasks such as central vacuuming, laundry, dropping freezer temperatures, or massive water pumping. The occupants will eventually become familiar with the availability of power, much like we as infants learned to flush a toilet. For instance, laundry and cleaning should be done in high wind conditions, when the wind generator is at peak output. The Earth Home generator will be located outdoors in a separate enclosure with its own starting battery. Estimates of yearly usage for the generator are about 125 hours/year. Useful features include an oil low-level cutoff switch and automatic choke. (See also Energy/Power section on Alcohol)

c. Mechanical Work from Generator Option

There are a number of tasks in the Earth Home System that would benefit from mechanical power such as can be obtained from a turning shaft. In the early days of the U.S., machine shops were operated by one motor that turned a long driveshaft above the floor. Any machine that needed power was attached to the spinning shaft and was operated using this single power source. The EH could use mechanical power to press croutons for fish food, grind flour, grind meat, and also run small tools directly.

d. Uni-Engine (See Uni-Engine section)

D. Storage of Electricity

1. Mechanical Energy Storage Systems

a. Weights/Water

Energy can also be stored with weight-lifting devices and water-pumping systems. However, these never enjoyed widespread use because of limitations due to temperature extremes and the mechanical problems of the support systems needed for lifting huge weights.

b. Flywheels

Flywheels are enjoying recent interest somewhat because of the use of superconductivity for the bearings. Argonne National Lab and others are working on super-efficient flywheels to store energy. They spin at very high speeds inside a vacuum chamber with ultra-efficient bearing design. However, flywheel technology for homes is still years off but shows significant promise.

Flywheels are being designed for the space station that are lighter and stronger than steel. They are using composites and advanced materials for fabrication.

The research on alternatives to the battery continues at a fast pace. However, the standard battery, in which weight is proportional to capacity, continues to be the most widely used type of storage method.

*Used in Earth Home

2. Battery Technology

a. Battery Charts/Types

Batteries are commonly used to store electricity in chemical form. For every amp-hour you use, approximately 1-1/4 amp-hours must be added to recharge the battery. The following two figures show most battery types that are commonly available, such as lead acid, nickel iron, nickel cadmium, etc.

b. Lead Acid and Care Required

In the past, lead acid batteries have been used primarily for automotive purposes. These batteries are not suitable for household electrical storage systems because of their limitations for "deep cycling" or complete discharge and recharge. Deep cycling batteries are similar to those in golf cart and trolling motor applications. They can tolerate almost complete discharge hundreds of times without harm. Many battery-powered homes used lead-acid batteries for storage. The following figure shows how to care for lead-acid batteries.

c. Ni-Cad Batteries

Another type of common battery is the nickel-cadmium, or "Ni-Cad" batteries. A positive feature is that their voltage stays at a very constant level throughout their discharge cycle. The voltage is slightly higher than lead-acid batteries. They can last 20 years or more but are much more costly, don't readily show level of charge, and can't be used with lead-acid batteries. These larger versions of the supermarket Ni Cad rechargeable batteries are available both new and used. (See Batteries file.)

d. Nickel-Iron and Gel-Cells

Nickel-Iron batteries have been around for 50 years or more. They are very similar to nickel-cadmium batteries in that they can withstand low temperatures. They have an extremely long life and their charge and discharge voltage characteristics are about the same. These batteries would be good for a low current application such as the Earth Home if they were available. The problem is that there is no dependable supply of nickel-iron batteries at present. Economy of mass production has not made the nickel-iron battery available in the marketplace as yet. Users have sought out other alternatives such as the gel-cell.

The massive amounts of care that lead-acid batteries require, plus heating and venting requirements, make the lead-calcium gel-cell an attractive alternative. Gel cell batteries have an electrolyte in gelatin-type form so water does not have to be added periodically. It also produces little hydrogen gasses and can be used in any position. ***This new generation of gel-cell batteries is a vast improvement over lead acid batteries***. However, the peak charging voltage should be limited to 13.7 volts and life expectancy is less. Gel-cell battery banks currently must be replaced every 8 years or so until battery technology is improved.

e. Earth Home Battery Bank

The Earth Home is using gel-cell batteries wired into a single “bank”. ***Battery banks for off-the-grid homes are typically designed to provide electricity for three days without either wind or adequate sunshine.***

Wiring of the battery bank should be in accordance with the next figure. This is done so all batteries will charge and discharge uniformly, to prevent sulfating, and to ensure longer life.

***Used in Earth Home**

System	Anode	Cathode	Theoretical battery		Practical battery		
			Voltage, V	Capacity, Ah/kg	Typical voltage, V	Capacity[a]	
						Wh/kg	Wh/dm³
Primary:							
Leclanche	Zn	MnO_2	1.6	230	1.2	65	175
Magnesium	Mg	MnO_2	2.0	270	1.5	100	195
Organic cathode	Mg	*m*-DNB	1.8	1,400	1.15	130	180
Alkaline MnO_2	Zn	MnO_2	1.5	230	1.15	65	200
Mercury	Zn	HgO	1.34	185	1.2	80	370
Mercad	Cd	HgO	0.9	165	0.85	45	175
Silver oxide	Zn	AgO	1.85	285	1.5	130	310
Zinc-air	Zn	Air (O_2)	1.6	815	1.1	200	190
Li-organic electrolyte	Li	[b]	2.1-5.4	130-660	1.8-3.2	250	400
Secondary:							
Lead-acid	Pb	PbO_2	2.1	55	2.0	37	70
Edison	Fe	Ni oxides	1.5	195	1.2	29	65
Nickel-cadmium	Cd	Ni oxides	1.35	165	1.2	33	60
Silver-zinc	Zn	AgO	1.85	285	1.5	100	170
Silver-cadmium	Cd	AgO	1.4	230	1.05	55	120
Zinc-nickel oxide	Zn	Ni oxides	1.75	185	1.6	55	110
Zinc-air[c]	Zn	Air (O_2)	1.6	815	1.1	150	155
Cadmium-air[c]	Cd	Air (O_2)	1.2	475	0.8	90	90
Zinc-O_2	Zn	O_2	1.6	610	1.1	130	120
H_2-O_2	H_2	O_2	1.23	3,000	0.8	45	65
Reserve:							
Cuprous chloride	Mg	CuCl	1.5	240	1.4	45	65[d]
Silver-chloride	Mg	AgCl	1.6	170	1.5	60	95[d]
Zinc-silver oxide	Zn	AgO	1.85	285	1.5	30	75[e]
Thermal	Ca	[b]	2.8	240	2.6	10	20[f]
Ammonia-activated	Mg	*m*-DNB	2.2	1,400	1.7	22	60[g]
High-	NA	S	2.1	685	1.8	200	[h]
temperature	Li	S	2.2	1,150	1.8	200	[i]
Solid electrolyte	Ag	Polyiodide	0.66	...	0.6	180	75[j]
Fuel cell:							
Hydrogen[c]	H_2	Air	1.23	26,000	0.7		[k]
Hydrazine[c]	N_2H_4	Air	1.5	2,100	0.7	800[b]	[l]
Methanol[c]	CH_2OH	Air	1.3	1,400	0.9	175[b]	185[m]

Delivered capacity when discharged at normal temperatures (20°C) at normal discharge rates.
Based on fuel consumption only.
Weight of air not considered in computation of watt hours.
Water-activated
Automatically activated; high rate discharge; 2- to 10-min rate.
Fused salt; heat-activated; high rate discharge; 2- to 10-min rate.
g Four-minute discharge rate.
h β-alumina electrolyte, 300°C operation.
i Fused salt; 350°C operation.
j Solid $RbAg_4I_5$ electrolyte.
k Several different cathode materials used.
l Fuel consumption is based on source of H_2.
m Based on methanol battery-fuel supply in situ.

Figure 105-BATTERY TYPES

*Used in Earth Home

COMPARISON OF SECONDARY BATTERIES					
System	Lead-acid (SLI, wound, gel)	Vented pocket plate Nickel-cadmium	Vented sintered plate Nickel-cadmium	Sealed wound Nickel-cadmium	Nickel Hydrogen
Chemistry: Anode Cathode Electrolyte	Pb PbO_2 H_2SO_4 (aqueous solution)	Cd NiOOH KOH (aqueous solution)	Cd NiOOH KOH (aqueous solution)	Cd NiOOH KOH (aqueous solution)	H_2 NiOOH KOH (aqueous solution)
Cell voltage Nominal Open-circuit Operating End	2.0 2.1 2.0-1.8 1.75	1.2 1.25 1.25-1.00 0.9	1.2 1.25 1.25-1.00 0.9	1.2 1.25 1.25-1.00 0.9	1.4 1.32 1.3-1.15 1.0
Operating temperature, (C)	-40 to 55	-20 to 45	-40 to 50	-40 to 70	0 to 50
Energy density at 20deg.C Wh/kg Wh/L	35 70	20 40	37 90	30 80	80 90
Calendar life years	2-8	8-25	3-10	2-5	—
Cycle life	200-700	500-2000	500-2000	500-2000	500-3000+
Self discharge % loss per month at 20deg.C	2-30	5	10	15-20	60
Advantages	Low cost; readily available; good high-rate, high and low temperature operation	Very rugged, can withstand physical and electrical abuse; good charge retention; lower cost	Rugged; excellent storage; good specific energy and high-rate and low temperature performance	Sealed, no maintenance; good low temperature and high rate performance, long cycle life	High energy density; long cycle life, can tolerate overcharge
Limitations	Relatively low cycle life; limited energy density; poor charge retention; hydrogen evolution	Low energy density	Higher cost	Higher initial cost than lead-acid	High cost; used for special military and aerospace applications
Major types available	Prismatic Cylindrical, wound cells 2-400 Ah	Prismatic cells; 5-1300 Ah	Prismatic cells 10-100 Ah	Button cells to 0.5 Ah; cylindrical cells to 10 Ah	Not commercially available

Figure 106-BATTERY COMPARISON CHART

*Used in Earth Home

HOW A BATTERY WORKS

1. A battery produces electricity as the result of a chemical reaction.
2. The sulfuric acid in the electrolyte combines with the positive and negative plates to form a new chemical compound called lead sulfate.
3. The amount of sulfuric acid consumed by the plates is proportional to the amount of electricity produced. Therefore, the more electricity produced, the less sulfuric acid remains in the electrolyte.
4. The gradual weakening of the electrolyte lets us measure, with a hydrometer, the amount of unused acid in the water, and thus how much potential energy is left.

HOW TO CHARGE A BATTERY

1. Before hooking charger up to the battery, make sure it is off or unplugged.
2. Connect the positive lead from the charger to the positive terminal of the battery and connect the negative lead from charger to the negative terminal of the battery.
3. A battery may be charged at any rate that does not cause the electrolyte temperature to exceed 125 degrees F.
4. A safe slow charge rate is 1/10 the electrical reference size on 12 volts and 1/5 the electrical reference size on 6 volts. Example: 12 volt battery with 60 amp reference charge at 6 amp rate. 6 volt battery with 60 amp reference charge at 12 amp charge rate.
5. A fully charged battery has a specific gravity of 1.265.
6. Maintain 1/4" to 1/2" of electrolyte above the tops of the separators. Add water only. Never add acid unless it has been spilled or dumped out accidentally.

CARE OF DRY CHARGE BATTERIES AND ACTIVATION

CAUTION: Dry charge batteries are sealed with a protective tape and a plastic seal or plug in each cell opening. Do not remove either prior to activation.

1. Store dry charge batteries in a cool dry place.
2. Keep dry charge electrolyte at room temperature.
3. Dry charge activation procedure—
   a) Remove and discard protective tape and plastic seals or plugs.
   b) Fill battery with 1.265 specific gravity electrolyte to 1/4" to 1/2" above separators.
   c) Charge 6 volt batteries at 30 amps for 20 minutes and 12 volt batteries at 15 amps for 20 minutes.
   d) After charging, be sure that electrolyte level is still 1/4" to 1/2" above separators.
   e) Use black or white vent caps to close openings after charging and when battery is ready to service. Do not use seals or plugs as battery might explode!

CARE OF WET CHARGED BATTERIES

1. A wet charged battery slowly discharges while in stock.
2. A wet battery will need recharging after 6 months in stock under normal conditions.
3. Minimize self-discharge by keeping your stock in a cool or cold place and away from direct sunlight and heat.
4. Your success in the battery business is governed to a large extent by the attention you give to batteries in stock. Dissatisfied customers result if you sell discharged batteries!
5. Boost charge and test all batteries when they are sold.
6. WARNING—DANGER! Batteries produce explosive gases. Keep sparks, flame, cigarettes away. Ventilate when charging or using in enclosed area. Shield eyes when working near batteries.

PROPER PROCEDURE FOR TESTING A BATTERY

WITH A MOTOROLA TESTER

A. With engine and all electrical loads off, connect red clip to the positive (+) terminal of the battery, black clip to the negative terminal.
B. Set 6-12 switch to 6 volt for 6 volt battery and 12 volt for 12 volt battery.
C. Set dial selector switch to "Voltage" and read voltage on the voltage scale of meter. If voltage is below 12.4 volts, the battery must be charged and then continue test.
D. Dial size of battery to proper position. If battery size is unknown, dial cubic inch displacement of engine the battery is used on. Set temperature switch to estimated temperature of battery. Turn selector switch to battery condition and read the red/green scale. If the dial indicator is in the green, the battery is good. If the indicator is in the red, the battery is bad *or* simply not large enough for the application.

TESTING PROCEDURE USING A HYDROMETER

A. Full charge equals 1.265 specific gravity.
B. Replace battery if there is 50 or more points variation between highest and lowest cell.

TESTING PROCEDURE USING A "LOAD" TESTER

A. Types of load testers vary widely. A safe rule of thumb is that a 12 volt battery under load should provide a minimum of 9 volts and sustain it for 10 seconds. A 6 volt battery should provide 4.5 volts and sustain it for 10 seconds.
B. Load testers create heat and can cause electrical sparks. Utmost care should be used when using a load tester, as a spark could cause an explosion.

TESTING STARTER DRAW USING MOTOROLA TESTER

A. After first determining battery condition proceed with starter test.
B. With tester connected to battery (red clip to positive terminal, black to negative terminal) set tester selector switch to "volt" setting. Disconnect coil wire and crank engine; indicator should not fall below the green "cranking" area on the voltage scale.

TESTING CHARGING SYSTEM USING MOTOROLA TESTER

A. After making the above test (starter draw) re-connect the coil wire and start engine. Indicator should ride in the green "charging" area. Undercharging will result in a discharged battery. Overcharging will destroy the battery.

CRANKING PERFORMANCE

The primary function of the battery is to provide power to crank the engine during starting. This requirement involves a large discharge in amperes over a short span of time.
Therefore, the CRANKING PERFORMANCE rate is defined as:
The discharge load in amperes which a new fully charged battery at 0°F (– 17.8°C) can deliver for 30 seconds and maintain a voltage of 1.2 volts per cell or higher.

RESERVE CAPACITY

A battery must provide emergency power for ignition, lights, etc. in the event of failure in the vehicle's battery recharging system. This requirement involves a discharge at normal temperature.
The RESERVE CAPACITY rating is defined as:
The number of minutes a new fully charged battery at 80°F (26.7°C) can be discharged at 25 amperes and maintain a voltage of 1.75 volts per cell or higher.

Figure 107-BATTERY BASICS

*Used in Earth Home

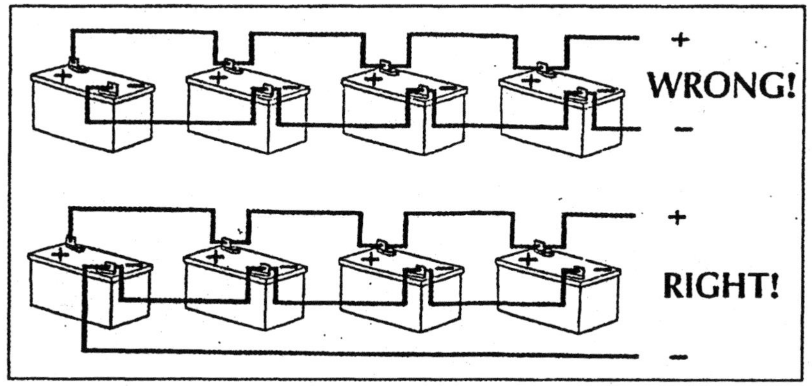

Figure 108-CORRECT BATTERY CONNECTIONS

3. Future Battery/Storage Technology

a. Paper/Polymer Battery

Research is being done on other types of batteries such as a paper battery. This is a much lighter version of the lead-acid battery. A new hybrid is also being developed called a "polymer battery". This battery is made of plastic and is being designed for specific low weight applications. Lithium polymer batteries are also being developed which exhibit the mechanical properties of a solid and the electrical properties of a fluid.

Research is constantly being done on new batteries specifically designed for electric cars by the U.S. Advanced Battery Consortium. So far, there has been little progress in reducing the weight and increasing power density. Given the huge potential of this market segment, more battery developments are sure to be in the future.

b. Nickel Metal Hydride Battery

Recently-developed nickel metal hydride batteries are being tested by GM Ovonic, LLC in the Chevrolet S-10 pickups. This NiMH battery provides more than twice the driving range of lead-acid batteries having the same weight. Saft is also working on them for Chrysler cars. (See Transportation-Batteries Section)

One recent improvement in small nickel metal hydride batteries has been developed at Rayovac. They have incorporated a pressure sensor inside the battery itself to stop charging if the pressure builds up past a certain point. Using this technology, the batteries can be recharged in 15 minutes. This is one of the fastest charging times available today.

c. Atomic/Radioactive Battery

Researchers at Cornell University (Ithaca, NY) may be capable of supplying power to remote sensors or implantable medical devices for decades by drawing energy from a minute amount of a radioisotope. As the isotope decays, it emits beta particles—but not hazardous alpha particles or gamma rays. The prototype comprises a 1 mm x 2 cm x 60 micron copper strip that is cantilevered above a thin film of radioactive nickel-63.

As the emitted electrons collect on the copper strip, a negative charge builds. At the same time, the isotope film, losing electrons, becomes positively charged. The attraction between the positive and negative plates bends the copper strip down. When the strip gets close enough to the isotope, current flows and equalizes the charge. The strip then springs up, and the process repeats. The moving cantilever could actuate a linear device directly, or

*Used in Earth Home

produce rotary motion using a cam or ratcheted wheel. Even though this research is still in its infancy, the atomic battery technology has attracted interest.

A related technology is called betavoltaics. This uses a silicon wafer to capture electrons from radioactive gas such as tritium. This new battery is based on the radioactive decay of nuclear materials. It is 10 times more powerful than similar prototypes and shows great promise.

d. Lithium-Ion Developments

The search for more compact and powerful batteries has driven scientists to develop innovative and effective ways of delivering power. Lithium batteries have a large advantage over both Ni-H2 and Ni-Cad batteries: They weigh less, take less space, and deliver more energy. There are lithium-polymer cells and lithium batteries with a liquid electrolyte.

Researchers at Sandia National Laboratories are in the process of developing silicon-graphite material that may double the capacity of current graphite-based battery anodes. This could lead to more powerful, smaller, and longer-lasting lithium-ion batteries.

e. "Combination" Battery (See Hydrogen section)

f. Hydrogen/Electrolysis "Battery" (See Hydrogen section)

g. Seebeck Effect Batteries

Scientists have developed tiny implantable semiconductor devices that are really not batteries but arrays of tiny elements that convert heat flow directly into electrical current. They are dependent on the temperature difference between the hot and cold side of the device. This difference is very small in the human body, but poses potential for scaling up to larger surfaces.

h. Ultracapacitors

One of the unique power devices being utilized for energy storage is the ultracapacitor. A capacitor is an electrical energy storage device consisting of two or more conducting electrodes separated from one another by an insulating dielectric. An ultracapacitor is an electrochemical energy storage device, which has extremely high volumetric capacitance energy due to high surface area electrodes, and very small electrode separation. Ultracapacitors have many advantages over batteries including:

1) Batteries can only be charged and discharged about 300 times while ultracapacitors can be charged and discharged over one million times.
2) High power density provides high power during surges, and the ability to absorb high power during recharging.
3) Ultracapacitors are rugged, reliable and free of any maintenance.
4) Have excellent low temperature characteristics and can be left indefinitely discharged.

E. Control/Distribution of Electricity

1. Charging Background

a. Battery "Balancing"

Keeping the PV panels and the wind generator producing electricity at a stable rate is very difficult. Therefore, it is necessary to add some mechanism to control electrical generation and provide a steady input to the battery storage bank. Batteries like to be charged <u>slowly</u>. This steady charging ensures longer battery life.

b. Electrical Charge Control

Battery chargers can be powered by a gas/propane generator source to provide an even voltage for uniform charging. Lower voltage batteries can be charged with approximately 30% of their capacity. (A 225 amp-hour battery can be charged with a 75-amp charger.) If the battery type will be changed at some future point, it is best to use a charger with a user-selectable voltage range. Nickel-cadmium batteries charge at a higher voltage (16.5 volts) than lead-acid (14.7 volts). Some people prefer Ni Cad's because they make 12-volt DC light bulbs brighter. However, the bulbs do not last as long.

c. PV Array

A photovoltaic array uses a small amount of electricity during the night or cloudy days when at rest. A blocking diode or "Shottky" diode is a sort of one-way gate that doesn't let the electricity into the panels. PV arrays should not use one because it "costs" about 3/4 of a volt to include it in the circuit when the panel is producing electricity. Modern charge controllers use a relay (electrical switch) to connect the array with the battery to eliminate this waste.

d. Earth Home Charge Control System

In a typical 12 volt DC application, charging takes place at approximately 14.7 volts, and reads 12.7 volts when the system is fully charged at rest. As you use electricity, the voltage on the battery gradually drops to about 10.6 volts -- an 80% discharged battery bank. A 5-hour slightly higher "equalizing charge" should be done at 2 to 6 month intervals to "tune up" the battery bank.

Any control system also has to deal with excess generation of electricity. For example, when the home is not being utilized or the occupants are on vacation, what happens when the wind generates electricity? A device called an "Enermaxer" will distribute electricity to the batteries and a "shunt" system. This shunt mechanism diverts excess energy to a heating device around the aerobic digester, a hydrogen production device, lights, the grain/ball mill, or a fan. This is a way to divert the excess electricity after the batteries are fully satisfied or charged. The "float voltage" can also be set depending on the season or temperature of the batteries. A float voltage is used to keep an idle battery healthy.

2. Earth Home Electrical Control Panel

a. Background of Control Panels

Electrical control systems normally include an indication of the amount of electricity being generated and the voltage of the entire system. Amperage or current is the amount of electricity flowing into or out of the batteries (amperes) and voltage is the "pressure" that the electricity exerts (volts), or state of charge. Both of these should be displayed on meters in the electrical panel. A control panel should be located in an accessible area such as a utility area to monitor the entire system. A visual system would help to develop "minimum electrical usage" habits. (I suggest that a hand-held digital multi-meter be used as an educational tool for anyone working with electricity even though the main control panel should show exactly what is going on at any one instant.) DC power is inherently much safer than AC power (no electrocutions; just blown fuses). (See 12-Volt Advantage article.)

b. Power Use Monitoring

The individual circuitry inside of the Earth Home II will be similar to 110-volt home circuits, with each circuit being fused separately. The wiring necessary to connect all of the outlets, appliances, controls, sensors, lights, and all the other electricity needs of the home is no small task. The total power needs of the home must be monitored from a central location not only to save energy, but to monitor the home's energy needs. (See Home Control section)

*Used in Earth Home

The home will be much more closely attached to the occupants because nature is used to the benefit of the occupants. Having the homeowners keep a close eye on nature will come as naturally as learning how to flush the toilet.

3. Home Automation

a. Background of Home Automation

Home control is loosely defined as electrical signals from a controlling device such as a computer directed to any number of devices in a home such as appliances, lights, furnace, valves, etc. The function is ***to save energy, save time, and/or control the functions of a home automatically***. The largest savings are in the HVAC system.

Signals can be inputs from a sensor such as a thermostat or outputs such as closing an air damper. These signals can be one of two kinds—digital and analog. A digital signal is either on or off, but an analog signal can be any amount of current or voltage -- depending on the device.

There have been many ways of wiring a home to achieve automatic control such as programmable logic controllers (PLC's), computers, CEBus, PLBus and X-10. These systems are quite expensive and may require A/D converters or special interfaces. The X-10 system needs 60-cycle AC power in order to trigger when the signals switch the device.

Swedish utilities are experimenting with e-box technology. This allows the homeowner to control virtually everything electronically, while at home or by long-distance. The system uses ordinary, fixed telephone lines, the Internet, and household electrical systems.

A more recent application of control is CAN or Controller Area Network. This control system is used on mobile equipment to approach a higher level of automation. Many manufacturers now offer entire mobile fieldbus systems. Chrysler and others are using multiplexed signals to control functions in an automobile. They use a primary and secondary system to control virtually every function inside of a vehicle.

b. Fieldbus Background

Fieldbus is a new digital communications network for linking field devices, such as controllers, actuators, and sensors. Its use not only reduces the cost of operations, but it is also aimed at achieving complete interchangeability and interoperability of products between different suppliers. Fieldbuses are so crucial that they have been described as the "fifth stage of the industrial revolution."

Manufacturers of sensors, switches, valves, and many other devices have had the trouble of using different methods to communicate with those devices. This method or "universal device interface technology" is evolving around the world in order to use any networking system and any control system. In the end, devices could be connected as easily as printers to a PC.

c. Fieldbus (Assortment) Chart

There has been more interest in developing a corporate-wide network-an extension of the technology being used elsewhere in manufacturing companies. Ethernet was the standardize backbone, and its TCP/IP protocol provided a link to the Internet. The focus now is on developing the final link between the factory floor the Internet. The following chart shows the relative popularity of fieldbus systems.

There has been an on-going and highly contentious search for a universal fieldbus system. Such a system has not been agreed upon, however, some standards are currently available, having been developed and supported by large manufacturers and end users.

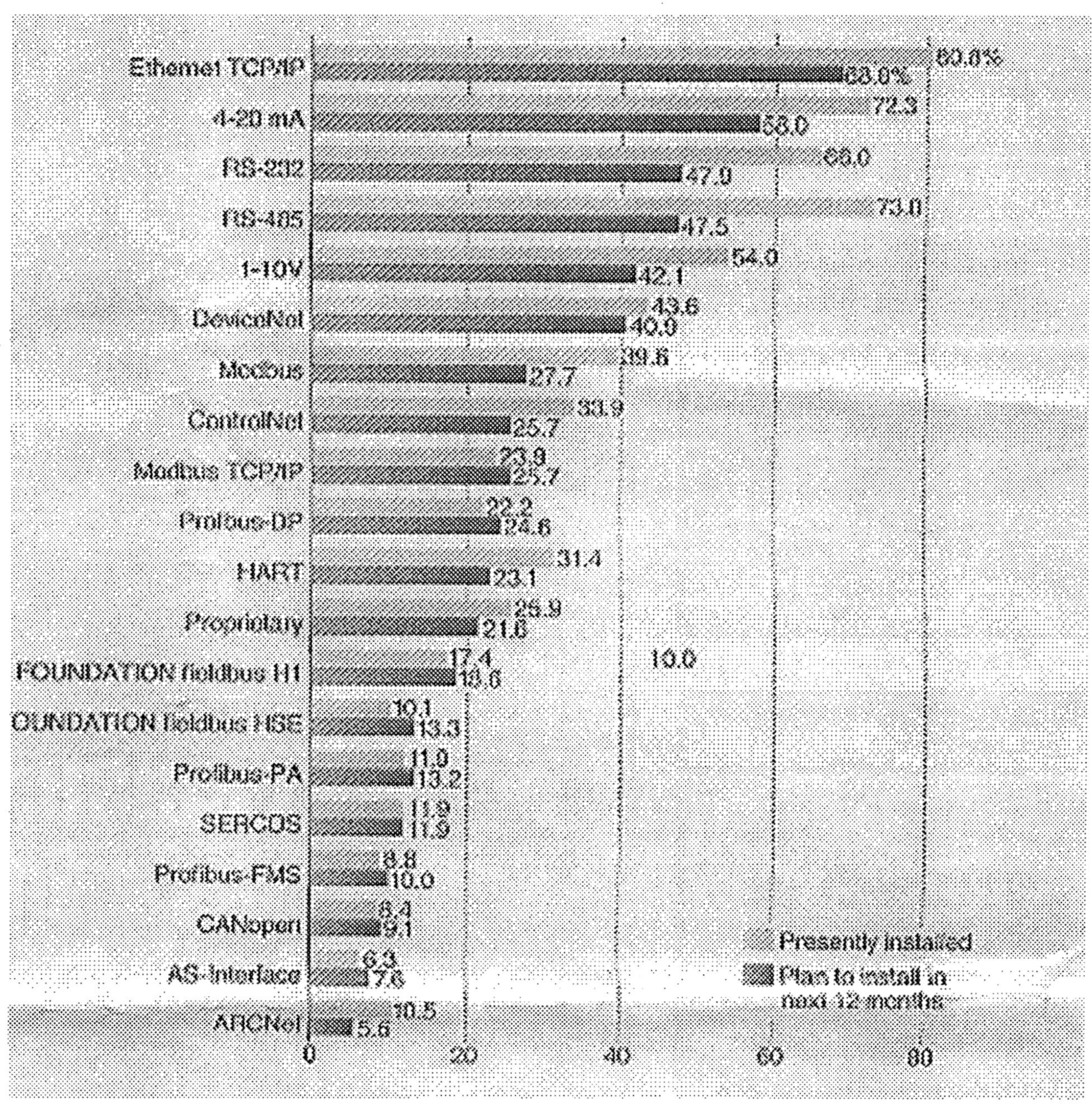

Figure 109-FIELDBUS TECHNOLOGIES

Over the years different network protocols have included; DeviceNet, Profibus-DP, Ethernet TCP/IP, EtherCAT, EtherNet/IP, AS-Interface, Interbus, CANOpen, CANBus, LonWorks, or Modbus. Depending on the application and the price, graduated, matching industrial communications systems such as Ethernet/IP, Profibus, and ASInterface offer the ideal preconditions of transparent networking in all areas of the production process.

Profibus, for example is a vendor-independent, open field bus standard for a wide range of applications in manufacturing and process control. For example, as of April 1999, Profibus, one of the market leaders, claims to have 2.5 million installed systems worldwide. The new international standard EN 50170 and EN 50254 ensure

*Used in Earth Home

the openness and vendor independence. The mix of fieldbus technology is confusing. The following graph shows a glimpse into how many systems are in place and the approximate popularity of each.

Over the years, end-users of devices are constantly looking for interoperability of devices/components so they can be used with any fieldbus system like the way they were able to do with 4-20 mA. Ethernet appears to have the most "openness" of the group.

d. Home Electronic Bus

Another emerging technology is the "Home Electronic Bus" system. This wiring method uses one bundle of wires to carry electricity and communications together. All electronic, entertainment, and communications devices can be accessed from the same outlet box similar to ones used to plug in a floor lamp. (See Electrical-Wiring files.) (See also Home Control files.)

e. Automotive Examples

In the automotive industry, control of electricity and devices has reached a high level of technology. Many devices are now controlled in the mechanics of the modern automobile. The following figure shows one example of the number of control devices inside an automobile. A model year 2000 economy car contains more than 50 small motors and a luxury vehicle has as many as 100 motors.

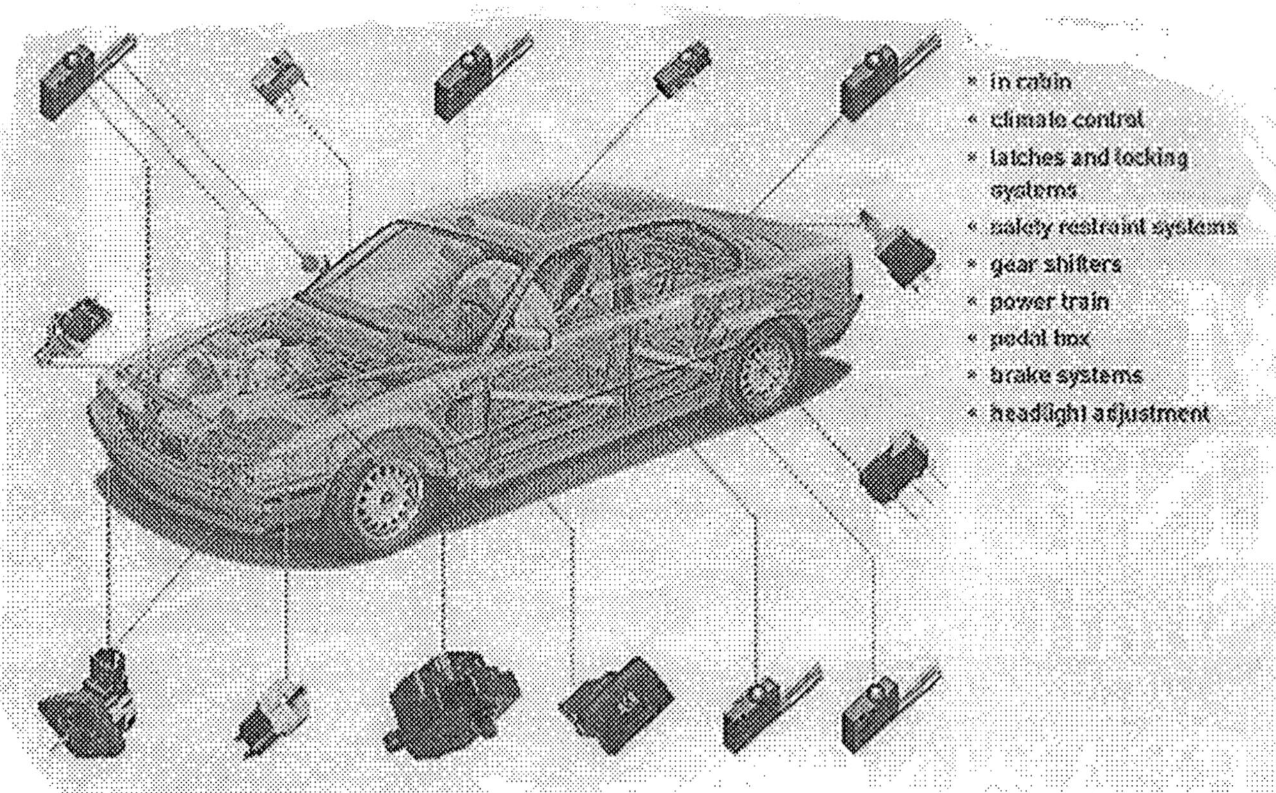

Figure 110-AUTOMOBILE CONTROLS

*Used in Earth Home

f. Aerospace Examples

Advanced sensors are currently being developed for unmanned aerial vehicles and robotic satellites. These new sensors will be specialty sensors that will enhance the activities of an automation operation. These new automated systems will replace the current system of operating the equipment from the ground. Tasks that are being automated are the parachute delivery systems from an automated guidance system.

g. Earth Home Automation

1. Importance of EH Automation

The Earth Home must function to serve the needs of its occupants. The Earth Home system would benefit greatly from some degree of automation due to the numbers of devices and functions that need regulation. The simple manual tasks such as irrigating plants, watering animals, adjusting the heat, and controlling the humidity/light levels would eat up much time and detract from a person's lifestyle. An automated system would greatly assist the family in performing repeatable tasks so they could concentrate on harvesting, cooking, or other tasks.

The Earth Home should be able to "sense" the outside conditions and react to it. Sensors for sound, vibration, liquid levels, temperature, flow, noise, etc. would be very beneficial. The EH should maintain light levels and temperature in the many areas of the structure. A seasonal "weather prediction" system may also be incorporated, so the home would react faster to unusual weather that may develop. The more that many of the routine functions of a controlled atmosphere are given to an automated system, the more time would be available by the family.

2. EH Automation Basics

The Earth Home is headed towards automobile sensor technology assisted with simple sensors. The auto industry has developed very advanced electronics technology (currently 12% of the value of an auto is in its electronics). (See Automotive Control section) Sensors can be made very simple if great accuracy is not needed. Separate wire runs may be necessary because of the electrical "noise" from motors, generators, fluorescent lights, capacitance, etc.

Above all, any automated control system control panel must be simple and easy to use. An inexpensive basic microprocessor chip could be used as the basis of the system. Current sensors for direct current would be at the heart of the energy conservation system. Currently only the CUI Stack, Inc. company manufactures a DC current sensor in the right sizes. (See Electricity-Sensors) Bluetooth wireless technology may also have application. (See Communication Section) It is also possible to pulse the 12 volt supply voltage intermittently to enable a sensor to sense how much current is passing in the wire. In this way, simpler and less expensive sensors could be employed.

3. Efficiency Improvements

Key to any system is not to use too much electricity for automation purposes. Recently, at least one solenoid valve company has introduced valves that draw only 2 watts of power as opposed to 17 watts in older versions. (See Valves-Solenoid Valves)

Recent improvements in piezoelectric devices have attracted much attention. Companies are now offering piezo-operated valves and piezo-actuated door locks. These devices draw much less power that their comparable solenoid devices. There is also work going on dealing with shock sensors, optical switches, and rotary torque transducers.

h. Home Automation Future

1. Inexpensive Laptop Technology

In early 2006, a project is expected to culminate in a laptop computer that costs less than $100 each. This significant effort is being accomplished first by dramatically lowering the cost of the display. This first-generation laptop machine will have a novel, dual-mode display that represents improvements to the LCD displays commonly found in inexpensive DVD players. These displays can be used in high-resolution black and white in bright sunlight—all at a cost of approximately $35. Second, they plan on getting the "fat" out of the systems. Current laptops have become obese—because about two-thirds of their software is used to manage the other third, which mostly does the same functions nine different ways. Projects like this one help to drive down the cost of future home automation systems.

2. Power Logic Technology/Hybrid Power Management (HPM)

Hybrid power management is defined as the integration of diverse power devices in an optimal configuration for virtually any application requiring power. Combining power control of all devices together makes for significant overall performance and efficiency. There are also many new power logic schemes that try to maximize battery life for many applications. Among them are LVC, ULP, and the newer AUP. AUP is short for Advanced Ultra-Low-Power logic. AUP has been promoted as the leader in power savings. There is much research in this field and promises significant battery power savings.

4. Earth Home Wiring

a. Wiring Chart for 12 Volt Systems

The wiring size of the Earth Home II has to be larger than is commonly used in a residential home, because low voltage requires larger wire in order to eliminate line losses (See the following figure). This is probably the most significant argument against 12-volt DC usage. However, I believe it is more than offset by the safety issue.

b. Electrical Outlets/Plugs

Standard 12-volt DC plugs (commonly used in cigarette lighters) are not used in Earth Home II because of the problems in quality. ***A better way of connecting electrical cords is to use a horizontal pin plug originally designed for 240 volts AC***. This plug uses two flat contacts in line and a ground pin below to make better contact and carry much higher current. (See Electricity-Wiring files.) (Also, see "12 Volt Advantage".) Recently, a good quality electrical outlet became available by the Marinco Company. This replaces the cheaper and lower quality cigarette-style plugs commonly used in automobiles. They will be used similar to the duplex outlets found in 110 volt homes.

F. Uses of Electricity—Lighting

1. History of Artificial Lighting Methods

Before electricity became available, the options for producing artificial light had hardly changed for thousands of years--essentially something had to be burned to provide light. Candles of tallow were used for a long time. At the end of the seventeenth century, lamps gave little more than one candlepower per wick, except at the expense of a smoky wick. There were wood burning utensils, float lamps, grease lamps, pan lamps, spout lamps, betty lamps, and lard oil lamps. They burned olive oil, vegetable oil, fish oil, whale oil, and lard oil. These simple lamps varied little all over the world from the early Greeks and Romans. Later alcohol, turpentine, candle wax, and finally kerosene was used.

Amps	Watts @ 12 V	#14	#12	#10	#8	#6	#4	#2	1/0	2/0	3/0
1	12	45.0	70.0	115	180	290	456	720	-	-	-
2	24	22.5	35.0	57.5	90.0	145	228	360	580	720	912
4	48	10.0	17.5	27.5	45.0	72.5	114	180	290	360	456
6	72	07.5	12.0	17.5	30.0	47.5	75.0	120	193	243	305
8	96	05.5	08.5	11.5	22.5	35.5	57.0	90.0	145	180	228
10	120	04.5	07.0	11.5	18.0	28.5	45.5	72.5	115	145	183
15	180	03.0	04.5	07.0	12.0	19.0	30.0	48.0	76.5	96.0	122
20	240	02.0	03.5	05.5	09.0	14.5	22.5	36.0	57.5	72.5	91
25	300	01.8	02.8	04.5	07.0	11.5	18.0	29.0	46.0	58.0	73
30	360	01.5	02.4	03.5	06.0	09.5	15.0	24.0	38.5	48.5	61
40	480	-	-	02.8	04.5	07.0	11.5	18.0	29.0	36.0	45
50	600	-	-	02.3	03.6	05.5	09.0	14.5	23.0	29.0	36
100		-	-	-	-	02.9	04.6	07.2	11.5	14.5	18
150		-	-	-	-	-	-	04.8	07.7	09.7	12
200		-	-	-	-	-	-	03.6	05.8	07.3	09

Figure 111-WIRE SIZING CHART

Maximum one-way distance for less than 2% voltage drop (for 12 volt circuits)

From about 1800-1850 there were over 500 patents for improvements in lighting techniques. There were camphene lamps, Argand lamps, and rushlights. In the 1800's, the kerosene lamp became popular in Europe. The light output was about 4 foot candles. (one foot-candle is the amount of light falling on a white paper 12 inches by 12 inches at a distance of 1 foot from a candle flame.) They took efficiency to the limit with their Kosmos burners and Matador flame-spreader burners. This technology basically spread the flame out and drafted it evenly as well. (Kerosene lanterns are still more efficient than propane lanterns.)

The Welsbach mantle, when used in a kerosene lamp, gave such a bright light that it allowed kerosene lamps to compete with electric light for another thirty years or so. Aladdin oil lamps achieved the equivalent illumination of a 60-watt incandescent bulb or 29 foot candles with 3,000 Btu/hr. The Aladdin lamps became cheaper to operate and became very popular. They tested at .0203 gallons of oil per hour when putting out 60 candlepower light. This was a 50 hour burn on one gallon of fuel!

Much later, burning acetylene (Mees burner), propane, or another gas inside of a silk wick (similar to Coleman lanterns) produced gaseous illumination at about 35 foot candles per wick depending on pressure. However, the

*Used in Earth Home

cost per foot-candle and the volume of gas used per foot-candle illumination was still high. Such a lantern also takes time and effort to light. In the summertime months, it would not be advantageous to use gas lighting indoors because of heat buildup. Propane lamps, such as the Humphrey Opalites, also use silk filaments that are quite fragile and often break. No "hard mantle" technology exists today. It is easy to see why electricity became very popular for lighting. The following figure shows how lighting developed up until the electric light.

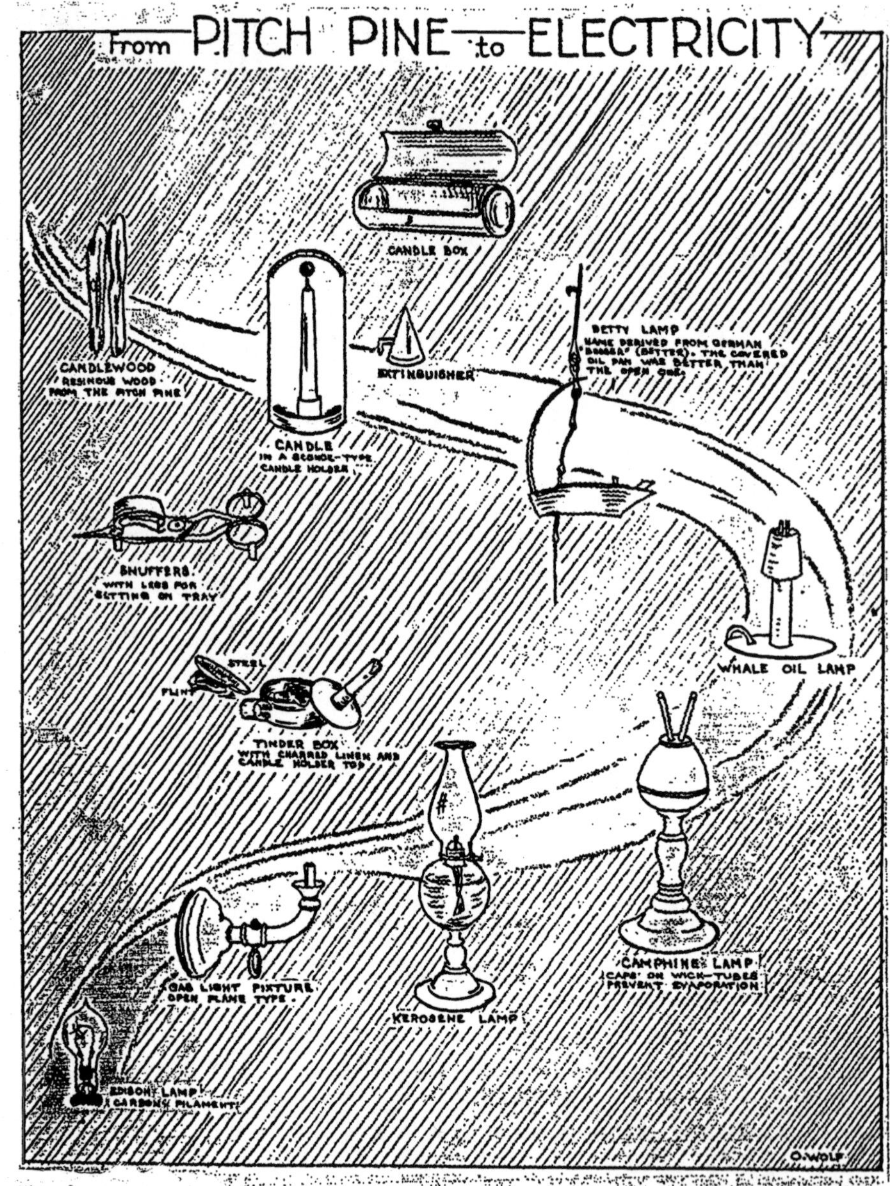

Primitive home lighting, of course, started with the **pine knots and splinters** from the resinous pine tree. The early Colonists called these splinters 'candlewood' and used them for illumination. The candlewood was placed in the corner of the fireplace on a flat stone and set afire.

Figure 112-EARLY LIGHTING TO ELECTRICITY

*Used in Earth Home

2. Electrical Lighting Background

Electricity is the cleanest and most versatile of all power generated. Statistics show that about 7% of an average home utility bill is for lighting. ***But lighting is the most important energy usage of all, because it gives us the convenience of instant light.*** In most countries of the world, electricity is several times more expensive than fossil fuels!

3. Typical Lighting Requirements

The following figures give lighting requirements for a typical home. These figures are similar to the IES Lighting Handbook figures.

4. High Efficiency Lighting Options

Electrical bulbs that are used to provide light in alternative energy systems are usually one of four different kinds: halogen, fluorescent, krypton, or incandescent. (See the following figure).

a. Incandescent Lighting Uses

Incandescent light bulbs are the most inefficient, but are also the most cost-effective. Incandescent lights should only be used in areas where they will be turned on and off frequently, and in areas of infrequent light usage, such as closets.

b. Fluorescent Lights

The kitchen is typically a high-use area, so fluorescent lighting should be considered there. Fluorescent lights can last 10 times longer than incandescent, and there are many new lighting products available which are very efficient. Fluorescent lighting should also be considered for the living and dining areas. The newer compact fluorescent lighting (CFL) is smaller and much more energy efficient.

c. Halogen lights

Halogen lights are used effectively in places like the bathroom and the bedroom, in which activities are carried on repeatedly for a short period of time. These would classify as a medium-use application. Halogens give 45% more light per watt than incandescent bulbs.

d. LED (Light-Emitting Diode) Lights

An LED generates light through an electronic process. Most LED's produce only one color of light. Recently, LED (light emitting diode) lights have came onto the market that screws into a normal light fixture. These new products put out much higher light levels than older LED products. They provide more light using less energy than many other options.

A new technology is called Photon Recycling Semiconductor Light-Emitting Diode (PRS-LED) and it is capable of two colors including white. This technology efficiently generates up to 300 lumens per watt.

The prevalence of LED's have dramatically increased with the creation of HB LEDs (high brightness light-emitting diodes). Also, white LEDs have been developed. These new versions offer longer lifetimes, improved reliability, compact packaging, and flexible optical designs.

*Used in Earth Home

Activity	Space Needed		Intensity Lumens/		Hours/ Day Needed	Energy Used	
	Meter^2	FT^2	Meter^2	FT^2		KJ	Watt-Hrs
Dining Area	4		150	14	.75	2.4	666
Kitchen							
Counter	2	21.5	300	27.9	3	9.5	2637
General	.5	5.4	750	69.7	1	2.0	555
Detailed	.75	8.1	300	27.9	.25	.3	83
Cooking--	.75	8.1	750	69.7	.25	.7	194
General	.5	5.4	300	27.9	.125	.1	27.8
Cooking--	.5	5.4	750	69.7	.25	.5	139
Intensive							
Sink--General							
Sink--Intensive							
Living Area							
General	5	53.8	75	7.0	4	7.9	2194
Reading	.2	2.2	300	27.9	2	.6	167
Sewing	.5	5.4	750	69.7	.25	.5	139
Recreation							
Music Study or	1	10.8	750	69.7	.75	3.0	833
Computer							
Work	2	21.5	750	69.7	.5	4.0	1110
Easel Hobbies							
(CONT. NEXT PAGE)							

Figure 113-COMPARATIVE LIGHTING NEEDS, PAGE 1

*Used in Earth Home

Activity	Space Needed		Intensity Lumens/		Hours/ Day Needed	Energy Used	
	Meter^2	FT^2	Meter^2	FT^2		KJ	Watt-Hrs
(CONT. FROM PREVIOUS PAGE)							
Laundry General Ironing	 1 3	 10.8 32.3	 300 300	 27.9 27.9	 .125 .5	 .2 2.4	 55.5 666
Bathroom Grooming	 3	 32.3	 300	 27.9	 2	 9.5	 264
Workbench General Detailed	 4 2	 43 21.5	 300 750	 27.9 69.7	 .25 .25	 1.6 1.0	 444 278
Sleep					8	0	
Empty House					7.5	0	
Total Daily Consumption						48	3324

Figure 114-COMPARATIVE LIGHTING NEEDS, PAGE 2

*Used in Earth Home

BULB TYPE	EFFICIENCY (LUMENS/WATT)	AVG. LIFE (HRS)	DIMMABLE?	RELATIVE PRICE
Standard Incandescent	12-20 over 40-150 watts	750 - 1,000	Yes	1x
Long-life Standard Incandescent	11-16 over 40-150 watts	1,500 - 3,500	Yes	1.5x - 2x
Krypton-filled Incandescent	2% to 5% increase over standard incandescent	750 - 1,000	Yes	1x
Krypton-filled Long-life	slightly lower than standard incandescent	1,500 - 3,500	Yes	1.5x
Infrared-reflective Coated Incandescent	29	2,500	Yes	10x
Tungsten-halogen Incandescent	16 to 19	2,200 - 3,500	Some	3x - 5x
Compact Fluorescent	35 to 60	10,000	No	10x - 30x
Circular Fluorescent Screw-in Type	30 to 60	12,000	No	10x - 15x

Figure 115-ENERGY-EFFICIENT LIGHT BULB CHART

*Used in Earth Home

e. Point-of-Use Lighting

A small point-of-use light, such as an Osram reading light, can be used where only a small area of illumination is needed, such as reading in bed or doing dishes. (A book can be read comfortably with illumination of only 50 foot candles.)

f. Reflectors and Dimming

Sometimes specular reflectors, improved dimming, and improved phosphors are also used. There are still many ways of providing adequate light that are yet unused and undiscovered for specific applications.

5. Occupancy Sensors

Occupancy sensors are electronic devices that turn on the lights when people enter a room and turn them off a set time after everyone leaves. They can be either ultrasonic or passive infrared. An ultrasonic sensor bounces a high frequency sound wave off of objects. It detects any change in the existing pattern of returning waves. Passive infrared detectors uses heat given off by the human body to trigger the switch. There is at least one 12-volt DC occupancy sensor on the market. (See Lighting files.) The use of occupancy sensors will lower the demand on the battery bank.

6. Earth Home Lighting

As earlier stated, one of the problems with direct battery-operated alternative energy lighting systems is that the lighting reflects the battery conditions. The lights will be slightly dimmer when the batteries are at a lower voltage, and will flicker somewhat when another load such as a light is turned on. I believe electronic surge devices can be developed to avoid this condition using "automotive-type" technology. Another method that also has possibilities is to physically locate individual batteries near the light bulb and charge from a central distribution area. These and other technologies have received little testing and evaluation simply because the demand is not great enough at present.

The Earth Home is designed to use as much natural lighting as possible to conserve electricity. One drawback to this, however, is the added heating and cooling costs associated with the lower R-value of windows.

7. Future Lighting Options

a. Fiberoptics

A fiberoptic system has been developed to actually channel the sunlight from outside through a cable and then re-focus it onto living space. (See Fiberoptic files.) However, as previously mentioned, this system has significant losses inside the cable, especially at certain wavelengths. (See also Fish/Worms/Insects section.)

b. High Intensity Discharge Lights

All lighting technologies excite atoms so that they produce photons. In the case of halogen bulbs and gas lanterns, heat is doing the exciting. In other technologies it is various forms of electricity or light that create the excitement.

Most cars currently use halogen bulbs in their headlights. The new "blue-ish" headlights are using a different technology called High Intensity Discharge (HID). Most HID lamps are in the form of mercury vapor and sodium vapor lights used as street lamps and as outdoor lighting for stadiums.

*Used in Earth Home

Mercury and sodium vapor lamps produce light using a technique similar to that used in fluorescent lamps. In fluorescent lamps a low-pressure mercury vapor produces lots of ultraviolet light that excites a phosphor coating the tube. In the case of mercury vapor lamps, it is a high-pressure gas. The distance between the electrodes is very short and the light is produced directly without the need for the phosphor.

In the case of the new HID headlights, the same high-pressure technology is used. The lamp is similar to a mercury vapor lamp. However, designers of the headlights had to solve one problem with normal mercury vapor lamps -- the fact that they have long start-up times. Xenon helps solve the start-up problem, as does a special controller. These headlights are expensive now, but mass production should bring the cost down eventually. This technology could be used to produce smaller 12 volt lights if the market was there for incentive.

c. Electroluminescence

There are recent studies on organic electroluminescence that may have low energy applications. They are using organic materials for low voltage active flat panel displays. There is always the chance that spin-off products will be discovered that will have commercial value.

G. Uses of Electricity—Motors

1. Motors Background

a. Motor Facts/History

Another major use of electricity if for electrical motors. In the United States, approximately 64% of all energy consumed is used simply to turn electrical motors. A full 33% of U.S. electrical energy consumption was for residential uses. There are 46 motors in an average American home, mostly in appliances.

As mentioned previously, all motors have a high starting torque, which means that a surge of electricity is necessary to overcome inertia and get the motor started. This can be as high as 2-3 times the running current. Some manufacturers are attempting to make electric motors more energy-efficient by developing "soft start" mechanisms. One such product is now available to lessen the starting torque of washing machine motors. (See Appliances file.)

b. Motor Efficiency

In the U.S. only abut 3% of the cost of an electrical motor over the product lifetime is the actual purchase cost. The vast majority of the expense of operating a motor is for the energy to run it. There has been a great increase in the number of motors that are more efficient. "Premium" efficient motors also run cooler, extending lifetimes and improving performance. This also helps the insulation life and extends the life of the bearings, which are responsible for more than half the failures for motors.

c. ECM Motors (See also Fan Efficiency section)

Also, electronically commutated AC motors (ECM's) are motors that more accurately adjust the energy input to the motor. This method allows the motor to draw only the current it needs to perform the task. ECM's in blower/fan HVAC applications can automatically adjust to varying static pressures. If a filter is plugging or duct constricted, it can adjust to these conditions. The ECM provides the most efficient, self-adjusting, and quiet operation of any motor currently available. Virtually every major manufacturer of HVAC equipment has, or is working on, an ECM product. I believe that similar technology can be developed for DC operation. (See also Fan Technology section.)

d. DC Motors

Most 12-volt DC motors have evolved from the automotive and/or recreational vehicle industry. ***These automotive motors were generally not designed to be energy-efficient.*** They were intended to be used for a short number of hours at a time and to be low in cost. Motor efficiency technology was generally not developed for 12-volt DC applications. (See Motors-DC file.) ***However, direct current motors are, by their basic design, more efficient than alternating current motors***. Also, DC motor speed can be regulated much more easily, simply by varying the amount of voltage to the motor. I feel that direct current motor development will expand greatly in the future.

e. Trolling Motor Technology

Trolling motors for propelling a fishing boat through the water is perhaps the most efficient use of 12-volt DC motors that exist currently. The trolling motor industry has been for the last 30 years developing more and more efficient motors that desire to make the battery last longer and longer. The efficient trolling motor and modifications of the motor will be used in EH research for mechanical movement needs.

2. Water Pumping (See also Water System-Pumping Waste section)

a. Water Pumping Options

Typically, water pumping is achieved by using electricity to drive a motor which in turn drives a pump impeller. There are many different types of water pumps, including diaphram pumps, centrifugal pumps, positive displacement pumps, piston pumps, circulating pumps, and metering pumps. (See Pumps - Water file.) Many of these pumps were developed for a specific flow rate, pressure, and end use.

Most of the pumps currently available are generally not designed specifically for energy efficiency. They were designed to be cheaply mass-produced and reasonably long lasting. Efficiency of water pumps did not become an advertising feature until the mid-1980's when pumping technology began to improve. This was probably due to more alternative and battery-operated homes that became more popular at that time.

Water pumps are used in the Earth Home for domestic pressurized water, HVAC circulation, and plant irrigation. Water pumping is a considerable use of electricity in the Earth Home, even though the entire design of the plumbing system relies as much as possible upon gravity flow.

b. Pump for Domestic Water Use

In the Earth Home system I used a Flojet pump wherever pressure was needed. It is a reliable twin diaphram pump that pumps 3 gallons a minute to about 35 psi, and uses 3 to 7 amps (amperes), depending on the pressure it's pumping against. A spare water pump is to be plumbed into the system for easy changeover in case the pump fails. The pump is somewhat noisy and will be mounted on dampening feet inside a soundproof enclosure.

c. Circulating Pump for HVAC

Circulating pumps use much less electricity than other kinds of pumps because they are designed for minimal pressure. This low energy-use pump is specifically designed to circulate water. It is classified as a "low head pump," meaning it pumps water to a limited height, but in great volumes.

d. Earth Home Circulating Pump

The efficient "Hartell" circulating pump is used for the first prototype Earth Home main heating, ventilating, and air conditioning (HVAC) system. Since water for this system requires only about 2 feet of head (or pressure), a modified "Venturi" system may help use the excess power to "pull" extra water with the main

*Used in Earth Home

stream. An air blow-off device manufacturer uses a similar principle to minimize the quantity of high-pressure air consumed in simply blow-cooling a part.

Recently the Laing Thermotech and the Wilo Stratos companies have also introduced low-head efficient circulating pumps that draw less than 10 watts of electricity. (See Pumps-Circulating) These pumps were developed in response to solar hydronic panel needs. These new efficient pumps will be used on the Earth Home II prototype.

e. Future Pumps—Circulating and Other

In the future, the EH will use a mixed-flow impeller pump as it becomes available. The Engineered Machined Products Company has combined characteristics of both centrifugal- and axial-flow pumps into the new design. This pump uses a venturi system of water flow originally designed to squeeze 3-7% more efficiency from an automobile engine.

Interestingly, medicine also provides an insight into very efficient pumping technologies. Efficient pumps are being developed by VAD (ventricular assist devices) development firms. They need to move blood inside the body using the least amount of electricity as possible. The DeBakey VAD from MicroMed Technology has only one moving part—the inducer impeller. These pumps are very expensive at present, but this technology may migrate into other technologies and products in the future.

3. Fan Technology

a. Background/History of Fans

The first mechanical air movers were steam-driven fans for venting coal mines, but it would take until the second half of the 20th century for forced air equipment to be extensively used in housing. Victorians used many ingenious methods of heating and venting buildings with natural convection. These non-powered gravity systems prevailed until the 1950s, except for summer cooling fans.

b. Fan/Blower/Compressor

Basically there are three ways to move air: a fan, a blower, and a compressor. Typically a fan only blows against a few inches of static pressure as in a duct. A blower "pushes" against approximately 10 inches of static pressure (inflatables), and a compressor compresses the air with a piston or a screw up to much higher pressures (factory compressed air). (See Air Compressors/Air Blowers/Air Fans file.) Compressors are rated in the unit PSI (pounds per square inch). Typically, blowers and compressors use more energy than fans. Because of this, more emphasis is given to specialized fans for moving air.

In looking at fans, I check rated capacity of a certain fan at zero static pressure. Static pressure is the measure of how strong a fan is at pushing against resistance in ductwork, for example. Most fans are rated at zero static pressure, or free air. When evaluating expected performance, I use the free air figure (cubic feet per minute) and multiplied it by .8 to get an approximation of air flow at .1 inch static pressure. This was done to get a more realistic view of what volume of air the fan will push. (See also Air Movement Section)

c. Fan Classifications/Types/Categories

There have been many attempts at moving air more efficiently. A closer look at the main categories of fans reveal three major types of fans: centrifugal, mixed flow, and axial. Within these categories there are many different fan variations that can be used to move air. ***Perhaps the most efficient fan for blowing air is called a backwardly-inclined fan***. (See following figure) Air moving technology is highly developed, and interested readers should reference Fan files.

*Used in Earth Home

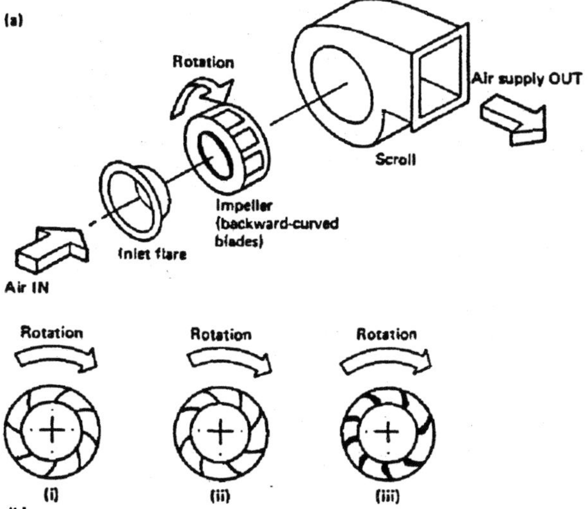

Centrifugal fans. (a) Elements of a centrifugal fan (motor drive not shown). (b) Types of centrifugal impeller: (i) Forward-curved blades, low cost, 60–70% efficient; (ii) backward-curved blades, more efficient 80–85%, higher pressure; (iii) aerodynamic backward-curved blades, most efficient 90%, quieter

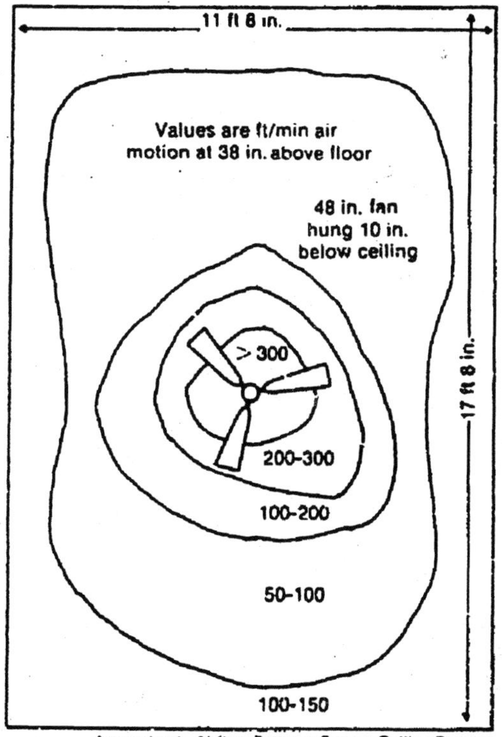

Approximate Airflow Patterns From a Ceiling Fan in a Room With No Furniture. Fan Speed Set at Maximum. Ceiling Height = 8 ft.

Figure 116-FAN TYPES

*Used in Earth Home

d. Home Air Movement Applications

There are <u>many</u> different air-moving applications inside a typical home. Some of these include; furnace blowers, bathroom exhaust fans, range hood exhausters, radon detection blowers, heat recovery ventilators (air-to-air heat exchangers), ceiling fans, cooling fans, window air conditioner fans, sun space exhausters, induced draft blowers (on combustion equipment), heat pump or air conditioning unit fans, clothes dryer fans, dehumidifier fans, air purifier fans, convection oven fans, high-speed vacuum cleaner blowers, attic fans, and simple hair dryers. ***So you can see that fans come in all sizes and shapes, and simply moving air is a considerable use of energy inside a home. Most of the fan efficiencies are very low, ranging from 1% to 10%,*** whereas the larger engineered air handlers range from 60% to 80% efficient. One of the most important fans in the home is the furnace fan.

e. Furnace Fans

Typically furnace fans exhibit an efficiency somewhere between poor at 7%, typical at 16%, and the best furnace fans are only 51% efficient. Studies have indicated a theoretically possible furnace fan efficiency of 69%. If furnace fans were 20% efficient with a poor furnace cabinet air flow design, the efficiency in terms of air moving load <u>external</u> to the furnace reduces the efficiency to about 7%. Individual exhausters are typically less than 2% efficient. The spread between the poor and the best equipment is in the order of 10 to 1.

Central forced air systems were originally designed for fan operation <u>only when heating</u> was required. When central cooling was added, operation times were extended. With increased attention on indoor air quality, continuous ventilation and filtration by recirculation have become more popular. Continuous recirculation has been further advanced with the growth in high efficiency filter installation, fresh air distribution, and preferences for steady, low background noise over intermittent fan operation. Equipment manufacturers are only now introducing products whose blowers can be "speed-controlled" efficiently.

f. Fan Efficiency

The potential for energy efficiency improvements of small air handlers is huge. Studies have also shown that improvements in impeller and housing combinations can also be dramatic. Up to <u>five-fold</u> improvements can be made by using currently available and just-emerging equipment. Variable or adjustable speed drives (ASD's) and DC electronically commutated motors (ECMs) as previously mentioned can also boost efficiency in part-load and variable flow conditions. (See Motors section.)

Some of these ECMs are available with electronic erasable, programmable, read-only memory (EEPROM) chips that allow a customized application to be used for motor control. This managed output produces dramatic reductions in input power when output needs are reduced. The result is almost constant efficiencies throughout the system.

Some of these increased efficiencies are due to the space program and NASA subcontractors. They have taken a fan motor and increased the RPM dramatically to get an increase in efficiency. Higher fundamental speeds mean higher efficiency. For example, an 1,800-RPM fan motor uses about 7% less electricity than a 1,200-RPM motor.

The annual electrical consumption (power required) of any air mover is a product of its flow rate times the total head (pressure) divided by aerodynamic efficiency for each speed setting over time. Many of the small electric air-moving devices have short run times, using very small relative amounts of energy. Infrequently operated devices, even with a high load similar to ***a vacuum cleaner, need not be anywhere as efficient as a more frequently run air mover of low load, such as a continuous exhaust fan or the furnace fan***.

***Used in Earth Home**

g. EH Large Diameter Circulating Fan

Recently there have been improvements in DC fans. One product, the he freestanding Endless Breeze fan features a three-speed permanent magnet motor that drives a 12-inch, 10-blade fan. The motor has a maximum electrical draw of less than three amps and is among the most efficient on the market.

The fan I will use in Earth Home II is a modification of a large diameter "circulating fan" or ceiling fan. The modifications include making the blade configuration backwardly-inclined and using a very efficient motor to drive fan blades. This motor uses an electronic system to feed back electricity when it's not being used so the fan will turn at a constant RPM. This particular motor only draws 250 milliamps of 12-volt electricity and was originally used as an aircraft component. I feel this technology will be used to develop much higher efficiency 12-volt DC fans and motors in the future. (See also Motors section.) The coils from the HVAC system will be retracted for higher efficiency when not needed. (See also Passive Ventilation section)

4. Earth Home Selected Motors

a. Refrigerator/Freezer Compressor Motor

Another big user of electricity in the home is the refrigerator/freezer compressor. ***The Earth Home refrigerator/freezer is designed to use a "Danfoss" compressor.*** The Danfoss is an efficient 12 volt DC compressor that powers the "Sun Frost" line of refrigerators and freezers that are commonly sold for "off the grid" uses. The Sun Frost has the condenser logically placed above the cabinet. It uses about 25 amp hours per day of 12-volt electricity, making it the most efficient compressor currently manufactured. The Danfoss models have recently been modified to use 134-A refrigerant, which is safer for the Earth's ozone layer.

The Earth Home is designed to use ducting and insulation methods to minimize energy use as much as possible. The high-efficiency freezer compressor should run much less than average because of added insulation surrounding the food chamber. The controller is designed to automatically cycle this compressor more when voltage is high (high winds or backup generator is running).

b. EH Central Vacuum Motor

The high-amperage vacuum motor should also be operated during these periods of high energy generation. The designed-in central vacuum system has the advantages of less noise, no residual dust, and greater convenience. This system will use a centrally located suction motor, permanent cyclonic filter, and pipes in the walls connecting 3 to 5 outlets throughout the house. A single 30-foot hose plugs into any outlet for cleaning. A common problem that has been associated with these systems can be the actual method of installation. The pipes should be angled correctly and provided with clean-out traps to prevent clogging. (See Appliance Vacuum Cleaner Section)

c. EH Fish Tank Back-up Aeration Motor

Another significant use of electricity in the Earth Home system is to provide additional or backup oxygen to the fish tank. Proper levels of oxygen in the water ensure that the fish can live, grow, and multiply. There are at least two different ways of providing aeration to the tanks. One is to use an efficient motor to spin a disc that sucks up and scatters small droplets across the surface of the water. This provides maximum contact with the air, so that the particles can absorb more oxygen. This motor must also be the same high efficiency type mentioned previously.

Another method to aerate the water is to pump air to the bottom of the tank inside a pipe, allowing the bubbles to bring some water up to the top with them. This was discussed earlier in the fish section and will be accomplished with mechanical air compression. (See also Wind-Powered Air Compressors section.)

d. EH Hydraulic Pump Motor/Power Tools

A 12-VDC "hydraulic pump" is designed to raise and lower the wind generator tower. A hydraulic pump compresses hydraulic fluid (similar to motor oil) in the same way as an air compressor. This compressed fluid is used to drive a cylinder similar to an air cylinder or the gas springs on automobile rear hatchbacks or trunks. Much stronger "push" on a device is achieved using this near non-compressible fluid. Due to the extensive counterweight, only a small amount of hydraulic power is necessary. A manual crank system will be used as a backup.

Another use for electricity is power tools. A number of battery-operated power tools are available. One tool series from Makita uses a 12-volt DC charger, and is used in the Earth Home. Commonly used power tools such as drills, saws, and sanders can also be used with a 12-volt charger. (See Appliances/Tools file.) (See Appliances/Sources section.)

If an AC appliance or tool is used much more often due to habits of homeowners, it can be retrofitted to use a 12-VDC motor. There is a vast selection of DC motors to choose from. (See DC Motors file.)

5. Future Motor Technology

a. Motor Efficiency Overview

Leading all electric motor types in power density and efficiency are brushless permanent magnet (PM) motors. A perfect motor would convert all input power to output power and have an efficiency rating of 100 percent. No motor achieves 100 percent conversion of electric input to mechanical output. There are always internal losses that reduce overall motor efficiency. A motor designer's task is to significantly reduce these losses.

An ironless brushless DC (BDC) motor still uses conventional copper wire windings but eliminates the need for soft iron or steel armature laminations to hold the windings. The ironless brush DC motor is comprised of a stationary magnetic field and the rotating armature eliminating a large part of the losses due to cogging but introducing higher resistance and power losses.

b. Linear Motors

Recently refrigerator manufacturers have been working on a linear compressor. The linear motor is being developed by LG Electronics among others. These efficient motors do not use a crank to convert rotary motion into reciprocating motion. Claims of energy reduction in order of 40 percent have been reported. Motor efficiency is one area where huge gains are possible. (See also ECM Section)

c. Wireless Winding Motor Technology

Electric motor manufacturers have traditionally employed round insulated copper wire in armature windings for both iron core and ironless brush DC motors. Ironless DC motors made with round insulated copper wire overcome many of the weaknesses of conventional iron core motors but are limited by copper packing density and larger magnetic air gaps.

However, a new technology is delivering even higher performance and efficiency electric motors in a family of slotless brushless DC servomotors. These motors utilize a new coil technology that gets rid of wire windings, substantially reducing eddy current, hysteresis losses and cogging, which contribute to power efficiency losses. The modern coreless circular copper coil increases copper density in the magnetic gap. This coil eliminates problems inherent in iron core and wire wound motors—thus making a motor more powerful. ThinGap Motor Technologies uses precision-machined copper sheet metal instead of circular wire to achieve a higher copper packing density and higher ratio of copper to total volume. It is utilized in both ironless PM brush and brushless motors.

VIII. DIETS AND FOOD

Before looking at specific diets and foods, it is beneficial to get a broad view of nourishment in general. Natu has a way to insure that each species is fed with appropriate food for its environment. Human beings are simi in many ways to other mammals.

A. Food Chains/Pyramids of Animals and Humans

1. Food Chain/Pyramid Description

In nature, the way that animals seek out their food is a complex procedure. Many people have put food sou into a form called a "food chain" or a "food pyramid". Note: the term "food pyramid" is more often referre as a diet for humans made up of selected foods. (See Predominant Cultural Diets section) The following fig depict various kinds of food chains/food pyramids. The further down an organism is on the pyramid, the n numerous its members. For example, there are many more plants and rodents to be eaten by larger animals. we move up the food chain we finally get to humans at the top, which have no natural predators.

In the Earth Home system, it is necessary to produce food for human beings by using other plants animals from lower levels on a food pyramid. The goal is that a four-person family unit obtains enough foc sustain them every day, throughout the year.

*Used in Earth Home

2. Food Energy Pyramid

A food energy pyramid. Each level is one-tenth the equivalent of the level below it. Every organism carries on activities that use or release most of the energy it obtains. Only a fraction of the energy is passed along in a food chain

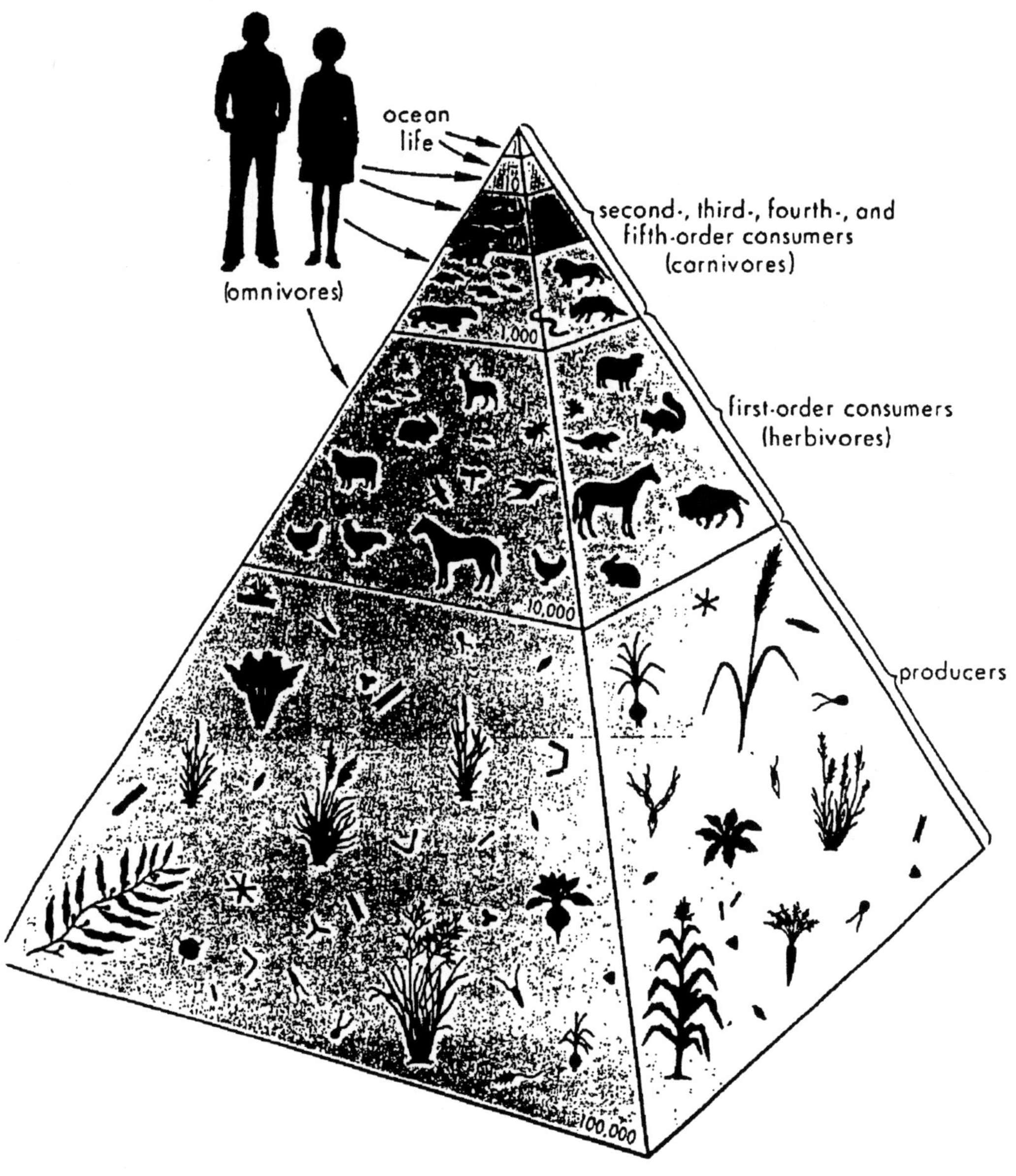

Figure 117-FOOD ENERGY PYRAMID

*Used in Earth Home

3. Food Cycles

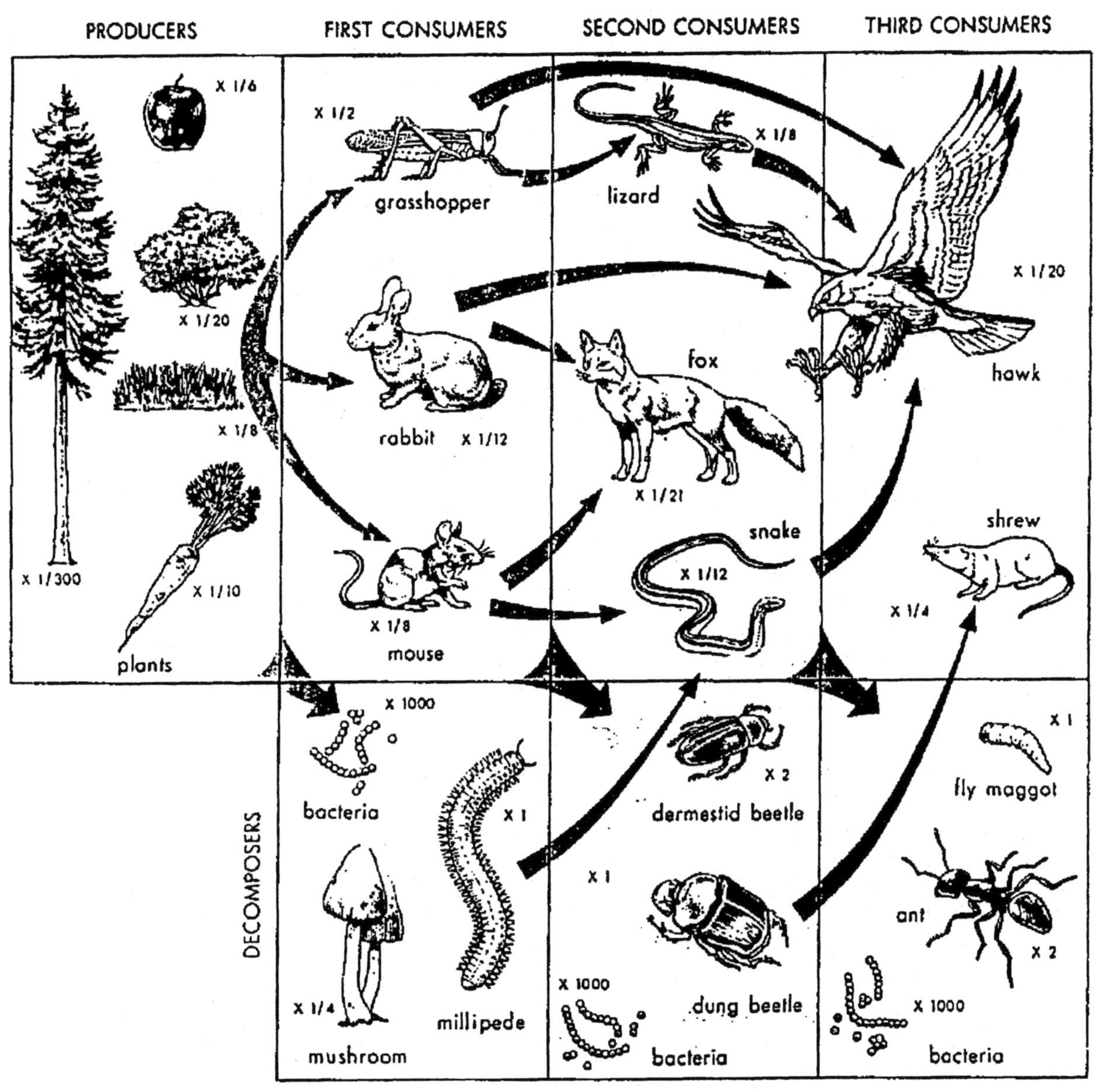

Figure 118-FOOD CYCLES

4. Simple Food Web

Figure 119-SIMPLE FOOD WEB

5. Zambie Food Web

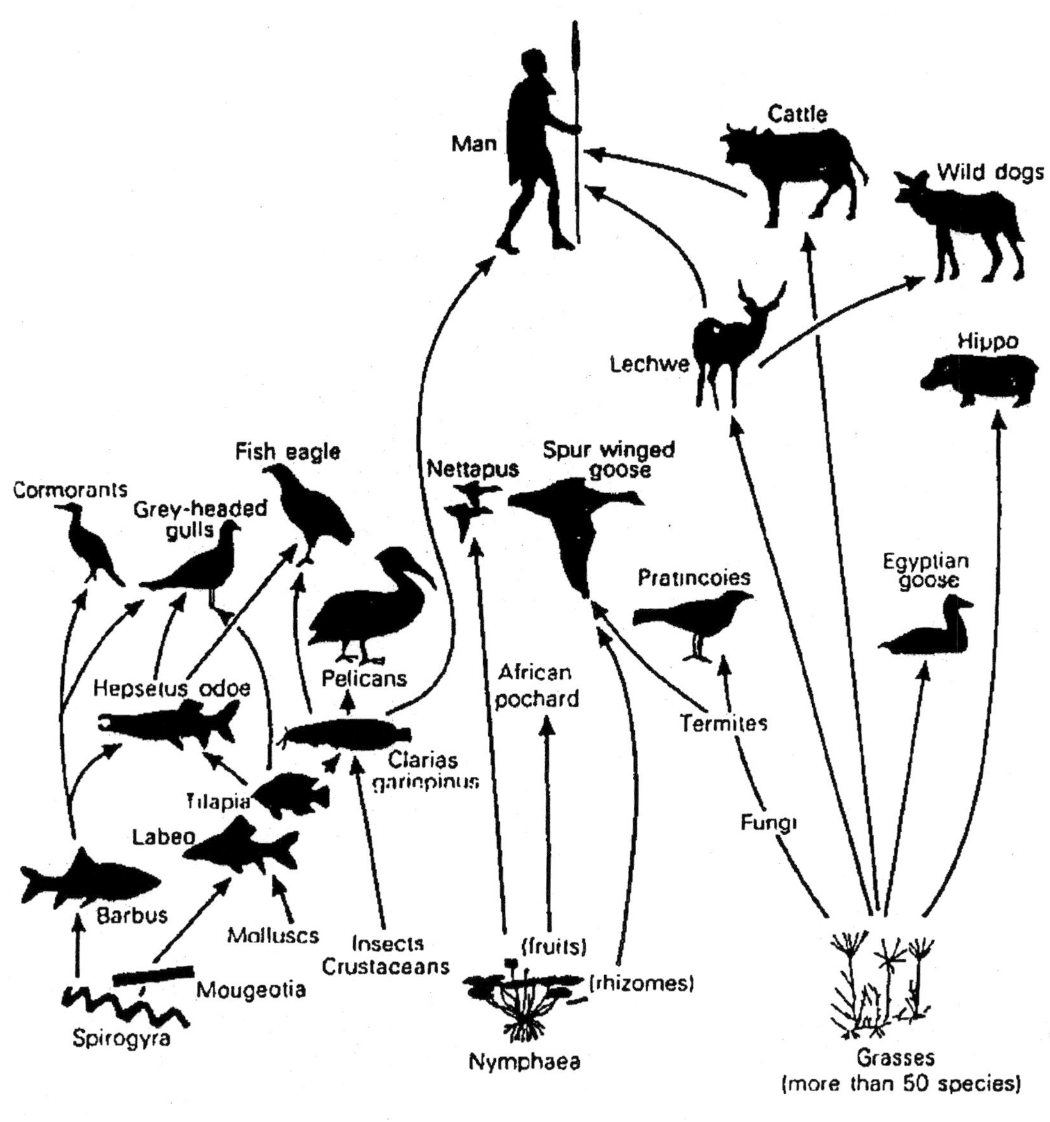

Generalised food web on the Kafue Flats of Zambie. Source: adapted from Handlos 1982 in Drijver & Marchand 1985.

Figure 120-ZAMBIE FOOD WEB

*Used in Earth Home

6. Detritis Food Chain

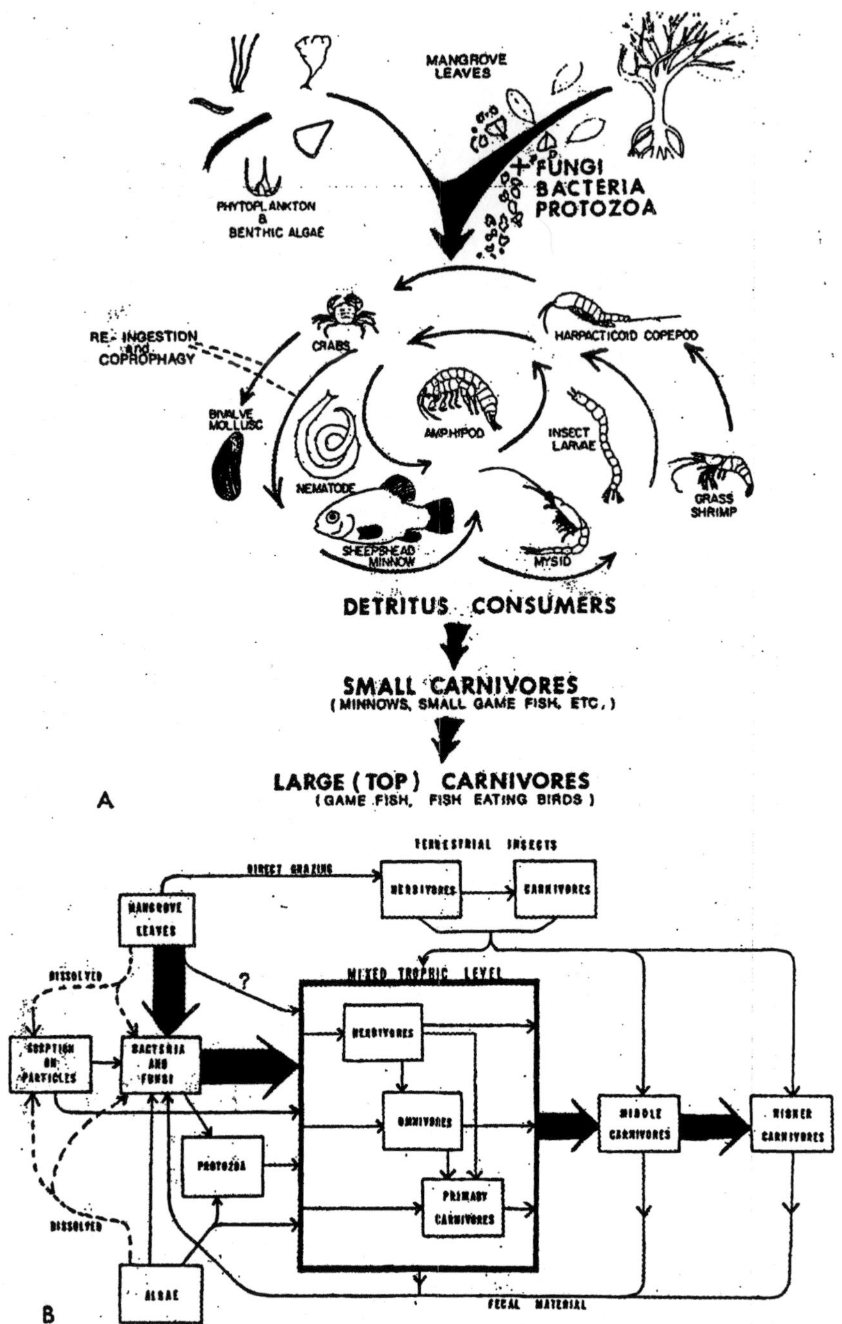

A detritus food chain based on mangrove leaves that fall into estuarine waters of south Florida. Leaf fragments acted on by saprotrophs and co by algae are eaten and reeaten (coprophagy) by a key group of small detritus c ers, which in turn provide the main food for game fish, herons, storks, and ibis. A ' model" of the food chain is shown in *A* and a "compartment model" in *B*. (R from W. E. Odum and Heald, 1975.)

Figure 121-DETRITUS FOOD CHAIN (IN SOUTH FLORIDA)

*Used in Earth Home

B. Anthropological Studies

1. Herbivorous or Carnivorous?

The studies of human food go back many thousands of years to prehistoric Neanderthal and Cro-Magnon peoples. Wherever human remains were found, there were almost always utensils, pottery, and animal bones. There exists an ongoing debate about whether our prehistoric ancestors were carnivorous or herbivorous in nature. Scientists study teeth and jaw structure for answers. They have also studied how intestinal enzymes break down food in an effort to determine if early humans were more efficient at digesting plants or animals.

Man's digestive tract is 12 times the length of his body for slow digestion of vegetables and fruits, which are known for slow decay. Carnivorous animals have very short bowels, 3 times the length of the body, for rapid expulsion of putrefactive bacteria from decomposing flesh.

It is generally agreed that the people of new and sparsely populated countries have been meat eaters, whereas the people of the older and more densely populated areas have been vegetarians. The latter group has been forced to eliminate most animals and to consume plants and grains directly in an effort to avoid famine.

2. Caveman/Paleolithic Diet

The earliest diet was the caveman diet or what is known today as the Paleolithic style diet. This hunter-gatherer diet consisted of wild game and gathered foods such as fruits, vegetables, nuts, and seeds as available on a seasonal basis. Most of the evidence suggests that early man was approximately 35% carnivorous and 65% herbivorous. The percent herbivorous increased as agriculture came into being. It is humorous that it has been postulated that farming was necessary to raise enough excess grain for alcohol fermentation.

Recent archeological findings suggest that these ancient ancestors of ours were a healthy bunch—tall, strong bones, and body structures like modern-day athletes. They appear to be most similar to ours in regard to stature, and as long as they survived accidents, infections, and childbirth, their longevity was similar to ours, but with much less chronic degenerative disease.

3. Aztec/Inca/Mayan

The Aztec and Inca cultures were highly developed thousands of years ago, but have since been almost completely obliterated. These cultures left us with drought-resistant and disease-tolerant plant species that survive in the southwest U.S. to this day. Much can be learned by looking at a small body of historical and archaeological evidence, but even more has completely vanished over the centuries.

The Mayan culture used products of the sea and corn as a principal grain. Again, little is known about the every day diet of these people. Some of the Spanish chroniclers reported that a few of the ancient Aztec emperors took full advantage of mineral salts available to them from certain lakes, ponds, and pools. They evaporated the water and used the mineral salts the way some people use vitamins.

4. Egyptian Mummies

Great amounts of research in the form of autopsies have been conducted on the many thousands of mummified remains of Egyptians unearthed over the years. The studies point to the fact that most of them seemed to have suffered from some of the same diet-related problems as Americans today. It appears that they had a diet similar to 20th century Americans.

There is evidence that a few of the pharaohs that lived somewhat longer had a diet of more fish and other forms of marine life and vegetation. They also showed very little disease patterns within their remains. This has been largely attributed to the generous supply of minerals they received from such water-derived food sources.

C. Historical Diets around the World

In order to design a food system to meet the Earth Home family's needs, it was beneficial to look around the world at the many varied diets that have been sustaining human life throughout history. Diets were initially based on availability of foods indigenous to locale—what could be grown or hunted, gathered, or caught.

1. Early Tribal Diets

Early tribes cooked food over an open fire. Whatever game was killed had the hair or feathers removed and then roasted over the open fire. Most of the animal, bird, or fish was eaten. Along with the meat often went some kind of starchy (storage) food such as cassava, sweet potatoes, or yams. Other foods were available on an opportunity or seasonal basis depending on the climate, season, and locale.

2. Early American Diets

American Indians had different diets depending on where they lived. The coastal Indians never faced the chronic starvation most less-settled tribes did. They relied primarily upon corn. A typical family of five ate 1344 pounds in one year or 65% of their caloric intake. Animal and birds constituted 10%, fish 9%, nuts and leguminous seeds 8%, eggs 1%, groundnuts and Jerusalem artichokes 2%, vegetables and fruits 4%, and acorns 1%. Beans, squash, pumpkins, and berries were the predominant cultivars because they stored so well.

When the Pilgrims landed on the New England coast in 1620, the diets of the local Indians contained no sugar, no salt, no milk, and no alcoholic beverages. Even honey was missing, since our honeybee is a European import. The "Three Sisters" (corn, squash, and beans) were staples of many of the indigenous peoples of the American continents before the advent of European colonization.

3. Primitive Diets around the World

In Africa, some tribes subsist entirely on porridge make of termites or midges. The Bedouin tribes of the Haohramaut in southern Arabia subsist solely on a diet of milk and meat. They care for animals and rely completely on them for survival. The Massai tribe of Africa, in the drier regions of the north, subsists on a diet of cow's blood and milk, which they mix together and drink. The Kaffir tribes of South Africa live almost exclusively on curdled milk called "amasi" or "leben". Another people called the Tuareg rely heavily on the camel for their subsistence. The Hunza natives of the mountainous region of Asia use sprouts for survival during the long, cold winters.

I believe that there is much more variation in the diets of human beings than most of us realize. Most of these diets have developed as a result of location, rainfall, temperature variations, and historical/cultural traditions. Later, disposable income played a part in diet selections.

4. Cultural Diet Pyramids of the World

Each culture has its own dietary patterns regarding what is eaten and how it is prepared. These patterns are very strong, as are tastes, food conditioning, and family influences. Both culture and environment affects eating patterns and diets/habits seem to run in families.

a. Cereal Grain Staple Diets

1. Porridge/Gruel History

One of the earliest methods of preparing cereals is the making of porridge and gruel. Ancient Egyptians commonly consumed slightly alcoholic gruel as a food. The Greeks coarse ground their barley and steeped it into a gruel called alphita. Hawaiian poi is another example of a gruel food. Mortar and pestles were used before grindstones to grind corn into a family dish and used throughout the Americas.

2. Starchy Food History/Importance

A culture's staple food around the world is usually a starchy food and bread of some sort is usually present. Cereal grain, as noted, is the most important single component of the world's food supply, accounting for between 30 and 70 percent of the food produced in all world regions. It is the major, and sometimes almost exclusive, source of food for many of the world's poorest people, supplying 60 to 75 percent of the total calories many of them consume.

It is generally agreed that a cereal diet can feed more people that a diet where the grain is used to make meat and then fed to the people. The word "bread" is mentioned more than 360 times in the Bible.

3. Eating Cereal Grain Development

One possible hypothesis on how the evolution of eating of cereal grains suggests the following sequence of events or steps:

1) Parched or popped cereals=cereal-heat
2) Gruel=cereal-heat-grinding-water
3) Unleavened bread=cereal-heat and/or grinding-water-heat
4) Leavened bread=cereal-heat-and/or grinding-water-yeast-heat
5) Beer=cereal-sprouting-drying-grinding-water-yeast

4. Bread Chemistry

Whole grains have constituted humanity's staple, primary food for thousands of years. Whole cereal grains contain a balance of protein, carbohydrates, fat, vitamins and other nutrients, and are especially high in niacin and other B-vitamins, as well as Vitamin A. The complex carbohydrates in whole grains are gradually and smoothly assimilated through the digestive organs, providing our bodies with a slow and steady source of energy.

b. Chinese/Japanese Diet

China contains more than one billion people-about a quarter of the Earth's population. What the Chinese people eat is the major diet of the world. That diet is primarily vegetarian, with usually only small amounts of animal foods consumed. They consistently eat polished white rice, cooked vegetables, mushrooms, tofu, and small amounts of meat, pork, or fish, with occasional poultry and eggs (a luxury).

Rice is a predominant part of many diets in the eastern and third world countries. Carbohydrates supply 80% of the calories in their diet. Large amounts of meat are rarely consumed at one meal. Fruits are eaten as they are available. Soybeans are used in a variety of ways-as tofu (soybean curd) or as soy sauce, a favorite flavoring. Milk products are consumed infrequently, mostly as yogurt, which spoils less easily. Pickled, smoked, and salted fish or meats are also common.

*Used in Earth Home

The Japanese diet is similar to the Chinese, except seafood is consumed in much higher quantities than in China. The close proximity to the ocean for the islanders accounts for the higher quantity of seafood. The Japanese are also fond of diversity in foods they eat. It is customary for a Japanese to consume 20 different foods in a single day and 100 different foods in one week's time.

c. Mediterranean Diet and Diet Pyramid

More studies are indicating that other diets around the world have advantages over the U.S. diet. For example, the Mediterranean diet has many advantages such as less heart disease. The following figure shows the "Mediterranean Food Pyramid". Notice the heavy reliance on pasta (carbohydrates). Carbohydrates are the cheapest, most efficient, and most readily available source of food energy in the world, since they are the main constituents of the foods that are the easiest to produce and obtainable throughout the world. Examples include grains, legumes, and potatoes.

d. Vegetarian Diet Pyramid

The next figure shows the vegetarian diet pyramid and physical activity as the base of good health. The fruits, vegetables, whole grains and legumes are the predominant portion of the pyramid. There are many notable vegetarians throughout history that include; Ben Franklin, Albert Schweitzer, Gandhi, Plato, Socrates, Leonardo da Vinci, and Leo Tolstoy.

e. Other Diet Pyramids

There are food pyramids for the Asian diet and the Latin diets. The Asian pyramid is closely related to the Chinese/Japanese diet. The Latin pyramid represents the actual traditional diet of a large portion of the human population. The other pyramids go further in that they recommend moderate exercise and alcohol consumption as elements of a healthy lifestyle.

D. Unusual Diets

1. Survival/Emergency Diets

a. Historical Accounts

1. Biblical Accounts

It is interesting to note that in 593 BC Ezekiel [4:9] wrote "take for yourself wheat, barley, beans, lentils, millet, and spelt and put them in one vessel and make bread of them for yourself. This Old Testament passage suggests sprouting and even 11 ounces per day quantities for a complete survival food. Essene bread is thin wafers made of wheat sprouts and was supposedly a major food source for the Jewish people leaving Egypt.

2. Rome/Greece/Egypt

Posca was the ordinary beverage of Roman soldiers, which they had to carry on all expeditions. It was made of vinegar and water, sweetened with sugar or honey. Homer is reputed to have prospered on a diet of honey, barley flour, wine, and cheese made from goat's milk. Honey and wheat were found in the Egyptian pyramids.

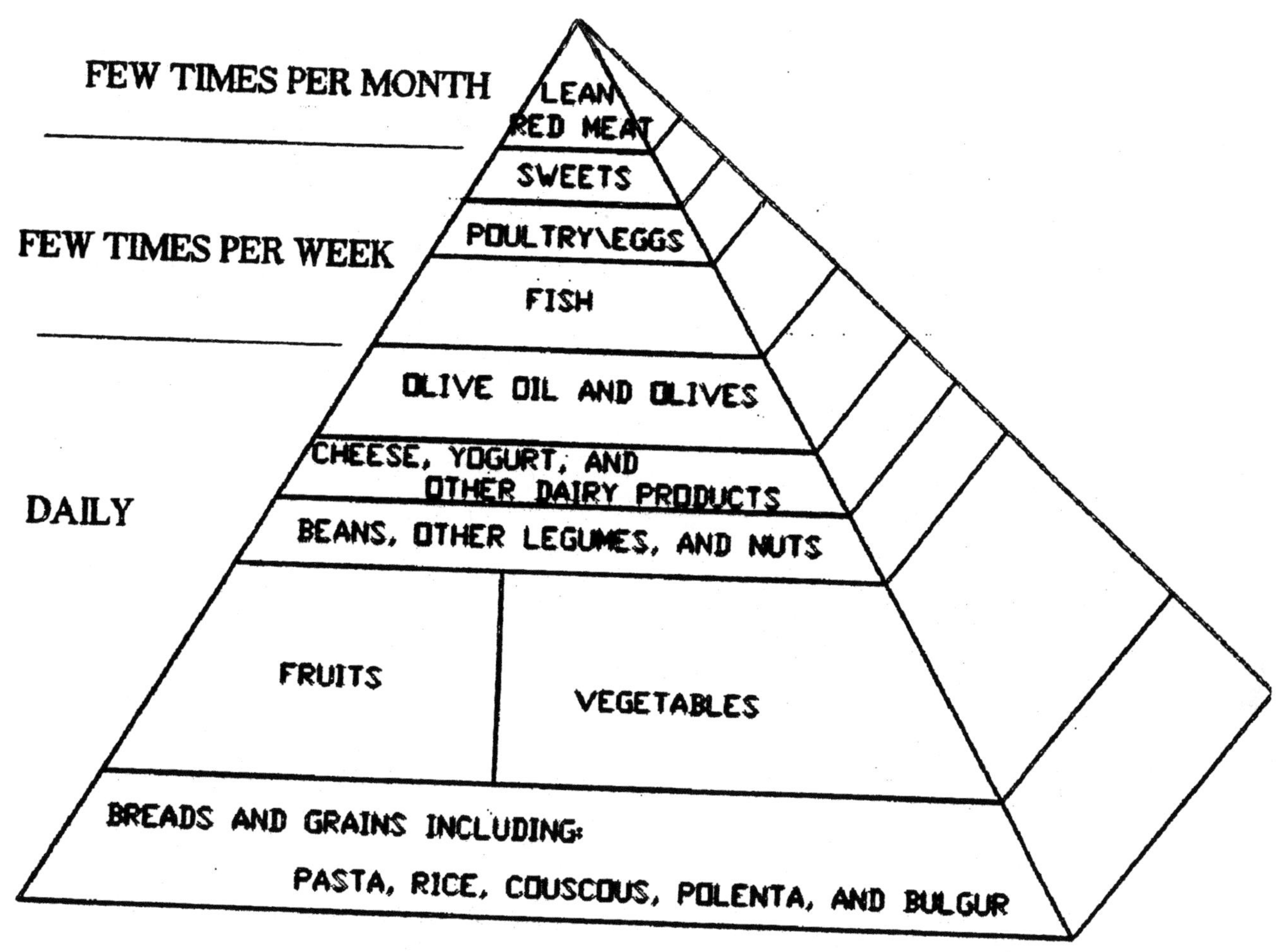

Figure 122-MEDITERRANEAN DIET

*Used in Earth Home

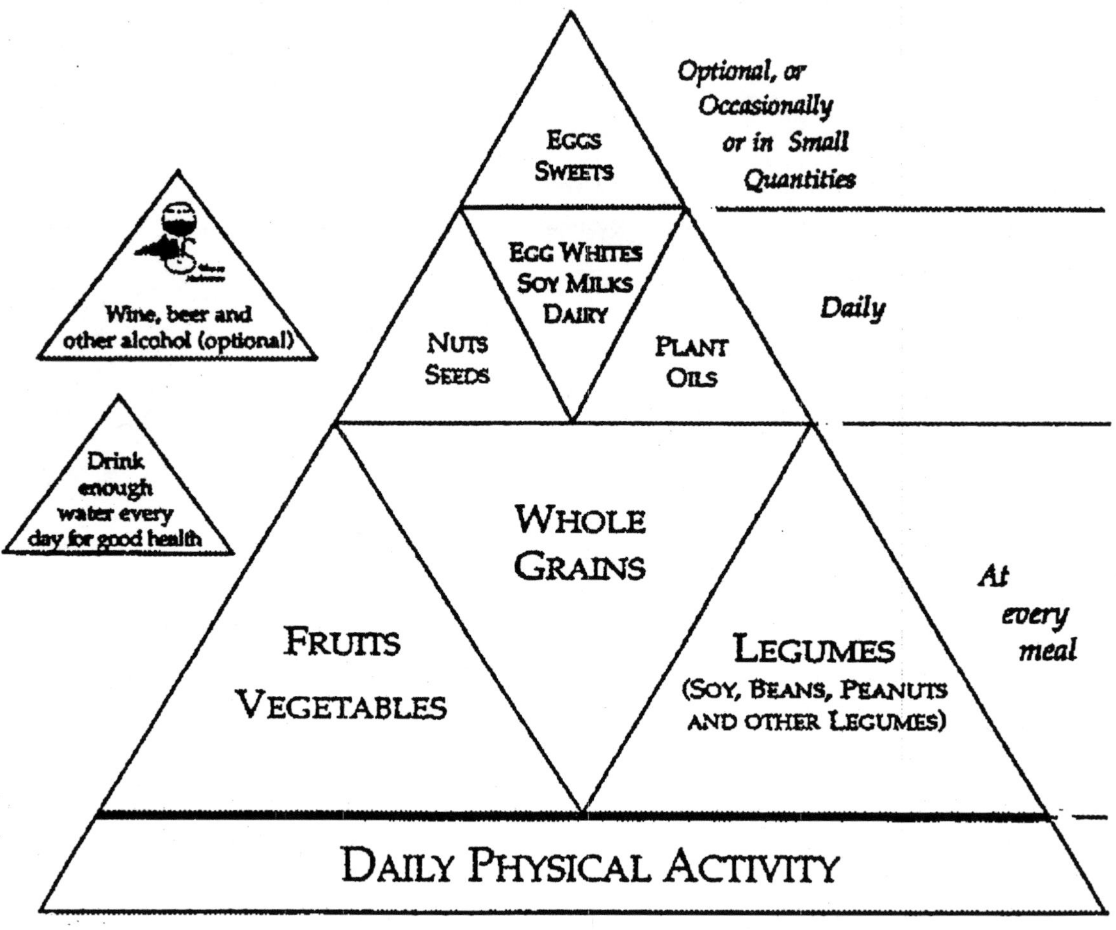

Figure 123-VEGETARIAN DIET PYRAMID

*Used in Earth Home

3. War Accounts

Wartime often brings out unusual diets based on necessity. Bomb shelters during World War II were stocked with honey and wheat germ because they don't spoil and people could survive on them for long periods of time. During the Civil War, troops short of rations found they could live indefinitely on sweet potatoes alone. The Japanese on Okinawa also raided sweet potato patches at night to survive.

The Guanches of the Canary Islands raised wheat and barley, parched them, pounded and/or ground them, and ate the resultant goffio as a staple. The Moroccan Berbers still use it as an emergency food and wartime ration.

4. Ships/Submarines

Captain Cook and his crew regularly consumed specially-formulated malt made by cooking sprouted beans on very low heat for a long time. They sailed for over three years without losing a single man to the wasting disease of scurvy. They drank a small amount of spruce beer for the same reason (vitamin C). Submarine crews also found sprouts the only fresh vegetable they could get when underwater for extended periods. The lost-at-sea diet usually made use of any sea creature available along with fresh water being the most important.

5. Africa/Survival

In the Sudan, people have consumed roots, leaves, caterpillars, frogs, locusts, bones, hides, and even heifer urine for survival. All of them are fermented, sun dried, and preserved for times of food shortage. They also make use of fermented bones, offal, and skins of animals in such products as jerbi-jerbi, lahmat-nimir, um-tibay, beirta, dodery, kaidu-digla, and adhum. In fact, about 60% of the fermented foods of Sudan are famine or survival foods.

Most "lost-in-the-wilderness-type" diets made use of buds on trees and shrubs, similar to the way deer would browse. It is said that a human can live without air for 3 minutes, without water for 3 days, and without food for 3 weeks.

6. Sprouts/Other

Sprouts have been responsible for much life-saving nourishment throughout history. During extremely difficult times, a family of seven survived a Utah winter by eating nothing but sprouts for six full months! No one suffered any ill effects, and during those six months the family was free from colds and disease.

b. Mormon Four Year's Supply

The Mormon 4 was originally created by the Mormon Church to provide one year of food for a typical member family. These four foods have also been suggested by many family preparedness/survival-type companies as the lowest cost, longest shelf life, and most nutritional foods. They are hard red winter wheat (seeds), honey, non-fat non-instant powdered dry milk, and salt. Some companies also suggest corn, pinto beans, and soy oil.

The phrase "a land flowing with mild and honey" is mentioned in the Bible seventy times. Wheat is constantly referred to in written history as "the staff of life."

c. Early American Traveler Diet

1. Klondike Gold Miners

New arrivals to the Klondike we required to have one years' supply of food including:

100 lbs. navy beans
150 lbs bacon
400 lbs. flour
25 lbs. sugar

*Used in Earth Home

10 lbs. baking powder
20 lbs. candles
25 lbs. hardtack
2 bottles Jamaica ginger
6 lbs laundry soap
2 suits heavy knit underwear

2. Pioneer Diet

When American pioneer families headed west in a covered wagon, they had to carry up to 2,000 pounds of belongings along with 6 months' supply of food. The wagon would be equipped with a very large wooden water barrel, another with cured meat in brine, and another with dried meat. The main food staple would be corn. Pioneers ate dried corn, cream corn, hull corn, dried corn mush, corn bread, and ground it up (corn meal) for flour and gravies. Other popular foods were doughnuts, bacon, eggs, dried meat, potatoes, rice, beans, and crackers. Yeast was used often for baking.

2. Longevity and Diet

a. Longevity/Aging Data

The three chief evils that hang over us are disease, old age, and death. A rule of thumb says that all mammals live about a billion heartbeats. The larger the mammal, the slower the heartbeat and the longer it lives. Only the tortoise lives longer than man at a maximum of 150 years old.

As we human beings age--our skin dries out, our hair thins and turns grey, and our sight and hearing dims. We get heavier and shorter, our muscles shrink, our joints stiffen, and our heart pumps blood less well. Our lungs will take in less oxygen, and our tissues will use the oxygen less efficiently. Kidney functions will slow and our endocrine glands secrete a lower level of hormones. Breasts sag, erections flag, and resistance to infection becomes a fraction of what it was. Reaction time is less, and memory becomes impaired. These effects are the last stages of development in us humans.

I do not get into the longevity discussion because *I believe it is not as important how long you live but how you live long*. There are many organizations that deal with longevity of humans in very scientific ways. One area of importance from a viewpoint of health is the colon health. Intestinal putrefaction causes the formation of many chemicals and substances which have a negative effect on the human body.

The diet of the Earth Home deals with health as a major focus and long life afterwards. However, the EH diet is very close to what some people would suggest if long life was the goal.

b. Long-Lived Culture Diets-Low Calorie

The quest for longer life is as old as life itself. From the ancient Greeks to Ponce de Leon and the modern research scientists--have searched for methods to keep death at arm's length for as long as possible. Life expectancy has risen from early twenties in Roman times, to mid-thirties at the time of the American Revolution, to forty only a hundred years ago, to almost eighty today. Some scientists believe the theoretical limit is 115 years based on the size of the skull relative to body weight. ***Scientists have already found a way to dramatically lengthen the life span in animals-eat less food!***

It has been reported that virtually all long-lived cultures that people have studied around the world live on a low calorie diet. These people include: the Hunzakuts of Pakistan (Hunzas in India), The Tibetans of Western China, the Georgians, the East Indian Todas, the Yucatan Indians, the Vilcamba of Ecuador, the Peruvians near Lake Titikaka, the Azurbaizanis (Abhasians) of the Soviet Union (Georgia), and the Okinawans of Japan. A Japanese village, Yuzurihara, also boasts many people living past 85 years old. However, later investigations failed to confirm some of their reputed longevities-except for the Okinawans.

The Okinawan diet, for the most part, consists of fresh uncooked food and is low in protein. Some of these cultures also drink mineral-rich water and/or oxygenated (alkaline) water located nearby. (See also Water-Ionizers) Cabbage is popular in the Eastern Europe diets in both raw and cooked forms and as fermented sauerkraut. Unleavened wholemeal bread, yogurt, beer, vegetables and spices, and a little meat are common foods of long-lived cultures. (It is also interesting that the longest-lived birds, the parrots, make regular visits to mineral-rich clay deposits along riverbanks.)

Part of the success of caloric (food) restriction stems from the fact that it takes a lot of energy to digest food and store excess calories, and the process itself creates free radicals. Reducing the number of free radicals reduces the rate of oxidation in the animals' cells, and thus slows down the process of aging.

The flip side of the coin is the peoples who have the lowest life expectancy. These include the Laplanders, Greenlanders, and Eskimos who live between 30 and 40 years. They live on a diet high in animal protein. This does suggest that any diet designed to specifically retard aging should contain very little protein. (See also Health/Medicinal/Weight Loss Diets section following)

3. NASA Diets

NASA has also looked into the subject of providing all a human's food and energy requirements from a closed space. These groups of studies have concentrated on the food needs for the crews of space stations, extended space travel, and missions on the surface of the moon and other planets. Experiments have been conducted with lunar soil or "regolith" and hydroponics to determine if a colony set up on the moon's surface could supply all of its food needs from a limited surface area.

NASA designs diets of about 2,800 calories per person, per day. It's interesting to note that in 1968 NASA gave this summary of its experiments:

> **"While experiments in life support learned from Mercury, Gemini, and Apollo flights have provided aerospace scientists with answers concurrent with the present state-of-the-art, no system has yet been devised which will provide man with the environment to sustain lengthy lunar visitation or interplanetary travel."**

Although NASA has not yet developed any completely closed life support systems, it continues to work on the various means necessary to develop such a system. Many of the published NASA studies deal with selected species under specific conditions, such as elevated light, elevated temperature, and/or CO_2 enrichment.

4. Biosphere II Diet

The Biosphere II project in Arizona recently opened up its doors and let out the eight people who had been living inside. The Biosphere II diet was predominantly made up of beans, rice, wheat, sorghum, sweet potatoes, white potatoes, and peanuts. These crops took 4 months to mature and ended up to be the staples of their diet. Most of the fat came from the peanut crop. There were some cabbage and carrots (cool weather crops) and plenty of beets in the winter months. They also had some bell peppers, eggplant, and chili peppers. Squashes were the most popular vegetable and they had an over supply of green leafy vegetables in the winter. In summer the mainstays were squashes and beans.

The spices that did the best were chives, oregano, basil, mint, thyme, and sage. They grew dill and fennel for the leaves and seeds. Ginger grew well with a continuous supply of chili peppers for a relish.

They had African pygmy goats because they can be bred all year long and give delicious milk. They crossed a jungle fowl with a "Silkie" chicken to get a foraging bird that was also good egg-layers and good mothers. But, they found that in order to get good egg production, it was necessary to feed them a lot of grain. The Vietnamese pot-bellied pig was their first choice in swine because they are very small, have a high fat content, don't eat too much, and have a delightful disposition. Afterwards, they looked for a smaller animal that eats a lot

*Used in Earth Home

of green leafy matter in their diet. They also noted that it took a lot of time to care for their animals. Overall, it took one-third of their days just to produce and prepare food.

The Biospherians' meat consumption consisted of about 6 ounces per week per person. They ate 3.5 ounces of goat meat, pork, chicken, or fish and one egg per week. They had to use all parts of the animals for maximum efficiency. The Tilapia fish production did not work out as planned. They consumed eight pounds of starch a day—rice, sweet potatoes, white potatoes, plantains, or taro. (The taro grew well and disease-free, but it had taste problems). They usually ate sourdough bread because they could not obtain yeast using their limited space. A large bowl of soup was always the main part of their lunch. Their diet was extremely restricted in that they had to grow all food in about a one-half acre parcel and they did not have a dedicated fish tank to produce fish for eating. (Incidentally, they complained of inadequate diet variation, feelings of confinement, and air quality problems.) Feasting (having a full stomach) once in awhile became very important to them. They kept trying new cooking recipes even when they ran out of ingredients by substituting the same type of ingredient (wet, dry, sweet, etc.).

5. Self-Sufficient Diets

Self-sufficiency in food has been a subject of experimentation by a vast number of home gardeners. A home gardener attempts to gain a small amount of self-sufficiency and control over food costs by planting a garden in their back yard. These gardens are dependent on the type of soil, amount of sunshine and shade, the climate in the region, taste preferences, and amount of space and time available. In many cases, the home gardener starts out with too many plant species, making it difficult to devote enough time to any one species. More experienced gardeners usually limit cultivar selection. (See plant selection section for more self-sufficient diet information).

There are other groups that are experimenting with complete self-sufficiency in food. Most of these projects are small, and are either individually oriented or have been centered on a publication or organization, such as *Mother Earth News* and *New Alchemy Institute*.

E. Modern Diets Overview

1. Average American Diet/SAD (See also Industrialized Food Problems Section)

a. American Diet Milestones

The past century has experienced a revolution in food manufacturing and consumption that has drastically affected the world's diet and attitude. The First World War brought us the existence of substances called vitamins. Below are more important milestones in U.S. diet study history.

-----1920 Dr. Royal Lee invented supplements
-----bacteria awareness brought us the FDA and USDA inspections
-----1940's gave us the "Recommended Daily Allowances" chart
-----1950's gave us supermarkets
-----1954 TV dinners came along
-----1956 gave us the four basic food groups
-----1960's brought vegetarianism
-----1968 the American Heart Association recommended limiting fat intake
-----1971 USDA established links between poor nutrition and all major health problems
-----1970's brought us many diets recommended by physicians
-----1980's saw many diet plans emerge
-----1990's gave us food labeling laws
-----1992 replaced the four food groups with the diet pyramid

Currently, most U.S. and industrialized nations of the world have adopted sophisticated and complex diets based on importation of great amounts and varieties of foods from other parts of the world.

b. U.S. Average Food Consumption

In the United States, we enjoy eating a great diversity of plants and animal products. We can purchase most foods almost any season, due to the great demand for those products. The human taste buds, the availability of disposable income, and modern food production methods allow us to enjoy this great variety of foods. The following figure is a graphic representation of the amounts of food that an average American family of four consumes in one year. Nearly 75% of the carbohydrates in the average American diet come from grains and refined sugar (132 pounds/year). The "fast sugar cycle" is reputed to be a significant cause of obesity in the United States.

The rest is divided about equally between potatoes, vegetables, fruits, and dairy products. A total of 89% of the American diet is fat and carbohydrate!

This chart was designed to illustrate how much and what types of food are consumed. ***The Earth Home system does not intend to grow the amounts of food and compositions that this chart represents***. It does, however, attempt to produce enough nutrition for the human body to carry out everyday activities.

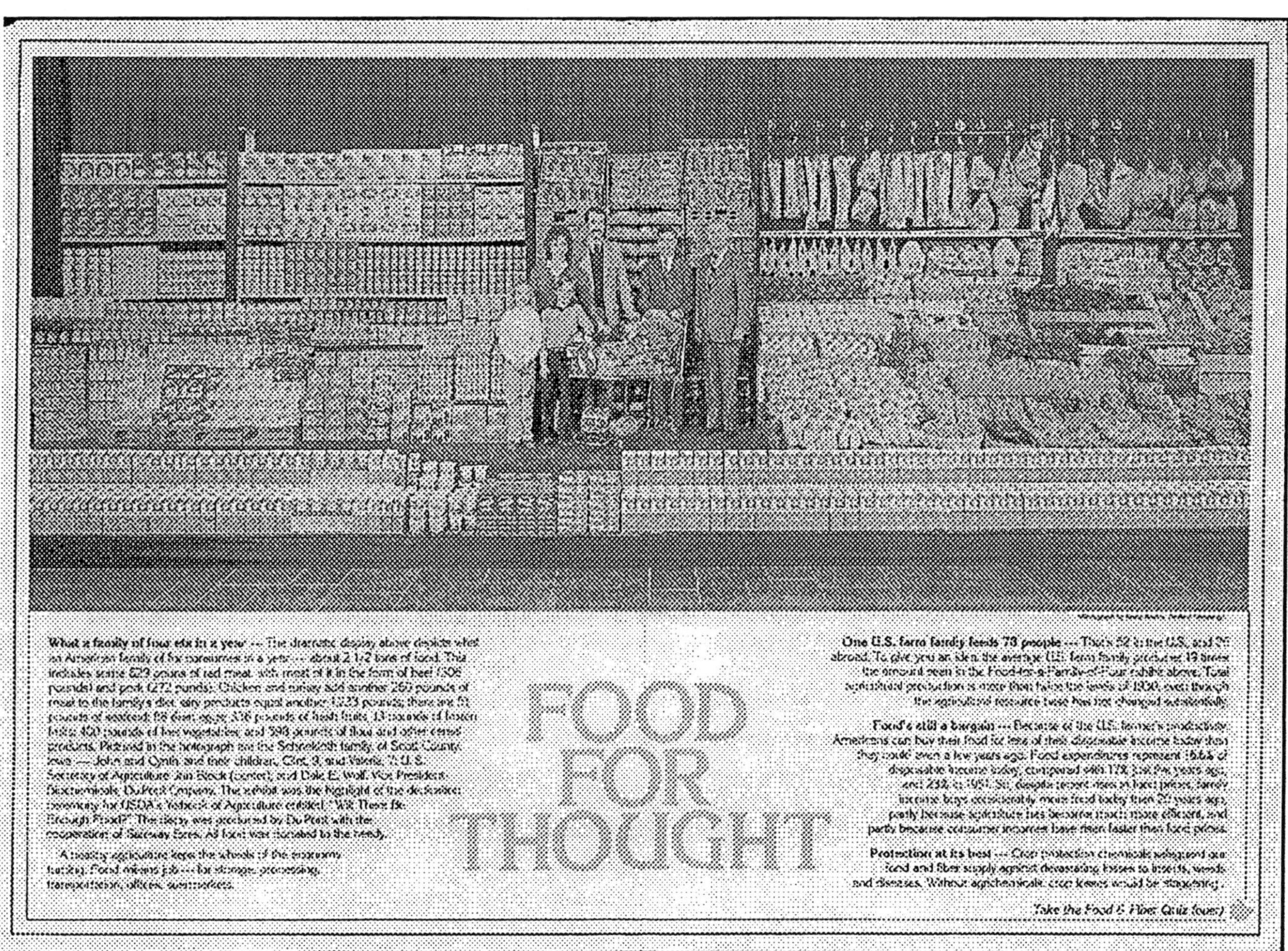

Figure 124-ANNUAL FOOD CONSUMPTION OF U.S. FAMILY

*Used in Earth Home

2. Meat Diets

a. Background/History

Throughout history, most people's diets have been primarily vegetarian, with meats eaten only occasionally. This is still true today throughout much of the world. It is just in the last century that the meat foods have been so heavily consumed in the Westernized cultures, such as North America, Australia, and the European countries. This is due mainly to the commercial herding, slaughtering, and packaging of flesh foods to make them readily available at the corner store.

b. Meat Consumption Patterns around the World

The following figure illustrates the worldwide consumption patterns of meat. (See also Nutritional Information-Protein Discussion section). Per capita meat consumption in the United States before 1941 was about 50 pounds; it is now over 150 pounds. Similar percentage increases have occurred in Japan and the other industrialized countries of the world.

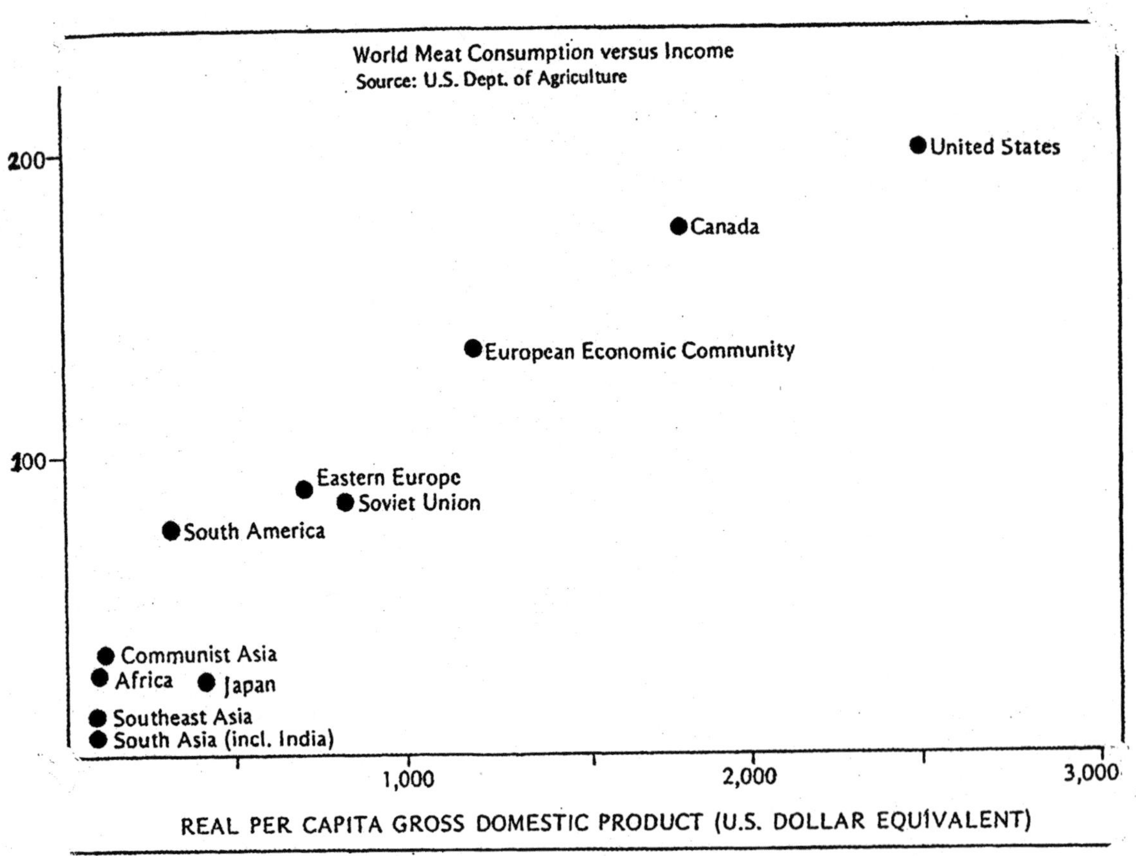

Figure 125-WORLD MEAT CONSUMPTION VS. INCOME

*Used in Earth Home

c. Land Area Used for Meat Diet vs. Vegetarian

Standard U.S. agricultural practice today requires from 45,000 square feet of land to 2 acres to feed a person on a high meat (American) diet, or about 10,000 square feet for a vegetarian. However, biointensive gardening can provide for a vegetarian's entire diet, plus the compost crops needed to sustain the system indefinitely, on only 2,000 to 4,000 square feet, even starting on low quality land.

3. Vegetarian Diets

a. Background and History

We probably all know someone who is vegetarian and very satisfied with their diet. Even the experts in sports medicine and athletes are now beginning to extol the virtues of a vegetarian regime high in raw foods.

b. Lacto-Ovo-Vegetarian

This is the most common of the vegetarian diets, one that does not include animal flesh but does use the by-products of the chicken and/or cow—eggs and milk products. Usually the vegetable foods are the largest part of the diet, which consists mainly of fruits, vegetables, grains, legumes, nuts, and seeds.

c. Biogenic Diet

The Biogenic diet is similar to the vegetarian diet. It consists of 40% fruit, 30% raw vegetables, and the rest grains, dried fruits, dairy products, seeds, and nuts. They believe fruit is ideal for ridding the body of its own wastes and environmental pollutants.

d. Vegan

This is the strict, or pure, form of vegetarianism. No animal products are consumed-only fruits, vegetables, legumes, grains, nuts and seeds. No eggs, cheese, yogurt, ice cream, butter, or other milk products are eaten. It is more difficult with this diet to obtain a balanced intake of all the nutrients that are needed during growth; however, it can be done.

e. Macrobiotic

Macrobiotics is a philosophy of life centered on a diet originally brought to this country from Japan by George Osawa. It has been expanded upon and shared with many by teachers and authors. A macrobiotic diet consists almost exclusively of cooked foods. Raw foods are felt to be difficult to digest and too cooling for our system. A minimum of fruits is consumed, less than 5 percent of the diet, and most of those should be cooked. Dairy foods and eggs are usually avoided. The only animal products recommended are whitefish such as halibut, trout, and sole, and these are also kept to less than 5 percent of the diet. Thus, it is primarily a vegetarian, almost vegan, diet, but it seems to contain more protein and nutrients than the standard vegetarian cuisine.

f. Miscellaneous Vegetarian Diets

Noodletarian or pasta diets are being used by some vegetarians. As the name implies, noodles are the mainstay of the diet with vegetables and other foods as a sideline. The making of noodles and the foods added to it are the center of the eating experience and takes some time for preparation.

Raw food diets consist of all uncooked fruits and vegetables. It is popular among those who wish to be cured from congestive maladies.

*Used in Earth Home

The diet called "natural hygiene" diet is an ancient raw foods diet supported by cleansing the colon and occasional fasting. This program and philosophy began with the Essenes, an ancient tribe of Jewish scholars.

Fruitarian diets attempt to satisfy subsistence solely on nature's gift of nourishment—fruits. However, fruits do not contain all the nutrients that human beings need to live, at least not on a long-term basis.

4. Health/Medicinal/Weight Loss Diets

Healthy eating is a timeless science, researched for thousands of years in many civilizations yet surprisingly neglected this century. Many different diet variations have received publicity over the last 30 years. These diets include high fiber diets, low fat diets, liquid diets, raw juice diets, high protein diets, and many more. There is always new scientific evidence in support of one diet or another.

a. Weight Loss Diets

In 1982, John Hopkins University researchers calculated that Americans had tried 29,068 schemes to lose weight. Researchers found that of eleven published diet plan books (the F-plan, Scarsdale, Pritikin, Richard Simmons, Atkins, Stillman, I Love New York, I Love America, Beverly Hills, Carbohydrate Craver's, and California diets), *none* provided a full 100 percent of the RDA for thirteen vitamins and minerals.

Some hospitals and clinics have offered their own version of weight loss diets. One example is the "New Mayo Clinic Diet". They give extensive instructions on when and what to eat to lose weight.

b. Raw Juice Diets

One of the most dramatic diets is the fresh raw juice diet for a period of time of two days to several weeks. Some of the results from this diet include improved facial tone; firmer body; healthier nails; and lowering of cholesterol, blood pressure, and uric acid levels. There are even reports of cures where no other medicine or foods have had any effect!

c. Protein Diets

Eating frwer carbohydrates was first written about in mid-1800 with a diet book called Banting's Letter on Corpulence. Low carbohydrate diets have recently been touted as the secret to losing weight and maintaining health. The Atkins, Scarsdale, and Stillman diets all recommend high protein intake. There is much research being done on gastric responses to foods and the associated wellness of the person. Experimental studies on long term high protein diets, however, point to kidney disease, shortened lifespan, and possible development of osteoporosis because of the higher rate of calcium excretion.

5. Low Carbohydrate Diets

a. South Beach Diet

Recently low carbohydrate diets have been very popular. The South Beach diet, for example, has attracted millions of loyal followers. Low-carb diets have a higher success ratio than most fad diets in the past. It is so popular that many foods have been introduced with lower carbohydrate levels to cater to the people on a low-carb diet.

b. Reversal Diet

The Reversal Diet basically says that Americans eat food in the wrong proportions. It basically reversed the percentages and specifies 70 percent carbohydrates and 10 percent fat. This diet also stresses lowering the cholesterol intake to a fraction of normal.

c. The "Perfect Diet"

If you skipped to this section, it will be a big disappointment! Massive amount of research effort is being put into finding the elusive "best diet". There are two things that I think would occur if we picked up the paper and found that scientists had found the secret to the ultimate human diet:

1) This diet could explain all the other diets and the effect on the human body.
2) Most of people would assume this to be another weight loss regimen!

What humans eat is sometimes more of a psychological issue than a physical one. Human food prejudices are often not related to logic or reason. For example, the tomato was raised for purely ornamental reasons for over two hundred years before someone discovered it was good to eat!

6. Low Fat Diets

a. Typical Low Fat Eating

Low fat diets have been popular for a long time. Many people report success with the simple avoidance of as much fats in the diet as possible. Many fast-foods and restaurants serve many kinds of food that is deep-fat fried.

b. The Life Choice Diet

The Life Choice Diet is a low-fat vegetarian way of eating with less than 10% calories from fat. Typically, this would be a diet with 15 to 25 grams of fat per day. The emphasis is on beans, fruits, vegetables, and whole grains, with processed foods and nonfat dairy products consumed in moderation. Simple sugars, alcohol, and fat are to be avoided.

7. Earth Home Diet Comparison Discussion

The Earth Home System diet can be adjusted to individual needs as necessary--high protein, high carbohydrate, high fiber, or whatever individual preferences there may be. The emphasis is on the quality of food, quantity eaten at one time, and the spacing between food groups. The much higher vitamin/mineral content should surpass any RDA requirements substantially because of the soil medium and the freshness.

I believe moderation in diet choices is a key element to a healthy diet. Also I think that each body is slightly different in terms of what is best for it. Even tiny diet variations can have different effects on each individual. (See Nutritional Information/Individual Needs section) Finding out about each person's unique dietary needs is very important to maximize well-being and health.

F. Industrialized Food Problems

1. History of Industrialized Diets

The American diet has been described as hydrogenated, de-fibered, de-germinated, defatted, re-fatted and manipulated by the food industry. An interesting fact is that when the industrial (mass produced/factory processed) or refined foods diet was introduced to different tribal cultures throughout the world, a general degradation of their health followed, usually within one generation. Tooth decay and diseases such as diabetes, cardiovascular disease, and cancer increased to levels that correlated with those industrialized societies. There are many different aspects to the industrialized diet that are separated as below.

2. Specific Food Group Issues

a. Dairy Products, Calcium, and Alternatives

Humans are the only animal to drink milk after they are weaned, and the only animal to drink another animal's milk. There is doubt whether the calcium in cow's milk can be assimilated by the human body—because of the heat of pasteurization. Researchers say that the organic calcium turns to an inorganic form similar to the calcium deposits in hard water. There is evidence that drinking milk contributes to colic, ear infections, allergies, diabetes, obesity, and many other illnesses. Eating a calcium-rich diet has been confused with drinking lots of milk, which also poses potential health concerns related to fat intake.

Raw nuts and seeds, whole grains, and leafy greens can provide adequate amounts of calcium in the diet. Good sources of calcium are broccoli, collard greens, turnip greens, soybeans, tofu, parsley, and sunflower seeds. As another alternative, a good quality of soy milk can be made from dry soybeans. It has been used in the Orient for centuries. Soybean milk has been shown to be an excellent food for babies where dairy milk was not available.

b. Refined Sugar

People in countries where sugar cane is produced and is eaten pure have healthy teeth. In the past twenty years, sugar consumption has increased from 12 kg. (26 pounds) per person to 67 kg. (150 pounds) per person per year. Compare this to the early 1900's when the average consumption was only 2.2 kg. (5 pounds) per person per year.

Refining of sugar has been implicated in a variety of diet-related illnesses. Generally, sugar is void of vitamins and minerals and fiber and has a deteriorating effect on your endocrine system. Because of this, sugar is considered one of the three major causes of degenerative disease. Sugar can fuel cancer cells, deplete us of calcium that sometimes leads to osteoporosis, cause tooth and gum decay, and can create extra cholesterol that hardens arteries and fattens the liver. Sugar has been implicated in problems with the immune system as well.

Your immune systems main defense is the activity of your white blood cells to remove invaders from your bloodstream in a process known as phagocytosis. One teaspoon of sugar will lower the phagocytic activity by 50 percent. Two teaspoons will lower this factor by 78 percent. Some people may average 33 teaspoons of sugar per day. Just think of what it is doing to your internal systems not to mention the calories.

Some diets point a finger at sugars as an undesirable "trigger" in the human body that starts the digestive process at the wrong speed at the wrong times. This has been called the "fast sugar cycle" and has been the subject of many studies. Some studies point to sugar as a poison that paralyzes the immune system. In my own research on diets, I have never run across research touting positive effects of refined sugar on human beings. Amusingly, a sign posted near the junk food machines in a major city zoo warns **"DO NOT FEED THIS FOOD TO THE ANIMALS OR THEY MAY GET SICK AND DIE!"**

c. High Fructose Corn Syrup

Over the last few years sucrose or cane sugar dropped in consumption from 81 percent of total market share and corn sweetener mainly in the form of high fructose corn syrup has increased from 18 percent of total market share to 55 percent. This change has occurred mainly because of the soft drink industry, because they use the high fructose corn syrup to sweeten their soft drinks.

High fructose corn syrup has been implicated in diet-related problems. A recent study at the University of Minnesota found that a diet high in fructose (as compared to glucose) elevates triglyceride levels in men shortly after eating, a phenomenon that has been linked to an increased risk of obesity and heart disease.

d. Fats/Anti-Nutrients

Today we consume, per capita, 100 percent more saturated fat and cholesterol, 250 percent more salt and refined sugar, and 1000 percent more "funny fats," described as isomers produced by hydrogenation. These fats act as kind of "anti-nutrients" either blocking the use of our essential nutrients or increasing our requirement for them.

We live in a world of caloric rich and nutritionally lacking foods. The result is diseases that are not genetic in origin, but the direct result of poor dietary and lifestyle choices.

3. General Food Content Issues

a. Pesticides/Herbicides

Pesticides and/or herbicides are also used routinely on agricultural products in many countries of the world. Organic food popularity is the consumer reaction to finding better quality foods.

b. Antibiotics/Steroids

Every year over 35 million pounds of antibiotics are consumed by humans, livestock, and poultry in the U.S. About half of all antibiotics and steroids produced (including testosterone) are fed to domestic animals for later commercial consumption. Humans may unknowingly consume second-hand antibiotics hidden in meat, poultry, and dairy products. The overall effect has not only been destruction of the healthful bacteria in the human intestinal tract, but also the establishment of strains of harmful bacteria that are resistant to antibiotics.

c. Vitamin/Mineral Deficiencies

1. "Green Harvest"

We routinely pick fruits and vegetables before they are ripe. This assures that the produce will arrive on the supermarket shelves before they can spoil. However, this process means that nature has not had a chance to mature the fruit to its prime and thus does not contain the full amount of nourishing ingredients.

2. Processing Losses

When wheat is processed into white flour, up to 40 percent of the vitamin C and from 65 to 85 percent of various B vitamins are depleted. In addition, 12 minerals are lost, including 59 percent of the magnesium and 72 percent of the zinc! You also lose significant amounts of other vitamins, protein, and fiber. All in all an appalling twenty-six essential nutrients are removed!

Cooking methods generally deplete about 50 percent of the less stable vitamins, especially vitamin C. This includes not just vegetables, but meat, which may lose up to half of its thiamin, B-6, and pantothenic acid during cooking. By the time you put cooked peas on the table, there may be only 44 percent of the original vitamin C (for fresh peas), 17 percent (for frozen peas), or as little as 6 percent (for canned peas). (See the following figure)

Canned and frozen foods have similar losses. Blanching before canning can destroy up to 60 percent of the vitamin C content, 40 percent of the riboflavin, and 30 percent of the thiamin. The sterilization process used in canned foods further destroys vitamins: for example, 39 percent of the vitamin A may be destroyed, and 69 percent of the remaining thiamin. While freezing itself seems preferable to canning, vitamin C may be depleted by about 25 percent. ***These losses are on top of the already lowered vitamin/mineral content due to soil depletion over the last 50 years!***

*Used in Earth Home

Losses of trace elements due to the refining of sugar.

Element	Raw-brown	Refined white	Molasses
Chromium, ppm	0.24-0.35	0.02-0.35	1.21
Cobalt, ppm	0.40	$<$0.05	1.26
Copper, ppm	1.34	0.57	2.21
Zinc, ppm	1.62	0.54	8.28
Ash%	3.2	0.11	8.0

Vitamin losses in the refining of whole wheat.

Vitamin	Wheat µg/g	White Flour µg/g	Germ µg/g	Millfeeds µg/g	Vitamin tablet* Required mg/day	mg
B_1 (Thiamine)	3.5	0.8†	22.0	17	1	10
B_2 (Riboflavin)	1.5	0.3†	5.5	4.2	1.2	10
B_3 (Niacin)	50.0	9.5†	80.0	150	10	100
B_6 (Pyridoxine)	1.7	0.5	12.0	7.2	2	5
Pantothenic acid	10.0	5.0	25.0	22	–	20
Folic acid	0.3	0.1	1.5	1.1	–	–
E (Tocopherol)	16	2.2	125.0	38	–	15 units
Gross energy, Kcal/g	4.4	4.3	5.1	4.7	–	–

*Theragran, high potency vitamins with minerals. As the average diet weighs 1.7 kg, to obtain µg/g or ppm divide value by 1.7 to compare with wheat.

†These three are replaced, along with iron. There are actually some 24 vitamins and bulk and trace elements partly removed from wheat during its refining to white flour; four are replaced.

Note: Millfeeds, which contain more of each vitamin than does whole wheat, and much more than white flour which humans eat, are fed to cattle and domestic animals, who must benefit greatly in many cases. Note the slight difference in calories; the higher level in germ comes from the oil.

Figure 126-VITAMIN LOSSES IN SUGAR AND WHOLE WHEAT

4. Fiber Deficiency

Most Americans do not get enough fiber in their diet which allows for proper use of the large intestine with associated elimination issues. Studies now confirm that natural dietary fiber not only works to keep the digestive system in order, it also acts to:

1) Keep fats and cholesterol in the blood at normal levels
2) Normalize insulin production by keeping blood sugar at appropriate levels and reducing "rebound" hunger half an hour after eating
3) Prevent cancer of the bowel
4) Help offset any tendency to irritable bowel syndrome and diverticulitis

Some of the best plant sources for fiber are lentils, peas, and spinach. It has been said that the salad is the master internal cleanser and "Mother Nature's Broom".

*Used in Earth Home

4 Specific Food Additives

A food additive is a substance or mixture of substances, other than basic foodstuffs, present in food as a result of any aspect of production, processing, storage, or packaging. The term does not include chance contaminants.

a. Chemicals

There are an estimated 140 chemicals in an average American meal. The average American consumes nearly 150 pounds of food additives each year, nearly 90 percent of it sugar. In 1980 almost 30 billion pounds of sweeteners were consumed by the public. Salt intake is about 15 pounds per year per person, while various other food additives account for another 5-10 pounds.

In 1958, the U.S. Congress approved the FDA's "Generally Recognized as Safe" (GRAS) list when it enacted the Delaney Clause. This required rigid testing for any new food additives—except several thousand that were already in use. The accepted list also included several thousand substances, such as salt, sugar, spices, vitamins, minerals, flavorings, preservatives, emulsifiers, thickening agents, colors, and so on. In 1977 a fairly extensive review of the GRAS list was undertaken and many of the additives are still being investigated. More than 415 selected common food additives were evaluated and only 305 were considered safe as of 1980.

Food processors use an estimated ten thousand chemicals they may add to what we eat. Some are deleterious, some are harmless, and some are beneficial. Every one of these chemicals used in food processing must serve one or more of the following purposes:

-Improve nutritional value
-Enhance quality or consumer acceptability
-Improve the keeping quality
-Make the food more readily available
-Facilitate its preparation

The majority of all food additives has nothing to do with nutritional value, but is used for other purposes.

b. Flavorings

Flavorings are the largest group of all additives—over 500 natural and 1500 synthetic. During the early days of history, people used mainly herbs and spices (whole or ground) to impart flavor to, or modify the flavor of foods. It was only in the Middle Ages that some extraction of plant materials started, followed by distillation of essential oils. More than 4,000 chemicals have been identified as flavoring substances. The flavor wheel as used by the industry contains green, fruity, citrus, minty, floral, spicy, woody, roasty, caramel, boullion, meaty, fatty, dairy, mushroom celery, and sulfurous tastes.

Many of the common foods consumed today have artificial flavorings in them. It is estimated that about 80% of all flavorings sold contain at least one synthetic compound, and this indicates the importance of synthetic flavor ingredients. For example, 80% of the world's vanillin is obtained from lignin in the sulphite waste stream of pulp mills. A significant number (30%) of Americans is estimated to have some kind of sensitivity to specific chemicals.

c. Preservatives

Preservatives are "antispoilants" used to help prevent microbiological spoilage and chemical deterioration. They are of many different types, which about one hundred are in common use. Preservatives for fatty products are called antioxidants, which prevent the production of off flavors and off odors. These include benzoic acid used in margarine and butylated hydroxyanisole (BHA) used in lard, shortenings, crackers, soup bases, and potato chips.

In bread, preservatives are "mold" and "rope" inhibitors. They include sodium and calcium propionate, sodium diacetate, and such substances as acetic acid and lactic acid. Sorbic acid and sodium and potassium salts are preservatives used in cheeses, syrups, and pie fillings. Preservatives used to prevent mold and fungus growth on citrus fruits are called "fungicides."

Sequestering agents, still another type of preservative, prevent physical or chemical changes that affect color, flavor, texture, or appearance. Ethylenediaminetetraacetic acid (EDTA) and its salts, for instance, are used to prevent the adverse affects of metals present in such products as soft drinks, where metal ions can cause clouding. Sequestrants used in dairy products to keep them "fresh and sweet" include sodium, calcium, and potassium salts of citric, tartaric, and rophosphoric acids. Other common multipurpose preservatives are sulfur dioxide gas, propyl gallate, and, of course, sugar, salt, and vinegar.

d. Many Other Additives

Added to the list above there may be acids, alkalies, buffers, neutralizers, moisture content controls (humectants), coloring agents, dies, physiologic activity controls (such as ethylene gas), bleaching agents, maturing agents, bread improvers, processing aids, sanitizing agents, emulsifiers, emulsion stabilizers, texturizers, fortifiers, antioxidants, deodorants, drying agents, extenders, gassers, hydrolizers, hydrogenators, disinfectants, neutralizers, anti-foaming agents, anti-caking agents, curers, waxes, coal tar, and more.

5. Specific Food Modifications/Processing Issues

a. Genetic Modifications (GM)

Throughout the world there are millions of acres of commercial farmland that is planted with genetically-modified seeds. Already, some 30,000 GM products are on supermarket shelves and they are not marked as such. They are made with ingredients produced from plants that have had genes from other plants or animals added to their own genetic makeup. Potatoes and tomatoes have a gene from fish added to help them withstand frosty weather! Genetically modified salmon grow 5 to 6 times faster than normal.

Society is debating the moral and ethics of such experimentation. It has been confirmed that Bt corn puts monarch caterpillars in risk. Over 50% of the soybeans, 35% of the corn, and 40% of the cotton grown in the US are genetically engineered. This causes some allergies, infertility, immune deficiencies, and other human health and environmental problems.

Surely companies can argue that the world needs new sources of food that can be economically grown. However, this text does not use or plan for improved cultivars using these methods. Cultivars with viable seed can be improved through the generations by observation and careful attention to details.

b. Irradiated Food

When food is irradiated, it is loaded onto a conveyor belt and passed through a radiation cell where it is showered with beams of ionizing radiation produced by high radioactive isotopes. The radiation can inhibit ripening and kill certain bacteria and molds that induce spoilage, so that food looks and tasted fresh for up to several weeks. The process does not make food radioactive and does not change the food's color or texture in most cases. Irradiation is being hotly debated recently.

6. Food Patterns and Disease

a. China Health Project

The China Health Project was a massive study comparing food patterns in relation to disease. The results are summarized in the following figure. The results go on to say that Chinese have lower cholesterol, lower heart disease, lower breast cancer, and lower colon cancer rates than Americans.

Nutrient	China	West
Total protein (g/day)	64	91
Plant protein (g/day)	60	27
Carbohydrate (g/day)	524	243
Fat (g/day)	43	114
% of calories from fat	15	43
Total calories/day	2,636	2,360
Dietary fiber (g/day)	45	10

Figure 127-CHINESE VS. AMERICAN NUTRIENTS

b. Diet-Related Diseases

There are 8 diseases attributed to deficiencies in food; beriberi, goiter, scurvy, rickets, eye trouble, and liver poisoning.

c. Standard American Diet (SAD) Problems

There are certain benefits to SAD such as;

1) There is a huge variety of wonderful foods available to nourish us.
2) Our race is growing bigger and stronger with each generation-mainly from the protein-rich and calcium-rich foods.

There are, however, certain nutritional problems associated with the Standard American Diet such as;

1) High Calorie
2) Low nutrient
3) Low fiber
4) High fat
5) Excess saturated fat
6) Excess hydrogenated oils
7) High Protein
8) Excess salt

*Used in Earth Home

9) Excess sugar
10) Excess alcohol
11) Excess milk foods
12) Excess meats
13) High vitamin D
14) Excess phosphorus

These nutritional problems have been linked to the following problems and diseases;

1) Coronary Heart Disease
2) High blood pressure
3) Heart Attacks
4) Strokes
5) Vascular insufficiency
6) Diabetes
7) Breast cancer
8) Colon cancer
9) Prostate cancer
10) Other cancers
11) Arthritis
12) Behavior problems/Crime
13) Obesity
14) Tooth Decay
15) Atherosclerosis

d. Diet-Related Disease History

The following are generally accepted diseases attributed to diet;

1) Cancer of the breast (one in three develops cancer of some kind)
2) Cancer of the colon
3) Diverticulitis
4) Heart disease (coronary heart disease accounts for nearly half of deaths in U.S.)
5) High blood pressure (hypertension occurs in 50 percent of individuals over 40 years old)
6) Irritable bowel syndrome
7) Non-insulin-dependent diabetes (16 million in the U.S.)
8) Obesity (80% of Americans)

The most common disease in which diet plays a major role is heart disease or atherosclerosis. Many studies have linked the incidence of heart disease with dietary intake of cholesterol and saturated fat. This alone is a major killer of Americans each year. If we feed a colony of young monkeys the American supermarket diet, within a few years these monkeys will develop all the modern diseases. It is often said that the U.S. is best with disease but not health.

G. RDA/Vitamins and Mineral Supplements

1. Diet Deficiencies/Trace Elements

National surveys give some inkling of the deficiencies in our diet. A government survey known as the HANES (Health and Nutrition Examination Survey) of 1971-72 showed that up to 50 percent of the general population received less than the recommended daily amounts (U.S. RDA's) of some vitamins and minerals. A preliminary report of the Department of Agriculture's Nationwide Food Consumption Survey of 1977-78 revealed that adolescents and young adults were most severely deficient in nutrients. But these surveys seldom indicate how critical the problem is since the RDA's, which serve as the yardstick, are set so low.

*Used in Earth Home

There is also evidence that trace elements are less prevalent in modern humans than in the past. The following figure shows evidence of this.

Trace elements in seawater and in man, ancient and modern.

Element	Sea Water ppb	Primitive Man ppm	Modern Man ppm	Principal Cause of Difference
'ssential				
Iron	3.4	60	60	
Zinc	15	33	33	
Rubidium	120	4.6	4.6	
Strontium	8000	4.6	4.6	
Fluorine	1300	37	37	
Copper	10	1.0	1.2	Copper pipes
Boron	4600	0.3	0.7	Vegetables and fruits
Bromine	65,000	1.0	2.9	Bromides? Fuels
Iodine	50	0.1-0.5	0.2	Salt iodized
Barium	6	0.3	0.3	
Manganese	1	0.4	0.2	Refined foods?
Selenium	4	0.2	0.2	
Chromium	2	0.6	0.09	Refined sugars and grains
Molybdenum	14	0.1	0.1	
Arsenic	3	0.05	0.1	Additives, weed killers
Cobalt	0.1	0.03	0.03	
Vanadium	5	0.1	0.3	Petroleum

Figure 128-TRACE ELEMENTS

2. (RDA) Recommended Daily Allowances Overview

a. (RDA) Recommended Daily Allowances History

The United States and other countries, including Russia and Sweden, have developed slightly different standards for human nutrition. In the United States this standard is called U.S. RDA (Recommended Daily Allowances). The RDA's were established in 1943 and are reviewed and published approximately every five years. This requirement has changed over the years to reflect new scientific evidence supporting the need for a given mineral or vitamin.

b. RDA Criteria

The RDA's are designed to satisfy the needs of a mythical "average healthy person," not the individual. The U.S. RDA does not vary with age or sex and is a single standard used by food manufacturers to give nutritional information about their products. The RDA's basis has six basic criteria:

1. The amount that apparently healthy people consume of the particular nutrient;
2. The amount needed to avoid a particular disease;
3. Physiological function adequacy in relation to the nutrient intake;
4. Nutrient-balance studies which measures nutritional status in relation to intake;
5. Studies of volunteers who were on controlled nutrient-deficient diets;
6. Extrapolation from animal experiments;

These official recommendations reflect levels needed to prevent well-defined deficiency diseases like scurvy, pellagra, and beriberi. (See also Vitamin/Mineral Deficiencies section) Although these diseases in their classical form are no longer a problem in our society, doctors continue to think in terms of small doses of vitamins.

For example, the U.S. RDA for vitamin C is 60 milligrams. This amount is more than enough to prevent scurvy, the disease that decimated the ranks of seamen deprived of fresh food on eighteenth-century voyages. In fact, 10 milligrams of ascorbic acid will do the job. But 60 milligrams of vitamin C may not be sufficient for optimal health.

c. Criticisms of RDA

Senator William Proxmire in 1974 said that "the RDA's have become powerful tools in shaping public policy. It is in the narrow economic interest of the industry to establish low official RDA's because the lower the RDA's the more nutritional their food products appear." He goes on to say that the Food and Nutrition Board was "heavily financed by the food industry." (See Vitamin/Mineral Losses in Processing section)

d. Non-RDA Diets

While it is true that there is the possibility that non-RDA or restricted diets may cause specific health problems, I don't feel that these diets can be ruled out in designing a self-sufficient diet. This is based in part on studies of the limited diets of some tribal societies throughout the world. RDA research still can't explain why a human mother's milk provides only 5% of its calories as protein and RDA diets cannot *ensure* optimum health!

3. U.S. Food Guide Pyramids

a. Food Guide Pyramid

The following figure shows the new "food guide pyramid" currently recommended by the U.S. (FDA/Department of Health/Nutrition Council). There have been no studies that I am aware of on the numbers of people actually adhering to these nutritional guidelines every day.

b. MyPyramid

In 2005 the U.S. government released a new version of the food guide pyramid. This new version is electronic and takes into account the sex and age of the person. A new feature is that it also mentions exercise as a key component to good health.

Food Guide Pyramid
A Guide to Daily Food Choices

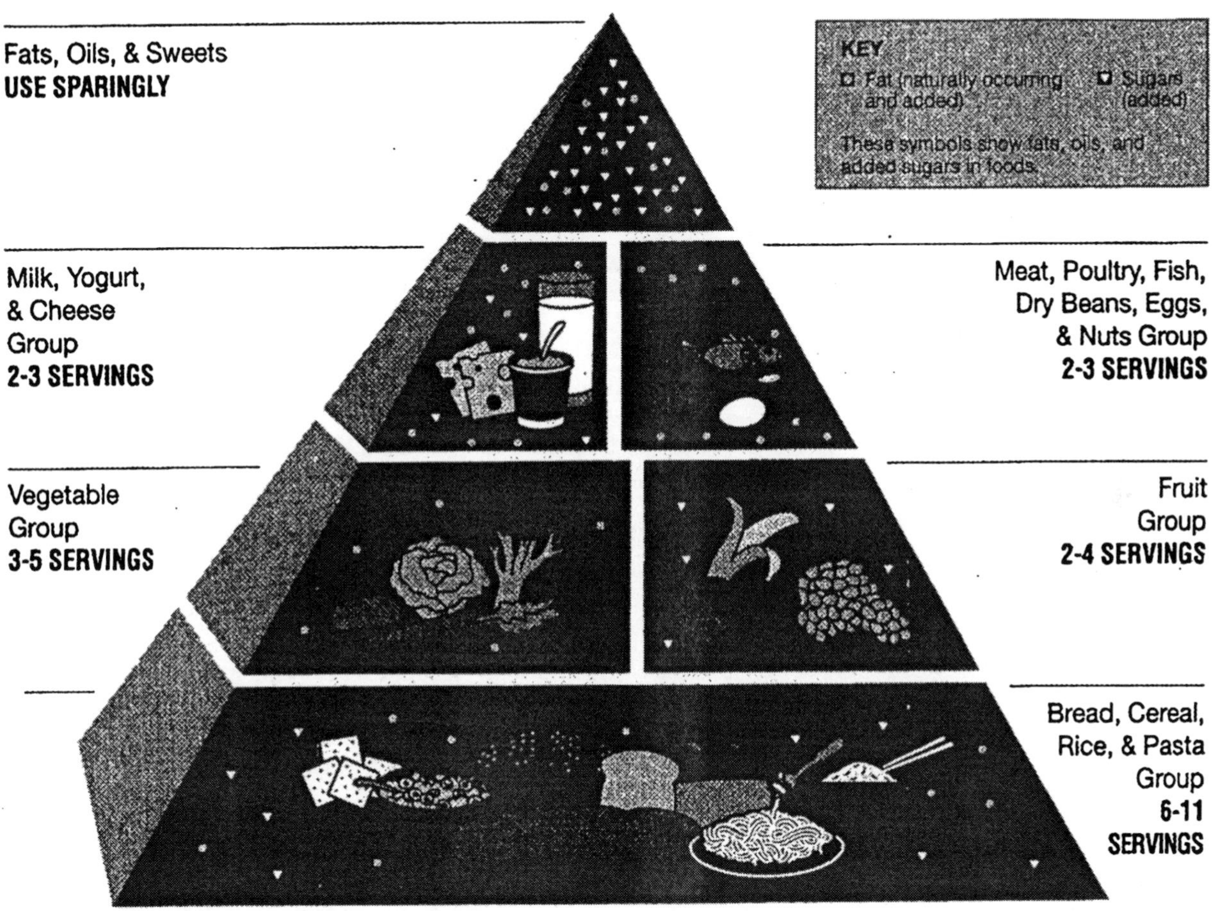

Figure 129-FOOD GUIDE PYRAMID

*Used in Earth Home

4. ODA (Optimum Daily Allowance)

The RDA's have been criticized as not looking at individual differences in diet. One study of laboratory rats showed that some needed up to 40 times as much vitamin A as others-even though they were inbred and are supposed to have a very similar heredity.

An optional nutrition guide is the ODA or Optimum Daily Allowance. This is a more personalized approach to nutritional needs. It weighs several factors: age; weight; family history; emotional, physical, and environmental stress. These amounts are often, although not always, in excess of the amounts in the RDA.

5. Vitamin and Mineral Supplemented Diets

a. Why Take Supplements?

It has been said that to derive the same amount of vitamins and minerals your grandparents did from food alone, you would have to consume six large meals per day! That is one incentive for people to take vitamin and mineral supplements such as blue-green algae and multivitamins. Another reason that people take supplements is to protect their bodies against the effects of a polluted environment. Recent research on free radical pathology supports the taking of supplements.

A tremendous amount of current research on nutrition has been focused on micronutrients--vitamin supplements. ***Nearly half of Americans now take vitamin and mineral supplements.*** Many Americans take them to ensure that they get enough of each element. Some of the most frequent chemicals deficient in most diets are calcium, silicon, and selenium. The term "cellular health" emphasizes the importance of nutrient supplementation for optimum health.

b. Evolution/Manufacture of Supplements

Commercial grade vitamin and mineral concentrates have historically been synthesized by the big pharmaceutical and chemical industries from the same starting material that drugs are made from; coal tar, petroleum products, animal by-products, waste and fecal matter, ground rocks, stones, shells, and metal. After that, they are then bulk sold to the various nutrient manufacturers who are just middlemen that do the mixing. Most of them assume that a vitamin is a vitamin. This idea is reinforced by the U.S.P.(United States Pharmacopoeia).

They say that if a product looks similar under a microscope, or in analysis, that it is the same regardless of what it is made out of. For instance, salicylic acid (U.S.P.) is considered identical whether it comes from wintergreen leaves or by boiling coal in carbolic and sulfuric acids. It also considers glycerin (U.S.P.) identical whether it is made from fresh vegetables, toxic minerals, or boiled down animal carcasses, cartilage, and feet. Basically, no one is grinding up fresh raw vegetables and organic grains to make vitamin pills!

Many recent suppliers of vitamin and mineral supplements extensively advertise the source of their products. The trend today is to know more about any particular diet supplement that a person is taking regularly.

c. Vitamins—Water Soluble/Fat Soluble

Vitamins can be separated into two broad groups: water-soluble and fat-soluble. The water-soluble vitamins include vitamin C and B vitamins. Water-soluble vitamins begin to be utilized be the body from the minute they are absorbed through your digestive system and must be replenished regularly. Since they are not stored, but quickly excreted from the body, toxicities are virtually unknown.

*Used in Earth Home

Fat-soluble vitamins, on the other hand, stay in the body for a longer period of time. Vitamins A, D, E, and K belong to this group. They are usually stored in fat (lipid) tissue, but some may also be stored in some organs, especially the liver. Therefore, you can have toxicity problems with some of the fat-soluble vitamins, but only when you take very large doses.

d. Minerals-Macro

Minerals can also be categorized into two groups: the "macro" or bulk minerals and the "micro" or trace minerals. The macro minerals (calcium, magnesium, and phosphorous) are needed in larger amounts than the trace minerals. Minerals are primarily stored in bone and muscle tissue.

Virtually all minerals used in nutrient manufacture are basically dirt. The iron, calcium, zinc, etc. are just mined ore, pulverized and powdered to a fine dust. These are still difficult to assimilate by our bodies. In fact, research tells us that minerals of this type are 99% inassimilable! In order to better use these minerals, the companies added pig digestive enzymes which chelates it. This was a way to make the body use more of the minerals.

e. Trace Minerals-Micro

Trace minerals include zinc, iron, copper, manganese, chromium, selenium, iodine, and potassium. ***Over the last 50 years the soil has given up most of its trace minerals.*** These minerals are only available in minute quantities and have not been replenished by fertilizing and composting. (See Soil Depletion Section) Modern science is just now finding out the health importance of some of these rare minerals and chemicals. Figure 92 shows the trace minerals in ancient man as opposed to modern man and some reasons for this difference.

f. Miscellaneous Supplements

It is interesting to note that historically, one supplement that has been proven to benefit the body is the simple **aspirin** tablet-and nobody seems to know exactly why! Aspirin was extracted from tree bark at least as far back as ancient Roman times. It is only in recent studies that this benefit is being called to question.

A recent major research study in Canada found an aspirin a day can actually increase the risk of stroke and heart attack in 40% of the people who take it. There are at least three other studies from Germany, Britain, and the U.S. that support this finding. Aspirin can also accelerate the breakdown of joint cartilage, cause gastrointestinal bleeding, and has been linked to eye damage.

5. "Natural" Supplementation

a. Colloidal Minerals

"Colloidal minerals" or plant-derived minerals have been gaining in popularity as a food supplement to give the body more than what it needs for trace minerals and other compounds. (See Vitamin/Mineral files) These minerals are in liquid form and much easier for the body to absorb since all minerals used by the body are "angstrom" sized. This is much smaller than can be broken down by other methods of mineral manufacture.

b. Eating Clay for Nourishment

Over two hundred cultures worldwide eat dirt on a daily basis. The dirt of choice for many is clay. In India, some pour tea into new-formed clay teacups, drink the tea, and then eat the cups. In South America, some cultures mix clay with honey and sugar as a sweet dessert, to be eaten after meals. In Europe, clay is sold for its gastrointestinal benefits and its purification properties. Eating clay is known as geophagy or pica and has been used as a famine food through history.

*Used in Earth Home

Animals are instinctively drawn to clay, often when it is in the form of mud. Deer, elk, coyote, and lynx gather in certain areas that contained clay. The animals lick the clay or, if injured, roll around in it to obtain relief from their injuries. Other animals that eat clay are brown and black bears, woodchucks, butterflies, lambs, rats and many other herbivorous animals.

There are seven groups of clay. They include kaolin, illite, smectite, chlorite, vermiculite, mixed-layer, and lath-form. The smectite includes montmorillonite minerals that contain very small particles. It is this group that is the most preferred group of minerals for ingestion. In particular, calcium montmorillonite seems to be the chemical of choice.

There are eight basic reasons why people eat clay. They include instinct, medicinal, detoxification, mineral supplementation/deficiency, religious rites, famine food, positive effect on pregnancy, and a delicacy among certain cultures.

c. Eating Sea Salt as Supplement

Sea salt contains 92 essential minerals that are found in the ocean. Twenty-four of these are known to be essential to maintain life. Salt is the single element required for the proper breakdown of plant carbohydrates into usable and assimilable human food. How and why the body uses many substances will continue to consume much research time.

H. Bodily Needs/Wants

1. Cell Chemistry/Functions

It has been known for a long time that there isn't a cell in the body that lasts longer than seven years. Most people are surprised to learn that the majority of cells do not live nearly as long. A body could grow several fingernails in a year; flesh cells take only two years to be replaced; blood cells are old in 14 days; and we rebuild a new heart every thirty days! We humans (along with the guinea pig, monkeys, apes, a type of bat, and a rare rat) do not have the ability to generate vitamin C in our livers. Constant chemical changes are taking place within the cells of our bodies every second of the day and night.

2. Body Needs

a. Six Nutrients Needed Regularly

The body needs six nutrients on a regular basis for energy, organ function, food utilization, cell growth and repair, and just plain good health. These nutrients are carbohydrates, proteins, fats, minerals, vitamins, and water.

Between 50,000 and 100,000 different chemicals go into the making and running of the human body. They interact with each other in ways so complex that they make the world's most advanced computer look like an abacus. Recent nutritionists say that the human body needs 60 minerals, 16 vitamins, 12 essential amino acids, and 3 essential fatty acids for perfect health.

b. Omega-3 Essential Fatty Acid (EFA)

Omega-3 is a group of cold-climate ultrapolyunsaturates including alpha linolenic acid that is very important to primates and man. It comes mainly from northern plants and fish. One-half to one teaspoon of linseed oil from flaxseed is one of the best sources for omega-3 EFA. It is marketed as "oil of flaxseed" supplement.

We have been systematically eliminating these for more than 60 years by food oil refining, cereal milling, and food selection patterns. The lack of this EFA in our diets has been linked to a myriad of diseases and health problems including heart disease and cancer. In fact, a deficiency of Omega-3 fatty acids is associated with over 50 common diseases!

c. Individual Needs

There are twenty-five documented inborn errors of metabolism, some of which can increase an individual's vitamin requirements by a factor of 10 to 1000. These have obvious symptoms and include Cooley's anemia (iron) and Wilson's disease (copper). Experiments have shown that it is highly probable that many individuals may have difficulties with specific nutrients on a more subtle scale which may not be so easily diagnosed. These may, however, diminish a person's quality of life and be implicated in future problems as serious as cancer and heart disease.

I believe that we all come into this world with our own individual biological blueprint and continue to change and undergo different life experiences, such as environmental pollution, stress, disease, drug therapy, and aging. Each of these has the potential for increasing our needs and/or interfering with the metabolism of nutrients. In particular, stress has been studied as a factor in changing nutritional needs of an individual.

Our bodies contain an inherent huge amount of tolerance for body punishment. When we eat foods that are "not good" for us or that is incompatible with our nutritional requirements and balance-we suffer. We are warned in subtle ways such as cramps, indigestion, diarrhea, drowsiness, or a general loss of energy. Most Americans are missing at least one essential nutrient in their bodies-most likely calcium, zinc, folic acid, magnesium, or vitamin A, C, E, or B_6. Diets many times slip into a state of being taken for granted and less important. I believe that the body is capable of "communicating" dietary needs by sudden, strong preferences for certain foods. (See Note on Eating "Mechanics" section)

d. Seasonal Needs/Wants

As with the animals, humans have seasonal preferences or diet shifts. Some people get an urge to eat more in the fall of the year supposedly in a reaction to cold weather approaching. This behavior is similar to the hibernation instinct in bears. Hot weather diets are heavy on fluids, raw foods, and low fat foods. Cool weather foods include more concentrated foods, cooked foods, and more oils and protein.

3. pH/Acid/Alkaline Interrelationships

a. Body Maintenance Functions

Our human body must maintain many constant functions. It has to keep in delicate balance all of the following functions:

1) The body temperature of 98.6 degrees F.
2) Acidity and alkalinity of the body fluids at pH 7.4
3) The concentration of certain chemicals dissolved in the body fluids.
4) The glucose level in the blood.
5) The amount of body fluids.
6) The levels of O2 and CO, in the blood.
7) The amount of blood in the body.

The organs, the inner fluid environment, and the cells are all dependent on each other. All these seemingly automatic checks and balances taking place constantly are an incredible testimony to the complexity of the human body.

b. pH Background

pH level is measured on a scale of 0 to 14. The midpoint, 7, is considered to be neutral; above 7 is alkaline and below 7 is acidic. The higher the number, the more alkaline--the lower the number, the more acidic.

The pH level varies in different areas of the body. For example, the pH of the blood should be at about 7.35-7.4, whereas the pH of stomach (gastric) juices range from 1.0 to 3.5. The intestines need an alkaline environment of 7.0 or higher for the various enzymes of the intestine to function properly. If the intestines are too acidic, then the enzymes cannot junction. This can create bacterial disturbances, congestion, and a breakdown of the intestinal wall. An overly acidic environment in the intestines can create various symptoms, including gas, constipation, diarrhea, bloating, colon irritation, and disease. Some health regimens suggest checking a person's urine daily for pH.

c. pH/Alkalinity Goal

Many diet practitioners recommend that a person eat at least 75% alkaline-forming foods. The average all-American diet consists of about 80% acid-forming foods which creates serious imbalances, toxicity, and congestion in the body. Because processed and refined foods are extremely acidic to our systems, the body creates a buffering system (a chemical process to protect the body from being harmed by the acids).

A mountain of literature suggests that maintaining an alkaline body chemistry will aid in keeping a healthy body. Negative events and certain foods will cause the body to become more acidic which invites attack by diseases. (See Medicine-Nutrition-Related Section) Alkaline water, which is produced by ionizers, also helps to keep the body in the alkaline range of pH.

4. Individual Differences in Food Needs

a. Unique Diet Background

No human being has the same fingerprints, lip prints, or voice prints. Everyone's cornea is different. No two people look 100% exactly alike. No two snowflakes or blades of grass are alike. It logically follows that all people's nutritional needs are not exactly the same as everyone else's.

b. Acid/Alkaline Body Chemistry Types

1. Metabolic Types/Characteristics

There is a theory that says there are two distinct types of body chemistry or body metabolic types. One is acid or sympathetic and the other is alkaline or parasympathetic. This theory is similar to the Chinese principle of duality, or yin and yang. These states reflect the human equilibrium which fluctuates throughout the day and year. The following characteristics describe an acid metabolic type:

1) Action-oriented
2) More nerve energy into energy production
3) Intellectual
4) Fast or catabolic metabolism
5) Lose weight easily, gain with difficulty
6) Prone to tension, constipation, or insomnia
7) Exercise-oriented
8) Energy improves with vitamin C
9) Minimum niacin reaction-heat flushing and tingling of the skin
10) Do better overall on an acid diet

*Used in Earth Home

These characteristics describe an alkaline metabolic type:

1) Inaction-oriented
2) More nerve energy into digestion and internal function
3) Intuitive
4) Slow, anabolic metabolism
5) Gain weight easily, lose with difficulty
6) Prone to lethargy, diarrhea, or insomnia
7) Exercise-avoidant
8) Little effect on energy with vitamin C
9) Big niacin reaction-heat flushing and tingling of the skin
10) Do better overall on an alkaline diet

2. Acid- and Alkaline-Producing Foods

Some acid foods include fruits, vegetables, sea vegetables, millet, seeds, salt, herbs, spices, wine. Some alkaline foods include meat, fish, eggs, beans, grains, nuts, food additives and drugs, beer, and whiskey. (See also Blood Group Specificity Section that follows)

The fact that a certain food measures with an acidic pH does not necessarily mean that the food influences our body to become more acidic. By acid forming or alkaline forming, nutritionists mean the condition foods cause in the body after being ingested. For example, limes, with a pH of 1.9, contain strong acid. However, they are an alkaline forming food.

c. Blood pH/Blood Type

1. Blood Type Theory

There is also a theory that is based on the standard A, B, and O blood grouping. The thought process says that your blood type is the key that unlocks the door to the mysteries of health, disease, longevity, physical vitality, and emotional strength. Your blood type determines your susceptibility to illness, which foods you should eat, and how you should exercise. It can be a factor in your energy levels, in the efficiency with which you "burn" calories, in your emotional response to stress, and perhaps even in your personality. The connection between blood type and diet may sound radical, but it is not. There has always been an incomplete comprehension of the process that is involved in the states of wellness or disease.

The blood type theory looks at the early movements and groupings of people originating at different places on earth. They have generally located where each blood group got its start. The variations, strengths, and weaknesses of each blood group can be seen as part of humanity's continual process of acclimating to different environmental challenges. Most of these challenges have involved the digestive and immune systems.

The theory centers on food lectins. Lectins are tiny proteins in foods, which selectively cause clumping of red blood cells, white blood cells, and cells of the gastro-intestinal tract. If a lectin is compatible with an individual's blood type, better health, immunity, and proper body weight are achieved. When a lectin is incompatible with one's blood type, inflammation occurs and, over time, may lead to food allergies or sensitivities and ultimately, in some cases degenerative diseases. Some cancer researchers have explored the role that food lectins plan in that disease.

Blood type testing related to diet, also known as dietary serotype testing, recognizes that people with different blood types have a genetic affinity of certain foods. The dietary serotype test also takes into account your Rh, MN, Lewis A/B group, and secretor status factors.

2. Blood Group Specificity-A,B,O

Blood group O, the first to evolve, represents the hunter/gatherer type. If you have O blood, you most likely produce large amounts of hydrochloric acid in your stomach, helping you to digest proteins. A diet high in meat, poultry, and fish protein would be ideal for you. Large amounts of fruits and vegetables are also healthful, for they help to balance your acid/alkaline levels. Corn, grains, and dairy products are likely to cause hives, hay fever, gas, bloating, and food allergies.

Blood group A represents the agrarian vegetarian societies that formed early in human history. Evolving later than the O's, the A's produce less hydrochloric acid, which means that protein from animal sources gives them more trouble. Instead, they do best on a diet of vegetables, fruits, grains, and nuts, with very small amounts of meat. Milk and cheese should be avoided altogether. Fruits and vegetables should be eaten raw, since cooking destroys the natural enzymes which help the body digest, absorb, and assimilate nutrients from food.

Blood group B, which evolved after O and A, reflects ancient herding and nomadic societies. People with blood group B, who tend to produce smaller amounts of hydrochloric acid, often need to take hydrochloric acid supplements and enzymes to handle the large amounts of animal protein typical of the standard American diet. Thanks to their genetic inheritance, people with B blood do best as ovo-lacto vegetarians, combining large amounts of fruits and vegetables with eggs, milk, and milk products. They do well to eat limited amounts of sunflower seeds and oil, sesame seeds and oil, chicken, buckwheat, and other foods containing larger amounts of agglutinins.

People with blood group AB, the last to evolve, produce smaller amounts of hydrochloric acid than do the O's, and may need hydrochloric acid and enzyme supplements if they eat large amounts of protein. Overall, they do well eating vegetables, fruits, grains, and seafood, with small amounts of milk and milk products included for flavor and variety. Those in the AB group should refrain from eating large amounts of red meat, chicken, tomatoes, potatoes, and foods high in lectins.

The theory goes on to mention what diseases and afflictions each blood type is prone to. They even further categorize and separate the blood types by having a genetic affinity for certain foods.

3. Blood pH Background

A healthy person's blood pH is 7.35 and a sick person's blood pH is 7.30. Although this is only .05 more acid, this condition invites trouble, since this slight acid increase allows tissues and organs to easily become inflamed. The blood is key to replacing worn-out parts all over the body and should not be underestimated in maintaining good health.

4. Chlorophyll/Hemoglobin Connection

The Nobel Prize Winner Dr. Hans Fischer in 1930 discovered that the green, proteinous compound found in the leaves of plants and grasses (chlorophyll) closely resembles hemoglobin, the pigment that gives human blood its color and oxygen-carrying capacity (See the following figure). The major difference is that chlorophyll has a core of magnesium and hemoglobin a core of iron. They are still looking at the body's possible capabilities to transform plant material into fats and tissue, similar to the way cattle get fat on nothing but green grass and water all summer.

There are also striking similarities between human blood serum and the mineral-rich seawater. Also bee's honey is strikingly similar to blood, except for the K and Na contents. I believe nutritional scientists are still in their infancy in looking at the human body's chemical needs.

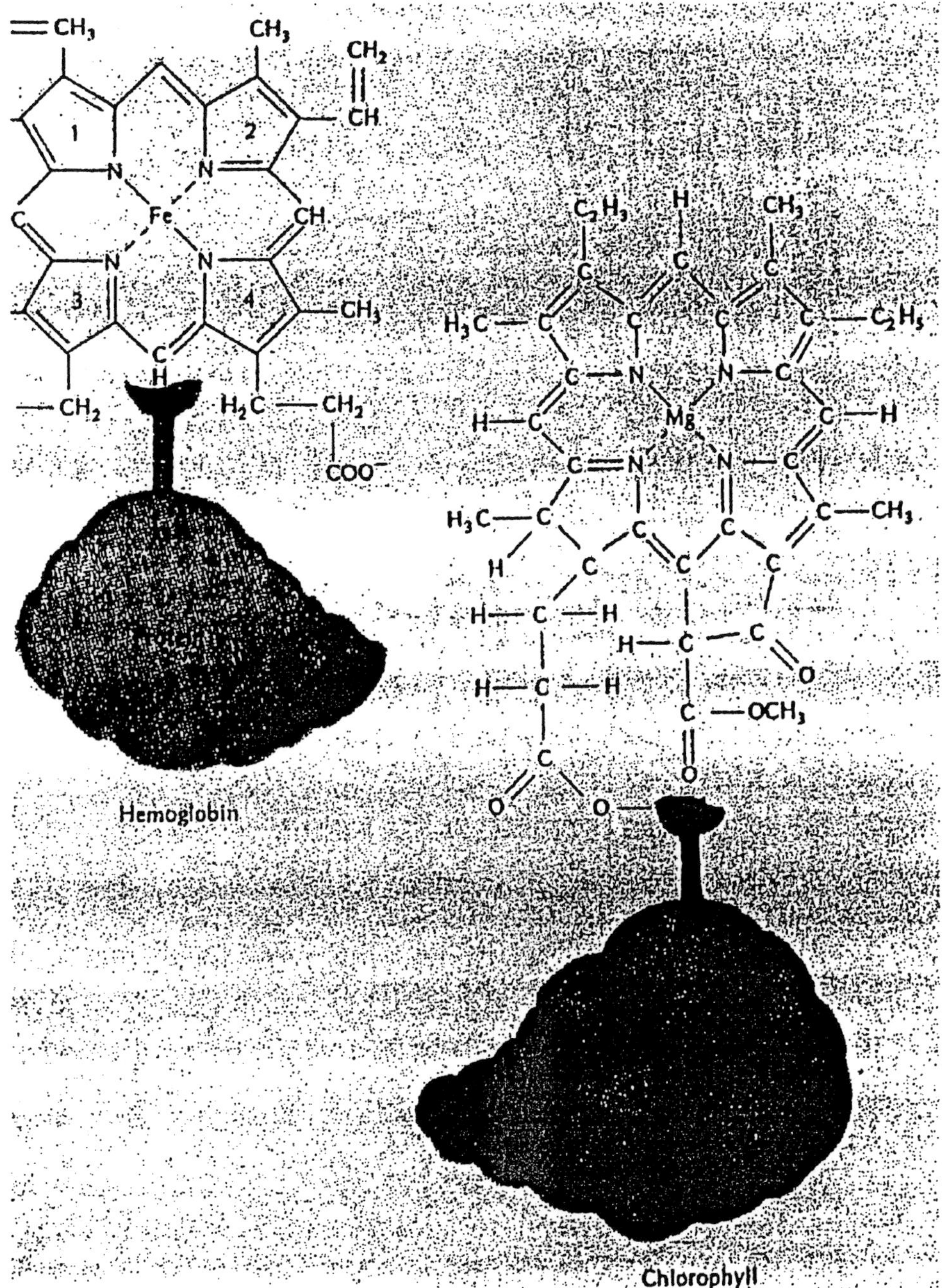

Comparison of Chlorophyll and Hemoglobin

Figure 130-CHLOROPHYLL/HEMOGLOBIN

*Used in Earth Home

d. Body Fluid Diagnosing

The modern human organism must cope with an unprecedented number of burdens on the job and at home. Stress, drug abuse, malnutrition, environmental pollution and disease engender a multiplicity of new health problems which overwhelm conventional diagnostic procedures. A new diagnostic technique has been developed in order to completely diagnose the health of the human body. Biological Terrain Assessment (BTA) analyzes blood, saliva, and urine. The specimens are tested with a device to determine pH, resistivity, and redox values of each of these fluids. This test logic suggests that the key to understanding physical health is to be found in observing the building blocks of life, which can be detected in the bodily fluids. (See also Acid/Alkaline Body Chemistry)

I. Healthy Diet Goals

1. Elements of a Healthy Diet

a. Food as Medicine

There is more and more interest in letting your food be your medicine. People are slowly realizing that food could achieve balance in the body--producing less acidity and more alkalinity in the blood and even calming the mind to lessen the impact of stress. There is an increasing body of scientific evidence that points to food as the *most important* chemical that we put into our bodies. (see Minor Health Care-Medical Nutrition)

b. Nutrients in Soil

1. Soil Nutrient History

At least 16 elements, called plant nutrients, are essential for plant growth. The first group includes three elements-carbon, hydrogen, and oxygen, which are over 90% of the basic building blocks of all plant compounds. Carbon dioxide and water supply them.

The 10% second group of essential elements, called macronutrients, consists of nitrogen, phosphorus, and potassium. sulfur, calcium, and magnesium. They are classified as macronutrients because they are used in relatively large quantities by plants and are normally supplied in ionic form in the soil. Nitrogen comes originally from the 78% nitrogen content in the air which plants cannot use in this form. Bacteria and leguminous plants take the nitrogen from the air (and hydrogen) and fix it in the plant roots or soil for plants to use.

The 1% last group of micronutrients is used in small quantities. This group includes iron, zinc, manganese, copper, boron, molybdenum, and chlorine, as well as trace amounts of others such as silicon and sodium.

Minerals are basic constituents of the earth's crust and plants "drink them up" from the soil enzymes and vitamins are produced in plant tissues. ***As mentioned earlier, most of the foods we eat are raised on the same soil for the last 30 years. Significant amounts of minerals have been removed from the soil.*** (See Pollution/Soil Problems) Typically only three (NPK) minerals are added back.

This results in vegetables with nutrients levels lower than they once were. One estimate show that the nutrients in the American food supply have declined on average 25-50% over the last 20 years based on an analysis of data on the USDA's Internet site. Levels of protein, calcium, phosphorus, iron, riboflavin, and vitamin C have all dropped—by as much as 38 percent.

Carrots may vary a hundred-fold in their concentration of carotene (vitamin A) and samples of fresh tomato juice have shown 16-fold differences in vitamin C! Vegetables grown in different parts of the country will vary in acidity and mineral content because of soil differences. Scientific tests show that organic fruits and vegetables contain up to three times more minerals and trace elements than inorganic produce. (See Vitamins/Minerals files) On top of that, about 60% of the U.S. produce is harvested several days before they are ripe and often treated to retard perishability.

In some African lands, pregnant women and their babies supplement their diet with soil from termite mounds that are enriched with calcium. These Banto women consume only one-fourth as much calcium as American women and avoid any calcium-deficiency problems such as osteoporosis. Thus, they bypass agricultural products that most of us depend on for calcium.

Historically, vitamins and minerals have also come from ingesting sea salt. Salt that has been made from evaporating sea salt contains many vitamins and minerals. Sea salt from the Celtic coast also contains other trace minerals and is commonly sold in health food stores.

2. Earth Home Soil Nutrients

The Earth Home System will have complete control of the soil medium so nutrients can be worked into the soil--giving the plants access to them. The nutrient content of the plants will then be much higher than the commercial variety. (Note that vegetables are generally a better source of minerals and fruit a better source of vitamins.) Plants can provide nutrition at a high level so those contemporary food groups can be combined.

2. Protein Needs Discussion

a. Protein Needs or Wants

It is often said that Americans eat too much protein. The World Health Organization recommends 40 grams of protein per day. The U.S. recommended dietary allowance (RDA) is 56 grams for men and 44 grams for women, yet the average consumption is 96 grams for men and 64 grams for women. It is reported that the amount of "complete" protein a person requires per day is about .015 ounces per pound of body weight. This comes to around 2 ounces (56 grams) per day, depending on the size of the person.

However, athletes have proven that they can train for and win international championships on a 50-gram protein diet instead of the usual 120 grams. ***The Earth Home diet will allow lowering to this level of protein by using meals with carbohydrates, starches and vegetables as a main portion, and protein served in smaller portions.*** The Earth Home diet will allow the option to be higher in vegetables and fiber, and low in fat. (See also Protein Diets)

b. Protein Sources—Plant vs. Animal

It is interesting to note that a full two-thirds of the world's protein supply is obtained from plant sources, while only one-third is from animal sources. Only 10% of the protein and calories we feed to our livestock is recovered in the meat we eat. Grain consumption directly accounts for about half the calories consumed in the world. Seventy-eight percent of all our grain goes to animals. It is said that if Americans ate half as much meat we would release enough food for the entire developing world! There are many arguments for some form of vegetarianism.

c. Protein Complementarity for Vegetarian Diets

A mixed vegetarian diet with or without eggs or dairy products can theoretically supply adequate protein, though it may take more effort than with the omnivorous diet. As long as the diet is not filled with a lot of sugars and other empty calories, the protein content is usually adequate. Protein combination, or complementarity, suggests mixing of two or more vegetable protein foods at a meal so as to provide sufficient levels of all the essential amino acids. Usually one or two of these amino acids may be low in each food, and mixing them at the same meal will mean that our body has what it needs to make new proteins. Some examples of incomplete proteins are: grains (low in lysine, isoleucine), legumes (low in tryptophan, methionine), seeds and nuts (low in lysine, isoleucine), and vegetables (vary-but most low in methionine, isoleucine).

3. Carbohydrates in the Diet

a. Types of Carbohydrates

Carbohydrates are the source of our energy. A carbohydrate consists of carbon, hydrogen, and oxygen. The formula of any of these compounds may be expressed as C (H2O). There are three types of carbohydrates. The simplest carbohydrates are the monosaccharides, of which the most important for us is glucose. Next are the disaccharides, which are made by two monosaccharide molecules joined together by an oxygen atom, with the elimination of a molecule of water. The most important disaccharides are sucrose (ordinary cane sugar), lactose, and maltose. The third type of carbohydrates are the polysaccharides, which have enormous molecules made of many monosaccharide units-about 10 for glycogen, 25 for starch, and 100 to 200 for cellulose.

b. Carbohydrate Digestion Speeds

Having small molecules, monosaccharides reach the intestinal wall and are absorbed directly into the body without any change of chemical compounds. Since disaccharides have slightly larger molecules, they must be broken down to monosaccharides by various enzymes. That is to say, sucrose will be broken down to glucose by invertase, maltose by maltase, and lactose by lactase. Then this simple sugar is absorbed through the intestinal wall. The absorption of monosaccharides and disaccharides very fast, and within a short time digested glucose enters the bloodstream. The polysaccharides take much longer.

4. Raw Foods for Health

a. Raw Food

1. Raw Food Research

Sweden, Finland, and Switzerland probably lead the world into research on the biochemical properties and physiological effects of raw foods. In Britain, Australia, New Zealand, and South Africa there are physicians and naturopaths who quietly heal their patients on raw vegetable diets. Raw foods are a part of their treatment for obesity, high blood pressure, diabetes, and even cancer. A very high order of the sun's energy is converted by plants through photosynthesis and then stored in them. Since the quality of this energy is degraded by all kinds of physical and chemical processes such as wilting, cooking, or processing, when we eat the fresh raw plants themselves we receive the very highest order of energy possible direct from our food. Some estimates put the percentage raw food at 60% to 75% in order to be effective.

2. Raw Food Benefits/Effects

When physicians and biochemists were asked why raw foods have such an energizing effect, they said several factors were responsible:

--A high-raw diet offers, in perfect and complementary combination, all the nutrients essential for maximum vitality at the whole body and at the cellular level.
--Raw foods cleanse the body of stored wastes and toxins that interfere with the proper functioning of cells and organs and lower energy levels.
--Raw foods increase the micro-electric potential of cells, improving your body's use of oxygen so that both muscles and brain are energized.
--Since a high raw diet is almost inevitably low in protein and low in fat it makes for better functioning overall. Too much fat slowly starves tissues of oxygen and too much protein exhausts the body's mineral reserves and creates an inordinate amount of toxic waste. Eating raw food is the manner of living for all other living creatures *except* man. Lipase is found only in raw foods. ***Cooking at 118 deg. F. or higher destroys lipase and all other enzymes.***

b. Raw Juices

Juicing consists of taking the edible part of fruits and vegetables and crushing or squeezing the mass until the pulp is separated from the juice portion. Interest in raw juices increased in the 19th century when humans were treating cancer diseases with fresh juice diets. Data suggests many other debilitating diseases were actually cured with only large amounts of fresh juice daily. There exist a number of books that say that all life on earth emanates from the green of the plant and that nothing is more therapeutic than green juices. Two to four glasses of fresh juice daily is an excellent source of vitamins, minerals, enzymes, purified water, proteins (amino acids), carbohydrates, and chlorophyll. In addition, they provide a source of cellulose and bioflavonoids.

Juices separate these elements, compounds, and the distilled water in the food from the fibers. This liquid food is digested quickly in a matter of minutes-rather than the normal hours. Also, digesting whole vegetables and food uses energy. Juices are intended to supplement the diet-not replace the body's need for fiber in foods such as whole grain breads, raw vegetables, etc. Some modern research suggests that the body can break down the cellular structure of raw vegetables and assimilate from 1-35% of the elements. When juiced, the figure climbs to about 92%.

c. Chlorophyll Benefits

When crude chlorophyll is fed to anemic rabbits, it restores normal red blood cell counts within 15 days and is apparently completely non-toxic. Chlorophyll has an impressive record of successfully treating all kinds of ailments of the body. It has the rare ability to internally "cleanse" the body and also to heal. (See Chlorophyll/Hemoglobin section) Chlorophyll also has been shown to be an excellent natural supplement—helping with slow bowel transit time, nourishing the friendly colon bacteria, and ridding of odorous gasses.

5. Live Food and Enzymes

a. Enzymes Explained

Enzymes are complex organic substances produced in plants and animals that catalyze (speed up) chemical reactions in cells and organs. There are many digestive enzymes in the body. Working with body fluids, they help to break down large chemical chains into smaller particles. The body is able to absorb these smaller food particles and utilize them. Without enzymes, the body functions would be too slow to sustain life.

The body's production of enzymes diminishes significantly with age. This is one of the many reasons why it is harder to lose weight as one gets older. Many serious diseases have been tied to enzyme deficiencies. These range from cancer, diabetes, heart disease, high blood pressure, lupus, and multiple sclerosis. Early skin aging can also be traced to enzyme deficiencies.

b. Enzymes Through History

Humans (and their domesticated animals) are the only creatures on earth that eat their food without its natural enzymes (i.e. cooked). Many people believe that this is one reason people suffer from cancer and other degenerative conditions that animals in the wild are free from. (See Vitamin/Mineral Losses in Processing/Cooking of Foods) The widest use of enzymes by man is the oriental cultures who utilize enzymes to produce miso, tofu, tempeh, and sake. Enzymes in the process of autolysis are also utilized in the diet of the Eskimo to "pre-digest" some of the food that they eat. They conserve their own enzymes by arranging for outside enzymes to help digest their food. Claims of surplus energy and a feeling of well-being have been reported.

c. Probiotics/Prebiotics

Probiotics are an important part of the complex world of foods that are good for health. Probiotics are foods that contain live bacteria. It is the bacteria and metabolites which they produce that give these probiotics their health promoting properties. The best known example of a probiotic is yogurt. The bacteria which are found in probiotic products such as yogurt, kefir, and fermented vegetables usually aren't found in the human intestine.

Fructooligosaccharides (FOS) have been known as prebiotics for some time, but have been joined by galactooligosaccharides and other digestion resistant carbohydrates. FOS are compounds made up of fructose sugar molecules linked together in long chains. They can be found naturally in such foods as Jerusalem artichoke tubers, onions, leeks, some grains, and honey. We are still learning about the benefits of bacteria and how they affect our health.

d. Enzyme Classes/Functions

Enzymes are catalysts that take amino acids and renew cells, make hormones, muscles, blood, and organs. They are activators in the chemical reactions that are continually taking place in our bodies. There are three classes of enzymes: metabolic enzymes, which run our bodies; digestive enzymes, which digest our food; and food enzymes from raw foods, which start food digestion. Vitamins function by and large as co-enzymes that also help us digest food. They are at the very foundation of all our bodily functions. Enzymes are what *makes* things happen, and happen faster. Without enzymes, you could not breathe, blink, or walk.

e. Benefits of Enzymes

Enzyme-rich foods such as sprouts, fresh vegetables, fruits, and their juices, are the most important factors in slowing the aging clock and also to inhibit potential carcinogens. Fermented cabbage (sauerkraut) also adds digestive enzymes. Live foods (particularly sprouts) have the capacity to strengthen the immune system and help us to lead long and healthy lives. It is the activity of enzymes that converts starches into sugars, proteins into amino acids, and fats into fatty acids inside the sprout. The food enzymes in sprouts not only work to digest themselves, but help the body to digest other foods as well.

f. Sources of Enzymes

When sprouts, for example, are eaten raw they are a good source of important food enzymes that aid in the digestion of starch, protein, and fat. The best sources of natural enzymes are apple cider vinegar, sprouts, honey, yogurt, and raw juices. The vinegar must be organic and not processed with high heat (such as distilled or pasteurized) which kills the enzymes.

They are sensitive to temperatures above 118 degrees F. Between 126 and 130 degrees F they are dead. Enzymes can be preserved at any low temperature without loss. ***We kill enzymes by baking, barbecuing, boiling, braising, brewing, broiling, charbroiling, frying, microwaving, sautéing, scalding, simmering, stewing, and toasting.***

g. Amino Acids

There are eight essential amino acids obtained in foods and another 12 that the body can build internally. The eight essential amino acids are lysine, leucine, tryptophan, phenylalanine, threonine, valine, and methionine.

6. Whole Foods

Whole foods are defined as foods that have no part removed and only minimally processed. It is by definition in much the same form as nature made it. Whole grains are a good example of a whole food. Whole foods are vastly superior in both taste and nutrition. Some foods with little traditional nutrient value (no protein and little vitamins and minerals) can have a substantial effect on health. The apple is one such food.

J. Earth Home Diet

1. Overview/Philosophy

a. Eat Alkaline-Forming Foods

A sick person is seldom happy, but a well person often is! A healthy body creates a happy mental state as well. A healthy diet cannot be underestimated in a person's overall happiness. Foods can be classified as acid-forming or alkaline-forming, even though they may not be acid or alkaline by themselves. The end result of eating a certain food is the important criteria.

b. Emphasize Plant Sources

In designing a system for a healthy diet and complete food self-sufficiency, I had to take into account the complex interdependency between plants, animals, and humans (see Plant Selection section). ***The Earth Home system is meant to use as many plant sources as possible for protein***. Plants are stressed wherever possible because of ease of production and "feed efficiency". Also, remember that two-thirds of the world's protein supply is presently obtained from plant sources, while only one-third is from animal sources.

A complete vegetarian diet can supposedly be grown on a quarter-acre of land (1 acre for a family of 4). The Earth Home diet is close to this estimate, with the addition of feed-efficient small animals, fish, fowl, and some eggs.

2. Food Groups-General

a. Soups and Stews

Soups and stews will be the mainstay of the EH diet. Soy flour thickeners will be used to add body and protein to these dishes. Protein such as fish, fowl, or eggs can be used in conjunction with these or in salads.

b. Leafy Green Salads

1. Leafy Greens

The leafy greens are probably the richest in nutrients of any foods in the vegetable kingdom. And usually the greener they are, the more nutritious they are. Salads will provide the bulk of the vegetable needs by mixing of many kinds of varying nutrients in leafy and other forms. Flavoring greens such as the tasty portions of leaves such as horseradish, nasturtium, lovage, and day lilies can be added.

2. Croutons/Sprouts/Toppings

Special "croutons" made from such things as comfrey, wheat, and soy products will be added. Barley leaves will also be added to the croutons for high vitamin and mineral content. Radishes will always be available because of their short maturity times. Roasted soybeans and fresh sprouts will be used to top the salad.

3. Oils

Vinegar and oil from soybeans and/or rapeseeds will be used to top the salads. Herb or vegetables will be added to the vinegar and allowed to age awhile to add flavor. Any excess oil that is made will be used for cooking such as fish. Some flax may be raised to produce nutritional linseed oil or flaxseed oil, which is a good source of cooking fat. Linseed oil has been used as a kitchen oil for thousands of years.

c. Fermented Foods

Sauerkraut and other kraut foods will be eaten regularly in the EH diet. These are shown to provide vitamin C and enzymes in the diet. Examples are lettuce kraut and mustard green kraut. (see Fermented Foods section)

d. Vegetable Juices

Juices will be a key player in the overall energy requirements of the family. Carrots with wheatgrass and sprouts in particular will provide a large part of the basic juice requirements. It contains a very high concentration of essential amino acids.

e. Pasta/Starches/Bread

Pastas will consist of wheat, soy, rapeseeds, broccoli meal, and artichoke products flavored with other herbs. Bread is a staple food in most cultures. (Wheat sourdough bread is mentioned in Egyptian history more than 4,000 years ago and can be made without yeast.) The use is intended to be similar to the japatis (chapatis) of Africa, baked injeras of Ethiopia, teff pancake, or tortillas. This combination bread/pancake should also minimize the use of utensils that would have to be washed. (Note that the EH is designed to have drying and grinding capabilities). Kudzu roots can also be made into starchy products and thickeners for soup. Kudzu has served as a famine food in Japan. The kudzu plants will be primarily used for animal fodder, though.

f. Meat/Meat Substitutes and Extenders

Protein sources such as fish, fowl, or eggs can be used for any meal but their use will be limited because of the "cost" in terms of effort to produce. Wheat gluten can be used as a close substitute for meat. It must be prepared before use and stored similar to meat. It can also be used as an extender and mixed up to 75% of the total volume. Beans can be used in a similar fashion.

Tofu is one of the most versatile of protein foods in the world. This fresh soybean curd can be stir-fried for a meat substitute or used as a cheese substitute.

g. Beverages/Tea

Tea is the most popular beverage in the world. EH beverages would consist of herbal teas for the most part such as Rosa Rugosa and alfalfa. Switchel was a refreshing drink commonly drank during haying season. It can be made with cold water and apple cider vinegar. This can be sweetened with honey if desired.

There are many possibilities to flavor water and sweeten. Just a few berries or juniper berries in a jug of water will flavor it if left for a few hours. Even soymilk would fill in for dairy products such as milk if the effort to make it was expended.

h. Raw Foods

Raw uncooked food would be used as snacks between meals. Vegetables and fruits that transport well would be better suited. (About 60% of the diet will be raw foods in salads, soups, stews, and "pita-style" sandwiches.)

*Used in Earth Home

i. Sweetener Options

Sweeteners are available and some are subject to location. Note that Jerusalem artichokes help reduce the craving for sweets!

1. Honey

Honey has historically been held in high regard for thousands of years. In fact, more than half of all remedies prescribed by Egyptian doctors contained honey! Pure honey is the only food that will not spoil.

2. Barley Malt Syrup

Also sprouted and ground grain can be used as a sweetener in place of honey. Germinated grains of barley yields maltose, which has been used as a sweetener for centuries. Barley malt syrup consists of mostly maltose (with some glucose) and contains significant amounts of protein starch and trace elements.

3. Stevia Rebaudiana

Another option for a sweetener is Stevia Rebaudiana. Stevia is a natural herb from the rain forests of Paraguay and has been used for 1500 years. It also possesses many medicinal healing properties and contains many nutrients (calcium, potassium, sodium, magnesium, zinc, rutin, iron, phosphorus, vitamins A and C, and more). It is one of the few sweeteners with a true alkaline pH level. Stevia has no calories and is much sweeter than sugar.

The purest form of Stevia is the whole leaf plant, ground into either a fine powder of extracted into a concentrated water-based extract. It can be grown inside and the leaves used in tea. About 8 plants should provide enough sweeteners for a typical family's needs. Japan is extensively using Stevia for much of their sweet needs.

4. Strawberries/Grapes

The Earth Home system has strawberries and grapes as fruits of choice because of the ease of growing, and the adaptability to various geographical locations.

5. Other Sweetener Options

If a topping is desired, soy butter can be used with honey added as a sweetener. It can be used similar to peanut butter. Also maple syrup can be made from many trees in addition to the maple tree. Box elder and birch trees also can be tapped for their sap, boiled down, and made into good sweeteners.

3. Sample Weekly Menu

It is said that it takes 21 days to break a habit. I believe that a human's eating habits could also be changed in that approximate length of time. The eating habits of an Earth Home family must reflect a change in habits. Natural combinations of foods will be the norm rather than relying on grease or sugar to provide the flavor. A variety of proteins, starches, fruits, and vegetables should be eaten. A sample menu follows.

a. Breakfast

-Wheat/soy flour pancakes with honey/maple syrup, bulgur (wheat) cereal, pan fried (toasted) japatis with grape jam, egg, herb tea, soymilk, strawberries, roasted wheat coffee substitute, rose hip tea are some possibilities.

b. Snacks

-Fruit **or** vegetables (not both) including carrot juice with wheatgrass and artichoke. The juice should be drunk on an empty stomach. The fruit such as grapes should be eaten raw.

*Used in Earth Home

c. Lunch

-Large bowl of soup or stew with fish, onions, garlic, and soybean flour stock. Vegetable leaf tortilla, with meat croutons and veggies.

d. Supper

-Large salad with sprouts, toasted soybeans, fresh vegetables, carrots, fowl (such as chicken) chunks, croutons made from comfrey and vegetable leaves, topped with vinegar flavored with garlic, chives, and basil. Wheat/soy tortillas, sourdough bread, and artichokes are examples of additions to the main course.

e. Seasonal

Sauerkraut, winter squash, sprouts, radishes, dried tomatoes, and alfalfa cuttings are all somewhat seasonal foods. Note that many of the exact recipes are yet to be developed.

4. Specific Cultivar/Food Information

a. Grapes

Grapes are one of the oldest fruits in history. Grape seeds were found in mummy cases in Egyptian tombs that were more than 3,000 years old. The Bible speaks of grape cultivation in the time of Noah. The variety selected must be a multi-purpose grape good for wine (vinegar), raisins for snacks, juice, and table use.

b. Comfrey

Comfrey is the only plant source of vitamin B_{12}. It contains "allantoin" in leaves and roots that are said to have qualities as a cell proliferant, demulcent, and astringent.

c. Cabbage

Cabbage is a calcium-rich healthy vegetable. It has been in cultivation for over 4,000 years. Cabbage provides a good source of natural enzymes for digestion. The best varieties are the reds or Chinese.

d. Garlic

Garlic is known as a natural antibiotic and also goes back thousands of years. Much literature has been written about this plant. Early pyramid builders ate garlic daily for endurance, while the Greeks used it to cure snakebite and pneumonia. During World War I, garlic was used extensively to prevent gangrene and to treat typhus and dysentery. Certain Slavic peoples still eat a clove of raw garlic with each meal during the winter months to prevent colds and flu. In 1858, Louis Pasteur confirmed that garlic juice killed bacteria in laboratory culture dishes, and modern research has confirmed garlic's ability to bolster the human immune system. Garlic is also high in selenium, which is an element that modern vegetables are sorely lacking because of soil depletion.

e. Carrots

Carrots are a superior source of Vitamin A and keeps very well. Much literature has been written about the health and healing qualities of carrot juice. Even racehorses are fed carrots for utmost performance.

*Used in Earth Home

f. Soybeans

1. Food Bean Soybeans

Soybeans are one of the oldest crops grown by man, and its first mention in Chinese records goes back a little beyond 2000 B.C. Soybeans are the only source of all the essential amino acids. The secret of any soybean dish is the proper seasoning, for the beans themselves are rather flat in taste and need added flavoring in the form of soy sauce, onions, or tomatoes. After fermenting with a mold, the soy beans become softer and more palatable, more nutritious, and better tasting.

Note: Before soybeans can be grown on new soil, it must be inoculated first with the bacterium they need to fix nitrogen or grow a small crop of soybeans the year before to inoculate.

2. Soy Products/Soy Sauce

Edible soybeans can be made into many different dishes such as tofu for a high protein source. Soymilk was supposedly made first in China during the second century BC. It has been used every since in Eastern Asia much like cow's milk in the West. (See also A Note on Dairy Products). Tempe, a curd cake made from fermented soy beans, is widely eaten as a meat substitute in Indonesia. Soy is possibly the food most often fermented.

The beans must first be soaked for 24 hours and then cooked in order to be used. A pressure cooker greatly reduces the cooking time.

Soy flour can be used in a 1 to 4 ratio with wheat flour when making most grain products. Note that soy sauce is difficult to make at home and is not included in diet at present.

g. Sprouts

Sprouts are a major part of the intended food source for the Earth Home. Sprouts are used more heavily in the wintertime when green or fresh vegetables such as carrots are harder to obtain. They would be used to top salads, ingredients in cooking, or in pitas. Sprouts can also be dried for a crunchy snack

1. Sprouting History

Ancient manuscripts tell us that the Chinese were regularly eating sprouts by about 3000 BC. (See Diets-Survival/Emergency Diet Section)

2. Advantages of Sprouting

Early Chinese writers say that sprouts could help cure bloating, muscular cramps, digestive problems, weak lungs, loss of nerve sensations, inflammation, rheumatism, and dropsy. Sprouts have been used to prevent scurvy (vitamin C) and supply adequate protein. A variety of sprouted seeds, beans, grains, and nuts provide complete protein-or all eight essential amino acids. They are also an excellent source of vitamins. (See also Plants-Sprouts file)

Besides their nutritional advantages, sprouted seeds, beans, and grains have several other significant attributes that make them an ideal addition to a diet and a prime food source.

Sprouts are:

1) Economical. One tablespoon of seeds will fill a quart jar with several ounces of delicious, ready-to-eat sprouts.
2) Ecological. The food value per unit produced is much higher than other foods.

*Used in Earth Home

3) Easy to store. Seeds can be stored in a few glass jars with air-tight lids and a cool, dark storage area for a year or more. After sprouting, they can be placed in plastic containers in the refrigerator.
4) Low in calories/fat. Sprouts are also simple sugars for quick energy.
5) Simple and quick. Sprouting takes minutes per day for 3 to 7 days.

Red winter wheat sprouts are probably the most nutritious, delicious and versatile of all the sprouted grains. High in fiber, protein, amino acids, vitamins A, C, B complex and E, niacin and pantothenic acid. Sprouted wheat is full of the sugar maltose and has a sweet, nutty flavor. It can be used in a wide variety of ways, including sprouted wheat breads and for making wheatgrass juice.

3. Sprouting Directions

Approximately one pound of beans, for example will produce about eight pounds of sprouts. The six rules of sprouting are:

1) Rinse often.
2) Keep them moist, not wet.
3) Keep them at room temperature.
4) Give them plenty of room to breathe.
5) Don't put too many in any one container.
6) Keep them covered-no light.

h. "Supergreens"

1. Wheatgrass Juice

Wheatgrass has the unique ability to sustain life in herbivorous mammals indefinitely. An example is beef cattle that eats nothing but green grass all summer and grows to a very large size. This particular strain was chosen over many others during testing by organizations that were specifically devoted to the health benefits of wheatgrass juice. Wheatgrass is one of the richest natural sources of vitamins A, complete B complex, B_{17}, C, E, and K. ***One ounce of wheatgrass juice is roughly equal to 2 ½ pounds of green leaf vegetables.***

Sprouted wheat that grows into wheatgrass about 8 inches long is a potent source of concentrated nutrition. As it grows, wheatgrass concentrates chlorophyll and other nutrients in preparation for becoming a big, fruitful plant. Wheatgrass itself is not digestible in our stomachs because it is too full of cellulose and other indigestible fibers. But when juiced and strained, all the nutrients are freed up and are readily assimilable by the body. And wheatgrass juice is also a very powerful body detoxifier.

2. Barley Leaves

When barley leaves are 10-14 inches high, they contain all the vitamins, minerals, and proteins necessary for the human diet, plus chlorophyll. They contain the small protein polypeptides that can be directly absorbed by the blood as well as a multitude of enzymes. They contain astounding amounts of vitamins and minerals that include; potassium, calcium, magnesium, iron, copper, phosphorus, manganese, zinc, beta carotene, B1, B2, B6, C, folic acid, and pantothenic acid. Green barley juice contains 11 times the calcium in cow's milk, nearly 5 times the iron in spinach, 7 times the vitamin C in oranges, and 80 mg of vitamin B_{12} per hundred grams. (see Vitamin C sources-Primary section)

i. Vitamin C Sources-Primary

Vitamin C in the diet comes from vegetable sources primarily. The diet must contain enough vitamin C to prevent scurvy and many health experts recommend larger amounts than recommended to fight off disease and colds.

1. Barley Leaves

Barley will be grown for alcohol production as well as the rich source of vitamin C in the young leaves. (See "Supergreens" section)

2. Acerola Cherries

Acerola cherry trees are to be grown inside the dining windows. Acerola cherries contain huge amounts of vitamin C and can be picked on an ongoing basis.

3. Sauerkraut/Lettuce Kraut

The fermentation process will be used to produce vitamin C as well as other food groups. (See Fermentation section)

4. Rosa Rugosa/Citrus

While it is possible to grow citrus trees in the EH, the growth rate is low and it is difficult in northern climates. Even Meyer dwarf lemon trees must be brought inside when the weather gets below 10 deg. F. Rosa Rugosa trees grown on the outside will provide some vitamin C.

5. Other Vegetables

Some other vegetables such as carrots have significant quantities of vitamin C in them. (See also "Supergreens" section above) It has been shown that cooking carrots frees up more vitamins and minerals from the woody parts than if they had been eaten raw.

j. Vinegar

1. Vinegar Background/History

A staple seasoning and ages-old medicinal throughout much of East Asia, vinegar, from the French meaning "sour wine" implies the use of grapes. However, grape vinegar has not played much of a role in Asian cooking. The Chinese, who were the first to make vinegar, used grains such as millet and barley, honey, fruits including peaches, dates, grapes, and cherries, and of course, rice. Vinegar has been used for over 10,000 years.

2. Making Vinegar

Vinegar can be made from maple syrup, grains, honey, grapes, apples, as well as many other things. Vinegar is made from alcohol by simply adding "mother of vinegar" enzymes. This moldy residue contains the living organisms that turn alcohol into vinegar. Making alcohol takes 1-6 weeks and vinegar takes a few months more. (See also Energy/Power section on Alcohol/Vinegar).

Apple cider vinegar has specifically been singled out as being the most important from a health point of view. Today, vinegar is employed as an antiseptic, internally and externally.

3. Vinegar Alternatives

An "alternative vinegar" can be made from the unfermented acidic juice of unripe grapes or apples. This "verijuice" was used in the same way as vinegar, and its milder flavor made it popular in many parts of the world. Another alternative vinegar is called alegar. It is made from sour ale or malt.

5. Limitations of Present Diet Design

a. Salt

The Earth Home system is not yet capable of providing 100% of the generally accepted human nutritional needs. At present, for example, the 6-12 pounds of salt which the average American eats every year cannot be generated inside the Earth Home (any sodium intake would lessen the body's need for salt). There are, however, "salt tolerant" plants which can survive in high-salt soil conditions. There is also a plant that, when raised in the salt-rich soil of coastal regions, will actually secrete salt through tiny buds on the surface of the leaves. Bluebill ducks also secrete excess salt from a gland on their bill when feeding in salty areas. It may be possible to reclaim and recycle salt in the diet using similar methods. (See Plants - Salt files.)

Note that soy sauce that is extensively used worldwide as a seasoning contains significant salt. There is no known way to produce soy sauce without adding salt.

b. Iodine

The Earth Home system cannot generate iodine, an additive to salt (except in canning salt) which is necessary for the proper functioning of the thyroid. Iodine can be added to the soil in dried seaweed from which it will be absorbed by plants and then replenished by compost. This cannot be done with salt, however, because adding it to the soil would harm or kill the plants.

c. Coffee/Caffeine

Coffee could either be purchased or substituted for. Among the coffee substitutes include chicory coffee, parsnip coffee, wheat coffee, beech nut coffee, garbonzo bean (chickpea) coffee, barley coffee, dandelion root coffee, okra seed coffee, acorn coffee, and rye coffee. Some people even use garden peas, burdock, carob, and other grains. Whole sorghum grains are roasted to almost charcoal in the form of galiya. These grains are then soaked in water and the steep water is used as a coffee substitute.

At least 100 species of plants contain caffeine. Half a dozen caffeine-containing plants are more widely used by mankind, primarily as beverages, than all the other herbal materials put together. Guarana seeds and yerba mate leaves also contain caffeine. Guarana usually refers to the dried paste made from the crushed seeds of the climbing shrub. Guarana has a relatively high caffeine content, ranging from 2.5 to 5% and averaging about 3.5%. Most of the caffeine plants are raised in a tropical climate. Related alkaloids to caffeine include the coca plant, ephedra, betel, and yohimbe.

d. Diet Variations/Palatability Changes

Today's modern taste buds are used to many different sensations-the palatability of some Earth Home food combinations is still being developed. The Biospherians faced similar challenges and overcame them in order to complete their mission. It is important to avoid significant "appetite fatigue" in any diet design. A small amount of interesting foods such as popcorn can provide relief from monotony. I believe that a rich and varied diet can play a large role in psychological and social life.

e. Ingredients/Spices/Condiments

Another limitation is the reduced number of ingredients for food preparation. However, if each EH family raised and bartered selected cultivars, the range of seasonings etc. would be greatly extended. Some ingredients for cooking can be substituted such as the American Indian custom of using clean, sifted wood ashes as a direct substitute for baking soda or baking powder.

*Used in Earth Home

A condiment called garum , nuoc-mam, or fish sauce can be used similar to soy sauces of the Orient. There are many other spices that can be grown in small spaces to add to the taste of foods such as horseradish with its distinctive taste.

J. Other Diet/Digestion Issues

1. Intestinal Health

a. Intestinal Health/Probiotics

The Russian bacteriologist, Elie Metchnikoff, 91 years ago documented a direct link between human longevity and the necessity of maintaining a healthy balance between those beneficial and pathological microorganisms residing within the human gut. He said this could be accomplished by consuming live, fermented foods. Another source of probiotic materials are what is referred to as homeostatic soil organisms (HSO). HSO's are beneficial bacteria which live in pure, nutrient-rich soil and are responsible for providing plants (vegetables and fruits) with those nutrients they require.

These organisms detoxify intestinal tracts, increase ability to absorb nutrients from food, and boosts immune systems. Furthermore they will be aggressive against pathological molds, yeasts, fungi, and parasites of all types which permeate human guts. They synthesize the B-complex vitamins, crowd out yeast and parasites, help regulate blood cholesterol levels, and produce antibiotic compounds.

The ratio of friendly microorganisms to harmful ones usually runs at 85% to 15%. Stool analysis shows that the average resident of North America possesses a pathogenic gut content of about 55%, so that he or she remains in a subclinical state of disease. A large number of commercial products used for digestive problems attest to this fact.

b. Toxin Elimination

A toxin is basically any substance that creates irritating and/or harmful effects in the body, undermining our health or stressing our biochemical or organ functions. This may result from drugs which have side effects, or from patterns of physiology that are different from our usual functioning. These free radicals irritate, inflame, age, and cause degeneration of body tissues. Toxicity occurs in our body when we take in more than we can utilize and eliminate. By getting enough of the antioxidant nutrients we help to neutralize free-radical molecules.

The diet is of course helped by the detoxification systems in place inside the body. These detoxification areas include the respiratory system (lungs, bronchial tubes, throat, sinuses, nose), gastrointestinal system (liver, gallbladder, colon, and whole GI tract), urinary system (kidneys, bladder, and urethra), and lymphatic system (lymph channels and lymph nodes). Note that colon cleansing is one of the most important parts of detoxification. (See Minor Health Care Section)

2. Eating "Mechanics"

a. Communicating Bodily Needs

I believe that the human body is capable of "communicating" dietary needs in subtle ways by a sudden, strong preference for certain foods. I think eating should imitate the blood's 80% alkaline and 20% acid ratio. The alkaline portion comes from about 6 vegetables and 2 fruits per day. The other 20% acid can come from acid, starches, and proteins.

*Used in Earth Home

b. Food Temperature

The stomach is a "barometer" of how you feel. As a general rule, I believe that all food and beverages should be served near room temperature. It takes energy to assimilate foods that are too hot or too cold. Some diets are based on the temperature of the food being eaten. (See Diet Section) Heating food too much destroys nutrients and leaches them into the cooking water. The small amount of this cooking 'broth" should be drank for the nutrients that it contains.

c. Chewing Food Slowly and Completely

Digestion begins in the mouth as we chew, or masticate, our food. Thorough mastication of food is of primary importance to assure that food completely mixes with oral digestive juices, initiating digestion.

The chewing habit greatly affects how efficiently we use food. The smaller particle makes it easier for the body to metabolize food. Colon hydrotherapists will see clients with whole food particles and other undigested bits of food coming out of their colon during colonic treatments.

History tells us that a common practice of the Jewish survivors of the German concentration camps was to chew their meager rations extremely well. Also it is known that eating *more slowly* results in less food being eaten.

d. Timing of Meals

I also believe that the spacing between snacks or meals has an effect on overall health. I believe that people should allow the stomach ample time to digest a meal before putting more food into it—but at the same time eat sooner than every 3 hours to keep the energy level up. After awhile the body "knows" when the previous snack has been completely used up. Also eating a large meal before bedtime should be avoided.

e. Food Combining Theories

Food combining might more aptly be described as "food separation". Food combining is the practice of eating foods from groups that are compatible based on the stomach and body's ability to assimilate them easily. The food groups are as follows:

--Acid fruits such as grapefruit, lemon, lime, oranges, pineapple, strawberries, tangerines, and tomatoes.
--Sweet fruits such as bananas, dates, figs, prunes, raisins, and dried fruits. Fruits take less than an hour to digest.
--Starches/carbohydrates such as dried beans, bread, cereals, chestnuts, corn, grains, Jerusalem artichokes, pasta, dried peas, potatoes, pumpkin, winter squash, and jams. Starches require 2 to 3 hours to digest.
--Proteins such as dairy products, eggs, fish, fowl, meat, nuts, seeds, soybeans and soy products, and tofu. Proteins take 4 hours to digest.
--Fats/oils such as avocado, butter, coconut, cream, margarine, olives; and oils made from avocado, corn, nuts, olive, safflower, seeds, and soy.
--Vegetables-all of them

The generally accepted rules of eating the above are as follows:

--Mix and match the foods within any single group as you like. You can have sweet fruits with sweet fruits, proteins with proteins, and so on.
--Enjoy vegetables at any meal. Most vegetables, which are relatively easy to digest, mix well with other foods, so you can enjoy them with almost any meal.
--Eat fruit alone. Fruit is rapidly digested in the stomach and small intestine. If it is mixed in with other foods that take longer to digest, such as meat, the fruit will be quickly broken up by digestive enzymes, but then forced to wait while the other foods are digested. While the fruit is waiting to move on through the digestive system, it ferments, releasing gas and causing other problems. Fruit should be kept moving quickly through the digestive

*Used in Earth Home

system, which is why it is best eaten by itself (and not with vegetables, grains, or other foods). Enjoy fruit two hours after a meal containing other foods, or ½ hour before.
--Separate sweet and acid fruits. Fruits are health-giving, nutrient-packed foods with but one disadvantage: Sweet fruits cannot be eaten with acid fruits. You can eat more than one acid or sweet fruit at a time, but do not mix the two types together, and do not eat fruits with other foods.
--Separate starches and proteins. The nutrients in the foods will be better digested and absorbed into the body if starches are not mixed with proteins. The old American "standby," meat and potatoes, is not a healthful mixture.
--Separate starches from fats and oils. Starches (such as rice, potatoes, and pasta) should not be mixed with fatty or oily foods.

When food-combining is properly done, it is claimed to help ensure easy digestion, fewer toxins produced by digestive difficulties, and a tremendous increase in energy resulting in better overall health. Some doctors claim that proper food combining and digestive enzyme support relieved about 90% of the digestive problems that plagued some clients. The following figures show the charts that are used when combining foods. There is also a "Modern Food Combining Pyramid" that looks much like the Food Guide pyramid.

The Hay diet is one diet that also stresses combining foods at the proper time. There are basically three rules to this diet. Firstly, separate starches from proteins. Secondly, try to eat half of your food that is fresh fruit, vegetables, and salads. The last item is simply to cut out any processed food.

The Hay diet and food-combining diets are based on the human digestive system and the transit time to pass through the digestive tract. Protein takes 4 to 8 hours, starch only takes 3 to 4 hours, fruit is gone in 20 to 40 minutes, and vegetables vary depending on the species and consistency.

f. Snacking

Snacking has become popular recently. An eating style called the "warrior diet" extols the virtues of taking small nourishment often. Reports of higher energy and increased feeling of well being is often heard.

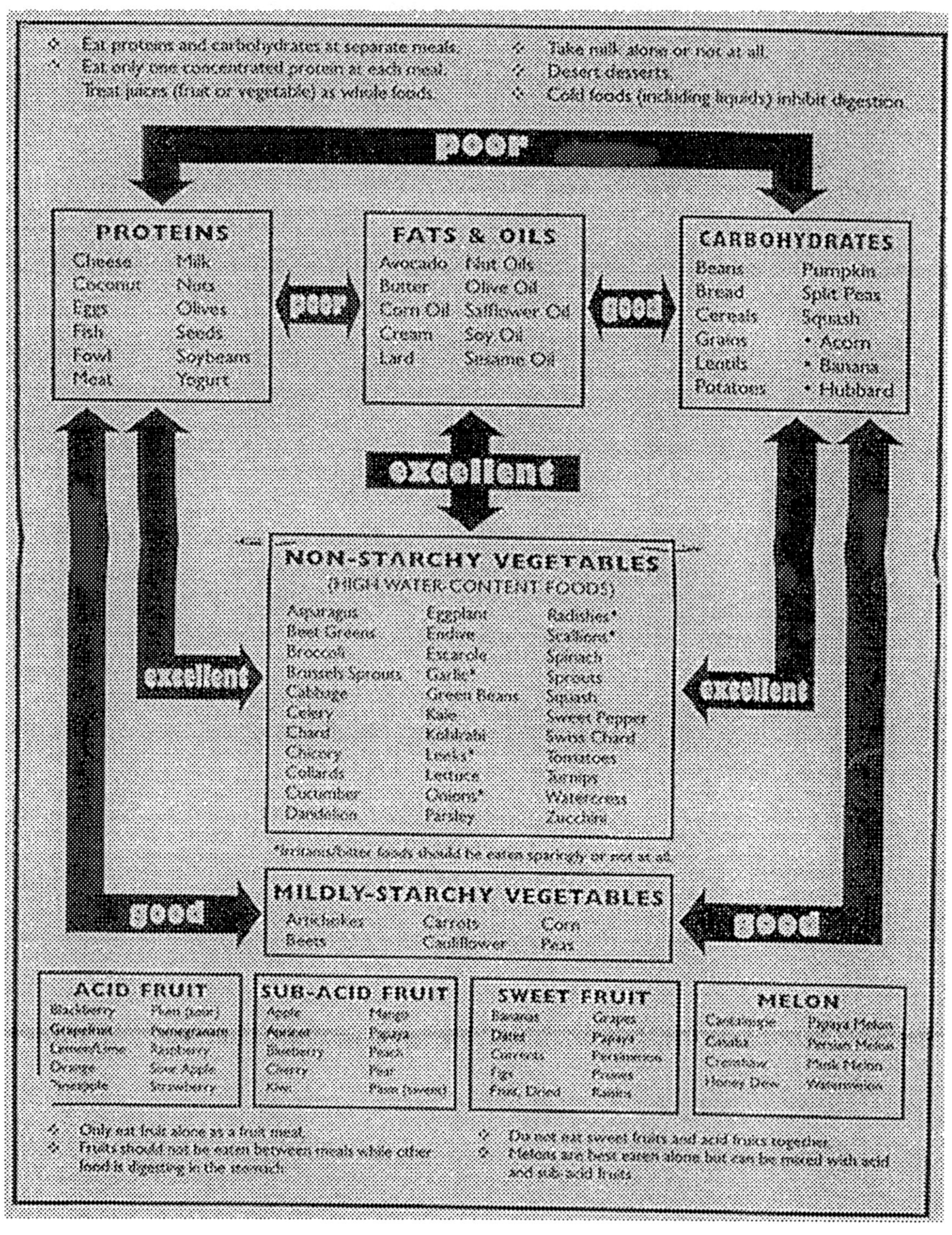

Figure 131-FOOD COMBINING CHART

*Used in Earth Home

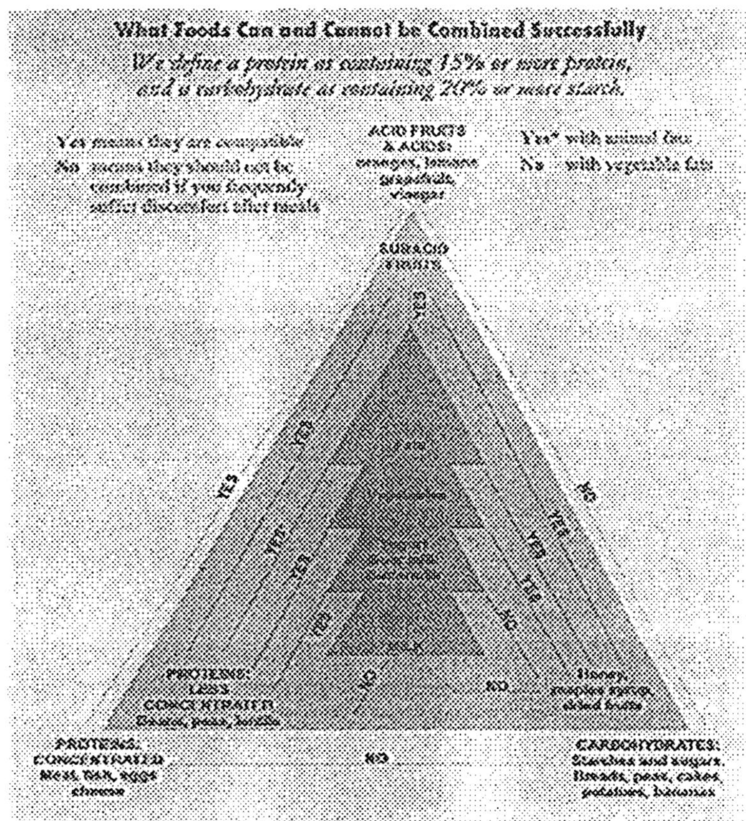

Correct Food Combining Chart

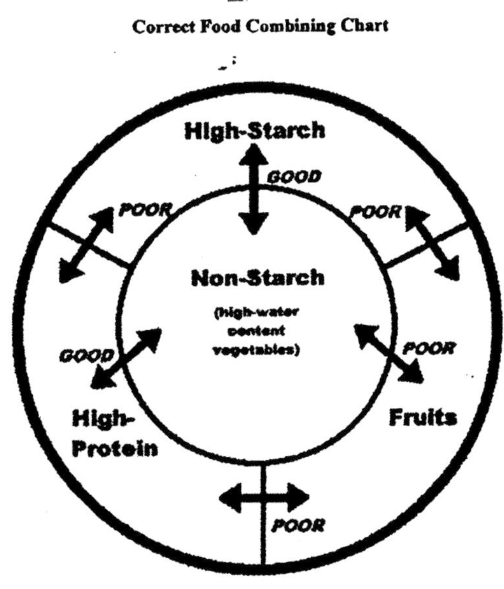

Figure 132-FOOD COMBINING CHARTS

*Used in Earth Home

*Used in Earth Home

IX. FOOD PRODUCTION TECHNOLOGIES

A. Species Used as Human Food Source

1. Traditional Plant Species

Of the approximately 500,000 species in the plant kingdom, prehistoric people ate 1,500 species of wild plants and about 500 species of domestically grown plants. Now, about 200 species are commonly grown in backyards for family consumption. (80% of homeowners currently garden.) Of these, 80 species are grown to sell by small gardeners, and only 20 species are extensively used for field cultivation.

Ninety-five percent of all human nutrition is derived from no more than 30 plants. Of these, 8 plants comprise over 75% of the total plant contribution to human energy. Only three crops -- wheat, rice, and maize (corn) -- account for three-quarters of our cereal consumption.

2. Traditional Animal Species

The vast majority of the foods that human beings consume come from 11 plant sources and 7 animal sources. We rely heavily on mass production of this small number of plants and animals for the world's food supply. ***Of the 150 or so nations of the world, there are only four nations that export more food than they import -- United States, Canada, Argentina, and Australia.***

3. Dangers of Limited Food Source

This reliance on a small number of species of plants and animals has a potentially catastrophic effect, as was experienced in the Potato Famine of 1847. The potato blight completely destroyed Ireland's potato crop. Of the 3 million people living in Ireland at the time, 1 million died and 1 million more moved to America. They had lost their diversity of plants, and had no back-up systems to feed themselves. This is further evidenced by the blight throughout the single-variety coffee plantations in Britain's Asian and African colonies that transformed the British into a nation of tea drinkers.

*Used in Earth Home

B. Plant Selection Criteria in Earth Home II

The plant species chosen for the Earth Home system were selected using a combination of the following:

1. Non-hybrids - Historical Overview.

All plants chosen for EH use are non-hybrid, open-pollinated cultivars. This is necessary because hybrid plants produce infertile seeds, or they produce qualities in the second and third generation that are drastically different from the first generation hybrid plant. This also goes for the new "genetically-engineered" plant species. -***Note that the eight major world food grains are all hybrids, requiring farmers to purchase seeds every year-***. This is done because of the higher productivity and specific disease-resistance of the hybrids. It is generally agreed that the world could not produce enough food if hybrids were not used.

These hybrids often depend on more water and fertilizers for their higher yield. Open-pollinated plants, however, often adapt to wider temperature fluctuations and variable watering schedules. Non-hybrid seeds are also viable for years (depending on species). Dutch seed companies have some excellent cultivars that do well in greenhouses, but almost all of them are hybrids.

2. Historical "Survival" Vegetables.

I have favored those plants that have sustained people throughout history. A complete discussion of those plant species is in Plants Selected section.

3. Small Size, Quick Growth.

Plants that grow to a large size are generally inefficient, because they put a lot of plant mass into stalks and roots, which are not used for human food. An efficient plant grows quickly in a small space. The following lists leaf growth rates for selected plants.

4. Low Light Levels.

Complete growth to seed without full sunlight is preferable. (See Growing Mechanics.) Plants grow at different rates. See the following figure for differences in growth rates for selected plants. "Shade-seeking" or "shade-tolerant" plants are preferred.

5. All Parts Edible.

Edible parts of the plant should make up a majority of the plant mass. If the roots, leaves, and stems were all used, this would be an efficient plant, and should be looked at closely. For example, the "winged bean" of Southeast Asia is used in salads, the leaves are eaten raw, and the roots and stems are chopped up for soups. This makes it a very efficient plant, from the standpoint of how much of the plant is actually used for human food. However, it does not do well in lower light levels inside the greenhouse.

6. High Nutrient Levels.

This is very important because the body needs many nutrients and vitamins to sustain it. The ability of a plant to gather many different nutrients from the soil and air and store them in edible parts is very important. Note: Vitamin B_{12} has only one plant source: comfrey. (See also Spirulina blue-green algae which is also a source of vitamin B_{12}) ***The hardest "nutrients" to produce are calories, riboflavin, calcium, and Vitamin A***.

*Used in Earth Home

DIFFERENCES IN LEAF PHOTOSYNTHESIS AMONG PLANTS	
PLANT	**Mg Co_2/dm^{-2}/hr^{-1}**
Tropical Grasses	70 - 80
Sugarcane	65 - 70
Corn, Sorghum	38 - 75
Rice	35 - 62
Sunflower	50 - 60
Cotton, Clover	24 - 45
Soybean, Sugar beet	25 - 40
Oats, Wheat, Barley	30 - 35
Alfalfa	20 - 50
Tobacco, Tomato	20 - 25
Most Vegetables	20 - 25
Trees, Fruits, Citrus	15 - 25

Note that Spirulina blue-green algae has photosynthetic efficiencies about 4 times more than land-based plant life!

Figure 133-LEAF GROWTH RATES

7. Sproutable Seeds.

In nature, many animals use seeds as a food source. ***Sprouts are a very important part of the Earth Home diet, because they are the best source of vitamins after sea vegetation. Sprouting a seed will increase its food value and vitamin content some threefold or more*** compared to the bare seed itself. They are easier to digest, having converted some of their fats and starches to vitamins and sugar. ***Sprouts can also provide food year round*** -- for salads, casseroles, and soups. They can also be roasted, ground up, and used to enrich bread and baked goods. (See Plants-Sprouts file.)

8. Taste Good Eaten Raw.

The criteria for selecting plants for the Earth Home are similar to those used by NASA, with the additional requirement that they taste good eaten raw. We know from experience that raw vegetables have higher vitamin content than when cooked or stored for any length of time. Also, energy is saved by not cooking.

9. Storage/Preservation Requirement

Some foods store better than others. The coastal Indians grew squash, corn, beans, and pumpkins for that reason. Modern times show us other methods such as drying and pickling which are adapted to a fixed storage location. (See Food—After Production section)

10. System Approach

a. Specific Plant "Specialty"

Many plant species have been tested for Earth Home use. (See Plants-Past Plantings files.) I found over the years that each plant has its own "claim to fame," whether it be high mineral content, high vitamin C content, quick growth, or all parts edible. Experimenters grow some plant species purely for one quality. ***Plants had to be chosen for the Earth Home on the basis of what they can do for the total system***. For example, rose hips (Rosa Rugosa) was chosen over citrus for a source of vitamin C because dwarf citrus and lemon trees would have a more difficult time maturing in an inside garden. (Nostradamos used rose hips as a primary ingredient in his treatment of black plague victims.)

Plants under consideration for future use in the Earth Home system include Stevia Rebaudiana. This plant contains no calories yet is 300 times sweeter than cane sugar. The Guarani Indians of Paraguay have used it for some 400 years. Also the radish is being used because it is a quick growing plant and possible future genetic variations may increase its vitamin content.

b. Multiple Cropping

The plant growing system for the Earth Home is designed around three crops per year, with a double cropping method. One crop will be grown and harvested quickly, while the second crop comes up underneath for later harvest. ***The Earth Home growing season is approximately February 21 through October 21***. Transplanting, root cuttings, and advanced gardening methods are not used, and are left for more advanced gardeners. Three crops are not grown in all places, due to the need for seed production. Some crops are grown to maturity for the seeds so they can be replanted, stored, or sprouted.

*Used in Earth Home

11. Plant Selection

a. NASA/CELSS Plants

It is interesting to note that NASA used the following plant list in 1988 on the CELSS program:

Legumes Soybeans Peanuts Pea Pods Split Peas Beans, Dry Chick Peas Tubers Potatoes Turnip Greens	Leaf Mustard Greens Kale Broccoli Grains Wheat Oats Corn Rice

Figure 134-NASA PLANTS LIST

The following comments relate to similar projects and NASA:

- After 1989, the NASA list was shortened to eight plants, and vitamin supplements were added to the diet. The plants were wheat, rice, sweet potatoes, soybeans, peanuts, lettuce, and sugar beets. They are also working on Spirulina blue-green algae for the CELSS system.
- A Russian study also listed radishes, turnips, cucumbers, and beets as good diet choices for extended space travel.

b. Balanced Diet/Survival Vegetables

The book, One Circle, by David Duhon, lists the following 14 plants as paramount to a balanced diet: collards, filberts, onions, leeks, garlic, parsley, parsnips, peanuts, potatoes, soybeans, sweet potatoes, sunflowers, turnips, and wheat.

Another study of "survival vegetables" listed the following as most important:

--Legumes: Lima beans, snap beans, soybeans, peas, butter peas.
--Tubers: Parsnips, turnips (and greens), sweet potatoes, rutabaga, Irish potatoes, beets with greens.
--Leaf: Chard, collards, kale, mustard, salsify, spinach.
--Herbs: Garlic.

*Used in Earth Home

It is interesting to note that the International Rescue Committee writes that only nine pounds of seed is needed to feed a refuge family for one year. The cultivars selected are generally site-specific (mostly tropical) and drought-resistant.

c. Comparison Discussion

There are elements common to most of these "survival vegetable" lists. Comparing the Earth Home plant list to NASA and others, I offer these comments:

a. The emphasis on legumes as a protein source in the earlier NASA list reflects the higher amount of protein that was commonly recommended prior to 1993.
b. Potatoes and sweet potatoes do not do well in a greenhouse without enhanced levels of light (such as NASA had intended). Also sweet potatoes are difficult to store for long periods of time.
c. Because seeds must be grown from year to year, kale and broccoli cannot be grown together because they cross-pollinate.
d. Peanuts are a long-season crop, and take up a lot of space.
e. Sugar beets and many tubers such as turnips rely on a wind to gradually force their roots into the soil, so they must be grown outside.
f. Typical lowland varieties of rice need to be submerged in water to grow, and also need to be rotated. They are usually transplanted during various growth stages. True upland rice varieties are banned from importation into the U.S. at present.
g. Little thought was given to growing leaves as fodder for animal food aboard spacecraft or space colonies.
h. Cucumbers were not chosen for the Earth Home because they are not space efficient and do not store well. Also, mushrooms were not chosen because they require very exacting growing conditions.
i. Outside gardening will be used for shading purposes and for hardy, space-intensive, sun-loving cultivars.

d. Earth Home Plants

The following figure shows plants selected for use in the Earth Home. A complete list of plant cultivars, with growing, harvesting, and related notes follows. (See also Complete Production Data section). (Exact planting locations are not included in this work). Generally, the fruit-setting varieties will be up front (south side), and the foliage plants will be 8 feet back on the V-trough. Legumes as companions will be used as much as possible to help soil fertility.

e. Plant Genetic Improvements

Improvements to the plants can be done by first choosing a suitable variety, providing good growing conditions, and discarding undesirable plants. The best plants are chosen for seed stock for the next year. This is the same method that has been used for centuries to improve a specific cultivar.

*Used in Earth Home

Legumes
Beans
Winged Beans

Tubers
Parsnips
Jerusalem
Artichokes **(outside)**
Carrots **(also outside)**
Sugar beets **(also outside)**
Onions **(also outside)**
Radish

Leaf
Mustard, Tendergreen
Collards
Swiss Chard
French Sorrel
Broccoli
Wheatgrass
Lettuce
Spinach

Grains
Quinoa **(outside)**
Wheat, Dwarf **(outside)**

Oil Plants
Rapeseed **(also outside)**

Sweeteners
Strawberries**(outside)**
Maple Syrup **(outside)**
Grapes **(outside)**
Stevia Rebaudiana

***Western Sun (inside)**
Tomatoes, Cherry

***Herbs (living space)**
Garlic
Basil
Thyme
Oregano
Chives
Lemon Balm
Parsley
Violets
Ecinacea

Perennials:
Asparagus
Rosa Rugosa
Dandelion

Rotated Crops:
Rapeseed
Quinoa
Soybeans
Squash
Cabbage
Alfalfa

Note: Inside plants unless marked.

Figure 135-EARTH HOME PLANT LIST

*Used in Earth Home

PLANTS - CURRENT PLANTINGS CATEGORIES

The following chart shows the plants to be used in the Earth Home system as of 2003 The categories with explanations are as follows:

1. **South Side Plants** -- These species will be planted along the entire 93' of the south glass. The perennials will remain in one spot and the others will be rotated with the soybeans. They are generally hardy and disease resistant cultivars.

2. **Western Sun Area Plants** -- Tomatoes are one popular plant that enjoys long days. By experimentation, they do better and mature earlier on the west side. Other plants will be added in the future.

3. **Earth Home Plants** -- These will be the bulk of the vegetables planted in the greenhouse east and west. Fruit-producing species up front (better light) and foliage plants on the vertical V-trough 5 feet behind the glass.

4. **Herbs** -- These herbs will be planted inside all year-round for seasoning as needed.

Figure 136-EARTH HOME PLANTS-CHART DESCRIPTION

*Used in Earth Home

EARTH HOME PLANTS
SOUTH SIDE PLANTS

PLANT	VARIETY/ QUALITIES/ SPROUTABLE (Y OR N)	SEED/SOIL/ CARE/ GROWING CONDITION	COMPANION/ DISEASE RESISTANCE	HARVEST/ PRESERVING/ USES/NOTES
OIL PLANTS				
Rapeseed	(Johnnies). Good in low light conditions Y	(See outside plants.)		Canola oil is made from one species
LEGUMES (NITROGEN FIXERS)				
Beans	Mung (Phaseous Mungo) Y	Grows good with anything, most vegetables	Similar to soybeans.	Grown in Orient for thousands of years.
Beans	(Phaseolus Vulgaris) Butterbean, Gurney's Top Crop Remus--MR by Park French, Giant Stringless (Vermont 111) Y		Beans with strawberries.	
(CONT. NEXT PAGE)				

Figure 137-EARTH HOME SOUTH SIDE PLANTS, PAGE 1

*Used in Earth Home

EARTH HOME PLANTS, CONT.
SOUTH SIDE PLANTS. CONT.

PLANT	VARIETY/ QUALITIES/ SPROUTABLE (Y OR N)	SEED/SOIL/ CARE/ GROWING CONDITION	COMPANION/ DISEASE RESISTANCE	HARVEST/ PRESERVING/ USES/NOTES
TUBERS				
Parsnip	(Pastinaca Sativa) Avon Resistor White Gem Can be planted under other crops--slow growing.	Can be left in soil until needed (south side with plenty of light).		Foliage and roots make a safe insect spray. Dig up a few good roots and plant next year for seed.
GRAIN PLANTS (STARCH)				
Quinoa	Very good protein source. Several ounces of seed per plant.	Freeze seed before planting. Grows very tall.		Remove saponin from seeds before using by rinsing. Goes back thousands of years.
(CONT. NEXT PAGE)				

Figure 138-EARTH HOME SOUTH SIDE PLANTS, PAGE 2

*Used in Earth Home

EARTH HOME PLANTS, CONT.
SOUTH SIDE PLANTS. CONT.

PLANT	VARIETY/ QUALITIES/ SPROUTABLE (Y OR N)	SEED/SOIL/ CARE/ GROWING CONDITION	COMPANION/ DISEASE RESISTANCE	HARVEST/ PRESERVING/ USES/NOTES
LEAF PLANTS				
Cabbage	Langedijker Bewaar Witte and Deense Witte Good Storage Variety			Sauerkraut/salads 6 month storage.
Lettuce/ Spinach				
Mustard, Tendergreen	(Brassica Perviridis) Broadleaf 6749-00 Vermont Y	40 days to maturity, water sparingly.	V-trough grown.	Grown in Western Europe for 4,000 years.
Parsley	(Petroselinum Crispum) Good vitamin A and C source. Perfection	Soak seeds 1 day before planting. Rich soil.	Chives	Grow larger amounts. Gather seeds early (seeds shatter).
Collards	(Brassica Oleracea) Nutritious--protein and calcium. Vates Morris Heading #232 Cooks Y	Heavy feeders--fertilize. Grow in cool area--near floor. Partial shade okay.		All leaves used. Two crops per year can be grown.
(CONT. NEXT PAGE)				

Figure 139-EARTH HOME SOUTH SIDE PLANTS, PAGE 3

*Used in Earth Home

EARTH HOME PLANTS, CONT.
SOUTH SIDE PLANTS. CONT.

PLANT	VARIETY/ QUALITIES/ SPROUTABLE (Y OR N)	SEED/SOIL/ CARE/ GROWING CONDITION	COMPANION/ DISEASE RESISTANCE	HARVEST/ PRESERVING/ USES/NOTES
LEAF PLANTS (CONT.)				
Chard, Swiss	(Brassica) Plant can be dug up and kept green a long time (harvested into winter). Rhubarb Red	Tolerates shade.	Free of insect and disease problems. Plant with bush beans.	Good green for fodder--chickens and animals. Harvest leaf stem all the way down to the base.
Sorrel French	(Rumex Slutatus) (milder) or Garden (Rumex Acetosa) Very high vitamin C. #461 Vermont Belleville	Grow on bottom shelf.		Teas, spices. Substitutes for vinegar in salads
Broccoli	(Brassica Oleracea) Leaves are more nutritious than heads. - Deckcio - Italian Green Calabrese)-Y Abundant Life - Early Purple Y	Grows well near glass or in V-troughs.	Companion: Onion, artichoke, beans, spinach. Tolerates shade. Don't plant near strawberries. Plant with lettuce in between.	Broccoli meal. Soak heads in salt water for 1/2 hour to remove any insects (1 tablespoon per quart). Cook like cabbage.
(CONT. NEXT PAGE)				

Figure 140-EARTH HOME SOUTH SIDE PLANTS, PAGE 4

*Used in Earth Home

EARTH HOME PLANTS. CONT.
WESTERN SUN AREA PLANTS

PLANT	VARIETY/ QUALITIES/ SPROUTABLE (Y OR N)	SEED/SOIL/ CARE/ GROWING CONDITION	COMPANION/ DISEASE RESISTANCE	HARVEST/ PRESERVING/ USES/NOTES
WESTERN SUN PLANTS				
Tomatoes	(Lycoperisicum) Vining or indeterminate best. Pixie, Tiny Tim, Sweet 100 (Cherry)	Water infrequently (once a week). Adequate phosphorous in soil to control white flies. Soil 9" diameter, 5 gallons or more. Grow in a wire cage 8' high/2' diameter, 6" apart. Leave 1 bottom sucker 1' tall and train 2 tops. Remove all other suckers (shoots) when 1" long. Trim past 5th truss (branch).	Grows good with chives, parsley, basil, beans, nasturiums. Must be hand pollinated by vibration when petals curl backwards every other day between 11 and 3 p.m., or water from overhead.	Mix pulp with water and ferment (good seeds drop to bottom). Tomatoes were raised for two hundred years before anyone discovered they were good to eat! Tomatoes can be cloned.

Figure 141-EARTH HOME WESTERN SUN PLANTS

*Used in Earth Home

EARTH HOME PLANTS. CONT.
EARTH HOME INSIDE PLANTS

The following herbs are to be basket-grown year-round in the south-facing dining room window of the Earth Home.

PLANT	VARIETY/ QUALITIES/ SPROUTABLE (Y OR N)	SEED/SOIL/ CARE/ GROWING CONDITION	COMPANION/ DISEASE RESISTANCE	HARVEST/ PRESERVING/ USES/NOTES
INSIDE PLANTS				
Garlic	(Allium Sativum) Pink (early), White variety, or Nichols top set. Perennial. Sutherland.	Started from bulbs. Water infrequently. When 12" high water less--bulbs develop.	Harvest when dry and store in a cool place.	6,000 years old. Grow lots of it for garlic spray for pest control.
Basil	(Ocimum Basilicum) Dark Opal	Pinch main stalks back early. Pinch flower buds. Water infrequently.	Harvest 6" above soil.	Repels mosquitoes and flies.
Thyme	Broad-leaved German Winter (Vermont)	High light level, sandy soil. Water infrequently. Bend over stem and put soil on top to keep plants young.	(Still used in some cough medicines.) Use sparingly. Dry for future use.	Harvest leaves during and after flowering.
(CONT. NEXT PAGE)				

Figure 142-EARTH HOME INSIDE PLANTS, PAGE 1

*Used in Earth Home

EARTH HOME PLANTS. CONT.
EARTH HOME INSIDE PLANTS, CONT.

The following herbs are to be basket-grown year-round in the south-facing dining room window of the Earth Home.

PLANT	VARIETY/ QUALITIES/ SPROUTABLE (Y OR N)	SEED/SOIL/ CARE/ GROWING CONDITION	COMPANION/ DISEASE RESISTANCE	HARVEST/ PRESERVING/ USES/NOTES
INSIDE PLANTS, CONT.				
Oregano		Full sun.		Harvest leaves during and after flowering.
Rosemary		Cold-tolerant to 40 deg. F.		
Lemon Balm (Labiatae Family)	Lemon flavor. Can reduce sugar requirements.	Nice large pot.	Flavor salads or tea.	
Sweet Bay		Cold-tolerant to 40 deg. F.		

Figure 143-EARTH HOME INSIDE PLANTS, PAGE 2

*Used in Earth Home

EARTH HOME PLANTS. CONT.
EARTH HOME EXTERIOR PLANTS
(Also Listed in South Side Plants)

PLANT	VARIETY/ QUALITIES/ SPROUTABLE (Y OR N)	SEED/SOIL/ CARE/ GROWING CONDITION	COMPANION/ DISEASE RESISTANCE	HARVEST/ PRESERVING/ USES/NOTES
EXTERIOR OIL PLANTS		(See South Side plants)		
Rapeseed	Y			Harvest seeds when dry.
EXTERIOR LEGUMES				
Beans--Soy (Glycene Soja, Glycine Max)	High protein. <u>Field Varieties</u>: Disoy, Early Hakucho, Okuhara Early <u>Veg. Varieties</u>: Giant Green, Kanrich, Royalty (See Stokes or Johnnies) Sprouts--Chico, Maple Arrow 0648B Y	Needs light. (See outside plants.)	Needs 500-1,000 lumens for seed growth. Few diseases. Grows good with anything.	Harvested as green beans. Mature dry beans. Roasted as snack food. Innoculant used on soil for first-time planting. Grown since 3,000 B.C. (Tempeh richest vegetarian source of B_{12}.)
(CONT. NEXT PAGE)				

Figure 144-EARTH HOME EXTERIOR PLANTS, PAGE 1

*Used in Earth Home

EARTH HOME PLANTS. CONT.
EARTH HOME EXTERIOR PLANTS, CONT.
(Also Listed in South Side Plants)

PLANT	VARIETY/ QUALITIES/ SPROUTABLE (Y OR N)	SEED/SOIL/ CARE/ GROWING CONDITION	COMPANION/ DISEASE RESISTANCE	HARVEST/ PRESERVING/ USES/NOTES
EXTERIOR TUBERS				
Artichoke, Jerusalem (Helianthus Tuberosus)	Upright stem--resists phototrophism. Tubers like potatoes, source of starch/ carbohydrates. Can be made into flour.	Contain insulin as carbohydrate--releases fructose. (See outside plants.)	Resistant to all pests and diseases. Tolerates shade. Companion to Brassicas, broccoli.	Must be dug when needed or in wet sand in cool root cellar (in refrigerator in airtight bags for 1 month). Harvest before top growth occurs. Native to North America. Leaves for fodder--Indians and settlers. (Can be used outside to shade greenhouse.) Alcohol can be made from artichoke stalks.
EXTERIOR GRAINS (STARCH)				
Wheat, Dwarf	Versatile. Yecoro Rojo Y		Use fresh-ground if possible (keep dry).	Grows 12" tall.
Teff	Disease Free ?	Excellent.		14% protein

Figure 145-EARTH HOME EXTERIOR PLANTS, PAGE 2

*Used in Earth Home

EARTH HOME PLANTS. CONT.
EARTH HOME PERENNIAL EXTERIOR PLANTS
(Grown around the Earth Home)

PLANT	VARIETY/ QUALITIES/ SPROUTABLE (Y OR N)	SEED/SOIL/ CARE/ GROWING CONDITION	COMPANION/ DISEASE RESISTANCE	HARVEST/ PRESERVING/ USES/NOTES
EXTERIOR SWEETENERS				
Strawberries Everbearing Dayneutral Variety	Varied diet. Tribute or Tristar from Nourse Farms or Gurney-- optional varieties are Aptos, Hecker, Brighton.	Lots of water, 7" between plants, lots of light (1,000 lumens), sandy soil. (See Strawberry Barrel.)	Don't plant near Brassicas. Okay with beans, spinach and lettuce.	Leaves for tea and salad greens. Don't plant near Brassicas
Grapes				
EXTERIOR TREES/ SHRUBS				
Maple, Boxelder, Juniper, Rose Hips				
(CONT. NEXT PAGE)				

Figure 146-EARTH HOME PERRENNIAL PLANTS, PAGE 1

EARTH HOME PLANTS. CONT.
EARTH HOME PERENNIAL EXTERIOR PLANTS, CONT.
(Grown around the Earth Home)

PLANT	VARIETY/ QUALITIES/ SPROUTABLE (Y OR N)	SEED/SOIL/ CARE/ GROWING CONDITION	COMPANION/ DISEASE RESISTANCE	HARVEST/ PRESERVING/ USES/NOTES
EXTERIOR LEAF PLANTS				
Chives (Allium Schoenoprasum)	Nichols, Garden Nursery Perennial.	Gravel in soil, approximately 5-gallon bucket.	Grows well with carrots, parsley, lettuce.	Pinch off flowers. 3,000 years old.
Asparagus	Variety: Mary Washington, grows very fast.	Perennial.		Shoots can be dried--rutin has medicinal uses. Seeds used as coffee substitute.

Figure 147-EARTH HOME PERRENNIAL PLANTS, PAGE 2

*Used in Earth Home

C. Plant Growing Options and Methods

There are a number of methods of growing plants that I looked at for the Earth Home:

1. Hydroponics.

I do not use hydroponics growing inside the Earth Home for a number of reasons. Even though, as the following figure shows, some of the earliest information on hydroponics made it appear to be a wonder method, some of the later books on hydroponics admit that it is possible to have the high growth and high production capabilities in a soil medium. I did not use hydroponics also because of the amount of energy needed to raise and lower the water for the plants, although there are methods of "trickle hydroponics" that claims to have a very low energy input.

Crop	Agricultural Yield Per Acre	Hydroponics Yield Per Acre
Rice	1,000 lb.	12,000 lb.
Wheat	600 lb.	5,000 lb.
Potatoes	22,000 lb.	150,000 lb.
Maize	1,500 lb.	8,000 lb.
Soybeans	600 lb.	1,500 lb.
Oats	850 lb.	3,000 lb.
Beets	9,000 lb.	20,000 lb.
Peas	2,000 lb.	14,000 lb.
Tomatoes	5-10 tons	180 tons

Figure 148-STUDY OF HYDROPONIC VS. AGRICULTURAL YIELD

Another reason why I didn't use hydroponics is that additional or secondary composting methods would be needed to recycle materials back into a nutrient solution. The recycled particle has to be a very fine mesh size to be pumped and absorbed into the hydroponics plant root system. (See Greenhouse Files for complete hydroponics discussion.) An under-soil modified hydroponics system may be tested for the outside plants, however.

2. Nutrient Spray System.

Experiments have been done using a mineral-rich and nutrient-rich water mixture sprayed directly on the leaves of the plants. Plants have the ability to absorb minerals and vitamins directly into the leaf, causing faster plant growth. Also, a 3,000 cycle per second "hum" has been used to "vibrate" or stimulate the plants to absorb nutrients much faster. Experiments have found that 3,000 hertz is the optimum frequency at which a plant opens up its leaf pores and takes in these minerals. Like hydroponics, the spray system also requires nutrients in a fine particle size.

3. CO_2 Enrichment.

a. CO_2 Benefits

Plants are 50% carbon. ***Studies have shown that raising the CO_2 (carbon dioxide) concentration*** from 300 parts per million (PPM) to 1,000 to 2,000 PPM ***can up to double yields***. Studies also show that the leaf surface should be "air-washed" sufficiently so the stagnating film of oxygen is replaced by CO_2. ***Research also shows that increasing airflow alone can dramatically increase production***. There are basically two ways to increase CO_2 concentrations in a greenhouse-compost or use CO_2 generators of some sort.

b. CO_2 from Composting

Compost provides a source of carbon dioxide by the natural decomposition of plant matter. (See Earth Home Greenhouse CO_2 Enrichment section) (See also Composting/Fertilization section.)

c. Limestone Source of CO_2

Limestone can be heated in a hot oven such as a furnace to release carbon dioxide. This system can be made renewable as the limestone is a "sponge" for the CO_2.

d. Exhaust CO_2 Generators.

The exhaust from an internal combustion engine such as a backup electrical generator can be filtered and used to increase CO_2 concentrations. Note that carbon dioxide is one of the "foods" for Spirulina. The propane backup generator or a future home electrical power source could be used. An easy way to measure CO_2 concentrations is to use a manual pump and disposable sample tubes. (See Greenhouse General files.)

e. EH Greenhouse CO_2 Enrichment.

The Earth Home will use composting as the primary CO_2 source. A good compost pile sealed and vented into the greenhouse area would increase the carbon dioxide concentration for about six weeks. The composting chamber is located below the level of the greenhouse and can be accessed from either the outside or the greenhouse itself. The carbon dioxide of gas can be ducted directly into the plant growing area or vented through the roof in times of hot weather when the air circulation requirements of the plants is paramount.

4. Greenhouse Advantages.

A significant amount of plants are to be grown inside in a greenhouse, rather than in an outside garden, for four basic reasons:

a. Climate Variation.

A person who relies solely on outside growing conditions is at the mercy of Mother Nature. Extreme hot and cold cycles have been prevalent for many years. Rainfall, hail, and winds can also be sporadic and dangerous for the plants.

b. Insect and Disease Control

It is easier to control insects in a confined space. Special care must be exercised to prevent spreading of diseases from the outside. ***The saying "a healthy plant is a disease-free plant" is very true***. Note: Companion planting and other methods are used so that one species of plant protects the species growing next to it by repelling pests. (See also Disease Control Section) Outside plants had to be chosen primarily for their disease resistance.

c. O_2/CO_2 interdependency

Plants give off oxygen and humans give off carbon dioxide. Plants and animals in the same growing space benefit each other using each other's by-products. The Earth Home design allows shared air between the plants and animals to provide a healthier environment for both.

d. Watering Control

Water is the "essence" of plants, and a closed environment where the water can be precisely controlled gives an advantage to the plant grower. Higher levels of humidity also greatly aid growth and lessen the need for watering. If possible, relative humidity should be kept between 45% and 60% to protect plants against many diseases.

e. Soil pH Control

The following lists pH preferences for a few common garden vegetables:

--Moderately Acid Soil (pH 4.0-6.0)
Blueberries, Blackberries, Cranberries, Raspberries, Rhubarb, Sweet Potatoes, watermelons,
--Slightly Acid Soil (pH 6.0-7.0)
Beans, Collards, Corn, Eggplant, Endive, Grape, Kale, Pea, Pepper, Pumpkin, Soybean, Strawberries, Squash, Tomato,
--Neutral to Alkaline Soil (pH 7.0-7.5)
Asparagus, Beet, Broccoli, Brussels Sprouts, Cabbage Cantaloupe, Carrot, Cauliflower, Celery, Cucumber, Lettuce, Onion, Spinach, Sunflower,

Plants should be grouped plants which thrive within the same pH range together in the same bed or row to make soil preparation and any pH adjustment easier.

5. Biointensive Outside Growing

a. Background/Description

The intensive closely spaced planting method in raised beds are to be used in the outdoors growing area. While widely spaced rows are convenient for machinery and harvesting, they provide poor microclimates for nourishing plants. Wide open areas between rows resemble deserts more than nature's gardens. They dry out quickly and provide an ideal space for weeds to grow in. Also, walking down the rows makes harvesting and weeding easy—but leads to rapid soil compaction.

The biointensive method uses double-dug, raised beds and intensive planting. The soil is richly composted and remains loose up to 24 inches deep, so plants can grow faster. This allows for easy weeding, good penetration and retention of water, and better utilization of fertilizers and composts. The beds take more time to prepare, but they require less time in the long run to maintain.

Biointensive methods are based on sophisticated principles dating back 4,000 years in China, 2,000 years in Greece, and 300 years in Europe. Biointensive agriculture is being practiced in 108 countries worldwide. These 3 to 5 foot wide mounds of closely spaced plants will quickly provide shade that helps to reduce weed infestations. Companion planting of different species that grow well together reduces insect infestations and helps create an effect that increases crop yield. Crop rotations will also be used. (see Companion Planting section)

b. Advantages of Intensive Mound System

The advantages of an intensive mound system include:

1) Soil builds up better than even nature can do.
2) Water consumption is a fraction of what other methods need, and energy consumption is much less
3) Can produce triple the yields of conventional methods and needs much less land area.

c. Fertilizers—Alternative Natural (See also Composting section)

1. Organic Material as Fertilizer

Almost any organic material can be made into fertilizer to assist in soil preparation. The NPK values for some commonly available natural materials are:

	N	P	K
Wood ashes	0	1.5	7
Alfalfa hay	2.5	.5	2.1
Fresh chicken manure	1.6	1.5	.9
Corn stalks	.8	.4	.9
Fish emulsion	5	2	2
Fresh grass clippings	1.2	.3	2
Leaf mold composted	.6	.2	.4
Maple leaves	.7	.1	.8
Fresh rabbit manure	2.4	1.4	.6
Sawdust	.2	0	.2
Straw	.7	.2	1.2

2. Marl/Clay as Fertilizer

Generations ago, farmers valued marl as a fertilizer for lime-deficient soils and as a soil conditioner for sandy soils. The lime in the clay-like marl cements sand grains together, so the soil can better retain heat and water. When added to clay soils, marl had the opposite effect: soil particles became less cohesive, allowing more air, heat, water and plant roots to penetrate. Scandinavian farmers, long familiar with these attributes, actively sought out marl deposits when they migrated to Wisconsin.

6. Vertical Gardening

a. Background/Description

It can be argued that vertical growing of plants started in the Hanging Gardens of Babylon. It has been practiced in various ways ever since. Vertical growing or vertical gardening can be loosely defined as using a small amount of space on the surface to support an upright system of growing medium with adequate access to sunlight or artificial light. Vertical gardening commonly utilizes hydroponics or soilless medium because of the lighter weight of the growing medium for root growth.

b. Products and Methods

Most of the vertical systems employ stacking containers that contain a combination of pearlite and vermiculite in various combinations. The containers can be expanded polystyrene (EPS), other plastic material, or even stainless steel sheeting. Some use a complete wall system made of lightweight concrete mixtures. (See Gardening-Vertical File)

c. Advantages of Vertical Methods

Vertically growing of plants most obvious advantage is the saving of floor space. Using the above-ground space that is normally underutilized results in dramatic increased in yields per square foot of floor space. Additional advantages include using greywater for watering. The greywater is normally introduced at the upper level of the plant wall and it trickles down through the root zone of the rest of the plants. The water is continually filtered until it reaches the bottom collection point.

Another advantage is that it evens out the temperature swings inside a greenhouse. This is because there is much greater mass that can be accessed by airflow. This increased density is similar to a large heat exchanger of sorts. This airflow can also be used for cooling in adequately designed systems.

d. Disadvantages of Vertical Methods

Most of the systems developed rely on hydroponics for culturing vegetables. This requires media, pumps, solution, timers, and energy to run the system. Also most of the systems recommend lettuce, tomatoes, greens, strawberries, and other herbs that do better using hydroponics. If a heavier media such as regular soil is used, it would tend to stress or even damage the fragile containers commonly used for vertical gardens.

e. EH Use of Vertical Methods

The Earth Home uses vertical methods in three places. The first place is the vertical Trombe wall as described in the next section. This wall uses more durable troughs that make it easier to change/mix the soil. The other area where vertical methods are employed is in the hanging herb containers inside the dining area. The third area where the advantages of vertical methods are used is in the animal area on the west side of the Earth Home. This method allows the tomato plants to be grown in an upward fashion on a trellis system. This saves valuable floor space for other uses.

D. Earth Home Greenhouse Growing Mechanics

1. EH Trombe Wall Soil V-Trough System.

a. Greenhouse Structural Overview

The Earth Home II is designed to use an 8 foot wide intensive growing area along the entire south side, except for the dining area. Vertical glass is used for glazing. Wooden beams, supports, and all wood components will use copper napthenate, cuprolignium (TM), or cuprinol preservative, which are more compatible with the high-humidity plant growing atmosphere.

In the present Earth Home design, the V-trough system on the south side is the main plant area. The west side will be used for growing plants such as tomatoes (with basil) that do better in the evening sun. The herbs will be grown next to the glass in the dining room, with a sheer nylon curtain over the window to help disperse the light into the room. Aluminized Mylar can also be used to reflect and spread the sunlight around the room.

b. Earth Home "V-Tough" System Details

1. Construction Details

In Earth Home I, I used a system of "stacked V-troughs". These are triangular troughs approximately 6 inches across at the top, and about 11 inches deep. Although most plant roots can go deeper, the vast majority of plant roots require less than 11 inches of soil for adequate growth (root zone).

Earth Home II will use a similar trough system—except that the roots will be allowed to go deeper into the back (See Earth Home II drawings for details). There will be a 3" wide layer of shared soil at the rear of the V-trough. Preliminary tests have been very successful.

2. Plant Growing Details

The vertical V-trough system will also make it easier to access the plants without bending over. Sunlight is spread throughout the levels of the V-trough system, allowing access by all plants. The plants bend towards the light and actually fall downward from the weight of growing. This is called "phototropism" and is designed into the growing method. Tests indicate that once the plant has stabilized in this configuration, plant growth continues.

Matte white paint reflects light back on the plants from the next trough and helps to spread the available sunlight onto the leaves. The smaller, sun-seeking, fruiting plants are placed in front in the sunlight, and the broader-leafed, shade-loving foliage plants are placed further back in the trough to absorb the rays of sun that make it through the other plants.

c. EH "V-Trough" Heat Transfer Overview

1. Providing Heat to the Soil

The V-trough system allows for the use of artificial heat to warm the soil by pumping hot water through tubing on the back surface of the trough. Studies have shown that warm soil (65°F) will produce plants even when the air temperature is considerably colder. It is better to rotate the soils so plants start with a "new" medium each time. Two-year soil rotation has been found to be adequate to grow healthy plants.

2. Getting Heat from the V-Trough

The water pipes can be used to extract heat from the soil as needed. As the pipes heat up, the water is circulated into a storage tank similar to active solar systems. This dual-use system is versatile and can be adjusted and maintained by the automation system. (see EH Home Automation section)

d. V-Trough Disassembly/Maintenance

The V-trough sides are removed and the soil can be blended while in a large mound. Compost can be added at this time also. Assembly is a matter of re-positioning the individual removable sides and putting the soil back into the V-trough.

*Used in Earth Home

2. Plant Growing Details

a. Seeds Overview

1. Seed Storage

The two greatest enemies of stored seeds are high temperature and high moisture. Seeds can be placed on screens in the hot sun or 90-95 deg. F. until the seeds break rather than bend when folded. This usually takes 7-8 days to reach about 10% moisture content. Seeds must be kept in stable, cool temperatures with low moisture. Sealed containers of glass or metal seem to work well. Seeds from all species can be kept for several years using this technique. Diatomaceous earth can also be added for additional pest protection.

2. Seed Planting

Seeds are planted directly in the soil, 1 seed diameter deep and watered heavily for the first week. Small seeds are covered with a light layer of sand to keep them moist. Allowing the soil to dry slightly before watering plants helps the roots go deeper. The plants in the Earth Home II are to be watered daily with a controlled system of automatic irrigation. Slightly warmed water will be used from a large coil of black plastic tubing. Shredded white mulch helps to reflect light and cuts down on evaporation loss from the soil.

The Earth Home design requires two seeds to be planted in place of every plant harvested, to compensate for the losses due to storage and germination. Planting two seeds will increase the likelihood that one plant will grow in the place of the one that was picked. (See Seed Viability Chart in Plants-Seed file.) It is a good idea to condition the seeds from storage by letting them pick up room moisture before putting them into the ground.

b. Cuttings

Advanced gardeners can also use cuttings to propagate selected varieties. Cuttings are the actual branches of a plant, which are put in soil and allowed to grow as a new plant or "clone." Typically the cutting is dipped into a root hormone such as indolebutyric acid, alphanaphthalene acetic acid, or commercial root hormone. Some old time growers split the lower part of the stem and inserted a kernel of oats before planting. The germinating of the oat was later found to release growth hormones.

3. Sunlight to Plants.

a. Sunlight Intensity

Full sunlight is approximately 10,000 foot-candles, while light on cloudy days is about 1,000 foot-candles. The rate of photosynthesis (food manufacture or growth) of plants is roughly proportional to the intensity of the sunlight, <u>up to</u> a maximum of about 1,300 foot-candles for short bushy plants and 2,300 for tall plants.

As previously mentioned, edible vegetable plants that grow in low light levels were selected over other varieties. There is very little information available on sunlight needs for vegetable plants. A level of 1,600 foot-candles was used as a baseline at the south glass, and 1000 foot-candles at a distance of 5 1/2 feet from the glass.

b. Overhead/Vertical Clear Panels

In order to increase the interior light levels above 750 foot-candles at about 5 feet from the vertical glass, opaque or white <u>overhead</u> panels must be used. There are three basic problems with near-horizontal, clear overhead panels that should be mentioned.

a. Hail damage can break panels.
b. Sealing problems necessitate increased maintenance over time. Wood, steel, caulk, aluminum, and glass all <u>expand</u> at a different rate.

*Used in Earth Home

c. An ingredient of sunlight, UV (ultraviolet) light degrades non-glass materials. Seven years is the approximate practical lifetime of most common polymer materials. (See Solar - Glazing.) Fluoropolymers such as Teflon and Tefzel can last much longer, but they are very expensive and are less resistant to tearing.

4. Irrigation Options.

Throughout the years of the Earth Home system research, I've tested a number of irrigation systems. They are as follows, with associated comments:

a. Drip Irrigation Systems.

These systems use small tubing that goes to individual plants. A small flow of water is delivered to the plant using intermittent controlled pressure. I've used seven different kinds of drip irrigation systems and I've had problems with six of them. Most of the problems are due to a slight variation of pressure, despite the claims of "pressure compensating" emitters. The pressure has to be exactly right in order for most of the drip irrigation system to perform well. The following figure lists some of the drip irrigation systems that are currently available and comments on each. (See also section that follows.)

b. Black Polyethylene "Grow Bag" System.

This system uses various sized plastic bags with holes punched in the bottom. Soil is so rare in Hawaii and Japan that many trees and shrubs are grown in these bags. The black surface soaks up the sun's rays to heat the soil and increase the growth rate. There is, however, difficulty in controlling the moisture in these bags.

c. Under-Surface "Sweating" Plugs.

I have tested the ceramic "sweating surface" plugs from Austria, and found that they do a good job of irrigating a plant up to about six weeks old. After this, the water requirements become more demanding, and the surface tension method of sucking the water through the tubing is not adequate. I find there has to be a certain amount of additional water pressure exerted to keep these ceramic elements operating. Also, the spaghetti tubing leading to the ceramic element is so small that bacteria and algae eventually plug it up.

d. Misting System.

I've experimented with water sprayed directly onto the leaves through a misting system, such as a spray nozzle. This system works well if the soil underneath the leaf system gets the excess runoff.

e. Earth Home Irrigation System

1. Primary Greywater Irrigation

I am currently using a dual irrigation system. The first system delivers waste water (greywater) from the Earth Home underneath the soil using Net-A-Film from Park Seed. The "under-soil" waste water system may be used without danger of disease or pathogen-causing bacteria on the leaves, because the leaves above the soil surface will not come in contact with these particles. Diluted detergent can be recycled in this way because most of the ingredients in the detergent, including phosphorous, are beneficial to plant growth. (See Plumbing - Greywater.) (See also Wash Water section.)

*Used in Earth Home

Irrigation Type	Company/Model	Comments/Opinions/Test Results
Drip	Global Rainbird Spears	clogs and waters non-uniformly
Fogger	RIS	Fine mist to increase humidity so plants need less watering -- requires high water pressure
Soaker Hose (Recycled Rubber)	Aquapore	non-uniform pore size causes uneven watering
Porous Ceramic	Wenninghaus (Blumat)	tubing too small, algae clogs flow
Tyvek Tubing	Irrigro	algae growth
Porous Tubing	Micropore	organic material clogs the pores, degrades more quickly in sunlight, susceptible to cuts and holes
Porous Tubing	Net-A-Film (Park Seed)	okay for organic fertilizers, durable

Figure 149-DRIP IRRIGATION SYSTEMS

2. Spray Water System

The second system uses a spray nozzle to direct filtered rainwater to foliage when necessary. The soil may become slightly compacted when water is sprayed upon it, as opposed to the under-soil system. Plants, however, like to have their leaves cleaned often. The amount of moisture that a plant gets is not the most important factor to growing plants. The controlling factor is when and where it gets the moisture. However, even more important than moisture is light and temperature. These two are the primary factors for growing plants. Recent research has shown that plants like to be soaked on an infrequent basis (once per week) more than daily small waterings. (See Watering Controls section)

3. Outside Irrigation

The outside plants, such as Jerusalem artichokes and quinoa, may need additional irrigation from below the soil surface. ***Irrigation from below ground has been shown to use only one twentieth (5%) of the water used in aboveground irrigation in arid climates.***

4. Watering Controls

Sensitive controls, sensors, and water moisture meters will help to determine when and how much water to use on the plants. Optimum levels of moisture will ensure that the crops will mature with maximum harvest potential.

*Used in Earth Home

f. Future Irrigation

The most accurate way of determining when soil needs irrigation is to measure what is called "soil tension," or, more accurately, pre-irrigation soil water tension. Most vegetable plants have a soil water tension in the range of .1 bar to 1 bar. This measurement can be made by measuring the amount of electrical current passing through ceramic disks under the soil. Other methods to measure soil moisture such as gypsum blocks and metallic probes have a shorter lifespan. These electrical signals are used to initiate the irrigation cycle. (See Irrigation files.) The following figure gives the optimal pre-irrigation soil water tension of various plants. From this chart and other studies, it was found that plants need irrigation at different depths and at different ages. Each species of plant has an optimal way to receive irrigation. The plant trough system in Earth Home II can segregate the various varieties of plants so that each individual species can be treated differently -- even when grown in the same greenhouse environment.

For irrigation purposes, the "root zone" is defined as the depth that the roots grow to get moisture. Most plants will have most of their roots close to the surface, though a few roots may grow very deep. Tomato plants, for example, will send a few shoots down ten feet if allowed. However, if the plant is not able to send shoots down that far, it will not be overly damaged.

5. Pollination.

a. Pollination Background

Pollination is the transfer of pollen from the anthers to the stigma of the flower in nature. This happens by action of the wind or by insects. Sometimes the advanced gardener may also assist with a watercolor brush or cotton swab. Studies have indicated dramatic increases in seed production when plants are insect-pollinated.

b. Honeybees as Pollinators

One third of all the food produced in the United States depends on honeybees for pollination. Honeybees are not the only insects to cross-pollinate flowers, but they are most important because they get pollen from one species at a time.

Normally, the smallest colony of honeybees that will keep warm is 4,000 to 5,000 bees and one queen. However, with artificial heat, a colony of 200 bees and one queen can constitute a colony. The hive is designed to be placed near the center of the greenhouse so they can travel both directions. The hive is perennial, and most of the bees will survive the winter if given back about 1/3 of their production of honey or boiled sugar beet juice. Their simple needs must be provided for except when they get their food in the form of nectar from flowering plants.

c. “Stingless” Honeybees

Most common honeybees possess a mean sting when provoked. Because of this, most growers do not manage beehives themselves. They have to call in professional beekeepers. Sometimes they find that hives are not available when they need them. However, there are 400 species of bees which have evolved without a sting. Whereas common honeybees collect mostly nectar from flowers, stingless honeybees collect mainly the pollen. This means that stingless honeybees are very good pollinators.

There is a long history of keeping stingless bees, going back to the ancient Mayan civilization of South America. Mayan beekeepers were harvesting honey from stingless honeybees more than a thousand years ago! The Australian stingless honeybee, Trigonia carbonaria, is a promising species being looked at to replace stinging varieties. It is known to be a good pollinator of macadamia trees and also quickly adapts to new plants it has not encountered before.

*Used in Earth Home

Crop	Tension (Centibar)
Celery	20 - 30
Melon	35 - 40
Lettuce	40 - 60
Strawberry	20 - 30
Cabbage	60 - 70
Cauliflower	60 - 70
Early Broccoli	45 - 55
Late Broccoli	60 - 70
Carrot	55 - 65
Green Onions	45 - 65
Dry Onions	55 - 65
Potatoes	30 - 50
Sweet Corn	50 - 100
Lemons	40
Oranges	20 - 100
Deciduous Fruit	50 - 80
Grapes	40 - 100
Avocado	50

Figure 150-OPTIMAL SOIL WATER TENSIONS

(Before irrigation)

Stingless honeybees also store honey, but not as much as common honeybees. For example Trigonia carbonaria produces only 800 ml (less than a liter) of honey per hive each year. Only half this small amount can be taken by the beekeeper. The rest must be left for the bees or they will die.

The number of stingless honeybees in a hive ranges from a few hundred to a few thousand. To overwinter in a cool climate, they need some form of heating. Japanese scientists have recently developed a heated beehive for stingless honeybees. The hive consists of two boxes. The bees live inside the inner box, which is usually made out of wood. The inner box has three compartments: one for feeding, one for food storage, and one for the brood. The outer box is insulated, and contains a heating element and a heat sensor. This keeps the hive at a constant temperature, even in the middle of winter.

d. Other Pollinators

Bumblebees (bombus sep.) have also been used as efficient pollinators. There are approximately 50 known species of bumblebees in North America. Mild-mannered species are generally used for pollination to avoid the possibility of aggressive behavior.

An advantage of bumblebees is that they will pollinate at lower temperatures than honeybees. Another advantage is that they visit more flowers per minute than do honey bees, making them very efficient. They know the difference between a pollinated flower and an unpollinated flower and are attracted to the scent of the unpollinated one.

One of the disadvantages to using bumblebees is that they are an annual society. This means that all of the bees die off except for an inseminated queen that hibernates and starts a new colony in the spring. Another disadvantage of bumblebees is that the colony is generally a very small size, with approximately 100 bees being the largest colony.

Other insects besides bumblebees such as beetles, flies, wasps, solitary bees, alkali bees (nomia melanderi), or leafcutter bees (megachile rotundata) sometimes go from one species to the next, making it more difficult for cross-pollination. Leafcutter bees have been used to pollinate many crops including alfalfa for many years. Leafcutter bees are more solitary and don't require as much care as honeybees. (See Insects-Bees file.) Leafcutter bees are also less dangerous and don't require the extensive equipment for care.

Other pollinators include andrenid bees, halictid bees, sweat bees, syrphid or hover flies, and blowflies. Blowflies have become popular in recent years because they are easy to handle, do not sting, and can be used in small numbers. Hummingbirds, butterflies, and moths are mostly interested in nectar and pollen from flower species.

e. Earth Home Pollinators

The vegetable species in the Earth Home are either self-pollinated or insect-pollinated. There are also "friendly" insects in the south plant growing area to help pollinate and to attack harmful insects. (See Insects/Biological Control files.) A small colony of honeybees (apis mellifera) will be used to pollinate the vegetable flowers in the Earth Home.

6. Composting (see separate Composting section)

7. Carbon Dioxide Enrichment (see CO_2 Enrichment section)

E. Animals in Earth Home

A small number of selected animal kingdom members will also be raised in the Earth Home. ***Preferred animals will be those that eat foods that human occupants do not-such as kitchen scraps, fish cleanings, fruit and vegetable cullings, and foliage.*** The rate at which an animal converts food into edible tissue for human consumption is called "feed efficiency".

1. High Feed Efficiency

One of the requirements of the animals is that they have a high feed efficiency (See the following figures). Many studies have been done on domesticated agricultural animals commonly used for food. However, some other animals not currently in widespread use have been studied and found to have a much higher feed to protein efficiency. (See Animals files.)

*Used in Earth Home

Disadvantages of plant proteins

It must be emphasized that the present review is restricted to the protein of the foodstuff and no attention is paid to the vitamins and minerals that accompany proteins from some sources but not others.

The disadvantages of plant proteins may be summarized as:—(1) In general they are lower in quality than are animal proteins; (2) Plant sources are usually bulky so that large quantities are needed to provide an adequate protein intake. The isolation of plant proteins can overcome this disadvantage. For example, a powder composed of 90% protein has been produced from groundnut in India, free from any distinctive taste, which can be emulsified with water (with the addition of 4 g sodium phosphate) to yield a liquid containing 80 g of protein per pint, compared with milk containing 18 g of protein per pint; (3) People prefer to eat meat. There is an unexplained preference for meat. When given free choice the number of vegetarians is very limited and some of them even produce foods, such as nut cutlets, which are an imitation of meat dishes. In an attempt to make greater use of available foods patents have been taken out for converting plant proteins to "synthetic" meat by extruding the protein in fibrous form, pressing to a block to simulate the texture of meat (the so-called chewable gel) and flavouring with meat extract or chicken extract; (4) Some pulses contain natural toxins, which means, although they can be removed by leaching or cooking, that further investigation is needed before such foods are advocated for large-scale consumption.

Advantages of plant proteins over animal proteins

(1) The outstanding advantage of plant sources of protein is that they yield a greater quantity of protein per acre of land (Table 2). About 10 times as much vegetable protein can be produced as animal protein from the same acreage. The efficiency of conversion of animal feed proteins to eggs or bacon is 15-30% and to milk 50-60%. This is the price we pay for a more concentrated protein, usually of higher biological value, and a desirable flavour.

(2) Greater quantities of plant proteins are available in world markets (Table 3) and when we normally speak of a protein shortage it is particularly of animal protein.

(3) Plant proteins are free from pathogens (usually).

TABLE 2
Land needed to produce 20 kg of protein in one year under various crops (acres)

Beans	0·1	Dairy cows	0·44 – 1·1
Grass	0·1 – 0·25	Fowls	1·4
Cereals	0·23	Sheep	0·8 – 1·9
Potatoes	0·27	Pigs	2·2
		Beef	1·0 – 2·5

(From "World Population and World Food Supplies" by Sir John Russell. George Allen & Unwin).

TABLE 2A
Conversion efficiency for proteins (Great Britain)

Milk	33%	
Eggs	37%	
Poultry meat	14%	
Petit poussin	25%	
Beef — winter	10%	least efficient — most desired by man
— grass	4·6%	
Lamb	12%	
Bacon	13%	
Pork	14 – 17%	

(4) There are no religious objections to plant proteins (with rare exceptions, e.g. the cow pea is not eaten in parts of Tanganyika). Apart from religious restrictions of beef and pig meat in several countries, there are regional restrictions on chickens, eggs and mutton for women and on fish during pregnancy, and certain local taboos on giving meat and fish to small children.

TABLE 3
World Production of major commodities (excluding U.S.S.R. and China) in million metric tons of protein

Wheat	16·5	
Maize	15·8	
Rice	7·4	
Barley	5·7	
Oats	4·9	
Pulses	6·0	Total vegetable protein 56·3
Milk	8·5	
Fish	5·7	
Meat	5·1	
Eggs	1·1	Total animal protein 20·4

(5) They are cheaper. In Mexico the farmer prefers to eat peas and beans and sell his eggs for money. With the money he can buy the peas and beans, which he finds more satisfying, although the nutritionist would advocate eating some of the eggs.

(6) On the open market plant proteins appear to be more accurately labelled than animal proteins. Certainly in the field of animal feedingstuffs it is not uncommon to find feather meal, crab meal and fish bone meal labelled fish meal, and meat and bone meals labelled meat meal.

Vegetarianism versus mixed diets

From the table of yields per acre it would appear that the answer to the protein shortage is vegetarianism. But in practice mixed farming has considerable advantages. For example, a report from India stated that when one-third of a farm was devoted to fodder crops for milch cattle, more wheat, cotton and sugar was obtained from the remaining area than had previously been obtained from the whole of the farm; due to the manuring of the ground.

A further point arises from the complementation in food consumption that exists between man and his animals. To quote Dr. Norman

Figure 151-PROTEIN CONVERSION EFFICIENCY

*Used in Earth Home

FEED TO FOOD EFFICIENCY RATING BY SPECIES OF ANIMALS, RANKED BY PROTEIN CONVERSION EFFICIENCY
(Based on Energy as TDN or DE and Crude Protein in Feed Eaten by Various Kinds of Animals Converted into Calories and Protein Content of Ready-to-Eat Human Food)

Species	Unit of Production (on foot)	Feed Required to Produce One Production Unit				Dressing Yield		Ready-to-Eat; Yield of Edible Product (meat and fish deboned and after cooking)				Feed Efficiency[1] (lb feed to produce one lb product)		Efficiency Rating			
		Pounds	TDN[2]	DE[3]	Protein	Percent	Net Left	As % of Raw Product (carcass)	Amount Remaining from One Unit of Production	Calorie[4]	Protein[4]			Calorie Efficiency[5]		Protein Efficiency[6]	
		(lb)	(lb)	(kcal)	(lb)	(%)	(lb)	(%)	(lb)	(kcal)	(lb)	(%)	(ratio)	(%)	(ratio)	(%)	(ratio)
Broiler....................	1 lb chicken	2.4[7]	1.94[8]	3,880	0.21[8]	72[9]	0.72	54[10]	0.39	274	0.11	41.7	2.4:1	7.1	14.2:1	52.4	1.9:1
Dairy cow..............	1 lb milk	1.11[7]	0.9[8]	1,800	0.1[8]	100	1.0	100	1.0	309	0.037	90.0	1.11:1	17.2	5.8:1	37.0	2.7:1
Turkey	1 lb turkey	5.2[7]	4.21[8]	8,420	0.46[8]	79.7[9]	0.797	57[11]	0.45	446	0.146	19.2	5.2:1	5.3	18.9:1	31.7	3.2:1
Layer.....................	1 lb eggs (8 eggs)	4.6[7]	3.73[8]	7,460	0.41[8]	100	1.0	100[12]	1.0[12]	616	0.106	21.8	4.6:1	8.3	12.1:1	25.9	3.9:1
Rabbit....................	1 lb fryer	3.0[13]	2.20	4,400	0.48	55[13]	0.55	79[13]	0.43	301	0.08	35.7	2.8:1	6.8	14.6:1	16.7	6.0:1
Fish......................	1 lb fish	1.6[14]	0.98	1,960	0.57	65[15]	0.65	57[16]	0.37	285	0.093	62.5	1.6:1	14.5	6.9:1	16.3	6.1:1
Hog (birth to 200 lb).........	1 lb pork	4.9[17]	3.67	7,340	0.69	70[18]	0.70	44[19]	0.31	341	0.088	20.4	4.9:1	4.6	21.5:1	12.7	7.8:1
Beef steer (yearling finishing period in feedlot)..........	1 lb beef	9.0[17]	5.85	11,700	0.90	58[18]	0.58	49[19]	0.28	342	0.085	11.1	9.0:1	2.9	34.2:1	9.4	10.6:1
Lamb (finishing period in feedlot)..................	1 lb lamb	8.0[17]	4.96	9,920	0.86	47[18]	0.47	40[19]	0.19	225	0.052	12.5	8.0:1	2.3	44.1:1	6.0	16.5:1

[1]Feed efficiency as used herein is based on pounds of feed required to produce 1 lb of product. Given in both percent and ratio.

[2]TDN pounds computed by multiplying pounds feed (column to left) times percent TDN in normal rations. Normal ration percent TDN taken from M.E. Ensminger's books and rations, except for following: dairy cow, layer, broiler, and turkey from *Agricultural Statistics 1974*, p. 358, Table 518. Fish based on averages recommended by Michigan and Minnesota Stations and U.S. Fish and Wildlife.

[3]Digestible Energy (DE) in this column given in kcal, which is 1 Calorie (written with a capital C), or 1,000 calories (written with a small c). Kilocalories computed from TDN values in column to immediate left as follows: 1 lb TDN = 2,000 kcal.

[4]From *Lessons on Meat*, National Live Stock and Meat Board, 1965.

[5]Kilocalories in ready-to-eat food ÷ kilocalories in feed consumed, converted to percentage. Loss = kcal in feed ÷ kcal in product.

[6]Protein in ready-to-eat food ÷ protein in feed consumed, converted to percentage. Loss = pounds protein in feed ÷ pounds protein in product.

[7]*Agricultural Statistics 1974*, p. 358, Table 518. Pounds feed per unit of production is expressed in equivalent feeding value of corn.

[8]Since pounds feed (column No. 2) per unit of production (column No. 1) is expressed in equivalent feeding value of corn, the values for corn were used in arriving at these computations. No. 2 corn values are TDN, 81%; protein, 8.9%. Hence, for the dairy cow 81% × 1.11 = 0.9 lb TDN; and 8.9% × 1.11 = 0.1 lb protein.

[9]*Marketing Poultry Products*, 5th Ed., by E. W. Benjamin et al., John Wiley & Sons, 1960, p. 147.

[10]*Factors Affecting Poultry Meat Yields*, University of Minnesota Sta. Bull. 476, 1964, p. 29, Table 11 (fricassee).

[11]Ibid. Page 28, Table 10.

[12]Calories and protein computed basis per egg; hence, the values herein are 100% and 1.0 lb, respectively.

[13]Based on information in *Commercial Rabbit Raising*, Ag. Hdbk. No. 309, USDA, 1966, and *A Handbook on Rabbit Raising*, by H. M. Butterfield, Washington State College Ext. Bull. No. 411, 1950.

[14]Data from report by Dr. Phillip J. Schaible, Michigan State University, *Feedstuffs*, April 15, 1967.

[15]*Industrial Fishery Technology*, ed. by Maurice E. Stansby, Reinhold Pub. Corp., 1963, Ch. 26, Table 26-1.

[16]Ibid. Reports that, "Dressed fish averages about 73% flesh, 21% bone, and 6% skin." In limited experiments conducted by A. Ensminger, it was found that there was a 22% cooking loss on filet of sole. Hence, these values -- 73% flesh from dressed fish, minus 22% cooking losses—give 57% yield of edible fish after cooking, as a percent of the raw, dressed product.

[17]Estimates by the authors.

[18]Ensminger, M. E., *The Stockman's Handbook*, 4th Ed., Sec. XII.

[19]Allowance made for both cutting and cooking losses following dressing. Thus, values are on a cooked, ready-to-eat basis of lean and marbled meat, exclusive of bone, gristle, and fat. Values provided by National Live Stock and Meat Board (personal communication of June 5, 1967, from Dr. Wm. C. Sherman, Director, Nutrition Research, to the senior author), and based on data from *The Nutritive Value of Cooked Meat*, by Ruth M. Leverton and George V. Odell, Misc. Pub. MP-49, Appendix C, March 1958).

Figure 152-FEED TO FOOD EFFICIENCY

Mostly high feed efficiency animals, such as fowl, piglets, and chevrotains, are to be used for the Earth Home system. Note that there is an average 90% loss of energy when plant food is turned into herbivore meat. (Rabbits and chickens cannot be grown in the same environment because of the diseases they transmit to one another and the incomplete nutritional benefits from rabbit meat.) Fish are probably the most efficient converters of feed to flesh, requiring from 2 to 4 pounds of basic feedstuffs to produce 1 pound of fish.

2. Large-Scale Animal Production Techniques

a. Chicken Production

In large-scale chicken production, for example, highly advanced techniques are used to care for them. Growers often raise 60 to 120 thousand chickens in one barn; automatically fed, watered, and cared for using automated equipment. ***This same type of automated feeding equipment will be used on a much smaller scale for Earth Home II.*** Grit for the chickens will have to be provided as well as extra calcium for egg production. This calcium can come from hydrated lime and/or recycled from other eggshells. Food for the chickens can be mixed from leaves, fish scraps, yard manure, and worms.

b. Calf Pen Example

Another example of large-scale efficiency in raising food for human beings is the use of small calf pens, in which the calves are confined and never allowed to walk about. The calves were fed a highly nutritious ration to gain weight quickly before slaughter. This produces a fast-growing animal with very tender meat. The Japanese have taken this system one step further by actually suspending their beef cattle in the air and feeding it without letting the feet touch the ground. The highest quality of beef in China and Japan is produced by "massaging" the live cow to tenderize the meat-*while it's hanging in the air.*

c. Earth Home Techniques

Human beings have developed very automated, efficient methods of growing animals for consumption. I feel that similar techniques can be effectively applied on a much smaller scale in a self-sufficient home. Many of the techniques and species to be used have never been experimented with to any extent.

3. Animals Production

a. Animals Discussion

I have compiled a list of animals that are under consideration for the Earth Home system. This is a comprehensive list assembled over a long period of time. Many were listed because of some unique quality or feature. Rodents, for example, can be fed to the fish or fowl and many have dual uses.

b. Animals under Consideration Chart

The following charts list some of the most efficient animals under consideration for the Earth Home. Descriptions and comments are included as necessary.

c. Animals Care/Feeding

The taste of animal tissue is greatly affected by the animal's diet. Feeding an animal a diet that human beings eat will produce meat that is highly palatable. Sodium chloride (salt) must be given to herbivores to help regulate body temperature. Insects are discussed in the Fish/Worm/Insect section that follows. Kudzu can be used to supply leaves to herbivorous animals. The kudzu grows very fast and has roots that are edible as well.

ANIMALS/ MAMMALS	SCIENTIFIC NAME	NOTES/COMMENTS
Goat	Nubian or pygmy (African)	Good milk goat. Gestation about 155 days. Can be bred at 8 months. Comes in heat late August or early September. 21 day cycle. Around the world, more people drink goat mild than cow milk. Needs ½ acre pasture per animal.
Pygmy goat/Pigs	Vietnamese drop-belly	50# (makes good pets) Friendly—eats almost anything. Pen may have to be ventilated for odors.
Sheep	Suffolk dorset or Nigerian	Gives milk also; 1 qt./day for 10 mos.; maximum maturity 1 year; 16-21 inches tall
Rabbit	Himalayan, Californian, and New Zealand White for meat. Flemish giant is bred for a prized pelt.	Many diseases when raised with chickens; pelts for clothing; 4 litters/year (84 offspring). If slaughtered at 5#/wt. yield of 420# protein/year. Rabbit manure has NPK of 7.0, 2.4, .6. Feed in evening. Rabbit meat is staple in the rest of the world. 3 does and 1 buck can provide one rabbit per week of protein.
Dog	Chow Chow (China)	Fed grain and pelts used for clothing.
Cavy (guinea pigs)	Family cavioae patagonian	Similar to tiny deer - free of disease, clean, odorless, already raised by Indians.
Chevrotain (mouse deer)	Family Malay tragulidae (order) genus tragulus	Favorite food of pythons; 5 mos. to maturity, artiodactyla, gestation 140-177 days, .7 to 8 KG, natives keep like pigs, nervous.
Bush antelope		Sometimes omnivorous.
(CONT. NEXT PAGE)		

Figure 153-ANIMALS IN EARTH HOME-MAMMALS

*Used in Earth Home

INVERTE-BRATES	SCIENTIFIC NAME	NOTES/COMMENTS
(CONT. FROM PREVIOUS PAGE)		
		--------Pheromones can be used to attract from great distances.
Sow bugs	Isopod, Negev desert species	They are vegetation "digesters" or "compost eaters"
Cockroach	Arenivaga erratica, Blattela germanica, Gyna kazungulana, Panesthia javanica	Lives in burrows of vertebrates - eats feces. Converts food to protein 3 times more efficient than pigs. These are the sub-group known as guanobies or feces eaters. Eats cellulose
Bees		Pollination/honey
Centipede	class chilopoda	Eats insects
Boxelder bug		Feeds on seed-bearing female boxelder trees with no harm to trees.
Common house fly		Pupae used for poultry food.
Meal worms		Feed to fish
Crickets		Food directly for humans or fish food, quick multipliers.
Grasshoppers		Already used by some scientists as human food.
Worms	Red worms, lumbricus rubellus (or Georgia Jumper)	Fed cornmeal or possibly animal manure, typically 53 to 72% proteins (dry wt.)
(CONT. NEXT PAGE)		

Figure 154-ANIMALS IN EARTH HOME-INVERTIBRATES

*Used in Earth Home

FISH/ WATER CREATURES	SCIENTIFIC NAME	NOTES/COMMENTS
(CONT. FROM PREVIOUS PAGE)		
Gambusia		These tiny fish eat mosquito larvae.
Rainbow Trout		Fed on human sewage. Feed conversion when young, 1# food/1# fish
Sponges		Water filters
Carp	Koi or grass carp	Easily spawned in captivity, wide temp. range (disease resistant).
Catfish	Channel	Withstands ½ the O_2 level, eats anything - typha water plant
Tilapia Mossambica		Needs warm water
Gouramis	Malaysia	1½ years to maturity, 4-8 years to spawn, raised in rain barrels in SE Asia.
Silver Salmon		1.62# food for 1# fish.
Ruffe	Gymnocephalus cernjus	Reproduce first year--thousands of eggs.
Leeches	Hirudidae	Food source for fish.
(CONT. NEXT PAGE)		

Figure 155-ANIMALS IN EARTH HOME-FISH/WATER

*Used in Earth Home

RODENTS	SCIENTIFIC NAME	NOTES/COMMENTS
(CONT. FROM PREVIOUS PAGE)		
Hamster	Give birth at 16 days old	Under consideration also.
Mouse	Muridae oxymycterus	O. Rutilans eats insects such as termites and cockroaches.
Pika	½# weight	
Gerbil	Mongolian or Saharan	28-day gestation, disease free, tolerates extreme hot and cold, eats salty leaves.
Fat sand rats		Eats salty succulent plants.
Bandicoot		Marsupial, gestation 12.5 days, 11.5 days adult.
Agouti	(also acouchi) dasyproctidae dasyprocta	Vegetarian, used as food now.
Lemming	Lemmus rodentia	Litters throughout the year: 16-23 day gestation.
Nutria		Small beaver, 8 months to maturity (130 days to maturity)
(CONT. NEXT PAGE)		

Figure 156-ANIMALS IN EARTH HOME-RODENTIA

BIRDS	SCIENTIFIC NAME	NOTES/COMMENTS
(CONT. FROM PREVIOUS PAGE)		
Goose/swan		Some species lay 1 egg/day if egg is removed. Much more fat in skin/tissue.
Chicken	Fayoumi Rhode Island Red/Sears Mini	Fast maturing, lay by 4 months of age, males 4.5 pounds, females 3.5 Avg. American east 55# chicken per year. Use 8-12 laying hens and one rooster. Sears Mini eats 20% less feed (60#/yr.) and produces an egg per day.
Turkey		Fast growing - eats many foods.
Quail	Coturnix (bobwhite also)	Omnivorous, food can be 1 plant--multi-eggs and meat, year round, lays at 6 weeks old. Quail outnumber chickens in Asia as source of eggs for eating. Eggs hatch in 23 days.
Ducklings	Campbell, muscovy, or White Pekin	Disease-free, extremely fast growing, eats insects, water constantly, forages for green plants in summer. 15 ducks and 2-3 drakes for a family of four. Produces 5-8 pounds of meat in 8-10 weeks. Much more fat in skin/tissue.
Jungle chickens		Native to India.
REPTILES		
Iguana		Two years to mature; eggs eaten for food also.

Figure 157-ANIMALS IN EARTH HOME-BIRDS

*Used in Earth Home

F. Raising Fish (Aquaculture)

Research has shown that the average family could provide all its animal protein requirements in a 3.000 gallon covered and heated pool full of Tilapia fish.

1. Mechanical/Electrical Systems

a. Tank/Filtration Designs

Fish are an intricate part of the Earth Home system. They can be raised efficiently in tanks (located on the west end of the Earth Home); using equipment modeled from current aquaculture projects in the southern United States and New England. The bottom of the fish tanks will be covered with a "water channel plenum" system covered with 2-3 inches of "pea gravel". Pea gravel is small rocks that provide a surface for aerobic bacteria that devour growth-inhibiting metabolites produced by fish. Air is introduced into the center tube connected to the bottom plenum. Rising bubbles create a flow of water toward the surface. Water near the bottom plenum system will be sucked down through the pea gravel. Bacteria thrive on nutrient-rich water flowing over the surface that is identical to most commercial aquariums.

When a new aquarium is fist set up, there will be very few bacteria. They will not multiply until there is something for them to feed on. Initially, only a few fish should be added to the tank to start the cycle with their waste products.

In any body of water, there is what is called a "nitrogen cycle". During this cycle, waste products from aquatic organisms, which are toxic to aquatic life, are converted into harmless nitrates, which are then absorbed by the plants. In the enclosed ecosystem of the fish tank, allowances must be made to enable this cycle to continue uninterrupted. Filtration and aeration must continue in order to effectively raise fish.

b. Power/Aeration Requirements

Power needed for aeration of the fish tanks comes from two sources. One is a wind-pumping system in back of the Earth Home, pumping air directly to the fish tank and aerobic digester. The second source comes from the battery bank which powers a low-wattage electrical motor connected to a spinning disk near the water's surface. Water is drawn up by centrifugal action, and thrown in small drops across the surface of the water. This increases the contact time between the water and the air, adding needed oxygen to the water.

There are a number of problems to be overcome with raising fish for food. ***Energy must be provided for aeration, water filtration, and any water pumping activity.*** Also, fish will stop growing when the stocking densities are too great. Fish naturally grow larger when raised in a larger tank. Sunlight must also be provided for adequate algae growth.

c. Lighting Requirements for Fish Tanks

Current design of Earth Home II will allow light to get into the fish tanks directly through the west side of the house. One interesting option I looked at for bringing light into the tanks is called a "Himawari". This is a concentrating solar collector system that focuses light inside a fiber optic cable and then directed anywhere. This is a somewhat inefficient system because some light is lost as it enters and leaves the fiber optic cable. However, the wavelengths of light from the cable seem to be much better for growing plants than natural sunlight. A similar concept was also evaluated for an interior lighting system but abandoned because of cost.

One recent advance by Department of Energy's Oak Ridge National Laboratory (ORNL) uses roof-mounted two-axis tracking concentrating collectors. These concentrators separate the visible and infrared portions of the sun's rays. Using large-diameter optical fibers, the device distributes visible light to interiors of buildings. The system converts infrared, or non-visible, portions of the solar spectrum into electricity. These and other advances will be utilized to provide more light for fish rearing.

***Used in Earth Home**

2. Fish Species Options

a. Herbivorous Fish

The tilapia mossambica has been the preferred, fast growing, warm water species for many aquaculture projects. Phytoplankton feeders such as blue tilapia have become more popular recently. The amurs (carp) are another logical choice, but grass carp, for example, won't breed in captivity.

b. Carnivorous Fish

Bluegill, catfish, perch, and crappie have also been used for fish culture. Trout requires water temperature below 60°F. Typically carnivorous fish are poor converters of food into flesh. The monks of old in Europe had carp in their stewponds. ***However, catfish is the species I have chosen because:***

a. They have a wide variation of diet: they eat almost anything.
b. They can thrive on one-half of the oxygen concentration that other fish need.
c. They don't slow down growth or succumb to diseases if the water temperature fluctuates up to 10°F.

For efficiency reasons, fish must be raised in "close quarters". The water surrounding them contains many fish waste products. Some irrigation systems have used fish tank water directly on plants, and have had good results because of the high fertilizer content in the water. The Earth Home plumbing system allows a portion of the roof water to replenish the fish tanks (for oxygenation) and to divert the overflow to either the aerobic digester or undersoil irrigation system.

3. Feeding Fish/Options

Some studies indicate that 55 fish, raised correctly, would supply a family of four with its minimum requirement of protein.

a. Worms/Minnows

Feeding fish a diet of worms exclusively would require five worms per day per fish, or 275 worms per day. This is a huge number of worms to raise effectively and substantially rules out feeding them exclusively.

Studies are underway to use an aquatic food chain inside the fish tank itself. For example, killifish such as the American Flagfish eat algae, live food, detritus, and bits of chopped meat and lettuce. They breed easily, grow fast, and could then be food for the catfish.

b. Rodents

Selected rodents may serve as another supplemental fish food. (See Animals file.) They can be raised on a variety of waste products, including waste vegetation from the greenhouse. They multiply rapidly and could provide food for fish and fowl. One example is using mice for feeding to fish and ducks.

There are many scientific studies on mice because of the ease to which they can be raised and the speed at which they multiply. Containment of the mice would be a primary concern when using for fish food.

*Used in Earth Home

c. Polyculture (Fowl Wastes into Tank)

Fish can also be directly fed waste products of certain fowl. In Asia, fish polyculture has been big business for many years (See the following figure). Fish are fed the waste products of ducklings and/or quail that are raised above the fish. Azolla/rice/fish and rice/azolla/pig/fish polyculture systems are being tested in China. Azolla/rice/duck systems are being looked at in Japan. A simplified polyculture system will be used in Earth Home II.

d. Insects as Fish Food

Insects in the Earth Home are designed to be utilized for waste control and human food as well as food for the fish. (See Future Food Production section). Insects will be of key importance for feeding fish. ***Ninety percent of the world's biomass is invertebrates, such as insects and worms***. This large portion of the Earth's creatures should be utilized at least to feed fish, thereby transforming protein into a form more palatable to human beings. (See Animals - Insects files.) (See Insects, Food Source files.)

Insects for fish food that are highly efficient include cockroaches, carrion beetles, and "guanobies" (native to bat caves). A mixture of insects can be blown down on the water's surface with a device known as a "Will-o-the-Wisp", or similar devices that capture insects. A semi-automated insect pellet feeder could be modified to feed insects such as mealworms from a special rearing area.

Another insect which is being considered is the box elder bug, which eats the female pollen sacks and other parts of the box elder, but causes little harm to the tree. A system of this kind may be tested using indoor vegetation such as dwarf or bonsai trees.

4. Pellets for Fish Feeding

a. Pellets/Alternative Fish Food Issues

There is also some research being done on "pelletizing" food scraps and vegetable greens to be used for fish food. However, the use of plant-derived materials such as legume seeds, different types of oilseed cake, leaf meals, leaf protein concentrates, and root tuber meals as fish feed ingredients is limited by the presence of a wide variety of antinutritional substances. Important among these are protease inhibitors, phytates, glucosinolates, saponins, tannins, lectins, oligosaccharides, and non-starch polysaccharides, phytoestrogens, alkaloids, antigenic compounds, gossypols, cyanogens, mimosine, cyclopropenoid fatty acids, canavanine, antivitamins, and phorbol esters. The effects of these substances on finfish can be substantial. Much testing is ongoing on alternative fish food.

The choice of fish species is paramount to finding an alternative food for them. Carnivorous fish require a diet of high protein content. These fish have very poor utilization of carbohydrate as an energy source, and some evidence is developing that the inclusion of certain types of carbohydrates in the diet is, in fact, detrimental. Soybean meal appears to be a reasonably good feed component for alternative aquaculture diets.

b. Nutrients Needed

Nutrients essential to fish are the same as those required by most other animals. These include water, proteins (amino acids), lipids (fats, oils, fatty acids), carbohydrates (sugars, starch), vitamins and minerals. (Note: Utilizing raw fish as a main ingredient in fish feeds has long been recognized to be harmful to the health and growth of fish due primarily to the presence of the anti-nutrient, thiaminase.)

Figure 158-POLYCULTURE PONDS

With few exceptions, feeding a single type of food is neither complete nor balanced and does not supply all the nutrients a fish might need in its diet. Hence, two or more ingredients should be mixed into homemade feed formulations. Feeds are formulated to be dry, with a final moisture content of 6-10%, semi-moist with 35-40% water or wet with 50-70% water content.

c. Main Ingredients

1. Proteins and Amino Acids (32-45%)

Soybean meal, legumes, and wheat gluten are excellent sources of protein.

*Used in Earth Home

2. Lipids. (4-28%)

Oils from vegetable oils such as canola, sunflower, and linseed are common sources of lipids in fish feeds.

3. Carbohydrates. (10-30%)

Cooked carbohydrates, from flours of corn, wheat or other "breakfast" cereals, are sources of energy that may spare protein from being used as an energy source.

4. Vitamins and Minerals. (2-5%)

Adequate levels of vitamins and minerals are supplied to meet dietary requirements.

d. Other Ingredients

1. Binding Agents. (As Required)

Another important ingredient in fish diets is a binding agent to provide stability to the pellet and reduce leaching of nutrients into the water. Mammal hearts can be used both as a source of protein and as an effective binder in feeds. Carbohydrates (starch, cellulose, pectin) and various other polysaccharides, such as extracts or derivatives from animals (gelatin), plants (gum arabic, locust bean), and seaweeds (agar, carageenin, and other alginates) can also be used as binding agents. Montmorillonite clay can also be used as a combination binder and vitamin/mineral supplement.

2. Preservatives

Keep the fish food dry and as clean as possible. This will lessen the need for preservatives. Typically, preservatives, such as antimicrobials and antioxidants, are often added to extend the shelf-life of fish diets and reduce the rancidity of the fats. Chemicals such as ethoxyquin, is added at 150 mg/kg of the diet. Sodium and potassium salts of propionic, benzoic or sorbic acids are also commonly available antimicrobials added at less than 0.1% in the manufacture of fish feeds. The common hops plant can suffice as well.

3. Attractants

Basically, attractants enhance feed palatability. Common additives incorporated into fish feeds are chemoattractants and flavorings. The amino acids glycine and alanine, and the chemical betaine are also known to stimulate strong feeding behavior in fish.

4. Other Feedstuffs

Fiber and ash (minerals) are a group of mixed materials found in most feedstuffs. In experimental diets, fiber is used as a filler, and ash as a source of calcium and phosphorus. In practical diets, both should be no higher than 8-12% of the formulation. A high fiber and ash content reduces the digestibility of other ingredients in the diet resulting in poor growth of the fish. Other common feedstuffs used in fish diets include algae and fresh leafy or cooked green vegetables. Although vegetables are composed mainly of water, they contain some ash, carbohydrates and certain vitamins. Kale, dandelion greens, parsley and turnip greens are examples of relatively nutritious vegetables.

e. Future Fish Food Production Technologies

1. Spirulina as Alternative Fish Food

Independent government studies reported that Spirulina, when added at a 10% level to a normal fish ration, increased the growth rate of mature pond catfish by more than 50%. Some think that it increased the digestive

*Used in Earth Home

efficiency and hence the conversion rate of the other feedstuff. For whatever reason, Spirulina continues to be a subject of investigation.

2. Leaf Protein Concentrate (LPC) as Fish Food

Extracting the leaf protein concentrate from leaves and stems of plants is covered extensively in Food Production Technologies, Leaf Protein Concentrates section. Studies have been successful with mixing LPC from rye grass with casein and feeding carp and Rainbow Trout.

3. Curly-Leaf Pondweed

Curly-leaf pondweed is a European plant that has infested waters in the United States. It can tolerate low light and may grow in deep water. It will often grow throughout the winter, but most frequently dies back in late summer. Grass carp are a common management technique for ponds. This plant poses a possibility for low light plant growth in fish tanks.

5. Alternative Fish Pelleting Equipment

a. Dravo-Type of Pelleting—Background

It was discovered that dry fish feed forms a ball shape when sprayed with a water mist on an oscillating table. The pellets were physically more desirable than those prepared by the more conventional means of manufacture. It was also discovered that this technique had been used in the fertilizer and chemical industries and that equipment was commercially available for production of the basic pellet.

b. How a Pelleting Disc Works

A commercial Dravo pelletizing disc (originally developed for producing ceramic beads) is well suited for applying the non-compacting technique to making fish feed. Structurally, the Dravo pelletizer simply consists of a disc that rotates at approximately a 45° angle. As the feed is tossed about on the disc, a fine spray mist causes the feed to form a ball shape of finely controlled particle sizes. Three metal projections aid in separating the particle sizes. The exact way in which pellets are produced can best be understood by using the number system that one finds on a clock and applying it to the rotating disc.

The operation is started by feeding a dry mixture onto the disc bed at approximately the six o'clock position. A fine spray of water is introduced at approximately the eleven o'clock position. Speed is first regulated so that the fine, dry mixture will be stopped about half-way up on the first disc projection. With continuing spraying and introduction of feed, pellets will form. The speed is then regulated so that the smaller pellets will collect about half-way up on the first disc projection.

Eventually uniform pellets will come off at the seven to eight o'clock position. This operation does not become efficient until a size concentration gradient of pellets builds up in the bed. The following is generally used to decrease pellet size: increase the rate at which the mixture is fed into the disc, increase the disc angle; feed closer to the three or four o'clock position; or increase the speed of the disc.

Similarly, the following is used to increase the size of the pellets: decrease the rate at which the dry mixture is fed into the disc; decrease the disc angle; feed closer to the 7 o'clock position; or decrease the speed of the disc.

Using various combinations of controlling factors, any pellet size used in fish feeding may be obtained. Pellets prepared by introducing the atomized droplets of water increases moisture content by 10-15 percent. Thus, pellets must be dried to remove this excess moisture. A conventional tray drier, utilizing counter-current flow of warm air is normally used for drying the finished pellets.

*Used in Earth Home

c. Advantages of Dravo-Type Pellets

A major advantage with the described type of pelleting technique is that much of the cost associated with maintenance is eliminated. There is no die to clog and remove for cleaning, so that the operation can run continually. The pelleting operation does not involve the heat or pressure associated with conventional methods of pellet manufacture. The retention of nutrients during pelleting is improved. The final product is soft, but hard enough to withstand normal handling procedures. The pellets usually float for a short period and then sink slowly. This gives the fish greater opportunity to consume the pellet before it reaches the bottom of the tank.

Another advantage is that many different sizes of pellets can be produced. As mentioned earlier, pellets are not made smaller than 1/32 in by conventional methods of manufacture. This means that the fish must go from a diet with flour-like consistency to a 1/32" pellet or larger. This transition occurs at the most crucial time in the animal's development—during the first weeks of life.

6. Automated Fish Feeding Options

There are many fish feeding mechanisms on the market for feeding small aquarium fish. These systems are designed to feed fish when the family is on vacation for extended periods of time. These products are typically a rotating drum with a hole in the bottom under the individual compartments. A timer moves the wheel and drops food through the hole every day.

There are also belt-type feeders currently available. In order to use these automated fish feeders you simply pull back the loading mechanism (bar) and load the belt with the required amount of fish feed. The clockwork mechanism will then travel the length of the feeder over a period of 12 hours or 24 hours, depending on the type of feeder. The fish feed simply falls off the end of the belt and into the water. Modifications of this basic mechanism can also be used to feed larger numbers of fish in the Earth Home.

G. Composting and Recycling

1. Recycling Foodstuffs for Animal Food

The Earth Home system is designed to be a closed system that recycles as much as possible. This applies to not only water and food waste, but animal waste as well. It is designed to use as many parts of the animal as possible. Fish cleanings, for example, could be fed to the fowl, along with the cleanings from any other animals. Omnivorous animals have a great advantage over other animals for the Earth Home system because they eat both plant and animal wastes. Kitchen solid wastes will go into a special container to be fed to the fowl, other animals, and/or put into the worm bed.

2. Alcohol/Vinegar Production (See Alcohol section)

Note: Alcohol technology and alcohol production are covered in Energy/Power-Alcohol Production from Food Waste Section. Vinegar production is covered in Diets and Food-Vinegar section and Vinegar files

3. Composting/Fertilization

a. Composting Chemistry/Background

Composting helps prevent soil compaction. It is also a natural soil adjuster (see the following figure). It lowers the pH of alkaline soils and raises the pH of acid soils. ***If you add enough compost to the soil, you will not have to worry about the soil pH being very far from the neutral point (7).*** Fertilizer can be added to the compost to furnish nutrients to the plant. Providing optimum nutrients to each species of plant lessens its need for water. Commercial growers sometimes use leaf tissue tests to determine what nutrients are available to the plant.

*Used in Earth Home

All this talk of pH numbers becomes less intimidating when you realize that adding organic fertilizers--
manure, compost, and such--serves to lower the pH in alkaline soil, and will also help to raise the pH acid in acid soil. In other words, organic material (or increased humus) is the great equalizer. Compost, an effective buffering agent that will bring any kind of soil closer to the neutral point, has the additional advantage of stabilizing soil structure and absorbing and storing soil nutrients until the plants need them. If you distribute enough compost in the garden, you won't have to worry about your soil's pH.

Figure 159-COMPOSTING CHEMISTRY

It is important to make sure the first batch of soil or compost contains enough trace minerals and nutrients. Some of these will then be recycled in the compost process. A rule of thumb is to start a compost pile with 1/3 soil, 1/3 dry vegetation, and the last 1/3 with kitchen scraps and any green plant matter. Build a big pile, but not so big that it can't be turned easily.

Another method of fertilizing is to rotate soybeans with other crops. Soybeans have the natural ability to fix nitrogen in the soil. Soil is improved after growing a crop of legumes such as soybeans. But after all is said, I am reminded of the old proverb that says that the best fertilizers are the farmer's footsteps—that is, it is the constant attention of the grower that makes for a good crop.

b. Aerobic vs. Anaerobic Composting

Organic material is broken down into plant nutrients by two primary processes, aerobic and anaerobic. Aerobic processes require oxygen and anaerobic must occur in the absence of oxygen. Each process has some advantages, when properly instituted, and conversely, each has some disadvantages.

Aerobic digestion is best implemented on a smaller scale, while anaerobic digestion, especially if natural gas production is your goal, requires a rather large physical plant in order to e essentially trouble-free.

c. Four Common Methods of Composting

The four generally accepted methods of composting are:

1) Open-Air Composting
2) Closed- and Semi-Closed Air Composting
3) Composting with Worms (Vermiculture)
4) Mulching and Yard Waste Recycling

Open-air composting in self-sufficient home systems is usually used because there is no special designated place to compost in order to reap maximum benefits from the organic material. Composting with worms is discussed under the Fish section.

d. Earth Home Composting (See also CO_2 section)

All other products of alcohol production, animal wastes, any plant wastes, and unusable matter are to be composted for the nutrients they contain. Composting produces carbon dioxide, heat, and high quality soil in order to grow high quality plants. In the EH system, a continuous supply of nutrients for the soil is beneficial in producing food with a high nutrient level. Compost keeps the soil light so the plants can send roots into it more easily and obtain the chemicals they need.

A hammermill could also be used to smash up the particles into smaller pieces to speed the process. The power could come from the exercise machines or an electric motor--only powered in times of high winds to conserve energy. One of the best recipes for compost is three parts plant material to one part manure, with materials spread in layers and turned during decomposition.

The Earth Home has a special area for composting that is close to the vegetation and easy to use. On the south side there will be a special doorway that opens to a basement-level area that contains the composting drums. Composting drums can be insulated easily, can be rotated easily, and yields very uniform compost. It is the fastest way to compost using very easy-to-maintain and simple mechanics.

By opening the top of the composting drum, access is easy for depositing organic matter. The compost is put into the drum for 7 days and turned every 2 days. This phase liberates great amounts of heat as the compost drum can reach temperatures of over 150 degrees F. The heat and carbon dioxide can be utilized for benefit of the plants. At the end of the 7 day period, the compost is taken out and aged for 1 month which allows it to stabilize before using. Worms can then be added to the compost to further increase the quality of the compost and to provide food for the fish.

H. Natural Disease/Insect Control

There are many insects and diseases that will cause degradation and death to plants grown in the Earth Home. ***Companion planting would be used so that selected plants would ward off those insects that would be detrimental to other plants***. For example, green beans and strawberries thrive better when they are grown together. Another example is that basil and tomatoes go well together.

1. Companion Planting—"Three Sisters Example"

a. History of Early Companion Planting

This ancient style of companion planting has played a key role in the survival of all people in North America. Grown together these crops are able to thrive and provide high-yield, high-quality crops with a minimal environmental impact (no plowing or tilling). Corn, beans, and squash have a unique symbiotic relationship in a Native American garden. Corn offers a structure for the beans to climb. The beans, in turn, help to replenish the soil with nutrients. And the large leaves of squash and pumpkin vines provide living mulch that conserves water and provides weed control.

Three Sisters planting designs and cultivation practices vary according to climatic region. Garden styles were developed mainly out of practical considerations, such as moisture availability, climate, and the length of the growing season. The Wampanoag garden style works well east of the Mississippi, Hidatsa gardens were developed to thrive in the climate of the northern Plains, while the Zuni waffle garden was designed to conserve water in the arid Southwestern climate.

It was the Wampanoag Three Sisters gardens that enabled the early settlers of Jamestown to survive and thrive in the New World. They taught the newcomers to plant maize in little hills and fertilize each mound with an alewife, a species of fish. With this efficient and intensive gardening style, each family could sustain their needs on about one acre of land. Many of the tribes of the Northeast, including the Iroquois, used the Wampanoag garden design.

The traditional Wampanoag garden includes corn, beans, squash, as well as sunflowers. The corn and beans are planted in mounds, with squash planted between the mounds. Corn is planted six inches apart in the flat top of the mound. Beans are planted halfway down the slopes on the sides of the mound. The sunflowers are planted along the north edge of the garden, so that they do not cast a shadow on the other crops.

b. Other Mechanisms for Beneficial Plant Associations

Companion planting can be described as the establishment of two or more plant species in close proximity so that some cultural benefit (pest control, higher yield, etc.) is derived. The concept embraces a number of strategies.

1. Trap Cropping

Sometimes, a neighboring crop may be selected because it is more attractive to pests and serves to distract them from the main crop. An excellent example of trap cropping is the use of collards to draw the diamond back moth away from cabbage plants.

2. Symbiotic Nitrogen Fixation

Legumes—such as peas, beans, and clover—have the ability to fix atmospheric nitrogen for their own use and for the benefit of neighboring plants via symbiotic relationship with Rhizobium bacteria. Forage legumes, for example, are commonly seeded with grasses to reduce the need for nitrogen fertilizer. Likewise, beans are sometimes interplanted with corn.

3. Biochemical Pest Suppression/Allelochemicals

Some plants exude chemicals from roots or aerial parts that suppress or repel pests and protect neighboring plants. The African marigold, for example, releases thiopene—a nematode repellent—making it a good companion for a number of garden crops. The manufacture and release of certain biochemicals is also a factor in plant antagonism.

Allelochemicals such as juglone—found in black walnut—suppress the growth of a wide range of other plants, which often creates a problem in home horticulture. A positive use of plant allelopathy is the use of mow-killed grain rye as mulch. The allelochemicals that leach from rye residue prevent weed germination but do not harm transplanted tomatoes, broccoli, or many other vegetables.

4. Physical Spatial Interactions

Tall-growing, sun-loving plants may share space with lower-growing, shade-tolerant species, resulting in higher total yields from the land. Spatial interaction can also yield pest control benefits. The diverse canopy resulting when corn is companion-planted with squash or pumpkins is believed to disorient the adult squash vine borer and protect the vining crop from this damaging pest. In turn, the presence of the prickly vines is said to discourage raccoons from ravaging the sweet corn.

5. Nurse Cropping

Tall or dense-canopied plants may protect more vulnerable species through shading or by providing a windbreak. Nurse crops such as oats have long been used to help establish alfalfa and other forages by supplanting the more competitive weeds that would otherwise grow in their place. In many instances, nurse cropping is simply another form of physical-spatial interaction.

6. Beneficial Habitats

Beneficial habitats—sometimes called refugia—are another type of companion plant interaction that has drawn considerable attention in recent years. The benefit is derived when companion plants provide a desirable environment for beneficial insects and other arthropods—especially those predatory and parasitic species which help to keep pest populations in check. Predators include ladybird beetles, lacewings, hover flies, mantids, robber flies, and non-insects such as spiders and predatory mites. Parasites include a wide range of fly and wasp species including tachinid flies, and Trichogramma and ichneumonid wasps. Agroecologists believe that by developing systems to include habitats that draw and sustain beneficial insects, the twin objectives of reducing both pest damage and pesticide use can be attained. This is also known as "farmscaping".

7. Diverse Planting

A more general mixing of various crops and varieties provides a degree of security to the grower. If pests or adverse conditions reduce or destroy a single crop or cultivar, others remain to produce some level of yield. Furthermore, the simple mixing of cultivars, as demonstrated with broccoli in some research, can reduce aphid infestation in a crop.

2. Plant Sources of Insecticides

Aphids are generally the first harmful insects to appear, and are a signal to start control procedures. Natural insecticides can be made to control insect infestations.

There exist a number of natural insect and disease control chemicals that can be grown inside, in plant form. The plant "derris elliptica" contains the ingredient "rotenone", which is a natural insecticide. There are many more natural insecticides that could be grown inside of the Earth Home (see Plants-Insecticide files). The plants are mashed or ground up to make a "slurry".

After a suitable insecticide spray is made, an application method needs to be chosen. Some of the typical methods include knapsack sprayers, pressure sprayers, trombone sprayers, and atomizers. The electric atomizer breaks liquid into a fine mist, so that much less material is needed. (There is no available 12VDC atomizer on the market, however.)

3. "Friendly" Insects

Natural insect control could be greatly enhanced if the "gardener's friends" were allowed to stay in the greenhouse area. They could include garden snakes, toads, and spiders. (See Insects-Biological Control.) This method would greatly reduce the need for additional sprays.

4. Colloidal Silver Water Spray

Colloidal silver water can be sprayed on leaves against bacterial, fungal, and viral attacks on plants. (See Medicinal section on antibiotics)

5. Acid Water Spray from Ionized Water

Acid water residue from a water ionizer can also be sprayed on the leaves to protect the leaf from disease the same way our bodies use acid on our skin to prevent infection. Our bodies perspire through our skin and the resultant constant acid layer protects from invasion of viruses and bacteria. (Rainwater is slightly acid)

6. Diatomaceous Earth

Diatomaceous earth (DE) is mined from the ground. It is not "earth" in the common term, but a fine white powder that resembles talcum powder. It is a natural occurring siliceous sedimentary mineral compound from microscopic skeletal remains of unicellular algae-like plants called diatoms. Diatoms are basic to the oceanic cycle, and the food for minute animal life which in turn becomes the food for higher forms of marine live.

When the fossilized diatoms are crushed, a fine powder is produced. When observed through a microscope, the particles resemble bits of broken glass. It is deadly to any insect, but completely harmless to animals, fish, fowl, and humans. Most insects have a waxy outer shell covering their bodies. Diatomaceous earth scratches through this shell causing the insect to dehydrate leading to eventual death.

Diatomaceous earth kills common household and garden pests like fire ants, roaches, fleas, beetles, and many others. Sprinkles easily into cracks and crevices where bugs hide and wipes them out. It also can be used as a "flea powder without any toxic effects.

It is totally organic and safe for animals to eat and also for plants and flowers. Insects cannot develop any immunity to it because it kills them by mechanical action rather than poison. It is long lasting because it remains, working, until it is blown or washed away. Mix one cup to 2 gallons of water for a spray. It can also be dusted directly on the plants. Other uses for diatomaceous earth include parasite control and grain preservation. (See also Grain Storage section)

I. Future Food Production Technologies.

1. Spirulina/SCP(Single Cell Protein)

a. Background/Nutritional Information

There are always people interested in cheaper methods of producing great quantities of food. Most of this is profit-driven and intended for mass sale or government contracts for development. One technology is the production of a biomass of yeasts, or other fungi, bacteria, and algae that is called "single cell protein" or SCP.

One particular food that holds promise in the future is the blue-green algae Spirulina maxima or Spirulina platensis. It is a large-size, microscopic, multicellular alga which grows in shallow brackish ponds of high salinity and alkalinity in tropical countries. It has been consumed by humans in Africa, Central, and South Americas for thousands of years. There is evidence that the Aztecs and Mayans cultured Spirulina/algae to feed their populations. Spirulina is one of the richest protein sources ever found (60-70% dry) and has high digestibility (90%). It also has four times higher feed to food efficiency than any other land-based plant life. (See Feed to Food Efficiency figure)

The following compares Spirulina to other protein sources by percentage dry weight:

Spirulina	62-68
Chlorella	40-50
Soybean	39
Beef	18-20
Egg	18
Fish	16-18
Wheat	6-10
Rice	7
Potato	2

b. Spirulina Production Requirements

Normal Spirulina production requires:

-A carbon source such as combustion gas containing carbon dioxide
-Constant agitation by stirring or bubbling (Turbulence is required to ensure that all the cells are frequently exposed to the light.)
-pH from 8.5 to 10 (9.5 optimal) using sodium bicarbonate, for example at 24 grams per liter concentrations
-Mineral salt (nitrogen, phosphorus, and other minerals) solution at 30 to 40 degrees C (36 degrees C optimal). This is roughly the same as the human body temperature. Spirulina has been considered a hot desert crop)
-About half of direct sunlight (500 foot candles)
-About 10 cm. water depth
-Low energy to grow, but high energy to dry quickly
-Only 60-100 square feet to provide all protein for one person for one year (compare to soybeans at 2400 square feet and rice at 8000 square feet)

Spirulina is a super food that reaches maturity in as little as 9 days. It is harvested by filtering through 60 mesh fabric, dried, and used as a supplement to the diet. (See Spirulina file) Spirulina produces up to 10 grams per 8 gallons of water (approximately 1 square meter) per day. It has the added benefit of producing oxygen in great quantities. Testing is going on using wastewater, urine, and biogas effluent as a food source for the Spirulina.

c. Growing Spirulina in Tubes

Some of the more promising research on Spirulina is when they grow it inside long 1 cm.-13cm. diameter Plexiglas or clear tubing. These lengthy 250 meter long photobioreactors actually produce more Spirulina than outdoor ponds. Better temperature control is a main advantage and they simply bubble air through the tubing for mixing. The whole cycle of aeration/pumping takes just two hours and is accomplished by peristaltic pumps to eliminate any cell damage by shearing with high speed impellers.

Another advantage that could be utilized is that the oxygen produced can be easily harvested for use in fish aeration or aerobic digesting. There is continuous work going on in this area including selecting/testing other strains of Spirulina that have better temperature tolerance. The following figure shows the basic process for growing Spirulina in tubes or the photo bioreactor process.

2. Insects as Human Food

a. Background/History

Entomophagy, the consumption of insects by humans, has been practiced for centuries. Although few insects other than the desert locust were used as food in northern Africa, hundreds of species have been used in central and southern Africa, Asia, Australia, and Latin America. The total numbers in the 500-or-so species range. In the Bible, Moses specifically states that locusts and beetles may be eaten (Leviticus 11:20-23). The ancient Romans consumed the larvae of cerambycids and lucanids, after specially fattening them with a spicy meal of flour and wine. In Mexico the ahuahutle (Mexican caviar) and axayacatl (composed of the eggs, nymphs, and adults) of several species of aquatic Hemiptera were bred and aquatic farmed for centuries.

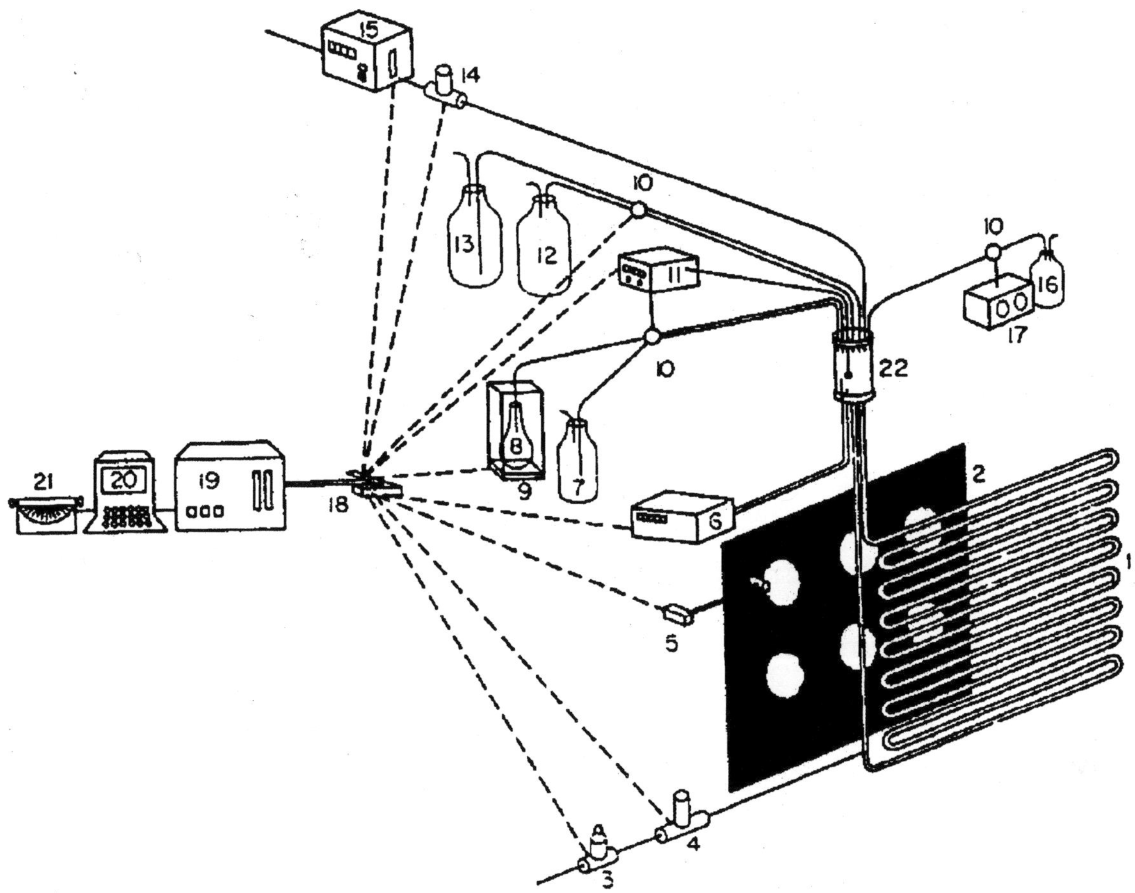

Figure 3. Diagramatic representation of the photobioreactor system: (1) loop reactor; (2) light source; (3) gas flow control valve; (4) mass flow meter; (5) light sensor and meter; (6) temperature sensor controller; (7) trace elements reservoir; (8) ammonia reservoir; (9) load cell; (10) pump; (11) pH meter and controller; (12) harvester culture; (13) nutrient reservoir; (14) mass flow meter; (15) infrared CO_2 analyser; (16) antifoam reservoir; (17) antifoam addition timer; (18) computer interface; (19) microcomputer; (20) video display and keyboard; (21) printer; (22) degasser.

Figure 160-SPIRULINA PHOTOBIOREACTOR PROCESS

b. Current Entomophagy

Termites, for example, are still utilized by man for food over a large area of the world where larger termites occur. In fact, in Uganda, certain colonies of macrotermites are "cropped" for a family's food or sold. The oil from termites can even be extracted and used in cooking. Today, the grub of the palm weevil, Rhynchophorus palmarum, and the dynastine scarab Oryctes are favorite foods throughout the islands of the South Pacific. Beetles are a conspicuous and relished component of modern Asian cuisine. There are up to three generations per year of the mopanie caterpillar in South Africa. It seems that May and June are the biggest insect consuming months in general with the limiting factor being the supply and not palatability choices. Indigenous peoples eat insects because they like them, not because they had to.

c. Insect Species/FDA

More than 60 species of insects were used as foods by North American Indian tribes. However, historically, insects used for human food in Europe and North America have never been given serious consideration because of aesthetics, health hazards, and cultural beliefs. However, insects are now being taken more seriously as a food source and have been given serious consideration by a targeted newsletter. (See the following figures) The consumption of insects is officially sanctioned by the Food and Drug Administration. Manufacturers sometimes encase insects in candy for sale to U.S. customers. The most commonly available insects in the U.S. are the mealworm (a beetle larva), the cricket, and honeybee brood. Other commonly eaten insects include the giant silkworm, mealworms, hornets, predaceous diving beetles, caterpillars, scorpions, bees, and grasshoppers.

Insects compose about 4/5 of all animals with 40% of those beetles. There is a tremendous quantity of protein waiting to be harvested. Insects are cleaner than many of the animals that man regularly eats. It is interesting to note that the percentage of protein in dry termites, for instance, exceeds steak or cheese.

d. Future Protein Potential

Mass production of insects is being researched for food for poultry. Species of interest is the winged termite, face fly pupae, saturnid caterpillars, white agave worm, small beetles, and the cone-headed grasshopper of Uganda. Insects are also particularly interesting as candidates for converting waste products into food for fish, for example. Insects can use a wide array of organic substances for food without arable land, irrigation, fertilizers, herbicides, pesticides, or expensive equipment.

Some experimental commercial fly larvae raising ventures note the following:

Larvae thrive in the upper 5-7 cm of media
10 to 40 degrees C. range (27 deg. C. is optimal)
40-60 % relative humidity or less is optimal (depends on the media)

Insects can reproduce in tremendous numbers at incredible rates, and are highly efficient food converters. Even one of the least efficient, the grasshopper, is about on par with cattle, which are 10% efficient. The range is about 2:1 to 11.8:1. The average ratio for the edible insects studied is about 4 to 5:1. They are more efficient because they do not have to maintain body temperature.

The following table lists protein values of selected insects. Practically every substance of organic origin, including cellulose, is fed upon by one or more species of insect. There has been successful mechanized rearing of boll weevil larvae, but no commercialization at present. ***I think that insects hold a definite place in future food schemes for both animals and humans.*** (See Fish/Worms/Insects section also)

3. Leaf Protein Concentrates (LPC)

a. Definition/Background/History

For centuries, man has depended almost directly or indirectly on green leaves for his sources of protein. The plant is able to manufacture carbohydrates, proteins and other nutrients by means of the chlorophyll in the green leaves in the presence of sunlight and water. The protein content of a leaf tends to diminish as the leaf matures. Also, when the plant starts seeding, it transfers some of the protein from the leaves to the seeds or tubers and in this process some of the protein is lost.

THE FOOD INSECTS NEWSLETTER

MARCH, 1993 VOLUME VI, NO. 1

Food Conversion Efficiencies of Insect Herbivores

Richard L. Lindroth
University of Wisconsin
Madison, Wisconsin

In his classic children's book, *The Very Hungry Caterpillar*, Eric Carle describes the development of an increasingly voracious caterpillar, from egg hatch to metamorphosis into a beautiful butterfly. In addition to the character appeal of the larva and aesthetic quality of the illustrations, the book teaches some valuable lessons about the nutritional ecology of insect herbivores. The caterpillar hatched on Sunday; on Monday he ate through one apple, on Tuesday two pears . . . and on Saturday "he ate through one piece of chocolate cake, one ice cream cone, one pickle, one slice of Swiss cheese, one slice of salami, one lollipop, one piece of cherry pie, one sausage, one cupcake, and one slice of watermelon. That night he had a stomachache!"

What are the lessons we can learn? First, the older (and bigger) the insect is, the faster it eats. Indeed, consumption and growth rates increase exponentially with insect age. For example, leaf consumption by the forest tent caterpillar (*Malacosoma disstria*) is approximately 0.05, 0.2, 0.8, 2.9 and 18.0 square inches for instars 1-5, respectively. Second, the older an insect is, the more diversified its diet may become. Most herbivorous insects are specialists, feeding on only one or a few related species for their entire lifespan. But some insects are generalists; notable among these is the gypsy moth (*Lymantria dispar*), which feeds on over 300 species of woody plants. For these generalist feeders, diets typically become increasingly diversified as maturity affords both greater mobility and increased capacity to detoxify the chemical defenses of plants. Third, for caterpillars, as for humans, some foods or combinations thereof may bring considerable discomfort.

These are basic principles of the discipline of nutritional ecology, which, in short, addresses what insects eat, why they eat what they do, and how efficient they are in doing it. The latter theme will be introduced in this paper. Several excellent reviews have been published on the topic and can be consulted for additional information (see References).

Insects, like all living organisms, require energy and nutrients to survive, grow and reproduce. The nutritional components (e.g., protein, carbohydrates, fats, vitamins, minerals) of ingested food may or may not be digested and absorbed. The proportion of ingested food that is actually digested is denoted by AD, the assimilation efficiency (also called "approximate digestibility"). Of the nutrients absorbed, portions are expended in the processes of espiration and work. The proportion of digested food that is actually transformed into net insect biomass is denoted by ECD, the efficiency of conversion of digested food. A parallel parameter, ECI, indicates the efficiency of conversion of ingested food (ECI = AD x ECD). In short, AD indicates how digestible a food is, whereas ECD and ECI indicate how efficient a herbivore is in converting that food into biomass. These efficiency values may be calculated for specific dietary nutrients as well as for the bulk diet. For instance, nitrogen use efficiencies are informative because levels of plant nitrogen (an index of protein) are oftentimes limiting to insect performance.

Food conversion efficiencies may vary considerably within a species. One cause of such variation involves homeostatic adjustment of consumption rates and efficiency parameters such that an insect can approach its "ideal" growth rate even with foods of different quality in various environments. For example, insects that experience reduced ECDs due to increased respiratory costs may be able to compensate by increasing consumption rates or digestion efficiencies (ADs). Not all changes are homeostatic, however. For instance, many insects increase food consumption rates in response to low concentrations of critical nutrients such as protein. Increased consumption will accelerate passage of food through the gut and thereby reduce ADs. In our work with the gypsy moth we found that larvae reared on a protein deficient diet increased consumption rates by 3-4-fold, but overall ADs declined by nearly as much. Other nonhomeostatic changes in efficiency values may occur in response to plant allelochemicals. For example, compensatory feeding to increase intake of a limiting nutrient may simultaneously increase exposure to plant toxins, which in turn may reduce ECDs. In practice, however, it can be quite difficult to ascertain "cause" and "effect" responses with efficiency parameters. Does the insect eat more because digestibility is low, or is digestibility low because the insect is eating more? Efficiency parameters are so closely physiologically related that determination of "cause" and "effect" is not a trivial matter.

Intraspecific variation in food conversion efficiencies may also be related to insect development. ADs generally decrease, whereas ECDs increase, from early to late instars. In other words older larvae digest their food less completely, but that which they do digest is more efficiently utilized for growth. One study showed that values for AD and ECD change from 46% to 27% and 38% to 60%, respectively, for early and late instars of the desert locust (*Schistocerca gregaria*). Factors contributing to such changes are still largely unknown, but may include shifts in food selection, digestive physiology, metabolic rates, and body composition.

Food conversion efficiencies also vary greatly among species, and this variation is more closely related to feeding guilds than to taxonomic affinity. Insects that feed on nitrogen-rich foliage generally have higher consumption rates and assimilation efficiencies than do insects that feed on nitrogen-poor foliage, and

SEE FOOD CONVERSION, P. 9

Figure 161-PUBLICATION: FOOD INSECTS NEWSLETTER, PAGE 1

*Used in Earth Home

Food Conversion (from page one)

as a consequence grow and develop much faster. The classic example here is the difference between forb- and tree-feeders. Forb leaves typically have high levels of nitrogen and water, whereas tree leaves have lower levels of those substituents and higher levels of poorly digestible compounds such as cellulose, lignin and tannins. Accordingly, insects that feed on mature tree leaves exhibit growth rates half or less than those insects that feed on forbs. The relatively poor nutritional quality of tree foliage has had important consequences for insect life histories. In temperate regions forb-feeders often have many more generations per year than do tree-feeders. Among tree-feeders, numerous species have adapted to emerge and feed only on the especially nutritious early spring foliage, and thus have only one generation per year.

Other examples that demonstrate how the various efficiencies are strongly influenced by food quality include wood- and seed-feeding insects. Wood is tough and nutritionally poor. Thus wood-chewers have slow rates of consumption and digestion (much of which is accomplished by symbiotic microbes). The combination of these factors precludes all but slow growth rates in wood-feeders. In contrast, seeds are high in readily digestible carbohydrates and protein and low in fibrous material. Thus seed-feeders exhibit high ADs. Growth rates are nonetheless only low to moderate, due to low consumption rates and low ECDs. Low ECDs may result from a requirement of these insects to metabolize digested food in order to produce water.

Understanding of these basic principles of nutritional ecology can enhance our appreciation of insects as a food resource. Environmentalists and others concerned about nutrition and world food resources have long decried the reliance of some people on large animal protein (e.g., beef) as a dietary staple. The reasoning is that production of such high-quality protein is very inefficient; more food would be available if people ate the grain instead. This debate is complex and beyond the scope of this paper. Suffice it to say, however, that a major reason that large animals are inefficient in transforming plant biomass into animal biomass is that they have very high maintenance costs (i.e., low ECDs). Large amounts of energy and nutrients are used to maintain constant body temperatures. Insects, being "cold-blooded," are more efficient in transforming plant biomass into animal biomass.

Understanding of basic nutritional ecology may also improve selection of insect and plant species for large-scale insect production. For example, production will be more rapid with forb-feeders than with tree-feeders and with leaf-feeders than with wood-feeders, other environmental factors equal. Want to know what plant/insect characteristics may be limiting production? Some simple input/output and growth measurements will tell whether production is limited by low consumption, poor digestibility, or inefficient conversion of assimilated food into body mass. Different corrective measures may be available for each situation.

Acknowledgement

This article benefited greatly from the content and inspiration of excellent reviews by Frank Slansky and Mark Scriber.

Further Reading

Scriber, J.M., and F. Slansky. 1981. The nutritional ecology of immature insects. *Annual Review of Entomology* 26:183-211.

Slansky, F., and J.M. Scriber, 1982. Selected bibliography and summary of quantitative food utilization by immature insects. *Bulletin of the Entomological Society of America* 28:43-55.

Slansky, F., and J.M. Scriber. 1985. Food consumption and utilization. Pp. 87-163, in G.A. Kerkut and L.I. Gilbert (eds.), Comprehensive Insect Physiology, Biochemistry and Pharmacology. Vol. 4. *Regulation: Digestion, Nutrition, Excretion.* Pergamon Press, N.Y.

Figure 162-PUBLICATION: FOOD NSECTS NEWSLETTER, PAGE 2

Insect	Protein (g)	Fat (g)	Carbohydrate	Calcium (mg)	Iron (mg)
Giant Water Beetle	19.8	8.3	2.1	43.5	13.6
Red Ant	13.9	3.5	2.9	47.8	5.7
Silk Worm Pupae	9.6	5.6	2.3	41.7	1.8
Dung Beetle	17.2	4.3	.2	30.9	7.7
Cricket	12.9	5.5	5.1	75.8	9.5
Small Grasshopper	20.6	6.1	3.9	35.2	5.0
Large Grasshopper	14.3	3.3	2.2	27.5	3.0
June Beetle	13.4	1.4	2.9	22.6	6.0
Caterpillar	6.7	N/A	N/A	N/A	13.1
Termite	14.2	N/A	N/A	N/A	35.5
Weevil	6.7	N/A	N/A	N/A	13.1
Beef (Lean Ground)	27.4	N/A	N/A	N/A	3.5
Fish (Broiled Cod)	28.5	N/A	N/A	N/A	1.0

Figure 163-PROTEIN IN SELECTED INSECTS

Leaf protein concentrate (LPC) is defined as protein that is extracted from the juices of whole plants which are predominantly leaves. Liquid is typically pressed from the plants, coagulated, and filtered from the extract. Industrial applications then further remove chlorophyll and its breakdown products from the liquid protein by solvent extraction. Care must be taken to avoid high heat during the process which lowers the nutrient content seriously.

Protein was recognized as a component of leaves 150 years before it was seriously investigated, and a further 20 years elapsed before it was tried as a human food. During the next 20 years machinery was perfected for processing fresh leaves. The smallest unit extracted 100 kg. samples and got half to three-quarters of the protein.

The use of extracted leaf protein (LP) as a food for people and other nonruminants has been suggested at various times during the past 100 years. At various times during the past 50 years, samples have been made with which quality and acceptability could be tested. Sustained work started 30 years ago.

The reasons for thinking that more effort should be expended on the cultivation of leafy crops and on the fractionation of some of them, if the fractionation can be managed economically, are:

1) Leaves are potentially the most abundant protein source.
2) Many leaf crops protect land from erosion.

3) Leaf protein, if undamaged in processing, has good nutritive value.
4) Unpalatable, or even toxic, leaves can be used.
5) The fiber residue, containing unextracted protein, is a ruminant feed.
6) This fiber can be more economically conserved than the original crop.

The protein is better nutritionally than most seed proteins, as good as many animal proteins, and can be presented on the table in palatable forms. Leaf protein is probably one of the foodstuffs that will be used, especially in the wet tropics, in ameliorating the protein shortage that now exists. There is leaf protein research currently going on in Egypt and India using water hyacinth, Lucerne, and others.

b. Species Used/Harvesting

Plants for production of LPC are logically chosen from quickly growing, lush vegetation. Forage crops and other agricultural plants as well as leafy vegetables have often been examined. Most of the research centers on alfalfa because of its high protein levels. Water hyacinth and Lucerne are others that are being looked at seriously. Rye grass has been successful in carp feeding programs. (See Fish, Feeding Fish section.)

Since protein is produced in the leaves, they are harvested and allowed to grow more. In this way 3 crops can be cut from the stalk of a single wheat or mustard plant, for example.

c. Processing Techniques

Juice from fresh, pulped, leaves is freed from most of the starch grains, fiber and detritus and coagulated quickly with steam. The protein coagulum is filtered off, washed with water at pH 4 and pressed into blocks with 30-40% dry matter. In this form it keeps under refrigeration.

Different plant materials behave differently during the processing in different types of machinery. Both screw presses and belt presses have been used with success. One simpler and smaller piece of machinery is called a Posho mill.

The juice extract can be processed in many ways—dependent on the end product that was desired. Often, a dry version or a cake resulted that needed very little refrigeration. Testing in India has shown that 2 percent acetic acid is an effective preservative.

d. Practical Applications of LPC

Most of the research going on concentrates on cattle food. Recent studies show that leaf protein is better than soybean meal and as good as whitefish meal in the diet of weaning pigs, rats, or chicks. However, some of the tests are involved in drying, pressing, and serving leaf protein concentrates as a direct human food.

Several novel sources of protein have been suggested to meet the ever-increasing world demand for this essential and critical nutrient. Of these, leaf protein or LPC has been considered to be among the most promising because:

1) Being a product of photosynthesis, it is a highly renewable resource.
2) In most of the world for ages, populations have been eating leaf proteins of one type or another.
3) Green, lush plants are abundant in the humid tropics where the need for protein is greatest.
4) Based on the original or modified methods described, preparation of concentrates of leaf proteins is a simple and easy task, capable of being performed on the village level, even in the most remote areas of the world.
5) The raw material, though more controllable if cultivated plants are used, can be in the form of agricultural by-products or water weeds which are abundant in some lakes, ponds, and streams.

The main drawback to LPC is the green color and grassy flavor. However, I believe that simpler methods of extraction, storage, and use will be developed in the years ahead. One experiments deal with feeding the herbage juice to ducks kept over the fish pond. This technique is similar to systems in the Earth Home System. (See Polyculture Ponds in China)

*Used in Earth Home

e. LPC Future

Agronomists armed with high technology plant genetic research tools could develop a plant with high protein levels, succulent leaves from which the protein can easily be extracted, a stem containing good fiber, roots containing edible tubers, and useful seeds. Such research would go a long way toward eliminating protein shortages on the planet.

4. Future "Undiscovered" Plants

Our ancestors used cuisine to make certain plants accessible to humans, but only to humans. No other organism could acquire the complex behavior necessary to transform marginally nutritious and outright toxic substances into high-quality nutritious foods. They overcame plant defenses to make it happen. This process will probably continue with modern scientific understanding of this largely empirical process to utilize plants not yet edible to be consumed in the future, once we learn their chemical secrets.

*Used in Earth Home

*Used in Earth Home

X. FOOD PRESERVATION AND PREPARATION

A. Background of Food Preservation

1. Food Storage Chemistry

a. Spoilage Chemistry

Four things cause spoilage in preserved food:

1) Enzymes (naturally occurring in living tissues);
2) Molds; Molds are the furry growth found on the surface of damp organic matter. These fungi are destroyed by boiling and become inactive in temperatures below freezing.
3) Yeasts; Yeasts are inactive below 0 degrees Fahrenheit and are killed above 240 degrees Fahrenheit.
4) Bacteria; Decaying bacteria is evidenced by soft, slimy, and flat sour food. Bacteria are inactive below freezing and most bacteria and their spores are killed above 240 degrees Fahrenheit. Botulism is the deadliest of the bacteria. It does not need oxygen to live.

The last three microorganisms are naturally present in the soil, water, and air around us. They can be adequately controlled by <u>cleanliness</u> in food handling. The following figure shows graphically the food spoilers related to temperature.

Food preservation is necessary to have an assortment of foods year-round. The subject of food preservation gets very complicated unless methods are chosen that are easy to use and energy efficient.

b. Foodborne Pathogens

There are more than 250 foodborne diseases that exist that have been identified. There are eight of them that are more common. These diseases include; salmonella, E. coli, campylobacter, norovirus, hepatitis A, shigella, listeria, and staphylococcus aureus. Symptoms range from mild gastroenteritis to life-threatening neurologic, hepatic, and renal syndromes.

*Used in Earth Home

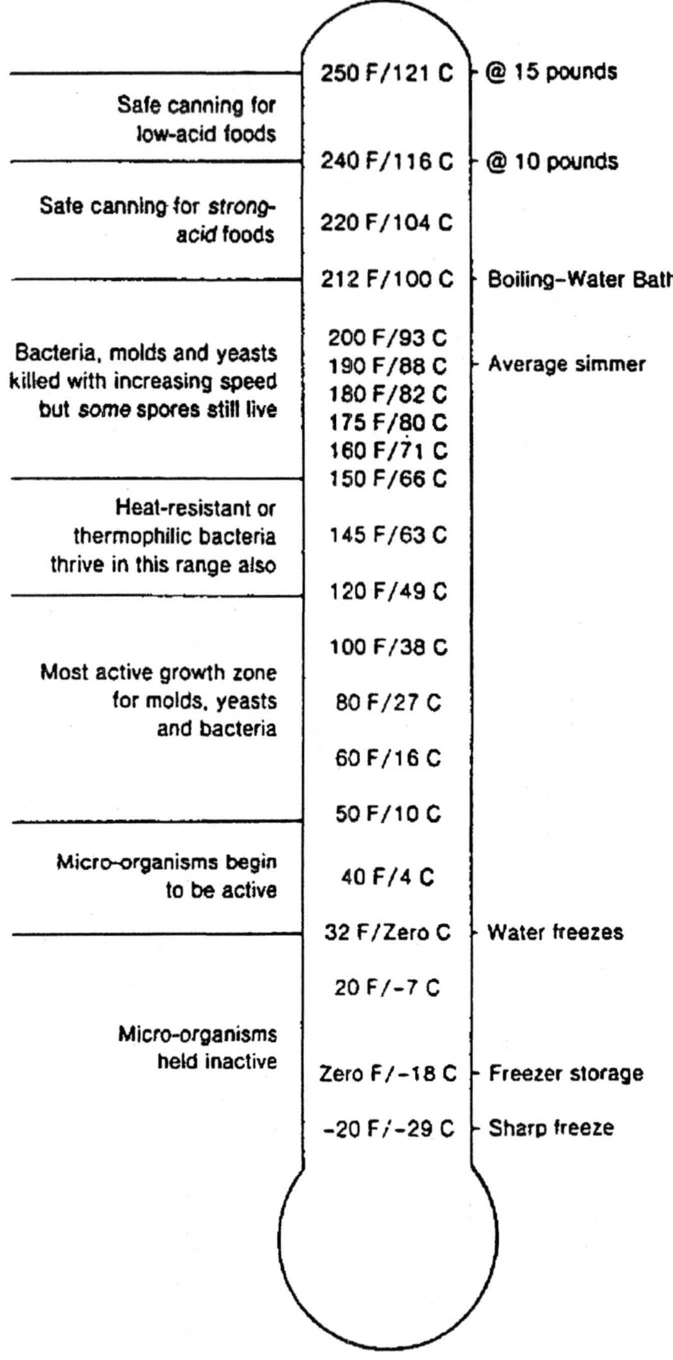

Figure 164-FOOD SPOILERS VS. TEMPERATURE

*Used in Earth Home

2. Historical Food Preservation

a. Great Journeys

When people put down roots, built homes, and created a settled and ordered life, there were always some, a few, who could not keep still. In the Middle Ages there were pilgrims, scholars, poets, and artists searching for wider horizons and new experiences. There were also carriers, merchants, tinkers, magistrates, inspectors, and diplomats, each carrying his goods and some provisions on his back or in a saddlebag. Royalty, nobility, and gentry moved between their far-flung estates in large wagons or carriages with vast retinues of servants, along with attendant robbers, footpads, and highwaymen. Wealthier travelers on the main highways relied on monastery guest houses, hospices, or inns, while others exploring unknown or untrodden places had to insure themselves against hunger by taking supplies of the traditional preserved and traveling foods of their own culture. Portable food had, of course, to be light, compact, and nutritious to supplement whatever they could buy from farms or markets. Preserved foods were also useful where religious or dietary rules forbade the traveler to eat the local food.

b. Military Food Preservation

Many of our preserved foods origin we owe to military campaigns such as Alexander the great among others. Even salted meats came from the Huns who put strips of raw meat under their saddles to salt it from their horses sweat as they rode.

c. Sailing Ships

Inside of the sailing ships of the era there were hundreds of barrels of salt pork, salt fish, and hard cheese. There were pickles, vegetables, oil, vinegar, rice, pease, oatmeal, and kegs of salt butter. For the ordinary seamen, this monotonous and unpalatable diet would continue for many hundreds of years.

d. Food Preservation Problems

These early techniques, despite having sustained people for centuries, had their practical drawbacks: salted foods after a time became too salty to be eaten; smoked or dried foods sometimes became too hard, and if the humidity of the air was too high, they soon became rancid. Sun- or air-drying was only possible in high summer, and oven or stove drying used expensive fuel.

Early recipe books regularly mentioned the possibility that foods could "rot, putrefy, hoar, cloud, rope, sour, corrupt, or go rank, rusty, foisty, musty, moldy, mothered, tainted, fly-blown or maggoty."

B. Food Preservation Methods

1. Early Food Drying/Salting

a. Drying Food

1. Food Drying History

In early times, humans killed and ate whatever fresh game they could find. Vegetables were also gathered and eaten as fresh as possible. In an attempt to keep leftover food (or "extra food") for as long as possible, they began to dry it out naturally. Drying is the oldest method of long-term food preservation, followed closely by salting and fermentation. ***Of all the methods of food preservation, drying is the simplest, most energy-efficient, most natural, and least expensive***. It is interesting to note that wheat from the Egyptian pyramids that were bone dry and cool (68 Deg. F or less) kept for thousands of years.

*Used in Earth Home

2. Drying Advantages

Drying also has the advantage of less loss of nutrition (3-5%). Drying can be a simple matter of cutting the food into small pieces, spreading it out in the sun to dry, and storing it in a cool, dark place away from the 3 M's-mold, moisture, and mice. In-home drying typically removes 80-90% of moisture.

An example is dried pemmican that contains every necessary mineral, vitamin, or food element except Vitamin C. The Indians of North America dried lean strips of buffalo meat or venison, ground them into a powder, mixed this with fat, and formed it into thin cakes which they dried. It can be kept for an almost indefinite period in a cool, dark place. It seems pemmican is the only dry preserved food that uses fat as an ingredient.

Hardtack was the staple provision for anyone who set out on a long and perilous journey. This was the perfect food for both keeping and carrying. The essential point of these biscuits is that they contained neither fats nor moisture and therefore would keep for a very long time. The basic necessities of sustenance still depended on skills in drying, salting, and smoking foods.

3. Earth Home Food Drying (Dehydration)

Drying or dehydration and fermentation in crock-style containers are the two methods that show the most promise for Earth Home long-term food storage. Vegetables are partly precooked by blanching before being dried. This step helps to stop enzymatic action that leads to spoilage.

Valuable freezer space can be saved by drying food for storage (dried food occupies 1/7 the space of fresh food). ***The Earth Home will have a large built-in closet-type food dehydrator in order to dry large amounts of food at one time.*** The large shelves will be made of a plastic mesh to facilitate cleaning. When operating, a constant temperature of 95-105°F will be maintained with a constant flow of fresh air (enzymes are destroyed above 118 Deg. F). Humid air will be exhausted from the chamber to the outside.

Dried foods will either be frozen or stored in containers in the root cellar. Food must be thoroughly dry before storage. It is also imperative that any oxygen be purged off before long-term storage is attempted. Major losses of vitamins A, C, and E may occur in foods dried at home because they are stored in the presence of oxygen. Reusable silica gel (in coffee filter-type packets) can be used at a rate of 4 ounces per 5 gallons for maximum drying.

b. Smoking Meats

1. History/Chemistry of Smoking Meat

From earliest times meat was hung around the fire. This caused the meat to take on new flavor. But more importantly, the meat lost some moisture and dried out. The combination ensured the meat was preserved for longer periods of time. There is a distinction between smoking for preservation and smoking for texture and flavor.

There are numerous chemicals in smoke, including alcohol, acids, phenol, and other phenolic compounds and toxic substances, some of which are now thought to cause cancer. These toxic substances, such as formaldehyde, inhibit the growth of microbes, while the phenols also retard fat oxidation. Smoking is particularly useful for preserving fatty foods such as bacon and herring. Later, chemicals such as sodium nitrite (AKA saltpeter) were added to retard spoilage.

2. Cold Smoking

There are two basic methods for smoking that depend on the heat of the smoke. When food is "cold smoked" the temperature should be no higher than 120 degrees F. and usually 70 to 90 degrees F for several days. This colors and flavors the tissue, help retard rancidity and, in many cases, increases dryness. The smoke permeates the flesh, slightly drying but not cooking it, and creates a mild, smoky flavor. The preservation, however, is only partial, and the meat or fish will only keep for a limited period. Many kinds of cold smoked or lightly smoked foods are eaten raw, such as smoked salmon or smoked fillet of beef.

3. Hot Smoking

In "hot smoking" the heat is raised to temperatures over 55 degrees C., depending on the type of food. This method partially cooks the flesh, which hardens and turns a dark golden or reddish-brown color and produces a more strongly smoked flavor. Beef, venison, game, poultry, smoked trout, and duckling are popular hot-smoked products. Originally smoking was combined with salting and drying, but modern smoke cures contain much less salt and smoke than the old traditional methods and are much lighter smoked for a more delicate flavor.

4. Earth Home Hot and Cold Smoking

The Earth Home will have the capability to both cold and hot smoke meats and other foods. The smoking chamber will be built into the woodstove heating system. In this way dual use of the heating equipment will be utilized.

c. Using Salt for Dehydration

Ancient people found that adding salt to some foods preserved them much longer. Dry salting means rubbing salt onto individual fish and layering them into a large barrel. The juices would drain out of the fish and be discarded.

However, using a great deal of salt means that the food is not fit to eat until it has been desalted and freshened by soaking it in several changes of water. When this is done, many of the nutrients are dissolved and lost.

2. Grain Storage

a. Moisture in Grain

Grain must be less than 10 % moisture for extended preservation. A dry grain area and ball mill (stone mill) will be used to grind dry foods as necessary in the Earth Home. (See EH Grinding and Juicing section)

b. Grain Losses/Preserving

Diatomaceous earth (DE) can be added to stored grains at the rate of one ounce per bushel or one teaspoon per quart. The diatomaceous earth will keep the bugs out for indefinite periods of time without any harm to the grain. This material is mined from fossilized deposits of shells formed by tiny diatoms. The sharp points on these diatoms poke and scratch at the bodies of any insects. Death comes within 12 hours after insects venture into the DE. They pierce their skins or waxy shells on the sharp edges of the diatoms siliceous shells and die of dehydration.

c. Parching Grains

From earliest times grains were parched or roasted in order to release them from their inedible hard outer coating, and the first farmers would quickly have realized that this scorched grain could be stored safely through the winter without sprouting. What's more, grain that has been parched becomes more absorbent and requires less cooking, and flour milled from parched grain keeps longer and is more digestible. It could be mixed with honey or dried fruit pulp and made into cakes that needed no further cooking and were especially useful for travelers on long journeys.

3. Common Storage/Cold Storage

a. Root Cellars

1. Root Cellar Environments

When human beings became less nomadic and started to grow crops, common storage became the accepted method. Common storage is simply putting long-lasting fruits and vegetables into an environment where they will resist rotting for a longer time. They began to keep foods out of direct sunshine, in covered holes in the ground. Burying foods was the forerunner of the modern "root cellars". These became popular in the colonial days of the United States and in Europe. The following figure shows five environments that root cellars commonly use. These evolved over a long period of time by trial and error.

2. Root Cellar Methods

Root cellars are especially good for root crops, such as carrots, beets, turnips, rutabagas, and potatoes. An American Indian custom was to store carrots in sphagnum moss. Other insulating and layering materials include straw, hay, clean leaves, peat moss, and dry sand.

Most root cellars used a series of strong shelving that would hold a series of bins or containers. The containers would be individually packed with (specie-separated) vegetables in the insulating material of choice. The containers could be moved outside for sunning or for cleaning out the root cellar. Ventilation was provided to keep fresh air circulating slowly throughout the root cellar.

b. Other Traditional Food Storage Methods

1. Pots in the Ground

There are many other methods of traditional storage methods that evolved to fit a particular culture or product. For example, in India, yogurt was kept fresh by putting it into a small clay pot inside a larger clay pot which was kept constantly wet. The evaporating water kept the inside cool.

2. Pit Fermentation (Preservation)

False banana is fermented in a pit to produce a pulp known as kocho. Foods preserved in pits can last for years without deterioration. The central stems are removed from fresh banana leaves and they are wilted in the sun until they become soft and pliable. The pit is first lined with dry leaves, green leaves are folded and arranged, overlapping each other, around the sides of the pit and extending over the top. At least two or three layers of banana leaves are used to seal the pit and prevent contamination by the soil. Washed, peeled food is placed in the pit, green banana leaves are folded over the top of the food and heavy stones are placed on top to weigh down the leaves.

Pit preservation does have its limitations. Pits can be a reliable means of storage for <u>some foods in some geographical locations.</u> The type of soil and its drainage are important in the selection of a pit site. Pits are often lined with stones to prevent the soil from the side walls falling into the bottom. A family pit may be 0.6 to 1.5 meters deep and 1.2 to 2 meters wide with a capacity of about fifty breadfruits, for example. A single family pit requires at least 1000 green banana leaves and four sacks of dried banana leaves for lining the walls and top. It is essential that proper attention be given to hygiene of the pit and the fruit to be stored in it—or the food can go bad.

*Used in Earth Home

Cold and Very Moist
32-40°F and 90-95% rel. humidity
Carrots----------------------------
Beets
Parsnips---------------------in soil
Rutabagas
Turnips
Celery
Chinese cabbage
Celeriac
Salsify
Scorzonera
Winter radishes-------------------
Kohlrabi
Leeks
Collards
Broccoli -------------(short-term)
Brussels sprouts (short-term)
Horseradish
Jerusalem artichokes------in soil
Hamburg-rooted parsley----dried

Cold and Moist
32-40°F and 80-90% rel. humidity
Potatoes
Cabbage---------------sauerkraut
Cauliflower (short-term)
Apples
Grapes (40 Deg.F)----raisins or common storage
Oranges
Pears
Quince
Endive, escarole
Grapefruit

Cool and Moist
40-50°F and 85-90% relative humidity
Cucumbers
Sweet peppers (45-550F)
Cantaloupe
Watermelon
Eggplant (50-600F)
Ripe tomatoes-------------dried or ?

Cool and Dry
35-40°F and 60-70% relative humidity
Garlic---------------------------dried
Onions----------------------------dried
Green soybeans in the pod----- (short-term)

Moderately Warm and Dry
50-60°F and 60-70% relative humidity
Dry hot peppers
Pumpkins
Winter squash-----------------------
Sweet potatoes
Green tomatoes (up to 70 Deg.F okay)

KEY:
----------------used in Earth Home

Figure 165-ROOT CELLAR ENVIRONMENTS

*Used in Earth Home

c. Cold Storage

It was probably by accident that early humans discovered that food kept longer if it was cold. Early food storage methods involved attempts to keep snow and ice for as long as possible into the summer. Pits were dug into the ground and insulated with straw or sawdust to keep food longer.

Later special insulated wooden cabinets were made to store the ice that was delivered to them. Hence the term "icebox" was used to describe these ice storage cabinets. (See Refrigeration section)

Some people used special boxes built around windows in the kitchen. These window box refrigerators kept food cold when outside temperatures were adequate for food storage. These could be used for several months of the year.

d. Earth Home Common Storage

The Earth Home II will use a modified root cellar system that will be connected to the kitchen space with a modified "dumb waiter" so that it can be accessed directly from the kitchen area. Modified versions of the five environments shown will be used to assist the food freezing function with the largest section used for carrots and root crops.

4. Canning Food

a. Canning History

Another food storage method that became popular in the early days of the United States was canning. Canning has been used for about 200 years. Canning began in the 19th century when Napoleon Bonaparte needed a way for his army to carry food for long periods. He offered a 12,000 franc prize to anyone who could help him out. In 1810 Nicholas Appert captured the prize with a paper on sterilization of food. This "boiling water bath" method was good for high-acid foods and was a great benefit for the early settlers in this country, allowing them to keep food for two years or longer at 65°F. This method made use of ceramic or glass jars with sealed covers. The jars were first sterilized by boiling. Hot food was put in them, covers were put on, and they were set aside to cool. The cooling of the contents created a vacuum that sucked the cover tightly against the jar opening. The food was thus sterilized and sealed for later use.

b. Canning Issues

Canning has disadvantages in that great numbers of jars are necessary to can sufficient quantities of food. Further disadvantages include lots of preparation time, lots of storage space, and heavy things to handle. The method also requires great amounts of energy and labor. Pressure canning using pressure canners was also needed for low-acid foods such as beans, peas, corn, and beets that required higher heat to kill microorganisms. High acid foods were prepared using only a high temperature water bath because yeasts and molds inherent to these foods nave a low heat resistance.

5. Pickling with Vinegar (Acetic)

a. Description of Pickling

Pickling is putting vegetables into a vinegar solution with herbs, etc. Throughout much of the world, pickling remains a regular part of home or village life. It is commonly used with cucumbers, peppers, onions, etc. (See also Fermenting Section) It can also be used to preserve eggs. The difference between pickling and fermentation is that acid (acetic acid from vinegar) is added o the food to encourage preservation, rather than occurring as a by-product of the fermentation process. (Note that pickles were always lacto-fermented in times past, and then transferred to vinegar solely to stabilize them for commercial purposes.)

b. Pickling Disadvantages

Compared with lactic fermentation, preserving with vinegar has two distinct disadvantages:

1) We miss out on certain benefits that derive from fermentation: the synthesis of enzymes and vitamins, easier digestion, and medicinal properties.
2) Foods taste very acidic and can only be eaten in small quantities.

Also, the limited amount of vinegar production that is included in the Earth Home system limits widespread use of the pickling method. Vinegar should be reserved for use as a salad topping on the vast number of salads.

6. Preserves

Canning of sweetened fruits has been done since the early days in the US. This method is included in the preceding canning section.

7. Lactic Fermentation (See separate Lactic section)

8. Refrigeration (See separate Refrigeration section)

C. Fermentation (Lactic) Techniques

1. Using Salt for Brining

a. Vegetable Brine Fermentation (4) Categories

The first category includes those pickled products prepared directly from vegetables without undergoing fermentation.

The second category includes those products fermented in a relatively weak brine solution. These include dill pickles and many vegetable blends consumed without further alteration. Bulky and whole vegetables and those with low water content are usually placed in brine solutions for fermentation.

The third category includes those vegetable products fermented in relatively high salt brine, such as salt stock pickles that are at a later date refreshed and converted to some type of finished pickle.

The fourth category includes those products prepared by dry salting with a relatively low salt content such as sauerkraut.

b. Brining Meat/Eggs

Historically, brining has been used as a method to preserve meat. Heavy concentrations of salt could preserve meats for long ocean voyages and military campaigns before the advent of refrigeration. The chemistry behind brining is actually pretty simple. Meat already contains salt water. Meat is soaked for many days in a very strong saltwater solution (1 cup per gallon) with the addition of sugar, spices, and other ingredients. This curing process binds the water in the meat or removes it altogether so it is not available for the growth of food-spoiling microorganisms.

Some foods, including eggs can be put into a mixture of salt and water (brine) for long periods of time. The Chinese soaked the eggs in brine for more than a month. The resulting egg, of a hard-boiled consistency with a bright orange yolk, will neither break nor spoil if properly handled.

c. Salt "Conservation" in EH

Historically, the salt and brine mixtures are discarded after each batch of meat was finished. Canning salt in the Earth Home is predominantly used for fermentation processes such as sauerkraut. This method insures that the salt is used more efficiently.

2. Salt and Sugar Added Fermentation

Salt and sugar can be added in combinations to produce a pickled leafy vegetable product. Pak-Gard-Dong is a fermented mustard leaf product made in Thailand. The mustard leaves are washed, wilted in the sun, mixed with salt, and packed into containers for 12 hours. The water is then drained and a 3% sugar solution added. They are again allowed to ferment for three to five days at room temperature.

a. Salt-Added Fermentation

Pak-Sian-Dong or Pak Sian is also cleaned and wilted in the sun for one to two hours. It is then placed in brine only and fermented for two to three days at room temperature. Wilted mustard cabbage is prepared in much the same manner.

Other pickled vegetables and fruits include bamboo shoots, beet root, red onions, ginger and papaya, carrots, turnips, bananas, sweet peppers, and cauliflower stalks.

b. Non-Salted Fermentation

Non salted lactic acid bacteria products include Gundruk (pickled leafy vegetable). Gundruk has been an important source of minerals particularly during the off-season when some diets consist of mostly starchy tubers and corn which tend to be low in minerals.

In the months of October and November, during the harvest of the first broad mustard, radish and cauliflower leaves, large quantities of leaves accumulate—much more than can be consumed fresh. These leaves are allowed to wilt for one or two days and then shredded with a knife or sickle. Shredded leaves are tightly packed in an earthenware pot and warm water (at about 30 deg. C) is added to cover all the leaves. The pot is then kept in a warm place. After five to seven days, a mild acidic taste indicates the end of fermentation and the Gundruk is removed and sun-dried. This process is similar to sauerkraut production except that no salt is added to the shredded leaves prior to Gundruk fermentation. The ambient temperature at the time of fermentation is about 18 deg. C.

3. Fermentation (Lactic) Overview

a. Fermentation History

In the Paleolithic age, fermentation emerged as another important technique. Fermentation, although naturally occurring, is one of the key processes our ancients harnessed to preserve food for longer durations and enabled survival. In the ancient world, where food sources were mostly local, having access to food in the lean winter season was a major problem for survival and fermentation helped solve that problem to a great extent.

Preparation of foods by the use of microorganisms predates the history of man. In many areas of the world fermentation is the only method used for preserving vegetables, and they are prepared almost entirely in the home. They probably originated from chance observations in which a set of environmental conditions prevailed and an acceptable food product resulted. In China, the use of microorganisms to convert agricultural commodities into foods and alcoholic beverages is an art which has 6,000-7,000 years of history-including the Chinese version of sauerkraut, paocai or yancai. They may have been the first to preserve food by this method. In Korea a blend of pickled mixed vegetables, called kimchi, is second only to rice in feeding the population.

*Used in Earth Home

According to early records, the northern Chinese, the probable originators of soybean sauces, also salted and fermented other protein sources such as fish and shellfish (as is done in Southeast Asia today)—even mutton, venison, hare and other animal meats—as a means of preserving them before soybeans were ever considered. It is conceivable that some early Chinese cooks mixed their food, millet, for example with a certain rabbit paste they preferred; others, with a paste made from fermented freshwater crab. In China today, because of its practicality, the soybean is the base of all these sauces.

b. Importance of Fermentation

The cultural heritage of virtually every civilization includes one of more fermented foods make by the souring action of microbes: leben (Egypt and Syria), taettemjolk (Scandinavia), matzoon (Armenia), dahi (India), and piner (Lapland). Fermented foods provided a major contribution to the diet in all parts of the world. Fermentation as a preserving technique was especially valuable in cool, damp climates where drying and associated dry salting and smoking were unreliable and where long, unproductive winters made it necessary for large amounts of foodstuffs to be preserved.

Now many fermented foods, because of their very distinctiveness and unpopularity with outsiders, have taken on cultural significance, and the enjoyment of them and involvement in the rituals of preparation and eating is part of belonging to a certain country or people.

c. Pit Fermentation Background

South Pacific pit fermentation is an ancient method of preserving starchy vegetables without the addition of salt. The raw materials undergo an acid fermentation within the pit, to produce a paste with good keeping qualities. Pit fermentations are also used in other parts of the world – for example in Ethiopia, where the false banana is fermented in a pit to produce a pulp known as kocho. Foods preserved in pits can last for years without deterioration; therefore pits provide a good, reliable cheap means of storage.

d. Pit Fermentation Technique

Root crops and bananas are peeled before being placed in the pit, while breadfruit are scraped and pierced. Food is left to ferment for three to six weeks, after which time it becomes soft, has a strong odor and a paste-like consistency. During fermentation, carbon dioxide builds up in the pit, creating an anaerobic atmosphere. As a result of bacterial activity, the temperature rises much higher than the ambient temperature. The pH of the fruit within the pit decreases from 6.7 to 3.7 within about four weeks. Inoculation of the fruit in the pit with lactic acid bacteria greatly speeds up the process. The fermented paste can be left in the pit and removed as required. Usually, it is removed and replaced with a second batch of fresh food to ferment. The fermented food is washed and fibrous material removed. It is then dried in the sun for several hours to remove the volatile odors, and pounded into a paste. Grated coconut or coconut cream and sugar may be added and the mixture is wrapped in banana leaves and either baked or boiled.

4. Chemistry of Fermentation

Fermentation is chemical changes in organic substances produced by the action of enzymes. Fermented foods may be defined as those foods which have been subjected to the action of micro-organisms or enzymes so that desirable biochemical changes cause significant modification to the food. Three important fermented foods are cheese (lactic), alcohol, and acetic when wine turns to vinegar. The concentration in this section will be on the lactic fermentation when salt is added to vegetables such as cabbage.

Fermentation occurs when only <u>small amounts</u> of pickling salt (approximately one pound for 40-50 pounds of cabbage) are used. Typically, salt is added at about ½-1 ½ percent by weight. In fermentation, bacteria change the sugars of the vegetables to lactic acid, and the acid (with the salt) prevents other spoilage organisms from growing. This lactic acid fermentation is the method used in making sauerkraut and other "sour" vegetables.

5. Advantages of Fermentation

Fermented foods have the following advantages:

1) Fermentation is a method of preservation
2) Fermentation may destroy undesirable factors in the raw product.
3) The fermented food may have an enhanced nutritional value and digestibility.
4) Fermentation may be used to salvage some products that could not otherwise be used for food.
5) Fermentation may improve the appearance of some foods.
6) Fermented foods may have a better flavor than the raw products.
7) Fermentation reduces cooking time.
8) Some fermented foods, e.g. beers and wines, are enjoyable (to some people).
9) Fermented foods may be safer.
10) Fermentation improves the texture of the food.
11) Fermentation helps solubilize some food components.
12) The methods used are inexpensive.

By fermentation, the food may be made more nutritious, more digestible, safer, or have better flavor. Fermentation is a relatively efficient low-energy preservation process which can increase product life and reduce the need for refrigeration or other energy-intensive operation in food preservation.

6. Fermentation Nutrition

Since the salting is so mild, both vegetable and juice may be eaten, and nearly all the nutrients are preserved. Fermented foods also supply vitamin B_{12} from bacteria to aid in vegetarian diets.

Virtually all plants can be fermented, but the classic vegetable for preserving in this way is the cabbage. The health-giving properties of sauerkraut have been well recognized for 200 years or more, and before vitamin C was discovered, it was a preventative or cure for scurvy. This was, of course, because cabbage ranks high among foods for vitamin C value. Even though two-thirds of the vitamin C is lost in fermenting and processing, there are still 16 mg. in a four ounce serving.

The well fermented kimchi has more lactic acid bacteria than yogurt. This bacteria 1s known to be especially good for the intestines and has anti-germ functions. Kimchi also contains acetic acid, amino acids and many vitamins.

7. Fermented Beverages

a. Background

Fruit and berry juices rapidly become alcoholic. Fermented beverages include wine, beer, sake', brandy, whisky, and non-alcoholic tea, coffee, and cocoa. These are of major importance throughout the world, particularly so where safe drinking water supplies cannot be guaranteed.

b. Fermented Beverage Choices

Rosel or russell is a fermented beet-vinegar used during the Jewish Passover, and to make a Russian-type beet soup. The liquid is clear, bright red, and has a winelike aroma.

Once there was even fermented tomato juice on the market. This pleasant effervescent acidic low-alcoholic beverage was discontinued after a short while. A forerunner of kvas from the USSR is the drink beryozovitsa. This ancient drink is made from the sap of the birch tree.

c. Nutrition in Alcoholic Beverages

Throughout the world, there are always versions of weak beer or gruel. The emphasis with these beverages is work-related nutrition and not inebriation. Examples include sorghum malt beverages such as merissa (an opaque beer), assaliya (clear beer), Kafir beer, and injera from the Sudan. Kafir beer is known to have added valuable B vitamins to the poor maize diet in many parts of Africa and helped to prevent the dietary disease of pellagra.

In northern Italy they make pachwai, a rice beer that may contain as much as 22 percent alcohol and is also used for its nutritional qualities.

Alcohol was not considered evil or inherently unhealthy by the ancient sages: indeed wine was used in ancient practice to dispel fatigue and enhance digestion, and there are detailed descriptions of alcoholic preparations for healing included in the classic texts. An endorsement of alcohol's beneficial use to humans, beer and wine became a part of almost every religion's sacraments, holidays, and feasts. Many monasteries continue their brewing pursuits to this day. If an average 12 ounce bottle of beer had a "Nutrition Facts" label, this is what if would say:

Beer contains 150 calories
Beer has no fat
Beer has no cholesterol
Beer is caffeine free
Beer contains 1 gram of protein and 13 grams of carbohydrates
Beer contains significant amounts of magnesium, selenium, potassium, phosphorus, and biotin
Beer is chock full of the B vitamins with impressive amounts of B3 (niacin), B5, B6, B9, with lesser amounts of B_1, B_2, and B_{12}
Beer is 92% water

d. Fermented Flavorings/Sauces/Condiments

The ancient Romans were very fond of a flavoring called "garum". Garum was made with the intestines of mackerel, small red mullet, sprats, or anchovies, macerated in salt in jars, and left in the sun for two to three months to autolyze. Autolyze means that the fish's own enzymes digest the proteins. The acidic concentrated juices "self-preserved" in the same way as a vinegar pickle, were then drained from this mush, sieved, and stored in amphorae. Not only thought delicious, it was also a "keeping" sauce full of essential nutrients. It retained its strong fishy taste almost indefinitely, and was so powerful that only a few drops were required, making it particularly useful for travelers. The military make a cheaper version called "muria" from inferior fish for soldiers to carry in their packs and dilute with water.

Several modern versions of this are popular in Nice called pissalat, nam pla or nuoc nam in Vietnam, and shottsuru in Japan. Related fermented fish sauces are still being produced in the Far East in vast quantities. Laos, Cambodia, and Philippines all have versions of fermented fish sauce.

8. Fermented Food Selection

a. Cabbage Sauerkraut

Cabbage has always had a peculiar place in the diet as an adjunct to make other foods more agreeable and digestible rather than for its own nutritional value. Cato, in his manuscript, De re rustica, written about 200 B.C., lauds cabbage as the most important vegetable that Romans had under cultivation. During a period beginning about 200 B.C., and continuing until about 450 A.D., it was the principle plant used in the Roman Empire for treatment of disease.

In most recipes, salt is weighed and applied at a 2.25% level to the shredded cabbage. Considerable attention has been given to efficient methods of distribution of salt-being fully as important as the amount of salt used. Also a fermentation temperature of 18.3 degrees C. is considered optimal. Sauerkraut takes 20-30 days for completion of fermentation.

b. Other Fermented Vegetables

Certain flavors such as sweet, sour, alcoholic, and meatlike appeal to large numbers of humans. Milks sour naturally. Over many centuries, people have developed tastes for such products that continue today. Other vegetables such as head lettuce, Chinese cabbage, rutabagas, cucumbers, sliced green tomatoes, radishes, turnips (and turnip tops), beets, peas, radishes, chard, and snap beans can also be made into kraut.

The fermentation of vegetables (sauerkraut, pickles, kim'chee/kimchi); grains (sourdough bread, kvass, kiesiel, kisra, koji); beans (miso, natto, tempeh) and fish are experiencing renewed interest. Examples of other fermented foods are cheese, mushrooms, bread, yogurt, soy sauce, fish sauce, pepperoni, kombucha, and gari. Around the world pickled foods such as sunki (pickled turnip leaves), achar tandal (cauliflower stalks), kanji (pickled carrots), pak-sian-dong, sayur asin (fermented wilted cabbage), and chai kiam are local specialties. Some of these foods do not take much time to prepare.

c. Fermented Leaves

An especially easy pickling task is called pickled mustard greens. It is also referred to as Borong Mostasa in the Philippines. Gundruk is a fermented and dried vegetable product of Nepal. It is produced by shredding the leaves of mustard, radish, and cauliflower leaves and placing them in an earthenware pot to ferment. After 5 to 7 days the leaves are removed and dried in the sun.

Lettuce kraut with 2-2 ½ percent salt is also easy to prepare. It is prepared in an earthenware crock pot similar to sauerkraut. Sometimes a layer of mineral oil is put over the surface of the fermentation preventing the growth of film yeasts. The oriental muchung kimchi is similar and made from the leaves of oriental radishes.

d. Meat Substitute

The green leaves of Cassia Obtusifolia are fermented to produce a food product, kawal, used by certain tribes of Sudan as a meat substitute. Following fermentation for 2 weeks, the product is sun dried and used when needed. Protein content of kawal is about 20% on dry matter basis. For reasons not fully understood, only the leaves of C. obtusifolia appear to yield a satisfactory product, and not logical choices like alfalfa.

9. Earth Home Fermentation-Lactic

a. Methods of Salt Preservation

Nearly all vegetable substances whether leafy, tuberous, or those containing seeds provide sufficient nutrients for the growth of lactic acid bacteria. The leafy vegetables sometimes may be low in total sugars; the root vegetables high in starch and sugar sometimes may be deficient in other nutrients; and some seed vegetables such as beans and peas may be so highly buffered that during fermentation a ;considerable amount of acid must be produced before a marked change in pH is attained.

1. Adding Salt to Vegetables

Dry salting, using a small amount of salt (2 ½ to 5 percent by weight), is usually employed for vegetables that are readily cut or shredded, that are high in water, and that contain enough readily fermentable sugar to support a vigorous fermentation. Cabbage, lettuce, and turnips are typical examples of vegetables that are salted in this manner. As a result of the action of the salt on the vegetable tissue, water is withdrawn which dissolves the salt and thereby forms brine.

Certain vegetables are best preserved when a large amount of salt (20 percent by weight) is used. Corn, lima beans, onions, and green peas are examples of vegetables considered to be in this group. The vegetables must be kept under the surface of the liquid with weighted covers to prevent spoilage.

2. Vegetables Covered with Brine

This method assumes a supply of brine or salt and water. Additional salt must be added to maintain the original brine concentration due to the water content of the vegetables. Brining is generally used for preserving bulky or whole vegetables and those that may be low in water content. Also, brining may be used to advantage where the effect of shrinkage on the shape and structure of the vegetables, caused by the use of dry salt, would be unduly severe. Common brined vegetables are snap beans, cauliflower, celery, corn on the cob, cucumbers, onions, and sweet peppers. Carrots have even been brined at 6.2 percent brine solution.

In Eastern Europe, salting vegetables has survived on a truly large scale up to the modern day. Red peppers, turnips, cauliflower florets, cabbage, red beets, small carrots, and artichokes are all dept in brine. Even some fruits, such as apples and pears, are preserved in this way. The Chinese salt apricots, eggplant, and even oranges!

For some vegetables a weak brine plus a small amount of vinegar is used. The addition of vinegar to the brine aids in bringing about a desirable fermentation and averts possible spoilage. Brine solutions have been used for soup stocks commercially.

b. Specific Fermentation Production

The Earth Home will use fermenting for sauerkraut and opportunistic crops as they ripen. Barley and cabbage is intended to be used in the EH system. (See also Pickling section)

1. Lettuce Kraut

Lettuce is one of the easier foods to put by. Lettuce kraut is made simply from the leaves of lettuce and common pickling salt.

2. Cabbage Sauerkraut

Sauerkraut is typically made from cabbage and salt also. It has been a staple of many people for generations and will be used in the Earth Home diet. (see Fermentation section).

3. Rejuvelac

Rejuvelac is a fermented grain drink or a fermented cabbage drink. It is high in the friendly bacteria (enzymes) that are so important for a healthy colon. The tonic can also be made from wheatberries, rye, barley, or millet. To make cabbage rejuvelac, simply blend some up with distilled water, cover, and let it set for 3 days at room temperature.

D. Refrigeration (See also Cooling System section)

1. Refrigeration/Freezing Background

a. Early Refrigeration Methods

Iceboxes were available beginning in the 1830's. Beginning in mid-1800, a couple of inventions became prominent in the science of food preservation and freezing. First was the absorption cycle that led to modern mechanized refrigeration. The first type of mechanized food freezing was a system called the "Icy Ball." Two canisters were connected by a pipe and partially filled with ammonia refrigerant (early refrigerants were ammonia, sulfur dioxide, and methyl chloride). One container was heated, driving the refrigerant to the other canister. This canister was then put inside a freezer compartment, and the heated canister was left exposed to the air. The refrigerant would gradually move back to the other canister, lowering the pressure and dropping the temperature inside the refrigerator compartment. In this way, a family could keep food cold for up to four hours before they had to remove and reheat one chamber of the Icy Ball.

A later adaptation of this method resulted in the early "Servel" refrigerators. They were absorption refrigerators that used a continuous heat source to drive the refrigerant around a loop. This refrigerator is still commonly used in remote cabins where there are no electrical lines. (See also Cooling: Mechanical/Absorption Systems section.)

b. Modern Refrigeration

History has shown that mechanical refrigeration has replaced food storage in cellars, iceboxes, and frequent shopping for fresh food. Beginning about 1930, compressors used a sealed piston to compress refrigerant (usually Freon). After it was compressed, it traveled through the condenser (on the outside of cabinet) where it gave up heat. It was then forced through a small "pitot" tube or restriction, and allowed to expand as it came out the other end. The refrigerant absorbed heat as it expanded and continued to move through the coils in the cooling chamber. After picking up heat from the cabinet, it was then compressed again and continued through the loop. This same concept is used for refrigerators, freezers, air conditioning units, and virtually all cooling mechanisms that use electricity for power.

Refrigerators account for up to 1/3 of electricity used in the home, and approximately 13 percent of total U.S. electric usage. The large size of typical refrigerators reflects the tendency to shop and store a week's food at one time.

c. Refrigeration/Freezing Chemistry

Freezing food at a temperature of around -18°C effectively kills many microbiological organisms, and prevents the growth of all others. Freezing is easy, fast, holds color/flavor/nutrients, safe, convenient, and is the least damaging method to preserve food. The main loss is vitamin C. The following figures show the length of time various foods can safely be kept frozen. As shown, this method of refrigeration greatly extends the usable life of foods. Freezers should be kept at 0°F or lower to minimize vitamin losses.

(Note that freezing food and then heating under vacuum to evaporate the ice into water vapor is called "freeze-drying". Freeze drying extends life much longer, but will not be covered here due to the excessive complicated technology, costs, and energy inputs.)

2. Refrigeration Options

a. Burning High Temperature Fuels (Absorption Cycle Refrigeration)

There are also a number of fuels including alcohol, kerosene, and methane that can be burned to provide these high temperatures. Kerosene refrigerators are commonly used in South American countries such as Venezuela.

Early American absorption refrigerators used propane gas because of its portability and versatility. Modern (absorption) gas refrigerators consume 5 to 11 gallons of propane per month. (See Alcohol and Propane file.)

b. Concentrated Solar Heat

In addition to electricity, there are methods of using heat to drive an absorption cycle device. Some refrigerators use solar heat to evaporate the refrigerant. However, it is necessary to heat the refrigerant to a much higher temperature than flat plate solar collectors can deliver. Systems have been developed to concentrate the heat on a pipe or point source for absorption mechanisms. (See Refrigerators File)

Commodity	Temp. (°F)	Rel. Humid. (%)	Approx. Length of Storage Period	Highest Freeze Point* (°F)	Water Content (%)	Specific Heat** (Btu/lb/ dg F.)
Artichokes, globe	32	90-95	1 month	29.9	83.7	0.87
Artichokes, Jerusalem	31-32	90-95	2-5 months	--	79.8	.84
Asparagus	***32-36	95	2-3 weeks	30.9	93.0	.94
Beans, green or snap	***40-45	90-95	7-10 days	30.7	88.9	.91
Beans, lima	***32-40	90	1-2 weeks***	31.0	66.5	.73
Beets, bunched	32	95	10-14 days	31.3	--	--
Beets, topped	32	95	3-5 months	30.3	87.6	.90
Broccoli, sprouting	32	90-95	10-14 days	30.9	89.9	.92
Brussels sprouts	32	90-95	3-5 weeks	30.5	84.9	.88
Cabbage, early	32	90-95	3-6 weeks	30.4	92.4	.94
Cabbage, late	32	90-95	3-4 months	30.4	92.4	.94
Cabbage, Chinese	32	90-95	1-2 months	--	95.0	.96
(CONT. NEXT PAGE)						

*Highest freezing points are from Whiteman, (739).
**Specific heat above freezing was calculated from Siebel's formula: S = 0.008 (percent water in food) + 0.20.
***See text.
****See text for cultivar differences.

Figure 166-FOOD FREEZING CHART, PAGE 1

*Used in Earth Home

Commodity	Temp. (°F)	Rel. Humid. (%)	Approx. Length of Storage Period	Highest Freeze Point* (°F)	Water Content (%)	Specific Heat** (Btu/lb/ dg F.)
(CONT. FROM PREVIOUS PAGE)						
Carrots, mature (topped)	32	90-95	4-5 months	29.5	88.2	.91
Carrots, immature (topped)	32	90-95	4-6 weeks	29.5	88.2	.91
Cauliflower	32	90-95	2-4 weeks	30.6	91.7	.93
Celeriac	32	90-95	3-4 months	30.3	88.4	.91
Celery	32	90-95	2-3 months	31.1	93.7	.95
Collards	32	90-95	10-14 days	30.6	86.9	.90
Corn, sweet	32	90-95	4-8 days	30.9	73.9	.79
Cucumbers	45-50	90-95	10-14 days	31.1	96.1	.97
Eggplants	45-50	90	1 week	30.6	92.7	.94
Endive and escarole	32	90-95	2-3 weeks	31.9	93.1	.95
Garlic, dry	32	65-70	6-7 months	30.5	61.3	.69
(CONT. NEXT PAGE)						

*Highest freezing points are from Whiteman, (739).

**Specific heat above freezing was calculated from Siebel's formula: S = 0.008 (percent water in food) + 0.20.

***See text.

****See text for cultivar differences.

Figure 167-FOOD FREEZING CHART, PAGE 2

*Used in Earth Home

Commodity	Temp. (°F)	Rel. Humid. (%)	Approx. Length of Storage Period	Highest Freeze Point* (°F)	Water Content (%)	Specific Heat** (Btu/lb/dg F.)
(CONT. FROM PREVIOUS PAGE)						
Ginger rhizomes	55	65	6 months	--	87.0	.90
Greens, leafy	32	90-95	10-14 days	--	--	--
Horseradish	30-32	90-95	10-12 months	28.7	74.6	.80
Kale	32	90-95	10-14 days	31.1	86.6	.89
Kohlrabi	32	90-95	2-4 weeks	30.2	90.3	.92
Leeks, green	32	90-95	1-3 months	30.7	85.4	.88
Lettuce	32	95	2-3 weeks	31.7	94.8	.96
Melons:						
- Cantaloupe (3/4-slip)	36-40	85-90	15 days	29.9	92.0	.94
- Cantaloupe (full-slip)	32-35	85-90	5-14 days	29.9	92.0	.94
(CONT. NEXT PAGE)						

*Highest freezing points are from Whiteman, (739).
**Specific heat above freezing was calculated from Siebel's formula: S = 0.008 (percent water in food) + 0.20.
***See text.
****See text for cultivar differences.

Figure 168-FOOD FREEZING CHART, PAGE 3

*Used in Earth Home

Commodity	Temp. (°F)	Rel. Humid. (%)	Approx. Length of Storage Period	Highest Freeze Point* (°F)	Water Content (%)	Specific Heat** (Btu/lb/ dg F.)
(CONT. FROM PREVIOUS PAGE)						
- Casaba	45-50	85-90	4-6 weeks	30.1	92.7	.94
- Crenshaw	45-50	85-90	2 weeks	30.1	92.7	.94
- Honey Dew	45-50	85-90	3-4 weeks	30.3	92.6	.94
- Persian	45-50	85-90	2 weeks	30.5	92.7	.94
- Watermelon	***40-50	80-85	2-3 weeks	31.3	92.6	.94
Mushrooms	32	90	3-4 days	30.4	91.1	.93
Okra	45-50	90-95	7-10 days	28.7	89.8	.92
Onions (dry) and onion sets	32	65-70	1-8 months****	30.6	87.5	.90
Onions, green	32	90-95	--	30.4	89.4	.91
Parsley	32	90-95	1-2 months	30.0	85.1	.88
Parsnips	32	90-95	2-6 months	30.4	78.6	.83
Peas, green	32	90-95	1-3 weeks	30.9	74.3	.79
(CONT. NEXT PAGE)						

*Highest freezing points are from Whiteman, (739).

**Specific heat above freezing was calculated from Siebel's formula: S = 0.008 (percent water in food) + 0.20.

***See text.

****See text for cultivar differences.

Figure 169-FOOD FREEZING CHART, PAGE 4

Commodity	Temp. (°F)	Rel. Humid. (%)	Approx. Length of Storage Period	Highest Freeze Point* (°F)	Water Content (%)	Specific Heat** (Btu/lb/ dg F.)
(CONT. FROM PREVIOUS PAGE)						
Peppers, chili (dry)	***32-50	60-70	6 months	--	12.0	.30
Peppers, sweet	45-50	90-95	2-3 weeks	30.7	92.4	.94
Potatoes, early crop	(***)	90	(***)	30.9	81.2	.85
Potatoes, later crop	(***)	90	(***)	30.9	77.8	.82
Pumpkins	50-55	70-75	2-3 months	30.5	90.5	.92
Radishes, spring	32	90-95	3-4 weeks	30.7	94.5	0.96
Radishes, winter	32	90-95	2-4 months	--	--	--
Rhubarb	32	95	2-4 weeks	30.3	94.9	.96
Rutabagas	32	90-95	2-4 months	30.1	89.1	.91
Salsify	32	90-95	--	30.0	79.1	.83
Spinach	32	90-95	10-14 days	31.5	92.7	.94
(CONT. NEXT PAGE)						

*Highest freezing points are from Whiteman, (739).
**Specific heat above freezing was calculated from Siebel's formula: S = 0.008 (percent water in food) + 0.20.
***See text.
****See text for cultivar differences.

Figure 170-FOOD FREEZING CHART, PAGE 5

Commodity	Temp. (°F)	Rel. Humid. (%)	Approx. Length of Storage Period	Highest Freeze Point* (°F)	Water Content (%)	Specific Heat** (Btu/lb/ dg F.)
(CONT. FROM PREVIOUS PAGE)						
Squashes, winter	50-55	****50-75	(***)	30.5	85.1	.88
Squashes, summer	32-50	90	5-14 days***	31.1	94.0	.95
Sweet potatoes	***55-60	85-90	4-6 months	29.7	68.5	.75
Tomatoes, mature-green	***55-70	85-90	1-3 weeks	31.0	93.0	.94
Tomatoes, ripe-firm	45-50	85-90	4-7 days	31.1	94.1	.95
Turnips	32	90-95	4-5 months	30.1	91.5	.93
Turnips, green	32	90-95	10-14 days	31.7	90.3	.92
Watercress	32-35	90-95	3-4 days	31.4	93.3	.95

*Highest freezing points are from Whiteman, (739).
**Specific heat above freezing was calculated from Siebel's formula: S = 0.008 (percent water in food) + 0.20.
***See text.
****See text for cultivar differences.

Figure 171-FOOD FREEZING CHART, PAGE 6

c. Electricity

If a mechanical compressor is used instead of heat, there are several ways to drive it including electrical motors and Stirling engines.(see Future Cooling-Stirling Refrigerators section) One of the requirements for efficient electrical mechanical cooling is to get the compressor going and keep it going using the minimum amount of electricity possible. Any electrical motor has what's referred to as "high starting torque". This means that two to three times as much electricity must be used to overcome inertia and get the motor to start running. Experimentation is being done on devices that lower starting torque. They are in the early stages of development, and only one or two devices are commercially available at the present time. (See Appliances file.)

3. Efficient Refrigeration Options

There are some recent developments that promise to aid the refrigeration process. Newer refrigerators have come out that use 50-90% of the energy requirements of a conventional one. Some of the technologies they use are; higher insulation levels; improved efficiency compressors; separate refrigerant loops for the refrigerator and freezer compartments; improved heat exchangers; and improved door seals. Vestfrost is one model that uses separate compressors. (See Refrigerator file.) Also rotary compressors are being marketed which claim 15% higher efficiency than the reciprocating models.

Sanyo has recently introduced a rotary two stage compressor that uses CO_2 refrigerant. This system will eventually make its way into smaller refrigeration units for the home.

4. Earth Home Refrigeration

As mentioned earlier, valuable freezer space can be saved by drying food for storage (dried food occupies 1/7 the space of fresh food. Freezer space is costly in terms of energy use and must be used for only a few select foods to conserve battery bank size and space. (Freezing of sweet products such as strawberries and grapes are minimized for this reason.)

a. Earth Home Refrigerator Compressor

As mentioned previously, The Earth Home refrigerator/freezer is designed to use a "Danfoss" compressor. A more thorough discussion is in Electricity-Selected Motors section.

b. Earth Home Refrigerator Plumbing/Ductwork

One method that has been used to gain efficiency for the freezer is to place it in an out-of-doors location (a garage or attached building) in cold climates. This greatly reduces the temperature differential that the freezer must overcome. Studies have shown that if a refrigerator is placed in a kitchen that is 5°C colder, electricity use will decrease by 30%. In the northern latitudes, it is still common to locate the freezer inside, even while the outside temperature may be 0°F. However, when this method is used without modifications, it can lead to frequent control cycling and condensation problems. The Earth Home is designed to bring outside cold air into a jacketed space around the freezer with a tiny air fan. The negative qualities of condensation and frequent cycling should be eliminated using this method.

The average duration of a refrigerator or freezer door opening is about 12 seconds. This is long enough to completely replace the cold air with warm air. Good habits of freezer and refrigerator use can greatly aid in lowering energy use. A separate isolated "transfer box" can be beneficial in pre-cooling and thawing items before they are put in the refrigerator or used. The backup generator will be used on an intermittent basis to drop the temperature of the freezer when adequate energy from the wind generator or solar panels is not available. Excess electricity can be used in other areas when the generator is running to maximize efficiency.

***Used in Earth Home**

5. Earth Home Night Cooler Tab (See EH Tabs section)

A night cooler is defined as thermal mass for the refrigerator/freezer functions. It is described in the EH Tabs section.

E. Future/High-Tech Food Preservation Technologies

1. Refrigerator Options

a. Stirling Refrigerator Compressor

Another option to drive a mechanical compressor is a "Stirling" engine. This engine uses heat to achieve mechanical motion. Stirling engines are discussed in Chapter I Power/Electrical section. (Note: For a discussion of helium as an alternative refrigerant, see the previous cooling section.

b. Thermoacoustics

Simply put, thermoacoustic effect is the conversion of heat energy to sound energy or vice versa. Utilizing the thermoacoustic effect, refrigerators can be developed that use heat as an energy source and have no moving parts. Recently, the DOE group at Los Alamos National Laboratory has developed a thermoacoustic heat engine that uses a variation of the Stirling cycle. Much work must still be done to achieve any commercially viable products.

2. High-Tech Options for Food Preservation

a. Ultra-High Pressurization (UHP) or (HPP)

Ultra-high pressurization or high pressure processing (HPP) of foods is a relatively new method. HPP has been used mainly for refrigerated and high-acid foods. It has also been called hydrostatic processing.

The first HPP applications were in heat-sensitive, value-added products. Foods "pasteurized" by HPP undergo pressures of up to 100,000 psi at or near ambient temperatures. The process involves packaging the food in a flexible pouch or container, then placing it in a chamber under ultra-high pressures for a few minutes.

Under these conditions, HPP was found to be effective in inactivating most vegetative pathogens commonly found in the foods. Commercially available UHP or HPP-processed products in Europe and Asia include juices, jams, jellies, meat and yogurt. There is significant commercial interest in development of this process for other foods.

b. Irradiation

In 1963, FDA approved irradiation to treat food. Initially, wheat and wheat flour were irradiated to eliminate insects. Over the years, irradiation has been approved in the United States for pork, spices, fruits, vegetables and poultry. Red meat joined the list with seafood in the making.

In irradiation, the food is exposed to a source of ionizing radiation. Irradiation is similar to X-rays in that there is no radioactivity.

c. Ozone (O_3)

Ozone (O_3) has been used for many years in municipal water treatment, aquarium environments, and other nonfood applications. In May 1997, ozone received GRAS (generally recognized as safe) status as a sanitizer of disinfectant for foods.

An unstable gas formed from oxygen, ozone decomposes into oxygen. As it does this, its high oxidizing potential leads to its disinfection potential. Bacteria are quickly destroyed, leaving behind oxygen. Ozone is a broad spectrum biocide. It will kill bacteria, viruses, and molds.

Ozone decomposes quickly and there is no residual for ingesting or buildup of residual compounds. Ozone's high reactivity means it must be generated on-site, as needed. This requires significant equipment.

d. Ohmic Heating

An advancement in thermal processing is ohmic heating. In principle, electric energy is transformed into thermal energy uniformly throughout the product. Ohmic heating employs electrodes immersed on a pipe. Product is pumped through the pipe as current flows between the electrodes. More rapid heating and better nutritional qualities are possible when compared with conventional in-can sterilization.

F. Earth Home Food Preparation Methods

The Earth Home lifestyle would entail more washing, peeling, and soaking than the average American diet. However, tools and appliances are available to help with these tasks. More mechanical aids could also be developed over the course of time.

1. Earth Home Grinding and Juicing

The Earth Home must also possess the capabilities to efficiently grind wheat, soybeans, fish scraps, chicken/fowl grit, and juices. Multi-purpose machines have been manufactured which combine most or all functions. Figure 136 lists juicers and grinders commercially available. They are listed together because juicers often come with grain grinding attachments.

The Earth Home is designed to use a bicycle-type mechanism powering the grinding mechanisms of commercial units. Most of them will need a modification to convert them to back-up 12 volt operation. However, the Welles Peoples Press uses hand-operated hydraulic action to squeeze vegetables and fruits without using any power at all (see Juicers file and Raw Juice section).

2. Earth Home Sprouting

The Earth is designed to have a built-in sprouter located in the kitchen cabinet area near the kitchen sink (for drainage after rinses). Because of the importance of sprouting in the Earth Home diet, sprouting trays will be rinsed and drained using partial automation techniques. Seed storage in small quantities can be located nearby. One pound of alfalfa seeds, for example, produces eight pounds of sprouts. (See Sprouting file and Sprouts section)

*Used in Earth Home

Name/Model of Grinder (Manual models)	Relative Cost	Fine/ Coarse Adjust Y=Yes N=No	Type: S=Stone B=Burr	Ability to be Motorized? Y=Yes N=No	G=Grains O=Oil Beans N=Nuts C=Corn B=Beans
Little Ark (Retsel)	2	Y	S & B	Y 90 RPM	G Option-O,B
Country Living Grain Mill	6	Y	B	Y	G Option-N,B
Back to Basics	1	Y	B	N	C,G
The Family Grain Mill DS630	3	Y	B	N	G
Corona King Convertible	2	Y	B	N	C,G
Diamant	12	Y	B	Y	O,B,C,G
Sunshine Nugget	2	Y	S	N	G
Marcato Grain Mill	2	N	B	N	G

Name/Model of Juicer(Manual models)	Relative Cost	V=Vegetables W=Wheatgrass
Miracle Manual MJ400	1	V,W
Wheateena Manual (Sundance Industries)	2	V,W
Chop-Rite Health Juice Extractor	3	V,W
Back to Basics	1	V,W
Lifestream	5	V,W
Welles Press (Hydraulic)	7	V,W
Fruit Press	1	V,W

Figure 172-COMMERCIAL MANUAL GRINDERS/JUICERS

*Used in Earth Home

3. Earth Home Flavorings

The taste of foods has always been important for most people. In the Earth Home system, significant flavors can be had using fermented fish sauce. These sauces can be used over vegetables, starches, or protein sources. The sauce can be made as salty as desired to add significant flavor to most dishes.

G. Cooking Method Options

Cooking food destroys over 80% of the nutrients. But we as a culture have placed emphasis on heating our food before we eat it. History has shown many methods to accomplish this.

1. Developing Countries Cooking Methods

a. 3 Stone Fire/Hearth (See also Heating section)

A common cooking method of many developing countries is the 3 stone fire or three-stone hearth. This was basically 3 stones arranged in a circle with a rock or steel plate on top. Fuel was put into the sides of the fire and the smoke bellowed out around the top. The vast majority of Kenya's population, for example, uses the above three-stone hearths. Wood is the principal fuel in rural areas while charcoal dominates urban households.

b. Mud Stoves (See Wok)

c. Traditional Metal Stove (TMS)

In urban areas, they use a charcoal-burning traditional metal stove (TMS). This stove is a small metal cylinder with a grate and 3 legs. These stoves are similar to the Ugandan "sigiri" and the all-metal "mbaula" of Malawi and Zambia. The metal versions are about 15-20 percent efficient at heating food.

d. Improvements in Basic Stoves

The Kenya Ceramic Jiko (KCJ) uses more ceramic in its construction for longer life. The Rocket Stove is another efficiency improvement on the basic concept without adding too much expense.

e. Biogas Stoves

One possible solution to the world cooking problem is to convert wood and other biomass to gas which can then be burned cleanly in a biogas stove with the correct amount of air. Gasification of wood (or other biomass) offers the possibility of cleaner, better controlled gas cooking for developing countries. There are cooking stoves being developed that generates gas using the "inverted downdraft gasifier" or simply "downdraft" principle. They are capable of producing 20-25% charcoal in one mode of operation. A typical biogas cookstove is illustrated in the following diagram.

f. Other "Fuel-Efficient Cookstove" Designs

There have been many attempts over the years to make traditional cooking stoves more efficient. To date, they have included; economical Indian chulhas, 1-pot Lougas, Tungku Lowons, Malawi mudstoves type C, new Kerens, and the Tandoors. There have also been attempts at adding "smokeless" to "efficiency" resulting in; HERL chulhas, improved Egyptians, Singer stoves, GS stoves, Ghanian stoves, Nepali chulhas (chula), Lorena stoves, the Hiko, the Maendeleo, the Kuni Mbili, the Wendelbro, and the Magan chulhas. There is only limited scientific testing to compare these stoves to each other. (See also Woodgas/Gasification section)

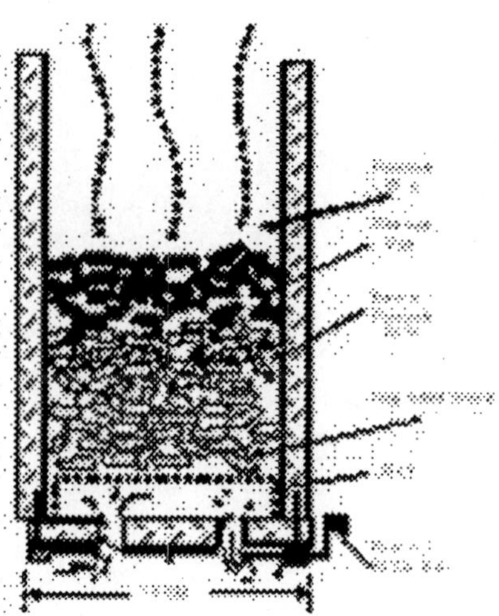

Figure 173-TYPICAL WOODGAS COOKSTOVE SCHEMATIC

2. Community Stew Pot/Dutch Oven.

Some small groups used a fire to heat up a perpetual stew pot. They pushed long wood sticks into the fire in "star" fashion to keep a small fire going continuously. ***It is interesting to note that 75% of the world's population uses wood for heating and cooking***. We have developed many ingenious ways to cook over a fire.

The Dutch oven is one of the most efficient cooking devices ever developed and was very popular in the American frontier. A Dutch oven was usually made of cast iron with a handle and cover. Food was put inside and slow-cooked similar to the modern crock pots.

3. Propane Cookstoves

Since 1850 the preferred means of cooking has been first gas, then electricity. Propane stoves use pressurized gas squirted through burner orifices. The size of the orifices can vary, depending on the BTU requirements of the burner. The burners spread the gas-air combination across the openings, which are then ignited and burned similar to candles. Many of these systems have a "pilot light" that is kept burning all the time. Each time a flame is desired, the pilot light ignites the gas as it travels to the burner. A common criticism of gas ranges is that a continuous pilot light uses up to 40% of the total gas requirement, because the pilot light remains on 24 hours a day. (See Propane Files.) A modern innovation in gas stove design is "piezo ignition". This is a special crystal that, under pressure, exerts a high electrical potential, creating a spark between positive and negative electrodes. Piezo ignition requires no energy input except the mechanical squeezing of the crystal to light the burner.

Burner design is critical when attempting to use a minimum amount of gaseous fuel. The width and height of the flame, size of the orifice, mass of the burners, distance between the burners, and the total number of burner ports are all critical in the design of an efficient burner. I feel that most modern burners use more holes than necessary. Recently, a sealed combustion gas range has been developed so much less products of combustion enter the air. (See Propane files.)

4. Pressure Cookers

One of the most energy efficient methods of cooking is a pressure cooker. This concept uses a cook pot with a sealable lid, into which is put a small amount of liquid and food. The entire container is heated to a certain temperature before the pressure relief valve opens, releasing excess steam from inside the container. Raising the pressure inside the cooker creates higher temperatures inside the pot to cook much faster. This method has been proven to be as quick as modern microwave cooking. It also has the added benefit of reaching temperatures high enough to kill all bacteria and spores.

5. Steaming

Steaming is another quick method of cooking vegetables that retains most of the nutrients. This method is very efficient because only a very small amount of water has to be heated, allowing the steam to do the cooking. The nutrient-rich water is then used as a broth or tea.

6. Hot Air Cooking

Another method of cooking that deserves mention for its efficiency is hot air cooking. In this method, steam and super heated air are generated inside a special cooking container. The super heated air whirls around the contents of the pot and cooks the food. At the present time, the hot air cookers are all electric-powered, but a modified model could be used on a stovetop.

7. Fireless Cooking/Hotbox Cooking

Hotbox, haybox, flameless oven, or fireless cooker means basically the same thing. Maintain a sufficiently high temperature (180 deg. F. or more) using insulation, and hot food will continue to cook. It will cook slower and more even without burning. This method was commonly used earlier in this century but has mostly been forgotten.

The advantages to fireless cooking are: thorough, burn-proof cooking without overcooking; hot meals first thing in the morning or night after work; arrival at parties, picnics and potlucks with piping-hot, ready-to-serve food; ready meals on long family road trips without stopping; nutrient loss reduction due to lower temperatures and less evaporation; fuel use reduction of 80%; elimination of need for power or fuel source during cooking; and a cooler kitchen in hot weather.

The Hawaiian luau uses basically the same concept when they place wrapped food into a pit of coals and covered it up for 12 hours or more. The insulated earth and the massive amounts of heat from the fire cooked the food slowly without losing moisture.

8. Solar Cooking

a. Solar Hot Boxes

Solar hot boxes or reflective ovens are sometimes used to cook foods. The sun's rays reflect into an insulated oven box and heats the food placed within. There are a few problems associated with this technology for Earth Home use. First, a south wall is preferred and the maximum attainable temperature is about 275 degrees Fahrenheit without concentration. Also these ovens work better in the "Southwest Heat Zone" where solar insolation is higher than anywhere in the U.S. (See EH Tabs section)

*Used in Earth Home

b. Parabolic Stand-Alone Cookers

These cookers use multiples of the sun's rays to achieve greater temperatures. These powerful solar cooking systems are generally based on parabolic reflectors. Among the most popular of these polished stainless steel collectors include the Scheffler reflector, SK 14, and the next generation, the Papillon. These are more user-friendly cookers that fold up for moving or storage. These collectors are increasing in popularity in India where there is an acute shortage of firewood for cooking fuel.

9. Wok/Mud Stove Combination

In the Orient, the "wok" or round bottomed method of cooking has been popular for centuries. Some of the early stoves, especially in Korea and Southeast Asia, used the wok as an integral part of the stove. Mud stoves were built to make efficient use of scarce wood and grasses. This type of stove was made out of clay or mud, with an open hole in the top for the cook pot or wok. In this way, a small amount of twigs or grass could be burned directly under the bottom of the pot. This is one of the most efficient uses of wood for cooking because the wood heats the food contents directly. The Earth Home system uses this technology as an integral part of the wood cook stove design. ***A special pot located in a hole in the top of the stove is used to cook meals with only a small amount of (wood) fuel***.

10. Cooking Pots Overview

a. Pots of Enamel, Copper, Glass, Ceramic

Enamel and copper pots leach out chemicals that may be damaging to human beings. Glass cookware is inert, but they can break more easily than metal. They also require more care not to quench from hot to cold very fast. Earthen (ceramic) pots can also leach toxic substances such as lead.

b. Stainless Steel Cookware

Stainless steel is made of iron and chrome, both of which the body can absorb healthfully. Stainless steel cookware is extremely durable, totally nonreactive, and noncorrodible. But, because stainless steel does not conduct and diffuse heat efficiently, it is usually joined to more conductive metals such as copper or aluminum. Stainless steel is easy to maintain and will last for generations.

c. Cast-Iron Cookware

Cast-iron cookware is also good for cooking because it maintains heat well and diffuses it evenly. The downside is that it is slow to heat up and cool down and can react with acidic or alkaline foods. Cast iron requires seasoning before being used for the first time, and the oil-seasoned surface must be maintained or it will rust.

11. Earth Home Cooking

a. Cooking Energy Discussion

Typically 15% of cooking energy actually ends up in the food; 85% heats up the hot plates, plans, cooking media, and surrounding air. Danish studies estimate that 90% of oven cooking only requires a very small (3-gallon) oven. ***The Earth Home system uses a combination of efficiency in burner/orifice design, efficiency in the cooking utensil design, and efficient cooking methods to gain maximum efficiency***. (See also Vitamin/Mineral Losses in Cooking section)

*Used in Earth Home

The actual amount of energy to cook a meal depends on a great number of variables. Statistics have shown that it takes 26 liters of gas to boil 1 liter of water. That translates into approximately 200 liters (7 cubic feet) of gas per day to cook three meals. (See also Gaseous Fuels Chart)

b. Cookstove/Burner Efficiency

Burner efficiency is controlled by adjusting the air-to-fuel ratio and the fuel injection system to allow for efficient combustion. If inefficient combustion occurs, soot may build up on surfaces and insulate it, so more heat will go unused. Inefficient combustion also produces more carbon monoxide.

c. Earth Home Cookstove Design

The Earth Home (backup propane) cookstove design will use three burners, a well-insulated oven, and a tiny warming burner. The warming burner uses a very small flame to keep a dish warm or at simmering temperature. To conserve energy and get the most benefit from the food, cooking techniques that preserve nutrients should be chosen. Earth Home cooking will stress baking, roasting, and steaming instead of frying or sautéing.

d. Continuous Hot Water Designs

The Earth Home as well as other homes share a common issue of needing boiling water in small quantities a few times each day. This hot water is needed for soups, beverages, washing, and showering. A steady access to hot water is provided from the combination hot water heater, distillation unit, and hot drinking water supply.

e. Future Cooking

As mentioned previously, hydrogen will be eventually generated from water and used for cooking as hydrogen technology matures. (See Energy/Power--Hydrogen section, Hydrogen files.) With minor modifications, most gas appliances can be used with hydrogen fuel.

f. Efficient Cooking Techniques

"Once-a-month" cooking techniques will be used as much as possible. Many meals are prepared at one time and frozen/refrigerated in smaller portions to be used over the course of the next couple of weeks or more. This not only saves energy, but valuable time for the family as well.

*Used in Earth Home

XI. RELATED TOPICS

A. Minor Health Care

Health care is a necessity for all families, whether self-sufficient or dependent. Earth Home system places the emphasis on prevention of diseases and illnesses, rather than their cure. It is often said that health depends on three basic factors: eating good, nourishing foods, absorbing those foods properly, and eliminating all the waste matter from your system.

1. Diet and Exercise Basics

a. Stressing Prevention of Disease

Western medicine doesn't offer much in the way of prevention. A famous English doctor said once that "There is but one cause of disease—poison, toxemia, most of which is created in the body by faulty living habits and faulty elimination". This is also the theory of the original naturopaths and is also known as the "unity of disease".

b. Eating Healthy Foods

One of the biggest advantages of the Earth Home system is providing very high quality, healthy foods to keep the body in good shape to help it resist many of the common maladies. Plants contain hundreds to thousands of substances called phytochemicals (plant chemicals) that may shield us from disease. Examples include anti-oxidants, sulforaphane, and genistein.

c. DRINK WATER!!

No living thing, whether living in water or on land, can live without water. No single body cell can sustain life without water. Of all of the many preventatives available, drinking water is the cheapest and most effective of all of them. Water has long been considered to have medicinal effects: Some 2,000 years ago the Greek physician Hippocrates recommended drinking plenty of water to prevent kidney stones. Chronic cellular dehydration painfully and prematurely kills. Its outward manifestations are often been labeled as diseases of unknown origin.

Every function of the body is monitored and pegged to the efficient flow of water. Since we have a gradually failing thirst sensation, we must remember to drink water. The adult body needs six to eight 8-ounce glasses of water a day (alcohol, coffee, tea, and caffeine-containing beverages do not count as water).

Some people claim that headaches are nature's way of telling you that the body is dehydrated and drinking a glass of water will make it go away. (See Water-Drinking section) In fact, water has been called the "forgotten nutrient."

Drinking water increases energy, improves digestion, lessens food cravings, moisturizes your skin, eases bladder problems, flushes out toxins, relieves tension, clears your head, eases constipation, improves cellulite, reduces fluid retention, and speeds healing. You can drink water between meals, half an hour before a meal, or sip it gradually over the day. However, drinking large amounts of water with meals can dilute the digestive juices and can lead to indigestion.

d. Exercise

1. Exercise Basics/Stomach Muscles

Exercise has been the cornerstone to health for a long time. There are theories that exercise is also good for the mind as well as nourishing the body. A chiropractor will often tell a patient that a stiff back is in many instances due to a lack of movement instead of working it too much or doing something wrong.

There are many proponents of keeping healthy and strong stomach muscles. These muscle groups are responsible for good posture and keeping the stomach area firm and in place. Some theorize that these muscles are more important for overall health than any other.

2. Earth Home Exercise Equipment (See also Exercise Equipment section)

Body movements and some degree of physical work are built into the Earth Home system. In addition, exercise equipment is used to grind grain/corn, Posho mill, hammermill, LPC press, and for back-up power. The press can also be used for squeezing sunflower seeds or linseed oil pressing. This will greatly aid in the normal health of muscle tissue.

e. Personal Hygiene

Simple washing of the hands and body on a regular basis does much to prevent disease and illness from attacking the body. Much research over many years on natural disasters such as flooding has shown that a lack of good personal hygiene greatly increases incidences of disease.

f. Attitude/Laughter

Simply avoiding most of the everyday stress of life in itself is reputed to have a major influence on health. There are many books written on the power of laughter on the human body. A positive attitude has a calming effect on the digestive system as well as the nervous system. However further work in this area is beyond the scope of this text.

2. Diagnosing Illness

a. "Modern" Medicine's Weaknesses

1. Modern Medicine Overview

Today conventional medicine is in a stage of frustration. Despite millions of dollars spent on pharmacological research, cancer, coronary disease, and other common health problems keep spreading like wildfire. In the old days the Indians had few diseases, and so there was not a demand for a large variety of medicines. A medicine man usually treated one special disease and treated it successfully. One reason why Indian medicine went by the wayside is that so many diseases came with the advent of the white man.

From the earliest to the present time, medical hucksters have found it ten times easier to relieve a man of ten dollars by acting on his superstitions than extracting one dollar from him by appealing to his reason and common sense. Only a tiny fraction of an American doctor's training is devoted to diet and nutrition.

2. Overuse of Antibiotics

Modern medicine has equipped nations with the ammo to quickly disarm many diseases that used to decimate populations. However, irresponsible use and unnecessary prescription of antibiotics has led to the rise of a stronger bacterial army. This misuse of antibiotics could be responsible for an evolutionary mutation in bacteria, resulting in their immunity to certain antimicrobial treatments.

According to the Centers for Disease Control and Prevention (CDC), ***close to 2 million patients each year in the United States acquire an infection while in the hospital. Seventy percent of the bacteria that cause these infections are resistant to at least one of the drugs most commonly used to treat them.***

3. More Statistics

According to the National Center for Health Statistics, among the 13 leading causes of death in the U.S. are medicinal drugs, infections in hospitals, and doctor-caused mistakes. The pharmaceutical industry has even come up with a term to describe side effects from too much pharmaceutical medication, "polypharmacy".

b. The Tongue as "Barometer of Toxins"

The tongue should be called "the Magic Mirror." The tongue reveals the great amount of toxic poison stored in the body. One of the means a doctor uses to diagnose a person is to say, "Let me see your tongue." When the doctor sees a white-coated tongue, he knows that person is in a highly toxic condition. This is one of the oldest methods of diagnosis used by doctors and alternative health professionals.

3. Fasting

a. Definition/Benefits of Fasting

Fasting-or going without food-is the stage where the body supports itself on the stored reserves within its tissues. *Note that fasting is defined here as the avoidance of solid food and the intake of liquids only*. Science is showing us that our bodies are capable of storing a huge amount of energy in our bodies. Starvation is the stage where all the reserves have been depleted and should be avoided. Controlled fasting has shown to be beneficial in many instances where other cures proved useless. Fasting copies the activity of nature's creatures when they are wounded, sick, hibernating, or in aestivation (sleeping throughout the summer in tropical climates.

Fasting has been touted as the single greatest natural healing therapy. Fasting is the oldest form of natural healing. Many authentic world healing systems, which include Ayurvedic, Unani Tibb, Chinese, Japanese, Sufi, Native American, and European folk medicines, utilize herbs, foods, and fasting to achieve balance and health. Internal cleansing is the foundation of preventative medicine.

b. History of Fasting

In human societies fasting has a long history dating back thousands of years. Many religions including Christianity, Judaism, and the Eastern religions, have encouraged fasting for a variety of reasons such as penitence, preparation for ceremony, purification, mourning, sacrifice and union with God, and the enhancement of knowledge and powers. Many cultures have also incorporated it into their writings and practices. North American Indians and Eskimos fast prior to being ordained for their priesthoods. Muslims fast for many reasons (before prayer, when ill, or when they wish to conjure). Eastern Yogis fast to achieve spiritual enlightenment. Jesus fasted forty days and nights.

c. Timing of Fasting

The two key times for natural cleansing are the times of transition into spring and autumn. In Chinese medicine, the transition time between the seasons is considered to be about ten days before and after the equinox or solstice. For spring, this period is about March 10 through April 1; for autumn, it is from about September 11 through October 2. In cooler climates, where spring weather begins later and autumn earlier, the fasting can be scheduled appropriately, as it is easier to do in warmer weather. With fasting, the body tends to cool down.

d. Cleansing Liquids/Juices

There are liquids that are especially formulated to help the body during and immediately after a fast. The cleansing liquids are often lemon juice and water with smaller amounts of maple syrup, cayenne pepper. When coming off from a fast, fresh fruit juices diluted with water makes the transition to solid foods easier. Many consider the cleansing of the colon an essential part of any fasting program. (See Colon Health/Cleansing section) Fasting clinics often also suggest that enemas be used daily, even up to several times a day.

4. Colon Health/Cleansing

a. Intestinal Bacteria/Flora

Intestinal flora is microorganisms that live, among other places, in the bowels of humans. There are a great many of these microscopic organisms in your body and they play a crucial role in health and disease. A healthy intestine rich in the proper bacteria leads to good bowel movements, vitamin processing, hormone production, and a long list of other health benefits.

Lactobacillus acidophilus is a healthful bacterial that lives in the colon. It inhibits the growth of disease-producing bacteria and is essential for normal digestion.

b. Constipation Problems with Health

For at least sixty years, a few nutritionists have been preaching the message that disease begins in the colon. At least five common diseases have been related to constipation: diverticulitis, appendicitis, hemorrhoids, hiatus hernia, and varicose veins. Each is caused by straining at stool to expel hard fecal matter.

In India they often treat schizophrenic patients with seven liters of saline. The saline causes them to have bowel movements. They have found that schizophrenics are heavily constipated, and after the treatment they noticeably improved. Also in a British study of 62 patients with diverticular disease who were chronically constipated, two tablespoons of bran daily as part of a high-fiber diet restored normal bowel function in all.

c. Colon Toxicity

Colon toxicity can be the underlying cause of many commonly reported problems including: constipation, headaches, hemorrhoids, backaches, arthritis, allergies, diarrhea skin problems, irritability, difficult weight loss, insomnia, hypertension, distended abdomen, chronic fatigue, depression, frequent colds, food cravings, foul body odor, bad breath/halitosis, asthma, prostate trouble, hypoglycemia, abdominal gas, and menstrual problems.

The typical industrialized diet has been criticized as leading to the build-up of old, putrefied fecal waste in the large intestine. This waste can block proper digestion, nutrient absorption, waste elimination and provides an excellent breeding ground for germs and parasites. We humans clean out our car and our home, so it is only natural to ask why we do not clean out ourselves from the inside out.

d. Five Ways to Colon Cleanse

The five major ways that one can cleanse their colon. These include: colon hydrotherapy (also known as colonic irrigations), enemas, herbal supplements, laxatives, and oxygen-based cleansers. Each of these treatments has their pros and cons.

e. History of Colon Hydrotherapy

Colon hydrotherapy was first recorded in 1500 B.C. in the Ebers Papyrus. Colon lavage was first recorded in the ancient Egyptian document, Ebers Papyrus, which dealt with the practice of medicine. These enemas were described as the infusion of aqueous (water) substances into the large intestine (bowel or colon) through the anus. In the fourth and fifth centuries B.C., Hippocrates reported using enemas for treating fevers. Pare, in 1600 A.D. offered the first recognized distinction between colon irrigation and the popular enema therapy of that age. The Essenes used water therapy to rid the colon of uncleanliness and the body of disease. Directions on how to take an enema is even in the Holy Bible in the book of John.

In modern times, colonic irrigation was quite popular among some physicians in the 1920's, 1930's, and the 1940's, and then it fell out of favor. Now, with safe, effective, and sterile equipment, colonic irrigation is once again being recognized as a valuable adjunct to health care.

Colonic irrigation with water is the most thorough form of colon cleansing. During a typical colon hydrotherapy session, about 25 to 35 gallons of water will be transferred in and out of the colon. Colon irrigation solutions may contain small amounts of baking soda, sea salt, or coffee.

f. Laxatives/Bulking Herbs

Herbal laxatives are commonly taken orally during fasting, and many formulas are available, as capsules or for making teas. These include cascara sagrada, senna leaves, licorice root, buckthorn, rhubarb root, aloe vera, and others. Psyllium seed or husks are also used as a bulking agent. (See also Perfect Diet section)

5. Oral Health

a. Oral/Dental Health Background

Oral health is systemic health. Gum tissue can be intact, as a complete barrier to bacteria. Or, it can allow microorganisms to enter the circulatory system, leading to stroke, heart attack, and other grave health conditions. Bleeding gums is an indicator of disease that can be caused by nutritional deficiencies, diabetes, alcohol, stress, smoking, hereditary factors, and other factors. Gum disease is not just bad breath, cavities, or loosened teeth. Brushing and flossing are insufficient remedies. Good nutrition, as well as effective nutritional supplements, is important in oral health as well as for general health. Your teeth are a reflection of your whole body. If you are healthy, your mouth will be healthy. Teeth, gums, and bone can heal.

b. Anti-Inflammatory Herbs

Oil of calendula has shown in studies to have anti-inflammatory properties and is helpful in wound and tissue repair such as mouth sores or after an extraction of a tooth. Clove oil is used for inflammation of the mouth and for toothache. It can be used as a mouthwash or a paste and placed in a tooth. A garlic clove has also been used for temporary toothache reduction.

c. Brushing Teeth

Bay, eucalyptus, oak, fir, and juniper twigs can be used for brushing teeth. The twigs contain volatile oils which stimulate blood circulation, tannins that tighten and cleanse gum tissue and other materials, such as vitamin C, which maintain healthy gums. In Asia, people often use twigs of the neem tree (Azadirachta indica). Other possibilities include using the roots of marshmallow, licorice, alfalfa, or horseradish.

d. Toothpaste

Herbal medicine abounds with great substitutes for store-bought toothpaste. Most effective natural tooth powders are warming, which promotes circulation in the gums; astringent, which tightens the gums; and detoxifying, which removes debris. Of course any preparation should also remove plaque.

A classic combination contains two parts powdered potassium alum, an astringent, and one part powdered salt. Prickly ash bark is a classic toothpowder from North America, and myrrh gum is widely used in Middle Eastern herbalism. Tea tree oil (very dilute) stimulates circulation and kills germs as well as a macrobiotic preparation of the ash of the calyx of the eggplant, which can cure toothache, pyorrhea, and other mouth and gum disorders.

e. Tongue Cleaning

And while you're concentrating on brushing and flossing, don't overlook the fact that cleaning the tongue is a critical part of maintaining oral health. Brush your tongue while brushing your teeth, or use a tongue scraper of sorts. Tongue cleaning reduces bad breath, and helps prevent plaque.

f. General Tooth/Gum Care

The tooth sockets are joints, and the teeth are essentially bones. Herbs that treat the skeleton and the joints when taken internally are good bets for long-term tooth health. Standouts include yellow dock root, alfalfa leaf, cinnamon bark, and turmeric root.

A gum massage can be used with a mixture containing five parts alum powder, two parts rock salt powder, three parts black pepper powder, and one part turmeric root powder. A gum pack can be made from rose petal, oak leaf, and carob powder. Amla works well as a mouth rinse and is considered to be a general rebuilder of oral health. One to two grams per day can be taken orally in capsules for long-term benefit to the teeth and gums. Herbs such as amla that support the healing and development of connective tissue when taken internally will always benefit the gums. They must saturate the whole body in order to work on the gums, the healing effect of these tonics takes longer to become apparent.

Most herbalists and natural healers recommend using warming, astringent, connective-tissue-healing herbs to enhance and maintain oral health. These herbs can be used as a rinse or applied as packs (a pinch of powder, wetted to a mush with a liquid such as water or vitamin E, and tucked next to the teeth). Bilberry fruit and hawthorn berry stabilize collagen, strengthening the gum tissue. Licorice root promotes anti-cavity action, reduces plaque, and has an antibacterial effect.

g. Mouthwash

Rinses are made by preparing an herb as tea in the usual way, or by simply stirring herb powder into water. Hold the rinse in the mouth for a few seconds or up to several minutes, gargle, and spit out. A daily mouth wash made from chaparral will help to prevent dental cavities. Another formula contains extracts of Echinacea, goldenseal, calendula, aloe, bloodroot, and grapefruit seed.

h. Periodontal Disease (PD)

Periodontal disease (PD) is a long-term, low-grade bacterial infection of the gums, bone, and ligaments that support the teeth and anchor them in the jaw. More than half of all people over 18 have some form of the disease. PD is a major, if not leading, cause of bad breath in American adults and is clearly the leading cause of tooth loss.

Turmeric capsules, goldenseal rinse, and nightly packs of a paste of turmeric powder, licorice root, and vitamin E can also be used for periodontal disease. Tinctures of Echinacea, eucalyptus, and myrrh as washes, or a gum massage with the oil of eucalyptus can also be used to treat PD.

i. Mouth/Canker Sores

Commonly called "canker sores," these mouth ulcers can be supremely painful. Canker sores are virtually always linked to food allergies and nutritional deficiencies, particularly iron, B12, and folic acid.

Since mouth ulcers stem from a breakdown in tissue structure, the herb gotu kola (Centella asiatica) can be quite effective. Gotu kola is widely known to heal wounds and promote connective tissue growth. The dose is one ounce dry weight of herb per day, brewed as tea. A recent study has also shown good results using a chamomile mouthwash in treating mouth ulcers caused by chemotherapy. Other rinses that can help include alum and cinchona bark and applying the powder of myrrh gum directly to the ulcer. However, probably the most outstanding herbal remedy for mouth sores is licorice root, a potent anti-inflammatory and tissue healer. Put a pinch of powder on the sore for relief.

6. Other Therapies

Note that all of the therapies mentioned here produce alkaline-forming reactions in the body. (See Individual Needs-Body Chemistry section)

a. Historical Therapies

<u>1. Homeopathy</u>

Homeopathy was invented in the early 1800's by Samuel Hahnemann. His system relies on using minute doses of what made you sick to heal you—usually in the form of plants and minerals. America is just rediscovering homeopathy, but it has continued to be popular in Europe. Roughly 40 percent of British doctors refer patients to homeopaths, and 40 percent of French doctors have studied homeopathy and are abler to prescribe it. Oligotherapy is related to homeopathy but involves the healing of illness by the presence and action of metallic ions in the body.

<u>2. Bee Venom Therapy (BVT)</u>

Apitherapy or bee venom therapy is mentioned in the Bible and it was practiced by Hippocrates. Modern medicine is just now investigating bee venom in the treatment of arthritis and multiple sclerosis. People long ago recognized the fact that beekeepers never got arthritis. This led to the successful practice of apitherapy or using actual honeybee stings for the treatment of arthritis and related illnesses. Bees are allowed to sting patients in increased numbers over several weeks to build up a sort of immunity. Often acupuncture points are used to administer stings.

<u>3. Ear Candling</u>

Ear candling is a technique where a 10 inch long hollow wax-impregnated cloth candle is inserted into the ear and burned for 10 minutes. Through convection, softer waxes and toxins are drawn out of the ear, oxidized and turned into vapors during the procedure. Ear candling is a technique dating back to the year 2500 B.C. This simple therapy can be effective in removing old and troubling blockages from the ear canal, without the use of solutions or probes. Ear candling cleanses the ear canal and sinus passages.

4. Hyperthermia

Hyperthermia is the raising of body temperature for treatment of cancers and tumors. As far back as 5,000 B.C., Egyptian doctors were treating tumors with heat. Hyperthermia for the whole body and parts of it are enjoying recent popularity using modern techniques and equipment.

b. Modern Alternative Medicine Therapies

1. "Mind" Therapies

Other "treatments" for human maladies include: hydrotherapy, sound therapy, color and music therapy, osteopathy, naturopathy, light therapy, dietetics, imagery, bodywork, ayurveda, hands-on therapy, essence therapy, aromatherapy, and relaxation techniques. There are also forms of meditation such as guided imagery, deep breathing, psychic surgery, radionics, hypnotherapy, and biofeedback. Most of these address the mind and the control that it has over the body.

2. Massage Therapies

There are also massage therapies such as rolfing, chiropractic, reiki, self massaging, aromatic massage, shiatsu, sports massage, Swedish massage, soft tissue work, spiritual healing, yoga, reflexology or zone therapy, tragering and many more. Recently BioMagnetic, TENS, and moxa therapies have been popular.

3. Far Infrared Waves (FIR)

During the last decade in Japan, people have been experimenting with far infrared wave technology (FIR) for healing as well as other uses such as cooking, drying, and heating. FIR wave treatment has been shown to be effective in expanding clogged-up capillary vessels and successfully dissolving the hidden toxins into the blood and eventually out of the body via urine and perspiration. The body perceives near infrared as heat and is absorbed near the skin. Far infrared waves (8 to 14 micron wavelength) penetrates deeper inside the body and promotes bioprocesses such as increased metabolism and increased blood circulation. It has been also used to treat arthritis and aching muscles.

4. Other Modern Therapies

There are also techniques such as astrology, medical intuitives, psycho-energetic healing, enneagram transformational coaching, spiritual counseling, vibrasound, Qigong, and many more. There are also various electrical modalities in current use such as: diathermy, galvanic, infrared, muscle stimulation, ultraviolet, ultrasound, electrical homeopathy, radionic, Rife, the violet ray, wet-cell battery, cold laser acupuncture, magnetic beds, and a whole assortment of very sensitive diagnostic devices.

c. Magnet Therapy

1. Bio Magnets

Therapeutic magnets have been used for decades. There have been many claims of how the magnetism actually works: In the field of biomagnetics, especially when applied to animals and humans, application of the south pole or a south pole-north-pole magnet scheme causes an aggregate south pole, or positive, charge in animal and human cells. The south pole does wonders for all kinds of plant life, but it is not safe for animals and humans. In therapy only the north pole touches animal or human tissue.

2. Magnets for Water Treatment

Magnetic water treatment (MWT) is simply the attachment (or insertion) of permanent magnets or electromagnetic devices to the incoming water pipe of a home or business. Magnets can be used to treat domestic water supplies as well as commercial and industrial applications such as boilers, cooling towers, etc. The process involves installing the magnetic system onto (or into) the water pipe leading from the water meter or well to your house or apparatus to be treated. Some applications call for installing the magnets on recirculating water lines (swimming pools and cooling towers for example). The magnets surrounding the water pipe create a magnetic force field that interacts with charged molecules in the water that surround suspended colloidal particles such as calcium (Ca), magnesium (Mg) and silica (Si02). As a result of this interaction, natural repulsion tendencies of these disbursed colloids are disturbed and a process of flocculation and possibly coagulation prevents scale producing minerals such as Ca and Mg from precipitating out to form scale in plumbing. Further, over time, existing scale in the system is eliminated.

3. Magnets for Agriculture

Magnetohydrodynamics, or MHD, is a branch of the science of the dynamics of matter moving in an electromagnetic field, especially where currents established in the matter by induction modify the field, so that the field and dynamics equations are

Numerous magnetic products claim to reduce the surface tension of the water, which gives greater solubility of minerals and deeper penetration into the soil and root system. Typically, over time, soil compacts. This restricts the root growth. When magnetism is used, the magnetized water de-clods and breaks up the compressed soil. This gives the roots of the plant or tree the freedom to grow and absorb nutrients more quickly.

B. Food "Medicines"/TCM

1. Traditional Chinese Medicine (TCM) Philosophy

a. TCM Philosophy

Traditional Chinese medicine or TCM studies the application of foods and natural nutriments as well as Chinese medical herbs to maintain health, strengthen the constitution, prevent and relieve diseases, quicken the rehabilitation, and slow down the process of aging. Foods and medical herbs are classified into "four tendencies". They are classified as either "cold", "hot", "warm", and "cool" according to their action and curative effects.

While Western medicine is great for trauma, emergencies, and acute care, Chinese medicine is a good choice for preventing illness, maintaining general health and treating most health conditions, if not all of them. Sometimes Chinese medicine can be life altering for people with conditions such as headaches, allergies, or asthma.

b. Foot Massage/Reflexology (See also Flooring section)

1. Reflexology Techniques

Reflexology is a method of stimulating reflex areas that correspond to each and every gland, organ, and part of the body by applying pressure with specific thumb, finger, and hand techniques. While those areas to be stimulated can be in the hands or ears, the bottom of the feet is the most common location. As yet there is no scientific proof of how or why reflexology works, it is generally understood that it works on energy channels in the body similar to the acupuncture meridian pathways. The following figure shows how the bottoms of the feet affect other parts of the body in reflexology. Recent scientific studies verified that walking on a cobblestone mat surface resulted in significant reductions in blood pressure and improvements in balance and physical performance among adults 60 and over.

2. Reflexology History

There are pictographs of work on feet and hands in Egypt—the first record of reflexology as physiotherapy. It is believed that the Egyptians had discovered the beneficial and pleasurable effects of manipulation and massage long ago.

In nearly every village in Taiwan they have built special paths of pebbles and every morning at 3 or 4 o'clock, people walk barefoot around the pebble path for a half hour before they go to work. China, Malaysia, Korea, and Germany also have many of these paths for reflexology therapy. (See also Flooring section)

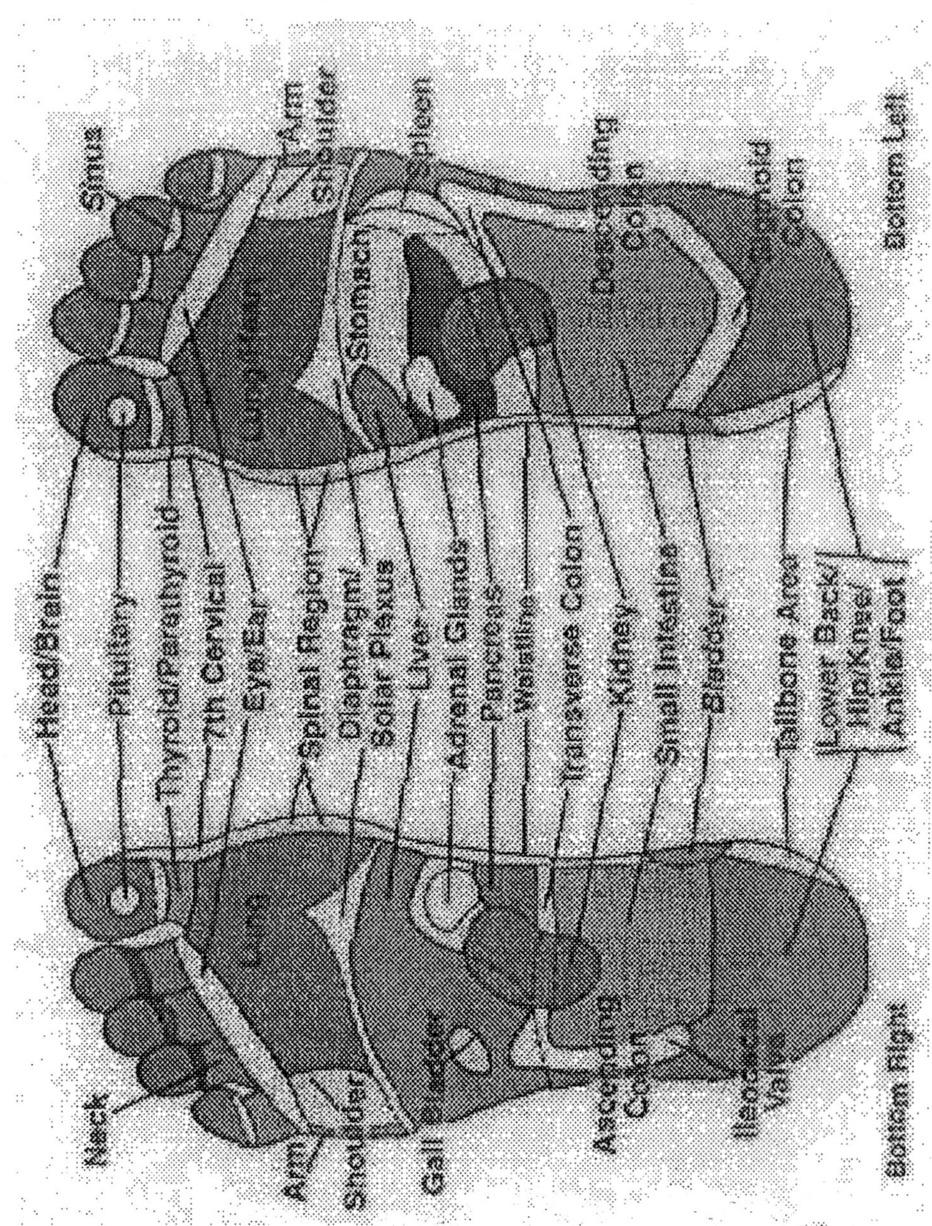

Figure 174-FOOT REFLEXOLOGY CHART

c. Acupuncture/Acupressure

Acupuncture/acupressure has been around for five thousand years, is practiced around the world, and has much scientific data to support claims. The Chinese view is that if there is pain, there is no free flow of blood; and if there is free flow of blood, there is no pain. Acupuncture is concerned with restoring proper energy flow to the various organs, glands, and tissues of the body on the premise that most diseases are the result of malfunction due to disrupted energetics.

2. Herbs

a. Herbs Background/History

In the Bible, herbs are mentioned for medicinal purposes twenty-seven times. The Talmud also identifies some 70 herbs and other plants as having medicinal properties—many for cures and others for prevention. The list includes olives, dates, pomegranates, garlic, hyssop, cumin, and other plants used mainly for food. Balm, figs, and oil are the only plant products mentioned in the Bible with reference to healing.

b. Tonics and Topical

Tonics and herbal remedies have the ability to preserve health in general and to keep the body from going bad. Using herbs to treat medicinal problems was common for literally thousands of years until the seventeenth century when the arts became "scientific." The botanical books ignored the medicinal properties of plants and the medical books contained no plant lore.

There are a number of plants that can easily be grown to assist with minor health care. One of these is aloe vera, which is used for burns and other skin problems. White willow has been used as an aspirin for many years and the flower of the skullcap is one of the best cures for insomnia.

c. Herbal Substitutions Chart

The following figure lists some common ailments, their modern prescriptions, and herbal substitutes for similar results.

d. Herbal Teas

There are also many herbal teas that claim to have medicinal powers. One such tea is Essiac (or Caisse's tea) which is made from sage and other ancient herbs. Red clover was used extensively in Europe for thousands of years to purify the blood. Buddhist readings told the Indian people to use herbalene for their tumors some 2500 years ago. The Indians and Mexicans made tea with Indian sage for blood purification to this day. Kudzu is a primary ingredient in many medicinal teas used in China today. Tea is one of the easiest methods to ingest herbs.

3. Antibiotics/Immune Boosters

a. Background/History

Antibiotics are a very important ingredient for continued good health. How many of us have asked for them when we feel sick from any illness? (See Plants - Medicinal files.)

*Used in Earth Home

HERBAL SUBSTITUTES FOR COMMON PHARMACEUTICALS

Ailment	Pharmaceutical	Herbal options
Acne	Retin-A, Tetracycline	Tea tree oil(external), calendula
Allergies	Synthetic antihistamines	Garlic, stinging nettle, *Ginkgo biloba*
Anxiety	Ativan, Xanax, Klonopin	Hops, kava-kava, valerian
Arthritic pain	Tylenol and other NSAIDs*	Cayenne (external), celery seed, ginger, turmeric
Athlete's foot	Griseofulvin	Tea tree oil, garlic, coffee grounds (all external)
Boils	Erythromycin	Tea tree oil, slippery elm (both external)
BPH (benign prostatic hyperplasia)	Hytrin, Proscar	Saw palmetto, evening primrose, stinging nettle, *Pygeum africanum, Serona repens*
Body odor	Commercial deodorants	Coriander, sage
Bronchitis	Atropine	Echinacea, garlic
Bruises	Analgesics	Arnica, St. John's wort, yarrow, plantain (all external)
Burns	Silvadene Cream	Aloe vera gel (external), calendula
Colds	Decongestants	Echinacea, ginger, lemon balm, garlic
Constipation	Laxatives	Flaxseed, psyllium, cascara sagrada
Cuts, scrapes, abscesses	Topical antibiotics	Tea tree oil, calendula, plantain, garlic (all external)
Depression (mild)	Prozac, Elavil, Trazodone, Zoloft	St. John's wort
Diarrhea	Imodium, Lomotil	Bilberry, raspberry
Dysmenorrhea (painful menstruation)	Naprosyn	Kava-kava, raspberry
Earache	Antibiotics	Echinacea, garlic, mullein
Eczema (itchy rash)	Corticosteroids	Chamomile
Atopic eczema (allergy-related rash)	Corticosteroids, sedatives, antihistamines	Evening primrose
Flu	Tylenol	Echinacea, elderberry
Gas	Mylanta, Gaviscon, Simethicone	Dill, fennel, peppermint
Gingivitis (gum inflammation)	Peridex	Chamomile, echinacea, sage
Halitosis (bad breath)	Listerine	Cardamom, parsley, peppermint
Hay fever	Antihistamines, decongestants	Stinging nettle
Headache	Aspirin, other NSAIDs*	Peppermint (external), feverfew, willow bark
Heartburn	Pepto-Bismol, Tums	Angelica, chamomile, peppermint
Hemorrhoids	Tucks	Plantain, witch hazel, calendula (all external)
Hepatitis	Interferon	Dandelion, milk thistle, turmeric
Herpes	Acyclovir	Lemon balm
High cholesterol	Mevacor	Garlic
Hives	Benadryl	Stinging nettle
Indigestion	Antacids, Reglan	Chamomile, ginger, peppermint
Insomnia	Halcion, Ativan	Chamomile, hops, lemon balm, valerian, evening primrose, kava-kava
Irregularity	Metamucil	Flaxseed, plantain, senna, psyllium
Lower back pain	Aspirin, analgesics	Cayenne (external), thyme
Male pattern baldness	Rogaine	Saw palmetto
Migraine	Cafergot, Sumatriptan, Verapamil	Feverfew
Motion sickness	Dramamine	Ginger
Nail fungus	Ketoconazole	Tea tree oil, garlic (both external)
Night blindness	Vitamin A	Bilberry
PMS	NSAIDs*, diuretics, analgesics	Chaste tree, evening primrose
Rhinitis (nasal inflamation)	Cromolyn, Vancenase	Echinacea
Shingles	Acyclovir	Cayenne (external), lemon balm
Sprain	NSAIDs*	Arnica, calendula
Stress	Diazepam	Kava-kava, valerian
Tinnitus (ringing ears)	Steroids	Ginkgo
Toothache	NSAIDs*	Cloves, willow bark
Urinary tract infection	Sulfa drugs	Cranberry, stinging nettle
Vaginitis	Clindamycin, Flagyl	Garlic, goldenseal

*NSAIDs are nonsteroidal anti-inflammatory drugs.
Source: Adapted from "Nature's Medicine—The Green Pharmacy," *Mother Earth News* (Dec/Jan 2000): 22-33, by James A. Duke, Ph.D.

Figure 175-HERBAL SUBSTITUTES

*Used in Earth Home

Interestingly, it is a fact that a large number of the prescription medicinal drugs used today throughout the world are derived from plant sources. These medicines are simply much stronger versions of the original plant, or a synthetic derivative that closely resembles the natural compound. Companies do this so they can patent the exact compound and exclusively sell it.

b. Garlic

Garlic has been used since the days of the Egyptians to treat wounds, infections, tumors, and intestinal parasites. Garlic's reputation as a powerful medical herb dates back to over 5,000 years. Its usage was recorded in King Tut's tomb. Roman gladiators ate garlic before combat and Roman nobleman gave garlic to their laborers and soldiers. During World War II, a time when antibiotics were scarce, garlic was placed in the wounds to prevent infection.

c. Astragalus/Echinacea

An herb native to China, astragalus (Astragalus membranaceous) has been used for more than 2,000 years. Astragalus appears to give the immune system a powerful boost. Teas, tablets, and other healing formulations are made from the plant's flat, yellowish root.

Taken as a tonic, astragalus is believed to build stamina and vitality. It has a reputation for improving overall health by helping the body to fight off viral and bacterial infections responsible for causing colds, the flu, bronchitis, and sinus infections. As an antioxidant, it helps to counteract cell damage caused by unstable oxygen molecules called free radicals. Many people undergoing cancer chemotherapy or radiation take astragalus to fortify their battered immune systems. It can be safely combined with many conventional medical treatments.

Results of archeological digs indicate that Native Americans may have used Echinacea for over 400 years to treat infections and wounds and as a general "cure-all." Echinacea has also been used throughout history to treat scarlet fever, syphilis, malaria, blood poisoning, and diphtheria. In the 1800's it became popular with the medical community in the United States and was a widely prescribed natural remedy for infections and inflammation.

Today, Echinacea is primarily used to reduce the symptoms and duration of the common cold and flu and to alleviate the symptoms associated with them, such as sore throat (pharyngitis), cough, and fever. Many herbalists also recommend Echinacea to help boost the activity of the immune system and to help the body fight infections

d. Aspilla

Another plant was discovered in Africa, called "aspilla." Studies found that chimpanzees do not get sick very often, taking daily doses of aspilla leaves to maintain health.

e. Other Immune Boosters

There are also antibiotic qualities in a number of plants that have not been widely written about. Some of these plants include taro (also known as dasheen), cocoyams, eddo (also known as colocasia esculenta), malanga, and yautia.

More than four thousand years ago, the Egyptians applied rotten moldy bread to control infected wounds. It took us until this century to find a similar antibiotic. They also used honey in their wound dressings. Honey breaks down into a common household disinfectant, hydrogen peroxide.

f. Other Antibiotics—Colloidal Silver

Silver has been used for healing for thousands of years. Ancient Greeks and Romans lined their eating and drinking vessels with silver. The word "silverware" came about because of silver's ability to kill germs on contact in 6 minutes or less. Silver was widely used as an antibiotic until the 1930's in this country. The advent of penicillin and the cost of silver combined to cause its use to decline.

Colloidal silver consists of sub-microscopic clusters of silver, held in a suspension of pure ionized water by a tiny electric charge placed on each particle. Illness causing organisms do not seem to build up a resistance to colloidal silver the way they do to pharmaceutical antibiotics. Colloidal silver also does not disturb the naturally occurring flora in the colon. The EPA's Poison Control Center reports a "no toxicity" listing for colloidal silver with no recorded side effects.

Coarser silver preparations are used in over 70% of all the burn centers in the U.SA normal antibiotic kills a few different disease organisms, but silver kills some 650! Silver is ingested in about a 5 PPM concentration in various amounts depending on condition. A tablespoon a day is a maintenance dose and a 16 ounce glass would treat a major illness. It is even sprayed topically for burns and skin problems. It is easily made by running 36-40 volts DC through distilled water using .999 pure silver electrodes and stored in amber glass containers.

g. Red Yeast Rice

Red yeast rice is a traditional food consumed throughout Asia for more than a thousand years. Rice is fermented naturally on a bed of cooked non-glutinous whole rice kernels. This food has gained recent support for its cholesterol-reducing qualities.

h. Other Food Medicines

There are many other food medicines that have benefited humans for thousands of years. Another example is curry that has value in the prevention of Alzheimer's disease. Curry powder is primarily turmeric. India has the lowest incidence of Alzheimer's in the world. Science is constantly finding herbs and other plants that contain medicine-like qualities.

C. Appliances

Products purchased off-the-shelf can sometimes be modified to fit a particular use. For example, a 12-volt DC hair dryer can be modified to function as a defroster for water pipes for the back window of a car. It is useful to show the vast numbers of gadgets available by separating them by categories. The following appliance categories were taken directly from the appliance list in the bibliography section. Refer there for addresses of specific manufacturers or distributors.

1. Household Appliances

a. Clothes Washing

There are a couple of options for clothes washing in the Earth Home system. One of them is called an Avanti wash machine. It's a small plastic washer with a 12-volt motor that shakes the clothes back and forth. (A manual washer/plunger is available for those who are into a little exercise when they wash clothes.)

For regular-sized machines, it is best at this time to have one modified to work on 12 volts. There are helpful books available that tell how to modify regular washers and dryers for 12 volt DC operation. A soft-start kit is also now available to retrofit washing machines. Manual "pullout-type" clothes dryers are also available. For extreme amounts of washing, older Maytag wash machines can be fitted with a small gasoline engine or power shaft.

b. Vacuum Cleaners/Floors

There are a number of options for cleaning the floors in the Earth Home system. A push sweeper, such as the Hoky, does an amazingly good job of cleaning debris off the floor. There are about 7 or 8 manufacturers of small hand-held 12-volt vacuum cleaners (none of which, however, are particularly powerful). The most powerful of these is the Metro, but the current draw is substantial. There is also a slightly larger canister vacuum cleaner that operates on the same principle as the Metro.

Many of these appliances use a cheaply made, commonly available Japanese-manufactured motor that is not rated for very long life. Eureka recently introduced a cordless vacuum cleaner that is very powerful, but recharges on 110-volt electricity. Note that Earth Home II is designed to use a central vacuum cleaner. (See Uses of Electricity section.)

c. Other Appliances

Singer has introduced a battery-operated, portable sewing machine. The old foot-operated Singers work very well and many are still used.

There is a 12-volt DC bed warmer that can be used either on top of or underneath the person to keep warm. This was made popular by over-the-road truckers. When the trucks pulled over with their engine running, the alternator would power the warmer to keep the bed warm. Note that resistance heating devices use electricity at an alarming rate!

There are small battery-operated plant moisture meters that tell when houseplants need watering. However, they are not very accurate and more complex systems are under development. The Earth Home system is designed to use the central system with the ceramic blocks in the greenhouse. (see Irrigation Section)

For those items that require batteries for portable power, there are many DC battery chargers available that charge A, AA, C, and D cells by using a 12 volt source. (Solar chargers are also available.)

2. Kitchen

For the kitchen, there are many devices that can be operated on 12 volt DC or batteries. They cover the full spectrum of 20th century appliances, including a gas match for lighting stoves, a piezo match (it strikes an arc by squeezing a crystal), a cordless can opener, a corn and grain mill, and even a blender.

There are also many heating devices for the kitchen such as fry pans, toasters, coffee makers and warmers. However, as mentioned previously, these appliances use excessive amounts of electricity. Earth Home-generated electricity should rarely be used for resistance heat in <u>any</u> form.

3. Bathroom

For the bathroom, there are cordless shavers by Remington and others. Several types of hair dryers and hair curlers are made to operate from 12 volt DC source.

4. Yard and Garden

Cordless grass shears, cordless chainsaw sharpeners, solar gate openers, solar fence chargers, and outdoor solar lights can be purchased. A hammermill could be operated in high wind conditions to break up the compost materials for faster decomposition.

*Used in Earth Home

5. Automotive

There is a baby bottle warmer available that plugs into a car outlet, a spark plug cleaner, and a 12 volt polisher and buffer for auto exteriors. There is also a burglar alarm system that makes extensive use of new technology. A car seat heats up when you plug it into the cigarette lighter outlet. This may be particularly useful in a northern climate.

Another type of automotive appliance is a propane engine heater. These heat water inside the engine block of an automobile, making it easier to start in cold weather. There are a couple of propane models that all operate effectively without electricity.

6. Garage/Tools

Makita makes a full line of cordless circular saws, jig saws, drills, and sanders. They make a charger that recharges portable batteries in one hour. Soldering irons and cordless screwdrivers can also be purchased. Milwaukee makes a 12-volt DC direct drive drill for heavy-duty industrial applications.

There are also tools that come equipped with gas-powered engines, such as drills, augers, and cut-off saws. These may be useful in remote areas for heavy-duty applications.

7. Industrial

There are many industrial products that do not require 110 volt electricity, most of which developed from a particular need. These products include a 55-gallon drum level alarm, an electric floor sweeper, a battery-operated scale, a cordless hydraulic pump, a Ridge hydraulic hand punch, a 7,000 lb. jack, a fuel transfer pump, lift magnets, strip chart recorders, and a gas alarm. There are a number of battery-operated hoists and winches, some of which are available from Sears. A 24-volt DC MIG welder is available, and there is even a portable X-ray machine that can be used without 110-volt power.

8. Business

Battery-operated laptop computers were introduced years ago. The manufacturers are constantly looking for ways to make the batteries last longer. There is also a thermal printer that works well with laptops, a battery-powered data logger to input most sensor types, and a cordless pencil sharpener available.

9. Sporting Goods

This area contains a number of devices, such as 12 volt DC trolling motors, battery-heated socks, and battery-heated gloves. There is a continued demand for these products in the marketplace.

10. Entertainment

There are many radios that use batteries, as most of you know. There are 12 volt black and white TVs and even a color model. There are portable compact-disc players and a VCR that requires 12 volt DC power. You can also purchase a kit to modify your turntable to use 12-volt DC power.

11. Medical

There are a few devices that use 12 volt DC, such as a blood pressure and pulse monitor and battery-operated thermometers in addition to the portable X-ray machine listed earlier. ***Each year there is an increase in the number of devices made to run on batteries***. Also, more 12-volt DC options are offered on many products. I

*Used in Earth Home

feel that there will be many more of these devices available in the future. The consumer is demanding portability and flexibility of use.

D. Transportation

1. Gasoline Automobile Efficiency

a. Chassis Options

There are also more efficient ways to use gasoline to power an internal combustion engine. The 3-wheel vehicles using Tecumseh engines were quite efficient (50-60 mpg). These could also be converted to propane if they used a 4-cycle engine. These vehicles enjoyed some popularity after OPEC, but consumer interest did not remain high enough to support continued production. There is, however, at least one automobile company offering a 4-wheel version of the original car. Some lighter and smaller recent automobiles are boasting mileage figures of 45+.

b. "Cute" Cars

Recently, the automobile companies have introduced smaller versions of traditional automobiles. Car models of what have been coined "cute" cars include the 2003 Audi A4 Cabriolet, BMW Mini Cooper, and the 2003 Saturn Ion. They are putting new safety features into the cars in order to sell more of them to the general public.

c. 42 Volt Systems

In the future, automakers are going to a 42 volt electrical system using an integrated starter/alternator. The extra jolt of power from these new systems makes camless valve actuation a real possibility. This could improve fuel economy by as much as 15% over normal vehicles.

d. Fuel-on-Demand Efficiency

Auto engineers are trying to cut all power requirements further by eliminating all devices that draw constant current. Fuel pumps are targeted as major users of electricity by circulating unused fuel back to the gas tank. Only using as much fuel as the engine needs would eliminate supplying power to the fuel pump when the engine does not need much gas such as idling.

e. Lean-Burn Vehicles

Lean-burn (high air-to-fuel) vehicles with their ultralow CO, emissions would probably dominate the roadways if it weren't for the voluminous NOx that they emit. The lack of a practical exhaust treatment that can meet current and anticipated NOx emission regulations, without a high cost to fuel efficiency, is perhaps the greatest roadblock to more widespread use of diesel and other lean-burn engines.

f. Direct Ignition (DI)

Recently introduced lean burn engines try for the best of both worlds. They wanted fuel efficiency and power. This resulted in Bosch's latest gasoline direct injection engine that runs in tow different modes, with a lean mixture injected in the compression stage for efficiency, or a rich mixture injected in the intake phase for power.

g. Stirling Engine Vehiclcs

In 1979 The AMC Spirit car powered by a Stirling engine was demonstrated. The car was the result of a cooperative effort on the part of General Motors, United Stirling, and a number of other companies. There exists a strong interest in this heat engine for automobiles.

2. Drive-by-Wire

a. Drive-by-Wire Background

In 2004 GM introduced its "Hy-Wire", a hydrogen-fueled, electricity-producing concept car. The car has a fuel cell producing about 126 horsepower. DaimlerChrysler, Ford, Honda, Toyota and others have spent billions on development of these types of cars. (See also Hydrogen section)

b. Drive-by-Wire Technology/Schematic

The following figure gives a glimpse into this new technology and the areas of a typical auto that is changed or affected by the new technology.

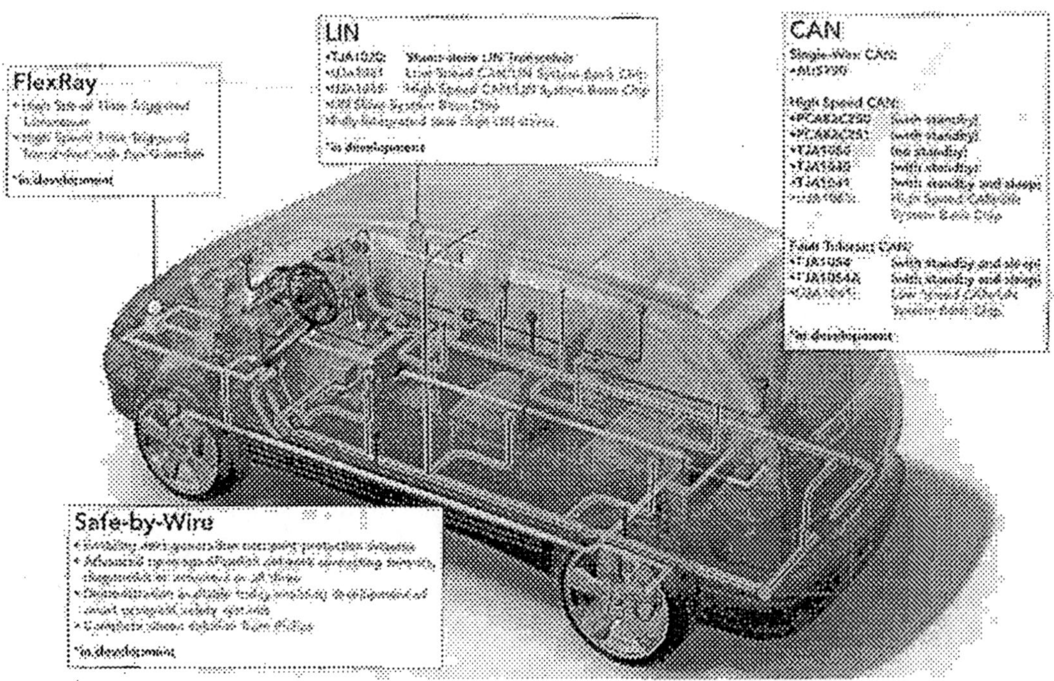

Figure 176-DRIVE-BY-WIRE SCHEMATIC

3. Hybrids/Alternative Fuels

a. Gas/Electric Hybrid Vehicle Overview

1. Background/History

Hybrid cars are powered by a combination of a small gas engine (internal combustion) and electricity. An electric motor powers the vehicle at all times. The electric motors are designed to generate electricity and recharge the batteries when the vehicle decelerates.

Gas/electric hybrid vehicles have become more common in the last few years. They combine the best qualities of both technologies and are experiencing the greatest product success of all of the above technologies. Toyota Prius is one of the first compacts with a hybrid electric/gasoline drive train.

2. Hydraulic Hybrid Powertrain

Like an electric hybrid vehicle, the new hydraulic hybrid powertrain will be powered by a gasoline or diesel primary power source and incorporate an engine that is about 25% smaller than that found in traditional vehicles. In the new hybrid hydraulic system, hydraulic accumulators, instead of electric motors/generators and batteries, are used to store energy and propel the vehicle.

b. Hydrogen-Fueled (See also Hydrogen section)

Engineers at Ford are testing a new hydrogen fuel internal combustion engine (H2ICE) that reduces noxious emissions by 99.7% compared to gasoline combustion engines of similar size and power. Ford's P2000 research vehicle emits mostly water vapor and a small amount of carbon dioxide from the exhaust. Test results indicate the new engine is 25 to 30% more efficient than its gasoline counterpart. Ford, Agua, and Clean Cities will place at least five hydrogen-powered Ford shuttles in Palm Springs, CA in 2006.

c. Alcohol/Gas Mix (E10, "E78", and E-85)

Ethanol is the most widely used biofuel in the world; technological advances have lowered the cost of its production and processing. Brazil boasts one of the largest green fuel programs in existence: petrol-only engines have been banned and replaced by engines that use pure ethanol or a 78-22 petrol-ethanol blend

About 90 percent of the ethanol produced in the United States is used to make "E10" or "gasohol" a mixture of 10 percent ethanol and 90 percent gasoline. Any gasoline-powered engine can use E10 but only specially made vehicles can run on E85.

E-85 is a blend of 85% denatured ethanol and 15% gasoline-like hydrocarbon primer. The goal is an ethanol-fueled vehicle with greater fuel economy and lower exhaust emissions, but with the drivability, performance, and consumer appeal of a conventional gasoline vehicle. Many states have E-85 programs and many new car models are equipped to burn E-85 fuel. Kentucky probably leads the country in this effort because of its numerous E-85 programs.

Vehicles that are able to burn this type of fuel are called flexible fuel vehicles (FFV). As of 2002, some 70,000 FFVs have been registered in Minnesota.

*Used in Earth Home

d. Biomass-Fueled Vehicles

1. Woodgas for Vehicle Background

Down-draft gasifiers in the 5-100 kw level were widely used in World War II for operating vehicles and trucks because of the relatively low tar levels. In operation, air is drawn down through a bed of burning wood, consuming the volatiles. The resulting gas then passes over the resulting charcoal and is reduced to a low energy fuel gas. However, since hot gases naturally rise, it is necessary to supply power to draw the gasses DOWN through the gasifier. (See also Woodgas section)

2. The World War II, Imbert Gasifier for Vehicles

A constricted hearth, downdraft gasifier is sometimes called the 'Imbert' gasifier after its inventor, Jacques Imbert; although, it has been commercially manufactured under various names. Such units were mass produced during World War II by many European automotive companies, including General Motors, Ford, and Mercedes-Benz. These units originally cost about $1500 each. However, after World War II began in 1939, it took six to eight months before factory-made gasifiers were generally available. Thousands of Europeans were saved from certain starvation by home-built, simple gasifier units made from washing machine tubs, old water heaters, and metal gas or oxygen cylinders. Surprisingly, the operation of these units was nearly as efficient as the factory-made units; however, the homemade units lasted for only about 20000 miles with many repairs, while the factory-made units operated, with few repairs, up to 100,000 miles. (See the following figure)

Figure 177-WWII WOODGAS AUTOMOBILES

3. Woodgas Vehicle History

Fuel shortages during WWII prompted searches for alternative fuels in England, Germany, Scandinavia and many other countries. One of the most unusual solutions involved the modification of vehicles for use with wood, charcoal, or coal. Typical modifications included: A) a gas generator; B) a gas reservoir; and C) carburetor modifications and additional plumbing to convey, filter, and meter the gas into the engine. ***Over a million gasifiers powered the civilian cars and trucks of Europe and Asia during WW II.***

*Used in Earth Home

4. Woodgas Vehicle Technology

All internal combustion engines actually run on vapor, not liquid. The liquid fuels used in gasoline engines are vaporized before they enter the combustion chamber above the pistons. In diesel engines, the fuel is sprayed into the combustion chamber as fine droplets which burn as they vaporize. The purpose of a gasifier, then, is to transform solid fuels into gaseous ones and to keep the gas free of harmful constituents.

The gas generator was an airtight vessel into which was introduced a charge of wood, charcoal, or anthracite coal. Heat was applied to the fuel either internally or externally to initiate a self-sustaining gasification of the fuel in an oxygen-deprived environment. The gas is produced by partial combustion of the wood. The resulting "woodgas" was piped to the reservoir, or in the case of small engines, directly to the engine carburetor.

In creating wood gas for fueling internal combustion engines, it is important that the gas not only be properly produced, but also preserved and not consumed until it is introduced into the engine where it may be appropriately burned. Wood-gas modified vehicles were therefore technically a "dual-fuel" vehicle in that a self-sustaining gasification of the wood charcoal, or coal required another fuel to start the process.

Gas reservoir sizes depended upon vehicle, engine, and gasifier size. Small vehicles and engines could be supplied directly from the gasifier, thus eliminating large reservoirs. Larger, more powerful vehicles required separate gas reservoirs to compensate for gasifier outputs which were less than the fuel consumption rate of the engine. These larger reservoirs usually took the form of gas bags that were attached to the roof or rear end of the vehicle. The largest mobile reservoirs were gas bags fitted to busses which were often several feet in diameter and as long as the vehicle.

4. Electric Vehicle Overview

a. Electric Vehicle Evolution

One method to get efficient transportation is to power the vehicle using electricity. The evolution of the electric vehicle was accelerated by the oil embargo of the early 1970's, pollution mandates, and recently because of the increased renewable/recyclable energy trend.

Electric car races have been held around the world for many years. They test new types of motors, solar cells, control systems, and aerodynamics of auto body designs. Recently an electric dragster, “Bad Amplitude”, set a new speed record of 127 mph.

General Motors is scheduled to debut its ParadiGM in 2004. This is intended to combine a V6 or inline four-cylinder engine with a pair of electric motors and a battery pack.

b. Automotive Battery Developments

1. Lead Acid Batteries

Electric and hybrid vehicles now use nickel metal-hybrid batteries as the electric power source. Although they are currently five to six times more expensive than valve-regulated leak-acid batteries (VRLA), they are preferred by electric-vehicle manufacturers because they last longer and have higher specific energy. The major concern of electric-vehicle developers regarding the use a lead-acid battery is their relatively short deep cycle life.

Battery development continues at a very fast pace with R&D on bipolar, zinc-air, and sodium-nickel-chloride batteries. (See Batteries-Future section) There are many publications and books dealing specifically with electric cars and will not be covered extensively in this text. The future of vehicles seems to be going toward fuel cells because of the lack of weight reductions in batteries.

2. Lithium Batteries

Lithium batteries are being used for motorcycles, cars, mopeds, lawnmowers, etc. The previous cost issues with lithium are being overcome with the advantage of light weight batteries that extend the cruising range of most vehicles. (See Batteries files)

c. Thermophotovoltaic Electric Hybrids

Automobiles are also being fitted with thermophotovoltaic generators. The 6.5 kW generator makes use of gallium antimonide photovoltaic cells surrounding a central emitter heated by a compressed natural gas flame to 1700 Kelvin. The infrared photons generated activate the PV cells to produce electricity that maintains a charge in the battery. This generator is very clean and quiet. This experimental vehicle uses a Unique Mobility 53 kW motor which is 92% efficiency through most of the operating regime. The motor is mounted end on to a single dry plate clutch assembly running in ball bearings in a separate housing designed to remove all thrust loading from the electric motor. The clutch assembly is mounted end on to a transversely mounted, four speed, wide ratio transaxle mounted between the rear wheels of the vehicle. The battery bank is composed of Saft Ni-Cad batteries. (See also Thermophotovoltaic section.)

5. Fuel Cell Developments (See also Fuel Cell section)

a. Hydrogen Fuel (See also Hydrogen section)

Daimler-Chrysler has set an $18,100 target price for its first fuel-cell-powered car—a version of the Mercedes-Benz. They expect fuel cell cars will account for up to 25% of the global market by 2020. Ford Motor Company also has plans to go to production with a direct hydrogen-powered fuel cell vehicle in 2004. BMW's 740h has an internal combustion engine that runs on either liquid hydrogen or gasoline, depending on availability.

Recently General Motors introduced its AUTOnomy concept car that will be powered by hydrogen-based fuel cells. They use Low-Rolling-Resistance tires to achieve the desired 300-mile range. Most major car companies now have fuel cell cars in their plans for the future. (See Automobile files.)

Cellex (Vancouver, Canada) has developed a compressed hydrogen system to replace lead-acid batteries in forklifts. The fuel cells run up to twice as long as batteries and require just 7 minutes for refueling.

b. Methanol-Driven Fuel Cells

Daimler-Chrysler plans to incorporate methanol-driven fuel cells into some cars in 2004. The company tested the technology in the NECAR 5 in Japan recently.

c. Borax-Driven Fuel Cells

Daimler-Chrysler has also said that it is developing technology to power vehicles with hydrogen fuel cells that use a mixture of sodium borohydride, commonly known as borax, and water. The borax and water deliver hydrogen to the fuel cell. The system has a longer range than any other fuel cell technology.

d. Fuel Cell Motorcycle

The ENV bike is a motorcycle with an on-board, portable, fully-functioning fuel cell. It is a recent product that demonstrates the real, everyday applicability of fuel cell technology. The Core fuel cell, which is completely detachable from the bike, is a radically compact and efficient fuel cell, capable of powering anything from a motorboat to a small cabin.

*Used in Earth Home

6. Continuously Variable Transmission (CVT) Technology

For many years, the "Holy Grail" of the transportation industry is to be the first to develop a reliable transmission that will continuously vary the torque and speed of an output shaft. There are many mechanical roadblocks to CVT development. There is a special show dedicated to development progress on this one subject. The Hybrid Transmission Congress meets regularly to continue developments and explore patents related to this important area of research.

UK-based NexxtDrive has recently introduced a DualDrive transmission that is also a continuously variable transmission (CVT) with two built-in motors to improve the drive's efficiency. It uses an epicyclic gear train transmission with four branches to combine the torques from the vehicle engine and one of two motors. One motor is high torque and the other is high speed.

7. Bicycle Technology (Human-Powered Vehicles)

a. Bicycle Electric Motor Developments

Emerson has recently put much research into fitting a bicycle with a highly efficient DC motor. The motor fits just inside the front hub of the bicycle and attains speeds of 25 mph. Other manufacturers are following this trend as well.

b. Bicycle Engine Developments

There is recently a tiny internal combustion engine gear set for bicycles that fits inside the front wheel. This light engine is pedal-started and assists after the bike has reached certain speed. (See Automobiles/Transportation files)

c. Recumbent Bicycles

Recumbent bicycles and tricycles have been on the market for many years. They have not been widely accepted as yet because of the cost. Some variations include rear wheel drive on a 3 wheel version, front wheel drive on a 3 wheel version, and many different variations on a 2 wheel model. Recumbents continue to make headway in the market due in some part to the aging population and risk of back and genital injuries in a standard upright bicycle.

E. Communication

1. Short-Wave

Besides the commonly used telephone, there are other methods of communicating using low technology. One of these is a short wave radio receiver, which can operate on 12 volt DC current. There are two methods of short wave radio communication. One of these is Morse Code, and the other is common voice communications, such as used on a walkie-talkie. Morse Code (a system of dots and dashes) can be used over a longer distance -- up to thousands of miles. Short wave voice communication is limited to 50 to 100 miles, depending on weather conditions. This system has interest for low technology self-sufficient communications, but there are regulations, training, and natural phenomenon that must be dealt with. For interest, the following figure shows the complete electromagnetic spectrum, with radio frequencies included.

The electromagnetic spectrum extends from short gamma rays through light waves to long radio waves. The spectrum diagrammed below gives the frequency and wavelength for the various waves. Frequencies are given in hertz and wavelengths in meters. The raised figures with the 10's are a way of abbreviating numbers. For example, 10^{15} hertz equals 1 followed by 15 zeroes, or 1,000,000,000,000,000 hertz. The numbers with a minus sign tell how many places the decimal point must be moved in front of the number. For example, 10^{-7} meters equals 0.0000001 meter.

Frequency in hertz

10^{23} 10^{21} 10^{18} 10^{15} 10^{12} 10^{9} 10^{6} 10^{3}

Gamma rays | X rays | Ultraviolet rays | Light | Infrared rays | Radio waves

10^{-14} 10^{-11} 10^{-8} 10^{-5} 10^{-2} 10^{1} 10^{4}

Wavelength in meters

The electromagnetic spectrum is continuous and, as a result, the different types of electromagnetic radiation grade into each other. The energy (in eV) is obtained by multiplying the frequency by the value of the Planck's constant in eV (= $4.14 \cdot 10^{-15}$).

Frequency (Hz)	Wavelength		Name	Typical source
10^{23}	$3 \cdot 10^{-13}$	cm	cosmic gamma rays	supernovae
10^{22}	$3 \cdot 10^{-12}$	cm	gamma rays	unstable atomic nuclei
10^{21}	$3 \cdot 10^{-11}$	cm	gamma rays hard x-rays	unstable atomic nuclei
10^{20}	$3 \cdot 10^{-10}$	cm	hard x-rays	inner atomic shell
10^{19}	$3 \cdot 10^{-9}$	cm	x-rays	electron impact on solids
10^{18}	$3 \cdot 10^{-8}$	cm	soft x-rays	electron impact on solids
10^{17}	$3 \cdot 10^{-7}$	cm	ultraviolet	atoms in discharges
10^{16}	$3 \cdot 10^{-6}$	cm	ultraviolet	atoms in discharges
10^{15}	0.3	µm	visible spectrum	atoms, molecules hot bodies
10^{14}	3	µm	infrared	molecules, hot bodies
10^{13}	30	µm	infrared	molecules, hot bodies
10^{12}	0.3	mm	far infrared	molecules, hot bodies
10^{11}	3	mm	microwaves	communication devices
10^{10}	3	cm	microwaves, radar	communication and detection devices
10^{9}	30	cm	radar	communication and detection devices
10^{8}	3	m	video, FM	television, FM radio
10^{7}	30	m	short-wave	short-wave radio
10^{6}	300	m	AM	AM radio
10^{5}	3	km	long-wave	long-wave radio
10^{4}	30	km	—	induction heating
10^{3}	300	km	—	induction heating
10^{2}	3,000	km	—	rotating electromagnets
10	30,000	km	—	rotating electromagnets
1	300,000	km	—	rotating electromagnets
0	infinite		dc current	batteries

The Major Ham Radio Bands

Frequency Range	*Meter Band*
1800 to 2000 kHz	160 meters
3500 to 4000 kHz	80 meters
7000 to 7300 kHz	40 meters
10100 to 10150 kHz	30 meters
14000 to 14350 kHz	20 meters
18068 to 18168 kHz	17 meters
21000 to 21450 kHz	15 meters
24890 to 24990 kHz	12 meters
28000 to 29700 kHz	10 meters
50 to 54 MHz	6 meters
144 to 148 MHz	2 meters
222 to 225 MHz	1.25 meters
420 to 450 MHz	70 centimeters
902 to 928 MHz	33 centimeters
1240 to 1300 MHz	23 centimeters

Figure 178-ELECTROMAGNETIC SPECTRUM AND RF

2. Wireless Technologies

a. Bluetooth

Bluetooth is the most recent in a string of available wireless technologies. IrDA, telemetry, 802.11, and home RF all preceded it. Bluetooth technology borrowed from the above technologies and was created by a consortium of electronics companies. One of the requirements is that it be able to transmit 10 meters in open air and 100 meters with an amplifier. Bluetooth specifies global 2.45 GHz radio wave band. (See also Home Control)

b. Emerging Technologies

A new wireless communication protocol called "nanotron" can transmit up to 60 meters. This new technology uses less energy to transmit than either Zigbee, Home RF 1.0, or IEEE 802.11b. This field promises to deliver new technologies due to the immense demand from consumers.

F. Toiletries

1. Soaps

Soap is necessary to cleanse the human body, and is usually purchased at a store. It can be made at home with lye and animal fat. There are three or four plants that can be grown to provide a measure of "de-wetting" of the water's surface to allow for the production of suds enabling one to shampoo and bathe. Currently, due to the availability of soap, none of these alternatives have been extensively researched and tested. (See Soap files.) (See Water System-Soap/Detergent Section)

2. Toilet Paper/Alternatives

The use of toilet paper is also a problem in any self-sufficient system, because it is difficult to do without. However, there are alternatives available. The Arab and many other cultures consider toilet paper ineffective for hygiene and have used water for hundreds of years. They typically use a squirter that can be reached from the toilet.

There is a Japanese squirter that uses a warmed water spray from a retractable tube located below the toilet seat. It is called the "Toto", and is available with optional features. (See Toilet files.) (See Toilet Waste section.)

3. Feminine Hygiene

Menstrual flow requires some form of sanitary protection from blood discharge. Through the ages, cotton rags have been used by women all over the world. They are messy and required cleaning. A modern invention called the Health Keeper uses a natural rubber molded cup to catch the fluid before it can escape the body. This is then emptied, rinsed, and replaced as needed. (See Medicine/Health files)

G. Clothing

1. History

When human life began on this earth, food and shelter were the two most important necessities. Immediately thereafter came clothing. The first materials used for it were fur, hide, skin, and leaves—all of them sheetlike, two-dimensional structures not too abundantly available and somewhat awkward to handle.

*Used in Earth Home

2. Animal Skins/Hides

Animal hides can be tanned by a couple of technologies. The most familiar is using chemicals such as tannic acid that comes from the bark of trees. This method is time consuming and requires tanks and hot water. An easier method uses salt to make hides into rugs, blankets, and clothing.

After the excess meat and fat has been scraped from the hide, tack it down in a sunny location. Cover with plain salt and rub into the hide. Let dry for three days and scrape off all the salt. Repeat two more times and the hide should be cured. Note that water is not used for cleaning again. This method does have the disadvantage of having excess salt on hand which would have to be obtained outside the EH System.

3. Woven Fabrics/Alternatives

It was a few thousand years ago that a very important invention was made: to manufacture two-dimensional systems (fabrics) from simple mono-dimensional elements (fibers). Fibers were readily available everywhere. They came from animals (wool, hair, and silk) or from plants (cotton, flax, hemp, and reeds). Yarns were made from the fibers by spinning and fabrics were made by weaving and knitting.

Clothing fabrics are extensively discussed in the previous Water-Clothes Washing Section. Some of the selected fabrics discussed are cotton, Tencel, and hemp. Cotton material and Tencel are difficult to grow and hemp requires extensive equipment to process into useable fabric. Perhaps the future will show more simple methods to process the hemp into clothing. (See also Hemp section)

H. Household Items/Miscellaneous

1. Background

Many products currently used or consumed in a typical home are disposable, as are many other consumer products in the 20th century. I feel that longer-lasting products should be used in order to preserve many of the resources we have on planet Earth. I feel that many of these durable products have already been designed, developed, and sold, but fell by the wayside during the last 50 years because of their expense and the transition to a dependent lifestyle. I believe we may have to re-assess the benefits of these products in the future.

2. Earth-Friendly Home Products Chart

The following figure gives examples of simple, low-energy, long-lasting, low-impact household items. This chart is to be used for reference purposes only and may not represent products currently available.

3. Cleaning Solvents

There are few earth-wise or make-at-home cleaning products available at the present time. 50-50 vinegar/water mix solution has been a popular option as mentioned earlier. The acetic acid in vinegar can be used as a stain remover and bleach. Vinegar can be made from many different plant sources as it is the next process after alcohol is made. Alcohol can be used as a solvent also. (See Home Care files for more earth-friendly products and information.) (See Alcohol Files.)

Turpentine is one of the solvents that may be able to be produced in a self-sufficient homestead. Turpentine is made from the resin or sap of pine trees. Most Pinus species "bleed" when the stem wood is cut or injured, but probably only a few dozen of approximately 100 species which exist has ever been tapped commercially as a source of resin for rosin and turpentine production. In all the others, poor yields and quality of the resin make it more difficult. Resin is collected after meticulous scarring of the tree and/or selected removal of some bark.

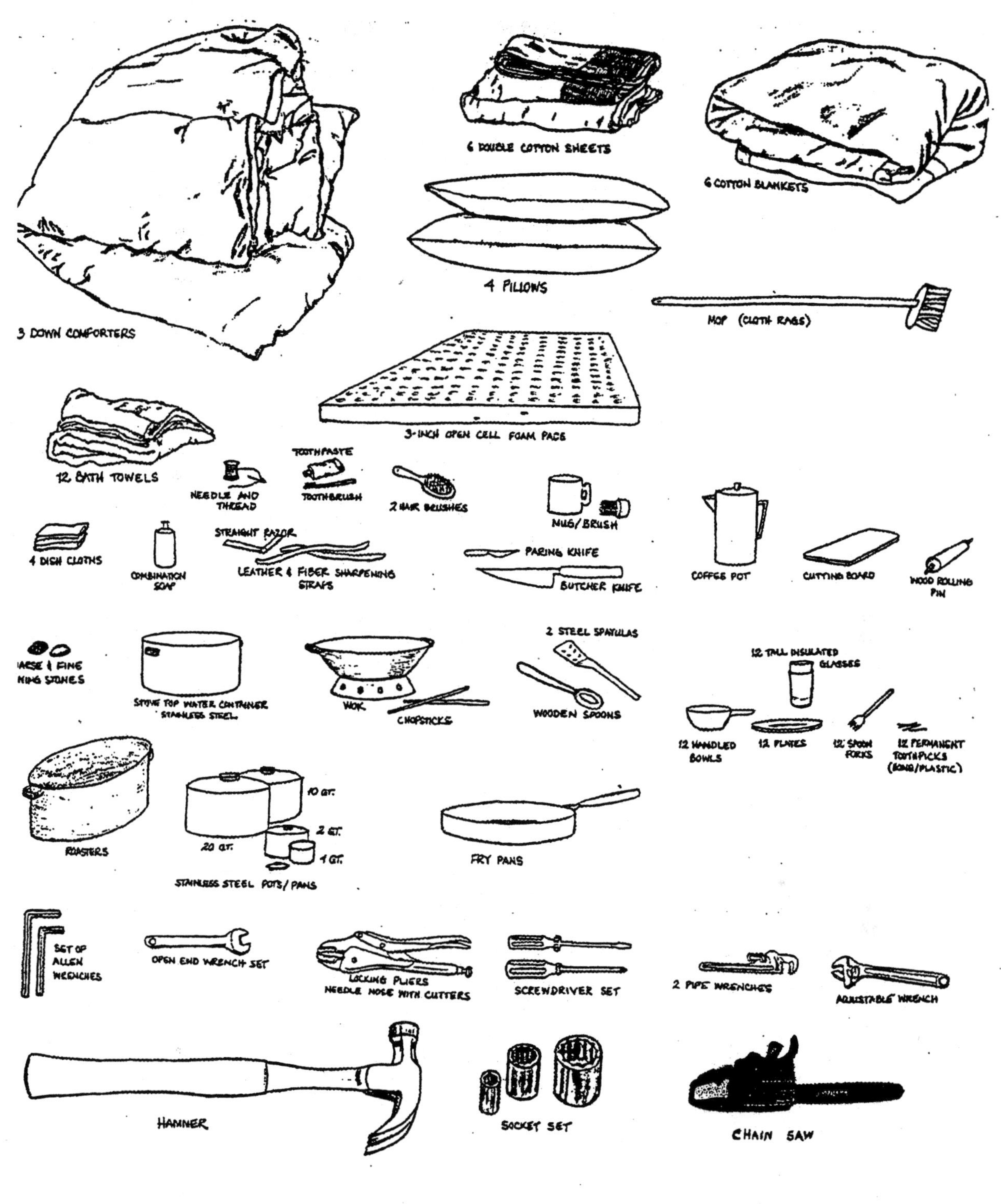

Figure 179-NATURAL EARTH HOME PRODUCTS

*Used in Earth Home

About 6 pounds of resin can be harvested from a tree in one year. In hotter weather, sap runs better and rain hampers sap flow. For more production sulfuric acid or other chemical is put on the tree to keep sap flowing. Distillation is the method used to extract the turpentine from the resin and rosin is the product remaining.

4. Pest Control

To make a natural rodent trap you need a 20-litre bucket or large clay pot, which holds water. Bury this in the ground near known rat holes or leading sites. Take a dry corn (maize) cob and cut off the ends. Push through it a thick wire, which is one meter long. Make sure the cob can spin freely. Fasten the cob in position in the center of the wire. Bend the wire as shown and push firmly into the ground on either side of the bucket (See following figure). Put a depth of at least 15cm of water in the bucket. Each evening, coat the corn cob with peanut butter, wetted flour or some other kind of food which will stick to the cob. Remove drowned rats each morning. The trap seems to work best during the new moon.

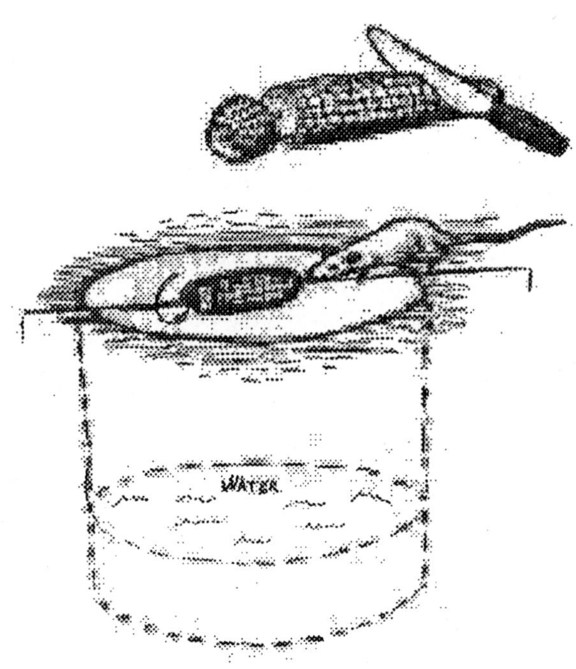

Figure 180-NATURAL RAT AND MOUSE TRAP

*Used in Earth Home

XII. PERSONAL MESSAGES

A. Conclusion

We live in an incredibly complex world. I do not think that we as a species are equipped to handle it very well. A *vast* bulk of knowledge always remains to be discovered.

We do not know everything about our own planet. Some of the great unknowns include: Atlantis; huge markings on the Mojave Desert and Peruvian plains of Nasca that can only be seen from aircraft; the Easter Island faces; the Bermuda Triangle; Stonehenge; Mystery Hill; the Mima mounds; Death Valley "Racetrack Rocks"; and pyramids all over the world. There are 18 sacred sites, seven symbolic landscapes, nine ancient cities, and five lost lands that we know very little about. Science has conflicting theories on the Siberian animals quick-frozen with fresh grass in their stomachs, and we still are baffled with crop circles.

Just recently, evidence suggests that the pyramids of Egypt were constructed using agglomerated stone (limestone cast like concrete), rather than carved and dragged blocks of natural limestone as virtually all of the textbooks depict.

Even though we may think that we are the "American Romans", history reveals doubts whether our 20th century represents the pinnacle of human achievement. I feel that humans have not learned everything in this world. Many people "pray" to technology—meaning that technology is all-powerful and all-knowing. They are many firm believers in the supremacy of modern technology and the "foolproof" dogma of the scientific method. Having known and lived technology for many years, I believe there are many limitations to human technological expertise. Most of the technology was developed for a certain purpose or product, and is rarely used to simply acquire knowledge, as in the case of "pure" science. ***I feel that our technology is very vulnerable to the forces of nature***.

I feel that we live in an age of discovery. ***We are constantly discovering new technologies (such as superconductivity) and even new species of plants and animals***. We can fly around the Earth in a matter of hours, rocket to the moon, clone ourselves, peer into the depths of the cell, alter genetics, and regulate most human body functions. ***But we are not evolved enough as a civilization and a species to develop a completely self-sufficient home***. I feel that this technology will succeed at some point in the future, but I am not sure who will do it. It may be me, my protégés in later years, someone influenced by my work, or an independent researcher in another part of the world.

***Used in Earth Home**

---------I wrote this in the hope that one of my contemporaries around the world will succeed at this endeavor, and that this collection of works will be of some benefit. I wish them the best of luck and hope for their success. Thank you very much for listening.

Sincerely,

Mel

Mel Moench

Max Planck once said that "an important scientific innovation rarely makes its way by gradually winning over and converting its opponents; it rarely happens that Saul becomes Paul. What does happen is that its opponents gradually die out and that the growing generation is familiarized with the idea from the beginning."

B. About the Author

Figure 1-ABOUT THE AUTHOR

Mel Moench

- Born January 31, 1950 on Perham, MN farm
- Coon Rapids, MN Senior High School - 1968
- Anoka-Ramsey State Junior College - 1969
- Bachelors in Mechanical/Industrial Engineering,
  University of Minnesota Institute of Technology - 1972
- Graduate work, Masters in Business Administration
  St. Cloud State University - 1974
- Registered Manufacturing Engineer - State of Minnesota
- Extensive hands-on experience in many mediums/materials
- Extensive prototyping/development work and "modifications"
- Started 3 business entities.
- Over thirty years engineering experience: Industrial/
  Mechanical/Manufacturing/Project/Design
- Research skills with three important tools:

  1. Telephone - ability to listen, talk, direct conversation, understand, and talk convincingly on the phone.
  2. Thomas Registers
  3. McMaster-Carr Catalog

Currently living in Howard Lake, Minnesota, and continuing to periodically update this publication and blueprints. He is searching for some individual and/or organization to assist in development/funding of Earth Home II. He is actively searching for a suitable location for construction, while testing/developing portions (sub-assemblies) of the total system.

....Louis Pasteur once said "CHANCE FAVORS THE PREPARED MIND".

SELECTED LIFE LESSONS

A friend of mine opened his wife's underwear drawer and picked up a silk paper wrapped package: "This, - he said - isn't any ordinary package." He unwrapped the box and stared at both the silk paper and the box. "She got this the first time we went to New York, 8 or 9 years ago. She has never put it on, was saving it for a special occasion. Well, I guess this is it. He got near the bed and placed the gift box next to the other clothing's he was taking to the funeral house, his wife had just died. He turned to me and said: "Never save something for a special occasion. Every day in your life is a special occasion". I still think those words changed my life.

Now I read more and clean less. I sit on the porch without worrying about anything. I spend more time with my family, and less at work. I understood that life should be a source of experience to be lived up to, not survived through. I no longer keep anything. I use crystal glasses every day. I'll wear new clothes to go to the supermarket, if I feel like it. I don't save my special perfume for special occasions; I use it whenever I want to. The words "Someday..." and "One Day..." are fading away from my dictionary. If it's worth seeing, listening or doing, I want to see, listen, or do it now.

I don't know what my friend's wife would have done if she knew she wouldn't be there the next morning, this nobody can tell. I think she might have called her relatives and closest friends. She might call old friends to make peace over past quarrels. I'd like to think she would go out for Chinese, her favorite food. It's these small things that I would regret not doing if I knew my time had come. I would regret it, because I would no longer see the friends I would meet, letters that I wanted to write...one of these days.

I would regret and feel sad, because I didn't say to my brothers and sisters, sons and daughters, not times enough at least, how much I love them. Now, I try not to delay, postpone or keep anything that could bring laughter and joy into our lives. And, on each morning, I say to myself that this could be a special day. Each day, each hour, each minute, is special.

WORDS TO LIVE BY

ONE. Give people more than they expect and do it cheerfully.
TWO. Marry a man/woman you love to talk to. As you get older, their conversational skills will be as important as any other.
THREE. Don't believe all you hear, spend all you have or sleep all you want.
FOUR. When you say, "I love you," mean it.
FIVE. When you say, "I'm sorry," look the person in the eye.
SIX. Be engaged at least six months before you get married.
SEVEN. Believe in love at first sight.
EIGHT. Never laugh at anyone's dream. People who don't have dreams don't have much.
NINE. Love deeply and passionately. You might get hurt but it's the only way to live life completely.
TEN. In disagreements, fight fairly—NO name calling.
ELEVEN. Don't judge people by their relatives.
TWELVE. Talk slowly but think quickly.
THIRTEEN. Remember that great love and great achievements involve great risk.
FOURTEEN. When you lose, don't lose the lesson.
FIFTEEN. Remember the three R's: Respect for self; Respect for others; and responsibility for all your actions.
SIXTEEN. Don't let a little dispute injure a great friendship.
SEVENTEEN. When you realize you've made a mistake, take immediate steps to correct it.
EIGHTEEN. When you think you want to change a decision, only do it once.
NINETEEN. Smile when picking up the phone. The caller will hear it in your voice.
TWENTY. Spend some time alone.
TWENTY-ONE. A true friend is someone who reaches for your hand and touches your heart.

FAVORITE SAYINGS, CONT.

The hardest part of any task is simply starting.

And Charlie Chaplain once said, “We are all amateurs: We don’t live long enough to be anything else!”

Mel Moench often says,...DETAILS, DETAILS!

"Life is NOT a journey to the grave with the intention of arriving safely in an attractive and well preserved body, but rather to skid in sideways, chocolate in one hand, thoughts of a true friend by your side, body thoroughly used up, totally worn out and screaming, 'WOO HOO - what a ride!!' "

C. Reader Feedback

The author wishes to extend an invitation to any interested people for written opinions, comments, and suggestions. Please send to address below, Attention: Mel Moench.

This book uses PC-based Microsoft Word software. Correspondence may also include 3.5" diskettes or CDs in preferred formats--.DXF, .WPD, .JPG, .DOC, or .TIF.

XIII. APPENDICES

A. Pictures of Earth Home I

The view above is 2-1700 gallon fish tanks (on either end), and the start of the water storage tank (cistern) on the left. The finished cistern held 10,000 gallons of rainwater. The square block area on the right is a water heat storage area

Figure 182-PICTURES OF EARTH HOME I

This view shows the upright floor trusses that are anchored to the surrounding soil. The steel cross-bands keep the structure from moving. The roof trusses extend over the cisterns for added water collection capacity. This framework stayed this way over an entire Minnesota winter.

The view on the left shows the home nearing completion. The ferrocement was applied directly over a paper/plastic film laminate. The windows on the south side are clearly visible. The tank on the south side is an experimental smoke scrubber. The view on the right is a view looking to the west after the scrubber and entry were removed a year later. The entry was relocated on the east side as shown.

Figure 182-PICTURES OF EARTH HOME I (Continued)

This view shows the first prototype of the V-Trough plant growing system. Notice the seedlings in each trough.

B. Earth Home II Energy Data (Available Soon)

Figure 183-EARTH HOME II DATA (AVAILABLE SOON)

C. Condensed Blueprints, CAD Drawings, Images of EH II

The following pages are part of the plans for Earth Home II. The original plans are hand drawn pencil sketches on 24" x 36" Mylar. They have been reduced and scanned. The first set of drawings are labeled "EH Blueprints", followed by a short explanation. These drawings are the most descriptive of the interior and systems.

Following the pencil sketches are CAD drawings done in AutoCAD software. The entire set of drawings has been scanned into .tif format and is included. They are labeled "CAD drawing Page 1 of 13". These represent the latest revisions to the EH structure.

Following the CAD drawings are .jpg computer images of the exterior of the Earth Home as depicted in the CAD drawings. The images were generated using AutoDesk Architectural Desktop and AudoDesk Studio Max software. They are labeled first with the direction in which the observer is located, followed by the direction the observer is looking. (North Hemisphere)

Note that no effort has been made to produce contractor-ready blueprints in this small page size. Full-size drawings are available. (See ordering information at end of book.) The entire set of plans are also drawn in 2D AutoCAD. Complete bill of materials will be available approximately spring 2007.

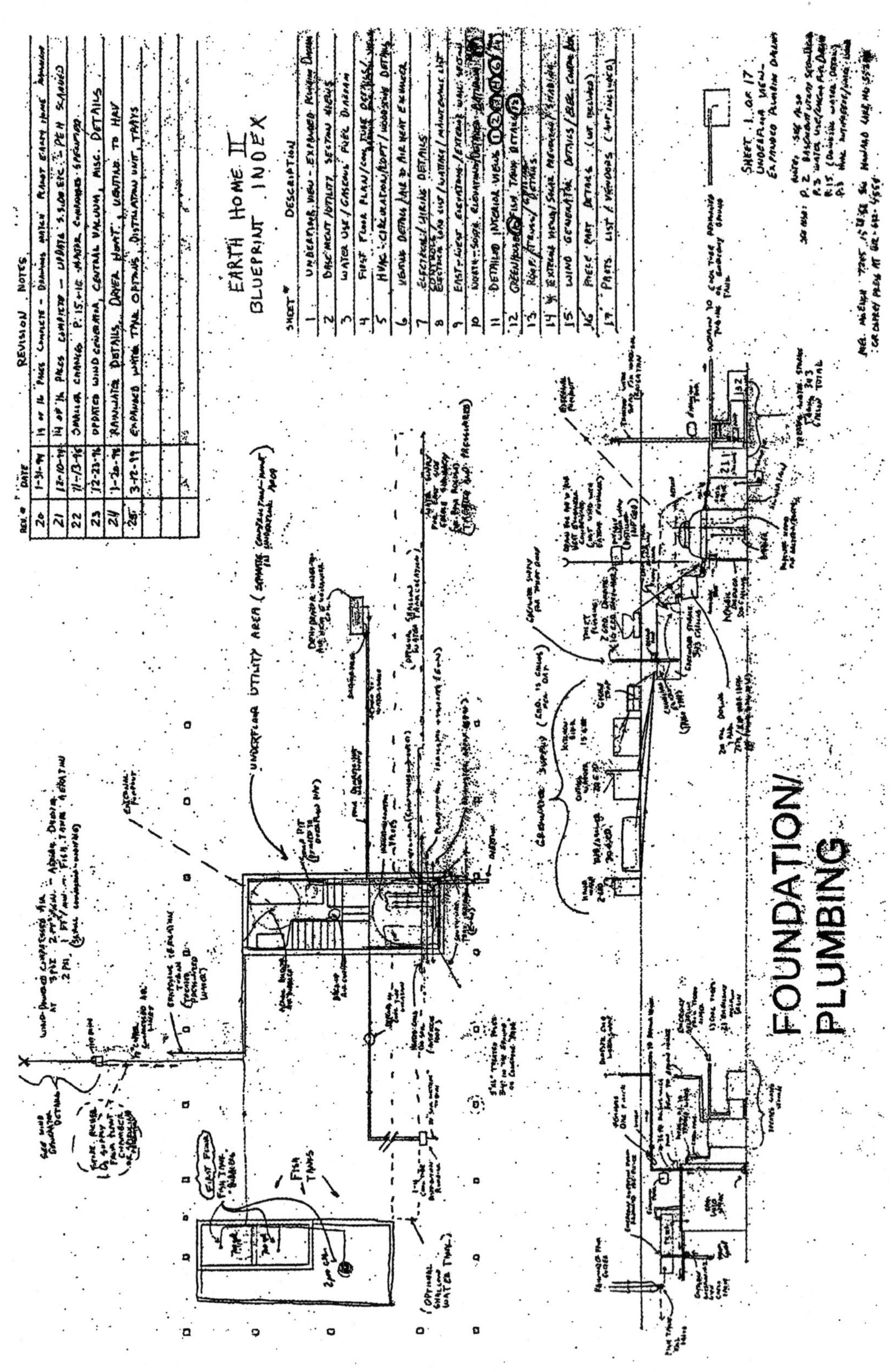

Figure 184-EH BLUEPRINT (FOUNDATION/PLUMBING)

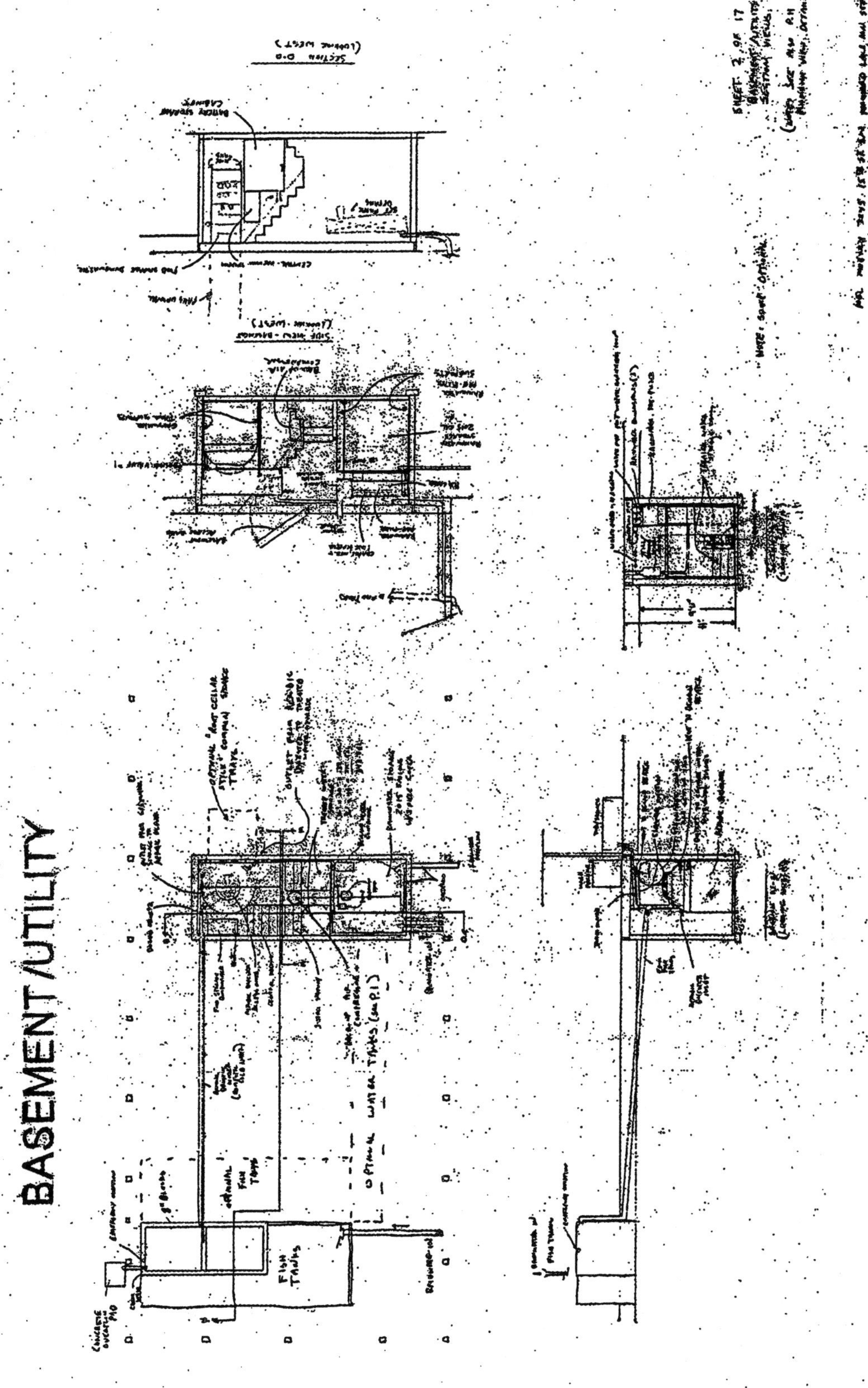

Figure 185-EH BLUEPRINT (BASEMENT/UTILITY)

*Used in Earth Home

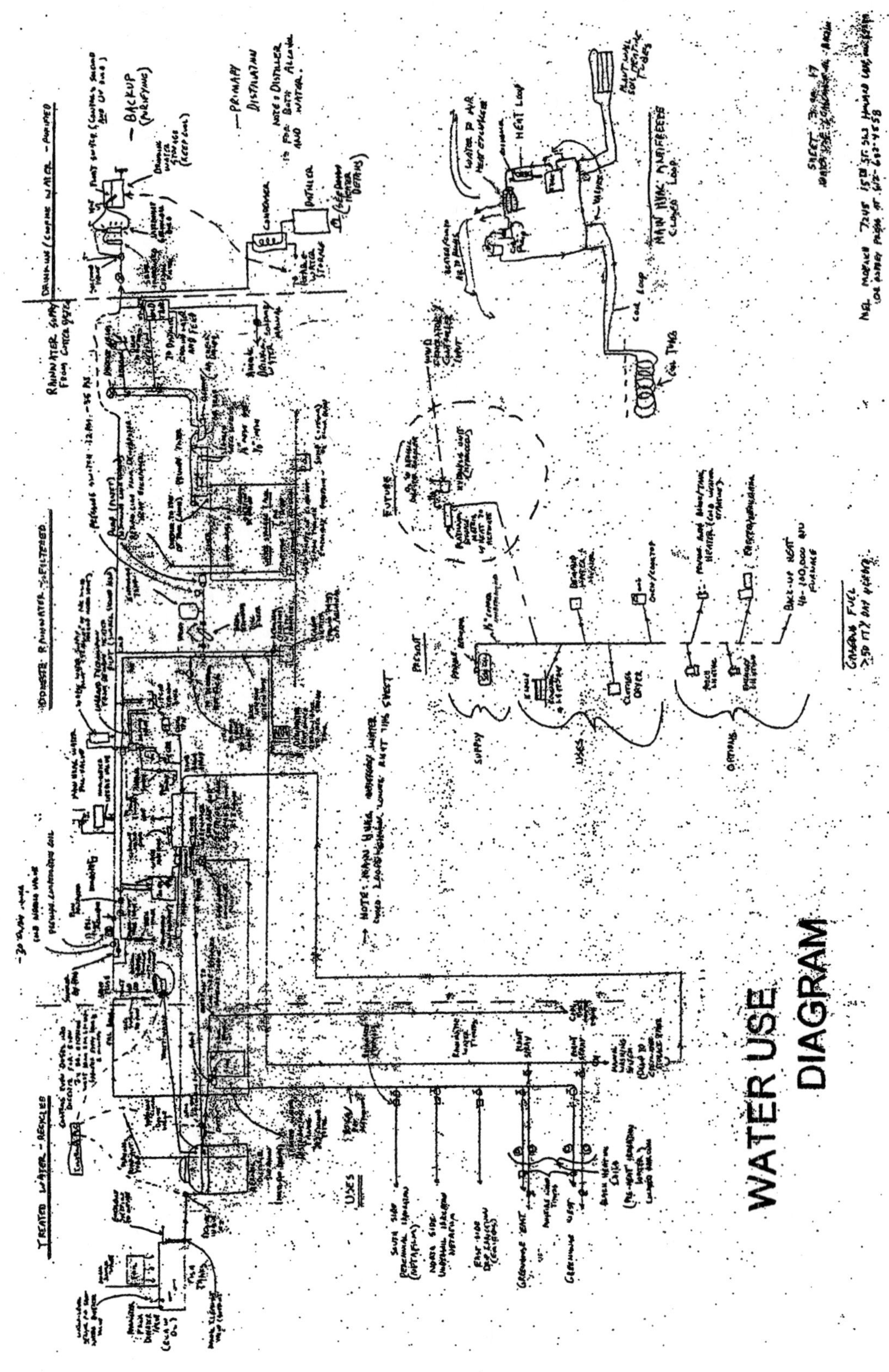

Figure 186-EH BLUEPRINT (WATER USE DIAGRAM)

*Used in Earth Home

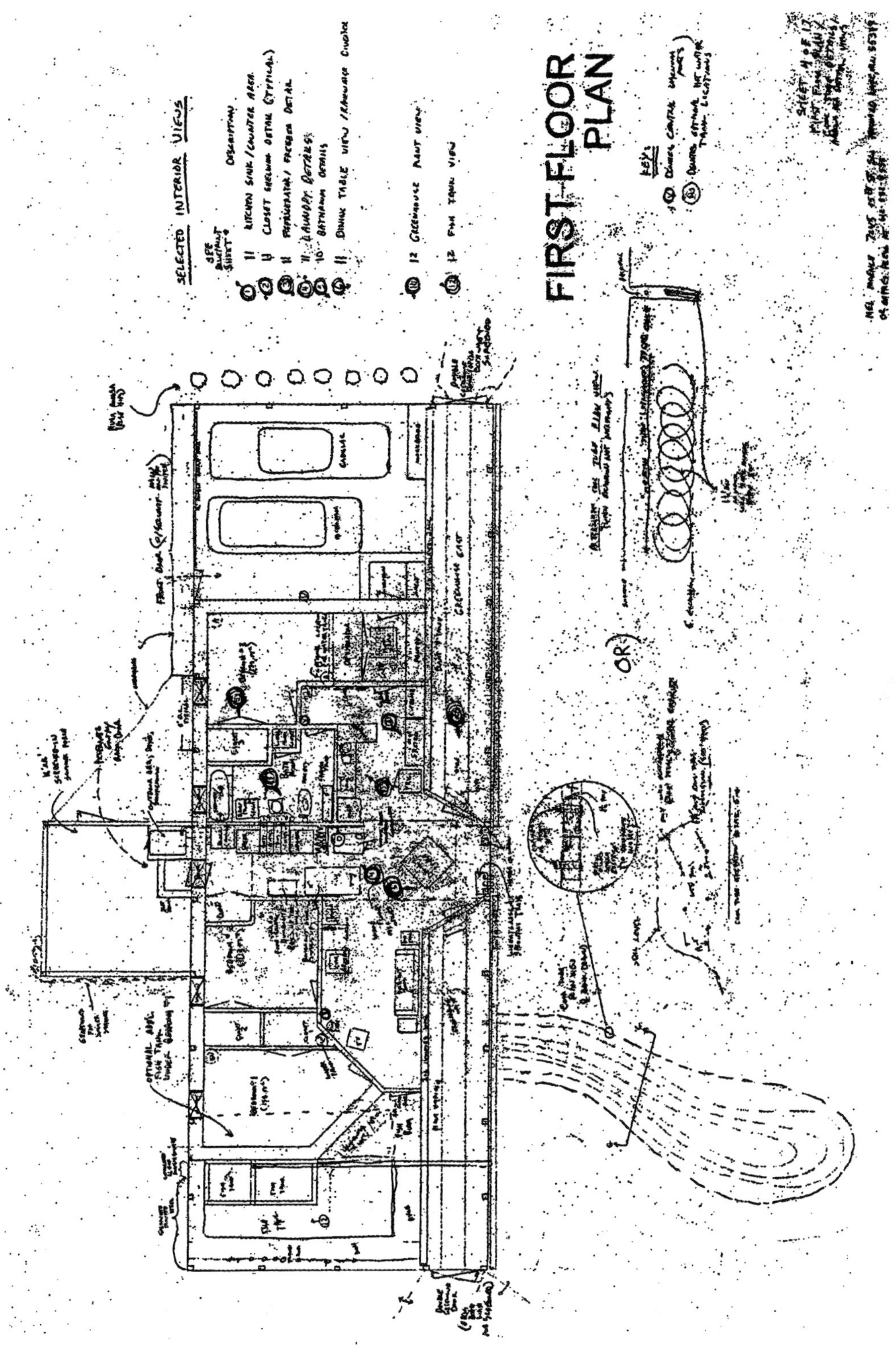

Figure 187-EH BLUEPRINT (FIRST FLOOR PLAN)

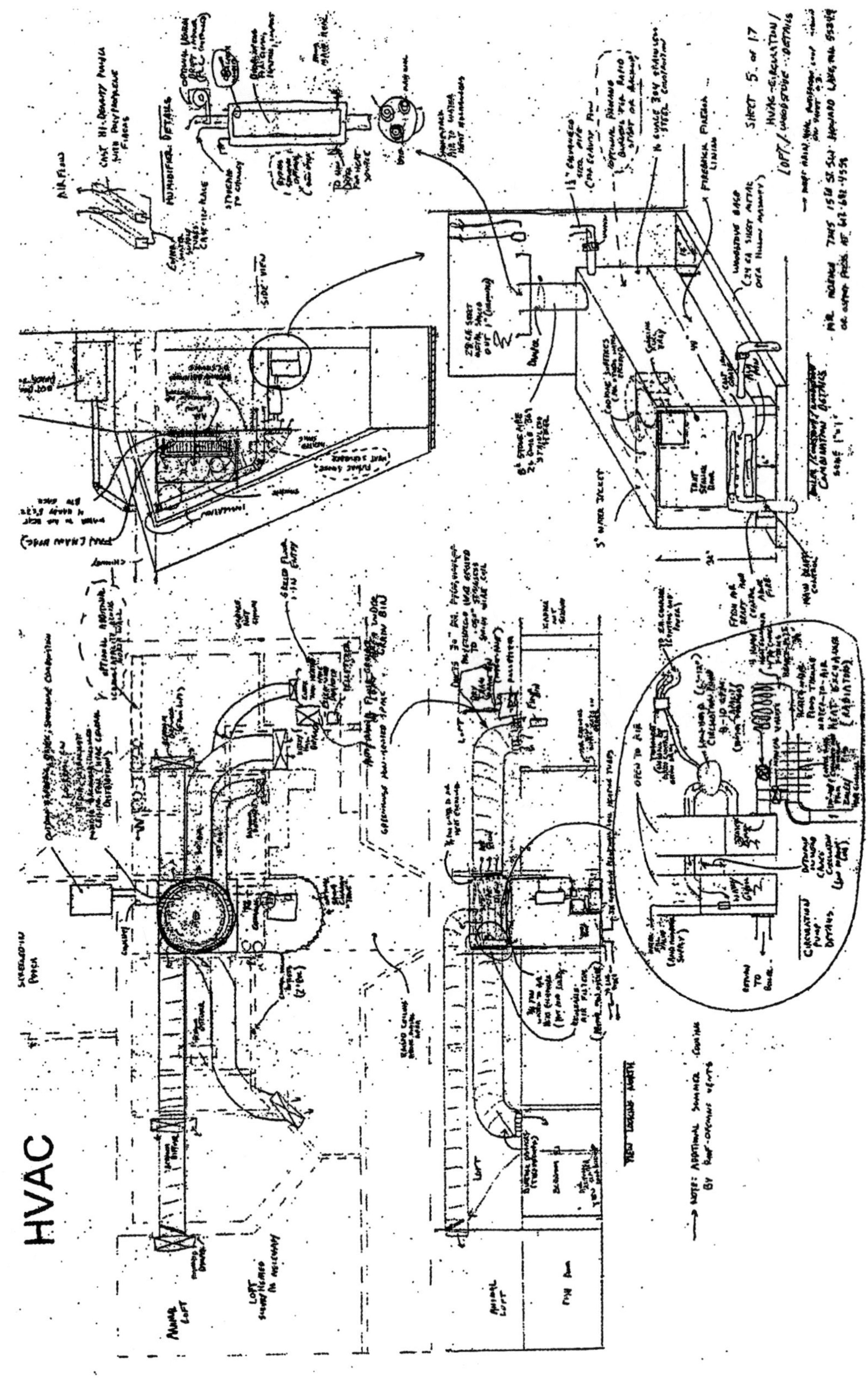

Figure 188-EH BLUEPRINT (HVAC)

*Used in Earth Home

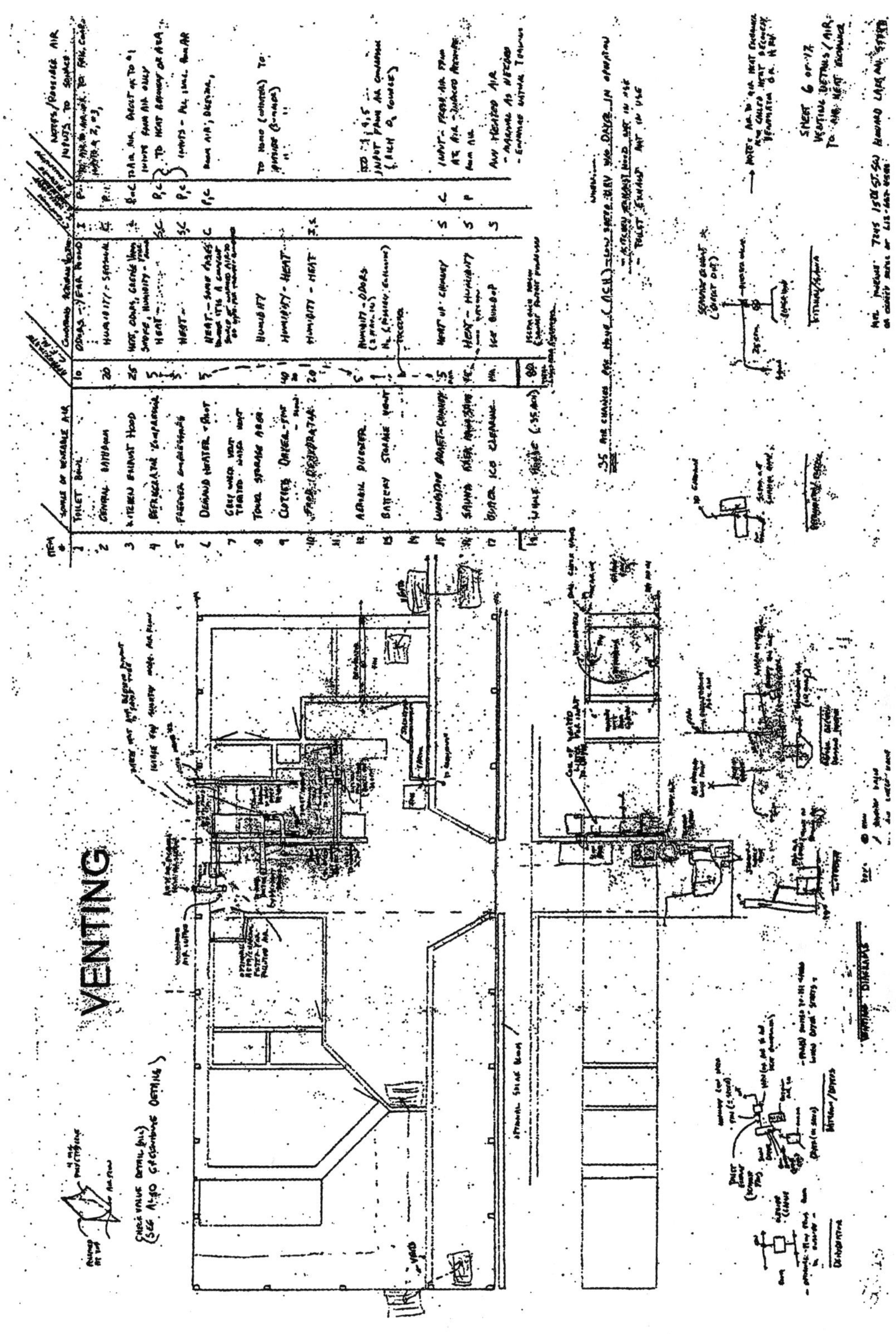

Figure 189-EH BLUEPRINT (VENTING)

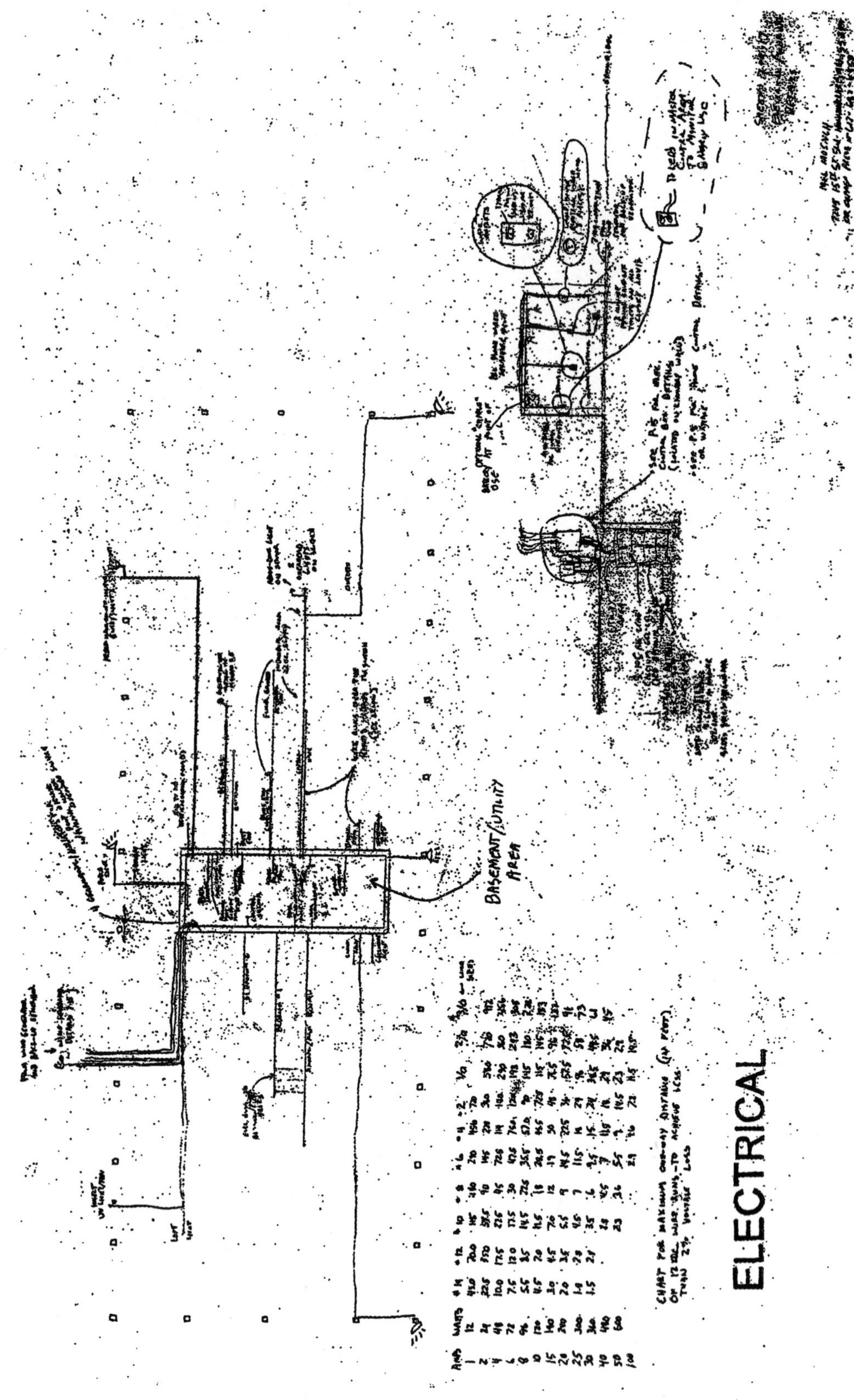

Figure 190-EH BLUEPRINT (ELECTRICAL)

*Used in Earth Home

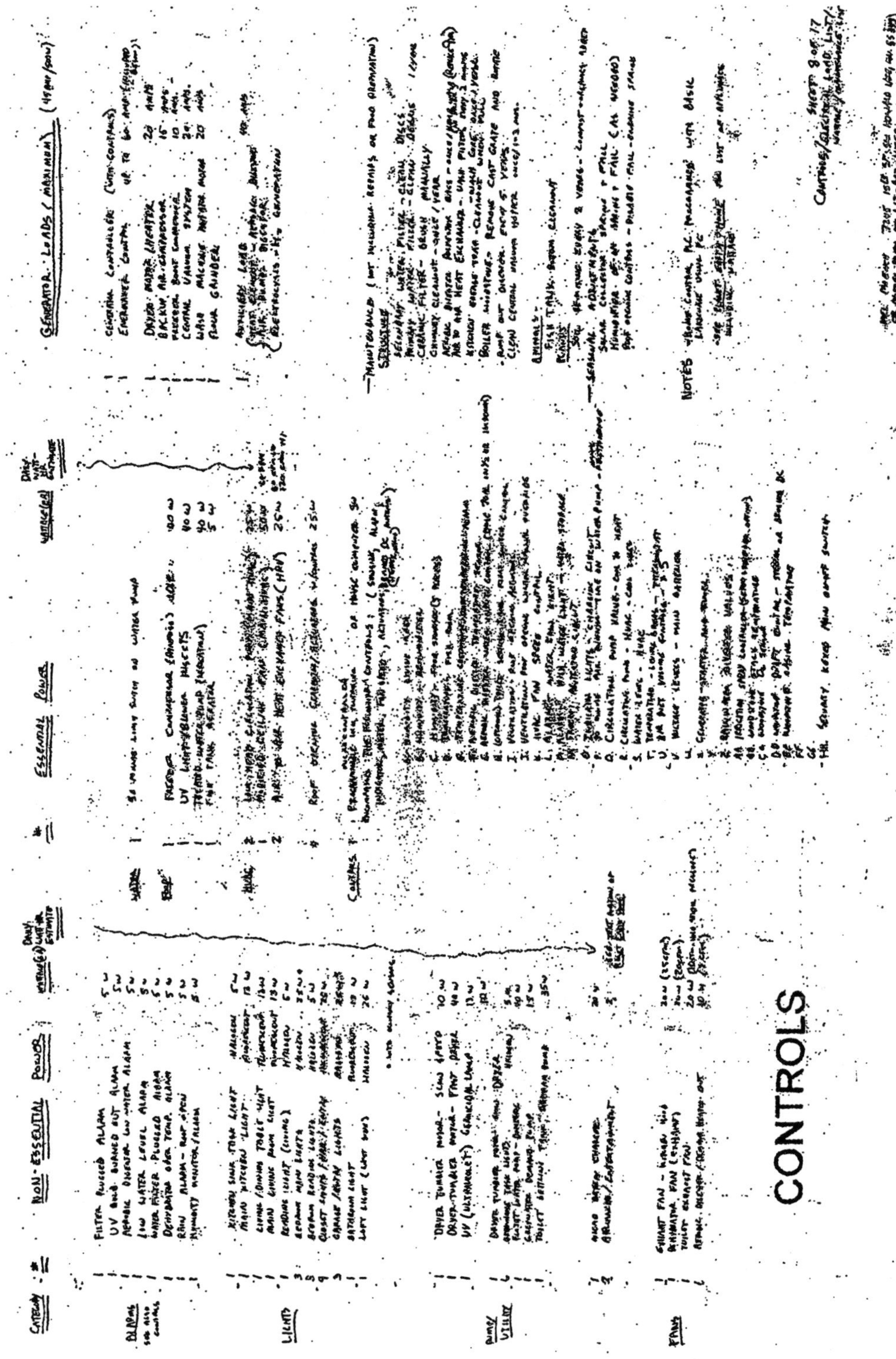

Figure 191-EH BLUEPRINT (CONTROLS)

*Used in Earth Home

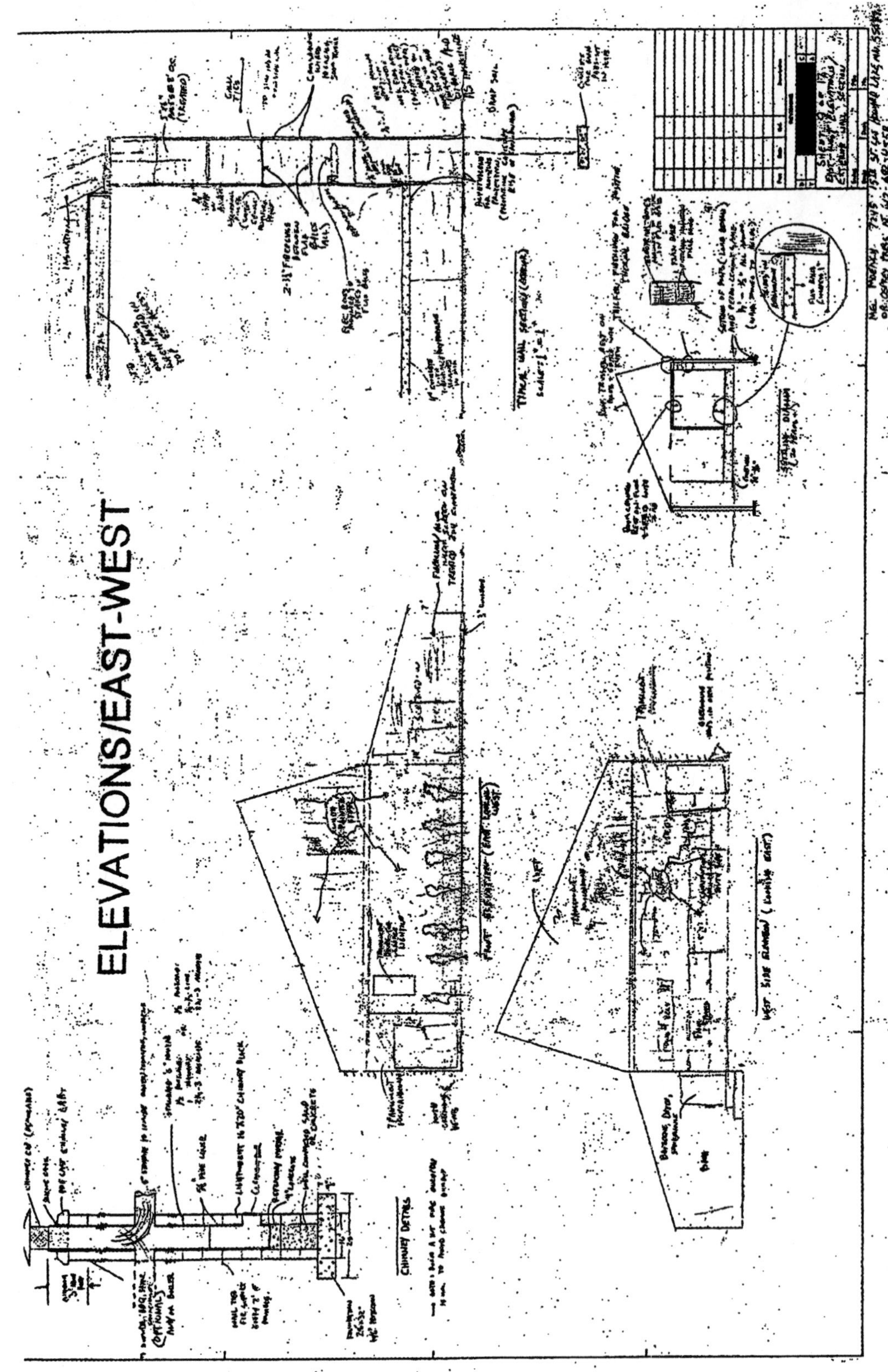

Figure 192-EH BLUEPRINT (ELEVATIONS/EAST-WEST)

*Used in Earth Home

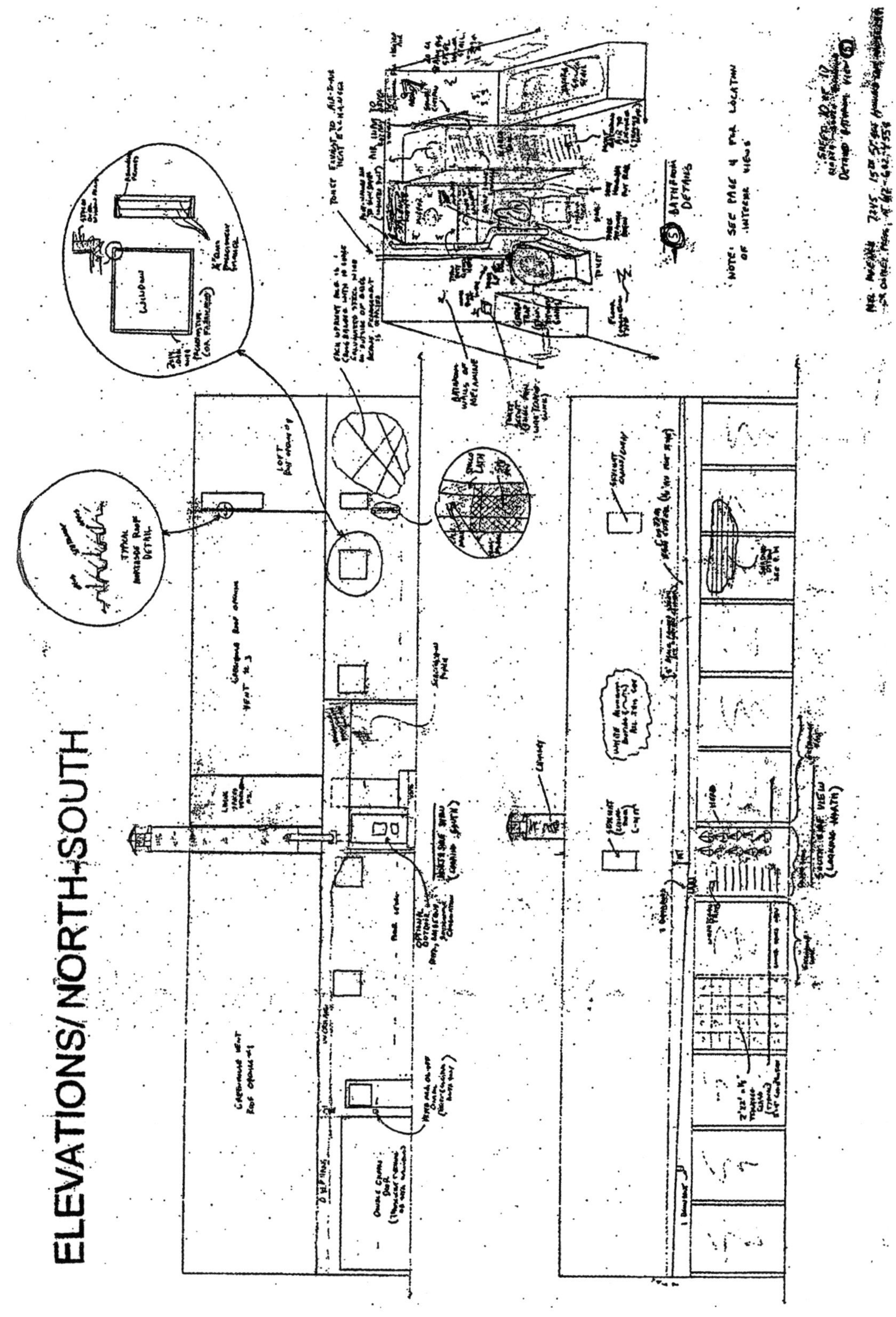

Figure 193-EH BLUEPRINT (ELEVATIONS/NORTH-SOUTH)

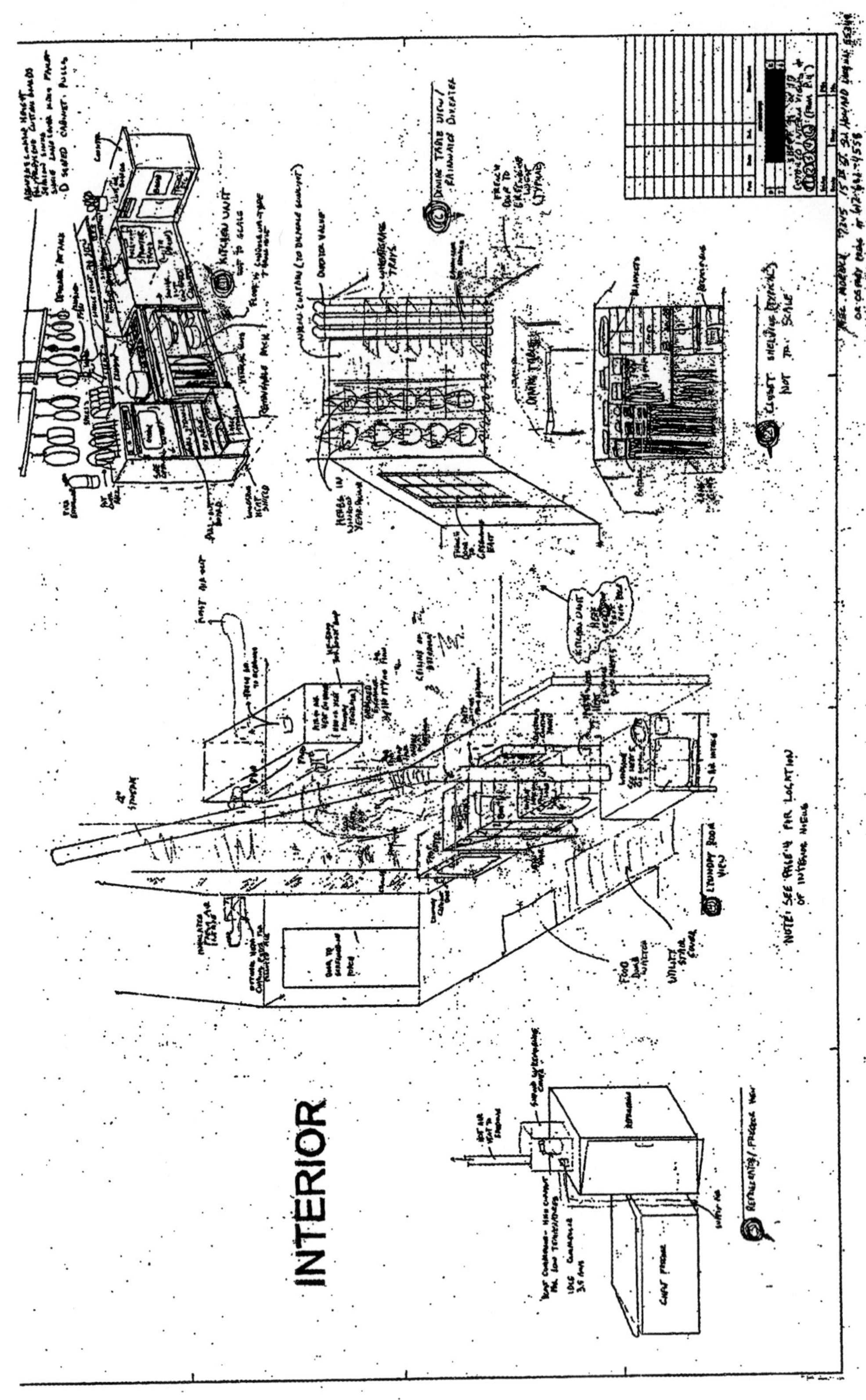

Figure 194-EH BLUEPRINT (INTERIOR)

*Used in Earth Home

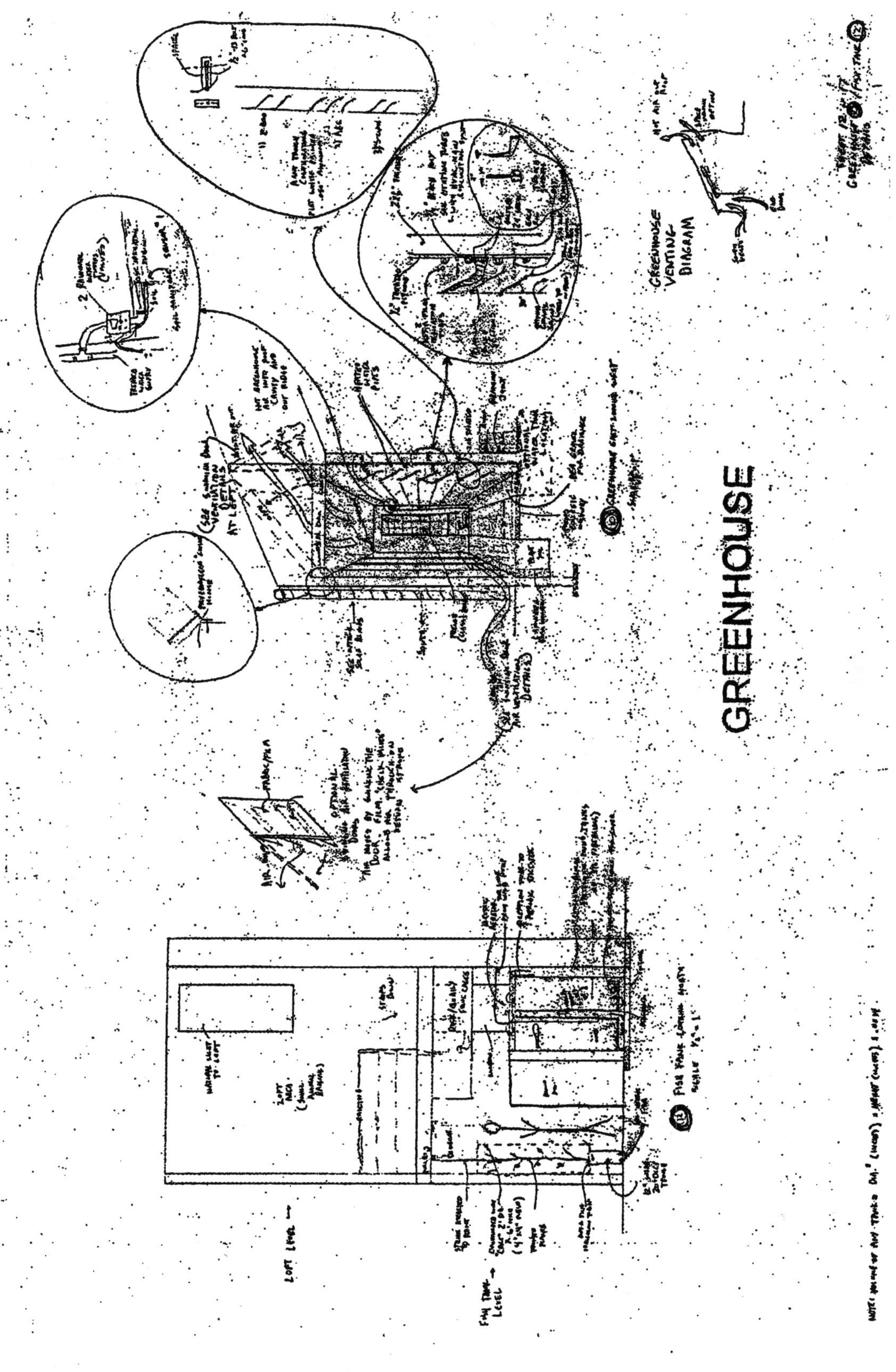

Figure 195-EH BLUEPRINT (GREENHOUSE)

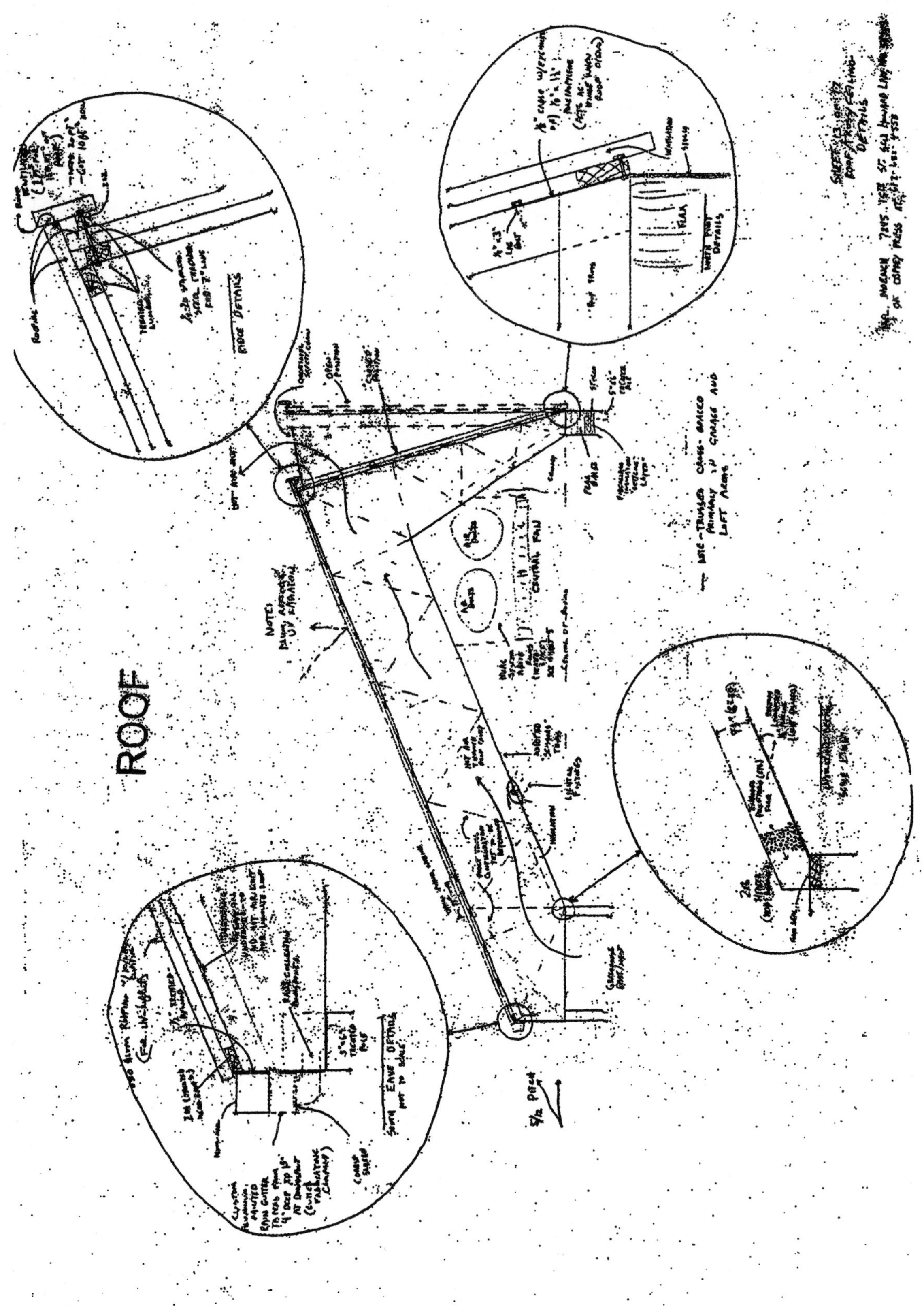

Figure 196-EH BLUEPRINT (ROOF)

*Used in Earth Home

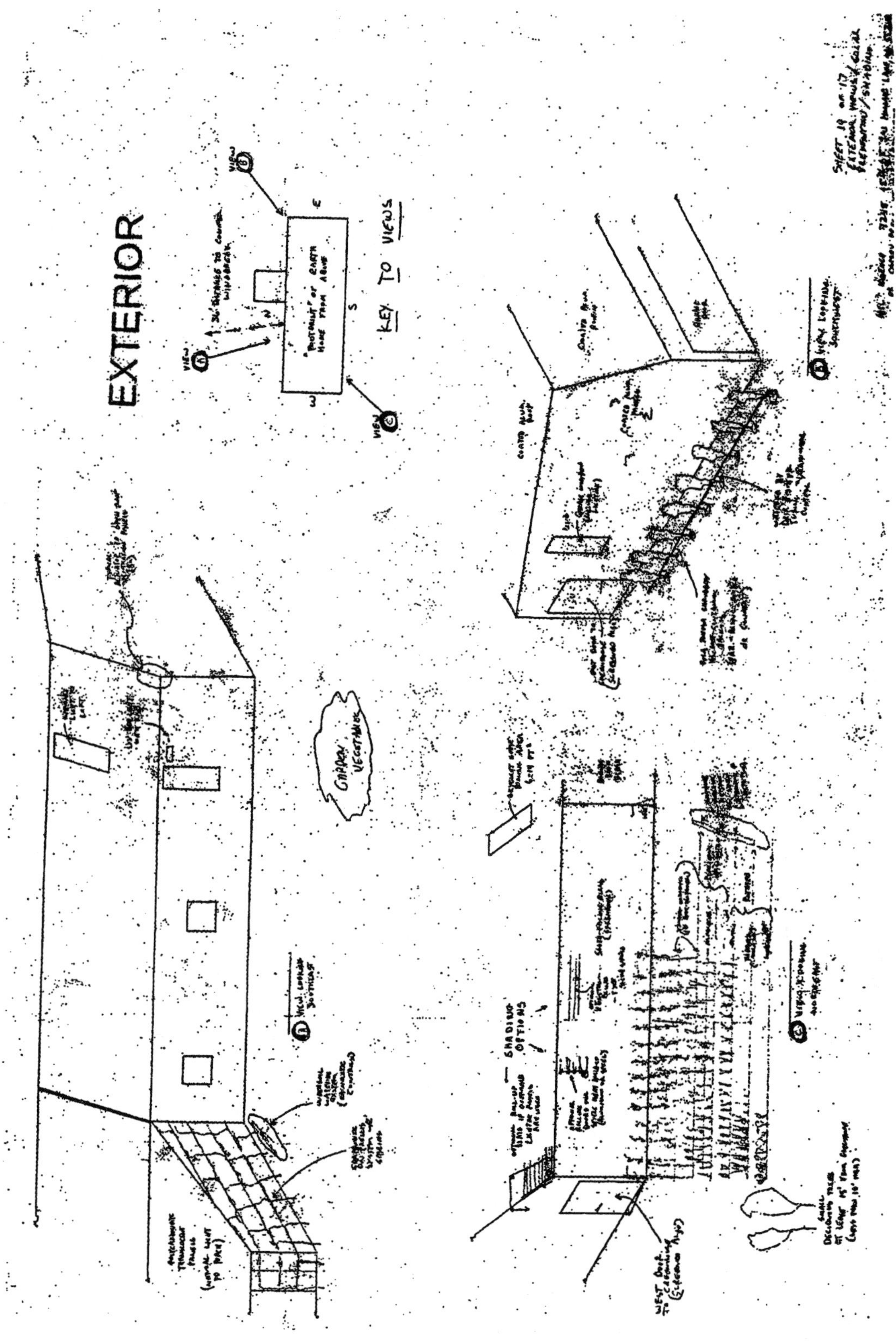

Figure 197-EH BLUEPRINT (EXTERIOR)

*Used in Earth Home

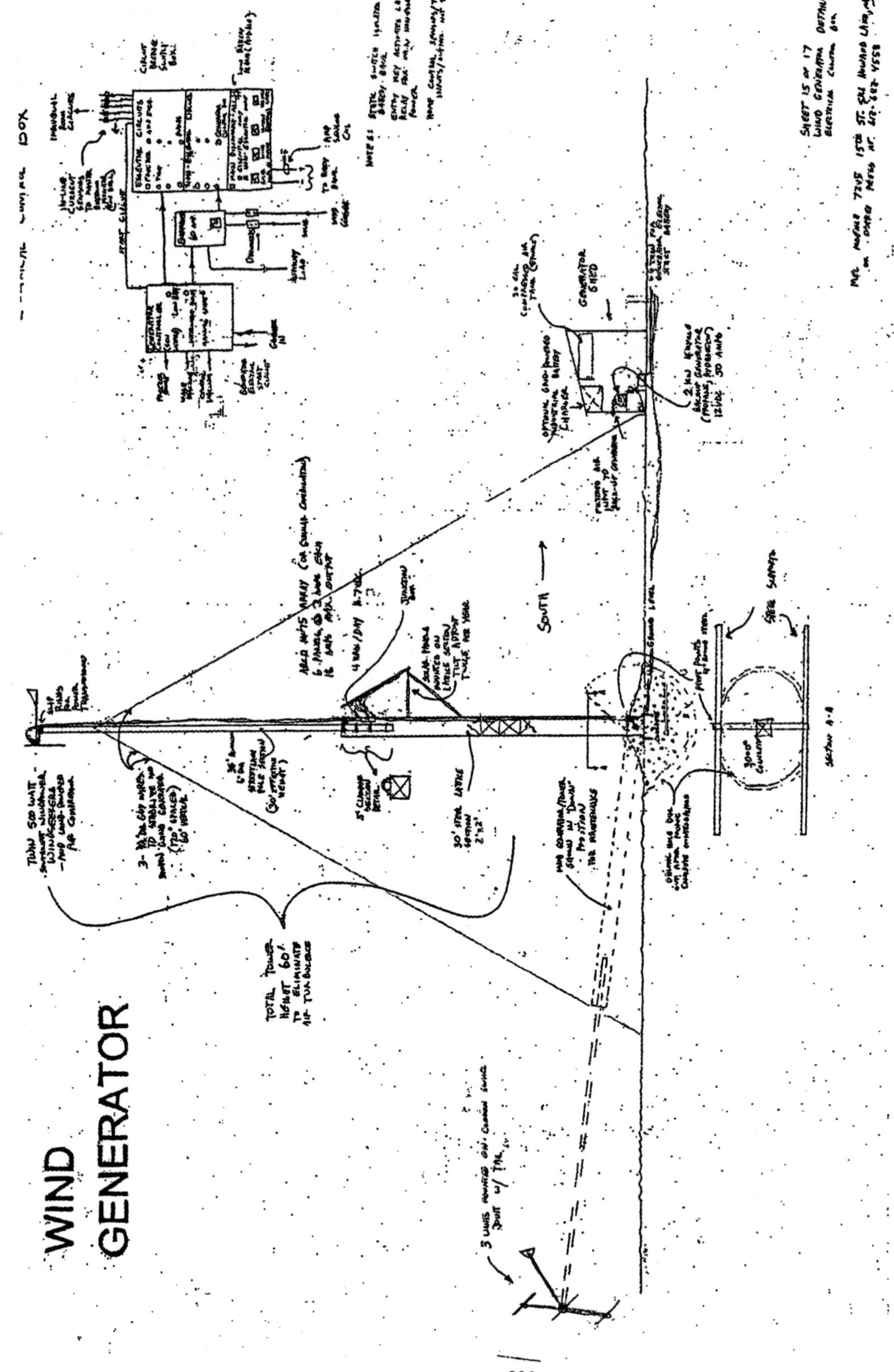

Figure 198-EH BLUEPRINT (WIND GENERATOR)

*Used in Earth Home

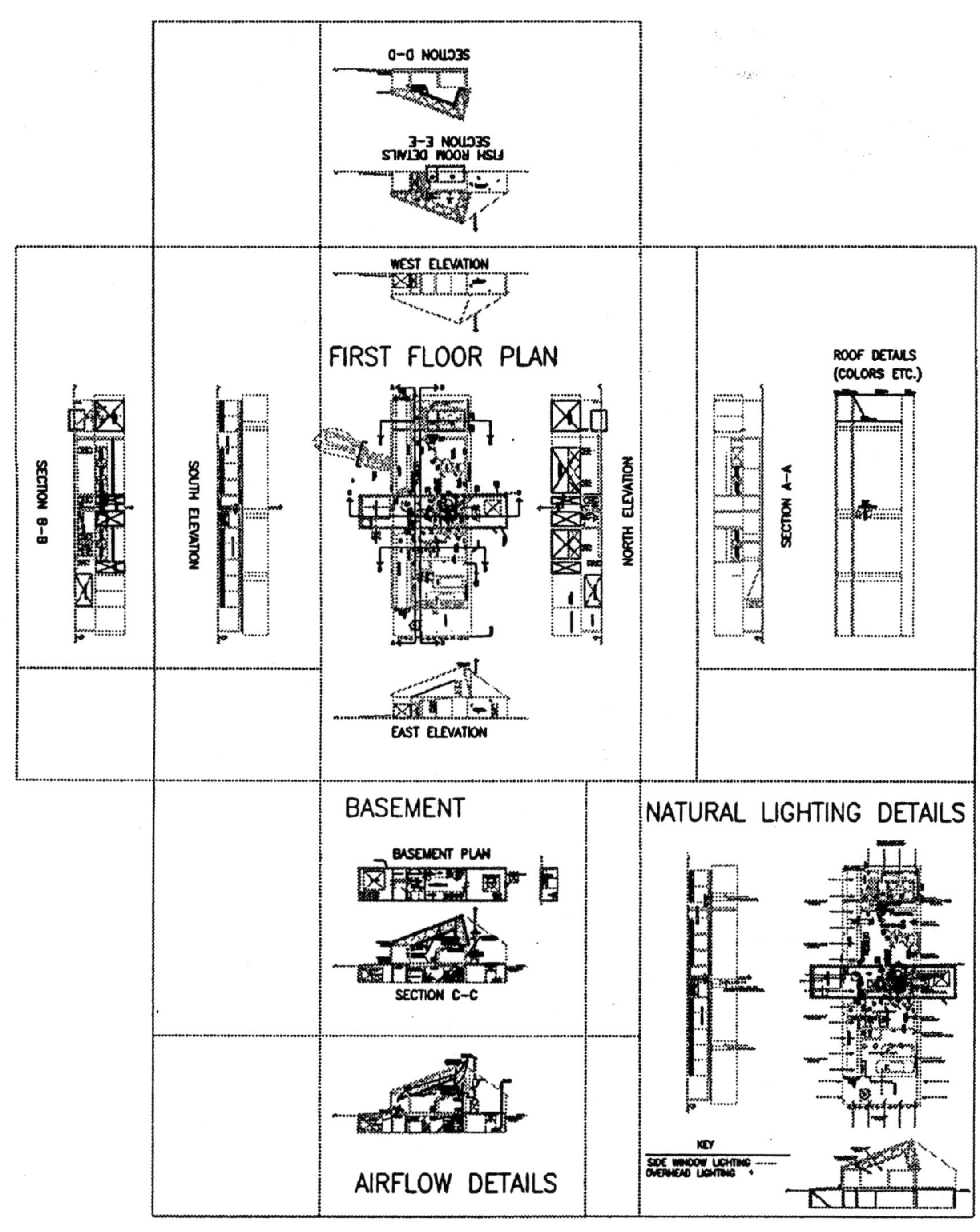

Figure 199-CAD DRAWING PAGE 1 OF 13

*Used in Earth Home

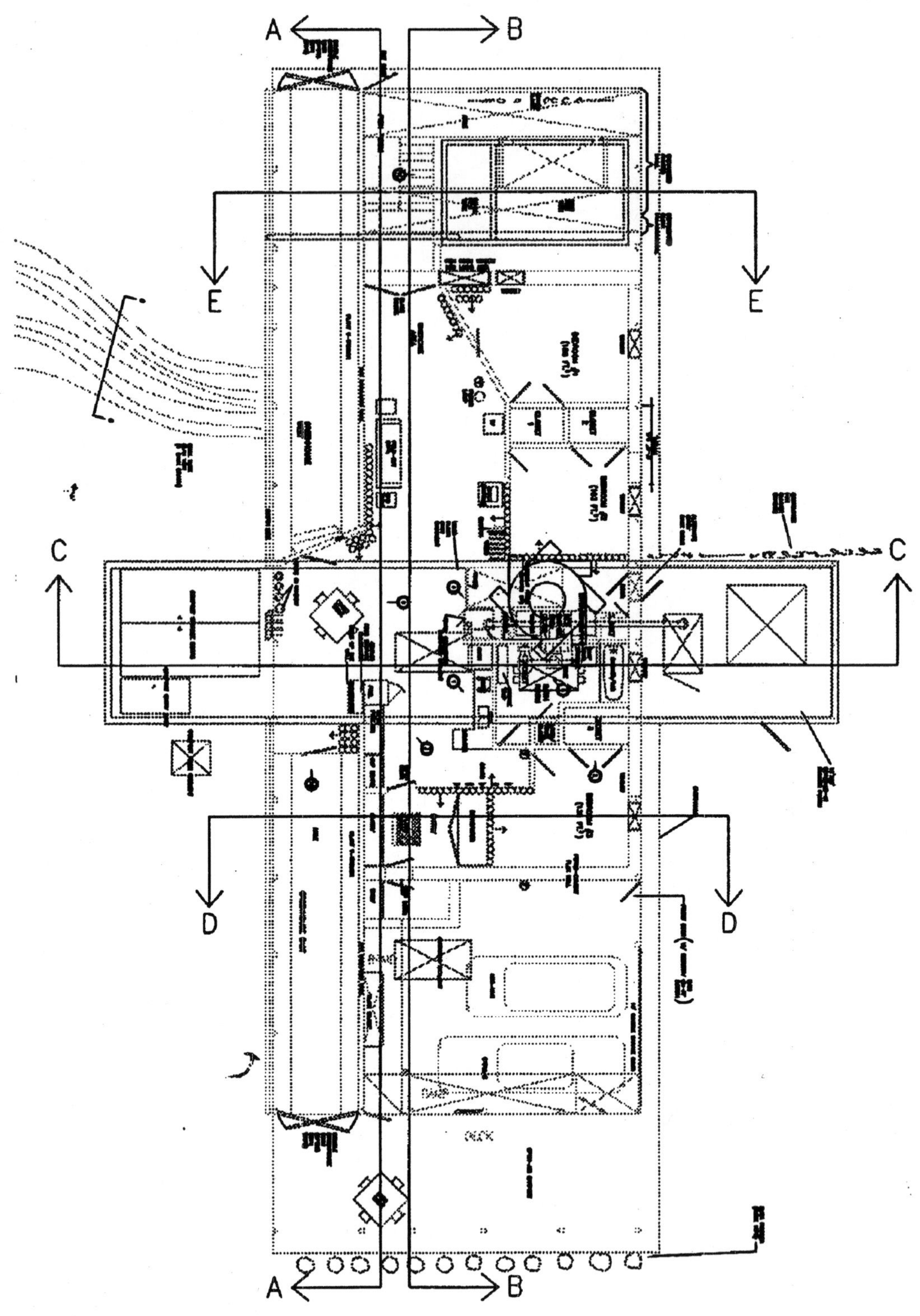

Figure 200-CAD DRAWING PAGE 2 OF 13

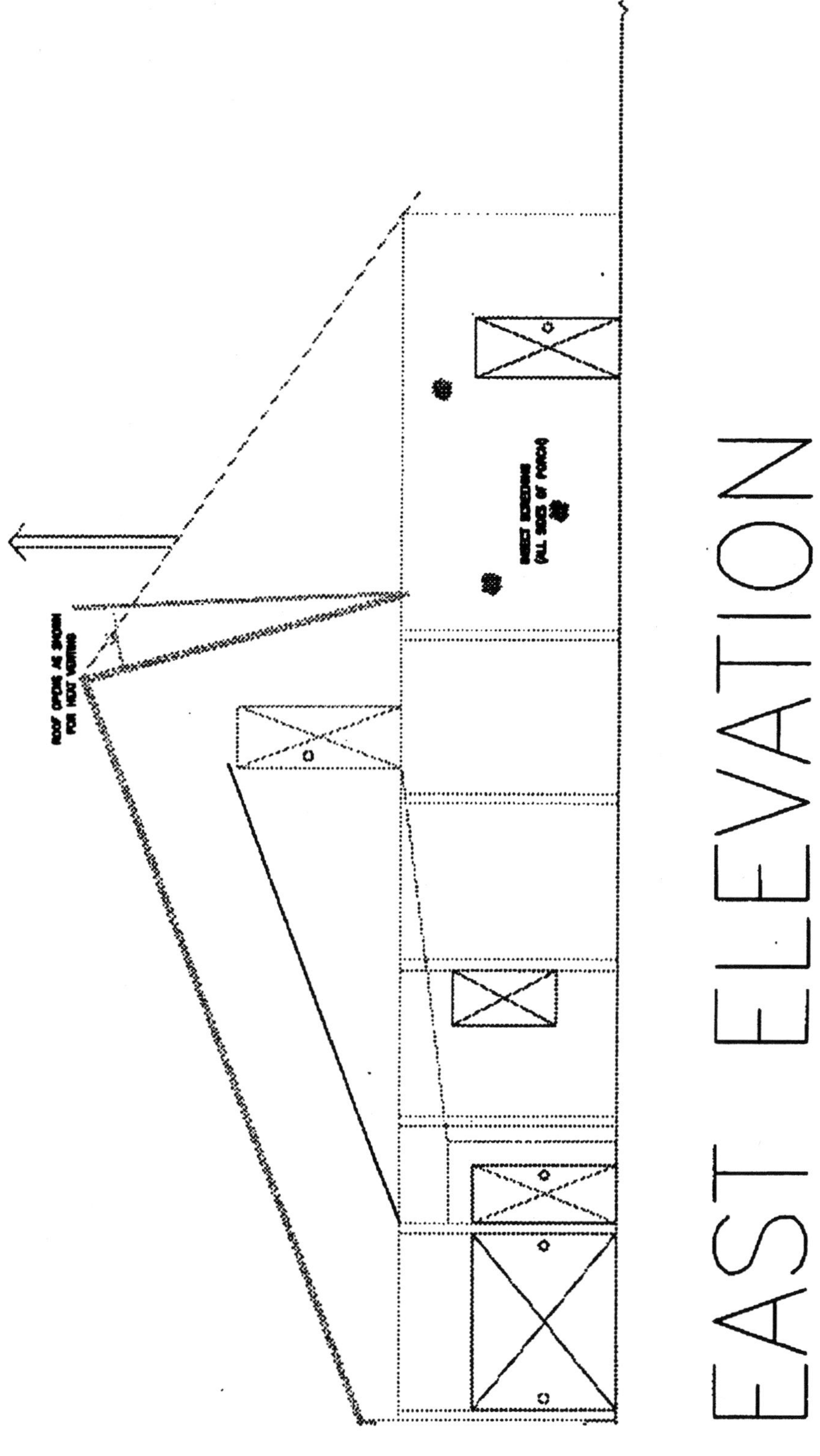

Figure 201-CAD DRAWING PAGE 3 OF 13

*Used in Earth Home

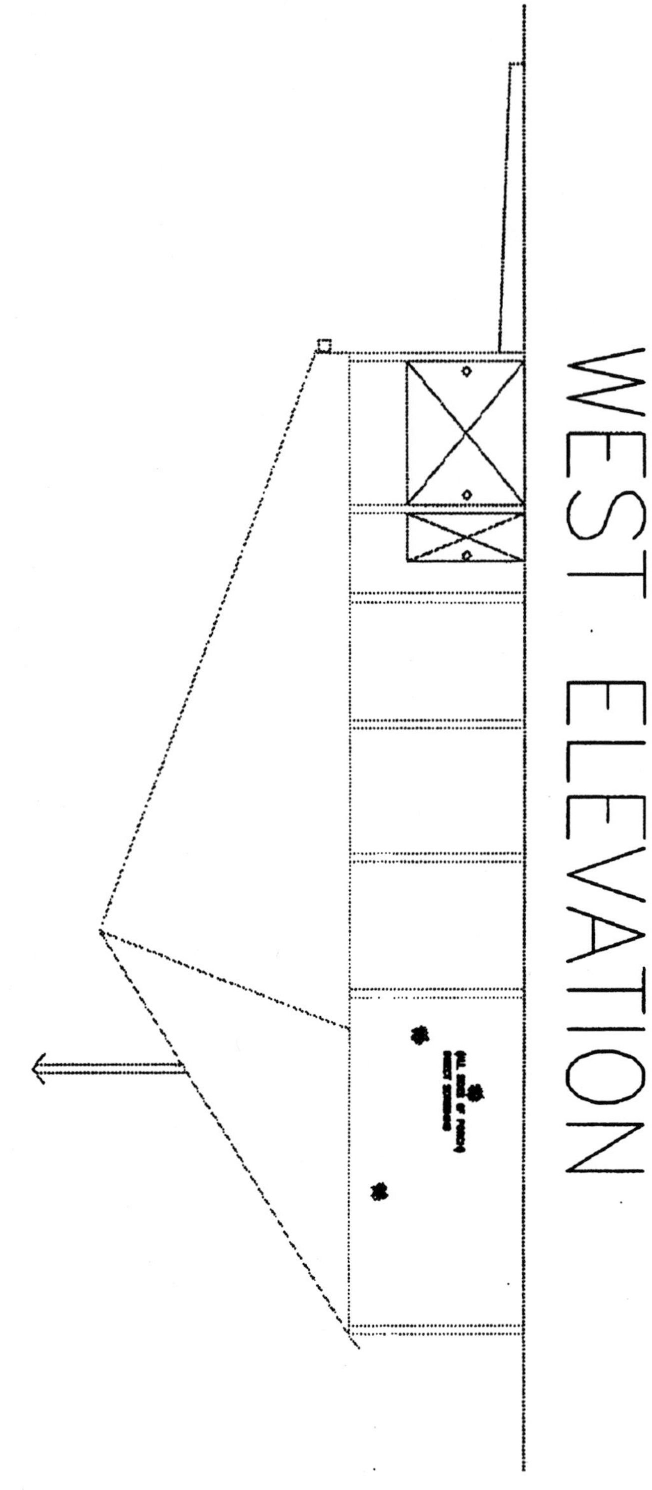

Figure 202-CAD DRAWING PAGE 4 OF 13

*Used in Earth Home

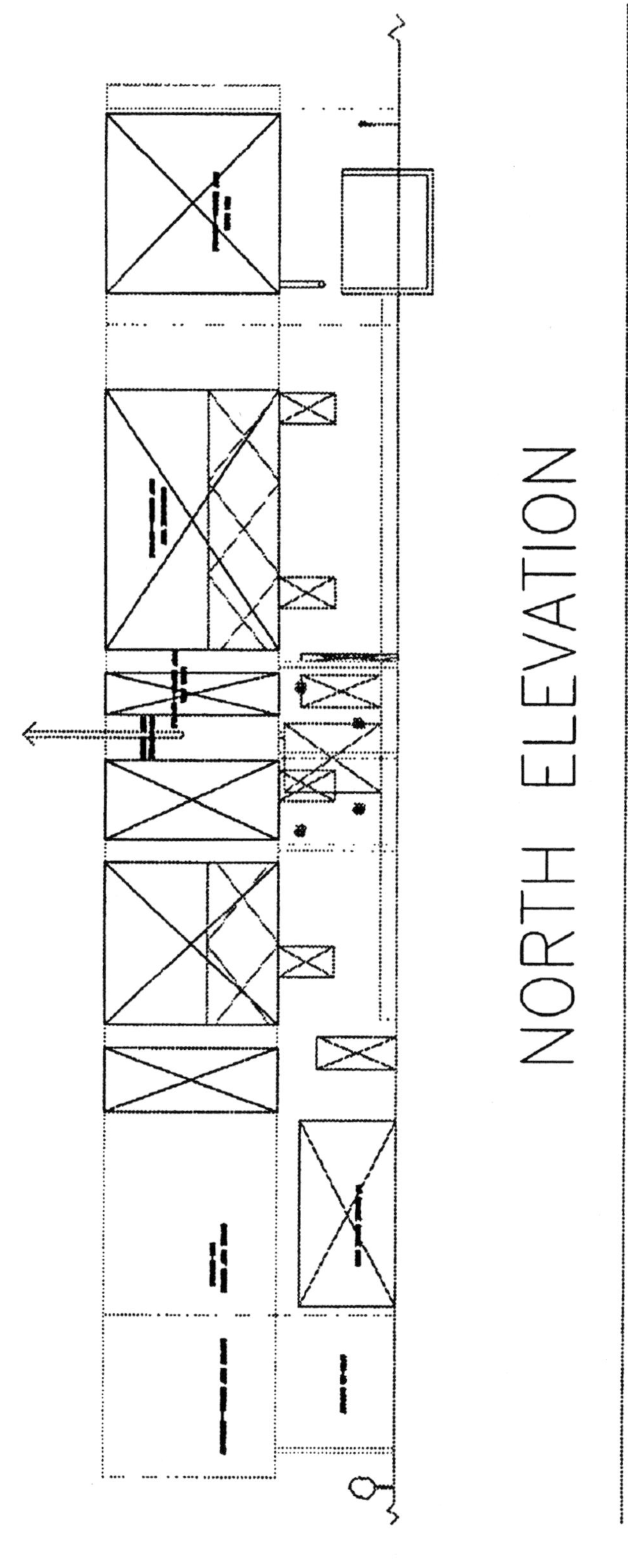

Figure 203-CAD DRAWING PAGE 5 OF 13

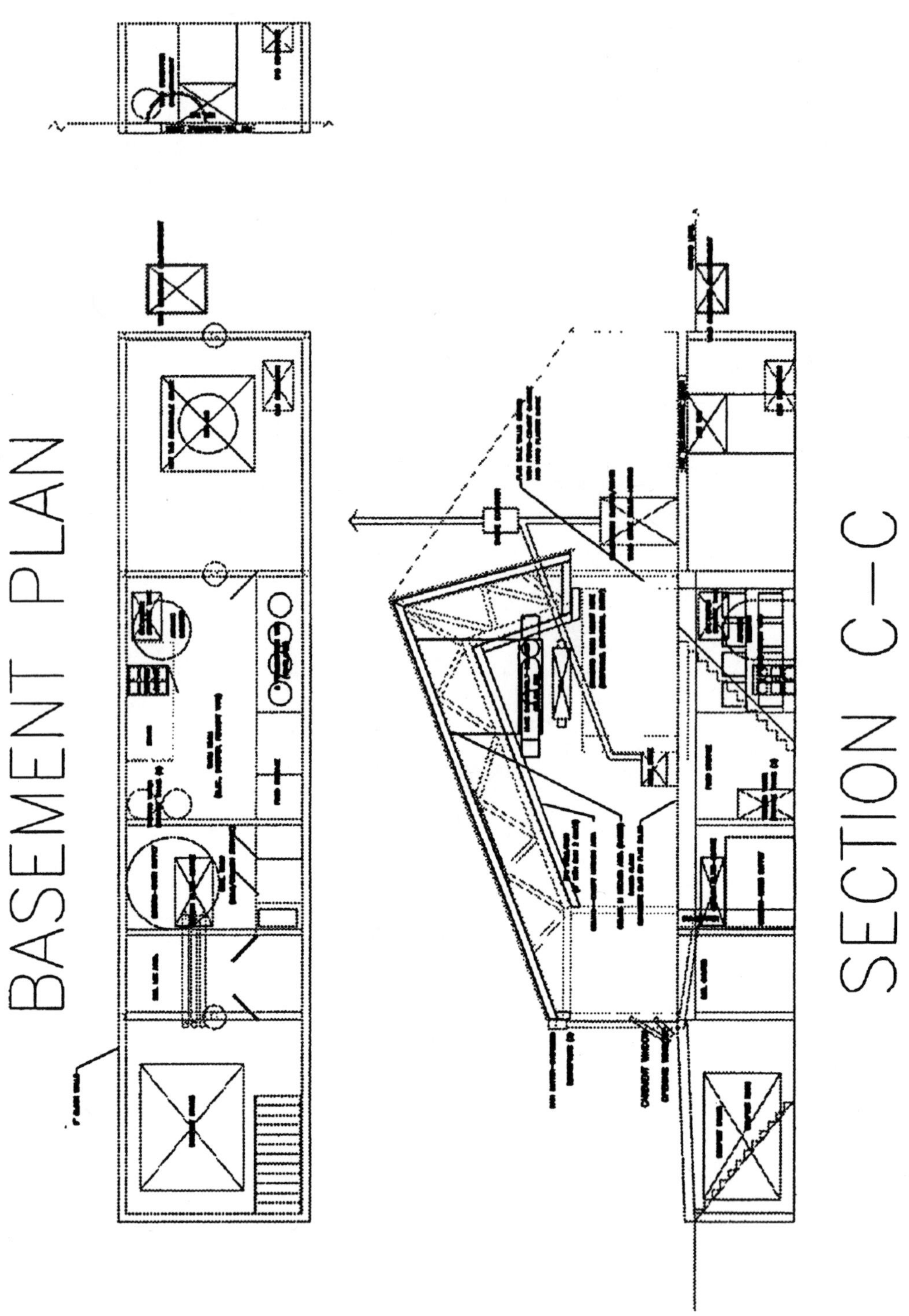

Figure 204-CAD DRAWING PAGE 6 OF 13

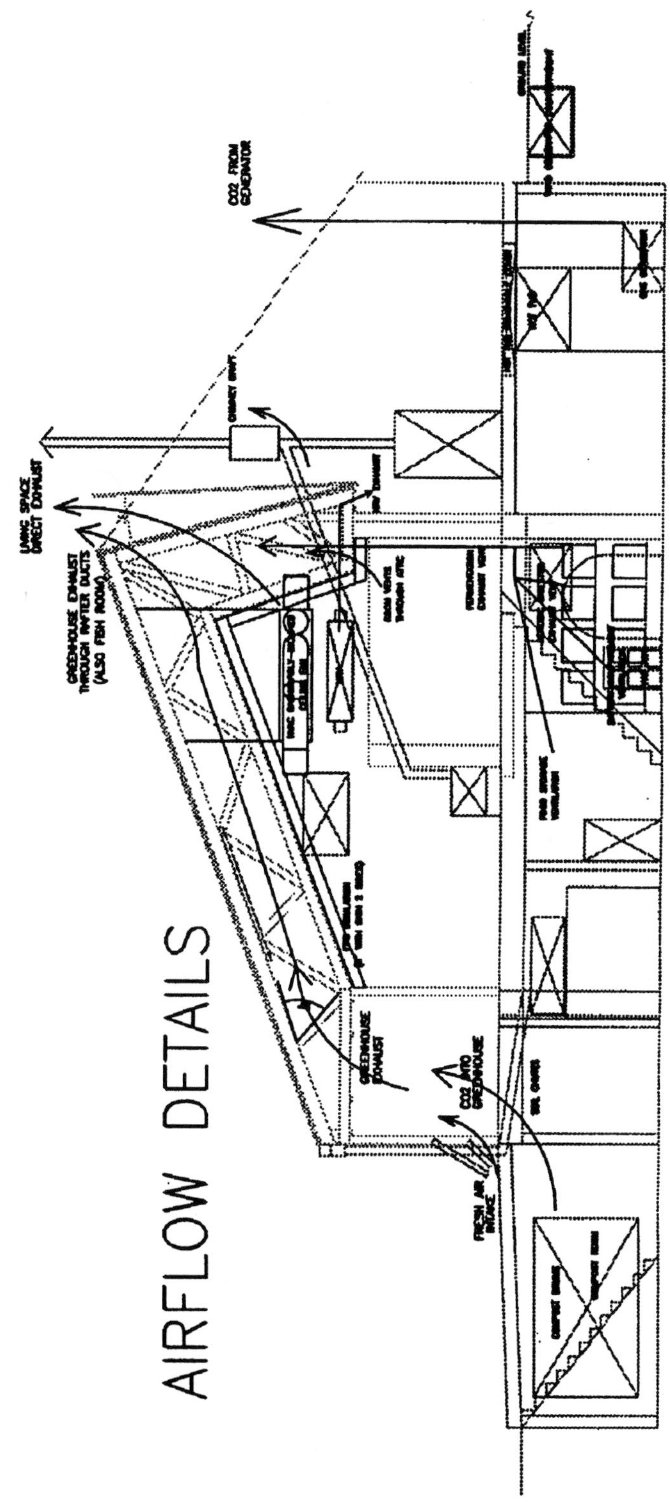

Figure 205-CAD DRAWING PAGE 7 OF 13

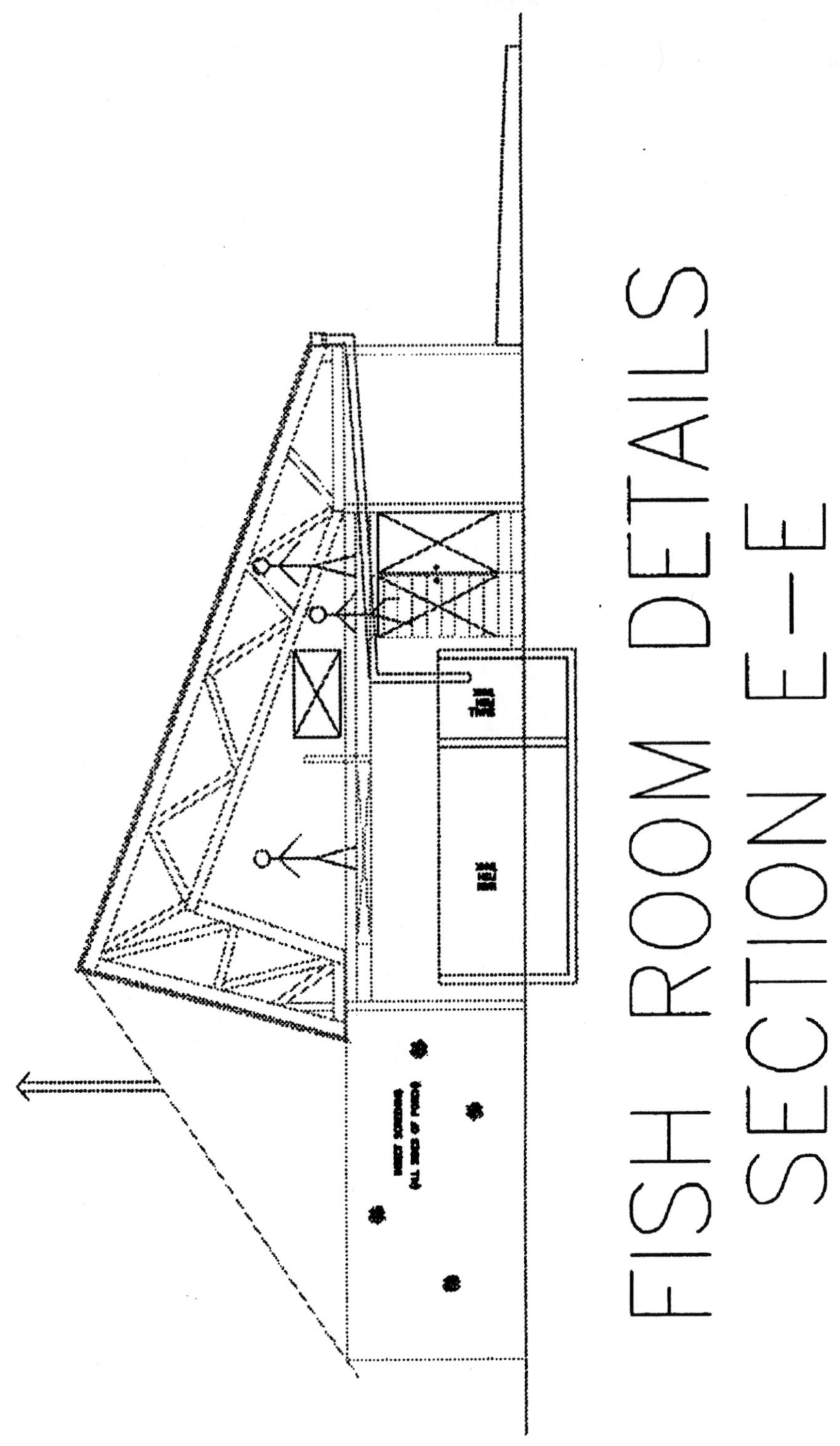

Figure 206-CAD DRAWING PAGE 8 OF 13

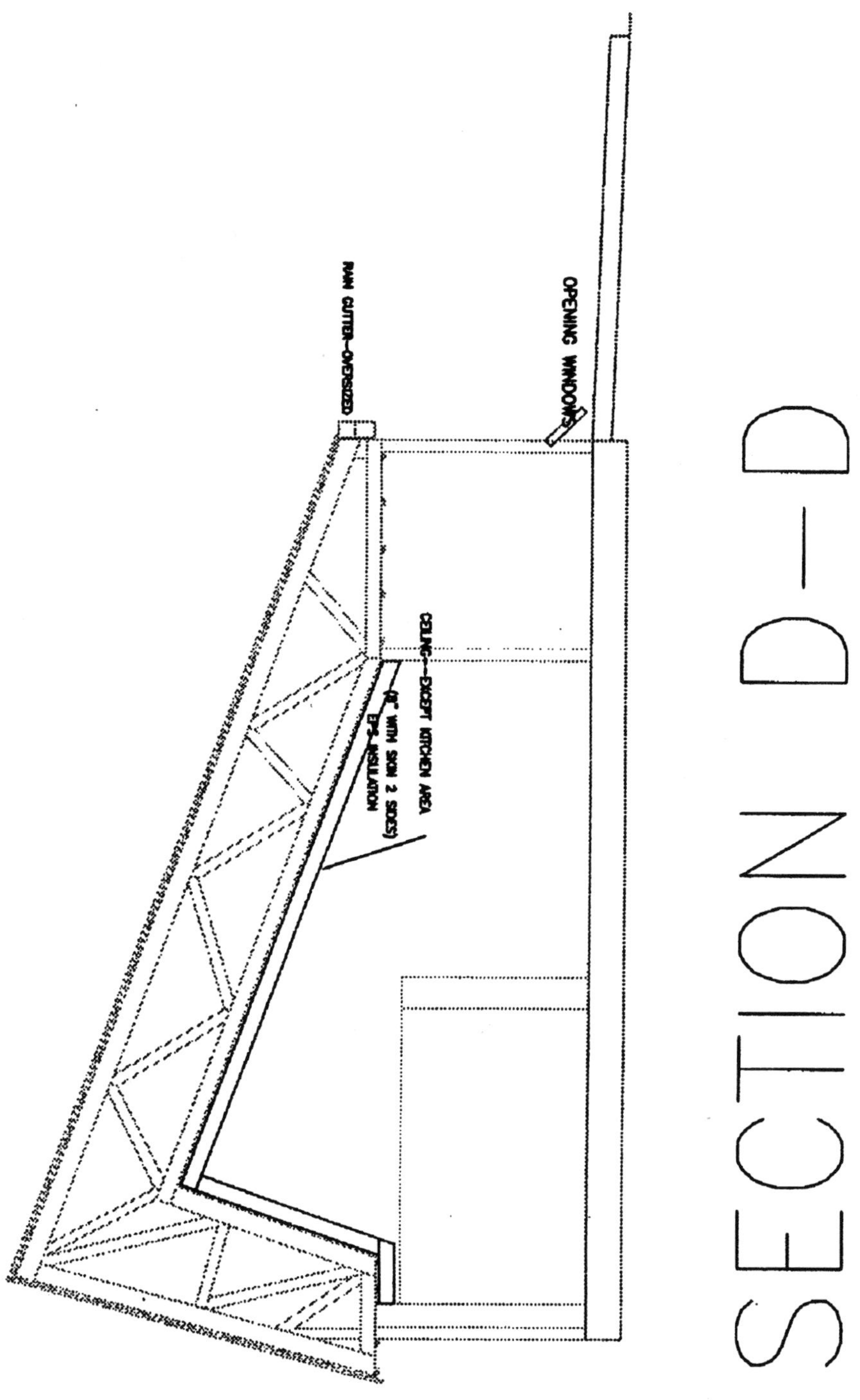

Figure 207-CAD DRAWING PAGE 9 OF 13

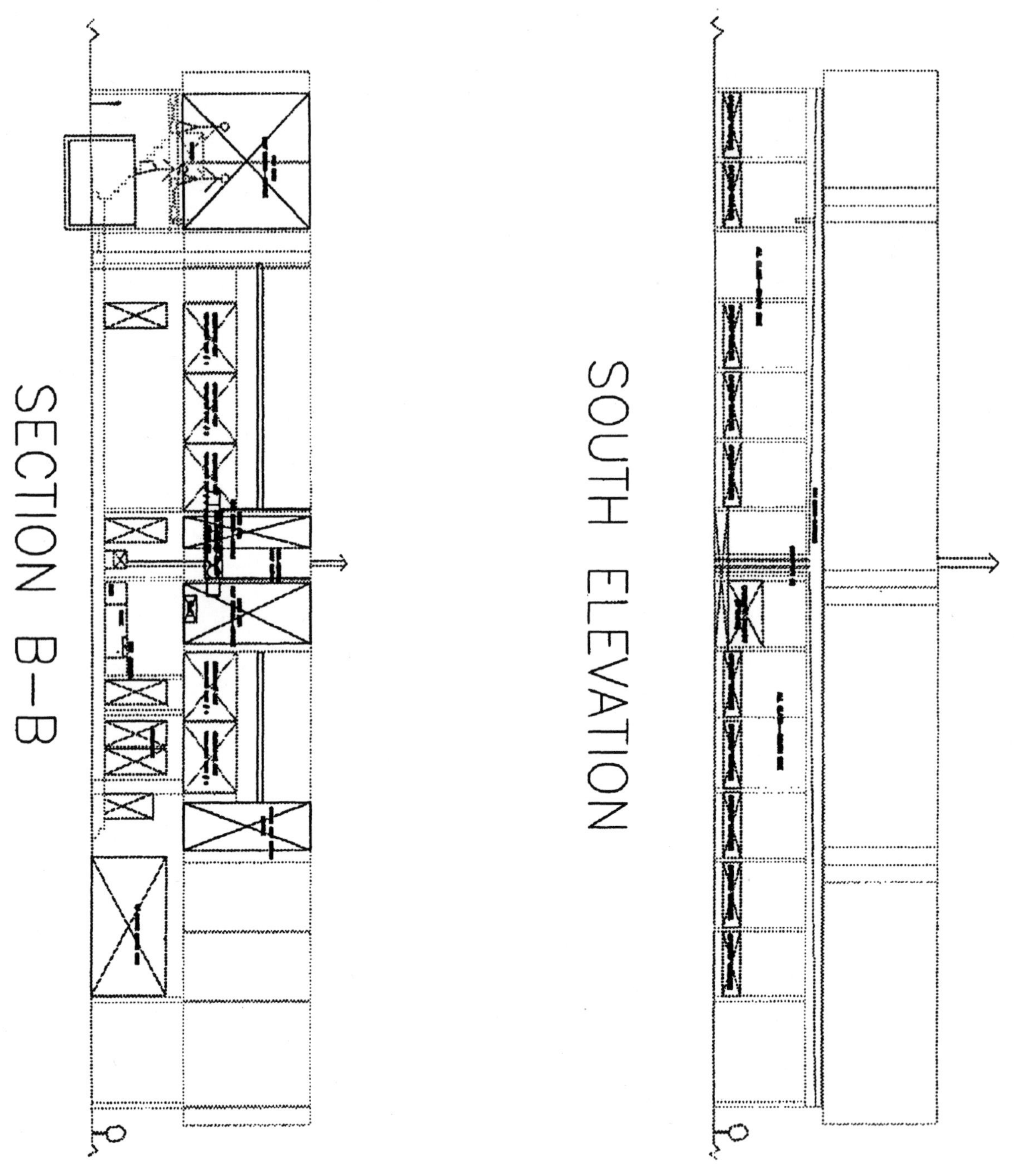

Figure 208-CAD DRAWING PAGE 10 OF 13

*Used in Earth Home

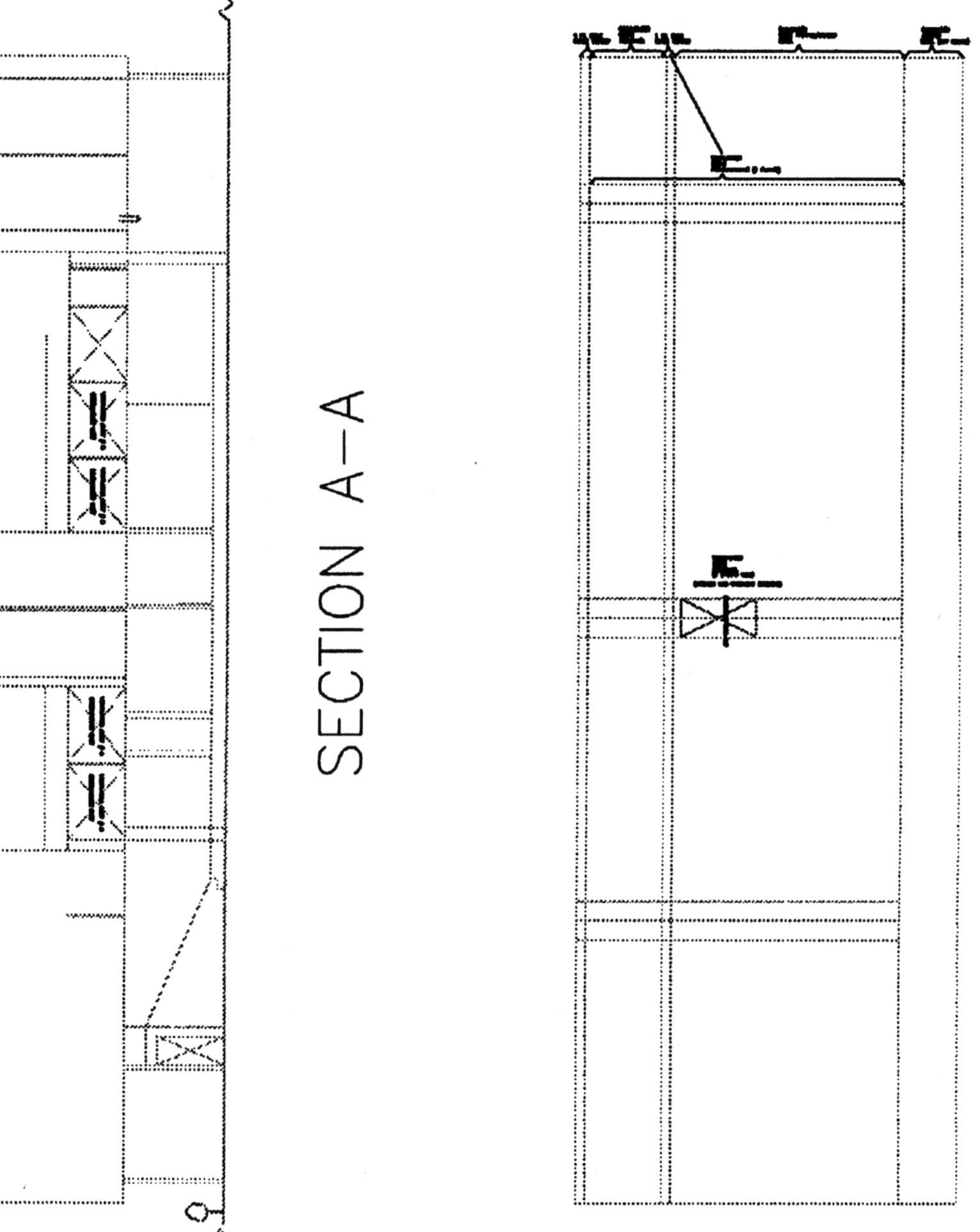

Figure 209-CAD DRAWING PAGE 11 OF 13

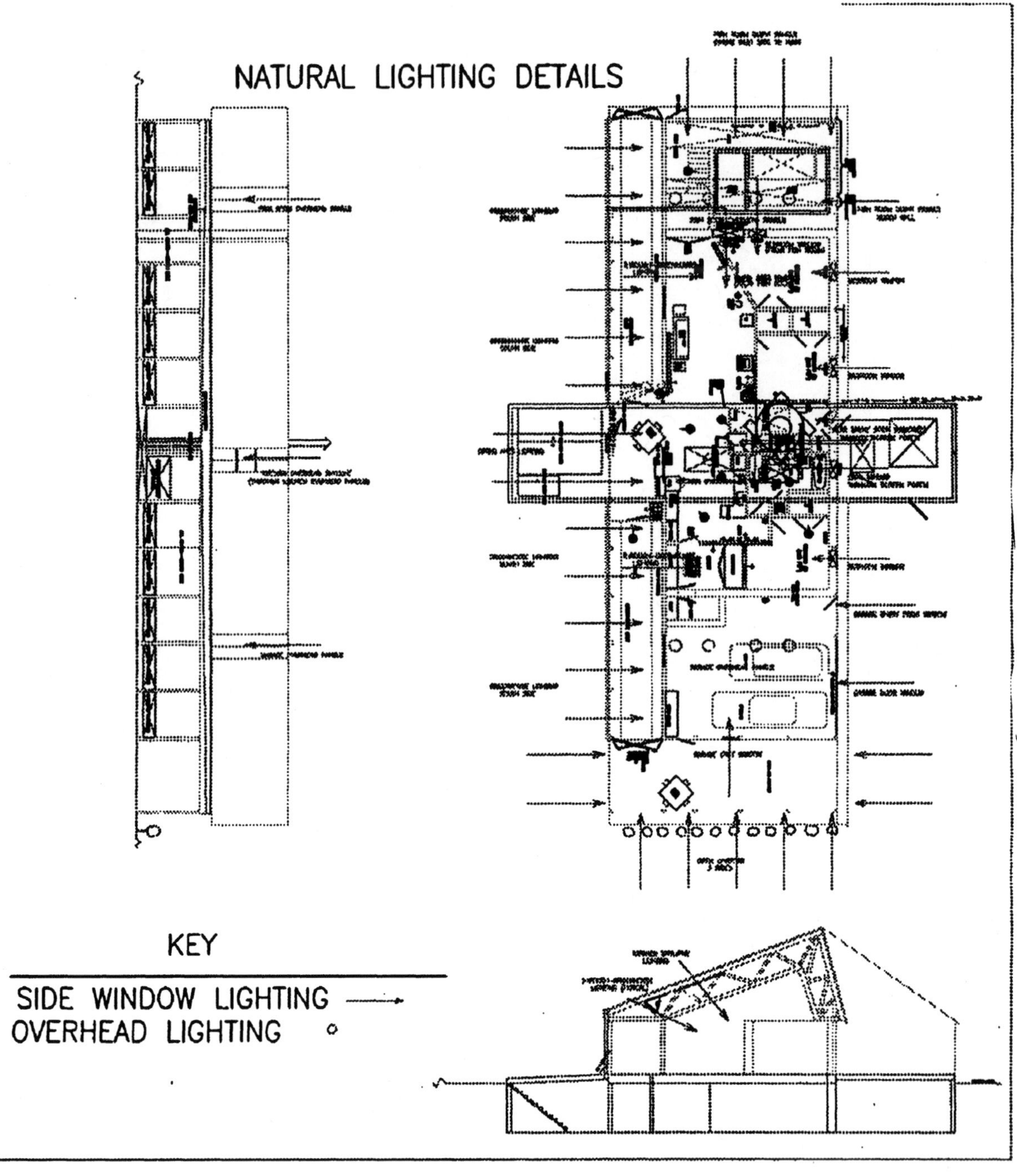

Figure 210-CAD DRAWING PAGE 12 OF 13

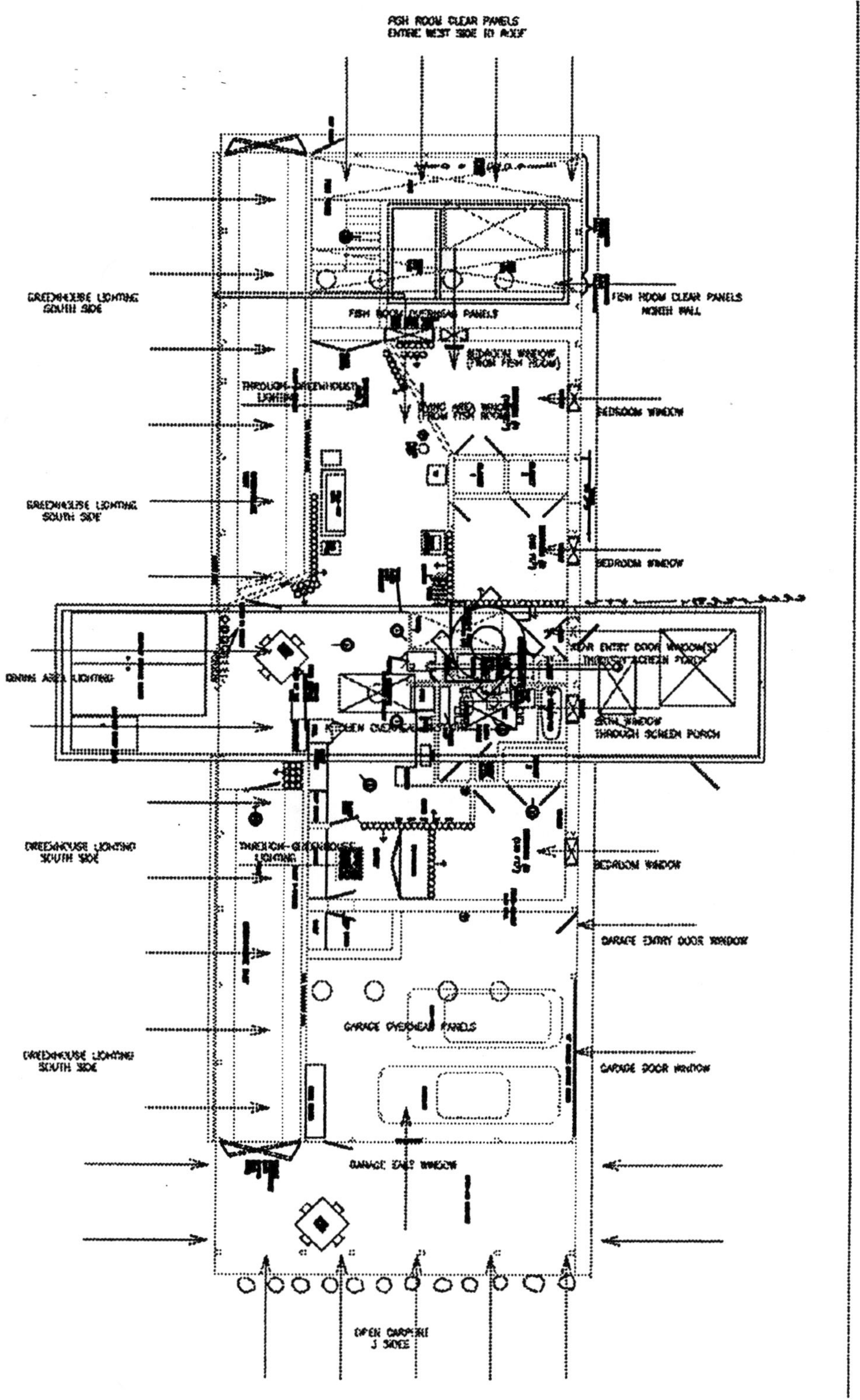

Figure 211-CAD DRAWING PAGE 13 OF 13

Figure 212-IMAGE SE LOOKING NW

Figure 213-IMAGE SE LOOKING WNW

*Used in Earth Home

Figure 214-IMAGE S LOOKING N

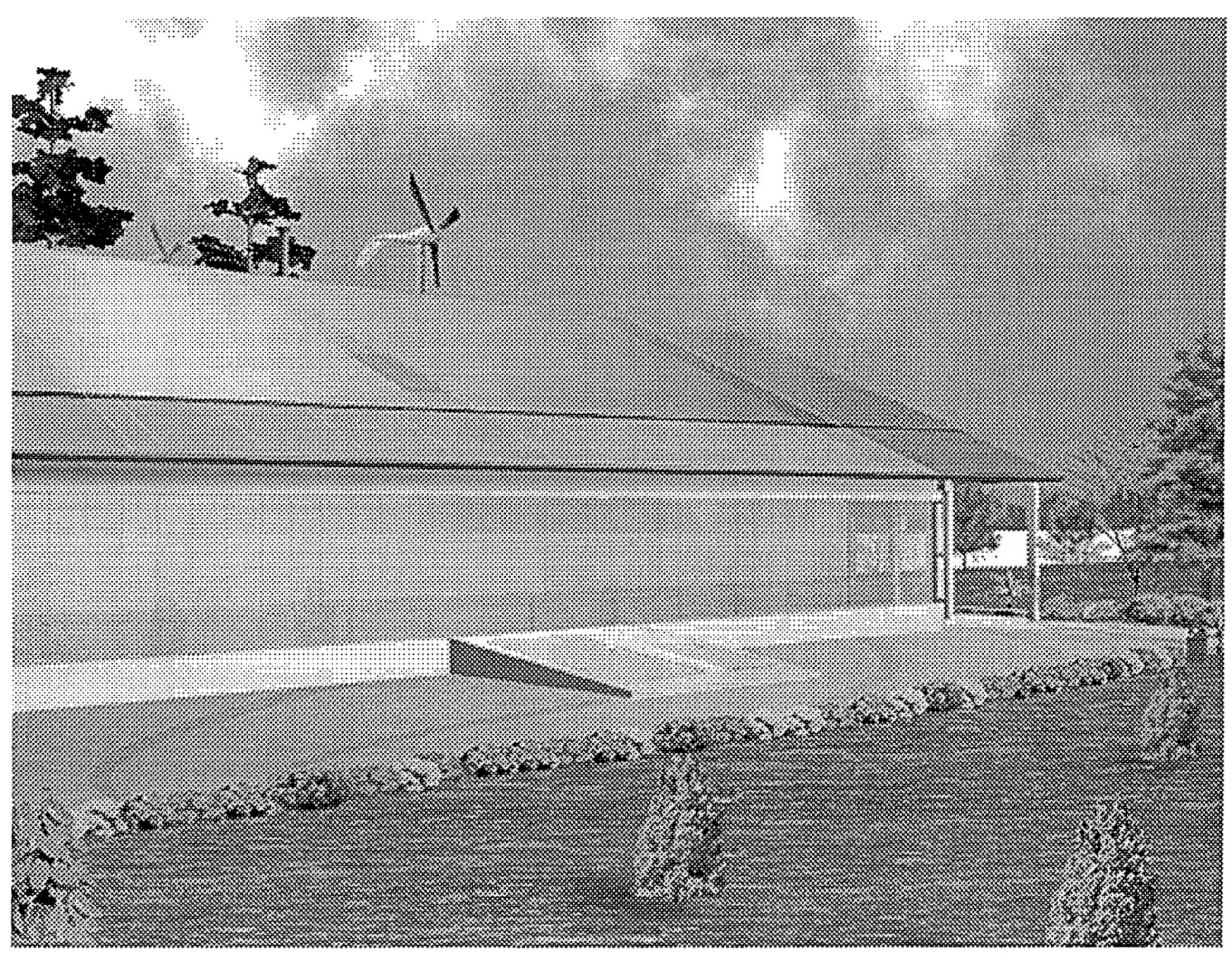

Figure 215-IMAGE SW LOOKING NE

*Used in Earth Home

Figure 216-IMAGE NW LOOKING SE

Figure 217-IMAGE NE LOOKING SW

*Used in Earth Home

Figure 218-IMAGE NE LOOKING SW

D. List of Sources for Products

__There are many appliances that operate on 12 volts DC__. They are available from many sources. Over the many years of this project, I have seen significant increases in the number of items that use either a battery source or a 12-volt DC source for power. Some of the best-known sources are:

1. New England Solar- 1-800-914-4131
2. Real Goods Trading Company - 1-800-762-7325
3. Alternative Engineering - 800-777-6609
4. Giam/Jade Mountain - 800-442-1972
5. Photocomm – 602-948-8003
6. Marine Supply – (any store)
7. Sierra Solar Systems – 888-667-6527
8. Hamilton Ferris Co. - 508-881-4602
9. Kansas Wind Power – 785-364-4407
10. Sunelco - 800-338-6844
11. Lehman's --- 330-857-5757
12. Direct from Manufacturers/Distributors
13. Online Solar, Inc. 877-226-5073
14. Northern Arizona Wind and Sun 800-383-0195

Many of the above have websites and catalogs online. Manufacturers sometimes sell directly to the public. In most cases, companies have local distributors that stock their products and may have an exclusive territory. If an intended user is an OEM (Original Equipment Manufacturer), the manufacturer will often sell the product (component) directly to them before the product (finished or assembled) is finally sold to the public.

E. Food Production Data

1. Prototype Diet per Person

__I have drawn elements from the diets of many cultures for the diet that I am designing for the Earth Home system__. This list shows an early model of the diet for the Earth Home System. I have since added maple syrup to the diet because maple trees or other trees producing a sweet sap are available world wide (with few limitations). Vinegar can also be made from maple sap. It's interesting to note that strawberries are included in the NASA CELSS diet because of the taste variation they provide.

4 pounds per week bread, pasta, crouton combination – carbohydrates
Vegetable, fruit, sprout, herb combinations -- much and varied
1/4 pound chicken, duck, or quail meat per week (8 fowl)
1/2 egg per day (from fowl)
1/4 pound fish per week (50 catfish)
1/2 teaspoon salt per day (purchased)
1/4 pound piglet/chevrotain meat per week
1 pound additional meat per week (see Animal files)
Rose hips, honey, garlic, vinegar, spices as needed
Preserved/dehydrated foods

PROTOTYPE EARTH HOME DIET—PER PERSON

*This diet has elements of Mediterranean and Far Eastern diets.
Note: The first Biosphere II produced 270 pounds of human food per week and 60 pounds of fodder for the animals.

*Used in Earth Home

2. Total Yield Data

Barley .2 acres yields 500 lb. (8712 square feet)
1 acre= 43,560 square feet
210 ft. X 210 ft. = 44,100 square feet.

Grains—1.095 pounds
Legumes—80 pounds
Eggs, dairy substitutes--50 pounds
Meat, Meat substitutes--20 pounds
Dry fruits, vegetables--30 pounds
Vegetable oil produced--40 pounds
Sprouting seeds--50 pounds
Yeasts—dry yeast, baking powder, baking soda—1 pound
Miscellaneous.—Spices, salt—5 pounds

Outside Perennials	**Number of Plants**	**Yield**	**Preservation method**
Rose hips	15	8 lb. hips	dried
Grapes	15	10 lb.	Dry as raisins
Alfalfa			Seeds in Bin
Maple Syrup	30 trees	20 qts./yr.	Keep in root cellar
White willow	1-2	Aspirin when needed	
Northern White Cedar	2-3	Spruce tea-vitamin C	Keep cool
Asparagus		6-10 week harvest	(plants last 20-30 years)

Figure 219-TOTAL YIELD DATA, PAGE 1

*Used in Earth Home

Cultivar	Sq. Ft. Planted	Yield	Preservation Method
Carrots			In Moss or Cold Storage
Cabbage	50 square feet	100 lb.	(Lasts 6 months) Cold storage/Sauerkraut
Wheat			Dried Seeds in Bin
Onions			Root Cellar
Beans	50 square feet		Cool/dry storage
Broccoli			
Parsley			Low light ok
Spinach	50 sq. ft. bottom shelf		Cut row to 1"-grow back
Lettuce	50 square feet	8 lb.	(winter density var.)
Winter Squash	Intercropped		Hung in Root Cellar
Soybeans	200 square feet	30 lb.	Dried Seeds in Bin
Rapeseed			Dried Seeds in Bin
Jerusalem Artichoke			Left in ground -Dig as needed

Animal/Fish/Fowl	Number of Each	Yield	Notes
Catfish	50 adults plus spawn		Feed vegetable. croutons
Bees	2-3 hives	60 lb/yr.	Give boiled sugar beets in winter
Quail		Eggs/flesh	Entrails/insects
Small Mammals			

Figure 220-TOTAL YIELD DATA CHART, PAGE 2

*Used in Earth Home

*Used in Earth Home

XIV. YELLOW PAGES BIBLIOGRAPHY

A. Yellow Pages Bibliography Information

1. Condensed List

The following is a condensed list of research information obtained from March 3, 1975 to the present. It is arranged categorically as much as possible.

2. No Endorsement

The manufacturers, books, product information, and articles are for reader interest only, and are not an endorsement. Where applicable, a product is identified that is used in current Earth Home design.

3. Consult Thomas Registers

Where a manufacturer is listed by name only and no address is given-the company has moved, changed name, or is no longer in business. Consult current Thomas Registers in your local library to find addresses or more information.

4. Emphasis

The emphasis in these file summaries is on 12 volt DC operation, small size, lightweight, efficient operation, and earth friendliness.

5. Terms Explanation

For an explanation to understand any of the terms, please consult the McGraw-Hill Dictionary of Scientific and Technical terms by Sybil P. Parker.

6. Overview of Project

The entire research project was mostly conducted with a sense of urgency with emphasis on constructing and testing rather than accurate documentation. It was only in the later years of this project where a full printed account of the research was determined to be beneficial. In many cases an article was saved without the periodical title or a paragraph from a book copied without the title/author page. Any omissions were purely accidental.

7. Bibliography Notes

The author wishes to acknowledge and thank all of the following organizations and authors who contributed to the information contained in this text. ***The yellow pages bibliography includes the bibliography***.

8. Index/Directory (See Table of Contents also)

Table of Contents to this section can befound in front of book also.

9. Website Notes

Appropriate websites are included in the section most related to the content.

10. Explanation of "*Used in Earth Home"

An asterisk in front of a listing means that the product is currently included in the materials list for the present design.

B. Index to Yellow Pages Bibliography

*Used in Earth Home

*Used in Earth Home

*Used in Earth Home

Actuators

New Scale Technologies, Inc.
10 East Main Street, Suite 301
Victor, NY 14564
Phone: (585) 924-4450
Fax: (585) 924-4468
sales@NewScaleTech.com
Squiggle linear motion piezoactuator

Eastern Air Devices
Dover, NH 03820
(603) 742-3330
all kinds

B.E.I. Motion Systems Co.
Kimco Magnetics
150 Vallecitos de Oro
San Marcos, CA 92069
all kinds

Warner Electric
Brake & Clutch Co.
449 Gardner Street
S. Beloit, IL 61080
Mini Actuators (linear)E050 low cost

Airpax/North American Philips Controls Corp.
Cheshire Industrial Park
Cheshire, CT 06410
tiny actuators

Burr Engineering and Development Co.
730 E. Michigan Avenue
P.O. Box 460
Battle Creek, MI 49016
(616) 965-2371
ball screw actuators

Saginaw Steering Gear Division
General Motors Corporation
Actuator Products Group
Saginaw, MI 48605
(517) 776-4123
12 VDC actuators

Adhesives-Caulk-Chemicals-Paint-Tape

Adhesives are substances that ensure a long-lasting bonding between various elements. Romans, for instance, used beeswax combined with pine wood tar as a waterproof adhesive for their ships. Glue can also be made from wheat flour.

Fox Industries, Inc.
3100 Falls Cliff Road
Baltimore, MD 21211
888.760.0369
410.243.8856
FAX 410.243.2701
Polyrea coatings

Epoxy Systems
352-489-1666 (Main Office - Info & Orders)
321-206-1833 (Orlando - Info & Orders)
352-465-3497 (Fax)
info@epoxy.com
Polyurea coatings

Sterling Supply Inc.
459 Harding St. N.E.
Minneapolis, MN 55413
612-331-5125
Casting resins/prototyping

Kindt-Collins Col
12651 Elmwood Avenue
Cleveland, OH 44111
(216) 252-4122
polyester casting compound

W.R. Grace and Co.
Organic Chemicals Div.
Lexington, Mass. 02173
(617) 861-6600
(add water to make foam)
FHP 2000 HP
FHP 3000 HP

Fiberglast Developments Corp.
1944 Neva Drive
Dayton, OH 45414-5598
(800) 821-3283
all casting products

Miller-Stephenson Chemical Co.
6348 Oakton Street
Morton Grove, IL 60053
(708) 966-2022
Tech. Serv. (800) 992-2424
epoxy - many kinds

3M Industrial Specialties Div.
3M Center Building, 220-7E-01
St. Paul, MN 55144
(612) 733-3300
bonding tapes, foam tapes

Industrial Tape & Supply
1061 King Industrial Drive
Marietta, GA 30062
(404) 422-1660
(800) 323-8273
many tapes

Solar Research
P.O. Box 869
Brighton, MI 48116
(313) 227-1151
TEDLAR, weather resistant tape

3M Contractor Products
Building 223-4N-06
3M Center
St. Paul, MN 55144-1000
sealing tapes

Jones Webbing and Tape Co. Inc.
170 Cherry Valley Avenue
West Hempstead, NY 11552
(516) 538-8668
narrow fabrics

Tape-Craft
Div. of NFA Corp.
17 South Hunter Street
Anniston, AL 36202
(205) 236-2535
webbing

American Cord and Webbing Co. Inc.

*Used in Earth Home

505 Eighth Avenue
New York, NY 10018
(212) 695-7340
cord, webbing

Indiana Mills and Mfg., Inc.
120 W. Main Street
Carmel, IN 46032
(317) 846-6631
straps, tie-downs

American Manufacturing Co.
206 Willow Avenue
Honesdale, PA 18431
(717) 253-5860
strapping

Northwest Fibr-Glass Supply, Inc.
3055 Columbia Avenue N.E.
Minneapolis, MN 55418
(612) 781-3494
(800) 544-1388
fiberglass and resins

Indeco Packaging Division
P.O. Box 1047
2410 Barnes Drive
San Marcos, TX 78667-1047
(512) 396-5814
polyester strapping

Horton Sales
Minneapolis, MN
strapping

Cyclop Strapping Corporation
Boot Road
Downington, PA 19335
(215) 873-0290
strapping

McMaster-Carr Supply
Chicago, IL
many adhesives

Camie-Campbell, Inc.
9225 Watson Industrial Park
St. Louis, MO 63126
(800) 325-9572
(314) 968-3222
spray lubricants and cleaners

Hardman, Inc.
600 Cortlandt Street
Belleville, NJ 07109
(201) 751-3000
epoxies

Cord Corp./Chemical Products Group
2000 West Grandview Boulevard
P.O. Box 10038
Erie, PA 16514
(814) 868-3611
structural adhesives

Bostik
Middleton, MA 01949
(617) 777-0100
adhesives

Cotronics Corp.
3379 Shore Parkway
Brooklyn, NY 11235
(718) 646-7996
hi-temp epoxy

H. B. Fuller Co.
Assembly Products Div.
5220 Main Street N.E.
Minneapolis, MN 55421
adhesives

Epoxy Technology, Inc.
14 Fortune Drive
P.O. Box 567
Billerica, MA 01821
(508) 667-3805
thermally conductive epoxy

Fulton Metallurgical Products Corp.
Box 188A
Saxonberg, PA 16056
self-cure acrylic plastic

Emerson & Cuming, Inc.
77 Dragon Court
Woburn, MA 01888
(617) 938-8630
conductive epoxy

Mameco
4475 East 17tth Street
Cleveland, OH 44128
(216) 752-4400
Distributed by:
Edwards Sales
6530 Cambridge Street
Minneapolis, MN 55426
(612) 929-6794
Vulkem polyurethane caulk

3M
Adhesives, Coatings & Sealers Div.
223-1N 3M Center
St. Paul, MN 55144-1000
plastic adhesive

The Kendall Co.
One Federal Street
Boston, MA 02101
(800) 225-2600
tapes

Flormel Adhesive Products, Inc.
214-26 - 41st Avenue
P.O. Box 608
Bayside, NY 11361
(212) 428-3755
tapes

Tapemark Co.
150 East Marie Avenue
West St. Paul, MN 55118
(612) 455-1611
(800) 328-0135
tapes

Chiswick Trading, Inc.
31 Union Avenue
Sudbury, MA 01776-0907
(800) 225-8708
polyethylene tape and plastic poly bags

National Coil Coaters Association
401 N. Michigan Avenue
Chicago, IL 60611-4267
(312) 644-6610
booklet "Joining Prepainted Metal with Adhesives"

Hexcel

*Used in Earth Home

Resins Group
P.O. Box 2197
20701 Nordhoff Street
Chatsworth, CA 91311
(818) 882-3022
epoxy resin systems

AFM Enterprises, Inc.
350 W. Ash Street, #700
San Diego, CA 92101
(619) 239-0321
non-toxic paints

Auro-Sinan Company - Natural Paints
P.O. Box 857
Davis, CA 95617
(916) 753-3104
non-toxic paints

Bio-Building
P.O. Box 1561, Bio-Building
Sebastopol, CA 95473
(707) 823-2569
non-toxic paints

Eco-Design, Inc.
1365 Rufina Circle
Santa Fe, NM 87501
(505) 438-3448
non-toxic paints

Weather-Bos Stains and Paint
13807 S.E. McLoughlin, #421
Milwaukie, OR 97222
(503) 786-7991
non-toxic paints

Kenyon Consumer Products
Peace Dale, RI 02883
water-based urethane

Pace Chemical Industries
779 S. LaGrange Avenue
Newbury Park, CA 91320
(805) 499-2911

Polyken Technologies
690 Canton Street
Westwood, MA 02090
(617) 320-1000
adhesive tape, aluminum foil

Pace Chemical Industries
3681 Sagunto Street, #104
P.O. Box 1946
Santa Ynez, CA 93460
(805) 686-0745
water-based acrylics

Glidden Insul-Aid
(216) 344-8000
low-perm primer

Sika Corporation
Suite A
2190 Gladstone Court
Glendale Heights, IL 60139
polyurethane caulk, sealants

Adobe/Rammed Earth

Foxfire Associates
PO Box 2153
Middleburg, VA 20117
540-687-4211
TerraBuilt adobe brick machine

Air

-Blowers

Ametek Rotron
Lamb Electric Division
627 Lake Street
Kent, OH 44240
(330) 673-3452
blowers--also mini blowers

Chicago Blower
1675 Glen Ellyn Road
Glendale Heights, IL 60139
(312) 858-2600
also fans

Brailsford & Co., Inc.
Milton Road
Rye, NY 10580
(914) 967-1820
miniature brushless blowers and air pumps

Lamson Corp.
Centrifugal Air Systems Division
P.O. Box 4857
Syracuse, NY 13221
(315) 432-5500
blowers

Sea Eagle
bellows pumps, cylindrical hand pumps

Dow Co. Products
P.O. Box 20522
Seattle, WA 98102
(206) 328-5521
12 VDC inflating pump

Paxton Centrifugal Blowers
Dept. D1
929 Olympic Blvd.
Santa Monica, CA 90404
(213) 394-2751
blowers

Thorgren Tool and Molding Co., Inc.
1100 Evans Avenue
Val Paraiso, IN 46383
blower wheels, fan blades

Tel Air Inc.
One Tec Air Drive
Willow Springs, IL 60480
(312) 839-1400
blower wheels and housings

Molded Products Co., Inc.
2820 North Sylvania
P.O. Box 7653
Fort Worth, TX 76111
(817) 838-6751
auto blowers

Fuji Electric Co.
Frassetto Industrial Park
6A Fassetto Way
Lincoln Park, NJ 07035
(201) 633-9000
ring compressors

E B M Industries
110 Hyde Road
P.O. Box 4009
Farmington, CT 06034-4009

*Used in Earth Home

(203) 674-1515
efficient blowers

Kaeser Compression Inc.
P.O. Box 946
Fredericksburg, VA 22404
(703) 898-5500
rotary blowers
Attwood Corporation
P.O. Box 230
Lowell, MI 49331
(616) 897-8358
bilge blowers

Air -Compressors

Sensydyne OEM Division
16333 Bay Vista Drive
Clearwater, Fl. 33760
800-451-9444
micro air pumps

Interflator
Culver City, CA
(213) 641-1240
* good, heavy duty compressor

Exter Engineering Inc.
4828 Howins Ferry Road
Baltimore, MD 21227
compressor

Coleman
Wichita, KS 67201
(316) 261-3200
uses Mabuchi motor, intermittent duty

Interdynamics
Edmund Scientific
101 East Gloucester Pike
Barrington, NJ 08007
compressor

Gast Mfg. Corp.
P.O. Box 97
Benton Harbor, MI 49022
(616) 926-6171
industrial ultra heavy duty (22 amps)
micro-diaphram 12 VDC

Bowjon
2829 Burton Avenue
Burbank, CA 91504
(213) 826-2620
wind-powered air pumping

LTD Commodities, Inc.
7300 McCormick Blvd.
Skokie, IL 60076
(312) 679-7240
compressor

Miracle Products, Inc.
From McMaster-Carr
Terryville, CT 06786
(203) 589-5758
uses electic drill for power (1800 RPM minimum)

Thomas
Power Air Division
1419 Illinois Avenue
Sheboygan, WI 53082-0029
(414) 457-4891
7.2 amps, all kinds vacuum pumps and
air compressors, industrial quality

K.J. Miller Corp.
2401 Gardner Road
Broadview, IL 60153
12-14 amps for pressurized water systems

Medo U.S.A. Inc.
808-C North Central Avenue
Wooddale, IL 60191
(312) 860-0500
linear motion industrial compressor,
many kinds
small air compressor

Vortec Corp.
use air pressure to make vacuum

Barnant Co.
28W092 Commercial Avenue
Barrington, IL 60010
(312) 381-7050
(800) 637-3739
air compressor/vacuum pump

True Value Hardware
Edmund Scientific
retail air compressors

"Whistler Air Command"
Distributed by:
Energy Answers
P.O. Box 24
Lake Bluff, IL 60044
(708) 234-2515, (800) 776-6761
air compressor and more

Microphor, Inc.
P.O. Box 490
Willits, CA 95490
(800) 358-8280
(707) 459-5563
"wobble" design with tank

KNF Neuberger, Inc.
Box 4060
Princeton, NJ
(609) 799-4350
micro diaphram pump

Gilian Inst. Corp.
8 Daws Highway
Wayne, NJ 07470
(201) 831-0440
micro air pumps

Smart Products, Inc.
111 East Brokaw Road
San Jose, CA 95112
(408) 436-0740
small diaphram air pumps - elec.

Aquaculture Research/Environmental Assoc.
P.O. Box 1303
1088 West Mowry Street
Homestead, FL 33090
fish tank aeration equipment

E.P. Industries
414 W. Walnut Street
El Segundo, CA 90245
(310) 322-1462
new efficient compressor

*Used in Earth Home

ASF Inc.
2100 Norcross Parkway, #120
Norcross, GA 30071
(404) 441-3611
miniature pumps

Air
-Cylinders

Clippard Inst. Lab
7390 Cole Rain Road
Cincinnati, OH 45239
(513) 521-4261
all kinds

Air & Hydraulic Power, Inc.
Box 159
555 Goffle Road
Wyckoff, NJ 07481-0159
(201) 447-1589
short stroke air cylinders

Mosier Ind. Inc.
325 Carr Drive
P.O. Box 189
Brookville, OH 45309
(513) 833-4033
rodless (enclosed)

Festo Corp.
395 Moreland Road
Hauppauge, NY 11788
(516) 435-0800
miniature non-rotating air cylinders

Kuhnke Inc.
1 East Highland Avenue
Atlantic Highlands, NJ 07716
(201) 291-3334
micro miniature cylinders

Fabro-Air Inc.
3716 NE 49th Road
Gainesville, FL 32609-1699
(904) 373-3578
gripping and other styles

Miller Fluid Power
7N015 York Road
Bensenville, IL 60106
(312) 766-3400
all styles

Bellofram Corporation
Blanchard Road
Burlington, Mass. 01803
(617) 272-2100
diaphram air cylinders

Firestone Ind. Prod. Co.
1700 Firestone Boulevard
Noblesville, IN 46060
(317) 773-0650
air stroke actuators (similar to small tires)

Air
-Fans

Fan-Tastic Vent Corp.
2083 S. Almont Ave.
Imlay City, MI 48444
(800) 521-0298
(810) 724-3818
www.fantasticvent.com
"Endless Breeze" fan

Ebm-Papst Inc.
Compact fans with Winglets
Low power and quieter.
www.ebmpapst.us

Sunon, Inc. 1075-A West Lambert road
Brea, CA 92821
www.sunon.com
no-wobble small fans

Revcor
Box 37169
Haltom City, TX 76117
www.revcor.com
8-16 inch fans

The HVLS Fan Co.
P.O. box 11307
Lexington, Ky. 40575
606-254-9921
High volume low speed ceiling fans

Pabst Mechatronic Corp.
Aquidneck Industrial Park
Newport, RI 02840
(401) 849-8810
brushless DC fans

Cincinnati Fan and Ventilator Co.
5345 Creek Road
Cincinnati, OH 45242
(513) 984-0600
fans and blowers

Airmaster Fan Co.
150 West North Street
Jackson, MI 49202
larger fans

Strobic Air Corp.
213 Bunting Avenue
Trenton, NJ 08611
(609) 396-8219
spot coolers

Buffalo Forge Co.
Buffalo, NY 14240
(716) 847-5121
larger fans and blowers

Reed Unit Fans inc.
P.O. Box 19466
New Orleans, LA 70119
larger exhaust fans

Aerovent Fan and Equipment Co.
P.O. Box 5067
Lansing, MI 48905
larger exhaust fans

Panasonic Industrial Co.
425 East Algonguin Road
Arlington Heights, IL 60005
(312) 981-4823
motors and DC brushless axial fans

Nidec-Torin
100 Franklin Drive
Torrington, CT 06790
(203) 482-4422
mid-size cabinet fans

*Used in Earth Home

ICX Fan Corp.
522 East Lambert Road
Brea, CA 92621
(714) 529-0868
cabinet fans

Canon USA Inc.
Electronic Components Divison
One Canon Plaza
Lake Success, NY 11042
(516) 488-6700
miniature fans

EG & G Rotron
Commercial Cooling Products Group
Shokan, NY 12481
(914) 657-6661
DC fans (muffin)

DC Densitron Corp.
Electro Magnetic Divison
P.O. Box 1318
Camden, SC 29020
(803) 432-5008
pancake fans (muffin)

Micronel
2142F Industrial Court
Vista, CA 92083
(619) 727-7400
miniature fans/motors and high pressure

Rocky Creek Hydro
2173 Rocky Creek Road
Colville, WA 99114
ceiling fans 12 VDC

Real Goods Trading Co.
12 VDC muffin fans, intake/exhaust fans

Thorgren Tool and Molding Co. Inc.
1100 Evans Avenue
Val Paraiso, IN 46383
(219) 432-1801
fan blades, blower blades

Air Turbine Propeller Co.
P.O. Box 218
Zelienople, PA 16063
propellers

H.A. Holden
1208 Harmon Place
Minneapolis, MN 55403
(800) 328-4662
fan blade replacement

Tec Air Inc.
8075 West Lake Street
Willow Springs, IL 60480
(312) 839-1400
blower wheels

Photocomm
930 Idaho Maryland Road
Grass Valley, CA 95945
distributor - ceiling fans and centrifugal

Air Drive
510 North First Street
Libertyville, IL 60048
(312) 367-0226
fan blades

Viron International
505 Hintz Road
Owosso, MI 48867-9603
(517) 723-8255
fans - all kinds

McMaster-Carr Supply
#2002K11
Venturi - blower/exhauster

Applied Energy Technology
P.O. Box 243
Highway 965 S
Cedar Rapids, IA 52410
solar attic fan

Kanalflakt Inc.
1712 Northgate Boulevard
Sarasota, FL 34234
(813) 359-3267
* quiet duct fans

Tech Development Inc.
6800 Poe Avenue
P.O. Box 1400-0
Dayton, OH 45414
(513) 898-9600
turbine air motors

Sutton Mfg. Co.
112 West Wilson Avenue
Norfolk, VA 23510
(804) 622-6313
8-inch blade, 12V 2.2 amps, 800 CFM

Panaflo (Panasolic)
Div. Matsushita Electric Corp. of America
Two Panasonic Way Panazip 7E-4
Secaucus, NJ 07094
(201) 392-4923
* efficient cabinet fan - "hydrowave" bearing

(800) 527-5247
#1230 tiny blower bellows

The Sharper Image
P.O. Box 7031
San Francisco, CA 94120-7031
"Vornado" aerodynamic fan

De Sta Co.
P.O. Box 2800
250 Park Street
Troy, MI 48007-2800
custom blower housings

Wm. W. Meyer & Sons, Inc.
8261 Elmwood Avenue
Skokie, IL 60077
(312) 463-5127
hand-cranked ventilation blower

Eastern Air Devices, Inc.
1 Progress Drive
Dover, NH 03820
(603) 742-3330
12 VDC blowers, 2" water 720 CFM

Air

-Misc.-Tools

Dwyer Instruments
Highway 212 at 12
P.O. Box 373
Michigan City, IN 46360

*Used in Earth Home

(219) 872-9141
low air pressure gauges, controls

Lee Co.
2 Pettipaug Road
Westbrook, CT 06498
(203) 399-6281
micro-miniature air solenoid valves

Airpot Corp.
27 Lois Street
Norwalk, CT 06851
(203) 846-2021
air pressure dashpots

Piab U.S.A., Inc.
65 Sharp Street
Hingham, MA 02043
(617) 337-6250
porous air mufflers

Caframo, Ltd.
P.O. Box 70
Wiarton, Ontario N0H 2T0
CANADA
(519) 534-1080
quiet, battery-operated fans

Air Logic Division
Fred Knapp Engraving Co.
5102 Douglas Avenue
Racine, WI 53402
miniature pressure regulators switches, fittings

Branford Vibrator Co.
Division of Electro Mechanics Inc.
P.O. Box 427
New Britain, CT 06051
air-driven vibrators

Martin Eng. Co.
U.S. Route 34
Neponset, IL 61345
air-driven vibrators

Haskell Inc.
100 East Graham Place
Burbank, CA 91502
(818) 843-4000
air-driven pumps, etc.

Gast
P.O. Box 97
Benton Harbor, MI 49022
(616) 926-6171
air - motors

Pneumatic Motor Mfg. Co.
P.O. Box 23386
Minneapolis, MN 55423
(612) 866-9302
air - motors

Micro Motors, Inc.
151 East Columbine Avenue
Santa Ana, CA 92707
(714) 546-4045
miniature air motors - air drills

Tachyon Corp
7232 Boone Avenue North
Minneapolis, MN 55428
(612) 533-2465
air motors

Tech Development Inc.
6800 Poe Avenue
P.O. Box 1400-0
Dayton, OH 45414
(513) 898-9600
air devices

Starion Products Corp.
Route 22
Robin Hill Ind. Park
Patterson, NY 12563
(914) 878-4411
air presses, rotary index tables

Navco
6880 Wynnwood Lane
Houston, TX 77008-5079
(713) 864-6303
air-driven vibrators

Monnier, Inc.
2034 Fruit Street
P.O. Box 409
Algonac, MI 48001
air filters, regulators, lubricators

Bellofram
St. Rt. 2
Newell, WV 26050
(304) 387-1200
air (pressure) regulator

Teledyne Sprague Eng.
19300 South Germart Avenue
P.O. Box 630
Gardena, CA 90247-0863
(213) 327-1610
air-powered booster pumps

Coventry Specialty Corp.
4 Ascutney Avenue
Westfield, MA 01085
small air-operated elec. switch

Angar Scientific Co.
52 Horsehill Road
Cedar Knolls, NJ 07927-2098
12 VDC subminiature air solenoid valves

Cob Industries Inc.
P.O. Box 870
Larchmont, NY 10538
(914) 834-9110
Spitznas air tools (chain saws, circular saws, etc.)

Sioux Tools Inc.
2901 Floyd Boulevard
Sioux City, IA 51102
air tools

Nitto Kohki Inc., U.S.A.
P.O. Box 129
Wooddale, IL 60191
(312) 860-9595
air tools

Cob Industries
Pneumatics Division
P.O. Box 361175
Melbourne, FL 32936-1175
(407) 723-3200
air-powered chain saw, drills, etc.

*Used in Earth Home

Alcohol (See Vinegar also)
-General

BioFuels
http://www.reap-canada.com/library.htm
biofuels website

Bread and BeerThe Early Use of Cereals in the Human Diet
Solomon Katz, Mary Voigt
Article on beer importance

Symposium: Did man once live by beer alone?
Am. Anthropol 1953 55 page 515-526

Wheat makes 2.7 gallons of alcohol per bushel, and corn makes 2.6 gallons per bushel

Sugars are easiest to convert to alcohol—followed
By starches and then cellulose
Enzymes are not required with sugars because
There are no starches to be broken down

How to Make Your Own Alcohol Fuels
Larry W. Carley
Book on do-it-yourself stills, etc.

Brazil's National Alcohol Program
F. Joseph Demetrius
Book on alcohol in Brazil

The Dept. of Energy's National Alternative fuels Hotline
800-423-1363
www.afdc.doe.gov

Bruce Jones
Mankato University
Alcohol expert
507-389-6700

Ethanol

"Solar Alcohol"
by Michael Wells Mandeville
book

20,000 U.S. Farmers Now Use On-farm Stills
excerpt

60% of Brazil's Vehicles Run on Alcohol
excerpt

Integrated Biofuels, Inc.
306 Foshay Tower
Minneapolis, MN 55402
alcohol consultants

Moonshining As A Fine Art (Excerpt)
book

MN Ethanol Commission
90 W. Plato Boulevard
St. Paul, MN 55107
(612) 297-2301
list of where to buy ethanol-blend fuel

No low-cost, small-scale, technology
for alcohol exists
Ethanol discussions -- information

All systems are labor intensive--need to watch temperature, time, pump, filtration, etc.

Alcohol in Cars "Cleans" Up Carburetor
. . . Particles Jam Existing Filter

"Moonshining" Is producing alcohol
information

Polyvinyl Alcohol (water-soluble alcohol)
article (see Toilet files)

Permaculture Two
Bill Mollison
Alcohol chapter

Continuous Ethanol Production from Jerusalem Artichoke Stalks Using Immobilized Cells of Kluyveromyces Marxianus
article

The Art of Home Brewing - Charlie Papizan
Book

Alcohol
-Yeast/Enzymes

Taka-Therm®
Diazyme® L-100
microbial enzymes

Need microbial enzymes for efficient
alcohol production in quantity such
as Taka-Therm® or Diazyme®

Allcoholase II
Alltech, Inc.
271 Gold Rush Road
Lexington, KY 40503
(606) 276-5331
enzyme

Yeast Culturing for the Homebrewer
Rog Leistad
Book on yeasts for making alcohol

Yeast Bank
Country Wines
Pittsburgh, PA
Store yeast in freezer product

Biological Principles in Fermentation
By J.C. Carr
Book on enzymes, etc.

Zymurgy magazine
Articles on yeast culture, etc.

Alkaline

Acid and Alkaline
Herman Aihara
Book on acid/alkaline forces at work in your body and diet

Alternative Energy
-Publications

http://www.daviddarling.info/encyclopedia/R/AE_renewable_energy.html
good "dictionary" for term/concept explanation

Green Building Resource Guide
John Hermannsson

*Used in Earth Home

Book on sources of renewable products etc.

Alternative Energy
-Suppliers/Retailers

bp solar
www.thesolar.biz
solar products
1-888-826-0939

Your Energy Company Inc.
1914 - 44 Avenue SW
Calgary, Alberta T2T 2N6 Canada
http://www.yourenergycompany.net

www.sustdev.org
sustainable development website

Big Frog Mountain
www.bigfrogmountain.com
solar, wind products

Animals

Note: Animals Chart is located in Food Production Section

Jay-Dee Industries
Dassel, MN 55325
automated laying houses

Dawn Electronics
1004 Mallory Way
Carson City, Nevada 89701
702-882-7721
Subminiature temperature-
Controlled heaters

Modern Meat
Orville Schell
book

Water Requirements

Sheep	-	2 gallons/day
Chickens	-	.1 gallon/day
Turkeys/Ducks	-	.25 gallon/day
Pigs	-	2-4 gallons/day

FEED CONVERSION TABLE

Livestock	33% to tissue (½ used by humans)
Laying hens	30%
Piglets	100% (up to 3 weeks) 72% (6 weeks)
Fish (38 week silver salmon)	52%
Young rainbow trout	100%

Feeds and nutrition
M.E. Ensminger and
C.G. Olentine

Source: Feed Efficiency Table

Raising Worms Commercially article

Efficiency of Feed Conversion article
T.C. Byerey

Animal excrement per 1,000 # live wt. chart

Chow Chow (dog from China) article

Kenaf leaves may contain up to 30% article on foodstuffs
protein (hibiscus cannabinus)

Appliances
-Automotive

www.HEBASTO.US
heated windshield wiper fluid to 150 deg. F

American Airlines
12V seat cover

Sears
spark plug cleaner, compressors, horns,
hot air rear window defroster, car vacuum

Penney's
12V emergency lights, coffee maker, air compressor,
auto vacuum

Veritechnology Electronics Corp.
P.O. Box 167
St. Joseph, MI 49085
G-force meter, engine analyzer

Coast-to-Coast - Douglas
car vacuum

J. C. Whitney
car vacuums

Oreck Corp.
100 Plantation Road
New Orleans, LA 70123
rechargeable flashlights, vacuum cleaner

J. C. Whitney
windshield washer fluid heater

Ambassador
car vacuum and oil changer

Handyman Jack Co.
manual jack

Appliances
-Bathroom/BR

LaBelle's, Wal-Mart
cordless razors

Prime Products
Paramount, CA 90723
hair dryer

Patented Products Co.
513 Market Street
P.O. Box A
Danville, OH 43014
(614) 599-6842
12 VDC bed warmer

Appliances
-Business

Syntest Corp.
40 Locke Drive
Marlboro, MA 01752
(617) 481-7827
12V thermal printer

Unavailable manufacturer
cordless pencil sharpener

Appliances
-Entertainment

TMK
- 9" color set
- 5" black and white set
12 VDC TV sets

Cobra Communications Product Group
Dynascan Corp.
6460 West Cortland Street
Chicago, IL 60635
portable telephones

Sears
TV sets

Appliances
-Garage/Tools

Cole Parmer Co.
Chicago, IL
propane torch and igniter

Fleet Farm
screwball hand drill

Fleet Farm
12 VDC trouble light

Ridge Tool Co.
400 Clark Street
Elyria, OH 44036
hydraulic punch

Eide Saw
1329 N.E. Tyler
Minneapolis, MN
(612) 789-3288
saw blades - all kinds

Jensen Tools and Alloys
4117 N. 44th Street
Phoenix, AZ 85018
12 VDC soldering iron

MM Newman Corp.
Phoenix, AZ
(602) 894-2188
12 VDC soldering iron

Makita - Blade & Decker
cordless tools - all kinds

Milwaukee
cordless screwdriver

Appliances
-Household

Miele dishwasher
640 kWh per year
Germany

Low electricity appliances - options for the future
Jorgen S. Norgard
(Denmark)

Convert automatic washers to 12 volts
David Copperfield
booklet

Convert dryers to 12 volts
David Copperfield
booklet

How to Make a Washing Machine
V.C. Pettit & Dr. K. Holtzclaw, A.I.D.
book

Metropolitan Vacuum Cleaner Co. Inc.
One Ramapo Avenue
Suffern, NY 10901
vacuum cleaner

Panasonic
Div. of Matsushita Electric Corp.
Home Appliance Div.
One Panasonic Way
Secaucus, NJ 07094
(201) 348-7000
hand-held vacuum cleaner

Avanti
8885 N.W. 23rd Street
Miami, FL 33172
(305) 592-7830
12 VDC wash machine

Royal Appliance Mfg. Co.
650 Alpha Drive
Cleveland, OH 44143
(800) 321-1134
"Dirt Devil" 12-volt vacuum

Sears
12 VDC refrigerators, fans, heaters

Dirt Devil by Royal
push sweeker

House Beautiful
Department GHSS 015
P.O. Box 2317
FDR Station
New York, NY 10150
battery-operated sewing machine

Singer
battery-operated sewing machine

Eureka
1201 East Bell
Bloomington, IL 61701
cordless upright vacuum

Real Goods Trading
wash machine, efficiency kits
Black & Decker
Space Light
(800) 257-6173
closet lights

Hoky
push sweeper

3M - Commercial Care Division
(800) 852-9722
model 4500, push floor sweeper

Central Vacuum Manufacturers:

* Beam Industries
P.O. Box 189

*Used in Earth Home

Webster City, IA 50595
(515) 832-4620

Broan Mfg.
P.O. Box 140
Hartford, WI 53027

Fasco Industries
P.O. Box 150
Fayetteville, NC 28302

Hoover Co.
101 E. Maple
North Canton, OH 44720

HP Products
512 W. Gorgas
Louisville, OH 44641

Lawrence Industries
P.O. Box 1838
Burlington, NC 27215

M&S Systems
2861 Congressman Lane
Dallas, TX 75220
(214) 358-3196

Nutone
Madison & Red Bank Roads
Cincinnati, OH 45227

Electrolux
Suite 900
2300 Windy Ridge Parkway
Marietta, GA 30067

Eureka
1201 E. Bell Street
Bloomington, IL 61701
(309) 828-2367

Vacuflo
H-P Products, Inc.
512 W. Gorgas Street
Louisville, OH 44641
(216) 875-5556
(800) 822-8356

Install A Central Vacuum
by Don Vandervort
Home Mechanix, February 1990, p. 48
article

Spencer Turbine Company
600 Day Hill Road
Windsor, CT 06095
(203) 688-8361
central vacuum manufacturer

Ecoworks
2326 Pickwick Road
Baltimore, MD 21207
(800) 466-9288
12 VDC photoelectric smoke detector

Asko Inc.
903 N. Bowser, #200
Richardson, TX 75081
Swedish washers/dryers

Staber System 2000
Staber Industries
4245 Arlington St. E.
Iverness, Fl. 34453

800-848-6250
110 VAC horizontal axis waster

Creda clothes washer from Twisted Oak
110 VAC 30 minute cycles

Equator combination washer
and drier from Twisted Oak

800-626-5944
Hand-operated clothes
pressure washer

Appliances -Industrial

YAG laser
Battery operated
Laserex 800-824-7444

Data Electronics, USA Inc.
17941 Sky Park Circle, Ste. H
Irvine, CA 92714
Battery-powered datalogger

O.S. Walker Company
Worcester, Ma.
800-962-4638
12 volt lift magnet

Strip chart recorders
EP-08380-66
Cole-Parmer
800-323-4340

Metro Equipment Corp.
P.O. Box 60248
Sunnyvale, CA 94088
battery-powered, digital scale

Penney's
12 VDC winch

Sears
12V polisher, buffer

Billy Goat Industries, Inc.
P.O. Box 308
1803 South Jefferson
Lee's Summit, MO 64063
(816) 524-9666
battery-operated floor sweeper

Pioneer Electric & Research Corp.
743 Circle Avenue
Forest Park, IL 60130
(312) 771-8242
battery strobe lights

MY-TE Products Inc.
3547 Massachusetts Avenue
Indianapolis, IN 46218
(317) 547-1341
12V winches

Arlyn Scales
199 Merrick Road
Lynbrook, NY 11563
battery bench top scale

OTC Power Team
2121 W. Bridge Street
Owatonna, MN 55060
(507) 455-7100

*Used in Earth Home

cordless hydraulic pump

Techni-Tool
Plymouth Mtg., PA
(215) 825-4990
battery-powered wire wrap tool

Kevex X-ray Tube Division
Box 66860
Scotts Valley, CA 95066
(408) 438-5940
portable X-ray machine

Cole-Parmer
12 VDC mini-chart recorder

Cole-Parmer
digital stroboscope

ARTX
4859 Factory Drive
Fairfield, OH 45014-1914
(513) 829-4244
air-powered vacuum

McMaster Carr Catalog
12 VDC fuel transistor pump

McMaster Carr/Fleet Farm
gas-powered cut-off saws,*
drills, and augers

Avdel Corp.
50 Lackawanna Avenue
Parsippany, NJ 07054
blind rivet tool - battery operated

Hand Held Products
P.O. Box 472388
Charlotte, NC 28247
battery bar code scanner

Intercomp
14465 23rd Avenue N.
Minneapolis, MN 55447
battery crane scale

Glenn Products
4111 N. Buchanan Circle, Unit 7
Pacheco, CA 94553
(510) 686-1788
battery-powered welder

Enerpac Div.
Applied Power, Inc.
13000 W. Silver Spring Drive
Butler, WI 53007
battery-powered hydraulic pump

Cole Parmer
(800) 323-4340
battery-operated magnetic stirrer

Batteryweld 200
12 VDC wirefeed welder
alternative energy engineering

Appliances
-Kitchen

Robert Bosch Corp.
2800 S. 25th Ave.
Broadview, IL 60153
800-866-2022
dishwasher

Asko, Inc.
PO Box 851805
Richardson, TX 75085
972-644-8595
#1475
dishwasher

P6785
800-251-9306
12 volt coffee maker

Retsel Corporation
McCammon, ID 83250
(208) 254-3325
grain mills

Oster Co.
cordless can opener

Futura
pressure cooker

Safe-T-Measures Co.
P.O. Box 1521
Culver City, CA 90232
baby bottle warmer

Current, Inc.
Colorado Springs, CO 80941
battery mini-mixer

King Refrigerator Corp.
76-02 Woodhaven Boulevard
Glendale, NY 11385
(718) 897-2200
mini-kitchens

Asko, Inc.
903 N. Bowser, #200
Richardson, TX 75081
dishwashers (Sweden)

Appliances
-Multiple Sources/Misc.

Dyson Cyclone vacuum cleaner
Does not need bags
Does not lose suction

The Most Energy Efficient Appliances
Booklet by ACEEE

12 Volt Products
756 Morning Glory Avenue
Holland, PA
many

Sears
special R.V. and camping equipment catalog

Penney's
many

Appliances
-Sporting Goods

Minnkota
trolling motor

Sporting goods - retail

*Used in Earth Home

trolling motors, depth finders

Appliances -Yard/Garden

tillers and cultivators article
Phil McCafferty
Consumer Digest
March/April 1997
Comparison of tillers
Rear-tine tillers

Tamarack
Route 1 Box 39
Exeland, WI 54835
Garden cultivator
(also available from Home-Health Resource
HCR 67, box 65
Mountain View, MO 65548
417-934-5454)

Wen Products Inc.
5810 Northwest Highway
Chicago, IL 60631
(312) 763-6060
chain saw

Black & Decker
cordless grass shears

Sears - Craftsman
cordless grass shears, battery-operated siphon pump,
chain saw sharpener

Sawtune®
chain saw sharpener

Dremel
Racine, WI 53401
chain saw sharpener

Granberg International
244 South 24th Street
Richmond, CA 94804
(415) 237-2099
(800) 258-9905
chain saw sharpener

Panama Pump Company
Hattersburg, MS
manual-spray tree marking--green

Tensen
Department 204
1218 N.W. Glisan
Portland, OR 97209
12V chain saw

Real Goods Trading Co.
push-type lawn mower and
rechargeable mower (Ryobi)

"Snapper"
gas lawn mower

Aquaculture (See Fish, Aquaculture)

Automobiles, Transportation

Globe Motors
www.globe-motors.com
937-228-3171
Drive-by-wire components

Big Cat
Orlando, FL.
800-521-2747
human-powered vehicles

Lithium Battery pack from Valence
Valence U-Charge
(doubles mileage on Prius)

Battery packs or Lithium-Ion
Ocean Server Technology, Inc.
www.ocean-server.com
508-678-0550

Intermittent Continuously Variable—
Hybrid Transmission Congress
CVT (continuously variable transmission)

bicycles
Patent Engineering
2610 Dexter
Denver, Co 80207
303-514-1991
Internal combustion engine gear set for bicycles

Hybrid Technologies
5001 East Bonanza Road
Suite 138-145
Las Vegas, NV 89110 USA
(888) 669-1808 Fax: (702) 926-9508
info@hybridtechnologies.com

Rosen Motors
Hybrid Electric Powertrain
Turbogenerator etc.
longman.awl.com/englishpages/

www.CleanAirChoice.org
800-642-5864
E85 program

NOTE: For electric car batteries, see Battery file.

Statistics
186 million autos in U.S.
1.96 trillion miles
Total % energy consumption 27%
(petroleum 62%)
Real Goods Catalog

Hydrogen - Electrolysis Plant
Riverside, CA
article

Design Engineering 4 Inc.
c/o John Plessinger
P.O. Box 143
Lebanon, OH 45036
(513) 932-3100
100 mpg car (gas)

Sinclair Vehicles Ltd.
Clive Sinclair
Motor Industry Research Association
electronic vehicle

D&A Vehicles, Inc.
606 NE Lincoln Avenue
St. Cloud, MN 56301
(612) 259-1403

*Used in Earth Home

(formerly Freeway)
"Minikin"

Hoxan Corp.
Phoebus III solar car

Rhoades Car Division
Rhoades National Corp.
100 Rhoades Lane
Hendersonville, TN 37075
(615) 822-2737
4-wheeled pedal car

Infinity Bicycles
Distributed by Hostel Shoppe
929 Main Street
Stevens Point, WI 54481
(715) 341-4340
recumbent bicycles

Taylor-Dunn Mfg. Co.
2114 W. Ball Road
Anaheim, CA 92804
electric towing vehicle

Coming Age of the Electric Vehicle
Fortune, March 8, 1993
article on electric vehicles

General Motors Electric Vehicle
Resource Center
432 North Saginaw Street, Suite 801
Flint, MI 48502
(800) 253-5328
electric vehicle program

American Flywheel Systems
Bellevue, WA
(206) 454-1818

Town Creek Industries, Inc.
41 East Patuxent Beach Road
California, MD 20619
(301) 863-9042
"electric wheel concept"

Electric Vehicle Directory
Philip Terpstra
book

Horizon Battery Technologies, Inc.
2809 IH 35 South
Box 788
San Marcos, TX 78667
(512) 753-6540
"Fiberglass Mat" batteries

Hughes Aircraft Co.
inductive charging system
"Design News"

Electrosource
Austin, TX
Horizon lead-acid cell

Autonomous Houses -Efficient Homes

Swedish Building Systems & Components Office
Swedish Trade Council USA
150 N. Michigan Avenue, Suite 1200
Chicago, IL 60611
(312) 781-6210

Earthship
Evolution Beyond Economics
Book on earthships
Michael Reynolds

Autonomous Houses -Non-Profit Associations

International Center for Sustainable Development
22923 Wildcat Road
Gaithersburg, MD 20882
301-428-1040
John Spears

Graviotas
A Village to Reinvent the World
Alan Weisman
Book on a South American village

The Sustainable Village
717 Poplar Ave.
Boulder, CO 80304
www.thesustainablevillage.com
Magazine
(888) 317-1600

Midwest Renewable Energy Fair
7558 Deer Road
Custer, Wi. 54423
Yearly Fair in Amherst, WI in June

Fraunhofer Institut Solare Energiesysteme
See SSSH on Internet
Solar Self-Sufficient Home in Germany
Adolf Goetzberger

The Self-Sufficient House
Frank Coffee
Book on Self-Sufficient Technologies

Nat. Center for Alternative Technology
In 1975 - Machynlleth (2400)
Wates built homes donated to Powys
wind-powered cottage

Masec - D.O.E. Contract
Mid America Solar Energy Complex
blue-prints/solar homes

CSIRO (Commonwealth Scientific and
Industrial Research Organization)
Victoria, Australia
research and publications

Foreign Building and Construction
Australia, Finland, India
literature

New Alchemy Institute (now dissolved)
John Todd
many publications, "The Ark" prototype,
research facility

Folkecenter for Renewable Energy
Denmark
literature/large facility

Solar Research Homes - Solar Heated Insulated House
South Carolina Agricultural Experiment Station
Clemson University
Clemson, South Carolina

*Used in Earth Home

literature

Brenda and Robert Vales
The Autonomous Home: Design and Planing for Self-Sufficiency
book on self sufficiency - 1975

Canmet Building Group
Energy, Mines, and Resources - Canada
580 Booth Street
Ottawa, Ontario K1A 0E4
CANADA
advanced houses program

Autonomous House Article
Popular Science, April 1980
article

Energy Efficient Building Association
North Central Technical College
1000 West Campus Drive
Wausau, WI 54401-1899
(715) 675-6331
building association

Autonomous Houses
-Private
Companies/Books

Build Your Ark!
How to Prepare for Self-Reliance in Uncertain Times
Geri Welzel Guidetti
Book on preparedness

Green Home
Planning and Building the Environmentally Advanced House
Wayne Grady
Book on homes

Self-Sufficiency
John Seymour
Book on complete self-sufficiency

Life Under Glass
Abigail Alling, Mark Nelson, with Sally Silverstone
Book--Inside story of Biosphere 2

Food Self-sufficiency
Walt Gullett and Jane Fellows Gullet
Book on traditional self-sufficient ways

The Energy Efficient Home
Steven Robinson with Fred S.Dubin
Book on solar, wood, and Wind

U-Bahn Earth Homes (underground)
Granite City, IL
private company

Big Outdoors People - Domes
2201 NE Kennedy Street
Minneapolis, MN 55413
private company (domes)

Ekosea Homes
San Francisco
design services

Enermodal Engineering, Ltd.
368 Philip Street
Waterloo, Ontario N2L 5J1
CANADA
(519) 884-6421
green home

Healthy House Building
John Bower
book

Guide To Resource Efficient Building Elements
Steve Loken

Ergonomic Living
Gordon Inkeles and Iris Schencke
book on user-friendly home design

Batteries/Chargers
-Batteries

Lithium Battery pack from Valence
Valence U-Charge
(doubles mileage on Prius)

Battery packs or Lithium-Ion
Ocean Server Technology, Inc.
www.ocean-server.com
508-678-0550

Gates Energy Battery
1050 South Broadway
P.O. Box 5887
Denver, CO 80217
(303) 744-4806
sealed gel-cell; all sizes

Globe Battery Division - Johnson Controls
5757 North Green Bay Avenue
P.O. Box 591
Milwaukee, WI 53201
(414) 228-2393
* GC12V100

Sonnenschein Batteries, Inc.
290 Pratt Street
Meriden, CT 06450
(203) 238-3088
* sealed-lead acid rechargeable "Prevailer"

GNB Batteries, Inc.
Automative Battery Div.
P.O. Box 43140
St. Paul, MN 55164
deep cycle

Hoppecke Battery Systems, Inc.
292 Main Street
Butler, NJ 07405
(201) 492-0045
fiber Ni-Cad battery (to 500 AH)

Douglas Battery Mfg. Co.
500 Battery Drive
Winston-Salem, NC 27107
(919) 788-7561
many sizes
Technacell by Elpower Corp.
2117 South Anne Street
Santa Anna, CA 92704
(714) 540-6155
mid-sized sealed lead acid

Power Sonic Corp.
P.O. Box 5242
3106 Spring Street
Redwood City, CA 94063

*Used in Earth Home

(415) 364-5001
mid size sealed lead acid

Real Goods Trading Co.
(also Pro-Cons on Ni Cad Batteries)
distributor of batteries

Alternative Energy Engineering
distributor of batteries

GS Japan Storage Battery (Portalac)
Distributed by:
Aristo Craft
Suite 562
200 Fifth Avenue
New York, NY 10010
Sealed Lead Calcium Co. Ltd.

Pacific West Supply Co.
P.O. Box 2116
Lake Oswego, OR 97035
(503) 835-1212
reconditioned large Ni-Cad

"Living on 12 Volts with Ample Power"
source book

Battery Book For Your PV Home
Fowler Solar Electric, Inc.
book

Utility-Free, Inc.
0050 Road 110
Glenwood Springs, CO 81601
(800) 766-5550
(303) 928-0846
Ni-Cad batteries

Pacific West Supply Co.
111723 S.W. 88th
Tigard, OR 97223
(503) 835-1212
Ni-Cad batteries

Batteries/Chargers -Battery Chargers/Controls

Microchip Technology
New battery monitor chipset

Todd Engineering Sales
3280 Hemisphere Loop, Suite 154
Tucson, AZ 85706
(602) 889-9333
* battery charger

Enermax Corporation
Russ Burkhardt
P.O. Box 1436
Ukiah, CA 95482
(707) 462-7604
* charge controller

Terado Corporation
1068 Raymond Avenue
St. Paul, MN 55108
(612) 646-2868
battery chargers

Lester Electrical of Nebraska, Inc.
625 West A Street
Lincoln, NE 68522
(402) 477-8988
chargers

Atec from
Alternative Energy Engineering
(800) 777-6609
chargers

National Railway Supply
7002 Hodgson Memorial Drive, Suite 201
Savannah, GA 31406
(800) 357-3572
(912) 356-5207
chargers

Todd Products Corp.
50 Emjay Boulevard
Brentwood, NY 11717
(516) 231-3366
* switcher power supplies

Benchmarq Microelectronics, Inc.
2611 Westgrove Road, Suite 109
Carrollton, TX 75006
(214) 407-0011
IC battery capacity monitor

Batteries/Chargers -Future

NASA
nickel/hydrogen cells

Matsushita
Elec. Ind. of NJ (Secaucus)
(201) 348-7000
paper batteries, available 1991

NASA
bipolar battery using conductive-fiber composite

NASA
multi kilowatt bipolar nickel/hydrogen battery

Alupower, Inc.
Subsidiary of Alcan Aluminum Ltd.
(underwater exploration)
salt water - aluminum alloy anode batter for underwater exploration

United States Advanced Battery Consortium
30200 Mound Road
P.O. Box 9010
Warren, MI 48090
(313) 947-1135
electric car battery research

Batteries/Chargers -Lithium

Lithium Battery pack from Valence
Valence U-Charge
(doubles mileage on Prius)

Battery packs or Lithium-Ion
Ocean Server Technology, Inc.
www.ocean-server.com
508-678-0550

Hybrid Technologies
5001 East Bonanza Road
Suite 138-145
Las Vegas, NV 89110 USA

*Used in Earth Home

(888) 669-1808 Fax: (702) 926-9508
info@hybridtechnologies.com

Batteries/Chargers -Rechargeables

Eveready
3636 S. Geyer Road, #250
Sunset Hills, MO 63127
(314) 821-3777

Gates Energy Products
(904) 462-3911

General Electric/Sanyo
(800) 626-2000
Capacity - "D" 1200, "C" 1200, "AA" 500
"AAA" 180, "9V" 65
Recharge Time - 14 hr.
Warranty - 1 year

Panasonic
One Panasonic Way
Secaucus, NJ 07094
(201) 348-9090

Rayovac
P.O. Box 4960
Madison, WI 53711
(608) 275-3340
(also reusable alkaline)

Sunlite Technologies
80 N. Broadway, #2008
Hicksville, NY 11801
(516) 433-2083

Batteries/Chargers -Related Topics

ACME Model Eng. Co.
654 Bergen Blvd.
Ridgefield, NJ
(201) WH3-7650
battery holders

Sure Power Products
7415 SE Johnson Creek Blvd.
Portland, OR 97206
(503) 777-4551
isolator

Pro-Start
special terminals for better connections

Zomeworks Corporation
P.O. Box 25805
1011A Sawmill Road N.W.
Albuquerque, NM 87125
(800) 279-6342
(505) 242-5354
special "cool" battery storage boxes (passive)

Batteries/Chargers -Smaller Batteries

NOTE: Small alkaline batteries have slightly higher voltages and are specified to be used in plant watering computers.

Tadiran Batteries
2 Seaview Blvd.
Port Washington, NY 11050
(516)6214980
small lithium batteries

Pro-Battery Inc.
3941 Oak Cliff Ind. Court
Atlanta, GA 30340-3408
(404) 449-5900
(800) 451-7171
9V rechargeable

Electro Chem Ind.
Div. of Wilson Great Batch Ltd.
10,000 Wehrle Drive
Clarence, NY 14031
(716) 759-6901
lithium batteries

Saft America Inc.
Advanced Battery Systems Div.
107 Beaver Court
Cockeysville, MD 21030
(301) 666-3200
lithium batteries

Harding Energy Systems, Inc.
826 Washington Avenue
Grand Haven, MI 49417
(616) 847-0989
rechargeable nickel-hydride "green" battery

Bees

Beeswax/natural wax candles produce no harmful carcinogens, burns longer and more uniformly, produces less soot, water soluble, and they are biodegradable. They are made from soybean oil and other vegetable waxes.

Bee in Balance
Amber Rose
Bee venom therapy book

Bee Venom
The Natural Curative for Arthritis and Rheumatism
Joseph Broadman

Health and the Honeybee
Charles Mraz
Book on the benefits of bees and bee products

Biodiesel

www.greasecar.com
www.greasel.com
WVO is waste vegetable oil

Biodiesel is vegetable oil used as fuel source
Most biodiesel is using recycled fast-food grease

Biofuel (See Alcohol)

Biogas (See Methane)

Bioshelter (see Autonomous Houses)

Blood/Blood Types (see also Food Combining)

Eat Right for Your Type

Blood type encyclopedia
Peter J. D'Adamo

The Food Combining/Blood Type Diet Solution
Dina Khader

Carbohydrates (See Plants-Grains, Plants-Tubers, or Plants-Legumes)

CHP (See Fuel Cells)

Clay

Terra Pond Koi Clay
Calcium montmorillonite clay used for pond lining

The Clay Cure
Ran Knishinsky
Book on natural healing

Our Earth, Our Cure
Raymond Dextreit
Book on clay materials for curing

The Healing Clay
Michael Abehsera
Book on clay packs

Get Well Naturally
Linda Clark
Book on clay

Cleaners

Oasis Biocompatible Cleaners
www.bio-pac.com
cleaner

soybean-based cleaner/degreaser
McMaster Carr catalog

Colloidal Silver

Colloidal Silver
The Natural Antibiotic Alternative
Zane Baranowski
Book on colloidal silver

Colon Therapy/Colonics

Detox for Life
Loree Taylor Jordan
Book on colonic hydrotherapy

Colon Health
The Key to a Vibgrant Life
Norman Walker
Book on colon therapy

www.colonic-association.com

www.colonhealth.net

Composting (see also Fish/Worms)

The Complete Book of Composting
by J.I. Rodale
book

The Spruce Creek Company
PO Box 106
Warriors Mark, PA
800-940-0187
info@sprucecreekrainsaver.com
composter

composters
www.sun-mar.com

Computers (See Home Automation)

Concrete

-Additives

Eabassoc Foamed Concrete
www.eabassoc.co.uk

Akona Corp.
Maple Plain, MN
many coatings/additives

Fibermesh
4019 Industry Drive
Chatanooga, TN 37416
(615) 892-7243
Distributed by:
National Minerals Corp.
P.O. Box 21326
St. Paul, MN 55121
(800) 437-5980
fibermix for concrete
Harbourite for stucco, mortar

Brock-White
Minneapolis, MN
chopped fiberglass

Englehard Corp.
220 W. Westerfield Ave.
Roselle Park, NJ 07204
908-245-9500
Cloncrete foaming liquid

Thoro Products
Thoroseal
7800 NW 38th Street
Miami, FL 33166
waterproof top coating

Concrete

-Alternatives

Grancrete LLC.
7110 Swindale Ct.
Mechanicsville, VA 23116
(804) 730-0023
Spray-on Concrete-like coatings

Dryvit Systems, Inc.
One Energy Way
PO Box 1014

West Warwick, RI 02893

Grancrete Spray-on Structural Cement
Casa Grande International
Mechanicsville, PA
Spray-on concrete

Concrete -Products

ICE Block is insulated concrete using polystyrene
www.a-1form.com

Sure Wall Producers Council
P.O. Box 241148
Charlotte, NC 28224
(704) 525-1621
cheap wall system

Licensee W.R. Bonsal Co.
P.O. Box 241148
Charlotte, NC 28224

Similar product in Mexico
Habitat for Humanity Housing Project
June 1990, Jimmy Carter work project
article
16-22 shovels sand
1 sack Portland (7 shovels)
2 shovels Masons
(Approx. 1 cement to 2 sand) approx. ratio
-- Keep damp - slow dry
stucco recipe

1 Lime
2 Portland
2½ sand
richer stucco recipe

washed silica sand
fine mesh
add Portland
add Masons
mortar recipe

Vulkem Products
Sold by: Mameco Int'l Inc.
4475 East 175th Street
Cleveland, OH 44128-3599
(216) 752-4400
polyurethane caulk

Earth System Inc.
Formworks Building, Inc.
P.O. Box 1509
Durango, CO
concrete forming of homes, etc.

Insteel Construction Systems, Inc.
2610 Sidney Lanier Drive
Brunswick, GA 31520
(912) 264-3772
concrete on wire - styrofoam construction

5 (sand and gravel)
1 cement
3/4 water
water-tight concrete (article also)

Concrete
A Homeowner's Illustrated Guide
David H. Jacobs, Jr.
book

The Mearl Corp.
220 W. Westfield Avenue
P.O. Box 208
Roselle Park, NJ 07204
(908) 245-9500
cellular concrete

Betostyrene Australia P/L
LVL 5, Suite 507
3 Smail Street
Broadway, 2007
AUSTRALIA
lightweight concrete

Build Your Own Ferrocement Water Tank
Donnie Schatzberg
book

Concrete Structure, Properties, and Materials
P. Kumar Mehta
Paulo J.M. Monteiro
book on concrete

Fox Industries, Inc.
3100 Falls Cliff Road
Baltimore, MD 21211
(301) 243-8856
corrosion-free concrete marine structures

Archibio concrete/flax slab
(see Flax)

Conferences

Sustainable Building Comference
SBIR

Cooking (See also Solar Cooking)

NOTE: See also Diet files.

Pressure cooking - Mirro
15 minutes max. cooking time for vegetables

Vita-Mix
8615 Usher Road
Cleveland, OH 44138
universal mixer

Poi - Tofu
soybean suggestions - article

Steaming times for fresh vegetables
chart

Bulgar
article

American Harvest
4064 Peavey Road
Minneapolis, MN 55318
(612) 448-4400
hot air cooker

The Smart Kitchen
David Goldbeck
book (bibliography)

Arrowroot powder is a thickener

(such as corn starch)
1 tablespoon/cup liquid
article

Grain beverage made from wheat and beet roots
coffee substitute

Percentage of calories from protein, fat and carbohydrates (vegetables, grains, legumes, nuts/seeds, fruits, dairy products and eggs, meats and fish)
chart

Cooling /Dehumidification -General

Munters Corporation
HumiCool division
PO Box 6428
Fort fMeyers, FL 33911
(41) 936-1555
Evaporative Cooling Elements

ConRoTec, Inc.
6 Raymond Ave.
Salem, N.H. 03079
603-893-2727
static mixers

Average temp of groundwater in U.S.
Chart-see text

2 story wind catcher
Wind catcher with underground shafts
Iraq and some Arab countries around Persian Gulf
article

TAH Industries, Inc.
107 North Gold Drive
Robbinsurle, NJ 08691
motionless (static) mixers

Kushi Institute Store
P.O. box 500
Becket, MA 01223-0500
800-645-8744
Pressure cookers and suribachis
(for grinding sprouts)

Chem-Mixx Technology
Div. of Tra-Con Inc.
55 North Street
Medford, MA 02155
(617) 395-7270
motionless (static) mixers

Kurt J. Lesker Co.
Technical Products Div.
1515 Worthington Avenue
Clairton, PA 15025
(412) 233-4200
(800) 451-9589
motionless (static) mixers

Cooling /Dehumidification -Desiccant Dehumidification

DryKor
www.drykor.com
desiccant dehumifiers

Advanced Desiccant Cooling and Dehumidifivation Program

ORNL NREL DOE

New thermal Technologies
12900 Automobile Blvd.
Suite 5
Clearwater, FL 33762
813-571-1888

Kathabar
PO Box 791
New Brunswick, NJ 08903
800-524-1370
Desiccant cooling

HTS Engineering
115 Norfinch Drive
North York, ON Canada
M3N 1W8
416-661-3400
Desiccant cooling

Chemineer, Inc.
125 Flagship Drive
North Andover, MA 01845
(508) 687-0101
motionless (static) mixers

Liquid Control Corp.
7576 Freedom Avenue NW
P.O. Box 2747
North Canton, OH 44720-0747
(216) 494-1313
motionless (static) mixers

Thermal Chimney
article

Moist sand is better conductor than dry soil
article

Cool tubes don't dehumidify or exhaust radon
article

Canada's air exhange standard is 1.5 air changes per hour
Energy Conservation Office
Atikokan, Ontario, CANADA

Mean Groundwater Temperatures
(International Ground Source Heat Pump Assn.)
Oklahoma State University
P.O. Box 1688
Stillwater, OK 74078
(800) 626-4747
(405) 744-5175
association/charts

Cryotech
6103 Orthoway
Fort Madison, IA 52627
(319) 372-6012
(800) 346-7237
GS4 heat transfer fluid

Moisture Control Handbook
Oak Ridge National Laboratory
by Joseph Lstiburek
NTIS
information source

Bionaire Corp.
90 Boroline Road
Allendale, NJ 07401
(800) 253-2764
digital humidity monitor

*Used in Earth Home

Handbook of Dehumidification Technology
by Brundreit, G.W.
information source

Evaporative Air Conditioning Handbook
by Dr. John R. Watt
information source

Solar-Regenerated Dessicant Dehumidification
Philip Haves
Texas Energy Development Fund
Report # EDF-064
report

"Sorbead R" Desiccant
Mobil Oil
drier-desiccant

Humidity Control
Ivan Stepnich
book

Cool Houses for Desert Suburbs
Jeffrey Cook
Arizona Solar Energy Commission
Project #78-1-01
book

Dial Manufacturing, Inc.
25 S. 51st Avenue
Phoenix, AZ 85043
(602) 278-1100
(800) 350-DIAL
evaporative cooler pumps - all

"Influence of Land Surface Conditions
on Groundwater Temperatures in
S.W. Suffolk County"
E. J. Pluhowski and I. H. Kantrowitz
Article

Cooling /Dehumidification -Evaporative Coolers

Coolerado Cooler
Idalex Technologies
Arvada, Colorado
www.idalex.com
Evaporative cooler-fans only

www.swampy.net
IceMystr and Icestrmystr 12 volt coolers

Bessam Mfg. Co. Inc.
grilles

Mission Mfg. Inc.
grilles

Flakt Products, Inc.
(Bahnson Co.)
atomizers

Pneumafil Corp.
P.O. Box 16348
Charlotte, NC 28216
large coolers

Buffalo Forge Co.
P.O. Box 985
Buffalo, NY 14240
large evaporative coolers

Quietaire
505 North Hutcheson
Houston, TX 77003
induction wall panel coolers

Energy Saver Mfg. Inc.
single-pad coolers

Air Plastics, Inc.
P.O. Box 42067
Cincinnati, OH 45242
"scrubber" type cooler

Air-Fan Engineering
rotary pad coolers

Essick Air Products
greenhouse coolers

Aerovent Fan and Equipment Co.
929 Terminal Road
Lansing, MI 48906
rigid-media greenhouse coolers

Acme Engineering and Mfg. Corp.
P.O. Box 978
Muskogee, OK 74401
cooling controls

Des Champs Laboratories, Inc.
P.O. Box 440
East Hanover, NJ 07936
plate-type indirect coolers

Norsaire Systems
indirect wheel-type

PHE, Pty. Ltd. (Dryconaire Pty. Ltd.)
23 Commercial Street
Marleston 5033
SOUTH AUSTRALIA
plastic - indirect

Byco Ltd.
window-sized coolers

Alternative Energy Resources
indirect

Mission Mfg. Inc.
3116 South 52nd Street
Tempe, AZ 85282
grilles - through attic

Goettl Air Conditioning, Inc.
drip coolers

Bonaire Industries, Ltd.
evaporative coolers

American Solar King Corporation
desiccant cooler

Mee Industries, Inc.
1629 South Del Mar Avenue
San Gabriel, CA 91776
fog coolers

Bacchus Industries, Inc.
P.O. Box 455
Sunland Park, NM 88063
solar-powered coolers

Photocomm, Inc.

*Used in Earth Home

7735 East Redfield Road
Scottsdale, AZ 85260
solar-powered coolers

William Lamb Co.
P.O. Box 4185
North Hollywood, CA 91607
solar-powered coolers

Research Products Corp.
P.O. Box 1467
Madison, WI 53701-1467
woven saturation pads

Arvin Industries
500 South 15th Street
Phoenix, AZ 85034
plastic indirect coolers

Aztech International, Ltd.
2417 Aztec Road N.E.
Albuquerque, NM 87107
indirect coolers

Vari-Cool
Division of H&C Metal Products
plastic tube - indirect

Di Peri Manufacturing Corp.
P.O. Box 793
Northridge, CA 91328
indirect

Energy Labs, Ltd.
P.O. Box 3089
Santa Fe Springs, CA 90670
indirect

Solar Electric Specialties Co.
P.O. Box 537
Willits, CA 95490
12V direct cooler

Quietaire
505 North Hutcheson
Houston, TX 77003
(713) 228-9421
greenhouse coolers

Solvay Performance Chemicals
41 West Putnam Avenue
Greenwich, CT 06830
(203) 629-7900
desiccants

Examining the Benefits of Desiccant Dehumidification
by James S. Fitzsimmons
February 18, 1993
Plant Engineering
article

Airflow Co.
295 Bailes Lane
Frederick, MD 21701
(301) 695-6500
desiccant dehumidifying equipment

Low Humidity Systems, Inc.
10117 Industrial Drive
Covington, GA 30209
(800) 553-6746
desiccant dehumidifiers

Sphinx Adsorbents, Inc.
58 Progress Avenue
Springfield, MA 01104
(413) 736-5020
bulk desiccants

Dehydrators/Driers

Leandre Poisson
Solar Survival
Box 118
Harrisville, NH 03450
build-it-yourself food dehydrator

How to Dry Fruits and Vegetables
At Home
by Food Editors of Farm Journal
source

American Harvest
P.O. Box 159
4064 Peavey Road
Chaska, MN 55318
(612) 448-4400
110V food dehydrator

Thomas Registers
commercial food dryers list

How to Dry Foods
Deanna DeLong
source, including sources

Drying Vegetables, Fruits and Herbs
Phyllis Hobson
source and how-to information

Food storage list
article

Energy-Free Food Storage
Jerry Minnich
source

The ABC's of Home Food Dehydrators
Barbara Oensley
source

Home Food Dehydrating
Jay and Shirley Bills
source

Ronco
110V dehydrator

Waring
110V dehydrator

Living Foods Dehydrators
3023 362nd S.E.
Fall City, WA 98024
(206) 222-5587
* dehydrator with Kevlar screening (tray material)

Waring Products
Division of Dynamics Corp. of America
283 Main Street
New Hartford, CT 06057
(203) 379-0731
110V dehydrator

Elmwood Sensors
500 Narragansett Park Drive
Pawtucket, R.I. 02861
Humidity Sensors

*Used in Earth Home

Desiccants

Superadsorbent Polymers
Bucholz and Peppas
Article on materials

United Desiccants
Colton, Ca.
909-825-1793

Cargoaire
79 Monroe Street
PO Box 640

Amesbury, Ma. 01913
800-843-5360
Desiccant Dehumidifiers

Advances in Desiccant Technologies
Davor Novosel
Article written for Gas Research Institute
Chicago, Il.
Includes 1M materials

The Basics of Commercial Desiccant Systems
Lewis G. Harriman III
Mason-Grant
Portsmouth, N.H.

The Potential for Solar Assisted Desiccant Cooling in the UK
at Warwick University
www.eng.warwick.ac.uk/~essix/thompson/solarac.ht

Diet (See Nutrition)

Distillation

Waterwise Model 1600
Non-Electric Distiller (stovetop/hotplate)
Leesburg, FL 34748
www.waterwise.com
352-787-5008

Earth Architecture

www.alternatives.com/cob-building
cob construction architecture

The Valley of Mud-Brick Architecture
Samar Damluji
Book of mud architecture

CalEarth
10376 Shangri La Avenue
Hesperia, CA 92345
760-244-0614
earth architecture

www.eartharchitecture.org
website dedicated to earthen construction methods

Earthship (see Autonomous Houses)

Elastomers

Dow Corning
Rep (Ellsworth Adhesive Systems)
9555 James Avenue South, Suite 260
Bloomington, MN 55431
888-1201
RTV rubber

Industrial Molded Rubber Products
15600 Medina Road
Plymouth, MN 55447
(612) 559-9061
polymer selection chart

Shell Chemical Co.
1415 West 22nd Street
Oak Brook, IL 60522
(312) 572-5500
"Kraton" thermoplastic rubber

Mobay Corporation
Inorganic Chemicals Division
Mobay Road
Pittsburgh, PA 15205-9741
(412) 777-2000
liquid silicone rubber

J.P. Stevens and Co., Inc.
Elastomeric Products Department
East Hampton, MA 01027
(413) 527-0700
polyurethane film

Ohio Rubber Company
Willooghby, OH 44094
(216) 942-0500
information on elastomers

Latex Products
Div. of Mid-State Enterprise, Inc.
155 Van Winkle Avenue
Hawthorne, NJ 07506-1593
(201) 427-6040
rubber bellows catalog

Rubber Corporation of America
2545 North Broad Street
Philadelphia, PA 19132
catalog of many rubber products

Elmhurst Rubber Co., Inc.
79-48 Albion Avenue
Elmhurst, NY 11373
(718) 899-3000
banding stock - natural and neoprene

Minor Rubber Co., Inc.
49 Ackerman Street
Bloomfield, NJ 07003-4299
(201) 338-6800
(800) 631-8574
bellows

Jim Donahue
(617) 872-4863
orthodontic bands

Loess Enterprises
1457 Iglehart Avenue

*Used in Earth Home

St. Paul, MN 55104
(612) 646-1385
plastisols

Unicast, Inc.
17 McFadden Road
P.O. Box 4627
Easton, PA 18043-4627
(215) 559-9998
urethanes

Boedicker Plastics
(800) 444-3485
urethanes

Electricity
-Automation (See Home Control)

Electricity
-Books

Boatowner's Mechanical and Electrical Manual
Nigel Calder
Book on self-contained power systems on a large boat

Electricity
-Buzzers

Hart Technological Ind.
303 East 43rd Street
Suite 19B
New York, NY 10017
(212) 697-6594
"Loud Mouth" security alarms

Universal Security Instruments, Inc.
10324 South Dolfield Road
Owings Mills, MD 21117
(301) 363-3000
vehicle security alarms

Murata Erie North America
2200 Lake Park Drive
Smyrna, GA 30080
(404) 433-7878
Piezo alarm

Projects Unlimited, Inc.
3680 Wyse Road
Dayton, OH 45414
(513) 890-1918
120DB siren

Electricity
-Controls/Pressure

Automatic Switch Co.
5009 Excelsior Boulevard
Minneapolis, MN 55416
(612) 925-5520
NJ - (201) 966-2000
pressure switches

Sensym
1255 Reamwood Avenue
Sunnyvale, CA 94089
(408) 744-1500
pressure sensors

Sigma-Netics, Inc.
Fairfield, NJ 07006
(201) 227-6327
pressure switch

Micro Pneumatic Logic, Inc.
2890 NW 62nd Street
Fort Lauderdale, FL 33309
(305) 973-6166
* air switch

IC Sensors
1701 McCarthy Boulevard
Milpitas, CA 95035
(408) 946-6693
PC mounted pressure sensors

Air Logic Division
Fred Knapp Engraving Co.
5102 Douglas Avenue
Racine, WI 53402
(414) 639-9035
(800) 558-5950
* low pressure air switches

World Magnetics
810 Hastings Street
Traverse City, MI 49684
(616) 946-3800
* low pressure switches

Orange Research, Inc.
140 Cascade Boulevard
Milford, CT 06460
(203) 877-5657
differential pressure gauge

Frank W. Murphy Mfr.
P.O. Box 470248
Tulsa, OK 74147
(918) 627-3550
pressure gauges

Coventry Specialty Corp.
4 Ascutney Avenue
Westfield, MA 01085
(413) 568-6355
* low pressure mini-switch

A.J. Atunes & Co.
1237 Capitol Drive
Addison, IL 60101
(312) 628-1790
low air pressure switches

Pres-Air-Trol Corp.
1009 West Boston Post Road
Mamaroneck, NY 10543
(914) 698-2026
* low pressure switches

Ametek Controls Division
860 Pennsylvania Boulevard
Feasterville, PA 19047
(215) 355-6900
compact pressure sensor

Sensym
1804 McCarthy Boulevard
Milpitas, CA 95035
(408) 954-1100
low-cost dip pressure sensors

Chicago Safety Products, Inc.
1237 Capitol Drive
Addison, IL 60101

*Used in Earth Home

(312) 543-8650
air pressure switch

United Electric Controls Co.
P.O. Box 9143
Watertown, MA 02272-9143
(617) 926-1000
miniature pressure switches

Setra Systems, Inc
159 Swanson Road
Boxborough, Mass. 01719
800-257-3872
miniature pressure transducers

Whitman General Corp.
41 Main Street
P.O. Box 65
Terryville, CT 06786
(203) 583-1847
miniature pressure switches

Dwyer Inst., Inc.
P.O. Box 373
Michigan City, IN 46360
(219) 879-8000
low pressure switches, etc.

Electricity -Controls-Humidity

Vaisala, Inc.
100 Commerce Way
Woburn, MA 01801
(781) 933-8029
humidity transmitters for dusty/humid

White Rogers Division
Emerson Electric
9797 Reavis Road
St. Louis, MO 63123
distributor - all kinds

Gem Products, Inc.
Garden Grove, CA 92641
90- 200C (GC 501) cold thermostat

Robertshaw Controls Co.
Fulton Sylphon Division
Knoxville, TN 37901
mechanical thermostats (liquid)

Custom Control Sensors, Inc.
2111 Plummer Street
Chatsworth, CA 91311
(818) 341-4610
custom

Hy-Cal Engineering
9650 Telstar Avenue
El Monte, CA 91734
surface mount temp/humidity sensor

Ranco Controls Division
601 West Fifth Avenue
Columbus, OH 43201
humidity sensor

Hycal
9650 Telstar Avenue
El Monte, CA 91731
(818) 444-4000
low-cost IC humidity sensor

Kele & Assoc.
P.O. Box 34817
Memphis, TN 38184
(901) 382-4300
humidity sensor

Thermodisc, Inc.
Subsidiary of Emerson Electric
1320 South Main Street
Mansfield, OH 44907
(419) 525-8500

National Semiconductor Corp.
2900 Semiconductor Drive
Santa Clara, CA 95052
tiny temperature sensor

Electricity -Controls-Temp

Dawn Electronics
(775) 882-7721
info@dawnelectronics.com
temp. controller without external controller
-surface mounted

Therm-o-Disc
1320 South Main St.
Mansfield, OH
(419) 525-8500
Accurate temperature control for water
Heaters, HVAC etc. (less overshoot)

Sauer Sunstrand
612-509-2088
S2X microcontroller

Control Products, Inc.
280 Ridgedale Avenue
East Hanover, NJ 07936
(201) 887-9400
thermal switches

Robertshaw Controls Co.
Uni-Line Division
4190 Temescal Street
Corona, CA 91720
(714) 734-2600
temperature switches

Inmark Corp.
147 West Cedar Street
Norwalk, CT 06854
(203) 866-8474
thermal circuit breaker

Selco Products Co.
7580 Stage Road
Buena Park, CA 90621
(213) 921-0681
(714) 521-8673
snap-action thermostats

Johnson Controls
temperature switches

Honeywell
7400 Metro Boulevard
Minneapolis, MN 55435
(612) 830-3858
return air controller

Airpax Corp.

*Used in Earth Home

Frederick Division
Husky Park
Frederick, MD 21701
(301) 663-5141
surface sensing and immersion thermostats

Fenwal, Inc.
Ashland, MA
temperature controllers

Electricity -Electronic Components

Selco Products Co.
Orange, CA
Thermisters with high precision

Electricity -Fuses/Breakers, Wiring

Marinco
(800) 767-8541
swdsales@marinco.com
30 amp DC Plug and Receptacle

Gould Shawmut
374 Merrimac Street
Newburyport, Mass 01950
(617) 462-6662
fuses, fuse blocks, most kinds of breakers

Euro plug
European outlet plug

Heineman Electric
P.O. Box 6800
Lawrenceville, NJ 08648-0800
(609) 882-4800
* push button breakers - most kinds

ETA Circuit Breakers
7400 North Croname Road
Chicago, IL 60648
(312) 647-8303
most kinds of breakers

Inmark Corp.
147 West Cedar Street
Norwalk, CT 06854
(203) 866-8474
weber circuit breakers

Relay Specialties, Inc.
13-00 Plaza Road
Fairlawn, NJ 07410
distributor-fuse blocks

Cole Hersee
20 Old Colony Avenue
South Boston, MA 02127-2467
(617) 268-2100
complete line

FIC Corporation
P.O. Box 2046
12216 Parklawn Drive
Rockville, MD 20852
(301) 881-8124
(800) 638-6594
fuses and fuse holders

Little Fuse
800 East Northwest Highway
Des Plaines, IL 60016
(312) 824-1188
(800) 227-0029
fuse blocks/indicator fuses

NASA Tech Brief
Spring 1983
Volume 7, No. 3
MFS-25172
solid state DC circuit breaker

Dennison Manufacturing Co.
Fastener Division
300 Howard Street
(617) 879-0511
(800) 225-5913
cable ties

National Tel-Tronics
State Road Hill
Meadville, PA 16335
(814) 724-6440
clamps and connectors

Mueller Electric Co.
1583 East 31st Street
Cleveland, OH 44114
(216) 771-3225
elec. clamps

Keystone Electronics Corp.
49 Bleecker Street
New York, NY 10012
(212) 475-4600
connectors, etc.

Hoffman Products
170 Allen Boulevard
Framingdale, NY 11735
(516) 293-5244
(800) 645-2014
crimp connectors

King Wire and Cable Corp.
179-45 100th Avenue
Jamaica, NY 11433
(800) 221-0144
wire and cable

Anderson Power Products
Division of High Voltage Engineering Co.
145 Newton Street
Boston, MA 02135
battery cable connectors

A.G. Busch & Co., Inc.
6060 Northwest Highway
Chicago, IL 60631
(312) 631-6216
12 VDC receptacles and plugs (triple outlet)

Plastic and Metal Products
1430 County Line Road
Huntindon Valley, PA 19006
(215) 322-2000
(800) 523-8928
distributor terminals/straps

Cole-Hersee
20 Old Colony Avenue
South Boston, MA 02127-2467
(617) 268-2100
most automotive - truck hardware

*Used in Earth Home

Bishop Graphics, Inc.
5388 Sterling Center Drive
P.O. Box 5007 EZ
Westlake Village, CA 91359-5007
(818) 991-2600
prototype circuit board - do it yourself

W.H. Brady Co. - Ind. Prod. Div.
2221 West Camden Road
P.O. Box 2131
Milwaukee, WI 53201
(414) 351-6630
wire markers

Midwest Components, Inc.
P.O. Box 787
1981 Port City Boulevard
Muskegon, MI 49443
(616) 777-2602
polymer current protector

Photron
77 West Commercial Street
Willits, CA 95490
(707) 459-3211
surge arrestors (lightning)

Thogus Products Co.
1374 West 117th Street
P.O. Box 682
Lakewood, OH 44107
(216) 226-4424
wiring clips

Heyco Molded Products, Inc.
Box 160
Kenilworth, NJ 07033
(201) 245-0033
wiring plugs and plastic hardware

Plastic and Metal Products Corp.
1430 County Line Road
Huntington Vallye, PA 19006
(215) 322-2000
(800) 523-8928
wiring products – all

Electricity -Inverters, Converters

The following are reasons why inverters are not used in Earth Home:

$ They lose 1% to 20% of power.

$ Require periodic servicing and replacement.

$ Expensive.

$ AC appliances are cheap but inefficient.

$ DC lighting does not interfere with TV or radio.

$ Do not produce a true sine save (60 cycle "humm")

$ DC car stereos use a fraction of power of AC models.

$ Some TV's have lines across the screen.

Powerstar
10011 N. Foothill Boulevard
Cupertino, CA 95014
(408) 973-8502
small inverter

Tripp-Lite
power supplies

Trace C-30A
charge controller

Enermaxer
P.O. Box 1436
Ukitah, CA 95482
* Enermaxer controller

J. Gordon Electronic Design, Inc.
7671 Central Avenue N.E.
Minneapolis, MN 55432
(612) 786-2405
custom electronic design

Air Castle
15941 Goldwin Place
South Field, MI 48075
(313) 557-7961
energy-efficient personal computers

Igloo
"Kool Mate"
AC/DC converter

Tumbler Technologies
19201 Phil Lane
Cupertino, CA 95014
(408) 996-8276
small inverters

Electricity -Meters

DC Ammeter
Bluesea.com
PN8248 model number

Datel, Inc.
11 Cabot Boulevard
Mansfield, Ma. 02048
508-339-3000
DC voltage monitors

Shurite Meters, Inc.
577 Grand Avenue
P.O. Box 1848
New Haven, CT 06508-1848
(203) 481-5721
amps, volts, battery condition meter

Simpson
853 Dundee Avenue
Elgin, IL 60120-3090
(312) 697-2260
complete line

Abbeon Cal, Inc.
123-213A Gray Avenue
Santa Barbara, CA 93101
many kinds

Emico
123 North Main Street
Dublin, PA 18917
(215) 249-9330
full line

Modutec, Inc.
920 Candia Road
Manchester, NH 03103

*Used in Earth Home

(603) 669-5121
battery conductor and full line

Prime Instruments
9805 Walford Avenue
Cleveland, OH 44102
(216) 651-0400
* battery charging meter and full line

Perfection Electronic Products Corp.
4850 Delemere Avenue
Royal Oak, MI 48073
(313) 280-1090
battery "fuel" gage

Curtis Instruments, Inc.
200 Kisco Avenue
Mt. Kisco, NY 10549
(914) 666-2971
battery, battery "fuel" gage

Altus Tech Corp.
11569 Encore Circle
Minnetonka, MN 55343
(612) 935-6595
battery energy gage

Anderson Power Products
Division of High Voltage Engineering
145 Newton Street
Boston, MA 02135
battery charge meter

Radio Shack - Micronta
multimeter w/10 AMP DC function

Extech Instruments Corp.
335 Bear Hill Road
Waltham, MA 02154
(617) 890-7440
multimeters, including foot-candle meter

Omnimeter by
Bobier Electronics, Inc.
P.O. Box 1545
512 - 37th Street
Parkersburg, WV 26201
(304) 485-7150
total house meter

Equus
digital voltmeter

F. W. Bell
6120 Hanging Moss Road
Orlando, FL 32807
(800) 775-2550
clip on amp meter

John Fluke Manufacturing Co.
P.O. Box C9090
Everett, WA 98206
testing meters

Beckman Industrial Corp.
630 Puente Street
Brea, CA 92621
(714) 773-8436
testing meters

Triplett
Bluffton, OH 45817-9987
(419) 358-5015
testing meters

Wal-Mart Stores
"Popular Mechanics" Multitester
low-cost meter with 10A DC range

Electricity
-Proximity Sensors

Hyde Park Electronics, Inc.
1875 Founders Drive
Dayton, OH 45420
(937) 252-2121

Electricity
-Relays

Standex
(513) 871-3777
reed relays

Allied Control
Telemechanique, Inc.
100 Relay Road
Plantsville, CT 06479
(203) 621-6771
generally PC-mounted

Schrack North America, Inc.
3 West Chester Plaza
Elmsford, NY 10520
(914) 592-1305
miniature

Guardian Electric Manufacturing Co.
1550 West Carroll Avenue
Chicago, IL 60607
(312) 243-1100
PC-mounted and open

Relay Specialties
13-00 Plaza Road
Fairlawn, NJ 07410
(800) 526-5376
(201) 797-3313
all kinds

Stancor Products
131 Godfrey Street
Logansport, IN 46947
(219) 722-2244
power relays, etc.

Potter & Brumfield
200 South Richland Creek Drive
Princeton, IN 47671-6001
all kinds - 30 amp

Antex Electronics
16100 South Figueroa Street
Gardena, CA 90248
(213) 532-3092
time delay relay

Aromat
250 Sheffield Street
Mountainside, NJ 07092
(201) 232-4260
* 30 A enclosed power relay

Robert Bosch Corp.
2800 South 25th Avenue
Broadview, IL 60153
(312) 865-5200
full line

*Used in Earth Home

Signaline
Div. of Time Mark Corp.
11440 East Pine Street
Tulsa, OK 74116
(918) 438-1220
time delay relay

Struthers-Dunn
512 Lambs Road
P.O. Box 901
Pitman, NJ 08071
(609) 589-7500
relays

Electricity -Sensors-Auto

Delphi Electronics
Delphi Harrison Thermal Systems
Fog sensing for auto industry
716-439-2293
www.delphiauto.com

Electricity -Sensors-Humidity/Fog

Delphi Electronics
Delphi Harrison Thermal Systems
Fog sensing for auto industry
716-439-2293
www.delphiauto.com

Electricity -Sensors-Misc.

Banner engineering Corp.
Tiny sensors such as photoelectric and machine vision

Kavlico, A solectron Company
Moorpark, CA
805-523-2000
OEM sensors-all

Optek Technology
Noncontact fluid sensor detects flow-optoelectronic
Carrolltown, TX

www.rbeelectronics.com
CS 880-DC Current Sensing Module

Emcore InSb Hall Sensors
For pulsed DC applications
www.emcore.com

Sensor Technology Ltd.
Banbury, Oxon, England
Optical switch using piezoelectrics

Murata Electronics North America Inc.
Smyrna, GA
770-436-1300
www.murata-northamerica.com
Shock sensor using piezoelectrics

Tokyo University of Agriculture and Technology
Rotary torque transducer
toyama@cc.tuat.ac.jp

Hamamatsu Corp.
360 Foothill Rd.
Bridgewater, NJ 08807
908-231-0960
S8369 Sun sensor for sun intensity sensing

Meder Electronic, Inc.
766 Falmouth Rd.
Box 2207
Mashpee, MA 02649
(508) 539-4088
www.meder.com
Liquid level sensors w/reed switches

Sunx Sensors
1207 Maple St.
West Des <pomes. IA 50265
(515) 225-0063
ultra-compact photoelectric sensors

Integrated Micromachines Incorporated
3360 East Foothill Blvd.
Pasadena, CA 91107
(888) 813-8880
miniature pressure sensor

Caddock Electronics Inc.
17271 N. Umpqua Hwy.
Roseburg, OR 97470
Current-sensing resistors

CUI Stack, Inc.
9640 SW Sunshine Ct.
Beaverton, Oregon 97005
503-643-4899
DC current sensors

Spectrol Electronics Corp.
4051 Greystrone Dr.
Ontario, Ca. 91761
909-923-3313
resistor fuel sensors

Current Ring Co.
P.O. Box 1525
Ballwin, MO 63022
(314) 227-4740
current indicator

United Elec. Controls Co.
85 School Street
Watertown, MA 02172
(617) 926-1000
pressure/temp switches

Cymatics, Inc.
P.O. Box 448
Naperville, IL 60566
(312) 420-7117
current sensors

Hitachi Motion Sensor Light
(Self-Care catalog)
1-800-345-3371
battery operated motion sensor light

Micro-Switch (Honeywell Division)
Freeport, IL 61032
(815) 235-6600
current sensor, 0-5 psi pressure transducer

Transamerica DeLaval Inc.
Cowles Road
P.O. Box 400
Plainville, CT 06062-0400
sensors and controls

Automatic Switch Co.
Florham Park, NJ 07932
(201) 966-2000

pressure/temp switches

Warner Electric
Brake and Clutch Co.
449 Gardner Street
South Beloit, IL 61080
(815) 389-3771
photo scanners

Systron Donner
Duncan Electronics Division
2865 Fairview Road
Costa Mesa, CA 92626
robotics controls

Electro National Corp.
Matthews Avenue
Canton, MS 39046
(601) 859-5511
DC current sensor and voltage sensor

Enmet Corp.
P.O. Box 979
Ann Arbor, MI 48106
(313) 761-1270
CO_2 detector

F.W. Bell
6120 Hanging Moss Road
Orlando, FL 32807
(407) 678-6900
DC current sensors

Lucas Novasensor
1055 Mission Court
Fremont, CA 94539
(510) 770-0645
pressure sensor

Force Imaging
3424 Touhy Avenue
Chicago, IL 60645
(800) 348-3240
(708) 674-7665
tiny force sensors

Electricity
-Sensors-Pressure

Omron Electronic Components
847-882-2288
MEMS technology
pressure sensor measuring .01 psi

All Sensors
www.allsensors.com
surface mount pressure sensors
408-225-4314

Beswick Engineering
Greenland, NH
Tiny pressure regulator

Urosolutions
Orlando, FL
407-447-1519
natural bladder pressure valve

Electricity
-Solenoids

GW Lisk Co., Inc.
Clifton Springs, NY 14432
(315) 462-2611
DC solenoids (push-pull)

Dliftronics, Inc.
2 South Street
Clifton Springs, NY 14432
(315) 462-9471
rotary solenoids

Relay Specialties, Inc.
13-00 Plaza Road
Fairlawn, NJ 07410
(201) 797-3313
(800) 526-5376
solenoids, relays

Kogyosha Co., Ltd.
179 Riveredge Road
Tenafly, NJ 07670
(201) 569-8769
solenoids

Deltrol Controls
2745 South 19th Street
Milwaukee, WI 53215
(414) 671-6800
solenoids

Electricity
-Switches
-----Float
-----Fluid
-----Miscellaneous
-----Pressure

Clark Solutions
Hudson, MA
.1-1.2 in. wc pressure range

Schurter
1-800-848-2600
piezo-effect electronic switches
hazard, explosion-proof

Standex Electronics
4538 Camberwell Road
Cincinnatti, Ohio 45209
(513) 871-3777
Reed switches for current measurement (with coiled wire)

Holly Solar Products
P.O. Box 864
Detaluma, CA 94952
(707) 763-6173
"conserve" switches, dimmer switch

McGill Manufacturing Co., Inc.
Valparaiso, IN 46383
heavy duty 4 pole switch

Control Products, Inc.
East Hanover, NJ 07936
(201) 887-9400
waterproof switches

Electro Switch Corporation
Weymouth, MA 02188
multi-position rotary switches

*Used in Earth Home

Fifth Dimension, Inc.
801 New York Avenue
Trenton, NJ 08638
(609) 393-8350
PC-mounted, tilt, delay switches

Cole Hersee
20 Old Colony Avenue
Boston, MA 02127-2467
(617) 268-2100
automotive - momentary, etc.

Heineman Electric Co.
P.O. Box 6800
Lawrenceville, NJ 08648-0800
(609) 882-4800
panel switch-fused and many others

EAO Switches Corp.
P.O. Box 552
198 Pepe's Farm Road
Milford, CT 06460
(203) 877-4577
many

Granzow, Inc.
6033 Kenley Lane
Charlotte, NC 28210
(704) 545-2200
(800) 222-5251
tapeswitches

Chicago Switch
1714 North Damen
Chicago, IL 60647
(312) 489-5500
many

Linemaster Switch Corp.
Plain Hill Road
Woodstock, CT U.S.A. 06281
(203) 974-1000
foot switches

Tapeswitch Corp. of America
100 Schmitt Boulevard
Farmingdale, NY 11735
(516) 694-6312
tape switches

Electric Switches, Inc.
2478 Fletcher Drive
Los Angeles, CA 90039
(800) 421-5588
full catalog - all

Illinois Lock Co.
305 West Hintz Road
Wheeling, IL 60090
(315) 537-1800
(800) 733-3907
key switches

Chicago Lock Co.
4311-T West Belmont Avenue
Chicago, IL 60641
(312) 282-7177
key switches

Medeco Security Locks, Inc.
P.O. Box 3075
Salem, VA 24153
(703) 380-5000
key switch locks

Berquist Co.
5300 Edina Ind. Boulevard
Minneapolis, MN 55435-3791
(612) 835-2522
membrane switches

Coventry Specialty Corporation
4 Ascutney Avenue
Westfield, MA 01085
(413) 568-6355
special

Fifth Dimension, Inc.
801 New York Avenue
Tranton, NJ 08638
PC-tilt switches

Otto Controls Division
2 East Main Street
Carpenters Ville, IL 60110
(708) 428-7171
many

Pres Air Trol Corp.
895 Mamaroneck Avenue
Mamaroneck, NY 10543
(914) 698-2026
* low pressure switches - air operated

Compac Engineering, Inc.
Box 9
Paradise, CA 95969
(916) 872-2040
switches

Revere Corporation of America
845 North Colony Road
P.O. Box 56
Wallingford, CT 06492
(203) 269-7701
switches

Madison Co.
9 Business Park Drive
Branford, CT 06405
(203) 488-4477
* submersible, BLE switches

Transamerica DeLaval, Inc.
Gems Sensors Division
Cowles Road
Plainville, CT 06062-9990
(203) 677-1311
* small float switches

Fluid Products Co., Inc.
14590 Martin Drive
Eden Prairie, MN 55344
(612) 937-2467
switches

Robertshaw Controls Co.
Uni-Line Division
Huntington Beach, CA 92647
SE 8000 023 sensitive water level

Riko Co., Ltd.
No. 2-52
Higashi 2-Chome
Nakanocho, Tondabayaski
Osaka 584 JAPAN
switches

Signal Systems International, Inc.

*Used in Earth Home

P.O. Box 470
Lavallette, NJ 08735
(201) 793-4668
switches

Chem Tec Equipment
234 SW 12th Avenue
Deerfield Beach, FL 33442
(305) 428-8259
switches

Electricity -Timers

Cole Parmer
digital timers - entire catalog

SSAC
P.O. Box 395
Liverpool, NY 13088
(315) 622-1000
whole catalog - 12 VDC time delay relays

DIEHL Time Controls
Borg Instruments, Inc.
902 Wisconsin Street
DeLavan, WI 53115
(414) 728-5531
24-hr. time switch 12 VDC

Deltrol Controls
2745 South 19th Street
Milwaukee, WI 53215
(414) 671-6800
timers - all kinds

Kessler - Ellis Products Co.
120 First Avenue
Atlantic Highlands, NJ 07716
(201) 291-0500
timers - all kinds

Valcor Engineering Corp.
2 Lawrence Road
Springfield, NJ 07081
(201) 467-8400
pulse timers

Texas Instruments, Inc.
Appliance Controls Marketing
300 North Main Street
Versailles, KY 40383
(606) 873-3161
low cost time delay relays

RBE Electronics
P.O. Box 1329
714 Corporation Street
Aberdeen, SD 57401
(800) 342-1912
(605) 226-2448
sold state timers

Artisan Electronics
5 Eastmans Road
Parsippany, NJ 07980
timing modules

Real Goods Trading Co.
#25-405, #25-401
programmable 12V timer .01 amp draw
outdoor lighting timer

Signaline
Div. of Time Mark Corp.
11440 East Pine Street
Tulsa, OK 74116
(918) 438-1220
time delay relay

Electricity -Wiring-General

Anderson Power Products
13 Pratts Junction Rd.
Sterling, MA 01564
(978) 422-3600
www.andersonpower.com
high amperage battery connectors

A. G. Busch & Co. Inc.
6060 Northwest Highway
Chicago, IL 60631-2950
(312) 631-6216
12 VDC plugs and receptacles

Thogus Products Co.
1374 West 117th Street
P.O. Box 682
Lakewood, OH 44107
(216) 226-4424
wiring clips

Heyco Molded Products Inc.
Box 160
Kenilworth, NJ 07033
(201) 245-0033
wiring plugs and plastic hardware

Plastic & Metal Products Corp.
1430 County Line Road
Huntingdon Valley, PA 19006
(215) 322-2000
(800) 523-8928
wiring products - all

Alternative Energy Source Book
From Real Goods Trading Co.
4 remote home kits (complete electrical power systems)
DC load and distribution centers

E-Z Circuit
Bishop Graphics, Inc.
Westlake Village, CA 91359
circuit board kit

W. H. Brady Co.
Industrial Products Div.
2221 W. Camden Road
P.O. Box 2131
Milwaukee, WI 53201
(414) 351-6630
wire markers

Dennison Mfg. Co.
Fastener Division
300 Howard Street
Framington, MA 01701
(800) 225-5913
cable ties

Cole Hersee
20 Old Colony Avenue
South Boston, MA 02127
(617) 268-2100
12V switches, etc.

Curtis Instruments Inc.

*Used in Earth Home

200 Kisco Avenue
Mt. Kisco, NY 10549
battery fuel gauge

Anderson Power Products
145 Newton Street
Boston, MA 02135
battery capacity gauge

King Wire and Cable
179-45 - 110th Avenue
Jamaica, NY 11433
(718) 657-4422
(800) 221-0144
wire, cable

Hoffman Products
170 Allen Boulevard
Farmingdale, NY 11735
(516) 293-5244
(800) 645-2014
connectors

A Car Battery Powers This Horse
September 1979
Popular Mechanics
article

Conical Electrical Connectors
- Align Easily
NASA article

Keystone Electronics Corp.
49 Bleecker Street
New York, NY 10012
(212) 475-4600
battery holders and misc.

Mueller Electric Co.
1583 E. 31st Street
Cleveland, OH 44114
(216) 771-5225
electrical clips, clamps

National Tel-Tronics
State Road Hill
Meadville, PA 16335
(814) 724-6440
battery and alligator clips

Canada Mortgage and Housing Corp.
home electronic bus project

Nu-Tek Plastics, Inc.
#25-11151 Horseshoe Way
Richmond, BC V7A 4S5
CANADA
(604) 272-5550
air-tight electrical boxes

Energy

-Publications

Refocus
International renewable energy magazine
www.re-focus.net

American Council for an Energy-Efficient Economy
1001 Connecticut Avenue, NW
Suite 801
Washington, DC 20036
www.aceee.org

Engines

-Related Products

Ingersoll - Rand
Power Tool Division
28 Kennedy Boulevard
East Brunswick, NJ 08816
air-powered starters

Start Master
Division of Sycon Corp.
P.O. Box 491
959 Cheney Avenue
Marion, OH 43302
(614) 382-5771
air-powered starters

Engines

-Small Engines

Teledyne Wisconsin Motor
4 stroke

Briggs & Stratton Corp.
Milwaukee, WI 53201
4 stroke

Tecumseh Products Co.
Engine & Gear Service Division
Grafton, WI 53024
(414) 377-2700
4 stroke

Enya Metal Products Co., Ltd
5-11-13 Toyotama-Kita, Nerima
Tokyo, JAPAN
.35, .40, .60 and .90 cu.in. engines

Saito Seisakusho, Ltd.
3-22-7 Tokagi, Ichikawa-ski
Chiba Prefecture, JAPAN
.30, .40, .45, .80, .90 and 1.2 engines

O.S. Engines Mfg. Co., Ltd.
6-15 3-chome, Imagawa
Higashisumihoshi-ku
Osaka 546, JAPAN
.40, .60, .80 and 1.2 engines

Magnum Engines
9 Andover CLose
Luton, Bedfordshire, ENGLAND LU4 9EQ
.91, 1.8 and 2.7 cu.in. engines

Condor Engines, Ltd.
1 Church Green, Roxwell
Chelmsford, Essex, ENGLAND
.91 cu.in. engines

Newstock Service Co.
45 Newport Street
Nelson, Lancashire BB9 7RW, ENGLAND
.60 R.V.E. engines

Webra Modellbau GmbH
Industriestrasse 287
D-8581 Weidenberg, WEST GERMANY
.87 cu.in. engines

Jamara Modelltechnik
Leutkirch 1, D-7970

*Used in Earth Home

WEST GERMANY
2.2 cu.in. engines

Kawasaki
650 Valley Park Drive
Shakopee, MN 55379
(612) 445-6060
2 stroke

Clinton Engines Corp.
Maquoketa, IA
engines

Fox Manufacturing Co.
5305 Towson Avenue
Fort Smith, AR 72901
(501) 646-1656
2 stroke tiny

Leisure Dynamics - Cox
4400 West 78th Street
Minneapolis, MN 55435
tiny

Roper - Everett H. Yost
RR #1, Box 37
Sauk City, WI 53583
(608) 643-3194
tiny

New Stock Service Co.
45 Newport STreet
Nelson, Lancs.
tiny 2 stroke

Trinden Manufacturing, Ltd.
P.O. Box 544 Canada Avenue
Huron Park, Ontario N0M 1YO
CANADA
(519) 228-6514
bicycle engine

Ryobi
4-cycle trimmer

Fabrics- (See also Films-Plastic)

-Cord, Webbing

Jones Webbing & Tape Co.
170 Cherry Valley Avenue
West Hepstead, NY 11552
(516) 538-8668
webbing

EON Corp.
2527 San Fernando Road
Los Angeles, CA 90065
(213) 223-1241
cord, lacing

Daburn Electronics & Cable Co.
70 Oak Street
Norwood, NJ 07648
(201) 768-5400
lacing, cord

Into the Wind
1408 Pearl Street
Boulder, CO 80302
kevlar kite string

Metalized Products
37 East Street
Winchester, Mass 01890
(617) 729-8300
aluminized polyethylene (space blanket) fabric

Indiana Mills & Mfg. Co.
120 West Main Street
Carmel, IN 46032
(317) 846-6631
straps, tie downs

Shelter-Rite
Division of Seaman Corp.
Millersburg, OH 44654
(216) 674-0040
(800) 521-7656
industrial coated fabrics

Snyder Mfg. Co., Ltd.
P.O. Box 188
3000 Progress Street
Dover, OH 44622
(216) 343-4450
laminated fabrics

Firestone Coated Fabrics Co.
American Fuel Cell and Coated Fabrics Co.
P.O. Box 887
Magnolia, AR 71753
rubber coated fabrics

Weblon, Inc.
Fox Island Road
P.O. Box 190
Port Chester, NY 10573
(914) 937-3900inflatable boat fabric
fabric

Internet
2730 Nevada Avenue North
Minneapolis, MN 55427
(612) 541-9690
plastic netting

W.L. Gore & Associates, Inc.
3 Blue Ball Road
P.O. Box 1130
Elkton, MD 21921-1130
(301) 398-6400
Gore-tex

American Waterproofing
New Haven, MO 63068
(314) 237-4404
polyester tent fabric

Tapetex
240 Commerce Drive
P.O. Box N
Rochester, NY 14623
(716) 334-0480
nylon fabrics

Hercules, Inc.
Northeastern Region
Marketing Center
Wilmington, Del. 19894
(362) 992-7000
light fabrics (bonding, etc.)

Apex Mills Corp.
168 Doughty Boulevard
P.O. Box 149
Inwood, NY 11696-0149
(516) 239-4400

light weight scrims, fabric

"Tencel" By
Courtaulds Fibers
P.O. Box 141
Axis, AL 36505
(spun by Burlington Knits)
solvent-spun cellulose (from trees)

Dura Cote Corp.
350 North Diamond Street
Ravenna, OH 44266
(216) 296-3486
vinyl-laminated reinforced fabrics

Viking Technical Rubber
P.O. Box 8236
163 Orange Avenue
West Haven, CT 06516
(203) 934-3401
hypalon coated nylon

Humphrys Textile Products, Inc.
1217-41 Carpenter Street
Philadelphia, PA 19147
(215) 463-3000
(800) 523-4503)
textile products (tarps, etc.)

STO-Cote Products, Inc.
Brawer 310
Richmond, IL 60071
(815) 675-2358
(800) 435-2621
woven products

Top Value Fabrics
316 South Range Line Road
Carmel, IN 46032
(317) 844-7496
tarps, etc.

Cyclop Strapping Corp.
Boot Road
Downingtown, PA 19335
(215) 873-0290
strapping

Indeco Packaging Division
P.O. Box 1047
2410 Barnes Drive
San Marcos, TX 78666
strapping

American Mfg. Co.
206 Willow Avenue
Huntsdale, PA 18431
(717) 253-5860
strapping buckles

DJ Associates, Inc.
8411 South Zero Street
Fort Smith, Ark. 72903
(501) 452-3987
buckles, fasteners

Armorlon Division
P.O. Box 33569
Houston, TX
(800) 231-6074
(woven poly) armorlon film

Griffolyn Division

Reef Ind., Inc.
P.O. Box 33248
Houston, TX 77233
reinforced plastic films and polytape

Humphrys Textile Products
Webb Mfg. Co.
1241 Carpenter Street
Philadelphia, PA 19147
(800) 523-4503
many

Raven Ind.
Box 1007
Sioux Falls, SD 57117
(800) 843-6840
(513) 568-4754
tarps, woven poly

The Hawaiian Hemp Co.
P.O. Box 2056
Pahoa, HI 96778
(808) 965-8600
hemp fabric products

Atkins & Pearce, Inc.
One Braid Way
Covington, KY 41017
(606) 356-2001
Vectran fiber (compare to Kevlar)

Hemp fiber (cannabis sativa)
one of the strongest fibers in the world--
also soil building plant

Fabrics-Cord Webbing
-High Temperature Fabrics

3M Ceramic Fiber Products
219-1 3M Center
St. Paul, MN 55101
Nextel 312

The Carborundum Co.
Insulation Division
P.O. Box 808
Niagra Falls, NY 14302
(716) 278-6221
fiberfrax

Delaware Assbestos/Rubber Co.
3645 North Smedley Street
Philadelphia, PA 19140
(215) 223-9500
fabric

Newtex
8050 Victor-Mendon Road
Victor, NY 14564
(800) 836-1001
hi-temp fabrics

Fans (See Air section)

Fasting

The Ancient Cookfire: How to Rejuvenate Body
And Spirit through seasonal Foods and Fasting
Carrie L'Esperance
Book on fasting and diet

*Used in Earth Home

The Miracle of Fasting
Paul Bragg
Book on fasting

Fats/Oils (See Animals, Plants-Legumes, or Plants-Grains)

Fermenting

http://www.fao.org/docrep/x0560e/x0560e11.htm
Pit preservation methods/fermentation

Microbiology of Food Fermentations
Carl S. Pederson
Book on the specifics of fermentation

Biological Principles in Fermentation
J.G. Carr
Book on fermentation

www.fao.org
fermenting information

Fermented Foods
A.H. Rose
Book on microbiology of fermented foods

Indigenous Fermented Food of Non-Western Origin
C.W. Hesseltine and Hwa L. Wang
J.Cramer
Book

Handbook of Indigenous Fermented Foods
Keith Steinkraus
book

Legume-Based Fermented Foods
N.R. Reddy, Merle Pierson, D.K. Salunkhe
book

Fermented Meats
G. Campbell-Platt and P.E. Cook
Book on fermented meat products

Beatrice Trum Hunter's fact/book on
Fermented Foods and Beverages-An Old Tradition
Keats Publishing, Inc.

Brine Preservation of Vegetables
J.L. Etchells, I.D. Jones, and M.A. Hoffman
Article on brine preservation

Indigenous Fermented Food of Non-Western Origin
Edited by C.W. Hesseltine and Hwa L. Wang
Fermented foods book-detailed

Fermented Foods of the World
By Geoffrey Campbell-Platt
Book on fermented foods

Handbook of Indigenous Fermented Foods
By Keith H. Steinkraus
Book on fermented foods

Saliva was used as a source of diastase (amylase) for conversion of starch to sugars in fermented alcoholic beverages such as Japanese sake and South American chicha

Fiberoptics

Norell, Inc.
3496 Winhoma Drive
P.O. Box 18382
Memphis, TN 38181
extruded acrylic rod

Esco Products, Inc.
171 Oak Ridge Road
Oak Ridge, NJ 07438
(201) 697-3700
lenses

Applied Products Corp.
96 Monroe Street
Bristol, PA 19007
(215) 785-1816
plastic lenses

Fiberoptics Technology, Inc.
1 Fiber Road
Pomfret, CT 06258
(203) 928-0443
industrial fiberoptics products

Rolyn Optics Co.
706 Arrow Grand Circle
Covina, CA 91722-2199
(818) 915-5707
(818) 915-5717
lenses and more

Himawari
Sumitomo Corp. of America (L.A. office)
444 South Flower Street
Los Angeles, CA 90071-2975
(213) 627-4783
fiberoptic concentrating lens apparatus

Large-Scale Optics
Trim Light Bulbs
Machine Design
April 12, 1979, p. 107
Tech. NASA briefs

Films-Plastic

-General

Continental Plastic Co.
Division of CPI, Inc.
452 Diens Drive
Wheeling, IL 60090
(312) 541-1960
films

Plastic Suppliers
Division of PlasticCorp
3330 Hollman Avenue
South Chicago Heights, IL 60411
(312) 493-8673
polystyrene film (window)

Flex-O-Glass, Inc.
1100 North Cicero Avenue
Chicago, IL 60651
polystyrene film

Signode
3650 West Lake Avenue
Glenview, IL 60025
(800) 323-2464
UV film stretch wrap

*Used in Earth Home

Interthor
1817 Beach Street
Broadview, IL 60153
(312) 345-1270
stretch wrapping

Insul Rib, Inc.
P.O. Box 447
Castle Rock, MN 55010
(612) 463-7009
"Polyvent" greenhouse tubes

Solar Stat
18920 N.E. Fifth Avenue
Miami, FL 33179
Window Film - (800) 783-0454
sun-control film (vinyl)

Clear-View Shade
6124 N. Broadway
Chicago, IL 60660
(312) 262-2360
sun-control film

Midwest Marketing
P.O. Box 2063
East Peoria, IL 61611
(309) 688-8858
many films

Madico, Inc.
64 Industrial Parkway
Woburn, MA 01888
(617) 935-7850
solar film manufacturer

Films-Plastic
-Related Items

Conwed - Plastics Division
P.O. Box 43237
St. Paul, MN 55164-0237
(612) 221-1260
birdnet plastic netting

Imtra
151 Mystic Avenue
Medford, MA 02155
(617) 391-5660
inflatable boat fabric

DuPont
Textile Fibers Department
Laurel Run Building
P.O. Box 80, 705
Wilmington, DE 19880-0705
"Reemay" and "Tyvek"

J.P. Stevens & Co.
Stevens Elastomeric/Roofing Systems
395 Pleasant Street
Northhampton, MA 01061-0658
(413) 586-8750
roof membranes

Owens-Corning Fiberglass Corp.
Fabric Structures Division
Fiberglass Tower
Toledo, OH 43659
(419) 248-8518
fabric structures material

Ross Daniels, Inc.
1720 Fuller Road
BOx 65430
West Des Moines, IA 50265
(515) 225-6471
plastic netting

Trans World Pacific Corp.
2133 Fourth Street
Berkeley, CA 94710
(415) 548-4434
(800) 227-1570
poly netting

Shelter Supply
1325 East 79th Street
Minneapolis, MN 55425
(612) 854-4266
(800) 328-4827
distributor of low moisture vapor barriers

3M Contractor Products
Building 223-4N-06
3M Center
St. Paul, MN 55144-1000
sealing tapes

Foam Tech
(612) 378-3113
polyethylene foam films (dist.)

Packaging Aids Corp.
469 Bryant Street
P.O. Box 77203
San Francisco, CA 94107
(415) 362-9902
poly tubing

Agratech
2131 Piedmont Way
Pittsburg, CA 94565
(415) 432-3399
poly fasteners

Filters
-Air

Airguard
3807 Bishop Lane
Louisville, Kentucky 40218
Phone: 502-969-2304
Toll Free: 1-800-999-3458
Fax: 502-961-0930
E-mail: mailbag@airguard.com
multi-stage filter media in fabric

filters-air
Camfil Farr
V-Bank Durafil air filters
More surface area

Filters
-Drinking Water Filtration Products

www.purennatural.com
www.naturalsolutions1.com
www.water4u.co.kr
www.sacredwater.org/sacred.html
water ionizers

Berkefeld
Doulton

Silver-impregnated ceramic
Search Internet for Berkefeld

National Safety Associates, Inc.
4260 East Raines Road
Memphis, TN 38118
activated charcoal

Keystone Filter Division
2385 North Pen Road
Box 380
Hatfield, PA 19440-0380
(215) 822-1963
silver/ceramic carbon combination

American Water Purification
1990 Olivera Road
Concord, CA 19520
(415) 825-9100
many units

Multi-Pure Corp.
9200 Deering Avenue
Chatsworth, CA 91311-5858
(818) 341-7377
many

Aquafine
25230 West Avenue Stanford
Valencia, CA 91355
(and McMaster-Carr)
(805) 257-4770
(800) 423-3015
* 12 VDC ultraviolet purifier

Dynion Water Systems Inc.
P.O. Box 34014
Omaha, NE 68134
(402) 571-3857
ceramic units

General Ecology Inc.
151 Sheree Boulevard
Lionville, PA 19353
(215) 363-7900
domestic filters

Katadyn U.S.A. Inc.
3020 North Scottsdale Road
Scottsdale, AZ 85251
(602) 990-3131
* silver ceramic

Bon-Del
3104 East Camelback Road, #110
Phoenix, AZ 85016-4595
(602) 277-8300
cartridge

Water Filter Fact Sheet
"Mother Earth News"
page 160
article and chart

Activated Carbon in Drinking Water Technology
book by AWWA Research Foundation

Carbon Adsorption Handbook
(Ann Arbor Science)
Paul N. Cheremisinoff
Fred Ellerbusch

Filters

-General

Ametek
Plymouth Products Div.
502 Indiana Avenue
Sheboygan, WI 53081
(414) 457-9435
many kinds

Osmonics, Inc.
5951 Clearwater Drive
Minnetonka, MN 55343
(612) 933-2277
silver membrane

Serfilco - Div. of Service Filtration Corp.
1415 Waukegan Road
Northbrook, IL 60062
(312) 498-1010
cartridge filters

Chlorine and boil
Reverse osmosis
Deionization
Distillation
Activated carbon
Sediment filter
Sand filters
article - filter options

Norman Equipment Co.
Filter Division
P.O. Box 1349
9850 South Industrial Dr.
Bridgeview, IL 60454
(312) 430-4000
filters

Methods for Solving Our Water Problems
Page 83
Real Goods Trading
Alternative Energy Sourcebook
article

Balston Filter Products
703 Massachusetts Avenue
P.O. Box C
Lexington, Mass. 02173
(617) 861-7240
(800) 343-4048
filters - many

Amiad U.S.A., Inc.
16735 Sticoy St., #109
Van Nuys, CA 91406
(818) 781-4055
irrigation filters - plastic and discs

Recovery Engineering
Minneapolis, MN
de-salting filter

Diversified Imports, Inc.
Corporate Park
1095 Towbin Avenue
P.O. Box 539
Lakewood, NJ 08701
(201) 363-2333
"Filtertap" disc unit

The K.J. Miller Corp.
2401 Gardner Road
Broadview, IL 60153
(312) 865-0800

*Used in Earth Home

water clarifier

Tetko Inc.
5050 Newport Dr., Suite 1
Rolling Meadows, IL 60008
stainless/plastic/woven screen

Plum Creek Mfg. Co.
P.O. Box 2
West Highway 20
Ainsworth, NE 69210
(402) 387-0347
reverse osmosis filters - drinking water

Hi Perm
Filter Equipment Corp.
140 East Merrick Road
P.O. Box 389
Freeport, NY 11520
(516) 379-7777
pool filters

Rustrap Mfg. Co.
P.O. Box 95
81 South Main
Edgerton, MN 56128
(507) 442-3451
rust removing filters

Oreck Corporation
100 Plantation Road
New Orleans, LA 70123
(800) 989-4200
electrostatic air filter

Rosedale Products, Inc. or
Flow Ezy Filters, Inc.
Box 1085
Ann Arbor, MI 48106
(313) 665-8201
cleanable wire filters

Keller Products inc.
Box 26
Lexington, Mass. 02173
(800) 352-8422
* cleanable disc filters

Arkal Beit-Zera
D.N. Emek Hayarden 15135
067-55331 ISRAEL

U.S. Solcor Irrigation
Distributor
16216 Raymer Street
Van Nuys, CA 91406
(818) 989-5911
* cleanable disc filters

Ron Vik Inc.
800 Colorado Avenue South
Minneapolis, MN 55416
(612) 545-0276
smaller strainers/wire cloth

Keller Products, Inc.
Box 26
Lexington, MA 02173
(800) 352-8422
* cleanable disc filters

Crane Co.
Cochrane Environmental Systems
800 - 3rd Avenue
P.O. Box 60191
King of Prussia, PA 19406
(215) 265-5050
filters

Heartland Promotions
Special Merchandising Headquarters
5023 Grover Street
Omaha, NE 68106-9957
(800) 851-6291
permanent furnace filter

Improvements
4944 Commerce Parkway
Cleveland, OH 44128
(800) 642-2112
permanent "electrostatic" air filters

Permatron Corp.
11400 Melrose Street
Franklin Park, IL 60131
permanent "electrostatic" air filters

Global Environmental Technologies
(800) 800-TERRA

Pure Air Systems, Inc.
701 Sundown Circle
Plainfield, IN 46168
HEPA filters

Fish/Aquaculture, Worms

-Feeding Fish

http://www.drydenaqua.com/feeders/clockwork_fish_feeders.htm
12-24 hour feeder (OK with pellets)
*used in Earth Home

http://www.milieu-nomics.com/how.html
DAF dissolved air flotation pumps

Nutrient Requirements of Fish
National Research Council
www.nap.edu

www.fao.org
Unconventional Feed ingredients for Fish Feed

feeding excreta to fish
www.aquatext.com
liquid manure

Freshwater Fish Pond Culture and Management
Marilyn Chakroff
Book on fish farming in Peace Corps

Red Manure Worm
Eisenia Foetida (770 soil temp)
- it reproduces rapidly and will eat almost any organic material at some stage of decay
article

Killifish for feeding fish

Fish Ailments and Diagnosis Chart
chart

Home Aquaculture
Van Gorder Strange
book

Gambusia east Mosquito larvae
article

*Used in Earth Home

Fish-attracting electrical current - experimental
non-traditional method - article

Cabellas
black light to attract insects

New Alchemy Institute
information source

Ecology of Compost
Daniel Dindal
information source

How to Hand Sort Worms
article

Worms Eat My Garbage
Mary Appelhof
information source

Leeches (Hirudinea)
Their Structure, Physiology, Ecology, and Embryology
by K. H. Mann
book

Biopharm U.S.A., Ltd.
701 East Bay Street
Box 1212
Charleston, SC 29403
(803) 742-3537
retail - leeches

#502 4-Day Fish Feeder
(800) 424-6255
(rotating drum drops pellets)

Fish/Aquaculture, Worms -Potential Fish for Raising

Pirarucu (redfish)
Amazon
Paiche (Peru)
Arapaima (British Buiana)
article

Gouramis (Malaysia)
raised in rain barrels
T. Pectoralis
article

Rice-fish polyculture
Chinese aquatic polyculture
gass carp and other carp
article

Freshwater shrimp and prawns
article

Mussels
article

Poly-prawns and catfish
- algae for food
article

Crawfish - 7 forages
article

Natural Chemicals, Inc.
P.O. Box 2446
Naples, FL 33939
"Crawler Caller"

Fish/Aquaculture, Worms -Sources for Fish

George Lukach
Central Minnesota Fish Farmers Association
Route 1
Buffalo, MN 55313
fish farming in your solar greenhouse

Amity Foundation
P.O. Box 11048
Eugene, OR 97440
source

DNR publications
- license to take fish from streams
- list of private fish hatchery licenses
source

The Catfish Institute
118 Hayden Court
P.O. Box 247
Belzoni, Miss. 39038
misc. products

Catfish Farmers of America
100 Highway 82E
Indianola, MS 38751
(601) 887-2699
source

Aeration methods
article

Method to smoke fish
Article

Fish/Aquaculture, Worms -Worms

Yelm Earthworms and Castings Farm
1477 Elliot Ave. W
Seattle, WA 98119
1-877-339-6767
www.yelmworms.com/vermicomposting

*Bowjon Wind compressors
888-ONSOLAR

Pacu-relative of the Piranha
Needs warm water

Hedlunds of Medford, Inc.
P.O. Box 305
Medford, WI 54451
120 VAC bug-attracting lights

Thoro System Products, Inc.
7800 NW 38th Street
Miami, FL 33166
(305) 592-2081
fish tank cement coatings

Old Boys Enterprises
4585 Schneider Drive
Oregon, WI 53575
black light fish tank, aeration products

*Used in Earth Home

Commerce Welding & Mfg. Co.
2200 Evanston
Dallas, TX 75208
12V aerator

AREA (Aquaculture Research/Environmental Associates)
P.O. Box 1303
Homestead, FL 33090
(305) 248-4205
full catalog - tank aeration/
fish raising equipment

Bex, Inc.
37709 Schoolcraft Road
Livonia, MI 48150-1009
(313) 464-8282
eductors for circulation

Turkey Mullein - poison fish
article

Fish tank sizes - measurement chart
article

Hydroponic hothouse
section notes on fish
book excerps

Appropriate Technology Transfer for Rural Areas
(ATTRA)
P.O. Box 3657
Fayetteville, AR 72702
(501) 442-9824
(800) 346-9140
good source, booklets on aquaculture
in closed/recirculating systems

ATTRA
Vegetarian fish such as grass carp grown
with crayfish
article

Flax/Straw/Fibers

Straw R 2.3 per inch

George Herrmann, Inc.
45 Nebury Street
Boston, Mass 02116-3197
(617) 426-1431
processed flax fibers for non-skid paint additive

F. Erv. Oelke
University of Minnesota
(612) 625-1211
flax expert

Kimbery Clark
13 South 4th Street
Grand Forks, ND 58201
(701) 746-8441
flax shive (waste product)

U.S. Borax
(312) 318-5400
borax (fireproof)

Ecusta - Marlin Caine
(701) 256-3550
* baled flax for linen

Also - Kenaf (Hibiscus Cannabinus) has been tried
in the southern U.S.
good fiber

M.W. Jenkins Sons, Inc.
P.O. Box 70
Cedar Grove, NJ
201-CE9-5150
fiber brushes - all kinds

Plants for People Book
Anna Lewington
p. 46 on Flax
article

Out on Bale, Ltd.
1037 E. Linden Street
Tucson, AZ 85719
(602) 624-1673
straw-bale construction

The Straw Bale House
Athena Swentzell Steen
Bill Steen
David Bainbridge
straw-bale book

Wirecraft Mfg.
St. Louis, MO 314-381-4445
Ty-Rite wire ties

U.S. Borax
Los Angeles
5 mol granular tech. Borax (fireproofing)

Flamort Chemical Company
746 Natoma Street
San Francisco, CA 94103
(415) 621-7825
WC (fireproofing)

A Straw/Bales/Mortar House
Demonstration Project
Prepared for Project Implementation Division
Policy Research and Programs Sector
Canadian Mortgage and Housing Corporation
by Louis Gagne
booklet

Archibio
1267, Lac Delignby
Mandeville, Quebec J0K 1L0
CANADA
(514) 835-4682
(514) 835-9040

Flooring

www.naturalcork.com
Cork flooring products

www/floorshop.com
natural cork flooring

Food

-Acid/Alkaline

Acid and Alkaline
By Herman Aihara
Book on pH of foods

Food

-Additives

*Used in Earth Home

A Consumer's Dictionary of Food Additives
Ruth Winter
Complete guide

Food

The Food Combining/Blood Type Diet Solution
Dina Khader

Food Combining
A Step-by-Step Guide
Kathryn Marsden

The Hay Diet Made Easy
Jackie Habgood

Food

-Storage/Preparation

Putting Food By
Janet Greene
Rugh Hertzberg
Beatrice Vaughn
Book on root cellars and more

Pickled, Potted, and Canned
Sue Shephard
How Food Preserving changed the world--book

Preserving the Fruits of the Earth
Stanley Schuler
Elizabeth Schuler
Book on preserving food

Root Cellaring
Mike and Nancy Bubel
book

Keeping Food Fresh
Old World Techniques & Recipes
The Gardeners and Farmers of Terre Vivante
Chelsea Green Publishing Company
Extensive food preservation book

Freezers (see Refrigerators)

Fuel Cells

-CHP/Fuel Cell Manufacturers

UTC Fuel Cells
Mfr. of key fuel cell systems

CellTech
Single-step hydrogen reformer
www.nixonpeabody.com

-Fuel Cell Technologies

Fuel Cell Summit 2005
Society of Manufacturing Engineers

Fuel Cell Systems Explained, Second Edition
John Wiley & Sons, 2003
Principles of fuel cells book

Electric Fuel Corporation
N.Y., N.Y.
Instant Power Charger

Small fuel cells for cell phones etc.--2003

Polyfuel
Menlo Park, CA
Small fuel cells for cell phones etc.--2003

Dais MEA (Membrane/Electrode Assembly)
www.dais.net

Northwest Power Systems
Fuel processors for PEM systems
(Proton Exchange Membrane)

Ballard
Developmental fuel cells
(early Fraunhofer)

Avista Corp.
1411 E. Mission St.
P.O. Box 3727
Spokane, Washington 99220-3727
509-495-4817

www2.thefuture.net
hydrogen sites

Northwest Power Systems
924 S.E. Wilson Ave., Suite F
Bend, OR 97702
541-383-3390

Energy Partners , L.C.
1501 Northpoint Parkway, Suite 102
West Palm Beach, FL 33407
561-688-0500

Plug Power
968 Albany-Shaker Road
Latham, NY 12110
518-782-7700

Fuel Cells

-Fuel Cell Mfrs.

Intelligent Energy
2955 Redondo Avenue
Long Beach, California 90806
562 997 3600
unitedstates@intelligent-energy.com
fuel cell bike

Ascent Power Systems, Inc.
8120 Shaffer parkwy
Littleton, CO 80127
www.itnes.com
solid oxide fuel cell using gasified biomass

Metallic Power
Steve Schaefer
2320 Camino Vida Roble
Carlsbad, CA 92009
760-476-8080
steve.schaefer@metallicpower.com
Zinc/Air regenerative fuel cell development

Furnishings

Milwaukee Metal Stamping

Milwaukee, WI 53214
(414) 476-2400
folding table

Freeform R&D
1539 Monrovia Avenue, UT-23
Newport Bech, CA 92663
sling-light camp chair

Garco Manufacturing Co.
2219-29 West Grand Avenue
Chicago, IL 60612
(312) 666-1688
folding tables

Telescope Folding Furniture Co. Inc.
Granville, NY 12832
(518) 642-1100
sun chairs, folding furniture

Texas Imperial American Inc.
Div. of Imperial American Co.
P.O. Box 878
Tyler, TX 75710
(214) 877-3435
lightweight furniture

Ambassador
blow-up bed/chair combo

Duralite Co. Inc.
2525 Firestone Avenue
Los Angeles, CA 90002
(213) 222-5207
sun chairs

Rattan Furniture
(Wicker)
article

Rattan Furniture
A Home Craftsman's Guide
Max and Charlotte Alth
book

Dellinger, Inc.
P.O. Drawer 273
Rome, GA 30162-0273
(706) 291-7402
custom non-toxic carpets

Gardening

-Information

Desert Gardening, Fruits and Vegetables
George Brookbank
Good section on tubers

Native American Gardening
Book by Michael J. Caduto and Joseph Bruchac

NOTE: See Also Greenhouse - General

The Complete Vegetable Gardeners Sourcebook
Duane and Karen Newcomb
book

The Organic Gardener's Handbook on
Vegetables, Fruits, Nuts and Herbs
Tanya Denckla
book

Grow More Vegetables
John Jeavons
book

The Bountiful Solar Greenhouse
Shane Smith
book

Secrets of Companion Planting
Louise Riotte
book

Organic Gardening Under Glass
George (Doc) and Kathy Abraham
book

How To Start On a Shoestring and Make A
Profit With Hydroponics
Hilmur L. Saffell
Book

Gardening

-Vertical

Verti-Gro, Inc.
800-955-6757
www.vertigro.com
Stackable foam containers and swivel systems

Hydro-Stacker
www.hydrostacker.com
Foam stacking containers

Growell Hydroponics Ltd.
www.growell.co.uk
vertical growing system with lights
Hydroponics inside a "cabinet" of sorts

www.holon.se/folke/projects...
Vertical wall examples simulating Permaculture

EasyGrower
www.easygrower.nl

Gasification (See Woodgas)

Gearing

The gears/gearing information is extensive and mostly comprised of product brochures and books.

Gears are generally available at industrial product companies in major cities. Consult Yellow Pages for details.

Generators

-Generator Manufacturers

Garlov Turbine
Moored power platforms
Helix-shaped vanes

Aquair Submersible Generator
www.nooutage.com
13 inch deep stream 6 mph equals 1.5 kw/day

E-Power portable DC chargers
Hamilton Ferris Co.
PO Box 126
Ashland, MA 01721
(508) 881-4602

Powermight
www.powermight.com

Sunpower, Inc.
PO Box 2625
Athens, OH. 45701
740-594-2221
"Biowatt"
Stirling Biomass fuel generator

Microturbines Technologies Inc.
86, Boul. Des Entreprises, Bureau 109
Boisbriand, Qc
J7G 2T3 514-435-5772
Small turbine generators producing power
From streams with one meter of head

Active power
11525 Stonehollow Drive, Suite 135
Austin, Texas 78705
512-836-6464
efficient flywheels for above turbines

Kubota diesel generators
Sold by Kansas Wind Power
785-364-4407

Aquabug Int'l Inc.
100 Merrick Road
Rockville Centre, NY 11570
(516) 536-8217
Now sold by:

Tanaka Kogyo Co. Ltd. (U.S.A.)
22121 Crystal Creek Blvd, SE
Bothell, WA 98021
(206) 481-2000
2 cycle 12V

Honda Motor Co.
* generators (quiet)

Sommer Electric Co., Inc.
1430 Louis Avenue
Elk Grove Village, IL 60007
(312) 569-2252
generators

Powermate
Ag-Tronic, Inc.
125 Airport Road
Kearney, NE 68847
(308) 237-2181
light generators

Electrical Generating Systems Assoc.
P.O. Box 9257
10251-D West Sample Road
Coral Springs, FL 33065
(305) 755-2677
trade association

Tanaka Ltd.
22322 20th Avenue S.E.
Bothell, WA 98021
(206) 481-2000
2-cycle generators

U.S. Motors Corp.
P.O. Box 758
Menomonee Falls, WI 53052
(414) 251-7724
generators

Genorak

P.O. Box 8
Waukesha, WI 53187
(414) 544-4811
gas generators

Onan Corporation
1400 73rd Avenue N.E.
Minneapolis, MN 55432
(612) 574-5000
full line--generators

Kohler Co.
Kohler, WI 53044
(414) 457-4441
LP and gas generators

American Honda Motor Co. Inc.
generators

Yamaha Motor Corp., U.S.A.
6555 Katella Avenue
Cypress, CA 90630
generators

Garretson Equipment Co. Inc.
P.O. Box 111
Mt. Pleasant, IA 52641
(319) 385-2203
LP conversion kits

Capstone
Allied Signal
Allison Engine
Elliott energy
Northern Research & Eng. (Ingersoll-Rand)
Microturbine manufacturers/developers

WINCO
225 S. Cordova Avenue
Le Center, MN 56057
(612) 357-6821
generators

T & J Manufacturing, Inc.
102 W. 5th Avenue
P.O. Box 200
Oshkosh, WI 54902

(414) 236-4200
(800) USA-POWER
generators

ACME North America Corp.
5203 W. 73rd Street
Minneapolis, MN 55439
(612) 835-2423
LP and gasoline generators

Coleman Powermate, Inc.
125 Airport Road
Kearney, NE 68848
(800) 445-1805
generators

Gillette Mfg. Inc.
1340 Wade Drive
Elkhart, IN 46514
(219) 264-9639
generators

ATI Power Products
1117 LaVelle
Alamogordo, NM 88310
(800) 545-5348
tiny battery charging generator

*Used in Earth Home

Hobart Welding Products
Troy, OH 45373
(513) 332-4000
generators

Kubota Tractor Corp.
3401 Del Amo Boulevard
P.O. Box 2992
Torrance, CA 90509
(310) 370-3370
generators

On-Site Power Generation
Gordon S. Johnson
reference book

Generators -Miscellaneous Products

NOTE: DC motors can be used as generators also.

*Generator remote start
800-626-5844

Startmaster
959 Cheney Avenue
P.O. Box 491
Marion, OH 43302
(614) 382-5771
air starters

Astro Flight Inc.
13311 Beach Avenue
Venice, CA 90291
(213) 821-6242
12 VDC motor-generator

Inland Motor
Specialty Products Div.
501 First Street
Radford, VA 24141
12 VDC alternators

Inertial Motors Corp.
280 North Broad Street
Doyelstown, PA 18901
12 VDC precision motor/generator

HTL Electrokinetics
P.O. Box 1500, 402 E. Gutierrez Street
Santa Barbara, CA 93102
(805) 963-2055
harmonic drive (speed increaser/reducer)

Harmonic Drive Division
51 Armory St.
Wakefield, Mass. 01880
(617) 245-7802

Dynetic Systems
19128 Industrial Blvd.
Elk River, MN 55330
(612) 441-4300
DC motors

Real Goods Trading Co.
Fossil-Fueled Generators
page 140
article

Alternative Energy Engineering
automated generator set control

Geothermal

NOTE: This category is included to show how various manufacturers design tubing "runs" in the earth.

This lists the manufacturers of geothermal equipment:

Addison Products
7050 Overland Road
Orlando, FL 32810
(407) 292-4400

Bard Manufacturing Co.
P.O. Box 607
Bryan, OH 43506
(419) 636-1194

Climate Control Inc.
881 Marcon Boulevard
Allentown, PA 18103
(215) 266-9500

Climate Master Inc.
P.O. Box 25788
Oklahoma City, OK 73179
(405) 745-6000

Command-Aire Corp.
P.O. Box 7916
Waco, TX 76714
(817) 840-3244

Florida Heat Pump Corp.
601 N.W. 65th Ct.
Ft. Lauderdale, FL 33309
(305) 776-5471
many kinds

Heat Controller
1900 Wellworth Avenue
Jackson, MI 49203
(517) 787-2100
water to air

Mammoth Refrigeration
13120-B County Road 6
Minneapolis, MN 55441
(612) 559-2711

Marvair
3570 American Drive
Atlanta, GA 30341
(404) 458-6643

Thermal Energy Transfer Corp.
1290 US 42 N.
Delaware, OH 43015
(614) 363-5002
(800) 468-3826

Water Furnace Intl.
9000 Conservation Way
Ft. Wayne, IN 46809
(219) 432-5667

Trane Co.
P.O. Box 7916
Waco, TX 76714-796

S&B Geothermal
c/o Bill Arzdorf
612-434-5162

*Used in Earth Home

heat pump systems (2,000 sq. ft. of
1" poly buried 8' deep)

Goats

5 goats need 10' x 12' shed and eat less than 1 cow!

Goats would require 4-5 acres of tillable land

Goats are clean, disease-free, and yields higher quality milk than a cow.

Greenhouse

-General

Greenhouse Gardeners Companion
Shane Smith
Extensive book on greenhouses

Add-on Solar Greenhouses and Sunspaces
Andrew M. Shapiro
book

Contractor Instruments
6488 Carlson Drive
Eden Prairie, MN. 55346
PHL-1 Light Intensity Meter
800-758-4822

Bayliss
(Superior Autovents, Ltd.)
heat piston vent openers

Thermofor
(Bramen Co.)
heat piston vent openers

Solarvent
(Dalen Products Inc.)
heat piston vent openers

Growing Food in Solar Greenhouses
Delores Wolfe
book

Thermal Shutters and Shades
William A. Shurcliff
book

Trade names of shutters and shades
article

Trade names of insulating plates and sheets
article

Willow Tea
(steep twigs for 48 hours and soak cutting for 24 hours before placing in soil--water with willow tea periodically)
home-made rooting hormone

Mee Industries, Inc.
4443 North Rowland Avenue
El Monte, CA 91731
(800) 732-5364
(818) 350-4180
misters, foggers

Soil sterilization
article

Shading requirements and products
articles

100% relative humidity and hydroponics combination (use 1/6 the water?)
article

Herrmidifier Co., Inc.
P.O. Box 11148
1812 Colonial Village Lane
Lancaster, PA 17605-1148
(717) 394-4021
humidification nozzles

CO_2 studies (enrichment)
many articles

spraying water on plants good against spider mites and white flies (sometimes)
article

Soil Science Simplified
Harpstead, Hole, and Benett
book

Polyvent Insul-Rib Inc.
Box 447
Castle Rock, MN 55010
(507) 663-0362
greenhouse glazing

Hydroponic Hot House
James B. DeKorne
book

National Draeger Inc.
101 Technology Drive
P.O. Box 120
Pittsburgh, PA 15230
(412) 787-8383
CO_2 measurement products

CEA Instruments, Inc.
16 Chestnut Street
Emerson, NJ 07630
CO_2 monitor, 0-5 V output or display

Sodium borate
environmentally responsible wood preservative

NISUS Corp.
101 Concord Street
Knoxville, TN 37919
(800) 264-0870
log home wood preservative, "Bora-Care"

Kele & Associates
P.O. Box 34817
Memphis, TN 38184
(901) 382-4300
infrared CO_2 sensor

Greenhouse

-Hydroponic Discussion

ADVANTAGES

Hydroponics	**Soil**
Higher yields Well suited to outdoor facilities (1/20th the water in Kalahari)	Theoretically possible but not in reality

*Used in Earth Home

Uses less water
Eliminates weeding and cultivation

Can be automated
Labor saving
Plants receive proper nutrition

More flexible with regard to mistakes in watering
Not as much electricity used

Can still be automated--but slightly more difficult feeding schedules don't vary as much

DISADVANTAGES

Best with only certain varieties of plants, namely:

- cucumbers
- tomatoes
- peppers
- lettuce

Does not produce CO_2 to help plant growth

Water quality must be calculated into nutrient solution (10-8-22 is all-purpose)

pH and EC (electrical conductivity) must be continuously monitored

Aggregate must be sterilized with 10% chlorine bleach

Some hydroponic systems need to be aggregated - more electrical energy

Only increases productivity by 20-25%, not 300%

Root crops such as carrots, beets, radishes, onions, turnips, parsnips don't do well

No easy method to use organic fertilizer - must be purchased

Some evidence to indicate more susceptibility to disease

NOTE: Hydroponics have been practiced for thousands of years.

- Marco Polo told of floating gardens in China
- Floating gardens along the Nile River
- Plants on rafts in Aztec lakes

Greywater

http://www.sydneywater.com.au/SavingWater/GreyWater/TreatmentOfGreywater.cfm
greywater site

Oasis Graywater Systems
http://www.oasisdesign.net

Drainfield Alternatives
http://www.formcell.com/

GFX
www.gfxtechnology.com
Greywater heat recovery system

Spartan Water Treatment
http://www.spartanwatertreatment.com/index.html
water treatment systems for industrial and municipal electrolytic organic destruction

www.greywater.com
greywater site

Gardens Alive
50 Beharrell St.
Concord, MA 01742
978-318-7033
www.ecotechusa.com
greywater site and store

Grinders (See also Juicers)

Lehmans
(261)-857-5441
Grinders and Juicers

R and R Mill Company
(435)-563-3333
Grinders and Juicers

Hardware

-Blind Rivets

Penn Engineering and Manufacturing Company
Banboro, PA 18916-1000
(215) 766-8853
thin sheets

B.F. Goodrich
Aerospace
150 Springside Drive
Akron, OH 44313-0501
(216) 374-2941
"Rivnuts"

Rexnord
Specialty Fasteners Division
3000 West Lomita Boulevard
Torrance, CA 90505
(213) 534-4400
inserts

Hardware

-Fasteners

Swiss Precision Instruments, Inc.
2206 Lively Boulevard
Elk Gove Village, IL 60007
(312) 981-1300
plastic thumb screw knobs

Rensen Products
Box 308
Ahmeek, MI 49901
molded inserts

Stimpson
1515 SW 13th Court
Pompano Beach, FL 33060
(305) 946-3500
rivets, ferrules, etc.

Davies Molding Company
4920 West Bloomingdale Avenue
Chicago, IL 60639-4562
(312) 622-8966
knobs, handles, cases

AGM Industries, Inc.
110 Shawmut Road
Canton, MA 02021
(617) 828-4705
steel weld pins

Goodlue E. Moore
2811 North Vermillion Street

*Used in Earth Home

Danville, IL 61832
(217) 446-7900
steel nail press - nuts

North & Judd Manufacturing, Inc.
699 Middle Street
Middletown, CT 06457
(203) 632-2600
metal snaps, pulleys

Sava Industries, Inc.
70 Riverdale Road
P.O. Box 30
Riverdale, NJ 07457
(201) 835-0882
cable assemblies

ALW
88 Century Drive
P.O. Box 1370
Woonsocket, RI 02895
(401) 762-5500
plastic snaps, buckles

Simmons Fasteners Co.
1750 North Broadway
Albany, NY 12201
(518) 463-4234
latches

Dzus Fastener Co.
425 Union Boulevard
West Ilsip, NY 11795
(516) 669-0494
latches, etc.

Corbin Cabinet Lock Division
Emhart Hardware Group
225 Episcopal Road
Berlin, CT 06037
catches

Erico Jones
P.O. Box 340
Dayton View Station
Dayton, OH 45406
(513) 276-5913
steel insulation fasteners

Bokers, Inc.
3104 Snelling Avenue South
Minneapolis, MN 55406-1937
(612) 729-9365
washers

Century Spring Co.
222 East 16th Street
Los Angeles, CA 90015
(800) 237-5225
(213) 749-1466
springs

Southco Fasteners
Concordville, PA 19331
(215) 459-4000
catches, hinges

Special-T Metals Co.
14740 West 101st Terrace
Cenexa, KS 66215
(913) 492-9500
alloy bolts, nuts

Camloc - Rexnord Specialty Fastener Division
601 Route 46 West
Hasbrouck Heights, NJ 07604
(201) 288-8300
latches

Carey Manufacturing Co. Inc.
105 Clark Drive, Dept. CC
E. Berlin, CT 06023
(203) 829-1803
catches

Hardware
-Hinges

Hartwell Commercial Division
950 South Richfield Road
Placentia, CA 92670
(714) 993-2752
hinges, catches

The Homer D. Bronson Company
Price Road, Route 8
Winsted, CT 06098
(203) 379-9901
hinges

Ono Industries, Inc.
26 North Avenue
Garwood, NJ 07027
(201) 789-2002
plastic hinges

Mid Lake Products and Manufacturing Co.
7349 Ravenna Avenue NE
P.O. Box 230
Louisville, OH 44641
(216) 875-4202
hinges

Flex-Fold
Westedge, Inc.
9 Surrey Lane
San Rafael, CA 94903
(415) 492-0272
urethane hinge

Hardware
-Knobs, Handles

Rogan Corporation
3455 Woodhead Drive
Northbrook, IL 60062
(708) 498-2300
(800) 423-1543
knobs - full line

O'Conner Engineered Products
160 Abbot Drive
Wheeling, IL 60090
(708) 459-9528
many kinds

Dimco-Gray Company
8200 South Suburban Road
Centerville, OH 45459
(513) 433-7600
knobs

Hardware
-Misc./Tools

Intech Power-Core
www.intechpower.com
201-767-8066
Poly cam followers

*Used in Earth Home

Tac Riveting Systems S.A.S.
20159 Milano (ITALY)
Via Thaon di Revel, 3
"accordion" blind rivet gun

Lapeer Manufacturing Company
3056 Davison Road
Lapeer, MI 45449
(313) 664-2964
toggle clamps

De Sta Co
P.O. Box 2800
250 Park Street
Troy, MI 48007-2800
(313) 589-2008
toggle clamps

Plastiglide Manufacturing Corporation
2701 West El Segundo Boulevard
P.O. Box 427
Hawthorne, CA 90250
(213) 777-8108
wheels, rollers

Impulse Mechanisms, Inc.
78-82 North Industry Court
Deer Park, NY 11729
(516) 586-5755
precision collar clamps

Capplugs Division
Buffalo, NY
(716) 876-9855
plastic plugs

AFM Corporation
P.O. Box 246
Excelsior, MN 55331-0246
(612) 474-0809
very long screws for stress-skin

Hardware

-Plastic Ties

Catamount Manufacturing, Inc.
P.O. Box 67
45 Francis Street
Leominister, MA 01453
(617) 537-6090
(800) 222-5969
wiring ties, fasteners

PMP Corporation
1430 County Line Road
Huntingdon Valley, PA 19006
(215) 322-2000
(800) 523-8928
distributor - many kinds

Product Components Corporation
30 Lorraine Avenue
Mt. Vernon, NY 10553
(914) 699-8640
distributor - many kinds

Niagara Plastics
7090 Edinboro Road
Erie, PA 16509
(814) 868-3671
plastic nuts and closures (caps)

Heyco Molded Products, Inc.
Box 160
Kenilworth, NJ 07033-0160
(201) 245-0033
nylon hole plugs and more

Micro Plastics, Inc.
Highway 178 North
Flippin, AR 72634
(501) 453-2261
many

Health (See Medicine/Health)

Heat

-Elements

www.hotronic.com
battery operated foot warmers w/controls

Heat

-Exchangers-Air to Air (HRV)

NOTE: Also called heat recovery ventilators (HRV's), recuperators, and regenerators

Therma-Stor Products
PO Box 8050
Madison, WI 53708
800-533-7533
HRV Mfr.

Vent-Aire systems
4850 Northpark Dr.
Colorado Springs, CO 80918
800-937-9080
HRV counter-flow

Automated Controls & Systems
500 East Higgins Road
Elkgrove, IL 60007
(312) 860-6860
cross flow, core only; many different sizes

Enercon Projects, Ltd.
607 Park Street
Regina, Saskatchewan S4N 5N1
CANADA
(306) 924-1551
large plastic counter flow w/variable speed fans

Flakt Products, Inc.
(for Svenska Flakt Fabriken)
P.O. Box 21500
Fort Lauderdale, FL 33335
(305) 524-6521
or
Semco Mfg. Inc.
P.O. Box 1797
Columbia, MO 65205
"Rexovent" aluminum cross flow w/fans

Melco Sales, Inc.
(for Mitsubishi Electric Corp.)
3030 East Victoria Street
Compton, CA 90221
(213) 537-7132
(800) 421-1132
cross flow w/paper, aluminum, or plastic cores w/fans

D.C. Heat Exchangers
RR #3
Saskatoon
Saskatchewan, CANADA
(306) 384-0208
lrg. plastic & plywood counter flow w/fans, can be home made

Nutech
511 McCormick Boulevard
London, Ontario N5W 4C8
CANADA
(519) 457-1904 or (204) 774-2223
full line

Lennox
400-T Norris Glen Road
Etobicoke, Ontario M9C 1H5
CANADA
full line

Air Changer Marketing
1297 Industrial Road
Cambridge, Ontario N3H 4T8
CANADA
(416) 673-0667 or (519) 653-7129
full line

Conservation Energy Systems, Inc.
2525 Wentz Avenue
Saskatoon, Saskatchewan S7K 2K9
CANADA
(306) 242-3663
(800) 667-3717
* full line

Environment Air, Ltd.
P.O. Box 10
Route 134
Cocagne, New Brunswick E3A 1K0
CANADA
(506) 576-6672
* full line

Dantherm Systems Division
208 East Adams Street Rockdale
Cambridge, WI 53523
(800) 368-4376
(608) 764-8300
heat exchangers

Heatex, Inc.
5100 Eden Avenue, Suite 101
Minneapolis, MN 55436
(612) 926-3999
heat exchangers

Xetex, Inc.
3600 East 28th Street
Minneapolis, MN 55406
(612) 724-3101
heat exchangers

Northern Scientific
P.O. Box D
Minot, ND 58702
build your own air to air heat exchangers

U-Learn Office
University of Saskatchewan
Saskatoon, Saskatchewan S7N 0W0
CANADA
book on air-to-air heat exchangers

Des Champs Laboratories Inc.
Box 440
17 Farinella Drive
East Hanover, NJ 07936
(210) 884-1460 or (703) 291-1111
heat exchangers

AirXchange, Inc.
401 V.F.W. Drive
Rockland, MA 02370
(617) 871-4816
Marketed by Honeywell
HRV manufacturer

American Aldes Ventilation Corporation
4539 Northgate Ct.
Sarasota, FL 33580
(813) 351-3441
HRV manufacturer

BossAire
1321 Tyler Street N.E.
Minneapolis, MN 55413
(612) 781-0179
HRV manufacturer

Enermatrix, Inc.
P.O. Box 466
Fargo, ND 58107
(701) 232-3330
HRV manufacturer

Les Industries Douvent Ltéé.
1375 Boul. Charest Ouest
(Suite 6)
Quebec PQ GIN 2E7
CANADA
HRV manufacturer

QDT. Ltd.
1000 Singleton Boulevard
Dallas, TX 75212-5214
(214) 741-1993
HRV manufacturer

Raydot, Inc.
145 Jackson Avenue
Cokato, MN 55321
HRV manufacturer

Star Heat Exchanger Corp.
B109-1772 Broadway Street
Port Coquitlam, BC V3C 2M8
CANADA
(604) 942-0525
HRV manufacturer

Trent Metals Ltd., Inc.
2040 Fisher Drive
Peterborough, Ontario K9J 6X6
CANADA
(705) 745-4736

Venmar Ventilation, Inc.
1715 Haggerty Street
Drummondville, PQ J2C 5P7
(800) 567-3855
(612) 854-0947

Broan Manufacturing Co., Inc.
926 West State Street
Hartford, WI 53027
(414) 673-4340

Vent-Aire
Engineering Development, Inc.

*Used in Earth Home

4850 Northpark Drive
Colorado Springs, CO 80918
(719) 599-9080
(800) 937-9080
HRV manufacturer

XchangeAir Corp.
7th and University Drive N.
P.O. Box 1565
Fargo, ND 58107
(701) 237-0491
HRV manufacturer

NewAire (Div. of Altech Energy)
7009 Raywood Road
Madison, WI 53713
(608) 221-4499
* HRV manufacturer (non-defrosting air care)

Super Insulated Houses and
Air-to-Air Heat Exchangers
William Shurcliff
book

Karlson Home Central Inc.
2605 Broadway Avenue
Evanston, IL 60201
HRV distributor of BAHCO (AB) of Sweden

Colchester Fan Mktg. Co. Ltd.
Hillbottom Road
Sands Industrial Estate
Highwycombe, Bucks HP12 4HR
ENGLAND
Indola R2000 crossflow exchanger

Temouex AB
Box 111
S 265 01
Astorp
SWEDEN
HRV manufacturer

Ener-Quip, Inc.
99 E. Kansas Street
Hackensack, NJ 07601
(201) 487-1015
HRV manufacturer

Berner International
P.O. Box 5205
New Castle, PA 16105
(412) 658-3551
HRV manufacturer

Aston Industries, Inc.
P.O. Box 220
St. Leonard d'Aston
Quebec J0C 1M0
CANADA
(819) 399-2175
HRV manufacturer

Airxchange Inc.
401 V.F.W. Drive
Rockland, MA 02370
(617) 871-4816
HRV manufacturer

ACS - Hoval
955 North Lively Boulevard
Wood Dale, IL 60191
(312) 860-6800
HRV manufacturer

Standex Energy Systems
1090 Legion Road
P.O. Box 1168
Detroit Lakes, MN 56501
(218) 847-9258
HRV manufacturer

Mountain Energy & Resources, Inc.
15800 W. Sixth Avenue
Golden, CO 80401
(303) 279-4971
HRV manufacturer

RB Kanalflakt
1121 Lewis Avenue
Sarasota, FL 33577
(813) 366-7505
HRV manufacturer

Home Ventilating Institute
Div. of Air Movement and Control Assoc. Inc.
30 W. University Drive
Arlington Heights, IL 60004
(708) 394-0150
association

Living Air
(612) 780-9388
HRV manufacturer

Home Ventilating Institute
Division of AMCA
30 W. University Drive
Arlington Heights, IL 60004
(708) 394-0150
HRV guidebook - HRV types

Heat -Exchangers-Water

Earthstar Energy Sysstems
PO Box 626
Waldoboro, MA 04572
800-323-6749
Water Heat Exchanger for Greywater heat reclaiming

Heat -Pipes

Heat Pipe Technology
Company making large heat pipes

Heat Pipes
P.D. Dunn
Book on heat pipes

Design and Technology of Heat Pies for Cooling and Heat Exchange
Calvin C. Silverstein
Book on heat pipes

Heat -Pumps

Federal Association for Heat Pumps (BWP) German

Heat Pump Manufacturers are not covered in this section. See Yellow Pages for HVAC installers. Heat pumps typically are large users of electricity.

Heaters, Water

*Used in Earth Home

Jay Baker
Direct Fire Technical, Inc.
2836 SE Loop 820
Fort Worth, TX 76140
817-568-8778
Direct-Fired Water heaters

Hemp

Hemp, Lifeline to the Future
Chris Conrad
Book on uses of hemp

Home Automation/Control -Automotive Applications

SEMAU-(smart electro-mechanical actuating units)
Filo concept car
Brake by wire from Brembo
SKF drive by wire applications

Saia-Burgess Inc.
627 East Maple, Suite 100
Troy, MI 48083
(248) 524-2701
www.automotiveassemblies.com
many applications

Home Automation/Control -Computer/PLC, Chipsets

Automation/Home control
Grid Connect, Inc.
800-843-1082
GC-CAN-USB adapter
CAN users to a PC
Prefers Devicenet or CANOpen protocol

Texas Instruments
TRF6900 chipset

Home Automation/Control -Misc. Products

Battery Power Management
Interstil Corp
Milpitas, CA
rbi.ims.ca/3846-523
power management chip

http://laptop.media.mit.edu/
laptop@media.mit.edu
One Laptop per Child
$100 wind-up laptop

Honeywell Hometronic
Comprehensive home automation system

Ono Ind. Inc.
R.D. #3, Box 7075

Micro/Sys Inc.
3730 Park Pl.
Montrose, CA 91020
(818) 244-4600
Small computers for possible home control

X-10 (USA) Inc.
185A LeGrand Avenue
Northvale, NJ 07647
(201) 784-9700
creator of X-10 controls

Microcontroller IDEA Book
Jan Axelson
book on basics of home control using chips

Elwood Corporation - Electronics Group
195 West Ryan Road
Oak Creek, WI 53154-4401
(414) 764-7500
phone transducer

Multiplexing Experts
Joe Zlomek
(305) 664-4218
David Cole
University of Michigan
(313) 764-5592

Sensors Magazine
Helmers Publishing, Inc.
174 Concord Street
P.O. Box 874
Petersborough, NH 03458
(603) 924-9631

Smart House
401 J. Prince George's Boulevard
Upper Marlboro, MD
(301) 249-6000
whole house control

Digi-Key Corporation
701 Brooks Avenue S.
Thief River Falls, MN 56701
(800) 344-4539
electronics catalog

Circuit Cellar Ink (magazine)
Suite 20
4 Park Street
Vemon, CT 06066
(860) 875-2751
computer applications/articles

Rockwell Automation
Allen-Bradley
1201 South Second Street
Milwaukee, WI 53204
(414) 382-2000
small PLC's

Allegro Microsystems, Inc.
115 Northeast Cutoff
Box 15036
Worcester, MA 01615
(508) 853-5000
IC's

U.S. Tec
470 South Pearl Street
Canandaigua, NY 14424
(716) 396-9680
home wiring network

Home Automation Systems, Inc.
Suite L4
151 Kalmus Drive
Costa Mesa, CA 92626
(800) 762-7846
complete catalog

*Used in Earth Home

Parallax, Inc.
3805 Antherton Road, #102
Rocklin, CA 95765
(916) 624-8333
basic computer

Tri-metric Associates
N78W14587 Appleton Ave.
Menomonee Falls, Wi. 53051
Tri-metric system monitor

Understanding Small Microcontrollers
James M. Sibigtroth
book

Motorola 68HC11
common microcontroller

SAE International
(Society of Automotive Engineers)
400 Commonwealth Drive
Warrendale, PA 15096
(412) 776-4841

Automotive Electronics Handbook
Ronald Jurgen
book

Chrysler Corporation
Fred Miesterfeld
auto multiplexing expert

Home Automation/Control -Software/Info

www.rbi.ims.ca/3878-511
AS-Interface fieldbus

www.rbi.ims.ca/3878-512
Fieldbus Foundation

www.rbi.ims.ca/3878-513
HART Communications Foundation

www.rbi.ims.ca/3878-514
Interbus

www.rbi.ims.ca/3878-515
Modbus

www.rbi.ims.ca/3878-516
ODVA

www.rbi.ims.ca/3878-517
Profibus Trade Organization

Omnipotence Software
1-423-745-0026
www.omnipotencesoftware.com
ECS

Home Care

Henley's Formulas for Home and Workshop
Edited by Gardner D. Hiscox
Book on home products etc.

Natural Cleaning for Your Home
Casey Kellar
Cleaning products book etc.

AFM Enterprises Inc.
1140 Stacy Court
Riverside, CA 92507
(909) 781-6860, 6861
earth-friendly products

Loofah gourds
sponges for washing

Clean & Green
Annie Berthold-Bond
book

List of sources of earth safe cleaners
article

Charcoal dust on damp cloth cleans teeth

Granny's Old Fashioned Products
P.O. Box 256
Arcadia, CA 91066
earth-friendly products

Coconut oil
surfactant

Citrus oil
universal cleaner

Loofah sponges (gourd)
washing dishes

Shaklee Products
literature

Home solvents
- non-polluting cleaners
article

Natural Animal
St. Augustine, FL
(800) 274-7387
soaps, etc.

The Natural Choice
E.C.O. Design Co.
1365 Rufina Circle
Santa Fe, NM 87501
(505) 438-3448
healthy home products

Espial
natural home care products

Vinegar for cleaning
article (50-50 w/water)

Minnesota Pollution Control Agency
(612) 296-6300
(800) 652-9747
Alternatives list
(toxic trash disposal guide)
- drain cleaner
- furniture polish
- oven cleaner

National Green Pages
Coop America
1850 M Street N.W., Suite 700
Washington, DC 20036
sources of Earth-friendly products
booklet

Hexametaphosphate potential bleach substitute
Dialog Search

*Used in Earth Home

Nontoxic, Natural, and Earthwise
Debra Lynn Dadd
book

Hose, Clamps, Fittings, Tubing

-Clamps

Rich Co. Plastics Co.
5825 North Tripp Avenue
Chicago, IL 60646
(312) 539-4060
plastic clamps

Tyton Corp.
7930 North Faulkner Road
Milwaukee, WI 53223
(414) 355-1130
"Snapper" plastic clamps

Heyco Molded Products
Box 160
Kenilworth, NJ 07033
(201) 245-0033
(800) 526-4182
plastic clamps

Breeze Clamp Products
100 Aero-Seal Drive
Saltsburg, PA 15681
(412) 639-3571
stainless clamps

DuPage Products Group
Precision Brand Products, Inc.
2250 Curtiss Street
Downers Grove, IL 60515
(312) 968-6900
steel and plastic clamps

Hose, Clamps, Fittings, Tubing

-Fittings

Colder Products Co.
2367 University Avenue
St. Paul, MN 55114
(612) 645-0091
quick disconnect couplers

Flojet Corp.
12 Morgan
Irvine, CA 92718
(714) 859-4945
fittings

Ark-Pas Products Inc.
Hwy 178 N
Flippin, AR 72634
(501) 453-2343
miniature hose fittings

Elton James Corp.
P.O. Box 948
Coveland, CO 80539-0948
miniature hose fittings

Newage Industries
Plastics Div.
2300 Maryland Road
Willow Grove, PA 19090
(215) 657-3151
fittings and tubing

Value Plastics Inc.
3350 Eastbrook Drive
Fort Collins, CO 80525
(303) 223-8306
miniature tubing, fittings

Boswick Engineering Co., Inc.
26 Brownville Avenue
Ipswich, Mass. 01938-2098
(508) 356-4392
(800) 354-5014
tiny swivel fittings

Cole Parmer Instrument Co.
7425 North Oak Park Avenue
Chicago, IL 60646
(312) 647-7800
(800) 323-4240
full line catalog

Hose, Clamps, Fittings, Tubing

-General

Cleveland Tubing, Inc.
PO Box 2698
Cleveland, Tennessee 37320
423-472-2554
Respiratory Hoses

Trickle Soak Systems
8733 Magnolia, Suite 109
Santee, CA 92071
(619) 449-6408
irrigation tubing

Drainage Industries
300 North Lilas Drive
Appleton, WI 54914
(414) 734-2665
culvert/drain pipe

Damerius - Switzerland
spaghetti tubing

Minor Rubber Co., Inc.
49 Ackerman Street
Bloomfield, NJ 07003-4299
(201) 338-6800
(800) 631-8574
rubber tubing and cord

Rehau
P.O. Box 1706
Edwards Ferry Road
Leesburg, VA 22075
(703) 777-5255
(800) 227-3800
miscellaneous

Smooth-Bor Plastics
23322 Del Lago Drive
Laguna Hills, CA 92653
(714) 581-9530
smooth bore corrugated hose

Smooth-Bor® Plastics
Laguna Hills, CA 92653
stylet 101
1 3/8" amd 1 1/4" ID waste hose

*Used in Earth Home

Ron-VIK
800 Colorado Avenue South
Minneapolis, MN 53416
(612) 545-0276
(800) 328-0598
nylon fittings

Advanced Technology Products (ATP)
P.O. Box 0195
Plain City, OH 43064-0195
(614) 873-5598
(spiral) urethane hose

Hose, Clamps, Fittings, Tubing

-Hose

Ono Ind. Inc.
R.D. #3, Box 7075
Jonestown, PA 17038
(717) 865-6619
poly sump hose

Petro Plastic Inc.
450 South Avenue
Garwood, NJ 07027
(201) 789-1200
poly sump hose

Smalands Listens
Box 154
57301 Transas
Vall Movagen 6
SWEDEN
silicone extruded hose

Inhome Ltd.
Sharston Road
Manchester M22 4th
ENGLAND
layflat tubing (cassette) hose

Rubber Corp. of America
2535 North Broad Street
Philadelphia, PA 19132
(215) 225-3700
many kinds of rubber hose

Hose, Clamps, Fittings, Tubing

-Tubing

Quest Eng. Inc.
2300 Edgewood Avenue South
St. Louis Park, MN 55426
(612) 546-4441
air tubing

Manville
P.O. Box 5108
Denver, CO 80217
coated fiberglass ducts, etc.

Fabricated Plastics, Inc.
Hanover Ave. & Horsehill Road
CN 1907
Morristown, NJ 07960-1907
(201) 539-4200
flexible hose

Wiremold Co.
60 Woodlawn Street
P.O. Box 10639
West Hartford, CT 06110-0639
flexible duct

Zeus Industrial Products
Foot of Thompson Street
Raritan, NJ 08869
(201) 526-0800
(800) 526-3842
teflon tubing

Norton Industrial Plastics
P.O. Box 350
Akron, OH 44309
(216) 798-9240
tygon tubing and more

Dayco Corp.
Dayflex Co.
Dayton, OH 45401
flex hose

Aero Rubber Co. Inc.
7501 West 99th Place
P.O. Box 1409
Bridgeview, IL 60455
(312) 430-4900
silicone tubing

Flexible Technologies
P.O. Box 5698 Station B
Greenville, SC 29606
(803) 288-7175
flexible hose

Parflex, Multitube Operations
Ravenna, OH 44266
poly pro tubing

Aetna Plastics Corp.
1702 St. Clair Avenue
Cleveland, OH 44144
(216) 781-4421
(800) 321-7004
tubing and connections

Wirsbo Company
5925 - 148th Street West
Apple Valley, MN 55124
(612) 891-2000
cross-linked polyethylene tubing

Human-Powered Vehicles
(See Automobile section)

Humidifiers

Bemis
P.O. Box 901
Sheboygan, WI 53085
(800) 558-7651
(414) 467-4621

Bionaire
90 Boroline Road
Allendale, NJ 07401
(800) 253-2764

Duracraft Corp.
355 Main Street
Whitinsville, MA 01588
(508) 234-4600

*Used in Earth Home

Emerson Moist Air
8400 Pershall Road
Hazelwood, MO 63042
(800) 237-6511

Holmes Products Corp.
233 Fortune Boulevard
Milford, MA 01757
(508) 634-8050

Kaz, Inc.
41 Cross Street
Hudson, NY 12534
(518) 828-0450

Sears Kenmore
Sears Tower
Chicago, IL 60684
(312) 875-2500

Toastmaster Inc.
1801 N. Stadium Boulevard
Columbia, MO 65202
(314) 445-8666

HVAC

-Dehumidifying

Cargoaire Engineering Corp.
79 Monroe Street
Amesbury, Mass. 01913
(617) 388-0600
industrial dehumidifiers thermostatic

Therma-Stor Products Group
P.O. Box 8050
2001 S. Stroughton Road
Madison, WI 53708
(800) 533-7533
(608) 222-5301
high-efficiency dehumidifiers

Hood and Co., Inc.
P.O. Box 181
Hamburg, PA 19526
(215) 562-3841
bimetal strips

Real Goods Trading
Chiller/heaters
(Absorption)
gas-powered air conditioners

Radiantec
P.O. Box 1111
Lyndonville, VT 05851
(802) 626-8045
(800) 451-7593
radiant underfloor heating systems

Humidity Control
by Ivan Stepnich
book

Wirsbo Company
5925 - 148th Street West
Apple Valley, MN 55124
(612) 891-2000
underfloor heating tubing

Heartland Promotions Inc.
Special Merchandising Headquarters
5023 Grover Street
Omaha, NE 68106-9957
(800) 851-6291
permanent reusable furnace filter

Improvements
4944 Commerce Parkway
Cleveland, OH 44128
(800) 642-2112
"electrostatic" cleanable air filter

Flexible Technologies
P.O. Box 888-T
Abbeville, SC 29620
* flexible air duct "Thermaflex"

Panametrics, Inc.
221 Crescent Street
Waltham, MA 02154-3497
(617) 899-2719
(800) 833-9438
* tiny relative humidity sensor

Newport Scientific, Inc.
8246 E. Sandy Court
Jessup, MD 20794-9632
(301) 498-6700
humidity sensor

Pure Air Systems
P.O. Box 418
Plainfield, IN 46168
(317) 839-9135
(800) 869-8025
whole house air filter

Better Heating - Cooling Control
35 Russo Place
P.O. Box 218
Berkeley Heights, NJ 07922
(201) 464-8200
hydronic heat advocates

HVAC

-General

NOTE: See also Filters for air filters
NOTE: See also Cooling-Dehumidification files

General Eastern Instruments
20 Commerce Way
Woburn Mass. 01801
617-938-7070
Capacitive Rel. Humidity Sensor

Korea's Tradition Floor Heating System - Ondol
article

DesignLife Products, Inc.
1516 North Orleans
Suite 4249
Chicago, Il. 60610
Drainout device to "venturi" water

Hudson Products Corporation
McDermott company
6464 Savoy Drive. Suite 800
Houston, Texas 77036
713-914-5930
Heat pipes and water-based fluid

Thermo VoltÔ from Photic Corp.
Dist. by Alternative Energy Engineering
Box 339 Briceland Star Rt.
Redway, CA 95560

*Used in Earth Home

(707) 923-2277
electricity from heat

Bon-Aire
P.O. Box 12
Marietta, NC 28362
(919) 628-6736
air filters

Heating Systems (Twintran)
3131 W. Chestnut Expressway
Springfield, MO 65802
(417) 864-6108
(800) 255-1996
under floor heating tubes

McMaster-Carr
#2171K11
humidifier - alum/mineral film

Ductulator Guide (Trade Co.)
booklet

Hydraulics

Parker-Hannifin
Hydraulic valves
8 watts of power

Sargent Controls
CEI Division
Oakhurst, CA
All-in-one hydraulic cylinder, pump, valves

SPX Fluid Power
Rockford, IL
Micro-Pack MP90 hydraulic power unit

Wanner Engineering, Inc.
1204 Chestnut Avenue
Minneapolis, MN 55403
(612) 332-5681
hydraulic pumps

Webster Electric Company
Fluid Power Division
1900 Clark Street
Racine, WI 53403
(414) 633-3511
DC power hydraulic systems

Ace Controls, Inc.
P.O. Box 71
Farmington, MI 48024
(313) 476-0213
hydraulic shock absorbers

Suntec Industries, Inc.
2210 Harrison Avenue
P.O. Box 7010
Rockford, IL 61125
(815) 226-3700
quiet hydraulic pump

Cook Manufacturing Corp.
3920 S. 13th
Duncan, OK 73533
(800) 654-3697
12 VDC hydraulic pump

Power Team
2121 West Bridge Street
P.O. Box 993
Owatonna, MN 55060
(507) 455-7100
hand and 12 VDC hydraulic pumps

Enerpac
Division of Applied Power, Inc.
13000 West Silver Spring Drive
Butler, WI 53007
(414) 781-6600
hydraulic tools

Hydrogen/Fuel Cells

The Hydrogen Economy
by Jeremy Rifkin
book on future of hydrogen

Midwest Research Institute
425 Volker Boulevard
Kansas City, MO 64110
816-753-7600
Sunlight directly into H and O2
Using photovoltaic-photoelectrochemical

Maxwell Technologies
Combining ultracapacitors with fuel cells

www.hydrogenconference.org
annual hydrogen conference

Renewable Energy Corporation
Los Alamos, New Mexico
Electricity and Hydrogen from concentrating collector
www.re-co2.com

The International Hydrogen Energy Forum
Hyforum 2004
Beijing, P.R. China

Hall, D.O.
Hydrogen Production by Algae and Isolated Chloroplasts
May 1977

Benemann, J.
Hydrogen and Methane Production Through Microbial Photosynthesis, in Living Systems as Energy Converters
North-Holland Publishing Company
Amsterdam 1977

Teledyne Electra Cell
Hydrgen generator

Billings Energy Corp.
Hydrogen Progress (Magazine)
Hydrogen Energy Industry Association
2000 East Billings Avenue
Provo, UT 84601
H_2 generators source for info

Matheson
P.O. Box "E"
1275 Valley Brook Avenue
Lyndhurst, NJ 07071
hydrogen gas

Laboratory Data Control
Div. of Milton Roy Co.
P.O. Box 10235
Riviera Beach, FL 33404
(305) 844-5241
H_2 generators

*Used in Earth Home

Fisher Scientific Co.
1600 Westglen Lake Avenue
Itasca, IL 60143
small H_2 kits

Gas Atmospheres
5353 West 161 Street
Cleveland, OH 44142
(216) 267-3350
large H_2 generators

DuPont Nafion perchlorinated polymers
Material for fuel cells in autos

Hydrogen, The Invisible Fire
by Patrick Kiernan
48 page booklet

Henes Products Corp.
4301 East Madison Street
Phoenix, AZ 85034
(602) 275-4126
water welder

The Barber Manufacturing Co.
22901 Aurora Road
P.O. Box 46217
Bedford Heights, OH 44146
(216) 439-1680
gas jets

Near Term Pathways Toward Hydrogen Energy
by Frank Lynch
Hydrogen Consultants, Inc.
technical paper

Matheson
P.O. Box 85
932 Paterson Plank Road
(201) 933-2400
H_2 generators

Teledyne Energy Systems
110 West Timonium Road
Timonium, MD 21093
(301) 252-8220
H_2 generators

Japanese H_2 burning car
Mazda's experimental car
H_2 experimental car

National Hydrogen Assoc.
1800 M Street N.W., Suite 300
Washington, DC 20036-5802
association

American Hydrogen Assoc.
219 S. Siesta Lane, Ste. 101
Tempe, AZ 85281
(602) 921-0433
association

The Phoenix Project: An Energy Transition
to Renewable Resources
H. W. Braun
book

Fuel From Water: Energy Independence with Hydrogen
Michael A. Peavey
(Formerly Hydrogen Home and Auto Fuel Conversion)
book

Haber Process: (A.K.A. Haber-Bosch)
Combine H_2 with ammonia to form liquid fuel--
transportation
information and articles

The Forever Fuel - The Story of Hydrogen
Peter Hoffman
book

American Association for Fuel Cells Newsletter
50 San Miguel Avenue
Daly City, CA 94015
fuel cells newsletter

Hydrogen Wind, Inc.
Route 2, Box 262
Lineville, IA 50147
(515) 876-5665
electrolyzer (H_2 & O_2 from electricity)

Hydrogen Transport and Storage in Engineered
Glass Microspheres
Glenn D. Rambach
paper

Energy Partners, Inc.
West Palm Beach, FL
hydrogen car

Inflatables

Avon Inflatables
79 East Jackson Street
Wilkes-Barre
Pennsylvania 18701
(717) 822-7185
boats/rafts

Aero Tec Laboratories
Spear Road Industrial Park
Ramsey, NJ 07446
(201) 825-1400
membrane products

Dry Dock Tackle Corporation
102 South Main
P.O. Box 412
Early, IA 50535
(712) 273-5591
inflatable pontoon boats

Bombard/Metzeler (Zodiac)
P.O. Box 400
Stevensville, MD 21666
(301) 643-4141
inflatable canoes and boats

Airlock Dock Seal
Division of O'Neal Tarpaulin Company
549 West Indianola Avenue
Youngstown, OH 44511
inflatable dock seal

Tuff Temp Corporation
P.O. Box 366
Fort Washington Industrial Park
Fort Washington, PA 19034
high temp woven (Kevlar)

Hope Webbing Company
P.O. Box 6387
Providence, RI 02940
woven sleeving

Atkins & Pearce
3865 Madison Pike

*Used in Earth Home

Covington, KY 41017
Kevlar tubing/sleeving

Halkey-Roberts Corporation
11600 Ninth Street North
St. Petersburg, FL 33702
(813) 577-1300
heat sealable valves, etc.

Thermoflex, Inc.
P.O. Box 1184
Salina, KS 67401
(913) 827-7201
structures fabric

Viking Technical Rubber
163 Orange Avenue
West Haven, CT 06516
(203) 934-3401
hypalon-coated nylon and polyester

Feathercraft
#4-1244 Cartwright Street
Granville Island
Vancouver, BC V6H 3R8
CANADA
(604) 681-8437--kayak kits, hypalon/Dacron

RPR Industries
P.O. Box 158
Apex, NC 27502
survival equipment (boats, etc.)

Insecticides
-Natural

Wood ashes - good against red spider, aphids on lettuce, cucumber beetles

Oak leaves burned for 1/2 hour helps control white fly.

Safer, Inc.
60 William Street
Wellesley, MA 02181
soap insecticide

B.T. (bacillus thuringensis)
Bacteria that parasitizes looper worms
Can be sprayed on

Common-Sense Pest Control
William Olkowski
book

GB Systems, Inc.
P.O. Box 19497
Boulder, CO 80308
beneficial insects

Insecticides
-Plants

NOTE: Always try soap first before other insecticides.

Fruit fly trap (beer)
article

Nasturium (and petunias)
repels bad insects

Flowering four o'clock (mirabilis jalapa)
possible mosquito repellent

Neem tree
insects avoid tree - insecticide article

Jicama (pachyrhizus erosus)
leaves, etc., contain rotenone

Sabadilla (insecticide)
article

Spearmint - bug repellent
article

Marigolds (calendula)
repels some pests

Ryania
insecticide

Recipes for botanical insecticides and repellents
article

Pest control plants:
Garlic - aphids, spider mites, weevils, Japanese beetle, onion flies
Pyrethrum (chrysanthemum cinerariae folium)
Basil - flies and mosquitoes
Catnip
Tobacco
Rhubarb
Tomato
Tree of Heaven

Ivory Liquid detergent at 1-2%
as good as commercial insecticides

Parsnip leaves and roots
safe insecticide

Insecticides:
-Derris elliptica - Rotenone (or cube barbasco or cube timbo)
-Tobacco - repels insects when intermixed with vegetables
-Sabadilla officinale (seeds)
-Pyrethrum - chrysanthemum cinerariae folium

-Savory - repels bean beetle

-PT 1200 resmethrin "synthetic pyrethrum" -lacewings, white flies control article

The Organic Gardener's Handbook of Natural
Insects and Disease Control
Ellis & Bradley
book

Rotenone - soak derris roots overnight, crush them, return to water and boil.

Hellebore - used same as derris.

Rue - repels the Japanese beetle.

Ryania - causes insects to stop feeding.

Sabadilla seeds used against grasshoppers, corn borer, codling moth, webworm, aphid, cabbage looper, and squash bug.

Biodynamic Greenhouse Management
by Heinz Grotzke
book

Bio-Dynamic Farming and Gardening Assoc.
P.O. Box 550
Kimberton, PA 19442
booklets and information

*Used in Earth Home

Insects

-Bees

Publication 1495 (1973) (Catalog A53-1495)
Alfalfa leafcutter bees for pollinating
alfalfa in Western Canada
by G. A. Hobbs
Agriculture Canada Information Services
Ottawa K1A OC7
CANADA
booklet

The Complete Guide to Beekeeping
Roger A Morse

First Lessons in Beekeeping
C.P. Dadant

The Art and Adventure of Beekeeping
Harry Aebi

Ken Richards
Research Scientist - Entomology
Agriculture Canada
Lethbridge, Alberta
CANADA
leafcutter bee booklet

R. W. Currie
University of Manitoba
Department of Entomology
Winnipeg 19, Manitoba R3T 2N2
CANADA
leafcutter bee research

Dennis Cash, Agronomist
Montana State University
Missoula, MT 59802
leafcutter bee information

Dorothy Murrell
Saskatchewan Agriculture and Food
McIntosh Mall
P.O. Box 3003
Prince Albert, CANADA S6V 6G1
(306) 953-2793
leafcutter bee specialist
(list of bee equipment suppliers)

Richard Gerhart
6346 Avon Belden Road
North Ridgeville, OH 44039
(216) 327-8056
bumblebees

Ron Bitner
Pioneer Hi Bred Int.
16645 Plum
Caldwell, ID 83605
(208) 467-3314
leafcutter bees

Insect Pollination of Crops
by John B. Free
book

Prairie Pollinating, Ltd.
Box 4042
Regina, Saskatchewan S4P 3R9
CANADA
(306) 949-3365
leafcutter bees

American Bee Journal
Hamilton, IL 62341
bee magazine

Bumblebees Demonstrate Their Pollinating Prowess
by Lee Rozelle and David Marshall
article, Greenhouse Product News

Bee Biology and Systematics Lab
Utah State University
Logan, UT 84322
(801) 750-2524
bee expertise

Dept. of Entomology
University of California
Davis, CA 95616
bee expertise

The Flight of the Bumblebee
Almond Facts
Jan/Feb 1993, p. 32
article

Insect Pollination of Crops
by John B. Free
book

Insects

-Biological Control

NOTE: Most good parasites are in the wasp family.

mosquito repellent
1 tsp soybean oil
¼ tsp. Palmolive liquid soap
1 cup water

A Guide to the Biological Control of Greenhouse Aphids
Mariam Klein & Linda Gilkeson
book

Common Sense Pest Control
Helga Olkowski
book

Natural Insect and Disease Control
Roger B. Yepsen, Jr.
(Rodale Press)
book

The Bug Book, Harmless Insect Controls
Helen and John Philbrick
book

Windowsill Ecology - Controlling Indoor Plant
Pests with Beneficial Insects
William H. Jordan
book

Handbook on Biological Control of Plant Pests
Cynthia Westcott, Editor
Brooklyn Botanic Garden
book

Handbook of Natural Insect and Disease Control
Barbara W. Ellis and Fern Marshall Bradley
book

Sources of Beneficial Insects
list

Plant Disease Handbook
Cynthia Westcott
book

Koppert Biological Systems (USA)
P.O. Box 39387
6346 Avon Belden Road
North Ridgeville, OH 44039
beneficial insects

Insects
-Food Source

Insects as Human Food
FS Bodenheimer
Classic book on insects for food

Improved Equipment and Techniques for Mechanizing the Boll Weevil Larval Rearing System
E.A. Harrell, W.D. Perkins, A.N. Sparks
ASAE 1980

The Human Use of Insects as Food and as Animal Feed
Gene R. DeFoliart
University of Wisconsin

Morgan, N.O. and H.J. Elby
Fly Protein Production from Mechanically Mixed Animal Wastes
Journal Entomology
Volume 10, P. 73-81
1975

Bee Brood as Food
Bee World May 1960
Vol. 41 No.5 p. 113-120

De Conconi, J.R.E/J.M. Pino Moreno....
Protein Content of Some Edible Insects in Mexico
Journal Ethnobiology 1984
Volume 4 p.61-72

Miller, B.F., J.S. Teotia
Digestion of Poultry Manure by Musca Domestica
Poultry Science 1974
Vol 15 p.231-234

Entertaining with Insects
Ronald L. Taylor, Barbara J Carter
Book on insect cookery

Insects: A Nutritional Alternative
Patricia A Dufour
The George Washington University Medical Center
1981
Prepared for NASA

The Production of Insects for Human Food
Robert Kok
McGill University-Quebec
514-398-7781
Article on insect mass production technologies

Different species selected based on these end uses.

A. Fed to poultry
B. Fed to fish
C. Fed to rodents
D. Fed to humans directly

The following insect families are under consideration in the Earth Home:

BOX ELDER BUGS
BEETLES - Some are flesh-eating (carrion beetles, dung, etc.)
LOCUSTS - Grasshopper family

Species	Country
Sphenarium	South Mexico
Schistocerca Gregaria (desert locust)	Algeria

CATERPILLAR/WORM

Species	Country
Belina Mopanie (Gonimbrasia)	Zimbabwe
Agave worms	Mexico City

COCKROACHES (Arenivaga Erratica)

Species	Notes	Country
Guanobies	eats feces such as bat guano	S.W. U.S.
Isopods Sow Bug	eats leaves and	compost piles –
Most organic matter		

The Food Insects Newsletter
Dept. of Entomology
545 Russell Laboratories
Univ. of Wisconsin, Madison
Madison, WI 53706
source:
Food Conversion
Efficiency Article
March 1993

Flesh-eating beetles in bat-filled cave (carrion beetles)
article

Rutabagas attract "bad" bugs
article

The Nutritional Value and Microbial Content of Dried Face Fly Pupae when used to Feed Chicks
Poultry Science 1980
Vol. 59 p. 2514-2518
Koo, S.I., T.A. Curran etc.

Crickets (raising for bait)
book excerp

House fly pupae fed to poultry
article

Insects as a protein source in sewage lagoon
article

Butterflies in My Stomach
by Ronald L. Taylor
book

Bee Culture
bee magazine

A. I. Root Co. (Publishers)
623 W. Liberty Street
Medina, OH 44256
(216) 725-6677

An Inordinate Fondness for BEETLES
Arthur V. Evans
Complete book on beetles

Helen M. Smith
World Conservation Monitoring Centre
219C Huntington Road
Cambridge CB3 0DL
ENGLAND
food insect researcher

American Avicultural Journals (Fowl)
list

The Biology of Termites
book

*Used in Earth Home

Insects of the World
Anthony Wootton
book

Insects - Their Biology and Cultural History
Bernhard Klausnitzer
book

African Termites
Tom Lisker
book

Insects

-Equipment

Koo, S.I., T.A. Curran etc.
The Nutritional Value and Microbial Content of Dried Face Fly Pupae When Fed to Chicks
Poultry Science 1980
Vol. 59 pp 2514-2518

Eby, H.J. and Dendy, W.L. 1976
An attempt to mechanize nutrient recovery from Animal waste by the use of house fly larvae
ASAE Technical Paper 76-6514

Miller, J.A., Schmidt, C.D., and Eschle, J.L. 1975
Systems for large scale rearing of the hornfly, Haematobia Irritans.
ASAE Technical Paper 75-4517
St. Joseph, MI

Elmer Hedlund Agency, Inc.
P.O. Box 305
Medford, WI 54451
(715) 748-4213
Or William Leader
(715) 748-5481
bug catchers

Old Boys Enterprises, Inc.
4585 Schneider Drive
Oregon, WI 53575
(608) 835-9416
bug catcher, black light trap

Bug-O-Matic
Zetts Fish Farm and Hatchery
Drifting, PA
345-5352
electrical bug catcher

F.E.I. Industries
bug catcher

In Southeast Asia they are attempting to breed the insect larvae of papilio polytes (lepidoptera) - a tropical butterfly (17 days to harvest)
WCMC

New York Entomological Society
insects on menu

Easy to build insect trap
article

World Conservation Monitoring Centre
219 Huntingdon Road
Cambridge CB3 ODL
UNITED KINGDOM
edible insects information

Pollination discussion
article

Bees as pollinators - discussion
article

Insulation

Neopor
BASF
Graphite flakes inside EPS
Less thermal radiation in walls

Vacuum Insulation Association
www.vacuuminsulate.org

Thermal Systems International,
Xenia, OH

VacuPanel, Inc.

Internet Information-Misc.

http://www.foodstorage.net/guides3.htm
how long food lasts in storage

Irrigation

-Controls

Gardeners Supply
800-234-6630
Moisture Sensing System
30-275

IRRI-TROL Manufacturing, Inc.
27940 Beale Court
Valencia, CA 91355
(805) 257-2333
moisture sensors

Rainmatic Corporation
P.O. Box 3321
Omaha, NE 68103
(800) 228-3615
* (battery) electronic water timer

Calsense
2075 Core Del Nogal South
Suite J
Carlsbad, CA 92009
(619) 438-0525
complex computer controls

Greywater Use in the Landscape
by: Rober Kourik
Also - Book on his drip system in Natural Garden magazine
217 San Anselmo Avenue
San Anselmo, CA 94960
(415) 456-5060
source - good book

Delmhorst Instrument Co.
51 Indian Lane East
P.O. Box 68
Towaco, NJ 07082
(201) 334-2557
moisture meters and ceramic blocks

Dayni Controls Manufacturing Co.
18414 Eddy Street
Northridge, CA 91325
(818) 349-8367

battery operated controls

Soil Moisture Equipment Corp.
P.O. Box 30025
Santa Barbara, CA 93105
(805) 964-3525
tensiometers/soil moisture blocks

Water Conservation Systems, Inc.
141 South Spring Street
Claremont, CA 91711
(714) 621-5805
irrigation controls

Systematic Irrigation Controls, Inc.
3190J Airport Loop Drive
Costa Mesa, CA 92626
(714) 850-0996
(800) 533-5157
irrigation controls

Irrometer Co.
8835 Philbin Drive
P.O. Box 2424
Riverside, CA 92503
(909) 689-1701
irrometers

Hendrickson Bros.
2931 Lester Avenue
Corona, CA 91719
(714) 737-6822
* flow controls

Irrigation
-Drip

RIS Irrigation Systems
1588 North Marshall Avenue
P.O. Box X
El Cajon, CA 92022-2246
(619) 562-2950
drip emitter systems

International Irrigation Systems
LPO 160
155 Third Avenue
Niagra Falls, NY 14304
"wet" tube micro-pore tubing systems

Thrifty Supply Co.
720 West Washington Street
Eureki, CA 95501
(707) 443-8095
(707) 485-5481
distributor

Pearls Garden Center
P.O. Box 213
Captain Cook, HA 96704
black "gro bags"

Spraying Systems Co.,
North Avenue at Schmale Road
Wheaton, IL 60188
(708) 665-5000
spray nozzles (see also TOILETS)

Trickle Soak Systems
8733 Magnolia, Suite 109
Santee, CA 92071
(714) 449-6408
distributor - many systems

Global Irrigation Corporation
7341 Whittier Avenue
Whittier, CA 90602
(213) 945-2287
drip emitters and more

Spears Manufacturing Co.
15853 Olden Street
P.O. Box 4428
Sylmar, CA 91342
(213) 367-6171
complete line

Weninger GMBH & Co., KG
Kunst Stoff-Kearmikwerk
A-6410 Telfs-Tirol
AUSTRIA
ceramic tubes (Blumat)

Rain Bird
145 North Grand Avenue
Glendora, CA 91740
(213) 963-9311
complete line

Gardeners Supply Co.
(Park Seed Co.)
128 Intervale Road
Burlington, VT 05401
(802) 863-1700
* Net-A-Film (also Hydro-Gro)

Roberts Irrigation Products, Inc.
700 Rancheros Drive
San Marcos, CA 92069
(800) 685-5557
Ro-drip

Drip In Irrigation Co.
4645 N. Bendel Avenue
Fresno, CA 93722
(800) 472-3747
(209) 275-1223
in-line emitters

Boca Automation, Inc.
P.O. Box 810444
Woodlands Station
Boca Raton, FL 33481
(407) 272-9838
automated indoor plant watering line

MPC Hydro Pro
2805 West Service Road
Eagan, MN 55121
(800) 672-3331
irrigation control

Irrigation
-Ionized water, Acidic water

acidic water produced from ionized water generators have been shown to promote plant growth
www.purennatural.com

Irrigation
-Miscellaneous Products

Bay World Trading, Ltd.
5 Third Street
Hearst Building, 1018

*Used in Earth Home

San Francisco, CA 94103
(415) 979-0656
(polyacrylamide) "Solid H_2O" (crystals that absorb water)

Spray-N-Grow
Foliar fertilizer

Ken-Bar
24 Gould Street
Reading, MA 01867
(617) 944-0003
crop covers/plastic mulches

Moisture Systems, Inc.
Melrose Park, IL 60160
porous rubber hose

Nelson 7719 North Pioneer Lane
Peoria, IL 61615
(309) 692-2200
hose and watering products

Gilmour Manufacturing Co.
A Subsidairy of Vermont American Corp.
Somerset, PA
insecticide and fertilizer injector

Melody Plant-Sentry
plays musical tune when plants need water

Mee Industries Inc.
4443 N. Rowland Avenue
El Monte, CA 91731
(800) 732-5364
(818) 350-4180
fogging nozzles and equipment

Moisture/light meter
H-9366
retail publication

CPN Company
2830 Howe Road
Martinez, CA 94553
(510) 228-9770
soil moisture tester

Irrigation

-Vertical (See Gardening, Vertical

Juicers/Juicing

Welles Peoples Press
From the Living Foods Marketplace
Hydraulic Juicer

Hand-Operated Juicers
209-277-8438

Aurora Hand Juicers

See juicebars.com for electric juicers

1 oz. of wheatgrass juice =2 ½ lbs. of green leaf vegetables

Hippocrates Health Institute

1443 Palmdale Court
West Palm Beach, Fl. 33411
561-471-8876
Juicing advocates

Leaf Protein Concentrates (LPC)

The Large-Scale Production of Protein from Leaf Extracts
J.E. Morrison and N.W. Pirie
Journal of the Science of Food and Agriculture
1961 vol. 12

American Protein Corp.

Ampcinc.com
Fao.org

Leaf Protein Concentrates
By Lehel Telek
Book on LPC

Leaf Protein as Solution to Protein Shortage in Developing Countries
Oke, D.L.
Journal Nutrition Diet
1969 article on LPC

Lighting

New electrodeless lamp design from Panasonic
Indium-halide and vane-type resonator

Optics and Wheels
Public Relations Staff
General Motors, Detroit
Book on lighting-especially auto

Flickering Flames
A History of Domestic Lighting through the Ages
Leroy Thwing
Book on history of human lighting

New Light on Old Lamps
Larry Freeman
History of many lamps and technology

LED lights
Real Goods Trading Co.
New LED's for more lighting applications

Patlite Corp.
3860 Del Amino Boulevard
Ste. 404
Torrence, Ca. 90503
310-214-5286
Tower LED Lights

*Hubbell
Milford, Ct.
203-882-4800
12 VDC Occupancy sensors

Gilway Technical Lamp
165 New Boston Street
Woburn, Mass. 01801
(617) 935-4442
halogen lamps

Carley Lamps, Inc.
1502 West 228th Street
Torrance, CA 90501
(213) 534-3860
Krypton flashlight bulbs up to 12V

UVP Inc.
5100 Walnut Grove Avenue
P.O. Box 1501
San Gabriel, CA 91778

*Used in Earth Home

(800) 452-6788
* UV lamps

Lo-Volt Lighting Division
Hi-Craft Metal Products
606 West 184th Street
Gardena, CA 90247
(213) 321-9683
lamps

Electrodex, Inc.
6209 17th Street East
Bradenton, FL 34203
(813) 756-4311
distributor all kinds

Bulbtronics
31-T Willow Park Center
P.O. Box 306
Farmingdale, NY 11735
(516) 249-2272
distributor of light bulbs

McLean Electronics, Inc.
10810 Talbert Avenue
Fountain Valley, CA 92708
(714) 963-5641
bulbs and fixtures

Xantech
13038 Saticoy Street
North Hollywood, CA 91605
(213) 982-6600
interior lights

Waldeman Lighting
1714 South Wolf Road
Wheeling, IL 60090
(312) 520-1060
12V machine/industrial lights

Sylvania
GTE Products Corp.
West Main Street
Hillsboro, NH 03244
(603) 464-5533
lamps - all kinds

Lunalite
accent lights for walkways

Rolls Ltd.
8 Proctor Street
Salem, MA 01970
(617) 745-3333
security lights and batteries

Sears Security Systems
ultrasonic motion detector

Gas Flames for Illumination
article

Infrared of NJ
P.O. Box 59
River Street Station
Paterson, NJ 07544
sensors to turn off lights (110 volt)

Sunalex Corp.
5955 Northwest 31st Avenue
Ft. Lauderdale, FL 33309
(305) 973-3230
energy-efficient ballasts

Northern Lites
P.O. Box 874
Towasket, WA 98855
adapters

Visual Communications Co., Inc.
7920-G Arjons Drive
San Diego, CA 92126
(619) 549-6900
(800) 522-5526
LED lenses and mounts

United Security Products, Inc.
2171 Research Drive
Livermore, CA 94550
(800) 227-1592
(415) 455-8866
alarms and sensors

Flashbaking
quartz lamp article

Dulux
Panasonic
Philips
Reflect-A-Star
Available from Real Goods Trading Co.
compact fluorescent reflector lamps

Coast to Coast
hand held spotlight

Material Flow Inc.
Chicago
200,000 candle power (CP)

Lectric Lites Co.
2504 West Vickery
Ft. Worth, TX 76102
2 amp strobe warning light 500,000 CP

Oreck Corp.
100 Plantation Raod
New Orleans, LA 70123
303,952 CP

Iota Engineering Co.
P.O. Box 11846
1301 E. Wieding Road
Tucson, AZ 85734
(602) 294-3292
efficient ballasts

Collins Dynamics
Aurora, CO
magnum 1,250,000 CP 8 amps

Ledtronics, Inc.
4009 Pacific Coast Highway
Torrance, CA 90505
(310) 549-9995
cluster LEDs

Lumex Opto/Components Inc.
292 E. Hellen Road
Palatine, IL 60067
(708) 359-2790
jumbo LEDs

Siemans Solar
P.O. Box 6032
Camarillo, CA 93011
"sensor" light - photo controlled

Terra Resources

*Used in Earth Home

2800 Wind Cave Court
Burnsville, MN 55337
(612) 882-4341
lighting and other products

Visible solar-ray supply system for space station
NASA article

Zane International
2026 - 10th Street
Boulder, CO 80302
(303) 444-7226
dimmers/light controls

The Brinkman Corp.
4215 McEwen Road
Dallas, TX 75244
(214) 387-4939
12V security lights and photo control

Photocomm
930 Idaho Maryland Road
Grass Valley, CA 95945
(916) 477-5121
(800) 544-6466
distributor

Solar Electric Specialties
P.O. Box 537
Willits, CA 95490
(707) 459-9496
solar-powered motion detector and full line

Alternative Energy Engineering
(800) 777-6609
12V low pressure sodium lights - security with photoswitch
battery-operated IR sensor light

Overton's
111 Red Banks Road
P.O. Box 8228
Greenville, NC 27835
(800) 334-6541
250,000 C.P. underwater halogen light and any boating accessories

Beacon Light Products
723 W. Taylor Avenue
Meridian, ID 83642
(208) 888-5905
dimmer discs

Leviton Mfg. Co.
59-25 Little Neck Parkway
Little Neck, NY 11362
ceiling-mount occupancy sensors

Heath Company
P.O. Box 1288
Benton Harbor, MI 49023
(616) 925-2896
occupancy sensors

Ushio America, Inc.
20101 S. Vermont Avenue
Torrance, CA 95002
(310) 329-1960
halogen lamps

Spectronics Corp.
956 Brush Hollow Road
P.O. Box 483
Westbury, NY 11590
(516) 333-4840
(800) 274-8888
battery-operated UV lamp

Elba Intl. Inc.
203 Lemon Creek Drive, Unit D
Walnut, CA 91789
(800) 626-3522
(909) 595-9881
ballasts

Extech Instruments Corp.
335 Bear Hill Road
Waltham, MA 02154-1020
(617) 890-7440
foot-candle meter

Lime (Building Lime)

Lime Mortar Render over Strawbale Construction
Francis Warren
Book on lime coatings

http://www.buildinglimesforum.org.uk/whyuselime.htm
website promoting lime as building material

Francis E Warren
West Coast College of TAFE, Balga
Lime plastering of straw bale homes

www.lime.org
National Lime Association
703-243-5463

Building Limes Forum
Michael Wingate
Books on Lime

Building with Lime
Stafford Holmes and Michael Wingate
Book on lime construction

Buildings of Earth and Straw-Structural Design for Rammed Earth and Straw-Bale Architecture
Bruce King
www.ecodesign.org

Small-Scale Lime Burning
A Practical Introduction
Michael Wingate
Book on making building lime

All About Lime: A Basic Information Guide for Natural Building
Charmaine R. Taylor
Book on natural cement

Natural Building with Lime Plasters, Mortars, and More
www.northcoast.com

National Lime Association
200 Glebe Road, Suite 800
Arlington, VA 22203
703-243-5463
Organization, information

Francis E. Warren
West Coast College of TAFE
Balga campus
Strawbale walls, plaster

Gary Boudreaux
Shahoma McAlister
Our Helping Hands

*Used in Earth Home

55 Beach Street

Ashland, OR 97520
541-482-7131
Lime Plasters, stucco

Willima Mallow
SRI
San Antonio, TX
Lime Paint developer

Lime Mortars Preparation and Use of Lime Mortar
Scottish Lime Centre
Edinburgh, Scotland

Lime and Other Alternative Cements
Edited by Neville Hill, Stafford Holmes, and David Mather
Compilation of articles

Longevity

The Prolongation of Life
Elie Metchnikoff
Book on aging and disease

The 120-year Diet
Roy Walford

The Anti-Aging Plan
Roy Walford
-Recipes also

Magnetism

http://www.magnetizer.com.au/foragriculture.html
agricultural magnetic product

http://www.wholly-water.com/Crop.Booster.htm
agricultural magnetic product

http://www.scalefighter.com/
magnetic water conditioner

http://clearwatergmx.com/
magnetic water products

Conquering Pain: The Art of Healing With Biomagnetism (Paperback)
by Peter A. Kulish

Mass (see Thermal Mass)

Medicine/Health -Allergies

Studies say children brought up on farms less prone to allergies
-internet article

Also animals, pets when young cuts risk of allergy suffering.

Medicine/Health -Colon Cleansing

Medicine/Health -Diet Related

Death by Prescription
Ray Strand
Book on dangers of modern medicine and hospitals

What Your Doctor Won't Tell You
Jane Heimlich
Book on diet

Cancer Battle Plan
Six Strategies for Beating Cancer From
A Recovered Hopeless Case
Book by
Anne Frahm with David Frahm

Reverse Aging
Sang Whang
Diet suggestions for alkalinity

This list may contain items not connected with Earth Home.

Alkalize or Die

Superior Health Through Proper Alkaline-Acid Balance
Theodore Baroody
Book on the effects of pH on diet and vagus nerve

The Layman's Course on Killing Cancer
book
They recommend condurago bark in a tea-3 tbl/day
From Inca civilization

Healthy Healing
An Alternative Healing Reference
Linda Rector-Page

Historically, Chinese doctors were paid when their patients were healthy with a lack of disease.

In 1988 only 24 out of 130 medical schools require future doctors to take courses in nutrition.

Thomas Edison once said "The doctor of the future will give no medicine, but will involve the patient in the proper use of food, fresh air, and exercise."

Fasting for the Health of It
Jean A Oswald
Herbert M. Shelton
Book on fasting

Lets Play Doctor
Joel Wallach
Mineral/Medicine Book

Merck Manual and PDR
Medical books

Medicine/Health -General

The Cure for all Diseases
Hulda Regehr Clark
Book about using electricity for health
Suggests each organism have a specific bandwith

How Indians Use Wild Plants
For Food, Medicine, and Crafts
Frances Densmore
Book on old remedies etc.

Ionized water
www.purennatural.com

Far infrared waves
Website www.kick-n-stuff.com

The Drug and Natural Medicine Advisor
By the editors of Time-Life Books
Book on alternative medications

Natural Healing Secrets
Brian Chichester
Book on alternative medicine

Ancient Healing Secrets
Dian Dincin Buchman
Book on alternative medicine

Health Keeper Inc.
83 Stonegate Drive
Kitchener, Ontario
Canada N2A 2Y8
519-896-8032
orderinfo@keeper.com

In the past 2,000 years more people have been treated with acupuncture than with all other health methods combined.

Making and Using Colloidal Silver
Mark Metcalf
Book on health benefits of c.s.

Colloidal Silver-the Natural Antibiotic Alternative
Zane Baranowski
Book

Alternative Medicines:
Acupuncture
Ayurvedic Medicine
Aromatherapy
Biochemics
Manipulation
Color Therapy
Laying-on-of-hands
Homeopathy
Hydrotherapy
Light Therapy
Macrobiotics
Megavitamin Therapy
Naturopathy
Negative Ion Therapy
Osteopathy

Pharmaceutical International
800-365-3698
mail order medications

Medicine/Health
-Oral Health

The Herbs of Life
Lesley Tierra
Book on healing herbs

The New Holistic Herbal
David Hoffmann
Book on oral health options

Planetary Herbology
Michael Tierra
Oral health suggestions

Ayurvedic Beauty Care
Melanie Sachs
Herbal alternatives

Yoga of Herbs
Vasant Lad
Book on alternative oral health techniques

Traditional Healers Handbook
Hakim Chrishti
Some dental herbs

The Oral Health Bible
Michael P. Bonner and Earl L. Mindell
Book on oral health

Methane

The Microbiology of Anaerobic Digesters
Michael Gerardi
Book on biogas and digesters

http://waste2profits.com
Methane equipment

Al Rutan
www.commonlink.com/~methane

Miscellaneous
-General

6000 Years in biblical Illustrations & Chronologies
4004 B.C. – A.D. 1997
Illustrated by Gustave Dore

Polyethylene bags-used
18" x 30"
800-543-3400

This list may contain items not connected with Earth Home.

"Global Change"
Newsletter by Pacific Institute
Oakland, Ca. 94612

Bic pens
Splatball, Inc. ph: (788-6392)
Protective blankets - clear, etc., OTC Power Team
ph: (800) 677-8326
Gripworks (hand grips) ph: (800) 827-4747
BBB information
Tie straps ph: (317) 846-6631
Electrical noise solutions
Shades - slatted
Biospere
Toad's semi-permeable membrane - moisture from air
Hose carriers - IGUS
Gortube - hose/cable carriers
Plastic boxes Davies Molding ph: (312) 622-8966
Posi-Pak expanded polystyrene
Shrinkwrap gun ph: (617) 281-1800
Igloo - polystyrene fish house
Round plate conveyors for - sewage (maybe) -
JEFFREY MANUFACTURING

Foam cushioning - JIFFY MANUFACTURING CO.
ph: (201) 688-9200
Lead foil ALUMAX ph: (314) 481-7000
Luffa sponges - SPECTER NATURAL SPONGE CO.
ph: (215) 855-3292
Japanese vs. American Technology article
Cans - FREUND CAN CO. - Chicago ph: (312) 224-4230
Typical wattage of household appliances
Energy uses chart - U.S. Total
Stoppers - Stevens ph: (413) 527-0700
Magnets - Bunting ph: 9316) 284-2020
Magnets - THE MAGNET STORE
ph: (800) 525-3536 (303) 688-3966
House heated with mirrors - article

*Used in Earth Home

Intermediate Technology Publications, Ltd.
Lettering - Varitronics
Bamboo - BOND MFG. CO. ph: (415) 229-0656
Linear transducer displacment (device) ph: (614) 594-7773
Pages on inverters - International Source Book
Tufoil - Like SLICK 50 ph: (800) 922-0075
Cylinders - propane and air pressure McDOWELL
ph: (814) 371-6550
Dynamark Imaging Systems - 3M
Unistrut catalog ph: (313) 721-4040
JEFFERSON ENERGY FOUNDATION
Casting - FIBER-GLAST DEVELOPMENT CORP.,
Dayton, OH ph: (513) 274-1159 (800) 821-3283
HUD publications
My Grip Grippers - tube fittings - JMES C. DENVER CO.

Air Castle
15926 Northville Road
Plymouth, MI 48170-4844
(313) 248-7135
high efficiency computers

V.I.T.A. (understanding technology series)
international Book of Low Technologies

Village Technology Handbook
Published by V.I.T.A.
1815 North Lynn Street, Suite 200
Arlington, VA 22209
International Book of Low Technologies

Midwest Renewable Energy Association/Fair
P.O. Box 249
16 Cross Street
Amherst, WI 54406
yearly fair

The Centre for Alternative Technology
Machynlleth
Powys
SY20 9AZ
U.K.

Back Home Magazine
P.O. Box 37
Mountain Home, NC 28758
hands-on magazine

Energy Answers
P.O. Box 24
Lake Bluff, IL 60044
(708) 234-2315
(800) 776-6761
energy products

National Renewable Energy Lab
Golden, CO
(303) 231-1000
government test lab

Dejashoe
made from recycled materials

Freezing point of sugar and salt solutions
chart

National Center for Appropriate Technology
(N.C.A.T.)
P.O. Box 3838
Butte, MT 59702
(406) 494-4572
(N.C.A.T.)

U.S. Department of Commerce
National Institute of Standards and Technology
Office of Technology Evaluation and Assessment
Gaithersburg, MD 20899-0001
energy-related inventions program

60 Most Popular
James T. Dulley
book (compilation of articles)

EOS Institute
580 Broadway, Suite 200
Laguna Beach, CA 92651
(714) 497-1896
organization

Energy Answers
P.O. Box 24
Lake Bluff, IL 60044
(800) 776-6761
(708) 234-2515
energy saving products

Conservation and Renewable Energy
Inquiry and Referral Service
P.O. Box 30048
Merrifield, VA 22116
(800) 523-2929
information source

Turning Up the Heat
Fred Pearce
book on climate change

The Mother Earth News
24 E. 23rd Street
Sussex, NY 10010
magazine

Folkecenter for Vedvarende (Alternative) Energy
Kammers Garosve 16
SDR. RDBY
DK 7760 Hurup Thy
DENMARK
Danish Research Institute

Canadian Mortgage and Housing Corp.
700 Montreal Road
Ottawa, ON K1A 0P7
CANADA
(613) 748-2000
Canadian Research Organization

Common Sense Architecture
by John S. Taylor
book

VITA
Volunteers in Technical Assistance
1600 Wilson Boulevard, Suite 500
Arlington, VA 22209
(703) 276-1914
organization

Miscellaneous -Medical

Women's health care
UV sunscreen ingredients
Medical book - Human Physiology and Mechanisms of Disease
Back care products
Dog first aid kit
Cool vest ILL DOVE INC. ph: 9302) 335-3911
Diffuse air vests - VORTEC, Cincinatti
ZEE MEDICAL ph: (612) 890-1321
Cool vest air-vest Racal Health ph: (301) 695-8200

*Used in Earth Home

Cool est - MSA
(412) 967-3000 or
(800) MSA-2222

Proflex Back Brod
Ergodyne
1410 Energy Park Drive
Suite One
St. Paul, MN 55108
(800) 225-8238
(612) 642-9889

Whizard
Box 336
Vermillian, OH 44089
(800) 321-8763
protective guard sleeves, gloves

Rehydration drink:
1 liter water
2 level tablespoons sugar <u>or</u> honey
1/4 teaspoon salt
1/4 teaspoon baking soda (or another 1/4 teaspoon salt)
from Village Technology Handbook

Motors-DC

<u>-General</u>

Faulhaber Group
www.micromo.com
tiny micromotors

Motion Tech Trends
Brushless PM motors advocate

EAD Motors
1 Progress Drive
Dover, NH 03820
603-742-3330
high power, compact motors

Maxon Precision brushless motors
High efficiency-minimal eddy current and Hysteresis losses.

Xtreme Energy, Inc.
www.xtreme-energy.com
12 volt slotless DC motors

Source Engineering, Inc.
408-980-9822
DC gearmotors-12 vdc

Warfield Electric
Dc motors for dragsters
www.warfieldelectric.com

NOTE: Most manufacturers carry motors in other voltages than 12 VDC

Dumore Corporation
1030 Veterans St.
Mauston, WI 53948

Energy-Wise Motor Design
Article in Design News 06.18.01 p. 79

Motor Appliance Corp. (MAC)
601 International Ave.
Washington, MO 63090
www.macmc.com
(636) 239-5652
enclosed BLDC motors

brushless, dust tight

Pittman
Harleysville, PA 19438
215-256-6601
Permanent magnet motors and gearmotors

Molon Motor and Coil Corp.
3737 Industrial Avenue
Rolling Meadows, IL 60008
847-253-6000
Custom Plastic DC Gearmotors
Mktg@molon.com

7 Myths about energy efficient motors
Article---Design News 8-16-99
Pages 59-61

Comair Rotron
2675 Custom House Ct.
San Ysidro, Ca. 92173
Tiny DC Motors

API Harowe
American Precision Industries
800-566-5274
Brushless DC motors

MFM Technonogy
200-13 Avenue
Ronkonkoma, N.Y., 11779
800-636-6867
2 wire brushless servo

RMB
"smoovy" by RMB
201-962-1111
smallest DC brushless motor
also miniature bearings

Densitron
Electromagnetic Division
P O. Box 1318
Camden, SC 29020
miniature

Surplus Center
1015 West "O" Street
P.O. Box 82209
Lincoln, NE 68501-2209
(800) 488-3417
(402) 474-4055
all kinds surplus

Servo Magnetics, Inc.
21541 Blythe Street
Chatsworth, CA 91304
800-45-servo
2 wire brushless DC tiny motors

Electronic Motion Control Assoc.
member list - source

Dynetic Systems
19128 Industrial Boulevard
Elk River, MN 55330
(612) 441-4300
DC motor - tachogenerators

Inertial Motors Corporation
280 North Broad Street
Doylestown, PA 18901
(215) 345-1010
low inertia motors

*Used in Earth Home

Motor Products Owosso Corporation
201 South Delaney Road
Owosso, MI 48867
(517) 725-5151
(800) 248-3841
blower motor

Fasco
505 Conestoga Boulevard
Cambridge, Ontario N1R 7P4
CANADA
or
Von Weisse Gear Company
500 Chesterfield Center
Suite 200
St. Louis, MO 63017
(314) 686-3622+
ceiling fan motors

Mabuchi Motor America Corporation
475 Park Avenue South (32 Street)
New York, NY 10016
(212) 686-3622
tiny, low-cost DC motors

Douglas International, Inc.
312 West State Street
Geneva, IL 60134
(312) 232-7419
small DC motors

Alsthom International, Inc.
Two Ram Ridge Road
Spring Valley, NY 10977
(914) 425-6908
DC servomotors

Sheller Globe Corporation
Leece - Neville Division
1374 East 51st Street
Cleveland, OH
(216) 431-0740
small

Hankscraft Motors
300 Wengel Drive
P.O. Box 120
Reedsburg, WI 53959
(608) 524-4341
(800) 808-2071
small gearmotors .5 amp.

Japan Electronics Mfr's Agency, Inc.
7550 North Kolmar
Skokie, IL 60076
(312) 679-2240
OEM motors - tiny

Hurst Manufacturing Corporation
Box 326
Princeton, IN 47670
(812) 385-2564
instrument motors, steppers

PMI Motors
Division of Kollmorgen Corporation
5 Aerial Way
Syosset, NY 11791
(516) 938-8000
thin permanent magnet motors

Clifton Precision
Broadway
Clifton Heights, PA 19018
(215) 622-1000
samariam cobalt motors

IMC Magnetics Corporation
Eastern Division
570 Main Street
Westbury, NY 11590
DC motors

Precision Mechanisms Corporation
44 Brooklyn Avenue
Westbury, NY 11590
tiny motor/switches combination

Panasonic Ind. Company
Division of Matsushita Electric Ind. Co., Ltd.
425 East Algongoin Road
Arlington Heights, IL 60005
(312) 981-4823
DC motors

Astromec, Inc.
2950 Arrowhead Drive
Carson City, NV 89706
(702) 883-9226
mini DC motor

Brevel Motors, Inc.
Broad and 16th Street
Carlstadt, NJ 07072
(201) 933-0220
DC motors

Oriental Motor U.S.A. Corporation
2701 Toledo Street, Suite 702
Torrance, CA 90503
(213) 515-2264
1/50 - 1/5 HP

Barber Colemans Company
Motor Division
1354 Clifford Avenue
P.O. Box 2940
Loves Park, IL 61132-2940
gearmotors

Namiki Precision Jewel Co., Ltd.
15 Essex Road
Century Plaza, 5th Floor
Paramus, NJ 07652
(201) 368-8310
small size

Fasco Ind., Inc.
Motor Division
1600 West Jackson Street
Ozark, MO 65721
(417) 485-2311
F.H.P. (fractional horsepower)

R.A.E. Corporation
5801 West Elm Street
McHenry, IL 60050
(815) 385-3500
custom and std. DC motors

Airpax - North American Philips Controls Co.
Chelshire Ind. Park
Cheshire, CT 06410
(203) 272-0301
precision

Micro Mo Electronics
742 2nd Avenue South
St. Petersburg, FL 33701

*Used in Earth Home

(813) 822-2529
small DC and gearheads

Buhler Products, Inc.
P.O. Box 33400
Raleigh, NC 27606-0400
(919) 469-8522
DC motors

Papst Mechatronic Corporation
Aquidneck Industrial Park
Newport, RI 02840
(401) 849-5930
DC motors and fans

Maxon Precision Motors, Inc.
838 Mitten Road
Burlingame, CA 94010
(415) 697-9614
(800) 865-7540
pancake motors-tiny
precision DC motors, .2-100 Watt
efficient motors-

Mamco Corporation
8630 Industrial Drive
P.O. Box 510
Fransville, WI 53126
(414) 886-9069
F.H.P. motors (up to 1/5 HP)

Twinco, Inc.
7620-3 Tyler Boulevard
Mentor, OH 44060
(216) 946-6309
2.7 amp DC motor

Reell Precision Manufacturing Corporation
1259 Wolters Boulevard
St. Paul, MN 55110
(612) 484-2447
small electric clutches

Inertia Dynamics, Inc.
146 Powder Mill Road
Collinsville, CT 06022
(203) 693-0231
clutches

Brailsford and Co., Inc.
Milton Road
Rye, NY 10580
(914) 967-1820
.1 amp diaphram pump blower

Semix, Inc.
4160 Technology Drive
Fremont, CA 94538
(415) 659-8800
step motor drive control

Dyna Pac Rotating Company
1630 South Industrial Road
Salt Lake City, UT 84104
collector rings

Energystics
872 E. Village Way
Alpine, UT 84004
efficient larger motors

BEI Motion Systems Company
Kimco Magnetics Division
150 Vall Ecitos de Oro
san Marcos, CA 92069

(619) 744-5671
DC motors

Parker Hannifin Corporation
Compumotor Division
1179 North McDowell Boulevard
Petaluma, CA U.S.A. 94952
(800) 358-9068
programmable motion control

Portescap U.S.
31 Fairfield Place
West Caldwell, NJ 07006
(201) 227-0322
DC micromotors

Scott Motors
1117 LaVelle Road
Alamogordo, NM 88310
(505) 434-0633
1/8 to 1 1/2 HP

W.W. Graingers (Dayton Brand)
F.H.P. motors

Astro Flight, Inc.
13311 Beach Avenue
Venice, CA 90291
(213) 821-6242
12 VDC airplane motors

Honeywell Disc. Inst. Subsidiary
102 East Baker Street
Costa Mesa, CA 92626
(714) 979-5300
encoders

Canon U.S.A., Inc.
Electronics COmponents Division
10 Nevada Drive
Lake Success, Long Island, NY 11042
(516) 488-6700
precision motors

Vee-Arc Corporation
West Boro, MA 01581
(617) 366-7451
adj. speed drives

Miniarik Manufacturing Division
321 east Boyd Street
Los Angeles, CA 90013
(213) 680-1444
speed controls

Arc Systems, Inc.
2090 Joshua's Path
Hauppauge, NY 11788
(516) 582-8020
DC motor with brake

Ametek
Lamb Electric Division
627 Lake Street
Kent, OH 44240
(216) 673-3451
brushless DC motors

Hathaway Corporation
10827 E. Marshall
Tulsa, OK 74116
(918) 438-7800
brushless DC motors

Panasonic (Panaflo)

*Used in Earth Home

Div. Matsushita Electric Corp. of America
Industrial Motor Department
Two Panasonic Way Panazip 7E-4
Secaucus, NJ 07094
(201) 392-4923
DC brushless fans with "hydrowave" bearings

Empire Magnets Inc.
5780B La Bath Avenue
P.O. Box 1908
Rohnert Park, CA 94928
(707) 584-2801
motion control motors

Hansen Corp. (Minebea)
P.O. Box 23
Princeton, IN 47670
(812) 385-3415
DC motors, steppers

Merkle-Korff Industries, Inc.
1776 Winthrop Drive
Des Plaines, IL 60018
(708) 296-8800
DC motors and gear motors

Transkoil Inc.
P.O. Box 9011
Valley Forge, PA 19485
(610) 539-4400
small brushless DC motors

Koford Engineering
445 Windy Point Drive
Glendale Heights, IL 60139
(630) 858-1162
miniature DC motors

Motors-DC

-Motion Control, Servo, Stepper

Motors-DC
ThinGap Corporation
2064 Eastman Avenue, suite 107
Ventura, CA 93003
805-477-7535
www.thingap.com

www.AllMotion.com
408-460-1345
tiny servos with onboard eeprom

Nippon Pulse America, Inc.
www.nipponpulse.com
540-633-1677
Linear servomotors (shaft motors)

MD Drive
Intelligent Motion Systems
Combine motor and drive

Northrop Brumman Poly-Scientific
Servo motors w/drive electronics attached

G&G Technology, Inc.
servomotors

Danaher Motion
45 Hazelwood Dr.
Amherst, NY 14228
800-566-5274
miniature step motors

www.dcpowersystems.com
motor controllers for dragster

Micro Mo Electronics
14881 Evergreen Ave.
Clearwater, FL 33762
www.micromo.com
(800) 851-5179
comprehensive miniature servo systems

Ogura Industrial Corp.
400 Cottontail Lane
Somerset, NJ 08873
(732) 271-7361
info@ogura-clutch.com
Micro electric clutch

Intelligent Motion Systems, Inc.
370 North Main Street
Marlborough, CT 06447
(860) 295-6102
www.imshome.com
Small motion control package
Hollow-core motors

Mushrooms

www.mycomasters.com
grow mushrooms with hydrogen peroxide

Natural Building

Nutrition

-Articles

B-12
article

Recommended Daily Intakes - East Asia
chart

Notes on energy values and nutrients
charts

NASA's balanced human diet from 8 species of plants and vitamins
NASA exerp

Balanced diet from plant sources
List

Dietary patterns
world map

Vitamins, minerals, etc.
chlorophyl dietary survey
article

Soybean products
chart

The Pritiken Promise
Pritiken Diet - low fat
book excerps

Hippocrates Health Institute
wheatgrass, etc.
articles

Food Pyramid, USDA
chart

50 grm/day protein needs for office job
RDA

Leaf protein as human food
article

Nutrition
-Books

the Food-Mood-Body Connection
Gary Null

The Woman's Encyclopedia of Natural Healing
Gary Null

Fit For Life
by: Harvey and Marilyn Diamond
-includes when to eat and in what order
-meat eating has increased 400% in the last 100 years
-carnivore vs. herbivore discussions
-eat much fruit
-RDA for protein 56 grams/day
book

Hydroponic Home Food Gardens
lists production from 16½'x12' greenhouse
book
Dr. Atkins' New Diet Revolution
Robert C. Atkins
Book on protein diets

The Zone
Barry Sears
Book on diets

Nutrition
-General

Comfrey can be roasted, ground, and used
as a coffee substitute
article

10 Appetite Cut Off Switches
September 1992
Prevention
article

Food Guide Pyramid Chart
USDA

World Meat Comsumption vs. Income Chart
Book of Tofu

Caloric values for vegetables
excerp from "Pritiken Promise"

Are You Eating Right?
article, consumer reports, October 1992, p. 644

U.S. Dietary Goals:
58% carbohydrates
12% protein
30% fats
from NASA files

Food and people - where does the truth lie?
S. H. Wittwer
Booklet
New arrivals to the Klondike we required to have one years' supply of food including:
100 lbs. navy beans
150 lbs bacon
400 lbs. flour
25 lbs. sugar
10 lbs. baking powder
20 lbs. candles
25 lbs. hardtack
2 bottles Jamaica ginger
6 lbs laundry soap
2 suits heavy knit underwear

Enzyme Nutrition
The Food Enzyme Concept
Edward Howell
Book on enzymes

Living Foods for Optimum Health
Brian R. Clement
Book on special diets

Design Your Own Vitamin and Mineral Program
Book on special diets and ODA

World Meat Comsumption vs. Income Chart
Book of Tofu

Caloric values for vegetables
excerp from "Pritiken Promise"

Are You Eating Right?
article, consumer reports, October 1992, p. 644

U.S. Dietary Goals:
58% carbohydrates
12% protein
30% fats
from NASA files

Food and people - where does the truth lie?
S. H. Wittwer
Booklet
New arrivals to the Klondike we required to have one years' supply of food including:
100 lbs. navy beans
150 lbs bacon
400 lbs. flour
25 lbs. sugar
10 lbs. baking powder
20 lbs. candles
25 lbs. hardtack
2 bottles Jamaica ginger
6 lbs laundry soap
2 suits heavy knit underwear

Enzyme Nutrition
The Food Enzyme Concept
Edward Howell
Book on enzymes

Living Foods for Optimum Health
Brian R. Clement
Book on special diets

Design Your Own Vitamin and Mineral Program
Book on special diets and ODA

World Meat Comsumption vs. Income Chart
Book of Tofu

Caloric values for vegetables
excerp from "Pritiken Promise"

Are You Eating Right?
article, consumer reports, October 1992, p. 644

U.S. Dietary Goals:
58% carbohydrates
12% protein
30% fats
from NASA files

Food and people - where does the truth lie?
S. H. Wittwer
Booklet
New arrivals to the Klondike we required to have one years' supply of food including:
100 lbs. navy beans
150 lbs bacon
400 lbs. flour
25 lbs. sugar
10 lbs. baking powder
20 lbs. candles
25 lbs. hardtack
2 bottles Jamaica ginger
6 lbs laundry soap
2 suits heavy knit underwear

Enzyme Nutrition
The Food Enzyme Concept
Edward Howell
Book on enzymes

Living Foods for Optimum Health
Brian R. Clement
Book on special diets

Design Your Own Vitamin and Mineral Program
Book on special diets and ODA

Ground up fish for topping on salad
article

RDA Protein U.S.
1941 70 gram
1968 65 gram
1980 56 gram

West Germany 115 gram

Rumania 110 gram

Netherlands, Poland 90 gram
recommended protein levels

Tempeh is the richest known vegetarian source of vitamin B_{12}
Tempeh information source

The Book of Tempeh
William Shurtleff and Akiko Aoyagi

Dried turnip leaf meal
Dried broccoli leaf meal
Can both be used to replace alfalfa meal
foodstuff article

May All Be Fed
John Robbins
book

The Power of Pasta
Olwen Woodier
book

Mediterranean Diet Pyramid
pasta-rich diet

Honey, garlic and vinegar home remedies
The Leader Co.
book

The Wellness Encyclopedia of Food and Nutrition
University of California/Berkeley
book on fresh food

U.S. Surgeon General reports up to 65% of all diseased could be prevented through proper nutrition

Raw Energy
Leslie and Susannah Kenton
Book on raw foods

Soil Science Simplified
Nature's Healing Grasses
H.E. Kirschner

Foods That Heal
Bernard Jensen

Back to Eden
Jethro Kloss
Book on natural foods

Honey, Garlic, and Vinegar
Patrick Quillin
Specialized book on these 3 foods

Fresh Vegetable and Fruit Juices
N.W. Walker
Book on Juicing

Protein Power
Dr. x
Early book on protein diets

5-Day Miracle Diet
Adele Puhn
Book

Papercrete

Building with Papercrete and Paper Adobe
Gordon Solberg
book

Papercrete News
Box 23-J
Radium Springs, NM 88054
Newsletter

Parasites

Diatomaceous earth
Can be used to kill larger parasites by ingesting
Also kills fleas and many garden pests

Fearsome Fauna
Roger M. Knutson
Book on parasites

Ther Parasite Menace
Skye Weintraub
Book on parasites

Overcoming Parasites: What You Need to Know
Ann Louise Gittleman
Book about parasites

Medical Parasitology
Markell and Voge
Book on parasites

Herbal Parasite Remedies
Hulda Regehr Clark
Book on parasite control

Guess What Came To Dinner—Parasites and your Health
Gittleman
Parasites book

Pasta

Korean sweet potato vermicelli
Long chewy noodles made with sweet potato starch

Bean thread noodles

Phase Change Materials (See Thermal Mass)

Photovoltaic

-Future Products

Efficient organic solar cells
www.princeton.edu

Plastic or paintable solar panels
Berkely University of California

Midwest Research Institute
425 Volker Boulevard
Kansas City, MO 64110
816-753-7600
Sunlight directly into H and O2
Using photovoltaic-photoelectrochemical

Photovoltaic

-General

Solmecs from Israel
Bifacial modules

Banner Engineering
PO Box 9414
Minneapolis, Mn. 55440
800-953-6392
DC photo sensors

Atlantis Energy
14790 Mosswood Ln.
Grass Valley, Ca. 95945
530-274-2743
PV roof tiles

Dinh Co.
P.O. Box 999
Alachua, FL 32615
(904) 462-3464
solar well pump system

Practical Photovoltaics
Richard Komp
Book

Just add Sunshine
J. Micheal Mooney
Book

Kyocera
Solar Systems Division
8611 Balboa Avenue
San Diego, CA
(619) 576-2600
solar modules

Arco Solar
P.O. Box 6032
Camarillo, CA 93010
(805) 388-6335
solar modules

Energy Emersion Devices (Sovonics)
1675 West Maple Road
Troy, MI 48084
* solar module

Solar Distributors:
-Carrizo Solar (505) 764-0345
-Photo Comm
-Real Goods Trading
-Alternative Energy Engr. (707) 923-2277
-Solar Electric (707) 586-1987
-Joel Davidson
-Sunlight Energy Corp. (602) 934-6492
-Atlantic Solar Power (301) 796-8094
-Northern Lights Solar (807) 597-4253
-Independent Power and Light (802) 888-7194
-Solar Mode (805) 486-1105
-Electron Connection (916) 475-3401
-Fowler Solar Electric (413) 238-8974

Sanyo Electric Co., Ltd.
Sumoto City
Hgoyo, JAPAN
smaller solar cells

Light Concentrating Fiberoptics
article

NASA
Converting RF to DC power
article

Real Goods Trading Co.
Tracking Collectors
Cost effective?
article

Solmate Solar Products
11648 Manor Road
Glen Arm, MD 21057
(410) 661-9880
PV controllers

National Renewable Energy Laboratory
1617 Cole Boulevard
Golden, CO 80401-3393
(303) 231-1243
coatings/reflector research

Siemens Solar
4650 Adohr Lane
Camarillo, CA 93010
(805) 482-6800
solar modules

Solarex
630 Solarex Court
Frederick, MD 21701
(301) 698-4218
solar modules

NAPS International
587-F North Ventu Park Road, Suite 508
Newbury Park, CA 91320

*Used in Earth Home

(805) 494-6657
solar modules

Mobil Solar Energy Corp.
4 Suburban Park Drive
Billerica, MA 01821
(508) 667-5900
solar for utilities

Star Power Intl. Ltd.
1016 Worldwide Industrial Centre
43 Shan Mei Street
Fotan, Shatin
HONG KONG
(852) 605-6451
solar products

Solec International
12533 Chadron Avenue
Hawthorne, CA 90250
(310) 970-0065
solar modules

Photovoltaic Energy Systems, Inc.
P.O. Box 290
Cassanova, VA 22017
(703) 788-9626
PV source book

American Solar Energy Society
2400 Central Avenue, G-1
Boulder, CO 80301
(303) 443-3130
association

A Guide to the Photovoltaic Revolution
by Paul D. Maycock and Edward N. Stirewalt
book

Sun Watt Corp.
RFD Box 751
Addison, ME 04606
(207) 497-2204
smaller panels

Midway Labs, Inc.
1818 East 71st Street
Chicago, IL 60649
power source modules

Photovoltaic
-Roof Panels

Websites of PV roof panels:

www.alwitra.de
www.laumanns.de
www.braas.de
www.pfleiderer-doch.de
www.sonnenstromag.de
www.rathscheck.de
www.rheinzink.de
www.rweschottsolar.de
www.solardachstein.de
www.sesol.de
www.solarwatt.de
www.starunity.ch
www.thyssen-solartec.com

Photovoltaic
-Trackers

Manufacturers of sun-tracking racks for solar cell panels:

Robbins Engineering
1641-25 McCulloch Boulevard
Lake Havasu City, AZ 86403
(602) 855-3670

Zomeworks Corp.
P.O. Box 25805
Albuquerque, NM 87125
(505) 242-5354
(800) 279-6342

Wattson Corp.
P.O. Box 751
614 - 2nd Street SW
Albuquerque, NM 87103
(505) 242-8024
PV tracker

Piezoelectric

See Elec. Sensors also

New Scale Technologies, Inc.
10 East Main Street, Suite 301
Victor, NY 14564
Phone: (585) 924-4450
Fax: (585) 924-4468
sales@NewScaleTech.com
Squiggle linear motion piezoactuator

NanoMuscle
2545 W. 10th St. Suite A
Antioch, CA 94109
925-776-4700
Shape memory alloys to produce movement.

Note: full plants chart located in body of text.

Plants
-Cellulose

Kudzu can be used for cellulostic alcohol production

Kudzu Kingdom Division of Suntop Inc.
www.kudzukingdom.com
seeds

Plants
-Future Research

Plants for People
Anna Lewington
alternative plants source

Brosimum Galactodendron
Brosimum Utile
"Cow Trees"
milk
alternative

Cuphea
article

Center for
Unusual Plants
- Biooptions

*Used in Earth Home

newsletter

Dictionary
of useful plants
American plants useful for food
book

Tropical agriculture - literature
article

Arracacia
article

Anona cherimola
article

The biology of Australian plants
article

Tamarind
article

Milk vetch
article

Edible leaves of the world
Ron Hurov
personal communication

Seed Head news
article

Rapoko - greens
article

Mangium casuarinas
article

Brazilian sassafras
article

Sea kale
article

Edible plants
article

Velvetleaf seeds
private communication

Alternative crops for Minnesota
government publication

Banana (plantation)
article

Plastic PHB
(polyhydroxy butyrate) in potato tubers
article

Baobab, monkey bread tree, adansonia L. Bobacaccae
article

Peruvian carrot
Arracacia xanta orrhiza
article

Oka
Oxalis crenata
Roots
article

African breadtree (isa quente)
Treculia decne Africana
article

Cyperus exculentus
Nut sedge
Chufa
article

Carob
article

Azolla - water fern
article

Fenugreek - trigonella
article

Maguey
article

Siratro - fodder crop
article

Weeds or foliage - 12 common
article

Lemon grass - cymbopogan citratus
article

Cowpea - foilage
NASA article

"Manna"
article
from reprint

New crop
symposium
reprint

Amaranth
ymposium
article

Seaweed
article

Algae
article

Stress in plants
- stress physiology
NASA reprint

Algae
article

Comfrey
article

Winged bean
article

Lentils
article

Jicama (contains rotenone)
article

Center for Alternative Plant and Animal Products
305 Alderman Hall
University of Minnesota
1970 Folwell Avenue
St. Paul, MN 55108
newsletter "Bio Options"

*Used in Earth Home

Chaya (cnidoscolus aconitifolius)
(perennial herb)
leaves high vitamin C and protein

These plants may find use in the Earth Home if they can be grown successfully:

Mangels - beta vulgaris
Yams - dioscorea esculenta (Chinese yam)
Taro or Yautia
- tops for greens
- root for Poi (fermented)
- xanthosoma sagittifolium
Ground-nuts - arachis hypocaea or arachis - American
Manihot utilissima - casaua (manioc)
Longhocarpus root (Peru) nicou utilis
Plantain musa paradisica
Esculenta psoralea or breadroot
Sago palm - starch
Bread fruit - artocarpus communis
Peppers - artocarpus altilis
Winged bean (dambala)
Leuceanna trees - for animal forage
Sea kale

Plants
-Grains (Cereal)

NOTE: See also Plants - Wheat (separate file)
NOTE: There are six major world cereal grains: rice, wheat, corn, grain sorghum, barley, and pearl millet.

www.growwheatgrass.com
*6 tray sprouter

Hulled barley for soups

Wildlife Nurseries
PO Box 2724
Oshkosh, Wisc. 54903
414-231-3780
Wild rice seeds

Rice
information

Quinoa Corp.
article

Upland rice
ackground articles

Southern Exposure Seed Exchange
PO Box 158
North Garden, Va. 22959
Upland and lowland rice

Grains article - misc.
article

Millet
article

Quinoa
article

Amaranth
article - contains good amount of calcium

Small-scale grain raising
book source

Amaranth, lupine, tritikale
articles

Misc. small grains
reprint

Buckwheat
article

About quinoa and amaranth
article

Drying grain with wooden blocks
Village Technology Handbook

West Africa Rice Development Association
Boite Postale 2551
Bouake 01, Cote D'Ivorie
information source

Amaranth Symposium
article

Teff - 14% protein - disease free
Montana State University
(406) 348-3400

Kamut Assoc. of North America
P.O. Box 691
Fort Benton, MT 59442
(406) 622-5436
Kamut grain

Making beer out of the "pa-shi-coquar-marsh" root in "The Old Fashioned Dutch Oven Cookbook"

Popped amaranth can be used as breading for baked fish and poultry

Plants
-Herbs, Spices, Tea

Dictionary of Herbs, Spices, Seasonings, and Natural
Carole Skelly

bay leaf
lemon thyme
4 pungent "Italian style" plants:
1. thyme
2. garlic
3. basil (oils)
4. oregano
basic seasoning

Mints--peppermint, lamb mint
teas

Chives--mild onion flavor
salads, fish

(perfection) parsley

Sorrel
High in vitamin C
1/2 cup provides 67% vitamin A of female; 57% vitamin C for adult
use as spice

The Edible Indoor Garden
Peggy Hardigree
book

Almost all hydroponic gardens contain the same herbs . . . dill, rosemary, tarragon, marjoram, basil, chervil, sage, thyme, and oregano

The Herb Society of America, Inc.
9019 Kirtland Chardon Road
Mentor, OH 44060
(216) 256-0514
herb seeds and publications

The Book of Tea and Herbs
Ministry of Information
tea/herb information

The Herbal Tea Garden
Marietta Marshall Marlin
tea/herb book

Sundance Roasting Co. Inc.
P.O. Box 1886
Sandpoint, ID 83864
(208) 265-2445
coffee substitute, "Barley Brew"

Essiac books
Snow/Klein and Cynthia Olsen:

http://essiac-info.org/recipe1.html

This makes a year's supply of essiac.

Herb	Weight		Form	% of Recipe
Burdock root	4.25 oz.	120g	pea-size cut	53%
Sheep sorrel	2.8 oz.	80g	powdered	36%
Slippery Elm bark	0.7 oz.	20g	powdered	9%
Turkey rhubarb root	0.18 oz.	5g	powdered	2%

1 cup herb mix + 2 gallons of water = about 224 liquid ounces of tea will fill fourteen 16-ounce pint bottles, or seven 32-ounce quart bottles.

1/2 cup herb mix + 1 gallon of water = about 112 liquid ounces of tea will fill seven 16-ounce bottles, or three and a half 32-ounce quart bottles.

1/4 cup herb mix + 1/2 gallon of water = about 56 liquid ounces of tea will fill three and a half 16-ounce bottles, or almost two 32-ounce quart bottles.

Supplies Needed:

Do not use anything made of aluminum.
Stainless steel kettle with lid (or glass, UK unchipped enamel, CND granite pot) Stainless steel sieve Large stainless steel or wood stirring utensil Stainless steel funnel or 2-cup glass measuring cup Glass bottles can be amber, colored or clear glass There are several ways to sterilize bottles

The water you use for making essiac tea should be as pure as possible. Don't use tap water. Most people use distilled water. Nice but not vital, you can "re-energize and re-oxygenate" distilled water by shaking it well or setting it in the sun for a few hours.

Preparation

Mix dry ingredients thoroughly.
Measure out desired amount of dry ingredients.
Pour proportionate amount of water into pot.
Bring water to a rolling boil with the lid on.
Stir dry ingredients into boiling water.
Replace lid and continue boiling at reduced heat for 10 minutes.
Turn off stove. Scrape down sides of pot and stir mixture thoroughly.
Replace lid, let pot sit and cool undisturbed for 10-12 hours (overnight).
Reheat to steaming hot, but do not let it boil.
Turn off heat and allow herbs to settle for a few minutes.
Pour hot liquid through sieve to catch sediment.
Use funnel to fill sterilized bottles, put lids on.
Allow bottles to cool, then tighten lids.
Store in dark cool place, always refrigerate an opened bottle.
Essiac contains no preservatives, discard if mold develops. "When in doubt, throw it out".
Unopened bottles can be stored in a cool, dark place, or keep all the bottles in the refrigerator. Don't freeze essiac or warm it up in a microwave (use hot water to dilute and warm it).

Directions for Use :

1 fluid ounce (30 ml) essiac tea per day, diluted in 2 fluid ounces (60 ml) hot water. This should be sipped, preferably at bedtime on an empty stomach. Food should not be eaten within one hour before/after drinking the tea.

As a daily tonic or to enhance the immune system: Take half a fluid ounce (15 ml) per day, diluted in one ounce hot water.

Plants

-Legumes

www.soyinfo.com
website on all soybean products

NOTE: See also Plants - Oil Plants.
NOTE: The major world legumes are: peas, beans, peanuts, and pulses.

Lupin seeds have been discovered in a pharaoh's tomb inside a 6,000-year-old pyramid
Lupin is a cool weather crop

Legumes in Tropical Environments
book

Snap bean
article

Legumes as leaf vegetables
article

Tropical Legumes - Resources for the Future
article

Pulses - many kinds
article

Soybeans
article

Making Soybean Oil
article

Dwarf beans
article

Tofu (made from soybean seeds)
book

Golden Gram (mung bean)

article

Lentils - lens esculenta
article

Marama beans
article

The Book of Tempeh
William Shurtleff and Akiko Aoyagi
book

Plants

-Medicinal, Hygiene, Diet

Hoxsey: The Quack Who Cured Cancer?
Documentary on medicinal plants

nitriloside
-plant which animals seek when
thety are ill
Graviola Essiac tea, artesimia, Tian Xian
Cancer treating drugs such as B17

Hoodia Gordonii (cactus)
Diet plant stops appetite

NOTE: A 1967 study revealed 25% of all prescription drugs in America are derived from plant sources.
NOTE: See also Home Care files.

Aloe vera
some UV protection and skin ointment

Diospyros usambarenis
wood toothbrushes and anti-bacterial juices

Diospyros whyteana
"chew sticks"

Poison ivy cure
article

Medicinal and aromatic plants
book reprint

Heather, myrrh, peppermint, eucalyptus, lavender, thyme, mint, and clove
inhibit bacteria

Rhubarb roots used as a laxative

The 5 Vital Secrets for a Healthy Life

Adele Puhn
Book

Nature's Gifts to Medicine
by L. Aikman in National Geographic,
September 1974
article

Elderberries
"Sambucol"
anti-viral (flu)

These plants have possible antibiotic qualities:

Meringo olifera
Alium
Garlic
Sauropus thangiana
Sarcandra glabra - bacteriostatic
Asp
St. John's Wort - inula thalynium (India)
Nasturiam
Avies laceocarp
Aspilia (or A. Chaenactis Douglasii (grass))--contains thiarubrine (an antibiotic)

These herbs have been used for thousands of years in China:

Chamomile flowers
headache

Fenugreek seeds
stomach pains

Black willow
aches/pains

Bear berry leaf
lower back pain

Valerian root
hypertension

Mullein
sinus

Juniper
prostate

Chickweed
weight loss

Eyebright herb
healthy eyes

Blue cohosh root
natural estrogen

Goldenseal root
healthy heart

Yellow duck root
improve circulation

A Modern Herbal
Mrs. M. Grieve

Thirty Plants That Can Save Your Life!
Douglas Schar
herb book

The New Holistic Herbal
David Hoffman
herb book - listed by illnesses

These plants need to be investigated for medicinal qualities:

Persimmon - bark
Frombego
Oaks
- Corkus
- Celogia
- Doublaseii - ground acorns

Asparagus

Health & Wellness Today
Philips Publishing
7811 Montrose Road
Potomac, MD 20854
"natural" medicine magazine

Melaleuca, Inc.
Idaho Falls, ID 83402
tea tree oil--from Australia

Ephedra (ephedrine)
used in China for 5,000 years as decongestant

White willow tree bark
(Salix Alba)
tea contains aspirin

Sunsource Health Products, Inc.
535 Lipoa Parkway, Ste. #110
Kihei, HI 96753
herbal products

Lemons, grapes, seeds and leaves, plumbs, cranberries, buckwheat, grapefruit, beans
source of bioflavonoids (such as pine forest bark "proanthocyanidian"

A New Super Antioxidant = Pycnogenol
Willa Vae Bowles
book

The New Super Antioxidant Plus
Richard A. Passwater
book

Plants
-NASA

Evaluation of candidate species for CELSS
NASA article

Toilets in NASA
NASA article

Biosphere II
notes on article

Plant diversity to support humans in a CELSS
microfiche

Use of higher plants
article

U.S. dietary goals
- 58% carbohydrates
- 12% protein
- 30% fats

recommended diets

Closed ecological systems
article

Closing an ecological system consisting of a mammal, algae, and non-photosynthetic organism
article

Plant productivity in controlled environments
article

Biogenerative life support system farming on the moon
NASA article

Seeding space
article

An overview of Japanese CELSS research
K. Nitta
article

Russian space program study - algae gasses hinder plants
microfiche

Controlled cultivation of higher plants (recycling wastes)
article

Plants
-Non-Edible/Misc.

(See also Plants, Oil Plants, Non-Edible)

Tea tree oil (leptospermum laevigatum)
article

Broussonetia papyrifera "Paper Mulberry"
paper substitute

Plants
-Oil Plants, Edible

The Soybean Book
Phylus Hobson
Book on the soybean

The Soybean Cookbook
Dorothea Van Gundy Jones
Book on the soybean

Sesame high in protein (55% oil)
article

Cottonseed oil
article

Minor oil species with high content of fatty acid example cuphea
list

Canola - rape
reprint

Sunflower seeds
article

Making soybean oil
article

Oils and fats - saturated
article

Oils and fats
article

Hemp oil (drying)
article

Oils and fats
complete biblography

Oils (classification/descriptions)

- Animal oil
  - fish/marine oils
  - land animal oil
- Fixed oils leave permanent greasy residue such as: vegetable oils, heavier mineral oils, animal oils
- Essential oils - characteristic oil
- Drying oil - form tough skin

The following plants are mentioned in literature as having some oil content:

1) Perilla, L.
2) Attalea Cohune
   article
3) Babassu (orbignya barbasiana) (slow growing)
   article
4) Muru Muru
5) Oiticica

*Used in Earth Home

Plants
-Oil Plants, Non-Edible

Tea tree oil (leptospermum laevigatum)
article

http://www.jatropha.de/system.htm
jatropha website

Plants
-Past Plantings, Research

Borage
B_{12}

Lettuce
iron source

Lotus, water chestnut
water plants

Sorrel - garden
vitamin C source

Spinach - winter Bloomsdale
perennial

Tomatoes
need western sun or overhead illumination

Vegetable Growing Handbook
Walter E. Splittstoesser
book

Plants
-Salt Plants

Spinach (in salt studies)
research

Halophytes
article

Plants in saline environments
research paper

Urine studies, sea water
study

Misc. salt tolerant plants
article

Rock-salt study
article

Salt tolerant plants
article

Salt secretion in aelaropus litoralis
reprint

Salinity tolerance
article

Extracting salt - salt in urine
article

Salty Plants
article

Salicornia grown in salt marshes
article

Saltbush (Atriplex Spp.) is good browse
feedstuffs article

Saltgrass (Distichlis Spp.) is of little forage value
feedstuffs article

Plants
-Seeds

NOTE: Seed catalogs in separate file.
NOTE: For past plantings, see Plants - Greenhouses.

Bountiful Gardens seed book
Ecology Action
5798 Ridgewood Road
Willits, CA 95490
www.bountifulgardens.org
(707) 459-6410

Home-Health resource
HCR 67, Box 65
Mountain View, MO 65548
Seeds and other health items

Quality Maintenance in Stored Grains & Seeds
Clyde M. Christensen and
Richard A Meronuck
Seed storage book

Saving Seeds
by Marc Rogers
source

Seed to Seed
by Suzanne Ashworth
source

4 crops of clover (grown inside)
forage

Seed catalogs
complete list

New Seed Starters Handbook
by Nancy Bubel
(list of seed catalogs)
source

Seed Germination
article

Soil temperature for seed germination
chart

Certified seed directory
article

Ongoing seed varieties and 1992 planting
results

U.S.S.R. study -- seeds
reprint

Seed Savers Yearbook literature
source

Companion planting - sowing your own seeds
article

Seeds - viability
chart

Planting chart

year by year

How long to save seeds
chart

Seed planting guide
chart

Greenhouse varieties
reprint

Companion planting
reprint

Seeds - extensive list
options

The Seed Finder
John Jeavons and Robin Leler
* open-pollinated seed book

Tropical seed companies list
photocopy

Seeds of the Earth
Patrick Mooney
book

Talcum powder is the base ingredient in rooting hormones
article

Willow bark can be used as a rooting hormone
article

Plants

-Sweeteners

NOTE: Sprouted wheat seeds can be used as sweetener substitute.

NOTE: Average American consumes 40 pounds of sugar in one year.

Stevia Rebaudiana
http://res.agr.ca/lond/pmrc/faq/Stevia
complete website on Stevia

Sugar Beets have 15% sugar

Strawberries
Put pine needles around them for acid
Eggshells discourage ants
Red pepper around them discourages insects

Syrup Trees
Bruce Thompson

Growing Berries and Grapes
Louise Riotte
Book on grape growing

Minnesota Grape Growers Association
35680 Hiway 61 Blvd.
Lake City, Mn. 55041
John Marshall
612-345-3531
Local grape varieties

Stevia Rebaudiana
reprints

Katemfe
article

Maple syrup - sucrose of 95-98% purity
two articles

Agua Miel - sap of the century plant

Sucrose
article

Strawberries
article

Mannitol
article

Sugar cane
(most calories from unit land area)
reprint

Sugar Cane
Frank Blackburn
book

Plants

-Tubers/Roots

NOTE: Four major world root crops are cassava, potato, sweet potato, and yams.

Kudzu: The Vine to Love or Hate
Nancy Basket
Book on Kudzu lore and more

Sweet potatoes
two articles

Desert Gardening, Fruits and Vegetables
George Brookbank
Good source for tubers

Taro grew well in Biosphere II
(disease-free) They peeled the taro
well to remove the non-edible oils.
It needed to cook a long time. They
Blended it into a soup or bean dish to
hide the distinctive taste.

Parsnips
* article

Tubers - general list of
article

Ulluco - ullucus tuberosos
article

Andean tuber crops, also oxalis tuberosa, tropaeolum tuberosum
article

Cultivation of minor tuber crops in Peru and Bolivia
article

African yam bean
girigari sphenostylis stenocarda
article

Taro (cocoyams)
article

Prairie potato, pomme blanche
psoralea esulenta
article

Cassava (manioc)
article

Mangel
article

*Used in Earth Home

Taro
article

Bread root
article

Plantain
article

Yam propagation
article

Prairie potato - Indian turnip
article

Groundnut
article

Growing Sweet Potatoes in Minnesota
article

Poi and taro
article

* Jerusalem artichoke
article

U.S. Patent #4,871,574
flour from Jerusalem artichokes

Jerusalem Artichokes, a Potential Fructose Crop for the Prairies
article

Zumbro, Inc.
138 West Front Street
Owatonna, MN 55060
(507) 455-0655
SunchokeÔ (artichoke) flour (10% added to noodles)

Wappato or sagittafolia
American Indian staple crop from the
"Old Fashioned Dutch Oven Cookbook"
cultivated in China

Plants

-Vitamin C

Acerola Cherry
May be grown indoors in very bright light.

Plants

-Wheat/Wheatgrass

Storage of Cereal Grains and Their Products
D.B. Sauer
Book on history of storage methods

Wheat for Man...Why and How
Vernice G. Rosenvall
Book on wheat

Make a Treat with Wheat
Hazel Richards
Recipe book using wheat

The Amazing Wheat Book
LeArta Moulton
Book on all the qualities of wheat

1 peck of wheat will feed 1 person for 2 weeks
4 oz. of wheat seed will plant 100sq.ft.
10x110 ft. will yield 1 bushel or 60 lbs.
4 oz. seeds will plant 10 sq. ft. and yield 1 lb.

How to Live on Wheat
John Hill
Book on basic wheat recipes

Make a treat With Wheat
Hazel Richards
Book on Wheat Recipes

Wheat bibliographies
article

Couscous
reprint

Dwarf wheat
NASA

Effect of temp on photosynthesis by maize and wheat
article

Wheat in high irradiance environments
reprint

Semi-dwarf wheat book
source

Growing wheat
source

Brewers yeast
article

Wheat - seeds of two varieties
reprint

International Maize and Wheat Center of Mexico
Mexico City, Mexico
research center

Growing wheat in optimal envinronment
article

Wheat Grass

Wheat grass - where to get seeds
article

Wheat grass - how to cultivate
article

Wheat grass - articles
article

Intermediate wheat grass or perrenial grass crop
article

Be Your Own Doctor
Ann Wigmore
book

National plant material directory
Hippocrates Health Institute
source

Wheat grass varieties
source

Techniques for creating rapid growth strains of wheat for human life support systems
USSR Space Life Sciences Digest article

Techniques for growing wheat
CELSS

*Used in Earth Home

International Maize and Wheat Improvement Center
Lisboa 27
Apartado Postal 6-641
00600 Mexico City, DF,
MEXICO
wheat research center

Plastics
-Mail Order/Retail

Eiler Plastics
7140 Madison Avenue W.
Golden Valley, MN 55427
full line

U.S. Plastics Croporation
1390 Neubrecht Road
Lima, OH 45801
(800) 537-9724
full line

Niagara Plastics Company
7090 Edinboro Road
Erie, PA 16509
(814) 868-3691
full line

Joseph T. Ryerson & Son, Inc.
P.O. Box 8000
Chicago, IL 60680
(Mpls. too)
(800) 242-2114
full line

Wedco Technology, Inc.
P.O. Box 99
Lovelady, TX 75851
powdered polyethylene (roto molding)

A. Schulman, Inc.
Northwestern Financial Center
7900 Xerxes Avenue South
Minneapolis, MN 55431
(612) 835-1601
powdered polyethylene (roto molding)

Philips 66 Company
P.O. Box 792
Passadena, TX 77501
(800) 231-1212
rotational molding powder

Precision Punch & Plastics
6100 Blue Circle Drive
Minnetonka, MN 55343
(612) 933-0993
full line

Aromat Plastics
11551 Rupp Drive
P.O. Box 1157
Burnsville, MN 55337-0157
(612) 890-4697
full line

Seelye Plastics, Inc.
9700 Newton Avenue S.
Minneapolis, MN 55431
full line

Plastics
-Natural Plastics

The only naturally-ocurring plastics are;

Shellac, Rubber, Asphalt, and Cellulose

Plastics
-Products

Product Components Corporation
30 Lorraine Avenue
Mt. Vernon, NY 10553
(914) 699-8640
hardware (see also Plumbing - Hardware Fasteners)

Cole Parmer
7425 North Oak Park Avenue
Chicago, IL 60648
(312) 647-7600
(800) 323-4340
many

Nibco, Inc.
P.O. Box 1167
Elkhart, IN 46515
industrial fittings

Aetna Plastics Corporation
1702 St. Clair Avenue
Cleveland, OH 44114
many industrial fittings, valves

Plastic Components, Inc. (Solidur Pacific Co.)
18179 SW Boones Ferry Road
Portland, OR 97227
(503) 620-9314
gears/bus hinges

Micro Plastics, Inc.
Highway 178 North
Flippin, AR 72634
(501) 453-2261
hardware and fasteners

Richco
5825 North Tripp Avenue
Chicago, IL 60646
(312) 539-4060
samples: (800) 621-1892
fasteners (clamps)

Afton Plastics
16455 20th Street South
P.O. Box 97
Lakeland, MN 55043
specialty plastics and machining

Laramy Products, Inc.
Routh 5N
Lyndonville, VT 05851
(802) 626-9328
welding torches

Memry Corp.
57 Commerce Drive
Brookfield, CT 06804
(203) 740-7311
user-moldable plastic (SMP)

Plastics
-Renewable

There is only one known renewable plastic and that is Cellulose Acetate. This material started the plastic technology revolution.

---Cellulose Background

Cellulose acetate was first prepared in 1865, but took another 29 years before it was made so it would not easily dissolve in common solvents. During World War 1, the technology was used for waterproofing and stiffening the fabrics covering airplane wings. 1919 saw the first cellulose-based yarn, called Celanese.

---Cellulose Technology from Wood Pulp

Commercially, cellulose acetate is made from processed wood pulp. The pulp is processed using acetic anhydride to form acetate flake from which products are made. Coming from wood pulp, means that unlike most man-made fibers, it comes from a renewable resource and is biodegradable. Another technique for producing cellulose acetate involved treating cotton with acetic acid, using sulfuric acid as a catalyst.

---Properties of Cellulose Acetate

Typical properties of cellulose acetate polymers include: good toughness, deep gloss, high transparency, and a feel that can be described as 'natural'.

---Modern Applications of Cellulose Acetate

Cellulose acetate fibers are used for textiles and clothing by many of the top designers in the world. Factors making this material suitable for this application include the fact that it is comfortable, breathable and absorbent. They can also be dyed in many different colors and combined with a range of other fibers such as rayon, cotton, wool, silk etc.

Early frames for spectacles were cut from sheets of cellulose acetate. While use of cellulose acetate has largely been superseded by injection molding with more modern thermoplastics, some up-market spectacles are still made in this way. This is most often the case when color blends/effect cannot be produced by injection molding. A popular example is the imitation tortoise shell effect.

Handles for tools have often been made with cellulose acetate. This material has been used for this application due to its natural feel and toughness. Cellulose triacetate has been a favorite material for photographic film since about 1940. A product called "safety film" exists that has been popular due to its resistance to combustion. Other applications of cellulose acetate include: wound dressings, personal hygiene products, absorbent cloths and wipes, specialty papers, and filter media, including cigarette filters.

Acetate is derived from cellulose (cellulose is a polysaccharide that is the chief constituent of all plant tissues and fibers) by deconstructing wood pulp into a purified fluffy white cellulose. The cellulose is then reacted with acetic acid (acetic acid is a colorless pungent liquid widely used in manufacturing plastics and pharmaceuticals) and acetic anhydride (acetic anhydride is a compound that is needed in order to refine opium into heroin) in the presence of sulfuric acid (sulfuric acid (H2SO4) is a highly corrosive acid made from sulfur dioxide; widely used in the chemical industry).

Plastics
-Resins/Misc.

Dyneon THV from
Dyneon LLC
Oakdale, MN
Low temperature fluorothermoplastic-clear film

Degradable Polymers Council
Society of Plastics Inductry
Suite 600K
1801 K Street N.W.
Washington, D.C. 20006
202-974-5200

List of Companies

Irradiated Plastics such as E-Beam Do Not Melt

Amoco Chemicals Corporation
700 East Randolph Drive
Chicago, IL 60601
(800) 621-4557
(312) 856-3414
Torlon

DuPont
Electronics Department
High Performance Filters
Wilmington, DE 19898
(800) 527-2601
Kapton

Poly Tech
Bloomington, MN
biodegradable plastic (corn meal)

How to identify plastics
article/chart

Plumbing
-Bidets

www.sandman.com
IntiMist electronic bidet

www.phess.ca
portable bidet

toilets/accessories/bidet attachments
search criteria for bidet attachments

Tushy Clean
www.juscuzz.com
bidet attachment for toilet seats

Plumbing
-Fixtures

EcoTrap
Waterless urinal using vegetable oil or mineral
www.waterless.com

American Standard
Lifetime water valves
Ceramic disc technology

Plumbing
-General

Cipax

Norwesco
Cistern Tanks
Dean Bennett Supply
800-621-4291

Plumbing Technology: Design and Installation
Lee Smith
Practical Plumbing book

Enertec
PO Box 85
Union City, Mi. 49094
517-741-5015
non-chemical water treatment system

*Used in Earth Home

The Bosworth Company
195 Anthony Street
East Providence, RI 02905
(401) 438-8411
hand pumps - diaphram

Captured Rainwater
Small Scale Water Supply Systems
by the State of California
Department of Water Resources
Bulletin 213
resource book

Residential Water Re-Use
by Murray Milne
California water Resources Center
Report #46, September 1979
resource book

Leonard Valve Company
Cranston, RI 02910-3817
(401) 431-1200
temp/pressure water mixing valve ± 10F

Valterra Products
720 Jessie Street
San Fernando, CA 91340
low cost gate valves

Water needs chart - animals, home, farm
resource chart

Dream Enterprises, Inc.
453 Hickory Hill Road
Sapulpa, OK 74066
(918) 224-9683
portable shower

APBW Manufacturing, Inc.
2417 West Lincoln
Phoenix, AZ 85005
(602) 258-3031
push button RV winterizing

Arens Controls, Inc.
2015 Greenleaf Street
Evanston, IL 60202
(312) 328-6905
push-pull cables

Molded Products, Inc.
1755 East Ninc Mile Road
Hazel Park, MI 48030
(313) 280-0680
nylon manifolds

Wescon Products, Inc.
2533 South West Street
P.O. Box 7710
Wichita, KS 67277
(316) 946-4280
push-pull cables

Elkay Manufacturing Co.
2222 Camden Court
Oak Brook, IL 60521
(312) 986-8484
SS (stainless steel) sinks, etc.

Schnitzer Alloy Products Co.
325 Pine Street
Elizabeth, NJ 07206
(201) 353-1300
(800) 631-7444
SS sinks

Legion Stainless Steel Sink Co.
P.O. Box 4300
Augusta, GA 30907-0300
(404) 738-9667
SS sink

Sani-Tech
P O. Box 1010
Ndover, NJ 07821
sanitary process tubing (make own fittings with machine)

Elson Thermoplastics
Division of Sekisui America Corp.
P.O. Box 240696
Charlotte, NC 28224
(704) 889-2431
PVC ball valves, etc.

Precision Fitting & Valve Co., Inc.
10365 West 70th Street
Eden Prairie, MN 55344
(612) 941-7753
(800) 874-1259
plastic fittings

ITT Jabsco
Bingley Road, Hoddesdon
Hertfordshire
EN11 OBU, ENGLAND
smaller accumulator tank

Reito®
Reitman Manufacturing Co.
10319 Pearmain Street
Oakland, CA 94603
(415) 638-8977
float valve

Symmons Industries, Inc.
31 Brooks Avenue
Braintree, MA 02184
(617) 848-2250
thermostactic water valve - high pressure

Bergen Cable Technologies
Gregg Street
P.O. Box 1300
Lodi, NJ 07644
(201) 487-3521
push-pull cables

Marine & Mobile Water Systems
6400 Marina Drive
Long Beach, CA 90803
(213) 598-9000
mobile water tanks

Plast-O-Matic
430 Routh 46
Totowa, NJ 07512
(201) 256-3000
plastic check valves

Watco Manufacturing Co.
7101 east 13th Street
Kansas City, MO 64126
(816) 231-6740
air vent valve (check)

Aetna Plastics Corp.
P.O. Box 03236
Cleveland, OH 44103
(216) 781-4421
plastic fittings

*Used in Earth Home

Amtrol, Inc.
West Warwick, RI 2893
* pressure tank accumulator

Colder Products Company
2367 University Avenue
St. Paul, MN 55114
(612) 645-0091
quick discount hose fittings

Tomlinson Industries
13700 Boradway
Cleveland, OH 44125
tap faucet

Smart Products
111 East Brokaw Road
San Jose, CA 95112
(408) 436-0740
(800) 255-0300
low pressure check valves and pump

Snap-Loc - Cedarberg Industries, Inc.
521 West 90th Street
Minneapolis, MN 55420
* pop together flexible hose

Flexcon Industries
300 Pond Street
Randolph, MA 02368
(617) 986-2424
diaphram expansion tanks

Quest Engineering, Inc.
2300 Edgewood Avenue South
St. Louis Park, MN 55426
(612) 546-4441
plastic caps (showerhead, etc.)

A.W. Cash Valve Mfg. Co.
666 East Wabash
Decatur, IL 62523
(217) 422-8574
* pressure regulators

Multi-Tech Precision Industry Co., Ltd.
P.O. Box 30-109
Taichung City TAIWAN, R.O.C.
fogging nozzles

Magline, Inc.
Pinconning, MI 48650
(517) 879-2411
alum. base with rollers

Amco Engineering Co.
3801 North Rose Street
Schiller Park, IL 60176-2190
(708) 671-6670
alum. framing

SGD Inc.
170 Vivian Avenue
Emerson, NJ 07630
horizontal drum gauge

Envirosense, Inc.
(800) 995-8801
Distributed by:
Delaney Linen Service
(800) 332-8406
(617) 926-9126
handwashing sensor

High-low shower
(800) 442-1972
(303) 449-6601
children/adult shower head

Europa "Swinger"
Resources Conservation
P.O. Box 71
Greenwich, CT 06836
(800) 243-2862
* swinging shower head and other products

Amtrol, Inc.
1400 Division Road
West Warwick, RI 02893

Note: Plumbing chart showing pipe sizes, etc. located in body of text.

Plumbing
-Greywater Systems

Cipax
by Enviroscope Inc.
Corona del Mar, CA 92625
80 gal./day greywater system

Clivus Multrum
One Eliot Square
Cambridge, MA 02138
(617) 491-0051
greywater filter and pipes

1" x 6" redwood planks burined in inverted "V" position
underground greywater distributor

Greywater irrigating rules
article

Greywater Use in the Landscape
Robert Kourik
book

Post and Beam Construction

Low-Cost Pole Building Construction
Ralph Wolfe
Book on post and beam construction

Monte Burch's Pole Building Projects: The Latest in Pole Construction Plans
Book on post and beam construction

Propane
-Demand Heaters

NOTE: Also called instantaneous water heaters.

Rinnai Corp.
Nice Enterprises
29312 Mission Boulevard
Hayward, CA 94544
(415) 881-5105

Pressure Cleaning Systems, Inc.
612 North 16th Avenue
Yakima, WA 98902
(509) 452-6607

Vaillant Corp.
2607 River Road

*Used in Earth Home

Cinnaminson, NJ 08077
(609) 786-2000

Paloma Industries, Inc.
1440 Howard Street
Elk Grove Village, IL 60007
* demand hot water heaters

Aquastar - Controlled Energy Corporation
Fiddlers Green
Waitsfield, VA 05673
(802) 496-4436
(800) 642-3111
* demand hot water heater modulates with warmer water input
(Earth Home with domestic hot water solar panel)

Myson, Inc.
P.O. Box 7789
Fredericksburg, VA 22404
(703) 371-4331
demand hot water heaters

Advanced Gas Technologies

International Technology Sales

Propane

-General

Athens Stove Works
P.O. Box 10
Athens, TN 37303
(615) 745-4332
Vesta® Hot Plates

Century - Primus
Century Tool & Mfg. Co.
1462 U.S. Rt. 20
Cherry Valley, IL 61016-188
(815) 332-4911
propane camping equipment

Amana Refrigeration
Amana, IA 52204
"pulse" propane furnaces

Detroit Radiant Products
1297 Terminal Avenue
Detroit, MI 48214
(313) 823-1074
infrared heaters

Atlanta Stove Works, Inc.
P.O. Box 5254
Atlanta, GA 30307
propane stoves

Marshall Brass Co.
450 Leggitt Road
Marshall, MI 49068
(616) 781-3901
(800) 447-9513
propane fittings - all

Suburban Mfg. Co.
P.O. Box 399
Dayton, TN 37321
(615) 775-2131
12 VDC propane camper furnaces

"Travel Star"
propane stove

IDEO - San Francisco

clean flat burner - propane

Mr. Stove, Ltd.
6118 Venice Boulevard, #102
Los Angeles, CA 90034
(213) 933-5777
propane stoves

Emerson
959 North Benson
Upland, CA 91786
(714) 958-7273
(800) 854-7933
wall thermostat

Therm X Corporation
P.O. Box 268, 835 South Frank Wood
Riedley, CA 93654
(209) 638-6824
propane stoves

Waywick Corporation
998 East Woodbridge
Detroit, MI 48207
(313) 568-1990
catyltic heaters

Worthington Cylinders
P.O. Box 391
Columbus, OH 43085
propane cylinders

Red-E-Hot Heaters
Master Specialty Co.
445 West Nixon Street
Savage, MN 55379
propane tank heaters - auto

Rego
4201 West Peterson Avenue
Chicago, IL 60646
LP gas serviceman manual

McDowell Mfg. Co.
Box 665
DuBois, PA 15801
(814) 371-6550
pressure cylinders

Aeroquip Industrial Division
1225 West Main Street
Van Wert. OH 45891
(419) 238-1190
propane hose

Duo Therm
2320 Industrial Parkway
Elkhart, IN 46515
(219) 295-5228
forced air propane furnaces

Propane Carburation Co., Inc.
2856 Hildebrandt
Roulus, MI 48174
(313) 946-8740
propane conversions

Atwood Mobile Products
4750 Hiawatha Drive
Rockford, IL 61103-1298
(815) 877-7461
mobile home products - stoves

National Propane Gas Association
1301 West 22nd Street

*Used in Earth Home

Oak Brook, IL 60521
(312) 573-4800
source of information

Suberb Hot Plate Co.
423 South Church Street
P.O. Box 99
Belleville, IL 62222
hot plate

Sunbeam Leisure Products Co.
Howard Bush Drive
Heosho, NO 64850
(417) 451-4550
propane products

Empire Stove Co.
Belleville, IL 62222
(800) 851-3153
propane stoves

Martin Industries
Gas Products Division
P.O. Box 128
Florence, AL 35651
propane stoves

Humphrey Opalite
propane lantern

Real Goods Trading
-"Piezo" lighters (electronic gas lighters)
-efficient gas stoves, 61-102 (universal orifice)
-Ecotherm direct vent heater 65-203

Peerless Gas Ranges
piezo light cookstoves

GPA liquified petroleum gas specifications
pamphlet

Canadian Gas Research Institute
55 Scarsdale Road
Don Mills, ON M3B ZR3
CANADA
(416) 447-6661
sealed combustion gas range

Gas Research Institute
8600 Bryn Mawr Avenue
Chicago, IL 60631
(312) 399-8100
efficient gas appliance research

Publications (see also individual sections)

-Ecology

the Ecologist (magazine)
Unit 18 Chelsea Wharf
15 Lots Road
London SW10 0QJ
www.theecologist.org

Publications

-Greenhouses

Publications

-Homesteading

Back Home

P.O. Box 70
Hendersonville, NC 28793

Publications

-Solar

Sun & Wind Energy
49-521/595514
Comprehensive solar magazine

Pumps

-Circulating

NOTE: A circulating pump is a "low-head" or low pressure pump that draws little current.

Hartell HEH Series Pump 12 volts 2' lift 3.6 gpm .5 amps
(2 required)
info@hartell.com

www.wilo.co.uk
Wilo Pumps
Less than 10 watts

Laing Thermotech, Inc.
1-619-575-7466
619-575-7466
www.lainginc.com
Laing D-Series Pumps
10 watts or less

Circulating Pump Types - S.I.D.
Static Impeller Driver
info

Taco, Inc.
1160 Cranston Street
Cranston, RI
(401) 942-8000
circulating pumps

Grundfos Pump Corp.
2555 N. Clovis Avenue
Clovis, CA
Model CP-43-75

March Manufacturing Inc.
1819 Pickwick Avenue
Glenview, IL 60025
(708) 729-5300
Model 809

Bell and Gossett
8200 N. Austin Avenue
Morton Grove, IL 60053
(800) 243-8160
circulating pumps

Amtrol Inc.
West Warwick, RI 02893
circulating pumps

Gorman - Rupp Industries
180 Hines Avenue
Bellville, OH 44813
(419) 886-3001
magnetic drive pumps

Dial Manufacturing Inc.
25 South 51st Avenue
Phoenix, AZ 85043
(602) 278-1100
(800) 350-DIAL

*Used in Earth Home

evaporative cooler pumps

Milton Roy Co.
Hartell Division
70 Industrial Drive
Ivyland, PA 18974
(215) 322-0730
* circulating pump CP-10B-12DC

Bell & Gossett Pumps
Mulcahy Co., Inc.
Minneapolis, MN
(612) 854-3621
circulating pumps, SLC-30, PR-102206

Beckett Corp.
2521 Willowbrook Road
Dallas, TX 75220
(214) 357-6421
condensate pumps

Solar Development Inc.
3607-A Prospect Avenue
Riviera Beach, FL 33404
(407) 842-8935
S.I.D. (static impeller driver)

Pumps

-Diaphram

www.clarksol.com
Clark Solutions
DC driven diaphragm pumps

T Squared Manufacturing Corp.
Fairfield, NJ
Compact diaphram Pump

Gast Mfg. Co.
Benton Harbor, Mi.
616-926-6171
.95 lpm, 8psi or 12.5 in. hg.

Flojet Corporation
12 Morgan
Irvine, CA 92718
(714) 859-4945
* 2000-12 duplex diaphram pump

KNF Neuberger
Two Black Forest Road
Trenton, N.J. 08691
609-890-8600
600 ml/min. diaphram pump
Micro-Diaphram pumps

Edson Pump Division
460 Industrial Park Road
New Bedford, MA 02745
(617) 995-9711
larger diaphram pumps

Aro Corporation
One Aro Center
Bryan, OH 43506-0151
(419) 636-4242
diaphram pump

Versa Matic Tool, Inc.
23 Cheswick Avenue
Cheswick, PA 15024
(412) 274-4940
diaphram pumps

Noria Company
P.O. Box 366
Chatsworth, CA 91311
RV pump, elec. Diaphram

Lowther Electric
18 Key Street
Eastport, ME 04631-1414
(207) 853-0960
submersible

Pumps

-Diaphram Air Driven

Versa-Matic Pump
6017 Enterprise Drive
Export, PA 15632
Air-driven diaphram pump

Bellofram
A Rexnord Company
Burlington, MA 01803
(617) 272-2100
(800) 225-1031
small double diaphram pump

Wilden Pump & Eng. Co.
22069 Van Buren Street
P.O. Box 845
Colton, CA 92324
(714) 783-0621
air operated diaphram pump

Warren Rupp-Houdaille, Inc.
800 North Main Street
P.O. Box 1568
Mansfield, OH 44901
(419) 524-8388
"Sandpiper" air operated diaphram

Pressed & Welded Products Co
216 East Grand Avenue
South San Francisco, CA 94080
(415) 588-5433
air driven diaphram

Graco Inc.
P.O. Box 1441
Minneapolis, MN 55440-1441
diaphram pumps - air

Pumps

-Hand, Foot, Miscellaneous

Reversing pump-drum
Exair Corp.
www.exair.com

Sea Dog Pump
Independent Natural Resources, Inc.
Eden Prairie, MN 55344
Wave pumps for swells and ocean waves

Implantable Pumps article
Medical Device & Diagnostic Industry
September 1997 p.56

Randolph Austin Co.
Manchaca, TX 78652-0955
(512) 282-1590
(800) 531-5263

*Used in Earth Home

(tubing pump) larger peristaltic

Lab Safety Equipment
3430 Palmer Drive
P.O. Box 1368
Janesville, WI 53547-1368
(800) 356-0783
distributor hand pumps

Bosworth Company (Guzzler)
195 Anthony Street
East Providence, RI 02914
(401) 438-8411
* hand diaphram pump

Dist. Imtra Corp./Whale East
30 Samuel Barnett Boulevard
New Bedford Industrial Park
New Bedford, MA 02745
(617) 990-2700
* hand/foot pumps, diverter valves

Finish Thompson, Inc.
921 Greengarden Road
Erie, PA 16501-1591
(814) 455-4478
drum pump

Advance Rubber Co.
3334 Washington Avenue North
Minneapolis, MN 55412
pump impellers

Norseman Marine, Inc.
169 Riverside Drive
Riverton, RI 02878
(401) 624-6671
hydraulic RAM

Serfilco
Division of Service Filtration Corp.
1234 Depot Street
Glenview, IL 60025
(312) 998-9300
barrel pumps

Industrial Safety
1390 Neubrecht Road
Lima, OH 45801
(800) 537-9721
distributor for barrel pumps

TAT Engineering Co.
360 Shaw Drive
North Branford, CT 06471
(203) 484-0429
"tubing" pump (larger peristaltic)

Crane Co.
eming Division
884 South Broadway
Salem, OH 44460
rotary hand pump

Philippines - agency article
foot bellows pump - handmade

Presto-Tek Corp.
4101 North Figeroa Street
Los Angeles, CA 90065
(213) 221-1178

High Lifter Water Systems
P.O. Box 29829
Oakland, CA 94604
(415) 763-0595
pump water with water

A.S.M. Industries, Inc.
7 Peters Road
P.O. Box 8
New Holland, PA 17557
(717) 6556-2161
hand pump - barrel

Copy
chain pump (washers)

Bowjon Intl. Co.
2829 Burton Avenue
Burbank, CA 91504
(213) 846-2620
wind-powered air pump to lift water

Copy
misc. hand pumps and diaphrams

Dinh Co.
P.O. Box 999
Alachua, FL 32615
(904) 462-3464)
solar well pump system

Real Goods Trading
sound-proofed "flow light" "Real" pump and chart field
serviceable pumps overview of pump application

UNICEF - manual semi-rotary irrigation pump for developing countries

Scot Division-Ardox, Corp.
P.O. Box 286
Cedarburg, WI 53012
(414) 377-7000
many kinds

Cimarron Mfg., Inc.
Route 2, Box 55
Selman, OK 73834
(800) 521-2268
(405) 727-4259
submersible pump

Canadian Agtechnology Partners
Div. of Zomeworks Corp.
Albuquerque, NM
(800) 279-SOLO

Pumps

-Heat (See Heat Pumps)

Pumps

-Mixed-flow Impeller

Engineered Machined Products
2701 N. 30th St.
Escanaba, MI 49829
906-786-8404
Higher efficiency pumps originally for vehicle cooling systems

Pumps

-Scroll

AC Engineering
Disposable sanitary pump of PPS material

*Used in Earth Home

Pumps
-Vacuum

NOTE: A vacuum pump sucks air out of a container to produce a vacuum.

PIAB USA
55 Accord Park Dr.
Rockland, MA 02370
(781) 792-0574
mini vacuum pump

Virtual Industries, Inc.
2130 Victor Place
Colorado springs, CO 80915
(719) 572-5504
miniature air vacuum pump

Clark Pump Solutions
55 Green St.
Clinton, MA 01510
Miniature rotary Pump pressure/vacuum

Pumps
-Water

DeBakey VAD
MicroMed Technology

WorldHeart Novacor VAD
VAD pump

Thoratec HeartMate II and XVE
VAD pump

Valcor Engineering Corp.
2 Lawrence Road
Springfield, NJ 07081
(201) 467-8400
mini metering pumps

Little Giant subsidiary of
Tecumseh Products Co.
3810 North Tulsa STreet
Oklahoma City, OK 73112
(405) 947-2511
complete line

Flotec, Inc.
14510 South Carmenita Road
Norwalk, CA 90650
(213) 921-1495
1/12 HP vane pump

Auto Components, Inc.
3201 West Soffel
Mel Rose Park, IL 60160
(219) 872-5150
windshield washer pump

Smart Products, Inc.
111 East Brokaw Road
San Jose, CA 95112
(408) 436-0740
(800) 338-0404
pump and check valves

Gelber Industries
7600 Gross Point Road
Skokie, IL 60077
(708) 965-1300
complete catalog - all pumps

Shurflo
1400 Cerritos Avenue East
Anaheim, CA 92805
(714) 533-7700
RV pumps and submersible

Dayton Electric Mfg. Co.
5959 West Howard Street
Chicago, IL 60648
1.8 amp Teel RV pump

Tuthill Pump Co. of California
2935 Kerner Boulevard
San Rafael, CA 94901
(415) 457-6330
magnetically sealed pumps

Photocomm
930 Idaho Maryland Road
Grass Valley, CA 95945
(800) 223-1931
(916) 477-5121
distributor - many kinds

Attwood Corporation
P.O. Box 230
Lowell, MI 49331
(616) 897-2290
bilge pumps

Omni Corp.
P.O. Box 305
South Holland, IL 60473
(312) 333-7330
(800) 323-8830
battery pump

Roberk Division
Parker Hamifin Corporation
88 Long Hill Cross Road
Shelton, CT
OEM windshield washer pumps

Arco Solar News - article
efficient swimming pool pump

Hypro
Division of Lear Siegler, Inc.
375 Fifth Avenue NW
St. Paul, MN 55112
precision shafted models

PFC Equipment, Inc.
P.O. Box 41037
Plymouth, MN 55447
(612) 424-2613
catalog of pumps

Dynatrol Industries, Inc.
38 Harbor View Avenue
Stamford, CT 06902
(203) 325-3536
small pump

K.J. Miller Corporation
22711 Cty. Rd. 14 East
Elkhart, IN 46514
pump

Brailsford & Co., Inc.
Milton Road
Rye, NY 10580
(914) 967-1820
tiny brushless pumps, blowers

*Used in Earth Home

Cole Parmer
peristatltic, gear pumps, 1/12 HP model

Solo/Fedco
WEST GERMANY
backpack hand pump sprayer

March Manufacturing, Inc.
1819 Pickwick Avenue
Glenview, IL 60025
(312) 729-5300
complete line

Gorman-Rupp Industries
Bellville, OH 44813
rotary vane pumps

ITT Jabsco - IT&T
1485 Dale Way
Costa Mesa, CA 92626
(714) 545-8251
complete catalog

Vanton Pump & Equipment Corp.
201 Sweetland Avenue
Hillside, NJ 07205
(201) 688-4216
flexible liner pumps

Micropump
1402 NE 136th Avenue
Vancouver, WA 98684
(206) 253-2008
precision metering pumps

Solar-Low-Flow
Solar Electric Specialties Co.
P.O. Box 537
Willits, CA 95490
(707) 459-9496
solar water pumping system

Goulds Pumps
P.O. Box 330
Seneca Falls, NY 13148
(315) 568-2811
sump pumps and specials

Greylor Co.
820 N.E. 24th Lane, Unit 10
Cape Coral, FL 33909
miniature pumps

Rule Industries, Inc.
70 Blanchard Road
Burlington, MA 01803
marine pumps

E.P. Industries
414 W. Walnut Street
El Segundo, CA 90245
(310) 322-1462

Radio/Communications

Yaesu U.S.A.
17210 Edwards Road
Cerritos, CA 90701
(213) 404-2700
amateur radio products

Morse Code (or "CW")
chart

Unimetrics
1Com
Ranger Communications
Kenwood
VHF marine radios, Ham transceivers

Cordon Wests Radio School
2414 College Drive
Costa Mesa, CA 92626
(714) 549-5000
school

Electromagnetic Spectrum with radio bands
reprint

West Marine
500 Westridge Drive
Watsonville, CA 95076
(800) 538-0775
VHF radios

Sony Corp. of America
Sony Drive
Park Ridge, NJ 07650
(201) 391-6111
12 VDC answering machine
TAM-30/TAM-50

Recipes

Note: More to be added in later editions

www.recipesource.com
preserved duck eggs (1000 year eggs)
the Regional Cooking of China
Margret Gin and Alfred E. Castle
Book on Chinese cuisine

Cruess, W.V. and Gilliland, R. 1939,
Lettuce Kraut and Juice
Fruit Prod. J. 18, 231-232, 251
Recipes for lettuce kraut

Eating In
From the Field to the Kitchen in Biosphere 2
Sally Silverstone

Back to Eden
Jethro Kloss
Good recipe book

The Anti-Aging Plan
Roy Walford
Recipes included in book

Refrigerators

-Manufacturers

Propane refrigerator
www.thenaturalhome.com

Conserv Refrigerators
Northern Arizona Wind and Sun
2725 E Lakin Drive
Flagstaff, AZ 86004
800-383-0195

Sundanze Refrigeration, Inc.
1320 Freeport Blvd. Suite 101
Sparks, NV 89431
775-331-6600

SunDanzer
Solar Refrigerators and Freezers
www.sundanzer.com
efficient models

Maytag
1 Dependability Square
Newton, IA 50208
515-792-7000
#RTD19EODA

Lehmans
(330) 857-5757
multi-fuel refrigerator
RC2000B gas/115v/12v

Koolatron Industries Ltd.
56 Harvester Avenue
Batavia, NY 14020
small ice chest type

Fogel Commercial Refrigerator Co.
5400 Eadom Street
Philadelphia, PA 19137
(215) 535-8300
thermoelectric ice chest

Dometic Sales Corp.
Executive Office
P.O. Box 490
Elkhart, IN 46515
(219) 294-2511
full line (including kerosene models)

Norcold Service Center
600 South Kuther Road
Sidney, OH 45365
full line

Sun Frost
P.O. Box 95518
Arcata, CA 95521
(707) 822-9095
$1,500-3,000 - efficient refrigerator

Zeo Power Co.
75 Middlesex Avenue
Natick, Mass. 01760
(617) 655-4125
solar powered

Avanti Products Div.
The Mackle Co.
Miami, FL 33152
tiny 110V refrigerator

Sibir
Switzerland
gas refrigerators

Low Keep Refrigeration
24651 Second Avenue
Otsego, MI 49078-9406
(616) 692-3015
12V freezers - refrigerators

Photocomm
930 Idaho Maryland Road
Grass Valley, CA 95945
(916) 477-5121
(800) 544-6466
distributor

Whirlpool
2000M-63
Benton Harbor, MI 49022-2892
"Greenfreeze" CFC-free refrigerators for Europe-see also below

Whirlpool
414 N. Peters Rd.
Knoxville, TN 37922
800-252-1301
#ED22DCXB with 134A
refrig/freezer combo

Vestfrost
DK-6705 Esbjerg 0
Spangsbjerg Malevej 100
DK-6705 Esbjergo 0
DENMARK
efficient refrigerators

Refrigerators -Miscellaneous

Storage of Foods
article

Refrigeration Habits
article

Sun Power Systems
1121 Lewis Avenue
Sarasota, FL 33577
(813) 366-3050
"Minto wheel" for power

"Icy Ball"
absorption refrigerator - basic
article

Cole Parmer
dry-ice maker from CO_2 cylinder

Panelcoil®
Dean Products Inc.
985 Dean Street
Brooklyn, NY 11238-3395
(718) 789-4444
heat transfer coils

Danfoss Inc.
P.O Box 606
16 McKee Drive
Mahwah, NJ 07430
(201) 529-4900
* efficient 12V compressor (they now have non-CFC refrigerants)

Dole Refrigerating Co.
1420 Higgs Road
P.O. Box 1009
Lewisburg, TN 37091
(800) 251-8990
cold plates

Epoxy Technology Inc.
14 Fortune Drive
Billerica, Mass. 01821
(617) 667-3805
cold transfer epoxy

NASA
Solar Refrigerators
article

Refrigeration Research
525 North Fifth Street
P.O. Box 869

*Used in Earth Home

Brighton, MI 48116
(313) 227-1151
complete refrigeration supplies

How Long to Freeze Food
Parade Magazine
page 12, April 17, 1991
article

Case Parts Co.
877 Monterey Pass Road
Monterey Park, CA 91754
(213) 729-6000
(800) 421-0271
commerical refrigeration parts

Vortec Corp.
10125 Carver Road
Cincinnati, OH 45242-9976
(513) 891-7474
(800) 441-7475
air cooling devices - compressed air

Igloo Corp.
P.O. Box 19322
Houston, TX 77224
small ice chest, etc.

Sanyo Electric Inc. (also San Diego)
200 Riser Road
Little Ferry, NJ 07643
(619) 560-1134
12 VDC refrigeration, absorption - lithium bromide

NASA
Ionic refrigerator
NPO-15288
article

Living on 12 Volts with Ample Power
Chapter 9
Breaking Bad Refrigerating Habits
article

Copeland Corp.
1675 W. Campbell Road
Sidney, OH 45365-0669
scroll compressors

R&D Magazine, December 1992, pp. 28-32
CFC Replacement Technologies
James Glanz
article - including stirling for refrigerant

Consul Gas Refrigerators
Alternative Energy Engineering
efficient gas refrigerator

Vestfrost: Spangsbjerg Molleves
Postbox 2079
Denmark - 6705 Esbjerg O Carsten Valentin
011-45-79-22-36
refrigerator

Renewable Energy (See also Alternative Energy)

Natural Home Heating: The Complete Guide to Renewable Energy Options
Greg Pahl

Renewable Energy for Home, Farm, and Business
Paul Gipe

Rigid Materials -Corrugated

Metawell
A Division of Cookson America
100 Minnesota Avenue
Unit 6
Warwick, RI 02888
(401) 732-6552
corrugated steel structural member

International Honeycomb Corporation
1149 Central Avenue
University Park, IL 60466
(312) 534-6595
corrugated paper laminate

Champion International Corporation
50-37th Avenue NE
Minneapolis, MN 55421
(612) 789-2485
corrugated box - thick

Convoy, Inc.
P.O. Box 8589
Canton, OH 44711
(216) 453-8163
impregnated corrugated boxes

Gaylord Container Corporation
10 man box shelter

Plascure
3022 88th Avenue
Zeeland, MI 49464
(616) 772-1220
honeycomb, polycarbonate ABS, etc.

Primex Plastics Corporation
Subsidiary of ICC Industries, Inc.
1235 North F Street
Richmond, IN 47374
(317) 966-7774
corrugated plastic

Diversiplast
7425 Laurel Avenue
Minneapolis, MN 55426
(612) 540-9709
corrugated plastic

Rigid Materials -Green Materials

Green Building Reslurce Guide
John Hermannsson
Complete resource guidebook

Rigid Materials -Foams, Stress-Skin

NOTE: It is said that stress-skin panels are earth-friendly because the chipboard does not use as much old-growth timber and the foams are now CFC-free.

Stress-Skin Panel Manufacturers

www.polybid.co.il
insulation boards

www.rastra.com

*Used in Earth Home

foam panels

www.nrc.ca/irc/newsletter

www.cancunshop.com/isorast/iso

AFM Corporation
P.O. Box 246
Excelsior, MN 55331
(612) 474-0809
(800) 255-0176

Advance Energy Tech.
P.O. Box 387
Clifton Park, NY 12065
(518) 371-2140

Atlas Industries
6 Willow Road
Ayer, MA 01432
(508) 772-0000

Branch River Foam Plastics
15 Thurber Boulevard
Smithfield, RI 02917
(401) 232-0270

Concept 2000 Homes

Enercept Inc.
3100 - 9th Avenue S.E.
Watertown, SD 57201
(605) 882-2222
(800) 658-3303

Fischer Corporation
1843 Northwest Parkway
Louisville, KY 40203
(502) 778-5577

Harmony Exchange
Route 2, Box 843
Boone, NC 28607
(704) 264-2314

Insul-Wall
11 Mosher Drive
Dartmouth
Nova Scotia B3B 1L8
(902) 465-7470

J-Deck Building Sys.
2587 Harrison Road
Columbus, OH 43204
(614) 274-7755

Marne Industries
P.O. Box 465
Grand Rapids, MI 49588
(616) 698-2001

Nascor Inc.
Nascor Business Park, Building A
Calgary, Alberta T2A 7P5
CANADA
(403) 248-9890

Poly Foam Inc.
116 Pine Street S.
Lester Prairie, MN 55354
(612) 395-2551

Pond Hill Homes

Radva Corporation
P.O. Box 2900
Radford, VA 24143
(703) 639-2458

Winter Panel Corporation
R.R. 5, Box 168B
Brattleboro, VT 05301
(802) 254-3435

Nature House, Inc.
Better Building Systems
563A Idaho Maryland Road
Grass Valley, CA 95945
(916) 477-8017

Rigid Materials
-Organic Panels

Adel Particleboard Sales
Adel, Georgia
888-633-7477
Medite II non-formaldehyde fiberboard

Phenix Biocomposites
PO Box 609
Mankato, MN 56002
507-388-3434
Biofiber wheat composite and others

Agriboard Industries
1500 S. Main St.
Fairfield, IA 52556
515-472-0363
Mfr. Wall panels

Strawboard
Glulam
Elie fiberboard
Woodstalk

Rigid Materials
-Retaining Walls

Environmental Plastics, Inc.
4981 Keelson Dr.
Columbus, OH 43232
614-861-2107
c-loc plastic retaining wall system

Presto Products
PO Box 2399
Appleton, WI 54913
800-548-3424
GEOWEB cellular confinement system

Rigid Materials
-SIP's

www.sipweb.com
SIP Directory
Construction, panels, design resources

Building with Structural Insulated Panels
Michael Morley
Book on SIP's

Rigid Materials
-Structural

Enviro Board Corp.

*Used in Earth Home

818-981-2290
4735 Sepulveda Blvd., Suite 356
Sherman Oaks, CA 91403
Fiberboard panels

Morrison Molded Fiberglass Co.
Box 580
400 Commonwealth Avenue
Bristol, VA 24203
(703) 699-1181
foam core fiberglass skin

Martin Fireproofing Georgia, Inc.
P.O. Box 768
Elberton, GA 30635
(404) 283-6942
structural cement fiber roof deck system

Hexcel
Los Angeles, CA
honeycomb aluminum

Louisiana Pacific Corp.
111 S.W. 5th Avenue
Portland, OR 97204
recycled paper/gypsum wall covering--fiberbond

Posi Pak
7703 Main Street NE
Minneapolis, MN 55432
(612) 571-1905
6" EPS (expanded polystyrene) foam

EPS
Energy Panel Structures
Grattinger, IA 51342
(712) 859-3219
large foam laminates

Harmony Exchange
Route 2, Box 843
Big Hill Road
Boone, NC 28607
(704) 264-2314
logs for log homes

Low-Cost Pole Building Construction
by Ralph Wolfe
book

Sodium borate
earth-friendly wood preserver

Nisus Corp.
101 Concord Street
Knoxville, TN 37919
(800) 264-0870
wood preserver

American Wood Preserves Assoc.
P.O. Box 286
Woodstock, MD 21163-0286
Wood Preserver's Trade Assoc.

Osmose Preserving Co.
980 Ellicott Street
Buffalo, NY 14209
wood pole preserving paste

Chapman Chemical Co.
P.O. Box 9158
Memphis, TN 38109
"Pol-No" wood pole preserving paste

"Fiberbond" from

Louisiana Pacific
111 S.W. Fifth Avenue
Portland, OR 97204
(503) 221-0800
recycled newsprint with gypsum

Pyramod Intl. Inc.
P.O. Box 2220
City of Industry, CA 91746
(818) 968-9501
agricultural fiber foam

Rigid Materials

-Wall Panels

Agriboard Industries
1500 S. Main St.
Fairfield, IA 52556
515-472-0363
Mfr. Wall panels

Eagle Panel Systems
PO Box 748
Florissant, MO 63032
800-643-3786
Mfr. Wall Panels

Universal Polymer
319 N. Main Ave.
Springfield, MO 65806
800-752-5403
EXCEL board and synthetic stucco

Roofing

-Glazing

NOTE: See also Solar - Glazing)

Johnson's Wholesale Florist
St. Paul, MN
distributor

Dynaglass Specialty Products and Services
P.O. Box 20909
San Jose, CA 95160-0909
(408) 997-6100
polycarbonate

Filon Div. of BP America
12333 South Van Nessane
P.O. Box 5006
Hawthorne, CA 90250
(213) 757-5141
Dist. API Supply 571-5100
Dist. Lauer 423-1651
* many profiles (fiberglass)

Resolite Div. of H.H. Robertson Co.
P.O. Box 338
Zelienople, PA 11063
(412) 452-6800
FRB and fasteners

Lexan/General Electric
One Plastics Avenue
Pittsfield, MA 01201
(800) 451-3147
ribbed polycarbonate

Dipcraft
(800) 245-6145
fiberglass

*Used in Earth Home

Roofing
-Miscellaneous, Information

Owens Corning
One Fiberglass Tower
Toledo, Ohio 43659
614-321-7731
Miraflex "itchless" fiberglass

Knox Lumber Co.
materials

L&J Agricultural Building
Liman Poast and Beam
Annandale, MN
274-8223
materials

Menard's
materials

Onduline USA Inc.
Route 9, Box 195
Fredericksburg, VA 22401
693-3616
corrugated asphalt roofing

Metal Building Manufacturers Assoc.
1300 Sumner Avenue
Cleveland, OH 44115-2851
(216) 241-7333
list of metal building manufacturers

Roof Consultants Institute
7424 Chapel Hill Road
Raleigh, NC 27607
(919) 859-0742
information source

Roofing Materials Guide
by National Roofing Contractors Association
source

National Coil Coaters Association
401 N. Michigan Avenue
Chicago, IL 60611-4267
(312) 644-6610
information source

Shelter Supply
1325 East 79th Street
Minneapolis, MN 55425
(800) 762-8399
(612) 854-4266
vapor barriers, etc.

Roofs and Roofing
J.A.C. Dunn
Country Journal
July/August 1993, p. 33
article

Roofing
-Reflective Foils

Rabar Products Inc.
3243 Blair Street
Cocoa, FL 32926
(407) 636-4104
* perforated foil/white

Innovative Insulation Inc.
2710 S.E. Loop 820
Fort Worth, TX 76140
(817) 551-5277
(800) 825-0123
bubble and others

Advanced Foil Systems
4471 E. Santa Ana Street, Suite F
Ontario, CA 91761
(714) 988-8365
(800) 287-4244
single layer

Thermonics International Inc.
4513 Old Shell Road
Mobile, AL 36608
(205) 343-7171
foil

Simplex Products Division
P O. Box 10
Adrian, MI 49221-0010
(517) 263-8881
poly mesh backed foil

Rich's Enterprises
2734 El Dorado Place
Snellville, CA 30278
(404) 979-9671
bubble, spray

Denny Products
3500 Gateway Drive
Pompano Beach, FL 33069
(800) 327-6616
(305) 971-3100
foil, etc.

Innovative Energy, Inc.
1119 W. 145th Avenue
Crown Point, IN 46307
(219) 662-0737
(800) 776-3645
many products

Reflective Insulation Supply, Inc.
P.O. Box 2846
Wichita, KS 67201-2846
(316) 265-6712
(800) 798-3645
bubble foil

Parsec, Inc.
P.O. Box 551477
Dallas, TX 75355-1477
(214) 341-6700
(800) 527-3454
tapes and foils

Solar Shield Inc.
1054 Branch Drive
Alpharetta, GA 30201
(404) 343-8091
radiant barrier

F1-Foil Co. Inc.
612 Bridgers Avenue W.
Auburndale, FL 33823
(813) 965-1846
many products

Popular Mechanics
September 1992, p. 60
"Radiant Barriers"
information source

*Used in Earth Home

Architecture
April 1993, p. 114
Radiant Heat Barriers
information source

Alfol Inc.
P.O. Box 7024
Charlotte, NC 28217
foil

Astro-Packing
11756 S. Austin Avenue
Alsip, IL 60482
foil

Denny Foil
foil

Eagle Shield
2006 N. Highway 360
Grand Prairie, TX 75050
foil

Energy Saver Imports
2150 W. 6th Avenue
Broomfield, CO 80020
foil

F1 Foil Co.
foil

Fortifiber Corp.
P.O. Box 959
Alttleboro, MA 02703
foil

K-Shield
7529 E. Woodside Cove
Scottsdale, AZ 85258
foil

Lamotite
2909 E. 79th Street
Cleveland, OH 44104
foil

Reflectix Inc.
P.O. Box 108
Markleville, IN 46056
foil

R-Fax
661 E. Monterey Avenue
Pomona, CA 91767
foil

Roofing

-Ridge Vent Manufacturers

Air Vent Inc.
4801 N. Prospect Road
Peoria Heights, IL 61614
(800) 247-8368
(309) 688-5020
ridge vents

Benjamin Obydyke
John Fitch Industrial Park
Warminster, PA 18974
(800) 346-7655
(215) 672-7200
ridge vents

Cor-A-Vent Inc.
16250 Petro Drive
Mishawaka, IN 46544
(800) 837-VENT
(219) 255-1910
ridge vents

Roofing

-Steel Panels

Corrugated Metals Inc.
P.O. Box 465
Jersey City, NJ 07303
(800) 631-3073
(201) 653-3370
profiles and load tables

Interstate Lumber
5517 145th Street North
Hugo, MN 55038
429-5381
retail

Pre-finished Metals
(708) 439-2210
Ceram-A-Sil coating, 82,000 psi

Menard
(612) 253-6170
Ceram-A-Sil coating, 82,000 psi

Flexospan, Inc.
253 Railroad Street
Box 515
Sandy Lake, PA 16145
(412) 376-7221
assorted profiles

Metal Sales Mfg. Corp.
22651 Industrial Boulevard
Rogers, MN 55374
(612) 428-8080
(800) 328-9316
Pro-Panel II and others

RPS Engineering
551 Stevenson Road
P.O. Box 333
South Elgin, IL 60177
(312) 931-1950
all profiles

Diversiplast
Frank Weis
590-9700
steel

Wheeling Corrugated Co.
1134 Market Street
Wheeling, WV 26003
(304) 234-2684
paneldrain, channeldrain profiles

Decrabond
2600 S. Loop W., Suite 230
Houston, TX 77054
(713) 664-2211

Follansbee Steel
Box 610
Follansbee, WV 26037
(800) 624-6906
metal roofing

*Used in Earth Home

National Coil Coaters Association
1900 Arch Street
Philadelphia, PA 19103
(215) 564-3484
association - source of information on all manufacturers

Morton International
1231 South Lincoln Street
Colton, CA 92324
(714) 825-6292
"Fluoro Ceram" coil coating

AEP Span
5100 East Grand
Dallas, TX 75223
(214) 827-1740
(800) 527-2503
aluminum, steel

Alcoa Building Products
P.O. Box 2527
Grand Rapids, MI 49501
(616) 459-3351
(513) 492-1111
complete roofing system, components, accessories, aluminum roofing

Atlanta Metal Products, Inc.
5700 Riverview Industrial Drive
Mableton, GA 30059
(404) 691-8500
steel, aluminum, copper

ATAS Aluminum Corp.
6612 Snowdrift Road
Allentown, PA 18106
(215) 395-8445
complete roofing system, components, accessories, steel, aluminum

Copper Sales, Inc.
1405 N. Highway 169
Minneapolis, MN 55441
(800) 426-7737
steel, aluminum, copper

Fabral/Alcan Building Products
3449 Hempland Road
Lancaster, PA 17601
(717) 397-2741
steel, aluminum

Ideal Roofing
1418 Michael Street
Ottawa, Ontario K1B 3R2
CANADA
(613) 746-3206
complete roofing system, components, accessories, steel, aluminum, copper

Kovach Metal Roof & Siding Systems
419 East Juanita Avenue
Mesa, AZ 85204
(602) 926-9292
steel, aluminum, copper

MBCI
14031 West Hardy
P.O. Box 38217
Houston, TX 77238
(713) 445-8555
complete roofing system, components, accessories, steel, aluminum, copper

McElroy Metal, Inc.
P.O. Box 1148
Shreveport, LA 71163
(318) 747-8000
components, accessories, steel, aluminum

Met-Tile, Inc.
P.O. Box 4268
Ontario, CA 91761
(714) 947-0311
complete roofing system, components, accessories, steel, aluminum

Reynolds Metals Co.
P.O. Box 27003
Richmond, VA 23261
(804) 281-2636
* components, accessories, steel, aluminum

Rib-Roof Industries, Inc.
2745 N. Locust Avenue
Rialto, CA 92376
(714) 875-8529
steel, aluminum

Southeastern Metals Mfg. Co.
11801 Industry Drive
P.O. Box 26347
Jacksonville, FL 32218
(800) 874-0335
(800) 342-1279
components, accessories, steel, aluminum, copper

Steelco - Metal Construction Products
P.O. Box 570
Salt Lake City, UT 84110
(800) 874-2404
components, accessories, steel, aluminum

Vincent Metals
700 - 25th Avenue S.E.
P.O. Box 360
Minneapolis, MN 55414
(612) 378-1131
components, steel, aluminum, copper

Zappone Manufacturing
North 2928 Pittsburgh
Spokane, WA 99207
aluminum, copper

Steelox Building Systems
P.O. Box 8181
Mason, OH 45040-8181
(800) STEELOX
steel roofing

Tile Master Roofing Systems
5972 Ambler Drive
Mississauga, Ontario L4W 2N3
CANADA
(905) 624-0953
steel roofing

Roofing

-Trusses/Info

Wright Lumber
trusses

Eng. Building Components
146 Washington Avenue S.
Hopkins, MN
(612) 935-4902
trusses

*Used in Earth Home

Local Lumber Co.
trusses

Menard Building
753-2611 (H)
253-6170 (W)
trusses

Knox
trusses

Emerich Wood Products
3115 - 162nd Lane
Anoka, MN 55304
(612) 427-4155
trusses

Commercial Low-slope Roofing Materials Guide
National Roofing Contractors Association
book

AFM Corporation
P.O. Box 246
Excelsior, MN 55331
(612) 474-0809
laminated I-beams

Truswal Systems Corporation
8925 Sterling Street, Suite 150
Irving, TX 75063
(214) 929-1100
trusses and floor trusses

Truss Mfg. Co.
Albertville, MN 62770
trusses

Trus Joist MacMillan
9777 West Chinden Boulevard
Boise, ID 83714
(208) 375-4450
trusses and "silent floor" joists

Sauerkraut

Sauer beans or green tomatoes-sliced
Wash green tomatoes, remove stem and core, slice thickly
Mix 4 oz. salt and 4 oz. (1/2 cup) vinegar with 5 lbs. of vegetables

Lettuce kraut-Los Angeles or iceberg

Scrubbers

NOTE: A scrubber is an air cleaning device.
NOTE: Smoke is a sub-micron aerosol.

Selas Fluid Processing Corporation
Five Sentry Parkway East
Suite 204
Belue Bell, PA 19422
(215) 834-0300
fume incinerators

Upgrading Scrubber Performance
by Edward Bloss
Plant Engineering Magazine
December 13, 1979, pg. 73
article on scrubbers - all

Heat Systems - Ultrasonics, Inc.
1938 New Highway
Farmingdale, NY 11735
(800) 645-9846
(516) 694-9555
scrubbers

Uni-Wash, Inc.
880 Fralick
Plymouth, MI 48170
(313) 451-2775
wet dust collectors

Tri-Mer Corporation
1400 Monroe Street
P.O. Box 730
Owosso, MI 48867
air pollution systems

Ametek
Lamb Electric Division
627 Lake Street
Kent, OH 44240
(216) 673-3451
combustion blowers (to 5000F)

Seasonings (See also Plants-Sweeteners, Herbs)

www.soyinfo.com
soybean information incl. soy sauce

Self-Sufficiency (See Autonomous Houses)

Soap

Readers Digest
"Back To Basics:
Soap making"
soap making article

Simmons
42295 Highway 36
Bridgeville, CA 95526
natural soap

Natural soap/shampoo:
Clethra flowers
Amole - roots
Soapwort - saponaria officinalis
Amole - tropical plants
Yulla - tropical plants
Soybean whey
Attalea cohune
Balanites aegyptiaca (small tree)
Atuqsara - phytolacca bogotensis
Quillaja - quillaja saponaria

SOAP: Making It, Enjoying It
by Ann Bramson
source book

The Natural Choice Catalog
ECO Design Co.
1365 Rufina Circle
Santa Fe, NM 87501
natural soaps (nettles and marigold)

Home soap making
article

Tallowberry
(Chinese vegetable tallow tree or sapium sebiferum)
natural soap

Soapwort roots were once pulverized, boiled, and used as a clothes bleach (bouncing bet)

Vegetable glycerine helps oil mix with water

Lanolin is removed from sheep's wool at no harm to the sheep

Spinach contains some saponin
possible soap

"Clean Power Plus"
(800) 424-6255
ceramic washing disks, wash clothes without soap

Solar

-Air Conditioning

China-America Technology Corp.(CTC)
Convent Ave at 138th St., J423
New York, N.Y. 10031
212-650-5606
212-650-5608 (f)
ctc@chinatech.com
solar air conditioning units

Solargenix
3501 Jamboree Rd
South Tower Suite 606
New Port Beach, CA 92660
(949) 856-2200
solar air conditioning

Meridian Energy Systems
2300 S. Lamar, Suite 107
Austin, TX 78704
512-448-0045
solar systems

All Research, Inc.
P.O. Box 3662
Princeton, NJ 08543
www.ailr.com
609-452-2950
Solar air conditioning units

Coolmax
78 West St
Torrensville, South Australia 5031
1300 729 573
http://www.coolmax.com.au/
evaporative air conditioners

OK Solar
347-624-5693
Solar evaporative coolers

Solar

-Coatings

Iowa Thin Film Technologies
Fabric for Army Tents that generate electricity

Ultrachem, Inc.
1400 North Walnut Street
Wilmington, DE 19899
chembrake 217-high temp oil

Revere Copper and Brass
P.O. Box 151
Rome, NY 13440
(315) 338-2022
absorber plates - liquid

Paul Mueller Company
P.O. Box 828
Springfield, MO 65801
(417) 831-3000
aluminum steel plates

Fafco, Inc.
255 Constitution Drive
Menlo Park, CA 94025
(415) 321-3650
plastic exchanger tubes

Residential Energy Systems, Inc.
5475 East Evans Avenue
Denver, CO 80222
(303) 753-0440
solar room additions

Conserval Systems, Inc.
2211 Main Street, Building B
Buffalo, NY 14214
(716) 835-4903
perforated aluminum wall cladding

Roper Eastern
9325 Snowden River Parkway
Columbia, MD 21046
(301) 730-8800
slats and tape

Birchwood Casey
7900 Fuller Road
Eden Prairie, MN 55344
(612) 927-1731
black metal stain

Roll-up Shutter Company
811 Main Street
Hopkins, MN 55343
(612) 931-0410
steel shutters

Solar

-Cooking

www.solarcooking.org

SK 14 cooker

Papillon cookers

Global Solar Energy Systems
www.globosol.ch

EG solar
www.eg-solar.de

Sun & Ice
www.sun-and-ice.de

Solar

-Exchangers/Coils

Geauga Company
Subsidiary of Carlisle Corporation
P.O. Box 459
401 South Street
Chardon, OH 44024
(216) 286-7111
custom plastic cooling coils

*Used in Earth Home

Bock Corporation
P.O. Box 551
Madison, WI 53703
(608) 257-2225
heat exchanger tubing

Solar

-Glazings

NOTE: See also Films - Plastic files.

Zomeworks Corporation
P.O, Box 712
Albuquerque, NM 87103
(505) 242-5354
"Beadwall" system

Solar Research
Division of Refrigeration Research
525 North Fifth Street
Brighton, MI 48116
(313) 227-1151
solar components catalog

J.R. Johnson Supply, Inc.
2582 Long Lake Road
St. Paul, MN 55113
(612) 636-1330
greenhouse supplies

Coburn
1650 Corporate Road West
Lakewood, NJ 08701
(201) 367-5511
metalized film, etc.

Exolite
Filon Corporation (fiberglass)
Lascolite
solar glazing

Suntek Inc.
6817 A Academy Parkway East
Albuquerque, NM 87109
(505) 345-4115
* cloud gel = "Smart Glazing"

Solar Components Division
Kalwall Corporation
88 Pine Street
Box 237
Manchester, NH 03103
(603) 668-8186
solar glazing and products

DuPont Company
Plastic Products and Resins Department
Wilmington, DE 19898
"Tedlar" film

Cy/Ro Industries
697 Route 46
Clifton, NJ 07015
double skinned acrylic sheet

Dow Chemical
Polystyrene film
Trycite® film

Flex-O-Glass, Inc.
1100 North Cicero Avenue
Chicago, IL 60651
(312) 379-7878
"Flex-O-Glass" (butyrate)

Copy - Article
air solar check value

Get Smart About Glazing
Popular Science, p. 76
article

Thomas Registers
Complete list - glazing
information source

Albert Lauer, Inc.
16700 Highway 3
Chippendale West
Rosemont, MN 55068
(612) 423-1651
Filon distributor

Solar Research
P.O. Box 869
Brighton, MI 48116
(313) 227-1151
Tedlar glazing and tape

Trade names of glazing materials
article

Norandex
8450 S. Bedford Road
P.O. Box 8000
Macidonia, OH 44056
(216) 468-2200
triple-glazed aluminum windows

Solar Research
P.O. Box 869
Brighton, MI 48116
(313) 227-1151
Microsorb collector coating

Bill's Shade and Blind Service, Inc.
755-765 East 69th Place at Cottage Drive
Chicago, IL 60637
493-5000
steel blind slats

Dale Peterson
Loveland Industries
Loveland, CO
(303) 667-6620
proprietary solar fluid

Eutectic Window Shades
Illinois Institute of Technology
eutectic salt louvers

Panel Coil
Dean Products, Inc.
985 Dean Street
Brooklyn, NY 11238
(212) 789-4444
absorber plates - liquid

Texas Division
Tranter®, Inc.
P.O. Box 2289
Wichita Falls, TX 76307
(817) 723-7125
absorber plates – liquid

Solar Sun, Inc.
644 West San Francisco
Santa Fe, NM 87501

*Used in Earth Home

(505) 982-8889
"Sun-clear" and "Vari-shade" coatings

Stewart Co. Inc.
3656 San Fernando Road
Glendale, CA 91204
"koolshade" shading system

Solar -Heating Manufacturers

www.sudarshansaur.com
evacuated tube solar collectors
Satish Vywhareay
Sudarshan saur Shakti
India
sudarsh@sancharnet.in

Thermo Technologies
Columbia, MD 21044
410-997-0778
evacuated heat pipe technologies
Solmecs
Omer Industrial Park
P.O. Box 3026
Omer 84965

Israel
Tel: 972-7-6900950
Fax: 972-7-6900953
www.pvsolmecs.com
Bifacial solar modules

AHS Energy Supply
1630 N. 63rd Street
Boulder, CO 80301
(303) 447-9193

American Energy Tech.
P.O. Box 1865
Green Cove Springs, FL 32043
(904) 284-0552

American Solar Network
5840 Gibbons Drive, #H
Carmichael, CA 95608
(916) 481-7200

BSAR Solar
980 Santa Estella
Solana Beach, CA 92075
(619) 259-8864
concentrating

Fine Products Co.
6248 Ogden Avenue
Berwyn, IL 60402
(708) 484-9299

Coyne Solar Mfg. Co.
P.O. Box 1120
San Juan Pueblo, NM 87566
(505) 852-2622

Fafco Inc.
2690 Middlefield Road
Redwood City, CA 94063
(415) 363-2690

Gull Industries
2127 S. First Street
San Jose, CA 95112
(408) 293-3523

(800) 748-6286

Hansen Energy Products
P.O. Box 1086
Rockland, ME 04841
(207) 594-4299
solar space - air

Heliodyne Inc.
4910 Seaport Avenue
Richmond, CA 94804
(510) 237-9614

Kimex International Tech.
4609 Old Gettysburg Road
Mechanicsburg, PA 17055
(717) 761-7757
air and water

Mor-Flo Industries
18450 S. Miles Road
Cleveland, OH 44128
(216) 663-7300
air and water

Nippon Electric Glass
650 E. Devon Avenue, Ste 110
Itaska, IL 60143-1264

Radco Products
2877 Industrial Parkway
Santa Maria, CA 93455
(805) 928-1881

Sage Advance Corp.
1001 Bertelsen Road
Eugene, OR 97402
(503) 485-1947
copper cricket

Solar Development Inc.
3607A Prospect Road
Riviera Beach, FL 33404
(407) 842-8935

Sun Earth Inc.

Sun Utility Network
5741 Engineer Drive
Huntington Beach, CA 92649
(714) 898-2084
vacuum type

Thermal Conversion Tech.
P.O. Box 3887
Sarasota, FL 34230
(813) 953-2177

U.S. Solar Corp.

Entech
P.O. Box 612246
Dallas-Ft. Worth, TX 75261
comb. PV and hot water

Industrial Solar Tech.
5775 W. 52nd Avenue
Denver, CO 80212

Luz International
924 Westwood Boulevard
Los Angeles, CA 90024

Science Applications Intl.

*Used in Earth Home

Solar Kinetics
10635 King William Drive
Dallas, TX 75220

Sunsteam
(505) 242-5354

U.S. Solar
(800) 279-6342

Zomeworks
P.O. Box 25805
1011A Sawmill Road N.W.
Albuquerque, NM 87125

Heliocol

Ramada Energy Systems

Sun Resource Energy Sys.

Arco/Siemens Solar
P.O. Box 6032
Camarillo, CA 93010
(805) 388-6351

Brinkman Corp.
4215 McEwen Road
Dallas, TX 75244
(214) 387-4939
solar lights

Intermatic
Intermatic Plaza
Spring Grove, IL 60081
(815) 675-2321
solar lights

Sunergy
P.O. Box 177
Princeton, NJ 08542
(609) 799-8800

American Solar Network, Ltd.
5840 Gibbons Drive, Suite H
Carmichael, CA 95608
(916) 481-7200
solar water heaters

Solar -Miscellaneous Information

The Passive Solar House
James Kachadorian
Book on solar homes

Passive Solar House Basics
Peter van Dresser
Book

The Self-Sufficient Solar House Freiburg
Advances in Solar Energy
1994 Volume IX 1994
Goetzberger, Adolf, Stahl, W. Bopp, G.
Complete article on the SSSH

Global Sun Oven
Solar cooker

Minnesota Guide to Waste Heat Recovery
Minnesota Energy Agency
Energy Conservation Division
980 American Center Building
150 East Kellog Boulevard
St. Paul, MN 55101
booklet

October 1978 RAIN Magazine, Page 17
simple solar ideas

Solar-powered Pump
NASA MFS-23996

D.O.E. Solar Energy for Heating and Cooling
OPA-008, 3-78

Argonne National Lab
6700 South Cass Avenue
Argonne, IL 60439
compound parabolic collector

American Solar Energy Society
2400 Central Avenue - Unit B-1
Boulder, CO 80301
"Solar Today" magazine

Renewable Energy News Digest
Rubby Sun Words
861 Central Parkway
Schenectady, NY 12309
(518) 372-1799
newsletter

Prototype Solar Heating System
NASA MFS-23916

Solar Rules of Thumb
article

Seasonal sun trajectory chart
alternative energy sourcebook

Solar Exp. Dwellings
American Society of Ag. Engineers
Rural Housing Research Unit
Clemson, SC
housing studies

Lightweight, Economical Solar Concentrator
NASA MFS-23727

Solar Powered Hot Water System
NASA NPO 14270

Heat Pipe
KSC-11311
NASA KSC-11311

Solar Energy International
P.O. Box 715
Carbondale, CO 81623

Total Energy Management
National Electrical MFRS Association
2101 L Street NW
Washington, DC 20037
(202) 457-8400
NEMA booklet

Solar Mind
759 South State Street, #81
Ukiah, CA 95482
Solar Source magazine

Real Goods Trading Co.
(Real Goods Solar Living Sourcebook)
California
-reading text with catalog
-Read Goods estimate of 50,000 solar homes in U.S.A.

*Used in Earth Home

-Seasonal sun trajectories at 400N latitude

Solar

-Miscellaneous Products

NOTE: For trackers see Photovoltaic files.

Sun & Wind Energy
49-521/595514
Comprehensive solar magazine

Evacuated Heat Pipe Technology
Thermo Technologies
5560 Sterrett Place Suite 115
Columbia, MD 21044
410-997-0778

Thermofor
Bramen Company, Inc.
Salem, MA 01970
(617) 745-7765
* thermal window openers

Sunnyside Solar (Distributor)
RD4 Box 808
Green River Road
Brattleboro, UT 05301
(802) 257-1482
(800) 346-3230
misc. solar products

Chicago Solar Corporation
5217 North Harlem
Chicago, IL 60656
(312) 774-7766
inflatable solar panels

Solar Research
Division of Refrigerator Research
525 North Fifth Street
Brighton, MI 48116
(313) 227-1151
solar components

Sunglo Solar
35 Litron Court
Concord, Ontario L4K 2S7
(416) 738-0300
solar hydronic systems

American Appliance Manufacturing Corp.
2341 Michigan Avenue
Santa Monica, CA 90404
(213) 829-1755
liquid systems

Solar Industries
Div. of Aquatherm, Inc.
1985 Rutgers University Builevard
Lakewood, NJ 08701
(808) 905-0440
(800) 227-7657
solar pool heaters

Solar Research
P.O. Box 869
Brighton, MI 48116
(313) 227-1151
refrigerant charged solar systems

Solar Gizer
P.O. Box 20142
Bloomington, MN 55420
(612) 941-8136
solar systems

Solarvent
Dahlem Products, Inc.
11110 Gilbert Drive
Knoxville, TN 37922
(615) 966-3256
thermal window openers

Sol-R-Veil, Inc.
635 West 23rd Street
New York, NY 10011
(212) 924-7200
motorized shade system

Zoneworks Corporation
P.O. Box 712
Albuquerque, NM 87103
solar systems and trackers

Suntime, Inc.P.O. Box H
101 Height Street
Belfort, ME 04915
collector system

Solar Resources, Inc.
solar rooms

Entropy, Ltd.
5735 Arapahoe Avenue
Boulder, CO 80303
(303) 443-5103
sun pumps, sun cycle

S.D.E.S.S.
P.O. Box 36
Crosby, MN 56441
(218) 546-5369
solar/wind retail

G-S Energy
108 Jefferson Avenue
Des Moines, IA 50314
(515) 243-7570
collector system

Sun-Tronics
Holly Solar Products
P.O. Box 864
Petaluma, CA 94952
(707) 763-6173
PV controls "conserve" switches

The Sunpipe Co.
P.O. Box 2223
Northbrook, IL 60065
(708) 272-6977
small "skylight"

Solatube
5825 Avenida Encinas, Suite 101
Carlsbad, CA 92008
(619) 929-6060
small "skylight"

Solar

-Storage

12 and 18 inch diameter
12 inch x 8 feet equals 47 gal. or 404 lbs
heat storage tubes of clear fiberglass
www.thenaturalhome.com

PSI Energy Storage Division

*Used in Earth Home

1533 Fenpark Drive
Fenton, MO 63026
(314) 343-7666
Thermol 81 energy storage rods (phase change)

Alkali Metal/Salt Storage
NASA NPO 16686

Texxor Corporation
Omaha, NE
"Heat cell" phase change drums

Air Salt/Gravity-Flow Solar Heating
NASA - LAR-12009

Thermal storage in aluminum/ammonium nitrate eutectic for solar space heating
University of Florida

Spices (See Plants-Herbs, Spices, Tea)

Spirulina/SCP

Food From Sunlight
Christopher Hills
Book on Spirulina

From open ponds to vertical alveolar panels: the Italian Experience in the development of reactors for the mass cultivation of phototrophic microorganisms
M.R. Tredici & R. Materassi
J.Appl. Phycol. 1992
Volume 4 pp 221-231

Article on the transition to closed tubes
For Spirulina production

The Spirulina Cookbook
Sonia Beasley
Book on how to use Spirulina

Rejuvenating the Body Through Fasting With Spirulina Plankton
Christopher Hills
Book on therapeutic uses for Spirulina

Food From Sunlight
Christopher Hills
Book on virtues of Spirulina

The Secrets of Spirulina: Medical Discoveries of Japanese Doctors
Christopher Hills, Naoharu Fujii
Japanese medical documentations

A Tubular Photobioreactor for Photosynthetic Production of Biomass from Carbon Dioxide: Design and Performance
S. John Pirt, Yuan Kun Lee, Marek R. Walach, Margaret Watts Pirt, Hushang H. M. Balyuzi, and Michael J. Bazin
Chem. Techn. Biotechnol. 1983
Vol. 33B p. 35-58

Production of Spirulina Biomass in Closed Photobioreactors
G.Torzillo, B. Pushparaj, F. Bocci, W. Balloni, R. Materassi, and G. Florenzano
Biomass 1986, Volume 11 p. 61-64

A Vertical Alveolar Panel (VAP) for Outdoor Mass Cultivation of Microalgae and Cyanobacteria
M.R. Tredici, P Carlozzi, G. Chini Zittelli & R Maserasssi,
1991 Biores. Technology Volume 38 P. 153-159

Novel Photobioreactors for the Mass Cultivation of Spirulina
Tredici, M. et al
April 1993
Bulletin de L'Institute Oceanographics
Article on growing Spirulina in tubes

Spirulina the Whole Food Revolution
Larry Switzer
Early book on Spirulina

Earthrise Company
800-949-7473
Spirulina powder and tablets

Growth of Spirulina maxima Algae in Effluents from Secondary Waste-Water Treatment Plants
N. Kosaric, H.T. Nguyen, and M.A. Bergougnou
University of Western Ontario
Biotechnology and Bioengineering Vol. XVI
Pages 881-896

Growth of Spirulina maxima in cow manure wastes
Gideon Oron-Israel
Biotechnol. Bioeng. 1979 Vol.21 2169-73

Amino Acid Composition and Microbial Contamination of Spirulina maxima, a Blue-Green Alga, Grown on the Effluent of Different Fermented Animal Wastes
Jung F Wu and Wilson G. Pond
Cornell University, Ithaca, New York
Bull. Environm. Contam. Toxicol. 27, 151-159 (1981)

Mass Culture of Spirulina using Low-cost Nutrients
C.V. Seshadri, and S. Thomas
Biotechnology Letters 1979 Vol.1 278-91

Production of Yeast Single-Cell Protein by Utilizing Food Wastes
Martin R. Okos
article

Biotechnology:An Overview
M.K. Goel
Book including info on single cell protein

Spirulina:Production & Potential
Ripley D. Fox
EDISUD
Book

Earth Food Spirulina
Robert Hendrikson
Book

Algoculture:Spurulina, Hope for a Hungry World
Ripley and Denise Fox
Book

Sprouting

NOTE: When seeds sprout vitamin content increases 10, 50, 100, 500 and 1,000%.
NOTE: There is 600% more food value in sprouts.
NOTE: Some 30 different seeds can be successfully sprouted.

Alfalfa	4-6 Hr. soak	3-5 days	1-1 ½"
Cabbage	4-6 Hr. soak	4-5 days	1"
Radish	4-6 Hr. soak	4-5 days	1"
Mung bean	12 Hr. soak	3-6 days	½"-1 ½"
Wheat	12 Hr. soak	2-3 days	¼"-½"

Above per half gallon jar

The Sprouting Book
Ann Wigmore
Book containing sprouting chart

Sprouting Publications
Micheal Linden
500-445-5519
The Sproutletter (publication)

The Sprout Garden
Mark Braunstein
Book on Sprouting

Life Sprouts
P.O. Box 150
Hyrum, Utah 84319
800-241-1516
Sprouting equip/supplies and more

Soybeans
40% protein, difficult to sprout, rinse 3-6 times/day, steam before eating

Mung beans

Garbonzos
Amaranth

Lentils

Alfalfa
smallest sprout, carotene, 35% protein, mild taste

Adzuki beans

Wheat

Automatic sprout grower
reprint

Radish
sproutable seeds

Turnip
sproutable seeds

Nutritional analysis of alfalfa and soybean sprouts
article

Natural Food Systems, Inc.
P.O. Box 1028
Pagosa Springs, CO 81147
(800) 874-2733
salad-a-day sprouting kits

Feel Like a Million
Catharyn Elwood
Book

The Sprout House
P.O. Box 1100
Great Barrington, MA 01230
(413) 528-5200
sprout kit

Life Sprouts
P.O. Box 150
Hyrum, Utah 84319
801-245-3891
800-241-1516

Steam/Vapor Cycles
-Steam Engines

Japan Trade Center
230 North Michigan Avenue
Chicago, IL 60601
(312) 726-4390
contacts for Japanese steam engine companies

Engineers and Engines
Donald D. Knowles, Editor
1118 N. Raynor Avenue
Joliet, IL 60435
small steam engine magazine

Steam Calliope Magazine
Panorama City, CA
steam publication

Light Steam Power Magazine
c/o Kirk Michael
Isle of Man
GREAT BRITAIN
steam magazine

Steam Power Quarterly
c/o Peter Scott-Brown
636 Ralston Street
Reno, NV 89503
steam power magazine

Live Steam Magazine
P O. Box 581
Traverse City, MI 49684
source

Steamboats and Modern Steam Launches
Howell North Publishing Co.
1050 Parker Street
Berkeley, CA 94622
12 volume collection

Steam/Vapor Cycles
-Steam Engines-
Contacts

These people have communicated by hand-written letters to me during the Earth Home project (and various sub-projects involving steam for power generation in a self-sufficient homestead such as Earth Home). These original letters are on file and are a direct part of the background research and findings.

Jerry Heermans
13925 SW River Lane
Rigard, OR 97223

Bob McIntyre
Rt. 2 Box 43
Newberg, OR 97132

Peter E. Moale
16 Harvard Court
Pleasant Hill, CA 94523

Paul R. Breisch
187 West Ridge Pike
Boyersford, PA 19468

G. Rosekilly Machinery
Box 752
San Mateo, CA 94401
(415) 343-3700

Bill Durham
3722 Bagley Avenue
Seattle, Washington

Bill Yallalee
58 Larkfield Maples Court
Santa Rosa, CA 95401

*Used in Earth Home

Steam/Vapor Cycles
-Steam Engine Companies

The following entries offer steam engine products to the public.

Sensible Steam Consultants
152 Von Goebels Lane
Branson, MO 65616
417-336-2869
www.geocities.com/researchtriangle/6362

Semple Engine Company, Inc.
P.O. Box 8354
St. Louis, MO 63124

Gordon Rose Killy Machinery
Box 752
San Mateo, CA 94401
(415) 343-3700

James D. Crank
J Dex Co.
1621 Palm Avenue
Redwood City, CA 94061
(415) 365-2005

Reitman Manufacturing Co.
10319 Pearmain Street
Oakland, CA 94603
638-8977

Paul R. Breisch
187 West Ridge Pike
Boywesford, PA 19468
(215) 489-9139

C. William Moore
Dayland Steam Engines
P.O. Box 756
Pleasanton, CA 94566
(415) 846-3008

Stuart Turner, Ltd.
Henley-on-Thames
Oxon, RG9 2AD

Coles Power Models
P.O. Box 788
Ventura, CA 93002

Reliable Industries, Inc.
3775 Wellman Line Road
Brown City, MI 48416

Tiny Power
c/o Eugene Goebel
P.O. Box G
Tehachapi, CA 93561
(805) 822-5944

William T. Blake Co.
P.O. Box 54
Canan Diagua, NY 14424
(315) 394-4931

Machin Knight & Sons
6 Avery Hill Road
Condon SE9 2BE ENGLAND

Caldwell Industries
603-609 East Davis Street
Luling, TX 78648

Stirling
-Automotive Applications

Ross Experimental
1660 West Henderon Road
Columubs, OH 43220
(614) 457-4104
Stirling kits

Society of Automotive Engineers
400 Commonwealth Drive
Warrendale, PA 15096
automotive Stirling engine

Philips Research Labs
Department Stelling Engines
N.V. Philips Gloeilampenfabrieken
Eindhoven, THE NETHERLANDS
automotive studies - Stirling

Stirling
-Books

The Stirling Engine Manual
James Rizzo
Volume 1 and 2

Making Stirling Engines
Andy Ross
Book on building Stirling Engines

Stirling
-Contacts

www.stirlingenergy.com/solar

Stirling Machine World
PO Box 66
Los Olivos, CA 93441
805-688-4849
stirmach@juno.com

SAIC USJVP
Prototype Dish/Stirling Engine
S. Kaneff
From ASES Solar Energy Forum

Ted Ledger
591 Windermere Avenue
Toronto 9, Ontario M6S 3L9
CANADA
older Stirling engine

UCLA Extension
109 95 Le Conte Avenue
Los Angeles, CA 90024
information pamphlet

University of Reading
Department of Engineering
c/o P.D. Dunn
Whiteknights, Reading
ENGLAND RG6 2AY
article on conversion to stirling with bibliography

ASME
United Engineering Center
345 east 47th Street
New york, NY

*Used in Earth Home

1/4 H.P. solar hot air engine articles

Jet Propulsion Labs
California Institute of Technology
4800 Oak Grove Drive
Pasadena, CA 91103
experimental engine for NASA

Stirling Cycle Machines
by G. Walker
book

Stirling Cycle Engines
by Andy Ross
book

Stirling Engine Newsletter
Editor Brad Ross
2303 Harris
Richland, WA 99352
newsletter

R&D Magazine
Dec. 1992, pp. 28-32
"CFC Replacement Technologies"
James Glanz
article (Stirling for refrigerator)

Peter Tailer
Windfarm Museum
RFD #2 Box 865
Vineyard Haven, MA
information

Mechanical Technology, Inc.
Sterling Engine Systems Division
968 Albany-Shaker Road
Latham, NY 12110
(518) 785-2344
Stirling research

Sunstrand Energy Systems
4747 Harrison Avenue
Rockford, IL 61101
(815) 226-6000
vapor cycle equipment

Stirling

-Products

STM Power
Advanced Stirling engine to convert waste heat and gas into electricity

Hoval AgroLyt Stirling
Wood-fired boiler

Stirling

-Small Stirling Engines

Stirling Engines in Solar Power Plants
www.rbi.ims.ca/4911-557
29% collector to grid efficiency

Sunpower, Inc.
PO Box 2625
Athens, OH. 45701
740-594-2221
"Biowatt"
Stirling Biomass fuel generator

Solar Engines
2937 West Indian School Road
Phoenix, AZ 85017
small Stirling kit and book

Stirling Power Systems
7101 Jackson Road
Ann Arbor, MI 48103
(313) 665-6767
Stirling info and engines

Sunpower, Inc.
6 Byard Street
Athens, OH 45701
(614) 594-2221
25 Watt model and prototypes

Martini Associates
2303 Harris Avenue
Richland, WA 99352
(509) 375-2251
model kits

An Introduction to Low Temperature
Differential Stirling Engines
James R. Senft
Book

Stirling Technology, Inc
9 Factory Street
Athens, OH 45701
(614) 594-2277
st. 5 engine

Wallace Minto Sunpower Systems, Inc.
1121 Lewis Avenue
Sarasota, FL 33577
(813) 366-3050
"Minto" wheel (see also refrigerator file)

Straw Bale (see Flax section)

(See flax, straw, fibers Section)
www.strawbalecentral.com

Survival

When Technology Fails
Matthew Stein
Comprehensive book on survival techniques

The Survival Handbook
Peter Darman
Survival technologies

Making the Best of Basics
James Talmage Stevens
Book on Family Preparedness

Tanks

-Fabricated

Hesco Barriers
Military explosion barriers

Weldmesh
Smorgon Steel
Galvanized steel mesh
Non-woven polypropylene geotextile fabric

Tanks

-Purchased

*Used in Earth Home

TCM (Traditional Chinese Medicine)

www.tcmcentral.com
TCM (Traditional Chinese Medicine) website

The Chinese Materia Medica
Xu Xiangcai

Thermal Mass

-Phase Change Materials

Merk KGaA Darmstadt
Eutectic salt PCM 72

Schumann Sasol Hamburg
Paraffin RT50

Thermal Mass

-Products

Styrofoam T-Mass Technology
www.dow.com/styrofoam/na/tmass1.htm

Thermal Mass

-Publications

Comfort in any Climate
Michael Reynolds
Book on thermal mass in construction
Earthships

Mass Walls Mean Thermal Comfort
hem.dis.an..gov/eehem/99/990515.html

Thermal Mass

-Research/Testing

Building Envelope Research
Oak Ridge National Laboratory
PO box 2008
Oak ridge, TN 37831-6070
865-574-0022
desjarlaisa@ornl.gov

Thermoacoustics

Journal of the Acoustical Society of America

http://civil.colorado.edu/~muehleis/thernoacs

Thermoelectric, Thermovoltaic

Tellurex Corp.
1248 Hastings
Traverse City, Mich. 49686
616-947-0110
www.tellurex.com
Z-Max module-efficient

Melcor
Materials Electronic Products Corporation
990 Spruce Street
Trenton, NJ 08648
(609) 393-4178
cooling modules

Global Thermoelectric Power Systems, Ltd.
P.O. Box 400
Bassano, Alberta T0J 0B0
CANADA
(403) 41-3512
information

National Renewable Energy Laboratory
1617 Cole Boulevard
Golden, CO 80401
TPV research

Marlow Industries, Inc.
10451 Vista Park Road
Dallas, TX 75238-1645
(214) 340-4900
information

Thermovolt from Photic Corporation
Distributed by Alternative Energy Engineering
Box 339 Briceland Star Rt.
Redway, CA 95560
(707) 923-2277
electricity from heat

G.E. Research & Development Center
Box 8
Schenectady, NY 12301
(518) 387-6374
"Seebeck Effect" thermoelectric generator

Thermophotovoltaic (TPV)

http://vri.etec.wwu.edu/tpv.htm
thermophotovoltaic research

Vehicle Research Institute
Western Washington University
Bellingham, WA 98225-9086
(360) 650-3045

JX Crystals, Inc.
1105 12th Ave. N.W. Suite A2
Issaquah, WA 98027
425 392 5237
www.jxcrystals.com/

Toilets

-Aerobic Digesters

Biocycle Pty. Ltd.
56A Old Barrenjoey Road
Avalon 2107, New South Wales
AUSTRALIA
61 2 918 9933
U.S. Distributor
Cliff Crocoll
Holland, MI
(616) 335-8262
combination aerobic and anaerobic (state-of-the-art)

Norweco
220 Repulita Street
Norwalk, OH 44857
(419) 668-4471
aerobic digesters

Chromoglass Corp.
Williamsport, PA 17701
(717) 326-3396

*Used in Earth Home

aerobic digesters

Aquarobic Ltd.
117 Pine Street
Chestertown, MD 21620
(301) 778-3279
aerobic digesters

Jet Inc.
750 Alpha Drive
Cleveland, OH 44143
(216) 442-9008
aerobic digesters

Multi-Flo Waste Treatment Systems, Inc.
2324 East River Road
Dayton, OH 45439
* aerobic digester

Nayadic Sciences, Inc.
1186 Winola Road
Clarks Summit, PA 18411
aerobic digester

Western Env & Engineering Corp.
823 Curtis Avenue
Columbux, OH 43203
aerobic dgester

Sun-Mar Corporation
5035 North Service Road, Unit C2
Burlington, Ontario L7L 5V2
CANADA
aerobic digesters

Toilets

-Bidet

TushyClean
Bathroom bidet conversion Kit
www.juscuzz.com

Toilets

-Books/Information

www.cromwell.intl.com/toilet
website on all toilets

The Toilet Papers
Recycling Waste and Conserving Water
By Sim Van der Ryn
Book on toilets of many kinds

Toilets

-Experimental Sewage Systems Information

Compost Toilet News
Star Route 3
Bath, ME 04530
source

Controlled Eutrophication
(using the sea - algae)
NASA article

Buckminster Fuller's
Dymaxion bathroom
(complete bathroom unit)
article

NASA toilet system
article

Water Hyacinths into Methane
article

Algae
article

Folkecenter for Vedurande Energy
DENMARK
P.O. Box 208
OK - 7760 Hurop Thy
DENMARK
alternative toilet systems

Reasons why composting toilet is not used in Earth Home
synopsis

Tecumseh
Tecumseh, MI
(517) 423-8411
rotary valve air compressor

Problems with dry toilet systems
correspondence

Urine, dung, discussion
(nitrogen, potash, fertilizer)
reprint

Septic Tank Practices
Peter Warshall
book

Homebuilders Guide to Aerobic
Wastewater Treatment
article

$ Nutrients in urine, feces
$ Composting methods
$ Bacterial count
articles

Compost Toilet News
Star Route 3
Bath, ME 04530
publication

Toilets in NASA Space Program
NASA files

Comparison of 4 kinds of home-site sewage treatment
chart

Weeds or tropical grasses have the highest weight gain (dry) per unit sunlight (followed by sugar cane and corn)
potential O_2 supply for aerobic toilet

Toilets

-Low Flush Toilet Manufacturers

NOTE: G.P.F. is gallons per flush.

Control Fluidics, Inc.
124 West Putnam Avenue
Greenwich, CT
(203) 661-5599
2 liter flush toilet

Raphael, Ltd.
P.O. Box 386
Brookfield, WI 53008-0386

*Used in Earth Home

I.S.G.P.F. floral designs

Control Fluidics Inc.
124 West Putnam Avenue
Greenwich, CT 06830
(201) 661-5599
.6 G.P.F.

Artesian Plumbing Products
201 E. Fifth Street
Mansfield, OH 44901
1.5 G.P.F.

Crane Plumbing
1235 Hartrey Avenue
Evanston, IL 60202
(708) 864-9777
1.5 G.P.F.

Eljer
17120 Dallas Parkway
Dallas, TX 75248
1.5 G.P.F. and full line

Universal-Rundle Corp.
217 North Mill Street
New Castle, PA 16103
(800) 955-0316
(412) 658-6631
1.5 G.P.F.

Microphor Inc.
P.O. Box 490
Willits, CA 95490
(800) 358-8280
(707) 459-5563
air-assisted .5 G.P.F. flush

Briggs Industries
4350 W. Cypress Street, Suite 800
Tampa, FL 33607
(813) 878-0178
1.5 G.P.F.

Porcher
13-160 Merchandise Mart
Chicago, IL 60654
(312) 923-0995
(800) 338-1756
1.6 G.P.F.

American Standard
P.O. Box 6820
Piscataway, NJ 08855
(800) 752-6292
1.5 G.P.F. full line

Kohler Co.
Kohler, WI 53044
(414) 457-4441
full line

Gerber Plumbing Fixtures Corp.
4656 W. Touhy Avenue
Chicago, IL 60646
(708) 675-6570
1.6 G.P.F.

Sun-Mar Corp.
5035 N. Service Road C2
Burlington, Ontario L7L 5V2
CANADA
(416) 332-1314
OR
900 Hertel Avenue
Buffalo, NY 14216
composting and low flush

Clivus Multrum, Inc.
1 Eliot Square
Cambridge, MA 02138
(617) 491-0051
(800) 4CLIVUS
composting, foam toilet "Nepon," plastic urinals

Peerless Pottery Inc.
P.O. Box 145
Rockport, IN 47635-0145
(800) 457-5785
many kinds

Control Fluidics, Inc.
124 W. Putnam Avenue
Greenwich, CT 06830
(203) 661-5599
"Fluidizer" toilet

Toilets

-Odor Control

Arizona Chemical Co.
1001 East Business Highway 98
Panama City, FL 32401
(904) 785-6700
(800) 526-5294
terpene (pine scent)

American Linen Supply
scents

Sani-Air Associates
1479 Glenn Avenue
Glenshaw, PA
(412) 486-2255
(800) 243-5689
scents

Huntington Labs of Canada
15 Victoria Crescent
Barmalea, Ontario L6T 1E3
CANADA
Formula 126 deodorant

Sea Breeze by
Rubbermaid
3124 Valley Avenue
Winchester, VA 22601
(703) 667-8700
odor release systems

Polyvinyl alcohol
(Exp. use to flush toilets (foam))
article

Commiphora myrrha
Commiphora abyssinica
plants with scent

Keystone Scent Conditioner
315-23 North Twelfth Street
Philadelphia, PA 19107
(215) 922-0345
scent blocks

Toilets

-Products

www.cromwell.intl.com/toilet/

*Used in Earth Home

site on world-wide toilet use

DYNO2 Reactor Dynamics
Forest Lake, MN 55025
Alternative plant-based wastewater system

In-Lieu toilet converter
For squatting position
www.nationaldrm.com/health/toilet.html
Sales@rotadyne.com.au
www.rotadyne.com.au

Natures Platform
www.naturesplatform.com
186 Westside Drive
Boone, NC 28607
828-297-7561
Squatting toilet converter

Aromat Corp.
1935 Lundy Ave.
San Jose, CA 95131
800-223-6247
Toilet seat-sophisticated
Similar to Japanese bidet-style

Envirovac, Inc.
1260 turret Dr.
Rockford, IL 61111
800-435-6951
Vacuum toilets-2 pint flush

Moore Products Co.
Spring Horse, PA 19477
flow controllers

Thetford Corp.
P.O. Box 1285
Ann Arbor, MI 48106
camping toilets

Mansfield Sanitary
Big Prairie, OH 44611
camping toilets

Sanitation Equipment Ltd.
35 Citron Court
Concord, Ontaio L4K 2S7
(416) 738-0055
flush-o-matic 1 qt. flush

Capitol Plastics of Ohio
Division of Dixico
333 Van Camp Road
P.O. Box 308
Bowling Green, OH 43402
portable toilet

Sealand Technology Inc.
P.O. Box 38
Big Prairie, OH 44611
* ceramic ball valve toilets

Century Tool and Mfg. Co.
1462 U.S. Route #20
P.O. Box 188
Cherry Valley, IL 61016
Mfr. Sanitation Equipment
35 Citron Court
Concorrd, Ontario L4K 2S7
CANADA
camping toilet (flap valve) 1 qt. flush, flush-o-matic

Sears (Pak-A-Potti)
camping toilets (slide valve)

Direct Solar Thermal-to-Electric
Energy Conversion Using Thermovoltaics
Nasa Lewis Research Center
article

Monogram Ind. Inc.
Sanitation Group
4030 Freeman Boulevard
Redondo Beach, CA 90278
(213) 973-0656
12 VDC recirculating toilets

Toto Kiki U.S.A.
415 West Taft Avenue
Unit A Orange, CA 92665
(714) 282-8686
"water wipe" toilet

N.A.I.S. Div. of Aromat
1935 Lundy Avenue
San Jose, CA 95131
(408) 433-3821
"water wipe" toilet

Thetford Corporation
7101 Jackson Road
P.O. Box 1285
Ann Arbor, MI 48106
camping toilets

Ark-Plas Products, Inc.
Highway 178 North
Flippin, AR 72634
(501) 453-8585
miniature hose fittings

Elton James Corp.
P.O. Box 948
Loveland, CO 80539-0948
(800) 443-0542
miniature hose fittings

Spray Engineering Co.
East Split Brook Road
Nashua, NH 03060
spray nozzles

Enviro Quip Corp.
Cincinnati, OH 45230
(800) 543-0489
diffusers, etc.

Eljer, Kohler, Rusco, Crane
bidets (see Low-Flush Toilets)

Marine & Mobile Water Systems
6400 Marina Drive
Long Beach, CA 90803
(213) 598-9000
smaller waste holding tanks

Whale
(gusher urchin pump)
* waste hand pumps (diaphram)

Bex, Inc.
37709 Schoolcraft Road
Livonia, MI 48150
(313) 464-8282
spray nozzles

Hyponex Corporation
Fort Wayne, IN 46801
brass syphon mixer (high flows)

*Used in Earth Home

Moisture Systems Inc. (Aquachem)
Wheeling, IL
fertilizer injector (container)

Spraying Systems Co.
North Avenue at Schmale Road
Wheaton, IL 60188
(312) 665-5000
* spray nozzles (all materials)

Enertech LJN Toys Ltd.
1107 Broadway
New York, NY 10010
squirt guns (mechanism)

Bell Industries
1081 Highway 36 East at JCT 61
St. Paul, MN 55109
12 VDC macerator pump

Mazzei Injector
Rt. 5 Box 453
Bakersfield, CA 93307
(905) 845-2076
accurate injectors

Sun-Mar Corp.
5035 N. Service Road, C9-10
Burlington, Ontario L7L 5V2
CANADA
(905) 332-1314
cottage toilets

Toilets

-Urine Separation

http://www.wost-man-ecology.se/double_flush.html

www.aquatron.se/us/function.us2.html
greywater site and urine separation

http://www.separett.com
alternative toilet systems and urine separation
also children separation system

http://www.ornplast.se/
urine separation systems

8 parts water to 1 part urine for above-ground disposal

http://www.aquatron.se/start.se.html

http://www.dubbletten.nu/dubblett-systemet/dubblett-systemet.htm

http://www.gustavsberg.com/Gustavsberg/ASP/Product.aspx?iSecID=1625&lev=3&lang=en-gb&iItmID=1182

http://www.oeko-toiletten.de/index.html

http://www.hyttetorget.no/category.php?categoryID=2&vera=1

Toilets

-Wastewater Systems

Eljen In-Drain
Passive Pre-treatment and Wastewater Systems
Pleated fabric systems.
800-266-4320
www.hdidistributors.com

Ultra-High Pressurization

-Products

Flow Pressure Systems

Flow (USA)

Valves

-Air-Operated Valves

Smart Parts paintball gun
6 msec valve closing

Richway Industries, Ltd.
P.O. Box 508
Janesville, Iowa 50647
319-987-2976
Airpinch
Air-operated pinch valves

Richway Industries, Ltd.
Janesville, Iowa 50647
800-553-2404
Airpinch valves(air pressure)

Valves

-Check Valves

Bio-Chem Valve, Inc.
85 Fulton St.
Boonton, NJ 07005
973-263-3001
Bio-Chek valve

Resenex Corporation
9614-F Cozycraft Ave.
Chatsworth, CA 91311
(818) 341-2525
www.resenex.com
Low Resistance High Flow check valves

Red Valve
700 N Bell Ave.
Carnegie, PA 15106
www.redvalve.com
one-piece molded check valves

The Lee Company
Westbrook, CT 06498-0424
Check valves-miniature steel

Circle Seal Controls
(Bivco Valves)
2301 Wardlow Circle
P.O. Box 3300
Corona, CA 91718
(909) 270-6200
check valves

Clayton Mark, Inc.
Rogers, AR 72757
check valve

Plast-O-Matic Valves Inc.
430 Route 46
Totowa, NJ 07512
(201) 256-3000
plastic check valve

Halkey-Roberts Corp.

*Used in Earth Home

37 Spring Valley Avenue
Paramus, NJ 07652
(201) 843-7700
syringe check valve

Miniature Precision Components, Inc.
Drawer "L"
Walworth, WI 53184
(414) 275-5791
miniature check and fittings

Valves

-Float Valves

O'Keefe Conntrols
Box Q
Trumbull, CT 06611
www.okee.com
(203) 261-8331
magnetic float-valve sensor

Valves

-Foot, Hand

Mead Fluid Dynamics
4114 N. Knox Avenue
Chicago, IL 60641
(312) 685-6800
air foot valves

Valves

-Manually Operated

Specialty Mfg. Co.
2356 University Avenue
St. Paul, MN 55114
(612) 646-6523
low-cost valves

Parker Hannifin Corporation
Brass Products Division
300 Parker Drive
Otsego, MI 49078
(616) 694-9411
plug valves

Hayward Industrial Products, Inc.
900 Fairmont Avenue
P.O. Box 18
Elizabeth, NJ 07207
(201) 351-5400
manual plastic valves

Hayward Industrial Products, Inc.
900 Fairmont Avenue
Elizabeth, NJ 07207
(201) 351-5400
Labcocks

Wandfluh of America Inc.
913 High Street
Mundelein, IL 60060
(708) 566-5700
12 VDC proportional valves

Valves

-Piezo-Operated

PBT Ltd.
Harlow, Essex, England
sales@servocell.com
low power door lock (Piezo)

Hoerbiger-Origa Corp.
Glendale Heights, IL
630-871-8300
usmarket@hoerbiger-origa.com
new piezo-operated valves

Valves

-Proportional

Electronic Control Valve
Engineered Machined Products
Thermostat-like valve for liquids

Valves

-Solenoid Valves

Asco Valve has introduced a 2 watt valve as opposed to the 17 watt versions
www.ascovalve.com

KIP Inc.
72 Spring Lane
Farmington, CT 06032
(800) 722-5547
Highflow Solwnoid Valve

Pneutronics
Hollis, NH
Microminiature fluid valve

Asco/Angar have merged (see below)

Microsol By
ITT General Controls Division
801 Allen Avenue
Glendale, CA 91201
(213) 842-6131
miniature solenoid valves

Lee Co.
2 Peitipaug Road
P.O. Box 424
Westbrook, CT 06498-0424
(203) 399-6281
ultra miniature valve - solenoid

Rainbird Sprinkler Mfg. Corp.
(800) 247-3782
sprinkler solenoid valve

Clippard Instrument Laboratory, Inc.
7360 Colerain Road
Cincinnati, OH 45239
(513) 521-4261
air valves and full line

The Johnson Corporation
Three Rivers, MI 49093
(616) 278-1715
direct-operated solenoid valves

Goyen Valve Corp.
25327 Avenue Stanford
Valencia, CA 91355
plastic body valves

Angar Scientific Co., Inc.
52 Horsehill Road
Cedar Knolls, NJ 07927-2098
(201) 538-9700
subminiature valves - Delrin and more

Automatic Switch Co.
5009 Excelsior Boulevard

*Used in Earth Home

Minneapolis, MN 55416
(612) 925-5520
full line

Snap-Tite Inc.
Valve Division
2953 West 12th Street
Erie, PA 16506
(814) 833-6131
plastic valves

Peter Paul Electronics Co. Inc.
P.O. Box 1180
480 John Downey Drive
New Britain, CT 06050-1180
(203) 229-4884
diaphram and full line

Red Valve Company, Inc.
P.O. Box 548
Carnegie, PA 15106
(412) 279-0044
control pinch valves

Burkert Contromatic Corp.
1574 N. Batavia Street
Orange, CA 92667
(714) 998-8071
(800) 325-1405
full line

Deltrol Controls
2745 South 19th Street
Milwaukee, WI 53215
(414) 671-6800
full line and dispenser valves

Datron Systems, Inc.
4585 Electronics Place
Los Angeles, CA 90039
(213) 247-7060
catching valves and full line

Smart Products, Inc.
111 East Brokaw Road
San Jose, CA 95112
(408) 436-0740
(800) 255-0300
full line

Herion
176 Thorn Hill Road
Warrendale, PA 15086
(412) 776-5577
full line

Valcor Scientific
2 Lawrence Road
Springfield, NJ 07081
(201) 467-8400
Teflon and stainless also

Honeywell
Skinner Valve Division
95 Edgewood Avenue
New Britain, CT
(203) 827-2300
full line plus proportional

Sporlan Valve Company
7525 Sussex Avenue
St. Louis, MO 63143
(314) 647-2775
* low amp draw

Humphrey Products
P.O. Box 2008
Kalamazoo, MI 49003
(616) 381-5500
air valves

Vertical Gardening

Topsy Turvey
Upside down tomato planter www.amazon.com

Hammacher Schlemmer
www.hammacher.com
upside-Down Tomato Garden

Vinegar (See Alcohol also)

Maple Sap makes good vinegar

Vinegar - recipes
article

Vinegar - other sources besides apples
article

Making vinegar - recipes
article

Making vinegar - at home and on farm
book

Good vinegar can be made from maple sap and Jerusalem artichoke stalks

Vitamins/Minerals (See also Clay)

-Trace Minerals

Healthy Water for

Healthy Water for a Longer Life
Martin Fox
Book on beneficial

Live Earth Products
PO Box 76
Emery, UT 84522
(801) 286-2222
Trace Mineral Fertilizer source

Richard Schulze
Consultant and SuperFood Mfr.
Vitamin and Mineral Supplements

www.traceminerals.com/coastal_cultures.html
website on mineral nutrition of coastal cultures

www.celtic-seasalt.com
website on the minerals in sea salt

The Grain and Salt Society
1-800-867-7258

The Hidden Power of Vitamins and Minerals
Jacques de Langre
Book on vitamins and minerals

Organic vegetables contain up to 3 times
More minerals and trace elements than inorganic
Produce— www.macrobiotics.org/minerals/html

*Used in Earth Home

Rockland Corporation
Live Earth Products
PO Box 76
Emery, Utah 84522
Colloidal minerals

Let's Play Doctor
Joel Wallach
Minerals/Medicine Book

Design Your Own Vitamin and Mineral Program
Shari Lieberman and Nancy Bruning
Book

Vitamins/Minerals
-Vitamin C

acerola berry contains the most potent source of natural vitamin C and bioflavanoids.

Vitamin C was made from Hemlock or white pine needles by the Iroquois Indians

Water
-As Medicine

Healthy Water for a Longer Life
Martin Fox
Book on beneficial qualities of water

Your Body's Many Cries for Water
F. Batmanghelidj
www.watercure.com

Water
-Condensed

www.fogquest.org
organization promoting water from fog

Water
-Distilled

193 Osborne Road
Fridley, Minnesota 55432
763-571-9001
http://www.hydrotechwater.com/Distillers/Precision%205-3%20Distiller.htm
counter top water distiller

http://www.sunlightsystems.com/index.php
UV water filters

SolAqua
P.O. Box 4976
El Paso, Texas 79914-4976
(915) 383-1485
http://www.solaqua.com/
solar water distillation

www.durastill.com/myths

Water
-Filters

www.rain-barrel.net
roofwashers, gutter strainers, downspout filters

AquaRain*
Gravity Filters for Drinking Water

*Used in Earth Home

*used in Earth Home

Water
-Rainwater

http://www.rainwaterharvesting.org/
site on rainwater/harvesting

http://www.rainwaterharvesting.com/
site on rainwater/harvesting

http://www.twdb.state.tx.us/assistance/conservation/alternative_technologies/rainwater_harvesting/rain.asp
site on rainwater/harvesting

http://www.rain-barrel.net/gutter-strainer.html
site on rainwater/harvesting

http://www.aboutrainwaterharvesting.com/
site on rainwater/harvesting

http://www.arcsa-usa.org/
site on rainwater/harvesting

http://seamlessgutters.com/Gutter-Strainers.htm
site on rainwater/harvesting

www.envireau.co.uk
rainwater accessories

www.arcsa-usa.org/suppliers
website of rainwater suppliers

www.aboutrainwaterharvesting.com
general site about rainwater collection and use

www.rain-barrel.net
rainwater harvesting guide

Websites (See Internet)

Wind Generator Technology
-Miscellaneous

NRG Systems
Anemometers
www.nrgsystems.com
802-482-2255

Sapphire vee bearings on
Kestrels anemometer

variable reluctance motors
used in the Electra motorcycles
They generate electricity as they stop—
Regenerative braking

Litton Poly-Scientific
1213 North Main St.
Blacksburg, Va. 24060
800-336-2112
Slip Rings

TFE Industries
148 Parkway
Kalamazoo, MI 49007
(616) 343-1341
(800) 253-4890
Teflon bearings

Tol-O-Matic

1028 South Third Street
Minneapolis, MN 55415
(612) 333-6605
industrial caliper disc brakes

National Telephone Supply Co.
5100 Superior Venue
Cleveland, OH 44103
(216) 361-0221
cable tools

Mercury Products
A Division of Dyneer Corporation
1201 Camden Avenue SW
Canton, OH 44706
(216) 456-3453
clutches

Loos and Company
Hardware and Tools Division
900 Industrial Boulevard
Naples, FL 33942
(813) 774-5667
cable ends

Gougeon Manufacturing Corp.
229 West Fifth Street
P.O. Box 32
Pinconning, MI 48650
(517) 879-5224
large blades

Maurey Manufacturing Corp.
2907 South Wabash Avenue
Chicago, IL 60616
(312) 326-6550
positive drives

Fairchild Manufacturing Co., Inc.
2300 South Concorde Road
Lafayette, IN 47902
(317) 474-3474
complex gears

Winsmith Division of UML Industries, Inc.
Springville, NY 14141
(716) 592-9311
gear reducers

Windpower for Home and Business
Paul Gipe
source book on wind

Browning Manufacturing Division
Emerson Electric Canada, Ltd.
Box 150
Markham, Ontario L3P 3S6
CANADA
(416) 294-9340
centrifugal clutches

Formsprag Division
Dana Corporation
801 East Industrial Drive
Mt. Pleasant, MI 48858
(517) 773-6921
centrifugal clutches

Hoboken Bolt and Screw Co.
1700 Willow Avenue
Hoboken, NJ 07030
cable

Bergen Wire Rope Co.
P.O. Box 1300
Gregg Street
Lodi, NJ 07644
(201) 487-3521
cable, assemblies

Meridian Laboratory
2415 Evergreen Road
P.O. Box 156
Middleton, WI 53562
(608) 836-7571
rotary contacts

Climax Metal Products Co.
30202 Lakeland Boulevard
Wickliffe, OH 44092
(216) 585-0300
(800) 722-0477
shaft collars

Igus Bearings, Inc.
P.O. Box 4349
East Providence, RI 02914
(401) 438-2200
(800) 521-5747
self-lube shaft bearings

Real Goods Trading Co.
California
$19 hand-held windspeed meter

Plastimatic
(201) 575-0038
(800) PLASTOR
plastic drive components

Rexnord Co.
2324 Curtiss Street
Downers Grove, IL 60515
(708) 969-1770
bearings

Thomson Industries, Inc.
Manhasset, NY 11030
nylon bearings

GBG Industries, Inc.
P.O. Box 286
South Park Street
Willimantic, CT 06226
(203) 456-1701
cable assemblies

All Line, Inc.
31 West 310 91st Street
Wheatland Industrial Park
Naperville, IL 60565
(312) 820-1800
wire rope, etc.

"Complete" list of worldwide
wind generators
copy on file

Reciprocating wire power transmission
for small water wheels
article

Wind Power Monthly
Reading, CA 96099
magazine

American Wind Energy Assoc.
777 N. Capitol Street NE, Suite 805
Washington, DC 20002
(202) 408-8988

*Used in Earth Home

association/wind resource maps

Doric Mfg. Co.
1800 South Acoma Street
Denver, CO 80223
(303) 744-2929
speed reducers

Wind Generator Technology -Wind Books

Wind Power for Home and Business
Paul Gipe
Book on wind energy and products

Wind Generator Technology -Wind Generated Compressed Air

Sparco piston-type compressors
Enertech

Bowjon

Wingen Company
Wind-powered water pump

Wind Generator Technology -Wind Generator Manufacturing Companies

NOTE: This list contains mostly manufacturers of 2 KW and smaller units.

Fortis wind turbine
1.4 kw size

Windside Production Ltd.
www.windside.com
vertical axis wind machines

Ropatec
Hybrid Engergy Solutions
Rotor-style wind generators
info@ropatec.com
750 watt and above

Bowjon Wind Compressor
(Winsmith)
888-onsolar
Sierra Solar Systems

Thermax
Box 3128
Burlington, VT 05401-3128
(802) 658-1096
Thermax "Windstream"

Bergey Windpower
2001 Priestley Avenue
Norman, OK 73069
(405) 364-4212
line of generators

Southwest Windpower
1855 Kaibab Lane, #5
Flagstaff, AZ 86001
(602) 779-9463
(520) 779-9463
* "Windseeker" 500

Bowjon
2829 Burton Avenue
Burank, CA 91504
(213) 846-2620
air/water pumping wind machine

LUMotors
Iroyston Road
Baldock, Herts, SG7 6N
Dist. by MMG Distribution Co., Inc.
34 Industrial Way Est
P.O. Box 1204
Eatontown, NJ 07727
(201) 389-4411
generator

World Power Technologies, Inc.
19 North Lake Avenue
Duluth, MN 55802
(218) 722-1492
complete line

Folkecenter for Vedvarende (alternative) Energy
Kammers Gardsve 16, SDR. RDBY
DK 7760 HURUP THY
DENMARK
Danish research institute

Soma Power, Ltd.
P.O. Box 226
Silverdale
Auckland
NEW ZEALAND
smaller generator

GJellerup Smed
V/Frede Sorensen
Kirkevaenget 3
7400 Herning
DENMARK
smaller plants

Widflower
Claus Nybroe
Stenbankevej 6
5771 Stenstup
DEMARK
(+45) 62 26 15 55
Danish wind generator co.

Sencenbaugh Wind Electric Co.
P.O. Box 11174
Palo Alto, CA 94306
(415) 964-1593
several models and literature

Bertoia Studio Ltd.
(Aesthetic Ecological Systems)
644 Main Street
Bally, PA 19503
systems

Carter Wind Systems, Inc.
1900 FM 369 South
Burkburnett, TX 76354
systems

Lake Michigan Wind & Sun
E 3971 Bluebird Road
Forestville, WI 54213
(414) 837-2267
new, used, repair many brands

Nature's Energy Technology
Systems

*Used in Earth Home

Northern Power Systems
1 North Wind Road
Moretown, VT 05660
(802) 496-2955
systems

Wind Baron
P.O. Box 3777
Flagstaff, AZ 86003
(800) 633-WIND
(602) 526-6400
systems

Roheico Int.
Gammel Hovedvej 5
Gribsvad
DK 5560 Aarup
tilt-down towers

Vergnet
6, rue Henri-Dunant
45140 Ingre
FRANCE

Wind Generator Technology -Wind Powered Compressed Air

Fleet Farm
Small compressor to keep ponds open using stone.

Wind Generator Technology -Vertical Axis

Oy Windside Production Ltd
www.windside.com

Ropatec Ag
Italy
www.ropatec.com
vertical axis wind machines

Marlec Engineering Co Ltd
United Kingdom
www.marlec.co.uk
vertical axis machines

Wood Stoves/Wood -Biomass

Frank Scott
Australian Biomass Thermal Systems
1/21 Angelo Street,
South Perth, Western Australia 6151
Low-grade fuel burner (stove)

Wood Stoves/Wood -Boilers

Hoval AgroLyt Stirling
Wood-fired boiler

Wood Stoves/Wood -Heat-Resistant Materials

Lime rich mortar
Until 1960 wood stoves and copper were built
With lime rich mortar because
It was unaffected by intense fire
And did not expand or contract

3M
Ceramic Materials Department
225-45 3M Center
St. Paul, MN 55144
(800) 328-1687
(612) 736-9390
heat expanding sheet

Zircar Fibrosis Ceramic Products
110 North Main Street
Florida, NY 10921
(914) 651-4481
ceramic fiber

Dow Corning
Pyrex Division
(Pyrex cooking containers)
Clear Pyrex cake pans, pie pans have been inserted into homemade wood stoves to enable one to "see" the flame - similar to a fireplace.
information

(See also FABRICS - HIGH TEMPERATURE)

Wood Stoves/Wood -Information

Fiber Fuels Institute
National Resources Research Institute
5013 Miller Trunk Highway
Duluth, MN 55811
(218) 720-4319
pellet stove information

Birch bark as wet/dry
fire starter material
personal contacts (B.W.C.A.)

Mudstove
Somali bucket stove
Electrostatic precipitator
Drawing of complete use of smoke from woodstove
articles

Ash wood
article

Georgia flatwood
article

Peterson Machine Shop
Little Falls, MN

Environmental Protection Agency
Washington, DC
1985 letter - EPA does <u>not</u> test wood stoves for efficiency - only rates them by category

Far East Clay
Wood stove with hole to heat pot directly, "smokeless"
article

Thomas Registers
One Penn Plaza
New York, NY 10117-0138
complete stoves - woodburning manufacturers' list

How To Design and Build Energy --
Efficient Fireplaces and Chimneys
Joseph D. Falcone
book

*Used in Earth Home

Fireplaces and Woodstoves
by Editors of Time-Life Books
book

Permacultures Books
theoretical wood stove design

The Harrowsmith Country Life Guide to
Wood Heat
Dirk Thomas
book

Wood Stoves/Wood -Masonry Stoves

NOTE: Masonry stoves are sometimes referred to as Russian fireplaces.

Envirotech
Division of Dietmeyer, Ward, & Stroud, Inc.
P.O. Box 323
Vashon Island, WA 98070
(800) 325-3629
(206) 463-3722
radiant fireplaces, "Russian fireplaces"

Hearth Products Assoc.
1101 Connecticut Avenue NW
Washington, DC 20036
(202) 857-1181

The Book of Masonry Stoves
David Lyle
source book

Envirotech
(800) 325-3629
radiant fireplaces and kits

The New Alberene Stone Company, Inc.
P.O. Box 300
Schuyler, VA 22969
(804) 831-2228
soapstone stoves - Tulikivi

Kickapoo Diversified Products, Inc.
1432 W. Kilbourn Avenue, #101
Milwaukee, WI 53233
(414) 933-6350

Wood Stoves/Wood -Pellets/Pellet Stoves

http://www.bixbyenergy.com/
pellet stoves

www.pelletheat.org
pellet burning website

www.rika.at
pellet stove manufacturer

Rika Pellet Stoves
www.rika.at/en/226

http://www.woodfuelpellets.com/wood-pellet-mill.html
small pelleting press
(220V 10HP motor)

American Freedom Fuels
PO Box 875
Tullahoma, TN 37388
1-931-607-3186
americanfreedomfuels@gmail.com

www.rhpl.co.uk/pelletmanufacture.htm
pellet manufacturing

Buhler (Canada) Inc.
16 Esna Park Drive, Unit 8
Markham, Ontario L3R 5X1
(905) 940-6910
Pellet mills

Bliss Industries, Inc.
P.O. Box 910, Ponca City, OK U.S.A. 74602
(580) 765-7787
www.bliss-industries.com
Pellet mills

Pelleting Concepts International, Inc.
5920 East Central, Suite 207
Wichita, KS 67208
(316) 686-3432

Pellet Fuels Institute
Organization for pellet manufacturers

http://www.fao.org/docrep/X5738E/x5738e3n.gif
pelletizing disc for lower power inputs
Dravo discs

Wood Stoves/Wood -Products

Pilgrim's Products
PO Box 63
Denison, KS. 66419
785-935-2900
Combination woodstove/water heater/oven

Thermo Volt TM
Photic Corporation
Dist. by Alternative Energy Engineering
Box 339 Briceland Star Rt.
Redway, CA 95560
(707) 923-2277
electricity from heat (see also Thermopile files)

Consolidated Dutchwest
P.O. Box 1019
Plymouth, MA 02360
(617) 747-1963
wood stove magazine

"Cor-Ten" steel
light pole steel

Corning
Technology Products Division
Corning Glass Works
Corning, NY 14831
(607) 874-9000
catalytic combustors

Sotz, Inc.
13664 Station Road
Columbia Station, OH 44028
wood stove parts

Condar Company
Box 6
Hiram, OH 44234
draft control manual

Ahrens Chimney Techniques

2000 Industrial Avenue
Sioux Falls,SD 57104
(800) 843-4417
chimney lining

Wilderness Woodheating Techniques
Box 8001
Fort St. John, BC V1J 5E6
CANADA
thermostat control

Lopi Stoves
Travis Industries, Inc.
10850 - 117th Place NE
Kirkland, WA 98033
woodstoves/fireplace inserts

Pacific Energy Woodstoves Ltd.
P.O. Box 29
Cobble Hill, British Columbia V0R 1L0
CANADA
wood stoves/fireplace inserts

Burn-Zol
P.O. Box 109-T
Dover, NJ 07801
(201) 361-5900
multi-fuel stoves

Vogelzang International Corp.
415 West 21st Street
Holland, MI 49423
(616) 396-1911
(800) 222-6950
barrel stove kits

Cabela's
Mail order magazine
EJ-25437-00
sheepherder's stove (lightweight)

Vermont Castings
Prince Street
Randolph, VT 05060
(802) 728-3181
stoves - all kinds

Jackes-Evans
4427 Geraldine Avenue
St. Louis, MO 63115
"Airtight" stoves

Energy King Stoves
Chippewa Welding Inc.
Route 5, Box 190
Chippewa Falls, WI 54729
(715) 723-9667
wood stoves and boilers

Kriss Water Treatment Eng.
(612) 722-8485
boiler water additives, "RP749"

KML Inc.
(414) 822-8592
boiler water additives

Wet Technology, Inc.
(612) 462-3162
boiler water additives

Wood Stoves/Wood -Woodgas Boilers

http://newhorizoncorp.com/offer.php?id=4
wood gasification boilers

Wood Stoves/Wood -Woodstove Comparison Chart (See body of text)

WOODSTOVE COMPARISON CHART
(see chart in body of text)

Wood Stoves/Wood -Woodstove Manufacturers

(See also comparison chart in body of text)

Capturing Heat
Book by the Aprovecho Research Center
Efficient and cheap woodstoves for cooking and heat

Rocket Stove
Winiarski Rocket Stove
Low-cost woodstove used in refugee camps
http://members.efn.org

NY Thermal Inc.
31 Industrial Drive
Sussex, New Brunswick
E4E 2R7 Canada
506-432-1130
www.nythermal.com
wood –fired boilers
gravity operation

Benjamin Heating Products
www.benjaminheating.com
wood-fired boilers
can be operated as gravity system

American Energy Systems
Countryside Multi-Fuel Corn/Pellet Stove

HAHSA Company
Heating and heat storage apparatus
Outside systems

Pilgrim's Products
PO Box 63
Denison, KS 66419
785-966-2900
combination woodstove, water heater, and cookstove

Clayton Mfg. Co., Inc.
112 Lind Street West
Mankato, MN 56001
(507) 345-3048
wood furnace

Johnson Mfg. & Sales
N 5499 County E
Ogdensburg, WI 54962
(414) 244-7581
smaller pellet stove

Aquatherm
Route 1, Box 1
Brooten, MN 56316
(800) 325-2760
stoker-fed boiler

*Used in Earth Home

Earth Sense Energy Systems
P.O. Box 1992
Appleton, WI 54913
(414) 734-6647
(800) 236-6647
corn-burning stove

Avalon
10850 - 117th Place NE
Kirkland, WA 98033
(206) 827-9505
wood stoves

Charmaster
2307 E. Highway 2 W.
Grand Rapids, MN 55744
(218) 326-6786

Central Boiler
Box 80
Greenbush, MN 56726
(218) 782-2575
outdoor boilers

Irwin Enterprises
346 Muddy Springs Road
Lexington, SC 29072
(803) 359-6737

Hardy Manufacturing Co.
Route 4, Box 156
Philadelphia, MS 39350
(601) 656-5866
* stainless steel outdoor furnaces

Long Manufacturing
11 Fairview Street
Tarboro, NC 27886
(919) 823-4151
Silent Flame

Phillips Co.
P.O. Box 1298
Clarksville, VA 23927
(804) 372-2818

Yukon Energy Corp.

Alpine Fireplaces
782 W. State Street
Lehi, UT 84043
(801) 768-8411

Dovre
401 Hankes Avenue
Aurora, IL 60505
(708) 844-3353
(800) DOVRE

Heatilator
1915 W. Saunders Street
Mt. Pleasant, IA 52641
(319) 385-9211
fireplaces

Heat-N-Glow
6665 W. Highway 13
Savage, MN 55378
(612) 890-8367
fireplaces

Majestic
1000 E. Market Street
Huntington, IN 46750
(219) 356-8000
fireplaces

Heatmor, Inc.
Highway 11 E. Box 787
Warroad, MN 56763
(218) 386-2769
stainless steel furnaces

Suburban Manufacturing
1200 N. Broadway
Dayton, TN 37321
(615) 775-2131

Superior Fireplaces
P.O. Box 2066
Fullerton, CA 92633
(714) 521-7302
fireplaces

Horstmann Industries (Royall)
301 Second Street
P.O. Box 66
Elroy, WI 53929
(608) 462-8431
boilers and wood stoves

Woodgas (AKA Gasification, Syngas)

http://www.dryfermentation.com/
dry fermentation technology

http://www.geocities.com/kenboak/wastewatts.html
woodgas discussion site

http://mitglied.lycos.de/cturare/gas.htm
good woodgas site

http://www2.whidbey.net/lighthook/woodgas.htm
woodgas site

www.waterwide.com/gasi.htm

http://www.green-trust.org/2000/biofuel/biofuel.htm

Synthetic Gas (see Woodgas)
Syngas (See Woodgas)

http://members.tripod.com/~cturare/lit.htm
gasification literature website

www.aboutbioenergy.info/technologies.html

www.woodgas.com

Thermogenics, Inc.
www.thermogenics.com
biomass/gasification/

www.woodgas.com/woodgas_cookstoves.htm
woodgas information site

www.woodgasllc.com
woodgas stove

http://journeytoforever.org/at_woodfire.html#woodgas
woodgas site

http://www.gengas.nu/byggbes/index.shtml

*Used in Earth Home

Wood gas as Engine Fuel
Mechanical Wood Products Branch
Forest Industries Division
FAO Forestry Department
ISBN 92-5-102436-7

http://www.fao.org/DOCREP/T0512E/T0512e00.htm
modern wood gasification technology

http://www.hotel.ymex.net/~s-20222/gengas/kg_eng.html
gas generation

http://members.tripod.com/~highforest/woodgas/woodfired.html
description with drawings

Alternatives to Fossil Fueled Engine/Generators
Clifford W. Mossberg

Woodgas for Engines and for Power
Homepower Magazine

History of Woodgas
Tom Reed of the Biomass Energy Foundation
http://www.woodgas.com/History.htm

Woodgas Powered VW's and Other Vehicles
http://www2.whidbey.net/
lighthook/woodgas.htm

http://www.repp.org/articles/static/1/1011975339_7.html

Briquette Presses for Alternate Fuel Use
Jason Dahlman with Charlie Forst

http://www.echotech.org/technical/technotes/Briquete.pdf
Design for a simple briquette/oil press

http://www.gengas.nu/byggbes/index.shtml

http://newhorizoncorp.com/offer.php?id=4
wood gasification boilers

Worms (See Fish section)

Note that worm raising is also known as vermicomposting.

XV. TEXT INDEX